SASKATCHEWAN 664

ALBERTA 696

BRITISH COLUMBIA 770

YUKON TERRITORY 907

NORTHWEST TERRITORIES 933

NUNAVUT 954

LANGUAGE 962

GLOSSARY 967

ACKNOWLEDGMENTS 970

INDEX 980

MAP LEGEND back page

METRIC CONVERSION inside back cover

Contents – Maps

8 Contents – Maps

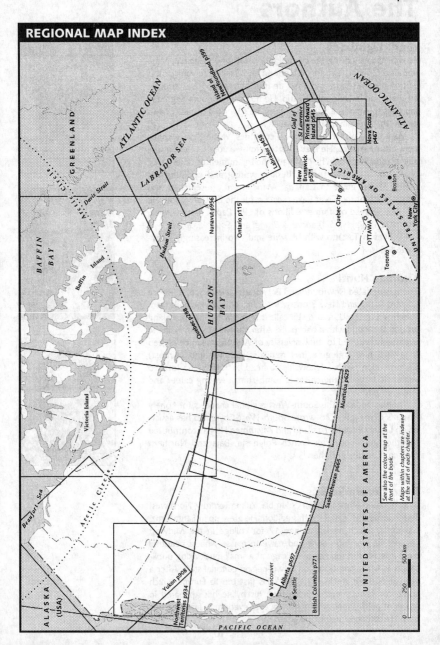

REGIONAL MAP INDEX

GREENLAND

Arctic Circle

ATLANTIC OCEAN

ATLANTIC OCEAN

Davis Strait

LABRADOR SEA

Island of Newfoundland p659

Labrador p538

St Gulf of Lawrence

Prince Edward Island p545

Nova Scotia p467

New Brunswick p571

Quebec City

OTTAWA

Boston

New York City

UNITED STATES OF AMERICA

BAFFIN BAY

Baffin Island

Hudson Strait

Nunavut p956

Ontario p115

HUDSON BAY

Quebec p888

Toronto

Manitoba p629

Victoria Island

Arctic Circle

Saskatchewan p665

Beaufort Sea

See also the colour map at the front of the book.

Maps within chapters are indexed at the start of each chapter.

UNITED STATES OF AMERICA

Yukon p908

Northwest Territories p934

British Columbia p771

Alberta p697

Vancouver

Seattle

ALASKA (USA)

PACIFIC OCEAN

0   250   500 km

The Authors

Mark Lightbody

As well as again being the co-ordinating author on *Canada*, Mark updated Quebec, Ontario, Manitoba and Saskatchewan for this edition. He was born and grew up in Montreal and was educated there and in London, Ontario. He holds an honours degree in journalism. Among a variety of jobs, he's worked in radio news and in the specialty graphics industry.

Mark has travelled in nearly 50 countries, visiting every continent but Antarctica. He made his first foray across Canada at the age of four. Since then he has made the trip numerous times using plane, train, car and thumb. Besides writing and updating the Lonely Planet guide to Canada, Mark recently researched and wrote much of the Great Lakes section for the LP *USA* guide. He has also worked on former editions of LP's *Papua New Guinea, Australia, Malaysia, Singapore & Brunei* and *South-East Asia*.

He lives in Toronto with his wife and two increasingly itchy-footed kids.

Thomas Huhti

Thomas updated Newfoundland & Labrador, Nova Scotia, Prince Edward Island and New Brunswick for this edition. He hails from Wisconsin in the USA and still calls it home when not barrelling around the world with a backpack. After studying in East Asia, he eventually returned to the University of Wisconsin, which agreed to award him a degree in Linguistics, English and (almost) Chinese, along with a fellowship to head back to China for two years. He travelled thereafter to jump-start a writing career and flee graduate school.

Thomas updated the South-West regional chapters for Lonely Planet's *China* guide, co-wrote *South-West China* and has assisted on Lonely Planet's *Thailand* and *Myanmar*. He has contributed to other guidebooks on French Polynesia, Baja and Northern Mexico, Canada, and the USA.

Ryan Ver Berkmoes

Ryan updated Alberta, British Columbia, Yukon Territory, Northwest Territories and Nunavut for this edition. He grew up in Santa Cruz, California, which he left at age 17 for college in the Midwest because he was too young and naive to realise what a beautiful place it is. His first job was in Chicago at a small muckraking publication as Managing Editor on a two-person editorial staff. After a year of 60-hour weeks, Ryan took his first trip to Europe which lasted for seven months. Since then his byline has appeared in scores of publications and he has covered everything from wars to bars. He definitely prefers the latter.

Among his work for Lonely Planet, he is the author of *Chicago*, co-wrote *Texas*, co-ordinated Germany for *Western Europe* and is co-ordinating *Russia, Ukraine & Belarus*. He and his journalist wife Sara Marley reside in London near the point of inspiration for noted musician Nigel Tufnel.

FROM THE AUTHORS

Mark Lightbody Canada, it seems, has earned the respect and admiration of travellers in greater numbers than ever. For me, this means more people to talk to, more businesses to check out, more places and activities to keep on top of. The country keeps getting bigger and the challenge to keep abreast greater.

In order to gain as much first-hand information as possible for this edition, I travelled over 20,000km on the roads, close to 3000km on the rails and only my feet know how many on the streets. I would like to once again thank Colleen Kennedy for research assistance and editorial help as well as suggestions and comments which, although usually appropriate, were not always well received. My father Alexander's unpaid but scrupulous proofreading resulted in a number of small but important corrections.

Greg Brockmann of Hostelling International offered generous support and Lloyd Jones of Backpackers' Canada supplied a wealth of friendly advice, encouragement and timely humour.

Special thanks also go to Dave Page and Pat Stuart in La Durantaye for food, drink and sharing their affection for Quebec. Best regards to Bill Macdonald in Winnipeg for his warm hospitality regardless of what time I bang on the door or what he's in the middle of, including writing his own book. I also appreciate the informative assistance of Vera Gould in Churchill. Thanks also go to Carolyn Hubbard and the rest of the LP staff for all manner of assistance. Thanks also to Diane and Alain Carpentier for always coming through with the details on details.

And of course, kudos are due to all the letter writers who supply such great and unbelievably varied information which can't be obtained other than by such personal experiences. I also appreciate all the useful tips travellers passed my way out on the road. Till next time ...

Thomas Huhti Many people built up their karma on me while I maxed out my assistance credit line. Canada possesses some of the most engaging and solicitous tourist reps, predisposed to help above and beyond the call.

The following went to even greater, astonishing lengths for me, for which I'm grateful: Jeanette Joudrey, Lunenburg; Michelle Brunet, Halifax; and somebody somewhere in government should appreciate Rachel James of St John's, Newfoundland and pay her the loads of money she's worth.

In civilian life, thanks to all the travellers I met who made the long roads more enjoyable. I wish you wind at your backs. The Long Island Murphys made the ferries especially fun. Don Hom was great help for Labrador. Thanks to my vigilant neighbour Kevin Mullaney; the support staff at WESLI; of course my family who never, ever get tired of me crashing on their couches; Joe 'Khun' Cummings for getting me into all this; Carolyn Hubbard and the rest of the LP US office, who were a pleasure to work with; and most of all to Hyeon for being there even when so far away.

Special mention goes to the CBC in all its incarnations. For help with the mojo through the more tedious miles thanks to Jimmy Lafave, JP Cormier, 54-40, Lucinda Williams and every single fiddle player of the Maritimes.

Ryan Ver Berkmoes I want to thank many people for their assistance starting with Laura Serena and Derek 'one more' Hemmes in Vancouver, Carol Maire and her bugs in Victoria, Susie Quarry in Prince George and Julia Ferguson and David Boyce in Prince Rupert. Mary Kellie was as amazing as the Queen Charlotte Islands. Sacha Veelbehr at Yoho National Park was inspired in her suggestions and Carter Fitzpatrick's enthusiasm was contagious. Ruth Roberts and Nim Singh paved the way from London.

In Alberta, Krista Rodger and Melody Kultgen were as gorgeous as their respective towns of Jasper and Banff. Gabi Wedin steered me clear of the dark side.

In the Yukon, Jim Kemshead and Mary Ellen McCaffery were gems. Peggy Amendola rendered invaluable assistance in Dawson City and Steve Halloran helped me discover Skagway away from the hordes. Maureen Cumming and Linda Mickle kept me afloat. Judith Venaas showed me the way in Inuvik and Mike Harrison and Martin Goodliffe were delights.

Kathie Adam, Vanessa Gagnon and Melissa-Ann Fletcher helped me mine Yellowknife where Joan Hirons was a splendid host. Cheri Kemp-Kinnear was unstinting in Nunavut and big thanks to Terry Jesudason in Resolute who drove me everywhere. Carsten Iwers, Doug Harvey and Jim Perrin were fun companions when things got weird.

I enjoyed working with my Lonely Planet compatriots on this project: Carolyn Hubbard (who made a critical FedEx move at the last moment), Mark Lightbody and Tom Huhti, plus Eric Kettunen who signed the contract. Finally thanks and love to Sara Marley who gave me reason to return home from my endless northern treks even if it meant I would take over another dining room table.

This Book

The first three editions were researched and updated by Mark Lightbody, the fourth and fifth editions were updated by Mark Lightbody and Tom Smallman, while the sixth edition was updated by Mark Lightbody, Dorinda Talbot and Jim DuFresne. For this edition Mark was joined by Thomas Huhti and Ryan Ver Berkmoes.

From the Publisher

The editing of this edition was coordinated by Craig MacKenzie in the Melbourne office. He was assisted by Clay Lucas, Chris Wyness, Anne Mulvaney and Rebecca Turner. The coordinating designer was Joelene Kowalski. She was assisted by Piotr Czaj-kowski, Paul Dawson, Mark Griffiths, Ann Jeffree and Chris Lee Ack. Joelene and Rachel Black produced the colour wraps, the cover is the work of Guillaume Roux while Celia Wood produced the colour country map. Kate Nolan and Matt King handled illustrative content, Quentin Frayne produced the Language chapter and Tim Uden's QuarkXPress expertise assisted layout.

THANKS
Many thanks to the travellers who used the last edition and wrote to us with helpful hints, advice and interesting anecdotes. Your names appear in the back of this book.

Foreword

ABOUT LONELY PLANET GUIDEBOOKS

The story begins with a classic travel adventure: Tony and Maureen Wheeler's 1972 journey across Europe and Asia to Australia. Useful information about the overland trail did not exist at that time, so Tony and Maureen published the first Lonely Planet guidebook to meet a growing need.

From a kitchen table, then from a tiny office in Melbourne (Australia), Lonely Planet has become the largest independent travel publisher in the world, an international company with offices in Melbourne, Oakland (USA), London (UK) and Paris (France).

Today Lonely Planet guidebooks cover the globe. There is an ever-growing list of books and there's information in a variety of forms and media. Some things haven't changed. The main aim is still to help make it possible for adventurous travellers to get out there – to explore and better understand the world.

At Lonely Planet we believe travellers can make a positive contribution to the countries they visit – if they respect their host communities and spend their money wisely. Since 1986 a percentage of the income from each book has been donated to aid projects and human rights campaigns.

Updates Lonely Planet thoroughly updates each guidebook as often as possible. This usually means there are around two years between editions, although for more unusual or more stable destinations the gap can be longer. Check the imprint page (following the colour map at the beginning of the book) for publication dates.

Between editions up-to-date information is available in two free newsletters – the paper *Planet Talk* and email *Comet* (to subscribe, contact any Lonely Planet office) – and on our Web site at www.lonelyplanet.com. The *Upgrades* section of the Web site covers a number of important and volatile destinations and is regularly updated by Lonely Planet authors. *Scoop* covers news and current affairs relevant to travellers. And, lastly, the *Thorn Tree* bulletin board and *Postcards* section of the site carry unverified, but fascinating, reports from travellers.

Correspondence The process of creating new editions begins with the letters, postcards and emails received from travellers. This correspondence often includes suggestions, criticisms and comments about the current editions. Interesting excerpts are immediately passed on via newsletters and the Web site, and everything goes to our authors to be verified when they're researching on the road. We're keen to get more feedback from organisations or individuals who represent communities visited by travellers.

Lonely Planet gathers information for everyone who's curious about the planet – and especially for those who explore it first-hand. Through guidebooks, phrasebooks, activity guides, maps, literature, newsletters, image library, TV series and Web site we act as an information exchange for a worldwide community of travellers.

Research Authors aim to gather sufficient practical information to enable travellers to make informed choices and to make the mechanics of a journey run smoothly. They also research historical and cultural background to help enrich the travel experience and allow travellers to understand and respond appropriately to cultural and environmental issues.

Authors don't stay in every hotel because that would mean spending a couple of months in each medium-sized city and, no, they don't eat at every restaurant because that would mean stretching belts beyond capacity. They do visit hotels and restaurants to check standards and prices, but feedback based on readers' direct experiences can be very helpful.

Many of our authors work undercover, others aren't so secretive. None of them accept freebies in exchange for positive write-ups. And none of our guidebooks contain any advertising.

Production Authors submit their raw manuscripts and maps to offices in Australia, USA, UK or France. Editors and cartographers – all experienced travellers themselves – then begin the process of assembling the pieces. When the book finally hits the shops, some things are already out of date, we start getting feedback from readers and the process begins again ...

WARNING & REQUEST

Things change – prices go up, schedules change, good places go bad and bad places go bankrupt – nothing stays the same. So, if you find things better or worse, recently opened or long since closed, please tell us and help make the next edition even more accurate and useful. We genuinely value all the feedback we receive. Julie Young coordinates a well travelled team that reads and acknowledges every letter, postcard and email and ensures that every morsel of information finds its way to the appropriate authors, editors and cartographers for verification.

Everyone who writes to us will find their name in the next edition of the appropriate guidebook. They will also receive the latest issue of *Planet Talk*, our quarterly printed newsletter, or *Comet*, our monthly email newsletter. Subscriptions to both newsletters are free. The very best contributions will be rewarded with a free guidebook.

Excerpts from your correspondence may appear in new editions of Lonely Planet guidebooks, the Lonely Planet Web site, *Planet Talk* or *Comet*, so please let us know if you *don't* want your letter published or your name acknowledged.

Send all correspondence to the Lonely Planet office closest to you:

Australia Locked Bag 1, Footscray, Victoria 3011
USA 150 Linden St, Oakland, CA 94607
UK 10a Spring Place, London NW5 3BH
France 1 rue du Dahomey, 75011 Paris

Or email us at: talk2us@lonelyplanet.com.au

For news, views and updates see our Web site: www.lonelyplanet.com

HOW TO USE A LONELY PLANET GUIDEBOOK

The best way to use a Lonely Planet guidebook is any way you choose. At Lonely Planet we believe the most memorable travel experiences are often those that are unexpected, and the finest discoveries are those you make yourself. Guidebooks are not intended to be used as if they provide a detailed set of infallible instructions!

Contents All Lonely Planet guidebooks follow roughly the same format. The Facts about the Destination chapters or sections give background information ranging from history to weather. Facts for the Visitor gives practical information on issues like visas and health. Getting There & Away gives a brief starting point for researching travel to and from the destination. Getting Around gives an overview of the transport options when you arrive.

The peculiar demands of each destination determine how subsequent chapters are broken up, but some things remain constant. We always start with background, then proceed to sights, places to stay, places to eat, entertainment, getting there and away, and getting around information – in that order.

Heading Hierarchy Lonely Planet headings are used in a strict hierarchical structure that can be visualised as a set of Russian dolls. Each heading (and its following text) is encompassed by any preceding heading that is higher on the hierarchical ladder.

Entry Points We do not assume guidebooks will be read from beginning to end, but that people will dip into them. The traditional entry points are the list of contents and the index. In addition, however, some books have a complete list of maps and an index map illustrating map coverage.

There may also be a colour map that shows highlights. These highlights are dealt with in greater detail in the Facts for the Visitor chapter, along with planning questions and suggested itineraries. Each chapter covering a geographical region usually begins with a locator map and another list of highlights. Once you find something of interest in a list of highlights, turn to the index.

Maps Maps play a crucial role in Lonely Planet guidebooks and include a huge amount of information. A legend is printed on the back page. We seek to have complete consistency between maps and text, and to have every important place in the text captured on a map. Map key numbers usually start in the top left corner.

> **Although inclusion in a guidebook usually implies a recommendation we cannot list every good place. Exclusion does not necessarily imply criticism. In fact there are a number of reasons why we might exclude a place – sometimes it is simply inappropriate to encourage an influx of travellers.**

Introduction

Canada is big, spacious, rugged, uncluttered and tremendously varied. You can stand in places where perhaps nobody else has ever stood and yet the cities are large and modern.

From the Atlantic Ocean it's over 7000km to the Pacific coast. In between you can enjoy a coffee and a croissant at a sidewalk café or canoe on a silent northern lake. You can peer down from the world's tallest structure or over the walls of a centuries-old fort. You can spy moose and bears in the forests or seals and whales in the oceans. You can hike amid snowcapped peaks or watch the sunset where it's an unobstructed 30km to the horizon.

Four very different seasons can bring the cold, harsh winters Canada is known for, but also sweltering summer days. Short explosive springs and intensely brilliant yellow-red autumns mean dramatic transitions.

It's said that the national personality has been shaped by the harsh realities of life in the northern frontier. Because the country is so young, a modern identity is still forming. But it's there, distinctly different from that of Canada's neighbour to the south.

The cultural mix of Canada is often described as a mosaic, not the melting pot of the USA. This patchwork of peoples is made up of British, French and many others, ranging from Europeans to those from Asia as well as the original Native peoples.

The Canadian dollar remains low compared with the US greenback, making exchange rates excellent for US citizens and many Europeans while holding steady for many other currencies. Inflation has been negligible for several years meaning relatively stable prices.

With its history, people, land and nature, Canada has a lot to offer the traveller.

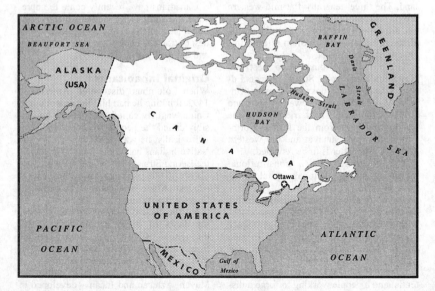

Facts about Canada

Canada is the second largest country in the world – nearly as big as all of Europe. Only Russia is larger. The population of over 30 million works out to close to just two people per sq km. In the countryside the population is very thinly spread – the average Canadian farm is 200 hectares in size.

Nearly 90% of Canadians, though, huddle along the 6379km southern border with the USA. It's the longest unguarded national boundary in the world. The southern region is, of course, the warmest, most hospitable area of the country and also has the best land and waterways. Three-quarters of the population lives in the towns and cities in this portion of the country. Toronto is the largest city with about 2.4 million residents.

The country is made up of 10 provinces and three northern territories. The four eastern coastal provinces are known as the Atlantic Provinces or the Maritime Provinces, the latter term often excluding Newfoundland. The three generally flat mid-western provinces are the prairies. Ontario and Quebec are collectively termed central Canada, although Canadians will often refer to this area as eastern Canada.

The provinces (from east to west) are Newfoundland, Nova Scotia, Prince Edward Island, New Brunswick, Quebec, Ontario, Manitoba, Saskatchewan, Alberta and British Columbia. The territories are the Yukon, and born from the former Northwest Territories, Nunavut and the Western Territory. The latter is to be renamed.

The government is a constitutional monarchy and the national capital is Ottawa, Ontario.

There are two official languages in the country, English and French. A movement within Quebec, the one predominantly French province, to separate from Canada and form a new country has waxed and waned since the mid-1960s.

Canada is a young country with great potential and a people working to forge a distinct national identity while struggling to hold the parts together.

HISTORY

Recorded Canadian history, while short relative to much of the world, is full of intrigue. Colourful, dramatic, tragic and wonderful occurrences and stories abound. Much of it has been well documented by historians and writers for those wishing to delve further.

In under several hundred years there has been the discovery and exploration of the country by Europeans. Their voyages and those of the settling pioneers are fascinating tales of the unveiling of a large part of the globe.

The aboriginal cultures the Europeans met and dealt with through the years of the fur-trade and beyond make up contrasting chapters of the story. Battles between the French and the British, and the British and the USA are other major themes.

Canadians have recently come to appreciate and admire their nation's history. National Historic Sites and buildings of every description can be found across the country and are well worth discovering.

Original Inhabitants

When Columbus 'discovered' America in 1492, thinking he had hit the lands south of China, vaguely called 'the Indies', he sensibly called the people he found 'Indians'.

Ironically, he was nearly correct, for the Native Indians had come from Asia, across the Bering Strait, after the last great Ice Age – about 15,000 years ago. The earliest known occupation site in Canada is the Bluefish Caves of the Yukon.

By the time Columbus arrived the descendants of these people had spread throughout the Americas, from Canada's frozen north to Tierra del Fuego at the southern tip of Argentina and Chile.

The major American Indian cultures – Mayan, Aztecan and Incan – developed in

Central and South America. Although no comparably sophisticated Indian societies sprang up in Canada, partially due to the climate, the Canadian Indian tribes had evolved dramatically through prehistory. When the Europeans arrived Native people across the country had developed a multitude of languages, customs, religious beliefs, trading patterns, arts and crafts, highly specialised skills, laws and government.

At this time, around the early 1500s, six distinct groupings of people could be discerned, each with its own language and customs. These six major groups are classified by their geographic location.

The Arctic peoples lived in the far north. The subarctic group was found across the country from Newfoundland to British Columbia. The eastern woodlands tribes lived across the top of the Great Lakes, along the St Lawrence River and in what was to become Nova Scotia, New Brunswick and Prince Edward Island. The plains people roamed across the prairies from Lake Winnipeg to the foothills of the Rocky Mountains. The plateau area covers those groups in central southern British Columbia and the north-west group ranges from Vancouver to Alaska along the Pacific coast and includes all the ocean islands of British Columbia.

Most of these peoples depended on hunting, fishing and gathering. The more complex societies lived either on the mild west coast or around the fertile southern Ontario and St Lawrence Valley region in the east. The Eastern Woodland Indians had developed agriculture and lived in more-or-less permanent settlements. The tribes of the north and midwest lived a more hand-to-mouth existence. The Inuit (meaning 'people', and once called the Eskimos) eked out an existence in a world virtually unchanged until the 1950s.

Within each grouping were numerous tribes which, in turn, comprised numbers of smaller bands who came together to winter or in times of celebration or hardship and when marriage partners were sought. Even today, 53 distinct indigenous languages are spoken and many of these have various dialects. Other languages are now extinct.

The existing languages fall into 11 broader families, most of which are independent from all the others. North America is generally considered to be one of the most complex linguistic regions in the world. Today, less than half of Canada's Native people can speak their original language.

The Inuit, who arrived from Asia after the forefathers of all other American Indians, are a separate people. There are about 100,000 Inuit in the Arctic areas of the USA, Russia, Greenland (Denmark) and Canada. Canada is home to roughly 25% of the total population.

The peaceful Inuit had little to do with the more southerly Indian groups and, other than meetings with European explorers around the north-east coast, remained in relative isolation. They were the last group of Native Canadians to give up the traditional, nomadic way of life, although even with more modern housing many remain primarily hunters. Despite having to face brutal weather conditions and frequent starvation, the Inuit were a remarkably healthy lot and the pristine conditions helped protect them from disease and sickness. The arrival of European infectious diseases reduced their numbers dramatically to the point where their very survival was in question.

Today they have increased to about 30,000 which is more than when the Europeans first showed up. The Beothuks of Newfoundland did not fare so well. They ceased to exist as a people when the last two women died in the early 1800s.

Across the rest of Canada, the explorers and pioneers, both intentionally and by accident, brought to an end the way of life of all Native people. The eastern tribes, such as those of the Iroquois Confederacy, had to side against each other with the French or English in their seemingly never-ending battles and ended up losing all their land.

The plains people, such as the Cree and Blackfoot, with their teepees, horses, bows and arrows and spectacular feathered headdresses – perhaps the archetypal North American Indian – were forced into the Europeans' world by the virtual extinction of the buffalo.

The west coast tribes such as the Haida were more fortunate, their isolation, strong tradition of independence and long, stable history affording some protection.

Overall, European discovery and settlement of the country reduced Native Indians from about 350,000 to 100,000. Through treaty arrangements, the formation of reservations (now called reserves) and strong policing, notably by the Royal Canadian Mounted Police (RCMP), the remaining groups were provided some measure of protection. Canada never had the all out wars and massacres that marred the clash of cultures in the USA.

European Exploration

The first European visitors to Canada were the Vikings from Iceland and Greenland. There is evidence that they settled in northern Newfoundland at the eastern edge of Canada around 1000 AD. How long they stayed, how much they explored and what happened to them is unknown.

It was around 1500 AD that the action around the Americas started to heat up. The Spanish, French, British and Italians all wanted in.

In Canada, it was the French who got first licks. After a few earlier exploratory visits by the Europeans in 1534, Jacques Cartier of France, a subject of Francis I, reached the gulf of the St Lawrence River and claimed all the surrounding area for France. It was probably from Cartier that Canada got its name. Originally *Kanata*, a Huron-Iroquois word for 'village' or 'small community', its derivative showed up in Cartier's journal. The name was used for the St Lawrence area and eventually became the official name of the new country.

The French didn't bother much with this new colony throughout the 1500s, but the pattern of economic development which began then has continued through to the present. This is, put bluntly and simply, the selling of its resources to whoever is buying, thus enabling the country to pay for everything else it needs. The first commodities prized by the French were the fish of the east coast and furs for the fashion-conscious of France.

Samuel de Champlain, another Frenchman, began further explorations in the early 1600s. He settled Quebec City, and Montreal was founded soon after in 1642 as a missionary outpost. Throughout the 17th century fur-trading companies dominated this new world. In 1663 Canada became a province of France. There were about 60,000 French settlers by then – the ancestors of a good percentage of today's French Canadians.

Throughout the 1600s the French fought the Native Indians, who soon realised that they were getting a raw deal in the fur trade and through development of their lands. The French kept busy, too, with further explorations. They built a long chain of forts down to Louisiana – another major settlement – in what is now southern USA. In the 1730s another of the major explorers, Pierre Gaultier de Varennes, Sieur de la Vérendrye, was responsible for another series of forts. This one stretched across the south of what are now the provinces of Ontario, Manitoba and Saskatchewan.

The Struggle for Power

Of course, the British weren't just sipping pints through all this. Though concentrating on the lands of America's east coast, the Hudson's Bay Company (still one of Canada's main department-store chains but now known simply as The Bay) had moved into the Hudson Bay area in northern Ontario around 1670.

The British soon muscled into settlements on the Canadian east coast. By 1713 they had control over much of Nova Scotia and Newfoundland. And then, for a while, there was peace.

In 1745 a British army from New England, in what is now the USA, moved north and captured a French fort in Nova Scotia. The struggle for control of the new land was on. What is known as the French and Indian War began in 1754 and the war in Europe known as the Seven Years' War began in 1756. The French held the upper hand for the first four years. In one of

Canada's most famous battles, the British defeated the French at Quebec City in 1759. Both General Wolfe, leader of the British, and the Marquis de Montcalm, who led the French, were killed in battle. After this major victory, the British turned the tide. At the Treaty of Paris in 1763, France handed Canada over to Britain.

The British, however, didn't quite know how to manage the newly acquired territory. The population was nearly exclusively French and at that time in Britain, Roman Catholics enjoyed very few rights – they couldn't vote or hold office. In 1774 the Quebec Act gave the French Canadians the right to their religion, the use of French civil law in court and the possibility of assuming political office. The British, however, maintained positions of power and influence in both politics and business. It was during this period that the seeds of the Quebec separatist movement were sown.

During the American Revolution (1775-83) against Britain, about 50,000 settlers – termed 'Loyalists' due to their loyalty to Britain – shifted north to Canada. They settled mainly in the Atlantic Provinces and Ontario.

This migration helped to balance the number of French and British in Canada. Soon after, Quebec and Ontario were formed with their own governors. Throughout the late 1700s and into the 1800s Canada's frontiers were pushed farther and farther afield. Sir Arthur Mackenzie explored the north (Mackenzie River) and much of British Columbia. Simon Fraser followed the river which was later named after him to the Pacific Ocean. David Thompson travelled the Columbia River, also in British Columbia. In 1812, Lord Selkirk formed a settlement of Scottish immigrants around the Red River Valley near Winnipeg, Manitoba.

Also in 1812, the last war between Canada and the USA, the War of 1812, began. Its causes were numerous, but the US attempt to take over its northern neighbour was only part of the campaign against Britain. Each side won a few battles, and in 1814 a draw was declared.

The Dominion Period

With the end of the US threat and the resulting confidence in themselves, many of the colonists became fed up with some aspects of British rule. Some spoke out for independence. In both Upper (Ontario) and Lower (Quebec) Canada, brief rebellions broke out. In 1840 both areas united under one government. But by this stage, the population in Upper (British, mainly) outnumbered that in Lower Canada (French) and wanted more than a half-say. The government became bogged down, with Britain attempting to work out something new.

Britain, of course, didn't want to lose Canada, as it had the USA, so it stepped lightly and decided on a confederation giving a central government some powers and the individual colonies others.

In 1867 the British North America Act (BNA Act) was passed by the British government. This established the Dominion of Canada and included Ontario, Quebec, Nova Scotia and New Brunswick. The BNA Act became Canada's equivalent to a constitution, though it was far less detailed and all-inclusive than that of the USA.

John Alexander Macdonald (known as Sir John A) became Canada's first prime minister. The total population was 3.5 million, nearly all living in the east and mostly on farms. It had been decided at the Act's signing in 1867 that other parts of the country should be included in the Dominion whenever possible.

The completion of the Canadian Pacific Railway – one of Canada's great historical sagas – joined the west coast with the east, linking those areas with the Dominion. By 1912 all provinces had become part of the central government except Newfoundland, which finally joined in 1949.

In the last few years of the 19th century Canada received large numbers of immigrants, mainly from Europe.

The government continued to grapple with French and British differences. These reached a peak during WWI, a conflict which Canada had entered immediately on Britain's behalf. In 1917, despite bitter

French opposition in Quebec, the Canadian government began a military draft.

The Modern Era

After WWI Canada slowly grew in stature and prosperity, and in 1931 became a voluntary member of the Commonwealth.

With the onset of WWII, Canada once again supported Britain, but this time also began defence agreements with the USA, and after the attack on Pearl Harbor, declared war on Japan.

In the years after WWII Canada experienced another massive wave of European immigration. The postwar period saw economic expansion and prosperity right across North America. The 1950s were a time of unprecedented wealth. The middle class mushroomed.

The 1960s brought social upheaval and social-welfare programs with their ideals and liberalism. Canada's first Bill of Rights was signed in 1960. Nuclear-power generators and US nuclear warheads became major issues in Canada.

The Quebec separatist movement attracted more attention. A small group used terrorism to press its point for an independent Quebec.

In 1967 the country celebrated its 100th anniversary with the World's Fair in Montreal – Expo – as one of the highlights.

Well known Pierre Elliot Trudeau, a Liberal, became Canada's prime minister in 1968 and, except for a brief period in 1979, held power until his retirement in 1984. Despite great initial support and international recognition, Trudeau was, to be kind, not a popular man at the end of his stay. In 1976 the Parti Québecois (PQ), advocating separatism, won the Quebec provincial election. Trudeau campaigned hard for a united Canada. In 1980 a Quebec referendum found that 60% of Quebeckers were against independence and the topic was more or less dropped.

Trudeau's leadership was also largely responsible for the formation of a Canadian Constitution, one of the last steps in full independence from Britain. It came into being in 1982 along with a Charter of Rights and Freedoms. Quebec, however, never ratified the agreement and it was passed without its participation. It wanted to be recognised as a 'distinct society' with special rights. Later talks to bring it into the fold and thus make the agreement more national have failed. Constitutional matters have largely been put aside for what many see as more practical, less divisive topics. The issue didn't go away, however, and played a part in the next startling election.

The 1984 election saw Brian Mulroney's Progressive Conservative party sweep into power with a tremendous nationwide majority, slamming the door on the Trudeau era. The 1988 World Economic Summit of the seven major industrial nations was held in Toronto and the winter Olympics were hosted in Calgary, each bringing greatly increased prestige and favourable attention to Canada's somewhat fragile international self-image. The government was re-elected to another five-year term in 1988.

Following the customary pattern this government, too, fell from grace with a loud thump. Among the major issues through the later Mulroney years were the very controversial free-trade alliance with the USA and the attempt to reach a consensus, known as the Meech Lake Accord, on overhauling the distinctions between provincial and federal powers, rights and jurisdictions. Another live wire was the introduction of a Goods and Services Tax (GST).

In 1993 and again in 1997, the Liberals, led by Quebecker Jean Chrétien, won elections handily. Chrétien, a one time associate of Trudeau, and known for his strong French accent, has been around a long time, knows the ropes and appeals with his apparent lack of artifice and posturing.

The USA pushed for, and got, an extension to the Free Trade Agreement (FTA) which included Mexico in the North American Free Trade Agreement (NAFTA). Big business likes the agreement but many Canadians see it as killing jobs rather than creating them.

Current issues include job creation and maintaining social programs such as a 'free'

universal Medicare system, unemployment insurance and welfare for the needy, of which Canadians are justifiably proud and protective. They are under an ever-increasing economic threat. The country's notoriously high taxes are also a contentious matter. Skirmishes continue between Canada and the USA regarding trade, especially in the realm of culture (books, television, radio).

Under the guidance of Lucien Bouchard (now PQ leader and premier of Quebec) Quebec independence sprang up again in the early 1990s and another referendum was held in Quebec. In late 1995 the 'No Side' once again won but you could barely wedge a ballot through the margin of victory. Despite Bouchard's popularity in Quebec, most people there are now currently in favour of Canadian unity. The possibility of Quebec forming a separate, distinct political entity at some point is always hovering over provincial-federal affairs and adversely affecting the economics of both.

Internationally, Canada maintains its position in NATO and as one of the so-called G-7 countries. (The G-7 group of Germany, France, USA, UK, Japan, Italy and Canada meets regularly to develop major economic policies.) In 1995 Canada won world headlines (and friends) over its hard line with Spain in the so-called fish wars. The disastrous depletion of Canada's once boundless fish stocks on both the Atlantic coast (cod) and then the Pacific coast (salmon) is a combined political, economic, environmental and emotional issue. In late 1995 Canada enacted some of the world's toughest anti-gun legislation.

The last couple of years have been uneventful politically with the Liberals content to softly cruise without rocking anybody's boat. The huge deficit has been decreased and the resulting impending tax cuts remain a dangling carrot in front of the electorate.

Canadian troops continue to be among the world's foremost peacekeepers, working not only in the Middle East, Cyprus and traditional trouble spots but also playing leading roles in Somalia, Kuwait and currently the provinces of former Yugoslavia.

GEOGRAPHY

Canada is about 7730km from east to west. Its only neighbour is the USA, which includes Alaska in the north-west. With such size the country can boast a tremendous variety of topography.

Though much of the land is lake and river-filled forest, there are mountains, plains and even a small desert. Canada has (or shares with the USA) seven of the world's largest lakes and also contains three of the globe's longest 20 rivers. The country is blessed with the most freshwater of any country. About 25% of the country is covered in forest. Canada's highest mountain, Mt Logan at 5951m, is found in the south-west Yukon.

Despite being bordered on three sides by oceans, Canada is not generally viewed as a maritime country. This is in part due to the large, central regions which contain the bulk of the population and dominate in so many ways. Also the Rocky Mountains and Niagara Falls, the country's two best known and most visited geographic features, are found inland.

From eastern Quebec to the eastern edge of the country, the Atlantic Ocean plays a major part in the population's day-to-day life and offers the visitor much to discover and explore. The same can be said of the Pacific Ocean and British Columbia to the west.

Canada can be divided into seven geographic regions each with its own characteristic scenery and landforms.

The far eastern area, the Appalachian Region, includes Newfoundland, Prince Edward Island, New Brunswick, Nova Scotia and the part of Quebec south of the St Lawrence River. The land is mainly hilly and wooded.

The St Lawrence-Great Lakes Lowland is roughly the area between Quebec City and Windsor, Ontario, and includes most of the country's large towns, cities and industry. In all, about half of Canada's population lives here. The land, originally forested, later nearly all used for farming, is generally flat.

Centrally, south of vast Hudson Bay, the most dominant characteristics of the Canadian map are the Hudson Bay and Arctic

Lowlands. This region is mainly flat, bog or muskeg – little-inhabited or visited, with the notable exception of Churchill, Manitoba.

Most of the north is taken up by the Canadian Shield, also known as the Precambrian Shield, formed 2.5 billion years ago. This geographic area covers all of northern Manitoba, Ontario and Quebec and stretches farther east across Labrador and west to the northern edge of Alberta. It's an enormous ancient, rocky, glacially sanded region of typical Canadian river and lake-filled timberland. It is also extremely rugged, cool and little-developed, with mining and logging the two primary ingredients in human settlement. This semi-remote area is best explored by visiting and/or camping in the government parks throughout the region.

The fifth region, the Great Plains, runs through Manitoba, Saskatchewan and parts of Alberta. The plains, formerly grasslands, make up a huge, flat region now responsible for Canada's abundant wheat crop.

The sixth geographic area is the Mountain or Western Cordillera Region covering British Columbia, the Yukon and parts of Alberta. Mountains dominate this region. The Rocky Mountains form the eastern edge of the area rising from 2000 to 4000m. Between them and the coastal peaks lie a series of lesser mountain ranges and valleys. Among the latter is the long, narrow valley called the Rocky Mountain Trench.

The interior of British Columbia consists of countless troughs, plateaus, hills, gorges, basins and river deltas. The province is by far the most scenically varied and spectacular in the country. Farther north, the 20 highest mountains in the country are found in the Yukon.

Lastly, there is the far north, the Arctic region. The northernmost section of the north is made up of islands frozen together for much of the year.

CLIMATE

Canada has four distinct seasons all of which occur right across the country although their arrival times vary. The single most significant factor in climate, and even

day-to-day weather, is latitude. In just a few hours travelling north by road, a drop (sometimes a considerable one) in temperature can often be felt.

The warmest area of Canada is along the US border. It's no accident that nearly everybody lives in this southernmost region. The overall warmest areas of the country are British Columbia's south and central coast and southern Ontario particularly around the Niagara Peninsula. These districts have the longest summers and the shortest winters.

July and August are the warmest months across the country and generally they are reasonably dry. Along the US border, summer temperatures are usually in the mid and upper 20°Cs. Each year there are a few days in the 30°Cs. Manitoba through to central British Columbia gets the hottest summer temperatures as well as the most sunshine. The west and east coasts are very wet with 2500mm of precipitation a year but much of that is through the winter months. The prairies are fairly dry all year but southeastern Canada including Montreal, Ottawa and Toronto can be quite humid in summer and damp in winter.

Ontario and Quebec have warm summers without a lot of rain. Southern Ontario can be hot in midsummer. The east coast is generally cooler than the rest of the country and can have more summer rain as well.

Summers in the Yukon, Northwest Territories (NWT) and Nunavut can be pleasantly warm and have the added benefit of extremely long daylight hours.

Outside the main cities, anywhere in Canada, nights are cool year-round.

Canadian winters are long. In more than two-thirds of the country the average January temperature is -18°C. The major cities are not consistently this cold but temperatures are generally below freezing. Except in the warmest areas, snowfall can be heavy especially from Toronto east. As a rule of thumb the farther north, the more snow. But only to a point, once past the central portion of the country, the dry conditions prevent snow fall of major accumulation. See the climate charts for more details on specific areas.

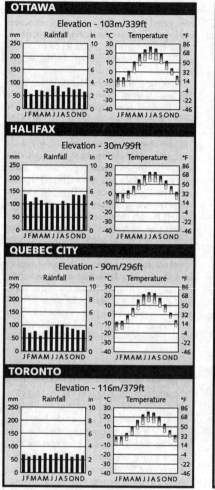

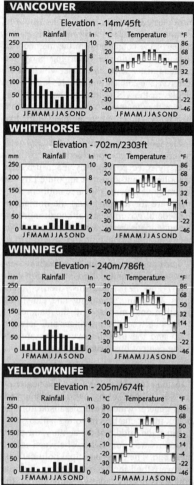

GOVERNMENT & POLITICS

The form of the government of Canada is a constitutional monarchy.

Canada is ruled by a parliamentary system with the head of state officially remaining the monarch of Britain. Within Canada the appointed governor general is the monarch's representative. The upper house, or Senate, also made up of appointees, is deemed to be the house of review regarding any potential legislation. Mostly it acts as a rubber stamp for the wishes of the elected lower house, or House of Commons. Senate reform, or its abolition, is an ongoing debate within the country.

The head of the political party with the most elected representatives in the House of Commons becomes the prime minister, the leader of the country. From the members of parliament within the governing party, the prime minister selects a cabinet which, in effect, runs the country and initiates legislation. Unlike in the USA, leaders can run for as long as they maintain popular support within their party. Governments are elected for five years, but elections can be called earlier.

The 10 provinces are essentially self-governing and are presided over by premiers, elected provincially. Each province has a lieutenant governor appointed by the federal government. The three northern territories are for the most part the domain of the federal government, although more independence is being sought and some has been granted to Nunavut, the eastern part of the Northwest Territories.

The constitution consists of both written proclamations under the Constitution Acts (1867 and 1932) and unwritten conventions. Updating, changing and clarifying constitutional matters and the balance of powers between the provinces and between them and the federal government are ongoing contentious issues.

Political Parties

Canadian voters were 'cranky' upon entering the 90s, as one losing politician lamented. This general widespread dissatisfaction has meant major changes in voting patterns.

Since the middle of the century, the party structure was somewhere between stable and staid. The three principal political parties were the Liberals (who for much of the country's history have virtually owned the reins of power), the Progressive Conservatives (not a lot unlike the Liberals but without the success) and the New Democratic Party (NDP; known by its opponents as the 'socialist menace').

The Progressive Conservatives (Tories) have been voted in every once in a while, apparently as an effort to keep the Liberals (Grits) somewhat humble and honest. The NDP has never formed a federal govern-

ment and always came up third. It has, however, ruled provincially in several provinces and generally accepts its opposition status, considering itself the 'conscience of the nation' keeping socialist-type initiatives on the burners.

After the 1993 Liberal landslide, the situation was altered more than anyone could have foretold. The Conservatives and NDP were close to being wiped off the political map and haven't recovered.

The Reform party based exclusively in the west, and espousing strong right-wing social, economic and political policies has taken over second place and is the Official Opposition. The Bloc Québecois (BQ), the Quebec independence-seeking party, is now ranked third. It has no members outside Quebec.

This line-up makes for a fractious parliament and a Liberal party without a serious threat.

Provincially, the three main parties remain the Liberals, the Progressive Conservatives and the NDP. In British Columbia the Social Credit Party periodically forms a government. The provincial parties generally keep their distance from their federal cousins and act independently from them. The voters,

Patriot Games

Canada's current flag was chosen in 1965 after 2000 public design entries were hotly debated in parliament. The side bars represent the ocean boundaries and are not blue because an important reason for the entire procedure was to show independence from Britain and France. Before the new flag was designed, between 1924 and 1965, the Red Ensign, which included a Union Jack, rippled over the country.

Each province also has its own flag, few of which would be recognised by most Canadians. The white and blue 'fleur de lys' of Quebec is probably an exception.

The national anthem, 'O Canada', was composed by Calixa Lavalée in 1880.

too, treat them differently and have elected the NDP in four provinces since the mid 1980s. The Parti Québecois (PQ), a Quebec provincial party, stresses Quebec rights and fuels the dream of separation.

ECONOMY

Canadians enjoy the high standard of living that major western countries are accustomed to and tend to take for granted. However, income and employment have fallen since the late 1980s so maintaining the wealth experienced by the previous generation is becoming ever more difficult, even elusive. Today nearly half the work force is women and by far the majority of households have two incomes, often by necessity.

The Canadian economy is based, as it always has been, on abundant natural resources. These natural renewable and nonrenewable riches include fish, timber and wood products, minerals, natural gas, oil and hydroelectricity. Although only 5% of the land is arable, the agricultural sector, primarily in wheat and barley, accounts for much of the Canadian export total.

Manufacturing has long been a weak component of the economy and today employs just 14% of the country's workers. The most important manufactured product is motor vehicles. Hi-tech industries and developers in the space and computer fields are playing increasing roles in the economy.

By far the largest part of the economy at a whopping 75% is in services which includes an enormous civil service. Banking, insurance, education, communication and consulting bring in foreign exchange. The rest of the service sector does not.

The country's major trading partner is the USA although business people are increasingly strengthening ties with Japan, China and all of the Pacific Rim. Mexico, too, is poised to become a major trading partner.

The high degree of foreign ownership of Canadian business has also been problematic, drawing profits away from the country. Overall, about 40% of the country's industry is owned by non-Canadians, led by US interests.

Currently unemployment hovers around 9% with regional variations, and the inflation rate is about 2%.

Canada has an immense 'underground economy'. This does not refer simply to various, more or less traditional, criminal activities but the hidden transactions of legitimate businesses done in order to avoid paying tax. Estimates of the extent of this underground economy range to over 20% of the country's internal economic output. This is a staggering amount of taxes going unpaid which means rates have to go up. This means people feel hard done by and so redouble their efforts to avoid paying. The car mechanic offers a tune-up, you offer to fix his plumbing; you stay at my B&B, I'll design you a brochure. The variations are infinite. There are even 'contra' or service-exchange clubs to join. All by word of mouth, of course.

Many transactions are done 'under the table', meaning paid for in cash with no bills, receipts, written guarantees or paperwork generated. Offering to pay cash usually results in a lower price as well as the tax saving.

POPULATION & PEOPLE

Canada's population is about 30.3 million (1998). About 35% of Canadians are of British stock. French descendants of the original pioneers long made up about 30% of the population but this now approaches 20% and continues to fall. By far the majority of people of French descent live in Quebec but there are large numbers in New Brunswick, Ontario and Manitoba.

The English-speaking population has grown mainly by immigration from Britain and the USA. Over 3.5 million Canadians are of Scottish or Irish ancestry.

Generally speaking, the French are Catholic, the British Protestant, but religion does not play a large part in Canadian life.

Early central and eastern European settlers went to the prairies but can now be found everywhere, particularly in the large cities. Canada's third largest ancestral ethnic group is German. Other major groups are Italian,

The Best Known Canadian of Them All

It's not a politician. Not an astronaut. Nor the discoverer of insulin. Not even a singer or a hockey star. The best known, most recognisable, most watched Canuck is Pamela Anderson (Lee), blonde bombshell, gracer of Playboy covers and feature of Baywatch reruns around the world. From Italy to India, fans can't get enough of her films, the latest news on her breast implants or relationship misadventures with Motley Crue rock musician Tommy Lee. Despite fame, if not glory, her too honest, self-deprecating reported quotes such as 'It's not like I'm a great actress or anything' indicate that the essential Canadian character remains intact.

By some accounts, her name has become the most significant on the Internet. It's used like a brand name, such as Coke, to attract surfers to Web sites, regardless of what product or service is being sold. On the Alta Vista search engine, Ms Lee gets 9000 hits a day. Reports indicate that there are 145,000 pages on the Net citing Pamela – including everything from dubious marketers to building supply companies. Now, that's a lot of drawing power. And with it, she's become the first cyber superstar.

Chinese, Ukrainian, Dutch, Greek, Polish and Scandinavian. In 1997, Chinese surpassed Italian as the third most common tongue in Canada. Since 1990, other Asians, and to a lesser degree, Latin Americans and blacks from the Caribbean have been immigrating in larger numbers. Four out of five immigrants have neither English nor French as their mother tongue. Canada also receives refugees from around the world. Unlike the early days of rapid expansion and settlement, today's arrivals head for the large cities. Toronto, the centre for international immigration, is one of the most cosmopolitan cities in the world.

Aboriginal Peoples

These now number about 470,000 Native Indians and 31,000 Inuit, vastly more than when Europeans first arrived. There are also about 450,000 Métis, the name used to denote those of mixed aboriginal and European blood. All together the three groups make up about 4% of Canada's total population. The majority are found in the Yukon, Northwest Territories and Ontario but every province has some aboriginal communities.

Inuit is the general name for the Eskimo peoples in Canada. This is their preferred name, as it distinguishes them from the Eskimo of Asia or the Aleuts of the Aleutian Islands.

Collectively the Indians, Inuit and Métis are also called Native Canadians. Another term which has gained currency is 'First Nations' which recognises the one-time independent status of individual aboriginal groups.

Since the early pioneering days the Native Indians' lot has been marked by sadness and tragedy. At first their numbers dropped dramatically with the influx of European diseases. Then they lost not only their power and traditions but also their land and eventually, in many cases, their self-respect.

There are about 2250 reserves scattered across Canada and 600 government registered Native Indian 'bands' which has become a political and organisational term. Every Native Indian is officially affiliated with a band. Some bands can own more than one reserve.

Over 70% of Native Indians live on these government reserves, most in poverty and on some form of government assistance. In the cities, with little education and few modern skills, many end up on the streets without a job or a place to live. Infant mortality, life expectancy, literacy, income and incarceration rates all compare unfavourably with those of other Canadians.

Native Indian leaders have, since the early 1980s, become more political, making

stands on constitutional matters, land claims and mineral rights. A range of national organisations such as the Assembly of First Nations keeps Native Indian interests from being pushed aside. It is through these channels, however slow-moving, that the Native Indian voice will make the changes it feels necessary. Most Canadians now feel the aboriginal peoples have had a raw deal and sympathise with many of their complaints.

This, however, has not so far resulted in the introduction of many concrete attempts to improve the situation. Increasingly, ugly, highly-publicised and potentially deadly confrontations have arisen across the country. Each summer Native Indian roadblocks and armed camps have erupted and disrupted the status quo. Accordingly, both provincial and federal governments are finding it less and less possible to ignore the state of affairs, and many issues regarding Native Indian rights and claims are currently before the courts. Among the issues to be dealt with is some form of self-government for aboriginal peoples. Native Indian schools to provide control over religious and language instruction and a Native Indian justice system are being discussed and slowly implemented on a district by district basis. Fishing and hunting rights and taxation are other debated subjects. Native Indians have also become more active in revitalisation movements which encourage original spirituality, culture, language and a respect for their history. Celebratory pow-wows, to which non-Native Indians are welcome, are now a regular cultural occurrence.

Note In North America, Indians from the Asian subcontinent are often called East Indians in order to distinguish them from the indigenous peoples. People from the Caribbean countries are sometimes referred to as West Indians.

EDUCATION

Under the jurisdiction of the provinces, Canada provides free education from elementary through to secondary school. Beyond that tuition must be paid in what are known as community colleges (CÉGEPS in Quebec) and universities, although the true cost is subsidised through taxes. Community colleges present one to three-year programs in a range of fields from graphic design to jewellery-making to nursing. These are taught under the broad categories of Arts, Business, Science and Technology, and Health Services. Universities provide higher academic and professional training.

At the early levels, there are two basic school systems, known as the public and the separate. Both are free and essentially the same but the latter is designed for Catholics and offers more religious education along with the three 'Rs'. Anyone can join either one but the two systems do split pretty much along religious denomination.

French-immersion programs, in which English-speaking children are taught all their courses in French, are quite popular across Canada.

There are also a number of private schools but no real private system. Schools in this category include alternative educational methods such as Waldorf and Montessori.

The education system has been under constant scrutiny in recent years. Many students leaving high school have fared poorly in international testing, have been called essentially illiterate by universities and, according to business leaders, are poorly prepared for jobs in industry.

In order to combat these shortcomings, a re-emphasis has been placed on the fundamentals and on standardised curriculums and testing.

Not quite half of all Canadians finish high school. About 10% have a university degree. Students from around the world attend Canadian universities.

ARTS
Literature

Canada has produced an impressive body of writing. Most of it has appeared since the 1940s.

Among the best known, most read poets are EJ Pratt, Earle Birney, Gwendolyn McEwen, Irving Layton, Leonard Cohen

From the Push-Up Bra to Instant Mashed Potato

If the push-up bra, Trivial Pursuit and instant mashed potato represent the ephemeral side of Canadian invention then insulin, Greenpeace and the paint roller must surely be of more enduring value.

Canadians can lay claim to quite an assortment of the products of human ingenuity, most of them worthwhile. The Native Indians have given the world snowshoes and the birch-bark canoe; the Inuit developed the winter parka and accompanying boots known as mukluks, and the kayak. More recent Canadian inventions include the electron microscope and the manipulable space arm used on the US space shuttle.

Canadians have been active in the food arena, too. Important research developed strains of wheat suitable to a variety of world climates. Pablum, a baby cereal, was created in Canada. The country's most important, best known fruit, the MacIntosh apple, comes from a wild apple tree found in Ontario which was reproduced through grafting. The chocolate bar was created by Ganong Brothers Ltd, which still produces bars and chocolates in St Stephen, New Brunswick. Canada Dry Ginger Ale is found throughout the world.

Other firsts include the paint roller (a simple yet great little device), the wireless photograph transmitter, the friction match, the chainsaw and the snowmobile. To clear snow, the rotating snowplough was created in 1911, and 10 years later the snowblower was devised.

Canadians have pioneered the development of short take-off and landing aircraft. For trains the observation car, known as the dome car, was designed in Canada.

The use of calcium carbide-acetylene gas for light was discovered by Canadian Thomas Wilson. It replaced kerosene, another Canadian invention, and led to the formation of the giant Union Carbide Company. Standard Time, adopted around the world, was devised in Canada.

In addition to the push-up bra, created by Canadelle in Montreal in 1963, Canada can also lay claim to the all-important clothes zipper.

Insulin was discovered by Banting and Best in 1921. Cobalt, the radiation source stronger than x-rays which is used to treat cancer around the world, was developed in Canada.

The first battery-less radio was invented in Canada in 1925. The first all-electric, battery-less radio station followed two years later, in Toronto; called CFRB, it's still transmitting and to this day is the most listened to in the country. IMAX large format films and technology were developed by a Canadian company.

Greenpeace, one of the world's predominant environmental groups, was founded in Vancouver. On the other hand, the green plastic garbage bag was also created in Canada.

Two Canadians devised that classic of the 1980s, Trivial Pursuit, a board game which swept the world, outselling even Monopoly. Over 50 million games have been sold.

The inexpensive Laser sailboat, popular around the globe, was designed by Canadians. Ice hockey was developed in the mid-1800s. And, to the chagrin of the country's US friends, it should be noted that the game of basketball was created by a Canadian.

The snowmobile is one of many Canadian firsts.

(who also wrote the less-known novels *Beautiful Losers* and *The Favourite Game*), bp Nichol for concrete poetry, Milton Acorn and Al Purdy. One of the world's favourite poems, the straight forward but poignant *In Flanders Fields* was written by Canadian soldier John McCrae in 1915.

Perhaps more familiar internationally are short-story and novel writers such as Margaret Atwood (equally famous as a poet), Morley Callaghan, Robertson Davies, Marion Engel, Timothy Findley, Margaret Laurence, WO Mitchell, Alice Munro, Michael Ondaatje, Mordecai Richler and Rudy Wiebe.

Who has Seen the Wind, WO Mitchell's best known book, is about a boy growing up in Weyburn, Saskatchewan, the birthplace of the author.

Humorist Stephen Leacock's *Sketches of a Little Town*, based on Orillia (a town at the north end of Lake Simcoe in Ontario), has been called the most Canadian book ever written.

Douglas Coupland in *Generation X*, *Shampoo Planet* and *Life After God* writes about the world of those in their 20s and 30s. William Gibson in work such as *Neuromancer* and *Count Zero* has a futuristic 'cyberpunk' perspective. His story, *Johnny Mnemonic*, was made into a Canadian film in 1995. WP Kinsella writes of contemporary Native Indian life as well as baseball and is best known for *Shoeless Joe*, which was made into the film *Field of Dreams* with Kevin Costner. *Dance Me Outside* was made into a feature length film with a Native Indian cast. Brian Moore's *Black Robe* is about Native Indian-European relations in the 17th century and has been filmed too. Rohinton Mistry has been heaped with international praise for his novels *Such a Long Journey* and *A Fine Balance*. Nino Ricci's excellent books, including *Lives of the Saints*, deal partially with being an immigrant in Canada. Also from the 1990s, Carol Shields' *The Stone Diaries* was another prize winner. Elizabeth Smart's *By Grand Central Station I Sat Down and Wept* is slight in size, powerful in impact.

Canada seems to produce writers who excel in the short story so an anthology of these would make a good introduction to Canadian fiction. For a short-story collection, try one of the anthologies published annually by Oberon Press or by Penguin.

English writer Malcolm Lowry spent most of his productive writing years in British Columbia, many of them in a basic shack on the beach near Vancouver.

French Quebec writers who are widely read in English include Anne Hebert, Marie-Claire Blais, Roch Carrier, Mavis Gallant and Gabrielle Roy. Extremely reclusive novelist Réjean Ducharme of Montreal is considered one of the major French language writers. His latest book is *Va Savoir*.

Two Native Indian writers are George Clutesi and Markoosie. The stories in Eden Robinson's *Trapline's* lay bare the realities of reserve life.

Most good bookstores have a Canadiana section with both fiction and nonfiction works. Two publishers specialising in Canadian fiction are Oberon and House of Anansi. McClelland & Stewart is an important, large Canadian publishing house.

For more information, consult *The Oxford Companion to Canadian Literature*.

Music

Canadian musicians have become increasingly and deservedly well known in the past few decades with many achieving international stature. The country has always tended to produce individualistic musicians who emphasise lyrics and personal sentiments. Many of the most established names have found it necessary to temporarily or permanently establish residency in the USA.

Canadian women once again hauled home a lot of shiny hardware from the 1999 Grammy music awards in Hollywood. Alanis Morisette from Ottawa bagged two, including best rock song for *Uninvited* from the movie *City of Angels*. Shania Twain, originally from Timmins, Ontario, scooped up two in the country music category. *You're Still the One* took best country song. Celine Dion, from

Native Indian Literature

One of the most exciting developments in Canadian literature is the increasing voice of Native Indian writers. Born from a need to tell the bloody colonial truth (it's not all log cabins and costumed workers) and a desire to share and celebrate the wealth of their own cultures, Native Indian work produced since the 1980s or so includes some powerful and challenging novels, stories, plays and poetry. It's literature that breaks new ground and old rules, much of it drawing from the rich Native Indian tradition of oral storytelling.

Some particularly strong work is being produced by women. Written initially as a letter to herself, Maria Campbell's autobiography *Halfbreed* was published in 1973 and became a best seller. Like other Native Indian writers, Campbell emphasises the need for authors to reclaim their own language. Many writers are angered at the appropriation of Native Indian stories by European authors. After having their land taken and their culture undermined, many saw the 'stealing' of their own stories as the last straw – the irony being that it is non-Native Indians who need those stories and the values they speak of the most.

The struggle for Native Indian self-determination was explored by Jeannette Armstrong in her internationally acclaimed novel *Slash*, published in 1985. Also successful was Beatrice Culleton's 1983 novel *In Search of April Raintree*, about the lives of two Métis girls. Another recommended novel is Ruby Slipperjack's *Honour the Sun*. Published in 1987, it charts the development of a young girl growing up in an isolated, fractured community. In 1992 she published *Silent Words*.

Thompson Highway has also been internationally recognised for his two very successful plays *The Rez Sisters* and *Dry Lips Oughta Move to Kapuskasing*. Though Highway, who sees theatre as a natural extension of the storytelling medium, is perhaps the most widely known Native Indian playwright, he is just one of many working across the country. In 1998 his first novel, *Kiss of the Fur Queen*, appeared. Ian Ross won the governor general's award for his play *FareWel*, which played in Toronto in 1998.

In 1996, Richard Van Kamp's *The Lesser Blessed* became the first Native novel written in the Northwest Territories.

Recent years have seen the publication of a number of excellent poetry and short story anthologies, too. *Achimoona*, published in 1985, contains short fiction by younger Native Indian writers. *All My Relations*, published in 1990, is a large collection of short stories edited by the writer Thomas King. The anthology *Seventh Generation*, edited by Heather Hodgson and published in 1989, contains a collection of contemporary Native Indian poetry.

Montreal, keeps rolling along with *My Heart Will Go On* from the movie *Titanic* winning Record of the Year and Female Pop Vocal Performance accolades.

Canadians have perhaps been best known in the field of folk and folk rock. Among the top names are Leonard Cohen, Bruce Cockburn, Gordon Lightfoot, Joni Mitchell, Stompin' Tom and Neil Young. In more of a country vein there are Patricia Conroy, George Fox, kd lang, Anne Murray, Prairie Oyster, Rita McNeil, and Ian and/or Sylvia Tyson.

Sort of between the two categories and current are Jann Arden, the Barenaked Ladies, Holly Cole, Blue Rodeo, the Cowboy Junkies, Kate & Anna McGarrigle and Sarah McLachlan.

In rock, big names include Brian Adams, Tom Cochrane, Amanda Marshall, Allanah Myles, Kim Mitchell, Our Lady Peace and The Tragically Hip.

continued on page 49

CANADA'S FLORA, FAUNA, GOVERNMENT PARKS & HERITAGE SITES

FLORA & FAUNA

FLORA

Canada's vegetation is considered young. Except for the west coast, the entire country was under ice 15,000 years ago making the forests across the country relatively new.

Canada comprises eight vegetation zones.

In the far north is the **Arctic tundra**. This area, north of the tree-line, contains essentially no trees or shrubs. In this mostly flat, barren, rocky region the most common plants are lichens and briefly blooming small wildflowers.

South of the tundra is the **boreal (northern) forest**, the largest vegetative zone, and perhaps the most typical, best known physical representation of Canada. By far the dominant vegetation of the country is forest and the boreal forest makes up the majority of all the woodlands. Within the vast, largely undeveloped boreal forest which stretches across the country the dominant tree species are the white and black spruce. In the east, balsam fir and jack pine are also common, in the west, alpine fir and lodgepole pine.

In the east, the **Great Lakes-St Lawrence River forest zone** is found south of the boreal forest. This forest is a mix of the more northerly coniferous (evergreen, softwood) trees and the deciduous (broadleaf, hardwood) trees more common in the southern portions of the country. In this region are the pines including the majestic white pine and spruces but also the maples, oaks, birches and others which supply the famous colours of Canadian autumns.

The sugar maple is one of Canada's best known symbols and the leaf appears on the country's flag. The sugar maples also produce edible maple syrup, a Canadian speciality worth sampling. In the southernmost areas there are walnut, hickory and beech trees as well as fruit trees.

The fourth region, the **Acadian forest** of New Brunswick, Prince Edward Island and Nova Scotia, is made up of red spruce, balsam fir, maple, yellow birch and some pine. It is not unlike the Great Lakes forest.

The **parkland zone** is the area between the eastern forests and the western prairies which begin in Manitoba. Trembling aspen is the dominant tree in this area.

NICHOLAS REUSS

Saxifrage flowering in tundra

G TAYLER

St Lawrence Islands National Park, Ontario

THOMAS HUHTI

Forest foliage in Fundy National Park, NB

PATRICK HORTON

Canola field, Alberta

COLLEEN KENNEDY

Fragrant water lily, Ontario

COLLEEN KENNEDY

Trillium, the provincial flower of Ontario

Manitoba, Saskatchewan and Alberta are best known for their flat **prairie grasslands**, the sixth zone, now mostly covered in cultivated grains. The grasslands once contained short, mixed and tall grass regions but these have all but disappeared. There are now protected pockets of native grasslands which can be visited, some of which are listed in the provincial chapters. Within these areas willow and aspen also grow.

British Columbia contains a richer variety of vegetation than elsewhere and also some of the country's most impressive flora. The **Rocky Mountain forest** consists of sub-alpine species such as Engelman spruce, alpine fir and larches. In areas of higher elevation there are lodgepole pine and aspen. Scattered around south-east BC, forests also contain some of the species found at the coast but here they do not attain the dramatic size seen farther west.

It is around the coastal areas though, in the **Pacific Coast forest**, that the truly awesome trees of the country may be seen. This last vegetation area is characterised by the ancient, gigantic western red cedar, Douglas fir, western hemlock and Sitka spruce. These are the forests which inspire the major environmentalist battles against the logging industry. These west-coast forests are the oldest in the country with some individual trees over 1000 years old.

Among the country's countless **wildflowers**, just a few favourites and commonly seen ones are mentioned here. For those with a keen interest, guidebooks are available.

Throughout the east, canoeists will appreciate the fragrant water lily, a large white flower with yellow centre surrounded by rounded flat leaves which sit on the water.

The trillium, the provincial flower of Ontario, is one of the most popular of wildflowers. Trilliums bloom in spring in shaded areas of the Ontario and Quebec woods, their large white or pink flowers often nearly carpeting whole sections of the forest floor. They grow about 20cm high and have three distinct petals.

The pitcher plant – seen from Saskatchewan to Newfoundland and Labrador in bogs – is carnivorous (ie it feeds on insects). The leaves collect rainwater. Insects are attracted to the plant by its purplish-red colour and odour. They fall down the slippery leaves

into the water where they drown and the plant then digests them. Even with all the protein the pitcher plant does not grow much taller than the length of an adult's hand.

The pickerel weed, with its deep-blue, purplish spiked flower and narrow, long, green leaves, grows around ponds and shallow streams from Ontario to Nova Scotia.

Loosestrife is a beautiful waist-high bright pinky purple plant seen along roadsides and in ditches and marshes across the country. Now considered a nuisance weed because of its rapid growth and spread which crowds out other native aquatic plants, it was once sold as a garden ornamental. Across the Maritimes the lupine (blue, pink or somewhere in between) grows wild in fields and by the roadsides.

Sea blush cast a pink glow over the rocks along the southern west coast in spring. Even the early explorers wrote about their beauty as they travelled the Strait of Juan de Fuca.

The bright-red, common Indian paintbrush supplies wonderful contrast to the blues and greys of the Rocky Mountains.

Those with a keen eye who enjoy the less travelled forest paths anywhere in the country may glimpse the Indian pipe or ghostly pipe. This uncommon plant forces its way up through the debris of the forest floor in shady moist areas. It is a ghostly, silvery white with no greenery and no coloured flowers. It grows about as long as a finger, with the top part nodding over (as in the shape of a pipe) when in bloom.

A delicious assortment of wild berries can be picked across the country. Blueberries are the most common and abundant. The blessed may happen upon a patch of wild raspberries, one of life's exalted moments. The forests, meadows and marsh areas all have plenty of other edible plants and mushrooms. They also have plenty of poisonous plants and mushrooms. Telling the difference is difficult at times even with years of experience and a good book. If in any doubt at all, don't take a chance. Some species can be fatal.

Less deadly but more irritating is the three-leaved but difficult to identify poison ivy found in wooded southern regions of the country. A brush against this small, nondescript plant will result in a skin reaction causing blisters and a very maddening itch.

Purple loosestrife, Ontario

Lupines, PEI

Wildflowers, Dinosaur PP, Alberta

FAUNA

Canada, with so much land and much of it relatively remote, has abundant wildlife yet conservation is an ongoing necessity. Campers and hikers can see a number of different animals in the wild. The following are some of the most interesting and/or most common:

Bears

These are Canada's largest and most dangerous animals. They are widely dispersed, and as there are four major types, most of the country is populated with at least one kind. For detailed information on the hazards of bears, see Dangers & Annoyances in the Facts for the Visitor chapter.

W LYNCH

Grizzly Bear, Glacier NP, BC

Grizzly Bear This is the most notorious bear and is found on the higher slopes of the Rocky and Selkirk mountains of British Columbia, Alberta and the Yukon. The grizzly is big – standing up to 275cm high. It can be recognised by the white ends of its brownish hair and the hump on the back behind its neck. It can't see well but makes up for that with its excellent senses of smell and hearing. To make matters worse, it's a very fast animal. The best thing about a grizzly is that it can't climb trees. Like other bears, it is normally afraid of people but can be unpredictable and is easily provoked.

Brown Bear Actually a black bear but brown in colour, the mostly nocturnal brown bear is found mainly in British Columbia, Alberta and the Yukon. Not to be confused with the brown bear of Europe and Asia which is closely related to the grizzly.

T W HALL

Black Bear, Banff NP, Alberta

Black Bear The most common of bears, the black is found all across Canada and is the one you'll most likely spot. The black bear often mooches around campgrounds, cottages and garbage dumps. It is usually less than 150cm high at the shoulders and 90kg in weight. It's active during the day and can climb trees.

Polar Bear The polar bear is very large – up to 680kg – with thick, white-ish fur. It is found only in the extreme north but can be viewed in Churchill, Manitoba and in zoos. A majestic animal, it is graceful in the water despite its size and apparent awkwardness. Due to hunting, it is now a protected animal.

Beaver

One of Canada's symbols, the beaver is an animal known for its industriousness, hence the expression 'busy as a beaver'. Found all across Canada, it is usually seen in the early morning or early evening paddling across a stream or lake with its head just above water. It chews down trees for food and for material with which to build its home. This home, a lodge, looks like a rounded pile of mud and sticks and is located in streams and ponds dammed off by the beaver.

Buffalo/Bison

The buffalo now exists only in government parks. It is a huge, heavy-shouldered, shaggy herbivore that once roamed the prairies in vast herds. Its near-extinction has become symbolic of the Europeans' effect on North American Indians and their environment. Technically, Canadian buffalo are bison, and there are two species, woodland and plains. Bison are now raised for their meat which occasionally shows up on menus.

Wolf

The wolf looks like a large, silver-grey dog. Its ferocious reputation is more misconception than fact. Hunting has pretty well banished this animal from the southern populated regions, but you may hear the wolf's howl late at night if you're in the bush. It usually hunts in packs and rarely harms humans.

Coyote

More widespread than the wolf, the coyote is smaller and more timid, with an eerie howl or series of yaps used for communicating. It is more scavenger than hunter and is sometimes the victim of massive poison-bait campaigns by western ranchers and farmers.

NICHOLAS REUSS

Polar Bear, Baffin Bay, Nunavut

W LYNCH

Bison, Wood Buffalo NP, Alberta

MARK LIGHTBODY

Young moose in the Yukon

W LYNCH

Caribou, Churchill, Manitoba

Deer

Various types of deer are plentiful in the woodlands of Canada, ranging across the entire width of the country. They are quiet and timid and the object of much hunting.

Moose This is one of the largest animals and again, a popular target for hunters. The moose is found in woods and forests all across Canada, particularly around swamps. Moose are, for the most part, a more northerly ranging animal than deer. They have large, thick antlers and are brown.

The moose is reclusive, generally solitary, and may be seen swimming to escape biting bugs. The male bellows in October and November in its search for a mate. At that time, their behaviour can be erratic and the normally timid moose can become aggressive. Both deer and moose can be road hazards, especially at night. Watch for them and the roadside signs warning of their presence.

Caribou The barren-ground caribou live in herds in the far north and are still used by some Inuit for food and for their hides. Their numbers are now carefully monitored as over-hunting and radioactive fallout from Chernobyl have affected them.

A full herd on its seasonal migration is said to be a wondrous sight. There are some small groups of woodland caribou in more southern areas such as the Gaspé Peninsula of Quebec and the Lake Superior region of Ontario. A close relative of the North American caribou is the reindeer found in Europe and Asia.

Elk The elk, a cousin of the European red deer, is also called the wapiti. They can be seen around the Rocky Mountains. They are striking animals and can appear quite tame often allowing visitors to approach for picture taking. This is not recommended as people have been attacked in either the rutting or calving seasons.

Rocky Mountain Goat

This goat is as close as you'll get to an all-Canadian animal. Found in British Columbia and the Yukon, it

MARK LIGHTBODY

Elk, Rocky Mountains, Alberta

is white and hairy, has horns and looks like an old man. Around populated areas it is quite tame. Generally though, it prefers the higher, more remote mountain regions. Part of its dietary intake is clay which aids its digestive system, and you might see one pawing at the ground and gobbling up clumps of earth.

Lynx

Another nearly exclusively Canadian animal, the lynx is a grey cat about 90cm long and found all across the undeveloped Canadian woodlands. It has a furry trim around its face and sharp pointed ears. The mainly nocturnal cat eats small animals. Although rarely seen, humans are its main enemy, largely by destroying its habitat.

Cougar

Larger, rarer and even less often seen than the lynx is the majestic cougar. Found in the forests of the west coast, it is a mostly nocturnal hunter and its favoured prey is the Columbian blacktail deer. Its numbers are increasing on Vancouver Island.

Skunk

The skunk resembles a large black cat but has a white stripe down its back and a big, bushy tail. It is seen everywhere – in woods, in larger city parks, even in residential suburbs and their household garbage. It's dangerous only in that its defence mechanism is the spraying out of the foulest, longest lasting, clothes-clinging smell you can imagine. The cure is a bath in tomato juice. Watch out!

Porcupine

A curious animal about 90cm long, the porcupine weighs 18kg. It is grey, lives in the woods across Canada and feeds mainly on bark and tree buds. Its protection from abuse are its hollow, barbed quills projecting from its body like long hair, which are easily dislodged, as many a dog will remember.

Mountain Goat, Rocky Mountains

MARK LIGHTBODY

Cougar, Yoho National Park, BC

W LYNCH

Porcupine

MARK LIGHTBODY

Birds

Five hundred species have been spotted in Canada but many of them are quite rare. One of the most notable among the feathered residents is the loon, a water bird with a mournful yet beautiful call which is often heard on the quieter lakes across the country in early morning or evening. It is most abundant in northern Ontario.

The great blue heron, one of the country's largest birds, is a wonder to see when it takes off. Seen in quiet marsh areas it is very timid, taking to flight at the least provocation.

Canada geese are seen across the country, especially during their spring and fall migration when the large V-shaped formations are not an unusual sight in the sky. Big, black and grey, these so-called honkers can be aggressive.

There are many species of duck, the mallard being the most common, the wood duck the most attractive and colourful. The whisky jack or grey jay, found mainly in the Rockies, is a fluffy, friendly and commonly seen bird that will eat out of your hand. Bald eagles and ospreys are large, impressive birds of prey. Owls may be seen or heard in wooded areas across the country. Sparrows are the most common garden songbirds. Finches, blue jays, chickadees and cardinals are also readily viewed and/or heard.

Around the coasts there is a very interesting array of marine birdlife including puffins and razorbills.

Whales & Seals

Whale watching is an inspiring, popular and successful commercial enterprise. A number of different species can be seen off the coast in British Columbia, in the St Lawrence River in Quebec, and in the Atlantic Ocean off the country's east coast. More details can be found in the text.

In the Atlantic Provinces the bloody, annual seal hunt (for pelts, boots, coats etc) diminished following the European Union's ban on imports. Indeed, tourists with the money can now fly out to the east-coast ice floes to see, touch and photograph the new-born calves.

J R GRAHAM
Scarlet tanger, Point Pelee NP, Ontario

W LYNCH
Arctic tern, Aulavik NP, NWT

MARK LIGHTBODY
Whale watching at Tadoussac, Quebec

Fish

Northern pike, bass, walleye and various trout varieties are the most common freshwater fish. There are several species of Pacific salmon which are prolific on the west coast. In the Atlantic Provinces and Quebec the Atlantic salmon is a highly sought after species. Arctic char, found only in the far north (and on some southern menus), is also fine eating. Fishing is a popular Canadian pastime and also attracts visitors in large numbers.

Off the coasts there is deep-sea fishing for both sport and table species.

Bearded seal

GOVERNMENT PARKS & HERITAGE SITES

Canada has 37 **national parks**, which have been developed to protect, preserve and make accessible a unique, special or otherwise interesting and significant environment. All of them are well worth visiting. Plans are to complete the system with 15 more. They are managed under a federal ministry department called Canadian Heritage-Parks Canada. Its office (☎ 819-997-0055) is at Room 10H2, 25 Eddy St, Hull, Quebec K1A 0M5. It doesn't provide much public information but does produce a free map brochure indicating where the parks are and giving their mailing addresses. This can be obtained by contacting the office. Further information can then be had by contacting the specific parks of interest.

Most parks have camping facilities. Several are close to major population centres and are heavily used, others are more remote and offer good wilderness opportunities. Many manage to combine both characteristics.

Some parks rent canoes and/or rowing boats. In parks with numerous lakes and rivers, a canoe is ideal; you can portage to different lakes. At other parks, bicycles may be rented. Many have established walking or longer hiking trails. The towns of Banff and Jasper are within the boundaries of the mountain parks of the same names.

Entrance fees to national parks vary from park to park and from nil to several dollars. Some offer free day-

Pukaskwa National Park, Ontario

Cape Breton Island, Nova Scotia

York Factory, National Historic Site, Man

Mont Tremblant Provincial Park, Quebec

use but charge, as they all do, for overnight camping. Some such as Cape Breton and the Rocky Mountain Parks have daily, multi-day and yearly permits. The latter type is good for any park in the system.

In addition to national parks, the system contains 750 **National Historic Sites** with 131 of special note being administered by the government. These are for 'day-use only' and present various aspects of Canadian history including forts, pioneer homesteads and battle sites. There are also seven nationally designated **Heritage Canals** and over two dozen **Heritage Rivers**.

For information on all the above contact Canadian Heritage-Parks Canada as listed. It also has offices in some cities such as Toronto.

For more information on the national and provincial parks, see Camping under Accommodation in the Facts for the Visitor chapter.

For Internet information check the site at www.parks canada.pch.gc.ca.

Provincial Parks

Each province runs its own system of parks and reserves. These can vary dramatically in size, accessibility, characteristics and main purpose. Some are developed for recreation, others to preserve something of historical interest, still others to protect wildlife or natural geographic features of particular beauty or uniqueness. They are much more numerous than national parks, with Ontario, for example, having 270.

Some provincial parks provide camping and other conveniences. In many provinces day-use is free and admission is charged only for those staying overnight. Most parks have knowledgeable staff who will answer questions and offer lectures, walks and other presentations. Some parks have a biologist or a naturalist on duty.

Provincial tourist boards and offices have free material available which provides some information on the parks under their jurisdiction. These outline camping facilities and basic features of the parks.

There is also a series of provincial historic sites across the country. These tend to be small and are meant, for the most part, to be visited for anywhere from a half-hour up to half a day.

Territorial Parks

The parks in the territories tend to be small, simple and inexpensive to visit. They are often best used for overnight camping although facilities may be minimal.

Crown Land, Reserves & Other Recreation Areas

Undeveloped crown land (government-owned land) can be used for hiking, canoeing and camping at no cost. Some national or provincial parks are adjacent to crown lands. Some crown land areas do have basic camp sites carved out of the woods or lake edges and/or portage routes and hiking paths.

Provincial nature reserves and designated wilderness areas can also generally be used by those seeking wilderness experiences. A careful scanning of provincial maps will often reveal some of these areas.

The BC Ministry of Forests produces a *Recreation Guide* and an excellent series of Forest District maps covering much of the province not part of any park system. Visitors are welcome to use these undeveloped areas. Information can be obtained at regional tourist offices.

Local people will be able to help with advice and access information. Be well equipped and be especially careful with fire when enjoying these undeveloped areas.

United Nations World Heritage Sites

In a world of ever increasing population and development, the permanent setting aside of specific areas around the world for international protection and appreciation by humankind is particularly timely and politically noble. In 1972 the UN's United Nations Educational, Scientific and Cultural Organisation (UNESCO) adopted The Convention Concerning the Protection of the World Cultural and Natural Heritage. Its mandate, signed by over 130 countries, is to identify and then help preserve the world's most valuable, unique and special cultural and natural wonders. Given growing threats of pollution, commercialisation, even tourism, UNESCO's intention is to help maintain the original characteristics and integrity of the designated areas through educational, technical and financial assistance.

Georgian Bay Islands National Park, Ont

Boya Lake Provincial Park, BC

Hattie Cove, Pukaskwa National Park, Ont

L'Anse-aux-Meadows, Newfoundland

Its work, it is hoped, will never end. To date, it has selected over 400 sites in more than 80 countries. They include America's Grand Canyon, Australia's Uluru (Ayers Rock), Ecuador's Galapagos Islands, England's Stonehenge and India's Taj Mahal. Canada is one of the 21 member representatives on the World Heritage Committee.

Canada has 12 sites designated by the World Heritage Convention. Of the eight of these that are natural, all are either national or provincial parks. They are: Gros Morne National Park, Wood Buffalo National Park, Dinosaur Provincial Park, Head-Smashed-In Buffalo Jump, Waterton Lakes National Park, Rocky Mountain National Parks, Kluane National Park and Nahanni National Park.

Four sites involve human endeavour: Quebec City, a European-style gem; L'Anse aux Meadows in Newfoundland, a 1000-year-old Viking camp; the seaside colonial town of Lunenburg, Nova Scotia; and Anthony Island with the historic Haida Indian settlement of Ninstints. This last is part of Gwaii Haanas National Park, on the Queen Charlotte Islands in British Columbia, which also has outstanding natural features. All are definitely worth visiting.

The entire central downtown core of **Quebec City** has been made a Heritage Site. The old part of town is the only walled city in North America. Within the stone ramparts, fortifications, churches, houses and countless original buildings preserve the development of the city from the 17th century. The future of Canada was decided here during the British-French colonial period. It's essentially a vibrant, living museum attractively situated overlooking the St Lawrence River.

L'Anse aux Meadows at the tip of Newfoundland's Northern Peninsula is a 1000-year-old Viking settlement. This is the oldest European habitation site in North America. There is evidence that they weren't newcomers though, that the site was occupied 4000 years before that by Archaic People. It's a wonderfully low key national park set at the edge of the Strait of Belle Isle across from Labrador in a rough, rocky northern environment. It doesn't look much different than when the Norse sailors first arrived. Some reconstruction brings the site alive.

Farther south but along the same road is **Gros Morne National Park**. It is scenically majestic with

mountains and fjords but qualifies for its outstanding scientifically valuable geographic characteristics. These include major evidence of plate tectonics and glaciation – the creation of the surface of the earth, in other words. There are barren lands, sandy beaches, wildlife and ancient human history to discover within its borders.

Lunenburg's hilly historic streets edge back from a protective harbour on Nova Scotia's jagged south shore. The old, central district was designated primarily for its largely unchanged character typifying an 18th century British colonial town. Lunenburg's tradition of wood-construction architecture has been maintained since the 1750s. In addition to the rows of fine homes, there are five central churches of note including Canada's oldest Presbyterian, dating from 1754, and the country's second oldest Anglican.

Aside from its well preserved architectural heritage, Lunenburg is the base for Atlantic Canada's largest deep-sea trawler fleet and home to the biggest fish-processing plant. It has also kept intact its shipbuilding reputation confirmed with the launching of the famous racing schooner *Bluenose* in 1921 and bolstered with its successor, *Bluenose II*, from the same yards in 1963.

In Alberta, way up north along the border with the Northwest Territories, is immense **Wood Buffalo National Park**, one of the world's largest parks. This wild, 45,000 sq km reserve is a critical wildlife habitat. It contains about 4000 bison – the world's largest, free-roaming herd. It is also the planet's only nesting site for the rare, endangered whooping crane. The subarctic mix of bog, forest, caves, and salt plains is home to thousands of waterfowl and a range of northern mammals and birds. The delta of the Peace and Athabaska rivers is among the world's largest inland deltas. This is a park on the grandest of scales.

Set on the floor of an ancient, tropical ocean, **Dinosaur Provincial Park** in eastern Alberta is virtually unrecognisable as part of Canada. The bizarre, convoluted, eroded terrain in dusty shades of ochre, sienna and brown contain secrets sunken and lost 75 million years past. Here in the glacially-sculpted badlands of the Red Deer River Valley is an unparalleled source of dinosaur fossils. Dozens of major museums around the world display specimens unearthed in this

Gros Morne National Park, Newfoundland

MARK LIGHTBODY

Dinosaur Provincial Park, Alberta

COLLEEN KENNEDY

MARK LIGHTBODY

Head-Smashed-In Buffalo Jump, Alberta

MARK LIGHTBODY

Emerald Lake in the Rockies, Alberta

park region. Guided interpretation and walking trails make accessible this fascinating area.

In the foothills of south-west Alberta, in the traditional lands of the Blackfoot Indian, is the intriguing **Head-Smashed-In Buffalo Jump**. It protects North America's oldest, largest and best preserved Native bison jump. Where the rocky ledges of the Porcupine Hills meet the plains, generations of Native People ingeniously hunted the revered herds of bison. An excellent interpretation centre and trails around the undisturbed site make this story of early Canada captivating.

The joint Canada-USA **Waterton-Glacier International Peace Park** straddles the Alberta-Montana border at the narrowest section of the Rocky Mountains. In Canada, it runs westward to the British Columbia border.

The joining of Canada's Waterton National Park with Montana's Glacier National Park in 1932 created the world's first international park. As a symbol for international cooperation in preserving places of global significance it has helped inspire the creation of other such parks.

The parks uniquely combine prairie landscape with lofty snowcapped peaks. Within a distance of just 1km, the dry, rolling hills of the southern Alberta plains rise dramatically to 3000m.

The lowlands support antelope and coyotes, the alpine meadows and slopes, mountain goats and grizzly bears. Deer are frequently seen in Crandall Mountain campground.

The scenic three Waterton Lakes wedged between mountains permit boat access to much of the park including excellent walking trails covering three vegetative zones. The park was originally the home of the Blackfoot people and Waterton has two National Historic Sites, western Canada's first commercial oil well and the Prince of Wales Hotel, a marvellous example of early mountain resort lodging featuring a timber-framed interior.

Glacier contains 50 smallish glaciers and is one of the USA's largest national parks.

Best known among Canada's Heritage Sites is the **Rocky Mountain Parks** straddling the Alberta-British Columbia border. Deservedly attention-getting and internationally famous, Banff and Jasper national parks are the main focus of the site. But

there are other significant components such as smaller, towering Mt Assiniboine Provincial Park, diverse Yoho National Park with the renowned Burgess Shale fossil beds, and BC's Mt Robson, at 3954m, the highest peak in the Rockies. To the south, Kootenay National Park is also included. Alpine meadows, glaciers, hot springs, rushing rivers – the list of outstanding features and the outdoor possibilities they present is stunning.

Off the coast of British Columbia sit the Queen Charlotte Islands, sometimes referred to as the Canadian Galapagos for the rich variety of life in and among the west-coast rainforest. The southern half of Moresby Island has become South Moresby Gwaii Hanaas National Park, managed in part by the native Haida Nation. Tiny **Anthony Island**, part of the park, is the most westerly of Canada's Heritage Sites. Ninstints, a former Haida village on the island, is regarded as the most significant of all Pacific Northwest Indian sites. It contains still standing totems and mortuary poles as well as longhouse vestiges and is believed to have been an inhabited area for 2000 years.

Featuring clean, uncluttered, unspoiled northern qualities is the south-western Yukon's **Kluane National Park**. Together with the adjacent Wrangell-St Elias Park of Alaska and the Tatshenshini-Alsek rivers of northern British Columbia, Kluane makes up one of the world's largest protected areas. It is also among the most untamed regions on earth. Another site of magnitudes, Kluane contains the world's largest non-polar icefields with glaciers from the time when Canada was uninhabited. In one of the two mountain chains sits secluded, aloof Mt Logan at 5951m, Canada's highest peak. Wildlife includes grizzly bears, moose, mountain goats, Dall sheep and sometimes caribou.

Tucked exclusively in the south-western corner of the Northwest Territories is remote mountainous **Nahanni National Park**, inaccessible by road. This Heritage Site of pristine, unbridled far northern wilds is dominated by the turbulent South Nahanni River, also classed a Canadian Heritage River. It cuts through awe-inspiring canyons from the tundra zones of rocky peaks to the forested valleys at its mouth on the Liard River. At Virginia Falls, it plunges over 90m, twice the height of Niagara. With hot springs along the way as well as abundant wildlife, a once in a lifetime river trip here is a dream for many.

Blizzard, Churchill, Manitoba

Kluane National Park, Yukon

W LYNCH

MARK LIGHTBODY

continued from page 32

Jeff Healy and Collin James both play scintillating blues guitar.

Among Quebec singers who are rarely heard outside that province, except perhaps in France, Gilles Vigneault could be the biggest name. Others are Michel Rivard and Daniel Lavois but there are many more. Montreal's Lhasa, singing in Spanish, surprises with her passionate global sound. The province has its own successful pop, rock and semi-traditional folk bands and artists.

The traditional Celtic-based music of the Atlantic Provinces remains popular in that region and efforts to hear some are recommended. The Barra MacNeils, the Rankins, Ashley McIassac, and the Irish Descendants bring this music to wider audiences. Loreena McKennitt has fashioned an Irish-based World Music sound all her own. Also from Ontario are the Irish traditionalists, Leahy. Buffy Sainte Marie was the first in an increasing line-up of Native Indian musicians which includes Inuit singer Susan Aglukark. First Nations is a record label producing Native Indian musicians. Two contemporary acts are Kastin and Lawrence Martin.

In the classical field, Canada's best known artists include guitarist Liona Boyd, the eccentric pianist Glenn Gould, soprano Teresa Stratus and composer R Murray Schafer.

Pianist Oscar Peterson is the country's highest profile jazz musician followed by jazz pianist and vocalist Diana Krall.

Film

Canadian film is well respected abroad primarily through the work of the National Film Board (NFB) whose productions are, perhaps surprisingly, little viewed and scarcely known at home. Each year the film board, formed in 1939, releases a combination of animation, documentary and dramatic films.

National Film Board offices can be found in many of the country's large cities. Films are often screened at these centres and, increasingly, videos of the vast collection can be rented.

Canada also has a commercial feature-length film industry. Its output is relatively small and the quality varies. In the past few years Quebec has been the most prolific and artistically successful in film. The better known movies are subtitled or dubbed into English. Denys Arcand's *Decline of the American Empire* and *Jesus of Montreal* were major critical successes. Others from Quebec include *Wind from Wyoming* by Andre Forcier, gritty *Night Zoo* directed by Jean Claude Lauzon and riotous *Perfectly Normal* by Yves Simoneau. *Black Robe*, directed by Australian Bruce Beresford, tells a story set in 17th century Quebec.

Norman Jewison, the director of *Moonstruck*, could be considered the father of English-language Canadian film directors. Among established English directors is David Cronenberg, known for *The Fly*, *Dead Ringers* and *Naked Lunch*. Another is Atom Egoyan with a series of off-beat, challenging films including the highly-praised *Exotica* and *Sweet Hereafter*. Bruce Macdonald has done *Highway 61* and *Road Kill*, two rock 'n' roll movies and *Dance Me Outside* about contemporary Native Indian life. Ron Mann makes full length entertaining documentaries such as *Comic Book Confidential* and *Twist*. *I've Heard the Mermaids Singing* by Patricia Rozema is a comedy-drama. *Margaret's Museum* by Mort Ransen takes place in Nova Scotia and won a handful of awards. *The Arrow* by Don McBreaty was a 1997 film based on the fascinating Avro Arrow fighter plane with some documentary footage. James Cameron, the director of *Titanic* is Canadian. Lesser known films and their makers can be seen at the major annual film festivals in Toronto, Montreal and Vancouver. Better video stores have a Canadian section.

Painting

Artists began painting Canada as early as the 1700s and their work has grown to encompass a wide variety of styles and international influences. One of the earliest distinctive Canadian painters was Cornelius Krieghoff who used the St Lawrence River area of Quebec as his subject matter. Out west Paul Kane

was equally captivated by the Native Indians and their way of life. Landscape painters travelled and explored the country often following the laying of railway lines.

Tom Thompson and the Group of Seven beginning just before WWI established the style and landscape subject matter which was to dominate Canadian art for about 30 years. The Group of Seven members are Franklin Carmichael, Frank Johnston (later replaced by AJ Casson), Lawren Harris, AY Jackson, Arthur Lismer, JEH MacDonald and Frederick Varley. Their work, drawn from the geography of the eastern Canadian lakelands, is still the country's best known both inside and outside Canada. Emily Carr in a similar tradition painted the west coast, its forests and Native Indian villages and totems.

In the 1950s, another group of painters, which included Jack Bush, Tom Hodgson and Harold Town helped bring new abstract influences into Canadian painting. Joyce Wieland and Michael Snow, two of the best known among more contemporary visual artists, grew out of this period. Well known realists include Ken Danby, Alex Colville, Christopher and Mary Pratt and, for nature studies, Robert Bateman.

As with the previous music and literature sections, this is but a very brief overview of some of the country's artists.

Native Indian Art

Among the country's most distinctive art is that of the Inuit of the north, particularly their sculptures and carvings. These also represent some of the more affordable pieces, although many of their prices too can range into the stratosphere for larger works by some well established artists.

Materials used for Inuit carvings include bone, ivory, antler and occasionally horn or wood. By far the most common, though, is a group of rock types known generically as soapstone. It includes the soft steatite and harder serpentine, argillite, dolomite and others. Quarried across the far north, the stone material can vary from black to grey to green and may be dull or highly polished.

Carving styles vary from one isolated community to the other across the far north, with some better known than others. Almost all work is done completely by hand with low-tech tools. Northern Quebec tends to produce realistic, naturalistic work such as birds or hunting scenes. Baffin Island sculpture is more detailed and finer, often with varying depictions of people. The central Arctic area art embraces spiritual themes, and whalebone is often employed.

As a result of interest and appreciation in Inuit carvings there are now mass-produced imitations which are widely seen and sold. Genuine works are always marked with a tag or sticker with an igloo symbol on it. Many are also signed by the artist. The type of retail outlet is also an indicator. A reputable store and not a souvenir kiosk will likely stock the real thing. Aside from the maker and the quality, imitations are not often even made of the true raw material and really are of no value or interest.

Inuit artists also produce prints which are highly regarded. Subject matter often is taken from mythology but other works depict traditional day-to-day activities, events and chores. Prices are best in the Northwest Territories and the Yukon.

The best of Native Indian art is also expressed in printmaking although there is some fine carving and basketry. Probably the country's best known Indian paintings are those by artist Norval Morrisseau. The carvings and totems of Bill Reid and Roy Henry Vickers from the west coast have established them as major international figures. Across the country much of what is sold as Native Indian art and craft is pretty cheap and tacky and a poor likeness to the work which was done at one time and to what can still be found with some effort.

Some of the most interesting and best quality items from either Inuit or Native Indian artisans are the clothes: moccasins *(mukluks)*, knitted sweaters (from Vancouver Island, known as Cowichan sweaters) and parkas (warm winter coats). Some interesting jewellery and beadwork can also be found.

SOCIETY & CONDUCT
Traditional Culture

Anthropologists divide Native Canadians into six cultural groupings each with their own religion, language family, lifestyle and geographic area. (See History earlier in this chapter.)

All had a system of beliefs in which there was no sharp division between the sacred and the secular.

Europeans did their best to crush the original cultures and together with disease, loss of land and means of livelihood, were largely successful. Despite somewhat intact traditions in the more remote communities, today the predominant religion is Christianity and English is the principal language.

Cultural rebirth with revival of song, dance, language programs, healing and ritual now accompanies the legal battles being waged across the country for land rights and political autonomy.

In pockets across the country there are followers of Pan-Indianism, a term used to describe the movement of resistance to white culture and its domination. It is essentially an inter-tribal political stand with some religious undercurrents.

Civil disobedience and confrontation with government occur sporadically across the country usually instigated by differences of opinion over Native rights.

For more information see Population & People earlier in this chapter.

RELIGION

Canada was settled by Christians, primarily French and Irish Roman Catholics and English and Scottish Protestants. Even today the largest single religious group is Catholic.

Within the Protestant group, the Anglicans form the largest denomination, followed by the United Church. Montreal, Toronto and Winnipeg have considerable Jewish populations. More recent immigration has brought Hinduism and Islam to Canada. The Sikhs in Vancouver have a sizable community, and is in fact the largest Sikh population outside India's Punjab province. The Chinese populations of Vancouver and Toronto maintain the Buddhist tradition. Canada also has small but determined pockets of rural, traditional religious sects such as those of the Mennonites, Hutterites and Doukhobors.

Regardless, formal religion plays an ever-diminishing role in Canadian life. Attendance at the established churches has declined steadily since WWII. Following in their peers' footsteps, the lack of interest in religion by the children of immigrants seems cause for some family strife.

Among the Native Indian population, most list their religion as Catholic, an indication of the efficiency of the early Jesuits. There is, however, a small but growing movement back to the original spiritual belief systems based on the natural world and the words of the ancestors.

Facts for the Visitor

PLANNING
When to Go

Spring, summer and autumn are all ideal for touring. The far north is best in summer as the roads are open, ferries can cross rivers and daylight hours are long. Many of the country's festivals are held over the summer, one notable exception being the Quebec Winter Carnival. If you're skiing and visiting the cities, a winter visit won't present any major hurdles. Winter tourism is increasing with many outfitters offering dog-sledding, nordic skiing and other winter outdoor activities. Also Canada's ballet, opera and symphony season runs through the winter months. You will, of course, need a different set of clothes.

The school summer holidays in Canada are from the end of June to Labour Day in early September. This is also the period when most people take their vacations. University students have a longer summer break running from some time in May to the beginning or middle of September.

March Break is a week-long intermission in studies for elementary and high school students across the country. The time taken each year varies with each province and school board but is sometime in the month of March. Many people take this as an opportune time for a holiday and all trains, planes and buses are generally very busy.

Note that outside the main summer season which runs roughly from mid-June to mid-September, many visitor-oriented facilities, attractions, sights and even accommodation may be closed. This is especially true in the Atlantic Provinces. Advantages are the slower pace, lack of crowds, lower prices and perhaps more time for the people serving you. Spring and autumn make a good compromise between the peak season and the cold of winter. For campers, though, July and August are the only reliably hot months. For more detail see the climate charts in the Facts about Canada chapter.

Maps

Good provincial road maps are available from the respective provincial tourist offices. Bookstores generally sell both provincial and city maps. Service stations often have road maps as well.

The Canada Map Office (☎ 613-952-7000, ☎ 1-800-465-6277, www.nrcan.gc.ca) produces topographic maps of anywhere in the country. The Web site lists its dealers across the country.

A store stocking thousands of road maps and topographical maps of Canada and the world is World of Maps & Travel Books (☎ 613-724-6776, ☎ 1-800-214-8524, www.worldofmaps.com), 1235 Wellington St, Ottawa, ON, K1Y 3A3. The store accepts orders by electronic mail and the Web site reviews new maps and publications.

Trailhead (☎ 416-862-0881), 61 Front St E, Toronto, ON, M5E 1B3, has a wide selection of maps of all kinds. Standard highway maps, city maps, fishing maps, nautical and aviation charts and topographic maps are all available. It will fill phone and mail orders.

What to Bring

Travellers to Canada have no real need for any special articles. Those with allergies or any particular medical ailments or conditions should bring their customary medicines and supplies. Extra prescription glasses and/or contact lenses are always a good idea. A small travel alarm clock is useful.

Those planning trips out of the summer season should bring a number of things to protect against cold. Layering of clothes is the most effective and the most practical way to keep warm. One thin and one thick sweater and something more or less windproof is recommended. On particularly cool days a T-shirt worn under a long sleeved-shirt and then a combination of the above is quite effective. Gloves, scarf and hat should be considered and are mandatory in winter.

Even in winter a bathing suit, which weighs next to nothing, is always good to throw in the pack. Aside from possible ocean and lake summer swimming there are city, hotel and motel pools of which some are heated, and some hotels have saunas. A collapsible umbrella is a very useful, practical accessory. A good, sturdy pair of walking shoes or boots is a good idea for all but the business traveller with no spare time.

For English-language speakers planning on spending some time in Quebec, a French/English dictionary or phrase book should be considered although these are available in Montreal.

Drivers travelling long distances should have a few basic tools, a spare tyre that has been checked for pressure, a first-aid kit and a torch (flashlight). A few favourite tapes may help pass the hours driving in remote areas where there's nothing on the radio but static.

TOURIST OFFICES

Due to government restructuring and cutbacks, there is no federal tourism department which supplies information to the public. All tourism information is handled by the individual provinces.

For basic help in planning a visit to Canada, see your closest Canadian embassy, consulate or high commission, listed later in this chapter under Embassies & Consulates. It can furnish details on entry requirements, the weather, duty regulations, and where to get travel information. The Canadian Tourism Commission produces a booklet with general information and addresses to contact for further information. Travel agents can also be consulted.

Provincial/Territory Tourist Offices

Each province has one or more major provincial tourist offices located within its borders. These may be in the major city, at provincial boundaries or at a major provincial attraction.

The provincial tourist offices can supply, at no charge, the basic information requirements including maps and guides on accommodation, campgrounds and attractions. They can also provide information on events scheduled for the current or upcoming year. On request, they will furnish more specialised information on, for example, a particular activity or an organised wilderness tour, however, they do not have detailed information on any given area of their province or territory. For this information, a city tourist office in your area of choice must be contacted by phone, mail or in person. Here is a list of provincial/territory tourist offices:

Alberta
(☎ 1-800-661-8888 free from anywhere in continental North America, www.discover alberta.com)
Alberta Tourism Partnership, 3rd Floor, 10155-102nd St, Edmonton, Alberta T5J 4G8
British Columbia
(☎ 1-800-663-6000 free from continental North America, Hawaii and parts of Alaska, www.tbc.gov.bc.ca)
Tourism British Columbia, Parliament Buildings, Victoria, British Columbia V8V 1X4
Manitoba
(☎ 1-800-665-0040 free from anywhere in continental North America, www.gov.mb.ca)
Travel Manitoba, Department SM5, 7th Floor, 155 Carlton St, Winnipeg, Manitoba R3C 3H8
New Brunswick
(☎ 1-800-561-0123 free from anywhere in continental North America, www.gov.nb.ca)
New Brunswick Tourism, Department of Economic Development & Tourism, PO Box 6000, Fredericton, New Brunswick E3B 5H1
Newfoundland & Labrador
(☎ 1-800-563-6353 free from continental North America, www.gov.nf.ca)
Newfoundland Department of Tourism, Culture & Recreation, PO Box 8730, St John's, Newfoundland A1B 4K2
Northwest Territories
(☎ 1-800-661-0788 free from anywhere in continental North America, www.nwttravel .nt.ca)
Northwest Territories Arctic Tourism, PO Box 610, Yellowknife, Northwest Territories X1A 2N5
Nova Scotia
(☎ 1-800-565-0000 free from anywhere in Canada, ☎ 1-800-341-6096 free from anywhere in the USA, www.explore.gov.ns.ca)

Tourism Nova Scotia, PO Box 130, Halifax, Nova Scotia B3J 2M7

Nunavut
  (☎ 1-800-491-7910 free from anywhere in continental North America, www.nunatour .nt.ca)
  Nunavut Tourism, PO Box 1450, Iqaluit, Nunavut, X0A 0H0

Ontario
  (☎ 1-800-668-2746 free from Canada, continental USA and Hawaii, ☎ 1-800-268-3736 in French, free from anywhere in Canada, www .travelinx.com)
  Tourism Ontario, 9th Floor, 1 Concorde Gate, Don Mills, Ontario M3C 3N6

Prince Edward Island
  (☎ 1-800-463-4734 free from continental North America, www.peiplay.com)
  Prince Edward Island Visitor Services, PO Box 940, Charlottetown, Prince Edward Island C1A 7M5

Quebec
  (☎ 1-800-363-7777 free from anywhere in continental North America, www.tourisme .gouv.qc.ca)
  Tourism Quebec, PO Box 979, Montreal, Quebec H3C 2W3

Saskatchewan
  (☎ 1-800-667-7191 free from anywhere in continental North America, www.sasktourism .com)
  Tourism Saskatchewan, 500-1900 Albert St, Regina, Saskatchewan S4P 4L9

Yukon
  (☎ 403-667-5340, www.touryukon.com)
  Tourism Yukon, PO Box 2703, Whitehorse, Yukon Territories Y1A 2C6

Local Tourist Offices

Each province in Canada has a governmental ministry or affiliate which is responsible for tourism and the major cities generally have an office for distributing provincial information.

In addition, most Canadian cities and towns have at least a seasonal local information office. Many of these are mentioned in the text.

The small, local tourist offices are clearly the best places for travellers seeking specialised information on a specific area. As a general rule the staff there will have little knowledge or information on other parts of the country.

VISAS & DOCUMENTS
Passport

Visitors from all countries but the USA need a passport. Two minor exceptions include people from Greenland (Denmark) and Saint Pierre & Miquelon (France) who do not need passports if they are entering from their areas of residence. All the above do need to have good identification, however, when visiting Canada.

For US and Canadian citizens, a driver's licence has traditionally been all that was required to prove residency but often this is no longer sufficient. A birth certificate or a certificate of citizenship or naturalisation, if not a passport, is recommended and may indeed be required in some cases before admission is granted.

US citizens arriving in Canada from somewhere other than the USA should have a passport. US citizens travelling in Canada may want to investigate the Canadian Nonresident Interprovince Motor Vehicle Liability Insurance Card – only available in the USA.

If you've rented a car, trailer or any other vehicle in the USA and you are driving it into Canada, bring a copy of the rental agreement to save any possible aggravation by border officials. The rental agreement should stipulate that taking the vehicle to Canada is permitted.

Visas

Visitors from nearly all western countries don't need visas. An exception is citizens of South Africa. Tourists from Hong Kong, Korea and Taiwan also need visas as do visitors from developing countries and residents of some Eastern European countries. Those from communist nations definitely need one too.

Visitor visas, which costs $75, are granted for a period of six months and are extendable for a fee. Extensions, at the same price, must be applied for at a Canadian Immigration Centre. Visa requirements change frequently and since visas must be obtained before arrival in Canada, check before you leave – Europeans included. A

separate visa is required for visitors intending to work or to go to school in Canada.

A passport and/or visa does not guarantee entry. Admission and duration of permitted stay is at the discretion of the immigration officer at the border. The decision is based on a number of factors, some of which you control, including: being of good health; being law abiding; having sufficient money; and possibly being in possession of a return ticket out of the country. This latter requirement will not often be asked of any legitimate traveller, especially from a western country.

If you are refused entry but have a visa you have the right of appeal at the Immigration Appeal Board at the port of entry. Those under 18 years old should have a letter from a parent or guardian.

Visa Extensions An application for a visa extension must be submitted one month before the current visa expires. The fee for an extension is $75. For more information and to obtain an application call or visit a Canadian Immigration Centre. These can be found in major cities. Requirements for receiving an extension include having a valid passport, an onward ticket and adequate finances.

Side Trips to the USA

Visitors to Canada who are planning to spend some time in the USA should be aware of a few things to avoid being met with disappointment. First, admission requirements to the USA when arriving by land can be significantly different than when arriving by air or sea from your country of origin. These regulations are also subject to rapid change; it's best never to assume. The duration of the visit, whether one afternoon or three months, is inconsequential; the same rules apply. The American assumption is that all visitors are attempting to become immigrants, a state of affairs they strongly seek to minimise.

Visitors to the USA from nearly all western countries do not need visas but there are exceptions, one being the Portuguese.

Residents of countries for whom US visas are necessary should get them at home. Visitors can apply for US visas in Canada but it is generally easier and quicker to apply at home and your chances of being refused are reduced. Visas cannot be obtained upon arrival in the USA. When getting a visa, ask for a multiple entry one as this may be useful.

Important Note People visiting the USA from countries whose citizens do *not* need a visa are subject to a $6 entry (visa waiver) fee at the border. It doesn't matter if you are going for an hour or a month. This fee is applicable regardless of your means of entry, including walking.

Most visitors to the USA (by air or sea) are required to have either a return or onward ticket in their possession. These tickets may be 'open', that is undated. Visitors entering the USA by land from Canada are not required to have any ticket but some show of finances may be required as well as some indication of a residence abroad, ie some document that shows you have a permanent address.

As mentioned, the border between Canada and the USA has tightened up even for citizens of either of these countries. Anyone travelling with young children should be aware of the extra need for good documentation. This is true whether on plane, bus, train or driving a vehicle. Because of the heightened fear of child abductions parents can find themselves in the unenviable position of having to prove that the baby in their arms is in fact their own.

This is particularly the case for male single parents but may affect anyone crossing the border without their spouse. In the latter case, a letter of consent, preferably notarised, from the missing partner should be considered. You may be asked to legally document custody of the child.

Commercial carriers such as Amtrak and Greyhound are facing threats of heavy fines for carrying passengers without sufficient documentation and so have been forced to be more strict in requiring proper identification for crossing the border in either direction. Any potential trouble can also be minimised by having valid passports for all members of the family.

Check that your entry permit to Canada, whatever it may be, includes multiple entry. For people holding passports from western countries multiple entry is generally given. But check, because if not, you may find your afternoon side trip across the border to the USA involuntarily extended when Canadian officials won't let you back in to Canada.

Also, the time spent on a side trip to the USA will be included as time spent in Canada for the purpose of your time allotment upon arrival. For example, if you have been given a six-month stay in Canada and after three months you spend one month in California, upon your return to Canada you will only be permitted to stay the remaining two months.

For those wishing to visit duty-free shops and perhaps take advantage of the prices, you must be in the USA for a minimum of 48 hours to be entitled to use them. The selection and prices at these shops has never been all that impressive anyway and the concept is a bit overrated. Smokers may find the cigarettes aren't a bad buy.

Border crossers should also note that foods such as meat, fish and eggs can be confiscated so eat your picnic before meeting the customs agent.

Travel Insurance

A travel insurance policy to cover theft, loss and medical problems is a wise idea. There is a wide variety of policies and your travel agent will have recommendations. The international student travel policies handled by STA Travel or other student travel organisations are usually good value. Some policies offer lower and higher medical expenses options but the higher one is chiefly for countries like the USA which have extremely high medical costs. Check the small print:

- Some policies specifically exclude 'dangerous activities' which can include scuba diving, motorcycling, even trekking. If such activities are on your agenda, you don't want that sort of policy. A locally acquired motorcycle licence may not be valid under your policy.
- You may prefer a policy which pays doctors or hospitals direct rather than you having to pay

on the spot and claim later. If you have to claim later make sure you keep all documentation. Some policies ask you to call back (reverse charges) to a centre in your home country where an immediate assessment of your problem is made.
- Check if the policy covers ambulances or an emergency flight home. If you have to stretch out you will need two seats and somebody has to pay for them.

Check to see if your health insurance covers you during a visit to Canada and the precise details, limitations and exclusions of that coverage. Medical, hospital and dental care is excellent but very expensive in Canada. The standard rate for a bed in a city hospital is at least $500 a day and up to $2000 a day in the major centres for nonresidents.

The largest seller of hospital and medical insurance to visitors to Canada is John Ingle Insurance. It offers hospital medical care (HMC) policies from a minimum of seven days to a maximum of one year with a possible renewal of one additional year. The 30-day basic coverage costs $90 for an adult under the age of 55, $110 for ages 55 to 64 and $130 above that. Family rates are available. Coverage includes the hospital rate, doctors' fees, extended health care and other features. Visitors to Canada are not covered for conditions which they had prior to arrival.

Be sure to inquire about coverage details if you intend to make side trips to the USA, Mexico, the Caribbean countries or others.

Ingle also offers insurance policies for foreign students (at reduced rates) and to those visiting Canada on working visas. Its policies may be very beneficial in filling in coverage gaps before either a government policy kicks in, in the case of students, or the employers' paid benefits begin, in the case of foreign workers. Again, the policies may vary depending where in the country you settle.

Ingle has offices in major cities across the country and representatives in the northern territories. The head office (☎ 416-340-0100, ☎ 1-800-387-4770) is at 438 University Ave, Suite 1200, Toronto, ON, M7Y 2Z1. It can supply information pamphlets in over 15

languages and staff in the office in Toronto even speak most of them. The pamphlet includes an application form and payment can be made before or after arrival in Canada. It can often be found at post offices, banks, chemists, doctors' offices and some shopping centres. Read the information carefully. There are exclusions, conditions etc which should be clearly understood. Also check the maximum amounts payable as different policies allow for greater payments.

There are many other companies offering travellers insurance so consult the Yellow Pages phone book.

EMBASSIES & CONSULATES
Canadian Embassies, High Commissions & Consulates

Australia
High Commission:
(☎ 02-6273-3844)
Commonwealth Ave, Canberra ACT 2600
Canadian Consulate General:
(☎ 02-9364-3000 or ☎ 02-9364-3050 for Visa Immigration Office)
111 Harrington St, Level 5, Quay West, Sydney, New South Wales 2000
Consulate:
(☎ 03-9811-9999)
123 Camberwell Rd, East Hawthorn, Melbourne, Victoria 3123
Consulate:
(☎ 08-9322-7930)
267 St George Terrace, 3rd Floor, Perth, Western Australia 6000
Denmark
Embassy:
(☎ 33-12-22-99)
Kr Bernikowsgade 1, 1105 Copenhagen K
France
Embassy:
(☎ 01-44-43-29-00)
35 Avenue Montaigne, 75008 Paris
Germany
Embassy:
(☎ 011-49-228-968-0)
Friedrich-Wilhelm-Strassa 18, 53113, Bonn, Germany
Ireland
Embassy:
(☎ 01-478-1988)
65-68 St Stephen's Green, Dublin 2 (Note: the immigration section of this office has closed.)

Italy
Embassy:
(☎ 06-44-59-81)
Via G B de Rossi 27, Rome 00161
Japan
Embassy:
(☎ 3408-2101)
3-38 Akasaka 7-chome, Minato-ku, Tokyo 107
Netherlands
Embassy:
(☎ 070-311-1600)
Sophialaan 7, 2514 SP The Hague
New Zealand
High Commission:
(☎ 4-473-9577)
61 Molesworth St, Thorndon, Wellington (Note: visa and immigration inquiries are handled by the Consulate General of Canada in Sydney, Australia.)
Spain
Embassy:
(☎ 1-431-4300)
Edificio Goya, Calle Nunez de Balboa 35, Madrid
Sweden
Embassy:
(☎ 8-453-3000)
Tegelbacken 4 (7th Floor), Stockholm
Switzerland
Embassy:
(☎ 31-357-3200)
Kirchenfeldstrasse 88, CH-3005 Berne
UK
High Commission:
(☎ 0171-258-6600)
Macdonald House, 1 Grosvenor Square, London W1X 0AB
USA
Consulate General:
(☎ 212-596-1683)
1251 Avenue of the Americas, New York City, New York 10020-1175 (Note: the Canadian Consulate Generals in Buffalo, Los Angeles and Seattle can provide visa information; and the Consulate Generals in Atlanta, Boston, Buffalo, Chicago, Dallas, Detroit, Los Angeles, Minneapolis, New York, Seattle and Washington have some tourist information. The only embassy is in Washington, DC.)

Embassies & Consulates in Canada

The principal diplomatic representations to Canada are in Ottawa and these are listed here. Other offices can be found in major cities and some of these are listed in the

relevant sections of the text. Those addresses not listed in the text can be found by looking in the Yellow Pages phone book.

Australia
  High Commission:
  (☎ 613-236-0841)
  50 O'Connor St, Ottawa, ON K1P 6L2
Austria
  Embassy:
  (☎ 613-789-1444)
  445 Wilbrod St, Ottawa, ON K1N 6M7
Belgium
  Embassy:
  (☎ 613-236-7267)
  80 Elgin St, Ottawa, ON K1P 1B7
Denmark
  Embassy:
  (☎ 613-562-1811)
  47 Clarence St, Ottawa, ON K1N 9K1
Finland
  Embassy:
  (☎ 613-236-2389)
  850-55 Metcalfe St, Ottawa, ON K1P 6L5
France
  Embassy:
  (☎ 613-789-1795)
  42 Sussex Drive, Ottawa, ON K1M 2C9
Germany
  Embassy:
  (☎ 613-232-1101)
  1 Waverley St, Ottawa, ON K2P 0T7
Greece
  Embassy:
  (☎ 613-238-6271)
  76-80 Maclaren St, Ottawa, ON K2P 0K6
Ireland
  Embassy:
  (☎ 613-233-6281)
  130 Albert St, Ottawa, ON K1A 0L6
Italy
  Embassy:
  (☎ 613-232-2401)
  275 Slater St, 21st Floor, Ottawa, ON K1P 5H9
Japan
  Embassy:
  (☎ 613-241-8541)
  255 Sussex Drive, Ottawa, ON K1N 9E6
Korea
  Embassy:
  (☎ 613-244-5010)
  150 Boteler St, Ottawa, ON K1A 5A6
Netherlands
  Embassy:
  (☎ 613-237-5030)
  350 Albert St, Ste 2020 Ottawa, ON K1R 1A4

New Zealand
  High Commission:
  (☎ 613-238-5991)
  727-99 Bank St, Ottawa, ON K1P 6G3
Norway
  Embassy:
  (☎ 613-238-6571)
  90 Sparks St, Ottawa, ON K1P 5B4
Russia
  Embassy:
  (☎ 613-235-4341)
  285 Charlotte St, Ottawa, ON K1N 8L5
South Africa
  High Commission:
  (☎ 613-744-0330)
  15 Sussex Drive, Ottawa, ON K1M 1M8
Spain
  Embassy:
  (☎ 613-747-2252)
  74 Stanley Ave, Ottawa, ON, K1M 1P4
Sweden
  Embassy:
  (☎ 613-241-8553)
  377 Dalhousie St, Ottawa, ON K1N 9N8
Switzerland
  Embassy:
  (☎ 613-235-1837)
  5 Marlborough Ave, Ottawa, ON, K1N 8E6
UK
  High Commission:
  (☎ 613-237-1530)
  80 Elgin St, Ottawa, ON K1P 5K7
USA
  Embassy:
  (☎ 613-238-5335)
  100 Wellington St, PO Box 866, Station B, Ottawa, ON K1P 5T1

CUSTOMS

How thoroughly customs will check you out upon arrival at a Canadian entry point depends on a number of things. First among them are point of departure, nationality and appearance. Arriving from countries known as drug sources or with a history of illegal immigration or refugees will add to the scrutiny. Always make sure the necessary papers are in order.

Travellers may find that different border personnel interpret the rules differently. Some are polite, others are rude. Arguing is of little use. If you are refused entry, and you feel it is unjust, the best course is simply to try again later (after a shift change) or

at a different border crossing. Young travellers may find rules strictly enforced.

If an agent wants to frisk or strip search you, you are entitled to be given a reason for their suspicion. If you wish to refuse, you can ask for legal counsel which may be available at airports and larger entry points.

Don't get caught bringing drugs into Canada. This warning includes marijuana and hashish, as they are termed narcotics in Canada. Sentences can be harsh.

Adults (age varies by province but is generally 19 years) can bring in 1.1L (40 ounces) of liquor or a case of 24 beers as well as 200 cigarettes, 50 cigars and 400g of tobacco (all cheaper in the USA). You can bring in gifts up to $60 in value.

Sporting goods, including 200 rounds of ammunition, cameras and film and two days' worth of food can also be brought in without trouble. Registering excessive or expensive sporting goods, cameras etc might save you some hassle when you leave, especially if you'll be crossing the Canadian-US border a number of times.

If you have a dog or cat you'll need proof that it's had a rabies shot in the past 36 months. For US citizens this is usually easy enough; for residents of other countries there may well be more involved procedures. If you must bring a pet from abroad, check with the Canadian government or a representative before arriving at the border.

For boaters, pleasure craft may enter Canada either on the trailer or in the water and stay for up to one year. An entry permit is required and is obtainable from the customs office at or near the point of entry. All boats powered by motors over 10hp must be licenced.

Pistols, fully automatic weapons and any firearms less than 66cm (26 inches) in length are not permitted into the country. Most rifles and shotguns will be admitted without a permit.

MONEY
Currency
Canadian currency is much like that of the USA with some noteworthy variations.

Coins come in one-cent (penny), five-cent (nickel), 10-cent (dime), 25-cent (quarter), $1 (loonie) and $2 (twoonie) pieces. The loonie is an 11-sided, gold-coloured coin known for the common loon (a species of waterbird) featured swimming on it. In 1996 the twoonie was introduced. It's a two-toned coin with a nickel outer ring and aluminum-bronze core featuring a polar bear. This means the phasing out of the $2 bill like the $1 bill before it. There is also a 50-cent coin but this is not regularly seen.

With the demise of the $2 bill, paper currency is found in $5, $10 and $20 denominations. The $50, $100 and larger bills are less common and could prove difficult to cash, especially in smaller businesses or at night. Service stations, for example, are sometimes reluctant to deal with larger bills. Canadian bills are all the same size but vary in their colours and images. Some denominations have two styles as older versions in good condition continue to circulate.

All prices quoted in this book are in Canadian dollars, unless stated otherwise.

Exchange Rates

country	unit	dollar
Australia	A$1	= C$0.97
euro	€1	= C$1.56
France	10FF	= C$2.38
Germany	DM1	= C$0.80
Ireland	IR£1	= C$1.98
Japan	¥100	= C$1.19
Netherlands	fl	= C$0.71
New Zealand	NZ$1	= C$0.82
UK	UK£1	= C$2.37
USA	US$1	= C$1.46

Changing Money
Changing money is best done at companies such as Thomas Cook or American Express which specialise in international transactions. In some of the larger cities these companies, and others, operate small exchange offices and booths along main streets.

The second option for changing money are the banks and trust companies. Lastly

there are hotels (always open at least), stores, attractions and service stations. The rates at the latter group are not likely to be in your favour.

American Express and Thomas Cook are the best travellers cheques to use in either US or Canadian dollars. Some smaller places don't know exchange rates, so you'll have to pay for a call to find the rate as well as the mailing charges. Some banks charge a couple of dollars to cash travellers cheques, so ask first. If a charge is levied be sure to cash several cheques as generally the charge remains the same no matter how many cheques are being cashed. Despite this service charge, banks usually offer better rates than places such as hotels, restaurants and visitor attractions. Personal cheques are rarely accepted at any commercial enterprise.

Banking hours are generally shorter than regular retail hours. Some banks have evening hours while others, more likely trust companies, are open on Saturday morning. For more information see Business Hours later in this chapter.

Automated Teller Machines Automated teller machines (ATMs) with Interac are common throughout Canada. Interac permits cardholders to withdraw money from their account at any bank machine. As well as being located at banks, they can be found in some grocery stores, service stations, variety stores, shopping centres, bus and train stations and elsewhere. Known in Canada as banking machines, these can be used day or night, any day of the week. Cards must be applied for at home through your own bank. Ask if the cards are good for use in the Canadian banking networks. Most Canadian ATMs will take cards from most foreign countries.

Be sure to obtain a list of addresses where banking machines can be found or the 1-800 toll-free telephone number which can be called to help locate one. Often tourist offices or any bank will be able to direct you to the nearest machine. Use of the Interac card has increased dramatically by travellers and is often the most convenient,

quickest way to replenish your cash. Bank cards are often used now instead of cash. With 'direct payment' the card is swiped through the retailer's scanner and your account is instantly debited.

Credit Cards Carrying a credit card is a good idea in Canada. Their use is widespread and they can serve a number of purposes. They are good identification and are more or less essential for use as security deposits for such things as renting a car or even a bicycle. They are perfect for using as a deposit when making reservations for accommodation, and even Hostelling International (HI) hostels will take credit-card reservations and payments. They can be used to book and purchase ferry tickets, airplane tickets or theatre tickets. Lastly, they can be used at banks to withdraw cash, termed cash advances.

Visa, MasterCard and American Express credit cards are honoured in most places in larger centres and many in the smaller cities and towns. American Express has the advantage of offering a free mail pick-up service at its offices. In tiny, out-of-the-way communities, the use of travellers cheques or cash is advisable.

Security
See Emergency later in this chapter for help with lost/stolen cards.

Costs
Finding a place to sleep and eat is not a lot different here than in Europe or other western countries. The Canadian lifestyle, like the Canadian personality, has been influenced by Britain and the USA but is somehow different from both. There are no formal social classes, but there are widely different incomes, and therefore a range in housing, eating and entertainment prices.

For many visitors, the biggest expense will be accommodation. There are, however, alternatives to the standard hotels which can make paying for a bed nothing to lose sleep over. The larger cities generally have the more expensive lodging prices, while those in country towns can be quite

reasonable. In the far north, accommodation rates are a little more than in the south, only sometimes outlandishly so.

The heavily touristed areas such as Niagara Falls and Quebec City tend not to have really inflated prices because the volume of places to stay means plenty of competition, particularly when it's not peak season. An exception is Banff in the Rocky Mountains which is costly. As a rule, accommodation prices are a little higher in the summer months. After this period, asking about a discount if one is not forthcoming is well worthwhile.

Food prices are lower than those in much of Western Europe but are higher than those in the USA and about parallel to those in Australia.

Gasoline prices vary from province to province but are always more than US rates, sometimes shockingly so, so remember to fill up before crossing the border if you are coming from the USA. Canada's gasoline prices are, however, lower than those in most of Europe. Within Canada the eastern provinces and the far north have the highest prices. Also, as a rule, the more isolated the service station, the higher the prices. Alberta has traditionally had the lowest prices. Of course, these prices reflect on all transportation costs.

Buses are almost always the least expensive form of public transport. Train fares, except when using one of the various special price rates, are moderate. Again, they are more expensive than US fares, less than European ones and comparable to those in Australia.

Inter-provincial airfares are high. Distances are great and the competition minimal. Again, always inquire about specials, excursion fares or last minute deals.

Inflation has been very low for several years, keeping prices fairly stable.

Prices Note In the text, train and plane fares given are the standard, one-way, no advance booking price. With advance booking, by even as little as five days, prices drop considerably. Planning ahead can save a *lot* of money. When flying, often return tickets are less than one-way fares, even if the return portion is not used, and booking two weeks in advance can mean additional savings.

Most prices that you see posted (and most found in the text) do not include taxes, which can add significantly to your costs. It's a good idea to ask if the price of something includes tax. See Consumer Taxes & Visitor Refunds later in this chapter.

Accommodation rates given are high season costs unless otherwise stated. Rates may vary seasonally $10 to $40.

Lodging and meal costs are outlined in the Accommodation and Food sections later.

Tipping

Normal tipping is 10 to 15% of the bill. Tips are usually given to cabbies, wait staff, hairdressers, barbers, hotel attendants and bellhops. Tipping helps for service in a bar, too, especially if a fat tip is given on the first order. After that you won't go thirsty all night.

A few restaurants have the gall to include a service charge on the bill. No tip should be added in these cases.

Consumer Taxes & Visitor Refunds

Provincial Tax In most of Canada, provincial sales tax must be paid on all things purchased. Alberta has a sales tax only on accommodation in hotels and motels, but the other provinces also have sales taxes on most items bought in shops and on food bought at restaurants and cafés. The Yukon, Northwest Territories and Nunavut have no consumer sales tax of their own.

Quebec and Manitoba allow partial rebates on accommodation tax and sales tax on goods being taken out of Canada. Check with a provincial tourist office for information and to obtain the necessary forms for reimbursement – it's worth the trouble on a tent, camera or similarly large purchase. Tax information is published in the provincial tourist information booklets.

Note that you need to send the original

receipts to obtain the tax refund. The originals are also required to receive the GST refunds. Get around this by applying first for the GST refund as the original receipts will be returned. Receipts are not returned from provincial refund offices. Some conditions apply and the form must be posted to the provincial tax office after you return home.

Goods & Services Tax Known as the Gouge and Screw Tax, the GST adds 7% to just about every product, service and transaction and is applied on top of the usual provincial sales tax. In Ontario, for example, this total can mean an additional 15% on a bill, so remember to factor it in before reaching the checkout cash register. Some provinces, such as Newfoundland and Nova Scotia, have now combined their provincial tax with the GST to make one general or Harmonized Sales Tax (HST) of about 15%.

For visitors or travellers who prepare their own food, note that there is no tax applied to groceries.

Some tourist homes (the small ones), guesthouses, B&Bs etc don't charge GST for rooms, and foreign visitors should try asking for an exemption from the GST on their hotel bill when making payment. If paid, the GST added to all other accommodation except camp sites is refundable.

A rebate or refund is available for visitors on accommodation and nonconsumable goods bought for use outside Canada, provided the goods are removed from the country within 60 days. Tax paid on services or transportation is not refundable. The value of the goods taxed must be over $100 and you must have original receipts. Credit-card slips and photocopies are not sufficient. Most 'tourist' or duty-free shops have a GST rebate booklet and mailing form or you can contact Revenue Canada, Custom, Excise & Taxation, Visitors' Rebate Program, Ottawa, Ontario K1A 1J5. The forms are also available at tourist information offices. The forms can also be used to apply for sales tax rebates on tax paid in the provinces of Quebec and Manitoba.

POST & COMMUNICATIONS
Post

The mail service is neither quick nor cheap but it's reliable. Canadian post offices will keep poste-restante mail for two weeks then return it to sender. Here's an example of how such mail should be addressed:

Your Name,
c/o General Delivery
Toronto, Ontario
Canada
M5W 1A0

A standard 1st-class air-mail letter is limited to 50g to North American destinations but as much as 500g to other international destinations. To the US, heavier mail can go by either surface or, more expensively, by air in small packet mail. Anything over 1kg goes by surface parcel post.

To other international destinations, letter packages, to a maximum of 2kg, can be sent by air. Small packet mail up to the same weight can go by either surface or air. Packages over 2kg are sent by parcel post and different rates apply. For full details go to a post office; full-page pamphlets which explain all the various options, categories, requirements and prices are available. Suffice it to say there are numerous methods for posting something, depending on the sender's time and money limitations: air, surface or a combination of these. Rates vary according to destination. Mail over 10kg goes surface only. For added security and speed there is registered mail and special delivery, and both surface and air mail for packages. Canada Post also offers an international courier-style service.

Some countries require a customs declaration on incoming parcels. Check at the post office.

Aside from the post offices themselves, stamps and postal services are often available at other outlets such as chemists (drug stores) and some small variety stores. Finding them is a matter of asking around. Hotel concessions also often stock stamps.

Here are some postal rates:

1st-class letter or postcard within Canada: 46 cents (up to 30g; includes GST)

1st-class letter or postcard to US: 55 cents (up to 30g, GST not included)

1st-class letter or postcard to other destinations: 95 cents (up to 20g, GST not included)

Aerogrammes (which are not common) cost the same.

Telephone

Canada has an excellent telephone system. Rates tend to be low for local use and rather costly (but decreasing) for long distances. Overall, the rates are about the same as in the USA but probably more expensive (at least for long distances) than in Europe. Public telephones are generally quite readily available and can be found in hotel lobbies, bars, restaurants, large department stores and many public buildings. Telephone booths can be found on street corners in cities and towns.

The basic rate of a call varies but is generally 25 cents for a local connection. If you wish to speak to an operator (dial ☎ 0) you will be connected free of charge. There is also no charge from a public phone for dialling ☎ 411, the telephone information number or for ☎ 911, the emergency number. For inquiries on long-distance calls, dial ☎ 1 (area code) 555-1212. This is also a free call.

Long-distance calls to anywhere in the world can be made from any phone but the rate varies depending on how it is done and when. A call made without the assistance of an operator is not only cheapest but quickest. This can be done if you know the area code as well as the number of the party to be reached. With operator assistance, calls in increasing order of cost are, station to station (no particular person to speak to required), collect (reverse charge) and person to person.

In Canada, long-distance rates are cheapest from 11 pm to 8 am daily. The second most economical time slot is from 6 pm to 11 pm daily, except Sunday when this rate runs from 8 am to 11 pm.

The most expensive time to call is from 8 am to 6 pm Monday to Friday.

Reductions can also apply to calls to the USA or overseas. All international rates and codes are listed in the front pages of the telephone book.

Important Note Many businesses, ferries, hotels, hostels and tourist offices etc operate toll free numbers which can be called at no cost, meaning no long-distance charges apply. These are great for making reservations etc.

These numbers begin with 800, 888, 877 or 777 and must be preceded with 1. Some of these numbers are good for anywhere in North America, others may be within Canada only and still others may cover just one province. You don't know until you try the number.

All Canadian business and residential phones are paid for on a flat monthly rate system – the number of calls made is immaterial. So don't feel guilty about the cost of using a friend's telephone to make local calls.

For those who will be using the telephone in hotels, motels, guesthouses, and other such places, note that most places charge a service fee for the use of the phone on a per call basis even for local calls. At maybe 50 cents per call, this can add up resulting in a bit of a shock on the final room bill, especially if you aren't expecting it.

Many Canadian businesses, tourist attractions and information offices use the cursed touch-tone menu information system. After dialling, the caller is given a range of options and recorded messages. This can be useful in learning the hours of operation of a museum, for example, but also frustrating because it's difficult to reach someone to whom you can direct specific questions.

There's a wide range of local and international phonecards. Lonely Planet's eKno Communication Card (see the insert at the back of this book) is aimed specifically at travellers and provides cheap international calls, a range of messaging services and free email – for local calls, you're usually better off with a local card. You can join online at www.ekno.lonelyplanet.com, or by phone

from Canada by dialling ☎ 1-800-294-3676. Once you have joined, to use eKno from Canada, dial ☎ 1-800-808-5773.

Fax & Telegraph

Fax machines accessible to the public are available at major hotels, city post offices and at a range of small businesses in major centres. For the last-named locations, check under facsimile, stationers or mail box services in the Yellow Pages. Facsimile messages are generally charged at $1 per page.

To send a telegram anywhere in Canada or overseas, contact AT&T Canada listed in the telephone directory.

Email & Internet Access

Email access is available at most large, corporate hotels. In addition, most cities and some smaller towns now have Internet cafés which offer on-line computer use at low rates. Many hostels also offer email availability.

INTERNET RESOURCES

Web sites for the provincial and territory tourist information offices are listed under Tourist Offices earlier. Many email addresses are given under specific accommodation places in the text.

For up to the minute general news try www.canoe.com. For information on some of the main sites in the country there is www.attractionscanada.com. Another general site is www.canada.com. The Council on International Educational Exchange can be reached at www.ciee.org.

For a peek at the world's weather check www.intellicast.com and for a site featuring Canadian music check www.canmusic.com.

Lonely Planet Publications is found at www.lonelyplanet.com.au with destination information and updates.

BOOKS

Canada has a small but quality publishing industry which is very active in promoting books by and about Canadians. For a brief guide to Canada's literature see the Arts section in the Facts about Canada chapter.

Travel

Canadian Lucy Izon's *Backpacker Journal* makes a handy, informative travel companion in which to keep your own diary and travel musings.

Jan Morris, a Welsh travel writer, who has written about many cities around the world, published *City to City* in 1990. Written after travelling Canada coast to coast it is a highly readable collection of essays of fact and opinion about 10 Canadian cities and their people. Note that this book was also published under the name *O Canada: Travels in an Unknown Country*.

Maple Leaf Rag is a quirky collection of travel essays by Stephen Brook. Stuart McLean in *Welcome Home: travels in small town Canada* reveals much about the character of small-town life and describes in a very approachable style some of the changes taking place within them.

Kildare Dobbs wrote of a bus trip across the country in *Ribbon of Highway: The Trans Canada Hwy Coast to Coast*. John and Martha Stradiotta describe the many, accessible varied national and provincial parks across the country in *The Road to Canada's Wild's: parks along the Trans Canada Hwy*. *Canada's National Parks – A Visitor's Guide* by Marylee Stephenson is the most complete guide to the country's national parks and provides all the essential information.

Gary and Joanie McGuffin have written *Where Rivers Run: a 6000-mile exploration of Canada by canoe*. Also for adventurers is *Freshwater Saga: memoirs of a lifetime of wilderness canoeing* by Eric Morse. *Lords of the Arctic: A journey among the polar bears* by Richard Davids is based in Churchill which many travellers may visit.

Farley Mowat, with such books as *Never Cry Wolf*, writes about the north, wildlife, nature and speaks for their conservation.

Wild is Always There: Canada through the eyes of foreign writers is a collection of pieces by a variety of writers who have spent some time in the country. It is edited by Greg Gatenby of Toronto who puts together writer

festivals and readings featuring writers from around the world.

The *French phrasebook* and the French *Quebec & Ontario* guidebook by Lonely Planet Publications are good references for visitors to those provinces.

People & Society

For more information on Canada's Native people try *Native Peoples and Cultures of Canada* by Allan Macmillan which includes both history and current issues.

The classic book on Canada's Native people, *The Indians of Canada* was written in 1932 by Diamond Jenness. Originally from New Zealand, the author's life is an amazing story in its own right as he spent years living with various indigenous people across the country. The book has been reprinted many times.

History

Pierre Berton is Canada's prime chronicler of the country's history. He has written on a wide range of subjects such as the gold rush, the railways and the Depression in an entertaining and informative way. Peter C Newman writes on Canadian business but has also produced an intriguing history of the Hudson's Bay Company, *Caesar's of the Wilderness*, beginning with the early fur-trading days.

A basic primer on the country's history is *The Penguin History of Canada* by Kenneth McNaught.

American William Vollman is in the midst of writing a massive, seven-volume fictional but well researched account of the clash of European and Native cultures in Canada. Within the collective, known as *Seven Dreams* is *Fathers and Crows* which outlines French expansion from Acadia. But these broad works, available from Penguin, are far more than dry history lessons.

General

Among academic writers, two who stand out are Northrop Frye for literary criticism and Marshall McLuhan for media analysis and theory.

John Robert Colombo has written a number of books of Canadian facts, figures and trivia and others on places in Canada such as *Canadian Literary Landmarks*. Mordecai Richler, well known for his fiction, also writes on a range of topics in his opinionated way. *Home Sweet Home: My Canadian Album* is a collection of essays on the country.

Ralph Nader (yes, the famous US consumer advocate) has put together an interesting and sometimes surprising list of many of Canada's achievements in the book *Canada Firsts*.

The *Canadian Encyclopedia* is a four-volume reference set published by Mel Hurtig and found in any decent Canadian library. It has a wealth of information on the country and is sold on CD-ROM.

Bookshops

Any store of reasonable size will have a Canadiana section covering both fiction and nonfiction titles. Other stores of note are mentioned in the text in the city sections. The country's two largest bookstore chains are SmithBooks and Coles which have merged and have giant outlets called Chapters. Another chain with huge stores is Indigo. Outside Quebec and New Brunswick, books written in French are generally available only at specialised shops which are found in most major cities.

NEWSPAPERS & MAGAZINES

The *Globe & Mail* newspaper, sometimes termed Canada's newspaper, is published in Toronto but is available across the country daily and provides a well written record of national affairs from politics to the arts. The *National Post* is also a quality national paper with an emphasis on business.

Other principal newspapers are the *Montreal Gazette*, *Ottawa Citizen*, *Toronto Star*, and *Vancouver Sun*.

In Quebec, readers of French should have a look at both the federalist *La Presse*, the largest circulation French daily and the separatist leaning *Le Devoir*, although there are other French dailies as well.

Maclean's is Canada's weekly news magazine. *Canadian Geographic* is a monthly with excellent articles and photography on a range of Canadian topics from wildlife to weather.

Shops specialising in magazines and newspapers from around the world can be found in many cities across the country. Staff of major hotels should be able to direct you to these central outlets although some hotels also stock a selection of foreign papers. A selection of international periodicals may also be available at airport kiosks.

RADIO & TV

The Canadian Broadcasting Corporation (CBC) with both national and regional broadcasts in both radio (on AM and FM bands) and TV can be seen or heard almost anywhere in the country including some of the more remote areas. It carries more Canadian content in music and information than any of the private broadcast companies. CBC Radio, in particular, is a fine service which unites listeners across the country with some of its programs.

Highly recommended is the This Morning show heard between 9 am and noon during weekdays. It's entertaining, educational and offers listeners a well rounded view of the nation's opinions.

Many private AM broadcasters in large cities have gone to so-called Talk Radio with a baiting host and opinionated listener/callers. Ask around and tune in for a quick earful of what some Canadians think of the day's hot topics. Two major stations you might try are CFRB 1010 in Toronto or CJAD 800 in Montreal.

FM stations tend to have fewer advertisements and specialise in one form of music, be it rock or classical.

The CBC also has a French radio and TV network, both going under the name Radio-Canada. These can also be tuned into anywhere across the country.

The other major national TV network is the Canadian Television Network (CTV). It is the main commercial channel broadcasting a mix of Canadian, US and national

programs. Its nightly national news show is seen across the country.

Canadians can readily tune into TV and radio stations from the USA and often do.

PHOTOGRAPHY & VIDEO

Camera shops in the major centres are good, well informed and stock a range of products. All films are available at these outlets. Stores in larger centres also provide the freshest film (always check the expiry date) and the best prices.

Transparency film (slides) has become difficult to get without going to a good camera shop. The same goes for digital and video camera equipment and supplies. Tapes are also available at Radio Shack, a cross-country electronic retailer. Chemists, department stores and corner convenience shops generally carry only basic Kodak and Fuji print film.

Most film in Canada is bought with processing not included. However, an exception is Kodachrome which can be purchased with processing included (the cheapest option) or finishing extra. The Kodachrome processing plant is in the USA and film can be mailed directly to them, or you can leave the film at a camera store where, for a modest fee, the delivery will be arranged. Black's is a good retail outlet found across the country except in Quebec. It sells a good selection of film and offers quick processing, too.

Carrying an extra battery for your built-in light meter is a good idea because you know the one you're using will die at the most inopportune time.

For photographing wildlife, a 100mm lens is useful and can be handheld. To get serious, you will need a 200mm telephoto lens and a tripod. Early morning and evening are the best times of day to spy animals in the wild.

Canadian airports use X-ray scanning machines for security which should pose no problems to most films. Any given roll should not be scanned more than half a dozen times to be on the safe side. With specialised film, for example film with an ASA

(ISO) of 400 or higher, X-ray damage is a real threat. For those who do not want to take a chance with any film, good camera shops offer lead-lined pouches which can hold several canisters of film and which provide total protection. And, no, they are not unduly heavy.

TIME

Canada spans six of the world's 24 time zones. As shown on the map, the eastern zone in Newfoundland is unusual in that it's only a half-hour different from the adjacent zone. The time difference from coast to coast is 4½ hours.

Canada uses Daylight Saving Time during summer. It begins on the last Sunday in April and ends on the last Sunday in October. It is one hour later than Standard Time, meaning a seemingly longer summer day. Saskatchewan is the exception, using Standard Time year-round.

For details of each provincial time zone see the Information section at the beginning of each province chapter.

Some examples for time comparisons are: if it's noon in Toronto (UST/GMT), it is 9 am in Vancouver or Los Angeles, 1 pm in Halifax, 5 pm in London, 2 am (the following day) in Tokyo, and 3 am (the following day) in Sydney.

ELECTRICITY

Canada, like the USA, operates on 110V, 60-cycle electric power. Non-North American visitors should bring a plug adapter if they wish to use their own small appliances such as razors, hairdryers etc. Canadian electrical goods come with either a two-pronged plug (the same as a US one) or sometimes a three-pronger with the added ground. Most sockets can accommodate both types of plugs.

WEIGHTS & MEASURES

Canada officially changed from imperial measurement to the metric system in the 1970s. Most citizens accepted this change only begrudgingly and even today both systems remain for many day-to-day uses.

All speed-limit signs are in metric – so do not go 100mph! Gasoline is sold in litres but items such as hamburger meat and potatoes

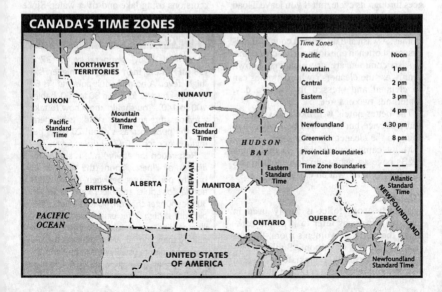

CANADA'S TIME ZONES

Time Zones	
Pacific	Noon
Mountain	1 pm
Central	2 pm
Eastern	3 pm
Atlantic	4 pm
Newfoundland	4.30 pm
Greenwich	8 pm
Provincial Boundaries	—·—
Time Zone Boundaries	— — —

NORTHWEST TERRITORIES

YUKON

NUNAVUT

Pacific Standard Time

Mountain Standard Time

Central Standard Time

HUDSON BAY

Eastern Standard Time

PACIFIC OCEAN

BRITISH COLUMBIA

ALBERTA

SASKATCHEWAN

MANITOBA

ONTARIO

QUEBEC

Atlantic Standard Time

NEWFOUNDLAND

UNITED STATES OF AMERICA

Newfoundland Standard Time

are still often sold by the pound. Radio stations will often give temperatures in both Celsius and Fahrenheit degrees.

The expensive changeover has really resulted in a bit of a mess. The old system can never be eliminated completely as long as the USA, Canada's largest trading partner, still uses its version of imperial measure.

For help in converting between the two systems, see the chart on the inside back cover of this book. Note that the US system, basically the same as the imperial, differs in liquid measurement, most significantly (for drivers) in the size of its gallons.

LAUNDRY

All cities and major towns have central storefronts known as laundromats (we use the term laundrettes in this book) with rows of coin-operated washing machines and dryers. These tend to be open every day until about 11 pm. There is rarely an attendant on the premises. Many laundrettes have machines which will dispense change and ones for dispensing soap. It is less trouble, more reliable, more convenient and cheaper to bring both. It's fine to go out for a coffee while the wash goes through its cycle, but if you leave a load too long it may be dumped on top of a machine when somebody takes it over for their clothes. A wash and dry costs a couple of dollars, most often in one dollar or 25-cent coins.

Also common are dry cleaners, known simply as 'the cleaners', where clothes can be cleaned and pressed in about a day, sometimes two or three.

The better hotels will likely have an in-house service but rates will be higher than going to the cleaners on your own.

Many campgrounds, hostels and some B&Bs have a washer and dryer that guests may use, generally at an extra fee.

TOILETS

That dirty word toilet is rarely used in Canada. Canadians refer to it as the bathroom, the men's or women's room, the rest room (!) or the washroom. Public washrooms are virtually nonexistent; instead visit a hotel, restaurant, museum etc.

HEALTH
Health Preparations

If you are embarking on a long trip make sure your teeth are OK. If you wear glasses take a spare pair and your prescription.

No jabs are required to visit Canada, except if you are coming from an infected area – immunisation against yellow fever is the most likely requirement. Some routine vaccinations are recommended nonetheless for all travellers. They include polio, tetanus and diphtheria, and sometimes measles, mumps and rubella. These vaccinations are usually administered during childhood, but some require booster shots.

It's a good idea to pack a basic medical kit (antiseptic solution, aspirin or paracetamol, band aids etc) even when your destination is a place like Canada where first-aid supplies are readily available. Don't forget any medication you are already taking.

Basic Rules

Water Purification Canadian tap water from coast to coast is safe to drink. The following information is for those who intend to be out in the woods or in the wilds on outdoor excursions using lake and river water. Since

---

Everyday Health

A normal body temperature is 37°C (98.6°F); more than 2°C (4°F) higher is a 'high' fever. A normal adult pulse rate is 60 to 80 per minute (children 80 to 100, babies 100 to 140). You should know how to take a temperature and a pulse rate. As a general rule the pulse increases about 20 beats per minute for each 1°C (2°F) rise in fever.

Respiration (breathing) rate is also an indicator of illness. Count the number of breaths per minute: between 12 and 20 is normal for adults and older children (up to 30 for younger children, 40 for babies). People with a high fever or serious respiratory illness (like pneumonia) breathe more quickly than normal. More than 40 shallow breaths a minute usually means pneumonia.

most extended adventure trips are taken in government parks, ask the ranger about local water quality. The simplest way of purifying water is to boil it thoroughly. Vigorously boiling for five minutes should be satisfactory even at high altitude. Remember that at high altitude water boils at a lower temperature, so germs are less likely to be killed.

Simple filtering will not remove all dangerous organisms, so if you cannot boil water it should be treated chemically. Chlorine tablets (Puritabs, Steritabs or other brand names) will kill many pathogens, but not giardia and amoebic cysts. Iodine is very effective in purifying water and is available in tablet form (such as Potable Aqua), but follow the directions carefully and, remember, too much iodine can be harmful.

Environmental Hazards

Sunburn & Windburn Sunburn and windburn should be primary concerns for anyone planning to spend time trekking or travelling over snow and ice. The sun will burn you even if you feel cold and the wind will cause dehydration and chafing of skin. Use a good sunscreen and a moisture cream on exposed skin, even on cloudy days. A hat provides added protection and zinc cream or some other barrier cream for your nose and lips is recommended if you're spending any time on ice or snow.

Reflection and glare from ice and snow can cause snow blindness so it's essential to use high-protection sunglasses for any sort of glacier visit or ski trip. Calamine lotion is good for mild sunburn.

Cold Despite the perception by some that Canada is a perpetually ice-bound wasteland, health problems due to extreme cold are not likely to be suffered by many people. On winter days when frost bite is a possibility (due almost always to a combination of low temperature and high wind, the result of which is a reading known as the wind-chill factor) you will be aware of it. Everybody will be discussing it, the radio will broadcast warnings about how many

minutes of exposed skin is acceptable and ... it will be bloody cold.

If you are in the mountains or the north, you should always be prepared for cold, wet or windy conditions even if you're just out walking or hitching.

Hypothermia occurs when the body loses heat faster than it can produce it and the core temperature of the body falls. It is surprisingly easy to progress from very cold to dangerously cold due to a combination of wind, wet clothing, fatigue and hunger, even if the air temperature is above freezing. It is best to dress in layers; silk, wool and some of the new artificial fibres are all good insulating materials. A hat is important, as a lot of heat is lost through the head. A strong, waterproof outer layer is essential, as keeping dry is vital. Carry basic supplies, including food containing simple sugars to generate heat quickly and take lots of fluid to drink.

Symptoms of hypothermia are exhaustion, numb skin (particularly toes and fingers), shivering, slurred speech, irrational or violent behaviour, lethargy, stumbling, dizzy spells, muscle cramps and violent bursts of energy. Irrationality may take the form of sufferers claiming they are warm and trying to take off their clothes.

To treat hypothermia, first get the person out of the wind and/or rain, remove their clothing if its wet and replace it with dry, warm clothing. Give them hot liquids – not alcohol – and some high-kilojoule, easily digestible food. Do not rub victims, instead allow them to slowly warm themselves. This should be enough for the early stages of hypothermia. If it has gone further it may be necessary to place victims in warm sleeping bags and get in with them.

Altitude Sickness Acute Mountain Sickness or AMS occurs at high altitude and can be fatal. The lack of oxygen at high altitudes affects most people to some extent.

A number of measures can be adopted to prevent acute mountain sickness:

• Ascend slowly – have frequent rest days, spending two to three nights at each rise of 1000m. If you reach a high altitude by

trekking, acclimatisation takes place gradually and you are less likely to be affected than if you fly direct.
- Drink extra fluids. The mountain air is dry and cold and moisture is lost as you breathe.
- Eat light, high-carbohydrate meals for more energy.
- Avoid alcohol as it may increase the risk of dehydration.
- Avoid sedatives.

Even with acclimatisation you may still have trouble adjusting. Headaches, nausea, dizziness, a dry cough, insomnia, breathlessness and loss of appetite are all signs to heed. Mild altitude problems will generally abate after a day or so but if the symptoms persist or become worse the only treatment is to descend. Even 500m can help. Increasing tiredness, confusion, and lack of coordination and balance are real danger signs. Any of these symptoms individually, even just a persistent headache, can be a warning.

There is no hard and fast rule as to how high is too high: AMS has been fatal at altitudes of 3000m, although 3500 to 4500m is the usual range. It is always wise to sleep at a lower altitude than the greatest height reached during the day.

Motion Sickness Eating lightly before and during a trip will reduce the chances of motion sickness. If you are prone to motion sickness try to find a place that minimises disturbance – near the wing on aircraft, close to midships on boats, near the centre on buses. Fresh air usually helps, reading or cigarette smoke doesn't. Commercial anti-motion-sickness preparations, which can cause drowsiness, have to be taken before the trip commences; when you're feeling sick it's too late. Ginger (available in capsule form) and peppermint (including mint-flavoured sweets) are natural preventatives.

Infectious Diseases

Giardiasis If you're going to backcountry camp, you should take precautions against an intestinal parasite *(Giardia lamblia)* which causes giardiasis, known colloqui-ally as 'beaver fever'. This intestinal parasite is present in contaminated water.

The symptoms are stomach cramps, nausea, a bloated stomach, watery, foul-smelling diarrhoea and frequent gas. Giardiasis can appear several weeks after you have been exposed to the parasite. The symptoms may disappear for a few days and then return; this can go on for several weeks.

You should seek medical advice if you think you have giardiasis or amoebic dysentery, but where this is not possible, tinidazole or metronidazole are the recommended drugs. Treatment is a 2g single dose of tinidazole or 250mg of metronidazole three times daily for five to 10 days.

Rabies This isn't a major problem, but rabies is something to be aware of when spending any time in the woods or undeveloped areas. Animals most likely affected are the squirrel, skunk, racoon, bat and, particularly, the fox. Paradoxically, all of the above animals have learned to adapt quite well to populated regions, and may be seen in city parks and recreation areas, wooded areas around rivers and streams and even along residential streets after dark. Especially on garbage nights!

Rabies is caused by a bite or scratch by an infected animal. Any bite, scratch or even lick from a mammal should be cleaned immediately and thoroughly. Scrub with soap and running water, and then clean with an alcohol or iodine solution. If there is any possibility that the animal is infected, medical help should be sought immediately. Even if the animal is not rabid, all bites should be treated seriously as they can become infected or can result in tetanus. A rabies vaccination is now available and should be considered if you are in a high-risk category – eg, if you intend to explore caves (bat bites could be dangerous) or work with animals.

Lyme Disease A minor threat but still something to be aware of is Lyme disease (doesn't it seem as though there's always something new out there to get you?).

Since the late 1980s each summer sees more of this disease although the vast majority of North American cases have occurred in the USA. The disease is really more of a condition transmitted by a certain species of deer tick, similar to a tick found on a dog but smaller. The tick infects the skin with the spirochaete bacterium which causes the disease. The disease was first identified on the continent in 1975 in Lyme, Connecticut, hence the name.

Most cases still go undetected, misdiagnosed or unreported. It is a difficult disease to diagnose because symptoms vary widely.

The illness usually begins with a spreading rash at the site of the tick bite and is accompanied by fever, headache, extreme fatigue, aching joints and muscles and mild neck stiffness. If untreated, these symptoms usually resolve over several weeks but over subsequent weeks or months disorders of the nervous system, heart and joints may develop. Treatment works best early in the illness. Medical help should be sought.

The best way to avoid the whole business is to take precautions in areas where it has been reported such as Turkey Point, Ontario.

If walking in the woods, cover the body as much as possible, use an insect repellent containing diethylmetatoluamide (DEET) and at the end of the day check yourself, children or pets for the ticks. DEET is not recommended for children, so a milder substitute will have to do. Chances are that you will not feel it if bitten. Of course, most ticks are not the right sort to pass on the disease and even most of the nasties do not carry the harmful bacteria.

Sexually Transmitted Diseases (STDs)
STDs include gonorrhoea, herpes and syphilis; sores, blisters or rashes around the genitals and discharges or pain when urinating are common symptoms. In some STDs, such as wart virus or chlamydia, symptoms may be less marked or not observed at all, especially in women. Chlamydia infection can cause infertility in men and women before any symptoms have been noticed. Syphilis symptoms eventually disappear completely but the disease continues and can cause severe problems in later years. While abstinence from sexual contact is the only 100% effective prevention, using condoms is also effective. The treatment of gonorrhoea and syphilis is with antibiotics. The different sexually transmitted diseases each require specific antibiotics.

HIV/AIDS Infection with the human immunodeficiency virus (HIV) may lead to acquired immune deficiency syndrome (AIDS), which is a fatal disease. Any exposure to blood, blood products or body fluids may put the individual at risk. The disease is often transmitted through sexual contact or dirty needles – vaccinations, acupuncture, tattooing and body piercing can be potentially as dangerous as intravenous drug use.

Fear of HIV infection should never preclude treatment for serious medical conditions.

Women's Health
Gynaecological Problems Antibiotic use, synthetic underwear, excessive sweating and contraceptive pills can lead to fungal vaginal infections, especially when travelling in hot climates. Fungal infections are characterised by a rash, itch and discharge and can be treated with a vinegar or lemon-juice douche, or with yoghurt. Nystatin, miconazole or clotrimazole pessaries or vaginal cream are the usual treatment. Maintaining good personal hygiene and wearing loose-fitting clothes and cotton underwear may help prevent these infections.

WOMEN TRAVELLERS
More and more, women are travelling alone in Canada. This goes for vacationers, visitors and women on business.

There are no overriding differences for men and women travelling in Canada and as a western country there are no particular cultural or traditional pitfalls of which females need to be aware.

As in so much of the world, though, women may face some sexism and the threat of violence is certainly felt more by women

than by men. The following tips to consider have been suggested by women.

When travelling alone, try to arrive at your destination before dark. If arriving at a bus or train station (bus stations in particular are often not in the best parts of town) take a taxi to the place where you're spending the night. In some of the larger cities, the bus and/or train station is connected to the subway system. Subways in Canada are clean and safe. Once close to your destination, catch a taxi from the subway stop.

Some parts of the downtown areas of major cities should be avoided at night especially on a Friday or Saturday. Where applicable, these areas are noted in the text.

If driving, keep your vehicle well maintained and don't get low on gasoline. If you do break down on the highway, especially at night, a large pre-made sign placed in the window reading 'Call Police' is not a bad idea. Such a sign will quickly result in calls and a cruiser on the way. Away from busy areas, it is not advisable for women alone to get out of their car and wait beside it, especially at night. Wait inside with the doors locked. In cities avoid underground parking lots, which are uniformly creepy.

It is rare indeed to see women alone hitching and it can't be recommended. Mixed sex couples are the better way for women to hitch a ride if they are determined to travel this way. For more information see Hitching in the Getting Around chapter.

Women alone may be more comfortable if their room is booked before they arrive in a new town. Many women prefer to simply use an initial with their surname and not to use a title when making reservations or appointments. Many of the chain hotels and motels have toll-free numbers which allow for reservations to be made in advance.

Hostels and B&Bs are good, safe choices. Many Canadian B&Bs are run by couples or women. In B&Bs and guesthouses, ask whether the rooms have locks – some do not.

When checking into a motel, ask to see the room first and make sure the doors and windows can be secured. Most motel rooms come with a telephone.

A few of the cheaper inner-city hotels listed in the text are not suitable for women alone. Where these places are mentioned it is suggested that accommodation should be sought elsewhere.

Unaccompanied women in nightclubs or bars will often find they get a lot of attention (and possibly drinks) whether they want it or not.

For women who enjoy the outdoors, the smell of perfumes and fragrant cosmetics attracts bears so, if you're likely to be in an area where they're around, it's best not to wear any. Insects, too, are said to find perfume a pleasant lure.

In Toronto, the Women's Counselling Referral & Education Centre (☎ 416-534-7501) at 525 Bloor St W can offer advice on a wide range of problems and questions.

Planned Parenthood can be contacted at ☎ 416-961-3200.

GAY & LESBIAN TRAVELLERS

As a generally tolerant country, Canada doesn't present any particular problems for homosexuals. Laws in Canada protect against discrimination on the basis of sexual orientation.

Montreal, Toronto and Vancouver have sizable gay communities with support groups, associations and any number of clubs and bars. Specialised bookstores and entertainment and news weeklies may also be found. In Toronto, *Xtra* magazine is a bi-weekly with a full range of information including advertisements for lodgings and other businesses which cater primarily to gays. It also publishes *Xtra West* in Vancouver and *Capitol Xtra* in Ottawa. Halifax has *Wayves* and Montreal *Fugues* which are similar. These magazines may be able to help with contacts in other parts of the country. All major cities have at least a dance club or two. Montreal, Toronto and Vancouver have celebratory Gay Pride Days which attract big crowds including straights.

In Toronto, call Gay Services – TAGL (☎ 416-964-6600) for information and counselling.

Columbia Fun Maps (www.funmaps.net) produces gay/lesbian oriented map/brochures for cities across North America. The Montreal guide, for example, also includes information on Quebec City.

The Male Accommodation Network (MAN; ☎ 514-933-7571) is a gay reservation lodging service with contacts around the major centres in Quebec, Ontario and Vancouver.

DISABLED TRAVELLERS

Canada has gone further than the vast majority of the world's countries in making day-to-day life less burdensome to the physically disabled, most notably the wheelchair bound. This process continues.

Most public buildings are wheelchair accessible, including major tourist offices. Ditto for major museums, art galleries and principal attractions. All the above and many restaurants also have washroom facilities suitable for wheelchairs. Major hotels are often equipped to deal with wheelchairs and some less-expensive motel chains such as the countrywide Comfort Inn (frequently mentioned through the text) has wheelchair access through ramps.

Many of the national and provincial parks have accessible interpretive centres and even some of the shorter nature trails and/or boardwalks have been developed with wheelchairs or self-propelled mobility aids in mind.

The VIA Rail system is prepared to accommodate the wheelchair-bound but advance notice of 48 hours should be given. All bus lines will assist passengers and take chairs or any other aids providing they collapse and will fit in the usual luggage compartments. And all Canadian airlines are accustomed to dealing with disabled passengers and provide early boarding and disembarking as standard practice.

In major cities, parking lots all have designated parking spots for the physically disabled, usually marked with a painted wheelchair. These spots, located closest to the door or access point of the place being visited, can not be used by others under threat of serious fine.

Car-rental agencies can provide special accessories such as handcontrols but again, advance notice is required. Toronto's public transportation system, the TTC, has a special bus service around town with lifts for wheelchairs.

The Canadian Parapalegic Association (☎ 416-422-5640) at 520 Sutherland Drive, Toronto M4G 3V9 can help with information on facilities for handicapped travellers in Canada.

SENIOR TRAVELLERS

Visitors over the age of 65, and sometimes 60, should take advantage of the many cost reductions they are offered in Canada. Canadians of this age are classed as 'seniors' and it is this term that is seen frequently. Seniors' discounts are offered on all means of transportation and can mean substantial savings. Many of the government parks have reduced rates as do most of the country's attractions, museums, historic sites, even movie houses. Some hotels and motels may provide a price reduction – it's always worth asking.

Elderhostel with branches in many countries is also found in Canada. It specialises in inexpensive, educational packages for those over 60 years of age. The standard type of program consists of mornings of talks and lectures followed by afternoon field trips and visits to related sights. Participants are accommodated in university dorms or the like. There is generally a full-package price which includes meals, lodging and some transportation. The courses are of varying lengths but may be several weeks long. Subject matter is drawn from a variety of interests including history, nature, geography and art. For more detailed information contact Elderhostel Canada (☎ 613-530-2222, ecmail@ elderhostel.org), 4 Catarqui St, Kingston, Ontario, K7K 1Z7.

From Toronto, Seniors Travel (☎ 416-322-1500) runs group tours for those over 50 to either eastern or western Canada during the summer. It is at 225 Eglinton Ave W, Toronto, Ontario M4R 1A9.

TRAVEL WITH CHILDREN

Almost all attractions in Canada offer child rates. Some hotels don't charge at all for young children. *Travel with Children*, Maureen Wheeler, Lonely Planet Publications, includes basic advice on travel health for younger children.

Always fit children with lifejackets during any boating/canoeing excursions. While camping or in remote areas be aware of how quickly children can become disoriented and lost. Also do not let kids stray where bears and cougars are known to exist. Ask park rangers if in any doubt. Never let children approach wild animals, no matter how cute and tame the animal appears.

DANGERS & ANNOYANCES

Check the Health section earlier in this chapter for possible health risks. See also Road Rules & Safety Precautions in the Getting Around chapter for tips about driving.

Urban Problems

Canadian cities have serious problems with homeless people and mental patients coping with little supervision or care. The numbers of beggars – young, old, male, female – often surprises and/or shocks both residents and visitors. Since the mid-1990s, the quantity of people living on the street has risen dramatically due to various social and political factors, although some of the young are poseurs. They generally present no danger, just a mix of emotions and concern.

Fire

When camping outside legitimate campgrounds do not start a fire. This is extremely dangerous and could cause untold amounts of devastation during the dry summer months.

In designated campgrounds make sure that anything that was burning is put out completely when you've finished with it, including cigarettes.

Bears

A serious problem encountered when you're camping in the woods is the animals – most importantly bears – who are always looking for an easy snack. Keep your food in nylon bags. Tie the sack to a rope and sling it over a branch away from your tent and away from the trunk of the tree as most bears can climb. Hoist it up high enough, about 3m, so a standing bear can't reach it. Don't leave food scraps around the site and never, ever keep food in the tent.

Don't try to get close-up photographs of bears and never come between a bear and its cubs. If you see any cubs, quietly and quickly disappear. If you do see a bear, try to get upwind so it can smell you and you won't startle it. While hiking through woods or in the mountains in bear country, some people wear a noise-maker, like a bell. Talking or singing is just as good. Whatever you do, don't feed bears – they lose their fear of people and eventually their lives to park wardens.

Blackflies & Mosquitoes

In the woods of Canada, particularly in the north, the blackflies and mosquitoes can be murder – they seems to get worse the farther north you get. There are tales of lost hikers going insane from the bugs. This is no joke – they can make you miserable. The effect of a bite (or sting, technically, by the mosquito) is a small itchy bump. The moment of attack is itself a very minor, passing pain. Some people are allergic to blackfly bites and will develop a fair bit of swelling. But other than the unsightly welt, there is no real danger. The potential trouble is in the cumulative effects of scores of them and even this hazard is mainly psychological.

As a rule, darker clothes are said to attract biting insects more than lighter ones. Perfume, too, evidently attracts the wrong kind of attention. Take 'bug juice' liquid or spray repellents. Two recommended names are Muskol and Off; the latter also has an extra strength version known as Deep Woods Off. An ingredient often used in repellents known as DEET should not be used on children. There are brands without it. Try to minimise the amount of skin exposed by wearing a long-sleeved shirt, long pants and a close-fitting hat or cap.

June is generally the worst month, and as the summer wears on the bugs disappear. The bugs are at their worst deep in the woods. In clearings, along shorelines or anywhere there's a breeze you'll be safe, except for the buzzing horseflies, which are basically teeth with wings.

Mosquitoes come out around sunset; building a fire will help keep them away. For campers, a tent with a zippered screen is pretty much a necessity.

If you do get lost and are being eaten alive, submerge your body in water if you are by a lake or river. This will enable you to think clearly about where you are and what to do. Lemon or orange peel rubbed on your skin will help if you're out of repellent.

Other Stings & Bites

Canada is relatively problem-free regarding stings and bites. There are no poisonous spiders or insects. Rattlesnakes do live in parts of Ontario, Alberta and British Columbia but are rarely seen – even by serious hikers – and actually are generally timid. Still the bite is a matter of concern and immediate medical attention is essential. The normal run of bees, wasps and hornets is found across the country. Those with allergies should carry kits outside of urban areas.

In some areas, sand gnats and 'no-see-ums', bugs so called because you never see them but rather just feel their bites, may be encountered. There is not much to be done about it; fortunately neither are overly common. Campers should have very finely meshed tents to prevent a possible night invasion of noseeums. This insect-generated horror really isn't so bad but it's better to hear the worst than to be caught off guard. Millions spend time in the bush each year and actually live to tell about it. And besides, this is the only kind of terrorism you have to concern yourself with in Canada – bugs are better than bombs.

Camp-Site Pests

Campers are unlikely to encounter bears but squirrels, chipmunks, mice and raccoons are common. And they all love human food. They will spend a lot of time tearing through any bags of food or garbage you leave about and even smack pots and pans around making a heck of a clatter in the middle of the night. The best defence is not to feed them, no matter how cute, and store all food securely.

EMERGENCY

In most of the country, particularly urban areas, telephone ☎ 911 for all police, fire, accident and medical emergencies. See under the province introductions for details. In all other areas or when in doubt, call ☎ 0 and ask the operator for assistance. You will

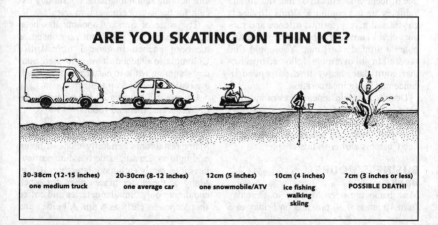

ARE YOU SKATING ON THIN ICE?

30-38cm (12-15 inches)	20-30cm (8-12 inches)	12cm (5 inches)	10cm (4 inches)	7cm (3 inches or less)
one medium truck	one average car	one snowmobile/ATV	ice fishing walking skiing	POSSIBLE DEATH!

then be put through to the appropriate service. Dialling ☎ 911 results in a faster response. For non-emergency police matters, consult the local telephone book for the number of the station.

Should your passport get lost or stolen, contact your nearest consulate. It will be able to issue a temporary replacement and inform you when and how to go about getting another. You may not need another depending on your travel plans. For lost or stolen travellers cheques, contact the issuer or its representative. Upon purchase of the cheques you should have received a list of telephone numbers to call in case of loss. To expedite matters, do record which cheques you cash as is suggested. If you supply a list of which cheques are gone, a refund should be forthcoming with minimal inconvenience.

If you plan to make an insurance claim be sure to contact the police and have them make a record of the theft. Ask for the reference number on the police report as the insurance company will want it.

If you lose your credit card or travellers cheques, call the salient emergency number: VISA (☎ 1-800-336-8472), MasterCard (☎ 1-800-361-3361) or American Express (☎ 1-800-221-7282).

LEGAL MATTERS

Visitors are unlikely to meet Canadian police officers. Spot checks on individuals and vehicles are not common. Drunk driving is considered a very serious offence and random checks are held at bar closing time and notably around Christmas. You could find yourself in jail overnight, followed by a further court date, heavy fine, suspended licence and more incarceration.

Despite possible appearances of indifference, recreational drugs are illegal and laws may be enforced at any time. Smuggling any drugs, including pot, is a serious crime. See Customs earlier in this chapter.

BUSINESS HOURS
Banks

Most banks are open Monday to Thursday from 10 am to 4.30 pm, and on Friday to 5

or 6 pm. Some banks are open Saturday morning. Trust companies open for longer hours, perhaps to 6 pm Monday to Friday and are often open Saturday from 10 am to 4 pm. Banks and trust companies are closed on Sunday and on holidays. Many banks now have ATMs, known as banking machines in Canada, which are accessible 24 hours a day.

Post Offices

Canada Post offices are open Monday to Friday, generally 9 am to 5 pm. Postal outlets in retails stores have longer hours.

Stores

Cities and their suburbs generally have the longest retail store hours. Opening time is usually from about 9 am with closing time around 6 pm. On Friday, and sometimes Thursday, shops are open until 9 pm. Shopping malls, plazas, large department stores and some downtown stores may remain open until 9 pm every day.

Larger centres have a limited number of stores which remain open 24 hours. The vast majority of these are convenience shops which sell basic groceries, cigarettes and newspapers. Also, some supermarkets remain open 24 hours as do some chemists (drug stores).

Shops in smaller centres generally have shorter hours with little evening shopping and nothing much available on Sunday except for basic groceries and movies.

The issue of Sunday opening has been hotly debated for years but no consensus has been reached. In general, from British Columbia to Quebec there is limited Sunday shopping while in eastern Canada shops are basically closed up tight.

On major highways 24-hour service stations sell gasoline and food.

Restaurants

Many restaurants generally close at about midnight as Canadians do not dine particularly late, rarely eating out later than 10 pm. Many of the better places open for lunch and dinner only. Smaller eateries and coffee shops open as early as 6 am. All cities and

many towns have restaurants that are open 24 hours.

Bars & Liquor Sales

Hours vary according to the province. Most bars, pubs and lounges open at noon and close at 1 or 2 am. In Ontario last call is 2 am. In Quebec laws are more liberal allowing bars to stay open until 3 or 4 am. The larger cities usually have after-hours bars which remain open for music or dancing but stop serving alcohol. West of Ontario there is 'off-sales' meaning bars and hotels are permitted to sell takeaway beer. In Alberta all alcohol is sold through private retailers, and in Quebec wine and beer can be bought at grocery stores and corner shops. In all other cases, alcohol must be bought through government retail stores.

The drinking age varies from province to province but the norm is 19 years old.

PUBLIC HOLIDAYS

Labour Day is an important holiday as this long weekend is unofficially seen as the end of summer. It marks the closing of many businesses, attractions and services, and the beginning of a change of hours of operation for many others.

Thanksgiving (the same as the American holiday, but held earlier) is really a harvest festival. The traditional meal includes roasted turkey.

Although not officially a holiday, Halloween, 31 October, is a significant and fun celebration. Based on a Celtic pagan tradition, Halloween is a time for costume parties. In larger cities, gays have adopted it as a major event and nightclubs are often the scene of wild masquerades.

National & Provincial Holidays

The following is a list of the main public holidays:

January
New Year's Day (1 January)

February-March
Alberta – Family Day, third Monday in February
Newfoundland – St Patrick's Day (Monday nearest 17 March), St George's Day (Monday nearest 23 April)

April-May
Easter (Good Friday, also Easter Monday for government and schools)
Victoria Day (Monday preceding May 24 except in the Atlantic Provinces)

June
Quebec – Fête Nationale, formerly known as Saint Jean Baptiste Day (24 June)
Newfoundland – Discovery Day (Monday nearest 24 June)

July
Canada Day, called Memorial Day in Newfoundland (1 July)
Newfoundland – Orangeman's Day (Monday nearest 13 July)

August
Yukon – Discovery Day (the third Monday in August)
All other provinces Civic Holiday (1 August or first Monday in August)

September-October
Labour Day (first Monday in September)
Thanksgiving (second Monday in October)

November-December
Remembrance Day (11 November – banks and government)
Christmas Day (25 December)
Boxing Day (26 December – many retailers open, other businesses closed)

SPECIAL EVENTS

Major events are listed in the text under the city or town where they occur. There are many others.

The provincial governments publish annual lists of events and special attractions as part of their tourism promotion packages. Each gives dates, locations and often brief descriptions. Local tourist departments may print up more detailed and extensive lists of their own, which include cultural and sporting exhibitions and happenings of all kinds. Military and historic celebrations, ethnic festivals and music shows are all included. Some provinces produce separate booklets for summer and winter events.

Major provincial and national holidays are usually cause for some celebration, especially

in summer when events often wrap up with a fireworks display. The 1 July Canada Day festivities are particularly noted for this with the skies lit up from coast to coast.

ACTIVITIES

Canada's greatest attribute is its natural environment. This, for the most part, is what it has to offer visitors and what makes it unique. Much of Canada's appeal lies in the range of physical activities such as hiking, canoeing, fishing, skiing and observing and photographing flora and fauna.

There are wilderness trips of all types, organised or self-directed. Provincial tourist offices have information on activities in their region and also details on the hundreds of private businesses, operators and outfitters offering adventure tours and trips. Many provinces have booklets and maps on canoeing and hiking. All have information on national and provincial parks, many of which can be highlights of a trip to Canada. Many of the national and provincial parks are detailed in the text (see the special section on Canada's Flora, Fauna and National Parks, or the province and territory chapters for more detail).

Activities of most interest to visitors are detailed below.

Hiking

Canada offers a range of walks and hikes that are long or short, rugged or gentle, mountain or coastal. Almost all of the country's trails, and certainly most of the best, are found in either the provincial or national parks.

The majority of parks have some type of walking path although some may be no more than a short nature trail. The larger the park, as a rule, the longer the trail. Some require one or more nights camping to complete. Conservation areas, wildlife reserves and sanctuaries often have marked trails.

Outside the federal and provincial park systems there are also some extended trails running through a mix of public and private lands.

Work is continuing on the Trans Canada Trail, a 15,000km crushed stone path winding from coast to coast with an offshoot from Calgary to Tuktoyaktuk on the Arctic Ocean. It will take about 300 days to cycle, 500 days to ride on horseback and 750 days to walk. For the current status and information on completed sections call the trail foundation at ☎ 1-800-465-3636 or visit www.tctrail.ca.

Throughout the text, parks with trails are discussed and some individual trails are outlined. Some highlights are:

- Killarney Provincial Park, Ontario
- Pukaskwa National Park on Lake Superior, Ontario
- Bruce Trail, Ontario which runs from Lake Ontario 700km north to Georgian Bay (see The Bruce Peninsula in the Ontario chapter for details)
- Voyageur Trail in Sault Ste Marie (see Gros Cap in the Ontario chapter for details)
- Gaspésie Park and Mont Tremblant Park, Quebec
- Gros Morne National Park, Newfoundland
- Dobson Trail, New Brunswick (see the Moncton section for details)
- Trail between St Martins and Fundy National Park (see St Martins in the New Brunswick chapter for details)
- Cape Breton National Park, Nova Scotia
- Prime hiking throughout the Rockies
- Coastal hike, Pacific Rim National Park, BC
- Historic gold-rush Chilkoot Trail, Yukon (see Klondike Highway in the Yukon Territory chapter for details)

Rock Climbing

Rock climbing has come out from under its rock and is now a possibility, even for novices. Group climbs, with instructors and equipment, are available across the country. Some areas to look into include:

- Collingwood, Ontario (with some trips out of Toronto)
- Sault Ste Marie and Thunder Bay, Ontario
- Banff and Jasper, Alberta
- Squamish, British Columbia

Canoeing

The possibilities for canoeing are almost limitless from an easy half-day paddle to

some of the most challenging white waters. Again, the government parks are a good place to start and many of them are quite accessible. Some parks provide outfitters able to supply all equipment, while at other parks private operators do much the same thing from just outside the park boundaries.

In major cities operators can be found who can help organise trips and you'll find excellent sporting-equipment stores. Provincial and territory tourist boards will be able to help with information on canoeing areas and outfitters. Better bookstores and outdoor stores sell good guides to canoeing in Canada.

Some of the country's main canoeing areas follow. Details for many can be found through the text.

* Kejimkujik National Park in Nova Scotia
* La Mauricie National Park, La Verendrye Provincial Park, Quebec
* Algonquin Provincial Park, Killarney Provincial Park and at Temagami, Ontario
* Prince Albert National Park, Saskatchewan
* Bowron Lake Provincial Park, Wells Gray Provincial Park, British Columbia; Nahanni National Park, Northwest Territories
* Yukon River, Yukon Territory

Kayaking
Both whitewater and sea-kayaking has increased markedly in recent years and rentals are widely available. Recommended areas include:

* Mingan Island National Park, Quebec
* Percé, Quebec
* Ottawa River, Ontario
* Vancouver Island and around the Gulf Islands, British Columbia

Fishing
Freshwater fishing is abundant and popular across the country with both residents and visitors. Casting a line is one of the country's basic outdoor activities. In winter many northern areas set up and rent 'huts', small wooden shacks, out on frozen lakes. Inside there is a bench, sometimes a heater, a hole in the ice and often more than a few bottles of beer.

Anglers must purchase fishing licences which vary in duration and price from province to province. Any tourist office can help with information and advice on where to buy one. At the same time pick up a guide to the various 'open' seasons for each species and also a guide to eating fish. In southern regions there are recommended consumption guidelines due to natural contaminants and pollution such as mercury which are important especially for pregnant women and young children. Also be sure to check on daily limits and if there are any bait restrictions. In some areas live minnows or other bait is prohibited.

Downhill Skiing & Snowboarding
There are four main alpine ski centres. They are located in Ontario, Quebec, Alberta and BC.

The provincial tourist boards produce guides to skiing, and travel agents can arrange full-package tours which include transportation and accommodation. As the country's major ski resorts are all close to cities, it is quite straightforward to travel on your own to the slopes for a day's skiing (rentals available) and head back to the city that same night. Highlights include:

* Between the towns of Barrie and Collingwood, Ontario
* The Laurentian Mountains, about a two hour drive north of Montreal and Quebec City. South of Montreal ski centres are part of the Appalachian Mountains, known to skiers in Vermont and New Hampshire.
* The Rocky Mountains provide truly international status skiing at Banff and Lake Louise, Alberta which have runs higher than any in the European Alps. Calgary is a two hour drive to the east.
* Whistler/Blackcomb, British Columbia, is a major resort which hosts international competitions. There is also good skiing in the Okanagan and Kootenay regions of the province.

Cross-Country Skiing
Each of the above alpine regions offers cross-country skiing although good trails or conditions can be found all across Canada.

Ecotourism & Soft Adventure Activities

With Canada's remote undeveloped areas and abundant wildlife, opportunities for nature appreciation and outdoor recreation are nearly limitless. Long before the environmental movement came to the forefront, Canada was into what is now referred to as ecotourism. Wilderness trips and lodges, outdoor resorts and remote escapes have long been a part of the travel possibilities on offer in Canada.

Since the mid-1980s, though, respect for the country's natural wonders has grown markedly, not only by Canadians but also by international travellers. Perhaps the perfect example of the new ecotourism (and one of the first) is the trips to Quebec's Magdalen Islands to see and photograph baby seals. It was publicity surrounding the bloody slaughter of the seal pups (activist Brigitte Bardot was seen on the ice floes with the seals and their hunters) which diminished the controversial hunt which had long been part of the fur fashion business.

Recent years have seen further changes, innovations and growth in the ecotourism movement, resulting in a much wider range of possibilities. These include hiking the west coast rainforest, whale watching and guided camping trips with instruction on plant ecology, geology and low-impact wilderness travel. Other trips specialise in the culture of Native people, running whitewater in rafts or photographing polar bears in Churchill.

Ecotours have connotations of being costly but this is no longer necessarily the case in Canada. An increasing number of good, small, inexpensive operators have sprung up and are discussed in the text under Organised Tours and Adventure Tours; see also the special section on Canada's flora, fauna, government parks and heritage sites.

Skating

Lacing up the blades for a glide on frozen rivers and ponds and outdoor rinks is a Canadian tradition. You can rent skates at rinks in some major cities such as Montreal, Toronto and Winnipeg.

COURSES

Students wishing to study formally in Canada (eg at a university) must get authorisation within their own country. This can take six months. Information should be obtained from the Canadian embassy or other government representative in your country of residence.

Major cities have privately run schools specialising in teaching English as a second language (ESL). These can be found through the Yellow Pages phone book. Some are on the Internet. For courses over three months long, a student visa is required. Some of these schools offer TOEFL English proficiency certificates used to gain entry into Canadian universities. Montreal has numerous schools for learning French.

Also within the cities, a tremendous range of work and/or recreational courses are available ranging from acupuncture to Web page design.

Many of the outdoor outfitters mentioned in the text offer short courses in canoeing, kayaking, rockclimbing and the like.

WORK

Work authorisations must be obtained outside Canada and may take six months. A work permit is valid for one specific job and one specific time, for one specific employer.

It is difficult to get a work permit; employment opportunities go first to Canadians. Those wishing to obtain a permit must get a validated job offer from an employer and take this to a Canadian Consulate or Embassy outside Canada.

Visitors to Canada are technically not able to work. However, employers hiring casual, temporary, service workers (hotel, bar, restaurant) and construction, farm or forestry workers often don't ask for the

permit. Visitors working here legally have Social Insurance numbers beginning with '9'. If you don't have this, and get caught, you will be told to leave the country.

Many young European women come to Canada as nannies. Japan has a program called Contact Canada which includes one-year work permits with pre-arranged work generally on farms. Many countries have agencies where details on these programs can be obtained.

Student Work Abroad Program (SWAP)

Of particular interest to Australian and New Zealand students may be the SWAP. Organised by STA Travel and the Canadian Federation of Students (CFS), the program allows Australians and New Zealanders between the ages of 18 and 25 to spend a year in Canada on a working holiday. This program only has space for 200 people a year and applicants must be enrolled in a post-secondary educational institution.

After an orientation program in Vancouver you find your own job with help from the CFS. Most jobs are in the service area – as waiters, bar attendants, cleaners and maids – particularly in the snowfields over winter, although SWAP participants have worked in other kinds of jobs ranging from farmhands to hotel porters. You are issued with a one-year, nonextendable visa which allows you to work anywhere in the country. 'Swappers' must be Australian or New Zealand citizens.

STA Travel arranges group departures at reduced fares leaving from most major Australian and New Zealand cities in November and December. Independent departures leave throughout the rest of the year. Participants are given orientation information and a copy of this Lonely Planet book prior to departure.

For full details in Australia contact an STA office or phone ☎ 131776. In New Zealand you can also contact any STA office or phone toll-free ☎ 0800-874773.

Working Holiday Program

This is another program, which is open to all Australians (the New Zealand program is under review) between the ages of 18 and 25 and they need not be enrolled in a post-secondary educational institution. This program has a quota of 3000 annually. Application forms can be obtained by contacting the Canadian Consulate General in Sydney, Australia. See Embassies & Consulates earlier in this chapter for the address or visit its Web site at www.canada.org.au. The minimum processing time for these applications is 12 weeks.

ACCOMMODATION
Camping

There are campgrounds all over Canada – federal, provincial and privately owned. Government sites are nearly always better and cheaper and, not surprisingly, fill up the quickest. Government parks are well laid out, green and well treed. They are usually quiet, situated to take advantage of the local landscape, and offer a program of events and talks. Private campgrounds are generally geared to trailers (caravans) and recreational vehicles (RVs). They often have more services available and swimming pools and other entertainment facilities.

In national parks, camping fees range from $10 to $19 for an unserviced site, and to as high as $23 for sites with services like electricity. There is usually a park entrance fee as well. See under Tourist Offices earlier for more information.

Provincial-park camping rates vary with each province but range from $10 to $22. Interior camping in the wilderness parks is always less, about $5 or $6. Commercial campgrounds are generally several dollars more expensive than those in either provincial or national parks.

Government parks start closing in early September for the winter. Dates vary according to the location. Some remain open for maintenance even when camping is finished and they might let you camp at a reduced rate. Other places, late in autumn or early in spring, are free. The gate is open and there is not a soul around. Still others block the road and you just can't enter the campgrounds although the park itself can

still be visited. So, out of the main summer season, you have to investigate but using the parks after official closing can save the hardy a fair bit of money.

There are also campgrounds every 150km or so along the Trans Canada Hwy.

Many people travel around the country camping and never pay a dime. For those with cars or vans, using roadside rest areas and picnic spots is recommended. If there are signs indicating no overnight camping, don't do something like set up a tent. If you're asleep in the car and a cop happens to wake you, just say you were driving, got tired, pulled over for a quick rest and fell asleep. For less chance of interruption, little side roads and logging roads off the highway are quiet and private.

Hostels

There are some excellent travellers hostels in Canada much like those found in countries around the world. The term hostel in Canada, however, has some unfortunate connotations for travellers as well as those running them and working in them. The term has long been and continues to be used in reference to both government and private shelters for the underprivileged, sick and abused. There are, for example, hostels for battered women who have been victimised by their partners and hostels for recovering drug addicts. So, if you get a sideways glance when you smilingly say you are on the way to spend the night at the hostel, you'll know why. Indicating travellers hostel or international hostel should help.

There are two hostelling groups operating in Canada geared to low-budget visitors. They represent the cheapest places to stay in the country and are where you'll probably meet the most travellers.

Visitors to Quebec are sometimes surprised to find the mixed-sex dorms common in Europe but not often seen elsewhere in Canada.

Hostelling International The oldest, best known and most established hostelling association is Hostelling International (HI) Canada. This national organisation is a member of the internationally known hostelling association.

The hostels are no longer called youth hostels, although they are sometimes still referred to in this way, but rather are known simply as hostels. Through the text of this book these hostels are referred to as HI Hostel. Their symbol is an evergreen tree and stylised house within a blue triangle.

HI Canada has about 70 hostels with members in all parts of the country. Nightly costs range from $10 to $23 with most around $16. At many, nonmembers can stay for an additional $2 to $5. A membership can quickly pay for itself and has now been built into the system so that after a few stays you automatically become a member.

In July and August space may be a problem at some Canadian hostels, particularly in the large cities and in some of the resort areas such as Banff, so calling ahead to make a reservation is a good idea. Reservations must be made more than 24 hours in advance and you need a credit card to pre-pay.

Note that reservations for North American hostels can be booked through hostels in Europe, Australia, New Zealand and Japan using computer systems and faxes. This can be convenient for those flying into 'gateway' cities who don't want to hassle for a bed upon arrival. Outside July and August, traffic thins and getting a bed should not be difficult. Many of the hostels are closed in winter.

In addition to the lower nightly rates, members can often take advantage of discounts offered by various businesses. Local hostels should have a list of where discounts are available. Guidebooks, sleeping sheets and other travel accessories can also be purchased at one of half a dozen hostel shops across the country. Some of the regional offices and hostels organise outdoor activities such as canoeing, climbing, skiing, hiking and city walks.

A yearly international membership costs $27 for an adult. Children under 17 stay free with a parent. Many hostels have family rooms set aside.

Contact Hostelling International (HI) Canada (☎ 613-237-7884, fax 613-237-7868, www.hostellingintl.ca), National Office, 400-205 Catherine St, Ottawa, Ontario K2P 1C3. Call ☎ 1-800-663-5777 for the booking network.

Backpackers' Hostels The second group is a network of independent hostels collectively known as Backpackers' Hostels Canada. Currently there are over 100 hostels in the network and a membership is not required to use the facilities. Its symbol is a circled howling wolf with a map of Canada in the background. For information, including a list of hostels, contact the Longhouse Village Hostel (☎ 807-983-2042, fax 807-983-2914, www.backpackers.ca), RR 13, Thunder Bay, Ontario, Canada, P7B 5E4. A self-addressed envelope and two international postal-reply coupons should be included with your request for information.

Aside from typical hostels, there also are campgrounds, campus and church facilities, organic farms, motels, retreats, and tourist homes which provide budget travellers with inexpensive accommodation. Several places offer an interesting work-for-stay system in which your labour means free room and board. A major benefit of Backpackers' is that while it has the main cities covered, it also offers accommodation in a range of smaller, out of the way locations where nothing else of the sort is available. This loose network has no formal standards so quality, atmosphere and approach varies a lot.

Many of the hostels are in regular contact with one another so a stay at one will turn up leads on others. The average price is about $15, and rooms for couples and families are often available.

A sort of sub-network of Backpackers' is the Pacific Rim Network (☎ 1-800-861-1366) which focuses on hostels of the Pacific Coast region.

Other Hostels In addition to these two organisations, totally independent hostels are found around the country, but their numbers are small. Most of these are found by word

of mouth. The province of British Columbia has an informal network of privately run hostels which charge about the same rates as the 'official' ones. Quebec, too, is most likely to have some of the unofficial variety.

YM-YWCA The familiar YM-YWCAs are for the most part slowly getting out of the accommodation end of their operations in Canada. They are tending to concentrate more on fitness, recreation and various other community-oriented programs. That said, many still offer good lodging in a style between that of a hostel and a hotel, but prices have been creeping up. In YM-YWCAs where complete renovations have occurred, costs can be as high as those of a mid-range hotel. One of the Vancouver Ys is a purpose-built hotel.

YM-YWCAs are clean and quiet and often have swimming pools and cheap cafeterias. They are also, as a rule, very central which is a big plus and they are open all year. Some offer hostel-style dormitory accommodation throughout the summer. Many are mentioned through the text under hostels in the accommodation sections.

The average price for men is from $25 to $38 a single, and usually a bit more for women. Sharing a double can bring the price down to quite a reasonable level. Also, some places permit couples and these doubles are fair value.

For information contact YMCA Canada (☎ 416-967-9622), 42 Charles St E, 6th Floor, Toronto, Ontario M4Y 1T4. A printed sheet on the country's Ys offering accommodation will be mailed out but the information is always outdated.

Universities Many Canadian universities rent out beds in their residence dormitories during the summer months. The 'season' runs approximately from May to some time in August with possible closures for such things as large academic conferences. Prices average $30 a day and, at many places, students are offered a further reduction. Campus residences are open to all including families and seniors.

Reservations are accepted but aren't necessary. Breakfasts are sometimes included in the price but if not, there is generally a cafeteria which offers low-priced meals. The other campus facilities, such as the swimming pool, are sometimes available to guests.

Directories of the various residences are sometimes published and may be available on the campus through the residence manager, the alumni association or general information.

Campus accommodation is listed in the text under hostels. This form of budget accommodation seems to be somewhat unknown in Canada and at most places finding a room even in peak season should not be a problem.

Efficiency Units

Efficiencies are also called housekeeping units or serviced apartments and are rooms with cooking facilities and light housekeeping. This type of room is often geared to business clients but can be especially helpful for travelling families.

Efficiencies are usually found at motels where some of the rooms have been converted or enlarged for this purpose and for which the owners can ask a few more dollars. A few guesthouse or B&Bs have a room or two with cooking facilities. Some hotels also offer such rooms usually calling them suites, although this broad term may not mean there is a kitchen.

In the country's larger cities some apartment complexes have also been set up to offer this type of lodging. Again, these suites are primarily aimed at the business traveller or those in town for a week or longer.

Guesthouses & Tourist Homes

Another alternative is the simple guesthouse or tourist home. These may be an extra room in someone's home but are more commonly commercial lodging houses. They are found mainly in places with a large tourist trade such as Niagara, Banff, Victoria, Quebec City and Montreal.

Rooms range in size and have varying amenities. Some include private bathrooms,

many do not. The standard cost is about $40 to $65 a double.

Some so-called tourist homes are really rooming houses rented more often by the week or month, and usually have shared kitchens.

B&Bs

B&Bs are an established part of the accommodation picture and continue to grow in number. They offer a more personal alternative to the standard traditional motel/hotel and are found throughout the country.

In many of the larger cities associations manage B&Bs, while in other places they are listed directly with tourist offices. Some operate as full-time businesses, others just provide their operators with part-time income for a few months in the summer.

Prices of B&Bs vary quite a bit, ranging roughly from $40 for a single to $100 a double with the average being from $55 to $75 for two people.

The more expensive ones generally provide more impressive furnishings and décor. Many are found in classic heritage houses. Rooms are almost always in the owner's home and are clean and well kept. Note that smoking is almost always prohibited (and banned in public places eg bars and restaurants, throughout British Columbia from 1 January 2000). Some places will take children and the odd one will allow a pet. Breakfast can vary from light or continental to a full breakfast of eggs, bacon, toast and coffee. It's worth inquiring about the breakfast before booking.

Several guidebooks dealing exclusively with B&Bs across the country are widely available in Canadian bookstores.

Hotels

Good, inexpensive hotels are not a Canadian strong point. Though there is a wide range of hotel types, the word usually means one of two things to a Canadian – a rather expensive place to stay or a cheap place to drink. Most new hotels are part of international chains and are designed for either the luxury market or for businesspeople.

Canadian liquor laws have historically been linked to renting beds, so the older, cheap hotels are often principally bars, and quite often low-class bars at that. Examples are found in number all over the country. For the impecunious, who don't mind some noise and a somewhat worn room, these hotels can come in handy.

Prices usually range from $25 to $35 a single, but rooms are often taken by more permanent guests on a monthly basis. There are some places in this category which are fine and which are mentioned in this book. They are not suitable for families or females travelling alone but couples and single males may find these basic hotels adequate, at least on occasion.

Between the new and the old hotels, there are places to be found in between. In some of the larger cities, in particular, you can still find good older, small hotels which mainly rent rooms. Prices vary with the amenities and location and range from about $35 to $75 for singles or doubles.

Two nationwide good-value hotel chains are Travelodge (☎ 1-800-578-7878) and Days Inn (☎ 1-800-329-7466) with about 60 locations each.

Motels

In Canada, like the USA (both lands of the automobile), motels are ubiquitous. Mostly they are simple and clean, if somewhat nondescript. Many can be found dotting the highways and clustered in groups on the outskirts of larger towns and cities. They usually range from $40 to $75 for singles or doubles.

Outside the cities motel prices drop so they can be a bargain, especially if there are two or more of you. Before entering a large city it's a good idea to get off the main route and onto one of the secondary roads. This is where you'll find motels as cheaply as they come. The less-travelled parts of the country tend to have lower prices, too.

Prices tend to go up in summer or when a special event is on. Off-season bargaining is definitely worthwhile and acceptable. This need not be haggling as in a Moroccan market; just a simple counter-offer will sometimes work. Unlike most better hotels, many motels remain 'mom and pop' operations and so retain more flexibility and often reflect more of the character of the owners.

The Choice motel/hotel chain – seen from coast to coast – includes the Comfort Inn (☎ 1-800-228-5150) and Econo Lodge (☎ 1-800-553-2666) lines. They are moderately priced, not the cheapest, not the most expensive but always reliable and good value. The rooms are plain and simple but spotless and always well maintained. The benefit of the chain system is that it allows for reserving a room anywhere through toll-free telephone numbers. Other links in the chain include Quality (☎ 1-800-228-5151) and the low-cost Rodeway (☎ 1-800-228-2000) inns.

Another oft-seen, quality chain is Super 8 Motels (☎ 1-800-800-8000).

Some motels offer 'suites'. This usually means there is a separate second bedroom (good for those with children) but may mean there is a sitting room with TV and chesterfield set apart from the bedroom. It may also mean there are some cooking facilities.

Farm Vacations

Each province has a farm or ranch vacation program enabling visitors to stay on working farms for a day, a week or even longer. The size and type of farm varies considerably, as do the activities you can take part in. There are usually chores to do and animals to tend. Rates range from roughly $40 to $45 for singles, $50 to $70 for doubles depending on meals taken. There are also family rates and reductions for children. Details of these programs are available from provincial tourist boards.

FOOD

Gastronomy in English-speaking Canada was, in general and with exceptions, long based on the British 'bland is beautiful' tradition. While there are still no distinctive national dishes or unique culinary delights, good food is certainly plentiful. The large numbers of varying ethnic groups

spread across the country continue to contribute to the epicurean palate.

In most cities it's not difficult to find a Greek, Italian, Mexican or Chinese restaurant. Small bistro-type places are found across the country with menus emphasising freshness, spices and the latest trends. They tend to fill the gap between the low-end 'greasy spoons' and the priciest restaurants. Many of these, as well as numerous soup, salad and sandwich bars, provide good-value lunches as they compete for office workers' appetites. In the country's largest cities, vegetarian restaurants, although not abundant, can be found. Such places may be known as natural food or health-food restaurants. East Indian restaurants also offer a selection of vegetarian dishes.

On the east coast of Canada, through all the Atlantic Provinces, deep-fried food is common; all too common for many. It does not hurt to ask for an alternative cooking method or pick from menus carefully.

The common 'spoons', the equivalent of the US diners, are found throughout Canada with names like 'George's' or 'Linda's Place'. Little changed since the 1930s, these small, basic places are the blue-collar workers' restaurants. Some are excellent, some bad news, but they're always cheap. There's usually a breakfast special until 11 am for about $4, followed by a couple of lunch specials. A fairly balanced, if functional, meal costs around $6.

Fruit is a bargain in summer and locally grown varieties such as apples, peaches and cherries are superb. In June watch for strawberries; in August, blueberries. Farmers' stands are often seen along highways and secondary roads.

Canada produces excellent cheeses, in particular, cheddars – mild, medium and old. Oka from Quebec is a more expensive, subtler and very tasty cheese developed by Trappist monks.

On both coasts, there is abundant seafood that is delicious and affordable. On the west coast the salmon, fresh or smoked, is a real treat, and crab is plentiful. The east coast has the less-known but highly esteemed freshwater Atlantic salmon. The Atlantic region is also famous for lobster and scallops. In the far north, Arctic char is a speciality. The king of inland fish is the walleye, often called pickerel.

One truly Canadian creation must be mentioned – the butter tart. This delectable little sweet can best be described as ... well, just get on the outside of one and you'll see.

French Food

Most of the country's few semi-original repasts come from the French of Quebec. French pea soup is thick, filling and delicious. The *tourtières* (meat pies) are worth sampling. Quebec is also the world's largest producer of maple syrup, made in the spring when the sap is running, and it's great on pancakes or ice cream.

French fries in Quebec, where they are known simply as *frites* or *patates*, are unbeatable, especially those bought at the small roadside chip wagons. *Poutine* is a variation with gravy and cheese curds.

Farther east into the Atlantic Provinces the Acadian French carry on some of their centuries-old culinary traditions in such dishes as rapie pie *(paté à la rapure)* – a type of meat pie (maybe beef, chicken or clam) topped with grated paste-like potato from which all the starch has been drawn.

Native Indian Food

Native Indian foods based on wild game such as deer (venison) and pheasant are something to sample if the opportunity presents itself. Buffalo meat, sold commercially in a few places, turns up on menus occasionally. It's lean and has more protein and less cholesterol than beef.

The fiddlehead is a distinctive green, only edible in springtime. It's primarily picked from the woodlands of the Maritime Provinces.

Wild rice, with its black husks and almost nutty flavour is very tasty and often accompanies Native Indian-style meals. Most of it is picked by hand around the Ontario and Manitoba borders but it's widely available in natural-food shops.

Markets

Many cities have farmers' markets where fresh produce can be bought at good prices. Roadside stands offering the crops of the season can be found in all rural areas. Corn is something to look for and is easy to prepare. On the coasts, seafood can often be purchased at the docks.

Prices

As with most things, food is costlier than in the USA. If you're from Europe, though, or are travelling with a strong currency, you'll find prices are reasonable.

Generally, for dinner, under $10 is a bargain and $15 to $25 is moderate. Lunches are a lot less, almost always under $10. Most of the places mentioned in this book fit into these categories but some costlier places are listed for treats and splurges.

DRINKS
Alcohol

Beer Canadian beer, in general, is good, not great. It's more flavourful and stronger than US brands and is always served cold. Lagers are by far the most popular beers but ales, light beers, porters and stouts are all available. The two big companies are Molson and Labatt, with the most popular beers being Molson Export and Canadian, and Labatt 50 and Blue.

A welcome trend is the continuing success of small breweries producing real or natural beers and pubs brewing their own for consumption on the premises. Both these breaks from tradition have grown rapidly across the country but are most evident in the large cities.

In a bar, a draught beer ranges from about $2.25 for a 340ml glass to $4.50 for a pint. Draught beer by the glass or pitcher is the cheapest way to drink. In places featuring live music, prices usually go up after the night's entertainment arrives. At retail outlets beer bought in cases works out to be about $1.40 for a bottle or a can.

Wine The past two decades have seen Canadian wine improve steadily and considerably.

Unfairly, the stigma often remains. True, the bottom-end wines are the domestics and they taste as cheap as the price. But most of the Canadian wineries also take great care with at least some of their labels.

The country has two main wine-producing regions, Ontario's Niagara Peninsula, with by far the largest share, and British Columbia's Okanagan Valley. Wineries can also be found in southern Quebec, elsewhere in Ontario (the Lake Erie Shoreline, and Pelee Island which is out in Lake Erie) and in Nova Scotia.

Most of these areas now have their own Vintners Quality Alliance (VQA) grading and classification system, meant to establish and maintain standards for the better wines in much the same way as is done in Europe. Wines sporting the VQA label are among the ones recommended to sample. A similar grading system is found in British Columbia.

Red, white, dry and sweet are all produced as are some sparkling wines, but the dry whites and the very expensive ice wines are Canada's best. Import duties keep foreign wine prices up to protect the Canadian wine industry but you can still get a pretty low-priced bottle of French or Californian wine.

Spirits Canada produces its own gins, vodkas, rums, liqueurs, brandies and coolers. But Canadian whisky, generally known in the country as rye, is the best known liquor and the one with the biggest reputation. Canadian Club and VO rye whisky are Canada's most famous drinks – good stuff. Rye is generally taken with ginger ale or soda but some like it straight with ice. Canadian whisky has been distilled since the mid-1800s and has been popular in the USA as well as Canada from the early days of production. Most of the high price of spirits in Canada is attributable to tax.

Nonalcoholic Drinks

The fruit-growing areas of Ontario, Quebec and British Columbia produce excellent apple and cherry ciders, some with alcohol, most without. In Quebec and the Atlantic Provinces, visitors may want to sample a local nonalcoholic brew called spruce beer.

It's produced in small batches by individuals and doesn't have a large commercial base but is sold in some local stores. It varies quite a bit and you can never be too sure what will happen when the cap comes off, but some people love the stuff.

Canadian mineral and spring waters are popular and readily available. Bottle waters from Europe, especially France, are also stocked.

A cup of standard coffee in Canada is not memorable but it isn't expensive either. If fresh it can be fairly decent. Restaurant coffee is almost always a filtered brew. In the western provinces it is not uncommon to be offered free refills (sometimes multiple) with every purchased cup. This is not the case in the rest of the country.

Quality coffee is now served at cafés such as The Second Cup and Starbucks across the country. Most offer espresso, cappuccino and the other European specialities. A respectable cup of coffee can also be found at the ubiquitous doughnut shops found everywhere across Canada.

Tea is also common and is served hot, unlike in the USA where tea often means iced lemon tea. In restaurants it is always

Hockey Night in Canada

For about 100 years ice hockey has brought out the passion in Canadians. No sport comes close to 'the world's fastest game' for a spot in a Canadian's heart. Now played in 20 countries, it is easily Canada's most important contribution to the world of sports.

The first match with rules (borrowed from field hockey, lacrosse and rugby) was played in Montreal in 1879 by McGill University students. Before that a version of the game had been played as early as the 1850s by British soldiers stationed in eastern Canada. In the 1880s several leagues were formed but the game really gained national attention in 1892, when the Canadian governor general, Frederick Arthur, Lord Stanley of Preston, donated a trophy to be given annually to the top Canadian team. The pursuit of the Stanley Cup by teams of the National Hockey League (NHL), which came into existence in 1917, has since become an annual quest.

Although almost all of the players were Canadian, cities in the USA became home to several teams, with the Boston Bruins being the first to join the NHL in 1924. Eventually the league consisted of teams in Montreal, Toronto, Boston, New York, Detroit and Chicago. This six team league existed until 1967, when it expanded to 12 teams; today it consists of 27 teams. More expansion in the USA is planned. Most people feel this growth has diluted the quality.

In the 1950s and 60s, hockey announcer Foster Hewitt could be heard across the country every Saturday night on the radio, and later on TV, as he called the game live from Maple Leaf Gardens in Toronto. Hewitt's 'play-by-play' of Hockey Night in Canada helped to establish hockey as the national game.

From this period on, hockey stars became not just household names, but Canadian legends. People still speak of the 'Rocket Richard riot', a time in the 1950s when the city of Montreal went berserk at having its Hall of Fame player, Maurice 'Rocket' Richard, suspended by league president Clarence Campbell. Some even say that this was the catalyst for the Quebec separatist movement!

During the 1980s superstar Wayne Gretzky became known around the world as he shattered every offensive record in the books. When he was transferred from Edmonton to Los Angeles in 1988, not only was it front page news across the country for days but also one politician brought it up in parliament, saying the trade should be prevented. It was said that

made with bags. It is often served in a small, steel pot which is impossible to pour without spilling.

ENTERTAINMENT

Entertainment in major Canadian cities is top rate. Theatre, ballet, opera and symphony orchestras can be enjoyed across the country. The main 'cultural' season is from November to May, however, first-rate productions are performed through the summer as well.

Toronto and Vancouver are the largest English-speaking cities and have particularly noteworthy theatre and dinner-theatre scenes. Montreal is the capital of French theatre and performance arts.

Nightclubs and bars present nightly jazz, blues, and rock of widely varying calibre. National and international names perform regularly in the main centres. Most large cities and towns have at least one comedy club. There are two widespread trends in city bars. The first is sports bars with numerous televisions for watching an array of live sporting events. The second is clubs featuring pool tables coupled with recorded music.

Casinos are increasingly numerous as governments seek new ways of raising revenue.

Hockey Night in Canada

Gretzky was as much a symbol of Canada as the beaver or the maple leaf. Gretzky retired in 1999, causing tears and homages across the country.

Now with excellent players and teams in such countries as Sweden, Finland, the Czech and Slovak republics and Russia, as well as semi-professional and college teams in the USA, international matchups are always close and many European players are drafted by NHL teams. Still, despite this influx of players from Europe and increased US influence and expansion, the majority of players in the NHL remain Canadian.

Although 'he shoots, he scores' is perhaps the most Canadian of phrases, hockey is also a game for girls and women. Women have played the game since its formative stages but in a much less organised fashion. In 1992 Manon Rhéaume from Quebec City, a goalie, became the first woman ever invited to a NHL training camp when the Tampa Bay Lightning offered her a try-out. She didn't make the team but was offered a contract to play with its minor-league team.

The most Canadian of sports

While amateur leagues are plentiful, there is still no professional women's league. The first Women's World Championship was held in 1990 and, incidentally, was won by Canada. Women's hockey is now included in the Winter Olympics; it's the same game but without body checking.

The Hockey Hall of Fame can be visited in Toronto and professional hockey games can be seen in many major Canadian cities. At any outdoor rink during the winter you are likely to find a pick-up game in progress. If you've got skates and a stick, you're in the game and a part of a Canadian tradition.

For more information on Canadian arts see the Arts section in the Facts about Canada chapter.

SPECTATOR SPORTS

Technically, Canada's official national sport is lacrosse, a Native Indian game similar to soccer but played with a small ball and sticks. Each stick has a woven leather basket in which the ball is caught and carried.

The sport that really creates passion, and is the de facto national game, is ice hockey. This is especially true in Quebec, home of the Montreal Canadiens, a hockey legend and one of the most consistently successful professional sports teams anywhere. If you're in Canada in winter, a National Hockey League (NHL) game is recommended. The season runs from October to April. There are teams in six Canadian cities and 27 teams altogether with the rest being located in US cities. Further expansion is planned. Although most of the players are from Canada, others come from the USA, Russia, Sweden, Finland and the Czech Republic. In Canada, NHL teams are found in Calgary, Edmonton, Montreal, Ottawa, Toronto, and Vancouver. Many other cities have minor league teams.

US-style football, with some modifications, is played in the Canadian Football League (CFL). There are teams in Calgary, Edmonton, Hamilton, Montreal, Toronto, Regina, Vancouver and Winnipeg. Although the Canadian game is faster and more interesting, fans seem to be deserting the game for the US version. The championship game, known as the Grey Cup, is played in late November.

Baseball is popular in Canada and there are two teams in the predominantly US-based major leagues – the Montreal Expos in the National League, and the Toronto Blue Jays in the American League. Toronto won the World Series Championship (in which the winning team of the National League plays the winning team of the American League) in 1992 and 1993. Minor league teams play in many cities across the country.

In 1995 Canada gained entry into the American professional basketball league, known as the National Basketball Association (NBA). The Toronto Raptors and Vancouver Grizzlies have become part of the sport's increasing popularity.

Soccer and rugby have never really caught on and are strictly small-time in Canada. Soccer, being one of the few remaining inexpensive sports to play, is part of many school curriculums, and park pick-up games are common. Rugby has a following in British Columbia and despite its low profile in the rest of the country, Canada has done well in international competition and the World Rugby Cup. With both sports, there are amateur and semi-professional teams and leagues found in some Canadian cities.

Canadian women have excelled at the highest levels in skiing, skating, golf, curling and numerous Olympic events. There are no major professional women's teams/leagues in the traditionally male-dominated spectator sports.

More details on spectator sports can be found in the city sections in the book. For information on participating in sports and all outdoor activities see Activities earlier in this chapter.

SHOPPING

Despite being a western consumer society largely filled with the goods of the international market place, Canada does offer the discriminating a number of interesting or unique things to buy.

Outdoor or camping specialists may turn up something you haven't seen before and some of the outdoor clothing is particularly good. Such products are not cheap but their longevity pays off.

For edibles, British Columbia smoked salmon is a real treat and from west coast outlets fresh salmon can be packed to take on flights home. In Quebec there is maple syrup and maple sugar which make different, inexpensive gifts. The wines of the Niagara region can be very good and advice is available at liquor outlets in southern Ontario. Rye whisky is a Canadian speciality.

Most good bookstores have a Canadiana section for books on Canada or Canadian

literature. Likewise, record shops offer tapes of Canadian music. Traditional, Celtic-based folk music is especially abundant in eastern Canada.

At art-gallery gift shops prints of the work of Canadian painters can be found. Wood carving has a long tradition in Quebec, notably at the town of Saint Jean Port Joli. Another area for this, but to a lesser degree, is along the French Shore of Nova Scotia. Also in Nova Scotia at Cheticamp you'll find some fine handmade rugs.

In the west, British Columbia jade can be bought in a number of ways including jewellery. Saskatchewan and Alberta have a western tradition which reveals itself in leatherwork – belts, vests, jackets, cowboy boots and hats can be good value.

Traditional Hudson's Bay blankets and coats of 100% wool can be bought at The Bay department stores run by Canada's oldest company. For both these items look for the tell-tale green, red, yellow and black stripes on a white background. Classic cloth lumberjack jackets in either red or blue checks are cheap and distinctive, if not elegant.

Roots, a high profile Canadian clothing company, with outlets across the country and products in major department stores, offers a range of fashionable, quality garments and accessories.

Crafts shows, flea markets and speciality shops showcase the work of Canadian artisans. Craftspeople such as potters, weavers, and jewellers turn out some fine work.

For information on the worthwhile Native arts and crafts to consider as purchases see Native Art under Arts in the Facts about Canada chapter. These represent some of the best value, most 'Canadian' souvenirs.

Shops designed to serve tourists at the country's attractions such as Niagara Falls are not the place to look for a meaningful keepsake. Canadiana kitsch in the form of plastic Mounties, cheap pseudo-Native Indian dolls, miniature beavers and tasteless T-shirts are good for a smirk and nothing more.

Readers have suggested visitors planning to stay the winter need not bring bulky, warm clothes with them. All major cities have second-hand clothing shops (such as Goodwill, Salvation Army and Value Mart) where good used wear of all sorts can be bought very cheaply.

Getting There & Away

AIR
Airports & Airlines
Major gateway cities (main entry points) are Dorval airport, Montreal; Pearson airport, Toronto; and Vancouver international airport. To a lesser extent Halifax international airport in Nova Scotia acts as gateway to eastern Canada. Major British, European, Australian and American airlines all fly into Canada as do the two domestic carriers, Air Canada and Canadian Airlines.

The most common way to enter Canada is via the USA. Many overseas flights to North America go to the USA, with New York, San Francisco and Los Angeles being the major destinations. You can then either fly to a major Canadian city such as Montreal or Vancouver, or catch a bus or train. Often though, flying directly into Canadian gateway cities can be more or less the same price as first arriving in US cities.

Buying Tickets
The lowest priced tickets are often found in cities that have the largest number of airlines passing through them such as New York, London, Athens, Bangkok, Hong Kong and Manila. If these departure points are not feasible, shop around the travel agents at home. There are often travel agencies which specialise in trips to North America and which will know of organised charters or good deals.

In London check out Trailfinders or STA Travel which are two agencies good for bargains. The latter has ties to many agencies on the continent.

One of the basics in air travel is that most airlines, particularly the larger ones (including the Canadian companies flying internationally), provide the greatest discount on return tickets rather than on one-way fares. Generally, one-way fares are no bargain and if they are less than a return, it is not by much. With both overseas flights and

domestic airlines, it is not uncommon for one-way tickets to cost more than returns.

Sales taxes and the GST may or may not be included in any airline ticket price quoted in Canada, so ask.

The USA
Flights between US and Canadian cities are abundant and frequent. Between larger cities there are generally direct flights. Montreal, Toronto and Vancouver are the busiest Canadian destinations but all major cities are plugged into the extensive North American system.

Canadian Airlines flies from Los Angeles, California, to Vancouver for US$205 plus taxes, one way.

Air Canada flies in and out of New York City to Montreal and Toronto. The one-way New York City to Toronto base fare is

US$330, but this can be dramatically lower depending on season and notice given. American Airlines also serves this route.

The *New York Times*, the *Chicago Tribune*, the *San Francisco Chronicle* and the *LA Times* produce weekly travel sections containing lots of ads with current airfares. You could also try the student travel service STA Travel, which has offices in all the major cities, or its Canadian counterpart CUTS (see the Getting Around chapter for details).

The UK & Continental Europe

The key to cross-Atlantic flights is timing. In either direction, the season is the price guide. That said, how high and low seasons are defined varies with particular airlines, the day of the week, the duration of the stay and other factors. Usually, the longer the stay, the higher the cost.

Many of Europe's major centres are served by either Canadian Airlines or Air Canada. They arrange return fares starting on either side of the Atlantic.

For example, Air Canada flies from London, Paris and Frankfurt (among many others) to Toronto. Fares vary a lot depending on the time of year, with the summer months and Christmas being the most expensive seasons. In any case an advance booking of 21 days is required for the best prices. From London, return fares can vary from as low as UK£356 in low season.

Air Canada flies one way London to St John's, Newfoundland twice a week for UK£415 or UK£830 return on a regular economy, no advance notice fare. With a 21-day advance booking this return fare drops to high season UK£515 and low season UK£401.

This is a flight to consider for a couple of reasons. It's one of the so-called open jaw return tickets which allow for landing in one city and departing from another, sometimes at no extra charge, sometimes with a small additional payment required. The fare to Toronto is the same price so you can fly into St John's, make your way across eastern Canada and head home from Toronto. Another benefit to this particular flight is

that transportation from mainland Canada to Newfoundland, for example, is costly and time-consuming. This way you start there and move to the rest of Canada without having to backtrack.

Canadian Airlines has London, Amsterdam and Frankfurt as major cities although it serves many other European cities, too. From Frankfurt midweek, midsummer the return ticket to Toronto costs DM1706. Its low-season rate is about 30% less. Prices are highest between 15 June and 15 August.

Both Canadian companies offer youth fares to Canada from Europe.

The British Airways direct one-way flight London to Montreal is UK£356 regular economy fare or double that for return. The advance booking return excursion fare is UK£584 midweek, midsummer. Youth and standby fares may be offered. Alternatively, British Airways offers a return to John F Kennedy Airport, New York City, for UK£310 (low season). From New York City, it's about an eight-hour bus ride or a 10-hour train ride to Montreal.

Stopover privileges in Canada for tickets like London-Montreal-Toronto-Vancouver-London are offered on some tickets.

departure	high season	low season
Frankfurt	DM1706	DM1194
London	£584	£401

Charters If you are travelling between Europe and Canada you might investigate these. Most charter trips with a Canadian connection are between Canada and Europe. Other Canadian charters connect to US destinations, mostly Florida or Hawaii (the sunspots), or to the Caribbean.

Private Canadian charter companies operate flights to various European countries. Often a good place to look in Canada is at the travel agencies in an ethnic part of a major city where immigrants are often seeking cheap trips back to the homeland.

Some of the bigger, better established charter companies and tour wholesalers in Canada work in conjunction with one of the

Air Travel Glossary

Baggage Allowance This will be written on your ticket and usually includes one 20kg item to go in the hold, plus one item of hand luggage.

Bucket Shops These are unbonded travel agencies specialising in discounted airline tickets.

Bumped Just because you have a confirmed seat doesn't mean you're going to get on the plane (see Overbooking).

Cancellation Penalties If you have to cancel or change a discounted ticket, there are often heavy penalties involved; insurance can sometimes be taken out against these penalties. Some airlines impose penalties on regular tickets as well, particularly against 'no-show' passengers.

Check-In Airlines ask you to check in a certain time ahead of the flight departure (usually one to two hours on international flights). If you fail to check in on time and the flight is overbooked, the airline can cancel your booking and give your seat to somebody else.

Confirmation Having a ticket written out with the flight and date you want doesn't mean you have a seat until the agent has checked with the airline that your status is 'OK' or confirmed. Meanwhile you could just be 'on request'.

Courier Fares Businesses often need to send urgent documents or freight securely and quickly. Courier companies hire people to accompany the package through customs and, in return, offer a discount ticket which is sometimes a phenomenal bargain. In effect, what the companies do is ship their freight as your luggage on regular commercial flights. This is a legitimate operation, but there are two shortcomings – the short turnaround time of the ticket (usually no longer than a month) and the limitation on your luggage allowance. You may have to surrender all your allowance and take only carry-on luggage.

Full Fares Airlines traditionally offer 1st class (coded F), business class (coded J) and economy class (coded Y) tickets. These days there are so many promotional and discounted fares available that few passengers pay full economy fare.

ITX An ITX, or 'independent inclusive tour excursion', is often available on tickets to popular holiday destinations. Officially it's a package deal combined with hotel accommodation, but many agents will sell you one of these for the flight only and give you phoney hotel vouchers in the unlikely event that you're challenged at the airport.

Lost Tickets If you lose your airline ticket an airline will usually treat it like a travellers cheque and, after inquiries, issue you with another one. Legally, however, an airline is entitled to treat it like cash and if you lose it then it's gone forever. Take good care of your tickets.

MCO An MCO, or 'miscellaneous charge order', is a voucher that looks like an airline ticket but carries no destination or date. It can be exchanged through any International Association of Travel Agents (IATA) airline for a ticket on a specific flight. It's a useful alternative to an onward ticket in those countries that demand one, and is more flexible than an ordinary ticket if you're unsure of your route.

No-Shows No-shows are passengers who fail to show up for their flight. Full-fare passengers who fail to turn up are sometimes entitled to travel on a later flight. The rest are penalised (see Cancellation Penalties).

On Request This is an unconfirmed booking for a flight.

Air Travel Glossary

Onward Tickets An entry requirement for many countries is that you have a ticket out of the country. If you're unsure of your next move, the easiest solution is to buy the cheapest onward ticket to a neighbouring country or a ticket from a reliable airline which can later be refunded if you do not use it.

Open Jaw Tickets These are return tickets where you fly out to one place but return from another. If available, this can save you backtracking to your arrival point.

Overbooking Airlines hate to fly empty seats and since every flight has some passengers who fail to show up, airlines often book more passengers than they have seats. Usually excess passengers make up for the no-shows, but occasionally somebody gets bumped. Guess who it is most likely to be? The passengers who check in late.

Point-to-Point Tickets These are discount tickets that can be bought on some routes in return for passengers waiving their rights to a stopover.

Promotional Fares These are officially discounted fares, available from travel agencies or direct from the airline.

Reconfirmation At least 72 hours prior to departure time of an onward or return flight, you must contact the airline and 'reconfirm' that you intend to be on the flight. If you don't do this the airline can delete your name from the passenger list and you could lose your seat.

Restrictions Discounted tickets often have various restrictions on them – such as needing to be paid for in advance and incurring a penalty to be altered. Others are restrictions on the minimum and maximum period you must be away, such as a minimum of 14 days or a maximum of one year.

Round-the-World Tickets RTW tickets give you a limited period (usually a year) in which to circumnavigate the globe. You can go anywhere the carrying airlines go, as long as you don't backtrack. The number of stopovers or total number of separate flights is decided before you set off and they usually cost a bit more than a basic return flight.

Stand-by This is a discounted ticket where you only fly if there is a seat free at the last moment. Stand-by fares are usually available only on domestic routes.

Transferred Tickets Airline tickets cannot be transferred from one person to another. Travellers sometimes try to sell the return half of their ticket, but officials can ask you to prove that you are the person named on the ticket. This is less likely to happen on domestic flights, but on an international flight tickets are compared with passports.

Travel Agencies Travel agencies vary widely and you should choose one that suits your needs. Some simply handle tours, while full-services agencies handle everything from tours and tickets to car rental and hotel bookings. If all you want is a ticket at the lowest possible price, then go to an agency specialising in discounted tickets.

Travel Periods Ticket prices vary with the time of year. There is a low (off-peak) season and a high (peak) season, and often a low-shoulder season and a high-shoulder season as well. Usually the fare depends on your outward flight – if you depart in the high season and return in the low season, you pay the high-season fare.

two principal Canadian airlines. An example is Air Canada Vacations which puts packages together in Europe for visitors to Canada. Canadian charter companies don't seem to have either an easy or a long life so the names change frequently. Two worth inquiring about are Canada 3000 and Air Transat. In Canada or abroad, travel agencies and university student offices should have some information on potential charter trips.

There are good charters from France to the province of Quebec.

Asia

From Asia it's often cheaper to fly first to the USA rather than directly to Canada. Singapore Airlines and Korean Airlines run cheap flights around the Pacific, ending on the USA's west coast.

Check in Singapore and in travel agencies in Bangkok and Kuala Lumpur. For example, from Bangkok to the USA's west coast, Thai Airways charges US$572 one-way and US$1113 return, Korean Airlines charges US$593 one-way and US$1071 return.

From Hong Kong, one-way fares to Los Angeles, San Francisco or Vancouver are also reasonable and usually cheaper than going the other way. The cheapest one-way fare to Los Angeles is around US$998, to Vancouver US$1086.

Australia & NZ

Canadian Airlines, United Airlines, Qantas and Air New Zealand offer regular flights to Vancouver from Australia and New Zealand.

Qantas offers standard economy airfares from Australia to Canada and there also are advance-purchase tickets available with varying conditions attached. These fares range from A$1795 in the low season to a high of A$2185.

From Auckland, Air New Zealand offers discounted advance-purchase airfares. Regular return fares to Vancouver start from NZ$2017 for a minimum stay of five days and must be purchased seven days in advance. A high season return fare is NZ$2167.

Coming from Australia, New Zealand or Asia, it's also possible to travel to Canada

via the USA. After arriving in Los Angeles, San Francisco, or possibly Seattle on the west coast, a train or bus will take you to Vancouver.

In addition, Qantas and Air New Zealand flights from Australia to US cities (in California), often include many stopovers in the Pacific – Fiji, Rarotonga, Hawaii and even Tahiti.

The fares given are only the airlines' official fares. You will find the best deals by shopping around the travel agencies.

Round-the-World Tickets

If you are covering a lot of distance, a Round-the-World (RTW) ticket could be worthwhile. A good ticket can include a lot of stops in places all over the world, with a maximum ticket validity of 12 months. Check out the huge variety of RTW tickets available.

Out of Canada, Air Canada in conjunction with other airlines, offers such tickets. Depending on which countries and therefore airlines you select, the price of the fare will change. Three that are regularly part of such a deal are Cathay Pacific, Qantas and Singapore Airlines. An average price is about C$3500 but the number of stopovers may be restricted or additional costs kick in. Side trips can be arranged in Europe at a reasonable cost. Similar fares are offered out of many countries but you should investigate in the country of first departure.

LEAVING CANADA
Departure Tax

Canada has a departure/airport tax which is levied on all international flights out of Canada. Almost all tickets out of Canada, whether purchased in Canada or abroad, should now have this cost built in. Tickets purchased in Europe or Down Under likely do. There may be some countries, however, where this is not done. If you did buy your ticket in another country and it didn't include departure tax, you will be asked for this tax after you pass through customs and immigration. Since you may have already changed all your money, if in doubt, ask about it beforehand.

In Vancouver there is an additional tax known as the airport improvement tax. A flight leaving Canada for a US destination is taxed at $10, every other international flight is taxed at $15. This tax is not included with the ticket price and must be paid at the airport. Montreal's Dorval airport is also considering an improvement tax.

Remember, too, that if you intend to apply for any GST rebate this is your last chance to get a form (see Consumer Taxes & Visitor Refunds in the Facts for the Visitor chapter for more details).

LAND
Bus

The US Greyhound bus network (☎ 1-800-231-2222) connects the major continental US cities with most major destinations in Canada but with a bus transfer at the border or nearest town to it. Note, however, that the multi-day passes (Ameripass) available in the USA cannot be used in Canada. If you're using a US pass, inquire as to how close you can get to your Canadian destination before having to buy a separate ticket.

Three cities in Canada are served by US Greyhound buses – Montreal, Toronto and Vancouver. The last trip taken on a US Greyhound pass can be used to travel to any of these three. New York to Montreal is eight hours, $US74 one way, Chicago to Toronto is 15 hours, $US76 one way and Seattle to Vancouver is $US20, four hours.

Other US bus lines run directly to some Canadian cities with no stop or need for a bus change.

Alaska's Gray Line Alaskon buses connect Fairbanks, Anchorage, Skagway and Haines in Alaska with Whitehorse in the Yukon. Alaska Direct Busline does the same routes.

Train

Amtrak has four routes between the USA and Canada. In the east, these are New York City to Montreal (10 hours, $US54 to $62 one way), New York City to Toronto (12 hours via Niagara Falls, $US65 to $US99 one way) and Chicago to Toronto (11½ hours, $US98 one way).

On the west coast, Amtrak connects Seattle to Vancouver (four hours, $US21 to $32 one way).

For information about fares and schedules contact Amtrak (☎ 1-800-872-7245, www.amtrak.com), 60 Massachusetts Ave NE, Washington, DC 20002, USA.

Car

The highway system of continental USA connects directly with the Canadian highway system along the border at numerous points, which then meet up with the Trans Canada Highway farther north.

During the summer months, Friday and Sunday can be very busy at major international border crossings with shoppers, vacationers and visitors all travelling at the same time. Delays can be especially bad on the holiday weekends in summer. Waits at these times can be hours, so avoid them if possible. Crossings that are particularly prone to lengthy queues are Windsor (Ontario) and Detroit (Michigan); Fort Erie (Ontario) and Buffalo (New York State); Niagara Falls (Ontario) and Niagara Falls (New York State); Quebec and Rouse's Point (New York State); and White Rock (British Columbia) and Blaine (Washington State). The small, secondary border points elsewhere are always quiet, sometimes so quiet the officers have nothing to do except tear your luggage apart.

Between the Yukon Territory and Alaska the main routes are the Alaska and Klondike highways and the Haines Road.

Visitors with US or British passports are allowed to bring their vehicles in for six months.

For important further information see Visas & Documents and Customs in the Facts for the Visitor chapter.

SEA
Ferry

On the east coast, Canada is connected with the USA by several ferries. Yarmouth, Nova Scotia, is linked to both Bar Harbor, Maine, and to Portland, Maine, in the USA with two different ferry routes. See the Yarmouth section in the Nova Scotia chapter for more

details. From the south end of Deer Island, New Brunswick in the Bay of Fundy, another ferry runs to Eastport, Maine. A ferry at the north end of Deer Island connects it to the New Brunswick mainland.

On the west coast there are ferries between Washington state and Victoria on Vancouver Island. From Port Hardy, on northern Vancouver Island, ferries also head north along the Inside Passage to Alaska. See the Getting There & Away sections for Port Hardy and Victoria in the British Columbia chapter.

Passenger Ships & Freighters

The standard reference for passenger ships is the *OAG Cruise and Ferry Guide* published by the Reed Travel Group (☎ 01582-600-111), Church St, Dunstable, Bedfordshire LU5 4HB, UK. Cunard's *Queen Elizabeth II* sails 20 times a year between Southampton in the UK and New York; the trip takes six nights one way.

Travel agents are the best source of information as some cruise lines do not sell directly to the public. Princess Cruises is one company with sailings from New England to east coast Canada and the St Lawrence River. Cunard Lines is another.

Seabourn Cruise Line/Cunard (☎ 1-800-929-9595), 55 Francisco St, San Francisco, California 94133, USA, offers cruises to and around eastern Canada from Boston

and New York. Both seven and 14-day trips are offered with stops in many Canadian ports ending up in Montreal. These trips are in the $1000 a day range.

American Canadian Caribbean Lines (☎ 1-800-556-7450) has a trip from New England up the Hudson River to Montreal and Quebec City. Many of the major lines cruise the Inside Passage and Alaska and these generally mean stops at either Vancouver or Victoria.

Adventure Canada (☎ 1-800-363-7566), 14 Front St, Mississauga, Ontario L5H 2C4, has east and west-coast cruises focussing on wildlife, history and the environment, including lectures and input by various guests on board.

A more adventurous, though not necessarily cheaper, alternative is as a paying passenger on a freighter. Freighters are more numerous than cruise ships and there are more routes from which to choose. Passenger freighters typically carry six to 12 passengers (more than 12 would require a doctor on board) and, though less luxurious than dedicated cruise ships, give you a real taste of life at sea.

The *ABC Passenger Shipping Guide* is a good source of information. Also contact the Cruise & Freighter Travel Association (☎ 1-800-872-8584), Box 580218-D1, Flushing, NY 11358, USA.

Getting Around

Whether using the train or bus network or a combination of both, visitors should remember that despite Canada's size, the population is small. In many ways this is an asset and part of the country's appeal, but can also mean that transportation is not always frequent, convenient or even available. Hopping on a bus or train on a whim, as may be possible in much of Europe, is not realistic here unless you're in one of the main population areas. However, as any traveller knows, the greater the hassle to get there, the less likely the place will be inundated by tourists.

Although quite a bit higher than in the USA, driving costs are reasonable with gasoline prices considerably lower than those in Europe.

Air fares are expensive, but for those with a little extra money and not much time, the odd flight may be useful.

Canadian University Travel Service For budget, young or student travellers, this service known as Travel CUTS (www.travel cuts.com) offers a wealth of information. This is Canada's student travel bureau with offices in Halifax, Ottawa, Toronto, Saskatoon, Edmonton and Vancouver. In Montreal it is called Voyages Campus. Some offices are on university campuses, others have central downtown storefronts.

To obtain student discounts you must have an International Student Identity Card (ISIC) available at these outlets. You must have proper ID though – this isn't Athens or Bangkok.

CUTS deals mostly in ways to get you out of Canada cheaply. It also sells European train passes, arranges working holidays and sets up language courses. It can, however, provide tickets and advice for getting around Canada.

Within Canada, CUTS can arrange tours and canoe trips and help with domestic flights. It has a *Discount Handbook* which

lists over 1000 stores and service establishments offering bargains to ISIC card holders.

AIR

The country has two major airlines both privately operated, Air Canada and Canadian Airlines International, usually referred to simply as Canadian. Both work in conjunction with a number of regional carriers known as partners to form widespread domestic networks.

Canadian Airlines is also linked financially and managerially with American Airlines of the USA. Air Canada has financial ties and agreements with Continental and United of the USA. These mean close working relationships and better connecting flights. Flights between the two countries are astoundingly numerous.

Air Canada partners in Canada include Air BC, Air Creebec (northern Ontario and northern Quebec), Air Nova, Air Ontario, Bearskin Airways, First Air (NWT) and NWT Air.

Many of the Canadian Airlines partners have been amalgamated into Canadian Regional Airlines. Within this group are Air Atlantic, Calm Air, Canadian North and Inter-Canadienne. These names may still be heard although the airlines do not formally exist – just their routes do.

There are also some independent regional and local airlines which tend to focus on small specialised regions, particularly in the north.

Canada 3000 is a charter airline which consistently offers good prices within Canada as well as for flights to US and Caribbean sun destinations. Inquire about them at travel agencies.

Together all these airlines cover most small cities and towns across the country. On smaller airlines it's worth inquiring about student rates though you will need an International Student Identity Card (ISIC).

Domestic flights tend to be costly. The prices and schedules of flights change and

fluctuate often. Phone an airline for information one week, and the next week it'll tell you something quite different. The best thing to do is shop around – directly with the airline or through a travel agent – and be flexible. Waiting a day or two or avoiding a weekend flight could save you a lot. If you have the time, advance-booking flights are usually the most economical.

Air Canada may be cheap for one flight, Canadian Airlines for another, although each keeps pretty well abreast of what the other is up to.

In order to keep down the price of air travel there are a few general rules to follow. First, plan in advance because the best bargains are excursion fares, pre-booked return flights with minimum and maximum stays. Flights booked at least seven days in advance are lower than spur-of-the-moment prices. Booking either 14 or 30 days in advance may well result in further reductions. Secondly, don't fly at peak times, that is between 7 am and 7 pm. Thirdly, be prepared to make stops; direct flights may cost more.

Both airlines offer year-round youth fares on domestic flights. On Air Canada and Canadian, those 24 years of age and younger are offered standby fares which mean reductions of about 30%. Photo ID is required. If you call in the morning the airline should be able to give you a good idea of what flight to try for.

Occasionally, there are short-term specials for promotion of a certain flight; these can be cheap but are irregular. Both Canadian airlines occasionally offer 'seat sales'.

Another thing to consider is getting a ticket from point A to B and stopping off in the middle. This can often be done for little more than the straight-through fare.

Canadian Airlines and Air Canada sometimes offer fly-drive packages which cover the air fare and car rental. The packages, only available on return flights, sometimes include accommodation. Other possibilities include reductions on cars, hotels and bus tours. The hotels used, however, are expensive. You just have to ask about the latest gimmicks and offers.

Travel agencies offer economical charters and package tours to various Canadian cities as well as to US destinations. These turn up throughout the year but especially over Christmas and through the summer holiday season. Book well in advance to take advantage of these specials. There's a varying minimum and maximum stay on charter flights. No student or youth fares are offered on these types of tickets.

Cheap tickets can be found in the classified ads of newspapers under Travel or Business Personals. These tickets are the unused half of a return ticket. Because return tickets are often the same price, or even cheaper, than one-way tickets, travellers will sell the unused half of a return ticket. These offers are also advertised on university and hostel noticeboards. It isn't strictly legal, as tickets are officially nontransferable, but it's done a lot.

Air fares in Canada are generally quoted as the base fare only and all taxes, including the GST, are an additional cost. Ticket agents will quickly total these for you, but you do need to ask. This is worth doing as taxes can add quite a bit to the bill, perhaps resulting in a rather nasty surprise. In Vancouver, passengers must pay an additional tax to help finance airport expansion. This is billed at $5 to fly within the province and $10 within the rest of the country. This tax is not added to the ticket price and must be paid at the airport. It can be paid with a credit card if you don't have the cash.

The standard no-notice one-way fares listed in this book should be used as a rough guide since prices fluctuate regularly and taxes change with new governments – both provincial and federal. Prices of regular economy flights go up for the high seasons of Christmas and summer.

Always confirm your bookings and ask for a specific seat number as this will guarantee you a seat on the plane.

BUS

Buses supply the most extensive transportation routes across the country. They go nearly everywhere and are normally cheaper than trains. Buses are usually clean,

safe and comfortable. They are also generally efficient and run on time.

The largest carrier is Greyhound with routes from Ottawa westwards. Other major companies include Voyageur in Ontario and Quebec, Orleans Express in eastern Quebec, SMT in New Brunswick, Acadian Lines in Nova Scotia and Roadcruiser in Newfoundland. There are other provincial, regional and local lines. Bus services are covered in the text.

Services are not exhaustive nor always convenient. Routes between any two given destinations may not be frequent and in some cases may not run daily, perhaps only two or three times a week. In more out of the way places there may be no service at all.

Some bus lines offer specials such as reduced return fares some of the time. Always ask as the policies often change.

On long trips the journey can usually be broken with stopovers but inquire if this is so and how many stops are permitted. A one-way ticket is usually good for 60 days and a return ticket is valid for a year.

A one-way ticket with stopovers can be cheaper than a pass and also be good for a longer period of time.

If a destination is beyond one company's territory and involves switching bus lines at some point, the connection is generally free. Through tickets are sold for many routes in central and eastern Canada but generally not westward into Greyhound territory.

Some bus lines offer student fares on some routes, so ask. For example, Voyageur Colonial provides student rates (ID required) for trips from Toronto to either Montreal or Ottawa. There's a deal on some routes for students where two free tickets are given with every four purchased. There is no student age limit.

Some bus companies in larger towns offer sightseeing tours ranging from one day to several weeks in length. Some include accommodation, meals and admission fees to attractions. You need to make reservations for these types of trips.

Bus Passes & Deals

There are some bus passes available in Canada which work much like the famous Eurail pass.

Greyhound has the Canada Travel Pass which allows for unlimited travel. This pass comes in seven ($246), 15 ($385), 30 ($449) and 60-day ($572) variations, tax included. Students and seniors can get 10% off. These are available all year except during major holiday times such as Christmas and Easter. The pass cannot be used on other bus lines with the exception of a connection to Montreal on Voyageur. You must buy the ticket at least a week before the first trip.

There are several other specials to consider. Any one-way ticket can include four stopovers along the way but you must specify them when buying the ticket and it must be used within 60 days. A return ticket good for one year permits 12 stopovers.

The Companion Fare Pass is very good if there are two people travelling together. One person pays full fare and the second person pays 50% of that. This applies to both one-way and return fares but must be purchased at least seven days prior to departure.

Lastly, there is the Family Fare with which each adult paying full fare can take one child aged up to 15 free. Extra children are billed at half fare from age three to seven, full fare from age eight and up. Children under age two are free. Again this requires a seven-day advance purchase.

Altogether different is the Route Pass which uses numerous linked bus lines for travel in Ontario and Quebec. It is good as far west as Sault Ste Marie.

The seven-day unlimited travel pass is $200, the 14-day is $230 and the 18-day goes for $288. Extra days are possible at a daily rate. The 18-day pass also includes New York City. There are some restrictions. For example you can't travel back and forth between two cities countless times. Also the passes are not valid during the Christmas season.

Travel agents in Europe may have Canadian bus passes for sale. Compare them carefully to those listed here. Representatives in

Europe say the bus passes in Canada are a better option.

Tips

All bus lines (except in rare cases) use the same central bus station in any given Canadian city so you can change bus lines or make connections at the same place. Buses are also convenient because reservations are not required. When one bus fills up, another is added so waiting hours for the next one is avoided. Always check this, however, as it may not be the case for all routes all the time. This does not apply unless you are getting on at the point of origin. For this reason, in a big city, if you have a choice of using the downtown station or a suburban stop, pick the downtown station. The bus may be full by the time it reaches the outskirts and you will be left waving goodbye. Seating is on a first-come, first-served basis.

Arrive at the station about an hour before the departure to purchase a ticket. Tickets can also be purchased up to several days in advance if this is convenient. Beware that advance tickets do not apply to any specific bus and do not guarantee a seat. You still must arrive early and line up for your bus. For a small fee, some bus lines will book you the seat of your choice.

On holiday weekends, especially Friday night or around major holidays such as Easter, the bus stations can get pretty crowded and chaotic. At these times arriving early or having bought a ticket beforehand is recommended.

On longer trips always ask if there is a direct or express bus. On some routes some buses go straight through while others stop seemingly everywhere and these trips can be interminable. The price is generally the same and you may save hours.

In summer, the air-conditioners on buses can be far too effective. Take a sweater on board. Smoking is not permitted.

Take your own picnic whenever possible as the long-distance buses stop at highway service-station restaurants where you pay an awful lot for plastic food.

Most of the larger bus stations have coin-operated luggage lockers. Many have small, simple cafeterias or restaurants for breakfasts and other basic, inexpensive meals. Some bus stations are not in the best areas of a city so some care should be taken after late-night arrivals.

Alternative Buses

The last few years have seen the very welcome development of small, innovative alternative transportation services geared to budget travellers and hostellers. These low-cost, high-convenience, good-fun companies started springing up in western Canada but now have eastern counterparts.

Services offered range from strictly transport to fully-fledged tours. Most fall somewhere in between, making the trip as meaningful as the destination. Some are just a few hours in duration, others go for weeks.

The following are a few examples. References to them and others can be found in the text under Organised Tours or Getting There & Away sections. Some are now represented at travel agencies overseas such as Travel CUTS, STA Travel and Carlson Wagonlit.

There are jump-on, jump-off adventure-hostel circuits in Quebec and Ontario with Moose Travel (☎ 1-888-816-6673, moosetc @sprint.ca). Major pick-up points are Montreal, Quebec, Ottawa and Toronto. The combination trip covering 3000km of very varied terrain costs $300 (transportation only). It could be done in six days, but taking 14 is recommended. It hits some feature sites but also gets to places difficult to reach without your own vehicle. Trips run from 1 May to 31 October. Canabus Tours (☎ 1-877-226-2287, www.canabus.com) runs seven-day hostel-based trips out of Toronto around southern Ontario. There are stops in cities, historic sites and, like Moose Travel, well selected outdoor locations for adventures such as whitewater rafting or provincial park canoeing. The season is May to November. As with Moose, passengers pay for the activities they select and can take advantage of the tour discounts.

Further Still (☎ 905-371-8747, www
.furtherstill.com) in Toronto and Niagara
Falls runs free-wheeling, easy-going, flexible two-week (one-way) trips to the east
coast and three-week adventures to the
west coast. The on-the-cheap packages include travel, hostel or camping overnight,
food and more. The east coast trip costs
about $800. There's about one trip a month
in each direction.

Tours can be picked up in Halifax or
Vancouver for the Toronto return.

In Calgary, Alberta, look for Hammerhead (☎ 403-260-0940, www.hammerhead
tours.com) for van day trips to fascinating
sites around southern Alberta. Trips are not
expensive but hostellers still get discounts.

Also based in Calgary is the Rocky Express run by True North Tours (☎ 403-275-
4979). It's a six day excursion running to a
series of hostels in the Rocky Mountains with
tons of opportunity for outdoor activities.

Moose Run (☎ 604-461-7402, www.
mooserun.com) operates a 10 day hop-on,
hop-off hostel to hostel bus circuit from
Vancouver, through central BC to the Rockies and back.

Bigfoots (☎ 1-888-244-6673) runs between Vancouver and Banff between April
and November with a hostel stop in between.

TRAIN

The railway was part of the formation of
Canada and has played a major role in the
country's history.

It was the promise of a rail connection
that brought the west into the Dominion of
Canada and it was the same line which
transported the first European settlers
across the country.

Because of the history of the Canadian
Pacific Railway (CPR) and the Canadian
National Railway (CNR) and because so
many have worked for them, Canadians
feel a special nationalistic attachment to
the 'ribbons of steel' from coast to coast.
Unfortunately, this does not mean they take
the train very often. Both major rail companies are out of the passenger business
and operate freight trains only.

VIA Rail

Despite lack of domestic support and slow
dismemberment of the network, Canada
still has a passenger train system extensive
enough to be useful as well as appealing.
VIA Rail (☎ 1-888-842-7245), a federal
government agency, operates most passenger trains in Canada. Exceptions include
some worthwhile train lines mentioned
below (or in the province text) and some
urban commuter trains. For the most part,
the word VIA has become synonymous
with train travel and the stations and their
roadside direction signs are labelled in this
way. VIA uses CPR and CNR trains and
lines but is responsible for the service.

Most of the country's major cities are
connected by rail, however, there are no
passenger trains in Newfoundland (on the
island) nor on Prince Edward Island. Some
routes provide the only overland travel option allowing passengers a glimpse of otherwise unseeable countryside.

Train service is best in the so-called Quebec City to Windsor, Ontario corridor. In this
densely populated area of the country, which
includes Montreal, Ottawa, Kingston,
Toronto and Niagara Falls, trains are frequent
and the service is quick. Meals are available
at extra cost but non-alcoholic drinks and free
snacks are brought to your seat. A first-class
option available in the 'corridor' includes
plush waiting areas, pre-boarding, deluxe
seating and complete meals. On some routes
there is food and bar service to your seat –
this food is quite good but not cheap. The
snack-bar food is usually lousy but the bar
car, when there is one, can be fun.

Generally, long-distance train travel is
more expensive than taking the bus and
reservations are important, especially on
weekends and holidays.

For train schedules and routes, pick up
the *National Timetable* booklet at any VIA
Rail station.

In smaller towns the station may only be
open at arrival and departure times and this
may not be every day. Also when telephon-
ing the station you may be speaking to
someone in a central location in another

part of the country who handles all questions and reservations.

The pricing policy at VIA Rail is essentially that every trip is considered a one-way fare. A return trip between points A and B is billed as a one-way fare A to B, and a one-way fare B to A. There are usually no return or excursion fares. There are, however, ways to reduce your costs considerably.

In the Quebec City to Windsor corridor, tickets are 40% off with five days notice but you can't travel on Friday or Sunday.

Everywhere else in Ontario and eastwards, travel on any day is discounted 40% if the trip is booked seven or more days in advance. The discount does not apply to trains linking the Maritimes to Quebec during the summer months, but does include trains within each of these areas all year. Note that there may be sales which do offer good discounts between Quebec and the Maritimes during summer.

In the provinces west of Ontario, ticket reductions of at least 25% are available from the beginning of October to the end of May with seven days or more advance notice. More than the minimum advance notice is recommended.

The reason for booking well ahead is that a limited number of seats are offered at the discount rates. Once they are gone, you're back into the full fare. Also note there are no discounts on holidays or on days around the major holidays such as Christmas. Children, seniors (over 60) and students with international cards are entitled to discounts any time. People with children should inquire about family fares which are offered at various times and can mean substantial savings.

Tip Quoted VIA fares, surprisingly, vary with the phone call even within the hour! It is worth trying several times over a day or two and then booking in when you hit a representative giving a low fare. On long trips, literally hundreds of dollars can be saved!

Long-Distance Travel A transcontinental train tour right across much of Canada passing through nearly all the provinces is pos-

sible by linking routes together. Taking approximately five days the journey rolls through vastly different scenery, some of it spectacular.

This can be a very pleasant, relaxing way to go, particularly if you have your own room. During the summer months this trip should be booked well in advance.

The longest continuous route in the country is from Toronto to Vancouver. VIA Rail calls this train the *Canadian*, in memory of CPR's original. The train looks like the 1950s stainless steel classic complete with the two-storey windowed 'dome' car for sightseeing. The route it takes passes through Sudbury, Sioux Lookout, Winnipeg, Saskatoon, Edmonton, Jasper and the Rocky Mountains. There are three of these four-day trips weekly.

The fare varies with the season. During high season from 1 June to 30 September the coach-seat fare is $555 including tax. In low season, the fare is $416. Both these rates are with a minimum seven-day advance booking.

If you want to begin farther east and go across the entire country, the train can be boarded in Halifax but you will have to change trains in Montreal and Toronto. The high-season fare from Halifax to Toronto is $225, so add that to the $555.

For all long-distance travel, VIA offers several types of cars and different sleeping arrangements ranging from semi-reclining seats, to upper and lower pull-out berths, to self-contained private roomettes of varying sizes. The price of any sleeping arrangement is added to the basic coach seat fare or Canrailpass. Discounts are also available on beds, with advance purchase.

Reservations for any type of sleeping arrangement beyond the basic seat should be made well in advance, several months if possible on popular routes such as Rocky Mountain trips.

If you're going long distances you may want to take some of your own food. Train meals can be expensive and, as mentioned, the snack food is not particularly good. In the west, booking any sleeping arrangement

other than the basic seat means getting all meals included. In the east it means getting breakfast.

Canrailpass For those who intend to travel a lot, or far, or both, VIA Rail offers the Canrailpass. The *National Timetable* booklet will help you plan your travels. The pass is available to anybody and is good for 12 days of coach-class travel within a 30 consecutive day period beginning on the day of the first trip.

The pass is good for any number of trips and stopovers from coast to coast. Reserving early is recommended, though, as the number of seats on the train set aside for pass holders is limited. You can buy the Canrailpass in Canada or in Europe (ask a travel agent or a VIA Rail outlet) but there's no difference in cost.

The Canrailpass comes in two price versions – low season and high season. Low season is from roughly 6 January to 31 May and from 1 October to 15 December. The cost with tax is $405 or $369 for those aged 24 and under, students or those 60 and over. High season is roughly 1 June to 30 September, when the pass with tax is $630 full fare or $565 for those in the specified age categories. For all passes, extra days can be purchased at additional cost.

Canrailpass holders may be entitled to discounts at a car-rental agency, at Gray Line for bus tours and at some hotels; inquire if these options are in effect.

Other Train Lines

Canada has a few, small, local train companies which may be of interest to the traveller and which are mentioned in the text. An example includes the Algoma Central Railway in Sault Ste Marie, Ontario which provides access to a northern wilderness area. Another is Ontario Northland which operates northwards from Toronto and includes the *Polar Bear Express* up to Moosonee on Hudson Bay.

The Quebec North Shore & Labrador Railway runs from Sept-Îles, Quebec north to Labrador.

British Columbia Rail runs from Vancouver north to Prince George.

The Rocky Mountaineer

The privately run Mountaineer is a tourist train operating through some of the country's finest western scenery including one route along the old CPR line through the southern Rockies connecting Banff, perhaps Canada's most spectacular stretch of track.

All trips run between Vancouver and Kamloops with variations to Jasper, Banff and Calgary. A range of side trips and tours is offered. Trips are offered from the beginning of May to the middle of October. Reservations should be made well in advance but seats can be available at any time. Prices are discounted for brief periods at the beginning and the end of the season.

The train is operated by Rocky Mountain Railtours (☎ 604-606-7200, ☎ 1-800-665-7245), 1150 Station St, 1st Floor, Vancouver, British Columbia V6A 2X7. See the Vancouver section in the British Columbia chapter for more details.

Amtrak

Amtrak is the US equivalent of VIA Rail. Good-value passes and information on Amtrak's services are available at many Canadian train stations. See the Train section in the Getting There & Away chapter for more details.

CAR

In many ways, driving is the best way to travel. You can go where and when you want, use secondary highways and roads and get off the beaten track. It's particularly good in summer when you can camp or even sleep in the car.

Canada's roads are good and well marked. In Quebec, non-French speakers may have some difficulty with the French-only signs. Getting hold of a decent provincial highway map is advisable. Provincial tourist offices have both provincial and national road maps – usually free. Service stations and variety stores sell similar maps.

There are few toll roads in the country although crossing some bridges requires a small payment.

The Trans Canada Hwy runs from St John's, Newfoundland across more than 7000km to Victoria, British Columbia. There are campgrounds and picnic stops all along the route, often within 100 to 150km of each other. Rural routes are among the smallest road categories; they're found in rural Canada and are marked RR1, RR7 etc.

Drivers expecting to travel long distances or to more out of the way areas may wish to bring along some audio tapes. The CBC radio network does cover much of the country but radio station options may be limited and in some areas nonexistent.

City rush hours – especially around 5 pm and on Friday – are bad, particularly in Montreal, Toronto and Vancouver. Toronto's main access routes are busy night and day and everybody is impatient. In Montreal, drivers possessing nerves of steel, abundant confidence and a devil-may-care attitude will fare best. To compound the fun there are no lines painted on the roads in some places and driving becomes a type of high speed free-for-all. Guess what? The province of Quebec has the highest accident rate in the country. All told, avoiding city driving anywhere as much as possible is recommended, regardless of the time. Walking or taking the bus is generally cheaper than paying costly parking fees, and it's a lot less wearing on your nerves.

Road Rules & Safety Precautions

Canadians drive on the right, as in the USA, but use the metric system for measuring distance: 90 to 100km/h = 60mph, 50km/h = 30mph. The speed limit on highways is usually 100km/h; in towns, it's 50km/h or less.

Road Distances (km)

	Calgary	Charlottetown	Edmonton	Fredericton	Halifax	Montreal	Ottawa	Quebec	Regina	St John's	Saskatoon	Thunder Bay	Toronto	Vancouver	Victoria	Whitehorse	Winnipeg	Yellowknife
Calgary	---																	
Charlottetown	4917	---																
Edmonton	299	4949	---															
Fredericton	4558	359	4598	---														
Halifax	5042	232	5082	346	---													
Montreal	3743	1184	3764	834	1318	---												
Ottawa	3553	1374	3574	1024	1508	190	---											
Quebec	4014	945	4035	586	912	270	460	---										
Regina	764	4163	785	3813	4297	2979	2789	3249	---									
St John's	6183	1294	6212	1622	1349	2448	2638	2208	5427	---								
Saskatoon	620	4421	528	4070	4554	3236	3046	3507	257	5684	---							
Thunder Bay	2050	2878	2071	2527	3011	1693	1503	1963	1286	4141	1543	---						
Toronto	3434	1724	3455	1373	1857	539	399	810	2670	2987	2927	1384	---					
Vancouver	1057	5985	1244	5634	6119	4801	4611	5071	1822	7248	1677	3108	4492	---				
Victoria	1123	6051	1310	5700	6185	4867	4677	5137	1888	7314	1743	3174	4558	66	---			
Whitehorse	2385	7034	2086	6684	7168	5850	5660	6120	2871	8298	2614	4157	5528	2697	2763	---		
Winnipeg	1336	3592	1357	3241	3726	2408	2218	2678	571	4855	829	715	2099	2232	2298	3524	---	
Yellowknife	1811	6460	1511	6109	6593	5275	5086	5546	2297	7723	2039	3582	4966	2411	2477	2704	2868	---

The use of seat belts is compulsory throughout Canada and the fines for not wearing them are heavy. All traffic violations in money-short Quebec will cost you plenty, so take it easy there. All provinces require motorcyclists to drive with the lights on and for them and their passengers to wear helmets.

Traffic in both directions must stop when stationary school buses have their red lights flashing – this means children are getting off and on. In cities with pedestrian crosswalks, cars must stop to allow pedestrians to cross.

Providing the way is clear, turning right at red lights (after first coming to a complete stop) is permitted in all provinces except Quebec.

Sleeping at roadside parks, picnic spots or other areas on the highways is OK, just don't set up a tent.

A valid driver's licence from any country is good in Canada for three months while an International Driving Permit, available in your home country, is cheap and good for one year almost anywhere in the world. You can't drive in Canada without auto insurance.

Driving in areas where there is heavy snow is best avoided but if you do, it may mean having to buy snow tyres. Many Canadian cars have four-season radial tyres. If you get stuck, don't stay in the car with the engine going; every year people die of carbon monoxide suffocation by doing this during big storms. A single candle burning in the car will keep it reasonably warm.

When driving in the north of the provinces, the Yukon Territory and the Northwest Territories, there can be long distances between service stations – try not to let your tank get much below half and always carry extra gasoline. Make sure the vehicle you're driving is in good condition and take along some tools, spare parts, water and food.

On the gravel roads the biggest problems are dust and flying stones from other vehicles. Keep a good distance from the vehicle in front of you and when you see an oncoming vehicle, slow down and keep well to the right (this also applies to ones overtaking you). Having a spare tyre, fan belt

and hoses is suggested. Some people use a bug and gravel screen, others also protect their gasoline tank and lights.

In much of the country, wildlife on the road such as deer and moose are a potential hazard. Most run-ins occur at night when animals are active and visibility is poor. In areas with roadside signs alerting drivers to possible animal crossings keep your eyes scanning both sides of the road and be prepared to stop or swerve. Often a vehicle's headlights will mesmerise the animal leaving it frozen in the middle of the road. Try flashing the lights or turning them off, as well as using the horn.

Rental

Car-rental agencies are abundant across the country. The main companies are Avis, Budget, Hertz and Tilden but there are many more. The biggies can all book cars for you at any outlet for any outlet. They also have rental desks and cars at almost all of the country's airports. To be certain of finding one and to save time, it is worthwhile making a reservation before your arrival.

Budget generally has the best rates among the new-car agencies and also provides good service. Rent-A-Wreck is a well known used-car rental agency and its prices are somewhat cheaper. Note that rates are not consistent within any company and each outlet is run independently. Rates vary from city to city, location to location. Downtown is usually cheaper than the airport.

Most companies have a daily rate of about $30 to $50 plus a kilometre fee. Others offer a flat rate which is nearly always better if you're travelling far.

Weekend rates are often the cheapest and can include extra days so building a schedule around this can save a lot of money. Weekends in car renting can mean three or even four days. For example, if you pick up a car Friday morning and return it before midnight Monday it may be billed as just three days.

Once a car has been rented you may be able to extend your rental at the given rate. Negotiation is possible. Also if renting for extended periods of time, say weeks, ask for

a discount beyond the weekly rate. Weekly rates are generally 10% less than daily rates.

Depending on the locations, it is possible to drop a car off at a different office than where it was picked up. In some places a fee, sometimes very high, is charged for this privilege.

Book early, especially for weekend use, and request a small, more economical car.

Beware that prices can be deceptive. The daily rate may be an enticing $29 but by the time you finish with insurance, gasoline (fill it up before taking it back or you pay the rental company's prices plus a fee for doing it), the number of kilometres, provincial sales tax, GST and any other bits and pieces, you can be handed a pretty surprising bill. So make sure you know all the extra costs.

Some companies offer vans and, with a number of people sharing, this can work out to be quite economical. These should be booked well in advance.

Count on needing a credit card to rent a car in Canada. Cash is not considered good enough. There may be some companies here and there who will rent to those without plastic but even after the hassle of finding one, expect more problems. First the company will need a few days (at least) to check you out. If you're not working, things can be sticky; bring a letter from an employer or banker if you can, and lots of good identification. You may also need to leave a deposit, sometimes as much as several hundred dollars a day. After all that you may still have to sign away your first child too. It's not worth the headache.

Some companies require you to be over 21 years of age, others over 26. You may be asked to buy extra insurance depending on your age, but the required premiums are not high. Insurance is generally optional. Check to see if your car insurance at home includes rentals or offers a rental clause. Doing it this way is cheaper than buying insurance from the rental agency.

Parents note, children under 18kg (40lbs) are required to be in a safety car seat which must be secured by a seat belt. The big-name rental companies can supply seats at a small daily rental fee. Out of the major cities it may take a couple of days for the outlet to come up with one but the cost is the same.

Recreational Vehicle Rental Renting recreational vehicles (RVs) or campervans, or various trailers (caravans) is another option. The RV market is big in the west with specialised agencies in Calgary, Edmonton and Whitehorse. Vancouver is the main centre but RVs can also be rented in Toronto and other central and eastern cities. They are popular with Europeans and should be booked before May for the summer. High season is most expensive with mid to large-size vehicles costing $180 to $220 a day. These are good for five to seven people and include six appliances. Make sure to ask for a diesel engine as this will save considerably on running costs. Cheaper campervans are also available but these should be booked even earlier.

A company to try is Canadream Campers (☎ 1-800-461-7368, www.canadream.com) with rentals in Toronto, Calgary, Vancouver and Whitehorse. It offers one-ways. Another is Go West Campers International (☎ 604-987-5288), 1577 Lloyd St, North Vancouver.

Buying a Car

Older cars can be bought quite cheaply in Canada. Look in the local newspaper or, in larger centres, the weekly *Buy & Sell Bargain Hunter Press*, *Auto Trader* or an equivalent, all of which can be bought at corner variety stores. Private deals are nearly always the most economical way to buy a car. Used-car businesses must mark up the prices in order to make a profit. Generally, North American cars are lower priced than Japanese and European cars.

For those who prefer a semi-scientific approach to car buying take a look at Phil Edmunston's excellent *Lemon-Aid*, an annual book published by the Canadian Automobile Protection Association. It is available in stores and libraries and details all the used cars on the market, rates them and gives rough price guidelines. Haggling over car prices, whether at a dealership or at someone's home, is the norm. Expect to knock

off hundreds or even a thousand dollars depending on the value of the car.

For a few months driving, a used car can be an excellent investment, especially if there are two of you. You can usually sell the car for nearly what you paid for it. A fairly decent older car should be available for under $4000. West coast cars last longer because salt does not have to be used on the roads in winter which means the cars rust less quickly.

You will need Canadian insurance. Bring a letter from you current company indicating your driving record. In addition to making a transaction easier, this might entitle you to some discount as it makes you a more credible risk. You will also need an international driver's licence. Call an insurance broker (check the Yellow Pages phone book) in Canada and they will find you a company offering temporary insurance, say three months. In order to get the insurance and then a plate for the vehicle, you will need an address in Canada. That of a friend, relative etc will suffice. You should also have your passport.

Insurance costs vary widely and can change dramatically from province to province. As a rule, the rates for women are noticeably less than for a man of comparable age and driving record. If you're planning a side trip to the USA, make sure the insurance you negotiate is valid over the border, too. Also remember that rates are linked to the age and type of car. A newer car may cost more to insure but may also be easier to sell.

Drive-Aways

One of the best driving deals is the uniquely North American Drive-Away system. The basic concept is that you drive someone's car for them to a specific destination. Usually the car belongs to someone who has been transferred for work and has had to fly, or doesn't have the time, patience or ability to drive a long distance. Arrangements are made through a Drive-Away agency in the major cities.

After the agency matches you up with a suitable car, you put down a deposit of $300 to $500 and are given a certain number of days to deliver the car. If you don't show up with the car in the allotted time, the police are notified. Most outlets suggest a route to take and may give you a very rough kilometre guideline.

You are not paid to deliver the car (but may be if you really hit the jackpot and someone's in a rush) and generally you pay for gasoline, although sometimes a portion or all of the gasoline costs are paid by the owner. With two or more people, this can be an especially great deal. The company will want to know who will be driving.

You'll require good identification, the deposit and a couple of photos. Look for Drive-Away companies under transportation or business personal ads in the newspaper classifieds or in the Yellow Pages under Drive-Away Automobiles. Some trips can take you across the border – from Montreal to Florida is a common route. About eight days is normal for a trip from the east to west coast. Try to get a smaller, newer car. They're less comfortable but cheaper on gasoline.

In summer when demand is highest, cars may be more difficult to obtain and you could be asked for a nonrefundable administrative payment, perhaps $100.

One thing to ask about is what happens if the car breaks down. Get this information in writing if possible. Generally minor car repairs of say $100 or less are paid by you. Keep the receipt and you will be reimbursed upon delivery. If bad luck strikes and a major repair is required there may be hassles. The agency might get in touch with the owner and ask how to proceed. This might take time and could involve some inconvenience.

Usually the cars offered with drive-aways are fairly new and in good working order. If not, the owner wouldn't be going to the bother and expense and would have just dumped the car. Occasionally you hear of a Jaguar or something similar available – class on a shoestring.

Some of these agencies are mentioned in city Getting There & Away sections.

Car Sharing

Allo Stop, started in Quebec, is a company which acts as an agency for car sharing. It

unites people looking for rides with people who have cars and are looking for company and someone to share gasoline expenses. It is a good service which has been around for years.

There are offices in Montreal, Quebec City, Toronto, Ottawa and many of the smaller towns around the province of Quebec. More information is given in the various chapters under Getting There & Away sections. Prices are good and destinations include Quebec, Ontario, farther afield in Canada and even down to New York City.

Call Allo Stop a couple of days before your planned trip and it will try to link you up with someone. Costs of the service are low.

Sometimes commercial van shuttle services arise which ply the routes between major cities such as Montreal, Toronto and Ottawa on a regular, scheduled basis. They charge far less than bus rates but are operating illegally. Also, insurance coverage may not be sufficient in cases of accident or emergency. They advertise in the classified section of entertainment weeklies.

Canadian Automobile Association

Known as the CAA this organisation, like its counterpart the American Automobile Association (AAA), provides assistance to member motorists (check in your country of origin to see if there are reciprocal agreements). The services provided include 24-hour emergency roadside assistance, trip planning and advice, and it can supply travellers cheques.

If you have a decent car the association's help may not be necessary, but if you have bought an older car to tour the country the fee may well be invaluable, and after one or two breakdowns will have paid for itself as towing charges are high.

For information contact the central Ontario office (☎ 1-800-268-3750), 60 Commerce Valley Drive E, Thornhill, Ontario, Canada L3T 7P9. Each province has its own regional office and branches can be found in most major cities and towns. An annual membership costs $85.

Gasoline

Gasoline (petrol) or simply gas (gaz in Quebec), varies in price across the country with the highest prices in the far north and on the east coast. In the east, the prices are highest in Quebec, Newfoundland and Labrador. Drivers approaching Quebec from Ontario should top up the tank before the border. Those arriving from the USA should always have a full tank as the low US prices will never be seen in Canada. Alberta's prices, with less tax, are fairly low, so it's a good idea to fill up there before hitting British Columbia.

In general, the big cities have the best prices so fill up in town. The more remote a place, the higher the price. Major highway service stations offer no bargains and often jack up the price on long weekends and at holiday time in order to fleece captive victims. Gasoline is always sold by the litre. On average a litre of gasoline costs about 60 cents, or about $2.70 per imperial gallon. The Canadian (imperial) gallon is one-fifth larger than the US gallon.

Credit cards are accepted at service stations, many of which are now self-service and will not accept large bills at night. The large cities have some service stations that are open 24 hours but you may have to search around. On the highways, truck stops stay open the longest hours and some have showers you can use.

BICYCLE

Most people can't really consider traversing vast regions, so it's best to concentrate on one area. Some of the most popular are around the Gaspé Peninsula in Quebec and all around the Atlantic Provinces, excluding Newfoundland. The Gaspé Peninsula is very hilly, Prince Edward Island is flat, and New Brunswick and Nova Scotia offer a fair bit of variety and are relatively small, with towns close together. You get a good mix of country and city. All these areas have good scenery.

In Ontario, the Bruce Peninsula is good for cycling as is the Thousand Islands Parkway area around Kingston.

The other major cycling area is around the Rocky Mountains and through British Columbia.

The provincial highway maps have more detail and secondary roads than the usual service-station maps. You can pick them up at tourist offices. Large bookshops have cycling guides. Provincial tourism offices and travel agencies can also help find companies which specialise in organising overnight and long-distance cycling trips. Bicycle shops are also good sources of information. Major cities have specialised stores where all manner of supplies and cycling gear can be purchased.

Off-road mountain biking is popular across the country, particularly in resort areas such as the Laurentian Mountains of Quebec and the Rockies. Rentals are available.

Some cities such as Edmonton, Montreal, Ottawa, Toronto and Vancouver have routes marked around town for bikes only. The extent of these routes varies considerably. Toronto's is minimal, Ottawa's is good.

VIA Rail allows passengers to take bicycles on trains with baggage cars for $15. This would mean pretty well any train going a fair distance. Local and commuter trains wouldn't be included.

Sending bikes on buses is possible, but expensive. They charge $10 for the box and then a weight and mileage fee. A five-hour trip with an average bike would cost about $70.

The major Canadian airlines have a flat fee of $65 for a one-way flight with just a bag supplied.

In all cases some disassembly is required and you must perform it.

For further information contact the Canadian Cycling Association (☎ 613-748-5629, www.canadian-cycling.com), 1600 James Naismith Drive, Suite 212 A, Gloucester, Ontario K1B 5N4. It can supply local contacts, trail information and much more.

Bicycle rentals, some routes, and events are discussed in the text. Most cyclists, at least for touring, wear helmets although this is not mandatory.

HITCHING

Readers' letters indicate there have been no problems hitching in Canada, however, hitching is never entirely safe in any country and we don't recommend it. Travellers who decide to hitch should understand that they are taking a small but potentially serious risk.

That said, hitching is good in Canada. It's not the UK, which is a hitchhiker's dream, but thumbing a ride is still a worthwhile option. Many travellers depend on hitching at least for a portion of their trip. Transportation can be expensive but more often lack of buses or trains means the thumb can fill in a gap in the most convenient way. And of course you meet people you would otherwise never speak to. Two people, one of each gender, is ideal. If you're three or more, or a single woman, forget it.

If you feel you've waited a long time to be picked up, remember that the ride you get may take you over 1500km.

Out of the big cities, stay on the main highways. Traffic can be very light on the smaller roads. Always get off where there's a service station or restaurant and not at a side road or farmer's gate.

Around towns and cities, pick your spots carefully. Stand where you can be seen and where a car can easily stop. A foreign T-shirt, like one with 'University of Stockholm' on it, might be useful. Some people find a cardboard sign with large clear letters naming their destination can be a help.

If you're going into a large city, make sure the ride is going all the way. If it's not, get dropped where you can catch a city bus, especially after dark. When leaving a city, it's best to take a bus out a little way.

You must stay off inter-city expressways, though the feeder ramps are OK. In Toronto and Vancouver particularly, the police will stop you on the expressway.

Hitching in town is not recommended. A lot of prostitutes employ this technique and it's generally considered that the inner-city hitcher is a less desirable breed than those out on the open roads, so most people ignore them.

It's illegal to hitch within some city limits; fines can be steep. Generally, the scruffier you look, the more ID and documents you should have to prove your identity should the police decide to question you.

Around the large cities there will be heavy traffic leaving on Friday and returning on Sunday. Despite the volume, hitching is difficult then because most cars are full with families. Weekdays are best, when you get salespeople and truckers on the road. Many companies forbid truck drivers to pick up people, though some do anyway.

If you're in a hurry, from Toronto to Vancouver shouldn't take longer than five days and has been done in three.

As early as the end of summer, nights can be very cold, depending where you are, and snow can fall in October in much of the country. Do not overestimate your luck.

One last tip – if you don't want to spend time in Northern Ontario, get a ride straight through from Sault Ste Marie to Thunder Bay. The same in reverse.

WALKING

See Activities in the Facts for the Visitor chapter for long-distance hiking trails including the Trans Canada Trail.

BOAT

With oceans at both ends of the country and a lake and river filled interior some boat travel is often called for.

On the east coast, major ferries link provinces and islands to the mainland. Nova Scotia is connected to Prince Edward Island. From Prince Edward Island, ferries connect with the Magdalen Islands of Quebec out in the Gulf of the St Lawrence. Nova Scotia is connected to Maine, USA, by two ferry routes and to New Brunswick across the Bay of Fundy by another.

Marine Atlantic (☎ 1-800-341-7981) connects Nova Scotia to Newfoundland. For information and reservations write to Marine Atlantic Reservations Bureau, 355 Purves St, North Sydney, Nova Scotia B2A 3V2. Details are found in the Getting There & Away sections of the port towns.

Other ferries run around the edges of Newfoundland and up to Labrador.

Along the St Lawrence River the north and south shore of central Quebec is connected at several points by ferry.

Across the country various boat tours and ferry services, both long and short, are discussed in the text.

On Canada's west coast, ferries connect mainland British Columbia with Vancouver Island, the Gulf Islands and the Queen Charlotte Islands. For schedules and fares contact BC Ferries (☎ 250-386-3431, www .bcferries.bc.ca) 1112 Fort St, Victoria, British Columbia V8V 4V2.

As a rule, ferry reservations need not be made more than two days in advance and can be done by telephone.

ORGANISED TOURS

Organised group tours are best arranged through bus companies, travel agencies or tour companies themselves. Many of the private specialised tour companies are listed in the tourist brochures available from provincial and territorial governments.

The larger transportation companies are reliable and they're your best bet if you want a general type of organised tour. Many of the larger regional bus companies offer trips of varying lengths, including transportation and accommodation. Some offer sightseeing as well.

Small companies offering low-cost, often nature-based, tours are discussed in the text. These can be found across the country offering a variety of adventure trips of different lengths and difficulty. Good camping stores often carry pamphlets put out by such companies. You can also pick them up at hostels and tourist offices.

Various private companies run tours throughout the Americas aimed primarily at 18 to 35-year-olds. These trips should generally be organised before arriving. Travel agents in your home country can help. Most of the trips are two to five weeks long and are city and sights oriented. Others are more slanted towards outdoor activities, with everything included but

sleeping bags. Some trips may split the time between Canada and the USA.

Two companies with established names are Trek America (☎ 1-800-221-0596, www .trekamerica.com) and Suntrek (☎ 1-800-786-8735, www.suntrek.com).

The Outward Bound Wilderness School, with offices in Vancouver and Toronto, runs good, rigorous outdoor adventure trips which are more like courses than holidays. Ranging from seven to 24 days, they take place in various rugged parts of the country; many programs include a solo portion. In Toronto the school (☎ 416-421-8111) is at 302-150 Laird Drive, M7Y 5R1 and will send out a pamphlet outlining its programs.

The Canadian Universities Travel Service Ltd (Travel CUTS), runs various trips and outings that include activities like hiking, cycling and canoeing. It can also arrange ski and sun-destination holidays. It has offices in every major city in Canada. In Toronto the office (☎ 416-979-2406) is at 187 College St, M5T 1P7.

Hostelling International (HI) Canada also runs some tours and special-event trips which feature hiking, cross-country (nordic) skiing etc. Check at hostels for organised activities.

Major museums and art galleries also sometimes run specialised educational/recreational tours, for example to the Canadian Arctic and the Inuit carvers. These trips, when available and with lectures included, are interesting but can also be very costly. If you have a particular interest a phone call may turn up the perfect opportunity.

Always make sure you know exactly what sort of tour you're getting and how much it will cost. If you have any doubts about the agency or the company it may be dealing with, pay your money into what is called the 'tour operators escrow account'. The law requires that this account number appear on tourist brochures (you may have to look hard). Doing this protects you and your money should the trip fall through for any reason. It's a good idea to pay by cheque because cash is always harder to get back; write the details of the tour, with destination and dates, on the front of the cheque. On the back write 'for deposit only'.

Ontario

The name 'Ontario' is derived from an Iroquois Indian word meaning 'rocks standing high near the water', probably referring to Niagara Falls.

Located smack in the middle of the country, Ontario is the centre of Canadian politics and economics, and much of the arts as well.

The country's largest city, Toronto, is here, as are Niagara Falls and Ottawa, Canada's capital. These three places alone make this region one of the most heavily visited in the country. Historic Kingston, located between Ottawa and Toronto, and some of the middle-sized towns to the west of Toronto, with their country flavour and varying attractions (such as the Shakespeare Theatre of Stratford and the German Oktoberfest of Kitchener), are also busy tourist centres.

Less visited, but equally representative of the province, are the beaches of Lake Huron and Georgian Bay – a shoreline made archetypally Canadian by the country's best known painters. Farther north again, accessible wilderness parks offer respite from the densely populated southern regions and provide opportunities to see the northern transitional and Boreal forests. The resource-based cities of Sudbury, Sault Ste Marie and Thunder Bay, each with their own attractions, are also good starting points for trips around the more rugged areas of Ontario, from the Lake Superior shoreline to as far north as James Bay, where you'll find one of the province's oldest settlements, Moosonee.

Ontario is the richest province with as much manufacturing as in all the other provinces combined. Despite that, agriculture is one of the most significant economic sectors. The north has tremendous mineral and forestry resources.

Ontario is traditionally conservative, politically and socially.

History

When Europeans arrived in the region, they found it settled and occupied by numerous

HIGHLIGHTS

Entered Confederation: 1 July 1867
Area: 1,068,587 sq km
Population: 11,411,547
Provincial Capital: Toronto

- Visit Canada's capital, Ottawa, with its numerous museums, art galleries and markets

- Get soaked while whitewater rafting down the Ottawa River

- Spend time in cosmopolitan Toronto, the country's largest city, where the CN Tower and a Blue Jays baseball game are 'musts'

- Be overwhelmed by Niagara Falls

- Raise a glass in the Niagara wine district

- Enjoy Shakespearean theatre at Stratford or the works of George Bernard Shaw at Niagara-on-the-Lake

- Celebrate Oktoberfest in Kitchener

- Canoe the lakes and rivers in Algonquin Provincial Park

- Explore the undeveloped timberlands above Lake Superior

Northern Ontario p253
Thunder Bay p278
Ontario South p116
Sault Ste Marie p267
Georgian Bay & Lakelands p237
Sudbury p256
Ottawa-Hull p120
Toronto p152
Downtown Toronto p156
Toronto Subway p189
Stratford p224
London p229
Kingston p139
Niagara Area p197
Niagara-on-the-Lake p199
Niagara Falls p205

Indian Nations. The Algonquin and Huron first dominated the southern portion of the province, but by the time of European exploration and trade in the 1700s, the Iroquois Confederacy, also known as the Five Nations, dominated the area south of Georgian Bay and east to Quebec. In the north and west, the Ojibway covered the lands north of the Great Lakes and west to the Cree territory of the prairies.

French explorers and traders in the 17th century were the first Europeans to see much of Ontario as they set up forts to link with the Mississippi. It wasn't until around 1775 with the arrival of the British Loyalists that large-scale settlement began. After the War of 1812 with the USA, British immigrants began to arrive in still larger numbers. By the end of the century specialised farming, industry and cities were growing markedly. At the end of each of the World Wars immigration rose with people coming from many countries of continental Europe.

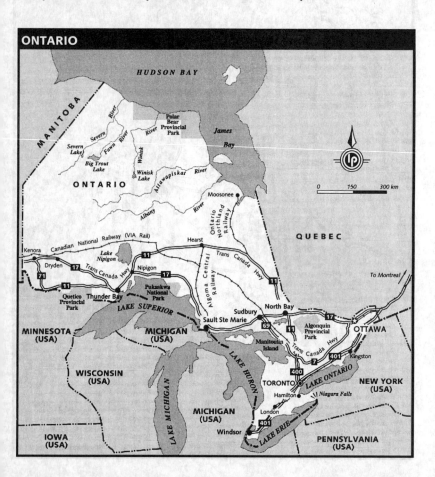

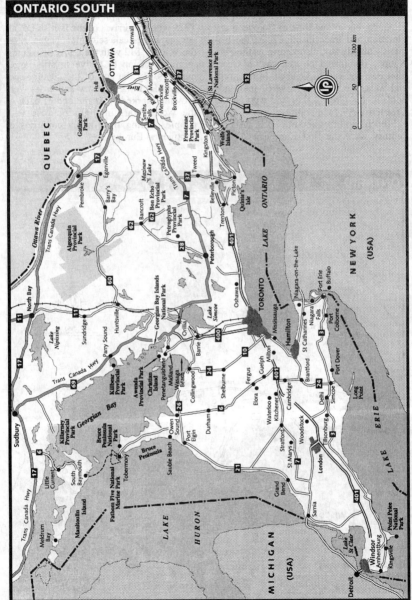

ONTARIO SOUTH

Ontario has a population of over 11 million, making it Canada's most populous province; it's also the most ethnically diverse.

Information
Provincial Symbols The provincial flower is the trillium, the provincial tree is the eastern white pine, and the as yet unofficial bird is the loon.

Tourist Offices Ontario Travel is the provincial tourism arm. It operates 10 year-round offices and several seasonal ones. Permanent offices can be found in Toronto, Niagara Falls, Windsor and at other major border crossings. The year-round general information number is ☎ 1-800-668-2746 from anywhere in North America. Ontario Travel produces a range of free publications from accommodation to events. Its mailing address is Queen's Park, Toronto M7A 2E5. City and regional tourist offices acting independently can be found around the province.

Telephone For emergency service dial ☎ 911 anywhere in the province.

Time Ontario is on Eastern Standard Time, except for the far western area which is on Central Time (matching neighbouring Manitoba). Thunder Bay is on Eastern Time and Kenora on Central Time.

Tax Ontario's provincial sales tax is 8%.

Activities
Despite urbanisation and development there remains much uncluttered, wooded lakeland and many quiet country towns surrounded by small market gardens. The northern regions contain vast areas of wilderness. The province offers fine camping, canoeing, hiking and whitewater rafting among other outdoor possibilities. A good place to start is one of the many excellent government parks. Details are outlined in the text.

Canoeing Ontario offers superb canoeing whether for a day or weeks. There are excellent routes in Algonquin and Killarney provincial parks as well as around Temagami. Details can be found in the text. For more information contact Canoe Ontario (☎ 416-426-7170, www.canoeontario.on.ca).

Cycling The Ontario Cycling Association (☎ 416-426-7242, www.ontariocycling.org) at 1185 Eglinton Ave E, Suite 408, Toronto, M3C 3C6, has a wealth of information on trails, associations, clubs etc. Southern Ontario has a number of bike paths on former train lines known as rail trails. The association can provide details.

Hiking Aside from the excellent walking in the provincial parks, long-distance trails are discussed in the text. See Bruce Trail under the Tobermory section and Voyageur Trail under the Sault Ste Marie section. Hike Ontario (☎ 416-426-7362, www3.sympatico.ca/hikers.net), 1185 Eglinton Ave Eglinton Ave E, Suite 411, Toronto, M3C 3C6, can offer more information.

Skiing Downhill skiing can be found north of Toronto in the Barrie area and, with higher, steeper runs, at Collingwood. The Gatineau Hills area around Ottawa has excellent cross-country skiing. Northern Ontario also offers some downhill.

Whitewater Rafting The Ottawa River in Eastern Ontario offers accessible river trips of the wild or mild variety. See under Ottawa and Around Ottawa for complete details.

Provincial Parks Ontario has 639 (some not yet developed) government parks ranging from simple day-use beaches to huge wilderness tracts. Tourist offices should have an information booklet. Also for information call the Ministry of Natural Resources (☎ 416-314-2000, www.mnr.gov.on.ca/mnr/parks).

Ottawa

Ottawa, the capital of the country, arouses in all Canadians the mixed emotions worthy of a nation's capital. It sits attractively on

the south bank of the Ottawa River at its confluence with the Rideau River. The gently rolling Gatineau Hills of Quebec are visible to the north.

The government is the largest employer, and the stately Gothic-style Parliament Buildings act as landmarks. Despite this, the city is now known as Silicon Valley North for its skilled computer, technology and telecommunications workforce.

The city attracts five million tourists a year, many to see just what the heck the capital is like. The abundance of museums and cultural activities is another enticement. And then, of course, in summer you can see the traditionally garbed Royal Canadian Mounted Police (RCMP), also known as the Mounties.

You may be surprised by the amount of French you hear around town. Quebec is just a stone's throw away, but probably just as important is the fact that most federal government workers are required to be bilingual.

Ottawa is not an exciting city but its streets, if not lively, are wide and clean; the air is not fouled by heavy industry. Everywhere people are jogging and cycling.

Hull (in Quebec), easily reached across the river, is smaller but is noted for its good restaurants and later nightlife.

Note that many of Ottawa's sights are closed on Monday.

History
In 1826 British troops founded the first settlement in order to build the Rideau Canal (linking the Ottawa River to Lake Ontario). First called Bytown, the name was changed in 1855, and Queen Victoria made it the capital in 1857. After WWII, the Paris city planner Jacques Greber was put in charge of plans to beautify Ottawa.

Orientation
This pleasant city of 315,000 residents is dotted with parks, and most of the land along the waterways is for recreational use. Ottawa's central core is quite compact, containing many of the places of interest, making walking a feasible method of getting about.

Downtown Ottawa is divided into eastern and western sections by the Rideau Canal.

On the western side, Wellington St is the principal east-west street and has Parliament Hill and many government buildings. The Ottawa River lies just to the north. One block south of Wellington St is Sparks St, a pedestrian mall with shops and fast-food outlets.

Bank St runs south and is the main shopping street, with many restaurants and several theatres.

Just to the west of the canal are Elgin St, and large Confederation Square with the National War Memorial in its centre. The large, French-looking palace is the Château Laurier hotel.

The Rideau Canal flows south through town, with walking and cycling paths at its edge. In winter the frozen canal is used for skating.

Gladstone Ave roughly marks the southern boundary of the downtown area. About 8km from the Château Laurier, the canal joins Dows Lake.

On the other side of the canal is Ottawa East, with Rideau St as the main street. The huge Rideau Centre is here, a three-level enclosed shopping mall with an overhead walkway across the street. North, between George and York Sts, is Byward Market.

Along Wellington St and up Sussex Drive are many 19th century buildings. Along Sussex Drive between George and St Patrick Sts, walking through the archways or alleys leads to a series of old connected courtyards, where you may find an outdoor café.

North up Sussex Drive and to the left (west) is Nepean Point. The view is well worth the short walk.

There are four bridges across to Hull. The Pont du Portage, which leads into Wellington St on the Ottawa side, is the one to take to end up in downtown Hull.

Information
Tourist Offices The new, efficient tourist office called Capital Infocentre (☎ 613-239-5000, ☎ 1-800-465-1867, www.capcan.ca) is at 90 Wellington St, opposite the Parliament Buildings. It's open every day

from 8.30 am to 9 pm from mid-May to the beginning of September and 9 am to 5 pm the rest of the year. There's parking in the World Exchange Plaza, one block south at 111 Albert St.

Hull has its own information office, on Rue Laurier on the corner of Boulevard St Laurent, near the Alexandra Bridge. There's another in City Hall, in downtown Hull.

The museums and attractions of Ottawa are often in a state of flux and are frequently closed, either being renovated, repaired, upgraded or moved. If there is something you really wish to see, it's a good idea to call first to find out its current status. Also note that admission at many of them is free one day or evening of the week.

Money Several banks can be found along Sparks St. Accu-Rate Foreign Exchange in the World Exchange Plaza, 2nd floor at 111 Albert St, has longer hours and sells travellers cheques. It's open Saturday.

Post & Communications There is a post office (☎ 613-734-7575) at 59 Sparks St.

Foreign Consulates See the Facts for the Visitor chapter for listings.

Travel Agencies Travel CUTS (☎ 613-526-8015) has a branch at Carleton University, south of the canal along Bronson Avenue.

Bookshops & Maps The World of Maps and Travel Books, (☎ 613-724-6776), 118 Holland Ave at Wellington St, has an excellent selection of maps (including topographical ones) and guidebooks. Books Canada (☎ 613-236-0629) at 71 Sparks St has a good Canadiana section. Chapters at 47 Rideau St is a good general store which is open every day.

Medical Services Ottawa General Hospital (☎ 613-737-7777) is at 501 Smyth Rd.

Dangers & Annoyances Nearly all day and night, the market area of Ottawa is busy. Late at night, however, it does get a bit of an edge to it, with some drug and prostitution traffic. Walking alone in the quieter areas in the wee hours should probably be avoided.

Parliament Hill

Federal government buildings dominate downtown Ottawa, especially those on Parliament Hill off Wellington St, near the canal.

The Parliament Building (☎ 613-239-5000) itself, with its Peace Tower and clock, is most striking. Beside it are East and West blocks, with their sharp, green, oxidised copper-topped roofing.

Inside the Parliament Building, the Commons and Senate sit and can be viewed when in session (which is not in summer). The interior is all hand-carved limestone and sandstone. See the beautiful library with its wood and wrought iron. Free 20 minute tours (☎ 613-996-0896) run frequently but reservations are required; be prepared for tight security, including metal detectors. In summer book the tour in the white tent out on the lawn; in winter there's a reservation desk inside.

When parliament is in session, Question Period in the House of Commons is a major attraction. It occurs early every afternoon and at 11 am on Friday. Admission is on a first come, first served basis.

At 10 am daily in summer, see the Changing of the Guard on the lawns – very colourful.

Pick up a free copy of the *Walking Tour of Parliament Hill*, which lists various details in and around the buildings.

At night during summer, there's a free sound and light show on Parliament Hill – one version is in English while the other is in French.

Supreme Court of Canada

This rather intimidating structure (☎ 613-995-5361) at 301 Wellington St is partially open to nonlitigants. Visitors can stroll around the grounds, lobby and courtroom from 9 am to 5 pm weekdays. During summer a visit can include a free tour given by a law student. Call for the schedule. The rest of the year, reservations are required for tours.

ONTARIO

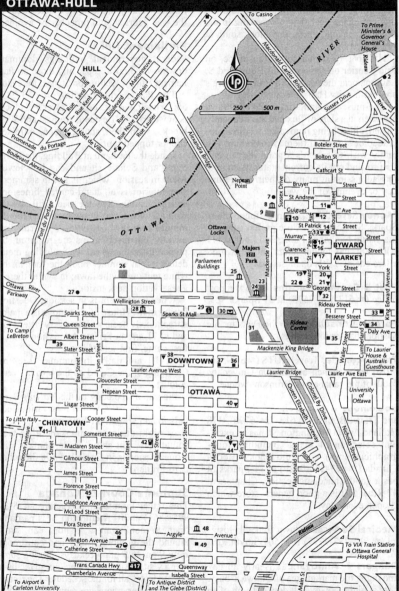

OTTAWA-HULL

To Casino

To Prime Minister's & Governor General's House

RIVER

Rideau River

Sussex Drive

HULL

Rue Papineau

Rue Laval

Rue Kent

Boulevard

Rue Notre Dame

Rue Champlain

Rue Laurier

Rue Hôtel de Ville

Promenade du Portage

Boulevard Alexandre Taché

Pont du Portage

3

5

6

Alexandra Bridge

0   250   500 m

Nepean Point

Boteler Street
Bolton St
Cathcart St
Bruyer
St Andrew   Street
Guigues   Ave
St Patrick
Murray
Clarence
York   Street
George   Street
Rideau Street

Dalhousie   Street

Parent Ave

BYWARD MARKET

7
8
9

10
11
12
13
14
15
16
17
18
19
20
21
22
32

33
34

King Edward Avenue

OTTAWA

Ottawa Locks

Majors Hill Park

Parliament Buildings

Mackenzie Ave

26

27

25
23
24

Wellington Street

28

Sparks St Mall

29
30

31

Rideau Centre

Besserer Street
Daly Ave

Cumberland St
Waller Street

35

To Laurier House & Australis Guesthouse

Mackenzie King Bridge

To Camp LeBreton

Sparks Street
Queen Street
Albert Street
Slater Street

39

Bay Street

Lyon Street

38
DOWNTOWN

37   36

Laurier Avenue West

Gloucester Street
Nepean Street

Laurier Bridge   Laurier Ave East

OTTAWA

40

University of Ottawa

Ottawa River Parkway

Lisgar Street

To Little Italy   CHINATOWN

Cooper Street

41

Somerset Street

Maclaren Street
Gilmour Street

42

Kent Street

Bank Street

O'Connor Street

Metcalfe Street

Elgin Street

43
44

Queen Elizabeth Driveway

Colonel By Drive

Cartier Street

Macdonald Street

Robert St

Nicholas Street

James Street
Florence Street

45

Gladstone Avenue
McLeod Street
Flora Street

46
47

Arlington Avenue
Catherine Street

Argyle   Avenue

48
49

Rideau   Canal

To VIA Train Station & Ottawa General Hospital

Bronson Avenue

Percy Street

Trans Canada Hwy   417

Chamberlain Avenue

Queensway

Isabella Street

Main St

To Airport & Carleton University

To Antique District and The Glebe (District)

ONTARIO

PLACES TO STAY	19	Zac's Diner	10	Basilica of Notre Dame
1 Couette et Croissants	20	Shawarma Place	14	Allo Stop
11 L'Auberge du Marché	21	Haveli	15	Rainbow Bistro
12 Auberge des Arts	32	Oregano's	18	Zaphod Beeblebrox
23 Château Laurier	38	Suisha Gardens	22	Byward Market
33 Quality Hotel	40	Dunn's Deli	24	Canadian Museum of
34 Gasthaus Switzerland Inn	41	Mekong Restaurant		Contemporary Photography
35 Ottawa International	43	Chez Jean Pierre	25	Bytown Museum
Hostel	44	The Ritz	26	Supreme Court of Canada
36 Lord Elgin Hotel	45	Roses Café	27	National Archives
37 Days Inn			28	Bank of Canada & Currency
39 Albert House Inn &	**OTHER**			Museum
Doral Inn	2	City Hall	29	Capital Infocentre Tourist
46 Voyageur Guest House	3	La Maison du Tourisme		Information
49 YM-YWCA	5	Maison du Citoyen	30	Post Office
		(Hull City Hall)	31	Confederation Square;
PLACES TO EAT	6	Canadian Museum of		National Arts Centre
4 Le Bistro		Civilisation	42	The Royal Oak
13 Domus Café	7	Royal Canadian Mint	47	Bus Terminal
16 Las Palmas	8	Canadian War Museum	48	Canadian Museum
17 Bagel Bagel	9	National Gallery		of Nature

Construction of the home for the highest court of the land was begun in 1939 but not completed until 1946. The grand entrance hall, 12m high, is certainly impressive.

National Archives of Canada

The mandate of this institution (☎ 613-463-2038) at 395 Wellington St, is to collect and preserve the documentation of Canada. The vast collection includes paintings, maps, photographs, diaries, letters, posters and even 60,000 cartoons and caricatures concerning Canadian history and people, culled from periodicals from the past two centuries. The exhibition rooms with varying displays are open daily, and are free.

At 136 St Patrick St, The National Archives in the Market (☎ 613-995-5138), by the corner of Sussex Drive at the edge of Byward Market, presents changing exhibits featuring segments of the vast collection. It's open from Wednesday to Sunday and is free.

National Gallery

The National Gallery (☎ 613-990-1985) is a must. As Canada's premier art gallery, it has an enormous collection of North American and European works in various media, all housed in an impressive building in the centre of town, at 380 Sussex Drive. It's just 15 minutes walk from the Parliament Buildings.

Opened in 1988, the striking glass and pink granite gallery overlooking the Ottawa River was designed by Moshe Safdie, who also created Montreal's Habitat (a unique apartment complex) and Quebec City's Musée de la Civilisation. He also renovated City Hall.

The numerous galleries, some arched and effectively coloured, display both classic and contemporary pieces, with the emphasis generally on Canadian artists. The USA and European collections do, however, contain examples from nearly all the heavyweights. The gallery also presents changing exhibits and special shows.

The excellent chronological display of Canadian painting and sculpture not only gives a history of Canadian art but also, in a real sense, provides an outline of the development of the country itself, beginning with the depictions of Native Indian life at the time the Europeans arrived.

For a recharging break, two pleasant courtyards offer the eyes a rest. Between them sits one of the gallery's most unusual

and most appealing components, the beautifully restored 1888 **Rideau St Chapel**, which was saved from destruction a few blocks away.

On level 2, along with the contemporary and international work, is the **Inuit Gallery**, and one room for the display of some of the extensive and fine photography collection.

The complex is large; you'll need a few hours and you'll still tire before seeing all the exhibits, let alone the changing film and video presentations, lectures and concerts. There's a pleasant café, a restaurant, and a very fine gift and bookshop. Underneath the gallery are two levels of parking.

Admission is free to all the permanent collections. An entry fee of around $8 is charged for special exhibitions. The gallery is open from 10 am to 6 pm daily in summer, except on Thursday, when it's open until 8 pm. The rest of the year, it's open Wednesday to Sunday from 10 am to 5 pm. It's closed on public holidays in winter.

Bytown Museum & the Ottawa Locks

Focusing on city history, Bytown Museum (☎ 613-234-4570) is in the oldest stone building in Ottawa. It's east of Parliament Hill, beside the canal – go down the stairs from Wellington St and back to the locks at the river. Used during construction of the canal for storing military equipment and money, it now contains artefacts and documents pertaining to local history.

On the ground floor, Parks Canada runs an exhibit about the building of the canal. The museum is open from the end of April to the middle of May. The hours are 10 am to 5 pm Monday to Saturday, and 1 to 5 pm Sunday. Admission is $2.50.

The series of locks at the edge of the Ottawa River in the Colonel By Valley, between the Château Laurier and the Parliament Buildings, marks the north end of the 198km Rideau Canal, which runs to Kingston and the St Lawrence River. Colonel By, who was put in charge of constructing the canal, set up his headquarters here in 1826. Though never fulfilling any military purpose, the canal was used commercially for a while and then fell into disuse. The locks are now maintained by the government as heritage parks.

Canadian Museum of Contemporary Photography

Wedged in between the Château Laurier and the canal, in a reconstructed railway tunnel at 1 Rideau Canal, the CMCP (☎ 613-990-8257) is the photo museum. Originally part of the National Film Board, this is where the still photography division houses its photographic research departments and the country's vast photographic archives.

Unfortunately, gallery space is limited, so you may want to check what's on before visiting. Exhibits are not always of Canadians' work and may not be of very much interest to the casual viewer unacquainted with esoteric approaches to the photographic medium. Shows change quarterly.

The gallery is open from May to October from 11 am to 5 pm daily (until 8 pm on Thursday), except Wednesday, when hours are just 4 to 8 pm. The rest of the year it keeps the same hours Wednesday to Sunday but is closed Monday and Tuesday. Admission is free.

Byward Market

The market is between George and York Sts, north of Rideau St. Opened in the 1840s, it's an interesting, busy renovated area where activity peaks on Saturday, market day. Farmers from west Quebec and the Ottawa Valley sell vegetables, fruit and flowers while speciality shops offer gourmet meats, seafood, baked goods and cheeses. Crafts are sold in the market building, and there are plenty of restaurants nearby.

Canadian War Museum

This museum (☎ 613-776-8600) at 330 Sussex Drive, with Canada's largest war-related collection, contains all manner of things military and traces Canadian military history. The life-sized replica of a WWI trench is good. You'll also see large displays, with sound and the museum also contains the country's largest collection of war art. A

major expansion and upgrading currently is underway. A new facility is planned for 2003 near the Aviation Museum.

The museum is open from 9.30 am to 5 pm daily (until 8 pm on Thursday) in summer, and from Tuesday to Sunday in winter. Admission is $3.50 for adults, $8 for families and free for veterans. It's free for everyone on Sunday morning.

Enthusiasts should ask about Vimy House, a warehouse for heavy artillery, which is open in summer. It's west along Wellington St at 221 Champagne Ave N (about 12 minutes by car).

Royal Canadian Mint

Next door to the War Museum is the mint (☎ 613-993-8990) at 320 Sussex Drive. No longer producing day-to-day coinage, it strikes special-edition coins, commemorative pieces, bullion investment coins and the like. Founded in 1908 and renovated in the mid-1980s, this imposing stone building has always been Canada's major refiner of gold. Tours are given by appointment; call to arrange one and see the process – from sheets of metal to bags of coins. It's open (in summer only) from 9 am to 4 pm Monday to Friday. Admission is $2, family $8. Sorry, no free samples.

The main circulation-coin mint is in Winnipeg, Manitoba.

Currency Museum

For those who like to look at money, you can see lots more of it at the Currency Museum (☎ 613-782-8914) in the Bank of Canada at 245 Sparks St. In summer, it's open Monday to Saturday and on Sunday afternoon. From September to May, it's closed Monday. Various displays tell the story of money through the ages, from whales' teeth to collectors' banknotes. Admission is free.

Basilica of Notre Dame

Built in 1839, this is one of the city's most impressive houses of worship. A pamphlet available at the door outlines the many features, including carvings, windows, the organ and the Gothic-style ceiling. It's on Guigues Ave, across from the National Gallery, in the Byward Market area.

Prime Minister's & Governor General's Houses

Both houses are north-east along Sussex Drive from the Basilica. Rideau Hall is off Princess Drive, the eastern extension of Sussex Drive.

You can view the outside of the present prime minister's house at 24 Sussex Drive and take a peek at the property. For security reasons, there is no strolling around the PM's grounds.

Rideau Hall (☎ 613-998-7113), the governor general's pad built in the early 1900s, is around the corner and up from the river, at 1 Sussex Drive. See the visitors centre which is open from April to the end of October approximately. There are 45-minute walking tours of the residence with stories of some of the goings-on over the years. Tours are offered through the day, in summer only, or you can stroll the grounds.

At the main gate there's the small Changing of the Guard ceremony, which happens on the hour throughout the day, from the end of June to the end of August.

Rockcliffe Village

Farther east along Sussex Drive, this is one of the poshest, most prestigious areas in the country. Behind the mansion doors live some very prominent Canadian citizens and many foreign diplomats.

Laurier House National Historic Site

This Victorian home at 335 Laurier Ave (☎ 613-992-8142), built in 1878, was the residence of two prime ministers: Wilfrid Laurier and the eccentric Mackenzie King. It's beautifully furnished throughout – don't miss the study on the top floor. Each of the two prime ministers is represented by mementoes and various possessions. Admission is $2.50.

From 1 April to 30 September it's open Tuesday to Saturday from 9 am to 5 pm (the rest of the year it opens at 10 am), and Sunday from 2 to 5 pm. An early morning visit

ONTARIO

is suggested (that is, before the tour buses arrive) so you'll have the knowledgeable guides all to yourself.

Canadian Museum of Nature

The Museum of Nature (☎ 613-566-4700) is housed in the attractive old Victorian building at 240 McLeod St on the corner of Metcalfe St, south of the downtown area. The four-storey building fostering an appreciation and understanding of nature includes a good section on the dinosaurs once found in Alberta. Also excellent are the realistic mammal and bird dioramas depicting Canadian wildlife. Major temporary exhibits on specific mammal, mineral or ecological subjects are a feature.

The Viola MacMillan Mineral Gallery is excellent, with some of the largest gems and minerals you're ever likely to see. The reproduction mine comes complete with a shaky elevator. The east-coast tidal zone recreation is also very realistic.

A separate section of the museum is geared to children. The museum also has a cafeteria.

The museum is open until 5 pm every day of the year, opening at 9.30 am in summer and at 10 am the rest of the year. On Thursday, hours are extended until 8 pm. Check for more extended hours during summer. Admission is $5, with special rates for seniors, kids and families. On Thursday, it's half-price from opening time to 5 pm and then free from 5 to 8 pm. It's free on 1 July, Canada Day.

From Confederation Square, take bus Nos 5, 6 or 14 down Elgin St. Walking from the Parliament Buildings takes about 20 minutes.

National Aviation Museum

This collection of over 100 aircraft is housed in a huge triangular building (about the size of four football fields) at Rockcliffe Airport (☎ 613-993-2010), about 5km north-east (along Rockcliffe Parkway) from the downtown area, near the river and the Canadian Forces base. See planes ranging from the Silver Dart of 1909 or the first turbo-powered Viscount passenger carrier right through to more recent jets. Peace and wartime planes are equally represented; included is the renowned Spitfire. The Cessna Crane is the very one your author's father (Alexander Lightbody) trained in for the RCAF.

Other exhibits include aviation-related video games and audiovisual presentations.

Admission is $5, less for seniors and kids, and it's free after 5 pm on Thursday. From May to September the museum is open daily from 9 am to 5 pm (until 9 pm on Thursday). In winter it's closed on Monday (unless it's a holiday). Call to check on opening hours, though, as they vary with attendance levels and the time of year.

National Museum of Science & Technology

This museum (☎ 613-991-3044) at 1867 St Laurent Blvd, on the corner of Russell Rd, has all kinds of participatory scientific learning exhibits. Try things out, test yourself, watch physical laws in action, see optical illusions. Also on display are farm machines, trains, model ships and stagecoaches. The bicycle and motorcycle collections are good. Higher-tech exhibits include computers and communication technologies. Make sure not to miss the incubator, where you can see live chicks in various stages of hatching.

The large display on space technology is interesting, with an assortment of Canadian space artefacts. An astronomy section has films and slides about the universe; on clear nights, take a peep through the large refracting telescope. Telephone reservations should be made for stargazing.

While popular with all age groups, this place is great for kids. Those without children may wish to avoid weekends and the increased numbers of young ones.

Admission is $6 for adults, less for students, seniors and children, with free parking. In summer, opening hours are 9 am to 6 pm daily (until 9 pm on Friday). It's free daily between 5 and 6 pm. After September it's closed on Monday. In winter it also closes earlier in the day.

Agricultural Museum

This Agriculture Canada government experimental farm (☎ 613-991-3044) at 930

Carling Ave is about 500 hectares of flowers, trees, shrubs and gardens. The site is used for research on all aspects of farming and horticulture. There are tours, or you can go walking on your own. The farm also has livestock and showcase herds of cattle, an observatory, a tropical greenhouse and arboretum. The latter is good for walking or having a picnic and is great in winter for tobogganing. The farm is linked to the rest of Ottawa's cycling routes. Admission is $3. The museum is closed in winter but the barn is open all year. Call regarding shows and special displays.

Antique District

Bank St south of the canal between Euclid and Cameron Aves has numerous antique and collectibles shops as well as cafés at which to ponder purchases.

Canadian Ski Museum

There's a small, specialised exhibit in the Trailhead store (☎ 613-722-3584) at 1960 Scott St, with a collection of equipment and memorabilia outlining the history of skiing. It's open Monday to Saturday from 9 am to 5 pm and Sunday 11 am to 5 pm; it's free.

Out of the City

A unique site is the Diefenbunker, a secret underground fort built in the early 1960s as a military/government refuge now reopened as a Cold War Museum (☎ 613-839-0007). The huge shelter was built to house 300 personnel for 30 days in case of nuclear attack. Displays include air-raid sirens and bombs. It's about 30 minutes drive, west of town at 3911 Carp Rd, in the village of Carp. Admission is high at $15 but includes a one hour tour and parking. It's open daily in summer, weekdays in winter. Call for details, times etc.

Even the Mounties have to practise, and the RCMP Stables & Practice Ground (☎ 613-993-3751) is where the musical ride pageant is perfected. The public is welcome to watch the practice sessions and the other equestrian displays held from time to time.

Every evening for a week sometime prior to Canada Day (1 July), there's a full musical

ride with band. Otherwise the daily evening practices are without the band and colourful uniforms. Also note that the ride is sometimes away on tour. Call for details. Tours of the stables are given Monday to Friday from 8.30 to 11 am and 1.30 to 3.30 pm.

The grounds are out of the centre. If travelling by car, take Sussex Drive east to Rockcliffe Parkway. At Birch St, turn right to the grounds. Bus route No 7 goes to the site. There's no admission fee.

This re-creation of a 19th century farm (☎ 613-825-4352), complete with costumed workers, is the Log Farm, 20km south-west of Parliament Hill off Cedarview Rd in Nepean. There are historical exhibits and activities. Special events occur sporadically through the year. The farm is open Wednesday to Sunday in summer but weekends only the rest of the year. Admission is by donation.

Where the Rideau River meets the canal south of town (at the junction of Colonel By St and Hog's Back Rd) are the Prince of Wales Falls and walking and cycling paths.

Activities

In summer, there are canoe and row-boat rentals for trips along the canal at Dows Lake Pavilion (☎ 613-232-1001), or at the marina on Hog's Back Rd (☎ 613-736-9894). Both are south of the city centre.

The city has an excellent parks system with a lot of inner-city green space. There are many walking, jogging and cycling trails as well as picnic areas. You'll even find some fishing. The tourist office has a sheet, with map, of all the parks and a description of each. Bicycle paths wind all over town; get a map of them. For rentals see the Getting Around section.

Surrounding the city on the east, south and west and connecting with the Ottawa River on each side is a broad strip of connected parkland known as the Greenbelt (☎ 613-239-5000). Within this area of woodlands, marsh and fields are nature trails, more bicycle paths, boardwalks and picnic areas. In the western Greenbelt, 20 minutes by vehicle from the downtown area off Richmond

Rd, the Stony Swamp Interpretive Centre has a staff naturalist, trails and displays about the area. It's open from Friday to Sunday. On the eastern side of the Greenbelt is another conservation area, Mer Bleue.

For whitewater rafting trips see Around Ottawa-Hull later in this chapter.

In winter there's skiing as close as 20km from town, in the Gatineau Hills. Two resorts with variously graded hills are Camp Fortune and Mont Cascades. Tow passes are more expensive on weekends. Gatineau Park has excellent cross-country ski trails with lodges along the way. In warm weather, the park is good for walking and picnicking.

Again in winter, the Rideau Canal is famous for skating along 5km of maintained ice. Rest spots on the way serve great doughnuts (known as beavertails) to go with the hot chocolate, although the beaver must be getting scarce judging by the prices. Ask at the tourist office about skate rentals.

Organised Tours

Gray Line (☎ 613-725-3047) offers a two hour tour of the city daily from May to November. Tickets are $20, available at its office in Confederation Square beside the National Arts Centre. All tours depart from here but there is hotel pick-up, too. It also does longer tours of the region and beyond.

Capital Double Decker & Trolley Tours (☎ 613-749-3666) has a few different options. Note that the trolley is just a bus decorated to look that way and that the vehicle is the only difference between the tours. The narrated $20 tour allows hop-on, hop-off privileges at 20 stops including some in Hull. The route takes at least two hours but you have the day to do it – a good way to get around. The straight two hour tour is $17 and there's a night version as well. Its ticket kiosk is at the north-east corner of Sparks and Metcalfe Sts.

Pegasus (☎ 613-731-1030) runs several day trips around Eastern Ontario, including the Thousand Islands, provincial parks and Kingston.

Paul's Boat Lines (☎ 613-235-8409) runs cruises on the Ottawa River and the Rideau Canal. Each takes about 1½ hours and costs

$12, less for kids. For tickets and information there's a dock at the Rideau Canal, across from the National Arts Centre.

The Ottawa Riverboat Company (☎ 613-562-4888) at the Ottawa Locks does much the same thing but along the river only. Meals are available on board.

Adventure/Alternative Tours Call the Adventure Zone (☎ 613-569-1400) for three and six-night summer packages covering area hostels, meals, biking, rafting and more. Moose Travel (☎ 1-888-816-6673) offers a popular budget travel jump-on, jump-off bus service with an Ontario circuit, one in Quebec and one combo trip. See Organised Tours under Toronto later in this chapter and the introductory Getting Around chapter for more details.

Special Events

Some of Ottawa's major events are:

February
Winterlude
This good and popular festival is held in early February. The three consecutive weekends of festivities centre mainly on or around frozen Dows Lake and the canal. The ice sculptures are really worth seeing.

May
Canadian Tulip Festival
This big annual event is held in late May, when the city is decorated with 200 types of tulips, mainly from Holland. Festivities include parades, regattas, car rallies, dances, concerts and fireworks.

June
Le Franco Festival
Held in June, this festival is good fun and an opportunity to see some of the country's French culture through music, crafts and more.

July-August
International Jazz Festival
This event lasts for 10 days at the end of July, with venues in Ottawa and Hull.
Central Canada Exhibition
This annual event is held towards the end of August and involves 10 days of displays, a carnival and entertainment. The exhibition is held at Lansdowne Park.

Ottawa Folk Festival
  This annual two-day music festival at the end of August is increasingly popular.

Places to Stay

Camping *Camp Le Breton (☎ 613-236-1251)* is an excellent campground practically right in the centre of town, west along Wellington St past the Parliament Buildings on the corner of Fleet and Booth Sts. It's designed primarily for cyclists and hikers and has 200 tent sites with no electric or water hook-ups. Sites are $7.50 per person with stays limited to five nights. It's open from mid-May to Labour Day. The city bus from the downtown area goes right to the campground, which is near the Ottawa River. Close to the campground are some rapids known as Chaudière Falls.

  Camp Hither Hills (☎ 613-822-0509, 5227 Bank St on Hwy 31) 10km south of the city limits charges $16 per tent.

  There are other places to camp both east and west of town on Hwy 17. The tourist office has lists of places in the Ottawa area, and there is camping in Gatineau Park, across the river in Quebec.

Hostels The HI *Ottawa International Hostel (☎ 613-235-2595, ☎ 1-800-461-8585, hicoe@magi.com, 75 Nicholas St)* in the old Ottawa jail – see the gallows at the back – is one of the best known hostels in the country. It has a very good, central location near the Parliament Buildings. Nicholas St is just east of the Rideau Canal, off Rideau St. There are 130 beds in the restored building, most of them in old cells – wake up behind bars.

  Prices are $17 for members, $21 for non-members. It's open all year but with 24-hour check-in from only April to October. Facilities include kitchen and laundry and a summer café. Reservations are recommended in midsummer and in February when the Winterlude festival is on. It has had some problems with cleanliness and organisation but is working at rectifying them.

  The No 4 bus from the bus station on the corner of Arlington and Kent Sts goes within

two blocks of the hostel. From the train station, the No 95 bus does the same thing.

  The *Regina Guest House & Hostel (☎ 613-241-0908, regina@wave.home.com, 205 Charlotte St)* is a fine alternative with a very friendly, helpful staff and spacious, clean premises with small dorms, couple and family rooms. Maximum capacity is 60 people. Dorms are $19 with HI membership, $23 without. Sleeping bags are not permitted. The only bummer is it's just open from May to the end of August when the students take over. There are bike rentals almost next door and a shuttle goes to Carman Trails hostel.

  The *YM-YWCA (☎ 613-237-1320, 180 Argyle Ave)* is on the corner of O'Connor St in the southern downtown area. Singles/doubles for either sex are $42/50 with a shared bathroom. More expensive singles with private bath are available. There's a cafeteria and a pool which guests can use.

  The *University of Ottawa (☎ 613-564-5400)* has open dormitories for visitors from May to August. Rates for singles/doubles are $22/35 for students, $33/40 for nonstudents. It has laundry facilities, a swimming pool, as well as a cafeteria with cheap meals. Go to Stanton Residence at 100 University St. The university is an easy walk south-east of the Parliament Buildings.

  Carleton University (☎ 613-520-5612), pretty central but south of the downtown core, has a residence offering summer rooms at 1233 Colonel By Drive. The price is $32 per person with breakfast included. Athletic facilities and full meal service are available. Families are welcome.

B&Bs & Inns The places listed here are central, but those away from downtown may be a bit cheaper. Almost all prices include either a continental or full breakfast. Smaller places with just a few rooms do not have to charge tax. Some locations offer perks such as fireplaces or swimming pools but nearly all have free parking.

  The Ottawa B&B Association (☎ 1-800-461-7889) is an organisation listing, promoting and booking such places. It lists city, suburban and country locations.

The *Voyageur Guest House (☎ 613-238-6445, 95 Arlington Ave)* is in a quiet residential street right behind the bus terminal and is the best low-priced place in town. Singles are $35 to $40, doubles $45 to $54 including breakfast. There are six clean rooms with shared bathrooms.

There are several places to check in the convenient Byward Market area north of Rideau St. The three mentioned here have parking. *Auberge des Arts (☎ 613-562-0909, 104 Guiges Ave)* has single/double rooms at $45/55 and English, French and Spanish are spoken. It serves healthful breakfasts and is air-conditioned. Down the street is *L'Auberge du Marché (☎ 613-241-6610, ☎ 1-800-465-0079, 87 Guigues Ave)*, a renovated older house with three rooms at $50/60 and full breakfast. Nearby, *Rainbow B&B (☎ 613-789-3286, 203 York Street)* is a gay-friendly place very close to the market. It has rooms with shared bath at $55/65 a single/double with full breakfast included.

In the downtown area, just east over the canal and south of Rideau St, is a pocket where many of the central guesthouses are found. Many in this posher neighbourhood are heritage houses or have some architectural distinction. It's a quiet, safe neighbourhood – with all the embassies around there's plenty of security. Amenities are more refined and the prices generally higher. The No 4 bus runs along Rideau St from the downtown area.

The comfy *Australis Guesthouse (☎ 613-235-8461, 35 Marlborough St)* is recommended for excellent breakfasts and helpful hosts Carol and Brian Waters. There are four rooms; singles/doubles with shared bathroom are from $48/60, rooms with a private bath from $70. The Waters offer a pick-up service from the train or bus station if arranged in advance. Marlborough St is south of Laurier, about a half-hour walk to the Parliament Buildings.

Comfortably and tastefully decorated *Brown's B&B (☎ 613-789-8320, 539 Besserer St)*, one street south of Rideau in the Sandy Hill District, is just a 15 minute walk to downtown. The standard double is

$65, with private bath the rate is $75/85. It's open all year and reservations are suggested from May to October.

Lampman House (☎ 613-241-3696, dgsy@compmore.net, 369 Daly Ave) is a Victorian house with three rooms at $45/65 with a full breakfast and rooftop deck – a good bargain. Daly Ave is two south of Rideau St.

The Swiss-style *Gasthaus Switzerland Inn (☎ 613-237-0335, ☎ 1-888-663-0000, 89 Daly Ave)* has one of the best locations in town, two blocks south of Rideau St and the market. From downtown, head south along Cumberland St to Daly Ave and it's near the north-east corner. The guesthouse has been created out of a large, old stone house and has 22 rooms, all with private bathroom. Single rooms go for $68 with a breakfast of muesli, bread, cheese and coffee. Doubles are $82. Prices go down a few dollars through the winter. The Swiss managers speak an impressive array of languages, including German and French.

Moving into the more deluxe inn category is *Auberge McGee's Inn (☎ 613-237-6089, 185 Daly St)* with 14 rooms in a restored Victorian mansion. Prices here begin at $72/80 and increase with the number of features. Some rooms have private bathrooms and a full breakfast is included.

On the downtown side of the canal is *Albert House Inn (☎ 613-236-4479, ☎ 1-800-267-1982, 478 Albert St)* with 17 well appointed rooms. It's more expensive with rooms starting at $80 and going over $100 but it has a good location, is a heritage home and offers all the comforts. And the breakfast menu is extensive.

If Ottawa seems booked up or you want to try staying across the river in Quebec, there are a few guesthouses in Hull.

Hotels In the middle range is the straightforward, just renovated *Quality Hotel (☎ 789-7511, ☎ 1-800-228-5151, 290 Rideau St)* close to downtown. Singles/doubles are from $75, kids are free.

The *Days Inn (☎ 613-237-9300, ☎ 1-800-329-7466, 123 Metcalfe St)* is good value with rooms starting from $79.

Close to the core is *Econolodge (☎ 613-789-3781, ☎ 1-800-263-0649, 475 Rideau)* with rooms in the $75/80 range with free parking and a restaurant.

The stately old *Lord Elgin Hotel (☎ 613-235-3333, ☎ 1-800-267-4298, 100 Elgin St)* at Laurier Ave (with free parking), has summer prices starting at $89.

The classic *Château Laurier (☎ 613-241-1414, ☎ 1-800-441-1414, 1 Rideau St)*, the castle-like place by the canal, is the city's best known hotel and a landmark in its own right. Rates are $129 to $169 and there's a large indoor swimming pool.

During summer, when Parliament is in recess and business traffic is light, many of the corporate-oriented downtown hotels offer very good daily and weekend specials. Even the Château Laurier offers discounts.

Efficiencies The central *Doral Inn (☎ 613-230-8055, 486 Albert St)* is well priced at $80/90 a single/double, plus a few house-keeping units (kitchenettes) at $10 more. The inn has a coffee shop and a swimming pool.

The *Capital Hill Motel & Suites (☎ 613-235-1413, 88 Albert St)* is similar but much larger. A room with two double beds, suitable for four people, goes for $96. With a kitchen, the same room is $120. Prices vary by the month.

Motels There are two main motel strips, one on each side of the downtown area. On the east side, look along Rideau St and its extension, Montreal Rd which leads east out of town.

The *Town House Motor Hotel (☎ 613-789-5555, ☎ 1-800-789-5555, 319 Rideau St)* is close to downtown, has free parking and charges from $65 for a double bed. *Parkway Motel (☎ 613-789-3781, 475 Rideau St)* has little character but isn't bad value and is close to downtown. Doubles are from $65, including breakfast in the inexpensive coffee shop.

The *Ottawa Inn (☎ 613-746-4641, 112 Montreal Rd)* is just a five minute drive to downtown. The 54 rooms range from $60/80. The *Travellers Inn (☎ 613-745-*

1531, 2098 Montreal Rd) charges from $60/70 a single/double and has a pool. The *Concorde Motel (☎ 613-745-2112, 333 Montreal Rd)* in Vanier is simpler and less expensive, with rooms from $45.

On the west side of town, check along Carling Ave, where there are numerous places to choose from about 10km from downtown. The basic *Stardust (☎ 613-828-2748, 2965 Carling Ave)* charges $50/55 for each of its 25 rooms. There are others closer to the centre which tend to be better but more costly.

Webb's Motel (☎ 613-728-1881, 1705 Carling Ave) is good at $67/72 and has its own restaurant.

Places to Eat

Byward Market Area The market is central, very popular and offers a good selection. During the warm months many of the eateries in the area have outdoor tables and on weekend mornings the place is hopping.

For breakfast try *Zak's Diner*, *(14 Byward St)*, a 1950s-style eatery which opens early and stays open late. It's usually busy and prices are reasonable.

Bagel Bagel (92 Clarence St) has full breakfasts at $3 and all sorts of bagel toppings and sandwiches, as well as salads and other light meals and deli items. It's open daily.

For inexpensive pasta dishes there is *Oregano's (cnr William & George Sts)*. There is an all-you-can-eat lunch ($7) or, for another dollar, an early-bird dinner (from 4.30 to 8 pm) of pasta, salad and soup. On Sunday the menu changes slightly and there's a brunch.

Another international choice is colourful *Las Palmas (111 Parent Ave)* which has been recommended for its Mexican food. The fajitas especially are not to be missed and most dishes are $9 to $12.

Shawarma Place (284 Dalhousie St) does the familiar Lebanese standards (felafels, shwarmas) well at very reasonable prices and is open late every day.

Excellent Indian food is dished up at the more upscale, sedate *Haveli (87 George St)*.

The tandoori chicken comes highly recommended. Meals are from $15.

Also in this category is the recommended *Domus Café (87 Murray St)*. Excellently prepared nouveau meals featuring fresh ingredients and an international slant are prepared daily but it's closed Sunday evening. Lunches are $9 to $13 and dinners about $25. BC salmon is often on the menu.

Lastly, in the Byward Market building, at the York St end, look for the stand selling 'beavertails' – hot, flat doughnuts which first became popular when sold to skaters along the canal in winter. There's a food fair in the big Rideau Centre on Rideau St and numerous cafés around the market building and on Clarence St.

Downtown Along Bank St and its side streets are numerous restaurants. *Suisha Gardens (208 Slater St)* near the corner of Bank St is a highly recommended Japanese place. The food is excellent (though somewhat westernised), the environment authentic and the service perfect. The best room is downstairs and to the left. Dinner for two is $35 before drinks and prices are lower at lunch.

There are several British-style pubs around; try the *Royal Oak (318 Bank St)* for British beer and food. It's friendly and you can play darts.

Kamal's (787 Bank St) has good and inexpensive Lebanese classics downstairs, a more formal dining room ($8 to $17) upstairs and is licensed. It's closed Sunday.

The 800 block of Bank is a lively area with cafés, shops and more.

Flippers (819 Bank St) by the corner of 4th Ave is a reliable fish restaurant with main courses from $10 to $16. It does a blackened fish dish every day.

Well established *Mexicali Rosa's (895 Bank St)* is pleasantly decorated and has tasty, moderately priced Tex-Mexican food.

Good, cheap, mainly vegetarian Indian food can be found at the unlikely named *Roses Café (523 Gladstone Ave)* between Bay and Lyon Sts. It's open only at meal times and closed Sunday at lunch. Most dishes are $6 to $7.

All through the downtown area and around the market, look for one of the numerous chip wagons, with names such as *Chipsy Rose*. They're excellent for french fries and hamburgers.

Chinatown, Little Italy & Area Ottawa has a small Chinatown with numerous restaurants within walking distance west of the centre. It's based around the corner of Bronson Ave and Somerset St W.

Ben Ben (697 Somerset St W) has good value lunches of Sichuan and Cantonese food at $6. Most dishes are $6 to $11 and it's open from 11 am to 11 pm daily. Also recommended is the *Mekong (637 Somerset St W)*, good for Vietnamese as well as Chinese dishes. Main meals are from $7 to $12.

The Somerset Heights area is a continuation of Chinatown along Somerset St around Booth Ave. It's a mix of Middle Eastern shops, Vietnamese places and more Chinese restaurants.

Nazareth (12 Lebreton St N) is a small Ethiopian place open daily. Full meals based on injera, an unleavened bread, with either meat or vegetarian side dishes are under $30 for two. Single dishes are $6 to $8.

A little farther west, a few blocks beyond Bronson St, Preston St which runs north-south has been designated Ottawa's Little Italy so you'll find plenty of Italian restaurants along this busy street.

Try the *Paticceria-Gelateria Italiana (200 Preston St)* for a dessert and coffee. *Joe's Italian Dressing (434 Preston St)* is an odd combo of Irish pub and Italian trattoria that works. Pizzas and pastas are about $10 and a range of brew is available.

Rideau St Across the canal from Wellington St, this area also has a number of eateries.

The difficult-to-find *Sitar (417A Rideau St)* is in the bottom of a high-rise building not far east from the canal. It's not cheap ($25 to $40 for two) but the Indian food is very good. It's closed Sunday at lunch.

Nate's (316 Rideau St) is something of a local institution. This Jewish delicatessen is renowned far and wide for its low

prices on basic food. The popular breakfast special is among the cheapest in the country ($2 for the works). Ask for the Rideau Rye – good bread for toast. The service is incredibly fast. It also serves things like blintzes and smoked meat. It's open and busy on Sunday.

Elgin St A stroll along Elgin St between Somerset and Frank Sts always turns up a couple of places to eat and it's popular for nightspots too. There are several outdoor patios, cafés and pubs.

The *Ritz (274 Elgin St)* is very good for Italian food; in fact, there's usually a line of people waiting to get in. Prices range from $7 to $14. *Dunn's Deli (220 Elgin St)* is open 24 hours for bagels and sandwiches.

For a splurge, *Chez Jean Pierre (210 Somerset St W)* is a high end French restaurant.

Entertainment
Music *Capital City* is the city's free entertainment weekly. *Capital Xtra* is similar but geared to gays. Also check Friday's *Ottawa Citizen* for complete club and entertainment listings.

Zaphod Beeblebrox (27 York St) is a popular eclectic place for everything from new-age rock to African music and rhythm and blues. Live bands play every Tuesday, Thursday, Friday and Saturday nights. It also has a good selection of small-brewery beers.

You can catch live blues every night of the week upstairs at the popular *Rainbow Bistro (76 Murray St)*. Nearby, the *Hotel Lafayette*, in Byward Market on York St, is good for its cheap draught beer day or night. It's your old basic hotel beer-parlour, but its character attracts a wide cross-section of people.

Barrymores (323 Bank St) features heavy rock and metal live on weekends.

Comfortable *Irene's Pub (885 Bank St)* often has live Celtic and folk music to go with the great variety of imported beers. Farther south, *Patty's Pub (1186 Bank St)* is a cosy Irish pub with music from Thursday to Saturday and an outdoor patio in summer.

The *Manx Pub (370 Elgin St)* is a small, casual, arty place with single malts and microbrewery beers. There's some live weekend folk music.

For more entertainment, see the Hull section.

Performing Arts The *National Arts Centre (NAC; ☎ 613-755-1111, 53 Elgin St)* has theatres for drama and opera and is home to the symphony orchestra. It also presents a range of concerts and films. It's on the banks of the canal, in Confederation Square.

Cinema There are two repertory theatres showing two films a night. The *Mayfair (☎ 613-730-3403, 1074 Bank St)* charges $7 for nonmembers for the double bill. The *Bytown Cinema (☎ 613-789-4600, 325 Rideau St)* between King Edward and Nelson Sts charges $8 per film for nonmembers.

Spectator Sports The Ottawa Senators plays NHL hockey in the Corel Centre in Kanata. For game and schedule information call ☎ 613-599-0300, and for tickets call ☎ 613-755-1166.

Getting There & Away
Air The airport is 20 minutes south of the city and is surprisingly small. The main airlines serving the city are Canadian Airlines (☎ 613-237-1380) and Air Canada (☎ 613-247-5000). Canadian Airlines destinations include Toronto ($260), Halifax ($495) and Winnipeg ($689). Advanced booked excursion fares (return) are much cheaper.

Bus Central Station for buses (☎ 613-238-5900) is at 265 Catherine St, near Bank St, about a dozen blocks south of the downtown area. The principal bus lines are Voyageur and Greyhound. One-way fares (tax included) include Toronto $55, Kingston $30, Montreal $27 and Sudbury $76. Students can get a third off the price for a book of tickets.

There are about six buses daily to Toronto, some of which are express and about 20 daily for Montreal. There are frequent departures for Kingston, Belleville, Sudbury and other towns.

Alternative Buses See under Organised Tours for information on budget hop-on, hop-off travel services like Moose Travel.

Train The VIA Rail station (☎ 613-244-8289) is 7km south-east of the downtown area. It's at 200 Tremblay Rd, near the junction of Alta Vista Rd and Hwy 417, just east of the Rideau Canal.

There are four trains a day to Toronto and to Montreal. One-way fares include Toronto $83, Kingston $36 and Montreal $39. By booking at least five days in advance you can save between 25% and 35% if you avoid peak days like Friday.

For trips west, say to Sudbury, there is no direct line and connections must be made in Toronto, so it's a long trip.

Car Tilden (☎ 613-232-3536) is at 226 Queen St and also at the airport. Their small-car rate is $45 per day with unlimited mileage or $209 per week, unlimited. Budget and Hertz are not as central as Tilden.

Ride Sharing Allo Stop (☎ 613-562-8248), a popular service in Montreal, Quebec City and Toronto which gets drivers together with passengers, has an office at 238 Dalhousie St in the market area. It shouldn't be difficult to get rides to Montreal ($10) or Toronto ($20).

Hitching Hitching is easy between Montreal and Ottawa but is convoluted if you're heading for Toronto. Going to Montreal, take the eastbound Montreal-Ogilvy bus on Rideau St; this leads to Hwy 17 East, where you can begin. For Toronto take Hwy 31 south to Hwy 401 near the town of Morrisburg. The busy Hwy 401 (probably the most travelled route in Canada) connects Toronto with Montreal and hitching is fairly common along the way. For a more rural trip, take Hwy 7 and 37 to Tweed and then to Belleville, then Hwy 401 from there.

Getting Around

To/From the Airport The cheapest way to get to the airport is by city bus. Take bus No 5 on Elgin St going south (away from

the river) to Billings Bridge Mall and then transfer to the No 96 to the airport. Or simply catch the No 96 as it runs along Slater downtown.

You can also try the Airport Shuttle Bus (☎ 613-736-9993), which leaves every half-hour on the half-hour from in front of the Château Laurier Hotel from about 5 am to midnight. It costs around $9 and takes about 25 minutes. The bus is not as frequent on weekends; ask about scheduling.

Bus Both Ottawa and Hull operate separate bus systems. A transfer is valid from one system to the other but may require an extra partial payment.

OC Transpo (☎ 613-741-4390) operates the Ottawa bus system which tends to be volatile, with frequent changes in routes and fares. Call for assistance – they're very helpful. The standard fare is $2.35 cash or cheaper tickets can be bought at corner stores around town. All Ottawa buses quit by around midnight; most quit earlier.

You can take the following buses from downtown to:

Bus terminal – No 4 south on Bank St or, more frequently, either the No 1 or No 7 stop within a block of the terminal
Train station – Transitway No 95 east on Slater St or the No 99 along Chamberlain
Museum of Nature – No 14 on Elgin St is good but Nos 99, 1, 4 and 7 all go within a block or so
Hull – No 8 west on Albert St, but only during the day; the Outaouais bus service runs to Rideau St from Hull and continues at night.

Car There is free parking in the World Exchange Plaza on weekends and it's always the best place to park when visiting the downtown tourist office, one block away.

Bicycle Ottawa is the best city in Canada for cyclists, with an extensive system of paths in and around town and through the parks. Get a bicycle route map from a tourist office.

For rentals try Cycle Tour Rent-A-Bike (☎ 613-241-4140) at the Château Laurier. It's open every day from May to September

and charges $20 per day. ID is required. It's at the rear parking of the hotel.

A second rental outlet is National Capital Rental (☎ 613-234-9770) at 75 Nicholas St in the hostel courtyard.

HULL

Across the river in Quebec, Hull (population 62,000) is as much the other half of Ottawa as it is a separate city (that's why it's included in the Ontario chapter of this book). It warrants a visit for more than the Canadian Museum of Civilization. Hull has its share of government offices, and workers cross the river in both directions each day, but the Hull side remains home to most of the area's French population. The architecture (at least the older stuff) is different, and you'll find some top restaurants here.

Promenade du Portage, easily found from either Pont du Portage or Alexandra Bridge, is the main downtown street.

The City Hall, known as Maison du Citoyen, is an attention-grabbing, dominating modern building with a 20m-high glass tower in the centre of town, at 25 Rue Laurier. It also contains an art gallery and a meditation centre (what English-speaking bureaucracy would do that?).

The tourist office for Hull (☎ 1-800-265-7822) is at 103 Rue Laurier, on the corner of Boulevard St Laurent just over the Alexandra Bridge. It's open every day, all year.

There is also a small tourist information desk in the Maison du Citoyen (☎ 819-595-7175) which is open every day in summer, weekdays only the rest of the year.

The Ottawa city bus and trolley tours include Hull in their circuits (see Organised Tours under Ottawa earlier in this chapter).

Hull is also the main city of the region of Quebec known as Outaouais (which is pronounced basically as though you were saying Ottawa with a French accent). The Quebec government has a booklet outlining the region's attractions and activities, mostly of the outdoor variety. There are some huge parks and reserves within a few hours drive of Hull.

Canadian Museum of Civilization

This is the area's feature museum (☎ 819-776-7000). It's in the large, striking complex with the copper domes at 100 Rue Laurier, on the river bank opposite the Parliament Buildings. Allow the best part of a day to seriously explore the place.

The museum is principally concerned with the history of Canada. The **Grand Hall** of the lower level, with its simulated forest and seashore, explores Native Indian cultures and offers explanations of the huge totems and other coastal Native Indian structures. The upper-level **History Hall** presents displays and realistic re-creations tracing the story of the European founding, voyages of the country's explorers, settlement

Native Indian vase

ONTARIO

and historical developments through to the 1880s. The Basque ship section, complete with the sound of creaking wood in the living quarters, brings to life the voyages undertaken to reach the New World. Also particularly good are the Acadian farm model and the replica of the early Quebec town square.

The entertaining and educational **Children's Museum** section includes some excellent interactive exhibits.

The main level consists of three halls containing temporary exhibits on varying aspects of human history, culture and art. The **Native Indian & Inuit Art Gallery** usually, but not always, offers various shows by Native Indian artists – painting, dance, crafts and more. Don't miss the chance to see the art of British Columbian Native Indians, especially that of the Haida.

Cineplus shows realistic large-format IMAX and OMNIMAX films. The ever-changing shows are extremely popular, with waits of two to three shows not uncommon, so arrive early for a ticket.

There is a good cafeteria which offers, among other things, sandwiches and a salad bar or economical full meals all served within view of the river and Parliament Hill. The museum bookstore and gift shop are worth a browse.

From May to October the museum is open every day; for the rest of the year it's closed on Monday. On Thursday it stays open until 9 pm, otherwise it closes at 6 pm during summer and an hour earlier the rest of the year. Admission is $8, less for seniors and kids; it's free from 9 am to noon on Sunday. A Cineplus ticket is extra; prices vary depending on the show but tend to be rather high. Again, it's less for kids and seniors. There's parking under the museum.

Casino de Hull

The other big site is the posh gambling hall with parking, docking facilities and a helipad. It's open daily from 11 am to 3 am and is somewhat dressy. It's north of the centre at 1 Boulevard du Casino, off the third exit after going over Macdonald Cartier Bridge from Ottawa.

Places to Stay

The tourist office can help locate a B&B. Prices are lower than the Ottawa average.

The *Couette et Croissants* (☎ 819-771-2200, 330 Rue Champlain) is a small, attractive B&B north-east of downtown. It's about 10 blocks north of the Canadian Museum of Civilization. Prices are $45/55 with shared bath.

Motels can be found along Boulevard Alexandre Taché, which runs beside the river to the west of downtown Hull after you come across the bridge from Ottawa. There are also some business-oriented hotels downtown.

Places to Eat

Le Bistro, on the Rue Aubry pedestrian mall just off the Promenade, is a café-bar serving light lunches for under $10. There's a variety of restaurants nearby along Rue Laval.

The central *Brasserie Le Vieux Hull (50 Rue Victoria)* in the Place du Portage office complex is an inexpensive tavern for a beer or two or a cheap meal, and there is a low-priced cafeteria geared to staff in the building, too.

Elegant *Café Henry Burger* (☎ 819-777-5646, 69 Rue Laurier) is one of the oldest restaurants in Canada. The expensive French menu changes with the seasons.

Entertainment

After 2 am, when the Ontario bars are closed, partygoers head across the river from Ottawa to Hull, where things are open until 3 am and later. Promenade du Portage, in the middle of the downtown area, has numerous nightspots, some with live music, some dressy.

Le Bistro, on Rue Aubry, attracts a casual and young crowd for loud dance music. East of Boulevard St Joseph is *Les Raftsmen (60 Rue St Raymond)* which has live music in a large, friendly, typically Québecois brasserie. It also has a menu of standard beer-hall fare at good prices, served until 9 pm.

Getting There & Away

Bus The Outaouais Bus System (☎ 819-770-3242) has buses which operate along

Rideau and Wellington Sts in Ottawa. From downtown Ottawa, bus Nos 33, 35 and 42 all go to Promenade du Portage.

Bicycle A bicycle route over the Alexandra Bridge from Ottawa connects with a trail system which goes around much of central Hull and to Ruisseau de la Brasserie (Brewery Creek), a park area east of downtown.

AROUND OTTAWA-HULL
Gatineau Park

Gatineau Park is a deservedly popular 36,000-hectare area of woods and lakes in the Gatineau Hills of Quebec, north-west of downtown Hull. It's only a 20 minute drive from the Parliament Buildings in Ottawa.

The visitors centre (☎ 819-827-2020) is at 33 Scott Rd, 12km from Parliament Hill, off Hwy 5. On weekends some roads may be closed to cars, and note that parking must be paid for at the more popular destinations such as Lac Meech and the King Estate.

The park has plenty of wildlife, including about 100 species of birds, as well as 150km of hiking trails and 90km of biking trails. **Lac Lapêche**, **Lac Meech** and **Lac Phillipe** have beaches for swimming and so are the most popular. The latter has a campground while there is canoe camping at Lapêche (canoes can be rented). You can fish in the lakes and streams, and the hiking trails are good for cross-country (nordic) skiing in winter. Small Pink Lake is pretty but is off limits for swimming. A boardwalk rims the lake for strolling. The lake is best during the week, when there are fewer people around. Lac Meech has a nude gay beach.

Also in the park is Kingsmere, the summer estate of William Lyon Mackenzie King, prime minister in the 1920s, late 1930s and early 1940s. Here he indulged his hobby of collecting ruins, both genuine and fake. In 1941, King had bits of London's House of Commons brought over after the German blitz. His home, **Moorside**, is now a museum. An astute politician, King was much interested in the occult and apparently talked to both his dead dog and deceased mother. There's a pleasant tearoom at Moorside, with

items such as cucumber sandwiches or blackforest ham on pumpernickel bread.

Fall Rhapsody in September or October, celebrates the brief but colourful season when the leaves change – a time when the maples and birches of the Gatineau Hills are having their last fling before winter. An arts festival is part of the affair, as are hot-air ballooning and various concerts and competitions. Events are held in the park, with a few around town as well. During Fall Rhapsody, there are cheap buses from Ottawa-Hull to various spots in Gatineau Park.

There is no public transport to the park. For access see Getting There & Away in the following Wakefield section.

Wakefield

This small historic town, just outside the park, is a mix of heritage buildings, restaurants, cafés and tourist-oriented shops. It's popular for day trips but many stay longer.

Places To Stay The HI *Carman Trails* hostel (☎ 819-459-3180, carman@magma.ca, Gatineau Park International Hostel) consistently gets great reviews. It makes an excellent base for exploring the park and is a fine retreat in its own right.

With 80 acres linked to the park, there is no end of outdoor possibilities. Cycling, hiking, canoeing and cross-country skiing are all available. Another option is the nearby jump and ripride (you've got to ask, but it's high and fast) at Great Canadian Bungee.

The hostel has its own licensed restaurant and organic greenhouses. Other features are a sauna, fireplace and family rooms. A dorm bed is $17 or $20 nonmember, and the hostel is open all year. Book ahead – capacity is 40.

You may be able to get picked up after getting off the Voyageur Maniwaki bus; call for details.

Getting There & Away The HCW Steam Train (☎ 819-778-7246) connects Hull to Wakefield. The 1907 train travels alongside the park, making one-day return excursions daily from early May to mid-October. Adult fare is $26 for the entertaining 64km round

trip. Reservations are recommended. In Wakefield, there's enough time for a meal or stroll. The station is at 165 Rue Deveault, north of central Hull.

Back Country Bus (☎ 613-851-7045) runs a daily (except Tuesday) shuttle between Ottawa, Hull, Gatineau Park trails, Carman Trails, Wakefield and area locations. The rates are very good and you can take skis, bikes, canoes etc. Call for details.

Whitewater Rafting Centres

North-west of Gatineau Park, there are several outfitters who use a turbulent section of the Ottawa River for rafting adventures. They range from a half-day trip to two-day adventures and run from roughly April to October. No experience is needed and the locations are less than two hours from Ottawa. Book ahead for weekends, as the trips fill up. Savings can be enjoyed by going on weekdays.

Recommended Esprit Rafting (☎ 1-800-596-7238), just over the Quebec border a few kilometres from Fort Coulonge, uses small, bouncy 14-foot, self-bailing rafts and has pick-up and delivery from the Ottawa Hostel and Carman Trails. A one-day rafting trip costs $85 with lunch and there is a whole range of other options such as four-day canoe trips and kayaking courses.

Good dorm accommodation is available at its rustic river lodge for $20 with breakfast and use of canoes and kayaks. You can also camp. All meals (the barbecue dinners are a treat) are offered.

Two other reliable organisations, both in Foresters Falls, Ontario, are OWL Rafting (☎ 1-800-461-7238) with both wild and mild trips (the latter being good for families) and Wilderness Tours (☎ 1-800-267-9166). Both offer meals, camping and more expensive cabin accommodation which should be booked ahead.

Eastern Ontario

West from Ottawa there are various routes through Ontario. Hwy 17, the Trans Canada Hwy, leads north-west to Pembroke, then continues to North Bay and on to Sudbury. This is the quickest way to western Canada.

From Pembroke there is another option. Hwy 60/62 leads west through the southern portion of Algonquin Park to Huntsville, where Hwy 11 runs north to North Bay and south to Toronto.

The southern route from Ottawa goes to the more populated southern region of Ontario, the St Lawrence River, the Great Lakes and Toronto. From Ottawa, Hwys 31 and 16 lead directly down to the 401, the expressway to Toronto.

A prettier, though slower drive is to take Hwy 7 west out of Ottawa going through Perth and as far as Hwy 37. From here Hwy 37 leads south through Tweed before dropping down to Hwy 401. This route is a standard itinerary and is a compromise between speed and aesthetics. Taking Hwy 7 any farther west really starts to add on the hours. Ottawa to Toronto on the Hwys 7 and 37 route takes about five hours.

ALGONQUIN PARK

The hilly eastern side of the park has some fine features, including the Barron Canyon which makes a great canoeing destination, and numerous waterfalls. There is a campground at the Achray access point on Grand Lake and many interior sites, including some beauties with a beach just a 20 minute paddle away. Call ☎ 705-633-5538 for reservations.

Algonquin Portage (☎ 613-735-1795) west of Pembroke on Route 6 (the road to Achray) rents tents, sleeping bags and canoes and has hostel accommodation, a shuttle service, food and gas.

Esprit Rafting (☎ 1-800-596-7238) is based near Pembroke, on the Ottawa River, east of Algonquin. It offers a one-day canoe trip down the Barron Canyon in Algonquin Park for $85 between May and October.

For more on Algonquin see the Georgian Bay & Lakelands section later in this chapter.

EGANVILLE

If you are in the region, this small town northwest of Ottawa is worth a stop for the nearby **Bonnechere Caves**. The caves and passages,

8km south-east, were the bottom of a tropical sea about 500 million years ago and contain fossils of animals from long before the dinosaur age. Pathways lead through parts of the extensive system, past fossil banks and stalactites. Tours are offered through summer.

MERRICKVILLE

South-west of Ottawa, Merrickville is a small, pleasant late 18th century town along the Rideau River/Canal route from Ottawa to Kingston. There are a couple of B&Bs in town, as well as some places to eat along St Lawrence St. A few craft and antique shops can also be found. In autumn the town's numerous artists host a studio tour.

Historic sites include the **locks** (dating from 1830) and the **blockhouse**, with its 1m-thick walls built by the British in 1832 to protect the canal in case of attack. The blockhouse is now a small museum.

SMITHS FALLS

Midway along the Rideau Canal system, Smiths Falls makes a good short stop. In addition to several minor sites, it's a focal point for the many recreational boats using the canal.

Smiths Falls has become known as much for the **Hershey Chocolate Factory** as for its history or its canal location. A free tour of the Canadian branch plant of this famous USA chocolate company based in Hershey, Pennsylvania is recommended. It isn't acceptable to dive into the undulating vats of liquid chocolate, but you can find out how chocolate bars are created and then start eating (discount prices offered). It's east of the centre on Hershey Drive off Hwy 43 East – just follow your nose – and is open every day. Tours are given weekdays only, but you can do it yourself.

The locks can be viewed in the middle of town and the best of the three small historical museums is the **Rideau Canal Museum**, in a 19th century mill at 34 Beckworth St S. Exhibits detail the history of the canal. The **Railway Museum** at 90 Mill St has some rolling stock as well as artefacts and documents and the **Heritage House Museum** reveals the life and times of a wealthy mill owner in the 1870s.

CORNWALL

Cornwall is the first city of any size in Ontario along the St Lawrence Valley and has the Seaway International Bridge to the USA. It was here in the 1870s that Thomas Edison, creator of the light bulb, helped set up the first factory lit by electricity.

Despite this corner of Ontario having Scottish and Loyalist ancestry, there is a good-sized French population in Cornwall.

The Pitt St Mall, in the centre of town, is a pedestrian-only two-block section of stores and gardens.

The **RH Saunders Energy Information Centre** has displays on the big, important hydroelectric facility here. It's open daily in July and August, on weekdays only in June. Tours of the power facilities at the dam are available. The **Inverarden Regency Cottage Museum** represents Ontario's finest example of Regency Cottage architecture. Built in 1816 by a retiring fur trader who had evidently done quite well, it's on the corner of Hwy 2 and Boundary Rd and is open from April to November.

Just out of town, on Cornwall Island, there is the **North American Travelling College Museum** focusing on the Cree, Iroquois and Ojibway Indians with artefacts and a replica village. It's closed weekends.

The bridge over to Massena, New York makes Cornwall another busy port of entry for US visitors.

In **Maxville**, to the north, Highland Games held at the beginning of August commemorate the region's Scottish heritage. **St Raphaels** has some interesting church ruins dating from 1815.

West of Cornwall, the **Long Sault Parkway** connects a series of parks and beaches along the river.

MORRISBURG & UPPER CANADA VILLAGE

This small town lies west of Cornwall on the St Lawrence River. Despite its small size, it's known far and wide for its good historic

site – Upper Canada Village (☎ 613-543-3704, ☎ 1-800-437-2233), the detailed recreation of a country town from the 1860s. About 40 buildings and costumed workers bring the past to life. There's a blacksmith's shop, inn and sawmill as well as a working farm, all set by the river.

You'll need at least several hours to fully explore the site, which is open from mid-May to roughly mid-October. Hours are 9.30 am to 5 pm. Admission is $13, less for kids and there's a $30 family rate.

Without transport, the village can be reached aboard buses running between Ottawa and Cornwall and on some buses which follow the Montreal to Toronto route. Many are direct, while others putt along, stopping at the smaller towns en route. Nearby **Crysler Battlefield Park** is a memorial to those who died fighting the USA in 1812.

Parks of the St Lawrence (☎ 613-543-3704, ☎ 1-800-437-2233), a government agency based in Morrisburg, runs Upper Canada Village, the **Upper Canada Migratory Bird Sanctuary** and **Fort Henry**, as well as many of the campgrounds and parks along the river between Cornwall and Kingston.

Hwy 2 along the river is slower to travel on but provides a more scenic trip than Hwy 401. It's used by many cyclists. There are numerous provincial parks along the way, especially east of town along the Long Sault Parkway. Going west there is a seaway-viewing platform at **Iroquois**.

There are about half a dozen motels in Morrisburg and four campgrounds. Among the latter is the *Upper Canada Migratory Bird Sanctuary Nature Awareness Campsite (☎ 613-543-3704, ☎ 1-800-437-2233)*. It's a little different from the average campground and is educational, too. Find it 14km east of town along Hwy 2. It has about 50 tent sites but few creature comforts.

PRESCOTT

Another 19th century town, Prescott is the site of the International Bridge to Ogdensburg, New York. The harbour area has been overhauled and has a busy marina, but there isn't anything of note for the traveller.

Just to the east of the downtown area and walkable from the centre is the **Fort Wellington National Historic Site** (☎ 613-925-2896). The original fort was built during the War of 1812. It was rebuilt in 1838 and served militarily until the 1920s. Some original fortifications remain, as does a blockhouse and the officers' quarters from the 1830s. During summer, guides in costume supplement the interpretive displays. In the third week of July, the fort hosts the country's largest military pageant, which includes mock battles in full regalia.

The fort is open daily from the end of May to 30 September. Also here, outside the grounds, are a few picnic tables with views of the river.

BROCKVILLE

A small community along the river, Brockville is a particularly attractive town, with its many old stone buildings and the classic-looking main street. The courthouse and jail in the centre of town date from 1842. During summer, many of the finest buildings are lit up, accentuating the slight resort flavour of this casual river port by the Thousand Islands. Cruises depart from the central waterfront area.

The **Brockville Museum** in historic Beecher House provides a look at the area's history and **Fulford Place**, a national historic site, is a 35-room mansion from the turn of the century. The other principal attraction, the **Brockville Railway Tunnel**, the oldest train tunnel in the country, is for buffs only.

For the Thousand Island Parkway area west of Brockville, see Around Kingston later in this chapter.

KINGSTON

Kingston (population 138,000) is a handsome town that retains much of its past through preservation of many historic buildings and defence structures. Built strategically where Lake Ontario flows into the St Lawrence River, it is a convenient stopping-off point almost exactly halfway between Montreal and Toronto,

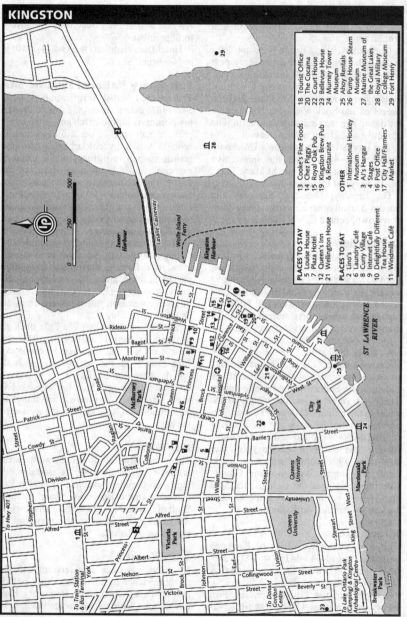

KINGSTON

PLACES TO STAY
5 Louise House
7 Plaza Hotel
12 Queen's Inn
21 Wellington House

PLACES TO EAT
2 Lino's
6 Laundry Café
8 Curry Village
9 Internet Café
10 Delightfully Different
   Tea House
11 Windmills Café

13 Cooke's Fine Foods
14 Chez Piggy
15 Royal Oak Pub
19 Kingston Brew Pub
   & Restaurant

OTHER
1 International Hockey
   Museum
3 Al's Hangar
4 Stages
16 Post Office
17 City Hall/Farmers'
   Market

18 Tourist Office
20 The Cocama
22 Court House
23 Bellevue House
24 Murney Tower
   Museum
25 Ahoy Rentals
26 Pump House Steam
   Museum
27 Marine Museum of
   the Great Lakes
28 Royal Military
   College Museum
29 Fort Henry

and it's not difficult to spend an interesting and enjoyable day or three in and around town.

Once a fur-trading depot, Kingston later became the principal British military post west of Quebec, and was the national capital for a while. The many 19th century buildings of local grey limestone and the streets of red-brick Victorian houses give the downtown area a distinctive charm. The attractive waterfront is also pleasant.

The city is home to Queen's University (founded in 1841) and the impressive cathedrals of St George and St Mary. There are also several large prisons.

On Tuesday, Thursday, Saturday and Sunday a small open-air market takes place downtown, behind City Hall on King St.

Orientation

The town lies a few kilometres south of Hwy 401. Princess St, the main street, runs right down to the St Lawrence River, along which are many fine old buildings. The whole city is low-rise, with few buildings higher than two or three storeys, and there aren't many modern structures either.

At the bottom of Princess St, Ontario St runs along the harbour by the start of the Rideau Canal to Ottawa. This is the old, much restored area, with a tourist office, old military battery and Martello tower. There are views across the mouth of the canal to the military college. The market is on the corner of Brock St and King St E.

King St leads out along the lake's shore towards the university. Here you'll see many fine 19th century houses and parkland. The impressive limestone County Courthouse is near the campus, facing a small park. Farther out is Lake Ontario Park, with camping and a small beach.

Information

The main downtown office of Kingston Tourism (☎ 613-548-4415, ☎ 1-888-855-4555) is at 209 Ontario St, across from City Hall in Confederation Park.

Away from the city centre, the Fort Henry Information Centre (☎ 613-542-7388) is at the fort, at the junction of Hwys 2 and 15. It's open only from May to September.

Hotel Dieu Hospital (☎ 613-544-3310) is at 166 Brock St.

Fort Henry National Historic Site

The restored British fortification (☎ 613-542-7388) dating from 1832 dominates the town from its hilltop perch and is the city's prime attraction. The beautiful structure is brought to life by colourfully uniformed guards trained in military drills, artillery exercises, and fife-and-drum music of the 1860s. Inside the fort you can peek into, among other things, a fully furnished officer's room and the commandant's quarters. Admission is $9, less for children, and includes a guided tour.

The soldiers put on displays periodically throughout the day. The best is the Commandant's Parade, performed daily at 3 pm. In addition, special events are held almost monthly. The fort is open daily through its season but is closed from 20 October to 20 May.

Without a car, the fort is a little difficult to reach, as there is no city bus. You can walk – it's not that far, over the causeway from town – but the last 500m or so is all uphill. Other than hoofing it, try to share a taxi and maybe get a ride back with a fellow visitor. Or if you have a few things to do around town, consider renting a bike for the day.

City Hall

The grand City Hall, in the downtown area, is one of the country's finest classical buildings – an excellent example of British Renaissance Tuscan Revival-style architecture! Built of limestone, it dates from 1843, when Kingston was capital of the then United Provinces of Canada.

Waterfront

Kingston was once a waterfront defence town; evidence of this is found in Confederation Park, which runs from City Hall down to the river, where yachts moor.

Brock St

Brock St was the middle of town in the 1800s, and many of the original shops still stand along it. It's worth a walk around. Take a look in Cooke's Fine Foods at 61 Brock St, a gourmet shop with old, wooden counters and a century-old, pressed-tin ceiling. There are lovely aromas and a curious assortment of goods and shoppers, including local professors drinking the fresh coffee at the back of the store.

Marine Museum of the Great Lakes

Farther east is the Marine Museum (☎ 613-542-2261) at 55 Ontario St. Kingston was long a centre for shipbuilding, and the museum is on the site of the shipyard. In 1678 the first vessel built on the Great Lakes was constructed here. Among its list of credits are ships built during the War of 1812. The museum details these and other aspects of the Great Lakes' history. The 3000-tonne icebreaker *Alexander Henry* can be boarded. In fact, you can sleep on board – it's operated as a B&B and is inexpensive (see Places to Stay). Admission to the museum is $4 or for $6.25 includes the ship and the pump house museum and there is a family rate. It's open daily from January to mid-December.

Pump House Steam Museum

This one-of-a-kind, completely restored, steam-run pump station (☎ 613-542-2261) at 23 Ontario St was first used in 1849. It now contains several engines and some scale models, all run on steam. It's open daily from the start of May to Labour Day. Admission is $4 but see above for the combo tickets. Train buffs will also want to see the 20 model trains from around the world displayed in a special exhibit room.

Macdonald Park

On the corner of Barrie St and King St E is Macdonald Park, right along Lake Ontario. Just offshore, in 1812, the British ship *Royal George* battled with the USA's USS *Oneida*. At the western end of the park is the **Murney Tower Museum**, in the Martello

tower from 1846. This round defence structure was part of the early riverside fortifications and is now a museum housing local military and historical titbits. Admission is $3. The museum is open daily from the end of May to the beginning of September. There are walking and bicycle paths along here and good swimming by the jetty.

On the corner of King St E and West St is **City Park** featuring a statue of Canada's first prime minister, Sir John Alexander Macdonald.

Bellevue House

This National Historic Site (☎ 613-545-8666) is a superbly maintained Tuscan-style mansion, which apparently means a very odd-shaped, balconied, brightly painted architect's field day. It works, though, and in the garden setting this is an impressive and interesting house. It was once the home of Sir John Alexander Macdonald. The mansion at 35 Centre St houses many good antiques. It's open daily during summer from 9 am to 6 pm and in winter from 10 am to 5 pm. Admission is $3.

Correctional Service of Canada Museum

Correctional Service is what Canadian bureaucrats call jails, and here is about as close as you'll get to finding out what they're like without doing something nasty. Located at 555 King St W, in the administration building across from the main prison, the museum (☎ 613-530-3122) has a fascinating collection of articles ranging from confiscated weapons to tools (and methods – like carved cafeteria trays) used in escapes. A visit is worthwhile – it's eye-opening, educational and free. It's open from May to September, Wednesday to Friday from 9 am to 4 pm and Saturday and Sunday from 10 am to 4 pm.

Royal Military College Museum

In the Fort Frederick Martello Tower on the grounds of the college (☎ 613-541-5010) is the Royal Military College Museum. This is the largest of the city's historic towers and

has a collection on the history of the century-old military college. You have to wonder how or why, but also here lies the small arms collection of General Porfirio Diaz, president of Mexico from 1886 to 1912. The museum is just east of town, off Hwy 2, and is open daily in summer.

International Hockey Museum
On the corner of Alfred and York Sts, this collection (☎ 613-544-2355) honours the history and stars of Canada's most loved sport. The displays include lots of memorabilia, photos and equipment. The museum is open daily mid-June to mid-September, but on weekend afternoons only for the rest of the year. Admission is $3.

Kingston Archaeological Centre
If you've been out along Hwy 401, you probably noticed the sedimentary rock outcrops, one of the few interesting things along that highway's entire length from Montreal to Toronto. The Kingston Archaeological Centre at 370 King St W, in the Tett Centre, has displays on the 8000-year human history of the area, featuring items dug from the surrounding landscape or found along the shoreline. It's open on weekdays and it's free.

Kingston Mills Lockstation Blockhouse
Away from the centre, up Kingston Mills Rd just north of Hwy 401, this restored blockhouse (☎ 613-359-5377) dates from 1839. The purpose of the lock station and what it was like to operate are part of the explanatory exhibits. The blockhouse is open daily through summer and is free.

Other Museums
There are several other specialised museums in or near Kingston (see Around Kingston later in this chapter), including one on county schools, one at the military base detailing the history of military communications and electronics, and others on such things as geology and mineralogy and art. The tourist office has details.

Wolfe Island
It's possible to have a free mini-cruise by taking the car ferry from Kingston to Wolfe Island. The 20 minute trip affords views of the city, the fort and a few of the Thousand Islands. Wolfe Island, the largest in the chain at 30km by 11km, lies halfway to the USA and is basically flat farmland, although many of its inhabitants now work in town.

There is not a lot to see on the island, but there is the *General Wolfe Hotel*, a short walk from the dock, with its three busy and highly regarded dining rooms. Prices are moderate to slightly expensive. There are also some moderately priced cabins on the island, B&Bs and a campground. On the Kingston side, the ferry terminal is at the intersection of Ontario and Barrack Sts. The ferry runs continuously every hour or so from 6.15 am to 1 am daily, taking about 50 vehicles at a time. From Wolfe Island, another ferry links Cape Vincent, New York, but a toll is charged on this segment if you have a car.

Organised Tours
The tourist office has a pamphlet with map for a self-guided walking tour of the older part of town.

Kingston by Bike Tours (☎ 613-542-0964) offers three-hour cycle tours of the city for $25, less if you have a bike.

During summer and autumn a Haunted Walk, featuring stories of hangings and grave robbers, leaves from the tourist information office every Tuesday to Saturday at 8 pm. The $8 tour takes about two hours.

On summer days, a trackless mini-train departs regularly from the tourist office area for a 50 minute tour of the central Kingston area.

Cruises Boat tours will take you around some of the islands; a couple of companies run daily trips in summer. Kingston 1000 Island Cruises (☎ 613-549-5544) has several choices. Its 1½ hour trip ($13) aboard the *Island Belle* takes you around the interesting Kingston shoreline with a commentary on some of the noteworthy sites. Throughout summer it offers two or three

trips a day, including three-hour cruises, leaving from the Island Queen dock, on Ontario St at the foot of Brock St. Departing from the same place is the *Island Queen* showboat, providing live family entertainment or a three hour evening cruise with a buffet dinner.

St Lawrence Cruise Lines (☎ 1-800-267-7868), 253 Ontario St, runs luxury cruises out of Kingston down the St Lawrence River to Ottawa, Montreal and Quebec City aboard the *Canadian Empress*. Trips last four, five or six nights and fares include all meals, entertainment and activities.

See Thousand Islands Parkway later in this chapter for more cruises.

Places to Stay

Camping *Hi-Lo Hickory* (☎ 613-385-2430, ☎ 1-800-400-7472) on Wolfe Island is reached by ferry from Kingston. The campground is about 12km east of the Kingston ferry terminal and has a beach. A bridge on the island's other side connects New York State.

Only 4km from downtown is recommended *Lake Ontario Park* (☎ 613-542-6574), which is operated by the city's parks department. It's west out along King St and is green, pretty quiet and there's a small weedy beach. A city bus runs from downtown right to the campground, from Monday to Saturday until 7.30 pm and on Friday until 10.30 pm.

KOA (Kampgrounds of America, seen all over North America) has a branch 1.6km north of Hwy 401 off Hwy 38 (☎ 613-546-6140). These places can be very plastic, having as little to do with camping as possible, and are also expensive, big and generally pretty busy. They cater mainly for trailers but have some tent sites.

Hostels HI operates a summer-only hostel at *Louise House* (☎ 613-531-8237 ext 400, 329 Johnson St), downtown. It's open 1 May to 20 August. The rest of the year this house from 1847 is a university residence. Rates are $18 for hostellers or $35/50 as a regular B&B.

B&Bs The Kingston & Area B&B Association (☎ 613-542-0214) runs a booking agency. There are about 40 participating homes in and around town. Tell it where you want to be and what your interests are and you'll be matched up suitably. Rates start at $40/50 for singles/doubles with full breakfast included, plus $10 to $15 extra for children. Cheaper rates are available for extended stays.

In summer, you can stay at a unique B&B on a moored, retired 64m icebreaker, the *Alexander Henry* (☎ 613-542-2261, www.marmus.ca), which is part of the downtown Marine Museum of the Great Lakes. Beds are in the former crew's quarters and a continental breakfast is served from the galley. You can wander all over the ship. It hasn't been gentrified at all – the vessel is plain, simple and functional and the 19 rooms are pretty much like those on a working ship. This partially explains the good prices, which start at $42 for a twin and go up to $65 if you want the captain's cabin.

Wellington House (☎ 613-544-9919, 60 Wellington St) has good rates at $40/50 with a full breakfast and shared bath.

O'Brien House (☎ 613-542-8660, 39 Glenaire Mews) up near the train station and north-west of the downtown area is a little less costly than the city norm. It's a B&B whose owner seems to particularly like overseas visitors. Singles/doubles cost $48/55, including a full breakfast and coffee or tea at any time. There are reduced rates for children.

Hotels The only remaining old cheapie is the *Plaza Hotel (46 Montreal St)* on the corner of Queen St. It exists basically for the downstairs bar but is not badly kept. It's no family place and is not recommended for single women, but it is cheap – $25/35 a single/double with private bathroom.

Totally different is the *Donald Gordon Centre* (☎ 613-533-2221, 421 Union St) affiliated with (and very near) Queen's University. The centre rents quiet, air-conditioned rooms for $70/80.

Offering more amenities, style and services is the **Queen's Inn** (☎ 613-546-0429, 125 Brock St) dating from 1839. It offers modern facilities in 17 rooms in a central setting. It's one of the oldest hotels in the country. Rooms vary from $90 to $110 in high season (April to November) and from $70 to $90 the rest of the year.

Motels *Comfort Inn* (☎ 613-549-5550, 1454 Princess St) is a two-storey place. Rooms are a couple of dollars cheaper upstairs and cost $68 to $82 for singles or doubles.

Cheaper is the **Hilltop** (☎ 613-542-3846, 2287 Princess St) where singles/doubles are $35/40 and up depending on season. There are many other motels on Princess St, and some along Hwy 2 on each side of town.

Places to Eat

Windmills Café (184 Princess St) serves very good vegetarian and meat dishes in pleasant surroundings. Lunch prices range from $6 to $8 and might include Thai Shrimp Salad or Warm Goat Cheese Torte. Dinner costs between $7 and $12. It's also open for breakfast and offers weekend brunch. Around the corner *Windmills To Go (19 Montreal St)* offers a good variety of takeout food.

The **Delightfully Different Tea House** *(222 Wellington St)* turns out excellent fresh sandwiches, salads and bagels for lunch, and muffins and the like for breakfast. It's only open from 7 am to 4 pm Monday to Friday but is worth getting to for a light meal and is very inexpensive. It's on the corner of Queen St.

Also for a sandwich lunch, snack, dessert or just a coffee, try the very good *Laundry Café (291 Princess St)*. The salads are noteworthy. It has an outdoor courtyard patio and is open late.

The *Kingston Brew Pub & Restaurant (34 Clarence St)* brews its own ales and lagers – try its Dragon's Breath Ale – and also has a good selection of nonhouse brands. It also makes its own wines and ciders, the first in Canada to do so. There are inexpensive tavern-style things to munch on and, interestingly, a daily curry. On the cor-ner of King St E and Brock St, near City Hall, the **Royal Oak Pub** serves food and British beers amid British-style décor.

You can get a fine Indian meal upstairs at *Curry Village (169A Princess St)*. Lunch specials begin at $6. At dinner, most dishes are $8 to $10. The menu includes biryanis, tandooris and a range of curries. It's open daily.

For a splurge there's *Chez Piggy (68 Princess St)* probably the city's best known restaurant, in a renovated early 19th century building, but really down a small alley off King St between Brock and Princess Sts. At lunch, from 11.30 am to 2 pm, soup and a sandwich or the good salads are not expensive. Dinners, starting at 6 pm, cost $10 to $18 for a main course, so the final bill can be quite high. There is also a Sunday brunch, with some items you don't see on a standard brunch menu (but again, it is definitely not for the budget-conscious). The restaurant is owned by a member of the 1960s US pop band, The Lovin' Spoonful. It's open daily.

Division St, towards Hwy 401, has a good cross-section of places representing the standard restaurant chains. *Lino's (cnr Division & Princess Sts)* serves the basics 24 hours a day.

For coffee, cake and computers, check the *Internet Café (303 Bagot St)* in the LaSalle Mews complex.

Entertainment

Bars & Clubs The *Cocama (178 Ontario St)* is a huge dance bar down near the water. It's styled after the Limelight in New York City. *AJ's Hangar (393 Princess St)* is a place to go for live rock and blues bands on weekends (or for a drink the rest of the week). *Stages (390 Princess St)* just across the road from AJ's is a popular dance club.

Kingston has quite a few British-style pubs. The *Toucan (76 Princess St)*, near King St, often has live music. *Tir nan Og (200 Ontario St)* has live Celtic music most nights with no cover charge.

Cinema The *Princess Court Cinema* (☎ 613-546-3456, 394 Princess St) is a good repertory movie house.

Shopping

Indigo at 259 Princess St is a good bookstore and has a café which even serves wine. Trailhead at 237 Princess St offers a quality selection of outdoor/camping equipment and supplies.

Getting There & Away

Bus The bus station (☎ 613-547-4916) is at 175 Counter St, a couple of kilometres south of Hwy 401, east off Division St. Services going to Toronto are frequent throughout the day (at least eight trips); to Montreal, buses are slightly less frequent. To Ottawa, there are buses each morning, afternoon and evening. Services also go to some of the smaller centres, such as Pembroke and Cornwall. The one-way fare to Montreal is $41, Ottawa $30 and Toronto $40.

Train The VIA Rail station (☎ 613-544-5600) is a long way north-west from the downtown area. There are five train services to Montreal daily, costing $53. To Ottawa ($36) there are four trains a day. To Toronto ($56) there are eight services daily. Discounts are offered on tickets purchased five days or more in advance.

Car Tilden (☎ 613-546-1145) at 2232 Princess St offers daily, weekly and longer car rentals.

Getting Around

Bus For information on buses, call Kingston Mobility (☎ 613-546-1181).

For getting into town from the bus station, there is a city bus stop across the street. Buses depart at a quarter to and a quarter past the hour.

From the train station, city bus No 1 stops on the corner of Princess and Counter Sts, just a short walk from the bus station.

Bicycle Rentals are available at Ahoy Rentals (☎ 613-545-7148), 23 Ontario St. Another choice is TBC Bike Rentals at 132 Ordnance St. The area is generally flat and both Hwys 2 and 5 have paved shoulders.

AROUND KINGSTON
Thousand Islands Parkway

East of Kingston between Gananoque (pronounced 'gan-an-ok-way') and Mallorytown Landing, a small road – the Thousand Islands Parkway – dips south of Hwy 401, runs along the river for 35km and then rejoins the highway. It makes a scenic and recommended side trip when travelling Hwy 401 in either direction.

The route offers picnic areas and good views out to many of the islands from the pastoral strip of shoreline. For information on lodging or activities call or visit the Chamber of Commerce in Gananoque (☎ 613-382-3250, ☎ 1-800-561-1595) at 2 King St E.

The waterfront here is lined with some tourist oriented shops in replica 19th century architecture.

The **Bikeway** bicycle path extends the full length of the parkway. Bicycles can be rented at several places including the 1000 Islands Camping Resort (☎ 613-659-3058) 8km east of Gananoque.

The St Lawrence Parks System maintains a series of recreational and historic places along this route and on Hwy 2 from Adolphustown to beyond Upper Canada Village at Morrisburg and all the way to Lancaster, near the Quebec border. Boat cruises around the islands depart from the two small towns of Rockport and Gananoque.

Some 16km east of Kingston, in a log house in Grass Creek Park, you'll find the **MacLachlan Woodworking Museum**. The museum uses an extensive collection of tools to outline the development of working in wood.

Close to the town of **Lansdowne** between Gananoque and Rockport is the busy bridge to New York State. The **Skydeck**, a 125m-high observation tower, is open every day from May to October. Its three decks provide great views over the river area. Admission is reasonable and there is a restaurant on the premises.

Along the parkway are privately run campgrounds, B&Bs, numerous motels, and some cottages to rent for longer stays.

There is a bit of an art colony in the area,

ONTARIO

and in autumn many of the local studios are open to the public. Ask the tourist office in Kingston or Gananoque for a list of the painters, sculptors, woodworkers, glass workers, weavers etc.

The Thousand Islands This scenic area just east of Kingston actually has more than 1000 islands which dot the river between the two national mainlands. In spring the islands undulate with the white blooms of the trillium, the provincial flower.

In Gananoque, the Gananoque Boat Line (☎ 613-382-2144) has one hour ($11) and three hour ($16) trips, daily in both July and August. It operates a reduced schedule in May, June, September and October. At impressive **Boldt Castle** you can get off for a closer look and return to Gananoque on a later boat. Passengers stopping at the castle, which was built in 1904 for Boldt's wife, are subject to US Customs regulations.

The Rockport Boat Line (☎ 613-659-3402) in Rockport also has trips out among the international islands at about the same prices. Trips depart from the dock 3km east of the Thousand Islands International Bridge frequently in peak season, less so in spring and autumn.

The autumn cruises with the coloured leaves as a backdrop are justly popular. A different angle is to do it all yourself on a rented houseboat. This can be a lot of fun, but is pricey unless you get several people together. If you want to look into it, try Houseboat Holidays (☎ 613-382-2842) in Gananoque and see Rideau Canal later in this chapter.

St Lawrence Islands National Park Within the gentle, green archipelago, is Canada's smallest national park (☎ 613-923-5261) consisting of 17 islands scattered along 80km of the river. At **Mallorytown Landing**, on the mainland, is the park headquarters with the interpretive and information centre, a walking trail and a beach.

Many of the islands have picnicking and camping, with minimal facilities, and 13 islands offer primitive camp sites accessible only by boat. Water taxis and boat rentals are available from the park headquarters and from many of the small towns along the parkway. Tourist offices or park headquarters will have information on what's available. National Park islands stretch from just off Mallorytown all the way down to Gananoque.

West of Kingston
West of town along the coast, Hwy 33 has been designated the Loyalist Parkway. It retraces the steps of the Loyalists who settled this area some 200 years ago after fleeing the American Revolution. The parkway runs for 94km from Kingston to Trenton, passing over Quinte's Isle.

Just west of Kingston, in Amherstview, **Fairfield Historical Park** runs along the shoreline. It includes **Fairfield House**, one of the province's oldest, built in 1793 by Loyalists from New England. North about 10km, in Odessa, the historic **Babcock Mill** is a working water-powered mill which again produces the baskets originally made here in the mid-19th century.

At **Adolphustown**, catch the continuously running short and free ferry over to Glenora (on Quinte's Isle) and continue on to Picton.

North of Kingston
North of Kingston is the **Rideau Lakes** region, an area of small towns, cottages, lodges and marinas with opportunities for fishing and camping. In a day's drive you can explore some of the smaller, rural Ontario villages.

Wilton has one of the many southern Ontario regional cheese factories with a retail outlet.

In the little town of **Yarker**, straight up Hwy 6 from Hwy 401, the *Waterfall Tea Room* is right on the river, by a waterfall, and has been recommended.

The region has attracted 'back-to-the-landers' and countercultural people. Their influences show up in the number of health food stores, craft outlets and bakeries. In **Tamsworth**, there is a big arts and crafts outlet which includes the *Devon Tea Room*. **Marlbank** is another similar town.

Frontenac Provincial Park (☎ 613-376-3489) straddles both the lowlands of southern

Ethnic Cleansing in the 18th Century

The issue of American independence from Britain divided the American colonies into two camps: the Patriots and the Loyalists. During the American Revolution of 1775 to 1783, the Loyalists maintained their allegiance to the British Crown. About one-third of the 13 colonies' population remained loyal to Britain. Severe laws were passed against them, forcing some 200,000 to leave during and after the revolution. Of those, between 50,000 and 60,000 fled to Canada, settling in the Maritimes, the Eastern Townships of Lower Canada (Quebec) and the St Lawrence-Lake Ontario region of Upper Canada (Ontario). Unknown to many today, not all were of British descent – they represented a mix of ethnic backgrounds. Regardless, their arrival strengthened Great Britain's hold on this part of its empire. In Nova Scotia, for example, the migration meant that the French no longer made up the majority of the population.

In this region, the Loyalists' arrival essentially meant the formation of the province of Ontario. Both the British and local governments were generous in their support, offering clothing, rations, and various aid and land grants.

Soon the Loyalists in Canada were not only self-sustaining but prosperous and powerful. Today their descendants make up a significant and influential segment of the Canadian population.

Loyalist sites can be seen in southern Quebec, the Gaspé Peninsula and, in particular, Saint John, New Brunswick and Shelburne, Nova Scotia.

Ontario and the more northern Canadian Shield, so the flora, fauna and geology of the park are mixed. The park is designed for overnight hikers and canoeists. There is no formal campground – rather, there are interior camp sites scattered through the park, accessible only on foot or by water. Though the park is large, there are relatively few sites. Trails and canoe routes have been mapped out.

The entrance and the information centre are at **Otter Lake**, off Hwy 5A north of Sydenham. The swimming is excellent, the bass fishing is pretty good and there are no bears to worry about. Frontenac Outfitter (☎ 613-376-6220) has canoes and is near the main entrance.

North-west from Kingston up Hwy 41 is **Bon Echo Provincial Park** (☎ 613-336-2228). One of the largest parks in Eastern Ontario, it's another good spot for canoeing. Some of the lakes are quite shallow and get very warm. There are walk-in and canoe-in camp sites or roadside campgrounds with facilities. At **Mazinaw Lake** there are Native Indian rock paintings on granite cliffs.

Rideau Canal The 150-year-old, 200km-long canal/river/lake system connects Kingston with Ottawa. The historical route is good for boating or canoeing trips, with parks, small towns, lakes and many places to stop en route. When travelling from one end to the other, boats must pass through 47 lock systems. The old defence buildings along the way have been restored.

After the War of 1812 there was a fear that there could be yet another war with the Americans. The Duke of Wellington decided to link Ottawa and Kingston with a canal in order to have a reliable communications and supply route between the two military centres. Although the canal is just 200km in length, its construction was a brutal affair, involving as many as 4000 men, battling malaria and the Canadian Shield, with some of the world's hardest rock. It climbs 84m from Ottawa over the Shield, then drops 49m to Lake Ontario. And guess what? Right! It never saw any military service.

It did prove useful later in the century for shipping goods around, but is now used mainly for recreation. *Houseboat Holidays*

(☎ 613-382-2842), based in Gananoque, rents houseboats for meandering along the canal. The boats sleep six to eight and come with all kitchen necessities. Prices start at $475 for a weekend when costs are considerably more than midweek.

Roads run parallel to much of the canal, so walking or cycling is also possible.

Rideau Trail The Rideau Trail is a 400km hiking-trail system which links Kingston with Ottawa. It passes through Westport, Smiths Falls and many conservation areas, traversing forests, fields and marshes as well as some stretches of road along the way. In Kingston call the Rideau Trail Association (☎ 613-545-0823). There are some historic sites on the route, and you'll see the Rideau Canal. There are also 64km of side loops. Most people use the route only for day trips, but longer trips and overnighting are possible. The main trail is marked by orange triangles, side trails are marked by blue triangles. The Rideau Trail Association, which has an office in Kingston, prints a map kit for the entire route. Between Kingston and Smiths Falls are numerous camping spots. The rest of the way, there is not as much provision for camping but there is commercial accommodation. Camping on private land is possible but get the owner's permission first.

BELLEVILLE & AROUND

There's not much for the visitor in Belleville, a town with 35,000 residents – it's more a departure point for Quinte's Isle to the south. In July, the Waterfront & Folklorama Festival is three days of events, music and shows.

Some 29km east of town, in Deseronto, Native Renaissance II Gallery & Shop (☎ 613-396-3255) has a sizable collection of Native Indian arts and crafts and a section where new ones are created. It's open every day and can be found on Hwy 49.

At Shannonville, in the same direction but just 12km from Belleville, the Mosport Speedway is the site of motorcycle and drag racing periodically through summer.

Mapledale Cheese sells excellent ched-

dar. It's north of Belleville up Hwy 37, roughly 10km north of Hwy 401.

Hwy 37 continues north through old Tweed to Hwy 7, which is the main route to Toronto from Ottawa. It's a bit slow, with only two lanes, but the scenery is good. There are a couple of parks along the way and several places to eat.

QUINTE'S ISLE

Irregularly shaped Quinte's Isle provides a quiet and scenic retreat from the bustle of much of southern Ontario. The rolling farmland is reminiscent of Prince Edward Island, and in fact Quinte's Isle is also known as Prince Edward County. Many of the little towns were settled in the 18th and 19th centuries. The cemeteries adjacent to the village churches reveal clues to these earlier times.

The island has been somewhat rediscovered and is slowly being developed for visitors, but hasn't changed very much yet.

Things to See & Do

Traffic is light on most of the island's roads, which lead past large old farmhouses and cultivated fields. The St Lawrence River is never far away and many routes offer good views. Fishing is quite good in the Bay of Quinte and the locals use the waters for sailing. The island is popular with cyclists – it's generally flat and some of the smaller roads are well shaded.

The excellent strawberry picking in late June draws many outsiders.

There are three provincial parks, including North Beach and the fine Sandbanks. Sandbanks (☎ 613-393-3319), the only one offering camping, is one of the most popular parks in the province. Book ahead – reservations are definitely required especially for weekends, when a fair bit of partying goes on. The park is divided into two sections: the Outlet (with an excellent strip of sandy beach) and Sandbanks itself (containing most of the area's sand dunes, some over three storeys high). There's a large undeveloped section at the end of the beach – good for walking and for exploring the dunes and backwaters.

On the other side of the island, **Lake on the Mountain**, the third park, is really nothing more than a picnic site but is worth a visit to see the unusual lake. It sits on one side of the road at a level actually higher than that of the road, while just across the street is a terrific view over Lake Ontario and some islands hundreds of metres below. Geologists are still speculating as to the lake's origins. The local Mohawk Indians have their own legends about the lake, which appears to have no source.

Picton This small town is the only town of any size on the island and has one of the six district museums. The main street's Chamber of Commerce (☎ 613-476-2421) has detailed maps of the island and some information on current accommodation. Get the walking-tour guide of Picton which leads you past some of the fine historic buildings in town. Another guide lists various island attractions, including **Bird House City**, with dozens of painted birdhouses (including a fire station and courthouse).

Tyendinaga Indian Reserve This is just off Quinte's Isle and is also mainly farmland. In mid-May the original coming of the Mohawks is re-enacted in full tribal dress.

Places to Stay
The area is best known for its camping. There are several commercial campgrounds nearby which, if you can't get in at Sandbanks, aren't quite as busy. The large one opposite the Outlet is geared mainly for recreational vehicles. There's also quite a nice one, good for tenting as well, out at the tip of Salmon Arm; it offers minimal facilities but great sunsets.

There are numerous resorts, cottages, motels and B&Bs covering a range of prices. For a day or two you're best off at a B&B, but for longer stays check into one of the simpler cabins or cottages. Some of the less costly places are situated in the Cherry Valley area. For B&B information contact Belleville Tourism (☎ 613-966-1333).

Isiah Tubbs Resort (☎ 613-393-2090), the most expensive place on the island, is

costly even by Toronto standards but the luxury facilities and very fine design keep visitors coming back.

If all the accommodation options are booked out, try the motels around Belleville's perimeter – it's not far to return to the island the following day.

TRENTON
Small Trenton is known as the starting point of the Trent-Severn Waterway, which runs 386km through 44 locks to Georgian Bay in Lake Huron. Yachties and sailors of every description follow this old Native Indian route each summer. **Presqu'ile Provincial Park** (☎ 613-475-4324) is west of town and south of Brighton. A popular feature is the immense beach, but birdwatchers make up a sizable portion of the campers. The park has a large adjacent marsh, which is home to many species and represents a migration pit stop to many more in spring and autumn. Boardwalks allow access to portions of the wetlands. The camping is good, too, with large, treed sites. At Beach 3, you can rent boats, sailboarding equipment and bicycles.

The Loyalist Parkway road route leads down onto Quinte's Isle and heads east.

Trent-Severn Waterway
The Trent-Severn Waterway cuts diagonally across southern Ontario cottage country, following rivers and lakes for 386km from Trenton (on Lake Ontario) to Georgian Bay at the mouth of the Severn River (near Port Severn and Honey Harbour). It travels through or near many of the region's best known resort areas, including the **Kawartha Lakes,** and **Lake Simcoe**.

Used a century ago for commerce, the system is now strictly recreational and is operated by Parks Canada. The water flow is regulated by a series of 125 dams along the route. The canal is opened for use in mid-May and closes in mid-October. A cruise ship plies the route, taking seven days. Shorter, four-day trips are also available. These are not cheap, but ask in Peterborough for details.

Several companies along the route rent houseboats by the weekend, by the week

or for longer periods. The boats come more or less fully equipped, some even have barbecues, and can accommodate up to eight people (six adults), which makes for not only a good party but also a more reasonably priced one. The trips are good for families, too, with separate sleeping rooms for the kids.

Egan Houseboat Rentals (☎ 705-799-5745), located at Egan Marine, RR4 in the village of Omemee, west of Peterborough on Route 7, is well established. Being right by the Kawartha Lakes gives you the option of hanging around the lakes or going all the way to Lake Simcoe.

Rates vary quite a bit, depending on timing, but start at about $500 for a weekend. On average, you will use about $120 worth of gasoline in a week.

Lake Ontario Waterfront Trail

Years of work through the 1990s by provincial and local governments, community groups and conservation authorities resulted in the opening of the 325km Lake Ontario Waterfront Trail, which stretches from Trenton through Toronto to Hamilton on the far western edge of Lake Ontario.

Suitable for walking, cycling and even roller-blading, the trail links 160 natural areas, 126 parks and dozens of museums, galleries and historic sites. Hundreds of organised activities, from sidewalk sales to jazz festivals, take place along the trail during summer. The Waterfront Regeneration Trust (☎ 416-314-8572) in Toronto can provide maps and information on trail events, or ask at the Trenton tourist office.

KAWARTHA LAKES

Many of the pretty towns in the Kawartha Lakes vacation region have a good restaurant or two and, usually, a couple of antique dealers – **Bobcaygeon** and **Fenelon Falls** are two that are worth dropping into if you're up this way (the former also hosts a big fiddle contest each July).

Nearby **Balsam Lake** is popular for swimming and fishing. At **Burleigh Falls**, who could resist a place called the *Lovesick*

Café? It's a typical country shop with food, souvenirs, fishing tackle and the like.

The district has some interesting parks as well. **Petroglyphs Provincial Park** (☎ 705-877-2552) has probably the best collection of prehistoric rock carvings in the country. Rediscovered in 1954, there are reportedly 900 figures and shapes carved into the park's limestone ridges. The portions of the collection which are easy to view are much smaller than the figure 900 might suggest, and though interesting, it is not an overwhelming site. The most visible have been enclosed to protect the rock from acid rain, a serious problem over much of Ontario. The area and small lake within the park remain important spiritual sites for the local Native Indians.

Serpent Mounds Provincial Park (☎ 705-295-6879) is the site of an ancient Native Indian burial ground. The **Warsaw Caves Conservation Area** contains tunnels eroded into limestone and walking trails.

Peterborough

Peterborough is a middle-sized town more or less at the centre of the Kawartha Lakes region. The older downtown area has some fine buildings; it's all very green, although the city seems in some danger of becoming a Toronto suburb. Trent University is another feature of the town's character.

The Trent-Severn Waterway passes through the large hydraulic-lift lock, a major landmark in town. A visitors centre shows how the locks along the system operate, and there is a working model. You can go on a trip through the locks into the Otonabee River or, if you're hooked, on a three or five-day cruise through the locks and along part of the system.

Canoeing is a popular activity. Possibilities include easy trips on the canal or, in spring, tougher whitewater trips on rivers in the area. From Peterborough, you can get to Serpent Mounds Provincial Park. Ask at the tourist office. The Ministry of Natural Resources publishes a map called *North Kawartha Canoe Routes*, which shows some possible trips and their portage distances.

Around Peterborough

South-east of Peterborough is **Century Village**, a pioneer village with costumed workers, demonstrations, and 20 buildings dating from 1820 to 1899.

A few kilometres north is **Lakefield**, a small town with a co-educational school; formerly a boys-only school, Lakefield was the school to which Queen Elizabeth II sent Prince Andrew.

About 900 Ojibway people reside on 400-hectare **Curve Lake Indian Reserve**, which is roughly 34km north of Peterborough. The reserve's Whetung Ojibway Arts & Crafts Gallery (☎ 705-657-3661) can be visited.

The log building contains both new and old examples of Native Indian art and the museum section has traditional pieces and valuable works from such artists as Norval Morrisseau. Some articles, including handmade jackets and baskets, can be bought.

The reserve, established in 1825, is off Curve Lake Rd, which runs out of Hwy 507.

NORTH OF KAWARTHA LAKES

Continuing north you come to a less busy, less populated, hilly region known as the Haliburton Highlands.

Hwy 507, leading up from Bobcaygeon through Catchacoma and Gooderham (which has a small waterfall), is perhaps the narrowest, oldest-looking highway in the province. It often looks more like a country lane.

Bancroft

A district centre, Bancroft is well known for its minerals and for the big gem festival held each August. Examples of 80% of the minerals found in Canada can be dug up in this area.

Maynooth

This small logging community about 20 minutes drive south of Algonquin Park's east gate, has the *Arlington Backpackers Hostel* (☎ *613-338-2080*, ☎ *1-800-595-8064*) in the old village hotel. Shared or private rooms are available.

Combermere

On Hwy 62 north from Bancroft is the **Madonna House Pioneer Museum** (☎ 705-756-3713), 18km south of Combermere. Run by a lay religious group operating a co-operative farm, the museum has displays on the area's early settlers. An adjoining gift shop sells a range of items, with the profits going to charity.

Barry's Bay

The old lumber town is now a supply centre for the cottagers in the area around **Lake Kaminiskeg**. It's also pretty close to **Algonquin Park** and is on the main highway to Ottawa. Odd as it may seem, this is the hub for a sizable Polish population, attracted to the hilly, green topography, which is much like that along the Baltic Sea in northern Poland. The town of **Wilno** in this area was the first Polish settlement in Canada. Nearby Killaloe, towards Ottawa, is a small centre for craftspeople and artisans.

The entire region has cottages for rent and lakeside resorts, but advance reservations are a very good idea. **Pembroke**, east at the Quebec border, is the nearest town of any size.

Toronto

Toronto is the largest city in Canada and the fourth largest in North America (after LA, Mexico and New York). Indeed, the size of its population, government and budget is greater than that of some Canadian provinces!

The five cities surrounding and adjacent to the relatively small city of Toronto proper amalgamated in 1998. This new city, locally dubbed the Megacity, with a population of 2.4 million, is now officially Toronto.

The urban sprawl beyond the new city boundaries is known as the Greater Toronto Area (GTA). The city and area continue to grow, due mainly to their popularity with new immigrants who arrive steadily from literally ever corner of the globe.

Toronto is well entrenched as the nation's financial, communications and business capital as well as being a primary focus for

ONTARIO

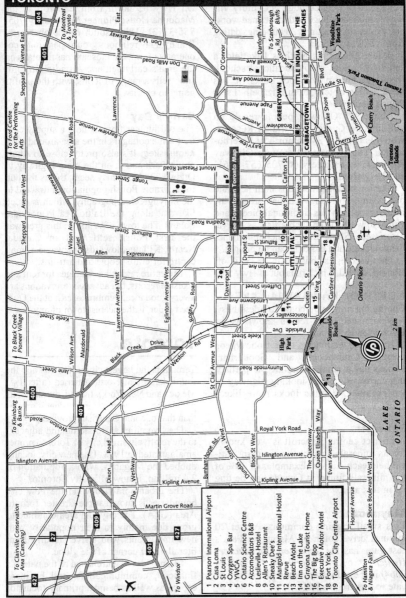

TORONTO

1 Pearson International Airport
2 Casa Loma
3 St Louis
4 Oxygen Spa Bar
5 YWCA
6 Ontario Science Centre
7 Accomodators B&B
8 Leslieville Hostel
9 Allen's Restaurant
10 Sneaky Dee's
11 Marigold International Hostel
12 Revue
13 Inn on the Lake
14 Beach Motel
15 Crayona Tourist Home
16 The Big Bop
17 Executive Motor Motel
18 Fort York
19 Toronto City Centre Airport

LAKE ONTARIO

0   1   2 km

English Canadian arts and culture. The recession of the early 1990s was (and continues to be) felt deeply but the city is not about to lose its prominence.

Two of the first things you'll notice about Toronto are the vibrancy and cleanliness of the downtown area (author Douglas Coupland describes Toronto as 'a city with the efficient, ordered feel of the Yellow Pages sprung to life in three dimensions, peppered with trees and veined with cold water').

These factors alone separate it from the bulk of large North American cities, but another great thing is that Toronto is safe. The streets are busy at night, with restaurants and entertainment places open and the downtown streetcars and subways generally used without hesitation. Of course, some prudence is always wise and women alone should take care after dark. There are some rougher parts of town, but these tend to be away from the centre and not where most visitors are likely to be.

There is a lot of central housing, part of an urban planning scheme which has kept a healthy balance between businesses and residences, making it a more livable city than many. Despite high costs, there are few areas of concentrated poverty. Toronto is one of the most expensive cities in North America in which to live, but fortunately this is not overly evident to visitors, for much of the cost is in real estate.

Throughout the city, various ethnic and immigrant groups have collected in fairly tight communities to form bustling, prosperous districts. These various neighbourhoods are one of the best and most distinctive aspects of the city and help to warm up the somewhat cold character of Toronto.

About 1970, the city scored points in its traditional rivalry with Montreal by surpassing it in size. Since this largely symbolic achievement, Toronto has grown in every way. It is the busiest Canadian port on the Great Lakes and is a major centre for banking, manufacturing and publishing. The Toronto Stock Exchange is one of North America's most important and the city is the provincial capital.

Tobacco lovers should know that Toronto has passed strict anti-smoking bylaws. Lighting up in virtually any indoor public place has been banned.

History

In the 17th century the Seneca Indians lived in the area. Étienne Brulé, on a trip with Samuel de Champlain in 1615, was the first European to see the site. The Native Indians did not particularly relish the visit, and it wasn't until around 1720 that the French established a fur-trading post and mission in what's now the west end of the city.

After years of hostility with the French, the British then took over. John Simcoe, lieutenant-governor of the new Upper Canada, chose Toronto as the capital in 1793 and it became known as York. Niagara-on-the-Lake had been the old capital.

During the War of 1812, the USA held York and burnt the Legislature. In retaliation, the British headed towards Washington and burnt the US political headquarters. Apparently the burn marks were painted over in white, leading to the name the 'White House'.

In 1814, when the war ended, York began to expand and stagecoach services began on Yonge St in 1828. In 1834, with William Lyon Mackenzie as the first mayor, York was renamed Toronto, a Native Indian name meaning 'meeting place'. During this time under conservative politicians, the city became known as 'Toronto the Good', a tag which only began to fade in the 1970s. Religious restraints and strong anti-vice laws (it was illegal to hire a horse on Sunday) were largely responsible for this. Not all that long ago, curtains were drawn in department-store windows on Sunday because window shopping was considered sinful, and movie theatres were also closed on the holy day.

Like many big cities, Toronto has had its great fire. In 1904 about five hectares of the inner city burned, levelling 122 buildings. Amazingly, no one was killed. The 1920s saw the first population boom, but in 1941 80% of the population was still Anglo-Celtic.

It was after WWII that the city began to change. Well over half-a-million immigrants have arrived since then, mainly Europeans. Italians make up the largest non-British ethnic group. The influx of new tongues, customs and food has livened up a place once thought to be a hopeless case.

Orientation

The land around Toronto is flat and the city tends to sprawl over a large area. Despite its size, the city's grid-style layout, with nearly all the streets running north-south and east-west, means it's easy to get oriented.

Yonge St (pronounced Young), the main north-south artery, is called the longest street in the world – it runs about 18km from Lake Ontario north to the city boundary, Steeles Ave, and beyond. The central downtown area is bounded by Front St to the south, Bloor St to the north, Spadina Ave to the west and Jarvis St to the east. Yonge St runs parallel to and in between Spadina Ave and Jarvis St, a few blocks from each of these. Street names change from 'East' to 'West' at Yonge St, and the street numbers begin there. Bloor St and College St (called Carlton St, east of Yonge St), which is about halfway between Bloor St and the lake, are the two main east-west streets.

At the foot of Yonge St and nearby York St is the lake and the redeveloped waterfront area called Harbourfront. The old docks have given way to restaurants, theatres, galleries, artists' workshops, stores, condominiums and some parkland all along Queen's Quay. The ferries for the Toronto Islands moor here, as do many private vessels.

A few blocks north is Front St, with Union Station (the VIA Rail terminal), the classic old Royal York Hotel, and the Hummingbird Centre, a theatre for the performing arts. Two blocks west of Union Station is the CN Tower and, next door, Skydome, the sports stadium. North of the Skydome, around Adelaide St W, Peter St and John St, is the Entertainment District.

Heading north from Union Station on Bay St to Queen St, you'll hit Nathan Phillips Square, site of rallies and concerts

and the unique City Hall buildings. To the east, the Victorian building dating from 1899 is the old City Hall, now used mainly for law courts. Check the gargoyles.

One block east is Yonge St, lined with stores, bars, restaurants and cinemas catering mainly to the young.

On Yonge St, between Dundas and Queen Sts, is the enormous modern shopping complex known as the Eaton Centre. The main tourist office is here, downstairs on level 1 by Eaton's department store. Farther east is an area known as Cabbagetown, a formerly run-down neighbourhood now renovated and trendy in sections but still retaining some of its earlier character. Go farther east, along Danforth Ave west of Pape Ave, to explore the restaurant-blessed Greek area of town.

On the west side of City Hall is Osgood Hall, home of the Law Society. Queen St W between University Ave and Spadina Ave and beyond to Bathurst St is busy with many restaurants and antique, book, record and distinctive clothing shops. A lot of young people involved in and on the fringes of the arts live in the area.

University Ave, lined with offices and trees, is Toronto's widest street and the location of most major parades. The lit beacon atop the stately Canada Life Building near the corner of University Ave and Queen St is a guide to the weather. The light at the top is colour-coded: green means clear, red means cloudy, flashing red means rain and flashing white means snow. If the tower lights are ascending, the temperature will rise; if they're descending it will cool. Temperatures are stable if the lights are on and static.

University Ave leads north to Queen's Park at College St and the provincial Parliament Buildings. To the west is the University of Toronto. North of the park the street is called Queen's Park Ave; it leads to Bloor St, where you'll find the city's principal museum, the Royal Ontario Museum.

North of Bloor St, Queen's Park Ave becomes Avenue Rd. Between here and Yonge St, fashionable, upmarket Yorkville was once at the vanguard of the 1960s folk music and drug scene.

West five blocks, Spadina Ave, once a strictly Jewish area, is the heart of Chinatown. Farther west, Dundas St W and College St are mainly Italian. Little Italy, west of Euclid along College St, has lots of outdoor cafés and is one of Toronto's most popular spots for eating and being seen. The more established Italian district, Corso Italia, runs along St Clair Ave W between Dufferin St and Lansdowne Ave.

Toronto is served by expressways on all four sides. Expect congestion. Along the lake, the Gardiner Expressway runs west into the Queen Elizabeth Way (QEW). The QEW goes to Niagara Falls. Just at the city's western border is Hwy 427, which runs north to the airport, and Hwy 401. Hwy 401 runs east-west above the downtown area, east to Montreal and west to Windsor, Ontario, which is opposite Detroit, USA. The often bumper to bumper segment of the 401 between Hwy 427 and Yonge St has been called the busiest stretch of road in North America after California's Santa Monica Freeway. On the eastern side of the city, the Don Valley Parkway connects Hwy 401 to the Gardiner Expressway at the southern edge of the city.

The city has been called Hollywood North and you may well come across one of a number of ongoing movie shoots around town.

Information
Tourist Offices The Toronto Visitor Information Centre (☎ 416-203-2500, ☎ 1-800-363-1990, www.tourism-toronto.com) has an office in the Queen's Quay terminal, down by the lake at Harbourfront between Yonge and York Sts. It's open all year from 9 am to 5 pm Monday to Friday. On weekends and holidays, someone will answer telephone questions. To get to the office, take the elevator (midway down the mall) up to the Galleria offices on level 5.

A second office, open daily from 8 am to 8 pm, is in the Convention Centre, 225 Front St W.

For information on other areas of Ontario as well as Toronto, the Ontario Travel Centre (☎ 416-314-0944, ☎ 1-800-668-2746 or ☎ 416-314-0956, ☎ 1-800-268-3736 for

French speakers) is located on level 1 (two below street level) of the Eaton Centre (which is at 220 Yonge St, on the corner of Dundas St). It's open the same hours as the shopping centre, from 10 am to 9 pm on weekdays, 9.30 am to 6 pm on Saturday and noon to 5 pm on Sunday.

Money Currencies International (☎ 416-977-1690), 2 Dundas St E at Yonge St, changes money and sells travellers cheques. Branches of the Bank of Montreal and the Canadian Bank of Commerce can be found on the corner of Yonge and Queen Sts.

Post & Communications Post restante mail can be picked up at General Delivery, 25 The Esplanade, Toronto M5W 1A0, Monday to Friday from 8 am to 5.45 pm (☎ 416-365-0656). There's a good post office at 31 Adelaide St E and numerous postal outlets in drugstores around town.

Travel Agencies For the purchase of tickets around the country and out of Canada, Travel CUTS (Canadian University Travel Services) is recommended. It has six offices in town, the main one (☎ 416-979-2406) being central at 187 College St. The staff will shop around for the best deal, and offer even better rates for young people (under age 26) and students. For the latter two groups, identification cards can be issued.

Alternatively, agencies such as the Last Minute Club (☎ 416-441-2582), which specialises in late sell-offs and the filling of flights and charters, may be worth a call. For flights to destinations such as Mexico or Florida, particularly during the Canadian winter, you could turn up a bargain.

Seeking out travel agencies in ethnic neighbourhoods can often turn up bargains back to the respective homelands.

The newspaper classifieds, especially the weekly *Now Magazine,* also list tickets for sale.

Bookshops & Maps The World's Biggest Bookstore at 20 Edward St, one block north of the Eaton Centre, is a browser's delight.

ONTARIO

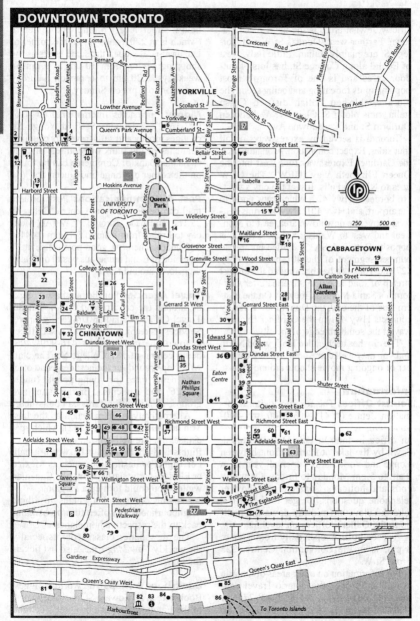

DOWNTOWN TORONTO

To Casa Loma

Brunswick Avenue
Spadina Road
Madison Avenue
Bernard Ave
Lowther Avenue
Bedford Rd
Avenue Road
Hazelton Ave

Crescent Road
Glen Road
Mount Pleasant Road
Rosedale Valley Rd
Elm Ave

YORKVILLE

Scollard St
Yorkville Ave
Cumberland St

Queen's Park Avenue

Bloor Street West
Charles Street

Bloor Street East

Isabella
Church Street
St

Dundonald St

Huron Street
St George Street

Hoskins Avenue

UNIVERSITY
OF TORONTO

Queen's Park Crescent

Harbord Street

Queen's Park

Wellesley Street

Maitland Street

CABBAGETOWN

Grosvenor Street
Grenville Street
Wood Street

Aberdeen Ave
Carlton Street

College Street

Allan
Gardens

Gerrard Street East

Huron Street
Beverley Street
McCaul Street
Bay Street
Yonge Street
Gerrard St West

Baldwin
St
Elm St

CHINATOWN

D'Arcy Street
Dundas Street West

Augusta Ave
Kensington Ave
Spadina Avenue

Edward St
Dundas Street West

University Avenue

**Eaton
Centre**

Bond St
Mutual Street
Sherbourne Street
Parliament Street

Shuter Street

Nathan
Phillips
Square

Victoria Street
Jarvis Street

Queen Street West

Queen Street East

Peter Street
John Street
Simcoe Street

Richmond Street West

Adelaide Street West

Richmond Street East
Adelaide Street East

Scott Street

Blue Jays Way
King Street West

King Street East

Clarence
Square

Wellington Street West

Wellington Street East

York Street
Bay Street

Front Street East
The Esplanade

Front Street West

P

Pedestrian
Walkway

Gardiner Expressway

Queen's Quay West

Queen's Quay East

Harbourfront

To Toronto Islands

0   250   500 m

DOWNTOWN TORONTO

ONTARIO

PLACES TO STAY					
1	Havinn	30	Swiss Chalet	40	Elgin & Wintergarden
3	Global Guesthouse	32	Swatow		Theatre Centre
6	Four Seasons	33	Pho Hung	41	Old City Hall
19	Aberdeen Guest House	42	Queen Mother	43	Bamboo Club
20	Days Inn	49	Alice Fazooli's	44	Horseshoe
26	Beverley Place	51	Zupa's Deli	45	Chicago's
28	Neill Wycik College Hotel	54	Peel Pub	46	Entertainment District
37	Bond Place	55	Old Ed's	47	Music Gallery
50	Canadiana International	61	Young Thailand	48	Montana's
	Guesthouse & Hostel	66	Wayne Gretzky's	53	Mountain Equipment
52	Global Village	73	Papillon		Co-op
	Backpackers	74	Spaghetti Factory	56	Royal Alexandra Theatre
57	Hilton			59	Post Office
58	Toronto Budget Hostel	**OTHER**		62	Montreal Bistro
60	HI Toronto Hostel	4	The Madison	63	St James Cathedral
64	Hotel Victoria	7	Metropolitan Toronto	65	Milano's
68	Strathcona		Reference Library	67	Second City
69	Royal York	9	Royal Ontario Museum	70	Hockey Hall of Fame
85	Westin Harbour Castle	10	Bata Shoe Museum	71	St Lawrence Market
		11	Brunswick Tavern	72	C'est What?
		12	TRANZAC	75	Hummingbird Centre
PLACES TO EAT		14	Parliament Buildings	76	General Delivery PO
2	By the Way	17	Woody's	77	Union Station
5	Master's Buffeteria	21	Free Times Café	78	Air Canada Centre
8	Green mango	23	Kensington Market	79	CN Tower
13	Kensington Kitchen	24	Grossman's	80	Skydome
15	The Mango	29	Sam the Record Man	81	Walter Carsen Centre
16	Papaya Hut	31	Bus Station	82	Pier Waterfront Museum
18	Bigliardi's	34	Art Gallery of Ontario	83	Queen's Quay Terminal,
22	Peter's Chung King	35	Museum for Textiles		Tourist Office & Premiere
25	Margarita's	36	Tourist Office		Dance Theatre
27	Ryerson Polytechnic	38	Pantages Theatre	84	York Quay Centre
	University Cafeteria	39	Massey Hall	86	Island Ferry Terminal

For travel books, guides, maps and a range of books on nature, camping and outdoor activities, see Open Air (☎ 416-363-0719), 25 Toronto St, near the corner of Adelaide St E and Yonge St; the door is downstairs off Toronto St.

Also for maps, check the basement of the Trailhead camping store (☎ 416-862-0881), 71 Front St E.

The Great Canadian News Co in BCE Place on the corner of Yonge and Front Sts has newspapers from around the world and a vast periodical selection. Librarie Champlain at 468 Queen St E is a good French bookstore.

Library The Metropolitan Toronto Reference Library (☎ 416-393-7000) is at 789 Yonge St, about a block north of Bloor St on the east side.

Medical Services Toronto Hospital (☎ 416-340-4611), is central at 200 Elizabeth St near University Ave.

Dangers & Annoyances The number of homeless people, beggars and car-window washers (known as squeegee kids) is appalling and comes as a shock to many visitors. These people are almost always harmless but are unsettling by their evidence of deep social problems.

The Jarvis and Sherbourne Sts area east of Yonge St are well known prostitution strolls. Women walking alone at night are likely to be hassled by curb-crawlers. The southern

section of Jarvis St, between Carlton and Queen Sts, and the streets nearby, should be avoided by everyone late at night.

CN Tower

The highest free-standing structure in the world, the CN Tower (☎ 416-360-8500) has become a symbol and landmark of Toronto. The tower is in the southern end of the city, near the lake, south of Front St W at John St. The top antenna was put in place by helicopter, making the tower 533m high. Its primary function is radio and TV communications but up at the top there is a restaurant, a bar and two observation decks. The one outside is windy, naturally, and not for those easily subject to vertigo.

On a good, clear day you can see for about 160km. On a hazy day, however, you won't be able to see a thing. At night it provides a spectacular view of the city lights. It's also worth bearing in mind that during the height of summer you may have to queue for up to two hours – going up and down.

A glass elevator whisks you up the outside of the tower. And for extra thrills there is a glass floor section on the main observation deck – stand on it and sweat!

The cost of a trip up plus entry to the main observation deck is $15 for adults (a further $4 to get to the top deck). A better deal is lunch or dinner at the 360 Revolving Restaurant (☎ 416-362-5411), because the elevator ticket price is waived. Lunch prices start at $17, dinner prices at around $25 but there is no lunch in winter. Sunday brunch is also offered. If you just want a drink in the bar (minimum $5) the elevator must be paid for.

The tower is open daily until 10 pm, an hour later on Saturday. The time and weather display at ground level is worth a look.

At the base of the tower are separate attractions directed toward the young. They include sophisticated simulator rides and a video arcade featuring the latest computer-generated games.

Other Views

For a pleasant and free view of the city, head to the rooftop bar of the Park Hyatt.

It's on the corner of Bloor St W and Avenue Road. You can sit under the sun and sip a cool one 18 floors above the masses. It's open from 2.30 pm until 1 am and there is an inside section, too.

Panorama, on the 51st floor of the Manulife Centre at 55 Bloor St W (on the corner of Bay St), is popular with a generally younger but mixed crowd. A beer costs around $4 up here. The lounge is open Monday to Saturday from noon to 2 am.

The upmarket Canoe Bar & Restaurant, 54 floors up atop the Toronto Dominion Bank Tower at 66 Wellington St W (corner of Bay St), offers fine views from Monday to Friday.

Skydome

Beside the CN Tower at 1 Blue Jays Way this dome-roofed sports stadium (☎ 416-341-3663) opened in 1989 and is best known for its fully retractable roof, the world's first such facility. The stadium, often referred to as simply the 'Dome', is used primarily for professional baseball and football but also stages concerts, trade shows and various other presentations.

Although far from eye-pleasing from the outside, the interior is strikingly impressive. It can be seen on the one hour tours which are offered every day between 11 am and 3 pm, events permitting. They're not cheap at $10. It's a bit rushed but quite thorough, offering a look at one of the box suites, the view from the stands and press section, a locker room (without athletes), a walk on the field and all sorts of informative statistics and titbits of information. Did you know that eight 747s would fit on the playing field and that the stadium uses enough electricity to light the province of Prince Edward Island?

Another way to see the place (and a game) is via one of the three restaurants at the stadium (see the Places to Eat section). For those with money (lots of it), rooms can be rented in the adjacent Skydome Hotel, with rooms overlooking the playing field.

A cheap seat to a Blue Jays baseball game is easily the least expensive way to

Hotel Hijinks

The hotel that's part of the Skydome became instantly notorious when, during one of the first Blue Jays baseball games, a couple in one of the upperfield side rooms – either forgetfully or rakishly – became involved in some sporting activity of their own with the lights on, much to the crowd's amusement. Such a performance was later repeated at another game. Since then, the hotel has insisted on signed waivers stipulating that there will be no such free double plays.

see the Skydome. (See Spectator Sports later in this chapter.)

Harbourfront

Harbourfront is a strip of lakefront land running from the foot of Bay St westward to roughly Bathurst St.

Once a run-down district of old warehouses, factories and under used docklands, the area was originally slated for redevelopment, primarily as parkland but with people and arts-oriented halls, theatres, galleries and workshops etc included.

Although this has happened to some degree, it is now generally acknowledged that construction was allowed to run amok and too much of the waterfront has been blighted by ugly condos.

For visitors, the centre of activity is the attractive York Quay at 235 Queen's Quay, where there's a tourist information office. Nearby is the du Maurier Theatre and Molson Place, a covered outdoor concert venue. There's a performance of some sort happening nearly every night and some presentations are free. For information on Harbourfront events call ☎ 416-973-3000. There are also a couple of nearby restaurants and a place or two for a drink. Boat tours depart from the shore here and many private boaters moor around the area.

Just to the east is the impressive looking Queen's Quay terminal, with the green glass

top. It's a refurbished 1927 warehouse containing some interesting speciality and gift shops, restaurants, the Premier Dance Theatre and, up above, offices and apartments.

Contemporary art is displayed in the Power Plant, an old power station near Queen's Quay.

On weekends the area is popular for a walk along the pier or a browse in the antique and junk market. Try the french fries from one of the many chip wagons. The Canoe School rents canoes, which can be used for an enjoyable paddle out around the harbour.

To visit Harbourfront, first get to Union Station, the train station on Front St, a few blocks north of the lake. The subway will take you this far south. From here, either walk south on York St or take the LRT streetcar which goes south, running along the Harbourfront area on Queen's Quay to Spadina Ave and then returning the same way. Service is continuous through the day and evening. Parking in the area can be a headache and/or costly, so seriously consider public transport.

Pier Waterfront Museum

This new museum (☎ 416-392-1765) at 245 Queen's Quay W at the waterfront, details shipping, boats, the harbour area and all things nautical through the city's history.

The two-storey exhibit has models, old ship relics and related articles. Admission is $8.50 and it's open daily but check hours in winter.

Toronto Islands

From the foot of Bay St near the Westin Harbour Castle hotel, you can take a 10 minute ferry ride out to the Toronto Islands. The three main ones are Ward, Centre and Hanlan's Point. Once mainly residential, the islands are largely public park and are very pleasant – particularly since there are no cars!

Centre Island has the most facilities, many summer events and the most people. Boats can be rented, and there is a small animal farm and an amusement area for kids. Beaches line the southern and western shores, and there are two licensed restaurants and some snack bars.

Hanlan's, to the west, is the best beach. You may see some nude sunbathing at Hanlan's south-western end – it's popular with gay men – but this is illegal, even though the law is only sporadically enforced. Inland from the beach are picnic tables and some barbecue pits. Towards the city, on Hanlan's Point, is a small airport.

Ward Island, the one on the east side, has quite a few houses inhabited all year. There is a small restaurant here for snacks and light lunches out on the lawn.

A ferry ride is as good as a harbour tour and offers good views of the city. Ferries (☎ 416-392-8193) to the islands run frequently in summer and cost $4 return, less for children and seniors. You can walk around the islands in under two hours. The cool breezes are great on a hot, sticky day, and it's pretty quiet during the week. Cycling along the islands' boardwalk on the southern shores isn't a bad way to spend some time. You can take bicycles on some of the ferries or rent them on Centre Island.

Because there is a year-round community living on Ward Island, the ferries run through the winter (though less frequently) and between September and May service only Ward. The other islands can be reached on foot, but note that pretty much everything else on the islands is shut tight. Good thing, too, because the winter wind over here is none too hospitable.

Ontario Place

This 40-hectare recreation complex (☎ 416-314-9900) is built on three artificial islands offshore from the Canadian National Exhibition (CNE) grounds, 955 Lake Shore Blvd W. The lake-edge setting, spacious design, numerous patios and outdoor activities can make a pleasant summer escape from the hot, crowded downtown streets but the privilege costs you $10. A large, popular children's play area where you can just let them go nuts is included. Other activities and attractions such as a water park with slides and a wading pool must be paid for separately or a $20 day pass is offered.

The futuristic buildings and parkland contain restaurants, beer gardens, the Molson Amphitheatre for concerts and an IMAX cinema (the Cinesphere), where 70mm films are shown on a six-storey-high curved screen. The IMAX prices are $7 to $9.

In summer there are nightly concerts at the amphitheatre, with everything from ballet to rock at usual performance prices (a ticket permits site entry for the whole day). At the western end is another stage with a waterfall as a curtain, where amateurs or lesser names perform free shows. Nearby is the 700m-long flume water slide with simulated rapids and tunnels.

The park is open from mid-May to October from 10.30 am to 1 am (until midnight on Sunday).

If you are driving, parking is a whopping $9. Take a subway or streetcar to Bathurst St and then the streetcar south down Bathurst St to the CNE exhibition grounds. Over summer months a shuttle bus runs from Union Station to the gate of Ontario Place and back frequently through the day. Take a sweater – even on a hot day it gets cold at night down by the water.

Also note that on rainy days many of the activities, restaurants etc may not operate.

Moored *outside* the eastern end of Ontario Place is the *Haida*, a destroyer, which is open to visitors.

Royal Ontario Museum (ROM)

The multidiscipline museum (☎ 416-586-5551) on the corner of Queen's Park Ave and Bloor St W is Canada's largest and has exhibits covering the natural sciences, the animal world, art and archaeology and, broadly, the history of humankind. The museum covers five floors, so a visit takes some time.

The collection of Chinese crafts, textiles and assorted arts is considered one of the best anywhere. The Egyptian, Greek, Roman and Etruscan civilisations are also represented. The dinosaur and mammalogy rooms are fascinating, with the latter containing a replica of part of an immense bat cave found in Jamaica. Another section outlines the history of trade between the east

and west, from the ancient caravan routes through to more modern times. The bird gallery, with a huge stuffed albatross and numerous display cabinets with pull-out drawers to explore, is very good.

The SR Perron Gem & Gold Room (actually four octagonal rooms), displays a dazzling collection of riches, including the 193-carat Star of Lanka Sapphire, a 776-carat behemoth opal from Australia and handfuls of rubies, diamonds and gold nuggets. They are made all the more appealing by the unique fibre-optic lighting system. In addition to these permanent exhibits there are often in-depth touring exhibits – these are generally excellent but a surcharge is added to the admission fee.

The museum, with restaurant, is open Monday to Saturday from 10 am to 6 pm, until 8 pm on Tuesday, and on Sunday from 11 am to 6 pm. Admission is $10 for adults, $5 for seniors and students, and free on Tuesday from 4.30 pm until closing time. Family rates are also offered. The subway is close by (Museum stop), but if you're driving there is parking on Bedford Rd, west of Avenue Rd north of Bloor St.

A ticket to the ROM also permits free entry to the Gardiner Museum.

George R Gardiner Museum of Ceramic Art

At 111 Queen's Park Ave, this museum (☎ 416-586-8080) is part of the ROM just across the street. The collection is divided into four periods of ceramic history: pre-Columbian, Italian majolica from the 15th and 16th centuries, English delftware of the 17th century and English porcelain of the 18th century. The pottery from Mexico and Peru done before the arrival of the Europeans is wonderful. It's quite an extensive collection spread over two floors. Admission costs $5 and opening hours are from 10 am to 5 pm Tuesday to Saturday and 11 am to 5 pm Sunday. Tuesday is free.

Art Gallery of Ontario (AGO)

This is one of the top three art galleries in the country (☎ 416-977-0414), the others being in Ottawa and Montreal. Though not the Louvre, it is excellent, and unless you have a lot of stamina, you'll need more than one trip to see it all. The gallery at 317 Dundas St W, two blocks west of University Ave, houses works (mainly paintings) from the 14th century to the present. There is also a Canadian section and rooms for changing exhibitions, which can sometimes be the highlight of a visit. The AGO is best known for its vast Henry Moore sculpture collection – one room holds about 20 of his major sculptures of the human form.

There is a cafeteria or pricey restaurant if you need a break and an excellent shop selling books, posters, crafts and jewellery. At the door, pick up a schedule of the gallery films, lectures, performances and concerts.

From May to October the gallery is open from noon to 9 pm Tuesday to Friday and from 10 am to 5.30 pm Saturday, Sunday and holidays. The rest of the year, it is also closed on Tuesday. It's open on holiday Mondays throughout the year.

Admission is pay what you can ($5 suggested, students and seniors $4). The excellent special shows, which run very regularly, are $10 and include the regular gallery.

Cinémathèque Ontario (☎ 416-923-3456) regularly screens top-quality cinema from around the world in Jackman Hall.

The Grange The Grange (☎ 416-977-0414) is a restored Georgian house adjoining the AGO. Admission is included with the gallery ticket. Authentic 19th century furniture and workers in period dress represent life in a 'gentleman's residence' of the time. Hours are noon to 4 pm Tuesday to Sunday and until 9 pm on Wednesday. The Grange looks onto a pleasant city park where Chinese people do their early morning Tai Chi.

Bata Shoe Museum

Designed to resemble a large and very stylish lidded shoebox, the Bata Shoe Museum (☎ 416-979-7799) has more to offer than you might imagine. Beginning with a set of footprints almost four million years old, and incorporating some neat interactive

displays, the general All About Shoes exhibit provides a fascinating look at human history and culture. From the gruesome to the gorgeous, every type of footwear imaginable is there. Upstairs there's a detailed look at 19th century women's shoes and an excellent exhibit devoted to the central role of bootmaking in Inuit culture.

The museum at 327 Bloor St W, opposite the St George subway, is open from 10 am to 5 pm Tuesday to Saturday (until 8 pm Thursday) and from noon to 5 pm Sunday. Admission is $6 and it's free on the first Tuesday of every month.

Museum for Textiles

Obscurely situated with no walk-in traffic at all, this excellent museum (☎ 416-599-5321) is highly recommended for anyone with the slightest interest in textiles. It's the only museum in the country to exclusively collect and display handmade textiles and tapestries from around the world. There are pieces from Latin America, Africa, Europe, South-East Asia and India.

The Tibetan collection is particularly fine, as is the one from Indonesia. In addition, there are changing shows of contemporary textiles.

The museum can be found (look hard, the door is tucked back from the street) at 55 Centre Ave (running south off Dundas St W in Chinatown between Bay St and University Ave), behind the Toronto City Hall. It's open Tuesday to Friday from 11 am to 5 pm, and from noon to 5 pm on weekends. Admission is $5.

Casa Loma

This is a 98-room medieval-style castle-cum-mansion built between 1911 and 1914 by Sir Henry Pellat, a very wealthy and evidently eccentric man. The mansion (☎ 416-923-1171) has been a tourist site since 1937, when the cost of upkeep became too much for its owner. The interior is sumptuous, built with the finest materials imported from around the world. Note especially the conservatory. Pellat even brought in stonemasons from Scotland to build the walls around the estate.

In summer, the 2.5 hectares of restored

gardens behind the castle are worth a visit in themselves. This area is open to the public (without the need to buy a ticket to the castle) on the first Monday of each month and every Tuesday from 4 pm to dusk.

At Christmas time, elaborate thematic indoor exhibits are put on, geared mainly to children.

Casa Loma is open every day from 10 am to 4 pm. A ticket costs $9 and parking at the site is $2.50 an hour. If you're lucky, you may find a spot in the surrounding neighbourhood; alternatively, consider using the subway; the Dupont subway station is within walking distance. The address is 1 Austin Terrace, off Spadina Ave. From the corner of Dupont and Bathurst Sts, it can be clearly seen, perched impressively above its surroundings.

Ontario Science Centre

The science centre (☎ 416-696-3127) has an interesting assortment of scientific and technological exhibits and demonstrations, most of which you can touch. You might even learn something, although it's best for children (but be warned, on weekends there are hundreds of them).

The approachable yet detail-conscious Living Earth exhibit includes a simulated rainforest, a limestone cave and an ocean ecosystem designed to encourage respect, knowledge and awe for the real thing.

The Information Highway allows you to explore the Internet and take a look at virtual reality. There is also a large-format OMNIMAX cinema.

To get to the science centre, which is located in a small ravine on the corner of Eglinton Ave E and Don Mills Rd, take the subway to Eglinton, transfer to the Eglinton E bus and get off at Don Mills Rd. The centre is open from 10 am to 6 pm daily. Admission is $10 for adults, $7 for children aged five to 10, and parking is $5. Family, youth and senior rates are available. Ticket packages which include films are available too.

Hockey Hall of Fame

Housed in the beautiful old Bank of Montreal building (from 1885) at the north-west

corner of Front and Yonge Sts, the Hockey Hall of Fame (☎ 416-360-7765) gives young and old fans all they could ask for, and more. And for visitors unfamiliar with the game, enough background and history is presented to perhaps help explain Canadians' passion for this, the fastest of sports. Included is hockey's biggest prize – the Stanley Cup (or a replica), a re-creation of the Montreal Canadiens' dressing room and all manner of interactive exhibits and activities. Admission is $10 for adults, less for seniors and kids. It's open every day, with extended evening hours on Friday in summer.

Children's Own Museum

The brand new kids museum (☎ 416-542-1492) at 90 Queen's Park beside the ROM, is geared to active, fun learning for two to eight year olds. The space is divided into various participatory areas such as the garden and construction site each with suitable play materials. Admission is $3.75 per person. It's open from 10 am to 5 pm (from noon to 5 pm Sunday) and closed Monday.

Police Museum

The police museum (☎ 416-808-7020), housed in the impressive headquarters building at 40 College St, displays a small collection of equipment, uniforms etc from 1834 to the present. The confiscated weapons display certainly gives pause. There are some interactive displays, details of some noteworthy cases, a police car and motorbike and an old jail cell. It's open daily and is free.

Redpath Sugar Museum

Along the waterfront at 95 Queen's Quay W a free museum (☎ 416-366-3561) is part of the large sugar mill. There is a film on the production of the sweet stuff, as well as exhibits of equipment. The museum is open Monday to Friday from 10 am to noon and 1 to 3.30 pm.

Toronto Dominion Gallery of Inuit Art

Housed on the mezzanine floor of the AETNA Tower of the Toronto Dominion Centre, on Wellington St between Bay and York Sts, this gallery (☎ 416-982-8473) displays a top-rate collection of far-northern art dating mainly from WWII to the present. It consists primarily of sculpture in stone and bone, which is the foremost form of Inuit art.

The gallery is free and is open daily. Hours are 8 am to 6 pm Monday to Friday, 10 am to 4 pm on weekends. Occasionally, you may find a rope across the door of the gallery. Just take it down and go in; the gallery is still open though there may well be no attendant. Free tours are given once a day on Tuesday and Thursday but can be arranged for any day – call and ask.

Stock Market Place

The city's stock exchange (☎ 416-947-4676) is Canada's largest and one of the most modern anywhere. Stock worth $100 million is bought and sold each day, so it's a fairly hectic place and one of the top 10 stock exchanges of the world – the only other North American exchange on the list being New York.

There is no longer a trading floor as it's all been computerised but the visitors centre has interactive displays which help demystify and explain the process of stock transactions. It's open on weekdays from 9 am to 4 pm. The stock exchange is at 130 King St W, on the north-east corner of King and York Sts, right in the centre of the city's financial district.

Chess Games Corner

Right in the heart of the city, on the corner of Yonge and Gould Sts, is the unofficial chess centre. Here through all kinds of weather, night and day, chess players and aficionados of every description gather to duel and bet. It all began with the late 'open highway' Joe Smolij in 1977, who can be found in the Guinness Book of Records as the world's fastest chess player.

Provincial Parliament Buildings

The attractive pinkish sandstone Legislature (☎ 416-325-7500) sits in Queen's Park, just north of College St on University Ave.

ONTARIO

The stately building was completed in 1892 and is kept in superb condition. Free tours are given frequently throughout the day, Monday to Friday until 4 pm; call for a schedule. For some home-grown entertainment, head for the visitors gallery when parliament is in session (roughly from October to December and February to June).

City Hall

In Nathan Phillips Square, on the corner of Queen and Bay Sts, this distinctive three-part building (☎ 416-392-7341) represented the beginning of Toronto becoming a grown-up city. It was completed in 1965 to Finnish architect Viljo Revell's award-winning design. The twin clamshell towers, with a flying saucer-style structure between them at the bottom, are unmistakable. Free tours are given frequently, Monday to Friday. The square out the front is a meeting place and the location for concerts, demonstrations and office-worker lunches.

In winter the attractive fountain pool becomes a popular artificial skating rink. Rental skates are available until 10 pm daily. It's a lot of fun; don't feel intimidated if you are a novice – you won't be alone. Immigrants from around the world are out there gingerly making strides towards assimilation.

Historic Sites

There isn't a lot for history buffs, as the city is so new, but the few small sites are well presented and the tourist office offers a printed guide to them. Many of these remaining old buildings stand where the old town of York was situated – in the southern portion of the city. Descriptions of some of the best sites follow. See also The Grange under the Art Gallery of Ontario earlier in this chapter.

Black Creek Pioneer Village A replica of an Ontario village a century ago, Black Creek Pioneer Village (☎ 416-736-1733) is the city's top historic attraction. It's about a half-hour drive from the downtown area, on the corner of Steeles Ave and Jane St in the north-west section of town, and is accessible by public transport.

Restored buildings and workers wearing authentic dress give a feeling of what rural life was like in the 19th century. Crafts and skills of the times are demonstrated, using the old tools and methods. One reader raved about the herb garden. You can buy the results of the cooking and baking. In one of the barns is a large toy museum and a wood-carving collection. It's open daily from May to December. Adult admission is $9. Special events are offered regularly through the season. There is parking, which is free – a rarity in Toronto, as you know by now.

Fort York The fort (☎ 416-392-6907) was established by the British in 1793 to protect the town, which was then called York. It was largely destroyed at the end of the 1812 War but was quickly rebuilt. Now restored, it has eight original log, stone and brick buildings. In summer, men decked out in 19th century British military uniforms carry out marches and drills, and fire musket volleys. The fort is open every day, from 9.30 am to 5 pm in summer and noon to 4 pm in winter. Admission is $5 for adults, less for kids and seniors. Free tours are given on the hour. It's on Garrison Rd, which runs off Fleet St W (which in turn is near the corner of Bathurst and Front Sts). Take the streetcar south on Bathurst St.

Mackenzie House Owned by William Lyon Mackenzie, the city's first mayor and the leader of a failed rebellion against the government, this mid-Victorian home (☎ 416-392-6915) is furnished with 19th century antiques. In the basement is an old print shop where (it's said) the machines can be heard mysteriously working some nights. The house is at 82 Bond St, a couple of blocks east of Yonge St, near Dundas St E. It's open daily, afternoons only, and admission is $3.50.

Spadina House This was the gracious mansion (☎ 416-392-6910) of local businessman James Austin. Built in 1866, the impressive interior contains fine furnishings and art collected over three generations. About 10 of its 35 rooms are open to the public. The family

gave the house to the historical board in 1982. The address is 285 Spadina Ave, just east of Casa Loma, and it's open daily, afternoons only. Admission is $5.

Campbell House Downtown on the corner of Queen St and University Ave, this house (☎ 416-597-0227) was once the residence of the chief justice of Upper Canada. It is a colonial-style brick mansion furnished in early 19th century fashion. The house is open daily (afternoons only on weekends) and admission is $3.50.

Colborne Lodge Situated in High Park, the lodge (☎ 416-392-6916) is a Regency-style cottage built in 1836. It contains many original furnishings, including possibly the first indoor flush toilet in the province. Informative tours are offered by the costumed staff and may include baking or craft demonstrations. In summer it's open Monday to Saturday from 9.30 am to 5 pm, and on Sunday from noon to 5 pm. Admission is $3.50.

Gibson House This Georgian-style house (☎ 416-395-7432) which belonged to a successful surveyor and politician offers a glimpse of daily life in the 1850s. Costumed workers demonstrate crafts and cooking and offer a tour around the house daily except Monday. Special activities are planned regularly through the year. On weekends it's only open in the afternoons. It's not far from the Sheppard subway stop in the far northern part of the city, at 5172 Yonge St north of Sheppard Ave. Admission is $3.

Churches The Anglican **Church of the Holy Trinity** (☎ 416-598-4521), hidden right downtown in behind the Eaton Centre on Trinity Square, is one of a kind. It's a funky, welcoming cross between a house of worship and a drop-in centre – everything a community oriented inner-city church should be. Opened in 1847, it was the first church in the city not to charge parishioners for pews. And it's been going its own way ever since. Don't miss the wonderful Christmas pageant tradition if you're in town in December. There is

no charge (a donation is suggested) but tickets are required – call for information.

On the corner of King and Church Sts, the town's first church was built in 1807. **St James' Cathedral**, built in 1853, now stands here, and is the country's tallest church. Nearby, on the corner of Queen and Parliament Sts, the first Catholic church was constructed in 1822. On this site, a second **St Paul's Anglican Church** now stands, one of Toronto's most impressive Renaissance-style buildings.

Montgomery's Inn Built in 1832 by an Irish military captain of the same name, Montgomery's Inn (☎ 416-394-8113) is a fine example of Loyalist architecture and has been restored to the period from 1830 to 1855. Afternoon tea is served, and costumed staff answer questions, bake bread and demonstrate crafts. Open daily, afternoons only, it's at 4709 Dundas St W, near Islington Ave, in the city's far western end. Admission is $3.

Enoch Turner Schoolhouse The school (☎ 416-863-0010) dates from 1848. It's a restored and simple one-room schoolhouse where kids are shown what the good old days were like. It was opened as the first free school so that the children of poorer citizens could learn the three Rs. You can visit it, free, when classes or other special events are not being held – call ahead and check the schedule. The address is 106 Trinity St, near the corner of King and Parliament Sts.

First Post Office Museum Toronto's first post office, dating from the 1830s, is at 260 Adelaide St E (☎ 416-865-1833). One of only two original city buildings remaining in its original location (the other is the Bank of Upper Canada), it has been designated a National Historic Site. Letters can still be sealed with wax by costumed employees and sent from here. It's open seven days a week.

University of Toronto The principal campus of the large, prestigious university is just west of the Queen's Park Parliament

Buildings, off College St at University Ave. The attractive grounds feature a range of architectural styles, from the University College building of 1859 to the present. Free walking tours of the campus are given on weekdays through summer months, departing from Hart House three times daily (weather permitting).

Other Historic Sites Todmorden Mills Historic Site, near the location of an important 1794 sawmill and gristmill on the Don River, preserves two houses, complete with period furnishings, and a brewery dating from around 1825. Also on the site is a train station (now a small railway museum) and a former paper mill (now used as a playhouse). The park is at 67 Pottery Rd and is open daily (except Monday) from May to December. A small admission fee is charged.

The large, red-brick houses found all over downtown Toronto were built around the 1920s. The taller, narrower ones, often with more ornately decorative features, are Victorian and mostly date from 1890 to 1900 – a few are older.

Markets

The city's prime one, **Kensington Market** is a colourful and lively multicultural, old-style market squeezed along Baldwin St and Augusta Ave off Spadina Ave, just south of College St and east of Bathurst St. It's open daily but is busiest on Saturday morning. The cheese shops are good, and there's all manner of fresh fruit and vegetables. You can bargain over prices. This was the heart of the city's Jewish area, but as you'll see, people from many countries have changed that. There are some excellent restaurants in the area, too. On Saturday, don't even think of driving down here.

The **St Lawrence Market** is at 92 Front St E (at Jarvis St) in what was Toronto's first City Hall, dating from 1844. Here nearly all the shoppers are of British ancestry and the atmosphere is closer to sedate – there may even be classical musicians playing. Although it's best on Saturday, with the farmer's stands, it's open every day but

Monday. The range and quality of produce – from fish to more rice varieties than you knew existed – is superb. On Sunday there is an antique and flea market here.

Just north of the old City Hall building is **St Lawrence Hall**. This public meeting hall from the 19th century, topped with a clock tower, is considered one of the city's finest old buildings.

The **Market Gallery** on the 2nd floor of the market building is the city's exhibition hall and displays good, rotating shows (paintings, photographs, documents, artefacts) on Toronto's history. It's free, but is closed on Monday, Tuesday and holidays.

The Harbourfront **Antique Market** at 390 Queen's Quay W features 100 booths selling collectibles. It's open Tuesday to Sunday with an additional outdoor section on Sunday.

Two major health-food stores are the Big Carrot Natural Food Market, 348 Danforth Ave, and the more central Baldwin Natural Foods, at 20½ Baldwin St.

City Neighbourhoods

Toronto has a wide variety of ethnic groups, some concentrated in neighbourhoods which offer outsiders glimpses of foreign cultures. Such areas are good for restaurants and several are mentioned in the Places to Eat section. Other neighbourhoods are mixed areas that preserve a distinctive character. Descriptions of a few of the most prominent districts follow.

Chinatown Toronto has a huge (and growing) Chinese population and the principal Chinatown area is right in the centre of town. The original old area runs along Dundas St W from Bay St, by the bus station, west to University Ave. There are many restaurants here, but this area is rather touristy and isn't really where the local Chinese shop.

The bigger and more interesting segment of Chinatown is farther west. Also on Dundas St W, it runs from Beverley St, near the Art Gallery, to Spadina Ave and a little beyond. Most of Spadina Ave, from south of Dundas St all the way north to College St

and then east and west for a bit along College St, is primarily Chinese.

Again there are lots of restaurants, but also variety and grocery stores, jobbers, herbalists, bakeries and places selling things recognizable only to the initiated. In addition to all the businesses, vendors often set up along the sidewalks. The area gets packed on weekends, when it's sharp with sounds and smells and the restaurants do good business. There are a few Japanese and more and more Vietnamese places in the neighbourhood.

There's a smaller, but equally busy, pocket of Chinese merchants and restaurants around Gerrard St and Broadview Ave in the city's east end.

Yorkville Once Toronto's small version of Greenwich Village or Haight-Ashbury, this old counter-cultural bastion is now the city's expensive boutique and gallery area. The district is central, just above Bloor St between Yonge St and Avenue Rd. It's centred around Cumberland St, Yorkville Ave and Hazelton Ave. Along the narrow, busy streets are many art galleries, cafés, restaurants, nightspots and glamorous shops. The boutiques of the enclosed Hazelton Lanes Shopping Centre are some of the most exclusive in the country.

The whole swish area can be pleasant in summer for its outdoor cafés and people-watching. It's worth a stroll but the pretension and snobbery can grate.

Still, there are some intriguing shops and the galleries present a range of work, several displaying or selling Inuit pieces (for big dollars).

Rosedale One of the city's wealthiest areas is just north-east of the corner of Yonge and Bloor Sts. Driving or walking up Sherbourne St, north of Bloor St, leads to Elm Ave where nearly every house on the north side is listed by the Historical Board as being of architectural or historical note. All the streets branching from Elm Ave contain some impressive domains, however. East along Elm Ave, Craigleigh Gardens is a small and elegant old park.

The Village Toronto's gaytown, known affectionately as the Ghetto, is based along Church St between Isabella and Grenville Sts and includes area sidestreets. Church St, around Wellesley St, has quite a few cafés and restaurants and a range of nightspots. It's generally a lively area but especially so on Saturday night.

Cabbagetown This district, east of Parliament St, was settled by Irish immigrants fleeing the potato famine of 1841 and became known as Cabbagetown because the sandy soil of the area provided ideal growing conditions for cabbages. It's now both a residential district (ranging from poor to comfortable) and a commercial district. As well as the differences between its denizens, the area is distinguished primarily by its 19th century Victorian terrace houses – possibly the richest concentration of fine Victorian architecture in North America.

Since the 1970s there has been considerable gentrification of this once rundown area. It's worth a stroll to peek at some of the beautifully renovated houses and their carefully tended gardens.

Cabbagetown is bounded roughly by Gerrard St E to the south, Wellesley St to the north, Parliament St to the west (which is the main business centre) and Sumach St to the east.

The necropolis off Sumach St at Winchester St is one of the city's oldest and most interesting cemeteries. Across the street is Riverdale Farm, a popular place for families and kids. It's run as a real working farm, with two barns to wander through and a selection of waterfowl and animals, some of which may permit a pat or two. It's a good place to start a walking tour of the area.

The Danforth In the east end of town along Danforth Ave, roughly between Pape and Woodbine Aves, is a large Greek community. Often called The Danforth, this has become one of the city's most popular dining areas, and warm summer nights in particular bring out serious crowds. There are many restaurants, a few smoky men's cafés,

and also some big, busy, colourful fruit, vegetable and flower stores which stay open into the night.

Little India Also out this way is Little India, with various worth-a-peek speciality stores, women in saris and the scent of spices in the air. There are also numerous restaurants situated here, many with very low prices. It's along Gerrard St E, just one block west of Coxwell Ave.

Corso Italia Italians, in number, are found in many parts of the city, but if there is one centre of the community it's probably on St Clair Ave W, east and west of the Dufferin St intersection. Here you'll find Italian movies, espresso cafés and pool halls. A secondary Italian area known as **Little Italy**, on College St west of Euclid Ave, is a good and trendier spot filling up fast with outdoor cafés, bars and small restaurants.

Nearby is a Portuguese neighbourhood, based along Dundas St W between Ossington and Dufferin Sts.

Markham Village As you approach the corner of Bloor and Markham Sts (one block west of Bathurst St), you'll see Toronto's most colourful, gaudy store, the zany Honest Ed's. Giant signs say things like 'Don't just stand there, buy something'. Hardly subtle but you won't believe the queues outside the door before opening time. Most patrons are from the nearby Italian and Portuguese districts. There are some good buys – cheap running shoes, T-shirts and various household necessities. With the money Eddie Mirvish has made, he has established a major reputation as a theatre impresario/entrepreneur. Markham St south from Bloor St, with its galleries, boutiques and bookshops, is mostly his or his son's doing.

There are some interesting little specialised import shops to browse in. David Mirvish Books has good sales on Sunday. Bloor St around this area is fun to stroll along, with numerous restaurants and bars, patronised mostly by a mix of students and immigrants.

Parks

High Park The city's biggest park is popular for picnics, walking, cycling and jogging. There is a small children's zoo, a lake where people fish in summer and skate in winter and a pool for swimming (which is free). Some parts of the park are manicured; other bits are left as natural woods. No cars are allowed on summer weekends.

Also in the park is **Colborne Lodge**, built by one of Toronto's first architects and now run as an historical site with costumed workers. It's open daily.

Not far from the swimming pool, on the main road through the park, there's the Grenadier Restaurant which serves a vast selection of quite good home-made meals at modest prices. The park is off Bloor St W at Parkside Drive and runs south down to Lake Shore Blvd, west of the CNE. The subway stop is either Keele or High Park.

Tommy Thompson Park & the Port Formerly called and often still known as the Leslie St Spit, this artificial landfill site is presided over by the Metro Toronto Conservation Authority (☎ 416-661-6600). It extends out into the lake and has unexpectedly become a phenomenal wildlife success. It was designed to both improve and develop shipping facilities but within a few years became the second largest ring-billed seagull nesting place in the world. Terns and other bird species nest here too, and you may spot many more types which drop by.

The area, a narrow 5km-long strip, is open to the public on weekends and holidays. Some construction work is still going on and marinas have been built on portions of it. The park is south of the corner of Queen St E and Leslie St, on the corner of Unwin Ave and Leslie St.

From April to October a free shuttle bus runs from the nearest bus stop, on Leslie St at Commissioners Rd (about three long blocks from the main gate), through the gate at the spit and down about halfway. It runs every half-hour from 9 am to 5 pm. At the far end (named Vicki Keith Point after a local long-distance swimmer), out by the

eastern edges of the Toronto Islands, there is a lighthouse and views to the city. The park closes at 6 pm. No vehicles are permitted, but many people use bicycles – the Martin Goodman Recreational Trail runs by in both directions.

At the gate there is a map and a bird checklist. Occasional portable toilets can be found along the main path. Although some small sections are wooded, note that there is very little shade, so be prepared in midsummer. Check the schedule at the gate for the free guided walks, which often have an ornithological (birding) or photography angle.

At the foot of industrial Cherry St, connected to Leslie St by Unwin St, the sandy, relatively quiet, poseur-free beach is popular with windsurfers and those seeking a cool breeze on hot days. There's a snack bar, a few barbecues among the trees and some walking paths along the shoreline.

The Port of Toronto is situated farther north along Cherry St towards Lake Shore Blvd. Freighters can be seen moored along the docks, but you can't get very close and there is no public access or viewing station. Off Cherry St, there is a small park at the end of Poulson St from where there is a fine view of the harbour, islands and the city skyline.

The Beaches & the Bluffs To residents, 'The Beach' is a rather wealthy, mainly professional neighbourhood along Queen St E at Woodbine Ave, down by the lakeshore. To everyone else, it's part of 'The Beaches' meaning the area, the beaches themselves and the parkland along the lake.

The sandy beaches are good for sunbathing and picnicking, the 3km boardwalk which edges the sand for strolling (or strutting, as the case may be). There's also a paved path for cycling and roller-skating. Water quality inhibits swimmers. You can rent sailboards, with or without lessons, and Sports World (☎ 416-693-7368), 2229 Queen St E, has rollerblades for hire at $15 (for 24 hours). At the west end, in Woodbine Beach Park, there's an excellent Olympic-size public swimming pool. There are quite a few places to eat nearby along

Queen St E. To get to The Beaches from downtown, take the Queen St streetcar.

About 5km farther east are the Scarborough Bluffs, cliffs of glacial deposits known as till, set in parkland at the lake edge. Erosion has created some odd shapes and has revealed layers of sediment that indicate five different glacial periods. There are paths here with good views over the lake. Below, in the lake itself, landfill has been used to form parkland, Bluffers Park, and boat-mooring space. To access Bluffers Park turn south off Kingston Rd at Brimley Rd.

If you want to be atop the cliffs (and you do), there are several parks which afford excellent views of the bluffs and panoramas of Lake Ontario. To reach one area worth visiting, for those with vehicles, turn south off Kingston Rd onto Scarboro Crescent and then Drake Crescent. Park here; the bluffs are within walking distance. Another excellent vantage point at the highest section of the bluffs (about 98m high) is at Cathedral Bluffs Park. Still farther east along Kingston Rd, turn south at Cathedral Bluffs Drive.

Not far (by vehicle) east of the park is the Guild Inn, with its large lakefront grounds and good views along the shoreline. In the garden there's a collection of sculptures, columns and gargoyles rescued from condemned buildings. Tea is served on the patio in the afternoon. The Guild Inn is on Guildwood Parkway, south from Kingston Rd at Livingstone Rd.

Other Parks Allan Gardens is an often-mentioned park that's rather overrated. Bounded by Carlton, Jarvis and Gerrard Sts, most of it is nothing more than a city block of grass interspersed with a few trees and benches. The highlight is the large, old, round-domed greenhouse filled with huge palms and flowering trees from around the world. It's open daily from 10 am to 5 pm and is free. After dark, the entire place is unsavoury enough not to be recommended and that includes even taking a short cut through the park.

Around the corner from Yonge St, west a few doors on the south side of Richmond St W

(beside little Temperance St) is the tiny **Clouds Conservatory**, an unexpected sanctuary in the downtown core. Built vertically as a 'modernist ruin' it features exposed steel, creeping vines, a waterfall and a mural to construction workers. It's only open from 10 am to 3 pm, Monday to Friday.

Though short on city parks, Toronto does have some substantial, largely natural parks in numerous ravines formed by rivers and streams running down to the lake. Start in **Edwards Gardens**, on the corner of Lawrence Ave E and Leslie St. It's a big, cultivated park with flower gardens, a pond and picnic sites. You can take a ravine walk from the gardens via **Wilket Creek Park**. The Science Centre backs onto the park here. Along Wilket Creek you can walk for hours all the way down to Victoria Park Ave, just north of Danforth Ave. Much of the way is through woodland.

From the corner of Yonge St and St Clair Ave, walk east to the bridge and the sign for the nature trail. This leads down into the **Don River Valley**, another good walk.

Toronto Zoo

This huge zoo (☎ 416-392-5900), with an excellent reputation, is one of the country's largest and best and continues to expand. There are around 5000 animals on the 283 hectares, some in natural-setting pens the size of football fields. Of course, with enclosures so large, it takes a lot of leg work to see it.

There is a small train that goes around the site (not in winter), but walking is best. You need a full day to see it all.

The animals are in five areas, each covering a major world geographical zone. There are outdoor sections, as well as simulated climates in indoor pavilions. A good idea is the black-light area that enables you to observe nocturnal animals. Other good exhibits include those allowing for underwater viewing of beavers, polar bears and seals. One area has displays especially geared to children, with some animals to touch and ponies to ride.

The zoo is on Meadowvale Rd, north of Hwy 401, at the eastern edge of the city. To get there using public transport, take the subway on the Bloor St line east to Kennedy, the last stop. From there get the No 86A Scarborough bus to the zoo. It's quite a trip – about 20 minutes on the subway from the centre of town and then about 40 minutes on the bus, plus waiting time.

Admission is $14, less for kids. Parking is $5 (free in winter). It's open daily in summer from 9 am to 7.30 pm, and in winter from 9.30 am to 4.30 pm. Call for the current schedule.

You may want to take your lunch, as McDonald's has an exclusive food contract for the grounds.

Paramount Canada's Wonderland

Wonderland (☎ 905-832-7000) is essentially a family-oriented amusement park with over 50 rides, including some killer roller coasters (one a looping inverted jet coaster which travels at 90km/h). In addition, there are also live shows, a five-hectare water park (bring a bathing suit) and loads of Hanna Barbera characters wandering around a huge kiddies area.

A one-day pass, good for most attractions and rides, is $38 plus tax, less for children and seniors. Straight admission to the grounds is $22 and there is also a grounds and coupon ticket good for some rides. Parking is another $7. Line-ups for rides can be lengthy.

Food available is run of the mill and expensive. Bringing a picnic is not a bad idea.

Concerts are held in summer at the Kingswood Theatre and tickets for these shows cost extra.

The park is open from approximately early June to early September, and on weekends a month before and after these dates. Opening hours are 10 am to 10 pm in peak season.

Wonderland is away from the centre of town, on Hwy 400, 10 minutes drive north of Hwy 401. Exit at Rutherford Rd if you're travelling north, at Major Mackenzie Drive if you're going south. There are express buses from Yorkdale and York Mills subway stations.

Activities

Cycling For cyclists (and roller-bladers), the Martin Goodman Trail is the place to go. This recreation route along the waterfront stretches from The Beaches in the east end, past Harbourfront and the downtown area, to the Humber River in the west end. From here, it connects with paths in parkland running northwards along the Humber. This section is a really fine ride. You can go at least as far as Eglinton Ave, and that's quite a few kilometres.

If you fancy a longer trek, the Martin Goodman Trail links into the Lake Ontario Waterfront Trail which stretches 325km from Hamilton to Trenton. Visit the tourist office for maps and pamphlets detailing sights along the way.

The Toronto Bicycling Network (☎ 416-766-1985) organises short, medium and long weekend trips (some overnight) throughout summer.

Water Sports Free swimming in public pools can be found in High Park, the Gus Ryder Pool (known as Sunnyside pool) south of the park at the lake on Lakeshore Drive, and in Woodbine Park at The Beaches in east-end Toronto, at the foot of Woodbine Ave. Many other city parks include pools but the three above are selected for their good locations, large size and popularity.

Sandy beaches, shady parks, a boardwalk and, on any hot summer day (especially on weekends), lots of people can also be found around The Beaches district (see attractions earlier). Kew Beach is the most popular section and the boardwalk goes through here. The same thing on a smaller scale can be enjoyed at Sunnyside Beach in the west end, south of High Park. Both are fun, relaxed and relaxing. Work continues to make the water fit to swim in.

There is windsurfing at The Beaches too; rentals are available in the Ashbridges Bay area at the western end of the beach.

Skating In winter there are good, free places to skate at City Hall and at Harbourfront, both with artificial ice and both with skate rentals. If it's been quite cold, there is also large, natural Grenadier Pond in High Park.

Organised Tours

Bus The reliable Gray Line (☎ 416-594-3310) runs a basic, two hour, inner-city tour for $25, less for seniors and children. Various other, more specialised tours lasting 2½ hours or more are offered, with site stops included. Passengers are picked up either from downtown hotels or the main bus terminal (610 Bay St). Tickets can be bought on the bus, or at the Gray Line desk in the Royal York Hotel, on York St across from the train station.

Olde Towne Tours (☎ 416-614-0999) uses pseudo-trolleys or double-decker buses for its hop-on, hop-off tours around town. The $25 ticket is good for 24 hours. They run from April to November.

Walking Civitas Cultural Resources (☎ 416-966-1550) offers three summer walking tours of the city focusing on history and architecture with interesting asides thrown in. Tours run on weekends only, taking about 1½ hours and costing $10. Call to reserve a spot and to check meeting times and places.

A Taste of the World (☎ 416-923-6813) runs various walking and cycling tours which delve into neighbourhood nooks and crannies; one visits the hidden ice-cream parlours of the city, another tries to unveil the mysteries of Chinatown.

Various historical walks are organised by volunteers from the Royal Ontario Museum from June to September. Jaunts take place, rain or shine, on Sunday afternoon and Wednesday evening. Call ☎ 416-586-5797 for details or pick up a brochure at the tourist office or ROM.

The University of Toronto (☎ 416-978-5000) runs free guided tours of the campus through summer, three times daily. This is the country's largest university and the campus has some fine buildings. Tours start from the map room in Hart House.

Boat Several companies run boat tours in and around the harbour and the islands. Most

depart from Harbourfront around Queen's Quay, John Quay and, especially, York Quay.

The main operator is Mariposa Cruise Lines (☎ 416-203-0178) with a variety of cruises, mostly seasonal. The one hour, basic, narrated tour of the harbour area is $12. Mariposa also offers more leisurely (and expensive) evening trips with buffet, cash bar and dancing. For all of the above, purchase tickets in advance at Queen's Quay Terminal, Pier Six.

Some privately owned sailing ships and schooners offer trips of varying duration as far as Niagara-on-the-Lake. Other boats are geared for fishing. Look around the docks at Harbourfront, you'll see signs and/or captains advertising their charters.

The island ferry has good views of the city and is very cheap. If you're visiting the islands, remember to check the time of the last return trip. In summer the ferries run about every half-hour but not very late at night. See Toronto Islands earlier in this chapter for more details.

Niagara & Adventure/Alternative There are quite a few Toronto-based companies offering out-of-town trips, activities and wilderness tours.

Gray Line (see above) has an all-day Niagara Falls trip for $100.

Better value is The Travel Express (☎ 416-861-9220) Niagara Falls trip via minibus for $60 which includes a ride on the *Maid of the Mist* or another attraction.

For budget travellers, JoJo Tours (☎ 416-201-6465) has a good one-day trip to Niagara Falls for $50 which includes a stop at a winery and Niagara-on-the-Lake. Tours operate all year with a price drop in the off-season. Pick-ups are made at all hostels from where you can book.

The Canadian Experience, operating through Hostelling International (☎ 416-971-4440, ☎ 1-800-668-4487), has been highly recommended by LP readers, and after taking some time off should be back in business. It runs a very full 2½-day trip which includes a visit to the reconstructed French mission Sainte-Marie Among the

Hurons near Georgian Bay, a hike along the spectacular Bruce Trail, a drive through some of Ontario's Mennonite towns and a look at Niagara Falls. Tours leave from the Toronto hostel once a week.

Free Spirit Tours (☎ 416-219-7562) has a similar trip with hiking and rock-climbing on the Bruce Peninsula with overnights at the Collingwood hostel. The small-group, three-day, two-night all-inclusive package is $175. Trips run from May to October and there are also winter programs.

For week-long adventure/outdoor activity tours call Canabus (☎ 416-977-8311, ☎ 1-877-226-2287, www.canabus.com) at 74 Gerrard St E. For about $300, the 24-seat buses take budgeters on a 1700km circuit of southern Ontario stopping for whitewater rafting, canoeing, hiking and various other geographic and cultural attractions. Travellers pay for the activities they wish and food. Accommodation is at hostels.

Moose Travel (☎ 905-853-4760, ☎ 1-888-816-6673, moosetc@sprint.ca) is a fun but practical combination of bus company and tour operator. It operates three jump-on, jump-off trips around Ontario and Quebec. The itineraries are well planned and researched allowing for a range of experiences – both city and wilds, active and contemplative – from historical sites to bungee jumping. Each route includes various stops and overnights at hostels, permitting a great deal of flexibility. The circuits' durations range from a minimum of three to six days long with most people taking seven to 14 days. Passengers pay only for transportation and add their own costs according to interests. Prices range from $180 to $300 depending on the trip and mileage covered. Trips run from May to October.

Further Still (☎ 905-371-8747, www.furtherstill.com) offers a few low-budget trips in its colourful (add a few brush strokes yourself) buses. It runs various concert/Ontario trips but specialises in two-week trips around eastern Canada or to the west coast. Accommodation en route is mainly camping or in hostels. The long trips run from May to October.

ONTARIO

For more information, also see the introductory Getting Around chapter.

For trips to Algonquin Park see under the park later.

Special Events

Some of the major events are:

May

Toronto International Powwow

The two day event celebrates Native Indian culture with dancers, costumes and crafts. It's at the Skydome in the middle of May.

June

Caravan

This is a nine-day event of cultural exchange during which ethnic groups offer music, dance and food native to their homelands. A passport ($15) entitles you to visit the 50 or so different ethnic pavilions set up around the city. Buses travel between the pavilions. The event takes place during the middle or end of June. Ask at the tourist office for a complete list of events and things to see and do.

Queen's Plate

The year's major horse race and one of North America's oldest (held since 1859), it is run at the Woodbine Racetrack (☎ 416-675-7223) around the end of June.

Gay Pride Day Parade

Always larger and more flamboyant, Gay Pride Day culminates in an outrageous downtown out-of-the-closet parade on Church St towards the end of June. People of all persuasions (not recommended for small children) come to watch floats and the participants and to generally party, with recent crowds estimated as high as 100,000.

Du Maurier Downtown Jazz Festival

The excellent and ever growing annual festival is held throughout the central city in June and early July, with a week of concerts day and night. The jazz is varied, featuring local, US and European players. More gospel, blues and world beat influences have been creeping into the mix. About a thousand musicians perform. Workshops, films and even jazz cruises are part of the event. Shows range from freebies on the streets, to nightclub performances, to concert hall recitals. Prices vary considerably but for the most part are pretty reasonable.

July

Soul & Blues Festival

This festival is conducted on weekends at Harbourfront.

International Picnic

At the beginning of July each year, to welcome summer, the huge picnic is held on Centre Island. Admission is free and there's music, dancing, contests and lots of food. It's very popular with the Italian community.

The Molson Indy

Toronto's only major car race is held in early or mid-July. Well known names from the international circuit compete in front of large crowds during the two days of practice and qualifying trials, with the big race on the last day of the three-day event. It's held in and around Exhibition Place and Lake Shore Blvd, in the south-central portion of the city. Get tickets early.

Fringe Theatre Festival

With over 400 performances in six venues over 10 days, generally in July, the festival (☎ 416-534-5919) has become a major theatrical hit. The participants are chosen by lottery, so the performances vary widely in style, format and quality. Expect the unexpected. Drama, comedy, musicals and cabaret-style shows are all part of the event. Ask at the tourist office for a program guide.

Mariposa Folk Festival

Begun in the early 1960's, Mariposa is a festival of mainly folk music but also includes bluegrass and American Indian music. Location and format vary annually; for current information call the Mariposa Folk Foundation (☎ 416-588-3655). Jam sessions and workshops are generally part of the multi-day event which takes place in July or August.

August

Caribana

This major West Indian festival held along Lake Shore Blvd W around the beginning of August, is primarily a weekend of reggae, steel drum, and calypso music and dance. The main attraction, however, is the huge parade featuring outrageous costumes à la carnival in Rio. The parade can have thousands of participants and take five hours or more to pass by. Other events and concerts are spread over the two weeks prior to the parade.

Canadian National Exhibition (CNE)

The CNE claims to be the oldest (from about 1900) and largest annual exhibition in the world. It includes agricultural and technical exhibits, concerts, displays, crafts, parades, an air show, a horse show, all manner of games and rides, and fireworks. The exhibition is held during the two weeks prior to, and including, the Labour Day holiday. The location is Exhibition Place on Lake Shore Blvd W.

September

International Film Festival

The annual festival is a prestigious and major international cinematic event. Usually held in September, it lasts about a week and a half and features films of all lengths and styles, as well as gala events and well known stars. Check the papers for special guides and reviews. You can obtain tickets for individual screenings or buy expensive, all-inclusive packages. Tickets do, however, sell out very quickly.

October

International Festival of Authors

Held in autumn (usually October) at Harbourfront, this is the largest literary event of its kind in the world. Dozens of well known novelists, poets and short-story writers gather to read and discuss their work. Each evening three or four writers are presented. Readings are also held through the year on a weekly basis, generally featuring less prominent authors.

Places to Stay

Rates in hotels fluctuate with demand and season, with summer being peak time. The high season rates are given.

Camping There are several camping/trailer grounds within 40km of the city. The tourist office has a complete list. One of the closest is the good *Indian Line Campground*, part of Clairville Conservation Area (☎ 416-661-6600). It's north up Indian Line Rd, which runs north-south on the east side of the airport. The campground, with 224 sites, is near Steeles Ave, which marks the northern edge of the city limits. This is probably the best place for tenters. The nightly rate is $18.

Also close to the city is *Glen Rouge Park* (☎ 416-392-2541), on Kingston Rd (Hwy 2) at Altona Rd, near Sheppard Ave E. It's on the lakefront, at the eastern border of Toronto and the town of Pickering. There are about 120 sites. Tent sites are $18 per night and it can be reached by public transit from downtown.

Hostels The HI *Toronto Hostel* (☎ 416-971-4440, ☎ 1-800-668-4487, thostel@hostelling int-gl.on.ca, 76 Church St) is very central in a former hotel. It's just north of Adelaide St E,

one block east of Yonge St. There are 170 beds and the usual facilities such as kitchen, laundry, lockers etc but also Internet facilities. A bonus is that it is air-conditioned. The larger dorms are $20 for members, a few dollars more for smaller ones, and there are couple ($50) and family rooms, too.

Global Village Backpakers (☎ 416-703-8540, ☎ 1-888-844-7875, www.globalback packers.com, 460 King St W) is a large, independent hostel with a great location on the corner of Spadina Ave by the edge of the entertainment district. There are nearly 200 beds but spread over many rooms in the former (storied) hotel so it's generally not cramped. There is a good lounge, a pleasant patio, Internet facilities and even a bar and travel agency on the premises. For a big place, it is well organised and management isn't loath to spending some money. Dorm beds are $23, less with hostel or student cards.

The *Canadiana International Guesthouse & Hostel* (☎ 416-598-9090, ☎ 1-877-215-1225, canadiana@inforamp.net, 42 Widmer St) was being built during research and is a new place to try. This small hostel with room for 46 in dorms or private single/double rooms is spread through two connecting Victorian houses with a great location in the entertainment district. It offers air-con, kitchen and linen. If things go as planned it could be a good, low-key addition to the hostel ($22) and budget hotel ($40 to $60) options.

Another good alternative is the independent *Leslieville Hostel* (☎ 416-461-7258, ☎ 1-800-280-3965, leslieville@sympatico.ca, 185 Leslie St), which consists of three houses, all close to each other in an east-end residential neighbourhood 4km from downtown. To get to the main hostel in Leslie St take a 20 minute streetcar ride along Queen St to Leslie St and walk north along Leslie. The streetcar operates 24 hours. The homy, casual hostels can accommodate up to 70 people. Most beds are in dormitories, but there are eight private rooms as well. Dorm beds are $18; private rooms are $35/45 a single/double. Breakfast is included. There are

kitchen and laundry facilities and free parking. Reservations are suggested in summer.

The *Toronto Budget Hostel* (☎ 416-703-3939, 223 Church St) adroitly took over the premises when the HI hostel left. The location is the same but that's about it and much of the international clientele has moved elsewhere. There are about 50 dorm beds at $21. Single/double rooms are $35/55 with tax. For $5, a crummy breakfast of coffee and doughnuts is offered.

The *Marigold International Hostel* (☎ 416-536-8824, marigoldhostel@hotmail.com, 2011 Dundas St W) is in the west end of town. It, too, is right on the streetcar line. Take either the College St or Dundas St cars from downtown for the 20 minute or so ride. On weekends the Dundas car is slow (and colourful) as it rolls through the heart of busy Chinatown. An alternative is the subway to the Dundas West stop, from where the Dundas streetcar begins its route eastbound, going right by the hostel.

The dormitory beds are $21. There are no cooking facilities but complimentary coffee and doughnuts are supplied each morning. There are around 40 beds and two rooms for couples. The rooms are small so it can get crowded and maintenance could improve. The door is generally locked until the 3 pm check-in but if you have spent the night you do not need to leave by any particular time – the door locks behind you. It's open all year.

For a smaller, quieter place more like a modest B&B than a hostel, *Havinn* (☎ 416-922-5220, ☎ 1-888-922-5220, 118 Spadina Rd) fits the bill. For $25 you get a real bed in a room with one or two others, max. And breakfast is included. There are kitchen facilities minus the stove but including microwave. Private rooms are $40/50. The main house on Spadina is conveniently located just north of Bloor and there is a second nearby. Both are simple and very clean. In summer reservations are a good idea and there is some parking.

The *YWCA* (☎ 416-923-8454, 80 Woodlawn Ave), for women only, is central near Yonge St. Singles/doubles are $47/62 and a dormitory bed costs $20. A continental breakfast is included and there's an inexpensive cafeteria. Discounts for stays of a week or longer are offered.

Most of the other hostels listed on the Internet are not recommended.

Colleges *Neill-Wycik College Hotel* (☎ 416-977-2320, ☎ 1-800-268-4358, 96 Gerrard St E) is a well located, apartment-style student residence by Ryerson Polytechnic University. From early May to late August the residence's rooms are rented out to short and long-term guests. Rooms are $35/60 and family rooms are available. There are laundry facilities and a student-run cafeteria for breakfasts. However, the building isn't air-conditioned so the small rooms can get very hot in mid-summer. Cleanliness can also be a bit of a problem.

Central *University of Toronto* (☎ 416-978-8735) rents rooms in a couple of college residences. The campus is by the corner of University Ave and College St. Rooms are available from the middle of May until late August. Rooms cost from $45 per person and include breakfast and maid service. There are good weekly rates.

B&Bs & Tourist Homes Between June and November reservations are suggested. In addition to the independent operators, there are B&B associations which check, list and book rooms in the participating homes. Indicate where you'd like to be and any other preferences and attempts will be made to find a particularly suitable host. There is generally no need to go to the agency – a telephone call should get things sorted.

The Downtown Toronto Association of B&B Guesthouses (☎ 416-368-1420) specialises in rooms downtown, mainly in renovated Victorian houses. Prices range from $45 singles and $55 for doubles. The mailing address is PO Box 190, Station B, Toronto, M5T 2W1.

Metropolitan B&B Registry (☎ 416-964-2566) is the largest outfit, with members in and out of town. The office is at 615 Mount Pleasant Rd, Suite 269, Toronto, M4S 3C5.

Toronto B&B Inc (☎ 416-588-8800) has about 25 members. There's no office to visit; if you're in town, just call. The mailing address is Box 269, 253 College St, Toronto M5T 1R5.

Global Guesthouse (☎ 416-923-4004, ☎ 1-800-387-4788, singer@inforamp.net, 9 Spadina Rd) has a great location just north of Bloor St W. The good-value rooms include parking, daily cleaning, cable TV, a telephone and maybe a painting by the owner. The 10 rooms fill up quickly. Singles/doubles are $49/59 with shared bath and $59/69 with private bath.

The spotless *Accommodators* (☎ 416-461-7095, 223 Strathmore Blvd) is in the east end near Greektown. The Greenwood subway stop is practically at the door. In summer, prices are $45/55 with continental breakfast and they drop even lower the rest of the year. There's a kitchen and deck for guests.

West of downtown is the simple *Candy Haven Tourist Home* (☎ 416-532-0651, 1233 King St W) right on the King St streetcar line; look for the sign which is right beside McDonald's. It's been around for decades and is quaintly old-fashioned. The elderly owner can tell you more than you want to know about the area. Singles/doubles with a shared bathroom are just $40/45.

Still farther west near Roncesvalles Ave is the *Grayona Tourist Home* (☎ 416-535-5443, 1546 King St W). It's a renovated old house run by Marie Taylor, a friendly and enthusiastic Australian. Singles are $45 to $50, doubles $60 to $65. Every room has a fridge and telephone and all but one a TV. Marginally more expensive rooms, which are good for families (there's even a cot), have cooking facilities. A large family room with bathroom and kitchen goes for $100 a night. Prices drop in the off-season. It's about 7km from downtown and although some of the visitors walk, there is a streetcar along King St which stops practically at the door.

More upmarket is the recommended *Beverley Place* (☎ 416-977-0077, 235 Beverley St) on a small north-south street running south from College St to Queen St W between University and Spadina Aves. China-

town, Queen St W and even the CN Tower are all within walking distance.

The house is a well restored, three-storey Victorian place dating from 1877, with lots of original features and wonderfully high ceilings. The entire place is furnished and decorated with interesting antiques and collectibles. An excellent breakfast is served at the large kitchen table overlooking a secluded garden patio.

The owner, Bill Ricciuto, also runs a similar house across the street. Guests staying here go to No 235 for breakfast. Prices for singles/doubles begin at $60/85. The 'Queen Room' (with an impressive bed) costs more, as does the 3rd floor, self-contained apartment with its own balcony and city view.

Aberdeen Ave runs west off Parliament St just north of Carlton St. Here there's *Aberdeen Guesthouse* (☎ 416-920-8697, ab erdeen@aol.com, 52 Aberdeen Ave), a small renovated Victorian home in the east-end area of Cabbagetown. There are three beautifully decorated rooms, with shared bathroom, from $80 to $90 single, $90 to $95 double. Breakfast is fabulous, the house is air-conditioned, there's a shady back garden and it's gay-friendly.

Hotels You can't say Toronto and budget hotels in the same breath. Unlike, say Montreal, visitors simply will not find one. There are, though, some good moderate central places with a bit of character.

The *Selby* (☎ 416-921-3142, ☎ 1-800-387-4788, 592 Sherbourne St), north of Wellesley St, best combines price with value. The turreted Victorian mansion, dating from 1882 and designated as a heritage site, has an interesting history. At one time it was a girls' school. Later, Ernest Hemingway lived here when he worked for the *Toronto Star* in his younger days, before heading to Paris.

The upgraded rooms cost $70 to $90 for either singles or doubles, depending on size, features and date. A continental breakfast is included. Reservations are recommended from May to October. The bar is popular with men from the local gay community but the hotel clientele is straight and gay. The

bar makes a lot of noise so ask for a quiet room or you won't sleep until very late.

The upgraded *Strathcona* (☎ 416-363-3321, ☎ 1-800-268-8304, 60 York St) is an old place with an excellent location very near the train station. It has all the usual amenities and yet, for the downtown area, is moderately priced at $95. There's a dining room, a coffee shop and a bar.

One of the best of the small, old downtown hotels is the *Victoria* (☎ 416-363-1666, ☎ 1-800-363-8228, 56 Yonge St) near *that* street's southern end. Refurbished throughout, it maintains such older features as a fine lobby. Prices are $100 to $120 for a single or double.

The more typical high-rise *Bond Place* (☎ 416-362-6061, 65 Dundas St E) has a great location near the Eaton Centre and is often busy with vacationers. Summer prices are $95.

More like a motel, but perfectly good and with parking, is the *Executive Motor Hotel* (☎ 416-504-7441, 621 King St W). The 75 rooms are priced at about $90 a double but dropping to $70 in the off-season. It's central and the King St streetcar goes right by.

The central *Days Inn* (☎ 416-977-6655, ☎ 1-800-329-7466, 30 Carlton St) has rooms for one or two people at $139 in summer and from $109 at less busy times. It's reliable and has other locations around the city.

Hotels – Top End Toronto has an abundance of large, modern hotels. There are many downtown, plenty around the city's edges and a good number around the airport. Many offer discount weekend packages but prices fluctuate.

The *Westin Harbour Castle* (☎ 416-869-1600, 1 Harbour Square) has a fine location near the bottom of Yonge St, right at the edge of the lake, opposite the Toronto Islands. The revolving restaurant offers good views over the city and lake. Rooms cost from $160.

The venerable *Royal York* (☎ 416-368-2511, ☎ 1-800-441-1414, 100 Front St) opposite the train station deserves mention. Among the top-class hotels, it's the oldest and has served people from rock stars to

royalty. Singles or doubles start at $169 and rise depending on vacancy levels.

Also well appointed, with a good reputation and a fine lobby area, the *Hilton* (☎ 416-869-3456, ☎ 1-800-445-8667, 145 Richmond St W) is right in the centre. Singles/doubles cost from $240.

The costliest rooms in town are found at the celebrities choice, the *Four Seasons* (☎ 416-964-0411, 21 Avenue Rd) in Yorkville where prices start at around $350 a night.

Apartment Hotels Although they can be reasonably priced, most places of this type are in the top-end category and tend to be geared towards the corporate client and business executive. Many have a minimum stay ranging from three days to a month.

Very central is the *Town Inn Hotel* (☎ 416-964-3311, 620 Church St) two blocks south of Bloor St. For the price of a hotel room, you can get a suite with kitchen. There is also a pool and sauna among the full amenities. A double is $125 a day, including a small breakfast.

Executive Travel Suites (☎ 905-273-9641) has four such properties in the downtown area, with prices starting at about $125 a day (with a three-day minimum stay). Each unit has a separate bedroom and living room and each building offers one or more extras, such as a pool, balconies, roof deck or restaurant.

Another place is the *Cromwell* (☎ 416-962-5604, 55 Isabella St). The minimum rental is for three days and rates for well equipped studios are from $65 a day for one or two people, with free parking. Larger units are available. This location is central but is also in one of the downtown prostitution districts. It is not generally a dangerous area but women alone at night may well be mistaken for being 'on the game'.

Motels For such a large city, Toronto is rather short on motels, so in summer they are often full. There are two main districts for motels in the city and others scattered throughout and around the perimeter.

On the west side of town, a shrinking motel strip (due to redevelopment) can be

found along the lake on Lake Shore Blvd W, informally known as 'the lakeshore'. Those remaining are mostly between the Humber River and Park Lawn Ave, just west of High Park. This district isn't too far from the downtown area, about 12km from Yonge St, and the streetcar lines run the whole way. To get there, take the Queen St or King St streetcar from downtown to Roncesvalles Ave and continue on the Queen St streetcar to the Humber River. Switch (for no charge) to the Humber streetcar, which goes along the lakeshore. The motels edge the shoreline, and several nearby parks on the waterfront offer cool breezes in summer and good views of the city and islands.

Farthest west, with the yellow sign, the **Beach Motel** (*☎ 416-259-3296, 2183 Lake Shore Blvd W*) is good. It has 40 rooms from $65 and is beside the entrance to a park. The large, modern, well maintained **Seahorse** (*☎ 416-255-4433, 2095 Lake Shore Blvd W*) is probably the most prosperous of the lot. It features rooms for the amorous, with waterbeds, lots of mirrors etc. And there is a swimming pool. The small, standard rooms are $70 but prices rise for the extras.

Nearby, the **Queensway Motel** (*☎ 416-252-5821, 638 The Queensway*) is sort of away from the main routes and may have rooms when others are full. Prices are considerably lower at $49 a double.

Back closer to town, before the start of the motel strip itself, there's the **Inn on the Lake** (*☎ 416-766-4392, 1926 Lake Shore Blvd W*). Prices start at $100.

Motels dot Lake Shore Blvd sporadically all the way along its course to Hamilton.

Several motels can be found along Dundas St W, west of Hwy 427 (which is in the suburban city of Mississauga rather than Toronto proper). From Lake Shore Blvd, go north up Hwy 427 and turn left at Dundas.

The other main motel district is on the east side of town, farther from the centre, on Kingston Rd which branches off Queen St E, east of Coxwell Ave, and later turns into the old Hwy 2 to Montreal. Motels start just east of Brimley Rd. Access to it is slower.

The Guildwood station of the GO train, a commuter service, is just east of the motel strip. It has parking, and trains run frequently into downtown. Alternatively, public transit can get you into town but is slower still. Many of these motels are now used by the government as overflow welfare accommodation. Those listed here rely on visitors for some or most of their clients.

The **Avon** (*☎ 416-267-0339, 2800 Kingston Rd*) just past Bluffers Park is an attractive looking place and friendly. A room with one double bed is $40 with TV and radio, and there is a heated pool. It's near Brimley Rd. Up Brimley Rd one block north at St Clair Ave, buses can be caught going to the subway system.

The **Park** (*☎ 416-261-7241, 3126 Kingston Rd*) charges $55 for one double bed. It's friendly, clean and well run.

Places to Eat

Toronto has a good selection of restaurants in all price categories and a wide variety to choose from, thanks to the many nationalities represented in the city. The following places are mostly central and accessible by public transport. They are listed according to area and cuisine categories.

Yonge St & Around Yonge St itself, though busy night and day, is not one of Toronto's prime restaurant districts. In the downtown centre, Yonge St has become swamped with fast-food franchises and cheap takeout counters. There are exceptions on and near Toronto's main street, but many places are geared more to lunch than dinner.

South of the Eaton Centre, Yonge St has always been a bit of a backwater, so we'll start with the centre itself and work north to Bloor St. Among the many places to eat in the huge shopping mall are a couple of busy pubs. At the Level 1 food court there are some way above average mall eateries. **Baguette Michel** offers a tasty array of sweets and breads as well as salads, sandwiches and really good coffee. **Ristorante Marchelino** has a range of fresh, international dishes all priced under $6.

Swiss Chalet (362 Yonge St) is an outlet of the popular Canadian roast chicken and chips chain. The meals are economical and tasty.

The large, crowded, noisy cafeteria at *Ryerson Polytechnic University* serves up reasonable meals at student prices. Food is served (at meal times only) in the cafeteria in Jorgenson Hall, which is on the corner of Gerrard St E and Victoria St.

At the hole-in-the-wall *Papaya Hut (513A Yonge St)* the home-made vegetable soup, the good sandwiches and the vast array of fruit drinks or smoothies provide an alternative to the nearby junk food.

Green Mango (707 Yonge St) serves up excellent Thai food every day but Sunday. It's fast, cheap (less than $6) and surprisingly good.

Young Thailand (81 Church St) is recommended for convivial atmosphere and classic Thai cuisine at reasonable prices. Northward, *The Mango (580 Church St)* has the best patio in The Village and serves simple food very well. A club sandwich of chicken and bacon on focaccia with a large salad and home-made dressing costs around $9. The mango margaritas are a trademark.

For a splurge on a good steak, try *Bigliardi's (☎ 416-922-9594, 463 Church St)*, an established, traditional steak house. Dinner for two will be over $100. Reservations are suggested for weekends.

Theatre/Entertainment District There are a clutch of new restaurants and nightclubs (some ferociously hip) to be found in this fickle, expanding galaxy north of the Skydome containing the Mirvish theatres and Roy Thompson Hall.

One newcomer likely to remain is the cavernous *Peel Pub (276 King St W)* of Montreal fame. It draws crowds with its great prices for any meal, $5 daily specials, cheap beer and light, friendly atmosphere. It's open from 6.30 am to 2.30 am every day.

Alice Fazooli's (294 Adelaide St W) is a popular party place featuring crab and Italian fare with a huge wine list to help wash it down. Most meals, with a starter, are under $25 at dinner.

For those in need of a smoked-meat sandwich in a small, busy, Jewish-style deli check *Zupa's Deli (342½ Adelaide St W)* east of Spadina. You'd have to be an alligator to get your mouth around one of these mega-sandwiches. It's closed on Sunday.

Wayne Gretzky's (99 Blue Jays Way), as in the hockey legend, is a pub/bar/restaurant with something for everyone. The food – lots of pastas as well as burgers – gets the job done but most people come for the busy, festive ambience and moderate prices.

There are several places in the Skydome itself. Among them is the *Hard Rock Café*. When no game is on, it runs as the regular sports bar that it is; you can simply go in for a hamburger and a beer and have a look at the playing field. It's open every day from lunch until late. During games, tables with views must be paid for.

The corner of King and Simcoe Sts is where the entertainment district Ed Mirvish single-handedly instigated began. Near his Royal Alexander and Princess of Wales theatres is his *Old Ed's* restaurant. It's famous more for its garish exterior and sumptuous interior of antiques and collectibles lit by dozens (hundreds?) of Tiffany lamps than for the food. Straightforward meals consist of quality meats, notably roast beef or steak, accompanied by forgettable instant potato and frozen vegetables. Dinners cost $13 to $19 and lunches to $10 and it's semi-dressy. The fish and chips (offered at lunch only) are very good and less expensive. After eating, check the museum/store upstairs – wow!

St Lawrence Market Farther east, past the Hummingbird Centre which is on Front St at Yonge, is this other busy (but less so) eating, entertainment and nightclub area popular with both visitors and residents. Toronto, like many Canadian cities of any size, has its *Spaghetti Factory (54 The Esplanade)*. The restaurant offers good value; meals start at $9 and are served in an interesting eclectic, colourful atmosphere popular with everybody, including families and teenagers. The lunch menu is even cheaper.

The *Papillon (☎ 416-363-0838, 16 Church St)* is a very comfortable French crêperie. Main dishes range from $9 to $18. In winter a fireplace adds ambience. It gets full when there are popular shows at the nearby Hummingbird theatre.

Queen St W Queen St W between Spadina and University is one of the lively central districts. Some places cater more to trend than to quality, but it's an interesting and varied area with some good and reasonably priced restaurants. One of the better and more stable eateries is the comfortable *Queen Mother (208 Queen St W)*. It offers a varied menu with a Thai influence for full meals and serves coffee and snacks all day. Complete dinners are about $25.

Many of the area's younger residents and more impecunious artists have moved farther west to between Spadina Ave and Bathurst St and beyond. The local Goths and vampires/Edwardians also stroll the area. Along here you'll find a range of new, small restaurants, clubs and speciality stores.

For a meal, snack or coffee at any time of day (or night) there's *Future Bakery (735 Queen St W)*. It's a very popular spot for cheese crêpes with sour cream, or perogies and sauerkraut (about $6), followed by pastries galore and bowls of café au lait.

Dufflet's is the creator of Toronto's best known desserts and has a small retail outlet with a couple of tables at 787 Queen St W. The chocolate cakes are unreal.

Small, cosy *Cities (859 Queen W)* serves up mainly traditional dishes making them seem totally modern with the tasteful use of fresh ingredients and understated flair. Main courses such as scallops are about $15 to $18.

Chinatown & Around The city's large Chinatown is based around the corner of Spadina Ave and Dundas St W and is home to scores of restaurants and Cantonese, Sichuan, Hunan and Mandarin food is all served. The district extends along Dundas St W, especially to the east of Spadina Ave and north up Spadina Ave to College St.

For tasty, inexpensive Chinese food in a variety of styles, including some fine spicy dishes, *Peter's Chung King* restaurant *(281 College St)* gets high marks. As well as superior food, the décor is a cut above the usual fluorescent and plastic, yet prices are no higher – around $25 to $35 for two. Longstanding *Lee Garden (331 Spadina Ave)* offers a consistently good and unusually varied Cantonese menu with dishes $6 to $10. It's open for dinner only. *Swatow (309 Spadina Ave)* is another good choice, with an extensive menu covering different Chinese regions.

Vietnamese places can also be found as some Chinese leave the central core for more suburban areas. *Pho Hung (350 Spadina Ave)* is highly recommended. It features an awesome array of soups from $5 to $7 which come with fresh greens. Some, featuring intestine, tendons and blood may be too authentic but many are delicious. The bowls of vermicelli with your choice of ingredients are an excellent meal at $5. It's open daily and a fair weather bonus is the patio.

An interesting street on the edge of Chinatown, which not too many out-of-towners get to, is Baldwin St running east off Spadina Ave about two blocks north of Dundas St. About three blocks from Spadina Ave towards the east end of Baldwin St is a small, low-key commercial and international restaurant enclave. Long a blend of Chinese and western counterculture, it's especially pleasant on summer evenings when many of the varied restaurants have outdoor patios.

Margarita's (14 Baldwin St) is a small, colourful cantina with the regular tortilla items at about $7 and more authentic meals at around $13. On weekends, it's open for dinner only.

Almost next door, the *Yung Sing Pastry Shop* specialises in Chinese sweets. Help yourself to Chinese tea. It's strictly takeaway but there's a shady picnic table in front of the shop. Also consider the Japanese deli for low-cost meals.

To the west of Spadina Ave, the market area on Kensington Ave and particularly on

Augusta Ave is busy during the day and has some small cheap cafés.

Annex/Bloor St W Bloor St W from Spadina Ave west to Bathurst St is a lively student area, with many restaurants, cafés, bookshops and the popular Bloor St Cinema.

If you're near Spadina and looking for a cheap place, there's *Master's Buffeteria (310 Bloor St W)*. It's in the University Faculty of Education Building. Mostly for students and staff, it's open from 7 am to 7 pm Monday to Friday. Cafeteria-style meals like lamb, sole and shepherd's pie are served at rock-bottom prices (under $5). Complete breakfasts are also available.

The Madison (14 Madison Ave) is a fine, four-tiered pub with lots of outdoor space and very good food.

By the Way (400 Bloor St W) is a small, comfortable bistro with an internationally-flavoured menu. The salads and pita sandwiches run $5 to $6, the main dishes about $10. Try the killer cakes, too.

Juice for Life (521 Bloor St W) is a city fave for its strictly vegetarian fare and absence of earnestness. The wholesome *and* tasty menu includes sandwiches, 'burgers' and pastas. There is also a vast array of smoothies and shakes to cure what ails. Prices are $5 to $10.

Casually elegant **Kensington Kitchen** *(124 Harbord St)* offers meals with a Middle Eastern/Mediterranean slant. Lunches are inexpensive, dinner for two with wine is about $45. During fine weather, take advantage of the wonderful patio.

Little Italy Based along College St west of Bathurst, Little Italy is a cool (as in hot) spot for eating, meeting and hanging out. *Kalendar Koffee House (546 College St)* is an intimate restaurant offering delicious things wrapped in pastry, as well as salads, soups, pasta dishes and big desserts. Main courses start at around $9. It also has a good selection of imported beer.

Always crowded, *Bar Italia (584 College St)* has lots of atmosphere, excellent Italian sandwiches at good prices and pool

tables upstairs. Complete dinners, including a glass of wine, start at $16.

Café Diplomatico (594 College St) is a busy restaurant and pizzeria with a large patio and particularly good cappuccino. It's open from 8 am till late seven days a week. For the best tartufo and Sicilian ice cream in town, head farther west to the *Sicilian Ice Cream Co (712 College St)*.

Greektown/Danforth The Greek area along Danforth Ave, east of the city centre between Pape and Woodbine Aves, is also a good place to get a meal. Most of the restaurants get very busy on summer weekend nights, when there's quite a festive air to the street. Casual, cheap souvlaki houses with a noisy, informal atmosphere but suitable for children are abundant. Eating early or after 9 pm is recommended if you want to avoid the crowds. Some places serve until the very wee hours.

A good, bustling, low-cost place – just look for the queue – is *Astoria (390 Danforth Ave)* where the kebab, rice, potato, salad combo is $12. It's near the Chester subway stop.

The popular *Ouzeri (500A Danforth Ave)* presents a range of slightly more sophisticated main courses and tapas amid colourfully trendy surroundings and fellow diners. Fresh sardines in mustard sauce with a Greek salad and a cold beer will cost around $16.

The comfortably upmarket *Pan (516 Danforth Ave)* is recommended for very well prepared meals featuring traditional Greek ingredients and flavourings. Open every day for dinner ($60 for two) only.

Since the 1960s, *Ellas (702 Pape Ave)* has carried on the tradition of the Greek standards, many on view as you enter. It also offers a lot of seafood. It's dressy with attentive, tablecloth service and dishes are from $15.

Little India There are good Indian restaurants scattered around town but for a wallet-friendly place with a side order of cultural experience, you can't beat *Little India*, based on Gerrard St E just west of Coxwell Ave.

ONTARIO

The *Madras Durbar (1386 Gerrard St E)* is a tiny, tattered, exclusively vegetarian place that serves South Indian dishes. The thali plate is a real taste sensation and makes a complete meal for $5! Masala dosas are offered for the same price here and at numerous other places. Note there is another restaurant down the street with the same name (just like India).

The long-established *Bar-Be-Que Hut (1455 Gerrard St E)* is plusher than most, has a selection of meat and vegetarian dishes and has live music Friday through Sunday nights. The half chicken tandoori is $9, biryani $11.

The quiet *Haandi (1401 Gerrard St E)* serves very good dishes from the extensive menu or offers cheap (lunch $7, dinner $8) buffets.

After dinner, pop into one of the shops for a paan made to order. With or without tobacco, this is a cheap, exotic mouthful.

Entertainment

Toronto is busy after dark, with countless nightspots, concerts, films, lectures and the country's largest theatre scene.

All three daily newspapers provide weekly entertainment listings. Check either the Thursday *Star* or the Friday *Sun* for full listings or the Saturday *Globe & Mail* for film and theatre. The city's most complete entertainment guide is provided by *Now* magazine, a good weekly tabloid-style paper available free around town. Find it at cinemas, restaurants, cafés, record stores and some street-corner newsboxes (where it must be paid for).

Bar hours are 11 am to 2 am, as they are all over Ontario. Numerous clubs stay open until 3 or 4 am without serving any more alcohol, and who knows how many illegal mercurial boozecans there are where pricey drinks can be had at all hours. Beer can be bought retail at Brewers Retail Stores, often marked as the Beer Store, and liquor and wine at Liquor Control Board of Ontario (LCBO) outlets.

Tickets Tri-tickets (☎ 416-504-7777) can usually get a ticket for any show or event,

sold-out or not. The classified sections of the *Sun* and *Star* newspapers also list tickets available for every event in town, from opera to Rolling Stones, hockey to baseball. For a price, any seat is yours.

Rush or same-day discounted tickets may be available at theatres for any given show. Also TO Tix sells half-price leftover theatre and dance tickets for shows the same day. It has a booth on the second level of the Eaton Centre. You must go in person. It's open afternoons only and closed Sunday and Monday.

Live Music *The Bamboo Club (☎ 416-593-5771, 312 Queen St W)* is very popular with lots of African and reggae sounds. It's always busy, with a 30-ish crowd. There's a rooftop patio to catch a breath and a kitchen serving tasty, spicy meals. Admission costs $5 to $10. *Chicago's (335 Queen St W)* offers live blues. The kitchen is open daily until 1 am and often there's no cover charge. Nearby is the classic *Horseshoe (☎ 416-598-4753, 370 Queen St W)*, which presents a mixture of rock, country, blues and rhythm and blues.

The *St Louis (2050 Yonge St)* often has good rhythm and blues or blues bands with dancing and there's no cover. *Lee's Palace (☎ 416-532-1598, 529 Bloor St W)* has long been good for current rock and pop.

Just down the street, *Grossman's (379 Spadina Ave)* is grubby but one of the cheapest places in town. Very good bands sometimes play here and there's usually an interesting, mixed crowd. Sunday afternoons and evenings are reserved for blues jams. Admission is free.

The *Brunswick (481 Bloor St W)* is a funky student hang-out, a bit like a pub and a bit like a fraternity house and often a lot of fun. There's live folk music at the *Free Times Café (☎ 416-967-1078, 320 College St)*.

For jazz, *C'est What (☎ 416-867-9499, 67 Front St E)* has a new act nearly every night. Another is the *Montreal Bistro (☎ 416-363-0179, 65 Sherbourne St)*. For more experimental music, there's the *Music Gallery (179 Richmond St W)*. There's no liquor served here.

Allen's Restaurant (143 Danforth Ave) has live Celtic music on Tuesday and Saturday nights. Sometimes there's a cover charge if the band is big.

The free *Island Club* at the western end of Ontario Place has great live Latin American music on Saturday night during summer. If this stuff doesn't get your feet tapping, you're probably dead.

Dance Clubs & Other Bars A range of nightclubs can be found around town but by far the most happening place is the booming entertainment district near the Skydome. Between Queen and Front Sts W, Richmond St W and Adelaide St W and the small streets of Duncan, John and Peter are packed with dance clubs. The area is jammed on weekends; the best way to find a place to your taste is to take a wander and check the people queuing to get in. Other busy streets are Blue Jays Way and from there King St W to John. For variety, some places in the area offer pool and more of a hip-pub atmosphere. Try *Montana's* on the corner of John and Richmond Sts, or showy *Milano's (325 King St W)*. For dancing, check *Industry (901 King St W)*.

Another busy, popular place for dancing with a twenties crowd is *The Big Bop (651 Queen St W)* on the corner of Bathurst St. *Sneaky Dee's* on the corner of College and Bathurst Sts is cheap and popular. For the older, better-heeled party goers, Yorkville has numerous places.

Woody's (467 Church St) is a very popular gay bar.

Those from Down Under may be interested to drop in at the *TRANZAC (Toronto Australia New Zealand Club; 292 Brunswick Ave)* where there is a bar open to all.

For a real gas, experimentalists will want to inhale the atmosphere of Canada's first oxygen bar. Modelled after the I-need-a-boost stations of Japan, the *Oxygen Spa Bar (2044 Yonge St)* hooks you up to a pure oxygen hose for 20 minutes for $16.

Cinema There are several repertory film houses around town. The *Bloor Cinema (☎ 416-532-6677, 506 Bloor St W)* is popu-

lar with the many students in the area. A wide variety of films is shown – US, European, old and new. Another venue is the *Revue (☎ 416-531-9959, 400 Roncesvalles Ave)* in the west end, which also features different films nearly every night.

Prices are a couple of dollars less than those at first-run theatres and are much lower for those with an inexpensive annual membership card.

Cinémathèque Ontario (☎ 416-968-3456) at the Art Gallery of Ontario also screens noncommercial films. IMAX movies can be seen at the *Ontario Place Cinesphere*.

The Festival Hall complex, on the corner of Richmond St W and John Sts has the latest in movie/IMAX/video arcade technology.

Also for first-run movies, the old *Eglinton (☎ 416-487-4721, 400 Eglinton Ave W)* north of downtown has a big screen and good sound. *Carlton Cinemas (☎ 416-598-2309, 20 Carlton St)* screens nonmainstream new releases.

Theatre There is plenty of first rate theatre in Toronto; only London and New York sell more tickets. Productions range from Broadway-type spectacles and musicals to Canadian contemporary dramas. Also big is dinner theatre.

Theatre costs vary widely. A dinner show costs $40 to $60 per person for a meal and show. The city's longest-running play is Agatha Christie's *The Mousetrap*, which has played at the *Toronto Truck Theatre (☎ 416-922-0084, 94 Belmont)* since 1976! A ticket is about $24. Many nonprofit theatres (eg Passe Muraille, Tarragon, Buddies in Bad Times) have one pay-what-you-can performance per week.

One of the more impressive theatres is the traditional *Royal Alexandra Theatre (☎ 416-872-1212, 264 King St W)*, which presents well established plays and performers. Next door is the lavish *Princess of Wales Theatre (☎ 416-872-1212)* with one of the largest stages in North America. It was built to accommodate the musical *Miss Saigon*.

Pantages (☎ 416-362-3218), with the long-running *Phantom of the Opera*, is a

classic 1920s central theatre worth visiting just for its gorgeous lobby. It's right downtown near the Eaton Centre. There are Saturday tours of the theatre for $4. The restored historic *Elgin and Wintergarden Theatre Centre (☎ 416-314-2901, 189 Yonge St)* is worth checking for its high profile productions. Tours are offered on Thursday and Saturday.

The Dream in High Park is a wonderful summer presentation in which a Shakespearean play is performed almost nightly through July and August with a donation requested ($5). The Canadian Stage's production and acting is top rate. For details, call its downtown theatre (☎ 416-367-8243). Shows begin at 8 pm, but go very early with a blanket and picnic or you'll be turned away.

Other Entertainment *Yuk Yuks (☎ 416-967-6425, 2335 Yonge St)* is a comedy club. The live acts are sometimes funny, sometimes gross, sometimes a joke. Admission ranges from $5 on some weekdays to $15 on weekend nights, when there are two of the two-hour shows. Dinner packages are also available. *Second City (☎ 416-343-0011, 56 Blue Jays Way)* has an excellent reputation for both its comedy shows and the people it develops.

The Toronto Symphony (☎ 416-593-4828) plays at *Roy Thompson Hall (60 Simcoe St)* not far from the CN Tower. A range of other, mainly classical concerts are presented here. In early autumn, the Canadian Opera Company performs at the *Hummingbird Centre (☎ 416-872-2267)* on Front St. The National Ballet of Canada has its own home at the *Walter Carsen Centre (☎ 416-345-9686, 470 Queen's Quay W)*.

The world renowned Tafelmusik orchestra performs baroque and classical music on period instruments in *Trinity-St Paul's United Church* at 427 Bloor St W.

The marvellous Recital Hall of the *Ford Centre for the Performing Arts (☎ 416-872-2222, 5040 Yonge St)* presents classical concerts by the world's top musicians and vocalists. The North York Centre subway station is nearby.

The city's oldest concert hall, *Massey Hall (☎ 416-872-4255, 178 Victoria St)* has excellent acoustics and is a wonderfully intimate and warm place to see a show, often folk or pop.

For dance, look into what's happening at Harbourfront's *Premiere Dance Theatre (207 Queen's Quay W)* in the Queen's Quay Terminal. The dance, symphony and opera seasons start in October or November and run through the winter.

Spectator Sports

The Toronto Blue Jays of Major League Baseball's American League play at the Skydome. The Jays won the World Series in 1992 and 1993 – the only times that baseball's top prize has been won by a non-US team.

Tickets can be bought by phone (☎ 416-341-1234) with a credit card, at the box office at gate 9 at the stadium or from a ticket outlet in the CIBC building on the corner of Bay and King Sts. Call ☎ 416-341-1111 for information, hours etc.

There are four price brackets. The cheap tickets are a mere $6 but are a long way away and are high above the field. Recommended are the $22 seats at the 500 level behind home plate. Try for somewhere between the 519 and 529 sections, through gates 7, 8 or 9. Those aged 14 and under are entitled to half-price tickets (except on the top-price seats) for Saturday games and all games with a 12.35 pm start.

Tickets are always available from scalpers at the stadium just prior to the game. After the game has started it is often possible to get tickets for less than face value.

Note that food and drink, especially beer, is expensive and that bottles or cans cannot be taken into the dome. Take a jacket as things cool off down here at night if the roof is open.

The Toronto Argonauts, of the professional Canadian Football League (CFL), also plays in the Skydome.

In winter, the National Hockey League Maple Leafs (☎ 416-977-1641) plays at the Air Canada Centre, on the corner of Bay St and Lake Shore Blvd (not far from

the Skydome). Tickets are hard to get at the box office, as every game is pretty well sold out, but they can be bought without difficulty from scalpers outside the door just before the game. Hockey tickets are costly, with the 'cheap' seats at $27.

The Toronto Raptors (☎ 416-366-3865) of the National Basketball Association also plays at the Air Canada Centre.

For horse racing, Woodbine Racetrack (☎ 416-675-7223) features thoroughbreds and standardbreds (harness racing) and is home to the prestigious Queen's Plate. It's north-west of downtown at 555 Rexdale Blvd. By public transport, take the subway to Islington and then catch the direct 'Race' bus. Admission is free and bets start at $2.

Shopping

You'll find an excellent range of camping gear and outdoor equipment in Toronto, most of it reasonably priced. Mountain Equipment Co-op at 400 King St W and Europe Bound across the street at 383 King St W are good for camping gear, tents, sleeping bags, packs, footwear and more. The latter rents tents and other gear.

Trailhead at 61 Front St E is another store with quality equipment.

For fine outdoor clothing, you should visit Tilley Endurables, a Canadian company which turns out some of the finest, toughest, low-maintenance threads imaginable. It's not cheap but it does last. There is a good outlet at the Queen's Quay terminal at Harbourfront but the main store is at 900 Don Mills Rd. Sam the Record Man at 347 Yonge St has a good selection of Canadian music from east coast traditional to rock.

Getting There & Away

Air The airport, Pearson International, is about 24km north-west of the downtown area in a part of the city known as Malton. This is actually a separate city, but you wouldn't know it from the continuous urban landscape. The major Canadian airlines fly in and out of Toronto, as do many of the internationals. Pearson is by far the busiest airport in the country.

The third terminal, known as Trillium Terminal, was the first in Canada to be developed, owned and operated by private interests rather than by the government. Distinguishing features include a Harrod's outlet. Food, drink and parking are costly, particularly at the Trillium Terminal.

When departing from the airport or picking someone up at arrivals, be sure to ask the terminal number. Signs on the roads into the airport direct you to each terminal and indicate which airlines they serve. Trillium is the main terminal for Canadian Airlines, American Airlines, British Airways, KLM, Lufthansa and Air France. Within the Trillium Terminal, Pier A handles domestic flights and Pier B handles international ones. Terminal 2 is home to Air Canada.

Some one-way fares on Air Canada (☎ 416-925-2311) are: Montreal $230, Halifax $380, and Calgary $620. Canadian Airlines (☎ 416-675-7587) has virtually the same prices, but they can both vary a lot.

Small Toronto City Centre Airport, on the lake at the foot of Bathurst St, is used by Air Canada commuter aircraft and private planes. The commuter flights are a lot quicker than the major flights because you're already downtown – and you get a better look at the city, too. There are flights to and from Montreal and Ottawa.

A shuttle bus, which is free for flight ticket-holders, runs from the Royal York Hotel down to the airport. The Union subway stop is across the street from the Royal York Hotel. Otherwise there is TTC service; take the streetcar south on Bathurst St to Lake Shore Blvd (generally known as Lake Shore Road or The Lakeshore). From there the airport is a two-block walk.

Depending on current conditions, it may be economical to skip over to Buffalo to take advantage of the periodically much cheaper US airfares. For example, a flight from Buffalo to Seattle could cost hundreds of dollars less than the fare from, say, Toronto to Vancouver. At either end, a short bus ride links the Canadian cities. In recent years, US fares have not warranted the expense of getting to Buffalo and the difference in the exchange rate.

Bus The coach terminal for out-of-town destinations is central on the corner of Bay and Dundas Sts, at the edge of Chinatown, one long block west of Yonge St. It's the station for the numerous bus lines which cover Ontario from Toronto. Students with international ID and seniors may get discounts.

For destinations in Eastern Ontario and north of Toronto call ☎ 416-393-7911. This number covers Voyageur, PMCL (Penetang-Midland Coach Lines), Canar, Ontario Northland and Trentway Wager bus companies. Collectively these lines serve Barrie, Huntsville, Montreal, Niagara Falls, North Bay, Orillia and Parry Sound as well as some US destinations, including New York.

Greyhound (☎ 416-367-8747) pretty much covers all of Ontario west of Toronto, including the Niagara region, Guelph, Kitchener, London, Windsor, Sudbury and beyond to western Canadian cities such as Winnipeg and Vancouver. It also operates the route to Peterborough and Ottawa and runs to Buffalo, Detroit and New York.

Smaller, local bus lines around Ontario connect to towns served by one or more of the above major carriers.

Some routes have slow, milk-run trips (which stop frequently) and other express, direct trips (which can be hours quicker). Ask about return tickets – some bus lines offer these at reduced rates.

There are five departures for Ottawa daily and the five hour trip costs $54 one way.

To Montreal, there are seven buses daily, one of them an overnighter, which leaves at 12.30 am. Tickets for Montreal cost $69.

To Niagara Falls, the two hour trip is $22 one way. A discounted same-day return ticket is offered too.

To Thunder Bay, buses depart at noon, 5 pm and 1 am ($138 one way, about 20 hours).

Lockers can be found on the lower level, and the upper floor has a restaurant. There's a bakery and café on the other side of Bay St. On the evening prior to a holiday or long weekend, expect crowds and arrive early to ensure getting a ticket before departure time.

Adjacent to the terminal, on the western side, is the bus station for (among other runs) the GO buses (☎ 416-869-3200), a government line which services many of the nearby surrounding towns, stopping frequently along the way. It's mainly used by commuters but goes a relatively long way (to Hamilton, for example) to the west of Toronto.

GO buses also go to the satellite communities of Barrie (to the north) and Oshawa (to the east), supplementing the regular bus service. Trips in these directions are not as frequent as the westbound ones and the downtown bus terminal is not used as the departure point. For Barrie, catch the GO bus at the Finch subway station during evening rush hour. For Oshawa, catch it at the York Mills subway, also during the end-of-day rush hour. In the morning the buses come into town.

Alternative Buses For information on budget/hostel bus routes and travel with people such as Canabus, Further Still and Moose Travel, see under Organised Tours earlier.

Train Grand old Union Station, for VIA Rail (☎ 416-366-8411) trains, is conveniently situated. It's on Front St (which runs east-west) at the south end of the city, at the bottom of University Ave, York and Bay Sts. The subway goes right into the station; the stop is called Union. Remember that five days notice drops the fares considerably. Students and seniors also get good discounts. The summer, high season rates are listed here.

There are frequent daily departures for Kingston, Montreal and Ottawa but fewer on weekends. One-way fares are Ottawa $89 tax included (four hours), and Montreal $99 (five hours). For Montreal, some trips are faster, with fewer stops than others.

To Sudbury, there are three trips weekly, departing on Tuesday, Thursday and Saturday ($82, 7½ hours). Note that for Sudbury, the train actually goes to Sudbury Junction, a station about 10km from the centre of town.

Other cities which can be reached by VIA include Niagara Falls and London.

Ontario Northland (☎ 416-314-3750) runs trains to northern Ontario destinations, including the *Polar Bear Express* to Moosonee.

Amtrak (☎ 1-800-872-7245) trains link Toronto with Buffalo, Chicago or New York City, with stops or other possible connections along the way. Amtrak offers good-value return fares. Reservations are needed for all trains.

The station has several restaurants, some fast-food outlets and a bar. Sometimes on the arrival level, just as you come out the gate from the train, a travellers aid booth is in operation to help with basic directions and to answer questions.

GO trains also use the station; see the upcoming Getting Around section.

Car If you're renting a car, be aware that many places require that you be at least 21 years old; for some places the minimum age is 23. There are countless rental agencies in the city but booking ahead, especially on holidays, is always recommended.

Wheels 4 Rent (☎ 416-585-7782) at 77 Nassau St, in Kensington Market off Spadina Ave, is central for used cars. If you have a credit card and are over 24, rates are excellent at $29 a day, including insurance, plus 9¢ per kilometre over the first 150km.

Also worth a call is No Frills (☎ 416-961-7500) at 374 Dupont St, between Spadina Ave and Bathurst St. Used cars cost from $20 a day (plus 12¢ per kilometre after the first 50km) for a compact vehicle. There are weekly and monthly rates, too. Insurance is extra, as it is at all places, and goes up as the driver's age decreases.

Tilden (☎ 416-364-4191, ☎ 1-800-227-7368), with an office in Union Station as well as several other downtown locations and one at the airport, is a more standard rental company and offers new cars. Its average rates start at $44 per day for the compacts with unlimited mileage. It offers weekend specials. Also available are child seats and ski racks.

Car Sharing & Drive-Aways Allo-Stop (☎ 416-975-9305), central at 398 Bloor St W, is a service based on a great idea – getting drivers and cars together with passengers. It mainly deals with trips to Montreal and Ottawa ($24), but other things come up

too, including rides to New York City and even to Florida. Give it a call a couple of days before you want to go and it may be able to line up a ride. Rates are very good.

For long-distance trips, there are driveaway cars – about half a dozen places are listed in the Yellow Pages (under Automobile). One company is Toronto Drive-Away Service (☎ 416-225-7754, www.toronto driveaway.com), with cars for Canadian and US destinations.

Also check the business personal columns in either the *Toronto Sun* or the *Star* and the travel ads in the weekly *Now* magazine entertainment tabloid. (See Drive-Aways in the introductory Getting Around chapter.)

Boat From the dock at 225 Queen's Quay E at Sherbourne St, the Hydrofoil Lake Jet Lines (☎ 416-214-4923, ☎ 1-800-313-3237) boats depart for a speedy, one hour boat trip to the Queenston Dock between Niagara Falls and Niagara-on-the-Lake. The $25 one-way fare includes a shuttle bus to either one. Call for schedule.

Hitching Thumbing is illegal on the expressways in the city. On city streets there's no problem but it's not commonly done, except by women offering their company for a price. You can hitch on Hwy 401 out of town or on the lead-in ramps in town.

If you're heading east for Montreal, the best bet is to take the city transit to roughly the corner of Port Union Rd and Hwy 401 in Scarborough, near the Toronto Zoo. To get there from downtown is a bit complicated and the fastest way takes about 1½ hours. Take the subway east to Kennedy stop. From there catch the Scarborough LRT (light rail transit) to the Lawrence East station. Transfer to the Lawrence East 54E bus. Go east to East Drive at Lawrence East. Transfer (free again) to the Rouge Hill No 13 bus to Hwy 401.

If you're going west, take the subway to Kipling. Transfer to the West Mall bus No 112 or 112B, and go to the corner of Carlingview Drive and International Blvd almost at Hwy 401. This is just at the city

limits, so you are okay on the highway, but it could be busy and difficult for cars to stop at rush hour. Public transit to this point takes about one hour from downtown.

If you're northbound, you're stuck. The best bet is to take the bus to Barrie and then hitch the rest of the way on Hwy 400 or Hwy 11, depending on your destination. The Trans Canada Hwy westbound can be picked up at Sudbury.

Getting Around

To/From the Airport There are several ways to get to the airport. The cheapest is to take the subway to Kipling on the east-west line. From there, take the Kipling or Martingrove bus (No 45 or 46) north up to Dixon Rd. With your transfer catch the Malton No 58A bus, which goes west to the airport. Reverse the same route to get downtown from the airport.

Alternatively, take the subway to the Lawrence West stop on the north-south Spadina-University line and from there catch the Malton No 58A bus.

The next method is easier, quicker and more costly. Between the airport and the Islington subway stop (one before Kipling) at the far western end of the Bloor Line there is a direct Airport Express (☎ 905-564-6333) bus. It leaves every 40 minutes or so, every day, takes half an hour and costs $7 one way. Another bus runs between the airport and the Yorkdale and York Mills subway stations. Each of these stops costs a bit more.

The Airport Express also operates buses every 20 minutes to and from the airport and major hotels, such as the Royal York and Sheraton as well as the bus and train stations and City Hall. The one-way fare is $12.50 and the trip takes about 80 minutes. These buses operate roughly between the hours of 5 am and 10.30 pm. The buses leave the airport terminals from outside the arrival levels.

Taxi fare from Yonge and Bloor Sts to the airport, about 45 minutes, is $40.

Toronto Transit Commission (TTC) The city has a good subway, bus and streetcar system (see the Toronto Subway map).

There's a 24 hour, recorded, route and fare information line on ☎ 416-393-8663, or for more specific information, call ☎ 416-393-4636. Regular adult fare is $2 cash, or 10 tickets (or tokens) for $17. Day passes are also available. Tickets or tokens (small dime-like coins) are available in the subway or at some convenience and corner variety stores. Once one fare is paid, you can transfer to any other bus, subway or streetcar within one hour at no extra charge. One ticket can get you anywhere the system goes. Get a transfer from the driver, or in the subway from the machine inside the turnstiles where you pay the fare.

The subway system is clean and fast. There is one east-west line, which goes along Bloor St/Danforth Ave, and two north-south lines, one up Yonge St and one along Spadina Ave, where some of the stops are decorated with the work of Canadian artists. The above-ground Scarborough RT train line connects the subway with the north-east part of the city, from the Victoria Park stop to the Scarborough Town Centre. The Harbourfront LRT (Light Rail Transit) car runs above and below ground from Union Station (on Front St) to Harbourfront, along Queens's Quay W to Spadina Ave and back again.

The subway runs until about 1.30 am and begins at 6 am (except on Sunday, when it starts at 9 am). Bus hours vary; some run late but are infrequent.

The Toronto system connects with bus routes in surrounding suburban cities such as Mississauga, Markham and Vaughan.

GO Train GO trains (☎ 416-869-3200) leave Union Station from 7 am to 11.30 pm daily, serving the suburbs of Toronto east to Whitby and west to Hamilton. Ticket inspection is random and on an honour system. Service is fast and steady through the day and frequent during weekday rush hours.

Streetcar Toronto is one of the few North American cities still using streetcars. They roll on St Clair Ave and on College, Dundas, Queen and King Sts, all of which run east-west and Spadina Ave, north-south.

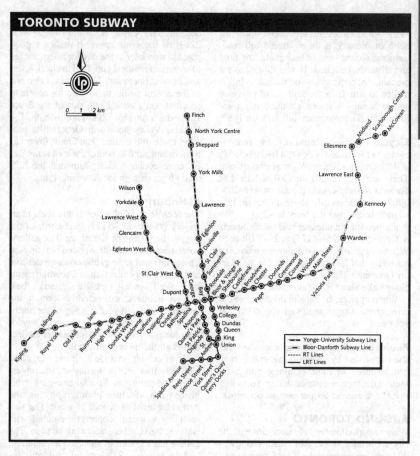

TORONTO SUBWAY

Finch
North York Centre
Sheppard
York Mills
Wilson
Yorkdale
Lawrence West
Glencairn
Eglinton West
Lawrence
Eglinton
Davisville
St Clair
Summerhill
Rosedale
Bloor & Yonge St
Castlefrank
Sherbourne
Broadview
St Clair West
Dupont
Chester
Donlands
Greenwood
Coxwell
Woodbine
Main Street
Victoria Park
Warden
Kennedy
Lawrence East
Ellesmere
Midland
Scarborough Centre
McCowan
Pape

St George
Bay
Spadina
Bathurst
Christie
Ossington
Dufferin
Lansdowne
Dundas West
Keele
High Park
Runnymede
Jane
Old Mill
Royal York
Idlington
Kipling

Museum
Queen's Park
St Patrick
Osgoode
St Andrew

Wellesley
College
Dundas
Queen
King
Union

Spadina Avenue
Rees Street
Simcoe Street
York Street
Queen's Quay
Ferry Docks

··· Yonge-University Subway Line
— Bloor-Danforth Subway Line
---- RT Lines
— LRT Lines

0 1 2 km

Car All over Ontario, you can turn right on a red light after first having made a full stop. All vehicles must stop for streetcars, behind the rear doors, while the streetcar is loading or unloading passengers. Pedestrians use the painted crosswalks across the street and traffic must stop for them. If you're driving, keep an eye out for these.

In Toronto, parking is expensive – usually about $2.50 to $3.50 for the first half-hour, then slightly less. Most places have a flat rate after 6 pm. Cheapest are the city of

Toronto municipal lots, which are scattered around the downtown area and marked by green signs.

Rush hours are impossible, so try and avoid them. And watch where you park during rush hours because the tow trucks show no mercy and getting your vehicle back will cost a bundle in cash and aggravation.

Traffic is generally horrendous around the edges of town and except for winter, construction never ends. Always budget extra time for delays.

ONTARIO

Hwy 407, running east-west from Markham to Mississauga for about 40km just north of the city, is an electronic toll road. Cameras record your licence plate, the time and distance travelled. If you don't have a prepaid electronic gizmo on the car, a bill is mailed to you. Bills are sent out of province and to some US states but there is no enforcement. The maximum bill for a car is $5.

Bicycle The most central place to rent bicycles is McBride Cycle (☎ 416-203-5651) at 180 Queen's Quay W, at Harbourfront. There are also rentals on Centre Island at Toronto Island Bicycle Rental (☎ 416-203-0009), on the south shore more or less straight back from the ferry landing.

Farther out but cheaper is Brown's Sports & Cycle (☎ 416-763-4176) at 2447 Bloor St W, near Jane St and on the subway route. It's not really that far from High Park or the Martin Goodman Trail for walkers and cyclists along Lake Shore Blvd (along the lakeshore).

When cycling, be careful on the streetcar rails; cross at right angles or you'll land on your ear.

Pedicab Pedicabs, deluxe bicycle rickshaws pedaled by sweating, fit young men can be hired in summer along Yonge St, around the theatre district, and in Yorkville. Prices are around $3 per person per block.

AROUND TORONTO

Within approximately 1½ hours' drive of the city are a large number of small, old towns that were once centres for local farming communities. Some of the country's best land is here, but working farms are giving way to urban sprawl and many of the old downtown areas are now surrounded by modern housing developments. Day trips around the district, especially on a Sunday, are popular. There is still some nice rolling landscape and a few conservation areas (essentially parks), used for walking or picnicking. Quite a few of the towns attract antique hunters, and craft and gift shops are plentiful.

North-west of Toronto, **Caledon** is one of the larger and closer examples and is set in

the Caledon Hills. Not far south-west of Caledon, in **Terra Cotta**, is an inn (☎ 905-873-2223) of the same name. It makes a good place to stop later in the day for afternoon tea of scones, cream and jam. Call to check hours and dates of operation. Terra Cotta is also one of the closest points to Toronto for access to an afternoon's walk along part of the **Bruce Trail**, which runs for 780km north-south. The **Hockley Valley** area near Orangeville provides more of the same. The **Credit River** has trout fishing, and in winter the area is not bad for cross-country skiing, although the hills aren't high enough for downhill skiing.

Kleinburg

The **McMichael Collection** is an excellent art gallery (☎ 905-893-1121), just north of the city, in the village of Kleinburg. The gallery, consisting of handmade wooden buildings in a pleasant rural setting, displays an extensive and impressive collection of Canadian paintings. Well represented are Canada's best known painters, collectively termed the Group of Seven. If you're going to see northern Ontario, where much of the group's work was done, a visit to the McMichael Collection is all the more worthwhile.

Other exhibits include Inuit and west coast Native Indian art. On display are sculptures, prints and paintings. Special changing exhibitions may feature photography or one particular artist or school of work. The surrounding wooded property is crossed with walking trails, where deer may be seen. The gallery has a book/gift shop and a restaurant.

Admission is $7, less for children, seniors and families. Schoolchildren often visit on weekday mornings. The gallery is open daily in summer, but is closed on Monday from mid-October to May. Opening hours are 10 am to 5 pm in the summer season, 10 am to 4 pm the rest of the year.

In Kleinburg itself, a rather pricey retreat from Toronto, there are numerous antique shops, small galleries, craft shops and places for a nosh.

Getting There & Away Kleinburg is 18km north from the corner of Islington

Ave and Hwy 401 in Toronto. To get there by car, go north up Hwy 427 to Hwy 27 and continue north. Turn right at Nashville Rd.

Public transportation is limited and a little awkward, but can be used. There is no service, though, on weekends or holidays. First, take the Toronto subway west to Islington on the east-west line. From there, catch bus No 37 north for around 35 minutes to Steeles Ave. At the intersection of Steeles and Islington Aves, transfer to the No 3 Vaughan bus. The only one of these of any use for those wishing to visit the gallery is at 8.45 am, so you must make this connection. The bus will take you to the gallery gate in about 20 minutes, from where it is a 10 minute walk in. On the way back, bus No 3 leaves at about 5 and 6 pm. To check details, call Vaughan Transit (☎ 905-832-2281).

Dunlap Observatory

Just north of the Toronto city limits, the Dunlap Observatory (☎ 905-884-2112) has what was once the world's second-largest telescope; it remains the biggest in Canada. From April to October, it's open to the public Saturday evenings at 9.30 pm. A brief introductory talk is given to accompany a slide show, which is then followed by a bit of stargazing through the scope.

The Magnificent Seven

The Group of Seven was a bunch of painters who came together in 1920 to celebrate the Canadian landscape in a new and vital way.

Fired by an almost adolescent enthusiasm, this all male group used its paint brushes to explore and capture on canvas the rugged wilderness of Canada. The energy they felt then can be seen today in some stunning paintings – vibrant, light-filled canvases of Canada's mountains, lakes, forests and townships.

This gung-ho group of painterly talent spent a lot of time traipsing the wilds of northern Ontario, capturing the landscape through the seasons and under all weather conditions. Favourite places included Algonquin Park, Georgian Bay, Lake Superior and Algoma. The Algoma Central Railway even converted an old boxcar into living quarters for the painters – a freight train would deposit them on a siding for a week or more and the intrepid painters would set off, on foot or by canoe, to paint from morning till night.

The original seven members (the group later expanded to become the Canadian Group of Painters) were Franklin Carmichael, Lawren Harris, AY Jackson, Frank Johnston (later replaced by AJ Casson), Arthur Lismer, JEH MacDonald and FH Varley. Although he died before the group was officially formed, the painter Tom Thompson was considered by other members as the group's leading light.

An experienced outdoorsman, Thompson drowned in 1917 just as he was producing some of his most powerful work. His deep connection to the land can be clearly seen in his vivid paintings. When the group took studios in Toronto (they sketched outside but produced finished work indoors), Thompson preferred working and living in his small rustic shack out the back. And as soon as the winter ice broke he'd be off to the great north.

The best places to see work by the Group of Seven are the McMichael Collection in the village of Kleinburg, north of Toronto, the Art Gallery of Ontario in Toronto, and the National Gallery of Canada in Ottawa.

Tom Thompson

The programs are free, but you must call ahead on a weekday for reservations. To reach the observatory, drive up Hwy 11 (the continuation of Yonge St) towards Richmond Hill; you'll see the white dome on the right. For public transportation, check with the TTC and its Vaughan Transit connections.

Cathedral of the Transfiguration

It seems nobody builds churches any more, especially on the grand old scale. But north of Toronto, straight up Hwy 404 from the city, at 10350 Woodbine Ave in the village of Gormley (near the town of Markham), there is one heck of an exception. Opened in 1987, this Slovak Byzantine Catholic cathedral (☎ 905-887-5706) is one of the country's largest, standing 62.7m high to the tip of its copper-topped spire. Based on a smaller version found in the Czech Republic, this is a 1000-seater church. One of the impressive features is the French-made main bell, ringing in at 16,650kg, second in size only to the one in Sacré Coeur in Paris. It's also the first cathedral in the western hemisphere to be blessed by a pope – John Paul II did the honours.

Pickering Nuclear Plant

About 40km east of Toronto on the Lake Ontario shoreline is this nuclear power station (☎ 905-839-1151), which has portions open to the public. Whether you're pro or con nuclear plants, you could find out something you didn't know. Free films, displays and a drive around the site explain the operation. It's open from 9 am to 4 pm Monday to Friday. Look for the signs on Hwy 401 – the plant is at the foot of Liverpool Rd. If your kids are born glowing in the dark, don't blame Lonely Planet.

Cullen Gardens & Miniature Village

About a 45 minute drive east from Toronto on Hwy 401, in the town of Whitby, is a 10-hectare site of carefully tended gardens which are interspersed with miniature models (☎ 905-668-6606). A path, which will take two or three hours to walk if you're looking at all the impressive detail, winds through the gardens past a village, modern suburban subdivision, farm and a scene from cottage country. The buildings, people and activities portrayed offer, in a sense, a glimpse of life in southern Ontario. The floral aspect of the gardens – although colourful and quite extensive – should not be confused with botanical gardens but, rather, should be viewed as the setting for the various scenes. The park appeals to a variety of people, particularly children.

The gardens are on Taunton Rd West, off Hwy 12 about 5km north along Hwy 401. They're open daily from the middle of April to the beginning of January. Admission is $10, less for children and seniors. When hunger strikes, there is a pleasant picnic and snack bar area (bring your own food) or a fairly pricey sit-down restaurant.

Canadian Automotive Museum

Farther east, near Oshawa (a centre for car assembly), this museum (☎ 905-576-1222) has a collection of 65 cars. Included are a Redpath Runabout from 1890, a Model T (of course) and various automotive memorabilia. It's at 99 Simcoe St S and is open daily all year. Admission is $5.

Parkwood Estate

Also in Oshawa, at 270 Simcoe St N, Parkwood (☎ 905-433-4311 from Toronto) is the estate of RS McLaughlin, who once ran the Canadian division of General Motors. The property consists of a 55-room mansion with antique furnishings, set amid large gardens. Admission is $6 and includes a guide. Afternoon tea is served outside during summer and in the conservatory during winter. Call for hours and days closed – they vary.

Local Conservation Areas

South-western Ontario is urban. To offset this somewhat, the government has designated many conservation areas – small nature parks for walking, picnicking and (sometimes) fishing, swimming and cross-country skiing. The quality and characteristics vary quite markedly. While some protect noteworthy geographic areas, others

are more historic in emphasis. Generally, they are not wild areas and some are not even pretty, but they are close to major centres and do offer some relief from concrete. The tourist office has a list of those around Toronto and within a 160km radius of town. The Metro Toronto Conservation Authority (☎ 416-661-6600) is responsible for their development and operation. Most areas are difficult to reach without a vehicle.

One place which makes a good, quick escape on a nice summer day is the large **Albion Hills Conservation Area**. It's primarily a quiet, wooded area with walking trails. In winter it allows for decent cross-country skiing. On the west side of town, take Indian Line (by the airport) north. It becomes Hwy 50, which then leads to the park.

Also in this region, near Kleinburg, is the **Kortright Centre for Conservation**. There are trails here, too, but it's more of a museum, with displays and demonstrations on resources, wildlife, ecology etc. It's open daily to 4 pm.

West of Toronto, near Milton, there are two conservation areas to consider visiting. **Crawford Lake** (☎ 905-854-0234) is one of the most interesting in the entire system. The deep, cool and pretty glacial lake set in the woods is surrounded by walking trails. Details on its formation and unique qualities are given in the well laid-out interpretive centre. Also on the site is a reconstructed 15th century Iroquoian long-house village.

Crawford Lake is open on weekends all year, and daily from May to October. It is 5km south of Hwy 401 down a road called Guelph Line. There is a snack bar and some picnic tables at the site. The Bruce Trail, described elsewhere (see Tobermory in the Georgian Bay & Lakelands section later in this chapter for details), also runs through the park.

In about the same general area is the **Mountsberg Conservation Area** (☎ 905-854-2276). To reach it, exit south off Hwy 401 at Guelph Line and continue to the No 9 Sideroad. Travel west to Town Line and turn north for 3.2km. It's 19km west of the town of Milton. The centre provides a series of

country-related educational programs throughout the year. One of the best is the maple syrup/sugaring-off demonstration put on each spring; it explains in detail the history, collection and production of this Canadian speciality (for more information about maple syrup see Lanaudière in the Quebec chapter).

South-Western Ontario

This designation covers everything south and west of Toronto to Lake Huron and Lake Erie, which border the USA. For the most part, the area is flat farmland – the only area in Ontario with little forest – and population density is high. With the warm climate and long growing season, this southern tip of Canada was settled early.

Arching around Lake Ontario is a continuous strip of urbanization. This 'Golden Horseshoe' helps make the region one of the most industrialised and wealthy in the country.

Hamilton, the largest city in the area, is a major steel town. Niagara, with its famous falls, is an important fruit-growing and wine-producing district.

Farther west, the soil becomes sandier and the main crop is tobacco, although this is changing as the Canadian cigarette market shrinks. Around Kitchener and London, the small towns are centres for the mixed farming of the region. Lake Erie and, especially, Lake Huron have sandy beaches. In some of the older country towns, crafts and antiques are available.

Windsor – like Detroit, Michigan, its counterpart across the river – is a centre for auto manufacturing.

Because the area is heavily populated and the USA is close by, attractions and parks do get busy in summer. In general, this is an area for people-related activities and pastimes, not for nature or rugged landscapes.

HAMILTON

Hamilton, sometimes referred to as Steeltown, is a heavily industrialised city of

about 319,000 residents. As the centre of Canada's iron and steel industry, with two major companies, Stelco and Dofasco, based here, it has a reputation for pollution.

Action has been taken to clean it up and work in this direction continues. Although the air cannot be compared to that of the far north (what can?), these days some of what one sees billowing from the many smoke-stacks is actually steam.

While Hamilton is obviously not a tourist mecca, there are nonetheless a few good things to see in and around town. As accommodation is modest, it's worth considering spending the night if you're planning a look around Niagara-on-the-Lake, which has high prices. Hamilton is halfway between Toronto and Niagara Falls.

Orientation

King St (one-way going west) and Main St (one-way going east, parallel to and one block south of King St) are the two main streets. King St has most of the downtown shops and restaurants. King and John Sts are the core of the downtown area. Jackson Square, on King St between Bay and James Sts, is a large, shopping complex that includes restaurants, cinemas and even an indoor skating rink. James St, at Jackson Square Park with its fountain, divides the east and west street designations. The Convention Centre (with an art gallery) is on the corner of King and McNab Sts. Just south across Main St is City Hall.

Information

The downtown central tourist office (☎ 905-546-2666, ☎ 1-800-263-8590) is at 127 King St E and operates seven days a week during summer. Other summer-only information booths are in busy visitors centres around the city, such as the Royal Botanical Gardens or the African Lion Safari.

Royal Botanical Gardens

The Royal Botanical Gardens – nearly 1000 hectares of flowers, natural park and wildlife sanctuary – is the big attraction in the area. It is one of the largest of its kind in the country

and only one of five in the world to be designated 'Royal'. The grounds are split into sections, with trails connecting some areas.

During spring, the Rock Garden is a highlight with its three hectares of rare trees and shrubs, waterfalls, ponds and 125,000 spring-flowering bulbs. From June to October thousands of roses, including many antique varieties, bloom in the Centennial Rose Garden. The arboretum boasts the world's largest lilac collection (what an olfactory treat), which is best in May.

The sanctuary takes up nearly half of the grounds and consists of trails winding through marsh and wooded ravines – a paradise for birdwatchers and home to deer, fox, muskrat and coyotes. There is also an interpretive centre and two restaurants at the gardens.

The site is between Hamilton and the suburban community of Burlington, on Plains Rd near the junction of Hwys 2 and 6. It's open daily all year but the outdoor areas have little to show from October to May and the price drops considerably. The regular admission is $7.

Art Gallery of Hamilton

The art gallery (☎ 905-527-6610), the province's third largest, is spacious and has a good selection of Canadian and international paintings. It also runs an interesting film series, with screenings mainly on weekends.

The gallery at 123 King St W is open Wednesday to Saturday from 10 am to 5 pm (until 9 pm on Thursday) and on Sunday from 1 to 5 pm.

Hamilton Place

In the same complex as the art gallery, this theatre-auditorium for the performing arts (☎ 905-546-3100) features shows of various types almost nightly, including regular performances by the Philharmonic and the Opera Company. Tours are available.

Dundurn Castle

One man's castle, Dundurn (☎ 905-546-2872) is actually a 36-room mansion once belonging to Sir Allan Napier McNab,

prime minister from 1854 to 1856 of what was then the United Provinces of Canada. It's furnished in mid-19th century style. The mansion is on York Blvd just out of town, about a 15 minute walk (or you can grab the York city bus). It's open daily all year, in the afternoon only from June to September. Admission is $6.

Concerts are held on the grounds through the summer. Also at the site is a military museum, with weapons and uniforms dating from the War of 1812.

Whitehern

At 41 Jackson St W (beside City Hall), this elegant mansion (☎ 905-546-2018), lived in by the prominent McQuesten family from 1852 to 1968, contains original furnishings and art works. It offers a peek into both the Victorian era and the life of the well-to-do. Also see the back garden. Admission is $3.50 and it's open afternoons only.

Football Hall of Fame & Museum

Canadian football is commemorated and promoted here through equipment, photos, trophies and the Grey Cup, football's top prize. The museum is at 58 Jackson St W; it's open all year, but closed Sunday and Monday. Call ☎ 905-528-7566 for more info.

Canadian Warplane Heritage Museum

The spacious museum (☎ 905-679-4183) is at 9280 Airport Rd just east of the airport. Its impressive collection contains about 25 vintage planes, including a restored Lancaster bomber from WWII. All are in flying condition. It's open daily and there's a cafeteria and gift shop. Adult admission is $9.

Many of the planes, together with newer ones from a variety of sources, are part of an excellent two-day air show held in mid-June. Flights are available in some of the vintage aircraft.

Museum of Steam & Technology

The old pumphouse (☎ 905-546-4797), dating from 1860, was built to supply clean water when cholera and typhus menaced

the city. These restored steam engines are among the largest in North America. Trimmed with mahogany and brass, they are rather attractive as objects. Also featured are photographs and engine exhibits. Admission costs $3 and the museum, at 900 Woodward Ave, is closed Monday all year and is open in the afternoon only from October to May.

Confederation Park

Not too far north of town on Centennial Parkway, this park contains Wild Waterworks, featuring a waterslide and a swimming pool with waves. There is also a beach along Lake Ontario, and picnic and camping facilities.

African Lion Safari

About 1000 animals and birds roam this vast, cageless park (☎ 905-623-2620, ☎ 1-800-461-9453). You drive through, sometimes getting very close to lions, tigers and other animals. Monkeys and others climb and grope all over the car, and for this reason those with particular pride in their vehicle are advised to use the park tour bus instead.

The park is not cheap ($17 for adults, $11 to $14 for children), but the whole thing can take a full afternoon and most people feel it's worth the money, especially if you have children with you. Try to make time for the live demonstrations such as the one on birds of prey.

African Lion Safari is open from April to October but weekends only in the shoulder seasons. The longest hours are in July and August, but even at that time of year it closes at 5.30 pm. The park is between Hamilton and Cambridge, on Hwy 8. For the daring, there is a campground at the site.

Lake Ontario Waterfront Trail

This recreational trail follows the shoreline of Lake Ontario for 350km from Trenton to Hamilton. It's good for walking, cycling and roller-blading and in summer there are dozens of organised outdoor activities and festivals along its length. Ask at the tourist office for a map and calendar of events or contact

www.waterfronttrust.com. It also connects to the Niagara River Recreational Trail.

Special Events

The Festival of Friends takes place each August in Gage Park and features music, crafts and foods from many countries.

Each June, in the town of Stoney Creek (south of Hamilton), an interesting spectacle is the re-enactment of a War of 1812 battle between British and USA soldiers. It's held at Stoney Creek Battlefield Park.

Places to Stay

Camping There are numerous local campgrounds, including one in Confederation Park (☎ 905-578-1644), just north of town on Centennial Parkway.

Hostels For low-budget lodgings, the *YMCA (☎ 905-529-7102, 79 James St)* has 172 rooms, for men only, at $28 a single. The *YWCA (☎ 905-522-9922, 75 McNab St)* is comparable, although much smaller, also with single rooms only at $27 including tax. Both have pools and inexpensive cafeterias.

B&Bs Central *Inchbury Street Bed & Breakfast (☎ 905-522-3520, 87 Inchbury St)* is next door to Dundurn Castle and a 15 minute walk from the Botanical Gardens. There are two rooms with shared bathroom at $50/60.

Haddo House (☎ 905-524-0071, 107 Aberdeen Ave), 1km from downtown, is a late 19th/early 20th century home offering two rooms complete with private bathroom. Singles/doubles are $80/85 and include a full breakfast. It's for adults only.

Hotels The *Budget Motor Inn (☎ 905-527-2708, 737 King St E)* has singles/doubles at $50. Also central is the *Visitors Inn (☎ 905-529-6979, 649 Main St W)* at $73/82 for singles/doubles.

Farther out, close to McMaster University, the *Mountainview Motel (☎ 905-528-7521, 1870 Main St W)* costs $45 for singles/doubles. More motels can be found on the outskirts east or west of town.

Places to Eat

In the downtown area King, John and James Sts offer numerous restaurants. The Jackson Square shopping mall includes many low-priced places to eat.

The casual, California-influenced *Fandango's Grill (146 James St S)* has meals under $15.

King St E has a few ethnic eateries as well as a café or two among its bars and skin-piercing parlours. *Taste of Bombay (234 King St E)* has a lunch buffet for $8.

A more pleasant area is Hess Village, two blocks west of the Convention Centre. The *Gown & Gavel (24 Hess St N)* is a British-style pub which serves light meals and beer under the umbrellas.

The *Lazy Flamingo (19 Hess St N)* has a casual atmosphere and a nice patio. The menu includes cheap pitas and some Mexican and vegetarian dishes.

Getting There & Away

The bus station (☎ 905-529-0196) is in the GO Centre, on the corner of James and Hunter Sts about three blocks south of the centre of town. Buses run to Toronto, Niagara Falls and Brantford.

Also here is the station for the GO commuter trains which run to Toronto and points in between.

Spectator Sports

The Hamilton Tiger Cats (☎ 905-527-1508) plays CFL football at the Ivor Wynn Stadium.

ST CATHARINES/WELLAND CANAL

Between Hamilton and the Niagara River, St Catharines is the major town of the Niagara fruit and wine-producing district.

In late September, the Niagara Grape & Wine Festival is held, with concerts, wine-and-cheese parties and a parade. In addition, activities are planned throughout the region.

The most noteworthy feature of the area is the historic Welland Canal, a bypass of Niagara Falls which connects Lake Ontario with Lake Erie. A series of locks along the 42km-long canal overcomes the

difference of about 100m in the lakes' water levels.

The canal was initiated in 1829 by local businessmen to promote trade and commerce. Now in its fourth incarnation and part of the St Lawrence Seaway, it is a vital link in international freight service, allowing shipping into the industrial heart of North America from the Atlantic Ocean.

The three principal cargoes that go through the canal are wheat, iron ore and coal. The average trip through the canal and its eight locks takes 12 hours.

Remnants of the first three canals (built in 1829, 1845 and 1887) can be seen at various points. The fourth version, still in use but with some modifications and additions, was built between 1914 and 1932.

At Lakeside Park, along the waterfront in **Port Dalhousie** (pronounced 'dal-oo-zey'), the early canals opened into Lake Ontario.

This old harbour area is now a blend of the new and historic, with a reconstructed wooden lock, the oldest and smallest jail in the province and a lighthouse set alongside contemporary bars and restaurants. For hikers, there is the Merritt Trail, a walk which stretches from Port Dalhousie in St Catharines to Port Colbourne, mainly following the Welland Canal. It is detailed in the Bruce Trail guidebook; see Tobermory later in this chapter. Local tourist offices will also have information.

At **Mountain View Park**, on the corner of Mountain and Bradley Sts, there are locks at the escarpment from the second canal, along with some other 19th century buildings.

For a more up-to-date look, visit the **Welland Canals Centre** (☎ 905-984-8880) at 1932 Government Rd also in St Catharines. It's at lock three of the currently used canal, and includes a museum with exhibits on the

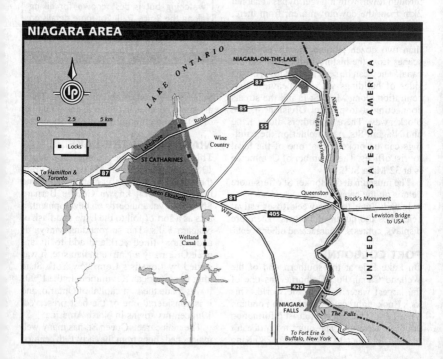

NIAGARA AREA

canal and its construction, a viewing platform and audiovisual displays on many aspects of the waterway. Ships from around the world may be seen on their way to and from the centre of North America and the Atlantic Ocean. Fifty million tonnes of cargo are transported through the canal annually. Open daily all year, the centre is off Glendale Ave (which exits from the Queen Elizabeth Hwy). Follow the signs to the locks. You can get a bite to eat and something to drink while you watch the ships. A daily shipping schedule is posted. There is also a lacrosse museum with details on Canada's oldest sport.

The last lock, number eight, is at Port Colborne (on Lake Erie).

WELLAND

Despite the predominance of agriculture in the region, Welland is primarily a steel town. A portion of the canal cuts right through town, with a larger bypass channel 2km from the downtown area; from there, international freighters can be viewed.

The city has become known for its more than two dozen painted murals depicting scenes from the history of the area and the canal. They can be seen around town on the sides of buildings with the heaviest concentration along Main St E and the streets connecting it to parallel Division St, one block away. There are others along King and Niagara Sts. A pamphlet on the paintings can be picked up at one of the local tourist offices. The Chamber of Commerce is at 32 Main St E.

The museum at 65 Hooker St offers more details on the canals.

In early June, the two-week Rose Festival celebrates the queen of flowers. There are displays, contests, a parade and other events.

PORT COLBORNE

On Lake Erie at the southern end of the Welland Canal, Port Colborne has one of the largest water locks in the world. This lock (lock eight) can be seen from Fountain View Park. The summer tourist information booth is here, too. The quiet town doesn't really offer much to see or do. At 280 King

---

The Niagara Escarpment

An escarpment is a steep rock face, or cliff of great length. The Niagara Escarpment, often referred to in southern Ontario, runs for 725km, with a maximum height of 335m. Once the shore of an ancient sea centred on what is now Michigan, USA, the escarpment begins in Ontario at the town of Queenston on the Niagara River. On its way north to Tobermory and Manitoulin Island it passes through or beside Hamilton, Collingwood and Owen Sound. A major outcropping of the escarpment can clearly be seen from Hwy 401 west of Oakville, at the Kelso Conservation Area.

The Niagara Escarpment Commission, through a series of parks and conservation areas, seeks to preserve the escarpment's natural beauty, flora and fauna. Now largely a recreation area, the escarpment is used for activities such as skiing and bird-watching but is best known for hiking along the Bruce Trail. For more details on the trail, see Tobermory under Georgian Bay & Lakelands in this chapter.

St is a small pioneer heritage village. There are some beaches in the area, and a number of cottage communities along the shoreline.

NIAGARA-ON-THE-LAKE

This small, attractive village (population 13,000) is about 20km downstream from the falls, and with its upmarket shops and restaurants, well known George Bernard Shaw Festival and curbs on development, it acts as a sort of foil to the hype and flash of Niagara Falls. The surrounding vineyards and history-filled parkland add to its appeal. Originally a Native Indian site, it was settled by Loyalists from New York State after the American Revolution. In the 1790s it was made the first capital of Ontario, and it is considered one of the best preserved, 19th century towns in North America.

The main street, Queen St, has many well maintained shops from the early 19th century.

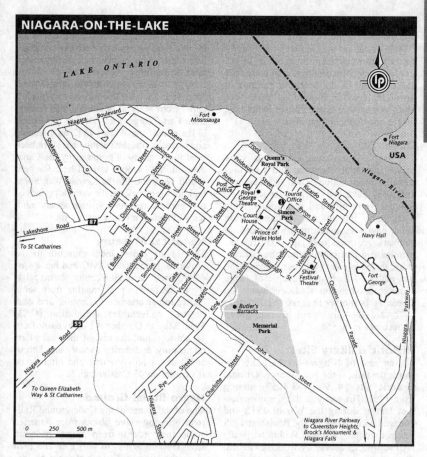

NIAGARA-ON-THE-LAKE

LAKE ONTARIO

Niagara Boulevard

Fort Mississauga

Shakespeare Avenue

Nassau

Queen Street

Johnson Street

Gage Street

Dorchester Street

Centre Street

William Street

Mary Street

Butler Street

Mississauga Street

Simcoe Street

Gate Street

Victoria Street

Regent Street

King Street

Prideaux Street

Post Office

Royal George Theatre

Court House

Queen's Royal Park

Front Street

Ricardo Street

Byron Street

Tourist Office

Simcoe Park

Picton St

Prince of Wales Hotel

Nelles St

Castlereagh St

Wellington St

Shaw Festival Theatre

Butler's Barracks

Memorial Park

Rye Street

Charlotte Street

Niagara Street

John Street

Fort Niagara

USA

Niagara River

Navy Hall

Fort George

Queens Parade

Niagara River Parkway

Lakeshore Road
To St Catharines

Niagara Stone Road
To Queen Elizabeth Way & St Catharines

Niagara River Parkway to Queenston Heights, Brock's Monument & Niagara Falls

0 250 500 m

87

55

The lakeside location, tree-lined streets and old houses make Niagara-on-the-Lake a nice place to see before or after the falls. The village does get very busy on good summer days, though generally only on the main street. Stroll down the side streets and you'll get a quiet taste of former times in a small, prosperous Ontario town.

Information

The tourist office (☎ 905-468-4263, www .niagara-on-the-lake.com) in the Chamber of Commerce, on the corner of King St and Prideaux/Byron Sts, is good, friendly and helpful and will book accommodation for you. From March to December the office is open every day; later in the year, the hours are shortened and it's closed on Sunday. On the eastern side of the downtown area towards Niagara Falls, King St crosses Queen St at large Simcoe Park, on the east side of Queen St.

Ask for the *Historic Guide*, a free pamphlet outlining in brief the town's history and a self-guided walking tour. It lists many

of the noteworthy structures around town and indicates them on a map.

Also ask about the Garden Tour (usually on the third weekend in June) put on by the Conservancy, which allows visitors a peek around some of the splendid gardens in town. In October, the annual B&B tour gives you another chance to see behind the fences and doors around town.

Queen St

The town's main street, Queen St, is the prime attraction. Restored and well preserved wooden buildings and shops contain antiques, bakeries, various specialities, Scottish souvenirs and restaurants. Note particularly the apothecary dating from 1866, now a museum, fitted with great old cabinets, remedies and jars. Also recommended is a jam sample from the Greaves store; the people here are fourth-generation jam-makers. There are a couple of fudge shops, too. The renovated courthouse, on Queen St, is another impressive building.

Towards the falls but still in town, Queen St becomes Picton St.

Historic Military Sites

To the east of Niagara-on-the-Lake, towards the falls, is the **Fort George National Historic Site** (☎ 905-468-4257), dating from 1797. The fort was the site of important battles during the War of 1812 and changed hands between the British and US forces a couple of times. Within the walls are the officers' quarters, a working kitchen, the powder magazine and storage houses. There isn't a lot to see, but the various costumed workers, particularly the soldiers performing different exercises, provide some atmosphere. Admission is $6 for adults (free after 4.15 pm). It's open daily to 5 pm from 1 April to 31 October.

Tucked behind the fort is **Navy Hall**, at the water's edge. Only one building remains of what was a sizable supply depot for British forts on the Great Lakes during the 18th century. It was destroyed during the War of 1812. The US Fort Niagara is across the river.

In a fine location on the west side of town at the opposite end of Ricardo/Front St are the minimal remains of **Fort Mississauga**. There are some plaques but no organised tours or facilities.

Also in town are **Butler's Barracks**, off John St at King St. Pedestrians can reach it either from Mary St or along a trail leading from Fort George. First used by the British at the end of the War of 1812 as a storage and barracks site, the location has since been used for a variety of purposes by the Canadian military. Troops trained here for both World Wars and for the Korean War. Some buildings remain from the various periods of use, and markers lead visitors around on a mini-Canadian military history tour.

Historical Museum

This is the oldest local museum in the province. It opened in 1907 and has a vast collection of early 20th century items relating to the town's past, ranging from some Native Indian artefacts to Loyalist and War-of-1812 collectables. Admission is $3. From May to October it's open daily from 10 am to 6 pm, the rest of the year afternoons only, and during January and February it opens only on weekend afternoons. It's central at 43 Castlereagh St.

Negro Burial Ground

One of the routes of the Underground Railroad bringing slave blacks from America across the border to freedom in Canada ran from Buffalo across to Fort Erie and then along the Niagara River to Niagara-on-the-Lake and St Catharines. At 494 Mississauga St is a plaque on the site of what was a Baptist Church and burial ground.

Whirlpool Jet

The only Niagara Falls-like attraction in town, the Whirlpool Jet (☎ 905-468-4800) is a boat which takes passengers on an hour-long trip through the rapids of the lower Niagara River. Reservations are required. Trips depart from 61 Melville St and passengers are advised to take a change of clothing. Tickets cost – brace yourself – $49.

Organised Tours

Short $5 walking tours of town leave from opposite the tourist office every hour from 11 am to 5 pm on Saturday and Sunday.

Niagara Bicycle Tours (☎ 905-468-1300) offers two daily tours of the area ($37) which take in wine tastings and visits to three of the major local wineries. It also

---

A Shaw Thing

The only festival in the world exclusively devoted to producing the plays of George Bernard Shaw and his contemporaries takes place in Niagara-on-the-Lake every year from April to October.

An internationally respected theatre festival, the Shaw Festival was founded in 1962 by a group of local residents led by Brian Doherty, a lawyer and dramatist who had a passion for theatre. The very first season consisted of eight performances of Shaw's *Candida* and *Don Juan in Hell* from *Man and Superman*.

Doherty chose Shaw because he was 'a great prophet of the 20th century', and because Shaw 'was the only outstanding playwright writing in English, with the obvious exception of Shakespeare, who produced a sufficient number of plays to support a festival'.

As well as producing Shaw's work, the festival aims to give space to a variety of plays not widely performed nowadays. These include Victorian drama, plays of continental Europe, classic US drama, musicals, and mystery and suspense plays.

The festival academy was established in 1985 primarily as a vehicle for the exchange of skills among the festival's ensemble of actors. Since then it has expanded to include various educational programs: there are specialised seminars held through the season and, on selected Saturdays, informal Lunchtime Conversations where the public can join in discussions with members of the Shaw Festival company.

Ten plays are performed every season in three theatres around town – the Court House Theatre, the Festival Theatre and the Royal George Theatre, a one-time vaudeville house and cinema. All three theatres are within walking distance of the town centre.

Tickets range from $22 up to $65 for the best seats in the house on Saturday night at the Festival Theatre. Cheaper rush seats go on sale at 9 am on the day of performance but are not available for Saturday shows. Students and seniors can get good reductions on some matinées, and weekday matinées are the cheapest. There are also brief lunchtime plays for $15.

The box office (☎ 905-468-2172) is open from 9 am to 8 pm every day from mid-April to mid-January. If you're planning to see a play call ☎ 1-800-511-7429 from anywhere in Canada or the USA, well in advance, and ask for the Shaw Festival guide. It will give you all the details, the year's performances and other useful information, as well as ticket order forms.

To hear the latest word on the festival, and on George Bernard Shaw and his plays 'about the beginning of the modern world', go to www.shawfest.com.

George Bernard Shaw

does a trip along the Niagara Escarpment and offers accommodation packages for one or two-day bicycle tours.

From the Navy Hall Dock at Fort George wood-fired steamship cruises depart hourly in summer. Adult fares for the river cruises cost $15.

Places to Stay

Accommodation is expensive and often booked out to boot. For many people, a few hours spent browsing around town will suffice before finding cheaper lodging elsewhere. When the Shaw Festival is on, lodging is even tighter so plan accordingly.

The town has some fine inns and several good hotels. By far the majority of the accommodation, though, is in the many cheaper B&Bs. This does not mean cheap, however, with rates averaging about $80 and rising a lot for a double. The tourist office has a free accommodation reservation service. Those listed here are central and reasonably priced.

The *Bunny Hutch* (☎ 905-468-3377, 305 Centre St) has rooms with shared bath at just $55/60 and that's with a full breakfast.

Henry & Irene's Guest House (☎ 905-468-3192, 285 William St), with rooms sharing the bath at $60 to $70 and a good breakfast, is also a bargain. Similarly priced is *Rose Cottage* (☎ 905-468-7572, 308 Victoria St), also in the downtown area. There's just one room and it comes with a private bath.

Also with reasonable rates is *Amberlea Guest House* (☎ 905-468-3749, 285 John St). There are two double rooms, both with private bathroom, at $85, and one twin with shared bathroom at $65. A single is $50. All include a full breakfast.

Carol's Saltbox (☎ 905-468-5423, 223 Gate St) is central with doubles at $80 including a full breakfast.

Among the pricier options (from $110) is the *Angel Inn* (☎ 905-468-3411), dating from 1823, one block south from Queen St on Regent St. The slightly older *Kiely House Inn* (☎ 905-468-4588, 209 Queen St) is a 13-room B&B. *Moffat Inn* (☎ 905-468-4116,

60 Picton St) is an attractive white-and-green place which offers all the amenities starting from $100.

Places to Eat

The *Stagecoach* (45 Queen St) is cheap, nontouristy and always busy. You can get a good-value breakfast before 11 am.

The *Epicurean* (84 Queen St) is a stylish cafeteria with very tasty food. Meals are $10 or less with a couple of vegetarian choices each day. There's also a small garden patio down the lane.

For a pub meal try the *Buttery* (19 Queen St), with a pleasant patio. Lunch starts at around $9. On Friday and Saturday nights, a Henry VIII-style feast is put on with entertainment, drink and victuals aplenty.

Fans Court, around the back at 135 Queen St, provides some fine ethnic diversion in this most Anglo of towns. It serves Chinese and Asian dishes, such as Singapore noodles with curry. Apart from the pleasant dining room, there are also a few tables outside in a small courtyard. Prices are moderate at lunch ($8), but the dinner menu rises to about $15 for main dishes.

The *Prince of Wales Hotel* (6 Picton St) has a good dining room for finer, more costly eating. Most of the other inns and hotels also have their own dining rooms. At the *Kiely House Inn* (209 Queen St) you can enjoy afternoon cream teas on the porch overlooking the golf course.

A few blocks from Queen St, Queen's Royal Park makes a good place for a picnic along the water.

Entertainment

In Simcoe Park, right in town, there are often free classical music concerts on Saturday during summer.

Getting There & Away

Bus There are no direct buses between Toronto and Niagara-on-the-Lake. From Toronto you must go to St Catherines or Niagara Falls (both daily) and then transfer.

Charterways Bus Lines runs between the St Catharines bus terminal and Niagara-on-

the-Lake twice each day three times a week. Here, the buses stop at Fort George.

From May through September a shuttle bus (☎ 1-800-667-0256) runs three times daily between Niagara-on-the-Lake and Niagara Falls for $10 or $15 return. From the middle of June to September it stops at the Fort George parking lot, which is walkable, or there's a free mini-bus which goes from there to the tourist office. There's one shuttle a day during winter. Check the times at the tourist office.

See Queenston under Niagara Parkway & Recreational Trail later for information on the high-speed hydrofoil from Toronto with a shuttle into Niagara-on-the-Lake.

Taxi Taxis to Niagara Falls charge $25 to $30.

Getting Around
Bicycle Cycling is a fine way to explore the area, and bicycles can be rented by the hour, half day or full day at 92A Picton St (☎ 905-468-0044), past the Moffat Inn. You can also hire rollerblades.

AROUND NIAGARA-ON-THE-LAKE
Vineyards & Wine Tours
The triangle between Beamsville, Niagara-on-the-Lake and Niagara Falls is Canada's most important wine-producing area. The moderate microclimate created by the escarpment and Lake Ontario is a big part of the area's success.

The ever-increasing number of wineries – there are now over two dozen – are producing some pretty fine wine. The better wines have a Vintner's Quality Alliance (VQA) designation.

Since the 1980s, wine producers have grown from operating an essentially small cottage industry to being internationally recognised vintners capable of turning out calibre vintages. Many offer visitors a look around and a taste. A full day can be enjoyed touring the countryside and emptying glasses. Three of the principal wines are riesling, chardonnay and gewurztraminer. Whites tend to dominate but reds are also produced. The

expensive icewines (sweet and fruity) have gained a lot of favourable attention. Many of the wineries are open year-round. Some of the commercial tour operators include a winery or two on their bus excursions; most of these operate out of Niagara Falls.

Area tourist offices have lists of the wineries and their locations. The Niagara Grape & Wine Festival takes place each September.

The following are among the best established:

The Reif Estate Winery
(☎ 905-468-7738) Located south of Niagara-on-the-Lake, between Line 2 and Line 3 on the Niagara Parkway. The winery, with tastings, is open every day of the year, as is the shop. Call for tour times.

Inniskillin Wine
(☎ 905-468-3554) Practically next door to Reif Estate, at Line 3. Open year-round, Inniskillin has developed a good reputation and is the leading award winner of the region. A display outlines the production process and history of wine-making in Niagara.

Hillebrand Estates Winery
(☎ 905-468-1723) On Hwy 55, south-west of town, Hillebrand Estates is a another with quality wines, tastings and tours.

Others worth considering are Konzelmann, Marynissen, Pillitteri and Stonechurch.

NIAGARA PARKWAY & RECREATIONAL TRAIL
A slow, 20km trip along the two-lane **Niagara Parkway** to Niagara Falls is most enjoyable. Along the way are parks, picnic areas, good views over the river and a couple of campgrounds, all of which make up part of the Niagara Parks Commission park system. It runs pretty well the entire length of the Niagara River, for 56km, from Niagara-on-the-Lake past the falls to Fort Erie. A 3m-wide paved recreational trail for cycling, jogging, walking or roller-skating runs the entire way, paralleling the parkway. It's excellent for either a short or long cycling excursion. The terrain is flat and the riverside scenery pleasant, and it's rarely very busy.

The trail can be easily divided into four sections, each of which would take around

one to two hours of leisurely pedalling. Historic and natural points of interest are marked with plaques. Perhaps best of all, in season, are the fresh-fruit stands with cold cherry ciders and juices. Ask at the tourist office for the Parks Commission's excellent Recreation Trail Map.

In the small village of Queenston, just before the Lewiston Bridge to the USA, is the **Laura Secord Homestead**. Laura, one of Canada's best known heroines (partly because of the chocolate company which bears her name), lived here, on the corner of Queenston and Partition Sts, during the War of 1812. At one point during the war, she hiked nearly 30km to warn the British soldiers of impending attack by the USA. The house can be visited for a small fee, which includes a chocolate sample. There's also a small candy shop on the premises. The rose garden out front is said to have been planted by Laura herself.

At the juncture of the Niagara Parkway and Queenston St (the main street in Queenston), by the War Memorial, is the **Samuel Weir Collection & Library of Art**. Weir had the house built as a live-in gallery and library in 1916 to house his remarkably extensive art, book and antique collection. He formed a foundation to administer the estate for public access, provided that he was buried on the front lawn (which, in due time, he was). It's free and open from May to October, from Wednesday to Saturday and Sunday afternoons.

In Mackenzie House, also in town, the **Mackenzie House Printery** has a collection highlighting printing and printing equipment as history. Displays detail historic newspapers, such as the *Colonial Advocate* edited by William Lyon Mackenzie, who later led the Upper Canada Rebellion.

Also in Queenston is the southern end of the Bruce Trail, which extends 780km to Tobermory on Georgian Bay. There are numerous access points in the Niagara and Hamilton areas. For more details on the trail, see Tobermory later in this chapter.

From the Queenston Dock, **Hydrofoil Lake Jet Lines** (☎ 1-800-313-3237) boats depart for a speedy, one hour boat trip to downtown Toronto ($25 one way). Coming from Toronto, the price includes a shuttle bus to Niagara Falls or to Niagara-on-the-Lake. Call for a schedule.

A little farther along the parkway is **Queenston Heights Park**, known for its large monument of Major General Brock. The winding inside stairwell will take you up 60m to a fabulous view. Also here is the Queenston Heights Restaurant, which itself has fine views of the river. Enjoy a summer beer on the balcony. This is not a bad place for a meal, either, although it's not in the low-budget category.

Near the restaurant is a monument to Laura Secord, and from here begins a 45 minute self-guided walking tour of the hillside, detailing the Battle of Queenston Heights. Pick up a copy of the good walking-tour booklet at any of the information offices. It explains some of the historical background, outlines the War of 1812 and describes how the British victory here was significant in Canada not becoming part of the USA. Interpreters are on hand at the huge **Brock Monument**, and the guidebook should be available there.

The Niagara Parkway continues through Niagara Falls and beyond, southbound. Attractions between Queenston and Niagara Falls, all of which can be reached on the Niagara Falls People Mover buses during the summer season, are covered in the Niagara Falls section below; there's an Around Niagara Falls section to cover the southern part of the route to Fort Erie.

NIAGARA FALLS

The roaring falls make this town one of Canada's top tourist destinations. It's a busy spot – about 12 million people visit annually and you'll hear and see people from all over the world.

The falls themselves, spanning the Niagara River between Ontario and upper New York State, are certainly impressive, particularly the Canadian Horseshoe Falls. They look good by day and by night, when colourful spotlights flicker across the misty foam. Even in winter, when the flow is partially

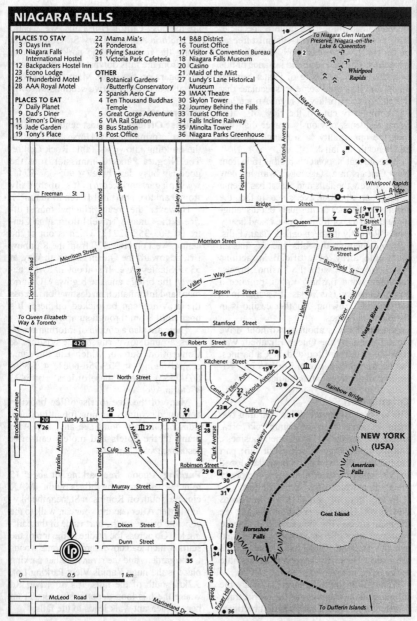

NIAGARA FALLS

PLACES TO STAY
3 Days Inn
10 Niagara Falls
   International Hostel
12 Backpackers Hostel Inn
23 Econo Lodge
25 Thunderbird Motel
28 AAA Royal Motel

PLACES TO EAT
7 Daily Planet
9 Dad's Diner
11 Simon's Diner
15 Jade Garden
19 Tony's Place

22 Mama Mia's
24 Ponderosa
26 Flying Saucer
31 Victoria Park Cafeteria

OTHER
1 Botanical Gardens
  /Butterfly Conservatory
2 Spanish Aero Car
4 Ten Thousand Buddhas
  Temple
5 Great Gorge Adventure
6 VIA Rail Station
8 Bus Station
13 Post Office

14 B&B District
16 Tourist Office
17 Visitor & Convention Bureau
18 Niagara Falls Museum
20 Casino
21 Maid of the Mist
27 Lundy's Lane Historical
   Museum
29 IMAX Theatre
30 Skylon Tower
32 Journey Behind the Falls
33 Tourist Office
34 Falls Incline Railway
35 Minolta Tower
36 Niagara Parks Greenhouse

hidden and the edges frozen solid – like a freeze-framed film – it's quite a spectacle. (But, as one reader warned – the mist freezes on contact!) Very occasionally the falls stop altogether. The first recorded instance of this occurred on the morning of Easter Sunday 1848, and it caused some to speculate that the end of the world was nigh. An ice jam had completely cut off the flow of water. Some residents, obviously braver than we, took the opportunity to scavenge the river bed beneath the falls!

It is said that Napoleon's brother rode from New Orleans in a stagecoach with his new bride to view the falls and that it has been a honeymoon attraction ever since. In fact, the town is sometimes humorously but disparagingly called a spot for newlyweds and nearly deads. Recently it's been called Viagra Falls.

Supplementing the falls, the city has an incredible array of artificial attractions which, together with the casino, hotels, restaurants and flashing lights, produce a sort of Canadian Las Vegas. It's a sight in itself and it's growing. Another casino is in the planning stages.

Niagara Falls is about a two hour drive from Toronto by the Queen Elizabeth Way (QEW), past Hamilton and St Catharines. Public transport between Toronto and Niagara Falls is frequent and quick.

Orientation

The town of Niagara Falls is split into two main sections: the older commercial area, where the locals go about their business, and the other largely tacky (but fun) part around the falls, which has been developed for visitors. The latter also has some pretty green areas which offer some contrast.

In the 'normal' part of town, known as downtown, Queen St and Victoria Ave are the main streets. The area around Bridge St, near the corner of Erie St, has both the train and bus stations. The international hostels are nearby. Generally, however, there is little to see or do in this part of town.

About 3km south along the river are the falls and all the trappings of the tourist trade – restaurants, hotels, shops and attractions.

In the vicinity of the falls, the main streets are the busy Clifton Hill, Falls Ave, Centre St, Victoria Ave and Ferry St. Going north along the river is scenic parkland, which runs from the falls downstream about 20km to Niagara-on-the-Lake. Many of the B&Bs are also between the two sections of town.

Information

Tourist Offices The most central place for tourist information is at Horseshoe Falls, in the building known as Table Rock Centre. The Niagara Parks Commission runs the good but busy desk here (☎ 905-356-2241, www.niagaraparks.com). It's open daily from 9 am to 6 pm (until 10 pm in summer).

However, the area's principal tourist office is the Ontario Travel Information Centre (☎ 905-358-3221), which is out of the centre, west on Hwy 420 from the Rainbow Bridge toward the Queen Elizabeth Way, at 5355 Stanley Ave. It's about halfway between the bridge and the highway. Ontario maps and information on destinations across the province can be picked up here. It's open until 8 pm through summer.

There are also a couple of information offices around town run by the Visitors & Convention Bureau, which use the same central phone (☎ 905-356-6061, ☎ 1-800-563-2557). One of these offices is at 5433 Victoria Ave.

Many of the free tourist office booklets contain discount coupons for attractions, rides etc. If you don't see any, ask. Also many of the hotels and motels can offer restaurant vouchers etc.

Parking A good, free parking lot about 15 minutes walk from the falls is by the IMAX cinema, south off Robinson St, near the Skylon Tower. After leaving your car, walk to the concrete bridge on the north side of the parking lot. Go across the bridge to the top of the stairs, which lead down through some woods to the gardens and the river. Another parking place is the huge Rapids View Parking Lot, 3.2km south of the falls. It's off River Rd where the bus loop depot is situated. From here, a pleasant walk leads to the falls.

Medical Services The Greater Niagara General Hospital (☎ 905-358-0171) is at 5546 Portage Rd.

The Falls

Some wags have said the falls are the brides' second disappointment, but the roaring water tumbling 56m is a grand sight – close up, just where the water begins to plunge down, is the most intense spot. Also good, and free, is the observation deck of the souvenir shop by the falls. (To get close to the falls and to get unobstructed photos, arrive early in the morning before the crowds.)

After checking all the angles at all times of day, you can try several services offering yet different approaches. Most close before the river partially freezes but all the jagged ice is another marvellous sight in itself. The best of them is the *Maid of the Mist* boat which takes passengers up to the falls for a view from the bottom – it's loud and wet and costs $10. Board the boat at the bottom of the incline railway at the foot of Clifton Hill. It sails from April to October.

From the Table Rock Centre right at the falls, you can pay $6 at Journey Behind the falls, don a plastic poncho and walk down through rock-cut tunnels for a close-up (wet) look from behind the falls and halfway down the cliff.

It's one way to cool off on a hot day, although the tunnels do get crowded and you should be prepared to wait in line for a brief turn beside the spray. The wall of water is thick enough to pretty well block out the light of day. A million people a year see the falls from this vantage point – as close as you can get without getting in a barrel. It's open all year.

Farther north along the river is the Great Gorge Adventure, an elevator to some rapids and whirlpools. Don't bother (see under Niagara Glen Nature Preserve later in this chapter). There also is a collection of pictures of the barrels and vessels that many of the wackos attempting to shoot the falls have used.

Surprisingly, a good proportion of those who have gone over purposely, suicides aside, do live to tell about it. But only one who took the trip accidentally has had the same good fortune. He was a seven-year-old boy from Tennessee who surged over from a tipped boat upstream and did it without even breaking a bone.

The 1980s was a particularly busy period, with five stunt people taking the plunge, all successfully. One of them said he did it to show teenagers there were thrills available without drugs (yeah, right). The first attempt of the 1990s, witnessed and photographed by startled visitors, was original. No conventional barrel here – it was over the edge in a kayak. He's now paddling the great whitewater in the sky.

In 1993, a local daredevil went over for the second time. For this outing he used a modified round diving bell, and became, apparently, the first person to do it twice and come up breathing. He said it was a bad one, though, and that he had hit hard. Among more recent escapades was the USA citizen who in 1995 attempted to jet ski over the falls with the help of a parachute. He might have made it if his parachute had opened. Ride Niagara, located under Rainbow Bridge, allows everyone to try the plunge via electronic simulation.

A little farther downstream, about 6km or 7km from Horseshoe Falls, is the Niagara Spanish Aero Car, last of the big four attractions. For $5, you ride a sort of gondola stretched 550m between two outcrops, both on the Canadian side, above a whirlpool created by the falls. It offers a pretty good angle of the river for a picture as it glides above the logs, tyres and various debris spinning in the eddies below. It also operates until the end of October.

Tickets can be bought separately for each of the above three land-based views, or buy the Explorer's Passport, a ticket for all three, which costs less than the total of the three individual tickets. It's not necessary to visit all three in the same day. The Explorer's Passport Plus also includes the People Mover Bus Pass.

Other Views

The Skylon Tower (☎ 905-356-2651) at 5200 Robinson St is the large, grey tower

ONTARIO

with yellow elevators running up the outside. There's an observation deck at about 250m, with both indoor and outdoor viewing. Aside from great views of the falls, both Toronto and Buffalo can be seen on clear days. The cost is $8. There are also a couple of dining rooms at the top, the more expensive of which revolves once per hour. The other one offers buffet-style breakfasts, lunches and dinners at more moderate (but not inexpensive) prices. In the revolving restaurant, the early-bird dinner special (4.30 pm and 5 pm sittings) saves some money.

The Minolta Tower (☎ 905-356-1501) at 6732 Oakes Drive is close to the falls and virtually overlooks the lip. The trip up is $7 or $9 for a day/night dual ticket. It has indoor/outdoor observation galleries and a revolving restaurant with spectacular views. An incline railway leads from the base of the tower down the hillside close to the falls.

The food served at both is not just an afterthought, and meals are well prepared, if straightforward.

Bridges

Two bridges run over the river to New York State: the Whirlpool Rapids Bridge and, closer to the falls, Rainbow Bridge, which celebrated its 50th year in 1991. You can walk or drive across to explore the falls from the USA side, but have your papers in order and all those who don't need visas to enter the USA (Canadians excepted) will be charged a $6 fee. Both pedestrians and drivers have to pay a bridge toll. It's 25¢ each way for walkers, $2 for cars.

Niagara Falls Museum

Established in 1827, this is the original of the many 'daredevil collections' of objects in which people have gone over the falls. As well as telling the stunt stories, there are displays of curios and artefacts from around the world, including Egyptian mummies and a dinosaur exhibit. The address is 5651 River Rd and the museum (☎ 905-356-2151) is open all year. Admission is $7 and a visit takes just 30 to 45 minutes.

Lundy's Lane Historical Museum

This seemingly out of place, conspicuously low-key museum (☎ 905-358-5082) sitting on the site of the 1814 Battle of Lundy's Lane, catalogues local pioneer and military history, notably the War of 1812. It's at 5180 Ferry St and has a very low admission fee. It's open all year, but weekdays only out of summer.

Clifton Hill

Clifton Hill is a street name but also refers more generally to the commercial part of the downtown area near the falls given over in sense-bombarding intensity to artificial attractions in Disney-like concentration. You name it – museums, galleries, displays such as Ripley's Believe It or Not, Tussaud's Wax Museum, Criminal's Hall of Fame (you get the drift) – they're all here. Looking is fun, but in most cases paying the entrance fee will leave you feeling like a sucker. Most don't live up to their own hype. Also in this bright and busy section are dozens of souvenir shops and restaurants.

Casino Niagara

The immensely successful gambling hall at 5705 Falls Ave is never closed. Free shuttle buses run to the door from hotels and attractions all over town.

Marineland

Of the many commercial attractions, this offers possibly the best dollar value. But Marineland (☎ 905-356-9565) *is* an aquarium with captive dolphins, sea lions and killer whales and hasn't escaped controversy. Admission includes kid-pleasing shows and a wildlife park containing bison, bears, deer and elk. There are also rides, including a roller coaster, all covered in the cost of admission. You may, however, want to take a picnic lunch with you – the restaurants here are expensive and offer a limited selection. Marineland is open daily April to October from 9 am to 6 pm. Entry is $21 for adults. It's roughly 2km from the falls, south on Portage Rd. There's camping nearby.

IMAX Theatre
The large-format (the screen is six storeys high) IMAX cinema (☎ 905-374-4629) at 6170 Buchanan Ave near the Skylon Tower, presents a 45 minute show about the falls, its history and some of the stunts that have been pulled in and over them. Shows run continually and cost $7.50. The price includes the adjacent Daredevil Museum.

Niagara Parks Greenhouse
Flowers and gardens are plentiful in and around Niagara Falls, which has moderate temperatures. The greenhouse and conservatory less than 1km south of the Horseshoe Falls provide a year-round floral display and are free. A bonus is the tropical birds.

The Old Scow
Across the street, rusting away in the river, the *Old Scow* is a steel barge which has been lodged on rocks waiting to be washed over the falls since 1918. So were the three men aboard when it broke free of the tug pulling it and drifted to within 750m of the brink. Without speedboats or helicopters, rescuing the men was some feat. Red Hill Senior, a local daredevil, climbed out hand over hand along a line that had been shot out from the roof of the waterside power-plant building. He was able to untangle the lines, allowing an attached buoy to reach the men, who climbed on and were pulled ashore.

Botanical Gardens & School of Horticulture Gardens
Also free for browsing are these fastidiously maintained 40 hectares. The school and gardens, which are open all year, are north along the Parkway towards Queenston, about 9km from Horseshoe Falls. A farther 2.5km north is the **floral clock**, which is over 12m in diametre. Beside the floral clock, don't miss the Centennial Lilac Gardens, which are at their fragrant best in late May.

Other flower gardens are at Queen Victoria Park (right beside the Canadian falls) and at Oakes Garden Theatre (opposite the Maid of the Mist Plaza, near the falls). Opposite the USA falls, Victoria Park also has varied and colourful floral displays through most of the year.

Butterfly Conservatory
In the conservatory (☎ 905-358-0025) at the Botanical Gardens, 2000 butterflies covering 50 species flutter about the flowers and visitors. Wearing white seems to attract them to land. In one area they can be seen making their way out of chrysalides. Admission is $7, half that for children. It's open daily.

Other Green Areas
Niagara Falls can be a fairly congested, urban experience, but there are some worthwhile quiet places to explore apart from the well tended areas of plant life listed above.

Niagara Glen Nature Preserve Top of the list and highly recommended, this is the only place where you can gain a sense of what the area was like before the arrival of Europeans. There are seven different walking trails here covering 4km, where the falls were situated 8000 years ago. The preserve is maintained by the Parks Commission (☎ 905-356-2241), which offers free guided walks four times a day through summer (July to early September). But the trails are always open to public use at no charge. The paths wind down the gorge, past huge boulders, icy cold caves, wildflowers and woods. Some people fish at the bottom from the shore. The river trail runs north to Pebbly Beach and south to the whirlpool, site of the Spanish Aero Car attraction. The whirlpool is an impressive sight from the Aero Car Terminal, but the size of the gorge itself isn't fully appreciated until seen from the shoreline. As noted above, there seems to be a lot of garbage trapped in the currents, mainly wood and tyres, often from cottage docks and boathouses, but remember that everything which leaves Lake Erie has to pass into the whirlpool. Officially, the excellent trails end here.

Going farther is dangerous and people have died. But some people do clamber over the rocks along the water's edge – to be safe, a good dozen or more metres back

from the water – upstream toward the falls. The area where the river flows (or rather shoots) into the whirlpool can be reached and is very dramatic. This is not easy walking; the rocks can be slippery and the river is hazardous. A local resident has said that from here, a further arduous 30 minutes leads to another set of even more overwhelming (and more dangerous) rapids. Twenty minutes beyond is the boardwalk for the Great Gorge Adventure. At this stage you can turn around, carry on for another five hours to a point close to the falls, or hop the Great Gorge elevator up to street level. Tickets evidently are not checked at the bottom because there are so few misfits who would take the time and effort to get down there on their own.

Walkers should take a snack and something to drink, for despite all the water, the Niagara is one river from which you do not want to drink – this region is one of the industrial centres of North America. The Niagara Glen Nature Preserve is 1km north of the Whirlpool Golf Course entrance on the Niagara Parkway (towards Niagara-on-the-Lake). The People Mover stops at the site, or in spring and autumn at the Spanish Aero Car, from where the glen is walkable (about 3km).

Dufferin Islands This series of small and interconnected artificial islands was created during the development of the hydro system. The area is green parkland, with walking paths and a short nature trail around the islands and through the woods. There are picnic tables, and a small area for swimming which is best for children (though anyone can be a kid if it's hot enough). The islands are less than 2km south of the falls, on the west side of the road. Entry is free. Another 250m south is King's Bridge Park with more picnic facilities and another small beach.

Ten Thousand Buddhas Temple
More tranquillity can be found at this totally out of context but intriguing Buddhist complex which was being built at 4303 River Rd

during research. Visitors are welcome to view the various sculptures and artworks from China and enjoy the calm environment.

Organised Tours
Double Deck (☎ 905-374-7423) offers bus tours on British red double-decker buses. For $35, one of the tours includes admission to three of the city's major attractions and stops at other free sites. You can stay on or get off at will, even taking two days to complete the tour. A second, 50km trip takes in many more of the things to see and travels further, taking about six hours. A third goes to Niagara-on-the-Lake and a winery.

Further Still (☎ 905-371-8747) operating through the hostel, offers alternative day trips in and around town.

More extravagant are the helicopter tours over the falls offered by Niagara Helicopters (☎ 905-357-5672) at 3731 Victoria Ave.

Special Events
The Blossom Festival is held in early or mid-May, when spring flowers bloom. Featured are parades and ethnic dances. For winter visitors, the annual Festival of Lights is a season of day and night events stretching from the end of November to the middle of February. The highlight is a series of spectacular night lighting displays set up along a 36km route.

Places to Stay
Accommodation is plentiful and, overall, prices aren't too bad, what with all the competition on both sides of the border. In summer, though, prices spike sharply upward. Outside the peak summer season, costs drop markedly, and through the winter there are some very good bargains with many of the hotels and motels offering two or three-day packages, often including meals and discounts on attractions. Checking the travel section of weekend newspapers in town or in Toronto will turn up some deals. Since a room is a room, many places offer enticements such as waterbeds, saunas, heart-shaped jacuzzis, FM stereos, movies etc for a 'dirty weekend' escape.

Prices vary by the day, season, demand and are higher on weekends and holidays (American *and* Canadian).

Camping There are campgrounds all around town. Three are on Lundy's Lane, leading out of Niagara Falls, and two are on Montrose Ave south-west of downtown. They are decidedly not primitive. *Niagara Glen View Campground (☎ 905-358-8689)*, with tent and electrical sites, is closest to the falls at Victoria Ave and River Rd, north of town toward Queenston. There are others along the Niagara Parkway farther north.

Hostels The popular HI *Niagara Falls International Hostel (☎ 905-357-0770, ☎ 1-888-749-0058, 4549 Cataract St)* is in a former commercial building in the old town close to the train and bus stations. Small Cataract St runs west off Bridge St near River Rd not far from the Whirlpool Rapids Bridge. The hostel has room for about 70 people and a bed costs $17. There's a good-sized kitchen, laundry facilities, lockers and a large lounge. On offer are bicycle rentals, and discounts for some of the museums and the *Maid of the Mist*.

A very good alternative is the nearby *Backpackers International Inn (☎ 905-357-4266, ☎ 1-800-891-7022, 4711 Zimmerman St)* in the huge, impressive house (mansion?) from 1896. There's a second entrance around the corner at 4219 Huron St. There are four-bed dorms for $15 and five rooms for couples at $40. The upstairs rooms, like those in a small European hotel, are particularly charming. The price includes bed sheets, towels and a morning coffee and muffin. Guests have use of kitchen facilities. Bicycles can be rented and there is pick-up at the train and bus stations.

Both hostels are open all year and during summer are regularly full.

B&Bs The B&Bs often offer the best accommodation value. The Visitors & Convention Bureau (☎ 905-356-6061) is the best of the tourist offices to try for accommodation assistance. When booking a room, check if the breakfast is continental or full.

There are quite a few B&Bs along convenient River Rd which links the falls area with old Niagara Falls downtown, 3km downriver. Another advantage is views of the river across the street.

Glen Mhor Guesthouse (☎ 905-354-2600, 5381 River Rd) has five rooms from $45 to $75 in season, $40 to $65 January to April. Shared bath lowers the price. A full breakfast is included. You can walk to the falls or bicycles are offered and they'll pick up at the bus and train station, free.

Also in the same price range is *Gretna Green (☎ 905-357-2081, 5077 River Rd)* just a little farther north.

Closer to the falls is *Butterfly Manor (☎ 905-358-8988, 4917 River Rd)* with four rooms from $60 double, full breakfast included.

The *Eastwood Tourist Lodge (☎ 905-354-8686, 5359 River Rd)* is in a fine old home with balconies overlooking the river. Each room is large with ensuite bath so prices are a little higher. English, German and Spanish are spoken.

There are several others in this area.

Hotels Hotels tend to be new and expensive. The *Europa (☎ 905-374-3231)* on the corner of Bridge St and Erie Ave, across from the train station, is a basic place with a night club downstairs which could be used by those travelling on the cheap in a pinch. Singles start at $19 but it's not recommended for single women.

Best buy among hotels is *Econo Lodge (☎ 905-356-2034, ☎ 1-800-424-4777, 5781 Victoria Ave)*. Prices range from $75 to $150 double determined by demand and it has good amenities. Other hotels are more costly.

Days Inn (☎ 1-800-263-7073) with three locations is also a reasonable and reliable choice. Try the one away from the centre a little at 4029 River Rd for lower prices. It offers excellent off-season packages.

Motels There are millions of them including many on a 7km strip along Lundy's Lane,

which leads west out from the falls and later becomes Hwy 20. There are scores more on Ferry, Murray and Stanley Sts. Prices vary from about $40 in the off-season to about $80 in July and August. They also range with the various honeymoon rooms, double-size bathtubs, waterbeds and other price-bumping features. You may be able to strike a deal if you're staying two, three or more nights.

Very near the lights of Clifton Hill and the restaurants, and under 30 minutes walk to the falls, is the central *AAA Royal Motel* (☎ 905-354-2632, *5284 Ferry St)*. The rooms are plain but fine and there is a small pool. Meal vouchers are offered to guests for discounts at several nearby eateries. Rates range from $40 to $85, with a double just $45 in June, before the big crowds arrive.

The better *Thunderbird Motel* (☎ 905-356-0541, *6019 Lundy's Lane)* has rooms from $35 all the way up to $90. There's also the small, tidy *Alpine Motel* (☎ 905-356-7016, *7742 Lundy's Lane)*. Its rates are $40 to $80 and it also has a pool. This street has literally dozens of other motels.

The quiet and tucked away *Maple Leaf* (☎ 905-354-0841, *6163 Buchanan Ave)* is nonetheless under two blocks from the falls. Prices for two people in one bed range from $40 to $90.

Similarly priced is the *USA Motel* (☎ 905-374-2621, *6541 Main St)* near George's Parkway.

Places to Eat

Finding food in Niagara Falls is no problem, and while the dining isn't great, it isn't bad either; most places provide pretty good value.

Inexpensive meals can be found at the *Victoria Park Cafeteria*, opposite the US falls, in the building complex in the park of the same name, run by the Parks Commission. On the 2nd floor is a more expensive restaurant and an outdoor beer garden where you can get smoked-meat sandwiches and hamburgers for around $6.

Around Clifton Hill and along Victoria or Stanley Aves, there are scads of restaurants. Japanese, German, Hungarian and, especially, ever-popular Italian eateries abound.

Many offer breakfast and/or lunch specials. Taking a leaflet from one of the hustlers on the street can lead to a good bargain.

Mama Mia's (5719 Victoria Ave) has been serving up standard Italian fare at moderate prices ($8 to $14) for many years.

Down a few doors, *Mai Vi (5713 Victoria Ave)* is a neat little place with well prepared Vietnamese dishes between $7 and $9.

Ponderosa (5329 Ferry St) is a budget steak house where all meals ($10 to $16) are accompanied by a huge help-yourself salad bar. Chicken and pasta are also available.

For fast food at any time of day, try the unmistakably shaped *Flying Saucer (6768 Lundy's Lane)*. There are breakfast specials from 6 am for 99¢. It's open daily until 3 am during the week and until 4 am Friday and Saturday.

There are also expensive restaurants in both the Skylon and Minolta Towers.

Between the falls and old downtown *Tony's Place (5467 Victoria Ave)* is a large, popular spot specialising in ribs and chicken. Regular à la carte dishes range from $8 to $16 and there is a lower-priced children's menu.

A pretty good Chinese meal for two can be had at *Jade Garden (5306 Victoria Ave)* for $25.

In the slow part of town (old downtown), the *Daily Planet (4573 Queen St)* has pub grub and Mexican accented snacks and is also a good place to grab a brew at nontourist prices.

Down near the hostels by the corner of River Rd is *Simon's (4116 Bridge St)*, the oldest restaurant (it looks it, with licence plates and knick knacks everywhere) in Niagara Falls. It offers cheap basics. Practically next door, *Dad's Diner* is very good for low-cost, complete breakfasts.

Getting There & Away

Bus The bus station (☎ 905-357-2133) is in the older part of town and away from the falls area, across the street from the train station, 14445 Bridge St on the corner of Erie Ave. This is the station for buses to other cities, but a shuttle to the falls and even bus tours depart from here.

For Toronto, service is frequent with a bus leaving about once an hour from early morning (around 5.30 am during the week) to about 10 pm, although on weekends there are fewer runs. The one-way fare is $22. The trip takes about two hours.

Shuttle buses run to Niagara-on-the-Lake three times daily during summer. Buses also depart for Buffalo, New York.

Train The station (☎ 1-800-361-1235) is in the older part of town on Bridge St at Erie Ave, close to this area's downtown section. There are two runs a day to Toronto – from Monday to Friday trains leave at 6.35 am and 5.15 pm; on Saturday and Sunday trains depart at 8.30 am and 5.15 pm. The trip takes about two hours and the one-way fare is $24. There are substantially reduced fares if you book five days in advance and also very good return tickets. There are two daily trains west to London and one to New York City.

Trips from Toronto See under Toronto Organised Tours.

Getting Around
Walking is best; most things to see are concentrated in a small area.

Bus For getting farther afield, there is the economical and efficient Niagara Parks People Mover bus system, which operates from the end of April to mid-October. It runs in a straight line from upstream beyond the falls, past the Greenhouse and Horseshoe Falls, along River Rd past both the Rainbow and Whirlpool bridges, north to the Niagara Spanish Aero Car attraction and, depending on the time of year, beyond to Queenston Heights Park. From there, it turns around then follows the same path 9km back. From the falls, it gets you close to either the bus or train station. One ticket is good for the whole day and you can get on and off as much as you like at any of the stops. For a low extra charge, transfers can be made to the regular city bus system. Such a connection will get you right to the door of the train or bus station. The People

Mover ticket is a bargain at $4.25 and can be purchased at most of the stops. Throughout summer, the bus runs daily from 9 am to 11 pm, but after 9 pm does not go farther out than the Rainbow Bridge. In spring and autumn the schedule is somewhat reduced, and in winter the system does not run at all.

Niagara Transit (☎ 905-356-1179) runs two similar shuttle services around town. One route, the Red Line Shuttle, goes around the bus and train stations then downtown and up Lundy's Lane. The other, the Blue Line Shuttle, runs from the Rapids View depot (at the southern end of the People Mover route, by the falls) along Portage Rd and around the downtown area. Both run half-hourly from 8.30 am to midnight. Free transfers can be made from these shuttles to any city bus. All-day shuttle passes for $4.50 or one way tickets can be bought from the driver. Both these routes cover many of the more popular sites and may be worth considering. They operate from May to October. After this time the regular city buses must be used.

Car Driving in and around the centre is nothing but a headache. Follow the signs to one of the several parking districts and stash the car for the day.

AROUND NIAGARA FALLS
See Around Niagara-on-the-Lake for details about the area between Niagara Falls and Niagara-on-the-Lake.

South from Niagara Falls, the Niagara Parkway, which begins at Niagara-on-the-Lake continues to Fort Erie, edged by parkland. The land along this strip is much flatter, the river clearly in view as the falls have not yet cut a gorge out of the river bed. But they are coming this way. Come back again in a few thousand years. There isn't much of interest here, as the road runs through residential districts, but there are certainly plenty of places to stop for a picnic or to rest in a shady spot by the water.

Fort Erie
The town of Fort Erie, situated where the Niagara River meets Lake Erie, across from

Buffalo, New York, is connected to the USA by the Peace Bridge. This is a major border-crossing point and buses from Toronto connecting with many eastern US cities use it. On summer weekends, expect queues. Some air travellers find it worthwhile to go by bus to Buffalo from Toronto and its vicinity to take advantage of sometimes cheaper US airfares.

The town is best visited for the reconstruction of **Fort Erie**, first built in 1764 and which the USA seized in 1814 before retreating. At the fort, a museum, military drills and uniformed soldiers can be seen. Admission is $4.

On Central Ave is the **Historical Railroad Museum**, with articles and a locomotive relating to the steam era of train travel. Fort Erie is also well known for its old, attractive horse-racing track. Races are held from May to October. The track is off the Queen Elizabeth Way at Bertie St. Slightly south of town is **Crystal Beach**, a small, rather run-down beach-cottage resort which is too bad because this is one of the warmest areas of the country, and the one with the longest summer.

BRANTFORD

West of Hamilton and surrounded for the most part by farmland, Brantford has an old, somewhat frayed downtown which is now being upgraded. It is known for several things which make for an interesting visit. Tourism Brantford (☎ 1-800-265-6299) is at 1 Sherwood Drive downtown.

The district has long been associated with Native Indians – Chief Joseph Brant was based here. He led the Six Nation Indians, who lived in an area stretching from here to parts of upper New York.

The **Brant County Museum** (☎ 519-752-2483) 57 Charlotte St, downtown, has exhibits mainly on the white settlers period through the 1930s. There is also information and artefacts on Brant and his people.

South-east of downtown about 3km are three worthwhile Indian sites. The **Woodland Cultural Centre Museum** (☎ 519-759-2650) at 84 Mohawk St has displays on the various aboriginal peoples of eastern

Canada and offers some history of the Six Nations Confederacy (it's closed on holidays). The confederacy, made up of the Mohawk, Seneca, Cayuga, Oneida, Onendaga and Tuscarora tribes, was a unifying cultural and political association which helped settle disputes between bands.

A few minutes away at 291 Mohawk St is **Her Majesty's Chapel of the Mohawks** (☎ 519-758-5444), the oldest Protestant church in Ontario and the world's only Royal Indian Chapel. It sits on what was an original village site. It's open every day from 1 July to Labour Day, and from Wednesday to Sunday the rest of the year.

North-east along Mohawk St leads to **Kanata**, a replica Iroquois village with longhouses which was being built when this book was being researched.

Brantford was also the home of Alexander Graham Bell, inventor of the telephone. The **Bell Homestead National Historic Site** (☎ 519-756-6220) at 94 Tutela Heights, displays some of his other inventions and is furnished the way it was when he lived in it. It's closed Monday.

The town is also known for local son Wayne Gretzky, the greatest ice-hockey player the world has yet produced. There are some additional attractions, such as **Myrtleville House**, dating from 1837, and the interesting **Octagon House**, now a restaurant.

The bus station (☎ 519-756-5011) is central at 64 Darling St. Buses connect to Toronto, London and, via Hamilton, Niagara Falls.

SIX NATIONS INDIAN RESERVE

To the south-east of Brantford, and larger than the city itself, is Ohsweken, the Six Nations of the Grand Iroquois reserve. It is one of the best known Indian communities in the country. Established in the late 18th century, it provides interested visitors with a glimpse of Native Indian culture.

Begin at **Odrohekta**, the gathering place, (☎ 519-758-5444) at the junction of Hwy 54 East and Chiefswood Rd. This centre has information as well as some cultural displays. Nearby, the home of poet E Pauline Johnson can be visited. Through the week

(and on weekends by appointment), tours are given of the reserve and its Band Council House, the seat of decision-making.

For overnighting, there is camping and the *Bear's Inn* (☎ 519-445-4133).

Various events are held through the year, including the Six Nations Pageant, a summer theatre program established in 1948 and an annual handicrafts sale in November.

The **Grand River Pow Wow**, held for two days in late July at the Chiefswood Tent & Trailer Park, is a major event with hundreds of colourful dancers, traditional drumming and singing as well as Native foods and craft sales.

ONTARIO AGRICULTURAL MUSEUM

With 30 buildings on 32 hectares of land, the museum (☎ 905-878-8151) brings to life the farming history of the area through demonstrations, displays, and costumed workers in historical settings. It's near Milton, 52km south-west of Toronto, about a 45 minute drive. Leave Hwy 401 at exit 320 and follow the signs. The museum is on Townline (also called Tremaine Rd), and is open daily from the middle of May to late September.

GUELPH

West on Hwy 401 from Toronto, Guelph is an old, attractive, middle-sized university town that's a nice place to live but does not have a lot to offer visitors. There are some fine houses along tree-lined streets, and the Speed River and downtown area is overseen by the dominant **Church of Our Lady**. The Eaton Centre shopping complex on the corner of Douglas and Wyndam Sts by historic St Georges Square marks the middle of town. Wyndam St is the main shopping district and also offers restaurants and places for a drink. Try the local Sleeman Brewery beers.

The **Farmers' Market** takes place by the square in the heart of town on Wednesday and Saturday mornings (Saturday only in the winter). Almost 100 vendors come in from the surrounding countryside to sell their produce. You'll also find an assortment of local craftspeople, artists and booksellers here.

The **Macdonald Stewart Art Centre**, at 358 Gordon St, often has good shows in its galleries, which specialise in Inuit and other Canadian art. It's open every afternoon, except Monday, and is free. It's also closed all of August.

McCrae House (☎ 519-836-1482) is the birthplace of John McCrae, the author of the antiwar poem *In Flanders Fields*, written during WWI, which every Canadian reads as a kid in school. The museum at 108 Water St is open every afternoon.

South of town is the **Donkey Sanctuary of Canada** (☎ 519-836-1697), a peaceful, pastoral refuge for abused and neglected donkeys. Only the hardest of hearts could fail to be charmed by these remarkably friendly, gentle and amusing equines. Visit Wednesday and Sunday from 1 May to 31 December. Donations ($3 to $4) welcomed. It's at 6981 Puslinch Concession Road, off Hwy 6 north from Hwy 401.

Through the summer, cheap accommodation can be found at the *University of Guelph* (☎ 519-824-4128). The campus is on Old Brock Rd (Hwy 6) at College Rd.

Near the main intersection of town (Wyndham and Quebec Sts) is the *Bookshelf Café (41 Quebec St)*. The front area contains a good bookshop and café, while the back portion is an excellent restaurant, although not in the low-budget category. There is also an outdoor patio, a bar and, upstairs, a repertory cinema. Less expensive for a good meal is *Latino's (51 Cork St E)* which features Latin American food and some vegetarian dishes. Most menu items are in the $8 range.

KORTRIGHT WATERFOWL PARK

The park (☎ 519-824-6729) has a mainly captive collection of Canadian and exotic waterfowl of about 1000 birds representing several dozen species. The wooded setting allows for natural and close observation.

It's open weekends and holidays from 1 March to 31 October and admission is $3.

The park is beside the Speed River south of Guelph at 305 Niska Rd. Niska is just west of the intersection of Hwy 6 (Hanlon Expressway) and Kortright Rd W.

ROCKWOOD CONSERVATION AREA

About 10km east of Rockwood along Hwy 7, Rockwood Conservation Area (☎ 519-856-9543) makes a good destination for an afternoon outdoors. It's definitely one of the best conservation areas within the Toronto area.

Admission is $5. The park offers swimming, canoeing and picnicking, but of most interest is the landscape itself. There are woods, cliffs, caves and glacial potholes, all of which can be explored on foot. Trails wind all through the park and canoes can be rented. There is also overnight camping available.

The Mennonites

The Mennonites are one of Canada's best known yet least understood religious minorities. Most people will tell you that Mennonites wear black, ride in horse-drawn carriages and, es-chewing modern life, work their farms in a traditional manner. And while basically true, these characteristics are only part of the story.

The Mennonites originated in Switzerland in the early 1500s as a Protestant sect among the Anabaptists. Forced from country to country due to their religious disagreements with the state, they arrived in Holland and took their name from one of their early Dutch leaders, Menno Simons. To escape persecution in Europe and to develop communities in rural settings, they took up William Penn's promise of religious freedom and began arriving in North America around 1640, settling in south-eastern Pennsylvania, where they are still a significant group. Most of North America's 250,000 Mennonites still live in that state. In the early 1800s, lured by the undeveloped and cheaper land of southern Ontario, some moved northwards.

There are about a dozen Mennonite groups or branches in Ontario, each with slightly different approaches, practices and principles. The Mennonite Church is the middle ground, with the numerous other branches either more or less liberal. The majority of Mennonites are moderates. Most visible are the stricter or 'plain' groups, known for their simple clothes. The women wear bonnets and a long, plain dress; the men tend to wear black and grow beards. Automobiles, much machinery and other trappings of modern life are shunned. The Old Order Mennonites are the strictest in their adherence to the traditions.

The Amish, who took their name from Jacob Ammon, a native of Switzerland, are another Mennonite branch. They split from the main body, believing Mennonites to be too worldly. Traditional Amish are the plainest of the plain; they won't even wear buttons on their clothes, considering them a vanity. They don't worship in a church, but hold rotating services in houses within the community. Homes are very spartan, with no carpets, curtains or wall pictures.

Despite their day-to-day differences, all the groups agree on a number of fundamentals, which include the freedom of conscience, separation of church and state, adult baptism, re-fusal to take oaths, practical piety and education stressing the moral and practical. Science is rejected by many, and the simple life esteemed. Mennonite and Amish communities are largely self-sufficient and they do no proselytising. Less than 10% of their followers were not born into Mennonite families.

Mennonite sites can be visited in Kitchener-Waterloo, St Jacob's and Elmira. It's not uncommon to see their carriages rolling along local roads or, on Sunday, parked by their country churches.

Many local stores and farmers' markets feature Mennonite goods. Perhaps the best known and most sought after of crafts are the beautiful, but pricey, bed quilts. The simple, well made furniture is also highly regarded. Their organic produce and meat has a market and the very good baked goods and jams are inexpensive and readily available.

In the village of Rockwood, an hour can be spent strolling along the main street, with its antique and junk shops, craft boutiques and eateries of various types.

Good, inexpensive food can be had at the *Out-to-Lunch* restaurant, open every day but Monday.

KITCHENER-WATERLOO

These twin cities – amalgamated to form one – are about an hour west of Toronto, in the heart of rural southern Ontario. About 55% of the 215,000 inhabitants are of German origin (which probably explains why Kitchener was originally named Berlin). The city also acts as a centre for the surrounding Amish and Mennonite religious farming communities.

It is these two factors that attract visitors and make the towns stand out from their neighbours. There is not a lot to see, and at a glance things here are much the same as in any other large town. However, it's worth a short visit, particularly if your timing is right and you arrive for Oktoberfest. The towns share two universities and therefore have quite a large number of young people.

Orientation

Kitchener is the southern portion of the twin cities and is nearly three times the size of Waterloo, but you can't really tell where one ends and the other begins. The downtown area refers to central Kitchener. King St is the main street and runs roughly north-south (even though it's called King St W and E); at the northern end it runs to the two universities and beyond.

The farmers' market on the corner of King and Frederick Sts marks the centre of downtown. This area of town has the train and bus stations, hotels and restaurants. King St runs south to Hwy 8, which continues to Hwy 401, west for Windsor and east for Toronto. Hwy 8 West, at the junction of King St, heads to Stratford.

The Uptown (downtown) area of Waterloo along King St N from Bridgeport Road north to William St W is a very pleasant district with various shops, restaurants, bars and nearby University of Waterloo.

It's 2.5km between the two downtown sections.

Information

Maps and information are available at the Kitchener-Waterloo Visitors & Convention Bureau (☎ 519-748-0800, ☎ 1-800-265-6959), south of the centre, at 2848 King St E. From June to the end of August, it's open from 9 am to 5 pm Monday to Wednesday, 9 am to 7 pm on Thursday and Friday and 10 am to 4 pm on weekends. The rest of the year, hours are 9 am to 5 pm Monday to Friday.

Farmers' Market

The central market is held downtown, on the corner of King St E and Frederick St. The market began in 1839 and features the products of the Amish and Mennonites – breads, jams, many cheeses and sausages, and handicrafts such as quilts, rugs, clothes and handmade toys. Whether they like it or not, it is the farmers themselves who are often the main attraction. Some of these religious people, whose ancestors were originally from Switzerland via Pennsylvania, live much as their grandparents did in the 19th century. There are also many merchants, including bakers, craftspeople and farmers, who aren't Mennonite. The market is held on Saturday from 6 am to 2 pm.

Across the street, on the corner of King and Benton Sts, a 23-bell glockenspiel rings at noon and at 5 pm.

Joseph Schneider Haus

At 466 Queen St S, not far from the market, this Heritage Canada site (☎ 519-742-7752) is the restored house of a prosperous German Mennonite. It's a museum depicting life in the mid-1850s, with demonstrations of day-to-day chores and skills. Through the summer, it's open every day; the rest of the year it's closed Monday and Tuesday. Note that it is shut completely for the last week in December and for the first six weeks of the new year. There is a nominal admission fee.

Woodside National Historic Site

This site (☎ 519-571-5684) contains the 100-year-old mansion where former prime minister William Lyon Mackenzie King (Canada's 10th prime minister) once lived. It has been restored and refurnished in upper-class 1890s style. The basement houses displays on the life of Mackenzie King. On weekends you can witness demonstrations of period crafts, music and cooking by guides in costume. The park is at 528 Wellington St N in Kitchener. It's open daily and admission is $3.

Universities of Waterloo & Wilfrid Laurier

In Waterloo, west off King St N on University Ave, these two universities sit right beside each other, and both have attractive, green campuses. The former is well regarded for its engineering; the latter specialises in economics. Waterloo has an art gallery, and the free **Museum & Archive of Games** (☎ 519-888-4424), which depicts the history of games around the world. Hours vary depending on exhibits.

Doon Heritage Crossroads

The Doon Heritage Crossroads (☎ 519-748-1914), south of Kitchener (20 minutes by vehicle or call for transit information), is a re-creation of a pioneer settlement circa 1914. The 23 buildings include a general store, workshops and a sawmill. There is also a model of an original Russian Mennonite village and a replica of an 1856 railway. To get to the site, go down King St, turn right on Fairway, left at Manitou St and left again at Homer Watson Blvd. Admission is $5, less for students, seniors and families. It's open daily from May through August and on weekdays during winter. Special events are often held on weekends.

The Centre in the Square

On the corner of Queen and Ellen Sts is this performing arts complex, with an art gallery and a theatre.

Homer Watson House & Gallery

One of Canada's first notable landscape painters is the subject of this quite small, specialised museum (☎ 519-748-4377). Watson (1855-1936) once lived here, and there are various pieces relating to his life and work. The museum at 1754 Old Mill Rd is open every afternoon from April to December (but is closed Monday).

Organised Tours

For getting around to some of the area attractions like St Jacob's or Elora, consider the quite reasonably priced half and full-day van trips offered by Town & Country Tours (☎ 519-743-3246).

Special Events

Some of the major events held here are:

May
Mennonite Relief Sale
It is a large sale of home-made foods and crafts and also includes a quilt auction. It's held on the last Saturday in May in New Hamburg, 19km west of Kitchener-Waterloo.

June
Summer Music Festival
This festival is four days of free or low-cost outdoor music concerts held at the end of June at venues around the downtown area.

August
Busker Carnival
An annual festival of street entertainers which takes place in late August. Some of these performers are very good and the whole thing is free.

October
Oktoberfest
The event of the year, Oktoberfest, the biggest of its kind in North America and said to be the largest outside of Germany, attracts 500,000 people annually. The nine-day festival starts in early to mid-October and includes 20 beer halls, German music and foods, and dancing. A huge parade wraps up the festivities on the last day. For more information, ring K-W Oktoberfest Inc (☎ 519-570-4267, www.oktoberfest.ca). Upon arrival, visit one of the reception areas for a map, tickets, information and all the details on how to tie on your stein so you don't lose it. Reservations for accommodation during the festival should be made well in advance. For getting around, there is a free bus in addition to the usual city buses.

Places to Stay

Hostels Backpackers' has a basic hostel here, the *Waterloo International Home Hostel* (☎ 519-725-5202, 102B Albert St), very close to the University of Waterloo. A bed is $15 but they are usually taken by students through the school year. The host, Joan, is a world-travelled author with a lot of unusual ideas she'll happily discuss.

The *University of Waterloo* (☎ 519-884-5400) has summer accommodation. The cost for singles/twins is $37/59 but $30 for a student single. Meals are available on the campus at several outlets. Free parking and use of the swimming pool are included. Buses run frequently to the campus. At *Wilfrid Laurier University* (☎ 519-884-1970), contact the housing officer at 75 University Ave West. Singles/doubles are $24/40. Rooms are available from 1 May to 15 August but are generally used by those attending conferences. The dining room is open in the summer, too.

B&Bs The tourist office can help with current B&Bs. *River Breeze* (☎ 519-653-6756, 248 Edgehill Drive) in Kitchener is good at $50 double with a full breakfast and a bonus is use of laundry facilities. It overlooks the Grand River and there is a pool, too.

During Oktoberfest many people rent out rooms. For information, call K-W Oktoberfest Inc (☎ 519-570-4267).

Hotels For the dollar-conscious, a central hotel is not on the cards. For those holding a different hand, the *Walper Terrace Hotel* (☎ 519-745-4321, 1 King St W) is central. It's an old place that has been restored and has won a heritage award. It has over 100 rooms, starting at $80/90 – not bad compared to the other top-end places in town. And there's a good deli right in the hotel, too.

Motels Motels are numerous, good and clean. Most of them are on Victoria St N (Hwy 7), which runs east-west off King St, just north of downtown Kitchener. One of the cheapest is the *Mayflower* (☎ 519-745-9493, 1189 Victoria St) which costs just $38 for singles or doubles. The *Victoria Motel* (☎ 519-742-7900, 1175 Victoria St N) is bigger, newer, more modern and has rooms at $52.

Places to Eat

There are many restaurants on or near King St in Kitchener. *Just Desserts* (273 King St W) has pizzas, pastas, sandwiches and desserts all under $10. *Howl at the Moon* (320 King St W) has something for everyone with finger foods, chicken, beef, kids menu, patio and live music. Most meals are under $15.

There are quite a few European delis in Kitchener. *Fiedlers* (197 King St E) is stacked full of cheeses, rye breads, sausages and salamis.

After the nose gets a whiff of the *Café Mozart* (53 Queen St S) the mouth will soon be munching on pastries, cakes or something covered with chocolate. It's not far from the bus station and is open until 10 pm (except Friday and Saturday nights, when it serves late-night snacks until midnight).

For solid German fare try the *Concordia Club* (429 Ottawa St S) for lunch or dinner. Live entertainment is included on Friday and Saturday nights but the restaurant is closed on Sunday. It's a popular site during Oktoberfest.

The Uptown area in Waterloo on King St N has numerous eateries and bars. The *Ali Baba* (130 King St N) is a steak house which has been in business since the 1960s.

Entertainment

Bars The *Heuther Hotel* on the corner of King and Princess Sts in Waterloo is a good brew pub despite one room featuring daytime strippers. Known far and wide, *Lulu's* is an immense, popular dance club on Hwy 8 in Kitchener, with what is said to be the world's longest bar. The *Circus Room* (☎ 519-743-0368, 729 King St E) draws a young crowd with live music Thursday to Sunday. *Id* is a free weekly with good club listings.

Entertainment Parks *Sportsworld* (☎ 519-653-4442, 100 Sportsworld Drive) is a massive entertainment park containing, among other diversions, a water slide, wave pool, go-kart track, video arcades and restaurants.

Various tickets are available. *Bingeman Park* (☎ *519-744-1555, 1380 Victoria St N)* on the Grand River offers much the same thing but also has 600 camp sites.

Getting There & Away

Bus The station (☎ 519-741-2600) is at 15 Charles St W in Kitchener, a five minute walk from the centre. There are frequent services to Guelph and Toronto and around five buses a day to London.

Train There are two VIA Rail (☎ 1-800-361-1235) trains a day to Toronto and one to London with a change for Windsor. The station is on the corner of Victoria and Weber Sts, an easy walk north of downtown Kitchener. See under St Jacob's for train service from Waterloo to this nearby Mennonite village.

AROUND KITCHENER-WATERLOO
St Jacobs

About 15km north of town (take King St N) is St Jacobs, a small historic village with a busy mix of traditional Mennonites and tourists. Numerous arts and crafts and gift shops housed in original buildings dating from the 19th century line the main street, King St.

See the **Meeting Place**, a very good interpretive centre on the Mennonites and their history at 33 King St. It's open daily through summer (afternoons only on Sunday). Through the winter it's closed weekdays. Admission is by donation.

At 8 Spring St, the **Maple Syrup Museum and Antique Market** has exhibits on the production of this Canadian speciality. The museum is open daily all year, except for Monday in January and February.

The **St Jacobs Farmers' Market** is a country version of the Kitchener farmers' market, with horse-and-buggy sheds still in place. It's 2km south of the village and is open Thursday from 7 am to 3 pm and Saturday from 7 am to 3 pm year-round. There's also a flea market here and on Tuesday and Thursday cattle are auctioned next door at the Livestock Exchange. More authentic

(and cheaper) is the less touristy Saturday **Waterloo Market** across the street.

For cheap brand-name goods check the nearby St Jacobs **Factory Outlet Mall**.

The St Jacobs B&B Association (☎ 519-664-2622) can fix you up with singles/doubles averaging $55/65. In town, *Benjamin's* (☎ *519-664-3731, 17 King St)* is an upmarket inn with a good dining room. The *Jakobstettel* (☎ *519-664-2208, 16 Isabella St)* deluxe guesthouse is another higher end, well established place to lay the head.

Whether you stay or not, a visit to the *Stone Crock Bakery* on King St near the corner of Albert St, should be considered.

The Waterloo-St Jacobs Railway (☎ 519-746-1950) operates a 1950s-style train between here and Waterloo from April to December but the schedule varies so call. A day pass is $9. In Waterloo, the station is at 10 Father Bauer Drive.

Elmira

Some 8km north of St Jacob's up Hwy 86 is Elmira. It's less touristy than St Jacob's; more a real, working country town but with a significant Mennonite population.

At 10 Church St W, the Old Town Village Craft Market has some Mennonite goods including fine quilts which are not cheap, as well as other crafts, furniture and antiques. Farther along at 58 Church St W, is the Elmira Mennonite Church and cemetery. Oddly juxtaposed are the modern, suburban-like townhouses across the street.

In spring, the Maple Syrup Festival, with street activities and pancake breakfasts, is considered the province's biggest and best attracting thousands of visitors.

The area has quite a few B&Bs, many on farms and with owners who speak German. To locate one, call the Elmira Chamber of Commerce (☎ 519-669-2605) at 5 First St. Rates start at $45/65 for singles/doubles.

There is no public transportation to Elmira.

About 7km east in **West Montrose** is the only covered bridge remaining in Ontario. It was built in 1889 and is known as the Kissing Bridge.

A Local Drive

Take Hwy 401 past Kitchener (going west) to the Doon exit and go to New Dundee. From there, travel north-west to Petersburg, where you'll find the Blue Moon Pub. Then on to St Agatha, with the church steeple, followed by St Clements and Lindwood – both are Mennonite towns with some interesting stores. Drive back east to Hawkersville, where there is a blacksmith's shop, and take a gravel road with fine scenery to St Jacobs. Continue north up to Elmira and over to West Montrose.

The Pub Crawl

Just west of Kitchener-Waterloo, four fine historic country taverns can be found in four neighbouring villages. Each one is from 1875 or earlier and offers atmosphere, good food and something to wash it down with. Begin in Petersburg, at the *Blue Moon* (☎ 519-634-8405), a Georgian-style inn dating from 1848. It's off Hwy 7 and 8 at Regional Rd 6 and 12.

Next stop to the west is *EJ's* (☎ 514-634-5711) in Baden, again with some intriguing original décor, including hand-painted ceiling tiles. In fine weather there is a patio as well. Beer from around the world is offered on tap.

Kennedy's Country Tavern (☎ 519-747-1313) is back east and north (not far from stop one – remember to designate a non-drinking driver, it's getting confusing). Kennedy's, in the village of St Agatha, has a bit of an Irish slant, although much of the food shows a German influence.

Last stop is the *Heidelberg Restaurant & Brew Pub* (☎ 519-699-4413) in Heidelberg, north from St Agatha, at the junction of Hwys 15 and 16. Here, in the middle of Mennonite country, a German country-style meal can be enjoyed with Bavarian beer brewed on the premises. The Heidelberg was built in 1838. Stops one and two are closed on Sunday. Call any one of them and ask about the bus tours which sometimes do the circuit.

Cambridge

South of Kitchener, Cambridge is an old mill town now grown large, set alongside the Speed and Grand rivers. There isn't much to see, but the redeveloped waterfront area known as Riverbank is pleasant and attracts shoppers. Many of the businesses once drawn by the power from the mill now contain factory outlets. Cambridge has a Scottish background, and this is celebrated with the annual summer Highland Games.

ELORA

Not far from Kitchener-Waterloo, north-west up Hwy 6 from Guelph, is this small, heavily touristed town. Named after Elora in India, with its famous cave temples, this was once a mill town using the falls on the Grand River, which runs through town. The falls, the old mill, the pleasant setting and the nearby gorge and park make the town a popular day trip for both out-of-province visitors and Ontarians.

The main streets are Metcalfe, Mill and Geddes Sts, all right by the mill and river.

There is a tourist office in the Elora Civic Centre, 1 MacDonald Square, at the junction of Metcalfe and Geddes Sts.

Things to See & Do

Not far from town at the **Elora Gorge Conservation Area** (☎ 519-846-9742) the Grand River flows through a deep limestone canyon. Much of the area is park, and trails lead to cliff views and caves at the water's edge. Riding the water in a tire tube is a fun way to spend a warm afternoon and rentals are available. There are also picnic areas in the park, camping and trout fishing.

The Grand River is also good for canoeing, and overnight trips are possible. You can paddle along the river all the way to Lake Erie. More information is available at the park.

About a dozen blocks east of town along Mill St E is the **Elora Quarry Conservation Area** – worth a look and, better, a swim.

Plenty of small stores in Elora offer crafts, jewellery, paintings and pottery, much of it produced by the numerous local artisans.

Special Events

The Elora Festival (☎ 519-846-0331), an annual music festival, is held during the last weeks of July and into the first two weeks

of August. The music is primarily classical (with an emphasis on choral works) or folk. Some of the concerts are held at the quarry, with performers playing in the middle of the water on a floating stage. On a warm summer night with the stage lit up, it really is an impressive experience.

Other events include the annual summer Antique Show & Sale, in May, the Open House Tour, when many of the older local houses are open to the public and the October Artist Studio Tour.

Places to Stay

There is a large campground at the *Elora Gorge Conservation Area* (☎ 519-846-9742) which, though usually full on holiday weekends, has a number of sites that can be reserved one week in advance.

There are quite a few B&Bs in and around town. For accommodation assistance, ring ☎ 519-846-9841 or visit the tourist office. Average price is $55 for two with breakfast.

One to try that's central and costs a little less than the rest is *Speers Home* (☎ 519-846-9744, 256 Geddes St) just off the main street. Rooms are $40/50 for singles/doubles. *Hornsby Home* (☎ 519-846-9763, 231 Queens St) gets great reviews and is also close to the centre with single/doubles from just $35/45.

The *Gingerbread House* (☎ 519-846-0521, 22 Metcalfe St) has rooms, but the deluxe features, special breakfasts, fine furnishings and décor put it into a considerably higher price bracket.

The *Elora Mill Inn* (☎ 519-846-5356, 77 Mill St W) is the prestige place to stay in town; it offers a convenient location, views of the river, fireplaces and a dining room but you may have to look in both pockets to pay the bill. Rooms start at $150.

Places to Eat

Elora Confectioner's Delicatessen (54 Metcalfe St) has fresh sandwiches and baked goods. The *Desert Rose Café* (130 Metcalfe St) is good for its Mexican-influenced menu under $10. The *Metcalfe Inn*, on the corner

of Mill and Metcalfe Sts, has an outdoor patio where beer is served.

Other places along Mill St, and the dining room of the *Mill Inn*, offer more expensive menus. At the back of *Leyanders* (40 Mill St), a store, is a quiet tearoom, good for afternoon cream tea with a view of the river.

Getting There & Away

The Greyhound bus connects north to Owen Sound and south to Toronto via Guelph. It stops at Little Katy Variety Store, central on Geddes St.

THE GRAND RIVER

Beginning near Georgian Bay, the Grand, a Canadian Heritage River, winds its way south through Elora, and continues just to the east of Kitchener-Waterloo, eventually emptying into Lake Erie. The Grand River watershed is the largest inland river system in the southern portion of the province. Aside from the gorge conservation area listed above, there are many other parks and conservation areas located along the southern sections of the river. Any one of them or local tourist offices should have a guide to recreational facilities along the Grand. Canoeing is possible in many sections (with rentals and shuttles); at others there are swimming facilities and walking trails.

For more information contact the Grand River Conservation Authority (☎ 519-621-2761) in Cambridge.

FERGUS

Fergus is Elora's neighbour and a quiet farming town. As the name suggests, the heritage here is Scottish, and this is best appreciated at the annual Highland Games, held during the second week of August. Included are Scottish dancing, pipe bands, foods, and sports events such as the caber toss. It is one of the largest Scottish festivals and Highland Games held in North America.

St Andrew St is the attractive main street. Many of the distinctive grey buildings are made of limestone and a town oddity is the painted fire hydrants. The tourist office is in the central Fergus Market Building along

with various shops. The **Templin Gardens** are in the centre of town, along the Grand River. A farmers' market is held on weekends.

Between Fergus and Elora Sts is the **Wellington County Museum**, with artefacts relating to the history of the county.

Like Elora, Fergus is quite busy, and accommodation is not overly abundant. In general, costs are a little lower here. *The Thompson's (☎ 519-843-4065, 360 Provost Lane)* is a B&B within walking distance of downtown. Prices are from \$40/50.

The *Riversedge Café* with a nice location behind the Market Building has sandwiches and a few vegetarian pasta dishes and burgers. It's open daily.

The Greyhound bus (☎ 1-800-661-8747) which goes to Guelph where connections for Toronto can be made stops at the Highland Inn, downtown.

STRATFORD

With a population of 29,000, this commercial centre surrounded by farmland is a fairly typical slow-paced, rural Ontario town except that it's consciously prettier than most and is home to the world-famous Shakespearean Festival. Many of the numerous older buildings in the attractive, architecturally interesting central area have been restored, and the layout along the river adds to the charm. Stratford's Avon River, with its swans and green lawns, together with the theatres help the town deliberately and successfully resemble Stratford-upon-Avon in England.

London is about 60km or a 45 minute drive south-west, and Toronto is about a two hour drive east.

Orientation

Ontario St is the main street and everything is close to it. At the foot of Huron St is the Perth County Courthouse, one of the town's most distinctive and dominant landmarks.

Information

There is a friendly, helpful and well informed tourist office (☎ 519-273-3352) on the corner of York and Erie Sts, in the heart of town. You can see pictures of guesthouses and peruse menus from many of the town's restaurants. You can also get a free parking sign for your car.

On fine days, heritage walks depart from the tourist office at 9.30 am Monday to Saturday from 1 July to Labour Day. With one of the descriptive maps available, you could do your own walking tour. One map, put out by the Local Architectural Conservation Advisory Committee, details some of the history and architecture of the downtown area. Don't miss out on a walk along the river where the park, lawns and theatres have been laid out in a charming and attractive manner.

Between November and May, information can be obtained from Tourism Stratford at 88 Wellington St.

The Gallery/Stratford

This is a good art gallery (☎ 519-271-5271) in a fine old building near Confederation Park, at 54 Romeo St N. Featured are changing international shows of modern painting, with the emphasis on Canadian works. Three shows are presented at any given time. The gallery is closed Monday mornings and admission is \$5.

Stratford-Perth Museum

Articles collected around the region from the turn of the century are on view at this small museum (☎ 519-271-5311) at 270 Water St. Admission is by donation. It's open from May to October from 10 am to 5 pm, but afternoons only Sunday and Monday.

Queen's Park

Down by the river, near the Festival Theatre, this park is good for a picnic or a walk. Footpaths from the theatre follow the river past Orr Dam and a stone bridge, dating from 1885, to the formal English flower garden.

Shakespearean Gardens

Just north of the courthouse by the stone bridge, these gardens on the site of an old wool mill run along the waterfront. Near the bridge is the mill's chimney and a bust of Shakespeare. Here and there, picnic tables can be found.

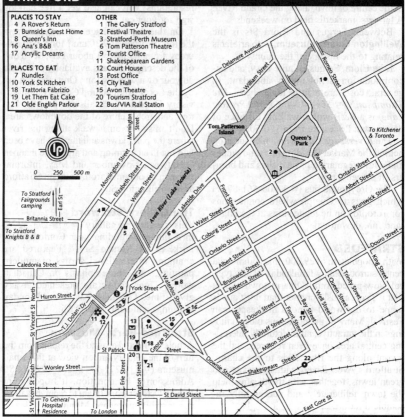

STRATFORD

PLACES TO STAY
4 A Rover's Return
5 Burnside Guest Home
8 Queen's Inn
16 Ana's B&B
17 Acrylic Dreams

PLACES TO EAT
7 Rundles
10 York St Kitchen
18 Trattoria Fabrizio
19 Let Them Eat Cake
21 Olde English Parlour

OTHER
1 The Gallery Stratford
2 Festival Theatre
3 Stratford-Perth Museum
6 Tom Patterson Theatre
9 Tourist Office
11 Shakespearean Gardens
12 Court House
13 Post Office
14 City Hall
15 Avon Theatre
20 Tourism Stratford
22 Bus/VIA Rail Station

Organised Tours

Festival Tours runs trips around town several times daily through summer, using red British double-decker buses. The tour lasts one hour. Ask at the tourist information office for details.

Boat Trips A small tour boat runs around the lake and beyond the Festival Building from behind the tourist office. The 35 minute trip costs $6 and the boat glides by parkland, houses, gardens and swans. Also at the dock, canoes and paddle boats can be rented.

Shakespearean Festival

Begun humbly in a tent in 1953, the shows attract international attention. The productions are first rate, as are the costumes, and respected actors are featured. The season runs from May to October each year. Tickets for plays cost between $37 and $67, depending on the day, seat and theatre, and go on sale mid-January.

By show time, nearly every performance is sold out. A limited number of rush seats are available at good reductions, and for

some performances, students and seniors are entitled to discounts. Less-costly tickets are available to the concerts, lectures (including a fine series with well known writers) and other productions, which are all part of the festival. Bargain-hunters should note that the two-for-one Tuesday performances offer good value.

Write for the festival booklet, which gives all the details on the year's performances, dates and prices. Also in the booklet is a request form for accommodation, so you can organise everything at once. Tickets are available from the box office at the Festival Theatre (☎ 1-800-567-1600), by mail at PO Box 520, Stratford, Ontario, N5A 6V2 or you can check www.stratford-festival.on.ca.

There are three theatres – all in town – that feature contemporary and modern drama and music, operas and works by the Bard. Main productions take place at the Festival Theatre, with its round, protruding stage. The Avon Theatre, seating 1100 people, is the secondary venue and the Tom Patterson Theatre is the smallest theatre.

Aside from the plays, there are a number of other interesting programs to consider, some of which are free; for others a small admission is charged. Among them are post-performance discussions with the actors, Sunday morning backstage tours, warehouse tours for a look at costumes etc. In addition, workshops and readings take place.

Places to Stay

Because of the number of visitors lured to town by the theatre, lodging is, thankfully, abundant. By far the majority of rooms are in B&Bs and the homes of residents with a spare room or two. In addition, in the higher price brackets there are several well appointed, traditional-style inns in refurbished, century-old hotels.

Camping There is camping at the *Stratford Fairgrounds* (☎ 519-271-5130, 20 Glastonbury Drive). The farmers' market and a number of other events take place here on the grounds, which are quite central, about seven blocks from the tourist office. There

is also camping in St Marys (see under that town later in this chapter).

B&Bs A good way to find an economical bed is to book through the Stratford Festival Accommodation Department (☎ 519-273-1600, ☎ 1-800-567-1600) at 55 Queen St. It will find a room in someone's home from as low as $35/38 a single/double if you have a ticket to a play. For a couple more dollars, breakfast can be included. Payment must be made in full when booking.

The Stratford & Area B&B Association (☎ 519-271-5644) does much the same thing, but not being part of the festival, its prices are higher and its members are trying to run viable businesses.

William St runs along the river, across from the downtown core. There you'll find the immaculate *Burnside Guest Home* (☎ 519-271-7076, 139 William St). A 15 minute walk will get you to any of the theatres or the downtown area. Singles cost $50 and doubles $65/70. There is also a cheaper but good hostel-style room downstairs for $25 per person. All rates include breakfast. Lester, the owner, is very knowledgeable about things to see and do around town.

A Rover's Return (☎ 519-273-3009, 132 Elizabeth St) has five rooms with shared bath economically priced at $45/60. It's a 10 minute walk to downtown.

Ana's B&B (☎ 519-273-7674, 48 Rebecca St) is near the Avon Theatre. Singles/doubles with a full breakfast are $45/65. The bathroom is shared.

Acrylic Dreams (☎ 519-271-7874, 66 Bay St) is an updated cottage from 1879 which has some pleasant little touches for guests. Costs are higher at $85/95.

In the same range is *Stratford Knights* (☎ 519-273-6089, 66 Britannia St). It's away from the centre a bit, on the other side of the river, off Mornington St. This fine old house has a pool in the yard, which guests can use. Doubles are $92 including a continental breakfast.

Hotels A possibility worth considering is a room at the *General Hospital Residence*

(*☎* 519-271-5084, 130 Youngs St), and no, you don't have to get hit by a car to qualify. Similar to university dorms, the small, neat rooms come with single or twin beds, a fridge and a sink. A single/twin is $50/55 and includes breakfast and taxes. Excellent weekly rates are offered. There are laundry and cooking facilities, a cafeteria and an outdoor swimming pool – all in all, a pretty fair bargain.

The historic *Queen's Inn* (*☎* 519-271-1400, *☎* 1-800-461-6450, 161 Ontario St), near Waterloo St, dates from the mid-1800s and is the oldest hotel in town. In summer prices range from $85 double. The popular standard room with full bath goes for $95.

Motels Motels are generally expensive. Try the *Noretta* (*☎* 519-271-6110), on Hwy 7 towards Kitchener. Rooms cost from $54 a double. *Majers Motel* (*☎* 519-271-2010), a little farther out, has rooms for about the same price. There are other motels along here, including the attractive but more costly *Rosecourt* (*☎* 519-271-6005, 599 Erie St).

Places to Eat
Near the tourist office, the *York St Kitchen* (41 York St) turns out excellent sandwiches ($5) and picnic plates which might include a bit of smoked salmon or corn on the cob. There is a takeout order window and the park by the river (right across the street) makes a good eating spot. It also has a few tables inside where you could try a lamb curry or pasta dish ($10).

Let Them Eat Cake (82 Wellington St) is good for a cheap breakfast or lunch or simply a dessert and coffee.

Visit *Trattoria Fabrizio* (71 Wellington St) for Italian sandwiches and pastas under $7. It also has various snacks, desserts and espresso.

As befits an English-style town, there are quite a few pubs about. *Stratford's Olde English Parlour* (101 Wellington St) has an outdoor patio. The *Queen's Inn* (161 Ontario St), with several different eating rooms, has a pub for inexpensive and standard menu items including a ploughman's lunch. The

Queen's Sunday and Wednesday evening buffets in the dining room are good. Dining rooms in some of the other inns also cater to the theatre crowd with more costly fare.

Expensive *Rundles* (9 Coburg St), where a dinner is about $55 before wine, has a good reputation.

Away from the centre, over the bridge and down Huron St about 2km, *Madelyn's Diner* (377 Huron St) is a friendly little place to have any meal. Breakfasts are served all day (from 7 am) and are good, as are the home-made pies. It's closed Sunday evening and all day Monday.

There are a few fast-food joints and a Chinese place on Ontario St heading out of town. For making your own picnic check the *Franz Kissling Delicatessen* (26 Wellington St).

Getting There & Away
Bus Several small bus lines servicing the region operate out of the VIA Rail station, which is quite central at 101 Shakespeare St, off Downie St about eight blocks from Ontario St. Cha-Co Trails (*☎* 519-271-7870) buses connect Stratford with Kitchener, from where you can go to Toronto. They also run buses to London and Windsor connections and some other southern Ontario towns.

Train There are two daily trains to Toronto from the VIA Rail station (*☎* 519-273-3234, *☎* 1-800-561-8630). Trains also go west to London or Sarnia, with connections for Windsor.

SHAKESPEARE
Some 12km east of Stratford along Hwy 8, this village is geared to visitors with the main street offering numerous antique, furniture and craft shops.

ST MARYS
To the west of Stratford, St Marys is a small Victorian crossroads with a former opera house and some fine stone homes as reminders of its good times last century.

The *Westover Inn* (*☎* 1-800-268-8243) tucked down Thomas St, and surrounded by

lawns and trees, is a quiet, five-star hotel with a dining room.

Several kilometres from town, off Hwy 7 and back towards Stratford, is the **Wildwood Conservation Area**. It isn't particularly attractive but you can camp or go for a quick swim. For better swimming, try the spring-fed limestone quarry just outside St Marys. It costs a couple of dollars and there are change rooms and a snack bar.

TILLSONBURG & DELHI

These two small towns are in the centre of a flat, sandy, tobacco-growing region. The number of smokers has been declining rapidly in Canada so various crop alternatives are being sought to keep the area productive. One of them is hemp.

On Hwy 3 west of Delhi there is the **Ontario Tobacco Museum**, with displays on the history and production of tobacco. It's open daily through summer, and on weekdays only the rest of the year.

For males, casual work picking tobacco starts in mid-August. Ask at the Canada Manpower offices in these towns. Jobs last roughly a month. It's hard work, but room and board are often thrown in with the wage and you can have a good time. Watch your valuables in the bunkhouse.

LAKE ERIE SHORELINE WEST

As the shallowest of the five Great Lakes, Erie long suffered the most with pollution. However, continuing environmental work has brought the waters back from the brink. Scattered along the lake's Canadian northern shoreline, from Windsor to Fort Erie, there are government parks, some with camping, some for day-use only. Most are busy on summer weekends.

Port Dover is a busy little summer resort with a beach, riverboat tours, numerous tourist shops, a lighthouse and the large, attractive *Erie Beach Hotel (☎ 519-583-1391)*, with popular dining rooms, right in the heart of town. This is also a centre for commercial lake fishing. Local restaurants specialise in Erie perch and walleye although some people are leery of eating any

of the lower Great Lakes catch due to possible chemical contamination. The Harbour Museum details the lake's fishing industry.

Turkey Point Provincial Park, and even more so, **Long Point** are good and popular. Despite an excellent beach at Long Point, the parks along the Lake Huron shoreline are superior for swimming. Also beware of deer ticks at Long Point; be sure to read the available information on these serious pests. Apart from these Lake Erie recreational areas, the region is mainly summer cottages, small towns and farmland. The shoreline itself is surprisingly scenic at points with cliffs edging turquoise waters.

Port Stanley has the agreeable atmosphere of an old, second rate summer tourist town that doesn't care to be overly pretentious. It also has enough happening to not need to pander obsequiously to its visitors.

It has a fine summer program at the Port Stanley Theatre, 302 Bridge St, several low-key restaurants, cafés and a pleasing waterfront location. There's a sandy beach and a large dock with plenty of commercial fishing vessel traffic.

A 14km portion of the old London and Port Stanley Railroad (☎ 519-782-3730) still operates, running north beyond the village of Union to St Thomas Parkside. A one hour trip costs $9 adult or you can go longer.

Some 11km west and 3km south of St Thomas, near the village of Iona, is the **Southwold Prehistoric Earthworks National Historic Site**. Surrounded by farmland are the earthwork remains of a double-walled Neutral Indian fort from around 1500-1650. It was once a village of about 600 people.

Farther west, **Point Pelee National Park** (☎ 519-322-2365), on the southernmost point of mainland Canada, is a top Lake Erie attraction. It's known for the thousands of birds that show up in spring and autumn on their migrations. Up to 342 species have been observed here – about 60% of all the species known in Canada. The fall migration of monarch butterflies is a highlight. The region also contains some plants found nowhere else in the country, such as the prickly pear cactus. There are numerous nature trails, a 1.5km

ONTARIO

boardwalk through the marsh, forest areas and sandy beaches within the park. Bicycles and canoes can be rented in summer although the park remains open all year.

To the east, the town of Wheatley has some accommodation and a provincial park where a violent storm swept much of the beach away in 1998. The camping area is good though. Note that during bird migration periods, this is a relatively busy area.

Hillman Marsh on the shoreline north of Point Pelee, offers good birdwatching, a nature centre and a walking trail.

Lakeside **Leamington**, north-east of the park, is Ontario's tomato capital and a major ketchup producer. There are several motels, B&Bs, and a seasonal tourist office on the main street. It's about 40km drive straight overland from Windsor, rather than around the lakeshore. *Do Drop In (☎ 519-326-5558, 202 Seacliff Drive W)* is a Swedish/English B&B. Rates are $35/50. For accommodation assistance call the Chamber of Commerce (☎ 519-326-2721) Monday through Friday.

From here and Kingsville, ferries run to the largest island in the lake, **Pelee Island**. Pelee (pronounced 'pee-lee') is halfway across to Ohio, and ferries run over to the USA side as well. Ferries run from March to the beginning of December. Tickets cost $7.50 each way for adults; cars are $17. For reservations and schedule call ☎ 1-800-661-2200. From the island, ferries run to Sandusky, Ohio.

The island is known for its good beaches and small vineyards. Visit the ruins of Vin Villa Winery and the old lighthouse. There are tours, with tastings, of Pelee Island Winery (☎ 519-724-2469). Quite a variety of wines are produced here, including Canadian champagne. There are a few restaurants on the island, inns, B&Bs and camping. Bicycles can be rented. During midsummer, ferries and accommodation should be booked in advance.

LONDON

London (population 320,000) is the most important town in the Lake Erie area and blends a fair bit of industry and manufac-

turing with its insurance company head offices and one of the country's largest universities. The overall ambience is quiet, clean and conservative.

Even though the town has its own Thames River, Hyde Park and Oxford St, that's the extent of the London, England resemblance. There are a few things to see in and around town, and it might prove a convenient stopover, as it lies roughly halfway between the US-Canadian border at Detroit-Windsor and Toronto.

Orientation

The main east-west street is Dundas St; Richmond St is the main north-south street. The central area is bounded by York St to the south, Talbot St to the west, Oxford St to the north and Waterloo St to the east. The northern end of Richmond St is the hip strip with a host of shops, eateries and cafés to hang out at. There are some pleasant tree-lined streets and elegant Victorian houses around the edges of the downtown area.

Information

There is a downtown tourist office (☎ 519-661-5000, ☎ 1-800-265-2602), on the main floor of City Hall, on Dufferin Ave on the corner of Wellington St. It's open from 8.30 am to 4.30 pm Monday to Friday.

A second office (with the same telephone number) is at 696 Wellington Rd S between Hwy 401 and Commissioners Rd heading north into town from the highway. It's open daily from 8 am to 8 pm in summer (weekends only otherwise) and also has provincial information.

London Museum of Archaeology & Lawson Indian Village

Both an educational and a research facility affiliated with the university, the museum (☎ 519-473-1360) displays materials and artefacts spanning 11,000 years of Native peoples' history in Ontario. Adjacent to the museum building is an active dig of a Neutral Indian village of about 500 years ago. Parts of the village, including a longhouse, have been reconstructed.

ONTARIO

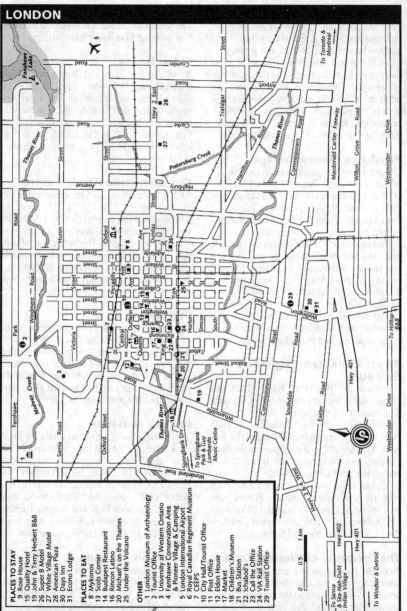

LONDON

PLACES TO STAY
9 Rose House
15 Quality Hotel
19 John & Terry Herbert B&B
26 Super 8 Motel
27 White Village Motel
28 American Plaza
30 Days Inn
31 Econo Lodge

PLACES TO EAT
8 Mykonos
13 Scots Corner
14 Budapest Restaurant
16 Rincon Latino
20 Michael's on the Thames
25 Under the Volcano

OTHER
1 London Museum of Archaeology
2 Tourist Office
3 University of Western Ontario
4 Fanshawe Conservation Area
  & Pioneer Village & Camping
5 London International Airport
6 Royal Canadian Regiment Museum
7 CEEPS
10 City Hall/Tourist Office
11 Post Office
12 Eldon House
17 Market
18 Children's Museum
21 Ichabod's
22 Call the Office
23 Bus Station
24 VIA Rail Station
29 Tourist Office

0   0.5   1 km

Special events are scheduled through the year and some displays in the museum are changed regularly. A gift shop offers crafts such as baskets, quill boxes and pottery.

Well worth a visit, the museum is open daily from 10 am to 5 pm. The Indian village is open daily from May to September. An adult ticket is $3.50 and there are senior, student and family rates. The address is 1600 Attawandaron Rd, north-west of the university. Take the Orchard No 31 bus from downtown.

Fanshawe Pioneer Village

On the eastern edge of the city, at the 22-building Pioneer Village (☎ 519-457-1296), staff in costume reveal skills and crafts and give a sense of pioneer village life in the 19th century. There is a tearoom at the site, or you can bring your own picnic.

Tickets are $5 for adults, less for students and kids, and there is a family rate too. The site is open Wednesday to Sunday from 10 am to 4.30 pm 1 May to 20 December. The entrance is off Fanshawe Park Rd just east of Clark Rd.

The adjoining Fanshawe Park is a conservation and recreation area with swimming, walking and picnicking areas.

Royal Canadian Regiment Museum

Known as the RCR (☎ 519-660-5102), this is the oldest infantry regiment in Canada. The museum has displays on its involvement in the North-West Rebellion of 1885 right through both World Wars and the Korean War. As well as the extensive displays, exhibits and dioramas, there is a gift shop with a range of military items.

The museum is at Wolseley Hall National Historic Site, on the Canadian Forces Base on Oxford St E (on the corner of Elizabeth St). Admission is free. It's closed on Monday. A visit takes one to 1½ hours.

The University of Western Ontario

North of the downtown area, the beautiful university campus is pleasant to stroll around. Western is one of the country's larger universities and is known particularly for its business, medical and engineering faculties. The tourist office has a self-guided walking-tour pamphlet outlining some history.

Eldon House

At 481 Ridout St N and dating from 1834, Eldon House (☎ 514-661-5169) is the city's oldest house and is now an historical museum, with period furnishings from the Victorian era. It's open afternoons only, from Tuesday to Sunday. On Tuesday it's free; otherwise a $3 charge applies. Afternoon tea is served.

Guy Lombardo Music Centre

At 205 Wonderland Rd S in Springbank Park, this museum (☎ 514-473-9003) honours the late musician and native son Guy Lombardo, well known across the continent for his New Year's Eve concerts. The collection of articles, including racing boats, and memorabilia outlines his career. Admission is $2. Note that the museum is open daily from May to September only, from 11 am to 5 pm.

Springbank Park

Located by the Thames on the western side of the city, Springbank is a huge, well tended park of lawns and gardens. Within the park is Storybook Gardens, a children's play area with figures from fairy tales and a small zoo. This area has a small admission charge but the park itself is free.

Banting Museum

This museum is in the house where Sir Frederick Banting, Nobel Prize winner and the co-discover of insulin, once lived and worked. The museum (☎ 514-673-1752) outlines the history of diabetes and displays include a doctor's office from the 1920s. The museum is at 442 Adelaide St N and is open Tuesday to Saturday from noon to 4.30 pm. Admission is $3 adult, less for students and seniors.

Children's Museum

Walkable from downtown, the London Regional Children's Museum (☎ 519-434-5726) at 21 Wharncliffe Rd S provides a variety of hands-on exhibits for kids to play

and learn with. It's open every day from 10 am to 5 pm (from noon Sunday) and admission is $4 child or adult.

Sifton Bog

This site is a little different – in fact, it's unique in southern Ontario. It's an acid bog which is home to a range of unusual plants and animals, including lemmings, shrews, the carnivorous sundew plant and nine varieties of orchids. Access to the bog can be gained off Oxford St between Hyde Park Rd and Sanatorium Rd. There is also a pedestrian gate into the bog from the Oakridge Shopping Mall parking lot.

Westminster Ponds

Also for nature-seekers, this area of woods, bogs and ponds supports a variety of wildlife, including foxes and herons. There is a viewing tower, and a boardwalk around some sections of the large undeveloped area. Two thousand years ago, indigenous people camped here. There is a trail into the area, heading east out of the tourist office on Wellington Rd S.

Ska-Nah-Doht Indian Village

Some 32km west of the city, Ska-Nah-Doht (☎ 519-264-2420) is a well done re-creation of a small Iroquois longhouse community of about 1000 years ago. Guided tours are available or you can wander about yourself. The village structures are encircled by a palisade. Outside the walls, crops the Indians would have grown have been planted and there are burial platforms. A museum supplies more information and contains some artefacts.

The site, on Hwy 2, is in the wooded Longwoods Road Conservation Area which has some walking trails. It's open from 9 am to 4 pm daily throughout summer. For the rest of the year, it's closed on weekends and holidays but call to confirm exact dates. Admission is $3. From London, take Hwy 402 to interchange 86 and then follow Hwy 2 west.

Organised Tours

Bus Tour Two-hour tours (☎ 519-661-5000) of the city aboard British double-decker buses depart from City Hall, 300 Dufferin Ave, twice daily from the end of June to the beginning of September. A ticket is $7.50.

Boat Cruise Departing from a landing in Springbank Park, the *London Princess* (☎ 519-473-0363) does a number of different cruises along the river. The basic trip lasts about 45 minutes and costs $7, with discounts for seniors, students and children. There are also Sunday brunch trips and evening dinner cruises. Reservations are a good idea. The season runs from the end of May to October.

Special Events

In the first week in June there is an International Air Show, and in mid-September, the Western Fair, a 10-day agricultural and amusement event. In mid-July, watch for the Home County Folk Festival. It's held in the centre of town, in Victoria Park. There are some pretty big names on stage over the course of the four-day event, and it's free. Dance, crafts and a range of inexpensive food are also featured.

Places to Stay

Camping Within the city limits, there is convenient camping at Fanshawe Conservation Area (☎ 519-451-2800) near the Pioneer Village. It's in the north-eastern section of town, off Fanshawe Park Rd, and is open from the end of April to mid-October.

Hostels During summer *Alumni House* (☎ 519-661-3814) at the University of Western Ontario rents rooms. It's at the Richmond Gates, the entrance into the campus from Richmond St. It costs $32 a single ($26 for students) with a continental breakfast. Be sure to call before arriving. The bus from downtown up Richmond St goes to the university gates, a short walk to the residence.

B&Bs The London & Area B&B Association (☎ 519-673-6797, 1035 Richmond St) has a list of places, averaging $40 single, $55 to $65 double.

Betty and Doug Rose offer three rooms in their 19th century home, *Rose House*

ONTARIO

(☎ 519-433-9978, 526 Dufferin Ave). It's central and costs from $40/55 a single/double with breakfast. The *Hilltop* (☎ 519-681-7841, 82 Compton Crescent) in the south section of the city is just $30 single. Doubles are $55.

Hotels The small, older downtown hotels tend to be alcoholic city. If you don't mind the ambience, there are a couple on Dundas St which are cheap.

Altogether different is the *Quality Hotel* (☎ 519-661-0233, 374 Dundas St) which is central and has its own restaurant. Rooms here are $70 to $80 with breakfast. At the same price, is the plain, no-frills *Super 8 Motel* (☎ 519-433-8161, 636 York St).

Motels For many visitors, the most convenient area to look will be along Wellington Rd, which leads north up from Hwy 401 to the centre of town.

Both *Days Inn* (☎ 519-681-1240, 1100 Wellington Rd S) and *Econo Lodge* (☎ 519-681-1550, 1170 Wellington Rd S) are clean, decent and reasonably priced. Prices at the former are $60, a bit more at the latter and rise a few dollars on weekends.

Cheaper are the smaller, independent motels along the Dundas St E commercial strip, on the east side of town leading to Hwy 2. It's about a 10 to 15 minute drive into downtown. They all seem to be run by East Indians.

A good, low-cost choice is the friendly *American Plaza* (☎ 519-451-2030, 2031 Dundas St E) at $40 single including tax, with a pool and a serviceable, if basic, room. The better *White Village* (☎ 519-451-5840, 1739 Dundas St E) charges $50 including tax.

Places to Eat

A good place to whet and satisfy the appetite is the excellent *market* in the centre of downtown, behind the Bay department store on the corner of Richmond and Dundas Sts. There's plenty of fresh produce, as well as cheeses and breads. A number of small counters also prepare food. It was being rebuilt during research.

The *Rincon Latino* (398 Richmond St) is a hole in the wall south of Dundas St, with excellent and dirt cheap Salvadoran food. Try the bean burrito and the genuine tamales wrapped in banana leaves.

The pleasant *Budapest Restaurant* (346 Dundas St) has been serving up Hungarian and European meals such as goulash, schnitzels and chicken paprika since the 1950s. Lunches are about $8, dinners $15.

On Dundas St at Wellington St, *Scots Corner* is a British-style pub.

For excellent Greek food and atmosphere try *Mykonos* (572 Adelaide St N) on the east side of town. Main courses (including a range of vegetarian dishes and lots of seafood) start at around $10. There's an outdoor patio and Greek music in the evenings.

Under the Volcano (300 Colborne St), named after Malcolm Lowry's great novel, is worth going to for its Mexican food. Dinner dishes are about $12. It's open every day (but not for lunch on Sunday).

Expensive, fine dining in a well appointed, oak-lined room overlooking the Thames River can be found at *Michael's on the Thames* (☎ 519-672-0111, 1 York St). Specialities are seafood and Chateaubriand.

Richmond St, north of Dufferin to Oxford St, is absolutely lined with cafés and various casual eateries.

Entertainment

London has always been a bit of a blues town, and though bars come and go, there is usually at least one place to hear some bar classics. Try the *Old Chicago Speak Easy & Grill* (153 Carling St) which runs off Richmond St between Dundas St and Queens Ave. *Ichabod's* (335 Richmond St) has dance music. *Call the Office* (216 York St) features alternative bands three nights a week and stays open till 3 am. The *CEEPS* (671 Richmond St) at Mill St is a perennial favourite drinking spot for under 30s.

Getting There & Away

Bus The Greyhound bus station (☎ 519-434-3991) is at 101 York St, on the corner of Talbot St, in central downtown. Eight

daily buses run to Toronto ($29) and four to Windsor.

Train The VIA Rail station (☎ 519-672-5722) is nearby, on York St at the foot of Richmond St. It serves Toronto at least half a dozen times a day, two trips going via Stratford. The standard Toronto train fare is $42. In the other direction, the train goes to Chicago via Sarnia or Windsor.

Getting Around

For fares and route information, the London Transit Commission (☎ 519-451-1347), the city bus service, has an office at 167 Dundas St, a couple of doors east of Richmond St.

ST THOMAS

South of London, St Thomas is a small farming community made a little more interesting by the fine Victorian and other period architecture. In the downtown area, City Hall, the Court House and St Thomas Church are all worth a look. Also for history buffs are the two small museums, one on pioneer life, the other on the military past in the vicinity. The Guildhouse Building (dating from 1912) at 180 Talbot St houses a number of arts and crafts stores and galleries.

St Thomas has another, not-so-agreeable claim to fame – it was here in 1885 that Jumbo, that famous circus elephant, was hit and killed by a train. The life-sized statue at the west end of town pays tribute to him.

WINDSOR

Windsor, with a population of 180,000, sits at the south-western tip of the province, south across the Detroit River from Detroit, Michigan. Like its US counterpoint, Windsor is primarily a car-making city. The inner cities, however, differ markedly. Reports from across the river suggest that the core has just about been given up for dead. In contrast, the cute little downtown area of Windsor is neat and clean, with an abundance of parks and gardens, especially along the river.

Windsor has another up on Detroit. In 1994 the city became home to the first casino in the province. Casino Windsor took in $100 million in its first three months of operation and has been attracting a daily attendance of about 20,000 ever since. No wonder Detroit wants one too.

Apart from the delights of the casino, Windsor doesn't have much to offer the visitor but it is a major international border crossing using either the Ambassador Bridge, or the tunnel which runs into Windsor's downtown. From here it is about a two hour drive to London, 4½ hours to Toronto. From Detroit, there are routes to Chicago.

The lively central area is around the junction of Riverside and Ouellette Sts. There are good views of the Detroit skyline, especially from Dieppe Gardens, which run right along the waterfront from the junction of these streets. Pitt and Chatham Sts are also important.

For information, there is a very helpful Ontario Travel Information Centre (☎ 519-973-1338) at 110 Park St E, just a few minutes walk from the bus station. It's open daily all year from 8.30 am to 4.30 pm, and until 8 pm during summer.

The International Freedom Festival combines Canada's 1 July national holiday with the 4 July celebrations in the USA for an event of parades, concerts and dances, with one of the continent's largest fireworks displays to end the affair.

Casino Windsor

The huge, posh casino (☎ 519-258-7878) and hotel complex overlooking the river at 445 Riverside Drive W forms the base for the city's central renewal. It offers gaming tables, including blackjack and roulette, and slot machines which take anything from 25¢ to $500. The minimum age of entry is 19 years. The casino is open all year, 24 hours a day.

There is also the Northern Belle Casino, a pseudo paddle wheeler on the riverfront at 350 Riverside Drive E.

Places to Stay

The *Nisbet Inn* (☎ *519-256-0465, 131 Elliott St W*), with a pub, is quite central and offers B&B at $55/65 a single/double.

Diotte Bed & Breakfast (☎ 519-256-3937, 427 Elm Ave) about five blocks west of the casino, has rooms from $50. A full breakfast is included. The tourist office has a complete list of B&Bs but most tend to be away from the centre.

The downtown *Travelodge (☎ 519-258-7774, 33 Riverside Drive E)* is central, very close to the casino and has singles/doubles for $70.

Most accommodation is in motels, and the place to look for moderately priced ones is in South Windsor, on Dougall Ave. For example, the *ABC (☎ 519-969-5090, 3048 Dougall Ave)* charges $55 single or double. More expensive and better is the *Cadillac Motel (☎ 519-969-9340, 2498 Dougall St)*. Rooms here start at $65.

Another area rich in motels is Huron Church Rd. The *Econo Lodge (☎ 519-966-8811, ☎ 1-800-553-2666, 2000 Huron Church Rd)* is 2km from the Ambassador Bridge.

Places to Eat

There's no shortage of eateries along Ouellette St, which runs down to Riverside Dr. *Beans Caffé*, on Ouellette on the corner of Pitt St offers light meals from $3, desserts and speciality coffees and is open until midnight.

The *Under the Corner Restaurant (309 Chatham St W)* which runs across Ouellette, is a really nice little place with an attached bakery. It's good for any meal and is very low-priced, especially for breakfast.

For seafood, try the *Old Fish Market (156 Chatham St W)* two blocks east of the casino. Dishes are $15 to $20.

A good place for a meal is in the Via Italia neighbourhood along Erie St between Howard Ave and Lincoln Rd. Among the many Italian restaurants try the casually classy *Spago Trattoria (614 Erie St)* for excellent sandwiches and salads. Pizza is also offered.

Ottawa St south-east of the core has a multi-ethnic flavour with a number of European restaurants including Polish and Hungarian and also an East Indian place.

Patrick O'Ryan's (25 Pitt St) is an Irish-type pub.

Getting There & Away

The bus station (☎ 514-254-7575) is central, on Chatham St, slightly east of Ouellette St. There are no long distance buses for US destinations. Take the Tunnel bus for $2.35 to the Detroit inner city bus terminal. From here connections can be made for other cities.

The VIA Rail station (☎ 519-256-5511) is about 3km east of the downtown core, on the corner of Walker and Wyandotte Sts. There are frequent trains to Toronto via London.

AMHERSTBURG

South of Windsor, where the Detroit River flowing from Lake St Clair, runs into Lake Erie, Amherstburg is a small, historic town.

Much of this history is outlined at the **Fort Malden National Historic Site**, along the river, at 100 Laird Ave. There are some remains of the British fort of 1840. Beginning with the arrival of the fur traders, the area was the focal point for a lot of tension between the French, Native Indians and English and, later, the Americans. Here during the War of 1812, General Brock (together with ally Shawnee Chief Tecumseh) discussed plans to take Detroit.

The **North American Black Historical Museum** has displays on both black history in North America in general and black settlement of the Windsor area in particular. It's at 277 King St W and is open Wednesday to Sunday from April to October.

Park House Museum, the oldest house in town, wasn't built here but rather it was ferried across the river in 1799 and is now furnished in 1850s style. It's at 214 Dalhousie St, and is open daily in summer but closed Monday and Saturday the rest of the year.

Also from here, ferries run to Canadian **Boblo Island**, where there is a huge amusement park which has been here for about 100 years. Boats also connect the island to Detroit. Moonlit night cruises run in midsummer.

LAKE HURON SHORELINE & AREA

North of Windsor, on the southern tip of Lake Huron, industrial **Sarnia** is the hub of Chemical Valley, a large, modern oil-and-chemical production and refining complex.

Black Settlement in Ontario

The stories of the French, the English and the Natives that settled this region of Canada are well known. But to these stories must be added a fourth – that of the many blacks who came to the region prior to the American Civil War (1861-65).

Essex and Kent counties, around Windsor and Chatham, make up one of the two regions of early black settlement in Canada (the other is around Halifax, Nova Scotia).

Windsor, as a terminal on the so-called Underground Railroad, was a gateway to freedom for thousands of former black slaves in pre-civil war USA. The railway was really just a network of people ('conductors') who aided, directed and fed the fleeing slaves as, each night, they followed the north star to the next 'station'.

Aside from the museum in Amherstburg, there are several sites in the region relating directly to this saga.

The John Freeman Walls Historic Site is located 1.5km north off Hwy 401 at exit 28 out of Windsor heading west. The site includes the log cabin built in 1876 by Walls, a fugitive slave from North Carolina. The Underground Railroad Museum is also here.

Farther west, visit the Raleigh Township Centennial Museum near Chatham, on County Rd 6 south of Hwy 401 after exiting at Bloomfield Rd. This museum concentrates on the lives of the black settlers who turned the Elgin Settlement into a new home and welcoming centre for others following in their footsteps.

In the town of Dresden is Uncle Tom's Cabin Historic Site. Uncle Tom was a fictional character in the controversial novel of the same name written by Harriet Beecher Stowe in 1852. It was based on the life of Josiah Henson, another southern black man. The site displays articles relating to the story and salient history.

Just how much the tales of the Underground Railway are ingrained in the hearts of black Americans was suggested a few years ago when the Toronto Argonaut football team outbid several American teams for the services of hot new rookie, Raghib 'Rocket' Ismail, just out of college. Ismail toured Toronto before deciding if he would join the Argonauts, and, sensing the region's racial tolerance, struck a deal with them. After Rocket signed for an obscene amount of money, reporters at the obligatory news conference asked his mother what she thought of the agreement. Her reply was that they were going to ride that train north to freedom.

Across the Bluewater Bridge over the St Clair River is Port Huron, Michigan.

South-east of Sarnia on Hwy 21 is the **Oil Museum of Canada**, a National Historic Site and the location of the first commercial oil well on the continent. Producing wells can be seen in the area, and the search for more oil continues.

Along Lake Huron as far up as Tobermory on the Bruce Peninsula are numerous and popular parks, good sandy beaches, cottages and summer resort towns. The water is warm and clean, the beaches broad and sandy.

At **Kettle Point**, about 40km north-east of Sarnia, is a 350-million-year-old attraction. Along the shoreline are a series of spherical rocks called kettles (to geologists, concretions). Some of these calcite formations, which sit on beds of softer shale, are nearly 1m in diameter. The rare kettles are found in other countries but are often underground, and this collection is considered top rate. Farther up the coast, south of Grand Bend, is the excellent **Pinery Provincial Park** (☎ 519-243-2220) with 1000 camp sites. The beach is 10km long and trails wind through the wooded

sections. Farther north is smaller Point Farms Park.

Grand Bend is a Lake Huron resort town. It's a lively place in summer, with a few places for a drink along the shoreline.

Acting as the regional centre, **Goderich** is a small, green and attractive town with a distinctive circular main street. It bills itself as the prettiest town in Ontario.

At dusk, view the 'world's best sunsets' from near the Governor's House & Historic Gaol Museum. It's set on a cliff on the town bluffs over the water. And these sunsets really are spectacular. Also in town, on West St, is a Marine Museum (with displays on shipping and the lake), the Huron County Pioneer Museum and the expensive, resorty *Benmiller Inn* (☎ 519-524-2191, ☎ 1-800-265-1711).

The nearby village of **Blyth** is home to a major summer theatre festival which features primarily Canadian plays, both new and old. A unique B&B in town is the *Blyth Station House* (☎ 519-523-9826) in the converted train station. Rooms, all with private bathroom, start at $70. Several restaurants can be found along Queen St, the main street.

See after Owen Sound in the following Georgian Bay & Lakelands section for details of the northern Lake Huron region as far as Manitoulin Island.

Georgian Bay & Lakelands

North of Toronto, the lakes and woods, towns, resorts, beaches and cottages, all presided over by magnificent Georgian Bay and its varied shoreline, make up the playground of southern Ontario.

The mostly wooded hills, scores of lakes and rivers and numerous parks are scattered in and around prime farmland, making for fine summer fishing, swimming, camping and lazing – just what the doctor ordered. In winter the area is busy with winter recreation: skiing, snowmobiling and lots of ice fishing. In September and October, people tour the region to see nature's annual, brilliantly coloured tree show. Despite the emphasis on outdoor activities, this is generally a busy and developed area. For more space or wilderness, head farther north, or to the larger parks such as Algonquin.

The district around Barrie and Lake Simcoe to Orillia and north-west to Penetanguishene, and then around Georgian Bay west to Collingwood, is known collectively as **Huronia**. The area north of Orillia (roughly between the towns of Gravenhurst and Huntsville along Hwy 11) and west to Georgian Bay is referred to as **Muskoka** or (incorrectly) as the Muskokas. The name is taken from one of the larger lakes of the region.

West from Collingwood along the south of Nottawasaga Bay, a smaller bay within Georgian Bay, is Owen Sound. Located at the southern entrance to the Bruce Peninsula, Owen Sound is the largest town in this area. The 'Bruce' is the narrow strip of land running north which divides Georgian Bay from the main body of huge Lake Huron. From the tip of the peninsula at Tobermory, ferries may be taken to Manitoulin Island, with connections to the mainland of northern Ontario.

The following text leads first from Barrie west and north to Manitoulin Island, around western Georgian Bay, and then from Barrie north and east through the Muskoka-Huronia region, around eastern Georgian Bay.

BARRIE

Barrie, about 1½ hours north of Toronto, is more or less the unofficial gateway to the big city's northward cottage country. On Friday afternoon, especially holiday summer weekends, expect a lot of traffic on Hwy 400, at least to Barrie and often beyond. Coming back into Toronto, the traffic is heavy on Sunday night.

There is nothing of particular note in Barrie itself, although the popular beach at Centennial Park (on Kempenfelt Bay of large Lake Simcoe) is convenient and generally busy.

The bus station (☎ 705-739-1500) is central, at 24 Maple Ave. From here buses go in all directions.

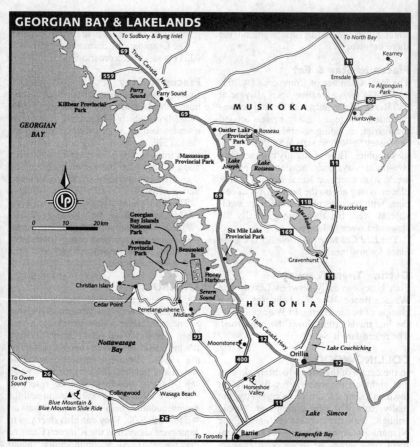

GEORGIAN BAY & LAKELANDS

Information

There's a large Ontario Travel Information Centre (☎ 705-725-7280, ☎ 1-800-668-2746) just south of Barrie at 21 Molson Park Drive at Hwy 400, with details on regional points of interest. It's open all year.

A smaller, more locally oriented tourist office can be found at 17A Mulcaster St.

WASAGA BEACH

Wasaga is the beach resort closest to Toronto. Around Wasaga Beach and the

strip of beaches (about 14km long) running up along the bay are hundreds of cottages, and several private campgrounds. The centre of activity is the decidedly unsubtle town of Wasaga Beach and its excellent beach (with fine swimming) at Wasaga Beach Provincial Park (day-use only). The park also has some fine, inland hiking.

A popular weekend spot, Wasaga Beach is nearly empty during the week. Some areas of the beach are more for families; others (like those around the snack bars) attract the

ONTARIO

younger crowd. Wasaga Beach has two water slides, including one right on the shore in town.

Places to Stay & Eat
The local Chamber of Commerce (☎ 705-429-2247) with an office open all year at 550 River Rd can help with finding accommodation. There are many motels around the district, including several along Main St or Mosley St. Rooms start at $45/55 for singles/doubles. They're slightly cheaper for a two-night stay, and cheaper still by the week. Also check on Rural Route 1. Other places to stay are on the beach. Lots of cottages with housekeeping facilities are available as well, but these are generally for stays of a week or longer.

The *Red Caboose (88 Main St)* is a good place for any meal.

Getting There & Away
Four buses run daily between Toronto and Wasaga Beach. It's a 2½ hour trip, with a change of bus in Barrie. In Wasaga Beach, the bus travels right down the main road. The return fare is $46.

COLLINGWOOD
In the centre of the Blue Mountain ski area and right on the water, this little resort town has a reputation for being pretty, but really isn't. The surroundings are scenic enough, with the highest sections of the Niagara Escarpment nearby. The escarpment runs south, all the way to Niagara Falls. The caves along it near town are heavily and misleadingly promoted; they are not what most people expect of that term, but are really more like overhangs. There is some good walking, however; the hour-long trail by the caves loops over interesting terrain and offers excellent views. An admission fee is charged to the area around the caves, with an additional charge to actually see the caves.

In summer, a chairlift runs to the top of Blue Mountain, from where there is a choice down of the chairlift, a slide-ride or cycling trails. The area is known for its 'blue' pottery, which is nice but not cheap. A bluegrass music festival is held here in summer.

The Chamber of Commerce (☎ 705-445-0221) is at 155 Hurontario St.

Places to Stay
Collingwood has an excellent Backpackers hostel, the *Blue Mountain Auberge (☎ 705-445-1497)*, which is open all year but is often booked out. It's on Rural Route 3, near the ski hills north of Craigleith – about 2½ hours from Toronto. There are about 60 beds and a kitchen in a chalet-style building. The sauna is a bonus. Rates are $17 in summer, $20 in winter.

There are plenty of motels too, including the *Milestone Motel (☎ 705-445-1041, 327 First St)* with rooms from $50. Of course, there are more expensive places in the area, including some resorts, lodges and inns with all the amenities.

SHELBURNE
A rather nondescript small southern Ontario country town between Toronto and Owen Sound, Shelburne comes alive once a year when it hosts the old-time fiddlers' contest. It's been held for two days in August since the 1950s. There's a parade, free music shows and ticketed concerts for the contest semi-finalists which should be reserved. For more information on the event and for accommodation help call the town hall on ☎ 519-925-2600. They can also steer you to campgrounds such as the Kinsmen Camp or Primrose Park. All accommodation should be reserved before the festival.

OWEN SOUND
Owen Sound, with a population of 22,000, is the largest town in the region, and if you're going north up the Bruce Peninsula toward Manitoulin Island, you'll pass by. It sits at the end of a deep bay, surrounded on three sides by the Niagara Escarpment.

Although still a working port, it is not the shipping centre it was from the 1880s to the first years of this century. In those early days, before the railway, the town rocked with brothels and bars, and was battled over

Skiing & Snowboarding North of Toronto

Though the region north of Toronto tends to have milder winters and the topography is considerably less dramatic than in either Quebec or around the Rockies, skiing is still a major winter activity. There are three main alpine centres, all offering daily equipment rental.

Closest to Toronto (about a two hour drive) is Horseshoe Valley (☎ 705-835-2790, or ☎ 416-283-2988 in Toronto). Take Hwy 400 up past Barrie to Horseshoe Valley Rd. Turn off and the ski hill is 6km east. This is the smallest and lowest in elevation of the three and ideal for kids, families, the inexperienced or the merely out of shape. It's open every day and has night skiing until 10 pm. Plenty of lifts (including a quad chair) mean the lines move quickly even on busy days. A plus here is that there is also a good system of nearly 40km of groomed cross-country trails. The trails close at 4.30 pm.

Mount St Louis Moonstone (☎ 705-835-2112, or ☎ 416-368-6900 in Toronto) is one of the province's top ski resorts, and the largest (in terms of the number of ski slopes) in southern Ontario. It's at the village of Coldwater, about 10 or 15 minutes north of Horseshoe Valley continuing on Hwy 400. Take exit 131 to the right. Features include snowmaking and two licensed lodges (no accommodation). There are 42 runs, ranging through easy to difficult, with a 160m vertical drop.

Blue Mountain Resorts (☎ 705-445-0231, or ☎ 416-869-3799 in Toronto) at Collingwood is considered the most challenging of southern Ontario's ski centres and, being relatively far north, tends to have more natural snow and a longer season. The vertical drop here is 216m, with the maximum run length 1200m. Lifts include quad, triple and double chairs.

Collingwood is about a 2½ hour drive from Toronto. The slopes are 13km west of town on Blue Mountain Rd. There's a daily bus service from Toronto.

Cross-country (nordic) skiing is considerably less expensive; entrance fees to most places are in the range of $7 to $10 for the day.

For cross-country skiing north of the city, there is the aforementioned Horseshoe Valley or, for a relatively wild, undisturbed winter wonderland, Awenda Provincial Park (☎ 705-549-2231) in Penetanguishene is recommended. Both are open daily.

Close to Toronto are two good places to consider for cross-country skiing. Albion Hills Conservation Area (☎ 905-880-4855) is 8km north of the town of Bolton, which is north-west of Toronto. Equipment can be hired and there are 26km of trails winding through the woods. End a good day here with a snack in the coffee shop.

A second choice is to ski the grounds of Seneca College (☎ 905-833-3333 ext 5024) at its King Campus, at 13990 Dufferin St, in King City. It offers 'old, used and abused' skis and boots for rent. Call for trail conditions. When there is a lot of snow, the trails are open every day, and they are good, winding through the woods. There is no public transportation to the campus.

For the ski conditions report phone ☎ 416-314-0988 in Toronto.

There are excellent skiing opportunities in Ontario.

by the believers – one intersection had a bar on each corner and was known as Damnation Corner; another had four churches and was called Salvation Corner. The latter seems to have won out, because the churches are still there. In fact, for 66 long years from 1906 to 1972, you couldn't buy alcohol here. There aren't too many merchant sailors on the waterfront now, but sections of it have been restored with marinas and restaurants.

Orientation & Information

The Sydenham River drifts through town, dividing it between east and west; the main street is Second Ave. There's a Visitor Information Centre (☎ 519-371-9833, ☎ 1-888-675-5555) at 1155 1st Ave W. You can get a folder from here or from City Hall detailing a two hour, self-guided historic walking tour of the city. A Saturday market is held beside City Hall.

Harrison Park

This large park is right in town, along the Sydenham River. It has picnic areas, trails, fishing and even camping.

Tom Thomson Memorial Art Gallery

Thomson was a contemporary of Canada's Group of Seven and is one of the country's best known painters. He grew up here and many of his works were done in this part of the country. The gallery (☎ 519-376-1932) at 840 First Ave W also displays the work of other Canadian painters. From June to September it's open Tuesday to Saturday from 10 am to 5 pm (until 9 pm Wednesday) and on Sunday from noon to 5 pm. Admission is by donation.

County of Grey & Owen Sound Museum

Here you can see exhibits on the area's geology and human history (☎ 519-376-3690). On display are a half-sized replica of an Ojibway Indian village, an 8m birchbark canoe and log cabin. The museum is at 975 Sixth St E.

Billy Bishop Heritage Museum

Home-town boy Billy Bishop, who became a flying ace in WWI, is honoured here. The museum (☎ 519-371-0031) is in the Bishop home, at 948 Third Ave W. Billy is buried in town, at the Greenwood Cemetery.

Marine & Rail Museum

In the old train station at 1165 First Ave W, next to the information centre, this museum details the transportation and shipbuilding history of Owen Sound.

Mill Dam & Fish Ladder

In spring and autumn, it's interesting to see the struggle that trout have to go through to reach their preferred spawning areas – this dam and ladder were set up to help them on their swim upstream. It's a couple of blocks south of downtown.

Kelso Beach

North of downtown is Kelso Beach, on Georgian Bay. Free concerts are held regularly here in summer.

Inglis Falls

Some 6km south of town, off Hwy 6, the Sydenham River falls over the Niagara Escarpment. The falls, a 24m drop, are set in a conservation area which is linked to the Bruce Trail. The trail runs from Tobermory south to the Niagara River. See under Tobermory later in this chapter for details. The segment by Owen Sound offers good views and springs, as well as the Inglis, Jones and Indian falls. It makes a nice half-day walk.

Special Events

The three-day Summerfolk music festival (☎ 519-371-2995), held annually around the second or third weekend of August, is a major North American festival of its kind. The event is held in Kelso Park, right along the water, and attracts crowds of up to 10,000. Musicians come from around the continent. Tickets cost around $20 a day – and each day is a full one. There's camping nearby.

Places to Stay

Camping Very conveniently, there are two municipal campgrounds right in town (☎ 519-371-9734). One is across the road from Kelso Beach, ideal for the music festival. Another is in *Harrison Park*, which charges $14 per site (without electricity), and you can use the heated pool – Georgian Bay is known for its cold water.

Motels Most accommodation is provided by motels. There are several on Ninth Ave, including the low-priced *Travellers Motel* (☎ 519-376-2680) with rooms from $42. The *Key Motel* (☎ 519-794-2350), 11km south of town on Hwys 6 and 10, is costlier but still in the moderate range, with rooms from $45 to $55.

Places to Eat

There are a few places along the waterfront and most offer fish. The *Marketside Café* (813 2nd Ave E) has good takeout sandwiches and salads. *Kelsey's* at the Heritage Place Mall, 16th St E, has a licensed patio and a range of finger foods and grilled meals from $8 to $16.

PORT ELGIN

Port Elgin is a little resort town on Lake Huron, west of Owen Sound. There are sandy beaches, the warm waters of Lake Huron, cottages and camping. **MacGregor Provincial Park**, with camping and some walking trails, is 5km south.

Farther south is the **Bruce Nuclear Plant**, which is controversial, of course, as are all nuclear plants in Canada. There are free tours and a film on nuclear power.

The **Saugeen River** has been divided up into canoeing sections ranging from 20 to 40km. Half-day and longer trips have been mapped out, with camping at several points along the river. A shorter trip is along the **Rankin River**.

SAUBLE BEACH

Sauble Beach is a summer resort with an excellent, sandy 11km beach, warm shallow waters and entertainment diversions.

The coast all along here is known for good sunsets.

There are plenty of hotels, motels and cottages for rent. Expect the many area campgrounds to be busy on summer weekends. Best is the *Sauble Falls Provincial Park* (☎ 519-422-1952). Reservations are a good idea. Farther north along the road are several commercial campgrounds although some of them tend to be noisy at night with young party goers – check with the neighbours if this is a concern!

A walk around some of the side streets of the downtown area sometimes turns up a guesthouse sign or a seasonal B&B. Cottages tend to be cheaper than motels. *Chilwell's Cottages* (☎ 519-422-1692, 31 Third Ave N) has six small cottages and is one of the cheapest at $40 for two people. Prices generally range from $45 to $80.

THE BRUCE PENINSULA

The Bruce, as it's known, is an 80km-long limestone outcropping at the north end of the Niagara Escarpment. Jutting into Lake Huron, it forms the western edge of Georgian Bay, splitting it away from the main body of the lake. This relatively undeveloped area of southern Ontario offers some striking scenery, mixing rocky, rugged shorelines, sandy beaches, lakeside cliffs and green woodlands. The north end has two national parks. From Tobermory (at the tip of the peninsula), ferries depart for Manitoulin Island. For regional information call the Bruce County Tourism Office (☎ 1-800-268-3838).

At Cape Croker, an Ojibway reserve north of Colpoy's Bay, about halfway up the peninsula, there's a secluded recommended campground. Nature tours are available and Native Indian crafts are offered for sale.

Dyer's Bay

If you have a car, a good scenic drive can be made via Dyer's Bay, which is about 20km south of Tobermory. From Hwy 6, take Dyer's side road into the village and then the road north-east along the coast. It's not long, but with Georgian Bay on one side and the limestone cliffs of the escarpment

on the other, it is impressive. The road ends at the Cabot Head Lighthouse. Before arriving there, you'll pass by the ruins of an old log flume where logs were sent over the edge. The road south of Dyer's Bay is also good, leading down to a 'flowerpot' known as the Devil's Monument. Flowerpots are top-heavy standing rock formations created by wave erosion. This secondary road continues to Lion's Head, where you can connect back with the main highway.

Dorcas Bay

On Lake Huron, 11km south of Tobermory, there is a preserve owned by the Federation of Ontario Naturalists. This undeveloped area attracts many walkers and photographers for its wildflowers – up to 41 species of orchids can be spotted. To reach the site, turn west from Hwy 11 towards Lake Huron. You're there when you reach the parking lot with a few picnic tables and a toilet.

Bruce Peninsula National Park

The park (☎ 519-596-2233) protects and makes accessible some of the best features on the entire peninsula. For hikers, campers and lovers of nature, it's not to be missed. The park has several unconnected components, with segments on both sides of the peninsula, including Cypress Lake, some of the Georgian Bay coastline, the Niagara Escarpment between Tobermory and Dyer's Bay, and a great section of the Bruce Trail along the shoreline cliffs. Cypress Lake, with the campground, swimming and some shorter walking trails, is the centre of most activity.

Tobermory

This unpretentious fishing and tourist village (population 900) sits at the northern tip of the Bruce Peninsula, which protrudes into Lake Huron. On one side of the peninsula are the cold, clear waters of Georgian Bay, and on the other the much warmer waters of Lake Huron.

There is not much to see in town itself, but it is a busy place in summer. The Manitoulin Island ferry docks here. Aside from having its own charms, many people driving

across Ontario and farther west cut through Manitoulin because it's quicker than driving around Georgian Bay. Tobermory marks the end of the 780km Bruce Trail and it is also a diving centre. The crystal-clear waters offshore contain more than 20 shipwrecks.

Activity is focused at the harbour area known as Little Tub. There's a Parks Canada centre here and a visitor information office (☎ 1-800-268-3838) just south of Little Tub on Hwy 6. Boats for tours of Flowerpot Island and all sorts of visiting yachts moor at Little Tub.

To reach Tobermory from the north, see under Manitoulin Island later in this chapter.

Fathom Five National Marine Park

This is Ontario's first partially underwater park (☎ 519-596-2233), developed to protect and make more accessible this intriguing offshore area, including the wrecks which lie in the park's waters, scattered between the many little islands.

About 5km offshore from Tobermory, **Flowerpot Island** is the best known, most visited portion of the park and is more easily enjoyed than the underwater attractions. The island, with its unusual, precarious-looking rock columns formed through years of erosion, can be visited by boat from mid-May to mid-October. There are various trails on the island, taking from a little over an hour for the shortest one to 2¼ hours for the more difficult. Look for the wild orchids. The island has cliffs, some picnic spots and six basic camp sites.

Reservations are needed for tenters, particularly on weekends, and you should bring all supplies with you, including water. Note that the mental image may not correspond with reality – there is little privacy, with boatloads of mainlanders arriving throughout the day. So much for the isolated island adventure.

Various companies and tugboats offer boat trips to the island allowing visitors to hop off and catch a later boat back. The cost is about $14; just ask around the harbour area. The glass-bottomed boat is the best known, but the waters are so clear that

wrecks can be seen simply by peering over the side of any boat. The last boat tours depart at around 5 pm. Tours don't run in poor weather conditions.

Bruce Trail Tobermory marks the northern end of this 780km footpath, which runs from Queenston (on the Niagara River) to this point (on the tip of the Bruce Peninsula, on Georgian Bay) over private and public lands. You can hike for an hour, a day or a week. The trail edges along the Niagara Escarpment, providing good scenery, though much of it is inaccessible from the road. UNESCO (United Nations Educational, Scientific and Cultural Organisation) has designated the Niagara Escarpment a World Biosphere Reserve – an area that although developed preserves essential ecological features.

The most northerly bit, from Dyer's Bay to Tobermory, is the most rugged and spectacular. A good day's walk within the national park is possible. You may even get a glimpse of the rare Ontario rattlesnakes, though the chance of seeing one is slight and they tend to be timid, so don't let their existence deter you from a hike.

The Bruce Trail Association (☎ 1-800-665-4452, www.brucetrail.org) puts out a detailed guide of the entire route for about $32, less for members. It's available in major bookstores. The mailing address is PO Box 857, Hamilton, L8N 3N9. Local tourist offices can tell you where there are access points.

Some parts of the trail are heavily used on summer weekends. Near Hamilton, at the southern end, there is a popular day walking area at Rattlesnake Point Conservation Area. Another southern one is at Terra Cotta, not far from Toronto. Yet another is at the forks of the Credit River.

There are designated areas for camping along the path, and in the gentler, busy southern sections there are some huts where you can even take a shower. In other sections there is accommodation in B&Bs or old inns. Prices start at $45/55 for singles/doubles. Remember the insect repellent, don't drink the water along the trail and bring good boots – much of the trail is wet and muddy.

Diving The waters here are excellent for scuba diving, with many wrecks, geological formations and clear water. The water is also very, very cold. Even for snorkelling a wet or dry suit is required. G & S Watersports (☎ 519-596-2200) at Little Tub in Tobermory hires out equipment and offers a variety of diving courses. To rent snorkel equipment, including a basic wetsuit, costs around $25. The Ontario government puts out a pamphlet listing dive sites with descriptions, depths and recommendations. It's available free at the tourist office.

In 1993 a large section of well preserved, 8000-year-old underwater forest was discovered at Colpoy's Bay. It is thought to have been submerged hundreds of years after the retreat of the last Ice Age, when the lake levels rose.

Other Activities Swimming in Georgian Bay in August can be good and warm, but not around here. Shallow Cypress Lake, in the park, is definitely a more sane choice. Farther south on the bay, at **Wasaga Beach** and **Penetanguishene**, the water is quite pleasant. The waters along the Lake Huron shoreline are also warm, even on the west side of the Bruce Peninsula, for example **Sauble Beach**. Huron Kayak Adventures (☎ 519-596-2950), based in Tobermory from mid-May to late-September, rents kayaks and offers tours and instruction.

Places to Stay *Tobermory Village Campground* (☎ 519-596-2689), 3km south of the village, has four basic rooms with shared bathroom for $35. Camping costs $18.

There are a dozen or so motels in and around Tobermory but prices are a little high in peak season and reservations are recommended for weekends and holidays. The *Harbourside Motel* (☎ 519-596-2422) overlooks Little Tub and has rooms from around $55 during the week. The *Peacock Villa Motel* (☎ 519-596-2242), in a secluded spot

ONTARIO

a short walk from the harbour, has rooms at comparable prices.

Places to Eat There are plenty of restaurants in Tobermory, all specialising in variations of whitefish. All the motels have dining rooms too. The *Ferry Dock* restaurant is a cheap and pleasant place for breakfast with tables overlooking Little Tub Harbour.

MANITOULIN ISLAND

The world's largest freshwater island, Manitoulin Island is basically a rural region of small farms. About a third of the population is Native Indian. Tourism has become the island's main moneymaker and many southerners own summer cottages here.

The island is about 140km long and 40km wide, with a scenic coastline, some sandy beaches, 100 lakes (including some large ones), lots of small towns and villages and numerous hiking trails. It has remained fairly undeveloped. Visitors will soon find out that part of the reason for this is the difficulty of getting to the island and, once there, in getting around. Transportation around the island is nonexistent but ask at the tourist offices for any tours which may have started up.

There are seasonal information offices in South Baymouth (where the ferry lands), Gore Bay, Mindemoya and Little Current (☎ 705-368-3021), the main one. West of the ferry landing, at the village of **Providence Bay**, is the island's largest beach. Also here is the well known *Schoolhouse Restaurant*. Beyond **Meldrum Bay**, at **Mississagi Point** on the far western tip of the island, an old lighthouse (from 1873) provides views over the strait. There is a campground here, as well as a restaurant and a museum in the old lighthouse-keeper's cottage. Meldrum Bay has an inn with a restaurant. Along the north side of the island from Meldrum Bay to Little Current is some of the best scenery.

Gore Bay, on the rocky north shore, has one of the island's five small museums, displaying articles relating to the island's early settlers. See the prisoners' dining-room table from the jail. From the eastern headland at the edge of town, the lookout offers fine views. On the other side of town, the headland has a lighthouse and a campground. One of the main beauty spots, **Bridal Veil Falls**, is 16km east.

The largest community is **Little Current** at the beginning of the causeway north to the mainland towards the town of Espanola. The main tourist office for the island is here and can help you find a B&B. Rates are not bad on the island, relative to the southern mainland. There are two viewpoints of note near town and one good walk. The Cup & Saucer Trail, 19km east of town, leads to the highest point on the island (351m), which has good views over the North Channel. Closer to town, 4km west and 16km south on Hwy 6, **McLeans Mountain** has a lookout with views towards the village of **Killarney**, on the mainland.

The **Wikwemikong Indian Reserve** is in the north-east part of Manitoulin Island. The Interpretive Centre (☎ 705-859-2385) has information on events and things to see.

Activities

Two principal attractions of the island for many visitors are the fishing and boating. There are several fishing camps around the island. For cruising, the 225km North Channel is superb. The scenery is great – one fjord, **Baie Finn**, is 15km long, with pure white quartzite cliffs.

There are quite a few hiking trails; the tourist offices have information.

Special Events

As mentioned, Manitoulin Island has a considerable Native Indian population. At the **Wikwemikong Reserve**, known as Wiky, the largest powwow (loosely translated as 'cultural festival') in the province is held on the first weekend in August, a three-day civic holiday. Native Indians from around the country participate. It's an all-inclusive event, with dancing and music, food and crafts.

Getting There & Away

Bus Getting to Tobermory or Manitoulin Island is a little difficult without a car. You must change buses in Owen Sound for the

Bruce Peninsula. From Toronto, and elsewhere, buses run frequently to Owen Sound but from there buses go to Tobermory on Friday, Saturday and Sunday in summer only. The complete trip takes almost the whole day. The schedule varies each year, so call for the latest information.

Greyhound goes all the way around Georgian Bay from Toronto to Espanola, and from there down to Little Current (on Manitoulin). There is no train service.

Ferry From Tobermory, the *Chi-Cheemaun* (☎ 1-800-265-3163) runs over to South Baymouth, on the southern edge of Manitoulin. It's not uncommon to have to wait in line for a crossing so reservations are strongly suggested. There are four crossings daily in midsummer, two in spring and autumn. From Tobermory, departure times are 7 am and 11.20 am, and 3.40 pm and 8 pm.

During the summer ferry season, mid-June to the beginning of September, the adult fare is $11. Cars cost $24. The 50km trip takes about 1¾ hours and there is a cafeteria on board.

Car The island makes a good short cut if you're heading to northern Ontario. Take the ferry from Tobermory, cross the island and then take the bridges to the north shore of Georgian Bay. The route can save you a few hours of driving around the bay and is pleasant, although more costly.

MIDLAND

North of Barrie, on the eastern side of Georgian Bay, is the small commercial centre of Midland (population 15,000), the most interesting of the Huronia region's towns. The Huron Indians first settled this area, and developed a confederacy to encourage cooperation among the neighbouring Native peoples. The established Huron settlements attracted the French explorers and, more critically, the Jesuit missionaries.

Midland has a number of worthwhile things to see. Unfortunately, even though the town is quite small, getting to the cluster of sites out of the centre is difficult without your own vehicle.

Information

For information, see the Chamber of Commerce (☎ 705-526-7884, ☎ 1-800-263-7745) at 208 King St, opposite the bus station, just south of the town dock.

Little Lake Park

South of Yonge St, a short walk from downtown, Little Lake Park has 100-year-old trees, a small lake and a sandy beach.

Huron Indian Village

Within the park, the Huron Indian village (☎ 705-526-2844) is a replica of what the Native Indian settlements may have been like 500 years ago (before the French Jesuits arrived on their soul-saving mission). The **Huronia Museum**, adjacent to the village site, has a good collection of Native Indian and pioneer artefacts (check The Slenderizer, circa 1958), as well as some paintings and sketches by members of the Group of Seven. A combined ticket to the museum and village is $5. It's open all year.

Sainte Marie among the Hurons

Away from the centre of town, this historic site (☎ 705-526-7838) reconstructs the 17th century Jesuit mission and tells the story of a rather bloody chapter in the book of Native Indian/European clashes. Graphic depictions of missionaries' deaths by torture were forever etched in the brains of older Canadians by now-discarded school history texts. **Martyrs' Shrine**, opposite the Sainte Marie complex, is a monument to six martyred missionaries and the site of pilgrimages each year. Even the pope showed up in 1984. Sainte Marie is 5km east of the town centre on Hwy 12. It's open daily from May to October and admission is $7.25. There's a café on the site.

Wye Marsh Wildlife Centre

Right next to the mission site, the centre (☎ 705-526-7809) provides boardwalks, trails and an observation deck over the

marsh and its abundant birdlife. Most notable of the feathered features are the trumpeter swans, once virtually wiped out in the area and now being brought back. The first hatching in the wild as part of this program took place in the spring of 1993. Displays provide information on the flora and fauna found in the area. Guided walks are offered free with admission ($6) and canoe trips through the marsh are also possible (for an extra $4). The site has a pleasant picnic area set amid indigenous gardens. It's open daily.

Organised Tours

From the town dock, 2½-hour boat tours depart aboard the *Miss Midland* (☎ 705-526-0161) for the inside passage to Georgian Bay and the islands around **Honey Harbour**. Cruises run from mid-May to mid-October, with two trips daily during summer months. A ticket is $14.

Places to Stay

The Chamber of Commerce has a list of B&Bs. There are a couple of central ones on King St, just across from the Huron village and museum. *B&B with the Artists (☎ 705-526-8102, 431 King St)* has singles/doubles at $45/55.

King's Motel (☎ 705-526-7744, 751 King St) on the main street running north to south, has rooms from $45.

Places to Eat

Riv Bistro (249 King St) serves moderately priced Greek food and good felafels. Down at the town dock there's a popular pub offering hamburgers, fries and salads.

Getting There & Away

Penetang & Midland Coach Lines (PMCL; ☎ 705-526-0161) connects to the main bus station in Toronto while also running to Penetanguishene.

PENETANGUISHENE

Slightly north of Midland, this town (pronounced 'pen-e-TANG-wish-een' but known as Penetang) is smaller but similarly historic. It has both a British and French popu-

lation and past. Early French voyageurs, fur traders, set up around the British military posts, and both communities stayed. There is an information office at 2 Main St (☎ 705-527-6484, ☎ 1-800-263-7745).

Discovery Harbour (☎ 705-549-8064) is a reconstructed naval base along Church St north of the centre. It was built by the British after the War of 1812 in case the USA forces came back for more, but they didn't. The site features eight reconstructed ships, 19th century naval buildings and costumed staff. In summer there are daily sailing programs aboard the two schooners *BEE* and *Tecumseth*.

For somewhere to eat, try *Captain Roberts' Table* down by the water.

Between Penetanguishene and Parry Sound (to the north), the waters of Georgian Bay are dotted with 30,000 islands – the highest concentration in the world. This and the nearby beaches make it somewhat of a boating and vacation destination, and the dock area is always busy in summer with locals and out-of-towners. Three-hour cruises, which are popular not only in summer but also in autumn, when the leaves are all reds and yellows, depart from here, Midland and Parry Sound.

AWENDA PROVINCIAL PARK

Awenda (☎ 705-549-2231), right at the end of the peninsula jutting into Georgian Bay, is relatively small but very good. It's busy with both day visitors and overnighters. The camp sites are large, treed and private.

There are four fine beaches, all connected by walking paths. The first one can be reached by car; the second and third are the sandiest. This is one of the few places around Georgian Bay where the water gets pleasantly warm.

There are also a couple of longer, less-used trails through the park, one offering a good view of the bay. Awenda is north of Penetanguishene, where food and other supplies should be bought. Firewood is sold at the park. Basic staples can be bought not too far from the park entrance but a vehicle is still needed.

Sometimes, particularly after heavy rain, water contamination from shoreline-dwelling beaver can result in bathers experiencing a nasty 'swimmer's itch'. It's worth asking about by phone before making the trip as the beaches are a main attraction of the park.

The camp sites cost $18, and reservations are advised for summer weekends (or arrive Friday morning). The roadside signs on the approach indicating that the park campground is full are not always accurate, so persevering can be worthwhile. By evening on a Friday, however, it may well be choc-a-bloc until Monday morning. The park office has a list of commercial campgrounds in the district if it's booked out when you arrive.

CHRISTIAN ISLAND

Off the north-west edge of the peninsula and connected by toll ferry, this island, part of an Ojibway reservation, is the site of the well preserved 350-year-old Fort Sainte Marie II. It was built by the Hurons in an attempt to protect themselves and some French soldiers and priests from the Iroquois. The Iroquois decided to starve them out. Inside, the Jesuits controlled the limited rations and exchanged food for the Hurons' attendance at mass. Within a year, 4000 Native Indians had starved to death, spelling the end of that band as a significant people in the area.

ORILLIA

Orillia at the north end of Lake Simcoe acts as the entrance to the Muskoka area and points beyond. Hwys 400 and 11 split just south of here and continue up to northern Ontario. It is also a major link in the Trent-Severn Canal System. From town, cruise boats ply the canal and Lake Couchiching.

Orillia was the home of Canada's well known humorist, Stephen Leacock. He wrote here and in 1919 built a huge house which is now a year-round museum. His *Sunshine Sketches of a Little Town*, based on Orillia, has been called the most Canadian book ever written.

The tourist office is at 150 Front St S. *Casino Rama* (☎ 1-888-817-7262), operated by the local Native Indian community

just outside of Orillia, is open every day, all day and night and provides a snowmobile parking area.

In a different vein there are four and eight-day canoe trips of Algonquin Park offered from June to mid-September by the Orillia Home Hostel (☎ 705-325-0970). All supplies are included, as is transportation to the lakes. The trips are always booked out, so call for details and reservations. The four-day excursion costs $170.

Places to Stay

There are about a dozen standard motels and inns. The area around the north end of Lake Simcoe also has three family-oriented provincial parks with camping. None of them offers much to do or dramatic scenery but all are busy, easy-going places. Bass Lake (☎ 705-326-7054) has a sandy beach, warm waters and a nature trail. There are also boat and canoe rentals, and fishing in the lake. The HI *Orillia Home Hostel (☎ 705-325-0970, 198 Borland St E)* is walkable from the bus station. There are 20 beds and some family rooms and the hostel is open all year. The basic rate is $13.

Places to Eat

For drivers heading north and in need of a snack, stop at *Webber's*, a hamburger joint so popular that a pedestrian bridge had to be put up to enable patrons to cross the highway. It's on Hwy 11, south of the Severn River.

GRAVENHURST, BRACEBRIDGE & HUNTSVILLE

These three towns, discussed from south to north, are the principal centres of Muskoka. They supply this older, well established and, in some sections, exclusive cottage country. All have numerous places to eat and many nearby motels and resorts.

In Gravenhurst is the **Bethune Memorial House**, in honour of China's favourite Canadian, Dr Norman Bethune, who travelled throughout China in the 1930s as a surgeon and educator and who died there in a small village. The house details this and other aspects of his career and life. Through the

summer, professional theatre is performed at the Muskoka Festival, in the restored Opera House. A restored 19th century steamship, the *Segwun* (☎ 705-687-6667) is based in Gravenhurst and provides summer cruises around some of the more well known Muskoka Lakes (including Lake Rosseau, with its 'millionaires' row' of summer retreats). The ship is the oldest operating steamship in North America and was used around the area before the days of the automobile. There is an office at Sagamo Park in Gravenhurst at 820 Bay St.

Other boats cruise around Lake Muskoka or Lake Joseph, including the *Lady Muskoka* departing from Bracebridge.

Huntsville is the last major place for supplies for those going into Algonquin Park. It's also the shopping area for those with summer places around the large Lake of Bays.

The Chamber of Commerce (☎ 705-789-4771) is central at 8 West St N.

Ontario Northland (☎ 1-800-461-8558) buses run from Toronto to Huntsville and Emsdale (near Kearney for canoeing). In Huntsville the buses use Huntsville Travel (☎ 705-789-6431), 3 Main St E, as a depot.

During the first three weeks of July, Huntsville hosts a Festival of the Arts (☎ 1-800-663-2787) which features classical music, jazz, theatre, dance and literary events.

ALGONQUIN PROVINCIAL PARK

Algonquin (☎ 705-633-5572) is Ontario's largest park and one of Canada's best known. Established in 1893, it is also the oldest park in the province. About 300km north of Toronto, it offers hundreds of lakes in approximately 7800 sq km of semi-wilderness. There are 1600km of charted canoe routes to explore, many of them interconnected by portage paths. The one road through the park, Hwy 60, runs through the southern edge. Off it are lodges, hiking trails and eight campgrounds, as well as wilderness outfitters who rent canoes and just about everything else. Maps are available at the park.

For camping reservations (strongly recommended) call ☎ 705-633-5538 (campgrounds or backcountry) as much ahead as possible.

If you want some peace and quiet and a bit of adventure, the park is highly recommended. Algonquin and the Temagami area represent the two wilderness regions closest to Toronto and southern Ontario and provide a good opportunity to experience what much of Canada is all about. There is a lot of wildlife in the park including bear, moose and wolves. The park is open every day, all year.

Hwy 60 can be taken through the park at no charge, but if you want to stop, a day fee of $7.50 is charged.

For more information, see under Eastern Ontario earlier in this chapter for a section of the park near Ottawa.

Information

Located 43km from the west gate of the park on Hwy 60, overlooking Sunday Creek, is the very good visitors centre (☎ 705-637-2828). Various displays and dioramas illustrate the park's wildlife, history and geology. The centre also contains an excellent bookstore, which includes cheap trail-guide brochures and a cafeteria. It's open every day from May to October, on weekends only the rest of the year.

On the reverse side of the canoe route map there is camping advice and a lot of interesting information about the park. (It's handy reading material when you're inside the tent waiting for a storm to pass.)

Near the East Gate is a logging museum. Be sure to read the pamphlet about bears thoroughly.

Canoeing

Summer weekends are a busy time for canoeing, so a system of admitting only a certain number of people at each canoe route access point has been established. Arrive early, or preferably book ahead. For reservations call the number above or write to the park at PO Box 219, Whitney, ON, K0J 2M0.

At two canoe-route access points off Hwy 60 within the park, Canoe Lake and Opeongo Lake, there are outfitters renting canoes (for about $22 a day) and gear. This is where most people begin a canoe trip into the park

ONTARIO

Canoeing is popular in Algonquin Provincial Park.

interior. To begin an interior trip from any other access point means transporting the canoe to it. (The interior refers to all areas of the park accessible only on foot or by canoe.) A good trip takes three to four days. The western access points – Nos 3, 4 and 5 on the Algonquin map – are good, with fewer people, smaller lakes and plenty of moose. The farther in you get by portaging, the more solitude you'll find. Also see under Around Ottawa for information on the park's east side. Most rental places have ropes and mounting pads to enable renters to carry the canoe on the roof of their vehicle. To be safe, it is a good idea to bring enough of your own rope to secure the canoe. Different types of canoes are available. The heavy aluminum ones are the cheapest but their weight makes them unsuitable for portaging. They are also noisy and the seats get hot in the sun. For paddling around the main lakes, though, they are fine and virtually indestructible. If you want to get into the interior, where carrying weight becomes an issue, pay the extra to get a kevlar canoe (which weighs in at about 30kg).

Water taxis (see the outfitter at Lake Opeongo) can whisk you up huge Lake Opeongo avoiding a long, rough paddle and getting you into the wilder areas. Reservations are suggested – check with your outfitter.

Hiking

There are some interesting hiking trails within the park, ranging from short half-hour jaunts around a marsh to treks of several days duration. Most of the short trails

and lookouts are just off or near Hwy 60 and so can be enjoyed as part of a day trip.

Outfitters & Tours

The Portage Store (☎ 705-633-5622, portage@inforamp.net) is based at Canoe Lake, 14km from the West Gate. It offers a full range of full or partial outfitting. A complete rental package with equipment and food for one day and night is $50. Guided trips are also available.

One of several outfitters based outside the park boundaries is Algonquin Outfitters (☎ 705-635-2243, canoe@muskoka.com) at Dwight by Oxtongue Lake, just outside the western edge of the park on Hwy 60. But it also has a base at Lake Opeongo in the park and an office in Huntsville. It can rent you *everything* you need for a trip, sells supplies and even offers guided trips. Daily canoe rates vary with the type (and weight) but range from $18 to $24.

Also recommended is Canoe Algonquin (☎ 705-636-5956) in Kearney, north of Huntsville. It rents kevlar canoes for just $18 a day, including paddles and life jackets. Tents, stoves and more can also be rented. Putting in at the nearby western access points gets you right into peace almost instantly. Book equipment in advance, especially in August. Call to find out about transportation from the Ontario Northland Toronto-Huntsville-Emsdale bus.

Call of the Wild (☎ 416-200-9453 in Toronto, ☎ 1-800-776-9453, www.call-wild.com) has various all-inclusive trips but the three-day, small-group guided canoe trip for $300 is the most popular. Meals, equipment and transportation from Toronto are included. Everyone helps with chores, setting up etc. It also offers three-day winter trips (not in tents) with doing your own dogsledding, snowshoeing and skiing options.

Another reliable canoe-package operator is Canadian Wilderness Trips (☎ 416-977-5763) at 243 College St, Toronto. It is owned by Travel CUTS and has worked with international visitors for many years. Short and long trips to various Ontario locations are offered. Voyageur Quest (contacted

through the Toronto HI hostel) does similar trips at about the same price.

Canadian Woodlands (☎ 416-515-0592) is a small outfit offering direct transport into Algonquin from downtown Toronto. Passengers can be dropped off at any access point along the Hwy 60 corridor which runs through the park. One-way/return costs are $40/75. Guided walks along some of the shorter trails are also offered. Trips run from June to September, leaving Toronto at 7.30 am Monday, Wednesday and Friday with an additional run on Sunday in July and August. A same-day return (which allows for around five hours in the park) costs $65 and includes the option of guided trips along some of the shorter trails. It also has a winter run for dogsledding. Call for details.

See under Orillia earlier in this chapter for the good-value canoe trips organised by the HI Orillia Home Hostel and under Eastern Ontario earlier in this chapter for other trip possibilities.

Moose Travel (see Organised Tours under Toronto earlier in this chapter) also makes pick-ups/drop-offs in the park.

Also ask about the park ranger-led programs including the wolf howls. These are offered through the season at various locations.

Places to Stay

Interior camping is $6.50 per person per night. At the campgrounds, where there are showers and real toilets, a site is about $18. Among the highway campgrounds, Mew Lake is suggested. It has its own warm lake for swimming, some fairly attractive camp sites by the far side of the lake away from the highway, some walking trails nearby, and a store within walking distance.

The park also has a series of very comfortable lodges but these are not budget category. There are modest motels and cabins on Hwy 60 outside the park borders.

Getting There & Away

Bus For those without vehicles but who want to do it independently, the park is accessible by bus during summer months. Take the Ontario Northland (☎ 416-393-7911) bus from the central Toronto bus station to the town of Huntsville. Transfer in Huntsville to a Hammond Transportation (☎ 705-645-5431) bus into the park along Hwy 60. Also see above under Canoe Algonquin and Canadian Woodlands in the Outfitters & Tours section.

According to one reader, it's relatively easy to hitch into Algonquin from Huntsville, particularly on weekends.

GEORGIAN BAY ISLANDS NATIONAL PARK

This park, consisting of 59 islands in Georgian Bay, has two completely separate sections. The principal segment is off Honey Harbour, north of Penetanguishene.

For park information there is an office (☎ 705-756-2415) near the grocery store. In summer, a relatively inexpensive shuttle service runs over to Beausoleil and water taxis can be taken to other islands.

Beausoleil Island is the largest island and park focal point, with campgrounds and an interpretive centre. Several of the other islands have primitive camping facilities. The islands are home to the eastern Massasauga rattlesnake, which is actually rather small and timid – and now endangered thanks to the proliferation of cottages and frightened men with axes.

Recreation includes swimming, diving, snorkelling and bass and pike fishing. Boating is also big in the area, what with all the islands and the Trent-Severn Canal system. Many boaters – and they range from those putting along in aluminum 14-footers (4m boats) to would-be kings in their floating palaces – tie up for a day or a night at the park islands, so they are fairly busy.

The park is really centred around the boating subculture and is otherwise not particularly interesting. For those seeking some sort of retreat, it is disappointingly busy and rather ostentatiously competitive. The water taxis are not cheap (from $28 one way) and, while providing some flexibility in destinations and schedules, still offer only limited access. Don't even think of taking a canoe out here – if the natural waves don't get you, one produced by a floating status symbol will.

Section two of the park, consisting of a number of smaller islands, is farther north up the bay, about halfway to Parry Sound. This section, although quieter, is inaccessible to those without their own vessels.

GEORGIAN BAY PROVINCIAL PARKS

Beginning with Six Mile Lake (☎ 705-756-2746) on Hwy 69 north of Port Severn, there is a series of very fine provincial parks along or near the bay. They make excellent stopping points on the way to Sudbury or fine destinations in themselves. Excellent Massasauga (use Oastler for information and rentals) is for canoeists only while Oastler (☎ 705-378-2401) has a campground and beach.

PARRY SOUND

Parry Sound sits about midway up Georgian Bay and is the largest of the small district supply towns between southern Georgian Bay and Sudbury. There's a tourist office (☎ 1-800-461-4261) on the east side of Hwy 69 about 10 minutes drive south of town. In town, there is a lookout tower with views over the bay. The town bills itself as the home of Bobby Orr who, for the uninitiated, was a superb ice-hockey player. He was a Boston Bruins defenceman in the 1960s and 70s who changed the role of that position forever with his offensive prowess.

Boat cruises around the 30,000 islands, on the *Island Queen* (☎ 705-746-2311), push off from Government Wharf. The trips are about three hours long, departing in the early afternoon, and run from June to October.

Parry Sound is also known for its excellent and popular summer classical-music festival called the Festival of the Sound.

There are dozens of motels and cottages for rent in the area and the tourist office can help with local B&Bs.

Close to Parry Sound and accessible by a one-lane swing bridge is one of the largest of the Georgian Bay islands. **Parry Island**, 18km long and 59km around, is home to about 350 Ojibway Indians. At Oak Point, on the tip of the island, there's a small campground (☎ 705-746-8041), a marina, a restaurant and

a craft shop. There are good views out to the surrounding islands and plenty of secluded coves to explore. Canoes can be rented.

KILLBEAR PROVINCIAL PARK

Lake Huron's Georgian Bay is huge, and grand enough to dwarf most of the world's waters. It's cool, deep, windy and majestic. The deeply indented, irregular shoreline along the eastern side, with its myriad islands, is trimmed by slabs of pink granite barely supporting wind-bent pine trees. This unique setting represents for many central Canadians the quintessential Canada. The works of the country's best known painters, the Group of Seven, have linked this landscape to the Canadian experience.

Killbear (☎ 705-342-5492) is one of the best places to see what it's all about. There is shoreline to explore, three short but good walking trails, numerous little hidden sandy beaches and camping. Of course, it's popular; in July and August call ahead to determine camping vacancies. To help ensure a quiet night consider asking for one of the radio-free campgrounds. Harold's Point is good. In September it may well be less than half-full. During autumn many visitors spend the day taking photographs and painting. May and June is also less busy. The park is highly recommended, even if an afternoon is all you have. From Parry Sound east to Burk's Falls is more lake and timberland with numerous cottages, both private and commercial. Out of season, things are quiet.

BYNG INLET

Packrat Lodge (☎ 705-383-0222, jenni mac@interlog.com) at 2 Tansy Lane, is a hostel and activity base with canoe, kayak and bike rentals and dorm lodging at $15. It also has couple/family space. It's open about June to October.

KILLARNEY PROVINCIAL PARK

Killarney (☎ 705-287-2800) is one of the province's most impressive parks, and a visit is highly recommended, even if only for a day's paddle. Its features are explored by foot or canoe. The members of Canada's

Group of Seven artists worked in the park, and a provincial artists' association was instrumental in its establishment. Note that the park is 60km from Hwy 69.

Because the lakes are relatively small, the maximum number of permitted overnight campers is low. The park's beauty is outstanding, so it's popular and often full. Try to go midweek, and make reservations, including booking a canoe, before arriving – call as far in advance as you can. Getting in on holiday weekends is nearly impossible.

The park is a uniquely mountainous forested area about 80km south-west of Sudbury, on the shores of Georgian Bay. It's one of Ontario's three wilderness parks and has few conveniences. There is excellent scenery, with birch and pine forest edged by the **La Cloche Mountains**. Some lakes are lined on one side by white quartz mountains and on the other side by more typical reddish granite.

The lakes themselves offer astoundingly clear water with remarkable visibility, but unfortunately this is in part due to acid rain. Indeed, some of the lakes were essentially dead, devoid of life but recovery is underway.

Portaging from lake to lake is relatively easy, as the trails tend to be short, at least for the first few, most-visited lakes. Two lakes could be explored from the dock at **Lake George**, making a fine day's outing for those without camping gear.

There is a campground at the park headquarters, on Lake George, and another at the village of **Killarney**, but to see more of the park, venture to the interior via portions of the 75km worth of portages. There are places for pitching a tent at most of the interior lakes.

Outfitters can be found along the road between the park and the village or in Killarney village. One to call is Killarney Outfitters (☎ 1-800-461-1117) with package trips available too.

The rustic but comfortable lodge, the **Sportsman's Inn** (☎ 1-800-282-1913), has rooms at $75 double, $65 in the adjacent motel-like section. There's a pub and sauna too. It's open all year.

Excellent fresh fish and chips can be had down at the dock area.

Northern Ontario

Northern Ontario is a vast, thinly populated region of lakes and forest. How large an area it is will quickly become evident if you're motoring around Lake Superior to or from Manitoba.

Commercial activity up here is almost all involved with natural resources – forestry and mining and their spin-offs. Sudbury is one of the world's major mining centres. Way up north beyond Sudbury, on James Bay, is the little town of Moosonee, one of the province's oldest European settlements, accessible by wilderness train. The big cities on the Great Lakes, Sault Ste Marie and Thunder Bay, are major shipping ports.

Outside the widely spaced towns, much of the land is wild, with clean waters and abundant wildlife. This is one of the best regions for really typically Canadian outdoor activities. The fishing and camping attract visitors from southern Ontario and the USA. Remember, summers are short.

NORTH BAY

North Bay, with a population of 57,000, sits at the eastern end of big Lake Nipissing. At about 350km north of Toronto, it is the southernmost of the north's major towns.

The Trans Canada Hwy, which connects Sudbury to the west and Ottawa to the east, passes through town.

North Bay is also an access point to the many mining towns above it which straddle the Quebec-Ontario border. There is also some fine wilderness in the area, which attracts outdoor enthusiasts.

Orientation

Main St is the main street; south of town it becomes Lakeshore Drive. The centre of town is found between Cassells and Fisher Sts. Ferguson is the principal cross-street, and runs from the waterfront east to the North Bay bypass (which connects Hwys 11 and 17). Lakeshore Drive going south turns into Hwy 11 for Toronto. Algonquin, leading north, becomes Hwy 11 for Timmins and also links to Hwy 17 east and west.

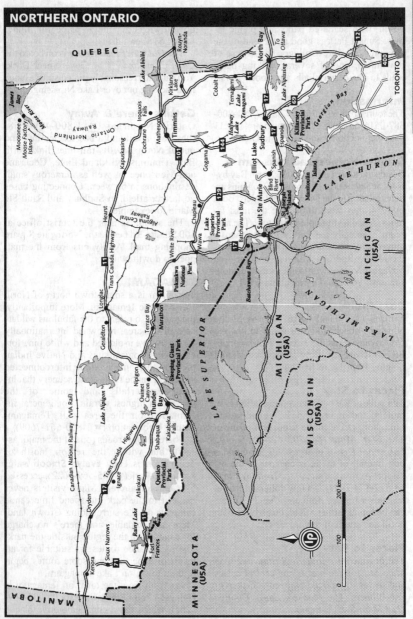

All along the shore in town is a sandy beach, with scattered parks and picnic tables. Sunset Park is good at the end of the day. At Canadore College, north-west of downtown, one of several walking paths leads to Duchesnay Falls and good views.

Information

The tourist office (☎ 705-472-8480, ☎ 1-800-387-0516) is south of downtown on Hwy 11 near the junction with Hwy 17 to Ottawa.

Dionne Homestead Museum

Beside the tourist office on the North Bay bypass, at Seymour St, the museum contains articles relating to the Dionne quintuplets. Born in 1934, they were to become the most famous Canadian multiple-birth story. The museum is actually the family log farmhouse, moved and restored. Also at this location is the Model Railroad Museum and the free Voyageur Village with some Native demonstrations. You could try a buffalo burger.

Boat Cruise

Cruises (☎ 705-494-8167) across Lake Nipissing aboard the *New Chief* follow the old voyageur paddle strokes to the Upper French River. A variety of trips are offered ranging from 1½ to five hours.

Places to Stay

The bulk of the city's accommodation is in motels and many can be found along Lakeshore Drive in the south end of town. The *Star Motel (☎ 705-472-3510, 405 Lakeshore Drive)* charges $50 for doubles but, like all of them, is cheaper in the off season. Across the street, the *Holiday Plaza (☎ 519-474-1431)* is a few dollars more but has newer rooms. Both are friendly. Others can be found farther afield, on Hwy 11 both north and south of town.

Places to Eat

The downtown *Windmill Restaurant (168 Main St E)* is the best of the central basics and serves low-priced barbecue chicken or fish dinners. The *Moose's Loose Change (134 Main St E)* is a pub.

Casey's (20 Maplewood St) north of downtown is a popular place for dinner (about $15) or a drink.

The *Old Chief Fish House* is on board the *Chief Commander I* by Government Dock. You can eat a reasonably priced simple lunch here looking out over Lake Nipissing.

Getting There & Away

Ontario Northland (☎ 1-800-461-8558) runs both a rail and a bus service into and out of North Bay. Its rail lines link North Bay, Timmins, Kirkland Lake, Cochrane and Moosonee, as well as numerous small destinations in between. Connecting buses go farther afield, to Sudbury and Sault Ste Marie for example.

The station is near the tourist office at 100 Station Rd beside the Northgate Square shopping mall. A city bus from the mall goes to downtown.

TEMAGAMI

Temagami is a small town north of North Bay on Lake Temagami. More importantly, the name also refers to the fabulous wilderness of the area, renowned internationally for its 300-year-old red and white pine forest, archaeological sites and Native Indian pictographs, an excellent interconnected system of canoe routes, and scenery that includes waterfalls and some of the province's highest terrain. For general information on the area call Temagami Tourist Information (☎ 1-800-661-7609).

There are few roads (one of the major assets), but within the region, north of Temagami, is **Lady Evelyn Smoothwater Provincial Park** (☎ 705-569-3622), accessed by canoe or aircraft. Many visitors never make it to the park but spend time canoe camping on the surrounding Crown land. Maps are available, and there's no charge for camping in the region outside the park. The local canoe routes are suitable for all levels of expertise, and some routes begin right in town, on Lake Temagami.

Just 2km from the town of Temagami is **Finlayson Point Provincial Park** (☎ 705-569-3205), which has a commemorative plaque

for English author Grey Owl, who lived with the local Ojibway Indians for several years and then convinced the world, through his writing on nature and its preservation, that he was a Native Indian himself. See boxed text 'Grey Owl at Home in the Wilderness' in the Saskatchewan chapter.

The town of Temagami is the park supply centre, where canoes can be rented and trips into the park organised, and where there are B&Bs, motels and restaurants.

The Shell service station has a restaurant, good for breakfasts and light meals. On Lakeshore, just along the waterfront, the Welcome Centre is worth a visit for its background information on the area and for the collection of canoes. It's open daily in July and August.

For all your canoeing, fishing or camping needs or for organising trips into the region, visit Smoothwater Outfitters (☎ 705-569-3539, www.smoothwater.com). It has a cabin in Temagami and the Wilderness Lodge (14km north on Hwy 11, then 1km west), where accommodation and meals are available. There is some hostel space and access to trails and canoe routes. Staff can suggest trips based on your skill and the amount of time available to you. Lady Evelyn Outfitting (☎ 705-569-2595, www.ladyevelyn.com) on Hwy 11 provides a similar service but has winter dog-sledding and a B&B.

Ontario Northland runs trains from Toronto to Temagami every day except Saturday. The fare is $76.

SUDBURY

Sudbury (population 92,000) sits on the rocky Precambrian Shield at the rim of the Sudbury Basin, a depression or crater formed two billion years ago. For over 100 years it has been supplying the world with nickel.

Inco Ltd, one of the world's largest nickel producers, is the town's biggest employer and was once its lifeblood. While still vitally important, Inco and its rival Falconbridge have seen their fortunes decline somewhat with the drop in international demand and price. But Sudbury, to escape the precarious one-industry town scenario, has

diversified. Provincial government decentralisation has meant the relocation to Sudbury of several major departments, such as Energy & Mines, and this has helped push things along in new directions.

The city has long had a reputation for ugliness. The rough, rocky landscape was debased for years by indiscriminate felling of trees and by merciless pollution from the mining and smelting operations. The result was a bleak, moonscape-like setting.

Much to Sudbury's credit, the worst of these characteristics have been (and are continuing to be) reversed. Indeed, the city has earned honours in environmental improvement, and with the development of parks and Inco's superstack to scatter emissions, the difference from years ago is impossible to miss. Some bleak areas do remain. From up at the Big Nickel park, the views indicate how barren the terrain can be around the mines. The lack of vegetation is mainly due to industrial discharges, but the naturally thin soil covering the rocky Canadian Shield never helped.

Still, most of the town is no longer strikingly desert-like, and in fact Sudbury is surrounded by a vast area of forests, hills and lakes, making it a centre for outdoor and sporting activities. On the east side of town, away from the mining operations, the land is green and wild-looking. There are over a dozen lakes just outside town, including large, attractive Ramsey Lake, at the southeast edge of the city.

The downtown core, however, lacks character and there really isn't much to see. Sudbury isn't a place worth making a major effort to get to, but if you're heading across country you'll probably pass through, and there are a few interesting things to see and do around the edges, mostly related to mining. Science North is a significant attraction.

The city has a large French population and a Scandinavian community.

Note that in July and August, the Sudbury region tends to be sunny and can be hot. However, it is generally dry and nights can cool off sharply.

SUDBURY

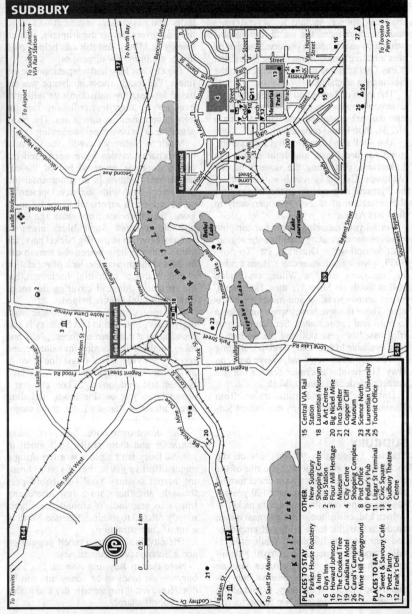

Enlargement

To Sudbury Junction
VIA Rail Station

To North Bay

Bancroft Drive

17

To Airport

To North Bay

Falconbridge Highway

Barrydowne Road

Lasalle Boulevard

Second Ave

Notre Dame St

Lake Ramsey

Bethel Lake

Lake Laurentian

Nepahwin Lake

69

543

To Toronto & Parry Sound

Van Horne Street

Shaughnessy St

Memorial Park

Brady Street

15

27

25 26

Kingsway

Howey Drive

Ramsey Lake Road

John St

Paris Street

Walford St

York St

Regent Street

See Enlargement

Notre Dame Avenue

Kathleen St

Lasalle Boulevard

Frood Rd

Regent St

Lorne St

Big Nickel Mine Drive

17

Elm Street West

Lorne St

Kelly Lake

To Sault Ste Marie

144

To Timmins

Balsam St

Godfrey Dr

N

0   0.5   1 km

PLACES TO STAY
5   Parker House Roastery
    & Inn
8   Days Inn
16 Howard Johnson
17 The Crooked Tree
19 Canadiana Motel
26 Carol's Campsite
27 Mine Hill Campground

PLACES TO EAT
6   Sweet & Savoury Café
9   Poetz Pantry
12 Frank's Deli

OTHER
1   New Sudbury
    Shopping Centre
2   Bus Station
3   Flour Mill Heritage
    Museum
4   City Centre
    Shopping Complex
7   Post Office
10 Pedlar's Pub
11 Lisgar St Terminal
13 Civic Square
14 Sudbury Theatre
    Centre
15 Central VIA Rail
    Station
18 Laurentian Museum
    & Art Centre
20 Big Nickel Mine
21 Inco Smelter
22 Copper Cliff
    Museum
23 Science North
24 Laurentian University
25 Tourist Office

Inuit Art, Toronto, Ontario

Six Nations Indian Reserve, Ontario

Redcoat, Fort York, Ontario

Toronto's central Harbourfront provides a range of activities.

Royal Ontario Museum exhibit, Toronto

CN Tower, Toronto, Ontario

Winter has its own appeal at Niagara Falls, Ontario.

The Sudbury Basin

The town of Sudbury sits on the southern rim of a ring of low hills outlining a unique and complex geological structure known as the Nickel Irruptive. The mines located around the outer rim of this boat-shaped crater produce much of the world's nickel, platinum, palladium and related metals, as well as large amounts of copper, gold, tellurium, selenium and sulphur. The inner basin area is roughly 60km long and 30km wide. Science North (☎ 705-522-3701 or ☎ 1-800-461-4898) has a show offering possible explanations for its formation (which include a volcano or a giant meteor).

Orientation

The main streets downtown are Elm St (running east-west) and Durham St (going north-south). The core runs along Elm St from Notre Dame Ave to Lorne St.

On Elm St is the City Centre shopping complex and the Holiday Inn. The post office is across the street. The local bus routes start nearby.

Elgin St, running south off Elm St, divides Elm St E from Elm St W. At its southern end is one of the two VIA Rail stations. As you head east on Elm St, at Notre Dame Ave you'll encounter the brown-bulbed Ukrainian church. Farther east the street changes names several times. It passes a commercial strip of service stations, fast-food restaurants, motels, and eventually becomes Hwy 17 to Ottawa.

South of town, Regent St becomes Hwy 69 for Toronto. It also passes through a long commercial district. Going west, Lorne St leads to Hwy 17, one branch of the Trans Canada Hwy. Along the way there are motels, the Big Nickel park, Inco Ltd, smelters and Copper Cliff. Hwy 11 running farther north over Lake Superior is another branch of the Trans Canada Hwy.

Laurentian University with good views, lies on a hill on the far side of Ramsey Lake, south-east from downtown along Ramsey Rd.

Information

The tourist office, the Rainbow Country Travel Association (☎ 705-522-0104, ☎ 1-800-465-6655), is inconveniently 10km south of town at 1984 Regent St S. It's open daily in summer but closed Sunday through the rest of the year.

Science North

The large participatory science centre (☎ 705-522-3701, ☎ 1-800-461-4898) at the southwestern end of Lake Ramsey is a major regional attraction. This museum complex is conspicuously housed in two snowflake-shaped buildings built into a rocky outcrop at the lake's edge, beside Alex Baumann Park (named after an Olympic swimmer native to Sudbury). Bell Park runs adjacent to the north, back toward downtown.

Inside, after you enter by tunnel through the 2.5-billion-year-old Canadian Shield, is a collection of exhibits and displays on subjects ranging from the universe to insects, communications to fitness, animal life to rocks. Visitors are welcome to get involved with the displays through the many computers, the hi-tech equipment and the helpful, knowledgeable staff, many of whom are from the university.

Some highlights are the white-quartz crystal displayed under a spotlight (looking like a lingam in an eastern temple), the excellent insect section (how about patting a tarantula?) and the bed of nails. The fitness test is fun but can be humbling. The display about the Sudbury Neutrino Observatory which is 2km underground away from downtown, is fascinating. The 3-D film presented in the pitch-black cave is also quite remarkable. There are major changing exhibits and an IMAX movie theatre.

Also in the complex is an inexpensive cafeteria, a restaurant, and a science and bookshop. At the swap shop, you can trade anything natural for anything else from nature's wonders.

Admission costs $10 at Science North or there is a value combination ticket which includes the Big Nickel and/or IMAX films. Opening hours are 9 am to 6 pm daily in

summer, till 5 pm in spring and autumn; from October to May, it's open from 10 am to 4 pm. The No 500 bus runs from the centre of town to Science North every day. Parking at Science North is $3!

Big Nickel Mine

Just west of town on Hwy 17 West, up on the hill, the Big Nickel (same ☎ as above) is the symbol of Sudbury. The huge nickel, however, is actually made of stainless steel. You can go down a 20m mine shaft, view equipment and see an exhibit of mining science, technology and history. Also in the mine is a vegetable garden and the country's only underground post office. The mine is open every day from mid-May to mid-October and keeps the same hours as Science North. Entry is $10, and city bus No 940 will get you there. From up at the Big Nickel, there's a good view of the surrounding area. The nickel can be viewed and photographed without buying a ticket.

Copper Cliff Museum

On Balsam St in Copper Cliff, where Inco has its operation, this pioneering log cabin (☎ 705-674-2453, ext 2453) with period furnishings and tools is open in June, July and August, from 10 am to 4 pm Tuesday to Sunday.

Flour Mill Heritage Museum

This is a similar place – a pioneer house (☎ 705-673-3141, ext 2453) with period implements, artefacts and furnishings from the late 19th century. The museum is at 514 Notre Dame Ave and is named after the three flour silos on this street. It's open from 10 am to 4.30 pm Tuesday to Friday and on Saturday afternoon, from mid-June to September.

Art Gallery of Sudbury

The art and museum centre (☎ 705-675-4871) features changing art shows, often the work of local artists. There is also a permanent display of articles relating to the region's history. The collection is housed in a former mansion at 251 John St, corner of Nelson St. It's open all year from Tuesday

to Sunday (afternoons only) and is closed on all holidays.

Bell Park

After all the serious Sudbury sites, perhaps a bit of relaxation is in order, and Bell Park, walkable from downtown, fits the bill. This large green area with sandy beaches offers swimming practically in the centre of town. It runs off Paris St south of downtown. Walk or drive toward Lake Ramsey and turn east on Facer St, beside the hospital. Walking paths follow the shore of the lake south all the way to Science North, and others continue north from the hospital.

Organised Tours

The *Cortina* (☎ 705-522-3701), a 70-seat passenger boat docked next to Science North, offers daily hour-long cruises around Ramsey Lake from May to September. Adult tickets are $10. The dock is part of a boardwalk which rims a portion of the lake.

Special Events

The Northern Lights Festival is a successful annual music event, featuring unknowns and rising stars from around the country. It takes place in early July in Bell Park. Other concerts and theatre are presented at Bell Park regularly through summer at the bandshell. It's on the corner of Paris and York Sts and overlooks Ramsey Lake.

Sudbury, with its rocky, sunny landscape is prime blueberry territory. A walk off the road anywhere in the region will probably turn up a few berries. Celebrating them is the annual Blueberry Festival, held in mid-July. There are lots of outdoor events, and public feedings such as pancake breakfasts.

Places to Stay

Camping Sudbury is surrounded by rugged, wooded, lake-filled land. There are quite a few government parks within about 50km of town. The best bet is *Windy Lake Provincial Park* (☎ 705-966-2315) 26km south of town. More commercial and designed for trailers and campers is *Carol's Campsite* (☎ 705-522-5570), just 8km

south of town on Hwy 69. *Halfway Lake Provincial Park (☎ 905-965-2702)* is about 90km out on Hwy 144 north-west of town.

Hostels *Laurentian University (☎ 705-673-6580)* on Ramsey Lake Rd rents rooms from mid-May to mid-August. Features include a cafeteria (which is closed on weekends) and use of the physical education facilities. The only problem is that the university is south-east of the downtown area, around the other side of Ramsey Lake. The views are good, though, and the area is pleasant and quiet. It costs $28/40 with tax. The No 500 bus from downtown runs to the university.

B&Bs *Parker House Roastery & Inn (☎ 705-674-2442, 259 Elm St)* is central and is a clean, comfortable bargain. Singles/doubles with shared bath are $45/60 in a nice room with a TV. Rooms with private facilities are available. Rates include a very good continental breakfast at the main floor café where the coffee beans are roasted daily.

Another good B&B is the more casual, homy *Crooked Tree (☎ 705-673-1352, 250 Edmund St)* between downtown and Science North. Rates are $40/50 with a full breakfast. Renate is a congenial hostess and the garden is a great place to plan the day.

Hotels The bottom-end *Ledo (☎ 705-673-7123)*, surrounded by a lot of gritty urban life, is on Elgin St opposite the train station. It can't really be recommended but may do for men looking hard for hostel rates. Ask in the bar about the rooms.

Moving up, a good choice is the central *Days Inn (☎ 705-674-7517, 117 Elm St W)* with clean, comfortable rooms for $70. Also central is the similar *Howard Johnson (☎ 705-675-1273, ☎ 1-800-461-1120, 390 Elgin St)* with rooms at $65, a deal. It's on the other side of downtown.

Motels The bulk of Sudbury's accommodation is in motels found around the edges of town.

Hwy 17 West is called Lorne St near town, and there are motels along it a few kilometres from the centre. At the standard *Canadiana (☎ 705-674-7585, 965 Lorne St)* single or doubles cost $45 and up.

The better, newer motels are found south of town on Hwy 69. The *Comfort Inn (☎ 705-522-1101)* is here at 2171 Regent St S, with rooms at $80. The *Brockdan Motor Hotel (☎ 705-522-5270)* is 5km south on Hwy 69. Rooms cost from $53.

There are other motels on Kingsway leading to Hwy 17 East. One is the *Ambassador (☎ 705-566-3601)* with rooms in the $82 range.

Places to Eat

Frank's (112 Durham St) is a deli near Larch St and is good, cheap and serves all three meals of the day.

The *Poetz Pantry (76 Cedar St)* is a small, colourfully casual café with a range of soups, salads, sweets and excellent sandwiches all under $6. It offers some good vegetarian fare, too. It's open 24 hours on Friday and closed Sunday.

The *Sweet & Savoury Café & Espresso Bar (50 Durham St)* is a quiet place with sandwiches under $5, lots of salads and various pasta dishes including Pad Thai for $7 to $9. It's closed Sunday. It also has occasional live jazz evenings. There's a health-food shop next door.

For good-value fresh seafood, *Seafoods North (1543 Paris St)* is in a small shopping plaza and is recommended. The front of the place is a seafood store; the restaurant, tucked at the back, offers chowder, fine fish and chips or good more complete dinners for about $10. It's just south of Walford St – too far to walk from downtown. Monday and Tuesday evenings are all-you-can-eat fish and chips.

Pat & Marios is away from the centre, on the corner of Lasalle Blvd and Barrydowne Rd, near two big shopping malls. This fairly dressy eating place is popular for Italian and finger foods in the $10 to $20 range.

For a bit of a splurge, consider the comfortable *Snowflake* restaurant at Science North overlooking Lake Ramsey. Main courses at dinner of between $12 and $16

include Arctic char or chicken. It's open daily from 11.30 am to 9.30 pm and has a full Sunday brunch.

The Friday or Saturday *Sudbury Star* newspaper lists the weekend restaurant specials and Sunday brunches.

Entertainment
Pedlar's Pub (63 Cedar St) is a friendly, Irishy pub with a good atmosphere and live music some nights. *Mingles (762 Notre Dame Ave)* is a dance club.

The *Sudbury Star* on Friday has complete club listings.

Getting There & Away
Air Air Canada and Canadian Airlines fly into the airport in the north-east corner of the city.

Bus The Greyhound Bus Depot (☎ 705-524-9900) is about 3km north of the downtown core at 854 Notre Dame Ave. This as also the station for Northland Ontario buses (same phone number), which run north to Timmins and south to Toronto.

There are three eastbound buses a day for North Bay/Ottawa/Montreal, and three a day westbound for Sault Ste Marie/Winnipeg/Vancouver. There are several buses a day southbound for Toronto; ask for the express trip.

One-way fares are Ottawa $77, Sault Ste Marie $46 and Toronto $60.

Train There are two VIA Rail stations servicing Sudbury, both at ☎ 1-800-361-1235. The original is conveniently situated on the corner of Minto and Elgin Sts, about 10 minutes walk from the centre of town. It's in the low, grey building that is mostly black roof.

Unfortunately, there's only one train which uses this station. The Budd car is the local nickname for the one-car train that makes the thrice-weekly trip from Sudbury through northern bush past Chapleau to White River, north of Lake Superior. The one-way fare is $73, but 25% off if you book seven days in advance. It's an inter-

esting eight hour trip through sparsely populated forest and lakeland. For many villages and settlements this is the only access. The train stops and starts as people along the way – often wilderness seekers with their canoes and gear – flag it down. A moose or bear on the track also means an unscheduled stop. There's lots of birdlife, including hill cranes and great blue herons. You might even do a bit of fishing or berry picking if you're stuck waiting for a freight train to pass. The train trip is popular in autumn to see the leaves.

The other trains, such as those for Toronto or westbound, use a less central station known as Sudbury Junction which is about 10km from the old downtown station. It is on Lasalle Blvd past Falconbridge Hwy, in the north-east section of town. Buses only go to within 1km of the station.

There are three trips a week to Toronto: on Monday, Wednesday and Friday. The one-way fare is $75 with taxes.

Going north and west, the route heads straight up through basic wilderness to Longlac, on to Sioux Lookout and eventually across the border to Winnipeg in Manitoba.

No direct route runs to Ottawa, so you must go via Toronto.

Car Renting a car may be useful in Sudbury. Tilden (☎ 705-560-1000) has the best rates and will pick you up. The address is 1150 Kingsway.

Hitching Hwy 17, which becomes Kingsway in town, goes east to Ottawa. Regent St runs south from town into Hwy 69 south to Toronto. If westbound, head out along Lorne St, which eventually becomes Hwy 17 West.

Getting Around
Bus For transit information call ☎ 705-675-3333. The city buses collect at the downtown transit centre on the corner of Notre Dame Ave and Elm St. Route 940 goes to the Copper Cliff Mine smelter site and the Big Nickel site, at quarter to and quarter past each hour.

NORTH OF SUDBURY
Halfway Lake Provincial Park
This is one of the many small, relatively developed parks with camping that surround Sudbury (☎ 705-965-2702). Within this park are various hiking trails of four, 10 and 34km in length, as well as several scenic lookouts. The park is about 90km northwest of Sudbury on Hwy 144.

Gogama
Continuing north up Hwy 144 about two-thirds of the way to Timmins, you reach the Arctic watershed, at Gogama, from where all rivers flow north to the Arctic Ocean. Did you notice it was getting a bit cool?

TIMMINS
Way up here in northern Ontario is the largest city in Canada – in area that is. The population is just 46,000.

Originally the centre of the most productive gold-mining area in the western hemisphere, Timmins still acts in the same capacity, but the local mines now work copper, zinc, silver, iron ore and talc as well as gold.

Kidd Creek Mines is the world's largest producer of silver and zinc and the main employer in town. One mine, now closed, was the country's deepest, going down nearly 2.5km. There are still over 2000km of underground workings in the area.

Forestry products are also important in this rough, rugged, cold region of primary industry. There are hundreds of lakes within the designated city limits, as well as several dozen registered trap lines.

The first Europeans to settle this area were from Poland, Croatia and the Ukraine and many of their progeny are still here. To them must be added numbers of Italians, Finns and Scots, all of whom came with the lure of gold in the 1920s.

As in much of north-eastern Ontario, there is quite a large French population in and around town, and Native Indians, the original inhabitants, are a significant ethnic group. A multicultural festival is held in June.

Orientation
Timmins is actually made up of a number of small communities, the more important of which, strung together running from west to east over a distance of about 10km, are Timmins proper, Schumacher, South Porcupine and Porcupine.

Hwy 101 passes through the centre of town (where it is known as Algonquin Blvd) on its way west to Lake Superior and east to Quebec. In town, the main streets are Third St (which runs parallel to the highway), Pine St and Cedar St. The central core is marked by the brick streets and old-style lampposts.

Information
The Chamber of Commerce (☎ 705-360-1900, ☎ 1-800-387-8466), east of town, on the main road in Schumacher, 916 Algonquin Blvd E, acts as the tourist office. In addition to the usual local information, it has details on numerous industrial tours of the Porcupine-Timmins area and sells the tickets for them.

Timmins Museum
In South Porcupine at 70 Legion Drive (near Algonquin Blvd E) this small but good museum (☎ 705-235-5066) doubles as an art gallery and exhibition centre, presenting changing exhibits ranging from paintings to masks to performances, and more. In the museum section, see the prospector's cabin, which gives an idea of the lives these people led. The history of the area is outlined. There is some old mining equipment outside, too. The museum is open every day (only afternoons on weekends).

Deadman's Point
Situated on Porcupine Lake in South Porcupine, Deadman's Point boasts the atmospheric cemetery where many of the town's people were buried after the great fire of 1911. There are excellent views over the lake.

The old storefronts of Schumacher, on First Ave between Pine St and Hollinger Lane, are being restored to the 1920s and 1930s period. This strip once had more bars per capita than anywhere else in the country.

Organised Tours

Gold Mine Tour The tour of the old Hollinger gold mine (☎ 705-267-6222, ☎ 1-800-387-8466) is the city's prime attraction. The mine was discovered in 1909 and was at one time the biggest producer in the western hemisphere – hundreds of millions of dollars worth of gold was dug out of here. The site has now been developed into a varied complex, with stores, a craft outlet, jewellery sales and a restaurant. The highlight remains the underground mine tour, which takes visitors down 50m in full mining gear and includes a rail ride and a simulated dynamite blast.

There are also some surface attractions worth seeing. Hollinger House is a relocated original worker's house; the company built these in number for the miners and their families. There are still a few in Timmins, a few blocks north of the highway. This one, though, holds artefacts and memorabilia of past eras. There is also an open-pit mine to see, and some trails past rocky outcrops from which minerals could be extracted. You can even try panning for gold.

All in all it's an interesting site although tickets for the full tour cost $17 but with reduced family rates. The tour lasts about 1½ hours and includes both underground and surface portions. Tickets can be purchased for the above-ground attractions separately for $8.

From May to October, tours run seven days a week and there are five a day. Tickets must be bought ahead of time at the Chamber of Commerce. Pants and flat shoes are essential, and take a warm sweater; other equipment is supplied. The mine is between Timmins and Schumacher on James Reid Rd, which is off the 'back road' from Timmins to South Porcupine.

Kidd Creek Metallurgical Site & Buffalo Tour Kidd Creek Mine runs tours of its concentrator and zinc smelter. It's a walking tour which shows how the valuable minerals – zinc, silver, lead and cadmium – are separated from the waste and then how the zinc is processed into shippable ingots. The same dress regulations apply as at the gold-mine tour. The tour, which lasts 2½ hours and costs $4, is only offered on Wednesday afternoon through July and August. Get information and tickets through the Chamber of Commerce. The site is 26km east of the centre of Timmins on Hwy 101.

Also at the Kidd Site, the employees keep a herd of bison which can often be seen from the road.

McChesney Lumber Tour This third industrial-site tour is a trip through the now fully automated sawmill by the Mattagami River, where it has been since the turn of the century. Follow the processing of a log to the cut lumber that consumers get at the store. The sawmill is central, just off Algonquin Blvd. Tickets here are also $4 and the tour is about one hour long. Reservations and tickets are through the Chamber of Commerce, which coordinates all the company tours.

On all the tours described, very young children are not permitted.

Pulp Mill Tour Tours are offered three times daily from Monday to Friday at the Abitibi-Price Pulp & Paper Mill in Iroquois Falls, north-east of Timmins. The mill is a major newsprint producer.

Places to Stay

East of town 35km and then north 3km is the recommended *Kettle Lakes Provincial Park* (☎ 705-363-3511), good for camping or a day trip to see the 20 or so small, round, glacial kettle lakes. You need a car to get here.

There are several motels on each side of town. On the east side, in South Porcupine, the *Regal* (☎ 705-235-3393) is reasonable with rooms from $45.

Both basic and good hotels can be found in town. At the agreeable *Venture Inn* (☎ 705-268-7171, ☎ 1-888-483-6887, 730 Algonquin Blvd E) a double sets you back $70.

Places to Eat

There are plenty of places along the highway between towns and several around the central streets of Timmins.

Bentley's *(36 Wilson Ave)* is recommended for soup-and-sandwich lunches. In Schumacher, the *McIntyre Community Centre (☎ 705-360-1758)* also known as the arena, serves a good breakfast. Later, sandwiches and various east European dishes are offered. The home-made pies and butter tarts are noteworthy. At the Italian *Porcupine Dante Club (☎ 705-264-3185, 172 Cedar St S)* you can get a satisfying, inexpensive Italian lunch or dinner – call to check the hours.

Casey's, east of town, is a popular chain restaurant and a place to have a beer. For a more expensive dinner out, try the *Airport Hotel*, an historic lodge out by Porcupine Lake in South Porcupine. Out the old lounge window you can see the runway – the lake. At one time this was a busy floatplane landing strip, hence the hotel name, and the bush pilots ate and slept at the lodge. A speciality is the fresh pickerel (walleye). There's still a flying school next to the lodge, so you may well see some landings and take-offs. Also, if you wander over, there are pilots who will, for a price, take visitors for a spin around in their planes. Try to get back in time for dessert.

Getting There & Away

Bus The train and bus stations (☎ 705-264-1377) are in the same building, at 1 Spruce Ave, not far from Algonquin Blvd. Ontario Northland has a daily bus service from Toronto via Sudbury. During summer, a bus runs from Timmins to Cochrane for the Polar Bear Express.

Train There is no train service into Timmins itself, although Ontario Northland does get as close as the town of Matheson. From there a bus makes the one hour trip into Timmins.

COCHRANE

Little Cochrane (population under 5000), roughly 100km north of Timmins, is the departure point for the *Polar Bear Express*. The large polar bear statue at the entrance to Cochrane symbolises the importance of the train to the town. Other attractions are the **Railway & Pioneer Museum**, with some early

railway, Native Indian and pioneer exhibits, the historical **Hunta Museum** and canoe tours. The tourist association (☎ 1-800-354-9948) can furnish more information.

Polar Bear Express

This is the best known rolling stock of the small Ontario Northland railway (☎ 1-800-268-9281). The *Polar Bear* heads north from Cochrane through northern wilderness to Moosonee, the oldest permanent settlement in the province, on the edge of James Bay (part of vast Hudson Bay). Three hundred years ago, this was the site of an important fur-trading centre.

Those taking the train have two choices. The *Polar Bear Express*, primarily for tourists or those in a hurry, provides a one-day return trip. It leaves early in the morning and returns late the same day, taking 4½ hours each way and allowing for a look around Moosonee and Moose Factory.

A slower local train, the *Little Bear*, caters to an odd mix of tourists, Native Indians, trappers and geologists. It does not return the same day meaning a minimum two-day trip.

The express runs daily (except Friday) from about 25 June to 5 September. The *Little Bear* operates all year but only three times a week.

The summer fare on both trains is $50 return (with tax), with reservations required. There are family, child and senior discounts. Trips can be booked from Ontario Northland Railway in Toronto, North Bay, Timmins or Cochrane or by phone. In Toronto, there is an information office in Union Station, the main train station, found on Front St.

Outside of the summer season, the fare nearly doubles. Simple lunches and snacks can be bought on the train but you're better off taking your own food for the trip. If you've driven to Cochrane, there is free parking beside the train station.

Ontario Northland also offers three, four and five-day packages (excluding most meals) out of North Bay and Toronto.

Visitors should know that despite the train's name, there are no polar bears in the region.

Places to Stay

Cochrane has several motels and Greenwater Provincial Park with camping. Drury Park, also with camping, is close to the train station. Note that the half-dozen motels tend to fill up in midsummer, so arrive early in the day or call ahead. The *Northern Lites Motel* (☎ 705-272-4281) at $64 a double has a handy restaurant/bar on the premises. Simpler *Motel Cochrane* (☎ 705-272-4253) is $40/52 with kitchenettes available.

Getting There & Away

From Cochrane, the Ontario Northland railway connects south with Timmins (via Matheson and a bus ride), North Bay and other regional towns. There are also buses between these points. The Ontario Northland train also runs between Toronto and Cochrane.

MOOSONEE

Moosonee, which sits near the tundra line with no road access, is as far north as most people ever get in eastern Canada. Once there, see the historic sites and the museums and, best of all, get out on the water on one of the boat tours.

Ontario Northland can supply information on things to do and places to stay. For a look at the true north, with tundra and polar bears, see under Churchill, Manitoba.

Moose Factory Island, out in Moose River, is the site of a Hudson's Bay Company trading post founded in 1672. It's 2km and 15 minutes from town by boat. Moose Factory itself is a community of about 1500 people, mainly Native Cree, at the far end of the island. Things to see include some buildings at the historic site, a cemetery, and the Anglican church dating from 1860 (with moosehide altar cloths and Cree prayer books). Also visit the Cree Interpretation Centre and Cree Village with crafts for sale.

Two Bay Tours (☎ 705-336-2944) offers several excursions including large 'freighter' canoe trips to the island. More costly and extensive tours are available which include the trip to the island, a bus tour around it and other optional side trips (eg to Ship Sands Island Bird Sanctuary, down the Moose River or out to James Bay).

Boat trips or the freighter canoes ($19) also take people upstream to **Fossil Island** where fossils over 300 million years old can be found.

On **Tidewater Island**, between the mainland and Moose Factory, is a provincial park. Trips here can be arranged and camping is possible.

Back in Moosonee, the other museum, **Revillon Frères Museum**, documents the Hudson's Bay Company's rival, the North West Company, which was based in Montreal. The James Bay Educational Centre also has some Cree crafts.

Another attraction is the sometimes visible aurora borealis (northern lights). Also in winter, dog sled trips are offered.

Places to Stay

There are a handful of places to stay, but they are not cheap. Rooms at the *Polar Bear Lodge* (☎ 705-336-2345) or *Moosonee Lodge* (☎ 705-336-2351) go for around $60/ 80 a single/double.

Reservations are pretty well a necessity wherever you stay. If camping, be prepared for a lot of mosquitoes and/or black flies.

NORTHERN ROUTE

Hwy 11 runs west from Cochrane, eventually connecting with Thunder Bay. The province's most northerly major road, it cuts across rough, scrubby forest through several mining towns. There are campgrounds along the way.

The principal town along the route is **Kapuskasing**, with its circular downtown centre. In town, a river tour-boat runs upstream to **Beaver Falls** providing historical and geological commentary and allowing for glimpses of local wildlife like beaver and muskrat.

Hearst, as noted in the Sault Ste Marie section, is the northern terminal of the Algoma Central Railway.

WEST OF SUDBURY

From Sudbury, Hwy 17 (the Trans Canada Hwy) runs along the north shore of Lake

Did You Say What I Thought You Did?

The way Espanola got its name is an intriguing tale. In about 1750, the Ojibway Indians of the district went on a raid down south, in what is now the USA but which at the time was under Spanish control. They brought back a captive woman who later taught her children Spanish. When French explorers arrived on the scene you can imagine their surprise to hear the familiar Spanish being spoken. They called the settlement Espanole which was subsequently anglicised to its present form.

Huron. There are a few things to see along the way if you wish to dawdle, and several smaller highways lead to more northern points. South of Espanola, Hwy 6 leads across Lake Huron's North Channel to Manitoulin Island.

Espanola

Espanola, the largest centre between Sudbury and Sault Ste Marie, is a pulp and paper town and acts as a gateway for the Manitoulin Island ferry. The island can be reached by road on this side but connects with southern Ontario by ferry (see Tobermory earlier in this chapter).

During July and August, EB Eddy Forest Products Ltd (☎ 1-800-663-6342) offers three different tours of its operations. Call for details and reservations or visit its information centre in Espanola. One trip lasts all day (nine hours) out in the bush, learning how the forest is managed. Good walking shoes are required.

Each of the other two tours is three hours in duration. One is through the pulp mill to see the paper-making process; the other is through a sawmill – the biggest this side of the Rocky Mountains. These last two tours are not open to kids under the age of 12 and safety gear (supplied) must be worn. Not every tour is offered every day, so be sure to check the schedule. All the tours are free.

There are standard motels and a few places for a bite.

Deer Trail

The Deer Trail refers to a driving route north from the highway at Serpent River through Elliot Lake, around a little-developed region along the Little White River and back south to Hwy 17 at Ironbridge.

Mississagi Provincial Park is about a third of the way around from Serpent River. At the park and at Flack Lake there are nature trails, the latter with good examples of fossils and a feature known as ripple rock. There are other areas of geological interest along the way, such as the tillite outcrops formed 1.5 million years ago found 4km north of the Elliot Lake uranium symbol.

Tourist offices in Serpent River or Blind River have a pamphlet/map indicating sites on the trail. There is also a lot of good canoeing in the district.

Elliot Lake

North of the Trans Canada Hwy, Elliot Lake is a mining town based mainly on uranium. It's a relatively new town, having been founded in 1954 when the ore was discovered. About a quarter of the population is French. With the tough times the local mining industry has been suffering, Elliot Lake has promoted itself as a fine retirement centre with a quiet, easy pace and low costs.

The **Nuclear & Mining Museum** (☎ 705-848-2084) features displays on the mining and applications of uranium but also has some area historical exhibits and a section on the wildlife of the region. The museum is open every day from June to September, on weekdays only the rest of the year.

Good views over the North Channel can be had from the Firetower Lookout, north of town 5km up the Milliken Mine access road.

Blind River

Blind River, sitting almost exactly halfway between Sudbury and Sault Ste Marie, is a good place to stop for a break. Though small, it's a neat and clean little town with a few good places to find a meal. On the east side of town is a large, helpful tourist office (☎ 1-800-263-2546), with information on the entire region.

Beside the information building is the **Timber Village Museum**, outlining the history of logging in the area. There are also some interesting items from the Mississagi people, the original Native Indian inhabitants.

The veneer mill south of town offers tours, and Huron Beach, 13km from Blind River, is a nice, sandy spot for a swim.

Places to Stay & Eat Camping is available near town; ask at the information office. Blind River also has five motels, and it's not likely they'll all be full. For food, *JR's* chip stand, beside the highway, has good burgers and fries, but there are several sit-down restaurants to choose from as well.

St Joseph Island

St Joseph lies in the channel between Michigan and Ontario, 50km east of Sault Ste Marie. It's a rural island visited for swimming and fishing and for the **Fort St Joseph National Historic Site**. The British fort ruins date from the turn of the 18th century and are staffed by workers in period costume. The reception centre (☎ 705-246-2664) displays Native Indian, military and fur-trade artefacts. A large bird sanctuary surrounds the fort. The fort is open from the end of May to the middle of October. Check at the Soo tourist office for complete details.

Also on the island is the **Museum Village**, housing 4000 island articles exhibited in six historic buildings varying from an old general store to a log school. Another thing to keep an eye out for are the so-called pudding stones – red, black and brown speckled white rocks. The jasper conglomerates (to rockhounds) found around the shoreline were named by English settlers (obviously hungry) who felt they resembled suet and berry pudding.

St Joseph has several private campgrounds, motels and B&Bs. The island is reached by a toll-free bridge off Hwy 17.

SAULT STE MARIE

'The Soo', as the city is called, sits strategically where Lake Huron and Lake Superior meet. Once a fur-trading outpost, the Soo is an industrial town important as a shipping centre, for here, on St Mary's River, is a series of locks which enables ships to navigate the seaway system farther west into vast Lake Superior.

Aside from the busy canal, the steel, pulp and paper, and lumber mills are major employers. The huge Algoma Steel mill, long one of the city's mainstays, has had to scale back considerably due to lost markets. Diversification has been assisted by the relocation of some provincial government offices from Toronto to the Soo.

The International Bridge connects the city with its twin in Michigan, USA. Going west to Winnipeg is slightly shorter via Michigan and Duluth than over the lake but is not as impressive.

With the bridge and the Trans Canada Hwy, the Soo is a convenient stopover and acts as a tourist supply centre. It is one of the more appealing of the northern cities, and there are some fine outdoor possibilities within range to complement it. With a population of around 79,000, it's the last big town until Thunder Bay to the west. Sudbury is 300km to the east, a drive of between three and four hours.

Orientation

The approach to Sault Ste Marie from the east or west is a long row of eateries, service stations and motels. Hwy 17 North (later west) becomes the Great Northern Rd and then Pim St in town. Hwy 17 East becomes Wellington St, which is the northern edge of the downtown core. If you're passing through, use the bypass to avoid traffic hassles.

For visitors this is a dream town in terms of convenience. The downtown area is quite small and pleasant, with pretty much

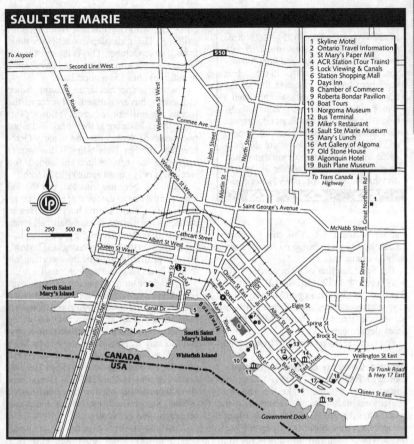

SAULT STE MARIE

To Airport
Second Line West
Korah Road
Wellington St West
John Street
North Street
Conmee Ave
Wellington St West
Mortin St
550
To Trans Canada Highway
Great Northern Rd
Saint George's Avenue
McNabb Street
Cathcart Street
Albert St West
Queen St West
Huron St
Canal Dr
Pim Street
North Saint Mary's Island
Canal Dr
St Mary's River
Boardwalk Dr
International Bridge
South Saint Mary's Island
Whitefish Island
CANADA
USA
Queen St East
Bruce Street
Elgin St
Spring St
Brock St
Wellington St East
To Trunk Road & Hwy 17 East
Queen St East
Dennis St
Bay Street
Foster Dr
East Street
Albert St East
Government Dock

0   250   500 m

1 Skyline Motel
2 Ontario Travel Information
3 St Mary's Paper Mill
4 ACR Station (Tour Trains)
5 Lock Viewing & Canals
6 Station Shopping Mall
7 Days Inn
8 Chamber of Commerce
9 Roberta Bondar Pavilion
10 Boat Tours
11 Norgoma Museum
12 Bus Terminal
13 Mike's Restaurant
14 Sault Ste Marie Museum
15 Mary's Lunch
16 Art Gallery of Algoma
17 Old Stone House
18 Algonquin Hotel
19 Bush Plane Museum

everything of interest either on or near the long, upgraded Queen St. South from Queen St is the restored waterfront area. This process continues, and the slow, thoughtful approach taken by the city is paying dividends in creating a central core popular with residents and visitors alike.

Many of the city's attractions, the bus station, the Station Mall (a large shopping centre) and several hotels are here, within walking distance of each other. Also in this general vicinity is the main tourist office.

A couple of buildings of particular note in town are the imposing courthouse in the middle of Queen St E and the Precious Blood Cathedral, constructed of local red-grey limestone in 1875 and originally a Jesuit mission. Queenstown refers to the renovated downtown core.

Information

The huge, modern Ontario Travel Information centre (☎ 705-945-6941) is at 261 Queen St W, at Huron St, by the International Bridge

What I Did on My Holidays

In 1836 Anna Jameson (1794-1860), from Ireland, left Toronto, where she lived with her attorney general husband Robert Jameson. She took off unescorted to the Detroit area; from there, she reached the Soo by boat, descended the rapids and attended a Native Indian assembly on Manitoulin Island. Through Georgian Bay and south to Lake Simcoe she travelled back to Toronto and later home to Britain, where she published an account of the trip entitled *Winter Studies and Summer Rambles in Canada*. And that was without a Lonely Planet guide.

leading to the USA. You can get maps, guides, advice and change money. It's open daily in summer.

The Soo Chamber of Commerce (☎ 705-949-7152, ☎ 1-800-461-6020) is at 334 Bay St downtown. It's open Monday to Friday. It also operates an information booth across the street in Station Mall by the Sears department store.

The General Hospital is at 941 Queen St E.

Agawa Canyon & the Algoma Central Railway

Together, these two make up the best known and most visited attraction in the area. The Agawa Canyon is a rugged wilderness area accessible only by the ACR trains. The 500km rail line due north from town to Hearst goes through a scenic area of mountains, waterfalls, valleys and forests. The route, constructed at the turn of the century, was originally built to bring raw materials into the industrial plants of Sault Ste Marie. Note that the best views are from the seats on the left-hand side of the train.

There are two options for passengers seeking access to the canyon and its surroundings.

The basic one-day visitor return trip to the canyon takes a full nine hours, with a two hour stopover for a quick walk, fishing or lunch on the floor of the canyon. There is a dining car on board and snacks and drinks are also available. An adult ticket costs $53, with considerable reductions for children. The train departs at 8 am daily from June to October. This is the most popular trip, so booking a couple of days (more in autumn) ahead is a good idea.

The trip is spectacular in autumn, when the leaves have changed colour and the forests are brilliant reds and yellows. Normally the colours are at their peak in the last two weeks of September and in early October. Yet another possibility is the winter snow-and-ice run, which is added (on weekends only) from January to March.

Secondly, there are trips that run the full length of the line to the town of **Hearst** (population 5500), about a nine hour trip. Hearst, perhaps surprisingly, is essentially a French town, with under 15% of the population listing English as their mother tongue. The town remains primarily engaged in lumbering, although it has its own small university.

Beyond the canyon, the track travels over less impressive flat, forested lakelands, various bridges and northern muskeg. This is a two-day trip with an overnight stay at the northern terminal. Alternatively, it's possible to stay in Hearst as long as you wish and return when ready, or not at all (mind you, there's not a lot happening in Hearst). There are motels and B&Bs in Hearst; ask about them at the tourist information centre in Sault Ste Marie. From Hearst, buses can be caught east or westbound.

The Hearst train is used by anglers, trappers, painters, lodge operators and their guests and various other local inhabitants and visitors. It stops anywhere you like or anywhere someone is standing and flagging it down, so obviously the going is slow, but some find the passengers a colourful lot and the train provides the only true access into the region.

The fare on this train is calculated by the zone of which there are six for the entire 500km route. Trip (not zone) costs range from $10 to $90.

Information on backpacking, canoeing, swimming, camping and lodges in the canyon and beyond is available at the train

station. All manner of supplies can be taken on board, including canoes, with 100lbs (30kg) free.

In Sault Ste Marie, the station (☎ 705-946-7300, ☎ 1-800-242-9287) is on the corner of Bay and Gore Sts, by the Station Shopping Mall in the centre of town. There is free parking at the station.

Canal National Historic Site

If Sudbury is rock city, the Soo is lock city. At the south-west corner of downtown, at the bottom of Huron St (by the International Bridge), are the locks linking Lake Superior to Lake Huron. Joining the two great lakes is the narrow St Mary's River, with its rapids. It is here that in 1895 the locks were built, enabling lake freighters to make the journey hundreds of extra kilometres inland.

Lake Superior is about 7m higher than Lake Huron. The often continuous lake traffic (about 80 freighters a day pass through in summer) can be watched from a viewing stand or from anywhere along the locks for no charge but they are a long way out, using the American locks. There are four US locks, and one Canadian lock, found in the narrow channel between North St Mary's Island and South St Mary's Island. The Canadian lock, built in 1895, is the oldest and is used only for recreational vessels.

Walk over the locks to South St Mary's Island, on which there is the circular Attikamek walking trail. The paths, winding through the woods and under the International Bridge, make a nice retreat, with views of the shorelines, rapids and ships. It's a good picnicking spot. Just south is Whitefish Island, from where for 2000 years the Ojibway Indians fished these plentiful waters. Fishing is still popular, and anglers can be seen all along the canal and around the islands.

Lock Tours Canada (☎ 705-253-9850) runs two-hour boat tours of the locks for $17. Boats depart downtown from behind the Bondar Pavilion beside the Holiday Inn. There are several trips daily in midsummer, fewer in spring and autumn. The boat goes through both the American and Canadian locks and is the only way to see the former

from Canada. You also get a bit of a waterfront tour.

Sea Lamprey Control Centre

Down at the locks is this small research centre where you can view some lamprey and the fish they victimise and learn more about these giant leeches. It's free, open Monday to Friday, in summer only, and is worth a look.

The Boardwalk

A boardwalk runs alongside the river off Bay St, behind the Station Shopping Mall, affording good views of the river and across to the USA. As well, there are places to fish and a number of city attractions to be found on or near the river. Near the foot of Elgin St, the large, white tent-like structure is the Roberta Bondar Pavilion, built to honour the Soo's very own astronaut. Doctor Roberta Lynn Bondar became Canada's first female astronaut aboard the Space Shuttle Discovery in 1992. The pavilion is the venue for regular concerts, exhibitions and, throughout summer, a farmers' market on Wednesday and Saturday mornings.

MS Norgama

The MS *Norgama*, now a museum (☎ 705-256-7447), was the last ship built for overnight passenger use on the Great Lakes. It's open daily from mid-May to mid-October for $2.50. The ship is moored at the Norgama Marine Park dock, near the Roberta Bondar Pavilion.

Ermatinger/Clergue Heritage Site

Ermatinger House (☎ 705-759-5443) was built in 1814 by a British fur trader and his Ojibway wife. It's the oldest stone house west of Toronto and was where many explorers, including Simon Fraser and Alexander Mackenzie, put up for the night. Inside, the house has been restored and contains 19th century furnishings. Someone there will answer questions. It's open every day in summer, from Monday to Friday during other seasons, and admission is $2. The museum is at 831 Queen St E, near the corner of Pim St.

ONTARIO

Bondar's Not Lost in Space

So what do you have to do to be the first and only woman on the Canadian astronaut team? If the remarkable Roberta Bondar is anything to go by, the answer is a lot.

Following Marc Garneau's achievement as first Canadian in space aboard a NASA shuttle flight in 1984, Bondar became the first Canadian woman to enter space, aboard the *Discovery* in 1992.

Bondar was born in Sault Ste Marie in 1945. Besides getting top marks, she was athlete of the year in her last year at high school. At university she gained a degree in zoology and agriculture while earning her pilot's licence and coaching the archery team. Continuing her education, she bagged a Masters in experimental pathology, then a Doctorate in neurobiology, and, just to stay well-rounded, finished off her Doctor of Medicine degree. For fun she parachuted and got her scuba diving certification.

Soon she was an assistant professor and head of a clinic treating patients with multiple sclerosis. But what she really wanted was to be an astronaut.

So, when the National Research Council of Canada decided to begin a space program, Bondar put her hand up, along with 4300 other Canadians. She was one of the six picked. You don't want to know about the training or the 12-hour days.

As a 'payload' scientist she carried out studies on board the shuttle related to the effects of weightlessness on the human body. One finding she noted was that you needed velcro to hold your head to the pillow (she's funny, too!). Upon returning to terra firma she wrote a book about her experiences, *Touching the Earth*, which included many of her own photographs. She calls herself an 'organised tornado'.

Roberta Bondar

Beside it is the Clergue Blockhouse, a house built atop a former powder magazine, where one of the city's most influential citizens once lived.

Bush Plane Heritage Centre

This two-in-one museum (☎ 705-945-6242) is in an old government hangar by the waterfront, on the corner of Bay and Pim Sts. The history of bush flying in Canada, a great story in itself, is tied closely to its role in forest-fire fighting. Many of the early small-plane pilots in the country were returning from the air force at the end of WWI. They also served in aerial mapping, surveying, medical assistance and rescuing. The museum has full-size planes on display, as well as some replicas, engines and parts. There are also maps,

photographs and a tent set up as it would have been in the bush.

The centre is open daily from May to October, but on weekends only the rest of the year. Admission is adults $5 and tours are offered.

Art Gallery of Algoma

This good local art gallery (☎ 705-949-9067) at 10 East St, next to the public library, is worth a visit. There's an education room, a gallery workshop and two exhibition rooms of changing work. It's open all year from 10 am to 5 pm Monday to Saturday. Admission is by donation.

Sault Ste Marie Museum

Housed in an Ontario heritage building at 690 Queen St E, on the corner of East St, this

small but well put-together museum (☎ 705-759-7278) has various displays representing Native Indians, exploration, fur trading, lumbering, geology and other aspects of the area. Another section, on the Inuit, is good. In the late 18th/early 19th century exhibits, the cigarettes recommended for asthma relief are a lark. The museum is open from 10 am to 5 pm daily in summer, Monday to Friday in other seasons. Admission is $2.

St Mary's Paper Mill
The large paper mill (☎ 705-942-6070) on Huron St, at the south-western edge of downtown, offers free walking tours on Tuesday and Thursday afternoons. Call ahead and register at the security gate.

Bellevue Park
On the water 2km east of town along Queen St E, near the university, is the city's largest park. There are some gardens and picnic areas.

Kinsmen Park
Known locally as Hiawatha Park, this is about a 10 minute drive from Great Northern Rd, north-west of downtown Sault Ste Marie. It's on Fifth Line, 3.4km east off Great Northern. The wooded area has walking and skiing trails and is free.

Tarentorous Fish Hatchery
Nearby off Landslide Rd (watch for signs on Great Northern Rd) is the hatchery (☎ 705-949-7271) which raises chinook salmon, rainbow trout and brown trout and releases them into the river and surrounding waters to develop and maintain major sport fishing in the district. And it seems to be working. The region has a good reputation and sizable fish are being taken right off the boardwalk in town.

Visitors may look around free from 9 am to 4 pm, daily from June to Labour Day and on weekdays only the rest of the year.

Gros Cap
About 20km west on Hwy 550 is this ridge about 150m above Lake Superior and Blue Water Park. Hike up the cliffs for excellent views of Lake Superior, where there's usually a ship or two cruising by. Or take the Voyageur Trail (marked by white slashes), which winds up along the ridge edge providing views of St Mary's River and the lake.

Beside the park is the *Blue Water Inn* (☎ 705-779-2530) for lodging or a meal. Ask about the weekend buffet fish fries. The inn is open in summer only.

Voyageur Hiking Trail
The partially completed Voyageur Hiking Trail will one day run between Manitoulin Island and Thunder Bay. The longest completed segment goes east from Gros Cap to Serpent River, a small village south of Elliot Lake on Hwy 108 along the North Channel of Lake Huron, a distance of about 200km. This is not an easy strolling path; obtain complete information from the Voyageur Trail Association, which has an office in Sault Ste Marie (☎ 705-253-5353, ☎ 1-800-393-5353).

Organised Tours
City Tour Hiawathaland Sightseeing Tours (☎ 705-759-6200) with a ticket booth on the waterfront, next to the Holiday Inn, runs two bus tours in summer. The double-decker bus city tour is a one hour trip costing $8.75. The other includes the American city.

Brewery Tour Northern Breweries (☎ 705-254-7373), downtown at 503 Bay St, offers free 45-minute tours of the facility and a chance to sample some of the various brews. This is one of the country's oldest beer companies and has been operating in northern Ontario since 1876.

Adventure Tours Experience North (☎ 1-888-463-5957) offers a range of multi-day canoe or kayak adventures including some in the Agawa canyon. Algoma Adventures (☎ 705-945-5032) runs various small group tours to area highlights. The van trips can include horse-riding and Indian rock paintings.

Special Events
The annual Tugboat Race, held on the St Mary's River on the weekend closest to the

1 July weekend, is a bit of good, silly fun. Competitors from both sides of the river dress up their boats with flags and banners and putt for prizes and prestige.

Places to Stay

A quirk here is that while July and August are typically busy, September and October are peak season for autumn train trips.

Camping There are several campgrounds close to town, though they are not rustic. *Ojibway Park (☎ 705-248-2671)* is a 10 minute drive east of Sault Ste Marie on Hwy 17 (called the Great Northern Rd in town). Tent sites cost $15 per night.

KOA (☎ 705-759-2344) tent and RV park is 8km north of town on Hwy 17. Turn west at the flashing amber light (Fifth Line). The park is on a river and is equipped with laundry, store and pool. Tent sites are $22 for two people.

A little farther (and a lot nicer) is *Pointe des Chênes (☎ 705-779-2696)* at the mouth of the St Mary's River with a good sandy beach. Go 12km west on Hwy 550 to Hwy 565, then 10km south past the airport to the community park. It takes about 25 minutes. There are 82 sites at $18.

Hostels HI has an affiliate here, the *Algonquin Hotel (☎ 705-253-2311, 864 Queen St E)*, a fine budget hotel for those with or without hostel membership. The central location is superb (on the corner of Pim St), within walking distance of just about everything. The rooms are plain, with no extras, but they're clean and each has at least a sink. Singles/twins are $22/30 with a hostel card, a dollar more without, plus tax. If four of you want to share a room, it's the same price as two. Drawbacks are no common area and no kitchen facilities. There's a bar downstairs for a cheap beer but there's no music so it's quiet in the rooms.

B&Bs *Amadata (☎ 705-945-6171, 376 MacDonald Ave)* is 3km north-west from downtown and is friendly and good. Rates are $40/45 with a continental breakfast and

a plus is the large guest sitting room with fridge, microwave and TV.

The *Top O' The Hill (☎ 705-253-9041, 40 Broos Rd)* is in the north-eastern section of the city, about a 10 minute drive from downtown. Prices, including full breakfast, are $45/65 with reservations suggested.

Another possibility is the conveniently central *St Christopher's Inn (☎ 705-759-0870, 923 Queen St E)*, a large Victorian place with rooms from $45/65 with breakfast. It's a short walk from the waterfront.

Hotels See the Hostels section for details of the budget-priced Algonquin Hotel.

Also central and good is the *Days Inn (☎ 705-759-8200, 320 Bay St)* right by the river. Singles/doubles here are $80/90. Facilities include a restaurant and a heated pool. Its Cellar Tap bar is the only brew pub in town.

Motels Sault Ste Marie's location means a lot of people passing and a plethora of motels. Most are on Hwy 17 either east or west of town, though some are downtown.

The *Shady Pines Motel (☎ 705-759-0088, 1587 Trunk Rd)*, 6km east on Hwy 17 East, is one of the cheapest. Though ugly at the front, it's actually good. Big rooms open onto a treed back yard with picnic tables and barbecues. Singles/doubles cost just $30/35.

Travellers Motel (☎ 705-946-4133, 859 Trunk Rd) is closer to town and has kitchenettes available. Standard doubles cost from $42. The pleasant looking *Holiday (☎ 705-759-8608, 435 Trunk Rd)* is $39/43.

Newer, more modern and pricier places can be found along Great Northern Rd, which leads north to the Trans Canada Hwy westbound.

The *Skyline Motel (☎ 705-942-1240, ☎ 1-800-461-2624, 232 Great Northern Rd)* charges $52/62 with a fridge in every room.

Comfort Inn (☎ 705-759-8000, ☎ 1-800-228-5150, 333 Great Northern Rd) charges $86/96. It's busy and part of a major chain.

Places to Eat

Most of the restaurants, many of which are the ubiquitous franchises, line the highway.

However, those listed here are mainly local establishments found in the city centre.

Queen St has a real assortment of good, atmospheric beaneries of the old lunch-counter type. The *Coral Coffee Shop (470 Queen St E)* near Spring St is a basic classic open Monday to Friday. It has cheap breakfasts and lunches of home-made soups, chilli and the like.

Tiny *Mike's (518 Queen St E)* with just half a dozen stools has been serving its regular customers home-made Italian since 1932. Meals are under $7 at this friendly place caught in a time warp. Near the corner of East St, the old-fashioned *Mary's Lunch (663 Queen St E)* serves its regulars lots of home-made stuff, including bread, and has the cheapest breakfast in town.

Two town specialities are lake trout and whitefish, and both turn up on menus all over Sault Ste Marie. *Muio's (685 Queen St E)* is a cheap place to sample them. It also offers daily specials, such as a complete meal with cabbage rolls for $8. It's open Sunday.

Italian food is very popular here. *Giovanni's (☎ 705-942-3050, 516 Great Northern Rd)* opens every day and has a good selection of lunches for $6 to $7 and dinners at $8 to $16. The latter includes an all-you-can-eat salad bar and bread. Reservations are suggested weekend nights.

Alpen Hof (674 Great Northern Rd), featuring the Alps design, is popular for its moderately-priced German dinners.

Queen St also has a couple of pubs.

Getting There & Away

Air There are regular Air Canada and Canadian Airlines flights to Sault Ste Marie.

Bus The bus station (☎ 705-949-4711) is downtown at 73 Brock St. There are three buses a day to Sudbury. From there, three buses daily depart for either Toronto or Ottawa. The through fare to Ottawa is $117, to Toronto $101. There are also three buses daily to Winnipeg at $134.

For buses to Detroit or Chicago, you must get to the city bus terminal. For details see Getting Around later.

Hitching The Soo is a major drop-off point for those thumbing east and west. In summer there are plenty of backpackers hanging around town. If you're going west, remember that it's a long way from Sault Ste Marie to Winnipeg, with little to see in between. Nights are cold and rides can be scarce. Try to get a through ride to Thunder Bay (715km) and then go on to Winnipeg from there.

Getting Around

To/From the Airport The airport is 13km west on Hwy 550, then 7km south on Hwy 565. There are airport buses between the airport and major hotels.

Bus The city bus terminal (☎ 705-759-5438) is on the corner of Queen and Dennis Sts. The Riverside bus from downtown goes east to Algoma University, near Belvedere Park. A city bus leaves from the terminal and goes over the bridge into the Soo, Michigan, USA. Taxis will also take you across the bridge. Check the current status but evidently the long-distance buses don't depart here but from St Ignace, Michigan, an hour away.

NORTH AROUND LAKE SUPERIOR

From Sault Ste Marie to Thunder Bay, the Trans Canada Hwy is one of the few roads cutting through the thinly populated northern Ontario wilds. The highway to Wawa is particularly scenic. This huge area is rough, lake-filled timberland. Development has been slow to penetrate and the abundant minerals and wildlife remain partially undisturbed. There are areas where there's logging, but these are rarely seen. You may see signs of forest fires, which are common each year.

This quiet and beautiful part of the country is presided over by awesome Lake Superior – once known as Gitche Gumee (Big Sea Water) to the Ojibway Indians. The largest of the five Great Lakes (and one of the world's largest lakes), it's sometimes pretty, sometimes brutal. Even today, there are disastrous shipwrecks when the lake gets angry, and according to a Canadian folk song, Superior 'never gives up her dead'.

Several of the Canadian Group of Seven painters were inspired to work here, and descriptions which reached the poet Henry Wadsworth Longfellow had the same effect on him. Along the highway are many provincial parks, which make good places to get a feel for the lake and surrounding forest.

Batchawana Bay

A relaxing afternoon or a full day can be spent north of town along the scenic shore of Lake Superior around Batchawana Bay. It's a 45 minute drive to **Chippewa Falls**, called the centrepoint of Canada with trails and the waterfalls. Agawa Indian Crafts, a well known landmark, is about 75km from the Soo. Other than the off-putting stacks of animal pelts, a browse is worthwhile.

Batchewana Provincial Park has camping and picnic spots but the park at Pancake Bay, also with camping, has a better beach although the water is cool. Park day passes are $7.50 per car. There are also motels, resorts and rental cottages.

Bears often hang around the Montreal River garbage dump, about 25km northwest of Batchawana Bay but it's gated most of the time preventing vehicle passage. If so, don't leave your car to have a look on foot.

Lake Superior Provincial Park

Hwy 17 runs for 80km through this large natural park north of Sault Ste Marie, so (luckily) you can't miss it. It's a beautiful park, with a few things to see even if you don't stay. The rugged scenery is good, with rivers in the wooded interior and a shoreline featuring rocky headlands and sandy beaches. Several of the aforementioned Group of Seven painters worked in the park.

The park (π 705-856-2284) has three campgrounds, short and long hiking trails usually accessible from the highway, and seven canoe routes. Naturalists give talks and guided walks. The park also offers fishing. Mammals include bears and be wary of moose on the road at night.

At **Agawa Bay**, see the Native Indian pictographs on the shoreline rocks, believed to commemorate a crossing of the lake. Note the crevices in the rocks along the path. Farther along, stop at **Sand River** and walk down to the beach. Though the water is cold, the beautiful sandy beach, long and empty, looks as if it's been lifted from a Caribbean island.

For access to the less-visited eastern side of the park, where there is no road, inquire about the train which runs along the far eastern edge. It can be caught at Frater at the southern end of the park or at Hawk Junction. The latter is a small village outside of the northern boundary of the park east of the town of Wawa. The train line is part of the Algoma Central Railway.

Distance hikers and canoeists should hope for good weather – this is one of the wettest areas in Ontario. Trails are often enveloped in mist or fog, which lends a primeval, spooky air to the woods. Interior camping costs a few dollars less than the campgrounds with their facilities.

Wawa

The name is an Ojibway word, meaning 'wild goose', bestowed on the town because of the thousands of geese which stop over on Lake Wawa during migrations. A huge steel goose by the tourist office marks the edge of town.

Wawa is in economic trouble as the iron mine, its mainstay, closed in 1998. Outdoor related tourism is picking up some of the slack and the town acts as a supply centre for the regional parks but there's nothing much to see. East of town, near the OPP police station, High Falls is a scenic picnic spot. Ask at the helpful tourist office about the numerous nearby hiking trails and treeless zone.

Motels are often full in summer; a good one to try is the *Lakewood Motel* (π 705-856-2774), 15km west of town at Catfish Lake. The *Pine Ridge Motel*, 5km west of Wawa, serves a decent meal.

Chapleau

Chapleau is a small logging and outdoors centre inland from Wawa. There are numerous provincial parks in the area, three within 80km. **Missinaibi Lake Park** (π 705-864-1710) is in the middle of **Chapleau Game Reserve**, the largest in the western

And You Thought He Wasn't Real

White River was apparently the original home of the bear which inspired AA Milne's *Winnie the Pooh* books. Evidently, a Canadian soldier got an orphaned bear cub here before his departure to Europe. Feeling lonely, he named it Winnipeg, after his home town. During WWI, it ended up at England's London Zoo, where it became quite popular, and was subsequently immortalised in fiction.

hemisphere. The boreal forest is ideal for wilderness camping, canoeing or fishing.

The tourist offices around the area have a listing of canoe routes. There are 12 trips ranging from one to 14 days, with five to 47 portages. The longest one is a river and lake circle route going through part of the reserve; it's good for viewing moose.

Tourist offices can also help with information on the many lodges and fly-in camps which operate in the area.

White River

Back on the Trans Canada Hwy, this is called the coldest place in Canada, with temperatures recorded as low as -50°C. Get your picture taken near the thermometer. There are a couple of moderately priced motels and VIA Rail connects the town to Sudbury. The station is on Winnipeg Rd, a short walk from the highway.

Pukaskwa National Park

Find out how tough you are. There is no road in this park (pronounced 'puk-a-saw') and access is by hiking or boat. From Heron Bay, off the Trans Canada Hwy near Marathon, is a small road, Hwy 627, which goes to the edge of the park at Hattie Cove. There is a small (67-site) campground and a visitor information centre (☎ 807-229-0801). For day-use, there is a picnic area, and swimming in a protected bay. In Superior itself, the water is cold and swells can be hazardous even for good swimmers.

The main attraction is the old 60km coastal hiking trail (one way), with primitive camping spots along the way. A shuttle can be arranged to take you one way. The terrain is rough but beautiful and the

weather is changeable, switching quickly from sun to storm. The trail is often wet and slippery, black flies and mosquitoes are guaranteed and bears are often a bother. Even the mice can be trouble, digging into unattended supplies. Good luck.

The interior offers some challenging canoeing, including runs down the Pukaskwa and the less difficult, more accessible White River. Facilities are operational from early June to late September but the park itself is open all year. Marathon has an outfitter.

Slate Islands Provincial Park

Offshore from the small town of **Terrace Bay** is this cluster of islands, home to the highest density of woodland caribou anywhere. The islands, without natural predators, support several hundred caribou which are studied by researchers looking into preserving the herds of mainland Ontario. Ask at the Terrace Bay tourist office for people who do boat trips to the islands to see or photograph the caribou. Camping is possible but the islands are 13km offshore so the trip is not cheap.

Nipigon

Nipigon sits at the mouth of the Nipigon River, where Hwy 11 meets Hwy 17, the Trans Canada. There really isn't anything of note, but it is interesting that this was the first European settlement on Superior's north shore. European traders established a fur-trading post here, in the middle of the traditional Ojibway lands. East of town along Hwy 17, look for the Kama Lookout, with good views of the Lake Superior shore. This segment of the highway is also known as the Terry Fox Courage Hwy.

ONTARIO

Ouimet Canyon Provincial Park

About 45km west of Nipigon and 40km east of Thunder Bay, this park features a great canyon 3km long and 150m both wide and deep. The walls on either side of the chasm are virtually perpendicular. Fences and viewing stations have been built right at the sheer edges for good, heart-pounding views. The canyon was scoured out during the last Ice Age and the bottom is home to some rare flora generally found only in Arctic regions. The canyon is definitely worth a quick stop; most times you'll find yourself alone. A 1km trail meanders around the top and there are some interpretive displays. The park is 12km from the Trans Canada. Officially, there's no camping and an admission fee is suggested.

Sleeping Giant Provincial Park

Part of the Sibley Peninsula, this large, natural and scenic park (☎ 807-977-2526) arcs 35km into Lake Superior. The setting and landscape are excellent, with woods, hills, shoreline and great views from several vantage points.

Look for foxes by the road on the way in at dusk. Moose also live in the park. Activities include swimming, fishing and camping, and there are some good walks, including one out along the top of the Sleeping Giant rock formation, from where there are fine views. One hike, taking a minimum of two days, cuts across most of the west coast of the peninsula.

The park makes a good stop if you don't want to go into town (about 45km) to sleep. At the very end of the peninsula is the tiny community of Silver Islet where the old mining store has been transformed into the *Silver Islet Store & Tea Room*. Pass Lake also has a restaurant.

THUNDER BAY

Edging the northern shores of Lake Superior, and known as 'the Lakehead', Thunder Bay

---

The Legend of the Sleeping Giant

An Ojibway legend tells the story of the formation of the Sleeping Giant. In one version, Nana-bijou, the spirit of the Deep Sea Water, showed the Ojibway a mine where silver could be found as reward for their peaceful, spiritual way of life. But, he said, if anyone should ever tell the white people of its source, they would forever be turned to stone.

Upon seeing the fine articles and jewellery made of silver, the Sioux, the Ojibway's historical enemy, sought to discover the metal's origins. When even torture failed to reveal the secret, the Sioux decided to send a man in disguise to live as an Ojibway. Eventually, he was led to the mine. On his way back to his people with the great news, the Sioux stopped at a white man's encampment.

The white men were enthralled upon seeing the silver sample he had with him. After being plied with alcohol, the Sioux agreed to take several of the men by canoe to the mine. A great storm came up, drowning everyone but the Sioux, whose canoe the Ojibway later found floating around aimlessly. When the weather cleared, the open bay had been partially blocked by a huge rock formation, and the Ojibway knew that Nana-bijou's words had come to be.

Another legend involves Mt Mackay. The Ojibway had become farmers and were growing wheat. One harvest, the crop was demolished by incessant flocks of blackbirds. The hunters were unable to replace the crop, due to early and heavy snowfalls.

The water froze, making fishing difficult, especially with the meagre bait available, and soon even this was gone. In desperation, the daughter of the chief cut strips from her legs to give the fishers for bait. Enough fish were caught to stave off mass starvation but the girl died. In her honour, a visiting priest had the men build the small chapel which still sits atop Mt Mackay. Each year at Thanksgiving, the chapel is visited and prayers are offered.

(population 114,000) is an amalgamation of the towns of Fort William and Port Arthur. Despite being so far inland, Thunder Bay is one of Canada's major ports and is as far westward as ships using the St Lawrence Seaway get this side of the border. The main cargo switching hands here is prairie wheat going to market. Although decreasing in importance, the docks have long been one of the world's major grain handlers.

The city, halfway between Sault Ste Marie and Winnipeg – 720km to either one – is a good stopping-off point. The place itself may not hold you long, but the setting is scenic and it makes a handy centre for experiencing some of the things to see and do in northern Ontario's rugged timberland.

The first Europeans here were a couple of Frenchmen who reached the area in 1662. For hundreds of years, this was a fur-trading settlement. In 1869 the Dawson, the pioneer's road westward, was begun. In 1882 the Canadian Pacific Railway arrived, and soon the prairie's first shipment of wheat was heading east.

Coming into town from the east on the Trans Canada Hwy, you'll pass mountains and see the city at the edge of the bay. Along the shoreline are pulp mills and grain elevators. Out in the harbour, ships are moored, and beyond is a long rock formation and an island or two. The unusually shaped mass of rock offshore, known as the Sleeping Giant, is important in Native Indian lore.

Orientation
Thunder Bay still has two distinct downtown areas, which are connected principally by Fort William Rd and Memorial Ave. The area between the two is pretty much a wasteland of fast-food outlets, the large Inter City Shopping Mall and little else.

Both downtown areas are rather drab, run-down and suffering from an economy long tied to dwindling resource-based industries. In Port Arthur (Thunder Bay North), closer to the lakeshore, main streets are Red River Rd and Cumberland St. Port Arthur's Landing, off Water St, is a redeveloped waterfront area and includes parkland.

The Pagoda tourist office is across the street. This half of Thunder Bay has a sizable Finnish population, which supports several specialised restaurants. Indeed, for a city its size, Thunder Bay has quite a large and varied ethnic population.

In Fort William (Thunder Bay South), main streets are May St and Victoria Ave. The Victoriaville shopping mall is at this corner and is where most of the Fort William action occurs.

On each side of Thunder Bay is a commercial motel/restaurant strip.

Information
Tourism Thunder Bay (☎ 807-983-2041, ☎ 1-800-667-8386) at the Terry Fox Lookout and Memorial about 6km east of town on Hwy 11/17 is open daily.

In Port Arthur, a central summer tourist office (☎ 807-684-3670) open daily, is in the 1910 Pagoda in the park on the corner of Red River Rd and Water St. In Fort William, you can get some information at City Hall, 500 Donald St E. There is also an information booth at Old Fort William. The tourist offices have pamphlets outlining architectural walking tours for both sections of town.

Port Arthur General Hospital is at 460 Court St N.

Old Fort William
Some of Thunder Bay's best known attractions are some distance from downtown, as is Old Fort William (☎ 807-473-2344), the city's feature site.

The old fort settlement, with 42 historic buildings spread over 50 hectares west of town, not far past the airport and off Broadway Ave, is worth getting to.

From 1803 to 1821, Fort William was the headquarters of the North West Fur Trading Company. Here the voyageurs and Native Indians did their trading, and settlers and explorers arrived from the east. In 1821, after much haggling and hassling, the company was absorbed by its chief rival, the Hudson's Bay Company, and Fort William declined.

The fort re-creates some aspects of the early, thriving days of the fur trade through

ONTARIO

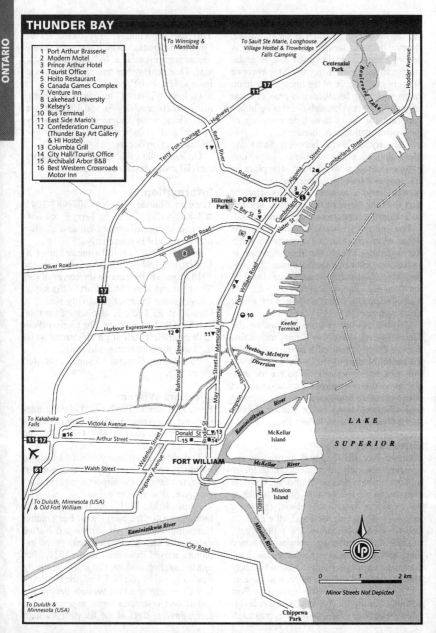

THUNDER BAY

1 Port Arthur Brasserie
2 Modern Motel
3 Prince Arthur Hotel
4 Tourist Office
5 Hoito Restaurant
6 Canada Games Complex
7 Venture Inn
8 Lakehead University
9 Kelsey's
10 Bus Terminal
11 East Side Mario's
12 Confederation Campus
    (Thunder Bay Art Gallery
    & HI Hostel)
13 Columbia Grill
14 City Hall/Tourist Office
15 Archibald Arbor B&B
16 Best Western Crossroads
    Motor Inn

To Winnipeg &
Manitoba

To Sault Ste Marie, Longhouse
Village Hostel & Trowbridge
Falls Camping

Centennial
Park

Hodder Avenue

Boulevard Lake

Terry Fox-Courage Highway

Red River Road

Algoma Street

Cumberland Street

PORT ARTHUR

Hillcrest
Park

Bay St

Cumberland St

Water St

Oliver Road

Oliver Road

Fort William Road

Memorial Avenue

Harbour Expressway

Keefer
Terminal

Neebing-McIntyre
Diversion

Balmoral Street

May Street

Simpson Street

Victoria Avenue

Donald St

Arthur Street

Waterloo Street

Kingsway Avenue

Walsh Street

FORT WILLIAM

To Kakabeka
Falls

To Duluth, Minnesota (USA)
& Old Fort William

Kaministikwia River

Kaministikwia River

City Road

McKellar River

McKellar
Island

LAKE
SUPERIOR

Mission
Island

108th Ave

Mission River

To Duluth &
Minnesota (USA)

Chippewa
Park

0   1   2 km

Minor Streets Not Depicted

buildings, tools, artefacts and documents. Workers in period dress demonstrate skills and crafts, perform historical re-enactments and will answer questions. Interesting displays include the Native Indian camp and the woodwork of the canoe building. Animals can be seen at the separate farm section.

In summer, free special-event days are held regularly. In mid-July the fort becomes the scene of the Great Rendezvous, a three-day festival which re-creates the annual meeting of North West employees, voyageurs, Native Indians and traders. In August, keep an eye open for the Ojibway Keeshigun, a weekend festival of Native Indian culture.

A thorough but relaxed visit to the fort can take half a day or more. Entry is $10, with family rates available. The fort is open daily from 10 am to 5 pm from mid-May to mid-October. Good, cheap home-made food (brick-oven bread and voyageur stew) is available in the fort's canteen.

Although the site is a long way out, the Neebing 10 city bus goes close to the fort, departing from the terminal in either Fort William or Port Arthur every hour; the last bus from the fort leaves at around 4.30 pm, but check.

Kakabeka Falls
Set in a provincial park 25km west of Thunder Bay off Hwy 17, the waterfalls, about 40m high, are worth a look. They're most impressive in spring, when the water in the river is at its highest, or after heavy rains. Sometimes the water flow is small, as it's dammed off for power. Walkways lead around and across the falls. Plaques tell the Ojibway legend of martyr Princess Green Mantle, who saved her village from the attacking Sioux by leading them over the falls.

Most people go to take pictures at the falls, but the park itself isn't bad, with camping, swimming at small beaches, and picnicking. Parking is $2 to see the falls, more for longer stays.

Mt Mackay
Mt Mackay is the tallest mountain in the area's north-western mountain chain, rising to about 350m and offering good views of Thunder Bay and environs. The lookout is on an Ojibway reserve and an admission of $5 per car is charged to use the winding road to the top. The view of the city is good, but for seeing the Sleeping Giant you're better off at the Terry Fox Lookout, off the Trans Canada Hwy.

Mt Mackay is south-west of Fort William. Take Edward St to City Rd, towards Chippewa Park, and follow the signs. The road to Mt Mackay cuts through a portion of the residential area of the reserve. At the top there is a snack bar and gift shop. A walking trail leads farther up to the peak. No city bus gets close enough to make public transportation to the mountain a viable option.

Terry Fox Monument
Overlooking the Sleeping Giant on Hwy 11/17 a few kilometres east of town, this 2.7m high statue, and the segment of the Trans Canada Hwy north-west of town, honours the young Canadian who, in the early 1980s while dying of cancer, ran halfway across Canada to raise money for cancer research. After having one leg amputated, he made it from Newfoundland to Thunder Bay, raising millions and becoming a national hero before finally succumbing. Each year, cities across the country and around the world hold Terry Fox Memorial Runs to raise further funds for his cause.

There is a good visitor information centre here.

Thunder Bay Museum
This small historical museum (☎ 807-623-0801), housed in the former police station at 425 Donald St E, contains Native Indian artefacts and a collection of odds and ends of local history. Topics covered include fur trading, mining and the early pioneers. There's also an Albertosaurus. The museum is not extensive but displays are well presented. It's open daily in summer. Admission is $2 (free on Saturday).

Thunder Bay Art Gallery
The gallery at Confederation College campus (☎ 807-577-6427), 1080 Keewatin St, off

Balmoral St, collects, preserves and displays contemporary art by Native Indians. Works include paintings, prints, masks, sculptures and more. There are displays from the permanent collection, as well as travelling exhibits, which usually feature non-Native Indian artists. Norval Morrisseau, perhaps Canada's best known Native Indian painter, was born in Thunder Bay and some of his work is on view. The gallery is open from noon to 8 pm Tuesday to Thursday, and from noon to 5 pm Friday to Sunday. Admission is $2. and it's closed Monday. The Northwood bus from Fort William goes to the campus door.

The Port

Thunder Bay Harbour is one of Canada's largest ports according to tonnes handled and once claimed the greatest complex of grain elevators in the world. Terminals, elevators and other storage and docking facilities stretch along 45km of central waterfront. Some are no longer used. At the Port Arthur shipyards, the huge freighters are repaired.

In the middle of the waterfront is the Keefer Complex, a cargo-handling facility where ships from around the world come and go. The terminal mainly handles resource materials and grains.

Mission Island

Despite the industrial look of the port, there is life down there among the terminals. On Mission Island, south-east of Arthur St, the Lakehead Region Conservation Authority has created a sanctuary for water birds. During the spring and autumn migrations, thousands of birds can sometimes be seen on the 40 hectares of wetlands. To get there, cross the bridge off Syndicate Ave S and follow the signs.

Prince Arthur's Landing

Located in Port Arthur, by the lake opposite the Pagoda tourist office, the landing is a waterfront redevelopment zone. It contains the marina, the dock, a small art gallery and gift shop. Also in the train station, on the 2nd floor, is a large layout created by the model railroad club.

Still, the site is primarily parkland. There are some walking paths which meander around three piers. Best is the one out to Wilson St Headland, with views of the lake and dock areas.

Parks

Centennial Park Centennial is a large, natural woodland park at the eastern edge of Port Arthur, near Hwy 17. It's alongside Current River, which flows into Boulevard Lake before entering Lake Superior. The park is over the Boulevard Lake Bridge just off Arundel St. Entry is free. There are nature trails along the river and through the woods. On the grounds is a simulated logging camp of 1910 – not much to see, but the log cabins and buildings themselves are good. A small museum has a cross-cut section of a 250-year-old white pine tree on display. Various dates in history are marked at the corresponding growth rings. It's amazing to think what has gone on while this tree quietly kept growing. You'll find canoes and boats for rent here as well. Up the road from the park is the Bluffs Scenic Lookout, for a view of the lake and shore.

International Friendship Gardens This good-sized city park is west of downtown Fort William, on Victoria Ave near Waterloo St. Various local ethnic groups, such as the Finns and the Hungarians, have erected monuments and statues. There is a pond and some flowers but no extensive gardens.

Hillcrest Park On High St, just to the west of Waverley Park near Red River Rd, Hillcrest has a lookout point for views of the harbour and to the Sleeping Giant.

Activities

Sauna Finnish saunas are popular in the region. Try one at Kanga's (☎ 705-344-6761), 379 Oliver Rd. It also offers some Finnish eats and good desserts.

Amethyst Hounding Amethyst (a variety of quartz) is a purple semiprecious stone that is found in several areas around Thunder

Bay. There are many superstitions surrounding amethyst, including the early Greek one that it prevents drunkenness. The ever-practical Greeks therefore often fashioned wine cups from the stone. It is mined from veins which run on or near the earth's surface, so looking for the stone and digging it out are relatively easy.

Within about 50km of the city are five sites where you can go looking for your own stones. Each site has some samples for sale if you should miss out on finding some. Shops in town sell jewellery and finished souvenir items made of the purple quartz. The tourist office has a list of all the mines and can direct you to stores around town which sell a range of stuff produced with the finished stone – mostly pretty tacky. The stone generally looks better raw.

Visits to all but one of the sites are free. You simply pay for the pieces you find and want to keep.

Thunder Bay Amethyst Mine Panorama (☎ 807-622-6908) is a huge property off East Loon Lake Rd, which is east of Hwy 587 South, about 50km east of town. The site is about 7km north of the Trans Canada Hwy, and the road is rough and steep in places. Entry is $2 and it's closed Sunday.

Three of the mine sites, all much smaller, are on Rd No 5 N, a little farther east than East Loon. Located 4km to 6km north up from the Trans Canada Hwy, the three mine entrances can't be missed. You are given a pail and shovel and pointed in the right direction, then you're on your own – see what you come up with. All the sites are open daily from May to October and each has a shop on the premises.

Organised Tours
Canoeing Wildwaters Nature Tours (☎ 807-767-2022), east of town on Dog Lake Rd, off Hwy 527 north, offers canoe expeditions of various lengths and costs. They include wildlife, photography and fishing trips. There are trips into Wabakimi, the large wilderness park north-west of Lake Nipigon, and expeditions that even go as far north as Hudson Bay.

The biologists at Blue Loon Adventures (☎ 807-767-6838, ☎ 1-888-846-0066, www .foxnet.net/~blueloon/) offer a range of day or longer outdoor trips including rafting, birding and biking from their tent camp about 45 minutes from town south along Hwy 61. Accommodation is $16 and meals are available.

Fishing Fishing charters into Lake Superior (for salmon and trout) are available from the Thunder Bay Marina. Trout fishing is possible in nearby rivers and streams; the tourist office has a list of local fishing spots put out by the Ministry of Natural Resources.

From Thunder Bay to Kenora, near the Manitoba border, there are almost limitless fishing camps and lodges. Many people fly in to remote lakes. Tourist offices will have more information on these wonderful sounding but pricey trips.

Special Events
For three days in mid-July Old Fort William hosts a re-creation of the Great Rendezvous, the annual get-together of North West Company employees, voyageurs, Native Indians and traders who congregated at the fort to trade pelts and generally carouse. Hundreds of appropriately dressed characters turn up to take part.

Harbourfest, also held in July, is an annual street festival centred around the marina. There's music, dancing, street theatre, markets and a firework display.

Mid-August sees the one-day Festa Italia, featuring food (of course), games and entertainment. It's held in the north-end Italian section of town.

Ask about the First Nation Powwow, featuring Native Indian dancers, held on Mt McKay around 1 July.

Places to Stay
Camping Thunder Bay is one of those happy places where good camping can be found close to the city.

On the east side of the city is *Trowbridge Falls* (☎ *807-683-6661*) off Hwy 11/17 about 500m north up Copenhagen Rd (near

the Terry Fox Monument). It's run by the City of Thunder Bay, as is the adjacent Centennial Park.

More commercial, and geared to RVs, is the **KOA** campground (☎ 807-683-6221) 3km east of the monument and visible from the Trans Canada. A site costs $16.

Farther east is excellent **Sleeping Giant Provincial Park** (☎ 807-977-2526), 32km off Hwy 11/17 (Trans Canada) down Hwy 587. **Pass Lake Campground** (☎ 807-977-2646) also on Hwy 587 is closer to the Trans Canada.

West out of town on Hwy 17 (the Trans Canada) there's good camping at **Kakabeka Falls Provincial Park** (☎ 807-473-9231).

There's also camping south-west of the city at **Chippewa Park** (☎ 807-623-3912) a short drive from Old Fort William. From the junction of Hwys 61 and 61B, go 3.2km on Hwy 61B to City Rd and look for the signs. The park is right on the lake.

Hostels The **Thunder Bay International Hostel** (☎ 807-983-2042, candu@microage-tb.com, 1594 Lakeshore Drive) at the Longhouse Village is excellent and open all year. It's a fair distance from town – 18km east along Lakeshore Drive – but is well worth the effort. The location is green and quiet, the atmosphere friendly and relaxed. The couple that run it, Lloyd and Willa Jones, are the driving force behind Backpackers Hostels Canada (see Accommodation in the Facts for the Visitor chapter for more information on this group). Write to them at RR13, Thunder Bay, P7B 5E4 for more information on this network, or you can check the website at www.backpackers.ca.

The Joneses are knowledgeable about things to do around town. There is swimming and walking near the hostel and ask about McKenzie Point, the waterfall in the woods and the lady nearby who sells fantastic smoked fish at good prices. Get the lake trout – mmm!

Basic food is available and guests can use the kitchen. Rooms and beds are scattered all over the property in a variety of units, including a large mobile home, cabins, the main house and even a couple of buses. The price is $17 per person, or a tent can be set up on the lawn for $11 per person or $17 for two. Couples and families can be accommodated.

There are no city buses to the hostel, so take the eastbound Greyhound bus from the terminal at 815 Fort William Rd. For $7 they'll take you along Lakeshore Drive to the hostel (or will at least let you off at Mackenzie Station Rd at the Trans Canada Hwy, from where it's a straight walk south of about a kilometre). Be sure to tell the driver where you're headed when you get on. There is a trip into town around noon and one back in the evening at around 7 pm, but ask about up-to-date scheduling.

From mid-May to mid-August, HI has rooms in **Sibley Hall Confederation College** (☎ 807-475-6381, 960 William St) north of downtown Fort William. It's very institutional with no common areas but cheap at $10/15 members/nonmembers.

There are beds available in the **Lakehead University Residence** (☎ 807-343-8612, 955 Oliver Rd) from 1 May to 20 August. Singles/twins cost $23/34. The university is between the two downtown areas and slightly west. The cross-town city bus goes past the campus.

B&Bs **Archibald Arbor** (☎ 807-622-3386, nthall@norlink.net, 222 South Archibald St) is very central in a renovated Fort William house. Singles/doubles are $35 to $55 with a continental breakfast. It's open all year.

Pinebrook (☎ 807-683-6114) is near the Terry Fox Monument east of town off Hwy 17. It's about a 15 minute drive, on a large, wooded property. Singles/doubles range from $45/50 to $65/75 with full breakfast. Features include nearby walking trails and a sauna. German is spoken.

Hotels The **Best Western Crossroads Motor Inn** (☎ 807-577-4241, ☎ 1-800-265-3253, 655 West Arthur St) in Prince Arthur is good value at $73/78 for singles/doubles.

Top of the list of the business hotels is the **Prince Arthur Hotel** (☎ 807-345-5411) on

the corner of Cumberland St and Red River Rd, right by the Pagoda tourist office. It's large, has several places to eat or drink and costs $77/85, less weekends or if you ask for the corporate rate. Some rooms look out over the lake.

The *Venture Inn* (☎ 807-345-2343, 450 Memorial Ave) is $80/90 and has a pool.

Motels There are two areas of heavy motel concentration, one on each side of the city. In Port Arthur look along Cumberland St N which leads from downtown into Hodder St, which then leads to the Expressway or Hwy 17 East. The motels are mainly found near the grain elevators along the lakefront.

The *Modern Motel* (☎ 807-344-4352, 430 Cumberland St N) is a very nice place with rooms at just $36 double.

The other motel district is along Arthur St, heading out of town from downtown Fort William past the airport. The *Ritz Motel* (☎ 807-623-8189, 2600 Arthur St E) is good and has some kitchenettes. Rooms cost $60/62 at this spacious property close to town.

There are a few motels side by side on Kingsway Ave, off Arthur St E, but these are priced higher than they're worth.

Places to Eat

Port Arthur The *Hoito* (314 Bay St) is a Finnish place set up about 1940. It is known for its economical home-made food served in plain surroundings. The large portions pack them in, even at lunch on the weekends. There are a couple of similar places in this Finnish neighbourhood, and around the corner on Secord St is a Finnish bakery.

Away from the central core (on the corner of Junot Ave) is the popular *Port Arthur Brasserie* (901 Red River Rd), a brew pub where, in addition to the usual meals, there's a Sunday brunch.

There are numerous restaurants on Memorial Ave which links the two parts of the city. Casual *Kelsey's* (805 Memorial Ave) or *East Side Mario's* (1170 Memorial Ave) are both geared to the young with most dinners under $15. The latter has numerous Italian dishes.

Fort William The *Columbia Grill & Tavern* (123 May St S) is a friendly, basic, all-purpose restaurant used by the locals. It gained some infamy in the early 1990s as the place where Laurie 'Bambi' Bembenek, the popular protagonist in one of North America's most captivating criminal cases, worked while on the run from US authorities. It's open daily from 8 am.

The *Cronos Bookstore Café* (433 Syndicate Ave S) is an arty, alternative sort of place and is a welcome addition for lunch or dinner. It's open until 6 pm Monday to Wednesday and until 11 pm Thursday to Saturday. It's good for inexpensive Greek or Middle Eastern fare or just a cappuccino.

Boston Pizza (217 Arthur St W) serves pasta and rib meals for about $15.

Victoria Mall, or the Victoria Centre, right in the centre of town, has a food fair.

The *Good News Café* is just outside the Victoria Mall in the parking loop about a block and a half north of the intersection of Arthur St W and Syndicate Sts. It serves up more substantial meals with flair and an international twist. Prices vary from $8 to $20. It's closed Sunday and Monday.

Entertainment

Fort William has several places to consider. *Dewar's Pub* (121 McKellar St) has an array of beer and fish and chips etc. *Armani's* (513 Victoria Ave E) is a somewhat dressy restaurant and nightclub with a casual rooftop bar in summer; it's not a bad place for a quiet beer.

The *Innplace* is a popular hotel bar for live pop and rock. It's in the Intowner hotel, on the corner of Arthur and Brodie Sts.

Getting There & Away

Air Thunder Bay Airport is about 15 minutes' drive south-west of town, at the junction of Hwy 11/17 (the Trans Canada Hwy) and Hwy 61 to Duluth, Minnesota and the USA. Air Canada (☎ 807-623-3313) and Canadian Airlines (☎ 807-577-6461) offer flights to Winnipeg ($295) and to Toronto ($355). Bearskin Airlines (☎ 807-475-0066) services the region and other northern parts of the province.

Bus The Greyhound Bus Depot (☎ 807-345-2194) is closer to Fort William but lies in between the two downtown areas, at 815 Fort William Rd (near the Inter City Shopping Mall). It's a long walk north from central Fort William; grab the city bus. The Mainline bus goes past the door as it runs between Fort William and Port Arthur.

For Winnipeg ($91) and points farther west, there are three buses a day, beginning early in the morning and running until the wee hours.

For Sault Ste Marie ($104) and points east, such as Toronto, there are also about three trips daily, and again the schedule is evenly spaced out over the 24 hours (with some departures at rather ungodly hours).

For Sudbury ($134), there is just one trip a day, departing in the early evening.

Four times a week buses go to Duluth, Minnesota.

The Grey Goose bus line runs to Fort Francis and, via the USA, to Manitoba.

Car Enterprise (☎ 807-344-2800) has cars from $33 per day with 200km free and will pick you up.

Budget Rent-a-Car (☎ 807-622-3366) at 230 Waterloo St S has weekend specials which may be useful. There are several agencies with desks at the airport.

A circular tour of northern Ontario can be made by car from Thunder Bay by backtracking to Lake Nipigon and following Hwy 11 (the most northerly provincial route) through Geraldton and Kapuskasing, returning south via Timmins, Sudbury or North Bay. Provincial parks are found at regular intervals along Hwy 11. Towns are small.

Hitching Westbound travellers should head out to Arthur St; the airport bus will take you to a good spot. Alternatively, if you can get to Hwy 102 (Red River Rd-Dawson Rd) on the north edge of Port Arthur, you save a few kilometres along Hwy 11/17 before the turnoff to Winnipeg. If you're eastbound, anywhere on Hwy 17 is OK. For $7 the eastbound Greyhound bus will take you to the edge of town, but tell the driver upon boarding where you want to get off because they don't like making surprise unscheduled stops.

Getting Around
To/From the Airport The major hotels, such as the Prince Arthur, have airport shuttle buses. The ride takes about 15 minutes.

A city bus, the 'Arthur' route, also goes from the Fort William side of town right to the door of the airport. It's much slower but costs less. Catch it anywhere on Arthur St.

Bus There is a good bus system which covers all areas of the city, and the drivers are some of the friendliest and most helpful in the country. Tell them we said so. For information call ☎ 807-684-3744.

In Fort William, the terminal for local buses is on the corner of May and Miles Sts. To get to the Port Arthur end of town, take the Memorial bus on May St or the Mainline bus along Fort William St (same thing going the opposite way).

In Port Arthur, the terminal is on the corner of Water and Camelot Sts (just down from Cumberland St), by the waterfront. The Pagoda tourist office is next door.

The cross-town bus from either end of Thunder Bay goes to the university. The Neebing bus goes to Old Fort William from the Fort William terminal.

City buses also go to and from the motel and fast-food strips on both sides of town.

WEST OF THUNDER BAY
Beyond Kakabeka, the traffic thins appreciably and the highway is not as scenic as east of Thunder Bay. At Shabaqua, the highway forks, the south branch leading to Atikokan and Fort Frances and the north branch heading for Kenora and the Manitoba border. The northern route is quicker. Along the Trans Canada Hwy from this point, moose are often seen, especially at night, so drive with caution and with your eyes frequently scanning the shoulders of the road. In the Upsala region, a sign indicates the Arctic watershed, from here, water flows north. Another marks the beginning of a new time zone – you save an hour going

west. Also note that you won't get much on the radio until you pick up Ignace stations.

Northern Route

Ignace Ignace has a number of motels and a couple of service station restaurants. It also has a large tourist office (on the west side of town, beside the old fire tower), good for regional information and for details on fishing and canoe routes, including the White Otter Lake district.

Bears hang out at the garbage dump on the east side of town, 2km north up Hwy 599 just past the golf and country club on the right-hand side. Unfortunately it's gated except Thursday to Monday, noon to 5 pm and evening is the best time to see them. Although generally pretty blasé about the presence of people, they are unpredictable, so walking in is not recommended. Bears may look clumsy but they can outdash any human – guaranteed.

South, between here and Atikokan, lies **White Otter Lake**, site of White Otter Castle, a locally well known oddity built in 1904 by a Scottish immigrant named Jimmy McQuat and now restored. He did it all by himself and nobody knows why – he was a bachelor, yet this is a huge timber place with a four-storey tower. It's on the north-western arm of the lake, accessible only by canoe.

Dryden Like so many of the towns in the region, Dryden is fishing crazy – you may see a service station offering free minnows with every tank of gasoline purchased. If you don't hunt or fish, there isn't much here for you. The Avenor paper mill, Dryden's major industry, offers interesting free tours on weekdays through summer. On the radio, listen for the Sunday morning church sermon broadcast in Cree.

Kenora Kenora, a pulp and paper town about 200km from Winnipeg, is the closest town of any size to the Manitoba border. It is a hub for much of the local tourist activity, which consists mainly of summer vacation cottages, fishing and hunting. Though slower, avoid the bypass and go through

town for the pretty setting along the convoluted shores of Lake of the Woods.

There is a visitors centre (☎ 1-800-535-4549) at 1500 Trans Canada Hwy East, about five minutes drive east from the central core, and another one about 20km west of town. Main St and Front St along the water are the main centres of activity.

The harbourfront area of downtown has been re-done to good effect; the marina is here, as are the docks for two-hour boat cruises out on the lake. Less expensive is the little shuttle over to **Coney Island** for an afternoon's swim at the best sandy beach near town. There are other nearby beaches, such as popular **Norman Beach**, about 3km from downtown, at the junction of Parsons St and the Trans Canada Hwy.

At 300 Main St S, in Memorial Park, the small but good **Lake of the Woods Museum** features local history, notably the period around the start of the 20th century when Kenora changed rapidly. Tours can be taken of the paper mill at 504 Ninth St N. History-based wall murals dot the downtown area.

There's an international sailing regatta in late July, held in and around the 14,000 islands in the lake. An annual folk festival takes place in early July.

Many Ojibway Indians live in the area and it is they who hand-pick the Canadian wild rice (manomin) which grows locally. It's easily available here or sold in health food stores across the country and is delicious.

Many Native Indian pictographs have been found around the Kenora area. These paintings, done on rock using berry juices, tree gums and sap, depict history and legends. Visitors are able to take part in a number of Ojibway events, including regional powwows.

There is camping just a few blocks from the centre of town, at Anicinabe Park on Sixth Ave S. It has showers, and there is a beach. Other provincial parks are nearby.

There are motel options along the highway. The *Whispering Pines* (☎ 807-548-4025), 10km east of town, has low-priced rooms, a beach and camping is available across the street.

Days Inn (☎ 807-468-2003, ☎ 1-800-465-1123, 920 Hwy 17 East) south of downtown has doubles at $75.

Places to eat can be found along Main St, and look for the chip wagons around town and by the waterfront.

Watch for the traditional *inukshuks* (stone figures) beside area highways.

Southern Route

Atikokan Once an iron-mining town, Atikokan is the supply centre for Quetico Park with two small museums, a number of motels and lodges and plenty of casual places to find a meal. The *Iron Mine* on Main St is a good restaurant and pub. Rockhounds may want to explore the interesting old mine sites of Steep Rock and Caland. Get a map at the tourist office, as the roads around the mines are rough and confusing.

Quetico Provincial Park This huge wilderness park (information ☎ 807-597-4602, reservations ☎ 807-597-2737), 100km long by 60km wide, is linked to the Boundary Waters Canoe Area in Minnesota. Quetico is undeveloped for the most part but has one major organised campground. It offers excellent canoeing (1500km of routes), primarily for those wanting peace and quiet. Portages tend to be short, averaging 400m. The use of motor boats is forbidden (except in a few areas by Native Indians) and you'll find no roads or logging within the park.

The park is a maze of lakes and rivers, with lots of wildlife and some Native Indian pictographs. Rocky shores and jack pines are typical of some parts, but there are large areas of bog in others and stands of red and white pine in others. The park can be accessed from several points, the principal one on the Canadian side being from the Dawson Trail campground, off Hwy 11, where there is an information pavilion. There are outfitters (for canoes and equipment) and maps available in and around the park. Quetico Discovery Tours (☎ 807-597-2621) offers a variety of packages into the park.

Fort Frances Situated on Rainy Lake opposite International Falls, Minnesota, this is a busy border-crossing point into the USA. Both sides are popular outdoor destinations, with countless lakes, cottages, fishing, camping etc. In town you can visit a paper mill, the town's main business. A causeway across **Rainy Lake** towards Atikokan offers great views of the lake.

The **Fort Frances Museum** (☎ 807-274-7891) examines Native Indian history and the fur trade, as well as more recent developments. The museum also operates **Fort St Pierre**, a replica fur-trading post and lookout tower at **Pither's Point Park**, on the eastern side of town. North Hwy 71 connects with Kenora and Winnipeg. East of town, Emo has the **Kay-Nah Chi-Wah-Nung Manitou Mounds**, the largest ancient burial mound site in Canada.

Grey Goose bus lines connects to Winnipeg or Thunder Bay.

Sioux Narrows About 80km south of Kenora, on the eastern side of Lake of the Woods, Sioux Narrows is a resort town. In addition to the regional residents, many US citizens and Winnipegers spend time here during summer. The town and its surroundings have a range of cottages, lodges, motels, campgrounds and houseboats for rent. Lake of the Woods fishing is renowned far and wide. Sioux Narrows Provincial Park (☎ 807-226-5223) has camping and contains some Native Indian pictographs.

Quebec

'Kebec', an Algonkian Indian word meaning 'where the river narrows', is the heart of French Canada. This is the country's largest province and with the vast majority of the population speaking French, visitors will soon realise that Quebec is unlike the rest of Canada and North America and that the differences go far beyond language. The unique culture is reflected in various aspects of life including architecture, music, food and religion.

Even Montreal (Montréal, pronounced 'mor-eh-al'), where English is still widely used, has a decidedly different air to other Canadian cities, while historic Quebec City is noticeably European. But much of the beauty and appeal of the province lies in distinct regions outside these two intriguing population centres. Scenic, unspoilt Charlevoix is a protected area of natural beauty. The Laurentian Mountains are a year-round resort. Estrie or the Eastern Townships south of Montreal, settled by Loyalists, is a gentle, quiet region of farms, lakes and inns. The Gaspé region in the east with its rugged shoreline scenery is one of the overlooked areas of the country. The northern forests with their huge parks offer some excellent and accessible wilderness. Much of the far north is only now being developed.

Quebec is generally at odds with the rest of English-speaking Canada, particularly in its politics. Most people are familiar with the movement advocating Quebec separation from the rest of Canada. This desire was first formally channelled into the elected Parti Québecois (PQ) in 1976, a separation-minded provincial party led by the late René Lévesque, a colourful, charismatic man. To the hardliners' dismay, enthusiasm waned in the 1980s and for some years separation was more or less a dead issue, deemed neither practical nor realistic.

As the 20th century ends, Quebec's leaving Canada in one form or another seems a possibility once again. This recent twist is

HIGHLIGHTS

Entered Confederation: 1 July 1867
Area: 1,540,687 sq km
Population: 7,333,283
Provincial Capital: Quebec City

- Visit Montreal with its unique, appealing mix of English and French culture

- Wander around historic Quebec City, the only walled city in North America

- Explore the Saguenay fjord and watch the whales off Tadoussac

- Experience the rugged, remote Mingan Archipelago

- Hike through the undeveloped parks of the rugged Gaspé Peninsula

- See Rocher Percé (Pierced Rock), one of Canada's most recognisable landmarks

- Ski and camp in the Laurentians

- Enjoy the mosaic of autumn colours in the Eastern Townships

- Be enticed by the Charlevoix blend of landscape and culture

QUEBEC

Quebec (South-East) p290
Gaspé Peninsula p377
Magdalen Islands/Îsles de la Madeleine p390
Tadoussac p364
Rivière-du-Loup p372
Island of Montreal p294
Downtown Montreal p297
Quebec City p329
Old Montreal p303
Old Quebec City p345
The Plateau & Area p319
Montreal Metro p326

in part due to Quebec's economic confidence which was in the doldrums for a number of years. But more so it is due to a sense that Quebec's differences and desires are neither understood nor appreciated by the rest of the country. Wrangling over constitutional matters and cultural differences regularly bring these issues and sentiments to critical debate across Canada.

For the past two federal elections, the Bloc Québecois party, which advocates separation, has dominated Quebec so completely that is has had enough seats to play a significant role in parliament.

It's former cause-inspiring leader, Lucien Bouchard, left the party and took over the PQ in 1996 determined to become leader of a new country. While he has had to divert attention to economic matters, Bouchard expends much of his energy on proceeding with the separation process.

Montrealers, both English and French, the vast majority of whom are federalists, have thrown an unsettling, unexpected notion at

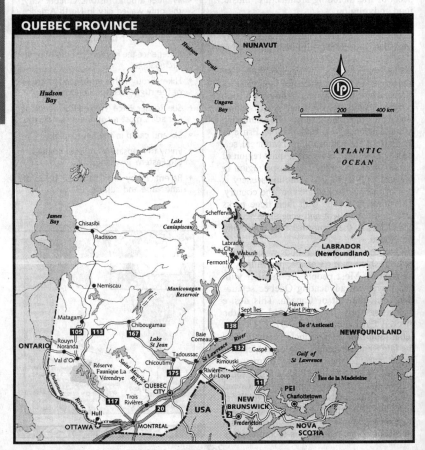

QUEBEC PROVINCE

JON DAVISON

Henry Moore sculpture, Museum of Arts, Toronto, Ontario

NICHOLAS REUSS

Inside Basilica Notre Dame, Montreal, Quebec

MARK LIGHTBODY

Percé Rock, Gaspé Peninsula, Quebec

The resort village of Mont Tremblant, Quebec

Bonsecours Market building, Montreal, Quebec

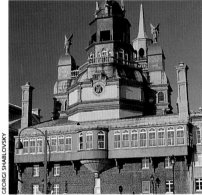

Notre Dame de Bonsecours, Montreal, Quebec

Views of Rue de la Commune, Old Montreal, Quebec

the PQ – that of partitioning themselves into their own political entity.

Regardless of the intensity of the debate, all this has no bearing on visitors or their ability to enjoy the province's separateness.

Economically, manufacturing is the prime industry. There are vast amounts of hydroelectric power and the province is the main paper producer in North America. Other important industries are aluminum, minerals, timber, tourism, dairy goods, apples and a local speciality, maple syrup.

Visitors should note that the farther east or north you travel the cooler the weather becomes. Even in midsummer an evening sweater may be required. Other than in the south-east, by September temperatures have dropped noticeably.

History

At the time of European exploration, the region along the St Lawrence River from Ontario to Quebec City was controlled by the Mohawks of the Iroquois Confederacy. North of and around Quebec City, the Montagnais were the principal aboriginal group. Farther north was and is Cree homeland and beyond that the Labrador Eskimo, Naskapi and Inuit peoples are dominant. The Montagnais and Naskapi are also known as Innu. Around the southern portion of the Gaspé Peninsula, the Micmacs, found around much of the Atlantic Provinces, were the principal aboriginal group. They still live in the region, although their numbers are small.

French explorer Jacques Cartier landed in Quebec City (then called Stadacona) and Montreal (then called Hochelaga) in 1534 (for information on the Native people see Population & People later in this chapter). Samuel de Champlain, also of France, first heard and recorded the word 'kebec' when he founded a settlement at Quebec City some 70 years later in 1608.

Through the rest of that century there were occasional disputes with the English, but by 1759 the English, with a final battle victory on the Plains of Abraham at Quebec, established themselves as the winners in the Canadian colony sweepstakes. From

this point on French political influence in the New World waned.

The coming of thousands of British Loyalists fleeing the American Revolution and its effects resulted in the formation of Upper (Ontario) and Lower (Quebec) Canada with almost all the French settlers in the latter region.

The inevitable struggles of power and status between the two language groups continued through the 1800s with Lower Canada joining the Canadian confederation as Quebec in 1867.

The early and middle portions of the 1900s saw Quebec change from a rural, agricultural society to an urban, industrialised one whose educational and cultural base, however, still relied upon the Catholic Church which wielded immense power and authority. About 90% of the population is Roman Catholic, though the Church's influence has declined sharply since the 1960s.

The 60s decade of questioning also brought the so-called Quiet Revolution during which all aspects of French society were scrutinised and overhauled.

During this period Quebec began to assert more independence nationally and internationally. At the same time, the Canadian government embarked on their ongoing quest to seek ways to ensure an harmonious, workable, long-term relationship between Quebec and the rest of the country. As part of this process, the national bilingualism policy was introduced. Just how difficult (impossible?) the task is has been painfully revealed over the last, sometimes bitter, three decades.

Today, the French dominate the province. Quebec is the only area of North America where people speaking French are in the majority.

Outside of Montreal, English residents are generally few, although parts of the Eastern Townships and the Gaspé and an area around the Ontario border near Hull still have English communities. Most immigrants arrive from French-speaking countries such as Haiti and Vietnam but line up with the Anglophone group politically.

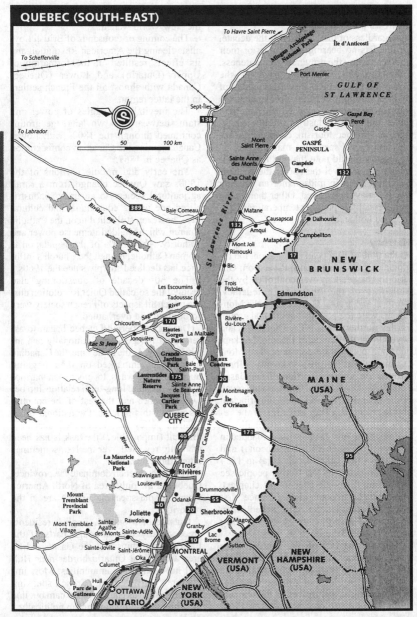

QUEBEC (SOUTH-EAST)

Information
Provincial Symbols Quebec's provincial flower is the white lily, and the provincial bird is the snowy owl.

Tourist Offices General provincial tourist information can be obtained from Tourisme Quebec by calling toll free ☎ 1-800-363-7777 from anywhere in Canada and the USA or checking www.tourisme.gouv.qc.ca. The mailing address is CP 979, Montreal, H3C 2W3.

There are few English signs or roadside markings in the province. Get hold of a good road map and watch for the conspicuous highway numbers and assorted symbols for attractions, ferries etc. The only hang-up is that the sometimes bizarrely obscure pictograms designed when bilingual signs were banned are often more use as passing-time riddles than travel aids.

For both accommodation assistance and reservations throughout the province, call Hospitalité Canada (☎ 1-800-665-1528). Accommodation in delightful small old hotels in the European mould abounds in Montreal and Quebec City and is relatively inexpensive.

Telephone For emergency service in Montreal and Laval dial ☎ 911. Elsewhere call the operator on ☎ 0.

Time Quebec is on Eastern Time except for the far north-eastern corner south of Labrador, which is on Atlantic Time.

Tax The provincial sales tax is 6.5%.

Activities
The Tourisme Quebec offices have general information booklets on parks, historic sites, outdoor activities and adventure tour operators.

Cycling This is good around Estrie and the Gaspé and more and more parks are developing mountain-bike trails. The province is working on creating the world's longest bike trail. The Green Trail, which will total 2400km, is partially complete. Mont Tremblant has mountain biking from novice to extreme. Vélo Quebec (☎ 514-521-8356) is a good information source.

Sea Kayaking Sea kayaking is increasingly popular along the north shore of the far eastern St Lawrence River area.

Skiing In winter, Quebec is one of North America's prime ski meccas with excellent slopes in the Laurentians north of Montreal and Quebec City and also south of Montreal close to the US border at Orford and Sutton. Tourisme Quebec has a *Ski Quebec* guide and a *Winter Getaway* booklet in which various hotel/ski packages are listed. There's excellent cross-country skiing at Parc de Gatineau and along the Petit Train du Nord trail in the Laurentians.

Whale Watching Whale observation trips are centred around Tadoussac and the Saguenay River.

Whitewater Rafting Whitewater rafting is popular along the Rivière Jacques Cartier near Quebec and the Rivière Rouge near Montreal.

Provincial Parks The mostly accessible parks preserve some of the best landscapes and features of southern Quebec. For information contact Les Parcs Quebec (☎ 1-800-561-1616) or pick up its booklet at tourist offices.

Wildlife Reserves Huge wildlife reserves (Réserves Fauniques) managed by the SEPAQ (☎ 1-800-665-6527) organisation offer the gamut of rugged outdoor pursuits. Pick up its information booklet at tourist offices. Reserves offer camping, canoeing, fishing, hiking and some mountain biking.

Montreal

Some cities take a bit of getting used to – you need time to know and appreciate them

Quebec and Separation: the Division Decision

One of Quebec's separatist leaders has said that until the independence issue is resolved relations between Quebec and the rest of the country will be like a never-ending trip to the dentist. Most Canadians agree with that assessment. Hey, there's something in common!

In Quebec, the idea of leaving Canada first became an organised political cause in the 1960s. Late in that decade, a small group of French-Canadian radicals used terrorism and bombings to impress their cause into the national consciousness. Since then, the movement has been peaceful. In the 1970s, the provincial elections were won for the first time by the Parti Québecois (PQ), whose stated policy is securing independence for Quebec.

But things in this province are never quite what they seem. Even with the separatist party in power, on the 1980 independence referendum 60% voted in favour of staying within Canada. In 1995 a second referendum under a revamped PQ party was held. Once again provincial voters opted to stay within Canada but the margin of victory was less than 1%. Immediately, there was talk of more referendums until the Yes side won; the matter became known as the 'neverendum'. Since then, though, polls reflect a softening of separatist leanings and so the third vote is indefinitely on hold.

To appease separatist leaning Québecois, the federal government has over the years transferred more and more of its powers to the provinces. Quebec has control over education, immigration and language. They have also been the beneficiary of a host of programs, grants, transfer payments and more, to the ire of much of the rest of the country. Yet, to the frustration of the rest of Canada, the province remains unsatisfied. English-speaking Canada often wonders what it is Québecois really want but there is no single answer and emotions, not logic, play a major role.

Anyone spending any time in Quebec quickly grasps that these people are not like other Canadians. The lifestyle, the mores, the beliefs and the attitudes, not to mention language, do indeed define a distinct society. English-speaking Canada sees it, visitors see it, and yet, without a border to reflect it, many French Québecois cannot. So they push to go it alone with a new country.

Other French Québecois do see their unique qualities. They want these preserved and feel threatened in a sea of Anglo-Canadian-American culture. They elect a party with an extreme view as extra protection, but don't want separation – just the power of the threat.

For others, the tussle between the heart (independence) and the head (stability) can never be resolved. While appreciating and respecting Canada, they conflictingly long both to stay and to leave, and their referendum opinions oscillate from one side to the other.

Canada maintains that if Quebec separates it will be with the province's portion of the national debt – billions of dollars. That promise and warnings of economic hardships brought on by large-scale unemployment, migration out of Quebec, and loss of federal services and tax money are met with both a shrug and a sigh.

Although it is unlikely blood will ever be spilt, it will certainly not be an entirely smooth transformation if separation does become a reality. For one thing, the Native peoples of Quebec, whose land claims take up about half of the province, have categorically voted against separation.

– but not Montreal. This city has an atmosphere all its own. It's a friendly, romantic place where couples kiss on the street and strangers talk to each other – an interesting and lively blend of things English and French, flavoured by the Canadian setting. There are about three million people in Greater Montreal – it's the second largest city in Canada after Toronto – and about 10% of all Canadians and 40% of Quebec's

population lives here. Two-thirds of the population are French, making it the largest French-speaking city outside Paris, but the downtown core is surprisingly English.

Since its founding, Montreal has been a major port and a hub for finance, business and transportation. It is also an arts centre, particularly for French culture. The four universities, two in each language, and numerous affiliates and colleges make it a major academic nucleus as well. It is becoming increasingly important in high-tech industry and research.

To the visitor, it is the mix of old with new and the *joie de vivre* that is most alluring. French culture prevails, giving the atmosphere a European tinge. The nightlife is great and there are 4000 restaurants in town.

The interaction of the English and the French gives Montreal some of its charm but is also responsible for some continuing conflict. The French may have long dominated the social spheres but traditionally it was the English who ran businesses, made decisions, held positions of power and accumulated wealth. As Québecois awareness grew, this changed, and the French are now well represented in all realms of life. In fact, some recent laws are reactionary in their discrimination against languages other than French. The English, and newer immigrants, are now voicing the need for balance and equality.

Regardless of these difficulties, Montreal exudes a warm, relaxed yet exciting ambience. It is as if the city itself has a pride and confidence in its own worth. Speak French if you can. If you can't, as long as you are not arrogantly defiant, you'll find most people helpful and likely to respond in English.

The city has a reputation for fashion savoir-faire, but this is not limited to the moneyed – a certain flair seems to come naturally to everyone.

Although the other seasons are temperate, a quick word about winter is in order. It can be cold, particularly in January, when the temperatures sometimes go as low as -40°C. There can be piles of snow too, although these don't disrupt things for long, and the Métro enables you to travel the city without taking one crisp breath of the outdoor air. The people are usually more gregarious when big storms hit, and afterwards, sunny skies make it all bearable.

History

Montreal's is a prominent and colourful chapter in the history of Canada. In many ways, the past is responsible for the politics here today. Before the French hit the scene, the Algonkian, Huron and Iroquois shared the area, not always peacefully. Jacques Cartier first visited in 1535 and found Hochelaga, an Iroquois village at the foot of the mountain. The first permanent European settlement didn't begin until 1642, when Sieur de Maisonneuve set up a religious mission named Ville Marie. The mountain had been named Mont Royal, which led to the city's present name. It soon became a fur-trading centre. The Native Indians weren't too thrilled with all this and attacks were a regular occurrence until just after 1700, when a treaty was signed. The fur trade boomed and Montreal became an exploration base. Today, Old Montreal preserves much of the city's 17th century past.

The British had been battling the French for some time and took Quebec City in 1759. The French moved their capital upstream to Montreal but that didn't last long. The British captured it in 1760 and settlers followed.

Soon the rebelling American colonies were after the city. In 1775 General Montgomery took Montreal without firing a shot. It was in the hands of the revolutionary forces only until the British beat back another group trying to take Quebec City, at which time the revolutionaries fled Montreal. In the mid-1800s Montreal was the capital of the United Provinces of Canada. The late 1800s saw a big boom and the shipping and rail lines brought prosperity. By 1900, Montreal was the commercial and cultural centre of Canada. In the early part of the 20th century there came a huge influx of Jewish Europeans – even today Montreal has the largest Jewish population in Canada.

QUEBEC

QUEBEC

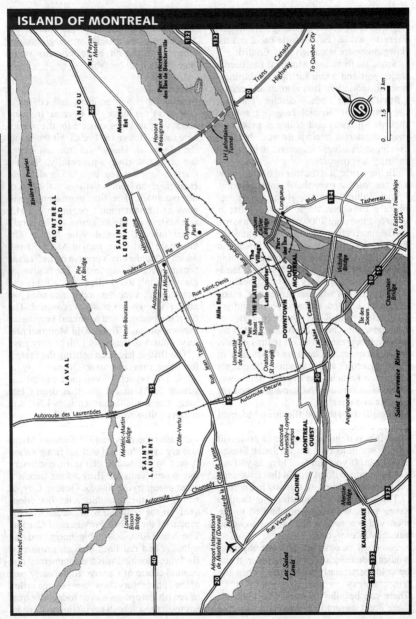

ISLAND OF MONTREAL

After both wars, immigrants of many nationalities arrived.

From the 1920s to the 1940s, Montreal gained a reputation as Sin City. This was due partially to Prohibition in the USA. Brothels, gambling houses and gangsters thrived and the nightlife was known far and wide; politicians and law-enforcers are said to have turned a blind eye. All this changed with the arrival of Jean Drapeau, who was elected mayor in 1954 and, except for a five-year period in the early 60s, was mayor right into the mid-80s. He cleaned up the city, encouraged redevelopment, and staged the World's Fair in 1967 and the Olympics in 1976. Still, he was touched by scandal and many dubbed him 'Emperor', claiming he was megalomaniacal. But Drapeau was popular and he certainly helped develop Montreal's international reputation.

For years, decades even, Montreal had been a stable city with little change in the downtown area. Since the late 1980s, however, that equanimity has dissolved as both redevelopment and modernisation strike markedly at points all over the downtown area. The changing and stylish look, a blend of European and North American forms, has sparked plenty of debate and continues to effect future projects and streetscapes.

Orientation

The city sits on an island roughly 40km long and 15km wide where the Ottawa River flows into the St Lawrence River. There are bridges connecting all sides with the mainland; this reinforces the impression of really not being on an island at all. Despite the size of the city and the size of the island, it's both easy to orient yourself and to get around Montreal.

In the middle of the island is Mont Royal, a 233m-high extinct volcano. The core of the city, which is actually quite small, is below this, in the south central section of the island. The city is full of fine architecture spanning eras and styles from the early 1800s to the present.

The downtown area is bounded by Rue Sherbrooke to the north, Avenue Atwater to the west, Rue Saint Antoine to the south and Boulevard Saint Laurent to the east. This is the busy area of skyscrapers, shops, restaurants, offices and luxury hotels.

The small park, Square Dorchester (formerly Dominion Square, and often still called that), marks the centre of downtown. The tourist office is on the north side along with the horse-drawn carriages, known as *calèches*, which can be taken around parts of town or up the mountain. On the southwest corner is the Windsor Station/Molson Centre complex, the hockey (and concert) arena built around the venerable old Canadian Pacific railway terminal.

The Cathedral of Montreal (Marie-Reine-du-Monde Cathédrale, or Mary Queen of the World Cathedral) with its pastel, gilt-trimmed interior is on the corner of Boulevard René Lévesque and Rue de la Cathédrale to the east of the square. Just to the east of the cathedral is the Queen Elizabeth Hotel below which is the VIA Rail Central Station.

Parallel to Rue Sainte Catherine, wide Boulevard René Lévesque is known for its tall towers. Place Ville Marie (sometimes referred to as the PVM) on the corner of Rue University across from the Queen Elizabeth Hotel, in the shape of a cross, is one of the city's best known buildings.

North, a block up Rue Peel from the square, is Rue Sainte Catherine, the principal east-west artery. North of Rue Sainte Catherine is Boulevard de Maisonneuve and then Rue Sherbrooke, the two other main east-west streets.

Sainte Catherine is one-way eastbound. It's the main shopping street with several department stores. At 705 Rue Sainte Catherine Ouest, by the corner of Rue University, is one of the city's largest shopping complexes, the modern showpiece Eaton Centre – almost an attraction in its own right. The Promenade de la Cathédrale is an underground portion of the complex which runs beneath a church. After a few tough years, Sainte Catherine is luring back major retailers and the vacancies and pinball arcades are decreasing. The numerous strip bars are a fixture – this is Montreal, after all.

QUEBEC

Avenue McGill College, running north off Rue Sainte Catherine, once a narrow student ghetto, presents an imposing boulevard edged with some of the city's newest corporate and retail architecture. Structures aside, the channel of space leading from the city's main street to the campus of McGill University and beyond to the mountain and its landmark cross is certainly impressive. A substantial number of statues and sculptures, including the eye-catching *Illuminated Crowd*, are found along the avenue.

Running north and south off Rue Sainte Catherine west of Rue Peel are Rue de la Montagne, Rue Crescent and Rue Bishop – a restaurant/nightlife district.

Walking uphill on Rue Peel for a number of blocks you'll come to Avenue des Pins, across which is the edge of Parc du Mont Royal. At the top of the staircase, the lookout provides excellent views of the city, the river and the surroundings to the south – great views day or night.

Other good vantage points for views over the city are the Olympic Stadium Tower (charging an admission fee), and the restaurant on top of the Radisson Hotel, 777 Rue University. There are also pretty good views from St Joseph's Oratory and from various points along the road around Mont Royal.

The area downtown and west to Loyola Campus on Rue Sherbrooke is pretty much English and residential. Westmount at the foot of the mountain is one of the city's wealthiest and most prestigious districts.

East of Rue Peel along Rue Sainte Catherine you'll see Square Phillips, a meeting place where guitarists busk and bask. Farther east, just past de Bleury, is Place des Arts, a complex for the performing arts. A few more blocks east is Boulevard Saint Laurent (St Lawrence Blvd) known as The Main. This is one of the city's best known streets, with an interesting history and ethnic mix, and lots of restaurants.

To the east of Boulevard Saint Laurent, Rue Sainte Catherine Ouest becomes Rue Sainte Catherine Est. East of Saint Laurent, streets are given the Est (East) designation, west of Saint Laurent they include the Ouest (West) designation in their name. All streets are divided in this way. East of Boulevard Saint Laurent the area has traditionally been predominantly French and it remains this way.

About seven blocks east (you can get a bus) is Saint Denis, the centre of a Paris-style café district sometimes called the Latin Quarter.

From Saint Denis east along Rue Sainte Catherine to Rue Papineau is Montreal's gay town known as The Village.

Two blocks east of Saint Denis is Rue Berri. Terminus Voyageur, the city's main bus station with US and Canadian destinations, is a block north on Rue Berri at Boulevard de Maisonneuve. A major transfer point of the Métro system, the Berri-UQAM station is also here and city buses roll in all directions from this subway stop.

Old Montreal is south-east of the downtown area; both Boulevard Saint Laurent and Rue Saint Denis lead into it.

There is a small but determined Chinatown clustered along Rue de la Gauchetière between Rue Saint Urbain and Boulevard Saint Laurent. Rue de la Gauchetière runs east-west past the train stations.

The streets of east-end Montreal and parts of the northern section are lined with distinctive two or three-storey apartment buildings with outside staircases. Such housing, peculiar to Montreal, was built in the 1920s and 30s. The stairs were put outside to save space inside.

Such an area is the engaging Plateau Mont Royal. Known simply as the Plateau, it attracts the young and/or hip.

Farther north along Boulevard Saint Laurent, between Avenue Laurier and Rue Bernard, the Mile End district contrasts tradition with chic.

Anywhere from lower Rue Saint Denis, north through the Plateau and up this far is great for merely wandering and seeing Montrealers busy at life. Saturday is the most lively day.

Street Names Montreal is a bilingual rather than a French-speaking city. The bulk

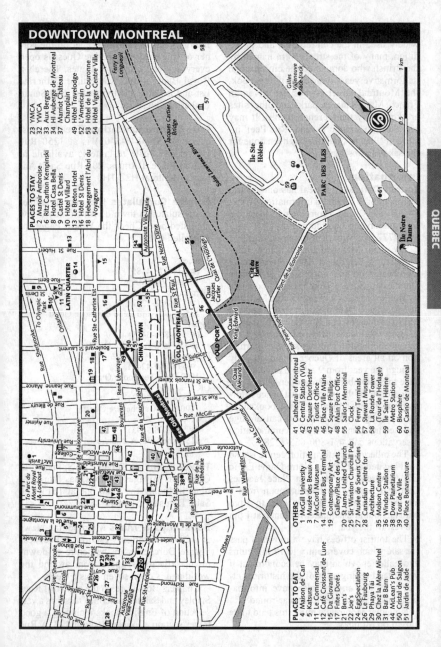

DOWNTOWN MONTREAL

QUEBEC

PLACES TO STAY
2 Manoir Ambroise
5 Ritz Carlton Kempinski
8 Hotel Casa Bella
10 Castel St Denis
13 Hôtel Villard
16 Le Breton Hotel
18 Hôtel St Denis
18 Hebergement l'Abri du Voyageur
23 YMCA
32 YWCA
33 Aux Berges
34 HI Auberge de Montreal
37 Marriot Chateau Champlain
49 Hotel Travelodge
52 L'Americain
53 Hôtel de la Couronne
54 Hôtel Viger Centre Ville

PLACES TO EAT
4 Maison de Cari
5 Katsura
11 Le Commensal
12 Café Croissant de Lune
15 Da Giovanni
17 Frites Dorés
21 Ben's
22 Joe's
23 Egg Spectation
26 Le Faubourg
29 Phaya Tai
30 Chez la Mère Michel
31 Bar B Barn
44 McLean's Pub
50 Cristal de Saigon
51 Jardin de Jade

OTHERS
1 McGill University
3 Musée des Beaux Arts
7 McCord Museum
14 Terminus Bus Terminal
19 Contemporary Art Gallery/Place des Arts
20 St James United Church
25 Sir Winston Churchill Pub
27 Musée de Soeurs Grises
28 Canadian Centre for Architecture
35 Molson Centre
36 Windsor Station
38 Dow Planetarium
39 Tour de Ville
40 Place Bonaventure
41 Cathedral of Montreal
42 Central Station (VIA)
43 Square Dorchester
45 Tourist Office
46 Place Ville Marie
47 Square Phillips
48 Main Post Office
55 Sailor's Memorial Clock
56 Ferry Terminals
57 Stewart Museum
58 La Ronde Tower (Tour de l'Horloge)
59 Île Saint Hélène
60 Metro Station
61 Casino de Montreal

of visitors are English-speaking, English is widely used in the central area, and in addition, many of the streets were named by the British who dominated the city through its formative years. However, in this book, the Montreal street names are given in French. Many squares, parks and other sites are known by their French names. It may seem a little strange to read 'Rue Peel' instead of 'Peel St', but this has been done for the sake of consistency.

Information

Tourist Offices Montreal has one central phone number for all its information offices (☎ 514-873-2015). From outside Montreal information can be obtained on (☎ 1-800-363-7777, www.tourism-montreal.org).

The main Montreal tourist office, Infotouriste, is central at 1001 Rue Square Dorchester on the north side of Square Dorchester. Square Dorchester is bounded by Boulevard René Lévesque, Rue Metcalfe and Rue Peel. Both the train station and the Métro are nearby and Rue Sainte Catherine is just a short walk away. Infotouriste is efficient and helpful and can supply information on all areas of Quebec. It's open daily through the year from 9 am to 6 pm but from June to September remains open until 7 pm. Aside from all the usual tourist office information, this centre also has a bookstore, moneychanger, souvenirs and can arrange sightseeing tours. For free accommodation reservations call ☎ 1-800-665-1528.

The other main information centre is also well located at 174 Rue Notre Dame Est in Old Montreal, not far from Place Jacques Cartier. It's busy but helpful, open from 9 am to 7 pm daily in season, 9 am to 5 pm with an hour and a quarter for lunch at 1 pm the rest of the year.

The tourist offices have a museum pass for sale which covers entry to 17 museums and galleries which may be economical if you intend seeing a lot of the historical attractions. The airports also have information kiosks which are open year-round.

Note that Montreal's museums tend to be closed on Monday.

Money For exchanging money, Currencies International at 1230 Rue Peel on the corner of Rue Sainte Catherine Ouest is open every day and offers good rates. There's a Royal Bank at 360 Rue Sainte Catherine Est and a Bank of Montreal at 670 Sainte Catherine Ouest.

Post & Communications The main post office (☎ 514-846-5401) is at 1250 Rue University. Poste restante is available at Station Place d'Armes, 201 Rue Saint Antoine, Montreal H2Z 1H0.

Foreign Consulates There are a number of consulates in town of which only a few are listed here. Check the Yellow Pages for a detailed list.

France
   (☎ 514-878-4385)
   1 Place Ville Marie
Germany
   (☎ 514-931-2277)
   1250 Boulevard Réné Lévesque Ouest
Japan
   (☎ 514-866-3429)
   600 de la Gauchetière Ouest
Netherlands
   (☎ 514-849-4247)
   1002 Rue Sherbrooke Ouest
UK
   (☎ 514-866-5863)
   1000 de la Gauchetière Ouest
USA
   (☎ 514-398-9695)
   1155 Rue Saint Alexandre

Travel Agencies Travel CUTS, known in Quebec as Voyages Campus, has five locations including the main one at 1613 Rue Saint Denis (☎ 514-843-8511).

Bookshops & Maps Metropolitan News at 1109 Rue Cypress, west off Rue Peel near Square Dorchester in the centre of downtown, sells newspapers from around the world and is open seven days a week.

Chapters Bookstore on the corner of Rues Stanley and Sainte Catherine Ouest has a vast selection of English books including a good travel section. Double Hook at 1235A Rue

Greene is a good English bookshop featuring Canadian writers. For French books check Librairie Champigny, 4380 Rue Saint Denis.

An excellent place for maps, English and French, as well as some travel books, is Aux Quartre Points Cardinaux, 551 Rue Ontario Est, north of the bus station.

Medical Services Although there is no real discrimination, the best hospital option for English patients is the Royal Victoria (☎ 514-842-1231) at 687 Rue des Pins Ouest (Pine West). For French patients, go to Hospital Notre Dame (☎ 514-281-6000), 1560 Rue Sherbrooke Est.

Warning Pedestrians, beware in Montreal! Might is right and drivers take full advantage of this. The careless may not get a second chance.

Downtown/Central
Musée des Beaux Arts (Fine Arts Museum) Beaux Arts (pronounced 'bose-ar') as it is known, is the city's main art gallery (☎ 514-285-1600), with both modern and pre-Columbian works. Europe, Africa, the Middle East and other areas are covered. There's also a display of Inuit art. The architectural style of the newer gallery annex across the street is also worth a look. The address is 1379-80 Rue Sherbrooke Ouest on the corner of Rue Crescent. It's open from 11 am to 6 pm and to 9 pm Wednesday if there is a special show on. Like many of Montreal's museums, this one is closed on Monday. Admission to the general permanent exhibits is free but there is often some sort of special show on too. Admission to these is around $10, students and seniors $5.

Contemporary Art Gallery Located in the centre of town by the Place des Arts Complex at 185 Rue Sainte Catherine Ouest, the gallery (☎ 514-847-6226) displays art from 1939 to the present with its substantial permanent collection and temporary shows.

It's the only public gallery in the country which specialises exclusively in contemporary art, and displays both Canadian and international work. On Tuesday and from Thursday to Sunday, the gallery is open from 11 am to 6 pm. On Wednesday it's open until 9 pm and is free from 6 pm onwards. It is closed on Monday. Admission is $6; students and seniors pay less. There is a simple restaurant within the gallery.

Canadian Centre for Architecture The centre (☎ 514-939-7026) is both a museum and working organisation promoting the understanding of architecture, its history and future.

The numerous exhibition rooms feature changing shows of local and international architecture, urban planning and landscape design. It may sound dry but most people will find at least some of the displays (incorporating models, drawings or photographs) of interest.

A portion of the centre has been created in and around Shaughnessay House, built as a home for a wealthy businessman in 1874 of the characteristic grey limestone seen so often around the city. Its 1st floor is interesting for the details and architectural features. A highlight is the solarium and the wonderfully ornate adjacent room with intricate woodwork and fireplace.

There is a busy bookstore here with books on famous architects and topics ranging from international styles to photography.

Don't miss the sculpture garden and lookout on the other side of Boulevard René Lévesque. About 15 sculptures of varying styles and sizes are scattered about a terrace overlooking parts of south Montreal. The old banks, mills etc seen below provide intriguing evidence of the centre's conviction that the study of architecture is the study of history and civilisation.

The centre is open Tuesday to Sunday from 11 am to 6 pm, until 8 pm on Thursday and closed on Monday. Admission is $5, $3 for students and seniors. On Thursday it's free all day for students and for everybody else from 5.30 to 8 pm. The address is central at 1920 Rue Baile near the corner of Boulevard René Lévesque and Fort. The Métro stop is Atwater and there is parking available.

QUEBEC

McCord Museum of Canadian History
The McCord is the city's main history museum (☎ 514-398-7100) but it's not large; budget 60 to 90 minutes for a visit. Located at 690 Rue Sherbrooke Ouest, the two-level museum is well laid out, with exhibits dealing, for the most part, with eastern Canada's early European settlement. One room exhibits the history of Quebec's Native people. The other displays highlight the museum's collection which includes early Canadian costume and textiles and folk art. There are permanent and changing exhibits.

A highlight of the 700,000 photograph collection are those by William Notman, who, with his sons, photographed Canadian people, places and activities from 1850 to about 1930.

The 2nd-floor room entitled 'Turning Point: Quebec 1900' neatly encapsulates French Canadian history in Quebec. The gift shop has some quality items and interesting reading material.

Admission is $8 (less for students) but free Saturday from 10 am to noon. Hours are 10 am to 5 pm; the museum is closed Monday.

If you tire before seeing the entire photo collection (don't panic – they're not all on display), there's a tearoom; but don't plan to eat a full meal as food prices are high.

McGill University On the corner of Rue University and Rue Sherbrooke, this is one of Canada's most prestigious universities. The campus is rather nice to stroll around, since it sits at the foot of the mountain. The **Redpath Museum** (☎ 514-398-4086) houses McGill's natural history collection, which includes animals, birds, fossils and rocks. It's free and open every day, except Friday and Saturday. On Sunday, it's only open in the afternoon.

Parc du Mont Royal Known as the mountain, this is the city's best and biggest park. It was laid out by the designer of New York's Central Park. The **Chalet Lookout** has great views of the city; you can walk up to it from downtown (see the Orientation section earlier for details), or drive most of

the way through the park and walk the rest. East of the lookout is the huge steel cross, lit up at night and visible from all over the city. Within the park is **Beaver Lake** (Lac des Castors), a depression-era 'make-work' project. The park has lots of trees and is used in summer for walking, jogging, picnicking and Frisbee throwing. In winter there is skating, tobogganing and cross-country skiing. There are walking trails, some with views. Calèches can be hired for rides up to the lookout or around the park's trails.

If you're driving here, take Rue Guy from the downtown area to Chemin de la Côte des Neiges and then look for signs. To the left is another small park called **Parc Summit**. There is another good lookout here; this one has good views of the western residential districts.

St Joseph's Oratory The impressive modern-style basilica (☎ 514-733-8211), completed in 1960 and based on and around a 1916 church, honours St Joseph, patron of healers and patron saint of Canada, and Brother André, a monk said to have had the power to cure illness. Piles of crutches testify to the strength of this belief. Brother André's heart, which is on view here – a display ranking with the weirdest – was stolen some years ago but was returned intact. The site, with a small museum dedicated to Brother André, is open daily and is free. Sundays include organ concerts at 3.30 pm.

The oratory dome, visible from anywhere in the south-west of Montreal, is at 3800 Chemin Queen Mary, off the western slope of Mont Royal. From downtown, take the Métro to Cotes des Neiges and then walk. For those seeking a quiet night, it is also possible to stay here (see Places to Stay later in this Montreal section for details).

Montreal Holocaust Memorial Centre
The centre (☎ 514-345-2605) at 5151 Chemin Cote Sainte Catherine honours the Jews who perished in WWII and aims not to let their fate be forgotten. It's open Monday to Friday, 10 am to 4 pm and is free.

Cathedral of Montreal Also called Marie-Reine-du-Monde (Mary, Queen of the World), the cathedral is a smaller version of, and is modelled on, St Peter's Basilica in Rome. It was built between 1870 and 1894 and sits on Boulevard René Lévesque on the corner of Rue Mansfield, just off Dorchester Square near the Queen Elizabeth Hotel. Note the unusual canopy over the altar.

St James United Church This church, at 463 Rue Sainte Catherine Ouest, is unusual in that the portals open onto the street but have stores and offices built in beside them. The church is actually behind the street.

Musée de Soeurs Grises (Grey Nuns Museum) Mentioned more for the building itself, rather than the small museum (☎ 514-937-9501), this is a fine example of early Quebec stone architecture, particularly of the numerous convents seen across the province. It's centrally located at 1185 Rue Saint Mathieu.

Founded by Sainte Marguerite d'Youville, this is home to the Grey Nuns, an active and hardy group from the colonial era. It was they who set out by canoe for what was to become Manitoba and founded a mission in St Boniface. That nunnery of 1850 is now a museum in the middle of the largest French community in western Canada.

The museum, open Wednesday to Sunday from 1.30 to 4.30 pm, contains Marguerite's tomb and some religious artefacts etc from the end of the 17th century.

Museum of Decorative Arts This new facility (☎ 514-284-1252) at 2200 Rue Crescent, features decorative art displays and handicrafts from the 20th century. The substantial collection includes glass, metal, furniture, as well as industrial and graphic design. It's open Tuesday to Sunday from 11 am to 6 pm and Wednesday to 9 pm. Admission is $4.

Mt Stephen Club Dating from 1880 and funded entirely by the George Stephen House Foundation, this Renaissance-style mansion (☎ 514-849-7338) was built for the man who gave it his name, the first president of the Canadian Pacific Railway. The 15 rooms inside are rich with quality materials and skilful artistry. Long the home of the private Mount Stephen Club, it is open to the public for $3 Sunday, noon to 4 pm except from mid-July to September. It's at 1440 Rue Drummond.

Montreal Stock Exchange Free tours are offered at this major trading centre (☎ 514-871-2424) weekdays year-round. The exchange specialises in derivatives and is the Canadian centre for this speculative portion of the market. The exchange is on the 4th floor at 800 Place Victoria. Ring for tour details, times and reservations.

Montreal Planetarium The planetarium (☎ 514-872-4530) is at 1000 Rue Saint Jacques Ouest near Windsor Station. It offers 50-minute programs on the stars, space and solar system which are usually good and interesting. The heavens are projected onto a dome above reclining seats. Admission costs $6.

Underground City To alleviate congestion and to escape the harsh winter, Montreal created a huge underground city in the city centre. Though much of it is actually underground, the term really covers anything connected by underground passageways. Thus you can go to the train stations, find a hotel, see a movie, eat out, go dancing or shopping, all without taking a step outside. There's about 30km of walking possible across the network!

The notion is functional and innovative, but there's really not much to see. The shops are all modern and most of the system looks no different from a contemporary shopping mall, the differences being this is bigger and has the Métro going through it.

Major building complexes like Place Ville Marie, Place Bonaventure, Place du Canada and the Molson Centre are all connected and within easy walking distance. Others, like Place des Arts and Complèxe Desjardins,

are a Métro ride away. The Eaton Centre is also part of the network. The tourist office has a good map of the entire system; it may prove useful on rainy or snowy days.

Old Montreal (Vieux Montréal)

This is the oldest section of the city, dating mainly from the 1700s. The main streets are Rue Notre Dame and Rue Saint Paul. The area is bounded by Rue McGill on the west, Rue Berri on the east, Rue Saint Antoine on the north and the river on the south, with Boulevard Saint Laurent dividing the area east from west. The Métro stops in Old Montreal are Place d'Armes or Champs de Mars.

The narrow, cobblestone streets divide old stone houses and buildings, many of which now house intimate little restaurants and clubs. Throughout the area are squares and churches and the waterfront is never far away. Old Montreal is a must for romantics, though it's unfortunately a bit crowded in peak season. With all the activity and history, it's a perfect area for just wandering where your feet take you. Do yourself a favour and don't bring your car down here – it's too busy and you won't find a parking spot.

Near **Hôtel de Ville** (City Hall) and the Rue Notre Dame tourist office is the square **Place Jacques Cartier**, which could be called the area's focal point. In summer, it's filled with visitors, vendors, horse-drawn carriages and musicians. At the tourist office ask for the *Old Montreal Walking Tour* booklet (in English or French) which is free and has all sorts of interesting historical titbits, and points out noteworthy spots.

The square **Place Royale** is where Ville Marie, Maisonneuve's first small fort-town, was built, when fighting with the Iroquois Confederacy was both lengthy and fierce. During the 17th and 18th centuries this was a marketplace. It's beside the Old Custom House at 150 Rue Saint Paul Ouest. The old **Bonsecours Market** building at 350 Rue Saint Paul Est is now set up with retail booths and craft/art displays. Many buildings are marked with informative plaques. Some descriptions of the highlights follow. Note that many of the sites offer family

rates. One oddity to look out for are the peregrine falcons that have been nesting on high building ledges around Old Montreal since the mid-1980s.

Place d'Armes & Basilica Notre Dame The other major square in the area is Place d'Armes. A monument to Maisonneuve stands in the middle. On the square at 110 Rue Notre Dame Ouest, is Basilica Notre Dame, which you shouldn't miss. Built in 1829 and big enough to hold 5000 people, the church has a magnificently rich interior. The masses around Christmas, particularly Christmas Eve, are worth a special trip. There's a small museum at the back.

Église de Notre Dame de Bonsecours This church is on Rue Saint Paul. It's also known as the Sailors' Church and has several models of wooden ships hanging from the ceiling. From the tower in the church there's a good view. The vignettes in the small museum are also quite good. They tell the story of Marguerite Bougeoys, the first teacher in Montreal and founder of the Congregation of Notre Dame order of nuns.

Pierre du Calvet House Across from the church at 405 Rue Bonsecours, Calvet House (☎ 514-282-1725), which dates from 1725, has been restored and is now a hotel and restaurant featuring the furnishings of that time.

Château de Ramezay At 280 Rue Notre Dame Est, across from the Hôtel de Ville, is the Château de Ramezay (☎ 514-861-3708) which was the home of the city's French governors for about 40 years in the early 1700s. The building has housed a great variety of things since, but is now a museum with a collection of artefacts, tools and miscellanea from Quebec's early history. The house is open daily in summer, closed Monday the rest of the year. Admission is $5, students $3.

Montreal History Centre Also in Old Montreal there's the Montreal History Centre (☎ 514-872-3207) in the old fire hall on

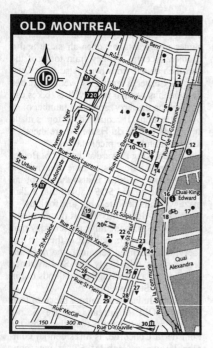

OLD MONTREAL

PLACES TO EAT
7 L'Usine de Spaghetti Parisienne
10 Chez Better
11 Le Père St Vincent
13 La Sauvagine
23 Café St Paul
26 Titanic
27 Gibby's

OTHER
1 Sir George Etienne National Historic Site
2 Église de Notre Dame de Bonsecours; Marguerite Bourgeoys Museum
3 Champ de Mars Métro Station
4 Hôtel de Ville
5 Château Ramezay
6 Bonsecours Market
8 Place Jacques Cartier
9 Infotouriste
12 Tourist Information
14 Les Deux Pierrots
15 Place d'Armes Metro Station
16 Tourist Information
17 IMAX Cinema
18 Vélo Aventure (bicycle rental)
19 Place d'Armes
20 Basilica Notre Dame
21 Centaur Theatre
22 Place Royale
24 Pointe à Callière
25 Place d'Youville
28 Montreal History Centre
29 Alternative Backpackers
30 Musée Marc Aurèle Fortin

QUEBEC

Place d'Youville. Audiovisuals and displays depict some of the city's history. It's open daily from 10 am to 5 pm May to September (closed Monday the rest of the year) and costs $4.50, less for students and seniors.

Musée Marc Aurèle Fortin Not too far away there's the Musée Marc Aurèle Fortin (☎ 514-845-6108) at 118 Rue Saint Pierre, which is less of a museum than a gallery dedicated to this Quebec landscape painter who lived from 1888 to 1970. He is especially known for his depictions of trees. Other painters are also represented in the changing exhibitions. This is closed on Monday throughout the year. Admission costs $4, students less.

Sir George-Étienne Cartier National Historic Site The site (☎ 514-283-2233) consists of two historic houses owned by the Cartier family. One details the life of the prominent 19th century lawyer and politician and the changes in society in his lifetime, and the other offers a glimpse of a middle-class home during the Victorian era. It's at 458 Rue Notre Dame Est. Admission is $3.50 and the site is open every day in summer, and from Wednesday to Sunday for the rest of the year. Short plays by costumed staff run periodically through the day.

Pointe-à-Callière (Museum of Archaeology & History) Built on the very spot where Sieur de Maisonneuve and Jeanne Mance founded the first European settlement, on the south side of Place Royale, this museum (☎ 514-872-9150) is an interesting

archaeological and historical study of the beginnings of the city of Montreal.

For the most part, the museum is underground, in the actual ruins of buildings and an ancient sewage/river system. The first European cemetery is here, established just a few years after the settlement itself. Grave sites can be seen presented like a working dig.

Artefacts are cleverly laid out on levels of shelving according to their time period just as they would be unearthed, the oldest items from Montreal's prehistory on the bottom. There are also a few interactive exhibits, the best of which is a video monitor which allows visitors to have a 'conversation' with some of the original inhabitants via a ghost-like image.

The lookout at the top of the tower in the new building provides an excellent view of the Old Port. The tower can be visited without paying the museum entry fee.

The museum is at 350 Place Royale; use the Place d'Armes Métro stop. It is open from Tuesday to Friday 10 am to 5 pm, Saturday and Sunday 11 am to 5 pm. Admission is $8 for adults, free for kids under 5.

Old Port (Vieux-Port) The Old Port waterfront is a district of riverside redevelopment east of Place Jacques Cartier which is still evolving and changing as construction and ideas continue. It covers 2.5km of riverfront and is based around four quays *(quais)* or piers. The Promenade du Vieux Port is a recreational path along the river from Rue Berri west to Rue McGill. An information booth (☎ 514-496-PORT) can be found at the entrance to Quai King Edward, pretty much in the centre of things. A number of the permanent features are listed here but each year, particularly through summer, the port features a range of different temporary exhibits, shows and events. Check prices of the main attractions as they are not cheap and may be prohibitive. Cruise boats, ferries, jet boats and speedboats all depart for tours of the river from the various docks.

At the far northern edge of the historic port on Victoria Pier is **Sailors' Memorial Clock Tower** (Tour de l'Horlage), now used as an

observation tower open to the public and with a history exhibit. Quai Jacques Cartier includes restaurants, an open-air stage and a handicraft centre. Trolley train tours of the port area depart from here. Also from Quai Jacques Cartier, a ferry goes over to **Parc des Îles** which is popular with cyclists (bikes can be taken on the ferry) and has a number of its own attractions. If requested, a stop is made at **Parc de la Cité du Havre**, where there's a restaurant and some picnic tables.

On Quai King Edward at the foot of Boulevard Saint Laurent is a large flea market *(marché aux puces)*. It is also the site of the IMAX Cinema and **SOS Labyrinthe**, a 2km maze which is definitely not just for kids.

At Quai Alexandra, a short distance east of Rue McGill, is the huge present-day port and container terminal. Also there is the Iberville Passenger Terminal, the dock for cruise ships which ply the St Lawrence River as far as the Magdalen Islands out in the Gulf of St Lawrence.

At Cité du Havre, a jutting piece of land between Old Montreal and Île Sainte Hélène connected with the island by the Pont de la Concorde, is a residential complex known as **Habitat 67**. It was constructed for the World's Fair as an example of a futuristic, more livable apartment block. It has aged well, is still appealing with its block modular look, and remains a popular, if not cheap, place to live.

Parc des Îles (The Islands Park)

South of the city in the St Lawrence River largely in the area between the Jacques Cartier and the Victoria bridges are Sainte Hélène and Notre Dame islands (☎ 514-872-4537). They were the site of the immensely successful 1967 World's Fair, Man & His World. For the event Île Sainte Hélène was considerably enlarged and Île Notre Dame was completely created with landfill. They are now primarily parkland though some vestiges remain of the fair and there are a number of other attractions of note.

There are several ways to get to the islands. If you're driving, one bridge, the Pont Jacques Cartier, leads to Île Sainte Hélène

and another, the Pont de la Concorde, to Île Notre Dame. Definitely consider taking the Métro to the Île Sainte Hélène stop instead as they hit you pretty hard for parking. From the Métro stop, where there is an information desk, there are buses (use a transfer) to both islands' attractions but you may find walking just as fast. Another possibility is to take the Water Shuttle (☎ 514-281-8000) across the river from the Old Port at Quai Jacques Cartier. The shuttle takes pedestrians and bikes for $3 one way. Or you could actually ride all the way from Old Montreal on the bike path for free.

Île Sainte Hélène At the extreme northern end of Île Sainte Hélène is **La Ronde**, the largest amusement park in the province with restaurants and bars as well as an assortment of games and rides. They include some impressive roller coasters – hold on to your stomach. The gentle mini-rail offers good views of the river and city. A variety of concerts and shows are held through summer, often including circus performances and excellent firework displays. A schedule is available.

Full admission to La Ronde including all the rides is $28. There is also a ticket to the grounds and shows at half the price which offers limited rides (not the scary ones).

During the last two weeks of May, La Ronde is open weekends only, from 11 am to 11 pm. Through the summer it's open daily from 11 am to midnight.

There are also some portions of an old fort near La Ronde. Inside the remaining stone ramparts is the **Stewart Museum** (☎ 514-861-6701) with artefacts and tools from Canada's past. Demonstrations are given by uniformed soldiers and others in period dress, and military parades are held daily in summer by the museum. Admission is $5 with free parking.

Walkways wind around the island, past gardens and among the old pavilions from the world's fair. One of them, the American Buckminster Fuller dome, is now the **Biosphere** (☎ 514-283-5000). This is an interpretation centre explaining the Great Lakes-St Lawrence River ecosystem. It is

designed to increase awareness about water and the need for its conservation. Using a range of exhibits and displays, topics include the world's water and pollution. It's open from 10 am to 5 pm (closed Monday) and admission is $6.50 with family rates.

Île Notre Dame This island which is largely parkland, has some attractions of its own. First among them is the **Casino de Montréal** (☎ 514-392-2746) which opened in 1993 and was so popular (and earning so much money) so quickly that expansion occurred almost instantly. It is open 24 hours daily and is busy pretty well continually. Weekend nights in particular can be hectic. There is a European-style section and a glitzier US-style area. Entry is free and non-alcoholic drinks are available at no charge. Liquor is served at bar prices. There is also an upmarket restaurant and a couple of bars. Dress during the day is casual but no jeans, sweat pants, shorts etc. After dinner, it's more formal with most people looking pretty smart but you needn't rent a gown or tux. Driving is not a great idea as the free parking fills up quickly. Instead, take the Métro to Île Sainte Hélène and from there catch the bus, free with a transfer, or walk. In summer there is a free shuttle bus from the Infotouriste office.

Also popular is the artificial **Plage des Îles** sandy beach (☎ 514-872-6093) with room for 5000 people. The water is filtered and treated with chemicals. There are picnic facilities and snack bars at the site. It's open every day from 24 June to Labour Day (the first Monday in September) from 10 am to 7 pm depending on the weather. The beach is closed on 'bad days', but be sure to call to check if it's open – their idea of a bad day may not be the same as yours. A ticket is $7.50, less for children. To get there take the Métro to Île Sainte Hélène and from there a bus runs to the beach.

Also on Île Notre Dame is the **Nautical Pavilion** (☎ 514-392-9761) based around the former Olympic rowing basin. In summer you can rent windsurfers and paddle boats but perhaps it's more fun in winter when the area becomes a huge skating rink. There are lockers

QUEBEC

and a snack bar and you can rent skates – a lot of fun. There is also some cross-country (nordic) skiing; equipment can also be rented. The centre is open until 9 pm daily.

Much of the surrounding grounds are parkland which you can stroll around for free. At the **Gilles Villeneuve race track** (named after a Quebec racing-car driver) the annual Formula 1 Grand Prix race is held.

Olympic Park & District

Ask any Montrealer and you'll find that the scandal, indignation and tales of corruption and government incompetence surrounding the buildings of the Olympic Sports Complex are as great as the structures themselves. Nevertheless, the complex (☎ 514-252-8687), created at enormous cost for the 1976 Olympic Games, is magnificent.

The showpiece is the multipurpose **Olympic Stadium** able to hold 80,000 spectators and often referred to as the 'Big O' or, more recently, 'The Big Owe'. A laughable litany of ongoing repairs has been required. It certainly is a grand structure, even if it did take until 1990 to get it finished.

In summer, it hosts major league professional baseball and it is also used for concerts and trade shows. All other visitors must take the tour.

A cable car runs up the arching **Montreal Tower** which overhangs the stadium to a glassed-in observation deck which provides outstanding views of the city and beyond for a distance of 80km. A ticket to the top is $9. Combination tickets which include a tour are available.

The **Sports Centre**, essentially a swimming complex, is also impressive with six pools including a 20m-deep scuba pool. Public swimming costs $3.50 at this huge facility.

The **Tourist Hall** at the cable car boarding station is a three-storey information centre with ticket office, restaurant and souvenir shop. Guided tours of the stadium in French and English (☎ 514-252-8687) leave here every day. The fee of $5.25 chisels away at the local citizens' debt. It's worth it for those with a special interest in either architecture or sport.

North of Rue Sherbrook Est are the Biodome, Botanical Gardens and Insectarium.

The entire site is in huge Parc Maisonneuve on the extreme eastern side of the city, off Rue Sherbrooke on the corner of Boulevard Pie IX. The address is 3200 Rue Viau. The Métro stop is Viau (pronounced 'vee o').

Biodome Housed in the former Velodrome cycling stadium at the Olympic Complex, the Biodome (☎ 514-868-3000), 4777 Avenue Pierre de Coubertin, is a captivating environmental museum which re-creates four distinct ecosystems and houses 4000 animals and 5000 plants. Under one roof visitors can enjoy, learn about and appreciate the necessity of the rainforest, the polar regions, the Laurentian Shield woodlands and the Gulf of St Lawrence ocean environment.

The rainforest section is particularly encompassing, with monkeys in huge live trees and alligators in rivers. Other highlights include the underwater views of riverscapes where ducks may be seen competing with fish for food, the ocean microcosm and colourful tidal pools. The penguins are a natural favourite, too.

Admission is $9.50 for adults, $7 for seniors and $4.75 for children; kids aged under six are free. A visit takes a good two hours. A two-day combination ticket is available for $21 which includes the Biodome, Botanical Gardens and Insectarium and the Montreal Tower.

It is a popular attraction, far exceeding attendance expectations. Plan to go on a weekday, if possible, and avoid midday. You can bring your own lunch, there are picnic tables near the cafeteria. The gift/bookshop is quite tempting – beware.

A free bus shuttle runs between here and the Botanical Gardens.

Botanical Gardens The 81-hectare gardens (☎ 514-872-1400) are the third largest in the world after those in London and Berlin. Some 26,000 types of plants are grown in 30 garden settings and various climate-controlled greenhouses. The collection of 700 orchid species is particularly

impressive, as are the Japanese Garden and bonsai and Chinese *penjing* with plants up to 100 years old. The Ming Dynasty-style Chinese Garden is also a must. Other displays change with the seasons and there are often special temporary exhibits.

The gardens are open every day from 9 am to 5 pm with extended hours in summer to 7 pm. In summer a ticket is $9 and includes the gardens, the greenhouses and the Insectarium. In the low season prices drop a couple of dollars. Also see the combination tickets available listed under the Biodome. The gardens are next to the Olympic Buildings in Parc Maisonneuve at 4101 Rue Sherbrooke Est; take the Métro to Pie IX. A shuttle bus runs to the Biodome at Olympic Park.

Insectarium Whether you love or hate the creepy crawlies, this collection (☎ 514-872-8753) of bugs from around the world will fascinate you. There's also a Canadian butterfly section. The site is at the Botanical Gardens and is included with the gardens ticket. It's open daily from 9 am to 7 pm in summer with winter hours slightly shorter.

Neighbourhoods & Districts
Lower Rue Saint Denis/Latin Quarter
Rue Saint Denis between Boulevard de Maisonneuve and Rue Sherbrooke, is the centre of a café, bistro and bar district with lots of open-air places and music bars. Though originally an all-student area, more expensive establishments are now part of the mix but the number of young people continues to make the nights especially lively. Snoop around in the side streets, too, where little bars can be discovered. There are also some good small hotels in the area.

French is the tongue generally spoken here but don't let that deter you – it's a good chance to practise.

Going south along Rue Saint Denis will lead you into Old Montreal.

North, up Rue Saint Denis just beyond Rue Sherbrooke, is Place Saint Louis, a small park dating from 1876 surrounded by fine Victorian homes built for the French elite of the time. West of the square is Rue Prince Arthur (see the following Boulevard Saint Laurent & the Plateau section). Saint Denis continues northward through the Plateau area.

Boulevard Saint Laurent & the Plateau
Away from the best known tourist haunts, the Plateau area is a multi-ethnic district of inexpensive housing, outdoor cafés, restaurants, discos, bars, and interesting, funky shops. The loosely defined area runs from Avenue des Pins north to about Boulevard Saint Joseph. Rue Saint Denis and Avenue du Parc mark the east and west edges. This energetic portion of Montreal, ignored a few years ago, is well worth exploring on foot.

Still called St Lawrence by some and known by many as The Main, always interesting Boulevard Saint Laurent is the principal commercial strip of the district. Running north-south, it divides the city into east and west, historically French and English, and has long reflected various nationalities.

Stores are topped by apartments in the two to four-storey rows that line both sides of the street. Around Rue Sainte Catherine it's a little sleazy (but entertaining), but from north of Sherbrooke it leads into the Plateau with a splash of upmarket shops and restaurants, and then past Avenue du Pins through a cornucopia of small businesses for countless blocks. Both Saint Denis and Saint Laurent pass through a mix of French, English and Portuguese communities with abundant bookshops, clothing stores, coffee shops and restaurants.

The area around and along Rue Prince Arthur is good for strolling and eating, as is the section farther north on and around Avenue Duluth.

Avenue du Mont Royal west of the Mont Royal Métro station for about 10 blocks to Saint Laurent contains numerous vintage and second-hand clothing stores for offbeat, street-fashion apparel. East of the Métro stop there are also some alternative shops, used-record stores and the like.

The Upper Main eventually leads to the Mile End area.

Mile End Upper Saint Laurent leads into this unusual neighbourhood bounded by Rue Laurier to the south, Rue Bernard to the north, Avenue Parc to the east and Saint Laurent itself to the west. It's a blend of French, Greek and traditional Hassidic Jews.

Many upper-class French, a growing segment of Montreal's population, live in the Outrement neighbourhood just to the east of Parc du Mont Royal. There is a smattering of pricey boutiques and restaurants along a portion of Avenue Laurier. Farther north, Rue Bernard has some noteworthy restaurants, bars and cafés. Avenue du Parc is the centre of the Greek community.

Little Italy Still farther north, Rue Saint Laurent leads into this slowly upgrading traditional Italian area. From the southern edge at Rue Saint Zotique, several restaurants and cafés can be found on Rue Saint Laurent for a couple of blocks northward. Rue Jean Talon marks the northern boundary, Rue Saint Denis the east and Rue Clark, the west.

Bustling Jean Talon Market has become a Montreal favourite and is really a cool place to be on Saturday.

The Village The city's homosexual community is revitalising Rue Sainte Catherine Est between Rue Saint Hubert and Rue Papineau. New restaurants and stores continue to open in this long neglected part of town which runs from Boulevard René Levesque north to Rue Sherbrooke. Numerous bars and nightclubs catering to gays and lesbians can be found in the district as well as specialised hotels and shops. The area around Rue Amherst and Boulevard de Maisonneuve has an increasing array of antique and speciality shops worth a browse.

There have been bashings in the neighbourhood. Take care and don't go wandering through parks alone in the middle of the night.

Markets

There are three fairly central markets. At **Atwater Market**, south on Avenue Atwater, below Rue Sainte Catherine at the Lachine

Canal, maple syrup is available, often from farmers who produce it. They can answer any questions about this traditional Quebec treat.

The **Marché de Maisonneuve** is on the corner of Rue Ontario and Avenue Létourneaux in the east end of the city.

More ethnically varied is the happening **Jean Talon Market** just south of Rue Jean Talon between Rue Henri Julien and Avenue Casgrain north of the Plateau in the middle of Little Italy.

Other Attractions

Lachine This suburb south-west of downtown Montreal is definitely worth a visit for its history, architecture and general ambience. It's not touristy, reveals a little of Montreal's roots and culture, and makes a very good day trip. The area with things to see is compact and nicely situated along Lac St Louis, a bulge in the river, about 10km from downtown.

The **Fur Trade in Lachine National Historic Site** (☎ 514-637-7433) is at 1255 Boulevard Saint Joseph on the corner of 12th Avenue along the pleasant waterfront. The museum tells the story of the fur trade in Canada, which was so critical to the development of the country. Trading was done right here because the rapids made further river navigation impossible. It's open daily in summer, from Wednesday to Sunday in autumn. Call for rates and exact times.

Nearby, on Boulevard Saint Joseph but down near 7th Avenue, is the **Lachine Canal National Historic Site** (☎ 514-283-6054, ☎ 514-637-7433). Admission is free to the exhibits on the canal's history and construction. Walking tours are given along the canal which was built for trade purposes. The site is open daily from mid-May to Labour Day.

At the **Lachine Museum** (☎ 514-634-3471) complex, 110 Chemin de LaSalle, is the oldest house in Montreal (from 1669). Also see (and smell) the old fur storage building from the original trading days. Adjacent to the museum is a huge waterfront sculpture garden containing around 30 pieces.

You may also like to wander a few of the side streets behind the impressive College

Sainte Anne nunnery or the City Hall, both along Boulevard Saint Joseph.

All of the above sites are within easy walking distance of each other.

The Lachine waterfront is accessible from Old Montreal along the cycling route beside the canal. You can also take the Métro to Angrignon and then the No 110 bus.

Kahnawake Indian Reserve South of Lachine where the Mercier Bridge meets the south shore there's the Kahnawake (pronounced 'gon-a-wok-ee') Indian Reserve where 6000 Mohawks live. Kahnawake Tourism (☎ 514-638-9699) has information on sites and events such as powwows.

There are a few things to see but the reserve, about 18km from central Montreal, looks pretty much like most suburbs, not like something from a Hollywood western movie.

The **Cultural Centre**, with an extensive library relating to the Six Nations of the Iroquois Confederacy, has a small display dealing principally with this reserve and its history. A $3 donation is suggested. It's open Monday to Friday.

The **Saint Francis Xavier Church** from 1717 has a small museum about the early Catholic missions. It's free and open daily from 10 am to noon and from 1 to 5 pm. Sunday mass at 11 am is sung in Mohawk.

In the Old Indian Village open daily in summer you can see craftwork and try some native foods. There are also several gift shops and galleries with arts and crafts.

Also in summer, the **Feast in the Forest** is an evening show of dance and song which reflects traditional celebrations. Dinner, comprised of some native dishes such as succotash, is included. Adult tickets are $20 and reservations are required.

Cheap cigarettes and alcohol may also be purchased on the reserve.

Canada's national game, lacrosse, is still popular here and you may see boys playing on the sports fields around town. The Mohawk team plays adult league games from May to July at the sports complex.

This reserve was the location of a major confrontation which lasted for months between the Mohawks and the Quebec and federal governments through the summer of 1990 which made headlines internationally. The residents' support of the Mohawks in Oka over their land dispute exploded into a symbolic stand against the continuing mistreatment of Native Indians across the country.

Cosmodome (Space Sciences Centre) This interactive museum (☎ 450-978-3600) concentrates on space and new technologies. Multi-media exhibits focus on the solar system, satellite communications, teledetection, space travel and related subjects.

The centre is about a 20 minute drive and can be reached by public transportation using the Métro and a connecting bus. It's at 2150 Autoroute des Laurentides in Laval, north of Montreal island.

Admission is $9, less for children and seniors and family rates are available. From 24 June to Labour Day, it is open daily from 10 am to 6 pm but closed Monday the rest of the year. The centre also runs well regarded one, two, three and five-day space camps, primarily aimed at youth who go through a sort of mini-NASA training.

St Lawrence Seaway The seaway system of locks, canals and dams opened in 1959 along the St Lawrence River enables ocean-going vessels to sail 3200km inland via the Great Lakes. Across Victoria Bridge from the city is an observation tower over the first locks of the system, the Saint Lambert Locks, where ships are raised/lowered 5m.

There are explanatory displays. The observation area is open from April to December between 9 am and 9.30 pm, and is free. In January, February and March the locks are closed – they're frozen like the river itself, until the spring thaw. The site can be reached by bike trail.

Canadian Railway Museum This museum (☎ 514-632-2410) is at 122A Rue Saint Pierre in Saint Constant, a district on the south shore near Châteauguay. The museum, with Canada's largest collection, has

examples of early locomotives, steam engines and passenger cars.

Admission is $4.50 and it's open daily from May to September and weekends to mid-October. To get there, take Champlain Bridge from town to Hwy 15, then Hwy 137 at the Châteauguay cut-off to Hwy 209.

Activities

Montreal is not bad for biking. Cycling maps can be bought at bookshops but also ask at tourist offices for freebies. One very fine route leads from the edge of Old Montreal, south-west all the way to Lachine along the old canal with a lot of history en route. Another route covers the Old Port area, and another Parc des Îles. All three are connected.

In the river north-east of downtown at Parc de Récréation des Îles-de-Boucherville there are 22km of trails around this string of island parks connected by bridges. To reach the islands by car, bike or ferry ask the tourist office for current details.

The light-hearted, good-time Tour des Îles on the first weekend in June is a major biking event which attracts about 50,000. Some riders wear wacky costumes in this long ride around the city. The organisers also set up Le Grand Tour, a longer ride around portions of the province.

There is year-round indoor ice skating at l'Amphitheatre Bell (☎ 514-395-0555) at 1000 Rue de La Gauchetière (Bonaventure Métro stop). Admission is $5 and skates can be rented.

See under Olympic Park and Parc des Îles for swimming and Mont Royal for winter and summer activities.

Organised Tours

Bus & Boat Gray Line (☎ 514-934-1222) at the tourist office on Square Dorchester operates 11 sightseeing tours. The basic city orientation tour takes 1½ hours, costs $17 and takes in some of the principal sights and the Mont Royal lookout. There are also tours aboard pseudo trolley buses. The deluxe bus trip is better value and costs $40 which includes admission into some of the attractions such as the Biodome. An eight hour all-day trip is $43. Another trip goes to the Laurentian Mountains north of Montreal.

Another company is Royal Tours (☎ 514-871-4733) also at 1001 Rue du Square Dorchester in the Infotouriste centre. It offers a lot of flexibility and you can choose from a number of options to customise the tour. On the summer Carousel tour, you can hop on and off the bus at different sights and take advantage of reduced admissions to some attractions. Like Gray Line, this is a reputable company.

The Amphi Tour (☎ 514-849-5181) offers a surprise – a bus tours the Old Port area for half an hour and then drives into the river! It then provides a port-area cruise for another half an hour. It operates daily from May to the end of October. The $18 tour departs from Quai King Edward and reservations are essential.

A couple of companies offer bouncing, soaking jet-boat trips through the nearby Lachine Rapids.

Lachine Rapids Tours (☎ 514-284-9607) at 105 de la Commune Ouest has 90-minute trips leaving from Old Montreal, costing $49. Smaller, faster, less expensive but shorter speedboat trips are also available. Rafting Hydrojet (☎ 514-767-2230) has rubber raft trips through the rapids for $34.

Cruises AML Cruises (☎ 514-842-3871) has river tours from Quai Victoria also called the Clock Tower Pier (Quai de l'Horloge), the pier at the foot of Rue Berri in Old Montreal. The basic trip around the port, Saint Helen's Island and the Boucherville Islands is $20. Longer sunset trips and later weekend night cruises with band, dancing and drinks are other options. Other choices are the cruise aboard the *New Orleans*, a Mississippi-style paddlewheeler and a one-day trip to Quebec City.

Tours aboard the smaller, comfortable and climate-controlled *Le Bateau Mouche* (☎ 514-849-9952), a more deluxe, Parisian-type vessel are also good. These tours depart Quai Jacques Cartier for the 90-minute narrated cruises. Call for details and reservations. Prices are slightly higher than AML's.

Walking Tickets for Old Montreal walking tours are available at the tourist office on Dorchester Square.

Adventure Windigo Aventure (☎ 514-948-4145) offers summer one-day canoe trips in Mont Tremblant Park including transportation, equipment, guide and lunch for $70, a pretty good bargain. They can also be taken from Tremblant Village. There are also kayaking and hiking trips to various destinations.

Globe-Trotter Aventure (☎ 514-598-7688) also offers good-value, small-group, outdoor trips from one to three days such as biking, canoeing and rockclimbing. One trip is to La Mauricie National Park which is otherwise difficult to reach without your own transport.

Moose Travel bus service through parts of Quebec and Ontario is listed under Getting There & Away later in this Montreal section.

Special Events
Some of the major festivals held in Montreal are:

January-February
Fête des Neiges
This is a winter festival held at the end of January and based around the Old Port and Parc des Îles.

March
Saint Patrick's Day
The city's major Saint Patrick's Day parade is a long-running tradition.

May-June
International Fireworks
Held from between the end of May into July on weekends, this fireworks competition lights up the skies.
Formula 1 Grand Prix
This major international event, the only Formula 1 race in North America, is held at the beginning of June (☎ 514-350-0000). Tickets must be pre-booked.
Montreal Jazz Festival
This is held at the end of June and the beginning of July and is a major event with both internationally-known and local players. Indoors and out, concerts are held at various places around town and many are free. There's usually quite a few performances around the

Saint Denis area. Accommodation may be tight at this time as this event is a big draw.
Fête Nationale
Formerly known as St Jean Baptiste Day (or Johnny Baptiste to the English speakers), this event is held each year on 24 June and includes a major parade and holiday. Originally a religious holiday then transformed into a strident Québecois political demonstration, it has become more of a feel-good, beginning-of-spring celebration with some optimistic Quebec nationalism thrown in.

July-September
Just for Laughs Comedy Festival
The bilingual comedy festival with both free and admission-charged performances is held in July. Over half a million attend with some 200 performers featured.
Divers/Cité
This gay event with a major parade is held in The Village at the beginning of August.
Montreal World Film Festival
This is held in mid to late August and early September with screenings at cinemas around town.

Several big cycling races are held through the summer including one around the island and one through the streets.

Places to Stay
Montreal, like Quebec City, is popular with tourists in summer, so rooms can be hard to find and cost more than during the rest of the year. The period around Christmas and New Year is also very busy.

Camping There's not too much camping close to town. As you come from the west, before you actually get on the island of Montreal, on Hwy 338 in Coteau du Lac (exit 17 from Hwy 20) is *KEA (☎ 514-763-5344)*. It's just off the highway around Dorion, about a 45 minute drive to downtown. Sites are $20 to $23.

Also 45 minutes drive west of Montreal is *Camping D'Aoust (☎ 514-458-7301)* on Hwy 342 in Hudson-Vaudreuil. Take exit 26 coming from Montreal, exit 22 coming from Ottawa from Hwy 40 (the Trans Canada Hwy) then it's 3km down the road on the right at 3844 Boulevard Hardwood. A tent site is $18.

South of the city there is a **KOA** *(Kampground of America;* ☎ *450-659-8626,* ☎ *1-800-562-9395, 130 Boulevard Monette)* in St Phillippe. Take exit 38 off Hwy 15. Others can be found about 20 minutes from town south on Hwy 15.

Hostels The large, central and well organised HI *Auberge de Montreal (*☎ *514-843-3317, 1030 Rue Mackay)* is south of Boulevard René Lévesque. For bookings call ☎ 1-800-461-8585. The Métro stop is Lucien L'Allelier. There are 250 beds and it's air-conditioned. Rooms vary with four to 10 beds and there are private rooms ($52/57 member/nonmember) and some for families. Dorm beds cost $16 and breakfast is offered in summer. It's open all year with check-in from 9.30 am to 2 am. Reservations are not a bad idea at any time but are strongly recommended from June through September when three weeks notice should be given. Walking tours of the city are offered and there is some parking. Shuttles are available to Mont Tremblant.

In Old Montreal is *Alternative Backpackers (*☎ *514-282-8069, info@Auberge-Alternative.qc.ca, 358 Rue Saint Pierre)* in a quiet street about a 10 minute walk from the Old Port. There are 48 beds spread over two very colourful, unusually laid out floors in this converted commercial space. Rates are $16, dropping to $14 in the off season. If required, a sheet is $2. Double rooms are $45 and there are cooking facilities. It's a short walk to the Square Victoria Métro stop.

Another good choice is *Le Gite du Parc Lafontaine (*☎ *514-522-3910,* ☎ *1-877-350-4483, www.hostelmontreal.com, 1250 Rue Sherbrooke Est)*, a hostel with an atmosphere more like that of a guesthouse or inn. The location, in a converted Victorian house, is very convenient with the main bus station about a 10 minute walk away and Rue Saint Denis very close. The park across the street presents frequent free shows. Dorm beds are $19, private rooms are $45/55 with tax and there are family rooms. Weekly rates are offered. Sheets and blankets are included as is a continental breakfast. It has kitchen and laundry facilities and can help in planning tours. It's open from 1 May to early September and is closed from 11 am to 3 pm. The place is very clean, bright and well run.

The same people operate the new *Le Gite du Plateau Mont Royal, (*☎ *514-284-1276 and above numbers, 185 Rue Sherbrooke Est)*. It's equally good, very clean, closer to the downtown core, and offers some self-contained units with cooking facilities. Prices are the same.

The *Hôtel de Paris and Auberge (*☎ *514-522-6861,* ☎ *1-800-567-7217, hdeparis@microtec.net, 901 Rue Sherbrooke Est)* is nearby. Primarily a fine, small hotel in a marvellous old turreted mansion, there is a hostel section in the basement with beds at $17 (summer rate) including cooking and laundry facilities. There is a good little café with *terrasse* (a patio) on the premises. Forty other hostel beds and self-contained apartment rooms are available across the street in a second property. Both hostel sections are popular and busy but are a bit cramped. See under European-Style Hotels for information on the good rooms upstairs.

Auberge Chez Jean (☎ *514-843-8279, 4136 Rue Henri Julien)* is a very casual place operated in Jean's private apartment home. The cost is $15 a night including breakfast. Guests share the small, busy space and kitchen. Out of peak season visitors may have a room to themselves. There is also a little garden/courtyard. The hostel is open all year and has a handy location north of Avenue Duluth, south of Rachel in the Plateau Mont Royal. Look for 'Jean' on the mailbox, it's the only sign. He's bilingual.

Open all year and very low-cost is the *Collége Francais (*☎ *514-270-4459, 5155 Ave de Gaspé)*, also called Vacances Canada 4 Saisons, with a range of cheap beds. Dorms go for as little as $11.50. There are rooms with four beds and a toilet, shower and sink at $12.50 per person or double rooms go for $15.50 per person. Inexpensive breakfasts are offered at a nearby restaurant or there is a cafeteria. Parking is available too. The college is near the corner of Avenue Laurier and Rue

Saint Denis, north-east of downtown. The Métro stop is Laurier, 300m east of Rue de Gaspé. Although there are hundreds of beds it's busy in summer so call ahead to check availability.

The *YMCA (☎ 514-849-8393, 1450 Rue Stanley)* is central and huge with 350 beds. Singles/doubles are from $35/54 and they take both sexes. The cheap cafeteria is open from 7 am to 8 pm weekdays, 8 am to 2 pm weekends.

At the *YWCA (☎ 514-866-9941, 1355 Boulevard René Lévesque Ouest)*, for women only, singles/doubles cost from $46/62 without bath or air-con and there is a kitchen on every floor. Good weekly rates are available. Beds in the four-bed dorms are $22. There is also a small restaurant and a pool which guests can use. On the Métro get off at the Peel stop.

Pretty inexpensive rooms are also available at *St Joseph's Oratory (☎ 514-733-8211, ext 2640)*. Singles/doubles cost $33/52 with breakfast. Go to Pavilion Jean 23rd at 4300 Chemin Queen Mary.

Universities *McGill University*, on the corner of Rue Sherbrooke and Rue University, opens its residences from 15 May to 15 August. The accommodation office (☎ 514-398-6367) is at 3935 Rue University. Singles (which is all there is) cost $38, for students $31, taxes included. There are cafeterias and laundry rooms. Rates go down with stays of more than one night and the weekly rates are good.

The residences of the *Loyola Campus (☎ 514-848-4756, 7141 Rue Sherbrooke Ouest)* of Concordia University are cheaper. This campus is in Montreal Ouest. Buses run along Rue Sherbrooke from the downtown area. The student rate is $21 per person, single or double. Nonstudents pay $28/42 for singles/doubles.

The *Université de Quebec à Montreal* residence (☎ 514-987-6669, ☎ 1-888-987-6699, 303 Boulevard René Levesque) offers rooms in a new building with a great location. Rates are $33/48 for nonstudents and readers have given it good reviews.

European-Style Hotels Most standard hotels in the city are costly. These independent tourist hotels are the alternative and there is a good, central assortment. Most of them are in the eastern portion of the downtown area. Nearly all are in older houses and buildings with 10 to 20 rooms. Quality ranges from the plain and functional to old-world-charm comfortable. Price is the best indicator of quality but sometimes just a few dollars can make quite a difference.

Practically all the smaller ones have a variety of rooms with price differences depending on facilities – whether it has a sink or toilet or a full bathroom. Air-con adds a few dollars too. Prices are highest from June to October.

A good district worth considering is the convenient Saint Denis bus station area where there are quite a few places offering good dollar value.

Castel Saint Denis (☎ 514-842-9719, 2099 Rue Saint Denis) is up the hill just south of Rue Sherbrooke. It's been renovated and redecorated a couple of times, and is clean and convenient, if not grand. Singles/doubles range from $40/50 without bath to $45/55 with bath before taxes.

In the café district, there's the larger more modern *Hôtel Saint Denis (☎ 514-849-4526, ☎ 1-800-363-3364, 1254 Rue Saint Denis)* with a range of 60 clean rooms starting at $49 a double in summer. Prices drop about $10 in the off season. It's got air-con and a restaurant.

Farther south on Rue Saint Denis between Sherbrooke and Old Montreal, the sprawling *L'Américain (☎ 514-849-0616, 1042 Rue Saint Denis)* has 60 rooms in a range of configurations. The basic ones with sink and TV are just $30/35; with private bath, cost rises to $40/45. Triples and quads are also available. None have air-con. The rooms on the top floor are reminiscent of those in tryst scenes in French movies. Montreal's gaytown is nearby and the hotel has become popular with out-of-towners who visit that part of the city, but straights also find the location convenient.

Cheaper rooms ($30) can be found at such places as the *Hôtel de la Couronne* (☎ 514-845-0901, 1029 Rue Saint Denis) across the street.

East of Rue Saint Denis there's *Le Breton* (☎ 514-524-7273, 1609 Rue Saint Hubert) in an excellent location on a pleasant street. It's beside the bus station. Singles or doubles go from $45 to $70 depending on size and amenities. Some rooms come with TV, shower or bath. There are many other small hotels nearby including plenty of cheap tourist rooms.

Farther south, on the corner of Avenue Viger, is the inexpensive but good *Hôtel Viger Centre Ville* (☎ 514-845-6058, ☎ 1-800-845-6058, 1001 Rue Saint Hubert). It has a wide variety of rooms from $45/48 singles/doubles. The least expensive of the 22 rooms come with sink, colour TV and fan. A continental breakfast is included and Old Montreal is within walking distance.

West of Rue Saint Denis there are places to stay on Rue Ontario. *Hôtel Villard* (☎ 514-845-9730, 307 Rue Ontario) has 14 good rooms with good prices, doubles ranging from $47 to $57. Singles are about $10 less.

On Avenue Hôtel de Ville, between Boulevard Saint Laurent and Rue Saint Denis, the *Hôtel Armor Manoir Sherbrooke* (☎ 514-845-0915, 1-800-203-5485, 157 Rue Sherbrooke Est) is the conversion of two fine Victorian houses into one hotel with 30 rooms. Both sections are busy with prices changing with the season and varying with the features. In summer, singles/doubles without bath are $50/65 with continental breakfast included. *Hôtel Pierre* (☎ 514-288-8519) is next door at No 169.

Hôtel de Paris (☎ 514-522-6861, ☎ 1-800-567-7217, 901 Rue Sherbrooke Est) is a turreted mansion with a wide range of upgraded rooms from budget at $60/65 in season to suites with kitchens at $120. The good standard rooms are $80. All have private bath. Additional people cost $7 and some rooms can accommodate six people. There is a fine little café on the premises and the location is excellent. In another building across the street apartments are rented by the week.

West of Rue Jeanne Mance is the 20-room totally upgraded stone *Hotel Casa Bella* (☎ 514-849-2777, ☎ 1-888-453-2777, 264 Rue Sherbrooke Ouest). The price range at this central hotel is quite wide with singles from $50 to $65, doubles from $50 to $85 with breakfast, air-con and parking.

There are also places around the central downtown area. Several can be found along Rue Sainte Catherine near Boulevard Saint Laurent, where the men, painted ladies and some in-betweens appear at about 6 pm.

The *Hebergement l'Abri du Voyageur* (☎ 514-849-2922, 9 Rue Sainte Catherine Ouest) is one of the best low-budget places in the province. The totally renovated hotel with original pine floors and exposed brick has 30 rooms, each with sink, fan and TV. High season rates are $40/50, low season $35/40 all including taxes. Additional people are $10. The front desk has a binder full of good information for visitors.

Villa de France (☎ 514-849-5043, 57 Rue Sainte Catherine Est) is also a well kept, friendly place which is quite OK if you're really on a budget, although it does rent by the hour. Without a bath, singles/doubles cost $35, with bath $45. Other places nearby tend to be more dubious.

Going west, the *Manoir Ambrose* (☎ 514-288-6922, 3422 Rue Stanley) is a very fine place in a more reputable and very central location. Singles range from $45 all the way up to $70, and doubles from $50 to $75. Compared to the sterile international hotels, its 22 rooms are a real bargain.

South of Boulevard René Lévesque, the *Aux Berges* (☎ 514-938-9393, 1070 Rue Mackay) serves gay male visitors exclusively. Rue Mackay is central but quiet and the hotel has all amenities. Rooms without bath are $65/80 including continental breakfast.

B&Bs Another alternative to the high-priced hotels are the B&Bs. Most are listed by agencies. If you're staying a while, it's worth asking about a weekly rate. Also inquire if the breakfast is full or continental.

B&B Downtown Network (☎ 514-289-9749, ☎ 1-800-267-5180) is an agency run

by Bob and Mariko Finkelstein which has been operating successfully for years. They have checked over 50 private homes for quality and hospitality beyond minimum requirements.

Hosts range from students to lawyers, the places from mansions with fireplaces in the bedrooms, to Victorian homes, to apartments filled with antiques. Rates are quite reasonable at $35 to $55 for singles, $45 to $65 for doubles and triples are available too. For information and reservations, call or write to 3458 Laval Avenue, Montreal, H2X 3C8. They speak Japanese.

A similar organisation is Montreal Oasis (☎ 514-935-2312) run by Swede Lena Blondel out of her own B&B at 3000 Chemin de Breslay (off Avenue Atwater just north of Rue Sherbrooke). Almost all of her participant homes are in older houses in the central core and they pride themselves on the quality of their breakfasts. Ask about the places on quiet and particularly attractive Rue Souvenir, which is perfectly located near Rue Sainte Catherine, or about the historic home in Old Montreal. Prices range from $40 to $70 a single, $55 to $90 a double and, again, triples are available. Most of the places welcome children.

Bienvenue B&B (☎ 514-844-5897, ☎ 1-800-227-5897, 3950 Avenue Laval) is a smaller agency which specialises in late 19th/early 20th century places around the interesting French area of Rue Saint Denis and Carré Saint Louis. Call or write to 3950 Avenue Laval, Montreal H2W 2J2. Avenue Laval is one block west of Rue Saint Denis and the office is a couple of blocks north of Rue Sherbrooke, a short walk from the Sherbrooke Métro stop. The owners, Carole Sirois and Allard Coté, operate a B&B themselves at the above address which is a great location very close to the Prince Arthur restaurant district.

Hotels & Efficiencies If you really like a more conventional, modern hotel but not the prices accompanying the usual downtown luxury choices there are a few possibilities. Many hotels also have lower weekend rates. Try the *Hotel Travelodge (☎ 514-874-9090, ☎ 1-800-363-6535, 50 Boulevard René Lévesque)* centrally located near Boulevard Saint Laurent. Rooms are in the $70 range.

Comfort Suites (☎ 514-878-2711, 1214 Rue Crescent) charges $125 for two people weekdays or $79 on weekends. Other middle priced hotels include the *Hôtel Montréal Crescent (☎ 514-938-9797, 1366 Boulevard René Lévesque)* with prices from $75 to $120.

The central *Le Riche Bourg (☎ 514-935-9224, ☎ 1-800-678-6323, 2170 Avenue Lincoln)* near Avenue Atwater has good-value studio, one and two-bedroom suites with kitchen. A small studio single or double is $94 or $79 on weekends. The hotel is very well equipped with pool and rooftop balcony and a restaurant and grocery store. Weekly rates are available.

The following hotels are in the expensive category. Despite the rather hefty prices, geared mainly to the business traveller, you will be charged outrageously for parking, telephone calls, drinks in the room fridge, and every other time you turn around. Some of the major hotels do have pretty good lower-priced weekend specials which may appeal to some for a splurge; prices are generally lower in summer when there is less commercial traffic.

Marriott Château Champlain (☎ 514-878-9000, ☎ 1-800-200-5909, 1 Place du Canada) has rooms from $100 to $175. Ask for a room facing Square Dorchester and the view will be quite good. There's a restaurant and Vegas-style revues are often presented.

Nearby is the *Bonaventure Hilton (☎ 514-878-2332, ☎ 1-800-445-8667, Place Bonaventure)* with rooms from $150 to $230.

The *Ritz Carlton Kempinski (☎ 514-842-4212, ☎ 1-800-363-0366, 1228 Rue Sherbrooke Ouest)* with rooms from $150 to $240, has long been a hotel of distinction and reputation. The penthouse suite here is the most expensive place to stay in Canada (and it's probably not too shabby either). This seems to be the hotel of choice for business, entertainment and, if it's not an oxymoron, political superstars.

QUEBEC

Motels Motels are not really a good choice in Montreal; they are not found in interesting areas and are rather costly. All charge less in the low season but rates listed here are summer ones.

An area of some concentration is along Rue Saint Jacques, south and parallel to Rue Sherbrooke, conveniently just a 10 minute drive west from the centre. Look around where Rue Cavendish runs into Rue Saint Jacques from Rue Sherbrooke. Coming from the west (from places like Dorval airport), Hwys 2 and 20 flow into Rue Saint Jacques. Be aware that some of the motels are short-stay only – like an hour.

Best of the lot, by far, is large, modern *Motel Le Chablis* (☎ 514-488-9561, 6951 *Rue Saint Jacques Ouest)* charging $80 to $125 single or double.

The basic *Colibri* (☎ 514-486-1167, 6960 *Rue Saint Jacques Ouest)* charges $40/45. It's the grey place behind Harvey's hamburger restaurant.

The *Motel Raphaël* (☎ 514-485-3344, 7455 *Rue Saint Jacques Ouest)* has been around forever and shows some wear but is still serviceable at $45 for doubles. It has a swimming pool and restaurant.

There are other quality places farther west, around Dorval airport.

In the east end of Montreal, *Le Paysan* (☎ 514-640-1415, 12400 *Rue Sherbrooke Est)* near Olympic Park is $54/65. *Le Marquis* (☎ 514-256-1621, 6720 *Rue Sherbrooke Est)* costs $50 and there are others in the area.

Other motels can be found on the south shore across the river on the mainland. Pont (bridge) Jacques Cartier leads into Boulevard Taschereau, also known as Hwy 134 Ouest.

La Parisienne (☎ 450-674-6291, 1277 *Boulevard Taschereau)* is close to the bridge. Singles/doubles cost $55. There are others much farther out in the 8000 number addresses.

West of here, at the foot of Pont Champlain, there are motels along Boulevard Marie Victorin. *Motel Champlain* (☎ 450-671-0066, 7600 *Boulevard Marie Victorin)* has rooms for $70.

Places to Eat

The French have long been responsible for Montreal's excellent restaurant reputation, which various immigrant groups have only added to over the years. Many places have lunch specials – always the best bargains – and at dinner, a table d'hôte or fixed-price complete dinner.

Many Montreal restaurants, generally in the lower and middle-price brackets, have a 'bring your own' wine policy. If you want to take advantage of this great idea and bring your own wine for a meal, you can get it in a *dépanneur* (convenience store) if there is no government outlet (known as SAQ) around or it's past their closing time. The price will be a bit higher at a store. Many restaurants, particularly the better ones, don't start to get busy until around 8 pm and will stay that way for a couple of hours. If you're an early eater in this city you may have the place to yourself.

Downtown/Central On the corner of Boulevard de Maisonneuve and Rue Metcalfe, *Ben's* is an institution. Montreal is known far and wide for its smoked meat and the Ben's name is familiar across the country. It's an informal deli, full of office workers at lunch time. Sandwiches are around $4, or $7 with french fries, pickle and coffee.

Throughout Quebec, there was a long tradition of 'men only' grubby drinking establishments known as taverns. These have been reincarnated as larger, brighter and cleaner establishments known as brasseries and open to all. The central area contains several that are busy at noon weekdays with office and retail workers. One to try is the old, wood-panelled *McLean's Pub (1210 Rue Peel)* with meals ranging from $6.

The *Bar B Barn (1201 Rue Guy)* is too small – it's usually packed at dinner, with a queue out the front – but it serves the best and biggest spareribs you've ever had. It's a comfortable, attractive place as well. The only other thing on the menu is chicken. This place offers honest value with meals costing from $11 to $17 and there's parking around the back.

QUEBEC

Nearby the **Phaya Tai** *(1235 Rue Guy)* offers tasty Thai food. Vegetarian main dishes are $7, seafood and meat dishes $8 to $12.

Rue de la Montagne and Rue Crescent offer a range of restaurants and cafés. Recommended is **EggSpectation** *(1313 Boulevard de Maisonneuve Ouest)*. This very attractive, comfortable, converted commercial space has excellent coffees and huge, delicious breakfasts and lunches of omelettes, crêpes or French toast for about $8. The French toast special with fruit and English cream is tough to beat. **Katsura** *(☎ 514-849-1172, 2170 Rue de la Montagne)* is a popular Japanese place with lunches $8 to $14 and an evening table d'hôte at $27 to $37.

Up from Rue Sainte Catherine is the well known, long-established **Joe's** *(1430 Rue Metcalfe)* steak house. Good steak dinners range from $10 to $17; including a baked potato or french fries and an excellent all-you-can-eat salad bar. For $8 you can have just the salad bar. All meals provide good value particularly the filet mignon special.

The cosy, casual **Maison de Cari** *(Curry House; 1433 Rue Bishop)* has dinners for about $15.

Very pricey, but mentioned because this is Montreal and people here like to eat, is **Chez La Mere Michel** *(☎ 514-934-0473, 1209 Rue Guy)*, a city institution renowned for fine French food. It's been around so long an entire generation knows it as Mother Michael's. Dinner for two will set you back roughly $120 including wine, tax and tip. The three-course lunches are a treat at $17. The service, the food, the style – everything is 1st class. Note that it is closed on Sunday and there is no lunch Saturday to Tuesday.

For a meal or making up your own, try shopping around **Le Faubourg** *(1616 Rue Sainte Catherine Ouest)*. This Parisian-style market/mall, which includes a bakery and liquor store, is devoted to food.

Old Montreal Old Montreal is a fine place to splurge. Menus, with prices, are generally posted outside. The charm of many of these establishments is in some measure the location and restaurant décor rather than purely gastronomic excellence. Also, because this is a major tourist area, prices tend to be a little high. Nonetheless, it is such a great area that a meal out should not be resisted too strongly.

Good for lingering over a meal is the French **La Sauvagine** *(115 Rue Saint Paul)* near the corner of Rue Saint Vincent. Lunch prices range from $7 to $10, dinners from $15 to $22. The Dover sole is good with lobster soup and escargot from the 'prix fixe' menu. If you need help with the French menu, the waiters will explain. The menu includes wild meats such as deer, caribou etc. The only drawback is the price of the wine.

Also comfortable is **Le Père St Vincent** *(431 Rue Saint Vincent)* with French meals from soup to dessert priced at $19 to $27. The tables are arranged in a series of small, intimate rooms in an old stone house.

A third option for a special meal (dinner only) is the long running **Gibby's** *(☎ 514-282-1837, 298 Place d'Youville)* which is popular with Montrealers as well as visitors. It's in a 200-year-old converted stable. The speciality is steak/roast beef and atmosphere and, though a meal is $30 to $50 per person, reservations are suggested, at least for weekends. And if you're going all the way, you could try the $250 wines.

There are inexpensive places in this busy part of town too. **L'Usine de Spaghetti Parisienne** *(273 Rue Saint Paul Est)* has meals from $9 to $15, including all the bread and salad you can eat. **Chez Better** *(160 Notre Dame Est)* has an array of sausages from mild to spicy and sauerkraut for $8, and imported beers.

The small **Café St Paul** *(143 Rue Saint Paul Ouest)* serves burgers and sandwiches under $5 but the club sandwich at $7.25 is really good. Well west of the busiest areas of Old Montreal and highly recommended is the **Titanic** *(445 Rue Saint Pierre)*, tucked in the basement. Catering to an established local clientele, the staff and atmosphere is friendly and casual but there is nothing nonchalant about the excellent food. Choose from an array of salads, creative sandwiches and pastas. A cream of vegetable soup, half

baguette brie and tomato sandwich and a coffee is $8. It's open from 8 am to 3 pm Monday to Friday and credit cards are not taken.

Saint Denis/Latin Quarter Area The *Café Croissant de Lune* on the east side of Rue Saint Denis, downstairs at No 1765 just south of Rue Ontario, is a great place for breakfast. A café au lait and one or two of the fresh sweet buns or croissants will hold you for a few hours.

There are several pubs on Rue Ontario Est at Saint Denis.

Le Commensal (1720 Rue Saint Denis) is open daily from 11 am to midnight and offers good self-serve vegetarian meals, salads and desserts priced by weight. It's highly recommended. While the food is good and the variety wide, keep an eye on how high you pile the plate or the cost will also mount up. An average meal is about $9. Outlets of this restaurant can also be found at 5043 Rue Saint Denis and 1204 Rue McGill College.

A well established, popular working-class, low-cost restaurant is *Da Giovanni (572 Rue Sainte Catherine Est)*. Spaghetti with garlic bread and Caesar salad is under $9. It's open from 7 am to 8 pm. There's another outlet at 690 Sainte Catherine Ouest.

In The Village, bright yellow *Nega Fulo (1257 Rue Amherst)* serves up spicy Brazilian/Cajun dinners ranging from $13 to $22 and lunches at $9.

The Main & the Plateau Just south of Rue Sainte Catherine on Boulevard Saint Laurent, known affectionately as The Main, are several of the city's best known french fries/hot dog places, such as *Frites Dorées*. Montrealers take these pedestrian items seriously and consequently they are produced with reasoned flair. Ask for 'toasté all dress' – everyone will understand and you'll get the full Quebec dog treatment, fully garnished with relish, mustard, onion and topped with chopped cabbage on a toasted bun.

These give way north of Rue Sherbrooke to some of the city's newest, slickest dining establishments. Among the many is elegant

Bueno Notte (3518 Rue Sherbrooke) serving excellent Italian fare. The table d'hôte is $27, the wines about $30.

Between the Latin Quarter and Plateau areas is Rue Prince Arthur, a small, old residential street a portion of which has been converted into a pleasant eating enclave. The restaurant segment runs west from Place Saint Louis on Rue Saint Denis (just north of Rue Sherbrooke) to a block west of Boulevard Saint Laurent. Many small, inexpensive mostly ethnic restaurants line the 'pedestrians only' street. Greek and Vietnamese restaurants are most prominent but there are also French and Polish places among others. Most of the restaurants here have a 'bring your own' wine policy. The Greek places specialise in a Montreal favourite, brochettes, known to many as kebabs. Generally the more traditional dishes such as moussaka are absent but vine leaves or spanokopita show up as appetisers and there is always Greek salad.

A fine Greek dinner can be had at *La Casa Grèque (200 Rue Prince Arthur Est)* for about $20 for two – excellent value.

For a bit of a splurge try *Akita (166 Rue Prince Arthur Est)*, a Japanese place that does everything well. Before 7.30 pm the set meal is a bargain. *Café Méliés (3682 Boulevard Saint Laurent)* in the Cinêma Parallèle is a pleasant, comfortable spot to break the stroll with a coffee or low-priced quiche or sandwich on a grilled baguette.

Schwartz's (3895 Boulevard Saint Laurent), farther north, is a must. It's a small, casual, friendly deli that's practically never closed. It is always packed and has absolutely the best smoked meat in town. It's made right on the premises and aged naturally without chemicals.

Avenue Duluth runs east-west off Boulevard Saint Laurent at about the No 4000 block. It's a narrow old street, once a red-light district, that has been redone as a restaurant centre much like Rue Prince Arthur. From just east of Boulevard Saint Laurent, running east to Rue Saint Denis and beyond, there are numerous good-value Greek, Italian and Asian eateries. A complete

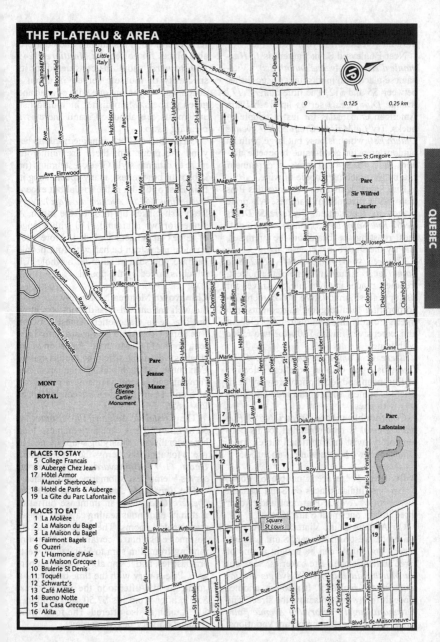

THE PLATEAU & AREA

QUEBEC

MONT
ROYAL

Parc
Sir Wilfred
Laurier

Parc
Jeanne
Mance

Georges
Étienne
Cartier
Monument

Parc
Lafontaine

Square
St Louis

PLACES TO STAY
5 College Francais
8 Auberge Chez Jean
17 Hôtel Armor
   Manoir Sherbrooke
18 Hotel de Paris & Auberge
19 La Gite du Parc Lafontaine

PLACES TO EAT
1 La Molière
2 La Maison du Bagel
3 La Maison du Bagel
4 Fairmont Bagels
6 Ouzeri
7 L'Harmonie d'Asie
9 La Maison Grecque
10 Brulerie St Denis
11 Toquél
12 Schwartz's
13 Café Méliés
14 Bueno Notte
15 La Casa Grecque
16 Akita

dinner at many of them is about $15. At almost all you can bring your own wine.

Near Boulevard Saint Laurent is *L' Harmonie d'Asie (65 Avenue Duluth Est)*, a Vietnamese place with moderately priced dishes between $5 and $12. The little *bakery (173 Avenue Duluth Est)* serves up fresh Latin American empanadas for just a couple of bucks. Try *La Maison Grèque (450 Avenue Duluth Est)* which is busy but large, with an outdoor area for good-value brochette dinners ($12 to $14). There's a dépanneur nearby for grabbing a bottle of wine.

Rue Saint Denis above Avenue des Pins also has a plethora of eateries. All price ranges are represented. *Brulerie St Denis (3967 Rue Saint Denis)* makes superb coffees, roasting the beans on the premises, and try the strawberry cheesecake.

Toqué! (☎ 514-499-2084, 3842 Rue Saint Denis) is currently one of the hottest, trendiest places in town and gets raves for its super fresh, innovative fusion menu incorporating local organic ingredients into internationally inspired dishes. It's elegant and expensive – in the $100-for-two range with wine.

Biere et Compagni (4352 Rue Saint Denis) is a pub with an excellent selection of European and local microbrewery beer. There is some standard pub grub and mussels with fries.

Comfortably urbane *Ouzeri (4690 Rue Saint Denis)* is recommended for its contemporary twist on traditional Greek food. Dinner for two before wine is about $35.

Mile End There are a couple of good, cheap East Indian places on Saint Laurent just north of Avenue Fairmont and two or three Italian ones near Saint Viateur.

On Avenue Saint Viateur and Avenue Fairmont, west of Boulevard Saint Laurent, superb hot bagels can be bought at one of three authentic open-fire bakeries. Seek out *La Maison du Bagel (158 Avenue St Viateur)* for the real deal. It also has another place farther west and across the street. The *Fairmont Bagel Factory (74 Avenue Fairmont)* offers more contemporary variations.

Rue Bernard, near Avenue du Parc, offers several good restaurants and comfortable places for coffee. *La Moulière (1249 Rue Bernard)* should be considered for its speciality of mussels served in about a dozen ways including one with cognac and green peppers. Main dishes including fish and meats are about $15 and there is a pleasant patio.

On Avenue du Parc, running north up beyond the mountain, there are numerous more traditional-style Greek restaurants (no kebabs or brochettes), many specialising in fish. Best of the lot is the casual but expensive *Milos (5357 Avenue du Parc)*. Very fresh fish makes up most of the menu. A dinner for two is around $110 with a range of Greek appetisers included. More economical meals can be had with four people because you select and order a whole fish which is priced by the pound.

Chinatown Montreal's Chinatown is small but well entrenched. The district is centred on Rue de la Gauchetière Ouest between Rue Saint Urbain and Boulevard Saint Laurent, north of Old Montreal. A portion of the street is closed to traffic. The food is mainly Cantonese although spicier Sichuan dishes show up and several Vietnamese places can be found. Many offer lunch specials from as low as $6.

The *Cristal de Saigon (1068 Boulevard Saint Laurent)* has cheap Vietnamese food but specialises in satisfying soups (a meal in itself) for about $6. Across the street, *Hoang Oanh (1071 Boulevard Saint Laurent)* serves Vietnamese submarine sandwiches.

The *Jardin de Jade (57 Rue La Gauchetière Ouest)* has an immense buffet to match its enormous seating capacity spread over several rooms. The food may not be gourmet class but it certainly is plentiful, ranging from dim sum to Sichuan to western pastries, and it's an all-you-can-eat bargain. Prices vary with the time of day; as a guide, in mid-afternoon the price is just $5.50, after 9 pm it's $7.50, and at dinner $11. Lunch is also offered. The food is the freshest on very busy Saturday.

QUEBEC

Entertainment

Montreal nightlife is good, varied and comes in two languages. Clubs serve alcohol until 3 am – the longest opening hours in Canada. Many bars don't start cooking until 10 or 11 pm; after that there will be queues to get in.

The *Mirror* is a free weekly entertainment newspaper which can be picked up around town. *Voir* is the French equivalent. The Saturday *Montreal Gazette* also has club and entertainment listings as does *La Presse*. *Fugues* is a free monthly booklet for gays. It's French but there are club listings for men and lesbians as well as other helpful information.

Call ☎ 514-925-1568 and you'll get an information line for theatre, show and event details.

Live Music & Dance Clubs Rue Crescent, Rue de la Montagne and Rue Bishop are lively at night; this has long been the area for the English nightlife, whereas the French tend to party on Saint Denis. It's fun just to wander either area at night, maybe have a beer and people-watch. A lot of the action has shifted to the Plateau with many clubs on upper Rue Saint Laurent and upper Saint Denis.

On Sunday afternoons in summer, considerable crowds collect for the hippie-like, percussion-based happenings at the edge of Parc Mont Royal. Go to the Georges Etienne Cartier monument opposite Parc Jeanne Mance at Avenue Parc and Avenue Duluth. There's usually some dancing, a few things to eat and a fun atmosphere to enjoy.

'Winnies', the *Sir Winston Churchill Pub (1459 Rue Crescent)*, is popular and has dancing. *Hurley's Irish Pub (1225 Rue Crescent)* with live music nightly is another favourite. *Thursdays (1449 Rue Crescent)* is a singles-style spot.

Sphynx (1426 Rue Stanley), an alternative/gothic/retro dance bar, has different recorded music nightly.

The *Salsathèque (1220 Rue Peel)* can be a fun place. It's a bright, busy, dressy place featuring large live Latin bands who pump out infectious Latin dance music. And if you like to see dancing, the patrons here will be a feast for your eyes.

The *Yellow Door Coffee House (☎ 514-398-6243, 3625 Rue Aylmer)* has survived from the 60s – US draft dodgers found refuge here. Folk music in a casual ambience is still presented but the schedule is erratic; call for upcoming concerts. It's closed through the summer.

The *Metropolis (59 Rue Sainte Catherine Est)* is the largest dance club in town, with bars spread over three floors and impressive sound and lighting systems but it's only open weekends.

Up in the Plateau Mont Royal there are a lot of clubs on Saint Laurent in the 4000 and 5000 blocks. The *Café Campus (57 Rue Prince Arthur Est)* is a popular student hang-out often with live bands, and *Rage (5116 Avenue Parc)* is popular with both live and recorded music. *Quai des Brumes (4481 Rue Saint Denis)* is a fine place for live blues and rock.

In Old Montreal, *Les Deux Pierrots (104 Rue Saint Paul)* is a huge, two-storey spot with local French singers and a casual atmosphere – and it's free.

There are numerous good spots for jazz in town. *L'Air du Temps (☎ 514-842-2003, 191 Rue Saint Paul Ouest)* is in Old Montreal on the corner of Rue Saint François Xavier. Solo music starts at 5 pm, groups after 9.30 pm; performers are mostly local musicians. There's no cover charge and the atmosphere and décor are pleasant.

At *Biddles (☎ 514-842-8656, 2060 Rue Aylmer)* you might get a standard trio, a swing band or a vocalist. There's no cover charge, and you can eat here too.

Other Bars For a sip with a view, there is the *Tour de Ville* near the top of the La Radisson Hotel, 777 Rue Université, between Rue Saint Jacques and Rue Saint Antoine. Drinks are costly but nursing one is kind of fun.

The upstairs *Comedyworks (1238 Rue Bishop)* presents standup comics, usually several in a night. Admission is charged. Mainly English-speaking, *Finnegan's Irish Pub & Grill (82 Rue Prince Arthur Est)* has

a vast selection of Irish draft beers and Scotch. *Fûtenbulle (273 Rue Bernard Ouest)* is a casual, busy beer bar featuring dozens of fine brews from around the world. *Le Swimming (3643 Boulevard Saint Laurent)* is one of the nicest of the many pool (as in billiards) bars in the Plateau area.

Visitors will notice that Montrealers support quite an array of straight and gay strip clubs where staff dancers, even couples, take it all off. It's been this way for years.

Cinema The trend is to huge, multi-screen (up to 30) complexes complete with video games, boutiques, cafés etc. Two major such emporiums are being constructed downtown on Rue Saint Catherine Ouest.

There remain several repertory film theatres usually offering double bills and midnight movies on weekends. These theatres are generally cheaper than the chains showing first runs but a membership may be required. Also call about the language version. *Cinema du Parc (☎ 514-287-7272, 3575 Avenue Parc)* at Rue Prince Arthur Ouest, closed during research but the owner hopes to open either here or elsewhere. It's the last English repertory cinema in town.

The *National Film Board (NFB; ☎ 514-283-9000, 1564 Rue Saint Denis)* is worth a visit for serious cinefiles. There are regular screenings or individual monitors where you can watch the film of your choice. There is also a huge Canadian video collection available.

There is an *IMAX (☎ 514-496-4629)* large-format theatre in the Vieux Port (Old Port) area of Montreal.

Theatre, Dance & More The *Centaur Theatre (☎ 514-288-3161, 453 Rue Saint François Xavier)* generally has the best in English presentations. Les Ballets Jazz de Montreal, a Montreal modern dance troupe, has a good reputation and often performs in the city. *Place des Arts (☎ 514-842-2112)*, Montreal's centre for the performing arts, presents an array of concerts, the symphony, L'Opera Montreal, and dance in three main theatres at the complex on Rue

Sainte Catherine Ouest on the corner of Rue Jeanne Mance.

If Montreal's internationally famed *Cirque de Soleil (☎ 514-722-3692)* animal-free circus is in town, a ticket is worth considering. The circus is based on acrobatics and a range of astounding acts of dexterity.

The *Casino de Montreal*, one of the 10 largest in the world, is open all day and night. For more details see under Île Notre Dame earlier in this Montreal section.

Spectator Sports

Although there are alternatives, for all intents and purposes sports in this town means hockey or hockey.

The Molson Centre (☎ 514-932-2582) on the corner of Rue Mountain and Rue Antoine beside Windsor Station replaced the legendary but smaller Montreal Forum in 1996 as home to the Canadiens. The 'Habs', as the team is called, of the NHL, are so popular it's been said that the crime rate goes down on game nights as people listen to the radio or watch it on TV in either French or English. A limited number of seats go on sale the first of the month for games during that month; call ☎ 514-790-1245. Otherwise seats are available through the legions of scalpers who begin lingering around the rink about noon on game days. Cost will depend on the opposition and importance of the game but all will be well above the list prices which range from $16 for a seat high in the rafters to $75 rink side. The season is from October to May.

The good, major league baseball team, the Montreal Expos of the National League, has a hard time drawing fans out to the Olympic Stadium. If you want to catch a game, tickets are available (☎ 514-790-1245) through the season from April to September starting at just $6. The stadium is at 4549 Avenue Pierre de Coubertin in Olympic Park.

The once defunct football team of the teetering Canadian Football League (CFL) is back as the Alouettes with games at the McGill University stadium (☎ 514-254-2400). The season runs from the end of June to November.

The National Film Board of Canada

The National Film Board of Canada (NFB) has a formidable reputation as a cultural organisation responsible for pioneering film-making in all its aspects. The board was established by the Canadian government in 1939 to make and distribute films that convey the country's social and cultural realities to both Canadian and international audiences. Over the years it has been the recipient of more than 3500 awards, including 10 Oscars.

The founder of the organisation, documentary film-maker John Grierson, wanted the NFB to become the 'eyes of Canada'. Today it remains the only public producer in the world with the equipment and infrastructure to produce films from script to screen. Films produced by the board are available to the public through a network of offices and libraries across Canada and in major cities around the world. Many are now available to rent on video.

The first genres the NFB excelled in were animation and documentary. In the 1940s animator Norman McLaren joined the organisation and, almost overnight, the NFB achieved an international reputation for its innovative animated films. Researchers are now using the latest software programs to produce increasingly sophisticated computer-assisted animation techniques.

The NFB's research and development department has been responsible for an impressive number of important film-making breakthroughs. In 1964 the board's invention of the battery-operated 16mm camera and lightweight synchronous sound recorder helped it to become the world leader in cinéma vérité, a direct 'warts and all' approach to the documentary which allows crews to work with a minimum of intrusion.

Working in documentary, education, animation and narrative genres, the NFB produces films on nearly every topic imaginable. Subject matter ranges from Inuit hunting to living with cancer to experimental abstractions. The overriding principles are to stimulate debate, present current issues, develop creativity and technology and, of course, entertain. There are some 9000 titles in the current catalogue fulfilling that mandate.

In the mid-1960s the NFB established the French Production Branch to produce films about the French community of Canada. Claude Jutra's 1971 film *Mon Oncle Antoine* has twice been chosen by critics as the best Canadian feature ever made. One of the board's priorities has been to make film-making accessible to under-represented groups.

In 1974 Studio D became the world's first production studio dedicated to making films by, for and about women. Some excellent films have been produced by Studio D, including Sherr Klein's *Not a Love Story: A Film About Pornography*, Terre Nash's *If You Love This Planet* (a documentary short which won an Oscar in 1983), Cynthia Scott's *The Company of Strangers* and Esther Valiquette's *Le Singe Bleu (A Measure of Your Passage)*. In 1990 Studio D created a production unit for Native Indian women, and in 1991 Studio One was established to give voice to Native Indian film-makers in general.

The head office of the NFB is in Ottawa and the operational headquarters are in Montreal. NFB films and videos can be ordered from anywhere in Canada on ☎ 800-267-7710. The Web site, at www.nfb.ca, contains a wealth of information. You can scan past titles, see what's in production and learn which films have been selected for inclusion at festivals around the world.

Horse-racing (with betting) can be seen at the Hippodrome (☎ 514-739-2741) at 7440 Boulevard Décarie most days but call for a schedule.

Shopping

The Canadian Guild of Crafts (☎ 514-849-6091) at 2025 Rue Peel, has a small and rather expensive collection of the work of

Quebec artisans and other Canadiana, as well as Inuit prints and carvings. It's free to look around.

Galerie Yves Laroche (☎ 514-393-1999) at 4 Rue Saint Paul Est on the corner of Boulevard Saint Laurent, has a fine varied collection of stone carvings. You can buy as well as look, but the pieces here are real collectibles and are not cheap.

Smokers, particularly Americans, could look for Cuban cigars – signs are seen in store windows frequently around town.

Getting There & Away

Air There are two airports. Fortunately, very convenient Dorval, 20km west of the centre of town, is used for almost all passenger flights. White elephant Mirabel airport, over 50km north-west of downtown, handles charters and cargo. Dorval has a user fee of $10 to finance upgrades. Expect to pay this upon departure.

A Canadian Airlines (☎ 514-847-2211) one-way fare to Halifax is $490 and to Winnipeg $720 before taxes. Air Canada (☎ 514-393-3333) has virtually the same prices.

Cheap tickets to Florida, Mexico and parts of the Caribbean are often available out of Montreal.

Bus The bus station (☎ 514-842-2281) is central at 505 Boulevard de Maisonneuve Est on the corner of Rue Berri, near Rue Saint Denis. It's right beside the Berri-UQAM Métro stop. The station serves Voyageur lines, Orléans Express, Trentway Wager and smaller Quebec regional bus companies.

Greyhound USA (☎ 514-287-1580) also uses the station. When dealing with Greyhound for US destinations, make sure you know which currency is being discussed.

Reservations are not required on any route but you should show up 45 minutes before departure to buy the ticket.

Buses for Ottawa leave every hour through the day for $28 and to Toronto (about seven services daily) for $74. On both these routes there are sometimes cheaper return fares offered, so ask.

Orléans Express operates most buses in

Quebec from Montreal eastwards. It has direct express runs to Quebec City and other slower trips which stop at smaller places along the way. Either way, a ticket is $37. Ask about possible return specials.

In winter, ask about companies providing ski-shuttle day trips to the Laurentians for either downhill or cross-country. One to try is Limocar (☎ 450-435-8899) with well priced trips to Mont Gabriel (with connections to nearby resorts) from the main bus station. Tickets include lift passes.

Train There are two train stations in the central area. You can walk underground from one to the other in 10 minutes. The main one, Central Station, below the Queen Elizabeth Hotel on the corner of Boulevard René Lévesque and Rue Mansfield, gets all VIA Rail (☎ 514-989-2626) passengers. Use the Bonaventure Métro station.

There are four trains a day to Ottawa and six trains a day to Toronto, starting at 6.45 am, less on weekends. Fares are: Ottawa $38, Toronto $90, and Quebec City $48 plus GST.

For information about US destinations call Amtrak (☎ 1-800-872-7245). Amtrak fares to New York vary depending on the month, day and how busy the route is. Cost varies from $US49 to $65 one way, with cheap returns available. Booking well ahead increases the chance of a low price. Remember when inquiring about fares to US destinations to check whether prices are being given in US dollars. They probably are.

Windsor Station on the corner of Rue Peel and Rue de la Gauchetière, a few blocks west from Central Station, is used for local commuter trains only. Use the same Métro stop.

Car The Trans Canada Hwy runs right through the city and Hwy 15 leads south to US 87 heading for New York. Hwy 401 joins Montreal to Toronto and beyond westward.

Car Rental Budget (☎ 514-866-7675) has offices around town, including one in Central Station downtown, and charges $40 per day with 200km free, 15¢ per kilometre over that for its economy cars. Tax is extra.

Tilden (☎ 514-878-2771), 1200 Rue Stanley, has similar rates.

For cheaper rates try Via Route (☎ 514-871-1166) at 1255 Rue Mackay, with vans as well as cars. Getting a small group together could be quite economical.

There are many other companies and outlets all over town and at both airports. Prices tend not to vary a heck of a lot but differences can be found among the weekend specials and other multiple-day offers.

Car Sharing & Alternative Buses Allo Stop (☎ 514-985-3032) at 4317 Rue Saint Denis is an agency that gets drivers and passengers together. Call a day ahead and tell it where you want to go or, if you're a driver, where you're going. Prices are considerably less than a bus ticket; it's $15 to Quebec City, for example. Allo Stop also goes to Toronto, New York and other cities. Passengers must pay a $6 membership fee, drivers slightly more. Those with cars can have some of their expenses paid by taking along passengers. Allo Stop has offices in Toronto, Ottawa, Quebec City and many other points around Quebec. This is an agency really worth checking.

Moose Travel (☎ 1-888-816-6673) operates a hostel/adventure/activity hop-on, hop-off bus service. One route leaves Montreal, goes to Quebec City, Tadoussac and loops back through the Laurentians. Another connects to Ottawa and Ontario destinations. See the introductory Getting Around chapter and under Toronto in the Ontario chapter for more details. Montreal hostels also have information.

Getting Around
To/From the Airport The cheapest and quickest way to Dorval airport is to take the Métro to Lionel-Groulx. Transfer to the No 211 bus outside. The first stop, about 15 to 25 minutes later, is the Dorval Bus Transfer Station. Switch here, with free transfer, to any No 204 bus which runs into the airport.

An alternative, at the same price but slower unless you are near one of these bus lines, is to take the Métro to Crémazie, then

catch bus No 100 west towards the airport and ask the driver to let you off to catch bus No 209, which will take you right in. The total cost for either of these routes is $1.75.

From the airport, catch the 204 East (Est) to the Dorval Bus Transfer Station and switch to the 211 Est. This will take you to the Métro. There is a maximum wait time of half an hour between buses, though most of the day waiting time will be much less. Bus Nos 204 and 211 run from 5 am to 1 am.

Autocar Connaisseur (☎ 514-934-1222) runs buses between Dorval and downtown luxury hotels for $9.50 one way and $17 return, taking a little under half an hour. They also go between Mirabel airport and downtown for $11 one way and $20 return. The latter trips take about 45 minutes.

Buses also connect the two airports and Dorval to the main bus station. A taxi from downtown to Dorval is roughly $25, from downtown to Mirabel a hefty $60.

Bus & Métro The city has a fairly widespread, convenient bus-Métro system (☎ 514-288-6287). The Métro is the name for the city's underground train system which runs on rubber tyres and is safe, clean, fast and quiet. The Métro runs until 1 am and some buses run even later. One ticket can get you anywhere in the city as it entitles you to a transfer to any connecting bus or subway train. On the buses get a transfer from the driver, and on the Métro from the machines past the turnstiles. A strip of six tickets is $8 or single tickets cost $1.85 each. Buses take tickets, transfers, or correct cash only.

Tourists can purchase day passes for $5 or three-day passes for $12.

If you are in town for a calendar month and plan to use public transit frequently consider the monthly pass. It can be shared as no picture is required.

Métro routes are shown on the tourist map and stops are indicated above ground by large blue signs with a white arrow pointing down. Berri-UQAM is the main intersecting station.

Car In town, most streets are one way and drivers are aggressive. Watch the action at

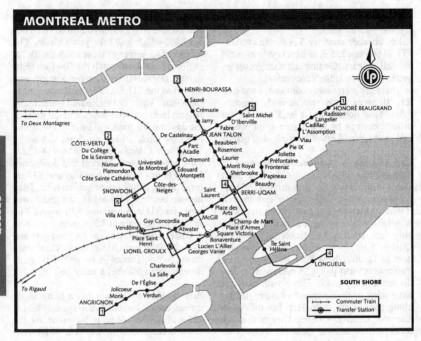

MONTREAL METRO

To Deux Montagnes

HENRI-BOURASSA
Sauvé
Crémazie
Jarry
Saint Michel
D'Iberville
De Castelnau
Fabre
JEAN TALON
CÔTE-VERTU
Du Collège
De la Savane
Parc
Acadie
Beaubien
Rosemont
Namur
Plamondon
Côte Sainte Catherine
Université
de Montreal
Outremont
Laurier
Mont Royal
Sherbrooke
Edouard
Montpetit
SNOWDON
Côte-des-
Neiges
Saint
Laurent
BERRI-UQAM
Villa Maria
Place des
Arts
Peel
McGill
Vendôme
Guy Concordia
Atwater
Champ de Mars
Place d'Armes
Square Victoria
Bonaventure
Place Saint
Henri
LIONEL GROULX
Lucien L'Allier
Georges Vanier
Île Saint
Hélène
Charlevoix
La Salle
De l'Église
To Rigaud
Jolicoeur
Monk
Verdun
ANGRIGNON
SOUTH SHORE
LONGUEUIL

HONORÉ BEAUGRAND
Radisson
Langelier
Cadillac
L'Assomption
Viau
Pie IX
Joliette
Préfontaine
Frontenac
Papineau
Beaudry

Commuter Train
Transfer Station

yellow lights. Driving the 'Metropolitan' (the Trans Canada Hwy, the No 40, through central Montreal) is an especially white-knuckle-inducing experience. Good luck. Don't drive to Old Montreal – the streets are narrow and busy and there is little parking. Pedestrians are fair game; cross walks mean little to Montreal drivers.

Bicycle For rentals or repairs, Vélo Aventure (☎ 514-847-0666) on Quai King Edward at the Old Port is recommended. It's open every day from May to October and has good bikes in good condition. Rollerblades (in-line skates) with all the padding necessary for novices are also offered. Rentals are by the hour or full-day and there are kids and family rates. Child trailers are available. Perhaps best of all, there is a major bike path going for miles from right at the door of the shop. Maps of

the city's bicycle paths, one of which circles the entire island, are available from Vélo.

A second rental outlet is Quadricycle (☎ 514-849-9953) at Quai Jacques Cartier.

Bicycles can be taken on the Métro in the last two carriages of the train and on the water shuttles over to Park des Îles.

Calèche These horse-drawn carriages, seen mainly around Square Dorchester, Old Montreal or up on the mountain, charge about $50 an hour with a four-person maximum. In winter, sleighs are used for trips up and around Mont Royal.

Around Montreal

OKA
This is a small town about 60km west of Montreal, where the Ottawa River meets the

St Lawrence River. It's on the north mainland shore, north of Dorion on the edge of Lac des Deux Montagnes which is really a bulge in the river. The place is well known for the Trappist monastery dating from the 1880s and the cheeses it produces. Cheese-producing has been largely taken over by business people and the monastery of 70 monks has been opened to visitors. There are religious artworks, a mountain with the Stages of the Cross and several old stone buildings. The chapel, gardens and boutique are all closed Sunday. A large park edges the waterfront with a popular sandy beach.

Oka became internationally known late in 1990 as the site of a major confrontation between Mohawk people and the federal and provincial governments. At first a local land squabble, this issue soon came to represent all the continuing problems such as land claims and self-government which Native Indians across the country would like to see properly resolved.

ROUGE RIVER

Not far north-west of Montreal near the Ontario border, is the well known Rouge, considered one of the best whitewater rivers in North America. Several companies offer day or weekend trips which most people reckon are a lot of fun. One to try is New World River Expeditions (☎ 1-800-361-5033) based in Calumet, Quebec (near Hawkesbury, Ontario) on the river. It's about an hour's drive from Montreal. The basic four or five hour-trip, offered April to October, is $80 and be prepared to go overboard. It also has two to five-day adventures. Facilities include camping, a lodge, pool, bar etc so you're not roughing it in the bush the whole time.

For more rafting, see Around Ottawa-Hull later.

SUCRERIE DE LA MONTAGNE

Situated in a maple forest, the sucrerie (☎ 450-451-0831), open all year, depicts a 1900s-era Quebec sugar shack where sap is converted to maple syrup and sugar. A visit includes a tour and explanation of the process, a meal and folk music. The lunch

package is $30, the dinner $40. It's an interesting, popular place although the focus is on the restaurant.

To get to the site, 70km west from downtown without a car, take the train to Rigaud and then it's about a $12 taxi ride. If driving take Hwy 40 west to 300 Rang Saint-Georges, Rigaud.

There are many seasonal sugar shacks through the Laurentians and Eastern Townships area tourist offices can steer you to one.

THE LAURENTIANS (LAURENTIDES)

Between 80km and 150km north of Montreal, this section of the ancient Laurentian Shield is a mountainous and rolling lake-sprinkled playground. The land proved a failure for lumber and mining, but when skiing caught on, so did the area as a resort-land. The district today is used not only for the best in eastern skiing but for camping, fishing and swimming in summer. Cycling is very popular with good distance trails and rougher mountain biking in many areas. The many picturesque French towns dominated by their church spires and the good scenery make it popular for just lazing and relaxing as well. Plentiful accommodation and restaurants provide a wide range of services, from elegant inns with fine dining rooms to modest motels.

The Autoroute Laurentienne, also known as Hwy 15, is the fastest route north from Montreal and is the way the buses go. The old Hwy 117 north is slower but more pleasant. A second major route goes northeast of Montreal to Joliette and then smaller roads continue farther north.

The better known towns and resorts are all clustered near the highways. Cottage country spreads out a little farther east and west. In general terms, the busy area ends at Mont Tremblant Provincial Park. The smaller villages on the upper areas of Hwy 117 are quiet and typically 'Laurentian'.

To find less-developed areas or to camp, you pretty much have to head for the big parks, as most of the region is privately owned. Outside the parks, campgrounds are generally privately owned too, and tend to be small and busy. Motels are next up the

economic scale; the lodges are generally (but not always) quite pricey.

The busiest times in the Laurentians are July, August, around Christmas, February and March. At other times, prices tend to be reduced, like the crowds. Autumn is a good season to visit, the hills are colourful and the cooler air is ideal for walking. The whole area (in all seasons) has a festive, relaxed atmosphere.

The area is served by Limocar Laurentides buses which leave from Montreal's main terminus. Stops are made in most main towns. In ski season, special buses operate to various hills; see under bus in Montreal's Getting There & Away section earlier in this chapter.

The P'Tit Train du Nord Linear Park is a 200km bicycle/walking/snowmobile trail stretching along an old rail line from Saint Jerome beyond Tremblant (about halfway) north to Mont Laurier. Many of the train stations have been restored. Tourist offices have maps and lists of the services along the route. Rentals are available in some towns and bus services transport bikes and riders to various points along the way. For more information and route planning, call the Laurentians tourist centre on ☎ 1-800-561-6673.

Year-round tourist information offices with accommodation assistance can be found in the villages of Saint Sauveur des Monts, Sainte Adèle, Sainte Agathe, Saint Jovite and at Mont Tremblant Village.

Saint Sauveur des Monts

Known simply as Saint Sauveur, this first stop-off on the way north, about 60km from Montreal, is a small pleasant resort town with four nearby ski hills. Summer or winter, day or night, the main street, Rue Principale, with its restaurants, cafés, bars and shops is busy. Stop in at *Boulangerie Page*, the bakery beside the church on Avenue de l'Eglise. Rue Saint Sauveur has B&B, hotel and motel accommodation. The aquatic park complex is a summer family attraction. **Morin Heights**, 10km north, is a tiny, mainly English village.

Mont Rolland

Mont Rolland is a recreation centre based at Mont Gabriel. There's excellent skiing in winter and in summer the mountain turns into a huge slide complex, a trend which many of the area's resorts have embraced.

The Rolland Paper Company, one of the oldest and most important paper makers in the country, is based here.

The *Auberge Mont Gabriel* on top of the mountain is one of the larger, more expensive lodges in the Laurentians.

Sainte Adèle

Sainte Adèle is perhaps the least attractive Laurentian town. The modern-looking centre has the Musée Village de Séraphin, a small re-created pioneer village. There is also a water slide complex.

Sainte Agathe des Monts

With about 6000 people, Sainte Agathe is the largest town in the Laurentians and a busy resort centre.

With numerous bars, cafés and restaurants, as well as shops for replenishing supplies, there is always plenty of activity yet the atmosphere is amiable.

At the edge of Lac des Sables, right in town, there is room for a picnic, and cruises of the lake depart from the wharf. Around the lake are busy sandy beaches, although admission is $5. There is camping at one of them, Plage Majer, south of town. Just 1km north of town, Village du Mont Castor is a modern townhouse development created in late 19th/early 20th century Quebécois style using full-size logs. At the end of July, watch for the annual music and dance festival.

Hwy 15 ends here and Hwy 117 continues north to Tremblant.

Places to Stay B&Bs, inns *(auberges)* and motels all tend to be quite busy, especially on weekends, so planning ahead is advisable. Very close to the centre by the lake is the B&B *La Villa Verra (☎ 819-326-0513, 246 Saint Venant)* with doubles at $70 and a good dining room. South of town are

Skiing & Snowboarding in the Laurentians

The Laurentians are without doubt one of the prime skiing regions in the country. The region has the hills, the snow, the scenery, the experience and, perhaps most of all, a relaxed, friendly sporting atmosphere that adds immeasurably to a day at the slopes.

With over 20 ski centres within 2½ hours of Montreal offering runs for the novice and the expert, the alpine skiing is convenient and varied enough to offer something for everyone. Over one-quarter of the 350 ski runs are now lit for night skiing – a wonderful experience, and often less busy than the trails through the day.

In a good winter skiing can be enjoyed for four months, with many lodges making artificial snow to complement what the sky provides. Although renowned for its downhill slopes, the region offers plenty of good cross-country skiing as well and this can be tried and enjoyed for considerably less money. Equipment can be rented at a couple of sport shops around Montreal (try the Yellow Pages telephone book or the tourist office) and, more commonly, at the ski centres up north. Arrive early in the day for the best selection and help in getting fitted out. Renting the whole package – boots, skis and poles – runs to about $25 for a full day, which isn't bad at all because the equipment tends to be good.

Tow prices vary from centre to centre but range from $25 to $44 a day, with most averaging about $30. Half-day tickets are sold at many resorts and a separate night-ski pass is available for less money. Children's tickets are also offered. Prices are lower during the week than at weekends and all prices rise for the period around Christmas and New Year.

Less than an hour from Montreal there are some fine places such as Saint Sauveur des Monts and, for beginners or the rusty, Olympia has a good selection of wide, easy runs. Go for it!

As a rough guide, the farther you go from Montreal, the more challenging the hills can become, although even resorts with deadly runs also offer some for novice or intermediate skiers so you don't have to get in over your head.

The grandaddy of them all is Mont Tremblant with the highest vertical drop in the Laurentians at 650m. The Mont Tremblant and Gray Rocks ski centres are huge, offering multiple runs. Travel down one side of the mountain in the morning and then, when the sun shifts, ski down the other side. The resort facilities here rival those of the Rockies.

The Mont Tremblant area has some 150km of mechanically set cross-country trails around the provincial park, Saint Jovite, and around the village of Mont Tremblant itself. Many of the trails even farther south, say at Mont Rolland, are interconnected and some have warming huts at intervals along the way.

some relatively modest motels such as the **Motel Clair Mont** (☎ 819-326-1444, 1591 Rue Principale) at $65 a double.

Val David

Close to Sainte Agathe but to the east off Hwy 15, Val David is a considerably smaller town that's become an arts and crafts centre. Studios and workshops can be visited, and stores sell a variety of handicrafts. A bike trail goes through town.

Places to Stay *Le Chalet Beaumont* (☎ 819-322-1972, 1451 Rue Beaumont) is an inn/HI hostel perched on a hill with great views. Hostel beds go from $15 and private rooms are about $50 for two. There are also family rooms. All meals are available or there is self-cooking. If you call ahead, you may be able to get picked up from the bus from Montreal and taken to the hostel. The village also has several B&Bs and motels.

QUEBEC

Saint Faustin/Lac Carré

Saint Faustin with a population of about 1400 is the base for Mont Blanc. In summer, the large Centre Educatif, a nature interpretive centre at Lac du Cordon with 35km of walking and hiking trails, can be visited. Guided walks are given detailing flora and fauna of the area and there is canoeing and camping. Admission is charged.

There is a maple-sugar shack here open in April and May where the production can be seen and the results sampled. Cabane à Sucre Millette (☎ 819-688-2101) is at 1357 Rue Saint Faustin.

The Pisciculture, a trout hatchery in a wooded setting just off Lac Carré at 747 Chemin de la Pisciculture, can also be visited. The fish raised here are used to restock the rivers and lakes of the Laurentians. Nearby, on the other side of small Lac Carré, there's a free public beach. North of town, roads lead past Lac Supérieur into Mont Tremblant Park.

Saint Jovite

With 4000 people, Saint Jovite is the last major town in the region and acts as a crossroad and supply centre for trips into the Mont Tremblant area with its many lakes and skiing. It's not particularly inviting but Rue Ouimet has numerous cafés and restaurants. The busy area incorporating traditional architecture is known as the Petit Hameau district. The Musée de la Faune at 635 Rue Limoges has a collection of stuffed indigenous animals.

Mont Tremblant

North of Saint Jovite, 146km from Montreal, is Tremblant – a three-part resort and park district which marks the northernmost point of the easily accessible Laurentian destinations.

Tremblant Village is the older, 'real' section with restaurants, accommodation, stores etc. About 4km to the east is Mont Tremblant itself. The mountain, with its 650m vertical drop, is the highest peak in the Laurentians. With over 60 runs it's the region's major ski centre. Intrawest, the company that developed Whistler in British Columbia into a world-class facility, has been totally overhauling the site since 1992. Millions of dollars have resulted in state-of-the-art ski facilities as well as golf courses, water sports, and a range of activities from cycling to tennis. A chair lift runs to the mountain peak in summer and winter. It's a major four-season resort with development continuing. The makeover has included construction of a traditional-look alpine township at the foot of the mountain that somewhat resembles an amusement park without rides. It includes hotels, condos, bars, and restaurants all in a pedestrian-only setting alongside pretty Lac Tremblant. It's known simply as Tremblant or 'the resort.'

To the east again is Mont Tremblant Provincial Park, a huge and lovely area of lakes and mountains with some facilities but much wilderness.

The tourist office (☎ 819-425-2434) is a few kilometres south of the village on the corner of Rue Principale and Montée Ryan. It's open daily all year. There are smaller offices at the resort village.

In Mont Tremblant Village, Chemin Principal is the main street, with several places for a bite or a drink. There's a beach at Lac Mercier at the western edge of the village; it costs $2 (waived if you're at the hostel). Bicycles and blades can be rented and a 10km blading/cycling path goes through town and over to the resort.

There are many trails (bike or foot) around Mont Tremblant and an excellent day can be had hiking around the peak; get a free map at the tourist office. The chair lift is $12 with discounts for hostellers. Tour boats cruise larger Lac Tremblant. When you're done, the resort village has a pretty fair brew pub, La Diable, among its numerous eateries.

In July, listen for the International Blues Festival. Aside from Mont Tremblant with the most ski runs and higher costs, there is Gray Rocks to the south of the lake. North of Tremblant, Labelle is a jumping off point for two undeveloped wildlife reserves as well as the western section of Tremblant Park.

Places to Stay Most accommodation is pricey, particularly at the resort complex. The new HI *Tremblant International Hostel* (☎ 819-425-6008, tremblant@hostelling montreal.com, www.hostellingmontreal.com /tremblant) has become an instant success and is often booked out. It's 1km from the village centre and 3km from the mountain on the main road. There are 80 beds beginning at $17.50 for the dorms (bed sheets included) and up to $40 for doubles. Breakfast costs $4.60, and there's a bar with a fireplace and pool table. If you stay here and at the hostel in Montreal there's a free shuttle bus between them in the 'peak' season – call the hostel for details.

Several B&Bs provide a somewhat reasonable choice. In the middle of the village is *Maison des Lauriers* (☎ 819-429-6006, 1926 Rue Principale) at $50/60 with breakfast. Closer to the lake and mountain is *Le Lupin* (☎ 819-425-5474, 127 Rue Pinoteau) in a log house. The simple rooms without private bath are $66 a double with full breakfast.

The tourist office can help locate a place, or consider staying at one of the nearby villages. Call ☎ 1-800-567-6760, a central reservation service which covers all budget categories.

Auberge Caribou in Lac Superior is moderately priced. With four people, one of the condos can be good value. In winter, the ski-package deals may be most economical but not at Christmas.

For camping you must get to Tremblant Park or there are alternatives in Saint Jovite, which is closer.

Getting There & Away Limocar buses run from Montreal to Saint Jovite Thursday to Saturday. From there, it is about a 10 minute drive to Tremblant but there is no public transport. See under hostel for shuttle information. Also ask about a shuttle bus which may soon link the village to the new resort/mountain area.

Mont Tremblant Provincial Park
The park is about 25km from Mont Tremblant. Opened as early as 1894, it's a huge

area – over 1500 sq km – of lakes, rivers, hills and woods which is divided into three sectors. Features include hiking and biking trails, canoe routes and wildlife. There are many campgrounds in the park, some with amenities but most are basic.

The most developed area is the Diable sector (closest to Mont Tremblant), north of Lac Superior, particularly around beautiful Lac Monroe. Roads are paved and some of the campgrounds have showers. At the lake, there is an information centre (☎ 819-688-2281) and canoes can be rented. There are numerous trails in the vicinity including a 30 minute walk to Diable Falls. Others cover many kilometres providing fine valley views.

Farther east, the Pimbina sector (☎ 819-424-2954) north of Saint Donat also has an information centre, rentals and campgrounds with some amenities. There is swimming at Lac Provost and hiking and biking trails nearby.

The wilder interior and eastern sections are accessible by unsurfaced roads some of which are rough old logging routes. Some camp sites are accessible only by foot or canoe. The more off-the-track areas abound in wildlife including bear and moose. With some effort, it's possible to have whole lakes to yourself, except for the wolves whose howls you hear at night. By late August, nights are cold.

Windigo Aventure (☎ 1-888-400-6161) offers one-day canoe trips from Tremblant Village or Montreal. It can be contacted through the hostels.

Saint Donat
North-east of Sainte Agathe, this little lakeside town is a supply centre for Mont Tremblant Park, which lies just to the north.

There are beaches on **Lac Archambault** and, in summer, 90-minute cruises around the lake.

Accommodation of all types can be found in and around town and is less expensive than in the towns along Hwy 117 to the west. Bars and cafés along the main streets are lively at night.

LANAUDIÈRE

Lanaudière refers to the region north-east of Montreal and, though it is essentially still 'up north' or 'the Laurentians', it has cultivated its own identity. Though still popular, without the quality ski hills and fewer large towns it is a less visited region. There are plenty of parks with walking trails over mountains and along rivers to enjoy. And food and lodging is noticeably cheaper than in the places farther west along the Autoroute. For any specific area information call the Lanaudière tourist office on ☎ 1-800-363-2788.

There is a lot of maple-syrup production in the area. In spring, many farmers allow visitors to the sugar shacks for a look-see and a taste. Sugar shacks can be found in Saint Esprit and Saint Jacques. Not to rush you, but it's said that, in time, acid rain could wipe out this traditional industry.

Joliette

Joliette is a principal town and centre for the local tobacco-growing industry. You may notice that in some areas the farmland is divided into long strips. This traditional way of dividing up the land is not seen outside Quebec.

The Art Museum, 145 Rue Wilfred Corbeil, is a major regional institution. Joliette is the site of the annual Festival International de Lanaudière, a major international, classical-music festival, which draws crowds of thousands to the 50 or so concerts which take place throughout the summer. Many events are held at the outdoor amphitheatre which has a capacity of 10,000.

At Parc des Chutes Monte à Peine (☎ 450-883-2245) along the Assomption River, there are waterfalls, walking trails and picnic areas. For directions to access points call the park or drop into the downtown tourist office.

Rawdon

Lakeside Rawdon has long been a local beauty spot. Trails and observation points wind along the central Ouareau River park with **Dorwin Falls**; an admission fee is charged. Nearby, there are rapids, other falls on the Rouge River and hilly, wooded areas

good for walking. Ask at the tourist office on 1st Ave.

Off 8th Avenue downtown is the public beach also requiring a ticket. Moore Canadiana Village is a re-created 1800s town complete with workers in costume. Most of the buildings are authentic (the schoolhouse is from 1835). Other attractions include a museum and art gallery.

Berthierville

To the east of Joliette on the St Lawrence River is Berthierville, the birthplace of Gilles Villeneuve, the Formula 1 racing car driver. A museum details his exciting career on the Grand Prix circuit.

EASTERN TOWNSHIPS (L'ESTRIE)

The Eastern Townships area (Les Cantons de l'Est), the 'Garden of Quebec', generally known as L'Estrie by the French, extends from Granby to the New Hampshire border. The area is appreciated for its rolling hills, green farmland, woods and lakes – an extension of the US Appalachian region. The area has long been based on its fertile soil and resources but high-tech industries are increasingly important.

It's a popular resort area year-round. In spring, 'sugaring off' – the tapping of trees for maple syrup, and then boiling and preparing it – takes place throughout the region. Summer brings fishing and swimming in the numerous lakes. During autumn, a good time to visit, colours are beautiful as the leaves change, and apple harvesting takes place with the attendant cider production. Skiing is a major winter activity with centres at Mont Orford and Sutton.

L'Estrie abounds in cottages and chalets both private and commercial, and inns. The region also has a reputation for its many fine but expensive dining rooms.

The Eastern Townships have a long history and, as evidenced by the place names, were predominantly English until the 1970s. Though originally occupied by the Abenakis Indians much of the region was first developed by Loyalists fleeing the USA after the revolution of 1776. Later in

the next century many Irish people arrived. Soon after, French settlers arrived to help with the expanding economy.

Many of the towns and villages are popular with antique-hunters; small craft shops and galleries line many a main street. Another lure is the area's growing reputation for its spas and health centres where the stressed-out can be treated like Hollywood stars for a couple of days. Around the countryside on the smaller roads keep an eye out for the remaining wooden covered bridges and the round barns.

There is a B&B program in the region (the tourist office will have the latest guide) and dozens of campgrounds. This region of the province is the only one where B&Bs make up the bulk of the accommodation but prices are not low. The more historic and deluxe choices offer supreme grace but prices rise accordingly.

The main L'Estrie tourist office (☎ 1-800-263-1068) is on the Autoroute (Hwy 10) south from Montreal at exit 68. It's open daily all year. Other offices can be found in Magog, Granby and Sherbrooke.

L'Estrie is one of the good cycling regions in the province and rentals are available in Magog, Orford, North Hatley and other places. Both cycling and B&B maps are for sale at the regional tourist offices. One major cycling trail begins at Granby and runs to Waterloo and there are other established routes. There is also some good hiking including a 140km long-distance trail network between Kingsbury and Mont Sutton. The district also produces some wines and most notably, mead, an ancient nectar made from fermented honey. A self-guided wine tour can be followed through the region.

Granby

This town is known far and wide for its zoo. It seems everybody in Quebec knows of it, even if they haven't seen it. All will say it's been there forever. Feature exhibits include the insectarium containing 100,000 little creatures, the reptile displays and a cave with nocturnal animals. It's a major zoo with 1000 animals and admission to match. An adult

Maple Syrup

Liquid, golden maple syrup is a traditional, all natural taste sensation. Quebec is the world's largest producer and Estrie, with its abundance of sugar-maple forests, has long been the centre of production.

It is believed the Native Indians, who had a spring date known as the sugar-making moon, passed their knowledge onto early pioneers. Production techniques vary but essentially in spring, when the sap begins to run, the trees are tapped and buckets hung from them to collect, drop by drop, the nearly clear sap. The liquid is then collected into large kettles and boiled at the 'sugar shack' for days, driving off most of the water. As it thickens, the colour becomes more intense and the sugar content rises to around 90%. It is then cooled, graded and bottled.

It is most often spread over vanilla ice cream or pancakes. A further refining results in maple sugar. The Montreal or regional Estrie tourist offices will be able to tell you where you can see a demonstration of the process in early spring.

Acid rain has adversely affected the maple forests of Quebec and there is concern over the future of this small-farm industry. Maple syrup is also produced in eastern and central Ontario and in New Brunswick.

ticket is $15. There is also good birdwatching at Lac Boivin Interpretation Centre.

Granby is also well endowed with highly respected restaurants and hosts a gastronomical festival every autumn.

Lac Brome (Knowlton)

Nearby, south of Hwy 10 on Hwy 243, is the town of Lac Brome on the lake of the same name. Seven former English Loyalist villages, including Knowlton, make up the town of 5000. Many of the main street's Victorian buildings have been restored and it's a bit of a tourist centre with craft and gift shops etc.

The good local history museum at 130 Lakeside St includes a tearoom. A favourite meal in this area is Lac Brome duck and it shows up frequently on the better menus.

Sutton

Farther south, Sutton is synonymous with its important ski hill, one of the area's highest. In summer, there are hiking trails in Sutton Park. The area around Sutton and south of Cowansville near the village of Dunham supports Quebec's wine industry and some of the wineries can be visited. This is also an important apple-growing region where casual work can be found in autumn. A 10km cycling path runs south to the US border.

At the natural environment park there is the decidedly nonregional llama-breeding farm where rides on the haughty creatures can be attempted.

The Sutton area, again, is well known for its comfortable country inns and fine restaurants, many of which specialise in using local produce.

The *Willow House* (☎ 514-538-0035, 30 Rue Western) is a B&B priced below average at $40/55.

Near the village of Sutton Junction, Rural Route (RR) 4, sits what was once the farm of Madame Benoît, Canada's best known chef. She appeared on national TV for many years and wrote numerous cookbooks.

Lac Champlain

Although essentially a US lake which divides Vermont from New York State, Lac Champlain does protrude into Quebec as well. Steeped in history, the area is popular with Canadian and US holidaymakers.

The lake is good for swimming and fishing and, in places, is scenic. At Plattsburgh, New York there is a good and busy beach, where on any summer weekend you'll find plenty of Québecois. The short ferry trip across part of the lake is quite pleasant and worth taking if you're travelling through the area.

Magog

Magog, sitting right at the northern tip of large Lac Memphrémagog, is an attractive town with 15,000 residents. The main street, Rue Principale, has a resort flavour with its many cafés, bars, bistros and restaurants.

The tourist office, 55 Cabana St, can help provide information about the area. Daily boat cruises lasting a little over two hours are offered around the lake in summer.

There are numerous places to stay in and around town, but most are motels in the singles/doubles $65/75 range. The 10 B&Bs around town charge about the same. Hotels tend to be even more pricey.

Lac Memphrémagog

This is the largest and best known lake in the L'Estrie area. Most of the lakefront properties are privately owned. Halfway down the lake at Saint Benoît-du-Lac is a **Benedictine monastery** where monks continue the tradition of the ancient Gregorian chant. Visitors can attend services and there's a hostel for men and another nearby at a nunnery for women if you want to stay. One of Quebec's cheeses – L'Ermite, a blue – is made and sold here. Also try to taste the cider the monks make. Call ☎ 819-843-4080 for information.

Rock Island, at the southern end of the lake, is a busy border crossing.

Mont Orford Provincial Park

Just out of Magog, this is a good but relatively small park (though the largest in the Eastern Townships). Dominated by Mont Orford (792m), the park is a skiing centre in winter but fills up quickly with campers in summer as well. You can swim, walk the trails and the chair lift operates throughout summer.

Each summer, the Orford Art Centre presents the Jeunesses Musicales du Canada music and art festival. The HI *Auberge la Grand Fugue* (☎ 819-843-8595) hostel on the wooded grounds of the centre is open from April to November. It's a very comfortable, spacious hostel with some rustic cabins which makes a good base for exploring the park. Bicycles can be rented. Call for transportation details from Magog where there is a bus station.

North Hatley

Just east of Magog, North Hatley sits at the north end of Lac Massawippi, the shape of which can lead to the waters quickly turning very rough. The village was a popular second home for wealthy US citizens who enjoyed the scenery but even more the lack of Prohibition during the 1920s. Many of these huge old places are now inns and B&Bs. Try the Massawippi dark beer at the *Le Pilsen* pub. There's an English theatre in town along with galleries and antique and craft stores.

Sherbrooke

Sherbrooke is the principal commercial centre of the region and a fair-sized city in its own right. It's a bilingual town with several small museums, a wide selection of restaurants and a pleasant central core lying between the Magog and Saint François rivers.

The tourist office (☎ 819-821-1919) is at 3010 Rue King Ouest. The 18km walking and cycling path along the Magog River known as Réseau Riverain, makes an agreeable stroll. It begins at the edge of the Magog River in Blanchard Park.

The **Musée des Beaux Arts** at 241 Rue Dufferin is a sizable art gallery open every afternoon except Monday. The annual local autumn fair is a big event held each August.

On the outskirts at Bromptonville, is the **Shrine of Beauvoir**, dating from 1920, a site of religious pilgrimages with good views over the city and the surrounding area. In **Lennoxville**, there's Bishop's, an English university. Also in Lennoxville are a couple of cottage breweries and some antique and craft shops to browse through. On Hwy 216 toward Stokes is the **Centre d'Interpretation de l'Abeille**, the Honey Bee Interpretive Centre, a research facility open for visitors with displays about the little buzzers and the honey they produce. Other nearby attractions include the Magog River Gorge and the Frontenac Hydroelectric Plant. A bike trail runs to North Hatley.

Places to Stay & Eat Here, as elsewhere around the Eastern Townships, the motels, hotels and inns are not at all cheap. Alternative B&Bs can be found through the local tourist office although these, too, in Sherbrooke are not inexpensive. In summer, rooms are also available at low rates at the university. *Motel L' Ermitage (☎ 1-888-569-5551, 1888 Rue King Ouest)* charges from $55 a double.

Two well established four-star eateries are *Au Petit Sabot* and *l'Élite*. For simpler fare there is the *Marie Antoinette (333 Rue King Ouest)*.

Getting There & Away The bus station (☎ 819-569-3656) is at 20 Rue King Ouest. Various small companies run to Montreal, Trois Rivières, Magog, Granby and other regional towns.

South-west of town, several of the smaller area highways join Hwy 55 which leads south to Rock Island, a small town which is the major entry point into the USA, close to the states of New York, Vermont, and New Hampshire. During summer, particularly on weekends, there can be major waits (as in hours) at this border. This is especially true going into Quebec as vehicles are checked for how much stuff was bought in the USA and duty collected. If possible find a smaller entry point, perhaps south of Coaticook.

East of Sherbrooke

East of Sherbrooke the rolling farmlands and historic cultured towns and villages give way to a much rougher, less-populated region of primary resource industry and untouched woodlands. Asbestos and Thetford Mines are mining centres. In the middle of the district is the large Frontenac Recreation Park for access into an unspoiled region. South of there, the Lac Mégantic area is a mix of mountains and scenic farmlands. Route 212 provides a scenic drive.

The south-eastern area is bounded by New Hampshire and Maine, USA.

MONTREAL TO QUEBEC CITY

Leaving Montreal behind, travelling east on Hwy 138, you begin to get a sense of what small-town Quebec is like. Stone houses with light blue trim and tin roofs,

silver-spired churches, ubiquitous chip wagons called *cantines* and main streets with shops built right to the road, are some characteristics. The best section is from Trois Rivières onwards to the north-east.

A much quicker route is Hwy 40, a four-lane expressway that can get you from Montreal to Quebec City in 2½ to three hours. There are not many services along this route, so watch your fuel levels.

From Montreal there is also one fast and one slow route along the south shore to Quebec City and beyond. The old Hwy 132 edges along the river but isn't as nice as its north shore counterpart (Hwy 138). The Trans Canada (Hwy 30) here is the fastest way to Quebec City but is boring until beyond Quebec, where it runs a little closer to the water. At Trois Rivières, you can cross the river.

Saint Antoine de Padoue Church

This is on the north side of the St Lawrence River in Louiseville. It would be hard to miss, but take a peek inside too; it's one of Canada's grandest churches. Next door, the seasonal tourist booth is helpful.

Odanak

Almost directly across the river from Louiseville is Odanak, a small Abénakis Indian village settled in the early 1600s. A museum right on Hwy 226 outlines their history and culture. It's open all year but not weekends November to April. Perhaps of even more interest is the annual powwow held the first Sunday of July.

Trois Rivières

Trois Rivières, over 350 years old and the largest town between Quebec's two main cities, is a major pulp and paper centre. Don't bother looking – there aren't three rivers. The name refers to the way the Maurice River divides as it approaches the St Lawrence.

The attractive **old section** based around Rue Notre Dame and Rue des Forges with its reminders of a long history, is small but good for a stroll. Cafés and bars are abundant in this lively area. Rue des Ursulines and Rue Radisson are also main central streets. The St Lawrence River borders the southern edge of the area. There is a year-round tourist office (☎ 819-375-1122) at 1457 Rue Notre Dame. Listen for the Blues Festival in July.

On Rue des Ursulines are several old houses now open to the public as small free museums and examples of various architectural styles. The **Ursuline Museum** at No 734 displays materials relating to the Ursuline Order of nuns who were prominent in the town's development. The **Manoir Boucher-de-Niverville**, an historic house at 168 Rue Bonaventure near the corner of Rue Hart has changing displays on the city's past.

The **Cathedrale de l'Assomption** at 362 Rue Bonaventure, built in 1858, is the only Westminster-style church on the continent and is open daily.

The large, new, central **Folk Arts & Traditions Museum** (☎ 819-372-0406) on the corner of Rue Laviolette and Rue Hart has three major components. The pre-history collection has displays on fossils, early pottery discoveries and local Native Indians. Another has a vast collection of traditional Québecois arts and crafts including textiles, furniture and toys. Lastly, the old prison on the site, used for 164 years, tells its grim story.

Two-hour **cruises** along the river aboard the MS *Jacques Cartier* depart from the dock in **Parc Portuaire** at the foot of Boulevard des Forges in the centre of the old town. Also in the park is the **Pulp & Paper Industry Exhibition Centre** worth seeing at $3 but ask if English has been added to the displays. There are no tours of the paper plant itself.

Just north of town is the **Saint Maurice Ironworks National Historic Park** (☎ 819-378-5116) which was the first major iron-ore operation in North America. Built in 1730, the forge ran sporadically, with a number of owners, until 1883. An information centre details the historic significance and also explains how the iron was produced and used ($4).

There is an HI hostel in town, *Auberge la Flotille (☎ 819-378-8010, 497 Rue Radisson)* where dorms cost members/nonmembers $15/18 and there are double and family rooms. A good, inexpensive breakfast is

available but there is also a communal kitchen and laundry facilities. Good, small tours are organised to local areas of interest. The hostel is about 10 minutes walk from the bus station. Several motels can be found on Boulevard Royal.

The old train station at 1075 Rue Champflour is now used solely for buses (☎ 819-374-2944); there is no train service. Voyageur Colonial and Orléans Express go to Montreal and Quebec City, Autobus Messier goes to Sherbrooke and other towns of the Eastern Townships.

Beyond the city, Hwy 138 becomes hilly with gradients up to 17%. There are lots of camping places along the way as well as stands offering fruit, cider and wood sculpture – an old Quebec folk art. The old-style double wooden swings on many a front lawn are popular in Quebec but rarely seen in the rest of Canada.

Shawinigan & Grand Mère
These medium-sized towns farther north up the Saint Maurice River are rather bleak, with little to hold the visitor. Both are industrial and pulp and paper has long been the backbone of the area. Both also have generating plants. At Shawinigan, you can visit the falls and see La Cité de l'Energie, a complex outlining and explaining the local industrial history. Exhibits, multimedia shows and a viewing tower focus on electricity, smelting and paper-making. There's a lot to see but it's $12.

Grand Mère has tourist information, and between 5th and 6th Aves, the rock in the shape of an old lady's head from which the town's name was derived. Boat tours out onto the river are available. If you're heading for any of the northerly parks, stock up here because the food and supply selection doesn't get any better farther north.

Between here and La Mauricie National Park there isn't much in the way of accommodation, so you're pretty much stuck with one of the few ordinary motels in Grand Mère or Shawinigan. In both places a decent meal can be had before or after venturing out with the canoe.

Orléans Express bus line runs north from Montreal and Trois Rivières into both centres.

La Mauricie National Park
North from Trois Rivières, up past Shawinigan and Grand Mère, La Mauricie National Park (☎ 819-538-3232) is the only national park among the many large provincial wilderness parks north of the St Lawrence River. The park is 220km northeast of Montreal.

The park covers 550 sq km, straddling northern evergreen forests and the more southerly hardwoods of the St Lawrence River Valley. The low, rounded Laurentian Mountains, probably the world's oldest, are part of the Canadian Shield that covers much of the province. Between these hills are many small lakes and valleys. Within the park, mammals include moose, fox, bear and beaver.

The park is excellent for canoeing. There are maps of five canoe routes, ranging in length from 14 to 84km, for beginners to experts. Canoes can be rented for about $20 a day at Lake Wapizagonke, itself scenic with sandy beaches, steep rocky cliffs and waterfalls. There's also fishing for trout and bass.

Hiking trails, guided nature walks and an interpretive centre are offered. The Route des Falaises hiking trail is a good one with fine scenery. Some of the trails go along or offer views of the Saint Maurice River, which is one of the last rivers in the province where logging companies still float down their timber to the mills. Along the edges of the river you can see the strays that get collected periodically.

There are three serviced campgrounds at $23 a night without power but firewood is included.

Interior camping (individual camp sites in the park interior accessible only by foot or canoe) is $16 a night (without wood; additional cost with) and you need to pre-plan your route and register. On holiday weekends in summer, calling ahead to check on availability or reserving is a good idea. Supplies are available in Grand Mère, but the selection is minimal; it's better to bring

QUEBEC

most stuff with you. There is good cross-country skiing in winter.

Two adjacent provincial parks also offer wilderness camping: one is to the north, one to the west, but road access is more difficult.

The English language is seldom spoken here, so be prepared to communicate in French. Hostellers should ask in Trois Rivières about package trips.

La Domaine Joly de Lotbinière

This is a stately museum on the south shore of the St Lawrence River, between Lotbinière and Sainte Croix on the way to Quebec City from Trois Rivières. It was built for Henri Gustave Joly de Lotbinière (1849-1908), once the premier of Quebec. Not only is this one of the most impressive manors built during the seigneurial period of Quebec, it remains nearly as it was in the mid-1800s. It's now a government-operated museum containing period furniture and furnishings, and the grounds and outbuildings are a real treat in themselves. Lunch and afternoon teas are served.

Quebec City

Quebec City, rich in history, culture and beauty, is the heart of French Canada. If you're anywhere in the eastern part of the country, make the effort to visit.

The town is unique in several ways, most noticeably in its European appearance and atmosphere. It has the charm of an old-world city. Old Montreal has this feel to some degree, as does the French Quarter in New Orleans, but nowhere in North America is the picture as complete. The entire old section of town, essentially a living museum, has been designated a UN World Heritage Site. Quebec City is a year-round tourist mecca but gets crowded in July and August.

As the seat of the provincial government and Laval Université, this is the centre of Québecois consciousness, in both its moderate and extreme manifestations. Quebec City has been the Canadian hub of French nationalist thought for hundreds of years

and many of today's 'intellectuals' and politicians speaking for independence are based here.

Although many people are bilingual, the vast majority are French-speaking and 94% have French ancestors. But this is a tourist town, ranking with Banff and Victoria as one of the country's most visited destinations, so English is spoken around the attractions and in shops. Speak French if you can, however, as this will make you more friends and enable you to feel more comfortable away from the busiest areas. Exhibits at national sites are bilingual while, unfortunately, some provincial attractions are labelled only in French. Before buying any ticket, it is good to ask.

The city is also an important port, lying where the Saint Charles River (Rivière Saint Charles) meets the St Lawrence River. It sits on top of and around a cliff, a wonderful setting with views over the St Lawrence River and the town of Lévis (pronounced not as in jeans but 'lev-ee') across the river.

Much of Quebec City's past is still visible. Its many churches, old stone houses and narrow streets make it an architectural gem. The old part of Quebec remains the only walled city in North America.

The climate in Quebec City must be mentioned as this is a city with both summer and winter attractions. Summers are much like those of Montreal or southern Ontario, though generally not as hot and always a bit shorter. The real difference is in winter when it gets cold.

There may also be mountains of snow if you're visiting in winter, especially during January and February. You can't take enough sweaters. Life does go on, however – the locals don't hibernate.

History

One of the continent's earliest settlements, the site of Quebec City was an Iroquois Indian village called 'Stadacone' when the French explorer Jacques Cartier landed here in 1534. The name 'Quebec' is derived from an Algonkian Indian word meaning 'the

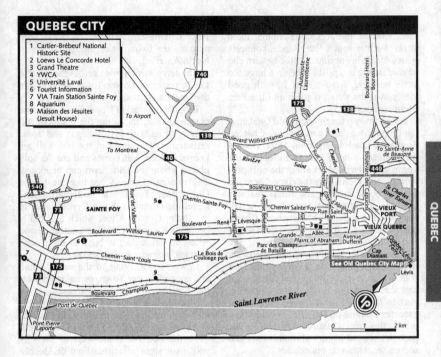

QUEBEC CITY

1 Cartier-Brébeuf National
   Historic Site
2 Loews Le Concorde Hotel
3 Grand Theatre
4 YWCA
5 Université Laval
6 Tourist Information
7 VIA Train Station Sainte Foy
8 Aquarium
9 Maison des Jésuites
   (Jesuit House)

QUEBEC

river narrows here'. Explorer Samuel de
Champlain founded the city for the French
in 1608 and built a fort in 1620.

The English successfully attacked in
1629, but Quebec was returned to the French
under a treaty and became the centre of New
France. Repeated English attacks followed.
In 1759 General Wolfe led the British to victory over Montcalm on the Plains of Abraham. This is one of North America's most
famous battles and virtually ended the conflict. In 1763 the Treaty of Paris gave Canada
to Britain. In 1775 the American revolutionaries had a go at capturing Quebec. They
were promptly turned back.

In 1791 the divisions of Upper Canada
(Ontario) and Lower Canada (Quebec and
the Atlantic Provinces) were created. In the
1800s Lower Canada became known as
Quebec and Quebec City was chosen as the
provincial capital.

Orientation

The city is surprisingly small, covering 93
sq km, with nearly all things of interest
packed into one compact corner. Since part
of the city sits on top of the cliffs of Cap
Diamant (Cape Diamond) and part lies
below, Quebec is divided into Upper Town
and Lower Town. The Citadelle, a fort and
famous landmark, stands on the highest
point of Cap Diamant overlooking the city.

Together these historic upper and lower
areas form the appealing Old City (Vieux
Québec). Just 10 sq km, this part of the city
contains nearly every essential attraction.
The best and maybe only way to orient
yourself in this area is to walk around. The
north-eastern end of Upper Town is still surrounded by a wall and is called Old Upper
Town. This area lies north of the Citadelle
on top of the plain. Rue Saint Jean is a main
street with many bars and restaurants.

Continuing south-east from Rue Saint Jean, Côte de la Fabrique is another main street. Farther south, Rue Buade, connects with Côte de la Fabrique. At the eastern end of Rue Buade is a post office, in a huge old stone building. Across from it, with good views over the water, is pleasant little Parc Montmorency.

A well known landmark in Old Quebec is the copper-topped, castle-style Château Frontenac hotel dating from 1892. Behind the château, a large boardwalk called the Terrasse Dufferin edges along the cliff providing good views over the river. There are always people strolling and often musicians and other street entertainers. Here you will also find the statue of Monsieur de Champlain who started it all. At the other (south) end is the wooden slide used during the winter carnival. From here, the boardwalk leads to the Promenade des Gouverneurs, a path which runs between the cliff's edge and the Citadelle. Beyond the Citadelle, outside the walls, is the huge park called Parc des Champs de Bataille. This is where the battles over Quebec took place. The park has several historical monuments and some sites within its boundaries.

For a look from higher up, go to the government building called Édifice Marie Guyart (☎ 418-644-9841) at 675 Boulevard René Lévesque. The observation deck with great views from the 31st floor is open from 10 am to 7 pm daily in summer (until 5 pm otherwise); it's $4. An alternative is the restaurant at the top of Loews Le Concorde Hôtel, 1225 Place Montcalm off Grande Allée, outside the wall.

Down below the Château Frontenac is Old Lower Town, the oldest section of the city, sitting mainly between the St Lawrence and St Charles rivers and hugging the cliffs of Cap Diamant.

The focal point of this small area, at the north-eastern edge of Old Quebec, is Place Royale. From here, you can walk (it's not hard, nor far) or take the funicular railway (elevator) for $1.50 one way to the top of the cliff of Upper Town. The funicular terminal in Lower Town is on Rue du Petit Champlain. Rue Sous le Cap and Rue du Petit Champlain, which are only 2.5m across, are two of the oldest streets in North America.

The ferry, which plies across the river to Lévis, docks in Lower Town not far from the Quebec Harbour.

Outside the wall in Upper Town are some places of note, including the National Assembly (Legislative Buildings) and some restaurants. The gates in the old wall are known in French as portes and are the only places where the Old Town can be exited. The two main streets heading west from Old Upper Town are Boulevard René Lévesque (formerly Saint Cyrille) and, to the south, Grande Allée, which eventually becomes Boulevard Wilfrid Laurier. Grand Allée, in particular, is busy at night with bars and numerous places to eat.

Lower Town, lying to the north, south and west of Upper Town, contains residential, business and industrial areas.

Much farther north in Lower Town are the highways leading east and west. In this section of the city you'll find some of the motels.

To the extreme south-west of the city you'll see signs for either Pont de Québec or Pont Pierre Laporte. Both bridges lead to the south shore.

Information

The main office is Centre Infotouriste (☎ 418-649-2608, ☎ 1-800-363-7777) at 12 Rue Sainte Anne on Place d'Armes, opposite the Château Frontenac hotel. The staff are bilingual and well supplied with maps and other information on the city and province. They can also help with booking accommodation. Most of the workers are friendly, considering the crowds they get at peak times. In summer it is open from 8.30 am to 7.30 pm daily; at other times it closes at 5 pm.

A second tourist office is at 215 Rue du Marché-Finlay (☎ 418-643-6631) in Lower Town. It's on a large square, Place de Paris, near the water, east of Place Royale and deals mainly with the Place Royale area.

Kiosk Frontenac, a booth on Terrasse Dufferin facing the Château Frontenac,

makes reservations for all city activities and is the starting point for some tours.

There is a post office outlet in the walled section of Upper Town, at the bottom of Rue Buade at No 3, opposite Parc Montmorency. The main post office is at 300 Rue Saint-Paul next to the train station.

Transchange at 43 Rue Buade is a central moneychanging office open daily.

Quebec has two French daily newspapers, *Le Soleil* and the *Journal du Quebec*.

Historic Quebec City Nearly every second building in Old Quebec is of some interest; a list of all the sites in this area would fill a book. For a more complete guide, ask at the tourist office for the walking-tour booklet. Following are some of the most significant sites in the old section as well as some outside the walls.

Historic Old Upper Town not only has most of the city's interesting accommodation and restaurants but also many of the important sites and attractions.

Old Upper Town

Citadelle The French started to build here in 1750 when bastions were constructed for storing gunpowder. The fort (☎ 418-694-2815) was completed by the British in 1820 after 30 years work and served as the eastern flank of the city's defence system. The irregularly sided structure sits on the plain over 100m up from the river at an appropriate vantage point.

Today the citadelle is the home base of Canada's Royal 22s (known in bastardised French as the Van Doos), a French regiment that developed quite a reputation through WWI, WWII and the Korean War. There is a museum outlining its history and a more general military museum containing documents, uniforms and models situated in a few different buildings including the old prison at the south-east end.

The entrance fee of $5 includes admission to these museums and a guided tour. Tours run April to November. The Changing of the Guard ceremony takes place at 10 am daily in summer. The Beating of the Retreat at 6 pm on Tuesday, Thursday, Saturday and Sunday during July and August is followed by the last tour. The citadelle is still considered a working military site so wandering around on your own is not permitted.

Parc des Champs de Bataille (Battlefields Park) This is the huge park running south-west from the citadelle. Its hills, gardens, monuments and trees make it pleasant now, however, the park was once a bloody battleground, the site of a conflict that may have determined the course of Canadian history. The part closest to the cliff is known as the Plains of Abraham and it was here in 1759 that the British finally defeated the French with both generals, Wolfe of the British and Montcalm of the French, dying in the process.

Walking or bus tours of the park depart from the new Discovery Pavilion (☎ 418-648-4071), 835 Avenue Wilfred Laurier, which introduces the park.

The National Battlefields Park Interpretive Centre focuses on the dramatic history of the park with a multi-media show. It is housed in the Musée du Québec.

The centre is open every day in summer but closed on Monday during the rest of the year. There are also two Martello Towers (small stone towers for coastal defence) in the park housing varying exhibits and a fountain with a lookout.

Musée du Québec (Quebec Museum) Towards the south-western end of the park at 1 Avenue Wolfe-Montcalm, is this museum/gallery (☎ 418-643-2150) with changing exhibits, mainly on Quebec's art but with major international touring exhibits, too. Encompassing three buildings, it shows both modern and more traditional art, ceramics and decorative works. The old prison nearby is now part of the gallery.

The museum opens longer hours in summer. It's open seven days from 10 am to 5.30 pm, except Wednesday when it stays open until 9.30 pm.

During other seasons, the museum is closed Monday. Opening hours are 10 am to 5.30 pm.

QUEBEC

During summer entry is $5.75 every day; during other seasons entry is the same price, but is free on Wednesday.

Fortifications of Quebec National Historic Site The largely restored old wall (ramparts) site (☎ 418-648-7016) can be visited for free. In fact, you can walk a complete circuit on top of the walls, 4.6km, all around the Old City. At the old Powder Building beside Porte Saint Louis, an interpretive centre has been set up, which provides a little information on the wall's history. Guided walks, with a fee, leave from the Frontenac Kiosk on Terrasse Dufferin.

Parc d'Artillerie Beside the wall at Porte Saint Jean, 2 Rue d'Auteuil, Parc d'Artillerie (☎ 418-648-4205), a National Historic Site, has been used militarily for centuries. A munitions factory built cartridges for the Canadian Forces here until 1964. It's now an interpretive centre with a scale model of Quebec City the way it was in the early 1800s. In the Dauphine Redoubt, there are costumes and displays about the soldiers for whom it was built during the French regime. The Redoubt, built between 1712 and 1748, is a defence structure designed to protect a prominent point. In this case, the edge of the hill could be well guarded by the soldiers within. In the officers' quarters there's a history lesson for children. Admission is $3 with family rates offered.

Musée du Fort This is a small museum (☎ 418-692-1759) at 10 Rue Sainte Anne near Place d'Armes, dealing with more provincial military history. With the aid of a large model of 18th century Quebec City, six sieges and battles are retold using sound and light (son et lumière). The half-hour show isn't bad, comes in English and French versions, and costs $6.50.

Musée Grévin Also facing Place d'Armes, the Musée Grévin, a wax museum (☎ 418-692-2289), depicts historical events and figures and contemporary cultural figures. Admission is $3, students $2.

Ursuline Convent & Museum This convent (☎ 418-694-0694) on Rue des Jardins is the oldest girls' school on the continent. There are several buildings on the estate, some restored. The Ursuline Museum, which you enter at 12 Rue Donnacona, deals with the Ursulines and their lives in the 1600s and 1700s, and also displays paintings, crafts, furniture and other belongings of the early French settlers. The skull of General Montcalm lies in the crypt of the chapel next door but is not on public display. Admission is $4, students $2.50. The convent, chapel and museum are open daily from 10 am to noon and 1.30 to 5 pm but closed on Sunday morning and Monday. It's also closed mornings in winter.

Nearby, on the same street, is the simple, elegant Anglican **Cathedral of the Holy Trinity**, built in 1804, which is open in summer from 9 am to 8 pm Monday to Friday, 10 am to 8 pm Saturday and 11 am to 6 pm Sunday.

Latin Quarter The Latin Quarter refers to a section of Old Upper Town surrounding the large **Quebec seminary** complex with its stone and wooden buildings, grassy, quiet quadrangles, a chapel and museum. The seminary was originally the site of the Laval Université which outgrew the space here and was moved in the 1960s to Sainte Foy, south-west of the downtown area. Many students still live along the old, narrow streets which look particularly Parisian. The focus of the site is the very good **Musée de l'Amerique Francais** (North American Francophone Museum; ☎ 418-692-2843), 2 Côte de la Fabrique. It's open daily in summer for $3 and contains various artefacts relating to French settlement and culture in the New World. Excellent changing exhibits are mounted in one of the seminary buildings. To enter the seminary grounds go to 9 Rue de l'Université.

Parc de l'Esplanade Just inside the Old City by Porte Saint Louis and Rue Saint Louis is this city park where many of the Quebec Winter Carnival's events are held.

Calèches, the horse-drawn carts for sight-seeing, line up for business along the edge of the park.

Other Things to See In the 1700s Upper Town began to grow after Lower Town was destroyed once too often in battle. **Place d'Armes** is the small square to the north of the Château Frontenac. It was once a military parade ground and is now a handy city orientation point.

Rue du Tresor is up, away from the water, off Place d'Armes. This narrow street, linking Rue Sainte Anne with Rue Buade, is jammed with painters and their wares – mostly kitsch stuff done for the tourists but some pretty good work too. At the end of Buade is the **Hôtel de Ville** (City Hall) dating from 1833. Next to the Hôtel de Ville, the park is used for shows and performances throughout summer, especially during festival time.

On the corner of Rue Buade and Rue Sainte Famille is the **Basilica of Notre Dame**, dating from 1647. The interior is ornate and contains paintings and treasures from the early French regime. How times change; there is now a bilingual, multimedia historical presentation shown in the cathedral – for $7.

Old Lower Town

The oldest section of Quebec City, like the Upper Town, is well worth exploring. Get down to it by walking down Côte de la Montagne street by Parc Montmorency. About halfway down on the right there is a shortcut – the break-neck staircase – that leads down to Rue du Petit Champlain. A second method is to follow the sidewalk beside the Musée du Fort toward the river and Lower Town and the staircase will lead you down. Alternatively, you can take the funicular from Terrasse Dufferin down; it also goes to Rue du Petit Champlain, to Louis Jolliet House. The house dates from 1683 and Jolliet lived in it when he wasn't off exploring the northern Mississippi. Rue du Petit Champlain, a busy, attractive street, is said to be the narrowest in North America and is also one of the oldest.

Place Royale This is the central and principal square of the Lower Town area with 400 years of history behind it. The name is now often used to refer to the district in general. When de Champlain founded Quebec, it was this bit of shoreline which was first settled. The entire area has been under renovation and restoration for years, and the work is now nearly complete.

The streets are full of visitors, people going to restaurants and cafés, and school children from around the province getting history lessons. There are historic sites to visit, galleries, craft shops and it's not uncommon to see a bride coming down the church steps either.

Also on the square are many buildings from the 1600s and 1700s, tourist shops (don't buy film here, it's too expensive!) and in the middle of a statue of Louis XIV. The information office (☎ 418-643-6631) at 215 Rue du Marché-Finlay can tell you of the many free events, concerts and shows which frequently take place in and around the Lower Town and has some historic exhibits.

Church of Notre Dame des Victoires Dating from 1688, this house of worship on the square is the oldest stone church in the province. It's built on the very spot where 80 years earlier de Champlain set up his 'Habitation', a small stockade. Hanging from the ceiling is a replica of a wooden ship, thought to be a good-luck charm for the ocean crossing and early battles with the Iroquois.

Royal Battery This is at the foot of Rue Sous le Fort, where a dozen cannons were set up in 1691 to protect the growing town. The Lower Town information office is just off the park here. The Canadian government has a coastguard base near the ferry terminal across the street.

Vieux Port (Old Port)

Built around the old harbour in Lower Town north and east of Place Royale, Vieux Port is a redeveloped multipurpose waterfront area still undergoing changes

and growth. It's a large, spacious assortment of government buildings, shops, condominiums and recreational facilities with no real focal point but a few things of interest to the visitor.

Near Place Royale at the river's edge you'll see the MV *Louis Jolliet* and other vessels offering cruises downriver to the waterfalls Chute Montmorency and Île d'Orléans. You'll get good views of the city, but you can also get them from the cheap ferry plying the river between town and Lévis. Near the wharf is the Musée de la Civilisation.

Strolling along the waterfront leads to the Agora, a large outdoor concert bowl and site of many summer shows and presentations. A little farther along is a warehouse-style building housing numerous boutiques. Nearby is a large naval training centre and by Bassin Louise, the free Naval Museum.

Musée de la Civilisation The large, striking waterfront museum (☎ 418-643-2158), 85 Rue Dalhousie, deals with both Quebec and broader historical and communication topics through permanent and changing exhibits. Human history and culture is explored through new and old artefacts and the creations of humankind.

It's spacious and well laid out. Aside from the static exhibits, it includes dance, music and other live performances.

It's definitely worth seeing and unlike many museums around the province there are English-speaking guides on hand. Admission is $7 (students $4) and it's open from 10 am to 7 pm daily from 24 June to Labour Day (the first Monday in September). The rest of the year it closes at 5 pm and it is not open at all on Monday. Note that on Tuesday out of the main season, it's free.

Old Port of Quebec Interpretation Centre A short distance away, housed in a building at 100 Rue Saint André, is the Old Port of Quebec Interpretation Centre, a National Historic Site (☎ 418-648-3300). It's a large, four-storey exhibition depicting the local 19th century shipbuilding and timber

industries, with good displays and often live demonstrations. Admission is $3 and it's open daily.

Antique Shop District Rue Saint Paul, north-west of the Place Royale near the Old Port Interpretation Centre, is the heart of an expanding antique quarter. From Place Royale, take Rue Saint Pierre towards the harbour and turn left at Rue Saint Paul. About a dozen shops here sell antiques, curiosities and old Québecois relics. There are also some good little cafés along this relatively quiet street. Right against the cliff on Côte de la Canoterie, you can walk up to Upper Town. Farther along at the waterfront on Rue Saint André, is the Farmers' Market on the right-hand side, and past that, the Gare du Palais train and bus station.

Outside the Walls
National Assembly Back in Upper Town, the home of the Provincial Legislature is just off Grande Allée, not far from Parc de l'Esplanade, on the corner of Ave Dufferin and Grand Allée Est. It's a castle-style structure dating from 1886.

There are free tours of the sumptuous interior from 9 am to 4.30 pm daily in summer, weekdays the rest of the year, with commentaries in English and French. The Assembly sits in the Blue Room. The Red Room, equally impressive, is no longer used as the Upper House. The restaurant is worth a look-see as well.

Grand Theatre On the corner of Boulevard René Lévesque Est and Rue Claire Fontaine is this grand three-storey building, home to the performing arts. The building's design and the gigantic epic mural in three parts – *Death, Space and Liberty* by Spaniard Jordi Bonet – are features. Unfortunately, you can't see the inside without a ticket to a show.

Le Bois de Coulonge Park Not far west of the Plains of Abraham is this large area dedicated to the plant world. Long the private property of a succession of Quebec's religious and political elite, the area of

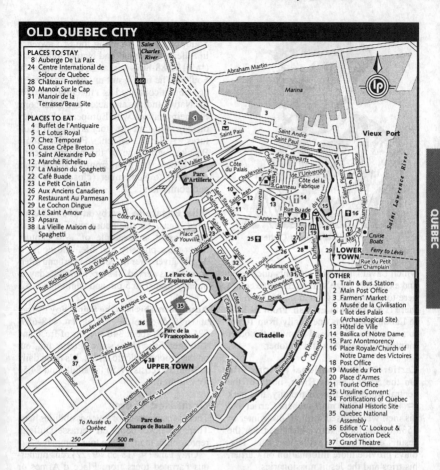

OLD QUEBEC CITY

PLACES TO STAY
8 Auberge De La Paix
24 Centre International de Sejour de Quebec
28 Château Frontenac
30 Manoir Sur le Cap
31 Manoir de la Terrasse/Beau Site

PLACES TO EAT
4 Buffet de l'Antiquaire
5 Le Lotus Royal
7 Chez Temporal
10 Casse Crêpe Breton
11 Saint Alexandre Pub
12 Marché Richelieu
17 La Maison du Spaghetti
22 Café Buade
23 Le Petit Coin Latin
26 Aux Anciens Canadiens
27 Restaurant Au Parmesan
29 Le Cochon Dingue
32 Le Saint Amour
33 Apsara
38 La Vieille Maison du Spaghetti

OTHER
1 Train & Bus Station
2 Main Post Office
3 Farmers' Market
6 Musée de la Civilisation
9 L'Îlot des Palais (Archaeological Site)
13 Hôtel de Ville
14 Basilica of Notre Dame
15 Parc Montmorency
16 Place Royale/Church of Notre Dame des Victoires
18 Post Office
19 Musée du Fort
20 Place d'Armes
21 Tourist Office
25 Ursuline Convent
34 Fortifications of Quebec National Historic Site
35 Quebec National Assembly
36 Edifice 'G' Lookout & Observation Deck
37 Grand Theatre

woods and extensive horticultural displays is open to the public. It's wedged between Boulevard Champlain and Chemin Saint Louis with access from the latter only.

JA Moisan Épicier This is known as the oldest grocery store in North America. It was established in 1871 and a timelessness pervades the air above the good selection of groceries and more, including maple syrup products. It's open every day at 699 Rue Saint Jean and is worth a look.

L'Îlot des Palais (Archaeological Site)
North of the upper walled section of Quebec City on the corner of Rue Saint Nicholas and Rue Vaillier – just a block south of Rue Saint Paul, a major street which runs into Boulevard Charest Est – is this rather interesting idea for an historic site (☎ 418-691-6092).

It's set up as a dig of the first city intendant's house, actually a palace. Platforms lead over foundations, firepits and outlines of several buildings from as early as 1669

French explorer Jacques Cartier

which Laval Université students uncovered and explored. There's an interpretive centre here to supply background information but there is not much in English. From 24 June to Labour Day, it is open daily from 10 am to 5 pm, free. It's closed Monday the other months between May and October.

Cartier-Brebeuf National Historic Site

On the Saint Charles River, north of the central walled section of the city, this park (☎ 418-648-4038) marks where Cartier and his men were nursed through the winter of 1535 by the local Native Indians. Later the Jesuits established a settlement here. Displays provide more information on Cartier, his trips and the Jesuit missionaries.

There is a full-scale replica of Cartier's ship and one of a Native Indian longhouse in the park's green but rather unauthentic-looking riverside setting. Throughout summer it is open every day from 10 am to 5 pm and entry costs $2.75. Native people may be on hand story-telling, demonstrating crafts etc. It's at 175 Rue de l'Espinay. From the downtown area take Rue de la Couronne north by car to the Laurentienne Expressway (Hwy 73 north) to the l'Espinay exit. Take the No 801 bus to Rue Julien from where you can walk to the park.

Maison des Jésuites (Jesuit House)

South of the centre along the St Lawrence in Sillery, this Jesuit and Native Indian site (☎ 418-688-8074) is at 2320 Chemin du Foulon. The first Jesuit mission was here in 1637 but it continued as a meeting place for the Native Indians and acted as a focal point for their relations with Europeans. Low-key displays illustrate the story and clash of cultures. A later resident, Francis Moore Brooke, wrote one of the country's early novels here. It's open from 11 am to 5 pm mid-May to September (closed Monday) and admission is $2.

Villa Bagatelle Nearby at 1563 Chemin Saint Louis, this fine house and English garden present an example of 19th century upper-class property and life. The house is largely given over to exhibiting art and afternoon tea is served. It's open Wednesday to Sunday from 1 to 5 pm and admission is $2.

Aquarium This is in the Sainte Foy district at 1675 Avenue des Hôtels (☎ 418-659-5264). It has about 340 species of fresh and saltwater fish. There's a cafeteria and, out on the grounds, picnic tables. It's open daily to 5 pm and costs $9.50 for adults and $4.50 for children.

Organised Tours

There is no shortage of tour possibilities here. There's a ticket booth on Terrasse Dufferin representing many of the tour companies.

Gray Line (☎ 418-653-9722) runs numerous narrated tours from Place d'Armes or picks up at hotels. A 1½ hour trip around town costs $14, and a four hour trip, to Sainte Anne de Beaupré, Chute Montmorency falls and a short visit to Île d'Orléans, is $32.

Adlard Tours (☎ 418-692-2358) conducts walking tours in English departing from the tourist office at 12 Rue Sainte Anne. The $12 guided walk takes over two hours.

Intégra (☎ 418-648-8424), 1105 Rue Saint Jean, or contacted through the HI hostel, runs small hiking and camping trips in the countryside surrounding Quebec City. Groups are small and the prices good, making access to

outdoor activities and historic and cultural sites fun and economical.

See under Getting Around for cycling tours.

River Cruises Boat tours are also plentiful. A variety of trips is offered on the big open-decked MV *Louis Jolliet*, which can carry 800 passengers. Tickets (☎ 418-692-1159) may be purchased at the kiosk on the board-walk behind the Château or at the booth along the waterfront near Place Royale.

The basic trip going downriver to Île d'Or-léans and Chute Montmorency with a bilin-gual guide costs $20 and the boat is jammed with people. There are evening trips with music and dancing for $23 with dinner op-tional. These cruises are popular so getting a ticket early is a good idea. Other possibilities include going all the way to Tadoussac. There's even an ice-breaker cruise in winter.

Another company with a smaller vessel, *Le Coudrier* (☎ 418-692-0107), does simi-lar 90-minute cruises around Quebec City and down the river for $15 and cheaper one-hour trips, too. There are also full day trips with a meal which include Grosse Île. For information call or see them at quay No 19 along the Old Port dock opposite the Agora.

The ferry over to Lévis is, in a sense, a short cruise and provides a great view of the Château and costs next to nothing.

Special Events

Some of the major festivals and celebra-tions held in Quebec City are:

February
Winter Carnival
This is a famous annual event unique to Que-bec City. The festival lasts for about 10 days in February, always including two weekends. If you want to go, organise the trip early as the city gets packed out (and bring lots of warm clothes). Featured are parades, ice sculptures, a snow slide, boat races, dances, music and lots of drinking. The carnival symbol and mascot is the frequently seen roly-poly snowman figure with a red hat called Bonhomme. The town goes berserk. If you take the train into Quebec City during Carnival, be prepared for a trip like no other. Activities take place all over Old

Town and the famous slide is on the Terrasse Dufferin behind the Château. In recent years, some celebrants have become overly unruly to the point of being problematic at times. Those with families may wish to inquire about par-ticipating in particular night-time festivities.

June
Les Nuits Black
This is a jazz and blues festival held at the end of the month with venues around town.

July
Summer Festival
This is held at the beginning and middle of July and consists basically of free shows and concerts throughout the town, including drama and dance. The tourist office should have a list of things going on. Most squares and parks in the Old City are the sites of some activity daily, especially the Parc de la Francophonie behind Hôtel de Ville at noon and in the evening.

August
Medieval Festival
Events with a medieval theme are featured dur-ing the popular five-day event held toward the beginning of the month on odd numbered years.
Quebec City Provincial Exhibition
Officially known as Expo Quebec, the Ex is held around the end of August each year and features commercial displays, agricultural competitions, handicrafts, a blackjack parlour, horse racing and midway, the latter a large carnival with 55 rides and games of chance. Nearly three-quarters of a million people visit each year. Parc de l'Ex-position (Exhibition Park) is north of the down-town area, off Route 175, Laurentienne.

Places to Stay

There are many, many places to stay in Que-bec City and generally the competition keeps the prices down to a reasonable level. The bulk of the good-value accommodation is in small European-style hotels. Motels and larger downtown hotels are expensive. As you'd expect in such a popular city, the best cheap places are often full. Look for a room before 2 pm or phone ahead for a reservation. Midsummer and Carnival time are especially busy particularly Friday and Saturday.

Outside the peak periods, prices do drop and you might get a break if you're stay-ing for more than a couple of days. Prices listed here are summer high-season rates.

For accommodation assistance, the tourist office is helpful. Do not take its occupancy information as gospel, however. It may have a place down as 'full' when in fact a call will turn up a room, after everybody else has ignored it. The tourist accommodation guide also doesn't list all the places – a wander around will turn up others.

Camping There are numerous campgrounds close to town. Excellent *Camping Municipal de Beauport* (☎ 418-666-2155) north of Quebec City is green, peaceful and just a 15 minute drive to the Old City. To get there, take Hwy 40 towards Montmorency to exit 321 and turn north. Follow the blue and white signs, the park is not too far. It costs $18 with a tent and $20 with trailer. There are also a few places on Hwy 138 going east from Quebec City through the Sainte Anne de Beaupré area including *Camping Mont Sainte Anne* (☎ 418-826-2323).

On the south shore, just 1km west from the Quebec bridge, is *Camping du Pont de Quebec* (☎ 418-831-0777) with simple tent sites as well as electrical hook-ups. There are many private campgrounds on this south shore road particularly west of Quebec City.

Hostels There are two well established and busy hostels here.

The HI *Centre International de Séjour de Quebec* (☎ 418-694-0775, ☎ 1-800-461-8585, 19 Rue Sainte Ursule) is central. Despite its great size with 245 beds, it's usually full in summer. Dorm bunks are $16 and there are some double and family rooms. The pleasant, economical cafeteria offers all three meals. The hostel-run activities are worth looking into and the helpful staff is knowledgeable about things to do and how to get around.

Auberge de la Paix (☎ 418-694-0735, 31 Rue Couillard) also well located, is relatively small and quiet. It's open all year and has 60 beds. The European-style building is marked with a peace sign. The cost is $18 with breakfast, and $2 extra if you need a sleeping sheet and blanket. There are two double rooms at $29 but management tends

to get grumpy if you ask about them. The doors close at 2 am. The location is perfect; there is a grocery store, a bar and restaurant all minutes away. It's best to arrive early in the morning to secure a bed. It's a short walk from the bus/train station but it's uphill all the way.

The *YWCA* (☎ 418-683-2155, 855 Avenue Holland) takes couples or single women. Singles/doubles cost $30/52 and there's a cafeteria and pool. The Y is often full, so reservations may be useful. Avenue Holland runs off Chemin Sainte Foy, which becomes Saint Jean in the old section. Bus No 7 along Chemin Sainte Foy goes past Avenue Holland. Walk south on Avenue Holland – it's not far.

The *Université Laval* (☎ 418-656-5632) between Chemin Sainte Foy and Boulevard Wilfrid Laurier to the east of Autoroute du Vallon, rents rooms in summer from May to mid-August. Rates are $33 for singles or $25 sharing a twin, with good student discounts. Bus No 800 from the Old City will get you there; it's about halfway between the bridges and the walled area.

Small Hotels Staying at one of the small, sometimes family-run hotels, often created out of an old house, adds to the charm of Quebec. Rates are good especially in rooms with shared bath and many places are now providing the morning meal. Many have some parking available but it usually comes with an extra charge.

Most of the cheaper lodging is in one specific area. This area is roughly bounded by Rue d'Auteuil on the west, Rue Sainte Anne to the north, the Château Frontenac to the east and Avenue Saint Denis to the south. Two streets abundant in accommodation are Rue Sainte Ursule and Rue Saint Louis. Rue Sainte Anne and Rue de la Porte are also good.

One of the best of the cheapies is *Auberge Saint Louis* (☎ 418-692-2424, 48 Rue Saint Louis). The 27 rooms start at a reasonable $55 a single or double but go up to $95 with a full breakfast included. Parking is available but costs extra.

Farther down the street is the more basic *Maison du Général* (☎ *418-694-1905, 72 Rue Saint Louis)*. There are 12 rooms which range in price from singles/doubles $33/38, without bath. As in many of these places, it's cheaper without TV, showers, the view or the biggest room. The cheaper rooms are sometimes noisier as they're often on the street but despite these drawbacks they always seem to be the ones to go first.

The super-renovated *Hôtel Le Clos Saint Louis* (☎ *418-694-1311*, ☎ *1-800-461-1311, 71 Rue Saint Louis)* has 29 rooms at $55 to $110 for singles or doubles when things are busy, dropping to $45 to $85 at other times. A continental breakfast is included.

Running off Rue Saint Louis is Rue Sainte Ursule, a pleasant, much quieter street. There are several places worth checking here. The prices at *Le Manoir La Salle* (☎ *418-692-9953, 18 Rue Sainte Ursule)* haven't risen in years. It has nine rooms at $30 to $40 for singles, $45 to $60 for doubles. Some may prefer the upstairs rooms to avoid having to go through the lobby to the bathroom, as is the case from the ground-floor rooms. Some kitchenettes are available.

La Maison Sainte Ursule (☎ *418-694-9794, 40 Rue Sainte Ursule)* looks and is more expensive, at $39 to $62 for singles and $48 to $89 for doubles. Kitchenettes are available here, too.

Across the street is *Maison Acadienne* (☎ *418-694-0280*, ☎ *1-800-463-0280, 43 Rue Sainte Ursule)*. Singles/doubles cost from $43/49 to $90/99 depending on the size of room and facilities. It's a good place and if you're lucky and have a small car you may get one of the parking spots around the back. A continental breakfast served out on the patio is available for $3.75.

Farther north-west off Rue Sainte Ursule is Rue Sainte Anne. *Maison Doyon* (☎ *418-694-1720, 109 Rue Sainte Anne)* has 17 rooms, all of which have been spruced up with baths replacing simple washbasins. Singles are $60 and a room for four adults goes for $110, simple breakfast included.

There are numerous places perfectly located by Parc des Governeurs to the south of the Château Frontenac. The *Manoir de la Terrasse/Beau Site* (☎ *418-694-1592, 4 and 6 Rue de la Porte)* is close to the boardwalk. Singles or doubles are the same price and range from $45 to $80. The lower-priced rooms represent excellent value. A continental breakfast is supplied, many rooms have their own balcony and there is a pleasant garden.

Manoir Sur le Cap (☎ *418-694-1987, 9 Avenue Sainte Geneviève)* has 15 rooms carved out of the old house, some with views of the park, others of the river and Lévis. Singles/doubles cost from $60 to large deluxe rooms with fireplace for up to $265!

Motels There are two major areas to look for motels and another area with several new, large hotel/motels. All are out of the Old City, but not really far and not difficult to reach. City buses run to these districts so whether you have a car or not, they may be the answer if you find everything booked up downtown. Prices, generally, are high.

Beauport A fruitful area is Beauport, a section of Quebec City to the north of the downtown area. You pass by on the way to Sainte Anne de Beaupré or on a trip along the northern coast. The easiest way to reach it if driving from the downtown area, is to head north up Avenue Dufferin to Hwy 440 eastbound. Then watch for exit signs to Boulevard Sainte Anne (Hwy 138). This is Beauport. There are places when the numbers hit the 500s and more in the 1000 area. At *Motel Chevalier* (☎ *418-661-3876, 1062 Boulevard Sainte Anne)* rooms cost from $50 to $60 for singles/doubles. *Motel de la Capitale* (☎ *418-663-0587, 1082 Boulevard Sainte Anne)* charges $60/65.

Nearby, there's *Motel Olympic* (☎ *418-667-8716, 1078 Boulevard Sainte Anne)* where prices range from $65 to an outrageous $90.

Boulevard Wilfrid Hamel A second area for motels is west of the centre on Boulevard Wilfrid Hamel, marked only as 'Hamel' on street signs. It's actually Hwy 138. To get to

this area from town, head north up Avenue Dufferin to Boulevard Charest Ouest (Hwy 440). Go west. At Henri IV go north to Hamel. If you're on Hwy 40, head south. It's about 7km from town in the airport district. *Motel Pierre (☎ 418-681-6191, 1640 Boulevard Hamel)* has rooms from $70 to $100. Most other options are farther west – there are three in the 3000 addressees and half a dozen in the 6000s. *Motel Le Sabier (☎ 418-871-8916, 3290 Boulevard Hamel)* charges from $50 to $80 for two people. *Comfort Inn (☎ 1-800-267-3837, 7320 Boulevard Hamel)* is in Sainte Foy. Rooms cost $95 for singles/doubles in this reliable Canada-wide chain.

Boulevard Wilfrid Laurier Lastly, there is Boulevard Wilfrid Laurier, west of the city. The *Motel l'Abitation (☎ 418-653-7267, 2828 Boulevard Wilfrid Laurier)* has good prices with doubles from $50 off season but up to $110 in season. There are a number of new, large hotels a little farther west with higher rates near Boulevard Henri IV, which runs into the bridges from the south shore.

Places to Eat

Restaurants are abundant and the quality high. On the down side, many eateries fall into the same upper-end category – good service, an attractive setting, a perfect splurge. But there are ways around eating a hole in your budget.

At dinner the set menus include soup, a roll, dessert and coffee. Many of these same dining rooms offer midday specials which aren't bad value at all. Some serve lunch until 3 pm and one place customarily offers it until 5.30 pm. Prices for the complete lunch can be as low as half the dinner cost although often portions are smaller.

The Upper Town restaurants, within the walls as a rule, offer the least price range and tend to be costly. Outside the wall or down in the quieter sections of Lower Town, less expensive and more casual places are easier to find. The ethnic restaurants also provide an alternative.

Old Upper Town One of the Old Town restaurants suitable for families is the *Café Buade (31 Rue Buade)* right in the middle of everything, just east of Rue des Jardins. In the downstairs section, a good full breakfast is $3.50. The lunch and dinner fare is similarly straightforward and moderately priced.

La Lunchonette (50 Côte de la Fabrique) is a bit of a rarity here – the small, basic diner with cheap breakfasts, including omelettes, and complete lunches featuring say, croque monsieur (grilled ham and cheese sandwich with egg-soaked bread), for $6.

For a more French-style breakfast there is *Le Petit Coin Latin (8½ Rue Sainte Ursule)* near Rue Saint Jean. Open every day, this small café has croissants, muffins, eggs, café au lait in a bowl (as it's served in parts of France) and low-priced lunch specials. It has an outdoor summer patio with a fixed-price dinner of $12 to $16. Located one block east of Rue Buade, *Chez Temporal (25 Rue Couillard)* is a little café which serves coffee, croissants and great salads. It's perfect for snacks, breakfasts and light meals. The café feels very French – a good place to sit in the morning and plan the day. Credit cards are not accepted here.

One of the main streets for restaurants is Rue Saint Jean. There are many places to eat as well as night spots scattered along here, both inside the wall and farther out. Near Côte du Palais, *Casse Crêpe Breton (1136 Rue Saint Jean)* is a small restaurant specialising in crêpes of many kinds, starting as low as $3.25. It's a favourite because it has been here for years and you can sit right up at the counter and watch them put the tasty crêpes together. The busy *Saint Alexandre Pub (1087 Rue Saint Jean)* has 200 kinds of beer and an array of pub-type grub.

To make your own meal try *Marché Richelieu (1097 Rue Saint Jean)* which offers breads from the in-house bakery, fruits, cheeses and even bottles of wine with screw top lids.

Quebec City is a fine place for a special dinner out at a good French restaurant. *Le Saint Amour (48A Rue Sainte Ursule)* has a $35 dinner table d'hôte, value lunch specials

and an excellent reputation. The menu offers about six meat and six fish dishes daily incorporating delicate sauces. The elegant setting includes an inner garden.

Another suggestion is *Aux Anciens Canadiens (34 Rue Saint Louis)* in Jacquet House, Quebec's City's oldest, dating from 1677. Aside from the historical aspect it is noteworthy for its reliance on traditional dishes and typically Québécois specialities. It costs no more than many of the upper-middle places and is one of the few with a distinctly different menu. Here one can sample such provincial fare as apple wine, pea soup, duck or trout followed by dessert of maple-syrup pie. The special table d'hôte menu offered from noon to 6 pm is fairly priced from $14 including a glass of wine or a beer.

For a menu of mainly Italian fare, *Restaurant au Parmesan (38 Rue Saint Louis)* is always busy and festive. Most dishes are from $15 to $22, the décor includes a vast bottle collection and there is live music.

Apsara (71 Rue d'Auteuil) has excellent Asian fare. Dishes are about $12 or a complete dinner for two will cost around $40. Down the street there's a cheap Lebanese spot, *Restaurant Liban (23 Rue d'Auteuil)*.

Old Lower Town *Le Cochon Dingue (46 Boulevard Champlain)* has a pig on its sign. At dinner French-style steak frîtes ($13) is a speciality. *La Maison du Spaghetti (40 Rue Marche Champlain)* with the attractive patio beneath the Château Frontenac is one of the best bargains in town with various pasta dishes including bread and salad from $10 ($8 at lunch). Don't bother with the indoor salad bar as it's very basic and the atmosphere outside is way better.

Along Rue Saint Paul, an old quiet street away from the main bustle, there are several inexpensive places. The *Buffet de l'Antiquaire (95 Rue Saint Paul)* is a small simple place for things like sandwiches or hamburgers at nontourist prices. It even has a few tables out on the pavement.

On Rue Sault au Matelot, which runs perpendicular to Rue Saint Paul, look for the *Le Lotus Royal (77 Rue Sault au Matelot)*

for Asian meals. This is one of the few places in town where there is a 'bring your own wine' policy. A full meal is about $17.

For a French place at lower prices than Upper Town consider *Le Vendome (36 Côte de la Montagne)* which has had a European-style menu since the 1950s. It's about $50 for two (before wine).

Outside the Wall West, along Grande Allée from Old Quebec, past the Quebec National Assembly and other government buildings, and just past Rue d'Artigny, is a popular and lively strip of over a dozen alfresco restaurants. They make a good spot for a beer or lunch if you're out near the Plains of Abraham and are packed at night. All have complete lunch specials for $7 to $10 (from soup to coffee) and at most places, dinners range from $12 to $22. *La Vieille Maison du Spaghetti (625 Grande Allée)* is a long-term favourite.

Rue Saint Jean, west beyond the gate, and its continuation Chemine Sainte Foy, house abundant bars, cafés, taverns and restaurants. This is a far less-touristed area, and prices are correspondingly lower. Walking and looking will turn up places all the way down to Avenue Cartier. There are Vietnamese, Lebanese and Mexican choices.

Le Commensal (860 Rue Saint Jean) has a wide selection of good vegetarian food paid for by weight. South just around the corner from Rue Saint Jean is *La Pailotte (821 Rue Scott)*, a good, casual (bring your own booze) Vietnamese place with complete dinners from $15.

Farther west, about six blocks, is Avenue Cartier. Southward, between Boulevard René Lévesque and Grand Allée, is a strip with a few interesting cafés, attractive pizza places and restaurants including Chinese and Indian.

Farmers' Market The market is on Rue Saint André in Old Lower Town near Bassin Louise, not too far from Vieux Port (Old Port) or the train station. Under the covered open-air building you'll find fresh bread, cheeses, fruit and vegetables. The best time to visit is busy Saturday morning.

QUEBEC

Entertainment

Though Quebec is small, it's active after dark with plenty of nightspots although many change faster than editions of this book. Many of the cafés and restaurants – some mentioned under the eating section – have live music at night. Much of the nightlife is in the Old City or just outside the walls. Bars stay open until around 3 or 4 am. *Voir* is a French entertainment paper appearing each Thursday with complete listings.

Rue Saint Jean is alive at night – this is where people strut. There are good places for just sitting and watching and places with music.

Folk clubs known as *boîtes à chanson* come and go along and around Rue Saint Jean and are generally cheap with a casual, relaxed atmosphere. Try *Chez son Père (24 Saint Stanislas)*.

At *Bar Le d'Auteuil (35 Rue d'Auteuil)* there is often live music. Next door, *Fourmi Atomik* is popular. *L'Inox (38 Rue Saint Andre)* in the Old Port area is the city's only brew pub and has a pleasant outdoor patio.

Some prefer the *Thomas Dunn* pub *(369 Rue Saint Paul)* with its 100 plus beer selection. *Jules & Jim (1060 Rue Cartier)* is decorated with stills from Truffault films and is a nice place for a drink. There are also lots of dance clubs around town but they change quickly, so ask.

The *Grand Théâtre de Québec (☎ 418-643-8131, 269 Boulevard René Lévesque Est)* is the city's main performing arts centre presenting classical concerts, dance and theatre among its shows.

Théâtre Capitole (☎ 418-694-4444, 972 Rue Saint Jean) is another performing arts centre.

Cinema *Cinema Le Clap (☎ 418-650-2527, 2360 Chemin Sainte Foy)* in Sainte Foy, shows English, French and other international films, many with sub-titles.

Théatre IMAX (☎ 418-627-4629, 5401 Boulevard des Galeries) shows large format and 3-D films featuring digital wrap-around sound.

Just Sitting The *restaurant/bar* at the top of the Loews Le Concorde Hôtel, 1225 Place Montcalm on the corner of Grande Allée, is good for views. Away from the clubs, if you just want to sit, *Terrasse Dufferin* behind the Château is perfect, as is the patio bar in the hotel.

Getting There & Away

Air The airport is west of town, off Hwy 40, near where Hwy 73 intersects it on its way north. Both Air Canada (☎ 418-692-0770) and Canadian Airlines (☎ 418-692-0912) serve Montreal, Ottawa and most major Canadian cities.

Bus The station (☎ 418-525-3000) is at 320 Rue Abraham Martin at the main train station. Orléans Express has buses to Montreal nearly every hour during the day and evening ($37). There are regular services to Rivière-du-Loup and then on to Edmundston, New Brunswick. The fare to Edmundston is $45. Rivière-du-Loup is the connecting point with SMT bus lines for destinations in Atlantic Canada. Intercar bus line runs up the north coast to Tadoussac ($33).

There are no direct buses to or from the USA. Most go via Montreal.

Train Odd as it may seem, small Quebec City has three train stations (☎ 418-692-3940). They all use the same phone number. The renovated and absolutely beautiful old Gare du Palais complete with bar and café on Rue Saint Paul in Lower Town is central and convenient. It is used for trains going to and from Montreal (daily, $38) and beyond Montreal westwards. Bus No 800 from Place d'Youville runs to the station. The station in Sainte Foy, south-west of the downtown area, by the bridges over to the south shore, is used by the same trains and is simply more convenient for residents on that side of the city.

Also of interest to travellers is the third station, the inconvenient one across the river on the south shore about 10km from the river in the town of Charny. This station is used primarily for trains heading eastward to the Gaspé Peninsula or the Maritimes. Some

Montreal trains also use it. Buses connect to Sainte Foy. To Moncton, New Brunswick there are daily trips, excluding Tuesday. It's an overnight trip, leaving at 10.30 pm and taking 12 hours. A ticket is $111.

Ask about transport to this new station.

Car All rental agencies here suggest booking two days ahead. Budget (☎ 418-692-3660) is at 29 Côte du Palais or there's an office at the airport. For compact vehicles the rate is $40 per weekday with 250km and $30 on a weekend day with 350km free. Ask what the insurance rate is.

Car Sharing Allo Stop (☎ 418-522-0056) at 467 Rue Saint Jean is an agency that gets drivers and passengers together. Membership for passengers is $6, then you pay a portion of the ride cost to the agency three hours before the trip, and the rest goes to the driver. It offers good deals, such as to Montreal $15, Ottawa $29, Toronto $41, New York (from Montreal) $65, and Gaspé $35. There are even rides all the way to Vancouver – especially in May.

Allo Stop also has offices at Rivière-du-Loup and Rimouski among others. If you'll be travelling around the province pick up a list of all its offices and phone numbers.

Ferry The ferry between Quebec City and Lévis runs constantly – all day and most of the night. The one-way fare is $1.25, less for kids and seniors and $3 for a car. You'll get good views of the river, cliffs, the Quebec skyline and Château Frontenac even if the cruise only lasts a few minutes. The terminal in Quebec City is in Place Royale, Lower Town.

Getting Around

To/From the Airport Autobus La Québecoise (☎ 418-570-5379) shuttles between downtown and the airport for $9. It leaves from major hotels, but will make pick-ups around town if you call at least one hour before flight time. A taxi is about $35. Ask if the bus service still runs to the Montreal airports.

Bus There is a recommended city bus system (☎ 418-627-2511) which costs $1.60

with transfer privileges. The buses even go out as far as Sainte Anne de Beaupré on the north shore. The terminal, Gare Centrale d'Autobus, is at 225 Boulevard Charest Est in Lower Town and will supply you with route maps and information or you can call the above telephone number. Many buses serving the Old Town area stop in at Place d'Youville (known locally as Carré d'Youville) just outside the wall on Rue Saint Jean. Bus No 800 goes to the central bus and train station.

Bus No 800 also goes from downtown to Laval Université.

Car In Quebec City, driving isn't worth the trouble; you can walk just about everywhere, the streets are narrow and crowded, and parking is an exercise in frustration. The tourist office has a handy map of city operated parking lots scattered around the central area and which don't gouge too much.

Bicycle Vélo Passe-sport (☎ 418-692-3643) at 77A Rue Sainte Anne in Old Upper Town has bicycles and rollerblades for rent. Bikes are $24 for 24 hours and hourly rates are offered. Various guided tours and adventures are available.

Cyclo Services (☎ 418-692-4052), with an office beside the Agora along the boardwalk close to the river in front of the Musée de la Civilisation, does the same thing.

There is a 25km cycling path running to Montmorency and the falls from the port area. Another 10km run goes north alongside the Saint Charles River.

Calèche Horse-drawn carriages (calèches) are nice but cost $60 for about 40 minutes.

Around Quebec City

NORTH SHORE

About 15km north-west of the city is the small town of **Wendake** which may be of interest as a half-day trip for those wishing to know more about the country's Native people. In the late 1600s, some Hurons, a

group native to the lands of Ontario, came to this region of Quebec to escape European disease epidemics and tribal conflicts.

Things to see in this decidedly nontraditional, modern town include the Notre Dame de Lorette Chapel of 1731 which contains some articles from the first Jesuit mission set up for the Hurons. The Maison Aroünne at 10 Rue Alexandre Duchesneau has a small collection of Native Indian artefacts. It is open weekdays all year, and weekends too in July and August, and is free.

The main attraction is **Onhoüa Chetek8e** (this is not a spelling error!) (☎ 418-842-4308), billed as a reconstructed Huron village. This it ain't, and the pseudo-teepee and totems are out of place. The longhouse and outdoor craft demonstrations, however, are good, particularly the traditionally Huron snowshoes and canoes. A visit is more worthwhile with a tour. Ask whether an English-speaking guide will be on hand.

A gift shop with books and tapes by Native Indian musicians and a restaurant serving traditional Native foods such as caribou, corn soup and bannock are part of the site at 575 Stanislas-Kosca St.

It's open from May to mid-October, daily from 9 am to 6 pm and a ticket is $5. Take the 800 bus from d'Youville Place to Terminus Charlesbourg. Transfer to the No 72 and stop at the Grand Teepee.

The Laurentians

As in Montreal, the Laurentians north of town are a summer/winter playground. **Lac Beauport** is one of the closest and most accessible resort lakes. **Stoneham** (☎ 418-848-2415) is a major downhill skiing centre spread over four mountains but the resort is busy in summer, too. The site is undergoing a massive $200 million redevelopment which will be comparable to Mont Tremblant's mega-upgrade. The *Auberge de Jeune Voyageur* (☎ 418-848-7650, 7600 Boulevard Talbot, Hwy 175) in Stoneham is a small, comfortable hostel with all meals available. There is walking and cycling close by. Call for transport information.

Buses run into Jacques Cartier Park from Quebec.

Laurentides Wildlife Reserve Provincial Park

Farther north up Hwy 175, about 40km from Quebec City, is this huge wilderness park with its wooded hills and mountains, and scores of lakes and streams. You can hike and fish and there are campgrounds along the road through the park. The road continues to Chicoutimi.

In the southern portion, **Jacques Cartier Park** (☎ 418-844-2358) is ideal for a quick escape from the city. In less than an hour's drive you can be camping, hiking trails or canoeing along the Jacques Cartier River. Near the entrance, an information centre provides details on the park's activities and services. Camping equipment, canoes and bikes can all be rented. In some backcountry sections simple overnight cabins have been set up. In winter there is cross-country skiing with shelter huts along some of the routes.

Île d'Orléans

East of Quebec, this 30km-long, green island has long had a reputation for its picture of traditional rural Quebec life. It offers good scenery and views and some of the villages are over 300 years old with examples of wooden or stone houses and cottages in Normandy style.

Though still primarily agricultural, a problem is its proximity to downtown Quebec. Aside from all the visitors, city folk are building more and more homes here, especially at the western end. It's certainly no longer just a sleepy, pastoral farming region. Still, there are some pleasing landscapes and there's lots of fruit, especially apples and strawberries. A view tower stands at the eastern tip.

There's a *campground* and the HI *Auberge le P'tit Bonheur* (☎ 418-829-2588) hostel in the middle of the south-side at Saint Jean. The island is linked to the mainland by a bridge at its north-west end and there is a tourist office here. For less changed rural-island escapes visit islands farther down the river.

Skiing & Snowboarding Near Quebec City

Excellent skiing is the main attraction of the Quebec City area during winter.

Mont Sainte Anne (☎ 418-827-4561), at 800m and with alpine runs down the northern, southern and western faces, is the premier ski centre in the region. Despite the obvious down-hill lure it also has a spectacular system of cross-country ski trails. Access to the cross-country area is 8km from the alpine centre on Route 360, in the village of Saint Ferreol les Neiges. For both types of skiing there are novice, intermediate and expert trails. The season runs from the end of November to the end of March. Numerous resorts, lodges and hotels can be found in and around the foot of the mountain. The tourist office provides publications detailing win-ter vacation packages which include hotel and ski passes. Meals and the shuttle bus to the lifts may also be options.

The second major downhill centre is Stoneham (☎ 418-848-2411) in the village of the same name on Hwy 175 north of Quebec City. With 26 alpine slopes, it is half the size of Mont Sainte Anne and ticket prices are about 25% less. It is undergoing a major expansion and redevelopment.

Smaller, less expensive alpine centres are Centre de Ski Le Relais at Lac Beauport and Mont Saint Castin, also at Lac Beauport. These too have snow-making and a range of lifts and slopes of varying degrees of difficulty.

All four resorts offer equipment rentals, lessons, child care, night skiing (a magical experi-ence) and lodging right on the hill. The latter is a luxury that must be paid for but there is plenty of accommodation near the centres; the week between Christmas and New Year's and during the March school break should be booked well in advance. There are other cross-country ski centres in the area in addition to Mont Sainte Anne, but a very good day can be had right in Quebec City in the Parc des Champs de Bataille. Where else can you ski on a battlefield that determined the future of a country?

Parc de la Chute Montmorency

About 7km east of Quebec City, along Hwy 138, just past the bridge for Île d'Orléans, are the Montmorency waterfalls, higher than those at Niagara but not nearly as impres-sive. They're set in a park with good walk-ing paths, stairs to the top of the falls, picnic grounds, an information centre with histori-cal and geological displays but also, in a case of total overkill, cable cars and heli-copter rides above the flowing water. There is some interesting history and it has been classed an historic site. A $7 admission is charged for the ride to the upper portions but you can walk the 487 stairs for nothing. There is a hefty parking fee as well although you can walk or cycle in for free. (A cycle path runs all the way to Quebec City.) The falls are accessible by city bus. Catch the No

800 at Carré d'Youville (Square) and trans-fer at the Beauport terminal, No 50 to the top of the falls, No 53 for the bottom.

Within the next 40km or so eastbound there are three other very impressive sets of waterfalls to consider. Also before Sainte Anne de Beaupré is the Bee Museum where mead is available.

Sainte Anne de Beaupré

This gaudy little tourist town is justly renowned for its immaculate and mammoth church. From the mid-1600s the village has been an important religious site. An annual pilgrimage takes place here in late July, at-tracting thousands of people when any nearby space becomes part of a huge camp. The beautiful basilica, begun in the late 1920s, replaced earlier chapels. Note the

many crutches inside the door. There's good tile-work on the floor, and stained glass and ceiling mosaics.

Check the hotel across the street. It's designed like a chapel, stained glass included – yuk! Yet it does have an inexpensive cafeteria.

Also in town are a museum, a monastery with a seminary, a few other churches and a stations of the cross walk. *Cyclorama of Jerusalem* is a 360-degree painting of Jerusalem on the day Jesus died ($6). There are several low-cost restaurants near the church.

Intercar bus line runs up the north shore from Quebec City and stops in town.

South, just a 10 minute drive toward Quebec, there's *Motel Spring (☎ 418-824-4953, 8520 Boulevard Sainte Anne, Hwy 138)* which is a good, clean, low-priced bilingual motel and restaurant. There are others closer to the centre.

About 3km north, towards Mont Sainte Anne, is *Auberge La Camarine (10947 Hwy 138 Est)*, a fine place for a splurge on a good French meal in an old Quebec-style house with complete dinners from $30.

Canyon Sainte Anne

Some 6km north-east of Beaupré on Hwy 138, in a deep chasm, are the 74m-high Sainte Anne waterfalls (☎ 418-827-4057) in a natural setting. You can walk around and across them via a series of steps, ledges and bridges for $6. Though busy, this is quite a pleasant spot – less developed and more dramatic than the falls at Montmorency. The water roars loudest in spring but autumn is grand with the surrounding red and gold of the maple leaves. The site, with restaurant, is open from May to the end of October. In July and August it's open from 8 am to 6 pm, otherwise 8.30 am to 5.30 pm.

Mont Sainte Anne Park

A little farther east, 50km from Quebec, Mont Sainte Anne Park (☎ 418-827-4561) is best known as a ski area – it's the number one hill near Quebec City and one of the top slopes in the province. There are about a dozen lifts. In summer, there is a gondola to the mountain's summit. Or if you're up to it, bicycle and hiking trails wind to the top. There is a campground, and surprisingly, it's not overly busy even in midsummer.

The Intercar bus line goes by the park en route to Charlevoix but not into it and the camping is quite a distance from the highway. In winter, there are dog sled trips available.

Les Sept Chutes

A few kilometres farther east are these waterfalls (☎ 418-826-3139) at a defunct hydroelectric station and a dam. Trails wind along the river past the various falls and through the woods and there is information about the old power-production facilities. There's a restaurant and picnic tables as well. Admission is $6.50 for adults.

Cap Tourmente National Wildlife Area

Beyond Cap Tourmente village, south off Hwy 138, along the riverside is this bird sanctuary. Flocks of snow geese come here in spring and autumn but many other species as well as a range of animals and plants make these wetlands home. There is an interpretation centre (watch for the hummingbirds) and meandering walking paths. The area is open every day from 9 am to 5 pm. Admission costs are low.

SOUTH SHORE
Lévis

There's not much here for the visitor. It's a cross between a smallish town and a suburb of Quebec City. The ferry ride over makes a mini-cruise and the views of Quebec are good. The train station here has closed; for train information see the Getting There & Away section of Quebec City.

Part of the way up the hill into town are the remains of a fort from where there are excellent views. Between 1865 and 1872 the British built three forts on the south shore cliffs to protect Quebec. One, known as Pointe-Lévis Fort No 1 has been restored and operates as a national historic site with guided tours. It's on the east side of Lévis in Lauzon.

Eastward

Leaving Quebec City, the landscape is pretty flat but looking across the river you can see the mountains and hills; the large one with the ski runs is Mont Sainte Anne. Going along Hwy 132 through the little towns, Île d'Orléans lies just offshore. Without offering anything of particular note, **Saint Michel** is particularly attractive and a quintessential example of small-town Quebec.

Montmagny

About 60km east of Lévis, along Hwy 132, Montmagny is the first main point of interest, primarily for two islands just offshore. The town is also of note for being on the migration route of the snow goose. Each spring and autumn thousands of these birds stopover on the shoreline around town. Birdwatchers can feast their eyes and enjoy the festival initiated by the geese.

At 45 du Bassin Nord in town is the **Migration Education Centre** (☎ 418-248-4565), a dual-purpose interpretive centre (☎ 418-248-9196) with exhibits on migration, both bird and human. The first portion is a display on the Great White Goose. The second presents the history of European migration at Grosse Île and the surrounding south shore through a sound and light show. There is an English version. Admission is $6.

The snow goose rests in Montmagny.

There is an extensive accordion collection at **Economusée de l'Accordeon** at 301 Boulevard Taché Est.

The Gare Fluviale or Marine Terminal in the centre of town on the waterfront has boats daily to Îsle Aux Grues and Grosse Île. Bikes and kayaks can be rented. A riverside bird sanctuary is adjacent.

In and around Montmagny there are numerous places to stay including lodges, motels and campgrounds. About a dozen places to eat can be found in town including the inexpensive bistro (or the costly dining room) in the *Manoir des Erables (220 Boulevard Taché Est)*.

Grosse Île and the **Irish Memorial National Historic Site** commemorate the significant role this small island has played in Canada's history. For 105 years, from 1832 until as late as 1937, Grosse Île was the major Canadian quarantine station for immigrants coming from Europe.

Through the 19th century and into the middle of the 20th, four million people passed through Quebec City en route to points across North America. Isolated Grosse Ile was meant to screen out those among the thousands of people of varying nationalities with typhus, cholera and the like. In attempting to perform this service it became, in a sense, a city of woe. One of its most tragic periods was the 15 years from 1832 when thousands of Irish died after taking the 'coffin ships' to escape the potato famine.

There are over 100 buildings or remains of buildings still on the historic site including churches, a school, the 'hotel' residences and hospital. And, of course, the cemeteries. Restoration is ongoing. There are half or full-day excursions but, in either case, reservations are required. For information call ☎ 1-800-463-6769 or ☎ 418-248-8888 in Montmagny. Bilingual guides are available from the reception centre to lead visitors around the site which is open from May to October.

From Montmagny there are several different operators who run boats the short distance over to the park. Croisières Lachance (☎ 1-888-476-7734), departing east down

the road at Berthier Sur Mer, is the main operator with a five hour trip at $32. This includes the park-guided tour of the site.

Taxi les Îles (☎ 1-888-755-2818) at the Montmagny dock is cheaper but check how long the trip is; docking here is more effected by tides. There is a cafeteria on the island or take a picnic.

The only inhabited island in the archipelago, small **Isle-aux-Grues** can also be visited. There are free ferry boats, pay water-taxi shuttles and bicycle rentals from the Montmagny dock. The island is mainly geared to those in need of a quick escape from the rat race and has a couple of costly inns and a restaurant. But a pleasant day can be spent cycling and walking on the 10km-long island and there is also a campground, several B&Bs and a café.

Saint Jean-Port-Joli

This small but spread-out town, with the big two-spired church right in the middle, is a centre for the Quebec art of woodcarving. Pretty well everything can be found along one street, Rue de Gaspé, including the central seasonal tourist office. The impressive church dates from 1890 and the priest's house next door was built even earlier in 1872.

Good examples of the woodcarvers' art can be seen in the **Musée des Anciens Canadiens** at 332 Ave de Gaspé Ouest with an admission of $4.50. The museum has work done by some of the best known local sculptors, past and present. There is a gift shop to browse without paying. It's open every day from May to November.

More recent carvings in the same style and in a variety of other styles can be seen in the many workshops and stores in and around town. Some carvers specialise in figures, others in religious themes, and still others in boats and ornate murals. Courses in carving can be taken as well. Other crafts produced and sold here are ceramics and textiles but they are distant seconds to the number of works in wood.

Faunart at 377 Ave de Gaspé Ouest, shows works of art, mainly dealing with animals, in many mediums by Denis D'Amours

and other Quebec artists. Admission is charged at this gallery/store.

At 322 Rue de Gaspé Ouest there's the **Maison Médard-Bourgault**, the former home of a wood carver who left reminders of his work on the walls and in the furnishings of the old house.

In and around the centre you'll also find a restaurant or two, a few motels and a B&B. On the west side is *Auberge du Faubourg*, a massive accommodation complex with a restaurant. Farther west is a good picnic area with views over the river. Campgrounds can be found in both directions out of town, closer heading east.

Orleans Express bus lines stop right in the centre of town at the SOS depanneur across the street from the church. There's a daily bus to Quebec City.

East along the St Lawrence River

East along the St Lawrence River from Quebec City are some of the most scenic landscapes in the province as the shoreline becomes more typical of that found in eastern Canada. With neat small farms and little villages dominated by the church – usually topped by a silver spire – this is rural Quebec. With few changes, life has been pretty much the same here for well over a century. You won't hear much English spoken in this part of the province.

From Quebec City you can take either the north or south shore up towards the Gaspé. Just don't take the super Hwy 20 from which you'll see nothing. The north side is discussed first followed by the attractions of the south shore.

There are ferries across the river at various points. The farther east you go, the wider the river becomes and the more costly the ferry.

Important Ferry Note Making ferry reservations can save you a lot of grief. They are often full so waiting standby for hours only to be turned away is no fun.

CHARLEVOIX (NORTH SHORE)

The north shore area is hillier, wilder and more dramatic than the south shore as the northern mountains come down close to the river. It also has the more physical points of interest.

Beyond Sainte Anne de Beaupré is the scenic coastal and mountain district known as Charlevoix. For 200 years this pastoral strip of hilly, flowery farmland counter-balanced with steep cliffs and woods wedged between northern wilderness and the river has been a summer retreat of the wealthy and privileged. Though vestiges of this remain and prices are on the high side it is now a more democratic destination.

UNESCO has classed it as a biosphere or heritage cultural and environmental region and this has meant worthwhile restrictions on the types of permitted developments.

It has long been a popular district with artists, and numerous galleries and craft shops may be found in the towns and villages. Inns and less-expensive B&Bs abound and there is no shortage of quality restaurants. Aside from summer visitors, people from Quebec City enjoy Charlevoix as a place for a weekend break or a short holiday destination. Beginning around the middle of September the autumn foliage is remarkable.

Due to its popularity as well as upper-class tradition (and quality), prices for food and lodging are higher here than elsewhere up the St Lawrence but the terrain and parks make a short visit worthwhile even for those on tight budgets. There is plenty of camping, and alternatives to the more costly places do exist. Intercar and Orléans Express buses serve the area stopping at many of the small as well as the larger towns.

Baie Saint Paul

Heading east along the St Lawrence River the first urban stop after Quebec City is Baie Saint Paul, with its old streets and big church. The year-round tourist office (☎ 418-435-4160) is on Hwy 132 west of town. Another (☎ 418-435-3681), open through the summer, is central in the Art Centre at 4 Rue Ambroise Fafard.

The main street of this attractive town, Rue Saint Jean Baptiste, is lined with historic houses some of which have been converted into galleries and restaurants. Artists' studios and craft shops are scattered around the side streets.

The Art Centre often has shows of Charlevoix painters. A major gallery is the Exposition Centre at 23 Rue Ambroise Fafard; entry is free. Another to have a peek at is at 58 Rue Saint Jean Baptiste. This house/museum is where a local painter, René Richard, lived and worked and played host to some of the country's most prominent painters through the mid-1900s.

The Natural History Centre west of town on Hwy 138 at the tourist office has displays on the flora and fauna and geography of the Charlevoix district. It's open all year and is free. It features exhibits on the massive meteorite that hit the district 350 million years ago. Many of the exhibits are described in French only but there are plenty of visuals.

For spending the night, there is the excellent *La Balcon Vert* (☎ 418-435-5587) east out of the centre up the hill, off Route (Hwy) 362. Watch for the signs. With its restaurant, bar, woodsy setting, chalets, dorms and campground it is a retreat, hotel and hostel all in one. And it has a fabulous view. It's open from about the end of May to the first week or so in October and makes a perfect base for exploring the region. A dorm bed is $16 and rates go down for stays of more than three nights. A private room or chalet for two is $40 and family rates are offered. The cafeteria has tasty, bargain-priced meals.

As the main town in the area, there are many hotels and B&Bs. *Gite du Voyageur* (☎ 418-435-3480, 44 Rue Amboise Fafard) is central and is a deal at $30/35 with breakfast. *Gite Chez Marie* (☎ 418-435-2927, 43 Rue Saint Joseph) is also modest at $35/45.

The immaculate red and silver *Auberge La Grande Maison* (☎ 418-435-5575, 160 Rue Saint Jean Baptiste), covered in flowers, is more costly with rooms from $50 to $130. This attractive place is central and has its own restaurant.

QUEBEC

About 20 minutes drive north of the centre is *Motels-Chalets Chez Laurent (☎ 418-435-3895, 1493 Boulevard de Laval, Hwy 138)* where singles/doubles in the motel units start at $50 and there are fully equipped chalet cottages available.

The central area has numerous enticing cafés and restaurants.

The bus station is at the side of the Le Village shopping centre on the corner of Rte de L'Equere and Boulevard Mgr de Laval. It's about a 20 minute walk to downtown.

Bicycles can be rented at Randonnées Nature Charlevoix, 41 Rue Saint Jean Baptiste, and an afternoon's cycle around the area should be considered. It also runs van tours in the area including around the meteorite crater's perimeter.

Around Baie Saint Paul

Quiet, rural Île aux Coudres is what many people disappointed in better known Île d'Orleans are looking for. It's the gentle, easy paced kind of place where you go to spend an afternoon and stay for days. Once the base for whale hunting, the island is now mainly farmland with a number of small low-key historic sites and a windmill. At the terminal there is an information booth. Bicycles are ideal for exploring the island and can be rented. The difficulty is that the bike rental place is 5km from the dock. Turn left at the blinking light after leaving the boat and keep walking. There are two campgrounds on the island and several motels and B&Bs.

Ferries run to the island from Saint Joseph de la Rive where there are a few places by the terminal to stay or to grab a bite. The pleasant trip takes 15 minutes and runs frequently, especially through summer months.

Hwy 381, north from Baie Saint Paul, runs along the edge of huge Laurentide Park offering good scenery and steep hills.

Excellent hiking and rugged topography can be found in Grands Jardins Provincial Park which encompasses an area of mountains and taiga (northern evergreen forest) and includes a caribou herd among the wildlife. The park is 35km from Baie Saint Paul and has the Thomas-Fortin information office (☎ 418-457-3945) at the entrance. There is camping or cottages in the park as well as bike and canoe rentals. There is little swimming but the hike up Mont de Lac des Cygnes (Swan Lake) is very fine and makes an excellent half-day outing. Sections of the park suffered a forest fire in the early 1990s and camping at Lac Athabaska amid the charred trunks certainly provides a unique perspective.

Going east along the St Lawrence, don't even consider taking Hwy 138 but take the coastal Hwy 362 which goes up and down hills beside the river. The scenery is superb around Les Éboulements, with farms running from the town's edge to the river. You may have to stop while a farmer leads cattle across the highway. Note the piles of wood used for the long winters and the many carving outlets.

Pointe-au-Pic

Seemingly a small, insignificant village, Pic was a holiday destination for the wealthy from as far as New York at the beginning of the 20th century. The scenery, the isolation and the trendiness had many building fine summer residences along the shore. One such resident was William-Howard Taft, who was a US president. Some of these large, impressive 'cottages' along Chemin des Falaises have now been converted into comfortable inns.

Today, the main attraction is the posh casino at the *Manoir Richelieu*. The huge, once elegant, romantic hotel dating from 1928 is now busy with bus loads of gamblers but is still worth a look. It offers one, two and three-day packages including some meals and entertainment but we're talking serious dollars. An exception to the prices is the Winston bar-restaurant on the ground floor with a low-cost breakfast – a good excuse for checking the place. The adjacent casino with gaming tables and slots is open daily until 3 am and has no admission fee. It's not overly formal but shorts and jeans are not acceptable.

The museum at 1 Chemin du Havre, offers a good view and exhibits on the life and times of Charlevoix. A major part of the museum is

the art gallery, which has a permanent display as well as changing shows which promote the works of local artists. The museum is open daily in summer from 10 am to 6 pm, with shortened hours at other times, and admission is $4, less for students.

Pointe-au-Pic has a considerable amount of accommodation, least expensive of which are the B&Bs. *La Maison Dufour-Bouchard* (☎ *418-665-4982, 18 Rue Laure Conan)* has doubles at just $45.

For a meal, or to savour some of the extremely impressive Belgian beer inventory, get comfortable at *La Douceurs Belges (121 Chemin des Falaises)*. This very attractive Belgian restaurant has main dishes in the $10 range and exotic brews from a few dollars less.

La Malbaie

La Malbaie, the second largest town in the region, sits in the middle of Charlevoix about 140km from Quebec City. There really isn't much to see and do here but there is a major tourist office at 630 Boulevard de Comport open daily which can help with information on the area and parks.

There are a couple of places for overnighters but nowhere near the number as in Pointe-au-Pic.

In Cap-à-l'Aigle, 10km east of town, is one of the top rated Charlevoix restaurants, the *Auberge des Peupliers* in a fine old house wrapped with a veranda. Lunches are about $20 and dinners $40 to $55. There is also a pricey B&B down the street, the *Maison Victoria* (☎ *418-665-1022)*.

Just east of this village on Hwy 138 is Les Quatre Vent, considered by many to be Canada's biggest and best private garden. It's only open four Saturdays a summer and tickets sell out. For information contact Centre Ecologique, 337 Highway 138, Saint Fidèle, Quebec G0T 1T0, or ☎ 418-434-2209.

About 44km north of La Malbaie is the impressive **Parc des Hautes-Gorges** (☎ 418-439-4402), a geographically and scenically intriguing area of mountains cut through by the Malbaie River. The sheer cliffs along the river reach 700m high at places.

Most of the road is unsurfaced and rough, making the drive over 1½ hours long. It leads to the gorge where there is an information centre with café and canoe rentals. The *campground* is often full but there are a number of undeveloped, cleared areas (sort of) where you can (barely) squeeze a tent in between the trees. The best sites, including some on stretches of beach, are reached by canoe.

Also departing from the information centre, 1½ hour cruises along the gorge cost $21. The same and more can be done by canoe. Many of those on cruises come as part of a one-day bus and boat package organised in Pointe-au-Pic. Call the park office for availability of other tours. Fine hiking trails crisscross much of the park. Take supplies with you.

Saint Siméon

The ferry (☎ 418-638-2856) to Rivière-du-Loup on the south shore departs from Saint Siméon. At this point in the river, a crossing is 65 minutes. It's in this area that the river, on its way to the Atlantic, begins to get salty. The ferry is comfortable with lounges, an information desk and a capacity of 100 vehicles. Whales may be seen if you're lucky. There are five trips a day during summer, three or four in spring and autumn, but the schedule varies according to the tides. Visitors with vehicles should be at the dock an hour before departure but for walk-ons this is not necessary. For prices see under South Shore later in this chapter.

The ferry terminal is in the centre of town. There is camping, a hostel and motels.

SAGUENAY RIVER & AREA

The Saguenay is the largest of eastern Canada's few fjords – a spectacular saltwater inlet, edged in part by steep cliffs and running to a depth of 500m along a crack in the earth's crust. Ocean-going ships can ply the deep black waters as far as Chicoutimi.

A federal marine park protects the river and the waters around where the Saguenay empties into the St Lawrence. The land surrounding the fjord and part of the shore

QUEBEC

north of Tadoussac is contained within the provincial Saguenay Park.

At the confluence of the Saguenay River and the St Lawrence, shrimp and capelin abound, attracting beluga, minke, finback, and even some humpback and blue whales. Now protected, the great beasts have sparked a revitalisation of the region and it has become one of the provinces most worthwhile visitor destinations. **Whale watching** and **fjord cruises** are the basis for all the activity. A range of whale-watching trips runs from the middle of May until mid-October but the surfacing giants can also be seen from shore at several locations. A community of the distinctive white beluga whales, normally found strictly in the far Arctic, live in and around the Saguenay River year-round. Once numbering 6000, only 550 beluga whales still remain and this area has become their refuge. In June, minkes and finbacks arrive from the Gulf of St Lawrence and, later in summer, the huge blue whale shows up to feed on the krill which is produced in copious amounts where the two rivers meet. August to October is generally the best whale-watching period. Seals and seabirds are abundant and porpoises and dolphins also frequent the region.

A range of cruises up the fjord are also offered. These trips upstream past the cliffs are interesting, as you lose your ability to judge size and distance against the rock walls.

Regardless of where you're headed if you're going out on the water take a lot of clothes no matter how hot it is on shore. It is always breezy on the rivers and the water temperature here is low, even in July. Also, the waters can become stormy very quickly.

The parklands alongside the Saguenay and St Lawrence are also well worth exploring and there are some very fine trails and walks to enjoy as well as various viewpoints and geological features.

Baie Sainte Catherine

Baie Sainte Catherine at the mouth of the Saguenay River marks the eastern end of the Charlevoix district and together with Tadoussac acts as a centre for exploring the majestic Saguenay and surrounding waters.

The main point of interest on this side of the river is the **Pointe Noire Coastal Station** up the hill from the ferry landing. This whale-study post (☎ 418-237-4383) where the two rivers meet has an exhibit, a slide show and films, and an observation deck with a telescope for views over the mouth of the river. The centre is open daily from June to September and then weekends only into the middle of October and is free. This is one of the best places, cruises included, to see belugas. They are often seen in the Saguenay very close to shore especially when the tide is coming in.

Of the many **boat cruises**, several of the larger operators with the bigger vessels are based at the small port here. Some can also be boarded in Tadoussac and tickets can be bought in either town. AML Cruises (☎ 418-237-4274), with three boats each taking hundreds of passengers, has whale-watching trips and excursions up into the fjord. The three hour whale trip runs from mid-May to mid-October and costs $32. In July and August, there is a 3½ hour cruise daily up the fjord to Cap Eternité for $30 or dinner/sunset trips. All its ships offer bars and all the extras.

Another major cruise company is Famille Dufour (☎ 1-800-463-5250) with similar trips. Information for all tours can be found at the dock.

See Tadoussac for information on the smaller vessels.

There is some accommodation in Baie Sainte Catherine and the surrounding area, mostly in fairly priced B&Bs. *Gîte aux Pignons Verts (☎ 418-237-4331, 526 Hwy 138)*, a B&B on the main street, charges $35/45. It's 3km from the dock area.

Hotel Motel Baie Sainte Catherine (☎ 418-237-4271, 294 Hwy 138) is a nice place with doubles about $50. Remember the area can be a busy place in midsummer so book a room early.

A couple of small, inexpensive eateries can be found along the highway here, too.

Through summer months, a ferry runs across the Saguenay to Tadoussac every 20 minutes from 8 am to 8 pm, then every 40 minutes. The free 10 minute trip is not as

frequent the rest of the year. It is not uncommon to see whales from the ferry.

Tadoussac

Across the Saguenay, Tadoussac, with a population of just 930, is about three times the size of Baie Sainte Catherine and though still a small town, acts as the regional centre. It's an attractive place and nearly all the numerous points of interest are within walking distance of each other. This is also headquarters for whale watching (May to October) and river trips around the Saguenay waters. See under Saguenay and Baie Sainte Catherine above for more information.

The tourist information office (☎ 418-235-4744) is at 197 Rue des Pionniers in the middle of town. The hours are from 8 am to 8 pm daily in summer, closed weekends otherwise. All the sites and boat trips operate seasonally, and from the end of October to spring Tadoussac pretty much shuts up and visitors are few.

The quay and waterfront area along Rue du Bord de l'Eau facing out to Tadoussac Bay has offices for the various **boat trip** operators although tickets can be purchased at numerous places around town. It may be best to scout around at the water having a look at the various boats before you decide. Whatever you're preference, try to wait for a calm day. Of all the factors affecting the success of a trip this could be the most significant. Whales are best seen and even heard when the sea is not too wavy and it makes the captain's work locating them easier. Rain or shine, early or late doesn't make much difference, it's largely a matter of luck but it's rare that no whales are seen. Having tried different size boats, each has advantages and disadvantages but overall, the Zodiacs are recommended. They are fast, quiet, manoeuvrable, generally can get the closest and every seat is good. Take a lot of clothes, especially early and late in the season; nobody is ever too hot. The small and medium size boats are the second choice; the MV *Pierre Chauvin* is good and includes bilingual (if you ask) narration. If it's very cold and you're not prepared or the water is rough or you have children this is a good bet. Rates are pretty standard at $35 for most trips and a little lower out of peak season. Kids are cheaper on the larger boats. For fjord trips see Baie Saint Catherine.

The **Marine Mammal Interpretive Centre** (CIMM) at 108 Rue de la Cale-Sèche is open daily from May to November and gives visitors some background information on the creatures found in local waters. Admission is $5.50 for adults.

Maison Chauvin at 157 Rue du Bord de l'Eau is a replica of the country's first fur-trading post and offers some history on the first transactions between Native Indians and Europeans. It, too, is open every day but through the warm months only.

Built in 1747 by the Jesuits, **La Vieille Chapelle**, on Rue Bord de l'Eau, is one of the oldest wooden churches in the country. It is also known as the Indian Chapel. The cemetery next door is worth a look, too.

The **Pisciculture** or fish hatchery, 115 Rue du Bateau Passeur, is operated by the provincial government to provide fish for the restocking of Quebec's salmon streams and rivers. It can be toured free. Some of the Parc du Saguenay's walking trails begin from behind the hatchery.

At 145 Rue du Bateau Passeur is the small specialised **Musée Maritime de Tadoussac** which through models, photographs and other artefacts outlines the sea-faring history of the area and shipping on the St Lawrence.

The conspicuous **Tadoussac Hotel**, a seemingly out-of-place, huge, old, attractive resort was built in 1941 and renovated in the mid-1980s. A walk through the lobby and around the grounds is certainly an experience.

There are some fine green areas around town for **walking**. From Pointe de l'Islet, a peninsular park at the southern edge of town, spying whales from the shore is possible. A walking trail beginning and ending from the Rue du Bord de l'Eau leads around the peninsula.

The **Parc du Saguenay**, beginning in Tadoussac, is a huge park which runs along both sides of the Saguenay River virtually all the way to Chicoutimi. There are numerous

QUEBEC

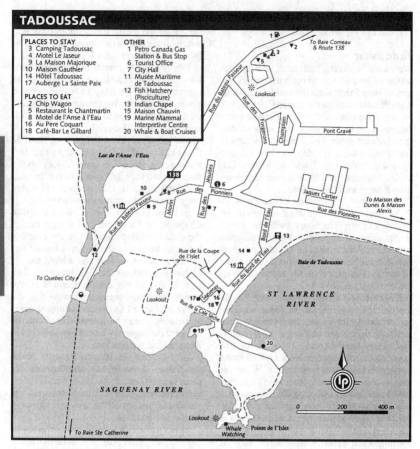

TADOUSSAC

PLACES TO STAY
3 Camping Tadoussac
4 Motel Le Jaseur
9 La Maison Majorique
10 Maison Gauthier
14 Hôtel Tadoussac
17 Auberge La Sainte Paix

PLACES TO EAT
2 Chip Wagon
5 Restaurant le Chantmartin
8 Motel de l'Anse à l'Eau
16 Au Pere Coquart
18 Café-Bar Le Gilbard

OTHER
1 Petro Canada Gas
Station & Bus Stop
6 Tourist Office
7 City Hall
11 Musée Maritime
de Tadoussac
12 Fish Hatchery
(Pisciculture)
13 Indian Chapel
15 Maison Chauvin
19 Marine Mammal
Interpretive Centre
20 Whale & Boat Cruises

good walks within it. For great views over the confluence of the rivers take the trails around the hill beginning across the street from the Fish Hatchery (Pisciculture). There's free parking. Longer trails running north begin across the street at the Pisciculture. Ask about them at the information office. The park includes the land all around Lac de l'Anse à l'Eau, the lake just north of town. One of the walking trails beginning at the Pisciculture leads along the edge of this lake where you can swim.

The park's mandate is to protect and promote the Saguenay, its waters, surroundings and wildlife. Affiliated interpretive centres are found at Pointe Noire in Baie Sainte Catherine (free) and at Cap de Bon Désir near Grandes Bergerons 22km north-east of Tadoussac up the St Lawrence. At both centres whales can be seen from shore and there are displays on the mammals of the sea. At the latter you can wander along the rocky shore, picnic and keep an eye out to sea for a fin. Naturalists can answer questions.

Between 5 and 6km north-east of Tadoussac, glaciers have sculpted massive sand dunes. The **Maison des Dunes Interpretive Centre** (☎ 418-235-4238) on Chemin du Moulin à Baude, part of the Parc du Saguenay, has information about their origins and is open daily from mid-June to the end of September. A walking trail leads 6km north-east along the beach and waterfront from the downtown area to the dunes. This recommended side trip can also be reached by car. A stroll at the shore here is virtually like being at the ocean with salt air, seaweed and marine creatures to observe. Climbing the lovely, immense sand dune along the beach is an aerobic challenge. The centre has detailed maps of the entire park with hiking trails, camp sites etc and can offer further information. These maps can also be bought at the tourist office.

Back in town, kayaks can be rented on the beach. At the beginning of June, Tadoussac hosts a music festival. In winter, ask at the hostel about dog-sled trips.

See under The North Coast & Area later in this chapter for more Tadoussac-related information.

Places to Stay *Camping Tadoussac* (☎ 418-235-4501) is 2km from the ferry on Hwy 138. During summer it is full nightly; arrive early in the morning to get one of the sandy sites. Don't miss the superb view from the playground.

For hostellers, year-round *La Maison Majorique* (☎ 418-235-4372, ☎ 1-800-461-8585, 158 Rue du Bateau-Passeur) is a large, casual, central HI hostel on the corner of Rue des Pionniers. It's the traditional-looking place with the red roof. Dorm beds cost $14 and good, informal banquet-style dinners are offered at $6. Breakfast is also available or you can use the kitchen yourself. It's been said the atmosphere is so congenial that a number of visitors meeting at the hostel have later married. There are now some tenting places, too.

During summer, there is a second place run by the same people, *Maison Alexis* (same telephone, 389 Rue des Pionniers),

about 1km east of town. It's smaller, quieter and much more low-key.

Tadoussac also has a range of rooms for rent in people's houses ($30 to $40 average), B&Bs ($50 to $60) and hotel-motels ($70 to $90). Most are central. Ask at the tourist office.

Auberge La Sainte Paix (☎ 418-235-4803, 102 Rue Saguenay) overlooking the river is a fine B&B choice. It's central, friendly, spacious and has a lovely garden. Guests can use the kitchen. Doubles are $55.

Another B&B to try is *Maison Gauthier* (☎ 418-235-4525, 159 Rue du Bateau Passeur). *Motel Le Jaseur* (☎ 418-235-4737, 414 Rue du Bateau Passeur) is the cheapest of the hotel-motels but is still costly at $75.

Places to Eat For a good, cheap breakfast check the restaurant at *Motel de l'Anse à l'Eau* on Rue des Pionniers near the corner of Rue Bateau Passeur.

Café-Bar Le Gibard on Bord de l'Eau, the main waterfront street, is a small, casual place for a coffee or beer, and whales can sometimes be seen from the window at high tide.

Au Pere Coquart (115 Coupe de L'Islet) is a pub-like place with a patio and sometimes live music. The sandwiches and salad ($7.50) are noteworthy and there are meats such as buffalo and caribou.

The *Chantmartin* beside the campground is a moderate, all-purpose place specialising in pizza (the vegetarian one is very good) but the menu is extensive.

Farther up the road on the same side don't miss the *chip wagon* (452 Rue du Bateau Passeur). It's run by connoisseur Claude Lapointe who knows life is a comic game but plays it seriously. He figures his fries can't be beat and he may be right. As you approach he'll say 'bonjour, Tremblay', betting that's your name so play along. The king of potatoes also knows a lot about the outdoors and enjoys a conversation.

For a splurge, the main dining room at the *Hotel Tadoussac* is a real treat complete with pianist and not unreasonable at $27 for the table d'hôte.

There's also a *bakery* (164 Rue Morin).

QUEBEC

Getting There & Away Intercar (☎ 418-235-4653) bus line connects Tadoussac from Quebec City along the north shore and runs as far as Baie Comeau. The Petro Canada gas station on Hwy 138 opposite the campground serves as the station. Autobus Tremblay & Tremblay runs up to Chicoutimi.

Up the Saguenay River

Just north-west of Tadoussac, Parc du Saguenay (Saguenay Park), which protects the river's edges almost all the way to Chicoutimi, begins. Aside from the cruises of the fjord departing from the quay in Tadoussac there are others from various points along the river. There is camping in the park and guesthouses in the nearby villages.

On either side of the Saguenay, the roads northward are a distance from the river but the wooded, hilly terrain interspersed with streams and cliffs make for a scenic trip. The east side is less developed, the west has access to more places of interest.

From the village of **Sacré Coeur**, 10km from Tadoussac on the east side of the river, a small road leads to L'Anse de Roche with a good view of the fjord and boat tours. There is also a campground here.

In the middle of the park on the west side of the Saguenay is pretty **L'Anse Saint John** from where there are daily cruises through the summer and guided kayak trips or rentals. The village has several B&Bs and camping. *Auberge Chez Monika* (☎ 418-272-3115, 12 Les Plateaux) is 4.7km from Hwy 170 (turn at the Centre Equestre sign). This small medicinal plant farm has a couple of hostel rooms and a kitchen. It's a very peaceful, secluded place with horse-riding next door. A mini-bus runs to the village from Chicoutimi (☎ 418-272-2897); there's no transport from Tadoussac. There are some good viewpoints and walking trails within a couple of kilometres. Farther west the area around Lac Ha! Ha! is where parts of the film *Black Robe* were filmed.

The main sites along the river are the cliff-side trails at **Cap Éternité** and Cap Trinité. Boat trips are also offered. At Cap Éternité, a rigorous hike, or rather a brutally long staircase, leads to a statue called Our Lady of Saguenay raised by a thankful, almost drowned soul in 1881.

Chicoutimi

Hilly Chicoutimi sits nestled between mountains on the west side of the Saguenay River about 1¼ hours from Tadoussac. Despite being one of the province's largest northern towns, working class Chicoutimi is quite small with a population of 65,000.

The tourist office (☎ 418-543-9778) is at 198 Rue Racine, the city's main street. There is not a lot to see around this ordinary town but the large number of students (there is a university and a community college known as a CÉGEP) livens things up.

La Pulperie (☎ 418-698-3100), 300 Rue Dubuc, was once the world's biggest pulp mill. Although no longer operating it can be visited and the site contains two of the city's other main attractions. See the **House of Arthur Villeneuve**. In the late 1950s when Monsieur Villeneuve retired as a local barber, he began painting. His depictions of the town and landscape along the river attracted a lot of attention and are now sold and collected around the world. The house, his former home, is a museum known not so much for the paintings it contains but for the painting it is. The entire house has been painted inside and out like a series of canvases in Villeneuve's bright, naive folk style. The **Musée du Saguenay-Lac Saint Jean** with displays on the history of the area including some Native Indian and Inuit artefacts is also here. The site is open from mid-June to Labour Day. Admission is $8.50.

The **Little White House** which held steady against the floods of 1996 and was made famous around the world by news photographs can be viewed on Rue Bosse a few blocks west of downtown by the Dubuc bridge.

From the redeveloped old harbour and market area, tour boats depart for trips down the Saguenay River.

The entire area is known for blueberries, a treat to try is the chocolate covered ones. Trappist monks make the best.

A Native Indian dream-catcher is among the artefacts on display in the Musée du Saguenay-Lac Saint Jean.

Places to Stay For low-budget accommodation try the *CÉGEP* (☎ 418-549-9520, 534 Rue Jacques Cartier Est) from May to mid-August. It's about 1.5km from the bus station.

Auberge Centre Ville (☎ 418-543-0253, 104 Rue Jacques Cartier) is a good, central place at $65 a double.

Another good value option is *Motel au Parasol* (☎ 418-543-7771, 1287 Boulevard Saguenay Est), with moderately priced rooms and a great view.

Places to Eat Rue Racine has numerous places to eat. *Au Café Croissant (398 Rue Racine Est)* is an inexpensive cafeteria-style place in the centre of town. *La Forchette (100 Morin)* just off Racine is cheap and open 24 hours for standard fare. Many other restaurants including the main chains, can be found on Boulevard Talbot and Boulevard Saguenay leading into town.

At night, the *Guinness Pub (455 Rue de l'Hotel Dieu)* is good and has a wide selection of beers. Along Rue Racine are several other places for raising a glass or kicking up the heels.

Getting There & Away Intercar bus line (☎ 418-543-1403) at 55 Rue Racine Est connects to Quebec and Montreal and to Jonquière. Buses also go to Tadoussac. L'Autobus L'Anse Saint Jean (☎ 418-543-1403) runs a van down the Saguenay to L'Anse Saint Jean.

Jonquière

West from Chicoutimi along Hwy 170, Jonquière is about the same size as Chicoutimi. It has an enormous aluminum smelter and two paper mills which can be visited. Get details from the tourist office.

Rue Saint Dominique, the main street, has a number of bars and cafés which are very busy at night. The lookout at the Shipshaw Dam is a good stop. Turn right after crossing the Aluminium Bridge north of downtown.

The hostel burnt in 1998; watch for a re-opening. There is inexpensive summer accommodation available at the *CÉGEP college* (☎ 418-542-0352, 2505 Rue Saint Hubert) and numerous motels.

Farther north, **Lac Saint Jean** is the source of the Saguenay. There's a wilderness park on the east side of the lake and at Sainte Monique the resort-like *Auberge Île du Repos* (☎ 418-347-5649). Encompassing a tiny island, the resort features hostel dorms, kitchen facilities, private chalet rooms, camping, a rather pricey restaurant, bar with 'name' live music (also pricey) and a beach with good swimming. There's no public transportation but it's popular with Québecois looking for some rest and recreation. The atmosphere depends a lot on who the other guests are.

On the west side at Mashteuiatsh, north of Roberval, is the **Pekuakamiulnuatsh Indian Reserve** (☎ 418-275-3750) with a museum.

The highway continues on through northern timberland and a huge nature reserve to the town of Chibougamou. From there the roads start to peter out (see The Far North section later in this chapter).

THE NORTH COAST & AREA

The scenic highway just east of Tadoussac leads to some of the same features found in town. About 12km out there is a lake with good swimming – watch for the parking lot on the left. A path leads through the woods to the beach.

At **Bergeronnes** is the bilingual **Cap de Bon Désir Interpretation Centre**, part of the Saguenay Park system. The rocky shoreline here is very good for whale watching and

QUEBEC

there are naturalists on hand, displays and a lighthouse. Admission is $4. Neptune Cruises has Zodiac whale trips. The benefit here is that you are closer to where the whales generally hang out so there is less travel time.

Large **Camping Bon Désir** (☎ 418-232-6297) in Bergeronnes is a very fine campground with views over the river and makes a great second choice if Tadoussac (25km away) is full.

Cheaper whale-watching trips also depart from the Montagnais native community of **Essipit** but the campground here is not good. The ferry from adjacent **Les Escoumins** makes a logical choice if you're going to Trois Pistoles and the Gaspé. There is a hostel (mainly geared to divers), a motel, a couple of places for a munch, a birdwatching lookout and kayak rentals.

Baie Comeau

Beyond Tadoussac on the north shore of the St Lawrence, the road continues north-east through hilly and less-populated areas to the ugly resource town of Baie Comeau. It's divided into east and west sectors with a combined population of 27,000.

There's nothing to see here but in a small part of the east sector (with the ferry) known as the **Quartier Saint Amélie** there is another of the grand north-shore hotels, Hôtel le Manoir. It's surrounded by a bland so-called heritage district with houses dating from the 1930s.

There are several motels on Boulevard Lasalle (Hwy 138, east sector). **Motel Amigo** (☎ 418-296-3131, 221 Boulevard Lasalle) is the most economical at $45.

Baie Comeau is one of the semi-remote industrial centres which seem to proliferate in this part of the country. As well as the pulp mill, there is a major grain elevator and the huge **Reynold's** aluminum smelter which runs free guided tours throughout summer, twice on weekday afternoons.

But most associate the town with hydropower because of the large projects along the Manicouagan River. Each of the three enormous **dams** operated by Hydro-Quebec – Manic Deux and Cinq – can be visited

free. The first dam is 50km north of town and the last one 200km north. The scope and scale of these projects will really boggle the eyes and mind.

From Baie Comeau, Hwy 389 runs north past the Manicouagan projects and then beyond to Wabush and Labrador City on the border of Quebec and Labrador, Newfoundland. For details of these similarly awesome towns and Labrador, see the Labrador section in the Newfoundland chapter. There is also some more information on travelling the road to Labrador in that section. The **Grouix Mountains**, about 120km north-west of Manic Cinq, reach as high as 1000m. This is a fascinating far-north landscape with lake-filled barrens and tundra.

Baie Comeau is connected by ferry to Matane across the river. For ferry details see Matane in the Gaspé Peninsula section later in this chapter.

Sept-Îles

Sept-Îles is the last town of any size along the north shore. It's a port city and international freighters make use of the docking facilities. In fact, despite the rather isolated location, this is Canada's second busiest port measured by tonnage.

Along the waterfront park, a boardwalk fronts the shoreline. The tourist office (☎ 418-962-1238), open all year, is nearby at 1401 Boulevard Laure Ouest.

Vieux Poste on Boulevard des Montagnais is a reconstructed trading post where the French dealt with the Montagnais Indians whose land this traditionally was. There is also the regional museum/art gallery. The Native Cultural Centre in a church at 1 Rue de la Reserve has some traditional crafts for sale and the Innu Museum, 290 Boulevard des Montagnais, provides more background.

The highlight is the offshore **Sept-Îles Archipelago Park** with its varied bird and sea life. There are various boat trips available. Île Grand Basque can be visited for camping, hiking, beaches and a few other things to see. Nature trails cross the island. Camping costs $10. There are frequent ferries which

cost $10, and water taxis to other places. Île du Corosol is a bird refuge.

Bicycles and kayaks can be rented at Rioux Velo, 391 Avenue Gamache. You can also take cod-fishing trips from Sept-Îles out among the many islands for about $15.

North-west of town is the huge, wild Reserve Faunique with camping.

The train from Sept-Îles permits access to part of Quebec's north and the western portions of Newfoundland's Labrador. See also the Labrador section of the Newfoundland chapter. The road continues eastward to Havre Saint Pierre.

Places to Stay There is an HI hostel, the *Auberge Internationale Le Tangon* (☎ 418-962-8180, 555 Rue Cartier) and half a dozen motels mostly in the expensive category. A B&B alternative is the *Gite des Iles* (☎ 418-962-6116, 50 Rue Thibeault) at $45. There are also private campgrounds.

Getting There & Away Autobus du Littoral (☎ 418-962-2126), 126 Rue Mgr Blance, runs buses between Baie Comeau and beyond Havre Saint Pierre stopping at Sept-Îles en route. From Baie Comeau buses connect with Quebec City.

The thrice-weekly train north from Sept-Îles to Schefferville via Labrador City, Labrador offers a fascinating trip through northern spruce forest and open tundra. The train crosses a 900m-long bridge, 50m over the Moisie River and past the 60m-high Tonkas Falls. The dome car is from the famous *Wabash Cannonball* train, a name often heard in US folk songs.

The route through the remote, rugged terrain was begun in 1950 and took 7000 workers four years to finish – a dirty job. These people had to be flown in, making the largest civilian airlift ever. For information in Sept-Îles call the Quebec and North Shore Railway on ☎ 418-968-7805. The station is at 100 Rue Retty.

Around Sept-Îles
A side trip from Sept-Îles (or Labrador City in Newfoundland) can be made to Fermont

(Quebec), a mining town 27km west of Labrador City, right on the provincial borders. Built in 1974, it has a unique design which consists of a 1.5km-long, five-storey arched building containing most of the town's commercial establishments. The housing is all built inside the windbreaking curve. Access is by the above-mentioned train which continues on to Schefferville, another mining town.

Havre Saint Pierre
The area from Sept-Îles to Île d'Anticosti and Natashquan is one of the province's remote regions now attracting more visitors for the wild undeveloped land, animal life and outdoor adventure.

This town is the jumping-off point for visits to the island national park just offshore. Visit the national park's reception and information centre at 975 Rue de l'Escale (☎ 418-538-3285). In the former Hudson's Bay Company store at 957 Rue de la Berge, the Cultural & Interpretive Centre is a museum on local history. The tourist office (☎ 418-538-2512) is here and so is the bus terminal.

On the eastern outskirts of town is *Camping Municipal* (☎ 418-538-2415). Some 15km out of town there is the *Auberge de la Minganie* hostel (☎ 418-538-2944), which can also help organise boat trips. Reservations are suggested. The bus from Sept-Îles will let you off at the hostel on its way to Havre Saint Pierre.

Gite 4 Saisons (☎ 418-538-1329, 1264 Rue Boréal) is a B&B. There are also a couple of inns and motels. In summer when the town is busy, some families in town rent out a room or two. Ask at the tourist office.

For the adventurous, Croisières Nordik, operated by Relais Nordik (☎ 1-800-463-0680), runs ferries from town to Île d'Anticosti and along the coast to Labrador.

Mingan Archipelago National Park
The park is made up of a string of 40 main islands no more than 2km from the mainland. A variety of seabirds can be seen and there are seals and whales. The major feature, though, is the appealing 'flowerpots'

QUEBEC

and other odd erosion-shaped limestone formations along the shores. Many visitors bring their own boats; kayaks are good, but a variety of commercial boat trips run from the mainland too. Some of the islands have hiking paths, picnic areas and/or wilderness camping sites. Fees are low but ask about drinking water. A second information office (☎ 418-538-3285) can be found at the marina, 1010 Rue de la Promenade.

To Labrador & Newfoundland

From Havre Saint Pierre, a ferry skips along the barren north shore servicing about 10 of the 15 little fishing villages. Recently, the road was extended to **Natashquan** which has quickly become a bit of a pilgrimage site. This little village is home to one of Quebec's most popular singers, Gilles Vigneault, and many wish to see how it inspires him. It's connected by bus from Havre Saint Pierre. Generally the people of this rugged, remote area, a mix of French and Montagnais Indian, eke out a living sometimes without even running water.

There are a couple of lodges and guesthouses but they are in the $50 double range. In English **Harrington Harbour**, lodging is often available in people's homes but it's a matter of asking around. Boat trips are possible to other islands. The ferry stops at Blanc Sablon, 2km from the 54th parallel and the border of Labrador. These ferries run from April to mid-January depending on the ice situation.

From Blanc Sablon another ferry can be caught over to Saint Barbe, Newfoundland. See the Newfoundland chapter for details. For more information on the Quebec ferry call Relais Nordik (☎ 1-800-463-0680) or ask in Havre Saint Pierre or Sept-Îles. The ferry costs are quite low as they are partially subsidised by the government.

Île d'Anticosti

This large island at the mouth of the St Lawrence, halfway between the Gaspé Peninsula and the north shore, is a natural wildlife reserve. It's a remote, heavily wooded, cliff-edged island with waterfalls,

canyons and good salmon rivers. For the first few editions of this book Île d'Anticosti remained practically totally unknown except to hunters attracted by the population of 120,000 white-tailed deer. Hunters who don't like to have to look too hard, it's presumed.

It now attracts more eco-sensitive visitors lured by its pristine ruggedness. About 150 species of birds have been recorded on the island and, as well as the canyons and waterfalls, there is a major cave to be explored. Services are increasing and include basic campgrounds.

Different companies and individuals privately owned Anticosti from 1680 to 1974. One of these was Henri Menier, a French chocolate whiz. Now there are about 300 residents, living mainly around Port Menier on the western tip, from where the island's lone road ventures to the interior.

Port Menier has a restaurant, lodging, tourist office, rental cars, gasoline and groceries. The Palaeontology Interpretation Centre has an assortment of fossils and the Eco-Museum has displays on the island's natural features.

There is a campground not far from Port Menier, towards West Point at the end of the island where there is a lighthouse. Potential campers should be well equipped and prepared for poor weather when planning trips anywhere in this region of the province.

L'Auberge Gîte L'Antique-Costi (☎ 418-535-0111, 26 Chemin de la Faune) is a fine place to stay with hostel beds at $17 and private rooms at $35/45 single/double breakfast included. There's a café-bar and big stone oven where pizzas are cooked over a wood fire. It's open from mid-June to mid-October.

Le Manoir du Passant (☎ 418-766-8608, 9 Rue Lebel) charges the same price. There are a couple of others as well as full-package resorts.

The one basic road leads along the north coast past a 4km-long canyon, Chute Vauréal waterfall and a couple of simple camping areas. Ask in town about the cave at Rivière a la Patate which can be explored.

A daily (except Sunday) ferry runs between here and Havre Saint Pierre on the

north coast of the Gulf of St Lawrence where the road eastward ends. It's operated by Relais Nordik (☎ 1-800-463-0680). The cost is $45 per adult and $65 for a car one way. A longer, less frequent ferry runs to Port Menier from Sept-Îles. There are also flights into Anticosti. Ailes de Gaspé (☎ 418-368-1995) has flights from Gaspé which are not bad value given the high ferry prices.

SOUTH SHORE
Rivière-du-Loup

Rivière-du-Loup, on the south shore of the St Lawrence River, is a pleasant surprise for many people. Although a small, second-level city in the middle of nowhere, it's a lively and attractive town with an appealing and distinctively Quebécois atmosphere. The massive stone church, Saint Ludger, in the upper portion of town dominates the skyline.

Much of the old town is built along winding, hilly streets offering views of the river to the mountains beyond. The location also makes it quite a busy stopping-off point for those going either through the Maritimes or farther east into the Gaspé region of Quebec. There is free parking all around the central area – look for the signs with the letter 'P' on them.

The main street, Rue Lafontaine, leads up the hill from Hwy 132 and Boulevard Hôtel de Ville. Many restaurants are found here.

The tourist office (☎ 418-862-1981) is at 189 Rue Hôtel de Ville on the corner of Rue Hôtel de Ville and Rue Saint Pierre. It's open every day in summer and from Monday to Friday the rest of the year. You can't miss it coming into town. There is another office on Hwy 20 just west of the city.

Things to See Across the street from the central tourist office is the **Musée du Bas Saint Laurent** (Museum of the Lower St Lawrence) at 300 Rue Saint Pierre on the corner of Boulevard Hôtel de Ville. The museum deals with local history and there's also a small art gallery. Admission is charged so note that all descriptions are in French.

Follow Rue Frontenac, east off Rue Lafontaine, for a few blocks and you'll reach **Parc des Chutes** based around some waterfalls formed by a drop in the Rivière-du-Loup. There are picnic tables, pedestrian bridges and trails leading around the river and falls.

The **Parc de la Croix** featuring an illuminated cross, another landmark and from which there are good views of the river, is easily seen but difficult to reach. From Chemin des Raymond turn left at Rue Alexandre, right at Rue Bernier and then left at Rue Sainte Claire. This is central and walkable from the centre of town.

Another **lookout**, less accessible without a vehicle, but with a great view of the St Lawrence and excellent at sunset is at the northern edge of town off Hwy 132 east past the large Auberge de la Pointe Hôtel within **Parc de la Pointe**.

Follow the street signs to the small parking lot. A short walk through the woods leads to the viewing platform. Below, the waterfront park is a popular place for a picnic. Farther west is a beach but the water is mighty nippy.

At 393 Rue Témiscouata are **Les Carillons**, a large collection of over 200 new and historic bells, some of which are enormous. All are oddly mounted and displayed on Hydro-Quebec pylons. The assortment can be visited daily in summer until 8 pm for a small fee which entitles you to ring the bells, from the smallest at 35kg to the two-tonne monster.

Ask at the tourist office about boat tours to two of the **Lower St Lawrence islands** which are protected nature sanctuaries. Lying just offshore, west from the city, the islands are good for walking and observing birds and seals. One has camping. Another company runs whale-watching excursions but the trips out of Tadoussac, where the whales are mainly found, are cheaper and use smaller boats. To the east, the river really begins to widen.

Places to Stay There is a convenient campground, *Camping Municipal*, next to Ave Cartier beside the Auberge de la Pointe Hôtel on the north side of town. It's geared to trailers as all sites have electricity but tents can be used.

QUEBEC

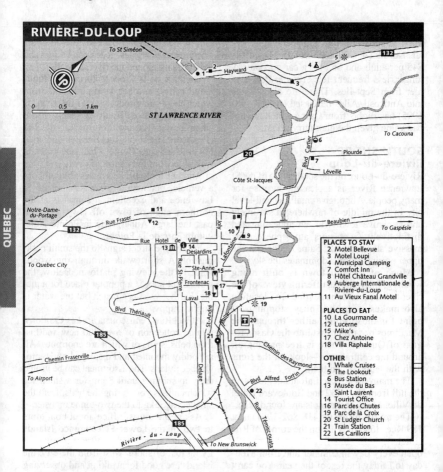

RIVIÈRE-DU-LOUP

PLACES TO STAY
2 Motel Bellevue
3 Motel Loupi
4 Municipal Camping
7 Comfort Inn
8 Hôtel Château Grandville
9 Auberge Internationale de Rivière-du-Loup
11 Au Vieux Fanal Motel

PLACES TO EAT
10 La Gourmande
12 Lucerne
15 Mike's
17 Chez Antoine
18 Villa Raphale

OTHER
1 Whale Cruises
5 The Lookout
6 Bus Station
13 Musée du Bas Saint Laurent
14 Tourist Office
16 Parc des Chutes
19 Parc de la Croix
20 St Ludger Church
21 Train Station
22 Les Carillons

The good HI hostel, *Auberge Internationale de Rivière-du-Loup* (☎ 418-862-7566, 46 Hotel de Ville), is central. Dorm beds are $16 for members and cheap breakfasts are available. Staff often organise good trips around the area.

Inexpensive lodging can also be found at the *CÉGEP college* (☎ 418-862-6903, 325 Rue Saint Pierre) which rents out its simple rooms at $20/35 throughout summer.

Also inexpensive is the interesting *Hôtel Château Grandville* (☎ 418-862-3551, 94 Rue Lafontaine) situated on the corner of Rue Iberville, with rooms at $55/60 for a single/double in summer. This is north of the centre of town and closer to the motel district.

A recommended B&B near the ferry terminal is *Le Tourelle* (☎ 418-860-3050, 180 Rue Mackay) charging $65 a double in a fine old house right by the sea.

Most accommodation is in motels, the majority of which are just north of Boulevard Hôtel de Ville on Rue Fraser. They are

scattered along here in both directions from the centre of town. Most are quite pricey but large and comfortable; some offer heated pools and good views of the river. They are all well kept and some are exceptional in appearance, the ultimate being the *Motel Loupi* (☎ 418-862-6898, 50 Rue de l'Ancrage) which is that rare breed – a motel which could be termed eccentrically spectacular. It's surrounded by immaculate terraced gardens complete with aviaries, a pool, swings, lawn chairs and a golf course. A double goes for $70 and up.

Au Vieux Fanal Motel (☎ 418-862-5255, 170 Rue Fraser) has views of the river and a heated swimming pool which is good for the typically cool evenings. A double costs $65.

Another fine place at the same price is the *Motel Bellevue* (☎ 418-862-5229) right beside the ferry terminal and overlooking the river. Some rooms have kitchenettes. The perfectly good *Comfort Inn* (☎ 418-867-4162, 85 Boulevard Cartier) is costlier but seems pedestrian in relation to the settings offered by the others. Along Boulevard Cartier there are cheaper options.

Places to Eat Many restaurants can be found along Rue Lafontaine along with a smattering of drinking places.

Mike's (364 Rue Lafontaine) is a classy submarine-sandwich shop but with a dining room instead of a plastic takeaway counter. The sandwiches, pastas and pizzas actually make a pretty tasty and inexpensive meal for between $6 and $10. It's on the corner of Rue Sainte Anne.

Chez Antoine (433 Rue Lafontaine) and, next door, the busier *Villa Raphaële* with more pasta dishes are both attractive, enticing places with more expensive ($16 to $25) complete dinners.

For breakfast head to *La Gourmande* (120 Rue Lafontaine). It's a café and bakery with bagels, croissants or toast, jam and coffee for $3. There are soups, salads and sandwiches at lunch.

A place for a casual dinner like steak frites and a beer is *l'Estaminet* (299 Rue Lafontaine).

The other major eating area is along Rue Fraser and serves the motel crowd. The *Lucerne* is a moderately priced place where you can comfortably take the kids.

Getting There & Away The bus station (☎ 418-862-4884), 83 Boulevard Cartier, beside the Comfort Inn, is a short walk from the centre. It's near the corner of Rue Fraser and Hwy 20, is open 24 hours a day and has coin lockers. Orléans Express runs west to Montreal, east to Gaspé and SMT goes south to Edmundston. Some trips are express, others local, meaning they stop at towns along the way.

VIA Rail (☎ 1-800-361-5390) connects to Quebec City and to Campbellton, New Brunswick via the Matapédia Valley. The station is on Rue Lafontaine at the top of the hill near the corner of Fraserville. It's closed except at train times which are in the middle of the night!

The ferry (☎ 418-862-5094) to Saint Siméon on the north shore runs from early morning to early evening and the trip takes 1¼ hours. About seven services a day run in summer costing $26 per car and $10 per adult. In mid-summer, the first (7 am) and the last (8 pm) trips of the day are offered at good discounts. There is a restaurant and bar on board.

Same-day return passenger-only fares – in other words a three hour cruise – are reasonable. Keep an eye out for whales on the crossing.

Boarding is on a first-come, first-served basis and hopeful passengers should be at the dock an hour before departure. This only applies to those with vehicles, walk-ons have no trouble arriving just before departure. The ferry, with a capacity of 100 vehicles, runs from April to January. Also offered is a five hour cruise to the mouth of the Saguenay and back. For pedestrians, there is no bus to the ferry terminal about 6km from the centre of town. If you want a cab try Taxi Capitol (☎ 418-862-6333).

Those without transport can have their ride requests broadcast over the ferry PA system before docking.

QUEBEC

Towards New Brunswick

Hwy 185 with its pulp. and paper mills and forests interspersed with farms provides a foretaste of New Brunswick. A highlight is the privilege of passing through and being able to say you've been to Saint Louis du Ha! Ha! ('Haha' is a French word traceable to the 15th century and meaning 'unexpected barrier' or 'dead end', says *Canadian Geographic*). Also pleasant is the beautiful, green rolling landscape around **Lac Temiscouta**.

There is some camping and, most notably around Cabano, a number of motels where, as is so typical of Quebec, the amenities include a bar. In Cabano itself with a large cardboard mill, there are a couple of restaurants on the one main street near the edge of the lake. Fort Ingall historic site was built in 1839 as protection from possible US attack.

In the heart of the Temiscouta region a recommended place to stay and eat is the *L'Auberge Marie Blanc (☎ 418-899-6747)* in Notre Dame du Lac. The address is 1112 Rue Commerciale. Built in 1905 by a lawyer for his mistress, Marie Blanc, the house has been operated as an inn since the early 1960s. It's open from the beginning of April until the end of October and the pricey dining room serves good food. Overnight rates are $65 a double. There's a beach and access to a 60km cycling trail along the lakeshore.

During summer a ferry runs across the lake but this remains a largely undeveloped area.

Trois Pistoles

Just east of Rivière-du-Loup, Hwy 20 ends and you must take the smaller 132. At L'Isle Verte there is a lot of seafood for sale and smokehouses offering their produce, mainly salmon. There is also a ferry over to rural Île Verte where there is a small community, cycling and accommodation.

A massive church dominates the town of Trois Pistoles and there's a good picnic site on the west side of town. If you want to linger, there are some eco-tour possibilities. Trips can be taken offshore to Île aux Basques which was used by Basque whalers in the 16th century and is now a reserve with a lot of birdlife. Kayaks can be rented

and guided paddling tours of the coast are offered. Also, cruises to the Saguenay area for whale watching depart Île Vert village if you can't make it to Tadoussac.

The new, distinct-looking **Parc de l'Adventure Basque** at 66 Avenue du Parc, is really a museum outlining the history of the Basques both in Europe and their trips to the new land. It's all in French but there is a good English booklet provided if you ask.

For campers, there is a central *Municipal Campground* with a pool or two other nearby campgrounds. There's a ferry (☎ 418-851-4676) going to Les Escoumins across the river on the north shore. The trip takes 1¼ hours and costs $26 per car, $12 per person. It runs from mid-May to mid-October, with three services a day in July and August when reservations are recommended.

The coast becomes more hilly and less populated as you head for the Gaspé Peninsula – it looks somewhat like the Scottish Highlands. To add to the similarity, people in the area, particularly between Saint Simon and Saint Fabien, cut and sell peat for garden fertiliser. The coast between Saint Fabien sur Mer and Bic is particularly scenic.

Bic

Bic was a little village in a beautiful setting a few kilometres from Rimouski but has now become a sort of suburb. There are some good coastal views in the area and there's a good picnic spot in the village.

A visit to **Parc Bic** is highly recommended. The park protects an unusual landscape of irregular, lumpy, conical mountains that edge the rough, rocky shoreline here. Numerous bays, coves and islands link land and sea. The transitional vegetation zone makes for an interesting mix of southern deciduous and northern boreal forest. The park is also rich in wildlife. Of most interest are the seabirds and the colony of grey and harbour seals offshore. Bring binoculars if you have them. The best place to see seals is at Pointe aux Epinettes; second best is Cap Caribou. Look on the half-submerged rocks at low tide.

Roads and walking trails (with a free map available in English) lead to mountain

tops and beaches and cut through portions of forest. Guided walks are offered. Bikes can be rented.

The park is divided into three sections. The middle one, Secteur Rivière du Sud-Ouest, has the seasonal interpretation centre and campground. Unfortunately, the campground, while attractive enough, sits in a bowl which amplifies the truck traffic noise all night long. Picnic sites can be found in various places. The park is easily big enough to spend a couple of days exploring and day-use is free. Note that it is officially closed from September to May but people do set up camp nearby and walk in during the day.

Boat tours around the river side of the park close to the seal and bird colonies are available.

Rimouski

Rimouski is a fairly large, growing industrial and oil-distribution town made lively in part by a sizable student population. The main street is Rue Saint Germain, which runs east and west from the principal cross street, Avenue Cathédrale. At this intersection is the Place des Veterans square where you will find the helpful tourist office (☎ 418-723-2322) at 50 Saint Germain Ouest.

Place des Veterans, marking the centre of town, is right by the highway near the **regional museum** in the neogothic **cathedral** from the 1850s. The museum, closed on Monday, presents varied and changing exhibits including the works of Canadian artists and a display on oceanography. The Maritime Institute is next door.

About 5km east of the tourist office, along Hwy 132, is **Maison Lamontagne**, an 18th century house now an historic site, set in parkland. It's open daily throughout summer and displays period furniture and other items and represents a now almost extinct style of construction.

About 10km east of town in Pointe au Père, past the ferry terminal, is **Le Musée de la Mer**, a maritime museum and lighthouse with displays on the *Empress of Ireland*. It sank offshore in 14 minutes becoming, after the *Titanic*, the worst ever maritime tragedy.

Admission is $5 and, as a National Historic Site, there is some English spoken at this worthwhile stop. The nature reserve here is a good place to look for coastal flora and fauna.

Some 30km south of town is the **Portes de l'Enfer** (Gates of Hell Canyon), a park with good walking alongside the canyon and its rushing waters.

Late summer is a good time to be passing through as the months of August, September and October each bring a different festival to the city.

After leaving Rimouski the land becomes noticeably more wooded as you enter the Gaspé region.

Places to Stay Rooms are available in the *CÉGEP college* (☎ 418-723-4636, 320 Rue Saint Louis) which is central. Singles/doubles are $21/28.

The spotless HI *Le Roupillon du Capitaine* (☎ 418-739-5152, 147 Route de Fleuve) is in Saint Luce about 15km north along the coast. The 125-year-old restored house with 36 beds is right across from the sea. Dorm beds with breakfast are $16.50 and private double rooms are $38. The Orleans Express bus will drop you off as it goes by.

Gites du Centre Ville (☎ 418-723-5289, 84 Rue Saint Pierre) is an attractive central B&B with doubles at $48.

There are plenty of motels especially on Rue Saint Germain Est and Ouest. Farther out westbound there are also a couple of places with small, simple individual cabins for rent.

Places to Eat East of Avenue Cathédrale on Rue Saint Germain there are three or four popular restaurants and bars with outdoor tables and live music. Avenue Cathédrale also has a number of eateries and nightspots.

The well established *Maison du Spaghetti* (35 Saint Germain Est) is open daily and offers Italian favourites including pizza. The basic spaghetti meal is $8.50. *Le Lotus* (143 Avenue Belzile) serves up very tasty Cambodian and Vietnamese fare; a good dinner is about $15. It's closed Monday.

West of the centre on Saint Germain Ouest just past Rue Saint Louis, *Les Halles*

is a complex with a deli, bakery, cheese shop, restaurant and more. *La Brulerie d'Ici* on the corner here serves great coffee.

Restaurant Marie Antoinette on the highway and open 24 hours is always reasonable with a selection of Canadian standards. Just east of town you'll see quite a few fish shops *(poissoneries)* where bargains can be had on sole, cod, Atlantic salmon, shrimps and the biggest lobsters seen outside a museum. Some 2.5kg brutes! Aside from fresh fish, many shops offer dried or smoked fish.

Getting There & Away The bus station (☎ 418-723-4923) is at 90 Avenue Leonidas, five lights east of the tourist office along Hwy 132. There are six buses daily to Quebec and Montreal and two for Percé.

Rimouski is on the VIA Rail line (☎ 1-800-361-5390) but this is about as far as it goes. At Mont Joli, the line heads for Campbellton, New Brunswick. The station is on Rue de l'Evêché two blocks east of the cathedral. It's open from 11.15 pm to 2.15 am daily, except Tuesday when it's closed, and Thursday 5 to 7 pm. Nice hours aren't they?

Allo Stop, the car/drive sharing agency, has an office here at 106 Rue Saint Germain Est in the bookstore.

One ferry (☎ 418-725-2725) runs to Forestville two to four times daily from May to November. Adult fare is $13 and $30 per car for the one-hour crossing.

A Relais Nordik ferry (☎ 1-800-463-0680) departs from here for the 11 hour crossing to Sept-Îles on the north shore. This is not one of the regular daily crossing points such as those west at Trois Pistoles or east at Matane. It runs just once a week, on Tuesday. The terminal is about 4km east of the tourist office.

Gaspé Peninsula

This is the rounded chunk of land that juts out north of New Brunswick into the Gulf of St Lawrence. To the people of Quebec it's 'La Gaspésie'. From west of Matane the characteristic features of the region really become evident: the trees and woods become

forests, the towns become smaller and farther apart, the weather becomes windier and cooler. The landscape is hilly and rocky with excellent views along the rough coastline.

The area is at least as impressive as the better known Cape Breton Island of Nova Scotia and much less crowded. There is less development and less organised tourism, which compensates for the fewer attractions and possible communication difficulties. At the eastern tip and around the south shore are a number of English communities so if French is a struggle, these will make a petit respite! The numerous parks are excellent for getting out into the rugged terrain or exploring the shoreline.

The Gaspé Peninsula is popular with cyclists, despite the hard climbs, and there are plenty of hostels, campgrounds and unoccupied woods to sleep in. All towns of any size have motels and there is a good number of guesthouses as well. Lots of seafood is available and the little trucks and chip wagons throughout the area make superb french fries and real meat hamburgers. You should expect cool evenings even in midsummer.

You may see some of these French signs so here's a quick rundown:

pain de ménage	–	home-made bread
gîte du passant	–	B&B
à vendre	–	for sale
des vers	–	worms (not a tasty snack)
bière froide	–	cold beer (available at most stores)
crêtons	–	a local pork pâté
miel	–	honey
sirop d'erable	–	maple syrup

Prices in the region are relatively low (except for gasoline) and a trip around this part of the country is highly recommended. A caution though – the region virtually shuts down visitor attractions between September and May (even Forillon National Park is open only seasonally). Parks can be visited for walking but services will be nonexistent.

SAINTE-FLAVIE
In Sainte-Flavie on Hwy 132 is a large, year-round information centre for the Gaspé

GASPÉ PENINSULA

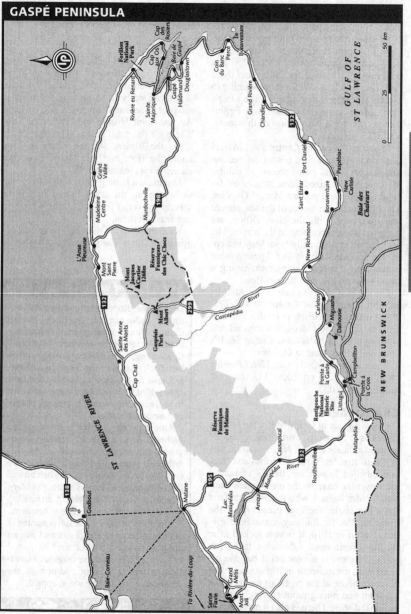

Peninsula. If you're here late in the season pick up one of the pamphlets which lists facilities that remain open until mid-October. Hwy 132 splits here; the southern portion goes past the larger town of Mont Joli and on through the Matapédia Valley directly to New Brunswick, useful for those wishing to bypass (recommended against) the Gaspé Peninsula. See the end of the Gaspé Peninsula section for a description of this route. VIA Rail goes this way.

In Sainte-Flavie, the **Centre d'Art Marcel Gagnon** is worth a visit. It's an inn, restaurant and art school based around an exhibit of some 80 life-sized stone statues by fecund sculptor and painter Marcel Gagnon. The figures, marching out of the sea, appear and disappear with the tide. Others are mounted on rafts bobbing in the waves. The centre itself is open daily from May to September and admission is free. There is other artwork on display. Aside from having a meal, you can just sit with a coffee.

On the east side of town is the **Atlantic Salmon Interpretative Centre** (☎ 418-775-2969) with various displays on this queen of fish, an aquarium, videos, a restaurant and walking trails. Admission is a steep $6. It's open daily from June to October.

There are four motels with *Motel Patrick* (☎ 418-775-8226) on Route 132 the most modestly priced.

GRAND MÉTIS
On the west side of Grand Métis, the **Jardins de Métis** is an oddity worth looking at. It's an immaculately tended, Japanese-style garden with streams, flowers, bushes and trees – all labelled. In addition, there's a fantastic view over the coast by the old wooden mansion. A Mrs Reford, who inherited the land from her uncle, the first president of the Canadian Pacific Railway, started the garden. Begun in 1910, it is now looked after by the government. Admission is $6 per adult and there is a joint ticket bargain offered with the museum in Rimouski. In the 37-room house at the centre of the park is a museum and dining room serving fish and regional dishes. There is also a more casual restaurant with views. The grounds, open from June to mid-October, close at 8 pm.

MATANE
A small, typical Québecois town, Matane makes a good stopover. There's an information office at the lighthouse off the highway, open daily in summer and weekdays all year. The small museum is also here. Avenue Saint Jérôme and Boulevard Saint Pierre are the main streets. The promenade along the Rivière Matane where it flows under the Hwy and into the St Lawrence makes for a pleasant stroll.

Matane is a fishing town with salmon and shrimp among the catch. In mid-June is the shrimp *(crevette)* festival, a time when you can feast on them.

Salmon go up the river here to spawn, beginning in June. The government has set up

---

Say a Prayer with Bathtub Mary

Despite the dropping attendance and declining influence of Quebec's Roman Catholic church, its iconography remains a pervasive part of the provincial landscape. Captivating, sometimes jarring, often beautiful, images of the Virgin or a bloodied Jesus on the cross both dot urban and rural settings. Inspirational statues look out to sea, mark the entrances to quiet villages and embellish gardens.

One type to look for is the so-called Bathtub Mary, a folk art tradition which graces the occasional roadside. An old-fashioned claw-footed bathtub is stood on end, usually one-quarter to one-half buried. Placed standing within it is a statue of Mary, mother of Jesus. The framing arched top thus forms a sort of protective encasement. Sometimes the edge of the tub is painted or otherwise adorned and plants and flowers are grown around the bottom.

All in all, any of these religious expressions makes a striking addition to the province's considerable visual appeal.

a monitoring system where you can see the fish heading upstream and learn something of this curious phenomenon. An information office (small fee) is in the little building by the dam, adjacent to the Parc des Îles and near the Hôtel de Ville at the top of Rue Saint Jerome. You may see salmon in the ladder beside the dam. Nearby in the park is an open-air theatre used for summer shows.

The large shrimp-processing and fish-packing plant (☎ 418-562-1273) at 1600 Matane Sur Mer can be visited free through the summer. Reservations are needed on weekends and fish can be bought, fresh or smoked.

Matane Wildlife Preserve

The preserve (☎ 418-562-3700) can be reached south of Matane off Hwy 195. It's a huge, wild area with camping, canoeing, hiking, fishing, boat rentals and abundant moose. The park closes in early September. The road continues on to New Brunswick but don't follow it. Go around the rest of the Gaspé Peninsula.

Places to Stay

There's good, quiet camping in the woods at huge *Camping de la Riviere Matane* (☎ 418-562-3414) on Route Louis Felix Dionne south-west of downtown. Follow the signs from the corner of Rue Parc Industriel and the highway for 3km.

An alternative is *Camping La Baleine* 6km west of town with the whale model by the roadside. It's basic but clean and a tent site in the field is $14.

Le Relais du Voyageur (☎ 418-562-3472, 75 Rue D'Amours) is a good-value central B&B with singles from just $21.

The modern-looking *Collège Matane* (☎ 418-562-1240 ext 2, 616 Ave Saint Redempteur) on the outskirts of town is another option for people on a tight budget. Rooms are offered to visitors through the summer months from about the same price.

Motels are the primary accommodation with many strung out along or near the highway. *Motel Le Beach* (☎ 418-562-1350, 1441 Rue Matane sur Mer) is $55.

Places to Eat

For the stomach, the all purpose *Café Aux Delices (109 Rue St Jean)* on the corner of Rue Saint Jerome in the centre of town is recommended. It has Italian, Canadian and Chinese food, good breakfasts and is open long hours every day.

Au Vieux Loup (389 Avenue Saint Jerome) is a decent brasserie and there's a popular pizza place next door. For good seafood in the $12 to $17 main course range there is *Les Délices de la Mer (50 Avenue d'Amours)*; no weekend lunches.

Le Vieux Rafiot (1415 Ave de Phare Ouest, Hwy 132) is the yellow and white place on the corner of Rue Parc Industriel. It's a casual sort of pub with plenty of seafood and good prices on shrimp dinners all summer long.

Getting There & Away

Bus Buses (☎ 418-562-4085) arrive and depart the Irving gas station at 521 Avenue du Phare Est (Hwy 132), 1.5km east of the centre. There are two buses a day for Gaspé and four a day for Quebec City.

Ferry The ferry (☎ 418-562-2500) link here to the north shore of the St Lawrence is the last in a series beginning at Quebec City and appearing periodically as the widening river travels north-eastwards to the sea. Call for information. Reservations are recommended. It runs all year.

The ferry is a large vessel capable of handling 600 passengers and 125 cars. To Baie Comeau, there are four services a day through the summer. The trip takes two hours and 20 minutes and costs about $38 per car and driver. Bicycles are free and there is a cheaper same-day return fare.

Another boat goes to Godbout, a small town a little farther west from Baie Comeau.

The ferry terminal is several kilometres west of the town centre.

CAP CHAT

At Cap Chat, enchantingly stretched along the water's edge complete with a big, sandy beach, the St Lawrence River meets the

QUEBEC

Gulf of St Lawrence. Rocher Cap Chat is a well known landmark. This rock, said to resemble a crouching cat and which gave the village its name, sits by the shore on the west side of town, about a 2km walk along the beach from the centre.

About 3km west of the central bridge is the odd looking hi-tech vertical axis windmill. Bilingual tours are offered. Call ☎ 418-786-5719 for schedule and rates.

Basic roads lead south inland to two different wildlife regions with camping. Lac Joffre, Lac Simoneau and Lac Paul are good for trout fishing.

Places to Stay & Eat

A good place to spend the night is the *Cabines Goémons sur Mer* (☎ *418-786-5715, 195 Rue Notre Dame Est*) right on the beach on the east side of town. The cabins have kitchens and go for $40 for one double bed.

Farther west, the smaller, simpler *Cabines Sky Line* (☎ *418-786-2626, 195 Rue Notre Dame Ouest*) costs only $30/32 for singles/doubles. Each of these cute little places is named after a planet and they're perfectly fine, though the location is not as good.

The *Motel Fleur de Lys* (☎ *418-786-5518, 184 Hwy 132 Est*) is a more modern choice and has a busy restaurant which serves all day and is good for breakfast.

SAINTE ANNE DES MONTS

Sainte Anne is not one of the prettier towns. But you can take advantage of it being a fishing centre by getting hold of some of the smoked or fresh fish for sale down by the dock opposite the church at the foot of Route du Parc. There is also a restaurant here. Beside the quay is Explorama (☎ 418-763-2500), a bilingual interpretation centre with exhibits on marine ecosystems and a large model of the Gaspé Peninsula. Admission is $6.

Immediately south of town is the Saint Anne River Nature Reserve (Réserve Faunique) which runs along the river and into Gaspésie Park. If you're heading into the park and need cash, there is an ATM in the Banque Nationale in the shopping centre on the corner of Boulevard Sainte Anne Ouest (Hwy 132) and Route du Parc.

For accommodation, there's the new hostel *L'échouerie* (☎ *418-763-1555, 1-800-461-8585, 295 1st Ave Est*) in a converted school. There are dorm beds, private rooms, kitchen, a café, transportation to Gaspésie Park – the works.

The Orléans Express bus stops at the Riôtel Monaco (a hotel) on Hwy 132 in the centre of town. It's a 2km walk to the hostel. Cross the street, go east to Route de Parc, then toward the church, then east along the river road.

GASPÉSIE PARK

From Sainte Anne des Monts, Hwy 299 runs south to the excellent Gaspésie Park (☎ 418-763-3301). It is a huge, rugged and undeveloped area of lakes, woods and mountains. There's lots of wildlife like deer and moose and the fishing is good but the highlight is the great hiking.

The Interpretive Centre (☎ 418-763-7811) is open daily from early June to Labour Day and, like the park itself, is free. Overnight camping is $15 in one of the four campgrounds. None of them is open past about 10 October but it is getting very cold by then anyway. Backcountry camping is also permitted. Maps and information on hiking trails are available at the centre, which is somewhat inconveniently located in the middle of the park in the section with the main facilities including a small grocery store.

Close by at **Gîte du Mont Albert** there is camping and a large, comfortable lodge (☎ 418-763-2288) with a highly praised restaurant. Singles/doubles in the hotel are $100. Prices start at $75 for chalets but rise way beyond that depending on location and size (some sleep eight). Bicycles can be rented. Campers can use the hotel pool for a small fee – there isn't much swimming in the park.

The roads leading through the park are rough and will take you to various hiking trails – some overnighters – and lookouts over the lumpy Chic Choc Mountains (Monts Chic Choc).

Mont Jacques Cartier (1270m) is the highest peak in this part of the country. It rises above the tree line and epitomises the conditions of the Gaspé Peninsula: cold, windy and often wet at the peak.

Hiking it takes about 3½ hours for the return trip, and is well worthwhile – the alpine scenery and views are fantastic and it is fairly common to see some of the herd of woodland caribou near the barren peaks munching on lichen. The trail is tightly regulated in order to protect the herd from being disturbed. These are the last of the caribou found this far south and conditions are very harsh. Do not approach or scare them. However, if you see some, you might try being quiet and raising your arms to form an antler shape. The curious caribou don't see too well and may actually walk toward you. Mont Jacques Cartier hikers can drive to a designated parking area at the basic La Galene campground along one of two routes each taking about 30 minutes from the Interpretation Centre where, alternatively, buses for $13 return can be boarded. They depart daily at 9 am. La Galene can also be reached from Mont Saint Pierre. From it, a $5 shuttle bus runs hikers 6km to the beginning of the trail. The first bus is at 10 am, the last leaves the trail at 4 pm and no one is permitted on the summit between the end of the afternoon and the next morning. Take warm clothing. The buses operate from near the end of June to about the second week in September. The mountain is open until the end of the month but you must walk in. This late in the year the temperatures at the top can be well below zero. At the peak, naturalists are on hand to answer questions and talk about the caribou.

You can also climb **Mont Albert**, a steeper, more rigorous trail despite the mountain not reaching the same elevation as Cartier. Also excellent and not busy is the trail by Lac aux Americains up to Mont Xalibu, a fine half-day return walk with superb alpine scenery at the peak with mountain lakes and a waterfall in view on the way.

It is not uncommon to see moose in the early morning or evening feeding at Lac Paul.

The main road enters the park at Sainte Anne des Monts. Another, less busy, rougher access road from Mont Saint Pierre meets it inside the park. A loop through the park is possible using both access points as connectors to the coastal highway (132). From mid-July to mid-August, a bus runs from the Riôtel Monaco in Sainte Anne des Monts to the park interpretation centre once a day in time for the Cartier shuttle.

MONT SAINT PIERRE

Not far from Sainte Anne des Monts on Hwy 132 is this little white village nestled in a short bay. The setting is spectacular with rocky outcrops on one side and a nearby crescent-shaped beach on the other. The sunsets are also noteworthy.

This small community, far from any big city, is famous for hang-gliding. Indeed, it is considered one of the best spots for the sport in North America.

Each year around the end of June is the two-week hang-gliding festival (La Fête du Vol Libre). A rough road goes to the summit of Mont Saint Pierre where there are three take-off stations and excellent views. A 4WD vehicle is required if you're not hoofing it up which takes an hour.

Carrefour Aventure, 106 Rue Prudent Cloutier, offers tours of the site and even rents hang-gliders to first-timers! It also rents sea kayaks and mountain bikes.

The cliffs east of town are etched with interesting rock patterns. The road runs along the bottom of the cliff and river's edge east (sometimes squeezed between the two) to about Gros Morne. Signs warn drivers to watch for both falling rocks and huge waves. Good luck.

Auberge Les Vagues (☎ 418-797-2851, 84 Rue Prudent Cloutier) is a hostel with room for 70 in summer. Dorm beds are $14 or there are double rooms for $38. In winter there is less space and prices rise due to heating considerations. There's a restaurant/bar or kitchen and for supplies, a grocery store down the street a few doors.

Alternatively, there is camping and several motel-hotels in town. The motel restaurant

QUEBEC

Au Delice (100 Rue P Cloutier) is open early for breakfast.

Gaspésie Park can be reached by unsurfaced road (watch for logging trucks!) from behind Mont Saint Pierre but having a good map is very helpful as the routes are not marked well.

EAST OF MONT SAINT PIERRE

East of Mont Saint Pierre look for good picnic areas with coastal views. There are also plenty of campgrounds, motels or cabins with cuisinettes (kitchenettes). At the many small villages watch for the signs for *pain frais* or *pain chaud* (fresh or hot bread).

At L'Anse Pleureuse, turn off to Murdochville for tours of its copper mine. Rivière la Madeleine and Grand Vallée are particularly beautiful villages with grand settings perfect for picture-taking. East of Cloridorme there is a good picnic site overlooking the Gulf of St Lawrence. Rivière au Renard is the largest fishing port in the Gaspé and the processing plant can be toured free. The industry is outlined at the Fishing Interpretation Centre at 1 Renard Est for $4. The tourist office is also here.

For those not visiting Forillon, Hwy 197 runs south cutting off the end of the peninsula. At L'Anse au Griffon watch for the house covered in big bugs. And where else have you seen a grocery-lingerie store? Talk about one-stop shopping!

CAP DES ROSIERS

This is a small, old and interesting little village on the north shore. The **graveyard**, right on the cliff, tells the town's history: how the English came from Guernsey and Jersey; how the Irish settlers were Kavanaghs, O'Connors etc; and how both groups mingled with the French. Generations later, the same names live on.

The **lighthouse**, built in 1858, is one of the highest in the country at 37m and is an historic site. It can be visited for a small admission fee.

Saltwater sport-fishing trips and whale-watching tours depart from the wharf (see under the following Forillon National Park section for details).

The **Chalets Cap Cabins** (☎ 418-892-5641), costing about $30, are pleasantly rustic with views over the bay. There's also a couple of motels and a few restaurants in town.

FORILLON NATIONAL PARK

The park (☎ 418-368-5505) lies at the extreme north-eastern tip of the peninsula and is well worth a stop for its rugged seaside terrain and wildlife. In the woods there are moose, deer and an increasing population of black bears. The shoreline cliffs attract numbers of seabirds, and offshore whales and seals are common.

There are good trails through the park, some with overnight camping. They range from rigorous 18km one-way trails taking six hours to easy 30-minute walks. The Parks Service naturalists offer information programs and free guided tours.

Two boat trips are offered. The MV *Felix Leclerc* (☎ 418-892-5629) departs from the quay at Cap des Rosiers for $15 and takes in the rocky cliffs, seabirds, seal colonies and possibly whales. The Zodiac *Norval* (☎ 418-892-5500) departs the harbour at Grand Grave for longer cruises costing $30 and concentrates on whales. Dolphins and porpoises are common. For both, inquire if the guide is bilingual (some are). Kayak trips also depart Grand Grave.

The northern coast consists of steep limestone cliffs – some as high as 200m – and long pebble beaches. See **Cap Bon Ami** for the best of this topography. There is a telescope for whale watching – good from May to October – and sometimes you can hear them surface. Seals are common all year just offshore. Look to the left.

The south coast has more beaches, some are sandy, and small coves. **Penouille Beach** is said to have the warmest waters. Petit Gaspé is the most popular organised campground as it is protected from sea breezes and it has hot showers too.

The hike along the southern shore to **Cap Gaspé** is easy and pleasant, with seashore

views. At the headlands, with a lighthouse, Percé Rock can be seen. Take the path one way and the road back, about two hours total. The famous US Appalachian Trail is being extended into Canada (see Matapédia Valley later in this chapter) to form the International Appalachian Trail (IAT). It will terminate at Cape Gaspé, the end of the mountain chain. Parts of the trail within the park are now open.

At **Grand Grave**, the Haymen & Sons store is an interesting place for a snoop around.

The entrance fee to the park is $3.50 per adult. A tent site without electricity is $22 at one of the three campgrounds and includes the admission fee. Through July and August book ahead (☎ 418-368-6050) or arrive by late morning.

CAP AUX OS

On the south side of Forillon National Park, Cape of Bones got its name because at one time whale bones often washed ashore here. Hostellers can use the village as a base for exploring the park, otherwise there is no reason to stop here. The **HI hostel** (☎ 418-892-5153, 2095 Boulevard Forillon) is good and friendly – it's one of the most established places in the province and has a fine view overlooking the bay. It's a fairly large three-storey place which can accommodate 56 people and is open all year. During summer, it is generally full. You gotta love Quebec hostels – first they surprise people by often having co-ed dorms and then here they have condom machines in the washroom. Is this preventative or suggestive? (There are some rooms for families.) It's open 24 hours and breakfast and dinner are available. There is a grocery store a few minutes walk away. The bus stops at the hostel throughout summer months. A drawback for those without vehicles is that it is a long way to any of the hiking trails, although bicycles can be rented.

GASPÉ

After all the little villages, the town, edged along the bay and after which the entire peninsula takes its name, seems pretty sizable. And it does have all the amenities. A fair bit of English is spoken too. Perhaps surprisingly, from here around the head of the peninsula and down along the Baie des Chaleurs, there are quite a few historic English-speaking towns which have stuck it out.

The **Jacques Cartier monument** at the north side of town right beside the highway, is worth a look. It's different and well done. It was here that the explorer landed in 1534, met the Iroquois and claimed the area for the king of France. With European condescension clearly evident, he took two sons of Chief Donnacona back to see Paris and later returned them. (They must have had a few stories to tell.) Beside the sculpture is a museum depicting the difficulties of those settling the Gaspé Peninsula, some maritime exhibits, crafts and a section on traditional foods. Admission costs $4. It's open daily in summer but afternoons only on weekends the rest of the year when it's closed Monday.

The **Cathédrale de Gaspé** is the only wooden cathedral in North America. A fresco commemorates the fourth centennial of Cartier's landing. It's at the top of Rue Jacques Cartier about a 15 minute walk from the museum.

Continuing in a religious vein, **Sanctuaire Notre Dame des Douleurs** is a church which has been a pilgrimage site since 1942. It's open daily from 7 am to 8.30 pm from early June to late October.

A good new attraction is the **Micmac Interpretation Site** (☎ 418-368-6005) next door at 783 Boulevard Pointe Navarre. Inside there are museum-like exhibits and outside, overlooking the bay, traditional village buildings. Interpreters explain hunting techniques, various activities, construction, lifestyle etc. Admission is $4 and a visit (with everything in English or French) takes at least an hour. It's open daily from June to October.

South of town there are beaches at Sandy Beach and Haldimand but the water is cool. There's camping by the Fort Ramsay Motel near the water.

For eating or sleeping most people will prefer to be in nearby Percé. But a place worth checking for a cheap bed through the summer is the central *CÉGEP de la Gaspésie*

(☎ 418-368-2749, 94 Rue Jacques Cartier). It is a regional college that rents its many residence rooms at reasonable rates. You can't miss it – it's the big red building with the cross. Otherwise there are numerous motels. A cheap breakfast can be had in any of the motel dining rooms.

DOUGLASTOWN

Like some of the other small English towns of the region, Douglastown was established by Loyalists. Their ancestors continue to fish and farm.

PERCÉ

Named after the immense offshore rock with the hole through it (one of Canada's best known landmarks), this town is the main tourist attraction of the Gaspé Peninsula. It's a pleasant, very pretty place and the **Rocher Percé** (Pierced Rock) is truly an impressive sight. It can be seen on the approach into town from either direction. The Pic de l'Aurore (Peak of Dawn) hill dominates the north end of town. Although you can walk the length of the main street in 30 minutes it's not hard to spend a couple of days or longer here. You can also walk out to the rock and around much of it at low tide. Tide-tables are posted at the tourist office.

Even in July and August, Percé is the only place on the peninsula that gets busy. June or September make good visiting times with the weather usually good, if not overly warm. By the middle of October, the town is shut up tight.

The tourist office (☎ 418-782-5448) is in the centre of town at 142 Hwy 132. It's open from the end of May to near the end of October. There's a laundrette at the wharf/shopping boutique complex nearly across the street from the tourist office. Hwy 132 toward Chandler (south) is termed westbound, toward Gaspé (north) eastbound.

Things To See & Do

The boat trips to green Île Bonaventure, an island bird sanctuary beyond Rocher Percé, are amazing value and highly recommended. For $12, one of a number of boats will take you out with a mini-tour of Percé, then around the cliffs of the island where seals may be seen and birds certainly will be, and then around to the dock. You can spend the day on the island walking the trails and catch a boat back later. A variety of seabirds nest on the island; over 200,000 birds can make some kind of noise (and smell)! The highlight is the gannet colony of 50,000, roosting on the cliffs just an arm's length from the trail. Among the boats, the small, slow, *Rocher Percé* or the ones run by Captain Ti-Jean are good and get very close to the attractions. The more modern ones can't and cost more. Go early in the morning to make the most of it. Boat tickets are sold all over town but can be purchased at the dock-side booths.

Wildlife Service rangers can answer questions and there is a small café but you'll enjoy it more if you take a picnic. Some intriguing hardy plant life can also be seen and the views are marvellous.

The service also runs the free **Wildlife Interpretive Centre**, 2km south of town on the Route d'Irlande and open from 9 am to 5 pm. There's a walking trail, film, aquariums and exhibits relating mainly to the seabirds. Naturalists are on hand to answer questions on the geology and flora and fauna of the area. Exhibits are bilingual.

Longer **whale-watching** boat tours are also available. Minke, blue, humpbacks but mainly dolphins and fin are species which frequent the area. The comfortable MV *Capitaine Duvall* charges $30 for the 2½ hour trip but the three-hour Zodiac trips ($35, less with hostel card) offered by Observation Littoral, 249 Hwy 132, are very good. Dress very warmly. Fishing trips can be arranged at the dock.

Behind the town are some interesting walks, for which the tourist office map is useful. Hike up to **Mont Sainte Anne** for a great view and to see the cave along the 3km path which begins behind the church.

Another area walking trail leads to the **Great Crevasse**, a deep crevice in the mountain behind the *Auberge de Gargantua Restaurant*. This 3km trail begins behind the restaurant which is 2km north-west of town.

Montmorency Falls, Quebec

St Lawrence River and harbour, Quebec City, Quebec

Whistler, Vancouver, BC

Whitewater rafting near Jasper, Alberta

Pedalling through Glacier National Park, BC

Surfing at Pacific Rim National Park, Vancouver Island, BC

The **Le Chafaud Museum**, opposite the tourist office, is more an art gallery featuring traditional and contemporary pieces. The changing shows often deal with local heritage and for the small admission can be worth seeing. A highlight is the ship's figurehead.

Kayaks and bicycles can be rented from Agaguk at its booth beside the swimming pool toward the south end of town. It also offers guided kayak trips and diving. There is an underwater park nearby.

Taxi Percé (☎ 418-782-2102), using a van, offers two-hour guided trips in and around town or full-day trips farther afield.

The main street has lots of souvenir shops selling glasswork, pottery and some good quilts.

At beaches north and south of town rock hounds can look for agate. Despite the publicity, there really isn't much left.

Places to Stay

Accommodation here is a pretty fair bargain although prices can spike sharply upward during midsummer when traffic is very heavy. Some days everything is gone by dinner time. Much of the budget category is in guesthouses in and around town. The tourist office will help in locating one, even calling places for you. There are also numerous campgrounds close at hand. Prices fluctuate with the season, the weather and the traffic.

Of the four convenient campgrounds, *Camping Côte Surprise*, 2km south of town, has the most spectacular views. Two others are nearby and one is in town.

The central *Auberge L'Annexe* (☎ 418-782-5055, 167 Route 132) on the ocean in perhaps the oldest building in town is a welcome addition for hostellers. The bright colours, licensed restaurant, patio and prices of just $12.50 have made this new hostel an instant hit. It's only open from June to September and the 30 beds fill up in peak season.

There are also good value guesthouses which are centrally located. *Maison Avenue House* (☎ 418-782-2954) is on Rue de l'Église, which runs off the main street in the middle of town. Before the church, you'll see this fine house with five rooms of varnished wood at just $23 a single, and from $30 to $35 a double. The rooms are clean and have sinks. The guesthouse is in an excellent location and both English and French are spoken. Also good and cheap is *Maison le Havre* (☎ 418-782-2374, 114 Hwy 132)*, formerly known as the Haven before the Quebec language laws kicked in making English signs difficult to live with. It's on the main street, with rooms from $25 to $40.

One serving breakfast is *Gite Rendez-vous* (☎ 416-782-5152, 84 Hwy 132)*. A double is $55.

Right in the centre of town, the green and white *Fleur de Lys* (☎ 418-782-5380, 1-800-399-5380)* is one of the most reasonably priced motels at $60 double with kitchen at peak times. The very central *Hotel-Motel Rocher Percé* (☎ 418-782-2330, ☎ 1-888-467-3723, 111 Hwy 132)* has hotel rooms at $50 for two, or more expensive motel rooms (some with kitchen).

South of the centre, there are several places with spectacular views at which to splurge. *Bonaventure sur Mer* (☎ 418-782-2166, ☎ 1-800-463-4212, 367 Hwy 132)* has rooms from $80 with breakfast.

There are many other places to stay, mostly motels but also some rustic cabins. The lower-priced ones are generally south of town.

Several kilometres north of town, *Auberge Au Coin de Banc et Chalets* (☎ 418-645-2907, 104 Hwy 132)* has rooms from $50, a swimming pool and restaurant.

Places to Eat

Many of the hotels and motels have their own dining rooms and most offer cheap breakfasts.

Les Fous de Basson is a casual recommended café slightly south of the centre of town on the main street (Hwy 132) beside the art gallery. It's good anytime – for just a coffee or whatever meal you're ready for. At dinner, specials start at $11 or there is

more expensive seafood and the atmosphere is warm. The menu also features a couple of vegetarian items. Some evenings live music is added.

Forgettable but inexpensive meals are available all day at *Auberge La Table à Roland (190 Hwy 132)* on the main street with pizza, spaghetti ($9), burgers etc.

You can get a very good evening meal at candle-lit *Resto-bar Le Matelot (7 Rue de l'Église)* which features seafood in the mid-price range. Later at night it's also a place to just have a beer and catch the night's entertainment.

There's also a *bakery (9 Rue Sainte Anne)*.

Entertainment

At night there is often folk music or jazz at *Les Fous de Basson Café*. The *Au Pic de l'Aurore* hotel often has live rock or blues weekends.

Getting There & Away

Bus Orléans Express (☎ 418-782-2140) buses link Percé to Matane, Rimouski and Quebec City once a day. They also go to Edmundston and Campbellton, New Brunswick via Carleton and the south shore of the peninsula twice daily. A ticket to Cap aux Os is $8.50, to Quebec City $71. The Petro Canada service station and depanneur (variety store) at the north end of the main street is used for the bus station.

Train From Montreal, VIA Rail (☎ 418-782-2747, ☎ 1-800-361-5390) serves the south side of the St Lawrence River with main stops at Lévis, Rivière-du-Loup, Rimouski and as far as Matane. The train then goes south through the Matapédia Valley and along the Baie des Chaleurs and up and around past Percé to the town of Gaspé. Many of the smaller places (along the entire route) are serviced. The one-way fare from Charny (Quebec City) to Percé for the 11 hour ride is $92 plus tax (less with seven-day advance) and it leaves Wednesday, Friday and Sunday. The station is 10km south of town at Anse à Beaufils. A taxi is about $11.

THE BAY SIDE

The south shore of the Gaspé Peninsula along the Baie des Chaleurs is quite different from the north coast. The land is flatter and less rocky and the weather warmer. Farming and various small industries are important here. Also, unlike on the north side, there are quite a few English towns. Much of the French population is descended from the original Acadian settlers. The numerous small villages almost run together edged along the coast. The inland area is virtually uninhabited.

Chandler

Long a pulp and paper town, Chandler is still based on the huge Abitibi-Price newsprint mill which can be toured for free. Freighters carry the finished product to South America and Europe from the town's own port facilities. At least they try to – the wreck of the Peruvian ship visible from shore indicates that they don't all make it. Chandler is a fairly large centre and has a couple of shopping malls.

Pabos Mills

The Le Bourg de Pabos archaeological site, dig and uniquely designed interpretation centre is in this French fishing village dating from the 1700s. Bilingual tours are offered from June to October and outline early fishing and settlement.

Port Daniel

Residents of this pretty, former Micmac settlement are of Scottish, Irish and Acadian backgrounds.

Secondary roads from town lead to the wildlife reserves of Port Daniel and Rivière Port Daniel.

Paspébiac

Descendants of Normans, Bretons and Basques live in this fishing town. The Banc de Paspebiac, a waterfront historic site, open daily throughout summer, depicts the early life of the village as a fishing port. There are tours around the site which has a restaurant and trade shops.

New Carlisle

One of the area's English towns, New Carlisle was founded by Loyalists and has some grand colonial homes. Hamilton House, 115 Rue Principale, from 1852, once home to the local member of Parliament, is open for tours. It's on the north side of the road at the east end of town. The house and grounds at 105 Rue Principale, once belonging to Judge Thompson, can also be visited.

Bonaventure

A small, pleasant Acadian town by the water and rocky beach, Bonaventure is the focal point for the area's farming community.

The Acadian museum, open all year, is worth a visit and has English bilingual booklets available to explain some of the tragic yet fascinating Acadian history. (For more on the Acadians see the New Brunswick chapter.) Visit the Les Cuis Fin de la Mer shop at 76 Hwy 132 Est, near the museum for an amazing array of items made of fish-skin leather. It's soft, supple and attractive and no, it doesn't smell. The cheap bookmarks make a good gift.

The new **Bioparc** houses a flora and fauna collection taken from around the peninsula ($10).

Near the museum on Avenue Grand Pré, the *Le Rendez-Vous* restaurant has good fresh-fish lunch specials Monday to Friday. The Orléans Express bus stops at the museum.

North of town, in **Saint Elzéar** (no public transportation) some of the oldest caves in the province were discovered in 1976.

A visit to the site (☎ 418-534-4335) is recommended but you won't be able to afford eating for a few days. The four hour trip, including safety equipment and a snack, is extensive and takes in the largest found variety of stalagmites and stalactites in Quebec. The cave is estimated to be 500,000 years old and it feels like it's never seen the sun. Warm clothing is essential or you'll freeze. Are you ready for the price now? It's $37 a ticket. Children aged 10 or more are admitted and their tickets are discounted. Reservations are required. A second cave is

$30. The caves are open from the beginning of June until the end of October.

There is a $2 museum which for some reason opens a month later and closes a month earlier. It has displays and bones and a slide show but the guided tour of the cave *(la grotte)* is the only real attraction.

New Richmond

Nestled in the bay near the mouths of two rivers New Richmond with a population of 4000 is another Loyalist centre. On Boulevard Perron Ouest, west of the downtown area is the **British Heritage Centre**, a small re-created Loyalist village of the late 1700s. It consists of an interpretive centre, houses, a general store, a lighthouse and other buildings. The centre, which is open daily from mid-June to September, also covers the influence of later Irish and Scottish immigrants.

Carleton

About half the size of New Richmond, Carleton has a pretty location on the water backed by rounded hills. The setting, the sandy beach and the relatively warm air and water of Chaleur Bay have made Carleton a mini-resort. This is where the people of the Gaspé come for a day at the beach and to hang out. There is a tourist office in the central City Hall (Hôtel de Ville).

From the docks there are boat excursions for fishing or sightseeing. At the central bird sanctuary, herons, terns, plovers and other shore birds can be observed along the sandbar. Walking paths and a road also lead behind the town to the top of Mont Saint Joseph which at 555m, provides fine views over the bay and across to New Brunswick. The oratory at the top can be visited and after the climb, the snack bar is a welcome sight.

The campground at La Pointe Tracadigash out on the jutting spit of land in front of town is excellent, with great views, miles of beach and swimming. Canoes can be rented nearby for birding and exploring the calm inner bay.

There are half-a-dozen motels which tend to be pricey. Some 8km east of town is the *Motel Carlton* (☎ 418-364-3288) with basic rooms at $40 a double and better ones at

nearly double that. All have perfect views of the sea which can be reached down a flight of stairs. Also economical is the *Auberge La Visite Surprise* (☎ 418-364-6553, 527 Boulevard Peron), a B&B on the main street.

The huge *Restaurant Le Heron* on the main street (you can't miss it) is a good, all-purpose eatery and the Orléans bus stops right out front. The train station is 1km from the centre, back against the mountains on Rue de la Gare. Good food is available with a beautiful setting down near the water at the more expensive *Café l'Independant*, specialising in fish. There is also a good picnic site.

Parc de Miguasha

The small peninsula south of Hwy 132 near Nouvelle, is renowned for its fossils. The park and Information Centre is set up around the 365-million-year-old fossil site and is free to visit. Guided walks take visitors through the museum and along a trail to the beach and the fossil filled cliffs. The site is open daily from June to October.

For those headed to Dalhousie, New Brunswick, a ferry just down the road from the park, makes a short cut by running across the Baie de Chaleurs. See Dalhousie in the New Brunswick chapter for details.

Pointe à la Garde

Although there is not really any village here, there is an excellent, year-round HI hostel on the highway, *Chateau Bahia* (☎ 418-788-2048, 152 Boulevard Perron). In addition to the building by the street (with dorms, $15), the manager has built a stunning wooden castle in the woods. Here there are double ($39), triple and family rooms and a dining room, where, during summer months, Jean, the host, offers banquet-style dinners. Good breakfasts are included in the overnight price. You can tent, too. The highway bus will stop 100m from the door if you ask the driver.

Pointe à la Croix/Listuguj

Formerly known as Restigouche, this has always been and remains a largely Micmac Indian community. Pointe à la Croix has a

few motels and shops, a seasonal tourist office and the bridge over to Campbellton, New Brunswick. The town runs on New Brunswick time.

Listuguj is the Micmac part of town. At 2 Riverside W is the **Micmac Museum** (☎ 418-788-5034) which outlines some aspects of their culture and history (before the Europeans arrival) and the gift shop sells crafts. Outdoor re-creations of traditional buildings were vandalized and may be replaced. Admission is $3. The Micmacs are found all around the Atlantic Provinces although their numbers are not large. These east coast Native Indians have traditionally produced fine basket work. The best pieces are seen in museums but modern versions can be viewed or purchased on the reserve here. Ask about summer events such as the powwow. Across the street, **Fort Listuguj** (☎ 418-788-1760) reveals a little of the post-contact period of Micmac history through demonstrations, food preparation and guided tours. Admission is $5 and there is a restaurant on site.

Restigouche National Historic Site

A few kilometres west of the bridge from Pointe à la Croix, the site (Parc Historique National La Bataille de la Restigouche, ☎ 418-788-5676) details the 1760 naval battle of Restigouche which pretty well put the kibosh on France's New World ambitions. An interpretive centre explains the battle's significance to the British and has salvaged articles and even parts of a sunken French frigate. The last few years of the war for control of the country are neatly chronicled. Don't miss the quote from Voltaire. The museum is open daily from early June until Thanksgiving in October. Admission is $4.

MATAPÉDIA VALLEY

From the village of Matapédia, Quebec, across the Restigouche River from the province of New Brunswick near Campbellton, the Matapédia Valley runs northward to Mont Joli or Matane on the St Lawrence River. This peaceful, pretty valley is unlike any other portion of the Gaspé Peninsula. Alongside the Matapédia River

and the railway line, traffic-free Hwy 132 passes through fertile farmland with a backdrop of green mountains for about 70km. Aside from the good farming, the valley differs from much of the rocky, more sparsely vegetated peninsula by supporting broad-leafed maple and elm trees which add a lot of colour in the autumn. The river is renowned for its salmon fishing for which expensive permits are required. There are several smallish towns along the way, a few sites to see and, around Lac Matapédia, a couple of picnic sites and a campground.

Matapédia

The *Auberge La Marmotte (☎ 418-865-2100, 13 Rue des Saumons)* has everything you need to make a worthwhile stop in this village where the Ristigouche and Matapédia rivers merge. There is economical lodging (from hostel dorms to family rooms), a good restaurant/bar, canoe and kayak rentals, guided tours of area rivers and trails and even Cuban cigars! The Appalachian Trail from New Brunswick and Maine passes by. It soon will connect to the far end of the peninsula (see Forillon). The bus and train both stop in town.

Routhierville

The first of several wooden bridges seen through the valley is in this small village. Some of them, known as settler's bridges, are covered, like the ones seen in greater abundance across New Brunswick. There's also a picnic site.

Causapscal

Causapscal is a good place for a stop on the trip through the valley. It's a pretty town with a traditional look, a beautiful stone church and many older houses with typical Québecois silver roofs.

The Causapscal and Matapédia rivers meet here. There are a couple of covered bridges south of town and, in the centre, a pedestrian-only suspension bridge across the Matapédia. Again, sawmills are the main economic focus and the smell or smoke from the processing chimneys is ever present.

There is a tourist office near the interesting **Matamajaw** historic site. This museum, once a salmon-fishing lodge, the outbuildings and much of the riverfront property were all part of a private fishing estate built in 1870 by Lord Mount Stephen of Canadian Pacific Railway fame. In the early part of the century a group of moneyed Canadian and US businesspeople bought the place and ran it as a private club for 60 years. Take a look in the lodge, some of which remains much the way it was – some people know how to live. Other rooms are devoted to the Atlantic salmon, the impetus for all this. The site is open from 10 June to 10 September from 9 am to 9 pm daily and costs $4.

About 15km north are some waterfalls and Les Marais, a **salmon pool** where fish can be seen swimming and jumping through much of the summer and autumn. Walking trails run along the river through the woods. Ask for directions, information and the sketchy map at the tourist office.

The Orléans Express bus, linking New Brunswick to the St Lawrence shore, stops at 122 Rue Saint Jacques Sud.

Places to Stay & Eat For spending the night or having dinner, there is the *Auberge La Coulée Douce (☎ 418-756-5270)* on the hill opposite the historic site. North of town is a campground and the *Motel Du Vallon (☎ 418-756-3433)* with doubles at $65, less out of season. There are also a few cheaper rooms to let where the bus stops.

Cantine Sportive at the south end of town is a good lunch bar.

Amqui

The largest town in the valley doesn't have much to recommend it. All the basic needs can be met, and north of town beyond the bridge is a campground. Towards the end of summer you may see people standing by the side of the road waving jars. They're selling locally picked wild hazelnuts *(noisettes)* which are not expensive. Around **Lac Matapédia** there are some viewpoints over the lake and picnic spots.

Magdalen Islands

Out in the Gulf of St Lawrence, closer to the Atlantic Provinces than to Quebec, lies this lovely 100km-long string of islands. The Magdalen Islands, or Îles de la Madeleine, comprise about a dozen islands, 120km north-east of Prince Edward Island, and most of them are linked by long sand spits. In fact, the islands are little more than spits themselves, so excellent sand beaches line the shores.

Because of their remoteness, the quiet life, the superb seashore scenery of carved red and grey cliffs and the great beaches, the islands have appeal and have become quite popular with visitors, although Québecois make up at least 90% of the tourists. Most people stay two to four days and this enables them to look around most of the islands.

More time can easily be spent walking the trails and beaches and exploring in depth.

The local people make their living mainly from fishing as they have always done but now the two months of busy tourism, July and August, are supplementing many an income. Sealing used to be important, but the commercial hunt has diminished under international pressure. Some former hunters are now taking tourists out on the ice in early spring to see and photograph the baby seals. The Magdalens are considered the best place for this. Although expensive as a single purpose excursion, they are becoming the basis for popular brief trips to the islands.

Over 90% of the population of 14,000 speak various French dialects, but many Scottish and Irish descendants live on Île d'Entrée and La Grosse Île. The towns and the people too, are sophisticated despite the remote, isolated nature of the islands.

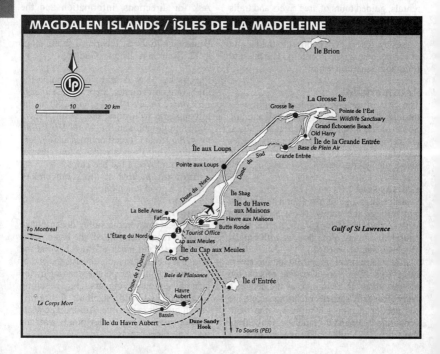

MAGDALEN ISLANDS / ÎSLES DE LA MADELEINE

Île Brion

La Grosse Île

Grosse Île

Pointe de l'Est
Wildlife Sanctuary

Grand Échouerie Beach
Old Harry

Île de la Grande Entrée
Base de Plein Air

Grande Entrée

Île aux Loups

Pointe aux Loups

Dune du Nord

Dune du Sud

Île Shag

Île du Havre aux Maisons

La Belle Anse

Fatima

Havre aux Maisons

Butte Ronde

Tourist Office

L'Étang du Nord

Cap aux Meules

Île du Cap aux Meules

Gros Cap

Gulf of St Lawrence

Dune de l'Ouest

Baie de Plaisance

Île d'Entrée

To Montreal

Le Corps Mort

Havre Aubert

Bassin

Île du Havre Aubert

Dune Sandy Hook

To Souris (PEI)

0   10   20 km

Restaurants and living rooms could easily be transplanted from downtown Montreal. Unlike many fishing or farming regions, the islands seem quite prosperous and don't really have the old-time feel, of say, Prince Edward Island. Food and accommodation prices can, but need not, reflect these characteristics.

The principal islands are Havre aux Maisons, which has its own airport, and Cap aux Meules. At the town of Cap aux Meules, the ferry from Souris, Prince Edward Island, ties in and there is an information office (☎ 418-986-2245).

Things to See & Do

Most of the islands' activities and sights revolve around the sea. Beach-strolling, and exploring lagoons, tidal pools and the cliff formations can take up days. More time can be spent searching out the best vistas, skirting around the secondary roads and poking around the fishing villages. The waters aren't tropical by any stretch of the imagination but are warmed (slightly) by the Gulf Stream. Swimming is possible in the open sea or, preferably, in some of the protected, shallow lagoons. Currents are strong and venturing far from shore is not advisable. With nearly constant breezes, windsurfing is good and several places offer boards and lessons.

Fishing expeditions can be arranged and diving on the reefs is possible.

There are also some historic points of interest such as the old churches and unusual traditional buildings such as the now disappearing hay barns. Also around the countryside look for the old smoke houses (marked on the islands' map) now disused but once part of the important herring industry. Keep an eye out for the many fine and distinctive houses dotting the largely barren terrain.

In the evenings during summer, you may be lucky to find a concert, a play, or an exhibition of some sort in one of the towns.

Special Events

At Grande Entrée, a lobster festival is held during the first week in July. Also in July watch for the annual sandcastle-building contests along a 2km stretch of beach on Havre Aubert.

Accommodation

From June to September the islands are busy and accommodation gets seriously scarce. If, upon arrival, you do not have a place booked (as most people appear to) go directly to the tourist office and have it find you something. After that first night and when settled a bit, you can always look around for something else. Before arrival, you could call the tourist office from Prince Edward Island and ask it to book a place in an area that appeals to you.

A good portion of the Magdalen Islands' accommodation is in people's homes or in cottages and trailers they rent out. These represent by far the most interesting and best value lodgings averaging $35 a single and $45 a double. The tourist office has a sheet listing many of these places but it is far from complete. The tourist office will call and book the ones it knows (including ones not on the list) for you, still others can be found by following roadside signs or just asking people. The residents are friendly and enjoy even a broken French-English conversation.

More commercial accommodation is being established all the time but remains mostly in motel form at often more than double the guesthouse rate. Cottages and cabins go for about $400 to $550 a week. The bulk of the places to stay are on either Cap aux Meules or Havre aux Maisons.

There are also about half a dozen campgrounds scattered around the islands. The campgrounds never seem full but remember this can be a wet and windy place. If you've got a cheap tent you're pushing your luck.

Food

Another of the islands' lures is the fresh seafood. One of the main catches is lobster; the lobster season runs from mid-May to mid-July. Snow crabs, scallops, mussels, perch and cod are other significant species. A local speciality available at many of the better restaurants is *pot-en-pot*, a dish of mixed fish and seafood in a sauce baked in its own pie crust. The adventurous eater

QUEBEC

may want to try seal meat which is served a couple of ways.

All the major villages have some sort of a restaurant but out of Cap aux Meules choices are limited. Cantines with burgers, hot dogs and fries are seen here and there.

Cap aux Meules

Cap aux Meules, the largest town of the islands, and with the ferry terminal, is the commercial centre of the archipelago. It's quite busy and modern which can be a little disconcerting for those looking for something else. This first glimpse is, however, atypical of the rest of the towns, villages and landscapes around the islands. Supplies, banking and any necessary reservations should all be taken care of here.

The islands' tourist office is a short distance from the ferry landing on the corner of Hwy 199 and Chemin du Debarcadere. There really isn't anything of note to see in Cap aux Meules but the town has more hotels and restaurants than any other one place in the Magdalen Islands. The rest of this island is also fairly densely populated.

Places to Stay & Eat The half-dozen hotels and motels are all rather pricey and, as Cap aux Meules isn't particularly interesting, you'd be better off finding something away from town in the spacious, scenic countryside. Of course if you're arriving late this may not be feasible but the tourist office has a list of local tourist homes which make a stay more pleasant and easier on the wallet. Try *Hébergement Village (☎ 418-986-4301, 385 Chemin Petipas)* which is just $30 single or double.

A number of inexpensive guesthouses can be found on the other side of the island in the Fatima or Étang du Nord areas. One place near the beach is *Lauretta Cyr (☎ 418-986-2302)*. Of course, nobody lives too far from the sea here.

Probably the least expensive place for dinner in town is the *Belle-Vue* with a choice of Chinese, Italian and some Canadian standards. More expensive and popular is the dressier *Pizza Patio* on the main

street, Chemin Principal, a few blocks south from the ferry terminal. *Casse Croûte Raymond* is good for breakfasts and fries and burgers. The *Auberge La Jetée (153 Rue Principale)* has something for everyone including some seafood.

La Belle Anse

The coastal area known as La Belle Anse on the north-west side of Cap aux Meules has some dramatic red cliffs and interesting coastal erosion features. There are some paths right along the cliffs offering excellent views. For a good and inexpensive meal go to the *Cooperative de Gros-Cap*, a lobster (*homard*) processing plant with a cafeteria-restaurant known as *La Factrie* upstairs with a large window overlooking the plant below. Just follow the road, Chemin de Gros Cap, north of the town of L'Étang du Nord. You needn't eat lobster; there is a selection of other seafood with soups and salad all reasonably priced. It's open from noon to 9 pm daily, Sunday 3 to 9 pm. In Fatima, the small plain looking *Decker Boy Restaurant* on Chemins les Caps, is cheap and good. Try one of the chowders.

North of La Belle Anse at the good sandy beach at Anse de l'Hôpital is a small complex of tourist-oriented shops and a snack bar.

Île du Havre Aubert

South of Cap aux Meules, connected by long strings of sand at points barely wider than the road, is the archipelago's largest island.

The most lively area of the town of **Havre Aubert** is known as La Grave, an old section by the water at the south-eastern tip of the island. The main street is lined with small craft and gift shops, some restaurants and many old houses. There is a theatre here for summer productions in French only.

On any rainy day the interesting aquarium is packed with visitors disturbed from their seaside activities. A pool with various creatures which can be handled is a major attraction. The **Musée de la Mer** has displays on shipwrecks and various aspects of

the islands' transportation and fishing history. Both are open daily in summer and have low admission fees.

Near town is the **Centre Nautique de l'Istorlet** with sail-boat and windsurfer courses and rentals. There is also a simple campground at the coastal property.

Places to Stay & Eat The *Auberge Chez Denis à François* (☎ *418-937-2371)* has six rooms; singles/doubles cost from $44/52 and meals are available in its restaurant which is open to nonguests.

In La Grave, the *Café de la Grave* is a good place for simple, inexpensive meals or a coffee and cake.

La Saline, open at lunch and dinner time only, is a pricier seafood restaurant where the local speciality, pot-en-pot, can be sampled.

Île du Havre aux Maisons

All told, probably the most scenic of the Magdalen Islands, Havre aux Maisons has a bit of everything. Definitely take the south shore road (Chemin des Montants) from Pointe Basse up around Butte Ronde and into a beautiful little valley. Excellent views, some traditional-style houses, smoke houses and a lighthouse are all seen along this route. There are several restaurants along the main road across the island.

Places to Stay & Eat For a place to stay on Havre aux Maisons, the *Auberge La P'tite Baie* (☎ *418-969-4073, 187 Rte 199)* is friendly and reasonably priced at $65 a double and meals are available. *Le Havre à William* (☎ *418-969-4513, 426 Chemin Lioseau)* has a guesthouse with rooms for just $20/30.

The coastal area around Dune du Sud is also attractive and there are some fine places to stay in the area including some little cottages right on the water by a beach with huge sandstone arches.

Pointe aux Loups

On either side of this small community in the middle of the long sand spits connecting the north and south islands are stretches of sand beaches and dunes. For a quick dip, the water is warmer on the lagoon side.

La Grosse Île

Scottish pioneers settled this, the principal English section of the Magdalen Islands. As soon as you arrive, you'll notice all the signs are in English. Despite generations of isolation, many of the local people barely speak a word of French. La Grosse Île, East Cape and Old Harry are the main communities.

Trinity Church, known for its stained glass depicting Jesus the fisherman, is worth a look. Out through the windows the eye captures the graves, the piles of lobster traps, some solitary houses and then the sea – the island's world in microcosm.

There is a commercial **saltmine** just off the main road en route to Old Harry. No tours are given but there is an information office open in the afternoon. Begun in 1983, the mine is 225m deep.

About 16km off La Grosse Île is **Île Brion**, an ecological reserve, once but no longer inhabited by humans. It remains home to 140 species of birds and much interesting vegetation. On days that are not too windy it can be visited. Even camping is possible, but for details call the tourist office.

Places to Stay Many of the people around La Grosse Île rent a room or two during summer but are not listed in the guides.

Île de l'Est

Linking La Grosse Île and Grande Entrée is this wild region which boasts the islands' most impressive beach. From Pointe Old Harry, **La Grande Échouerie Beach** extends, a curving sweep of pale sand, about 5km down Île de l'Est. A short road with parking areas and trails stretching down to the beach begins near the Old Harry harbour. From Hwy 199 (through Île de l'Est which, other than the beach is entirely a national wildlife refuge area) a few turn-offs lead to hiking paths.

Île de la Grande Entrée

On this island stop at Old Harry, a fishing wharf with about 10 boats and some

spectacular shoreline cliffs, portions of which contain caves. Walruses once inhabited the area but they were slaughtered indiscriminately. Sea Cow Lane is the site of the former walrus landing.

In the other direction from Old Harry don't miss **Saint Peter's by the Sea**, a beautiful, peaceful little church overlooking the sea and bounded by graves, belonging almost exclusively to members of the Clark and Clarke families. It's open to visitors and well worth a visit. On a breezy day the inside offers a quiet stillness broken only by the creaking rafters. It is all wood, including a richly carved door honouring drowned fishermen.

Across the street is a fine area for watching the sea explode into sparkling bits up onto the rugged, rocky shoreline.

The **Seal Interpretation Centre**, 377 Rte 199, is open daily in summer, with a range of exhibits including references to the very controversial annual seal hunt.

Places to Stay & Eat *Club Vacances 'Les Iles'* (☎ 418-985-2833) is a resort built around the island's nature and the activities it affords: walking, windsurfing, boat tours, birdwatching etc. Package deals include rooms, all meals and organised activities. The same package is offered to tenters at a discount. Very little English seems to be spoken. If you just want to put up a tent, the fee is $14 a night and anybody can use the cafeteria-style restaurant. Activities are also offered on an individual basis.

At the far tip of the island are more colourful fishing boats to check along the docks and a couple of places to eat. Best is the *Restaurant du CEPIM* where lobster is cheap and other seafood is offered.

Île d'Entrée

This is the one inhabited island not interconnected by land with the others. A ferry links it to the port at Cap aux Meules. The boat runs twice a day from Monday to Saturday: once early in the morning and once in mid-afternoon. Board in front of the coastguard building. The ferry crossing takes be-

tween 30 and 60 minutes. The virtually treeless island has an English-speaking population of around 175 and is primarily a fishing community. It's about 4km long and less than 1km wide with walking trails leading over much of it.

The gentler western section supports some farms before ending in high red cliffs. The eastern section is mountainous with the highest point, Big Hill, at 174m above sea level. A trail from Post Office Road leads up to the views from the top.

There is one guesthouse, *Chez McLean* (☎ 418-986-4541) on the island, with cooking facilities, but call before arriving if you wish to stay. Also on the island are a couple of grocery stores and one basic snack bar.

Getting There & Away

Air Canadian Airlines flies in daily from Halifax; Air Alliance has two flights a day from Montreal, Quebec City, Gaspé and other points.

Ferry The cheapest and most common way to get to the Magdalen Islands is by ferry from Souris on Prince Edward Island. The boat leaves daily at 2 pm but out of July and August, check the schedule. During midsummer's peak season, there are additional trips at 2 am Saturday to Monday, nonetheless, they too will be packed.

In midsummer, reservations are strongly recommended. Make them by calling ☎ 418-986-3278 or ☎ 1-888-986-3278. If not, arrive at least two hours ahead of time. That's *at least* two hours. The boat, the MV *Lucy Maud Montgomery*, with a capacity of 90 vehicles and 300 passengers is always completely full. If after waiting in line for hours you do not get aboard, you'll be given a reservation for the very next ferry only.

For the return trip, reservations can also be made. It's advisable to do this on arrival or not long after. In peak season there will be at least several days worth of returning passengers choc-a-bloc as soon as you arrive. The return to Prince Edward Island

departs at 8 am, except on Tuesday when it leaves at 8 pm. Again, the seasonal supplementary trip is at night.

This is not a cheap trip. The cost is $35 per person for the five hour, 223km cruise. It's the car fee that really kills you though. That's another $66. And these are both one-way fares only. Campers, trailers etc are still more costly. Bicycles can be taken for $8. Credit cards are accepted for payment.

The ship is well appointed, however, with a surprisingly inexpensive cafeteria. For those with a little extra money there is also a white-tablecloth dining room with meals in the $17 to $22 range and a full course (from soup to dessert) table d'hôte which is not bad value. The ship has some outdoor decks, various inner lounges and a bar with live entertainment.

Passenger boats operated by the same line cruise to the islands down the St Lawrence River from Montreal, but are expensive. There is also a passenger and cargo ship once a week from Montreal, which is less costly but still over $370 one way. The CTMA *Voyageur* taking cargo and 15 passengers departs Montreal once a week for Cap aux Meules and returns four days later. In Montreal call ☎ 514-937-7656. Meals are included in the price of the ticket. In the off-peak tourist season the price drops by about one third.

Getting Around

Five of the main islands are linked by road but distances are small and cycling is not uncommon. Bicycles can be rented at Le Pedallier in Cap aux Meules. The office is closed Sunday.

There is a guided bus tour of the islands available out of Cap aux Meules and taxis will take you to specific parts of the island. Also, cars and motorcycles can be rented in Cap aux Meules or at the airport.

A ferry connects Île d'Entrée with the two principal islands.

One boat tour operator, Excursions en Mer, in Cap aux Meules, offers day-trips to Île d'Entrée, fishing/lobster excursions and trips around the coast to see the cliffs. Sea kayaks can be rented at Adventure Plein Air in Étang du Nord.

The Far North

Wherever you are in Canada, the north or far north are ambiguous terms. For the vast majority of people, two hours north of Montreal – or a few hours drive north from almost any of the country's major cities – is considered the north. In Quebec, certainly, straying more than a couple of hundred miles beyond the main population centres puts you in the land of the boreal forest. And yet, if you travel as far north as possible on the most remote route in the middle of nowhere you might get halfway up the province. The north is an immense and sparsely populated region, the most northerly sections of which are dotted with tiny Inuit and Native Indian settlements here and there accessible only by bush plane. The developed areas are based on massive industrial operations – mining, forestry and hydro-electricity.

Much of the accessible north has already been discussed in the text. These regions from west to east include the areas north of Baie Comeau connected by road to Labrador; Sept Îles with its train into Labrador and beyond; and the far eastern Gulf of St Lawrence with a sketchy road system and ferry access to Labrador. Many of the parks discussed between Quebec City and the Saguenay River are as far north as most people ever get. This section outlines some possibilities in the north-west up to James Bay. Most tourism in the far north involves very expensive fly-in camps specialising in fishing and hunting. Some operators are now offering cultural and ecotours of various types but again they are prohibitively costly. For these trips inquire at tourist information offices in Montreal or Quebec. To experience wilderness and the northern coniferous forest, the various parks and reserves are the place to go. Most people visiting the James Bay area go to get a look at the colossal power stations. Hotels/motels in the region are not cheap but as a rule not way out of line and there are plenty of

campgrounds. The roads are discussed below. Canadian Regional Airlines and Air Creebec serve many of the north's major towns. Note that you should carry cash or a credit card. Residents also suggest you use a lip balm as it's very dry.

LA VÉRENDRYE RESERVE

North-west of Montreal, Highway 117 leads past Mont Tremblant Park into this massive, almost untouched wildlife reserve about six or so hours later. The wilderness canoeists who make up the majority of visitors tend to sigh and go into silent rapture when asked about it. Some supplies can be obtained in Mont Laurier or Maniwaki (south toward Ottawa) but most should be brought in. The interpretation centre at the park's south end has information on trails and canoe routes. The park has two campgrounds.

VAL D'OR

With a population of 24,500 this is a major town and centre for the local mining and forestry industries. The Mining Village of Bourlamaque is a re-created log village from the gold rush period. Surface operations can be toured and underground visits descending a 90m mine shaft are an option ($15). There are numerous motels and a nearby campground. The tourist office has a list of B&Bs.

ROUYN NORANDA

To the west, this copper mining and smelting town is slightly larger than Val d'Or. Free tours of the Horne Smelter, one of the world's largest producers, can be taken in summer. There is also a reconstructed historic site here detailing the settlement era.

Nearby are several areas to enjoy nature such as Parc Aiguebelle. There are car rental agencies in town.

South of town, a main highway runs along the Ontario border to Temiscaming which is connected to North Bay and hence southern Ontario.

JAMES BAY

North of Val d'Or, past Amos and the many satellite villages, the surfaced road continues through wilderness to **Matagami**. This mining town is based on copper and zinc. Free tours are offered at the Noranda site. There are two motels in town and camping.

From here the so-called Route de la Baie James, also paved, travels 620km to Chisasibi on the waters of James Bay. Side roads on the way lead to Native Indian villages. Enroute are designated picnic spots, viewpoints and numerous lakes to stop at. You'll have lots of time because the sun doesn't set until 10.30 pm or later in summer. The James Bay Municipality (MBJ in French) tourist office (☎ 819-739-2030) is at km 6 (6km out of town) along this road. Ask here about the gasoline stations and to reserve a site at one of the campgrounds. It is important to have accommodation prebooked. Campgrounds are located at km 38 and km 582 on the main road.

The MBJ, lying between the 49th and 50th parallels, covers a fifth of the province and is twice the size of England. At about the tip of James Bay, the forest gives way to the taiga vegetative zone. The true tundra is much farther north, well beyond any road access.

The region began to open up in the mid-1970s with the commencement of work on the mega hydro-electric projects. The roads and all the recent settlements are related to these ongoing controversial developments. Local Native peoples have long objected to the dams, mass flooding and resulting radical environmental changes. In the early 1990s, the Cree very successfully lobbied in New York, Quebec's main customer for power. Some projects have been scaled back and others shelved, at least for now.

Radisson, with 700 people, is the area's main town. From the vantage point in town much of the surrounding territory can be seen. To the east lies the string of reservoirs and massive power stations. A road, hundreds of kilometres long stretching three-quarters of the way to Labrador, connects them. La Grand 2, (now also called Robert Bourassa Centre, after a former premier) just west of Radisson, produces half of Quebec's electricity. Free tours of the enormous

site are given but reservations are required. They must be made 48 hours in advance through the MBJ tourist office in Matagami or at the Hydro-Quebec Information Centre in Radisson.

There are two hotels and a campground. South of town about 30km is the other main road campground. The average temperature in July is 14°C.

Chisasibi, a Cree settlement on the coast at the mouth of La Grand Rivière also has an expensive motel. La Grande 1, another power station, can be visited on the way. Again reservations must be made beforehand.

The other main road in the region is the unsurfaced Route du Nord (the North Route) which runs south-east off the Route de la Baie James, above Matagami, 437km to Chibougamou. Before driving this lonely stretch ask about conditions and services.

Gasoline is available at the Cree village of Nemiscau (Nemaska).

CHIBOUGAMOU

North-east of Val d'Or, Hwy 113 cuts through the forest toward central Quebec all the way to Chibougamou. It's a long, isolated trip, so take extra supplies. There is camping at Lebel sur Quevillon, a pulp and paper town. Canoes can be rented at the lake. Once in Chibougamou there are a few motels and hotels with attached restaurants and a campground.

From town, the road continues 200km through a reserve and past the Cree village of Mistissini before ending at Lac Albanel.

South of Chibougamou, Hwy 187 runs through Ashuapmushuan Wildlife Reserve, which has camping, to Lac Saint Jean and Chicoutimi. There are no towns until nearly Lac Saint John.

Newfoundland & Labrador

Two distinct geographic areas make up this singular political entity but the residents will remind you that Newfoundland (pronounced 'new-fen-LAND') is Newfoundland and Labrador is Labrador. The former is the island section of the province, the latter the larger northern mainland portion and each is always referred to separately. Though they have much in common, there are cultural, historical, geological and developmental differences.

By far the majority of the population lives in more accessible Newfoundland and this is the region most visitors see.

Newfoundland has a unique character, and even a brief encounter with it is gratifying. It's a rugged, weather-beaten land at the edge of Canada, heavily influenced by the sea and the conditions of the not-too-distant far north.

From the often foggy shores, generations of fishers have headed out to sea and the waters legendary for cod and dozens of other kinds of fish. This more than anything has determined the life and culture of the province.

On the Grand Banks, lying south-east off the most populated region (the Avalon Peninsula), fishing boats gather from around the world as they have done since before Columbus even saw the 'New Land'.

Unfortunately, the huge, modern, hi-tech, floating factories now used by some nations, together with illegal practices, are a far cry from the traditional Newfoundland family trawler.

The 1990s have seen the inevitable result of this with drastically reduced catches and the end of work for tens of thousands of Newfoundlanders in the fishing industry. It is hoped the decimated cod schools will return and that in the meantime other species, particularly lobster, can help to tide people over. Fish farming is also being attempted but for many people the old way of life, relying on the sea, is gone for good.

All of Labrador and the northern portions of the island are part of the Laurentian

HIGHLIGHTS

Entered Confederation: 31 March 1949
Area: 404,520 sq km
Population: 544,500
Provincial Capital: St John's

- Walk the hilly streets of St John's, the oldest city in North America

- Enjoy traditional music and satirical theatre at local clubs found around the province

- View the icebergs around Twillingate and Notre Dame Bay

- Hike along the fjords in Gros Morne National Park

- Visit a 1000-year-old Viking settlement at L'Anse-aux-Meadows National Historic Park

- Discover the isolated fishing villages, called outports, along the shores of Labrador

- Explore northern Labrador's remote grandeur and be overwhelmed by the solitude

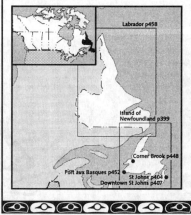

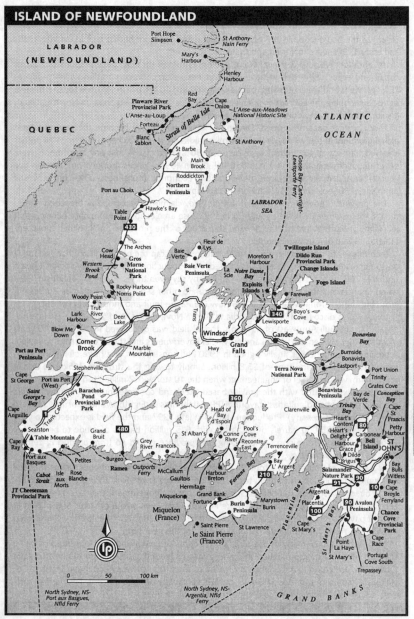

ISLAND OF NEWFOUNDLAND

**LABRADOR
(NEWFOUNDLAND)**

QUEBEC

Port Hope
Simpson

St Anthony-
Nain Ferry

Mary's
Harbour

Henley
Harbour

Red
Bay

Cape
Onion

L'Anse-aux-Meadows
National Historic Site

**Pinware River
Provincial Park**

L'Anse-au-Loup

Forteau

Strait of Belle Isle

Blanc
Sablon

St Barbe

St Anthony

Main
Brook

Roddickton

Port au Choix

**Northern
Peninsula**

Table
Point

Hawke's Bay

430

The Arches

Fleur de
Lys

Baie
Verte

La
Scie

Moreton's
Harbour

Twillingate Island

**Dildo Run
Provincial Park**

Change Islands

Cow
Head

**Gros
Morne
National
Park**

*Western
Brook
Pond*

**Baie Verte
Peninsula**

*Notre Dame
Bay*

Fogo Island

Rocky Harbour
Norris Point

Woody Point

Trut
River

Lark
Harbour

Deer
Lake

Blow Me
Down

**Corner
Brook**

1

Trans

Canada

**Port au Port
Peninsula**

Marble
Mountain

Hwy

Cape
St George

Stephenville

Port au Port
(West)

**Barachois
Pond
Provincial Park**

*Saint
George's
Bay*

Cape
Anguille

Searston

Trans Canada Hwy

▲ Table Mountain

Grand
Bruit

480

Grey
River

Francois

360

Head of
Bay
d'Espoir

St Alban's

Pool's
Cove

Conne
River

Recontre
East

Cape
Ray

Port aux
Basques

*Cabot
Strait*

Petites

Isle
aux
Morts

Rose
Blanche

Ramea

Burgeo

*Outports
Ferry*

McCallum

Gaultois

Hermitage

Harbour
Breton

Bay
L'Argent

210

Terrenceville

Miquelon

Grand Bank

Fortune

**Burin
Peninsula**

Burin

Marystown

**JT Cheeseman
Provincial Park**

Miquelon
(France)

Saint Pierre

St Lawrence

Ile Saint Pierre
(France)

Cape
St Mary's

Placentia Bay

Argentia

Placentia

100

Cape
St Mary's

*ATLANTIC
OCEAN*

*Goose Bay-Cartwright-
Lewisporte Ferry*

*LABRADOR
SEA*

La
Scie

Exploits
Islands

Farewell

340

Boyo's
Cove

Lewisporte

Windsor

**Grand
Falls**

Gander

**Terra Nova
National Park**

*Bonavista
Bay*

Burnside
Bonavista

Eastport

Port Union

Grates Cove

**Bonavista
Peninsula**

Bay de
Verde

*Conception
Bay*

Clarenville

Heart's
Content

Heart's
Delight

Harbour
Grace

*Trinity
Bay*

Trinity

Carbonear

Bell
Island

Dildo

Brigus

80

Cape
St Francis

Petty
Harbour

**ST
JOHN'S**

90

10

Salamander
Nature Park

91

Bay
Bulls

Witless
Bay

Cape
Broyle

Ferryland

1

90

**Avalon
Peninsula**

**Chance
Cove
Provincial
Park**

Cape
Race

Point
La Haye

Portugal
Cove South

St Mary's

Trepassey

St Mary's Bay

Fortune Bay

0   50   100 km

*North Sydney, NS-
Port aux Basques,
Nfld Ferry*

*North Sydney, NS-
Argentia, Nfld
Ferry*

GRAND   BANKS

NEWFOUNDLAND & LABRADOR

All the Money in the World

Easing all the bad economic news Newfoundland and Labrador had to face in the late 1980s and early 1990s were major oil and mineral discoveries.

In Labrador's Voiseys Bay near Nain, geologists turned up rich concentrations of copper, cobalt and especially nickel. Inco, the huge mineral extraction corporation which produces 27% of the world's nickel metal, paid an astonishing C$4.3 billion in 1996 for the mineral rights; developing the Labrador site and constructing a smelter at Argentia on Newfoundland, it said, would cost an additional US$1.5 billion.

Though what became termed 'Diamond Fields' could easily become the second-largest nickel producer in the world, as the new millennium drew near bickering between all parties involved had scaled the project back by up to 50%. Inco claims that any agreements were never unconditional and that a world nickel glut in 1998 – prices dropped one-third in five years – would make large-scale development economic foolishness. The company still promises 1700 jobs and US$1.1 billion in development.

The provincial government is far from pleased, claiming the company breached agreements; the issue was volatile enough to nearly cause an election. The province believes that Inco simply wants to extract the ore and ship it out of the province, an absolutely unacceptable tenet in previous agreements.

Inco refuses to back down, and even threatened to scrap the project altogether and move on to mine sites in Indonesia and New Caledonia. Production at Voiseys Bay couldn't begin until late 2001 – two crucial years late – and many say even this is egregious optimism. Even when financial numbers are agreed upon, there are other serious concerns to be addressed, including the environmental impact and how the native Inuit and Innu would benefit.

Oil was also discovered in Newfoundland's Terra Nova region. And then there is Hibernia. Located in the Bull Arm west of St John's, the oil field was discovered in 1979 but 10 years of wrangling between the federal and provincial governments and the oil companies followed. A binding agreement was finally signed in 1990 and construction of a huge oil rig and loading system began to the tune of $5.8 billion. Simply towing the structure 315km to its site off Bull Arm was a marvel of engineering; when the 10 storey, 1.2 million ton production platform was finally mated with the gravity based, steel and concrete foundation, news media shamelessly quoted dignitaries' favourite PR catchphrase: 'Eighth Wonder of the Modern World' (capitals necessary). Production started in late 1997 and the field is expected to yield an average of 135,000 barrels of oil a day, with 615 million barrels of crude to be tapped. Within two years of the onset of pumping, the province would go from producing zero to 36% of Canada's crude oil.

There were of course detractors. To counter the provincial government's claims that the entire project would contribute up to 18,100 'person-years' of work and some US$2.15 billion in direct investment, opponents pointed out that the government spent over a US$1 billion in direct grants, guaranteed far more in loans, and even wrote off over $50 million in interest payments (to the oil industry!). Deals signed with Ottawa in the 1980s will also keep most of the money flowing into national coffers for the near term.

More interestingly, many of the 600,000 residents of Newfoundland, long tired of being the butt of jokes (not to mention misconceptions of federal assistance policy) by mainland Canadians, are going to experience a windfall of sorts from the new economic linchpin. Sociologists, reporters and especially politicians have already noted a nascent 'Newfie nationalism', which to some may be more important than black gold.

Shield, one of the earliest geological formations on earth – possibly the only area unchanged from times predating the appearance of animals on the planet.

Across the province, in both sections, the interior is mostly forested wilderness with many peat bogs and countless lakes and rivers. Almost all the people live along the coast, with its many isolated fjords, bays and coves.

History

In 1497, John Cabot sailed around the shores of Newfoundland in the employ of Henry VII of England. Not long after explorers under the flags of France and Portugal were also in the area. Thanks to tales of cod stocks so prolific that one could nearly walk on water, by the 15th and 16th centuries fishers from those countries, as well as Basques and Spaniards, regularly plied the offshore waters.

In 1583, Sir Humphrey Gilbert claimed Newfoundland for England and small settlements began developing over the next 200 years. Some autonomy was granted in about 1830.

The province has a rich aviation history hosting 40 pioneering transatlantic flights between 1919 and 1937 including those of Charles Lindbergh and Amelia Earhart.

During WWII, Canada, Britain and the USA all set up military bases and airports.

The province was the last to join Canada, doing so in 1949, a relatively recent date which surprises most visitors. By this time, fishing had become more modernised and pulp and paper, iron ore and hydro power had all added to the province's development.

Climate

Newfoundland's weather is cool throughout the year, Labrador's especially so, with the Arctic currents and north winds. There's heavy precipitation all year too, mainly around the coasts where fog and wind is common. Summer is short but July and August are generally quite warm. The sunniest and driest places are the central, inland areas.

Economy

The economies of Newfoundland and Labrador experienced an upheaval in the 1990s. Years of overfishing depleted the essential cod stocks to the point that, in 1992, federal fisheries officials imposed a ban on cod fishing off eastern Newfoundland. A year later the moratorium was extended to southern Newfoundland in an effort to give the cod fishery a good chance to recover. The ban, however, devastated a province that was already enduring a 20% unemployment rate. More than 30,000 fishers were put out of work and in many small coastal villages as many as 80% of the families were on a government assistance program called TAGS.

Tempering the bad news were major oil and mineral discoveries. In Labrador's Voiseys Bay, near Nain, massive deposits of nickel, copper and cobalt have been located. Development of these resources has so far been impeded by political and economic debate as well as Native concerns.

The vast oilfields of Hibernia, located offshore near the Grand Banks and east of St John's, began production in the late 1990s.

Population & People

The people, of mainly English and Irish descent, have developed a distinct culture. Perhaps the most noticeable difference is the language with its strong lilting inflections, distinctive accent, unique slang and colourful idiom. A look at the map reveals descriptive and light-hearted names such as Nick's Nose Cove, Come-by-Chance, Main Tickle and Cow Head. To people in the rest of the country the residents of 'The Rock' are known humorously as Newfies, and though they are often the butt of Canadian humour there is no real malice meant. It's generally accepted that they are among the friendliest and most quick-witted of Canadians. (Which is not to say Newfoundlanders always appreciate the humour.)

Other peoples have played prominent roles in the development of this land. The Vikings landed and established a settlement in 1000 AD. Inuit and Native Indian bands were calling the area home long before that,

and historic sites mark some of these settlements. Newfoundland proper, the island portion of the province, was the site of one of the most tragic of all North American encounters between the early Europeans and the original inhabitants. The Beothuks lived and travelled across much of the province for about 500 years. In the early 1800s the last of the group died, victims of white diseases, hostility and bad luck. Today, Labrador is still inhabited mainly by Inuit peoples and in smaller numbers the Innu Indian people.

Information

Tourist Offices The Department of Tourism, Culture and Recreation (☎ 1-800-563-6353, fax 709-729-0057, info@tourism.gov.nf.ca, public.gov.nf.ca/tourism) oversees tourism promotion and publishes a series of guides. Its mailing address is Visitor Services Section, PO Box 8730, St John's, A1B 4K2.

Tourist information booths across the province are known as chalets. At information chalets you can buy good provincial highway maps ($3).

Telephone For emergency service in the St John's and surrounding area dial ☎ 911. Elsewhere, call the operator on ☎ 0.

Time The island portion of the province is on Newfoundland Time which is 30 minutes ahead of Atlantic Time. The south-eastern portion of Labrador from south of Cartwright and down along the Strait of Belle Isle uses Newfoundland Time. Northern (from Cartwright and northwards), central and eastern Labrador are all on Atlantic Time.

In summer, the province uses daylight savings time as do all provinces except Saskatchewan.

The expression '... and a half-hour later in Newfoundland', taken from the central Canadian broadcast media schedules, has become a regularly used comic interjection with an infinite number of possible applications.

Tax In Atlantic Canada there is a Harmonized Sales Tax (HST). It's a consumer tax that includes provincial sales tax and the federal GST. In Newfoundland & Labrador this tax totals 15%.

Activities

Outdoor possibilities are wide ranging and the tourism department publishes a guide outlining many of them. There is excellent hiking and camping in the national and provincial parks. When in season, whale and iceberg watching are popular on the north and east coasts. Note that iceberg season is generally mid-April through mid-June, while whales appear mid-July and after. Many regions provide excellent wildlife observation, with moose and caribou two of the most interesting animals to watch. Freshwater fishing can be enjoyed across the province. Hydrophiles have begun to discover the nearly unlimited kayaking and canoeing opportunities.

Sometime between April and June each year the province celebrates St George's Day.

Traditional Celtic-style music remains popular and numerous folk festivals are held around the province during the summer months.

Accommodation

Accommodation prices are much like those in the rest of Canada but there is less variety of places to stay. Labrador's prices tend to be higher and the choices fewer. Scattered about the province are small, family-run guesthouses known as 'hospitality homes'. These are often the best choice for both price and fun. Often they are the only choice. Some are like small rooming houses and others, probably the majority, are just an extra room in a family's home. The tourist office publishes lists but they are never complete. In some of the small, out of the way spots the pub manager might be able to suggest a couple of names.

Motels are generally fairly new and reliable but more expensive and fairly uniform. The larger towns offer hotels as well.

Opportunities to camp are pervasive. In 1997 Newfoundland privatised all but 10 provincial camping parks; long-term effects on quality at ex-provincial parks have yet to

be seen. Note that facilities at many provincial parks are minimal, including a lack of showers or serviced sites for recreational vehicles. A provincial camping reservation hotline (☎ 1-800-866-2267) has been set up for provincial parks.

There are also some privately run campgrounds but nowhere near as many as you'll find in many other provinces. Still, it is rarely a problem to find a decent place to pitch a tent. However, potential tenters should have reasonably decent equipment as the weather doesn't allow for a casual hammock-in-the-tree style of camping.

All provincial tourist chalets – and an increasing number of local information offices – provide free phones to arrange lodging for the night.

Getting Around

Getting around the province presents some peculiar problems. The ever-growing road network connects major towns and most of the regions of interest to visitors but remains sketchy in many areas. Outside the two cities of St John's and Corner Brook and a few large towns, such as Gander and Port aux Basques, communities are small and the visitor traffic is light. Except for the one transisland route, the public bus system consists of a series of small, regional services that usually connect with one or more major points. Although not extensive, this system works pretty well and will get most people to where they want to go.

There is no train service on the island but one line in western Labrador still operates.

The 905km-long Trans Canada Hwy is the only road linking St John's, the capital, to Port aux Basques on the other side of the island. It is a long haul from St John's to Port aux Basques, a 10 to 12-hour drive, but there are a few places worth stopping at on the way, and several towns break up the trip.

For many of the small, isolated coastal villages known as outports, the only means of transportation and connection with the rest of the province is by boat. Some of these villages are connected by a surprisingly inexpensive ferry service which runs regularly in a couple of areas and is for passengers and freight only. A trip along one of these routes provides a chance to see some of the most remote communities in North America. Visitors are few, but mainstream culture is seeping in at an ever-increasing rate.

For more information on outports and their connecting ferry services see the Outports section later in this chapter.

ST JOHN'S

St John's, the province's capital and largest town with a metropolitan population of 175,000 is not to be confused with Saint John (no 's'), New Brunswick. It is a city that manages to feel like a town – invigorating yet warm, busy yet homy, modern centre and fishing village.

Its splendid geographical location and its tumultuous, romantic history make St John's an inviting tourist destination.

As the oldest city in North America and Britain's first overseas colony, the establishment of St John's has been said to mark the birth of the British Empire.

St John's rises in a series of steps, sloping up from the waterfront. Everywhere there are stairs, narrow alleys and winding streets. Several of the downtown roads are lined with colourful, pastel clapboard town houses – the kind found all over the province.

The land is inhospitable, the weather not much better and the economy still pretty much dependent on the whims of the sea. This will undoubtedly alter with the oilfield's exploitation (see Economy earlier in this chapter) and the past few years have seen some quickening of controversial downtown development.

History

John Cabot in 1497 was the first to find the excellent and protective harbour that led to the city's development. As it's the closest point to Europe in the New World and because the famous Grand Banks teemed with fish offshore, a European settlement sprang up in 1528. Unfortunately, this brought to an end not only the lifestyle but the very existence of the Beothuk Indians.

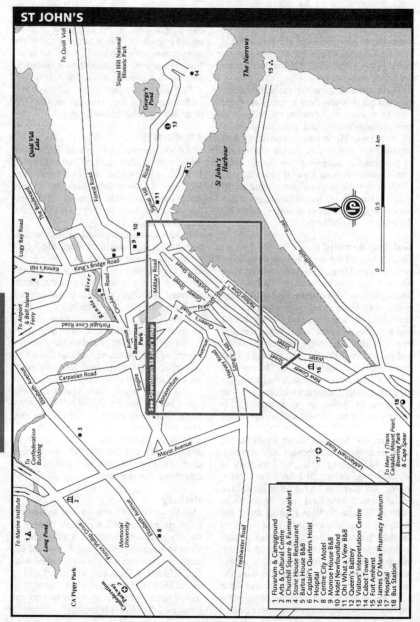

ST JOHN'S

To Quidi Vidi

Signal Hill National Historic Park

The Narrows

George's Pond

St John's Harbour

Quidi Vidi Lake

The Boulevard

Logy Bay Road

Forest Road

Signal Hill Road

Kenna's Hill

King's Bridge Road

Rennie's River

Circular Road

Portugal Cove Road

Southside Road

To Airport & Bell Island Ferry

Military Road

Gower Street

Duckworth Street

Prescott Street

Queen's Road

Harbour Drive

Water Street

New Gower Street

Springdale Street

Avenue

Bannerman Park

Empire Avenue

Carpasian Road

Queen's Road

Long's Hill

Harvey Road

Bonaventure Avenue

Mayor Avenue

Elizabeth Avenue

To Confederation Building

To Marine Institute

Prince Philip Drive

Long Pond

CA Pippy Park

Confederation Parkway

Memorial University

Elizabeth Avenue

Freshwater Road

LeMarchant Road

To Hwy 1 (Trans Canada), Mount Pearl, Bowring Park & Cape Spear

See Downtown St John's map

0   0.5   1 km

1 Fluvarium & Campground
2 Arts & Cultural Centre
3 Churchill Square & Farmer's Market
4 Stone House Restaurant
5 Bartra House B&B
6 Captain's Quarters Hotel
7 Hospital
8 Centre City Motel
9 Monroe House B&B
10 Hotel Newfoundland
11 Oh! What a View B&B
12 Queen's Battery
13 Visitors' Interpretation Centre
14 Cabot Tower
15 Fort Amherst
16 James O'Mara Pharmacy Museum
17 Hospital
18 Bus Station

NEWFOUNDLAND & LABRADOR

From its inception, the settlement was the scene of battles, raids, fires, pirating, deprivations and celebrations.

The Dutch attacked in 1665. The French ruled on three occasions, but each time the English regained the settlement from them. Its location has inspired more than trade, warfare and greed, however. The first transatlantic wireless cable was received here; 40 pioneering aeroplane crossings – including Earhart's and Lindbergh's – used the site, and even Pan Am's inaugural transatlantic flight touched here.

The wharves have been lined with ships for hundreds of years and still are, acting as service stations to fishing vessels from around the world. As befits a port of adventurers and turbulent events, the tradition of raising a glass is well established. Eighty taverns were well in use as long ago as 1775, and in the early 1800s rum was imported to the tune of over a million litres annually. Today the city might well lay claim to having the most watering holes per capita (likely disputed by Halifax).

In 1892 the Great Fire, lit by a dropped pipe, burned down more than half the town. In 1992 another major downtown fire burned a considerable section of Harvey Rd and its many old houses.

The city has an infill housing policy which stipulates that new housing be designed to blend in with the existing historic character of the street. Examples of this may be seen on New Gower St east of the City Hall.

Orientation

The main streets are Harbour Drive which runs right along the bay; Water St, lined with shops, restaurants and bars, one street up; and Duckworth St, farther up still from the waterfront. The rest of the city continues to rise, rather steeply, up the hill away from the sea. It's said that everyone in town has strong legs.

In town, the east end of Gower St is noted for its many multicoloured Victorian terrace houses. These attractive old English and Irish-style houses are now protected for their historic character. Although central, Gower

St – not to be confused with New Gower St – is a little tricky to find but it runs parallel to, and in between Duckworth St and Queen's Rd immediately behind the Anglican Cathedral and then north-eastwards.

Beside City Hall, located on New Gower St near Adelaide St, is the oft-photographed 'Mile 0' sign marking the start of the Trans Canada Hwy.

At the north-eastern end of Water St is the small Harbourside Park, with a monument to Sir Humphrey Gilbert. His landing near here on 5 August 1583 marked the founding of Newfoundland and Britain's overseas empire. Lord Nelson and Captain Bligh also landed here. Across the street in a sharply rising park there's a War Memorial and benches with views.

Farther east is the unmistakable Signal Hill, looming over both the harbour and the

St John's on Ice

A sight that almost equals seeing a 40 ton humpback whale breaching is a five storey iceberg silently sailing past St John's Harbour. Greenland glaciers produce up to 40,000 icebergs annually and the prime viewing area in Newfoundland is around Twillingate Island in Notre Dame Bay; an average of 370 icebergs drift as far south as St John's each year, in some years even more. In 1984 a total of 2200 reached the city.

The typical iceberg is 30m high and weighs 204,000 tons with only one-eighth of it appearing above the water. Icebergs are often classified as 'slob ice', a thick slush of small ice pieces; 'bergy bits', or small icebergs; and 'growlers', icebergs that are particularly dangerous because of their low profile and instability.

The iceberg season in St John's extends from May to June with an occasional iceberg appearing in early July. The best places to see them are at Signal Hill and Cape Spear.

A big one nearby puts a noticeable chill in the air.

NEWFOUNDLAND & LABRADOR

downtown area. At its base is a small group of houses known as the Battery, one of the oldest sections of the city. Note that this section is inaccessible by car.

Ships from many countries moor along the waterfront by Harbour Drive. Among the most commonly seen flags are the Russian, Spanish and Japanese.

For a view over the area, drive or walk to the top of the brown car park building across the street.

Information

Tourist Offices St John's does *not* have a provincial tourist office; the staff at the city offices try their best to help out on Newfoundland information, but they're really not set up to do so.

The Tourist Commission's **main office** (☎ 709-576-8106, www.city.st-johns.nf.ca) is in the City Hall Annex on New Gower St. It's open Monday to Friday from 9 am to 4.30 pm. But through the summer months there is a much better **information office** (☎ 709-576-8514) set up in an old railway car on Harbour Drive on the waterfront right in downtown. It's open daily from 8.30 am to 5.30 pm.

There is also an information desk at the airport.

For drivers, a provincial **information chalet** (☎ 709-227-5272) is found right off the ferry at Argentia. It's open daily during the summer from 10 am to 6 pm Monday, Wednesday, Friday and Sunday, from 6 am to 6 pm other days. Another chalet is found in Whitbourne, (☎ 709-759-2170) 70km west of the city at the junction of the Trans Canada Hwy and Hwy 100 from Argentia. It's open daily during the summer from 8.30 am to 8 pm.

Money Several major banks can be found along central Water St; all have ATM kiosks and most are accessible 24 hours.

Post There is a post office at 354 Water St.

Internet Access Wordplay Books (www .wordplay.com) at 221 Duckworth St has Internet access for $5 per hour.

Travel Agencies Travel CUTS (☎ 709-737-7926) has an office in the Thompson Student Centre at Memorial University.

Bookshops Breakwater Books at 100 Water St has a large and excellent selection of titles on the city and Newfoundland.

Medical Services St Clare's Mercy Hospital (☎ 709-778-3111) is central at 154 LeMarchant Rd.

Newfoundland Museum

The small but decent museum (☎ 709-729-2329), 285 Duckworth St, has a few relics and a skeleton – the only remains anywhere – from the extinct Beothuk Indian tribe who once lived here. Also on display are exhibits about the Vikings and the history of St John's. Also there is a life jacket worn by a steward on the *Titanic*. The museum is open from 9 am to 5 pm Tuesday through Friday (Thursday till 9 pm) and weekends 10 am to 6 pm. Admission is free.

Murray Premises

The fully renovated Murray Premises on Water St and Beck's Cove is one of the oldest warehouses in the city. It was built in the 1840s, somehow escaped the fire of 1892 and today is a National Historic Site, where the original timber and brick can be seen. Among the many shops and restaurants is the **Newfoundland Science Center** (☎ 709-754-0823), a hands-on science experiment for kids. Exhibits change three times yearly. Hours are Monday through Friday from 10 am to 5 pm, Saturday until 6 pm, Sunday noon to 5 pm; admission is $4.50, $3.50 students and seniors, free for children under five.

James O'Mara Pharmacy Museum

At 488 Water St in Apothecary Hall, the original Art Nouveau building, the pharmacy museum (☎ 709-753-5877) is a replica of an 1885 drug store (chemist's) complete with vintage fixtures, cabinets, equipment and medicines. It's open from mid-June to mid-September only and is free. Hours are 11 am to 5 pm daily.

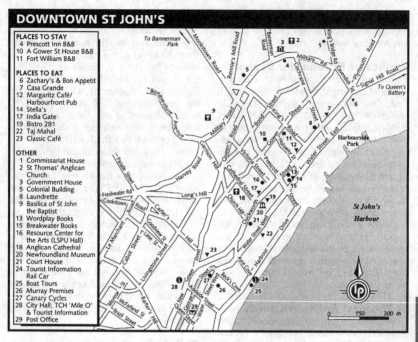

DOWNTOWN ST JOHN'S

PLACES TO STAY
4 Prescott Inn B&B
10 A Gower St House B&B
11 Fort William B&B

PLACES TO EAT
6 Zachary's & Bon Appetit
7 Casa Grande
12 Margaritz Café/
   Harbourfront Pub
14 Stella's
17 India Gate
19 Bistro 281
22 Taj Mahal
23 Classic Café

OTHER
1 Commissariat House
2 St Thomas' Anglican
  Church
3 Government House
4 Colonial Building
8 Laundrette
9 Basilica of St John
  the Baptist
13 Wordplay Books
15 Breakwater Books
16 Resource Center for
   the Arts (LSPU Hall)
18 Anglican Cathedral
20 Newfoundland Museum
21 Court House
24 Tourist Information
   Rail Car
25 Boat Tours
26 Murray Premises
27 Canary Cycles
28 City Hall; TCH 'Mile O'
   & Tourist Information
29 Post Office

St John's
Harbour

Harbourside
Park

0   150   300 m

NEWFOUNDLAND & LABRADOR

Court House

By the Newfoundland Museum, the working courthouse on Duckworth St dates from 1904 and in the late 1980s had a major facelift. Now appearing pretty much as it did when it first opened, it is one of the more imposing buildings in town.

City Hall

On New Gower St, five blocks west of the court house (Duckworth St runs into New Gower St), is the new City Hall and 'Mile 0' sign, from where the Trans Canada Hwy starts westwards on its 7775km-long journey right across Canada to Victoria, British Columbia.

Masonic Temple

On Cathedral St, up the hill from the Newfoundland Museum on Duckworth St, is the striking, renovated temple from 1897, now a private men's club and also home to a dinner theatre troupe.

Anglican Cathedral

Just across the street from the temple is the Anglican Cathedral of St John the Baptist (☎ 709-726-5677), 22 Church St, serving Canada's oldest parish (1699). Now a National Historic Site, the Gothic-style church had its cornerstone laid in 1834. It was gutted in the Great Fire of 1892 and then rebuilt within the remaining exterior walls by 1905. Inside, note the stone walls, wooden ceilings and long, thin stained-glass windows. Some museum-quality British cathedral artefacts are preserved in one room. To enter, go to the side facing the harbour and into the doorway by the toilet. Ring the bell and someone will probably come to let you in. Tours are offered at 10 am Monday through Saturday, 12.30 pm Sunday, May to

October. Admission is free. The cathedral also has a tearoom open from 2.30 to 4.30 pm, Monday through Friday.

Basilica of St John the Baptist

Farther north up Church St to Garrison Hill, and then right on Military Rd, you'll find this twin-spired Roman Catholic church (☎ 709-754-2170), also a National Historic Site and once the largest church in North America. Built in 1855, it's considerably more impressive from the outside than the cathedral and, in fact, the Gothic façade in the shape of a Latin cross dominates the cityscape. Inside, however, it's rather plain although the polychrome Italianate ceiling with gold-leaf highlights will catch the eye's attention as will the pipe organ. There is a small museum on the premises which has articles relating to the history of the church. Free tours are offered from 10 am to 5 pm Monday through Saturday in summer.

St Thomas' Anglican Church

Opened in 1836, this wooden church (☎ 709-576-6632) is the oldest in St John's, famous for surviving both St John's 19th century conflagrations. It's located on the corner of Military and King's Bridge Rds.

Signal Hill National Historic Park

The view alone makes this site a must. East of town along Duckworth St, this park rises up the hill forming the cliff edge along the channel into St John's Harbour. Halfway up the road from the end of Duckworth St is the Visitors' Interpretive Centre (☎ 709-772-5367) with a small museum featuring audiovisual displays on Newfoundland's history.

During the Battle of Signal Hill in 1762 the British took St John's which pretty much ended French control of North America. **Queen's Battery** farther up the hill has some cannons and the remains of the British battery of the late 1700s. **Cabot Tower** at the top of the hill honours John Cabot's arrival in 1497. Built in 1900, this tower was where Marconi received the first transatlantic message in 1901 – the wireless broadcast

was sent from Cornwall, England. There are guides and displays in the tower; an amateur radio society still operates a station from the tower in summer.

From July to mid-August Signal Hill is the site of British military drills called a Tattoo. Each Wednesday, Thursday, Saturday, and Sunday at 3.30 and 7 pm 60 to 80 soldiers dressed as a Royal Newfoundland Company go through their routines for the crowd on hand on a field next to the visitors centre. They end the demonstration by firing the historic cannons.

Admission into the visitors centre/museum is $2.25 or $5.50 per family but Cabot Tower and the rest of the park are free. Signal Hill is open daily in summer until 8 pm.

Highly recommended in either direction is the 1.7km walking trail connecting Cabot Tower with the Battery section of town down in the harbour. Going up, the trip takes about 90 minutes and climbs almost 200m. This walk should not be considered in winter, when any ice lingers, in heavy fog, or at night. A slight stumble and it's a long way down.

Fort Amherst

Across the Narrows is the remains of this fort which includes a lighthouse that was put into operation in 1810 as the first light in Newfoundland. There are also remains of WWII gun batteries here and some incredible views of the rugged coastline. From Water St, head west of the bus depot and turn south at the first light to cross Waterford River. Follow the signs to Fort Amherst. You end up parking just before Amherst and walking through the cliffside village about 200m to the fort. Admission is free.

Commissariat House

On King's Bridge Rd near Gower St, Commissariat House (☎ 709-729-6730) is the late-Georgian mansion used by the supplies officer of the British military. It was later used as a church rectory, nursing home and children's hospital. Now restored to reflect the style of the 1830s with many period pieces, a tearoom is also inside. The house

is open daily in summer from 10 am to 5.30 pm. Admission is free.

Colonial Building

This building, on Military Rd, was the seat of the provincial legislature from 1850 to 1960 and today houses the Provincial Archives among other things. It's built of white limestone from Cork, Ireland which was formerly used as ships' ballast. The building (☎ 709-729-3065) is open in summer Monday to Friday from 9 am to 4.15 pm and admission is free.

Government House

Built in 1830 (at a cost four times that of the US White House, built in the same year), Government House is beside Bannerman Park close to Commissariat House. The house was once the official residence of the governor of Newfoundland until it became part of Canada and since then the lieutenant-governors have called it home. Tours of the house aren't available but on the ground floor you can sign the guest book.

CA Pippy Park

The dominant feature of the north-western edge of downtown is the huge 1343-hectare CA Pippy Park (☎ 709-737-3655). Within the park, recreational facilities include walking trails, picnic areas and playgrounds.

At Long Pond marsh the birdwatching is good and mammals such as moose can sometimes be spotted in areas of the park. There is also a campground and snack bar.

The province's only university, **Memorial University** is here. The university's Botanical Garden at Oxen Pond, at the western edge of the park off Mt Scio Rd, about a 10 minute drive, is both a cultivated garden and nature reserve.

Together, these two areas provide visitors with an excellent introduction to the province's flora and varying natural habitats including boreal forest and bogs. The garden area is open from 10 am to 5 pm daily May through November, and admission is $1, less for seniors and children. Guided tours are given at 3 pm Sunday.

Fluvarium Also in CA Pippy Park the Freshwater Resource Centre is the striking hexagonal balconied building across the street from the campground. The main feature is the 25m fluvarium (☎ 709-754-3474), a glass-sided cross-section of a 'living' river, the only public fluvarium in North America. Viewers can peer through large windows to observe the natural, undisturbed goings-on beneath the surface of Nagle's Hill Brook. Numerous brown trout and the occasional eel can be seen. If the weather has been unsettled with high winds or if there has been any rain, the water becomes so cloudy that virtually nothing can be seen through the murkiness.

Within the centre are exhibits that closely examine plants, insects and fish of freshwater ecosystems and a demonstrative fish hatchery. Outside there are interpretive trails; it's possible to walk all the way to Quidi Vidi Lake from here.

In summer the centre is open daily from 9 am to 6 pm with a feeding time scheduled at 4 pm. Tours are offered hourly except at 4 pm. The rest of the year it is closed on Wednesday, Sunday morning and the daily hours are reduced. The rates are $4, less for seniors and children and a ticket includes a tour. The site is run by a nonprofit environmental awareness group which has done some fine work along the Rennie River and Quidi Vidi Lake.

Arts & Cultural Centre

The Arts and Cultural Centre (☎ 709-7729-3900) complex about 2km north-west from the downtown area on Prince Phillip Drive, beside the university, contains the Art Gallery of Newfoundland and Labrador (☎ 709-737-8209). The art gallery displays mainly contemporary Newfoundland and Canadian painting and sculpture. It's free and open from Tuesday to Sunday, noon to 5 pm and on Thursday and Friday nights also from 7 to 10 pm. There is a theatre at the complex which hosts events during summer.

Confederation Building

Just off Prince Phillip Drive, north-east of the arts centre, is the 12-storey home of the

provincial government. You can visit the building and the small military museum inside for free. It's closed on weekends.

Marine Institute

Although misleadingly named, the Marine Institute (☎ 709-778-0372) may be considered more worthwhile than the Freshwater Resource Centre, featuring primarily interactive exhibits. There is enough for a visit of over an hour with exhibits on such matters as fibre optics, magnets, a real-size shipbridge, and the world's largest flume tank.

The institute is open daily with tours available in summer at 1.30 and 3 pm Monday through Friday. Also at the site is the province's only planetarium which presents its own shows featuring the heavens. The address is 155 Ridge Rd (at the top of the hill) in CA Pippy Park. You can only visit on a weekday tour (summer only) but there is no fee.

Bowring Park

South-west of the downtown area off Pitts Memorial Drive on Waterford Bridge Rd, this is another popular large city park. A couple of streams and walkways meander through the park. The Peter Pan statue is a replica of the famous one in Kensington Gardens in London, England and was made by the same sculptor.

Ocean Sciences Centre

Tours can be undertaken at this research unit (☎ 709-737-3706), which is part of Memorial University's science department. Ongoing research examines the life cycle of salmon, seal navigation, ocean currents and many other aspects of life in the colder ocean regions. There is a visitor interpretive centre and guided tours of the facility which take about an hour. Seals can be seen and there is a hands-on tank where various creatures can be touched.

It's open daily from 10 am to 6 pm in July and August and tours are offered every half-hour until 5 pm; otherwise late May through 1 September tours are scaled back. April-May and September-November tours are available from 1 to 4 pm Sunday only. Part of the tour is outside so bring appropriate clothes and footwear. Admission is $4.50, $3.50 for children. The centre is about 8km north of town just before Logy Bay at the end of Marine Lab Rd on the ocean. From town take Logy Bay Rd (Route 30) and then follow Marine Drive. There is no public transport to get here.

Cape Spear

A 15 minute drive south-east of the city is Cape Spear, the most easterly point in North America. The area is preserved as the Cape Spear National Historical Site and located here is an 1835 lighthouse that has been refurbished inside, an interpretive centre (☎ 709-772-5367) and the heavy gun batteries and magazines built in 1941 to protect the harbour during WWII. There is also a trail system that takes you along the edge of the headland cliffs, past 'the most easterly point' observation deck and up to one of the oldest lighthouses in Newfoundland. From there you can continue all the way to Maddox and Petty Harbour if you wish.

The coastal scenery at this spot is spectacular and through much of the summer there is an opportunity to spot whales. The interpretive centre is open from 10 am to 6 pm daily mid-June through Labour Day and a lighthouse fee is $2.25, $1.75 seniors, $1.25 ages 6 to 16, and $5.50 families. Everything else is free. You reach the cape from Water St by crossing the Waterford River west of the bus station and then following Blackhead Road for 11km.

Quidi Vidi

Over Signal Hill, away from town, is the tiny, picturesque village of Quidi Vidi (pronounced 'kiddie viddie'). This little fishing port has the oldest cottage in North America. **Mallard Cottage** (☎ 709-576-2266) dates back to the early 1700s and is now a National Heritage Site and an antique shop. Hours to tour it in summer are from 10 am to 6 pm daily except Tuesday. The rest of the year it's open from 10.30 am to 5.30 pm. Admission is 50¢.

Quidi Vidi also has a new microbrewery on site in an old fish processing plant. Summer tours (with tastings of the three offerings) start hourly from 10 am to 4 pm Tuesday through Saturday in summer, cost $1 and are popular.

You can walk to the village from Signal Hill in about 20 minutes or go around by road from St John's. Take Forest Rd, which runs along the lake and then turns into Quidi Vidi Village Rd. Note that driving is hazardous on these narrow streets and locals would rather you parked on the outskirts and walked in.

Quidi Vidi Battery Built in 1762, this provincial historic site (☎ 709-729-0592) is up the hill from the village, guarding the bay. The French built it after taking St John's. It was later taken by the British and remained in military service into the 1800s. Unfortunately it had also closed at last check and no word was available on whether it would reopen.

Quidi Vidi Lake Inland from the village, this lake is the site of the St John's Regatta, which is held on the first Wednesday in August. Started in 1818, it's probably the oldest continuing sporting competition in North America.

The Regatta Museum (☎ 709-576-8058) is on the 2nd floor of the boathouse at the lake.

The Rennies River flowing into the west end of the lake is an excellent trout stream.

Hiking

The **Grand Concourse** is an ambitious 100km-long network of trails slated to be completed in 2000 linking St John's with Mount Pearl and Paradise via downtown sidewalks, trails, river corridors, and old railway beds. Most hiking is done in the CA Pippy Park or Quidi Vidi Lake areas. Maps ($1) can be found at magazine stands and hotel gift shops, and street signs will be colour-coded to map trails.

Organised Tours

For a relatively small city, St John's has an extraordinary number of tours available.

On Land McCarthy's Party (☎ 709-781-2244), a well established tour operator, offers three different excursions. The three hour tour of the city costing $20 is good, but really doesn't provide too much that you can't do yourself for free. The other two, one to Cape Spear and one in the opposite direction along Marine Drive, are more worthwhile. Plenty of humour, interesting historical titbits and general information on the people and province is woven into the commentary.

Uniformed multilingual guides and double-decker buses ply a St John's tour with British Island Tours (☎ 709-738-8687). For $20 it takes in everything *except* Signal Hill. Three-hour tours depart at 9.30 am and 1.30 pm and they offer free shuttle service to and from lodgings.

Legend Tours (☎ 709-753-1497) also covers St John's, Cape Spear and the Marine Drive area and has received many favourable reviews for its $25 city tours. Discovery Tours (☎ 709-722-4533) has $85 half-day tours of the Avalon Peninsula, $95 to Trinity, and overnight packages to the Burin Peninsula.

One popular newer offering is the **Haunted Hike** (☎ 709-576-2087), sort of an alternative local history heavy on the supernatural. Tours are at 9.30 pm Tuesday through Thursday June through August and cost $5.

Starting at around $10 for a walkabout tour, On Your Own Tours (☎ 709-753-5353) offers perhaps the most flexible option, since you design your own itinerary, from a half-day walking tour to a two-day provincial trip.

On Sea Other tours are done by boat, departing from near the railroad car information office or from communities south of St John's along the coast. Most charge about the same rate, around $25 to $35, though some do offer student and senior discounts, so shop around. And try to pick a calm day as it allows the boat to travel farther. It can get rough and cold, so take warm clothes – it may be balmy in the protected harbour but it's quite a different story once outside the Narrows. A sip of the Screech may help.

Dee Jay Charters (☎ 709-753-8687) is at the harbour near the railcar tourist chalet. It runs a good-value three hour trip from the waterfront out to sea in search of icebergs in June, whales in July and August, and seabirds anytime, for $25, children half price. If the big highlights are not in the neighbourhood there is still birdwatching and sightseeing along the coast and you'll go by Quidi Vidi. Three trips are offered daily.

Island Rendezvous (☎ 709-747-7253, ☎ 1-800-504-1066) based in suburban Mount Pearl, but operating out of the village of Garden Cove two hours from town, has a one-of-a-kind trip. Popular with local residents, the two-day adventure visits one of the many now abandoned outport communities. Visitors are taken by boat to Woody Island, virtually a ghost town except for some people who use it as a base for seasonal fishing. Visitors are put up in a large old house run as a hospitality home. The days are spent poking around the old town and island and on a boat tour of Placentia Bay, a glimpse into the traditional fishing village way of life as well as offering escape from what has replaced it. The cost is around $130 and the office is at 42 McCrath St in Mount Pearl.

Sea kayaking is now also possible out of St John's. Eastern Edge Outfitters (☎ 709-782-1465) has one-day tours for $120 as well as a number of multi-day tours. It also offers courses.

There are several charters in St John's offering 'tall ship' outings from the waterfront. Both J&B Schooner Tours (☎ 709-753-7245) and Adventure Tours (☎ 709-726-5000) are on Pier 6 and offer several daily tours for more than two hours for $30 on different boats.

Special Events

Only major festivals are listed here.

June
Discovery Days
The celebrations are held from around 18 June for two days to commemorate the city's birthday. Festivities include concerts (any Newfoundland event includes music), a parade, street dance and sporting events.

July-September
Craft Fair
The Newfoundland and Labrador craft fair is held twice annually, at the end of July and November, in St John's Memorial Stadium.

George Street Festival
Featuring music of all kinds this festival, performed on central George St, is held around the end of July.

The Provincial Folk Festival
This three-day event, which takes place annually around the first week of August, has great music and should not to be missed. Dancers and storytellers also perform in their respective traditions.

Royal St John's Regatta
What probably began as a bet among a few fishers to see who could row faster is now the oldest continuous sporting event in North America. The regatta officially began in 1825 and is held on the first Wednesday of August. The entire town closes up that day and everybody heads to the shores of Quidi Vidi Lake to watch.

Places to Stay

Camping Conveniently located right in the city by the university there is camping 1 May to 30 September in *CA Pippy Park* (☎ 709-737-3669). The charge is $9 for tenting, $14 for unserviced sites and $20 for serviced ones. The campground is off Higgins Line at the north-western side of the park near the Confederation Building.

The nearest provincial park with camping is *Butter Pot*, 30km to the west along the Trans Canada Hwy. Unserviced sites in a very pleasant wooded setting cost $9. There is a beach, interpretive centre and trails including an easy climb up Butter Pot Hill.

Hostels The hostel situation is extremely changeable and usually minimal, but check with the tourist office.

A new hostel to check out is the *Hostel on the Hill* (☎ 709-754-7658, 65 Long's Hill St) which is centrally located. Shared singles are $15 and doubles $29.

There are rooms for rent at *Hatcher House* at Memorial University (☎ 709-737-7590, ext 20) through the summer months from mid-May to mid-August. Singles cost $15/20 for students/nonstudents with even cheaper doubles. Weekly rates are offered

and all meals are available. There are buses to town but you can walk in less than half an hour, even if the roads are not direct. From the campus Newtown Rd leads downtown.

The owners of *Travellers B&B Hostel* (☎ 709-437-5627), who have travelled on the cheap themselves, rent out a couple of rooms in their house on a large property about a 10 minute drive north of the centre on Pine Line by Torbay. There's no public transportation but if you play your cards nicely someone may pick you up. The price is $25 including breakfast. The grounds are large enough to accommodate tents. Call Donna or Jerry for availability of beds and exact location.

The tourist office has one or two other options, usually used in summer, but they're generally not cheap.

Tourist Homes & B&Bs Aside from the established places listed here, the tourist office should have an up-to-date list of places available in people's homes. There are usually places not mentioned in the printed provincial accommodation guides. At the time of writing there was rumoured to be a new cheaper (around $25) B&B set to open near the Commissariat House along Forest Rd.

Centrally located near the Anglican Cathedral is *A Gower St House* (☎ 754-0047, ☎ 1-800-563-3959, 180 Gower St). All the rooms are good and half come with private bathroom while one has a balcony. Singles begin at $40 with a full breakfast which may include some traditional fare. Other benefits here include the use of kitchen, laundry and parking facilities.

Nearby, the *Fort William B&B* (☎ 709-726-3161, 5 Gower St) is open all year with singles/doubles $50/65 and one housekeeping unit at slightly higher cost.

Oh! What a View (☎ 709-576-7063, 184 Signal Hill Rd) is recommended as a neat, clean B&B with a spectacular view over the harbour and city from two decks. There are four rooms at $65 and up including a continental breakfast of bread and muffins. Two of the rooms are in the basement but they are modern and comfortable. City buses run

nearby but it's only a 10 minute walk into town. It's open summers only.

The *Prescott Inn* (☎ 709-753-7733, ☎ 1-888-263-3768, 19 Military Rd) is a long-running B&B centrally situated on the north-eastern side of the downtown area. It's a well kept old house with balconies looking out over the harbour. There are rooms, suites and furnished apartments from $45 to $105 with full breakfast included. Seniors get a 10% discount.

More upmarket is *Monroe House* (☎ 709-754-0610, 8A Forest Rd), behind the Hotel Newfoundland. It was once the home of the Newfoundland prime minister. The six rooms are spacious and tastefully decorated, the breakfasts substantial and in the evening there's complimentary wine. It's on a quiet street just a few minutes walk from the centre. If you are seeking some creature comforts and a little pampering this fits the bill at $74 and up.

Also good for those on a slightly higher budget is *Bartra House* (☎ 709-722-8282, 28 Circular Rd), with one room with shared bath for $69 and three gorgeous suites from $99 in a designated heritage structure.

Out of downtown there's the low-priced *Fireside Guesthouse* (☎ 709-726-0237, 28 Wicklow St) near the Avalon Mall Shopping Centre and the university. Call for directions. Including a full breakfast, singles/doubles cost $35/40, making it one of the better deals, and it's just a short walk to an indoor swimming pool.

Hotels Hotels are not St John's strong point but with good guesthouses this shouldn't pose problems. As a rule the hotels are fairly pricey and business-oriented but there are still some good, inexpensive places around town.

For a central and low-cost place, there's *Captain's Quarters* (☎ 709-576-7173, 2 King's Bridge Rd) across the street from the Commissariat House. There are 20 rooms with small but clean singles/doubles starting at $40/45 for a good shared bath. On the first floor there is a small pub with dartboards and fireplaces.

NEWFOUNDLAND & LABRADOR

The historic *Hotel Newfoundland* (☎ 709-726-4980, ☎ 1-800-441-1414) with the imposing stone façade on Cavendish Square at the end of Duckworth St is the top-end classic in town. Run by Canadian Pacific Hotels, it's $145 (up to $600!) for singles/doubles during summer but there are special rates for weekends.

About 6km from downtown is *Hotel St John's* (☎ 709-722-9330, ☎ 1-800-563-2489, 102 Kenmount Rd). About a third of its 85 rooms come with kitchen facilities. Singles/doubles go for $75/85 and up. Also on this road is the *Best Western Travellers Inn* (☎ 709-722-5540, ☎ 1-800-261-5540, 199 Kenmount Rd), one of the same chain. They're fairly standard, reliable mid-range hotels. Here prices are $75/85 and children stay free.

Motels The *Centre City Motel* (☎ 709-726-0092, 389 Elizabeth Ave) near the university is a clean place with singles/doubles at $46/66. It has a restaurant and pub.

Greenwood Lodge & Motel (☎ 709-364-5300) towards Mount Pearl, off Route 60, is close to town. It has a games room and laundry facilities. Singles are $45.

Not as costly is the *Crossroads Motel* (☎ 709-368-3191) at the junction of Routes 1 and 60 at $45/60 a single/double.

Places to Eat

The city has a good array of places 'to have a scoff' to use a local term for eating. Duckworth and Water Sts in particular have many eateries. Every other storefront here seems to be a restaurant or café offering something slightly different than the one before.

A local dish is called 'brewis', a blend of fish, onion and a bread-like mix that's soaked overnight. Another local speciality is cod tongues which are really closer to cheeks. They're often served deep-fried with very unimpressive results but, if you can, try them pan-fried.

The *Classic Café (364 Duckworth St)* is open 24 hours. This is an excellent place, featuring a wide selection of seafood, fresh-baked goods and good prices. For $10 you

can get a large basket of steamed mussels and two beers. A lobster dinner special costs $13 with a coupon from the tourist office. Coffee and a giant muffin is $2.50 and there are always $6 to $8 lunch specials like grilled salmon.

At 188-190 Duckworth St are the comfortable *Margaritz*, a popular pasta and eclectic casual nouvelle cuisine place; and *Harbourfront Pub* with good all-day breakfasts and a few Newfoundland dishes. Just up the street are two new places that are highly recommended by locals. *Bon Appetit (71 Duckworth St)* is a casual French restaurant with a pleasant outdoor patio overlooking the harbour, while at *Zachary's* next door you can order a traditional breakfast of fish cakes and toast for $4. Finer French dining is found up the street at *Bistro 281 (281 Duckworth St)* where the seafood and lamb specialities cost $15 to $25.

Keep in mind that many of the pubs, including those on George St, serve very reasonable midday meals. *The Duke of Duckworth (325 Duckworth St)* is just one of many quiet English-style pubs that offer meat pies, sausages and sauerkraut or soup-and-sandwich combinations for under $6.

Smaller, cosy *Stella's (cnr St John's Place & Water Sts)* is the best bet for vegetarian food, serving natural foods and vegetarian plates in the $7 to $12 range. The Caesar salad is good.

St John's has (or used to have) some of the best fish and chips anywhere. People often bad mouth cod but it is *the* fish in this part of the world and fresh out of the sea it's excellent. These days with the lack of fish and the moratorium on fishing, getting fresh cod is not always possible. Sometimes the restaurants have it, at other times they must use frozen imported cod, which given the once boundless local stocks is enough to make you wince.

For a quick sampling head to the junction of Harvey, LeMarchant and Freshwater Rds, a short walk from the centre, where you'll find several choices, among them the ever popular *Ches's (5 Freshwater Rd)*; the *Big R (69 Harvey)*; *Scamper's (1 LeMarchant)*;

or the nearby *Leo's (27 Freshwater Rd)*. At any of them you can take away a plate for under $8.

Casa Grande (108 Duckworth St) is a nicely decorated Mexican restaurant. It holds about 10 small wooden tables encircled by wicker chairs and has dishes from around $8 and full dinners for $12.

For an East Indian meal try the *India Gate (286 Duckworth St)* which has an all-you-can-eat lunch buffet Monday to Friday from 11 am to 2 pm for $8. Others prefer the Indian food at the *Taj Mahal (203 Water St)*.

For fine dining, the *Stone House Restaurant (☎ 709-753-2380, 8 Kenna's Hill)* has long been considered the number one choice. Specialities at this expensive restaurant are seafood, game and traditional Newfoundland dishes. It's in one of the city's oldest homes. Reservations are recommended. For dinner with the best view in the city, head to the *Cabot Club* in the Hotel Newfoundland. Watching the lights emerge around the harbour at dusk is spectacular. Dinners range from $18 to $24.

Lastly, you may want to check out the *farmers' markets* which feature local produce for sale on Saturday throughout the summer. There's a very small all-day market at Churchill Square off Elizabeth Ave near the university.

Entertainment

St John's is a lot of fun at night. Political correctness in the sphere of alcohol is pleasantly absent in these parts and makes a refreshing change from the ever present didacticism found in much of Canada. The elsewhere often forbidden 'happy hour' here becomes stretched to a laughable misnomer lasting from as early as 11 am to as late at 7.30 pm! Two for one specials abound across town and establishments are busy through the day especially on weekends.

George St is pretty crazy with crowds and queues at a variety of bars and is closed nightly at 10 pm to vehicle traffic, with the exception of the police and taxi drivers. These raucous places party on till 3 am. For a complete rundown of the music and bar

scene in St John's, pick up a free copy of *Moonlighting* or *Beam* found in bars and restaurants.

The *Corner Stone* on the corner of Queen St has videos and live rock, *Sundance* has a large outdoor deck. *Jungle Jim's* has a 46-ounce frozen concoction called a Jumbo Hurricane and there is blues and jazz at *Fat Cat*.

Ship's Inn (245 Duckworth St) down the steps beside the Arts Council is good with live music and *Schroeder's Piano Bar* on Bates Hill is an interesting little place.

There are also many Irish pubs offering live traditional music, including *Erin's Pub (184 Water St)* which has live Irish music six nights a week in summer, four nights in winter; and *Blarney Stone* in the George St stretch. Wednesday night is a sure night for live music at the Blarney Stone.

Live theatre or dance performances are staged regularly at the *Arts and Cultural Centre (☎ 709-729-3900)* on Confederation Parkway. The *Resource Center for the Arts (☎ 753-4531, LSPU Hall, 3 Victoria St)* presents work by local playwrights.

In August, you can head out to Logy Bay where, across from the Ocean Sciences Centre, is the theatre for *Shakespeare By The Sea (☎ 709-576-0980)*.

Getting There & Away

Air Air Canada (☎ 709-726-7880) to Halifax costs $548 one way, to Montreal $730. Canadian Airlines (☎ 709-576-0274) flies to the same places. One example: Charlottetown for $545. Obviously round-trip tickets (and pre-planning) save you considerably. Canada 3000 has dirt cheap flights – one way to Halifax $150 for example – but you'll need to reserve far in advance. The two biggies work with Air Nova and Inter-Canadien respectively for local flights. For flights solely within the province also try Interprovincial Airlines (☎ 709-576-1666) and Air Labrador (☎ 709-753-5593, ☎ 709-896-3387).

Bus The bus system is a little confusing but if you can track things down it can work fairly well for you. The system, unlike that in other provinces, isn't monopolised by

one or two operators but consists of a lot of small local and regional services.

The main bus station is at the far southwest end of town at 495 Water St, underneath the overpass. It's about a 20 minute walk from town. Call before you trudge, as many of the cross-island services will tell you where to meet them if they don't pick you up.

DRL (☎ 709-738-8088) operates just one route but it's the province's main one, running across Newfoundland along the Trans Canada Hwy to Port aux Basques and stopping at most every place along the way. To Port aux Basques there's one bus daily at 7.45 am from the university's Education Building which costs $90 one way. The trip takes about 14 hours.

For Argentia, Placentia and Freshwater there is Newhook's Transportation (☎ 709-726-4876, ☎ 709-227-2552 in Placentia), 13 Queen St, which runs buses daily down to the south-west Avalon Peninsula ($18 to Argentia, 1½ hours); buses are supposed to await ferry arrivals but call first. Molloy's Taxi (☎ 709-722-4249) runs down the east coast of the Avalon to Trepassey. Fleetline Bus Service (☎ 709-722-2608) goes to Carbonear and the lower Conception Bay area daily except Sunday; to Carbonear it's $11. Call first as this schedule changes at a whim.

Shirran's (☎ 709-722-8032) runs up to the Bonavista Peninsula area for $25 but it drops you on the highway, not in Bonavista. Venture Bus Lines (☎ 709-722-4249) goes to the peninsula, but you can only get to Southern Bay ($20) halfway up the peninsula.

North Eastern (☎ 709-747-0492) goes to Twillingate for $47.

On the Burin Peninsula Cheeseman's Bus Service (☎ 709-753-7022) goes to Marystown at 3.30 pm daily for $15; and Foote's Taxi (☎ 709-832-0491, ☎ 1-800-866-1181) goes all the way to Fortune at 4 pm for $30. North Shore Bus Lines (☎ 709-722-5218) runs up to Old Perlican. Contact the tourist bureau for information on new services.

The only train is in Labrador.

Taxi Share-taxis also run between St John's and the ferry terminal. In Argentia you can make dockside arrangements for getting to St John's.

Ferry The Marine Atlantic ferry for North Sydney, Nova Scotia, docks at Argentia on the south-west coast of the Avalon Peninsula. The MV *Joseph & Clara Smallwood* goes in each direction three times a week and runs from mid-June to mid-September only. It departs Argentia on Tuesday, Thursday and Saturday at 9 am, and North Sydney on Monday, Wednesday and Friday at 2.30 pm from 1 July to 31 August. Late June and early September, the Tuesday-Wednesday trips don't run. The crossing time is 14 hours, less if you have calm seas. An adult ticket is $54, a bicycle $18, and a car $122. Rooms and beds are extra. You can take the less expensive ferry to Port aux Basques and then drive across the province twice but with gasoline at 66¢ to 70¢ a litre, calculate the savings first. From Argentia to Nova Scotia – and on the afternoon ferry from Port aux Basques to Nova Scotia – you arrive around midnight and definitely need to make a reservation for a room in advance.

Passengers can enjoy the movie theatre, a bar with live band, a tourist booth, a children's play area, even miniature golf on the top deck – in short, the works. On the night trips most people flake out anywhere they can including all over the floor. Bring a blanket or sleeping bag and join the slumber party.

In July or August reservations are a good idea in either direction; call ☎ 902-794-5254 in North Sydney from anywhere in Canada or ☎ 709-227-2431 in and around eastern Newfoundland. In the USA or Canada, call toll-free ☎ 1-800-341-7981; the website is www.marine-atlantic.ca. Usually one or two days notice is all that is necessary though you may not get a cabin or dorm berth.

If you're in a car, you may get a free car wash as you board the ferry back to the Canadian mainland. This is to get rid of two bug varieties harmful to potatoes and found only in Newfoundland.

Southern shores outside Port aux Basques, Newfoundland

THOMAS HUHTI

Port Riche lighthouse, Newfoundland

THOMAS HUHTI

Rose Blanche fishing village, Newfoundland

THOMAS HUHTI

Vista from Signal Hill, St John's, Newfoundland

Car If you want a car when arriving at the airport (or in town) make sure you reserve. Rates are about the same as anywhere else in Canada.

Budget (☎ 709-747-1234) is at 954 Topsail Rd; Dollar (☎ 709-722-7300) at 497 Kentmount Rd; and Rent-A-Wreck (☎ 753-2277) with cheaper, used cars is at 43 Pippy Place and 933 Topsail Rd. Rent-A-Wreck has small compacts for $32 a day plus 100km free; it also has free pick up and delivery.

If you drive a car one way between St John's and Port aux Basques, you'll have to pay a return charge of at least $200.

Getting Around

To/From the Airport There is no city bus to the airport which is about 6km north of town on Route 40 going towards Portugal Cove. Going by taxi, at about $12, is the only way. The official airport service is by Dave Gulliver Cabs (☎ 709-722-0003). Inquire about sharing and if you're lucky it may be cheaper.

Bus The St John's Transportation Commission runs the Metrobus (☎ 709-722-9400) city bus system. Schedules are printed in the Yellow Pages phone book. There are a few bus routes in and around town and together they cover most areas; No 3 does the central area. By transferring from this one to an adjoining loop, say the No 12 going west, you can get a pretty good city tour for just a couple of dollars. For hitching south on Avalon Peninsula, catch Nos 150 or 8 that will take you to Bay Bulls Rd. For the Trans Canada Hwy, take No 9 out to Avalon Mall.

The fare is $1.50 per ride. If you're in town for a while a 10-ride Metropass is $12.50.

Bicycle Hills and crazy intersections are not a cyclist's only nightmare in the city. Here, the sewer grates run *parallel* with the road; thus, unless you want a bent rim and broken arm, pay strict attention.

For two wheels, try Canary Cycles (☎ 709-579-5972) at 294 Water St. Top-of-the-line

mountain bikes are $13 for two hours, $20 for a day or $30 for two days.

AROUND ST JOHN'S

Marine Drive, north of St John's up towards Torbay, goes past nice coastal scenery. There are rocky beaches at both Middle Cove and Outer Cove – good for a walk or picnic.

Offshore around **Torbay** is a good whale-watching area; one or two lost puffins may also be around. Marine Drive ends at Pouch Cove but a gravel road continues to Cape St Francis for good views. West of town, head to Topsail for a great view of Conception Bay and some of its islands.

West of St John's is the day trip-worthy **Bell Island**, reached by a 20 minute drive and a 20 minute ferry (6.45 am to 11.15 pm; $1.50, $2.50 including car). The *Theatre of the Mine* (☎ 709-576-6463) recreates the life of the 'submarine' miners who actually toiled in shafts under the seabed. Tickets are $10 to $15 and reservations are advisable. Take warm clothes and do not wear good shoes. The rest of the island sports a pleasant melange of beaches, coastal scenery, lighthouses, and trails; there are several B&Bs and a trailer park.

Some 10km south of St John's is **Petty Harbour**, filled with weathered boats, wharves and sheds on stilts and surrounded by high rocky hills. Several production companies have used it for movie settings. If you want to spend the night, *Orca Inn* (☎ 709-747-9676) has four rooms at $45/50.

In **Goulds**, at the junction of Hwy 10 and the road to Petty Harbour, don't miss *Bidgood's*, a supermarket with a twist. It's known for its Newfoundland specialities, especially with locals, who stock up on their favourite items before returning to jobs on the mainland. Where else can you buy caribou steak, moose in a jar or sealmeat pie? Depending on the time of year the selection may also include cod tongues, saltfish or lobster. There are jars of the province's distinctive jams – try partridgeberry or the elite of the island's berries, bakeapple. It's open daily, and until 9 pm on Thursday and Friday.

Bay Bulls and **Witless Bay** are excellent places from which to observe birds. Three islands off Witless Bay and southward are preserved as the Witless Bay Ecological Reserve and represent one of the top seabird breeding areas in eastern North America. Every summer more than a million pairs of seabirds gather to breed, including puffins, kittiwakes, murres, cormorants and storm petrels. Several operators run highly recommended trips out to the colonies.

No one is permitted on the islands but the boats do get close enough for you to consider taking ear plugs as well as a camera and binoculars. The din overhead is incredible. The best months for visiting are June and July which is also good for whale watching – humpback and minke are fairly common here. Whales are seen in the vicinity until early August and the humpback is the most spectacular of all whales for its breaching performances. If you really hit the jackpot, an iceberg might be thrown in too.

Gatherall's (☎ 1-800-419-4253) runs a wildlife boat tour in Bay Bulls on the North Side Rd with several trips daily that include whale watching and the bird colonies. The cost for the 2½ hour trip is $28. Also offering whale-sighting and seabird tours is O'Brien's (☎ 709-753-4850) out of Bay Bulls. Tours depart several times daily during summer and cost $30 to $35. O'Brien's also runs a shuttle bus from major hotels in St John's and charges an additional $10 for the ride. In Witless Bay, Murphy's Bird Island Tours (☎ 334-2002) charges $25 for the trip. One of the cheaper and quicker ways to see aquatic life is through Seabird Puffin & Whale Tours (☎ 709-334-2098) or Ocean Adventure Tours (☎ 709-334-3998), operating out of Bauline East south of Witless Bay. Here from 8 am to around 8 pm consistent $15 ($10 for children under 12) departures head for Great Island, just a 10 minute water jaunt from the docks.

On Hwy 10 in Witless Bay there is a Tourist Chalet, open 9 am to 8 pm daily.

AROUND THE AVALON PENINSULA

The peninsula, more like an island hanging onto the rest of the province by a thin strip of land, is the most densely populated area of Newfoundland as nearly half its population lives here.

Conception Bay is lined with scores of small communities, but all around the coast you'll find fishing villages.

At Argentia in the south-west is the ferry depot connecting with Nova Scotia. The **tourist office** (☎ 709-227-5272) can suggest driving and camping tours of the peninsula.

For hikers, when completed the epic **East Coast Trail** will stretch 270km from Cape St Francis all the way to Cape Race, making use of existing coastal trails and bucolic rural paths. At the time of writing, two-thirds of the trail had been completed; a 50km segment also connects with the 50km D'Iberville Trail in the Avalon Wilderness Area (See the following Southern Avalon section.) The East Coast Trail Association (☎ 709-738-4453) has information.

Southern Avalon

Despite its proximity to St John's this section of the province is very good for viewing wildlife and has several good parks.

Down the coast there is excellent camping at **La Manche Provincial Park** (☎ 709-685-1823), 53km south of St John's. The park has 70 camp sites, many of them overlooking La Manche Pond, along with a day use area and beach. A tent site is $9 a night. There are also two scenic trails that begin in the campground. The first is a 15 minute walk from the day use area to a small waterfall. The second follows the fire-exit track from site No 59 to the remains of La Manche, a fishing village that was destroyed in 1966 by a fierce winter storm. It's about a 30 minute hike one way.

At Cape Broyle, some 20km south, there's Wilderness Newfoundland Adventures (☎ 709-747-6353), which has three-hour, half-day, full-day, and sunset sea kayak trips from $50.

South a few kilometres along Hwy 10 is **Ferryland**, site of one of the earliest English settlements in North America, dating to 1621 when Sir George Calvert, who later became Lord Baltimore, established a village, the Colony of Avalon. The town lasted

The World's First Flush Toilet

The digs at Ferryland have turned up some interesting artefacts, including, say archaeologists, what is probably the world's first flush toilet, dating back to the 1620s. Among the remains that have turned up from Lord Baltimore's colony is a privy that was strategically situated on the shoreline with a hole above the sea. Twice a day the high tide came in and 'flushed' the contents away into the ocean, leaving nothing but a little salt water on the seat.

for a few years before the long cold winters sent Calvert to Maryland in search of warmer weather. Other English families followed, however, and maintained the colony until 1673 when a Dutch raid destroyed most of the town.

The courthouse has a small local **museum** but most visitors will want to head to the **Colony of Avalon Interpretation Centre** (☎ 709-432-3200), opposite the playing field and open from 9 am to 7 pm daily June through August, till 5.30 pm in September and October. Displayed inside are many of the artefacts that have been recovered and preserved. Admission is $3.

From the centre it's a short walk to the four main dig areas and the field laboratory where everything from axes to bowls are being recovered and restored. Workers are at the dig sites from 8 am to 4.30 pm Monday through Friday and 8 am to 12.30 pm some Saturdays.

There is also an 1870 lighthouse that can be reached along a dirt road from the dig sites or you can climb the Gaze. The towering hill sits beyond the community museum and was so named by early settlers who used to climb it to watch for approaching warships or to escape the frequent pillages the area experienced. The view on a clear day is worth the climb.

The *Downs Inn* (☎ 709-432-2808) has 10 rooms at $45/55, including breakfast. The *Irish Loop* serves up cheap but excellent

seafood. The *Colony Cafe* sits in the centre of Ferryland for tasty and somewhat expensive seafood. Note the historical murals on the walls detailing a 1694 French invasion.

In the interior of the peninsula is the huge **Avalon Wilderness Reserve** with an increasingly large herd of woodland caribou now numbering about 100,000. Permits, available at the La Manche Provincial Park office, are required to visit the area for hiking or canoeing. Caribou, however, can sometimes be seen right at the edge of Hwy 10. There are two posted areas for caribou crossings. The first is a 30km stretch between Chance Cove Provincial Park and Portugal Cove South and the second a 20km stretch between Trepassey and St Stephens. The former section near Portugal Cove South is particularly rife with caribou; one local reportedly stopped counting at 85 one morning. Unfortunately, days are rarely without thick fog; the Portugal Cove area holds an unofficial world record for most foggy days in a row. As migrating animals, caribou tend to move en masse and often you spot the animals grazing in groups of 10 to 30. Even spotting a lone individual is a real treat as they are quite impressive beasts and are rarely seen by those not living in the far north of Canada, Russia or Finland.

At Portugal Cove South, taking the Cape Race exit brings you, after 16km, to the 5km-long **Mistaken Point Ecological Reserve**, in which 620-million-year-old multicelled marine fossils have been found, easily the oldest in North America. It's being considered for World Heritage Site status by UNESCO. Where the road ends to the east is Cape Race, where a lighthouse keeper received the *Titanic's* fateful last message.

Camping is possible at **Chance Cove Provincial Park** (☎ 709-729-2424) south of Cappahayden. The campground is almost 7km towards the coast from Hwy 10 and little more than a gravel parking area for those with recreational vehicles. Tenters can walk up the bluff for an exceptional camp site overlooking the cove. These are some of the most scenic camp sites on the Avalon Peninsula and, even better, are now free. Also

working out of the campground is Chance Cove Diving and Venture Tours (☎ 709-363-2257), which offers both whale-watching tours and diving tours. Within a short distance of the cove is a large concentration of wrecks only 36m deep. The rates are $30 per dive or $10 for a whale-watching trip.

Trepassey was the launching place of Amelia Earhart's renowned first-woman-across-the-Atlantic flight in 1928. In town, besides a diminutive **museum** open in July and August ($1) you'll find a large food store, a commercial campground, the *Northwest B&B* (☎ 709-438-2888) with singles/doubles for $40 and the *Trepassey Motel* (☎ 709-438-2934) with 10 rooms for $55/59.

The area from St Vincent's to St Mary's provides an excellent chance of seeing whales, particularly the humpback which feeds close to shore. Halfway between the two villages is **Point La Haye Natural Scenic Attraction**, a sweeping pebbled beach overlooking St Mary's Bay. The lighthouse isn't much more than a light atop scaffolding. There are no official camp sites here but people occasionally camp on the beach.

On Hwy 90, **Salmonier Nature Park** (☎ 709-229-7888) is in the centre of the Avalon Peninsula, 12km south of the junction with Hwy 1. Here you can see many animals found in the province, enclosed in the park's natural settings. A marked 2.5km trail through the woods takes you past the animals – moose, caribou, beaver – as well as indigenous flora. There is also an interpretive centre with exhibits and touch displays for children. The park is open daily June to mid-October from noon to 7 pm.

Moose on the Loose

Though the moose is a fairly common animal across the country it is mainly found in the less populated, heavily forested northern regions. Nowhere in Canada are you as likely to see one as in Newfoundland. There are some 40,000 of them here and many of them live close to towns and roads including the Trans Canada Hwy. This, of course, increases the chances of getting a good look at one but also presents some hazards. There is more than one moose-vehicle collision per day across the province, and smacking into a beast the height of a horse weighing 400kg and with antlers nearly 2m across is more wildlife than most people care for.

Moose tend to like the highways for a number of reasons. The open space makes walking easy, there is usually more breeze and fewer insects, and in spring the salt from winter de-icing makes a nice treat. For these reasons they also enjoy the train tracks, a habit which decreased their population at the rate of some 2000 per year until the train service was discontinued.

The areas of heaviest concentration are well marked and signs should be heeded, particularly when travelling after dark, which is when most accidents occur. Ninety per cent of the run-ins take place between 11 pm and 4 am. If you do see a moose on or beside the road, slow down and, if it doesn't want to move, approach slowly with the lights off as they seem to get mesmerised by the beams.

Get out and take pictures if you like; moose are generally not aggressive and are very impressive, if unusual looking, animals. They can be unpredictable, however, and anything of this size should not be approached too closely or startled. During rutting (mating) season in October and November the males (bulls) can become very belligerent and downright ornery; it's a good time to stay in the car and well out of their way.

Calves are born in the spring, and throughout the summer it is not uncommon to see a cow moose with her young. Females and their young do not have antlers. An adult male grows a 'rack' of antlers each summer, only to have it fall off each autumn.

Conception Bay

Like the rest of eastern Newfoundland, Conception Bay is rich in history and coastal scenery (and well populated as befits its name). Much of the early history of Canada was played out here. **Bay de Verde** in the north can be reached in half a day's drive from St John's. But, if time permits, there are places to stay. Fleetline Bus Service (☎ 709-722-2608) connects St John's with Carbonear with a daily bus, except Sunday, and makes stops along the way.

Despite its small size, **Brigus**, 80km west from St John's, has quite a reputation for its pleasing old European atmosphere. A former resident, Captain Robert Bartlett, was renowned as one of the foremost Arctic explorers in the 20th century. He made more than 20 expeditions into the region, including one in 1909 during which he cleared a trail in the ice that enabled US Commander Robert Peary to make his celebrated dash to the North Pole. Bartlett's house, Hawthorne Cottage, is a National Historic Site and museum open daily during summer from 10 am to 8 pm and there is a $2.25 admission fee.

Also in town is the Ye Olde Stone Barn Museum which has a set of displays on Brigus' 200-year history. It's open daily from 10 am to 6 pm and admission is $1. Nearby is the Brigus Tunnel that was cut through rock in 1860 so Bartlett could easily access his ship in the deep water cove on the other side.

There is more accommodation here than anywhere else on Conception Bay. The ***Brittoner*** (*☎ 709-528-3412, 12 Water St)* is right in the middle of things with singles/doubles for $50/55 including full breakfast. The rooms at the ***Cabot Inn*** (*☎ 709-528-4959),* not far away and still in the village centre, are $10 cheaper. For a bite to eat or afternoon tea there's *North St Cafe*.

North along Hwy 70, you'll quickly come to the turn-off to Hibbs Cove, 9km to the east at the end of Port de Grave Peninsula. Along the peninsula you'll see a very active fishing harbour. In the town of Port de Grave the *fish market* sells everything from cod tongues and crab to salt fish, salmon and scallops.

Hibbs Cove at the end is another picturesque harbour and home of the Fishermen's Museum (☎ 709-786-3912). The small complex consists of a museum with pictures and artefacts depicting the trade at the start of the 20th century, a fishermen's home built in 1900, and a one-room schoolhouse. Hours are 10 am to noon and 1 to 5 pm daily (except Sunday when it is open afternoons only) from the end of June to early September. Admission price is $2, children 50¢.

Up past Cupid's, where the first official English settlement of Newfoundland was attempted in 1610, is **Harbour Grace** where the Spanish and French, and pirates, had been since the early 1500s. The old Customs House – on the site of an erstwhile pirate headquarters – is now the Conception Bay Museum with three floors of exhibits, including one on the aviation history of the area. Hours are 11.30 am to 4.30 pm daily and admission is free.

Many of the first attempts to fly across the Atlantic began in Harbour Grace beginning in 1919. In 1932, four years after her flight from Trepassey on the Avalon Peninsula to Europe, Amelia Earhart took off from here and became the first woman to cross the Atlantic solo. The airstrip is designated an historic site.

Carbonear Island has had a tumultuous history with international battles, pirate intrigues, shipwrecks and more recently, sealhunt controversy. Carbonear Island is designated an historic site and there are many examples of old architecture in town. The annual Conception Bay Folk Festival here is not to be missed.

EJ Pratt (1883-1964), one of Canada's best known poets, was born in Western Bay and a national historic plaque here commemorates him.

Farther north up the coast, **Northern Bay Sands Park** (☎ 709-584-3465), an ex-provincial park, has beautiful beaches. On the inland side is a good spot for freshwater swimming as the ocean is far too cold. The park has a 60 site campground with tent sites for $9 a night.

At Bears Cove, near **Bay de Verde**, a short walk leads to dramatic views. **Baccalieu Island Ecological Reserve** offshore has 11 species of seabirds which breed here, including three million pairs of Leach's Storm Petrel, the largest such colony in the world. Where Hwy 70 ends at the tip of the peninsula the countryside around **Grates Cove** features hundreds of rock walls used to wall vegetable gardens and pen livestock; the entirety is now a designated National Historic Site.

Trinity Bay

On the other side of the peninsula along Trinity Bay are several towns which exemplify wonderful Newfoundland place names. How about the absolutely lovely Heart's Delight or Heart's Content?

In **Heart's Content**, the Cable Station Provincial Historic Site tells the story of when the first transatlantic cable was laid here in 1866 and how the community played an important role in transatlantic communications for the next 100 years. The site is open from 10.30 am to 5.30 pm daily June through mid-October and admission is free.

In **Heart's Delight** is *Farm House Hospitality Home (☎ 709-588-2393)*. There are three rooms, one with a private bath, and rates begin at $40/45 with a light breakfast. Heart's Content has the small, more costly *Legge's Motel (☎ 709-538-2929)* which consists of seven self-contained housekeeping units and two cheaper simple motel-style rooms. Rates are $45/65 for singles/doubles.

At the bottom of Trinity Bay, **Dildo** (when you stop sniggering) is a good spot for whale watching. Pothead whales come in by the school and humpbacks, a larger species, can also be seen in summer. Both can be viewed even from the shore. The **Dildo Interpretation Center** (☎ 709-582-2687) has exhibits on the area's 19th century codfish hatchery as well as the ongoing Dorset Eskimo archaeological dig on Dildo Island. It's open daily during summer and admission is free. In South Dildo is the Whaling and Sealing Museum (☎ 709-582-2282), open from 11 am to 5 pm Monday through Friday. Admission is $1.

Argentia

The south-west portion of the Avalon Peninsula is known primarily for Argentia with the large ferry terminal for boats to Nova Scotia. For ferry information see the St John's section earlier in this chapter. Newhook's Transportation connects both Argentia (☎ 709-227-2552) and Placentia with St John's by road. If you have a vehicle, it's 130km to St John's or a good 90 minute drive.

The ferry arrives around 5 am so you shouldn't need to get a room since there's not much to see. You pass one motel along Hwy 100 in Argentia, but it is a less than desirable place to stay. **Fitzgerald's Pond Park** (☎ 709-227-4488), 25km north along Hwy 100, has 24 sites and turns its day-use area into additional camp sites when the campground becomes full. The rate is $10 for the unserviced sites.

Placentia

Nearby in Placentia, settled in 1662, are the remains of a French fort at **Castle Hill National Historic Site** (☎ 709-227-2401), with a visitors centre and fine views. In the early 1800s Placentia – then Plaisance – was the French capital of Newfoundland and French attacks on the British at St John's were based from here. The site is open from 8.30 am to 8 pm daily during summer and until 4.30 pm the rest of the year. Admission is $2.50.

The old graveyard by the Anglican church offers more history as does the **O'Reilly Heritage House** (☎ 709-227-5568), 48 Riverside Drive. In a home built in 1902 and restored in 1989, it also acts as a local museum offering details of both the house and the area. It's open June to September from 9 am to 8 pm Monday through Friday and noon to 8 pm on weekends. Admission is free. The courthouse and Roman Catholic church are other notable historic buildings. A boardwalk runs along the waterfront and there is a beach.

Near Placentia there is a section of the coast which is forested, a rather unusual sight here as so much of the entire provincial coastline is barren and rocky. Placentia has one hotel and two B&Bs. The *Harold Hotel (☎ 709-227-2107)* on Main St 5km

from the ferry terminal has rooms at $52/58 and a restaurant.

Cape St Mary's

At the southern tip of the peninsula is **St Mary's Ecological Reserve**, an excellent place for glimpsing seabirds. An unpaved road leads the 16km from Route 100 into the sanctuary where there is an interpretive centre (☎ 709-729-2431) and a lighthouse. A 30 minute walk from there takes you to views of Bird Rock, the third largest gannet-nesting site in North America. Its near-vertical cliffs rise more than 100m from the sea and provide ideal nesting conditions during summer for some 53,000 seabirds, including kittiwakes, murres and razorbills. During summer guides are present to answer questions. The interpretive centre is open daily from 9 am to 7 pm 2 May through 31 October. The reserve itself is free, but the centre has a $3 admission, less for children, and a $7 family pass.

Eastern Newfoundland

This is the smallest region of the province and consists of the area just west of the Avalon Peninsula on the edge of the main body of the island. Geographically it is also distinguished from the central portion of the province by the jutting peninsulas at each end: the Bonavista to the north and the Burin to the south.

The ferry for the islands of Saint Pierre and Miquelon departs from Fortune in the south. To this day, the islands are French possessions and certainly not in name only.

BONAVISTA PENINSULA

The Bonavista Peninsula has many flyspeck traditional fishing communities including some of the oldest in the province. Some people claim that historic Trinity is the oldest town in North America. Several companies around the peninsula offer boat tours and Terra Nova National Park preserves a section of the peninsula in its natural state.

Clarenville

This is the access point to the peninsula and it's best to pass right through. The town does have a full range of services for travellers including large food stores, a laundrette and a handful of hotels and B&Bs. The *Island View Hospitality Home* (☎ 709-466-2062) just north of Clarenville on Hwy 230 charges $39/45.

Up the Coast

Hwy 235, along the edge of **Southern Bay**, has some splendid water views and a picnic spot with a view at Jiggin' Head Park. Along the beaches here and around the Avalon Peninsula in late June and early July, millions of capelin – a small silver fish – get washed ashore by the tides. This is partially due to the spawning cycle and partially to being chased by hungry cod. People go down with buckets and bags to scoop up a free meal.

Bonavista

This largish town of 5000 residents is at the end of the peninsula where John Cabot landed on 24 June, 1497, and first saw the 'new found land'. Later he drifted down to St John's harbour and stopped there. For his troubles King Henry VII of England rewarded him with the royal sum of £10. It wasn't until the 1600s that Bonavista became a permanent village and from then on through the 1700s, the British and French battled over it like they did for other settlements along the coast.

Government tourist information says that street names are 'as rare as hen's teeth' and you'll likely get lost but it's tiny so you can walk it.

At the old courthouse is a whipping post where instant justice could be meted out. Most visitors come for the **Ryan Premises National Historic Site**, an assemblage of six refurbished 19th century outport fishing buildings originally used to grade, cure, barrel and store salted fish. An interpretive centre (☎ 709-468-1600) features displays and exhibits. The site is open daily from 10 am to 6 pm mid-June through mid-October. Admission is $2.50, less for seniors, and $6 for a family.

NEWFOUNDLAND & LABRADOR

In the centre of town the **Mockbeggar Property** is the restored home of F Gordon Bradley, Newfoundland's first representative to the Canadian Senate. A number of buildings dot the premises. Hours are 10 am to 5.30 pm daily during summer and admission is free.

Just up the road from here is *The Matthew*, a replica of the ship Cabot sailed into Bonavista. You can board the ship daily in summer from 9 am to 7 pm for $2, $1 students.

The **Cape Bonavista Lighthouse** dating from 1843 has been restored and is now a provincial historic site with period-garbed guides. Hours are 10 am to 5.30 pm daily during summer and admission is free. Nearby is **Landfall Park** with its statue of John Cabot. You can look into Landfall Boat Tours (☎ 709-468-2744) which operates on the cape and has three boat tours a day of the coastline. The two-hour tours are $30.

Dungeon Provincial Park is the site of an unusual rock formation on the shoreline. The park itself is little more than a parking area and an interpretive display but from the top of these headland cliffs you can view a handful of sea stacks along the coastline of Spillar's Cove. More impressive is the Dungeon, a hole along the shoreline that is 250m in circumference, 15m deep and has two channels where the sea roars in and out. In early summer whales may be seen off the coast.

Outside of town at the village of Maberly on Hwy 238 you can get views of an offshore island where thousands of seabirds roost. Principal species are puffins, kittiwakes and murres.

Places to Stay There are a handful of B&Bs in the city, including *White's B&B (☎ 709-468-7018)* at $40/45 which has bike rentals. Camping is not allowed officially at Dungeon Provincial Park. The nearest campground is the large *Paradise Farm Trailer Park (☎ 709-468-1150)*, 7km away on Hwy 230, part of a 65-acre farm, which has tent sites from $9.

Getting There & Away Two bus lines run up the peninsula, but not all the way into

Thousands of puffins can be seen near Maberly.

Bonavista. Venture Bus Lines (☎ 709-722-4249) leaves Southern Bay at 7.30 am daily and then leaves St John's at 5.10 pm for the return trip. This costs $20.

Shirran's (☎ 709-722-8032) runs farther up the peninsula for $25.

Port Union

The Fisherman's Protective Union was formed here in 1910 and a monument honours its founder. The province's largest fish-processing plant is here and one of Newfoundland's largest trawler fleets is still struggling to survive the cod moratorium in this ice-free port. For history of the town and fishing industry check out the Port Union Museum in the former train station. It's open from 11 am to 6 pm Tuesday through Sunday. The home of Sir William Ford Coaker, founder of the union, is now a small museum known as the **Bungalow** (☎ 709-469-2728), full of period artefacts. It's open daily mid-June through September. Admission is $4.

Trinity

First visited by Portuguese explorer Corte-Real in 1500 and established as a town in 1580, Trinity might be the oldest town on the entire continent. Many buildings along the town's narrow streets have been restored or

renovated and indeed, much of the diminutive town has national heritage designation. The Interpretive Centre (☎ 709-729-0592), open from 10 am to 5.30 pm daily in summer, has information on the history, houses and buildings in town.

From there swing past **Green Family Forge**, a blacksmith museum. They have been forging iron pieces here for shipbuilders since 1750 with the present building dating back to 1895. Hours are 10 am to 7.30 pm daily in summer, lesser times the rest of the year. Admission here is $2 though for $3 you can get access to the Trinity Museum and Garland Mansion.

Trinity Museum has over 2000 local artefacts as well as the oldest fire engine in North America, dating to 1811. The **Garland Mansion** is a Georgian brick house and home of the first speaker of the House of Assembly. Both of these are open the same hours as the forge. **Hiscock House Provincial Historic Site** is a restored merchant's home, furnished to the 1910 period. Hours are 10 am to 5.30 pm. **Ryan Building** is another provincial historic site that has been restored to portray the general store owned by the Ryan family from 1902 to 1952. Hours are 10 am to 5.30 pm and there is no admission fee. Finally, venture out to **Fort Point**, where you'll find four cannons embedded in the ground, the remains of the British fortification in 1745.

One of the more entertaining aspects of Trinity is the **Rising Tide Theatre** (☎ 709-464-3232, ☎ 709-738-3256 in St John's, ☎ 1-888-464-1100), which performs Wednesday, Saturday and Sunday at 2 pm near the Interpretive Centre. It's an outdoor drama on the history of the area with a Ryan slant. Tickets are $6 and worth it. This is part of 'Theatre in the Bight', a three-month-long historical pageant of different theatrical forms in and around Trinity.

Every Wednesday night at 10.30 pm at **Rocky's Place** you can experience traditional dancing.

Organised Tours Atlantic Adventures (☎ 709-781-2255) uses a sailboat for its whale-watching tours. Several are offered a day

and the cost is $35 for the 2½ hour sail. Ocean Contact (☎ 709-464-3269), a whale-watching and research organisation, offers whale-watching expeditions ($44) in a 9m rigid hull inflatable and all-inclusive, expensive multi-day trips in its larger boat.

Places to Stay & Eat Ocean Contact operates from the historic and popular *Village Inn* (☎ 709-464-3269), which has singles/doubles from $50. Films and slides on whales and other sea life can be seen.

An alternative option is *Trinity Cabins* (☎ 709-464-3657), with housekeeping cabins in the $42 to $50 range for two people. There's a swimming pool or, for the brave, a beach nearby.

There are also now a half-dozen B&Bs, and $50 is the cheapest you'll likely find in summer. The more modest is the *Beach B&B* (☎ 709-464-3695) for $50, while *Campbell House* (☎ 709-464-3377) is a beautifully restored historic house with rooms at $80 to $100. In the village of Port Rexton, 10 minutes south-east, is *Just Like Home* (☎ 709-464-3338) with rooms from $45. *Fisher's Loft* (☎ 709-464-3240) in Rexton starts at $75 and has garnered good reviews.

Campers can head 5km up Hwy 236 to pitch a tent at *Lockston Path Provincial Park* (☎ 709-464-3553) where the 22 unserviced sites are $11 a night. For something even cheaper, as in free, head to *Trinity Loop Fun Park* (☎ 709-464-2171). This is a touristy haven of ferris wheels, pony rides and a miniature train. It has large gravel areas where it allows anybody, especially RVers, to camp for free. Within the complex is a store, restaurant and a laundrette in a boxcar.

The best meal in town is at *Eriksen Premises* (☎ 709-464-3698) which is also a hospitality house with rooms from $70. The delightful little gourmet restaurant on the first floor consists of two small rooms, offering afternoon tea or dinners ranging from $9 to $15. Slightly cheaper seafood can be found at the marina restaurant, from where the Atlantic Adventures sailboat embarks.

NEWFOUNDLAND & LABRADOR

Terra Nova National Park

This east coast park (☎ 709-533-2801), 240km west of St John's and 80km east of Gander, is split by the Trans Canada Hwy and typifies the regional geography. The rocky, jagged coastline on beautiful Bonavista Bay gives way to long bays, inland lakes, ponds, bogs and hilly woods. There's canoeing, kayaking, fishing, hiking, camping, sandy beaches, even swimming in Sandy Pond. Lots of wildlife may be seen – moose, bear, beaver, otter and bald eagles – and, from May to August, icebergs are commonly viewed off the coast.

There's a new **Marine Interpretation Centre** north of Newman Sound. Literally dozens of different hands-on exhibits, computers, and other displays can easily take up a whole morning. Hours are 9 am to 5 pm May through October, till 9 pm June through August. The centre also has the *Starfish Eatery* with lots of good seafood.

Vehicle entry fee into Terra Nova National Park is $3.25 a day per adult, $6.50/19.50 one day/four days for a family. The park's main campground is *Newman Sound*, where sites are $14 to $16 a day. Also located here is *Newman Sound Service Center* (☎ 709-533-9133) with groceries, a laundrette and bicycle rentals. At the north end of the park is *Malady Head Campground* where sites are $12 a night. Even though there are 570 sites, on weekends in summer arrive a bit early.

Commercial lodging can be found outside the park, most notably at Eastport at the north end and Port Blandford in the south. *White Sails Inn & Cabins* (☎ 709-677-3400) in Eastport has two-person units that begin at $40.

Organised Tours Departing from behind the Marine Interpretation Centre are excellent trips with Ocean Watch Tours (☎ 709-533-6024). One 2½ hour trip explores the fjords and islands and sometimes stops in at old abandoned outports. It departs daily at 12.30 and 3.30 pm and the cost is $26. Another working research trip specialises more in wildlife and seeks out whales, seals, and birds. It leaves Newman Sound at 9 am and is $28 per person. An outport sunset cruise departs at 7 pm and costs $28. With advance notice, bilingual guides can be arranged.

Also here is Terra Nova Adventures (☎ 709-533-9797, ☎ 1-888-533-8687), with hour-long kayaking primers Saturday at 1 pm for $25 or popular 2½ hour tours four times daily for $45. A full-day tour costs $120. One of the guides here speaks German.

Technically out of the park in Burnside but popular with parkgoers nonetheless are boat tours to visit the archaeological sites of the Quarry, the largest aboriginal quarry ever found, and The Beaches, the largest Beothuk settlement discovered, including the only Beothuk grave found. Tour boats take 20 minutes; while waiting, you can visit the field laboratory in Burnside daily from 10 am to 8 pm. If you book early enough, you can even help scientists dig.

Hiking & Canoeing Terra Nova has 14 trails totalling nearly 100km. There are some excellent day hikes in the park. The Malady Head Trail is a round trip of 4km to the edge of a headland cliff with stunning views of Southwest Arm and Broad Cove. Sandy Pond Trail is an easy 3km loop around the pond and through a bog. From Newman Sound Campground you can hike the Coastal Trail and see marine life along the shoreline. There's also the 9km Old Trails network of small trails from Sandy Cove to the historic fishing community of Salvage, a mixture of gentle and demanding hikes.

There are eight total backcountry locations, six accessible via trail, canoe or water taxi from the Marine Interpretation Centre; another two are canoe-in only via the Sandy Pond-Dunphy's Canoe Route, a 10km paddle that has one short portage. Canoes can be rented at Sandy Pond, where the canoe trails begin. Two more canoe trails exist, totalling 17km one way. The camp sites are $8 per party and you must obtain a backcountry permit from the Newman Sound information kiosk, the Marine Centre, or the Administration Building in the off season. Reservations are a good idea in summer,

particularly the Sandy Pond-Dunphy's route. To avoid backtracking, Ocean Watch will also drop backpackers at the Newman Sound outports during its regular trips. That would reduce the trek to South Board Cove to 17.5km and to Minchin Cove to 14km.

The grandaddy of all backpacking opportunities is the Outport Loop, a 50km epic trek which will ultimately link up several of the existing backcountry trails. New for this edition are trail extensions from South Broad Cove to a new camp site at Lions Den, then continuing to Park Harbour. Most of the trail is finished but parts are unfinished and unmarked – not to mention mucky and wet. Only serious and prepared hikers should try the whole loop. It is possible to cheat via a water taxi.

BURIN PENINSULA

This southern peninsula has been the base for European fishing boats since the 1500s. The Grand Banks off the peninsula (part of the continental shelf) teem with fish. Or at least they did until the early 1990s when stocks plummeted.

Getting There & Away

Sadly the southern coast Marine Atlantic ferry, which used to skip along the province from Port aux Basques to Terrenceville on the Burin Peninsula, was suspended in the mid 1990s. Terrenceville, already depressed from the moratorium on cod fishing, was hit hard by the loss of the ferry business and subsequently lost its bus service to St John's.

Without a vehicle, the only transportation to the peninsula is through van service from St John's. Cheeseman's Bus Service (☎ 709-753-7022) goes to Marystown at 3.30 pm daily for $15; the return trip is at 8 am. Foote's Taxi (☎ 709-832-0491, ☎ 1-800-866-1181) goes all the way to Fortune at 4 pm for $30; the return trip is at 8 am.

The MV *Northern Whale* ferries passengers and freight between Bay L'Argent, Recontre East, and Pool's Cove across Fortune Bay. But Bay L'Argent is far north of the highlights on the Burin Peninsula and Pool's Cove is far, far from Harbour Breton,

or anything else really. If you do go, no buses service Pool's Cove; you'll have to contact Hickey's Bus Service (☎ 709-885-2523) which services Harbour Breton and Grand Falls-Windsor. The ferry is daily in summer; all told getting to Pool's Cove from Bay L'Argent would take you over three hours and cost $6.50.

Marystown

Although the largest town on the peninsula, there is not much here for the visitor but Marystown does have a laundrette, food stores – even a *McDonald's*. A huge hotel is here, along with a few cheaper B&Bs, including the *Bayside B&B* (☎ 709-279-3286), with rooms from $40. There is also a tourist centre on Hwy 210 that is open daily from 8.30 am to 9 pm Monday through Friday and 10 am to 9 pm on the weekends. You can camp and swim at *Frenchman's Cove Provincial Park* (☎ 709-826-2753) 11km away at Garnish. Sites are $9 a night.

Burin

Settled by fishers from Europe in the 1700s, Burin is one of the oldest towns on the south coast. It is actually a picturesque series of villages sparsely scattered around coves and lumpy, treeless hills.

Burin is still struggling to maintain its important role in the Grand Banks and has a major trawler repair facility as well as a processing plant. Crab and lobster fishing have kept many of the trawlers afloat during the cod moratorium.

In the town of Burin itself, there is the free **Heritage House**, on the corner of Main and Union Sts, which consists of two historical homes and a small park dotted with marine engines and winches. It's open daily from noon to 8.30 pm in summer. Nearby is **Captain Cook's Lookout Trail**, picked up by turning off Main St at St Patrick's Elementary School and following the side street to its end. It's a 20 minute walk to the top.

St Lawrence

St Lawrence is a mining town with the only deposits of fluorospar in Canada. It was

once the world's largest producer and although this is no longer the case, the mine still operates and the **St Lawrence Miner's Museum**, right on Hwy 220, outlines its history. It's open daily during the summer.

From St Lawrence to Lawn, Hwy 220 rises steadily over a series of hills and ridges to provide some grand views of the coast and numerous opportunities to hike to the top of rocky knobs for an even better view. There are small community parks with free camping at both Point au Gaul and Point May. *Point May Park* is an especially scenic spot to spend the night. Located right on Hwy 220 north of the town towards Grand Bank, the small park overlooks the French islands. The only facilities here are a pair of outhouses and a parking lot.

Grand Bank

Its role now diminished, this was one of the main centres of the early Grand Banks fishery. The Burin Peninsula long served as the base for the famous Banks fishing grounds. You can pick up the brochure *Grand Bank Heritage Walk* for a self-guided walk through town that will explain the varied 1880s architecture of the homes, churches and Water St storefronts. Hikers will like the **Marine Hike**, a 6km trail leaving from Christian's Road off Hwy 220 and tracing Admiral's Beach. Another 5km trail climbs 108m to the top of Bennett's Hill and proffers grand vistas.

The **Southern Newfoundland Seamen's Museum** (☎ 709-832-1484), on Marine Drive at the edge of town, depicts both the era of the banking schooner and the changes in

The Grand Banks

The fabulous portion of the Atlantic Ocean known as the Grand Banks, lying just south-east and south-west of Cape Race at the southern part of the Avalon Peninsula, is one of the prime reasons why anybody ever bothered with the New World. After 500 years of serious plundering it remains one of the world's best fishing grounds. However, in the early 1990s the warning bells finally went off when it was realised that the dominant species, cod, had finally been reduced to alarmingly small numbers. Biologists, fishers and government have now combined forces to work out a plan to allow the stocks to replenish.

The banks are a series of submarine plateaus stretching from north-west to south-east about 80km out to sea from Cape Race. They cover an area about 500km long by 300km wide with a depth ranging from 5 to 350m. Though mostly in the Labrador Current, the waters are met by the Gulf Stream and this blending of the warm and cold gives rise to the legendary fogs. It also helps plankton (tiny marine plants and animals) to thrive and it is this food source that results in the millions of fish.

The main catch has always been cod but there is also halibut, flounder and herring, among others. Boats come from around the world to fill their hulls, notably from Norway, Japan, Portugal, Spain and Russia. Canada has imposed restrictions and regulations but has an impossible task in trying to enforce its limits and authority.

It was in 1497 that John Cabot, an Italian working for England, first put down a net and couldn't believe his eyes when he saw it bulging with fish. It wasn't long before other Europeans began to arrive and set up fishing communities on the shores of Newfoundland. As well as the fog, nasty storms and marauding icebergs are hazards that fishers have had to contend with through the centuries.

In the past 20 years oil has been discovered in parts of the Banks, raising another potential threat to this unique biological resource.

fishery over the years. Its collection of model sailing ships is impressive. Hours are 9 am to 4.30 pm Monday through Friday and 10 am to 6 pm Sunday. Admission is free. Also in town is **George C Harris House** at 16 Water St with rooms housing local artefacts. It's open daily from 10 am to 8 pm and is free.

If you're spending the night in Grand Bank, the imposing but pleasant *Thorndyke* (☎ 709-832-0820, 33 Water St), a designated historic home, makes a fine place to stay. It's busy, so call for reservations. From the roof there are views over the town and bay and there also is a restaurant on the premises. Rooms are $45 for singles or doubles. If you don't stay, tours are available for $5. The very understated *Crosswinds* (☎ 709-832-0430) has a dozen basic but comfortable rooms from $30.

There are a handful of takeaways and small restaurants in town and on Saturday in July and August the *Burin Peninsula Producers Market* is staged from 9 am to 2 pm on the old school grounds at 4 Main St.

At 3 pm Wednesday through Sunday in summer are the *Living Interpretation* historical dramas, affiliated with Trinity's Rising Ride Theater. Tickets cost $5 to $7 and some include lunch.

Fortune

Fortune is the jumping-off point for trips to Saint Pierre and Miquelon and 20,000 people a year pass through on their way to the islands. Aside from looking after visitors, many of the townspeople are employed at the large fish-processing plant. There is also a shipbuilding and repair depot.

The *Fair Isle Motel* (☎ 709-832-1010) with 10 rooms at $60 a single or double is currently your only option in town.

Saint Pierre & Miquelon

Once called the 'Islands of 11,000 Virgins', these two dabs of land, lying 16km west off Newfoundland's Burin Peninsula, belong to France. The tiny islands represent the only French holdings left in North America. The 6000 residents drink French wine, eat baguettes and pay for it in francs.

First claimed by France in the 1500s, the islands were turned over to the British along with Cape Breton after the Seven Years' War. They were then ceded to the French by the British in 1783 under the Treaty of Paris. Battles over fishing rights continued with Newfoundland and the islands changing hands a couple of times until 1815. Since then they have remained under French control. The disputes persist, however, and in 1989 there was a fairly serious flare-up with France getting involved in the bickering over territorial fishing limits.

An interesting aside is Saint Pierre's role during the Prohibition period in the USA. Canada would legally export what amounted to oceans of booze to the French island where US rum runners would pick it up to take home.

As in so much of Atlantic Canada, the main source of livelihood has always been fishing and the supplying of fishing boats. Closing much of the region's fishery, most notably the moratorium on cod fishing, has seriously undermined the economic viability of the islands. France has been paying some compensation to those put out of work and aims to boost the tourism industry. France is building a new airport able to accommodate jumbo jets, and plans are being made to develop casinos to lure even more visitors.

The archipelago consists of numerous islands. Saint Pierre, although not the largest, is the principal one; it's the most populated and its town of the same name is the largest on the islands.

Miquelon is actually two islands separated by a narrow isthmus of sand. The northern section, Great Miquelon, has most of the people and a small town. The southern island called Langlade or Little Miquelon is quite wild. The remaining islands are all very small.

Canadian and US visitors need neither passports nor visas for a visit, but good ID such as a birth certificate or driver's licence

with photograph is recommended. For citizens of the European Union (EU), Switzerland and Japan, passports are required. All other nationals need both a passport and a visa.

Note that the time on the islands is half an hour ahead of Newfoundland time. Also keep in mind that making a phone call from Newfoundland to the islands is an international call as far as the long distance carriers are concerned and the area code for the French islands is ☎ 508. They'll gladly take Canadian money on the islands but prices are usually quoted in francs. One dollar is worth roughly 3½ francs. And you'll need every scrap of money as this place is prohibitively expensive. On the plus side is the duty-free shop for alcohol, cigarettes etc. *There are no cash machines on the islands!*

Information

The Saint Pierre Tourist office (known as ART; ☎ 412222 or ☎ 1-800-565-5118 off the islands) can provide a complete accommodation listing. Calling to the islands is like calling overseas. Other than any 800 numbers, you must dial 011 508, the country and area codes before the local number.

Things to See

In Saint Pierre you can see the **museum** which outlines the island's history and the cathedral. Also, visit the interesting **French cemetery**.

Outside town there is a lighthouse at **Gallantry Head** and good views from Cap aux Basques. Out in the harbour, a 10 minute boat ride away, is **Île aux Marins** with a small museum. You can take a bilingual guided tour around the island which had its own fishing village at the start of the 20th century.

Miquelon, 45km away, is less visited and less developed. The people here are largely of Acadian background while Saint Pierre's inhabitants are French (mainly from Brittany and Normandy) and Basque.

The village of **Miquelon**, centred around the church, is at the northern tip of the island.

From nearby l'**Étang de Mirande**, a walking trail leads to a lookout and waterfall.

From the bridge in town a scenic 25km road leads across the isthmus to **Langlade**. The island of Langlade remains pretty much the same as it has always been. There are some summer cottages but no year-round inhabitants – human ones, that is. There are some wild horses and smaller animals such as rabbits, and around the rocky edges and lagoons you'll see seals and birds.

Special Events

Several annual holidays and festivals occur in July and August. Bastille Day is on 14 July. On 4 August, Jacques Cartier's arrival in the islands in 1536 is celebrated. The following week, a two-day festival on Miquelon recalls the Acadian heritage and, later in the month, another two-day event on Saint Pierre celebrates the Basque heritage. From mid-July to the end of August folk dances are often held in Saint Pierre's square.

Places to Stay & Eat

Saint Pierre has around a dozen hotels, guesthouses or pensions which are more reasonably priced and which generally provide breakfast. Accommodation can be tight in the high season so you may want to check before you go.

Hotel Robert (☎ *508-412419*) is situated on the waterfront and is the largest place with 54 rooms that go for 430/530FF. Pensions include *Louis Vigneau B&B* (☎ *508-412042, 12 rue Amiral Musekier*) with five rooms at 180/220FF; and the *Bernard Arrossamena* (☎ *508-414086, 16 rue Georges-Daguerre*) with all rooms at 230FF. At a couple of these places meals are available.

Miquelon has its own tourist office (☎ 508-416187), one hotel *Motel Miquelon* (☎ *508-416310*) near the ocean with rooms from 325FF, as well as two pensions and small campgrounds at *l'Étang de Mirande* and *Le Cap* near town.

As might be expected on French islands, restaurants are numerous relative to the size of the population, and the food is good. In both Saint Pierre and Miquelon there are several places serving traditional French food. *Chez Dutin* on Saint Pierre is worth a

try. Saint Pierre has more choice and a number of less expensive places for sandwiches, pizza and the like. *Le Maringoiun'fre* has good crêpes.

Getting There & Away

Air Air Saint Pierre (☎ 508-414748 out of the islands) flies from St John's ($123, 45 minutes), Montreal, Halifax and Sydney (Nova Scotia) April through October. Information and reservations can be had through Canadian Airlines International. More connections should be added with the arrival of a new airport.

Ferry Definitely double check times and companies before arriving in Fortune. From Monday through Saturday May to around Labour Day there is a ferry leaving St Pierre at 1.30 pm and returning from Fortune at 2.45 pm. This is a one hour trip. Labour Day through December it's weekends only. On two Saturdays per month in summer a day trip is still possible with the ferry departing St Pierre at 8 am and 5 pm and leaving Fortune at 9 am and 6 pm. A second ferry runs in peak times, leaving Fortune at 8 am and returning at 3 pm; this one costs the same but takes two hours. Technically this would allow a quick, quick day trip, especially on Wednesday, when the ferry departs St Pierre at around 5 pm. A day trip to Miquelon alone is available Sunday in peak season; it departs Fortune at 7.30 am, returning at 3 pm.

Lloyd Lake's Travel Ltd (☎ 832-2006, ☎ 1-800-563-2006) operates the ferries and has an office right at the dock in Fortune. Round-trip passage is $65 per adult and $33 for children. For just a day trip on those special Saturday ferries it's $50 per adult, $30 per child. Reservations are required.

St Pierre Tours, with offices in both St John's and Fortune, offers various package tours which includes ferry crossings, room and continental breakfast. It's $117 per person based on double occupancy of a room for a night at Hotel Robert. For round-trip transport from St John's, it's another $100 each person. You can call St Pierre Tours at

Fortune (☎ 709-832-0429) or stop at its office in St John's (☎ 709-722-3892), 116 Duckworth St.

Getting Around

Between the Islands The MV *Anahitra* travels to and from Miquelon Tuesday, Friday and Sunday twice daily. The rest of the year there is only one trip daily. The return fare is 120FF, less for children, and the trip takes about an hour. Other ferries ply the hour-long route to Langlade (90FF round trip) and Île aux Marins (20FF round trip).

Around the Islands In Saint Pierre rent a 'rosalie', a four-wheeled bicycle that comes in two sizes; two and four-person models are available. There are regular bicycles as well, or small motorbikes. In both Saint Pierre and Miquelon, tours on horseback are offered.

Also on Saint Pierre there are tours by bus and mini-train, and on Miquelon a bus trip takes visitors around the island and across the isthmus to Langlade. In a couple of days much can be seen on foot. If you're in the market for a tour, shop around, as there are many options.

Central Newfoundland

The vast, little-populated central area is the largest geographic region of the island portion of the province. From Lewisporte, ferries depart for Labrador. The southern area is mostly inaccessible, lake-filled woodland. One road leads down to the coast linking many small remote villages to the rest of the province.

GANDER

Gander, with a population of 13,000, is at the crossroads of the east-west Trans Canada Hwy and Hwy 330 which leads to Notre Dame Bay. It is a convenient stopping point whichever way you're going.

Gander served the first regular transatlantic flights and then, during WWII, was a

major link for planes on their way to Europe. The first formation of bombers made in the USA for the UK left here in February 1940. The location was chosen because it is close to Europe but far enough inland to be free of the coastal fog that often plagues St John's.

Numerous USA and Canadian airlines also used it for transatlantic flights beginning in the 1930s. The airport, a major Aeroflot refuelling stop, was long known as the site of thousands of defections from Russia, Cuba and former Eastern Bloc countries – the plane touched down and passengers asked for political asylum. These days it is more likely the hopeful arrivals will seek refugee status which permits them to stay in Canada until their case is heard.

There is a tourist chalet (☎ 709-256-7110) on the Trans Canada Hwy at the central exit into town and it's open from 9 am to 9 pm daily during summer.

Aviation Attractions

Aviation attractions have all been consolidated just west of the tourist chalet at the **North Atlantic Aviation Museum** (☎ 709-256-2923). Exhibits detail Newfoundland air contributions to WWII, a history of navigation, the Battle of Britain, and numerous reconstructions of planes and controls. Hours are 9 am to 9 pm in summer, lesser times the rest of the year. Admission is $3 adults, less for seniors and children.

At the airport (☎ 709-256-3905) is a small aviation display and a huge tapestry depicting the history of flight. It's in the passengers waiting lounge but, if you don't have a ticket, ask the security officials and they'll let you in for a look. Some have received an impromptu tour of the ATC Tower and/or Gander Flight Training, though advance notice is requested.

The **Silent Witness Monument**, just east of town, south off the Trans Canada Hwy, tenderly marks the site of an horrendous early morning crash in December 1985 in which 248 US soldiers returning home from the Middle East for Christmas were killed along with eight crew members. The possible causes are still debated.

From the tourist chalet a path leads to the **Thomas Howe Demonstration Forest** with 2km of trails through forest and wetlands; this is where the US plane went down. The swathe of forest taken out by the crash is astounding. You can also wander down to Gander Lake from the tourist chalet.

Places to Stay

There is a campground just a few kilometres north of town at *Jonathan's Pond Park* (☎ 709-424-3007) with $10 sites, and another at *Square Pond Park* (☎ 709-533-2738) 28km east of Gander where tent sites are $10 a night.

There are numerous motels, mostly chains, on the highway but they're decidedly pricey. The exception to this is *Skipper's Inn* (☎ 709-256-2534) where there is a dining room and rooms for $45/50. The spiffy *Hotel Gander* (☎ 709-256-3931 or ☎ 1-800-563-2988 in Canada) is also along the highway and has absolutely everything you could want in services; it's known for its dining room. Rooms start at $65.

Places to Eat

On Airport Drive in town are the usual fast-food outlets. The lavishly decorated Chinese restaurant, *Highlight*, is better. It's in the little mall strip on the corner of Elizabeth St and Airport Blvd.

Continuing east on Airport Blvd towards the airport, just beside the Gander mall is the *Bread Shoppe (136 Bennet St)*. This is a good bakery with a wide selection of breads and pastries and tables for its morning coffee drinkers.

Getting There & Away

Gander is a main stop for DRL (☎ 709-651-3434) which maintains a ticket office at the airport. A bus for St John's departs there at 5.02 pm daily while the bus for Port aux Basques departs at 12.46 pm daily.

NOTRE DAME BAY & AROUND

This coastal area north of Gander is the highlight of Central Newfoundland. About 80 little villages are found around the bay

nestled in small coves or clinging to the rocky shoreline. From Gander there are two road loops – one through Lewisporte, the other eastward to Wesleyville – which make good circular tours.

Offshore is a large cluster of islands, including Fogo, New World and Twillingate, which should not be missed and where whales and icebergs may be seen.

Change Islands

These two islands, reached by ferry from Farewell at the end of what seems a long road from the main highway, don't change much, name notwithstanding. There are five 25 minute trips in each direction daily costing $6 per car and driver and $2.50 per person round trip. From Farewell the first ferry leaves at 7.45 am, the last at 9.15 pm with the others scattered evenly through the day. Check schedules at the ferry office (☎ 709-627-3492) or, better, one of the B&Bs on the islands as the times change *often*.

The two main Change Islands with a population of just 500 or so are connected by a short causeway at the northern end where the largest village is located. The islands are quiet with many traditional wooden houses and some old fishing-related buildings painted in a red-ochre colour common to the area. At the northern end is a small store and one of the two places to stay, the well-regarded *Seven Oaks Island Inn & Cottages* (☎ 709-621-3256). Singles/doubles cost $49/59 while the two-bedroom cottages are $85. Meals are available and boat tours can be arranged. The island also has a small B&B – *Hart's* (☎ 709-621-3133) – run by the mayor! Rooms are $46. About 15 minutes from the ferry terminal is *TLP Restaurant & Bakery*.

Boat tours are also available from Change Islands Adventure Tours (☎ 709-621-3106), which has four two-hour cruises daily Monday through Saturday, three on Sunday, and sunset cruises if enough people show interest. Rates are $15.

Fogo Island

Fogo, just to the east of Notre Dame Bay, is the largest of the area's islands. It is just 25km long. Tread carefully because the Canadian Flat Earth Society has stated that Fogo is at the edge of the world! Indeed, it's claimed that Brimstone Head is one of the four corners of the earth. Standing here looking out to sea it's not difficult to agree. Boat tours can be arranged through aptly named Flat Earth Boat Tours (☎ 709-266-2745) in Fogo.

Like the Change Islands, Fogo is reached by ferry from Farewell. There are five services daily leaving from 8.15 am to 9 pm. The fare is $7.50 for car and driver, $2.50 for adult passengers round trip. This trip takes about 50 minutes. Again, check with the ferry office (☎ 709-627-3492) as it is flexible.

The island has an interesting history being first settled by Europeans in the 1680s. There are about 10 villages on the island, together making up a population of about 4500. There are a couple of fine walking trails, a sandy beach at Sandy Cove and a small herd of caribou and some free roaming ponies on the island. At Burnt Point is a lighthouse. Several fish plants are on the island and visitors can have a look around them.

Icebergs can often be seen and in July there's a folk festival. A heritage house, once the residence of a merchant, has been converted into the small free **Bleak House Museum** in Fogo; the town also has the reconstructed free **School House Museum**. Little Seldom has two buildings at the marina which house the **Marine Interpretation Centre**, full of local heritage displays. Picking berries is also a treasured pastime here.

Places to Stay For those wishing to stay, *Payne's Hospitality Home* (☎ 709-266-2359) is the cheapest at $29 and up. *Fogo Island Motel* (☎ 709-266-2556) back in Fogo has rooms at $55/60; as an oddity their lounge claims the largest dance floor east of Montreal. Two or three more B&Bs and a hotel round out the options. It's a good idea to book ahead before arriving in July and early August. In Fogo, there is *Beaches Bar & Grill* for seafood and traditional Newfoundland dishes.

NEWFOUNDLAND & LABRADOR

New World Island

From the mainland, causeways almost imperceptibly connect Chapel Island, tiny Strong's Island, New World and Twillingate islands.

At **Newville** the tourist office is open 9 am to 9 pm daily during the summer and has maps of the area and a sheet describing some of the trails and walks on Twillingate.

Dildo Run Provincial Park (☎ 709-629-3350) is central with camping and picnicking, set in a wooded area by a bay. Due to currents, swimming is not recommended. Sites are $11.

The western section of New World Island is far less visited and has some of the area's older houses in the small fishing villages clinging to the rough, rocky edges of the sea. At **Moreton's Harbour** is a small museum in an old-style house furnished in much the manner it would have been when the town was a prosperous fishing centre. It's open daily from 10 am to 8 pm except at lunch and dinner.

There are several very small parks around where picnicking and even camping are possible although facilities are minimal. One of them is **Wild Cove Park**, 2km north of Moreton's Harbour on the road to Tizzard's Harbour. The facilities amount to a single picnic table and a pair of doorless outhouses but the cove is extremely scenic.

Twillingate Island

Actually consisting of two islands, north and south Twillingate, this is the area in all of Notre Dame Bay that gets the most attention and deservedly so. It's stunningly beautiful, with every turn of the road revealing new ocean vistas, colourful fishing wharves or tidy groups of pastel houses perched on cliffs and outcrops.

The **Long Point Lighthouse** is a spectacular place with dramatic views of the coastal cliffs. This is an ideal place to watch for icebergs which are fairly common in May and June and not unusual in July. Places around Twillingate even sell the ice; you can get it in your drinks.

You can visit the 114-year-old lighthouse and a guide will lead you up the winding stairs of 44 steps to the top where you can enjoy the 360-degree view or watch the light flashing. Hours are 10 am to 8 pm Monday through Saturday and 4 to 7 pm on Sunday. Admission is free.

In Twillingate town is the **Twillingate Museum** (☎ 709-884-2825) in what was formerly the Anglican rectory. Twillingate, one of the oldest towns in this part of the province, was settled by British merchants in the mid-1700s. One room displays articles brought back from around the world by local sea captains and includes a cabinet from India, a hurdy-gurdy from Germany and an Australian boomerang. Another room details the seal hunt and its controversy. Hours are 10 am to 9 pm daily from 1 June to 30 September; some Sundays it may open later. Admission is $1. Next door is **St Peter's Church** which dates from 1844 and is one of the oldest wooden churches in Newfoundland.

Twillingate Adventure Tours (☎ 709-884-5999, ☎ 1-888-447-8687) is an exceedingly friendly operation with two-hour iceberg tours (possibly whales and seabirds too) departing from the wharf; generally three tours depart daily, each costing $25.

Durrell Don't neglect to tour around unbelievably scenic Durrell. Many of the two-storey, box-like wooden houses are over 100 years old. The **Iceberg Shop** in a barn from the 1860s is an interpretation centre on the first floor and a craft shop on the top floor. Twillingate Island Tours (☎ 709-884-2242) also operates from the shop, offering three highly recommended boat trips a day to view icebergs and whales along the jagged local shores. The cost is $25 for adults, $15 for children. Across the road is the *Cod Trappers* restaurant – good for reasonably priced seafood.

Also here is the **Durrell Museum** perched way up on a hill. It has displays on what the fishing community of the early 1900s was like. It's open daily from 11 am to 9 pm and admission is 50¢. Even better than the museum are the views from this high point. Bring your lunch; there are a couple of picnic tables outside.

Fish, Fun & Folk Festival Held each year during the last week of July, the festival is a 'don't miss' event. The four-day festival features traditional music and dance, some of which goes back to the 16th century. There are fishing exhibits, lots of great food and crafts as well. This is a busy time of year what with the possibility of whales and icebergs lurking offshore, so book early if it is at all possible.

Places to Stay *Sea Breeze Municipal Park* beside the Long Point Lighthouse is a glorious, very inexpensive – though primitive – place to bed down. The unserviced sites are $4 a night and the park includes a picnic shelter and hiking trails to highpoints overlooking the coast.

The *Hillside B&B* (☎ 709-884-5761, 5 Young's Lane), just up the hill from the Iceberg Shop, is a house built in 1874. It features fine views of the harbour and lighthouse. Singles/doubles are $40 with a light breakfast. Nearby is *Toulin-guent Inn* (☎ 709-884-2080, 56 Main St) right on the water with three rooms at $45/55.

The *Anchor Inn* (☎ 709-884-2776), with views from on top of a hill, has some rooms in the lodge, some more motel-style rooms and some with cooking facilities at $55/60, but for $5 more housekeeping units are offered. There is also a dining room.

Harbour Lights Inn (☎ 709-884-2763) is the newest lodge, an historical house that was renovated in 1995. It's located right on the harbour and charges $50 and up, light breakfast included. It's popular, so call ahead. South of town at Little Harbour is *Beach Rock B&B* (☎ 709-884-2292) at $35/45.

Places to Eat The *R&J* has fish and chips and a great view of one of the many harbours. The *Anchor Inn* has a dining room and bar. There is also a Chinese restaurant, takeout cafés and foodstores in town. One of the newer local cafés is *Marg's Kitchen* in the Beach Rock B&B.

You could also get dinner and a show at the *Fisher Players Dinner Theatre* (☎ 709-884-5415, ☎ 1-888-287-7884) which serves Newfoundland food at 7 pm Monday through Saturday, followed by a show.

AROUND TWILLINGATE

From Twillingate the road leads through Birchy Bay past timber and farming districts once roamed by the Beothuk Indians. The newest provincial interpretive centre, at Boyd's Cove, is devoted to the extinct tribe. The **Beothuk Interpretation Centre** (☎ 709-729-0592) features displays, exhibits and a video theatre that explain the archaeological discoveries of a nearby Beothuk village. From the centre you can then walk a short trail to the sites of the digs. The centre is open from 10 am to 5.30 pm daily during

Beothuk Indians

Scattered around much of north-central Newfoundland, the Beothuks, a distinct cultural group, inhabited the area from about 500 years ago until 1829, when the last woman died. It was they, their faces painted red with ochre, who were first dubbed 'redmen' by the arriving Europeans, a name that was soon to be applied to all the Native peoples of North America.

Semi-nomadic, they travelled the rivers, notably the Exploits, in birch bark canoes between the inland lakes and the sea at Notre Dame Bay. They were not a violent people and there weren't large numbers of them. As a result of hostility, firepower, and diseases from white people, the ultimate tragedy unfolded. Before anybody had enough gumption or time it was realised there was just a handful of Beothuk Indians left. By the early 1800s there were only two women alive to leave what knowledge they could.

Both the Mary March Museum and a re-created village in Grand Falls outline what is known of the Beothuks. The Newfoundland museum in St John's also has a display, including a skeleton – the only known remains anywhere. The Beothuk Trail, Hwy 380, leads through some of their former lands.

summer and admission is free. From Hwy 340 head along the road to South Boyd's Cove to reach it in 2km.

LEWISPORTE

With a population of 4500, Lewisporte is the largest town along the coast and is known primarily for its ferry terminal. Other than the boats, there really isn't much reason to visit – though as a distribution centre it does have all the goods and services.

The **Bye The Bay Museum & Craft Shop** (☎ 709-535-2844) in the large wooden Women's Institute Building on Main St displays articles from the area's history, including a long, colourful handmade rug depicting various facets in the life and times of Lewisporte. Hours in the summer are 9 am to 5 pm daily, except Sunday, with extended hours possible in July and August. It closes from noon to 1 pm. Admission is 50¢.

Several people offer boat trips to the quiet, rocky **Exploits Islands** where local people have summer cottages, whereas Caribou Adventure Tours (☎ 709-535-8379) runs a safari-like trip to observe woodland caribou as well as canoe, mountain bike, and backpacking trips.

Places to Stay & Eat

You can camp in town at **Sunset Hideaway Campground** (☎ 709-535-0560), which features showers and a swimming area or at **Notre Dame Provincial Park** (☎ 709-535-2379) 14km from town on the Trans Canada Hwy. Both are $9 a night but keep in mind that Notre Dame will often fill up during summer.

There are three guesthouses right on Main St. **Northgate B&B** (☎ 709-535-2258, 106 Main St), a short walk from the ferry terminal, is $40/50 including a breakfast of bread, muffins and homemade jams. On the way into town from Hwy 341 is **Brittany Inns** (☎ 709-535-2533) with 37 hotel, motel and housekeeping rooms from $59. There is a dining room.

For other places to eat try the mall near the junction of Hwys 340 and 341. Fast food places are pretty much everywhere. There is

a bakery here and a Sobey's grocery store which could be useful if you're getting on board one of the ferries. On Main St the **Oriental Restaurant** has dinners for under $7.

Getting There & Away

Bus The DRL bus running between Port aux Basques and St John's makes stops at Notre Dame Junction at the Edison Irving service station (☎ 709-535-6749) south of town on Trans Canada Hwy. The bus for St John's departs at 3.54 pm daily and the one for Port aux Basques at 1.25 pm. This is about 16km from town and the ferry dock. Taxis meet the bus arrivals.

Ferry The ferries out of Lewisporte which go to Happy Valley-Goose Bay, Labrador, are run by Coastal Labrador Marine Services. Information and reservations for them can be obtained through the provincial tourism information office (☎ 1-800-563-6353).

The car-carrying ferry (☎ 709-535-6876) goes to Cartwright on the Labrador coast then on through Hamilton Inlet to large Lake Melville (which the Vikings may have visited) and on to Happy Valley-Goose Bay in the heart of Labrador where there is an important military base.

With a vehicle you can go from here across central Labrador to Churchill Falls and beyond to Labrador City at the Quebec border. The road continues south through Quebec to Baie Comeau.

The ferry to Goose Bay is a serious ride taking about 38 hours and only making the one stop en route. A variation is the direct trip with no stop in Cartwright. This knocks about three hours off the total travel time.

A one-way ticket is $97; add $160 for a car. Reduced rates are offered for children and seniors. Cabins are available at additional charge; the cheapest dorm berth is $38. There are two ferries a week in each direction (one direct, one with the stop) from mid-June to approximately mid-September that depart every four days: first the direct, then the one with the stop four days later etc. The direct boat leaves at 10 pm (no meal the first night, so eat first), the latter at 4 pm.

Tickets might be available on the same day, but – especially in summer – they make no promises, and if you have a car you're likely out of luck.

If you are driving, you can leave your car at the ferry terminal in Lewisporte. There is a security guard but a waiver must be signed discounting responsibility.

Arrive 90 minutes before departure in either Lewisporte or Happy Valley-Goose Bay.

GRAND FALLS & WINDSOR

These two small towns sit in pulp and paper country. Actually Windsor seems more like a suburb of Grand Falls and it is the latter which is of more interest to the visitor.

There's a tourist chalet information booth (☎ 709-489-6332) on the highway about 2km west of town and it's open from 8 am to 8 pm. The **Mary March Museum** (☎ 709-292-4522), on the corner of Cromer Ave and St Catherine St, is particularly worthy and among other things outlines the life of the extinct Beothuk Indians. The museum is open daily from 9 am to 5 pm weekdays and 12.30 to 5 pm on the weekends, 10 am to 6 pm in July and August, and is free.

Adjacent to the museum set in the woods is a re-creation of a Beothuk Indian village. It's open from 10 am to 7 pm daily and admission is $2.

Overlooking the Grand Falls, a series of rapids and small cascades, is the **Salmonid Interpretation Centre**. The centre itself has exhibits and displays covering the biology and history of the Atlantic salmon. There is also an observation deck where you can watch the fish struggle upstream during its spawning run. Hours are 8 am to dusk during summer and admission is $3. You reach the centre from the downtown area by crossing the Exploits River from Scott St then following the signs.

Not far west of town, **Beothuk Park** has an exhibit simulating a late 19th/early 20th century logging camp. The exhibit is free and is open from 10 am to 5.30 pm.

Places to Stay & Eat

Camping is available at Beothuk Park, 2km west of town. A tent site costs $9. There are a couple of expensive motels in town or the *Poplar Inn (☎ 709-489-2546, 22 Poplar Rd)*, a B&B at a lesser rate with singles/doubles at $45 and up. As such, it fills up fast. Poplar Rd runs off Lincoln Rd behind the Mt Peyton Hotel. The DRL stop is walkable, about 3km away. On the way to the city centre is the newly redone *Hotel Robin Hood (☎ 709-489-5324, 78 Lincoln Rd)* with rooms for $69/79.

Grand Falls' city centre is Church Rd and High St but most of the commercial district is now on the north side of the Trans Canada Hwy along Cromer Ave. Here you will find the fast-food chains, large foodstores and malls. Out by the tourist chalet is *Loung's Restaurant* with a $7 Chinese buffet served daily.

Getting There & Away

The DRL bus stops at the Highliner Inn west of town.

SOUTH OF GRAND FALLS

Hwy 360 runs 130km through the centre of the province to the south coast. It's a long way down to the first settlements at the end of **Bay d'Espoir**, a huge fjord. The cliffs at **Morrisville** offer the best views. **St Alban's** is the main town and is connected with Grand Falls by bus. **Conne River** is a Micmac Indian town. There are a few motels and a campground around the end of the bay.

Going farther south you'll find a concentration of small, remote fishing villages. The scenery along Hwy 364 is particularly impressive, as are the aesthetics around **Harbour Breton**. Shutterbugs will definitely dig the place.

Places to Stay & Eat

Harbour Breton has a motel, the *Southern Port (☎ 709-885-2283)*, with rooms from $60 and the only dining room in town. A better choice is found in little English Harbour West at the *Olde Oven Inn (☎ 709-888-3461)* where singles/doubles are $40/50. The town is noted for its knitted sweaters. In Head of Bay d'Espoir there are three motels, generally charging $60 or more. The exception is

Pardy Cove Cottages (☎ 709-882-2233) with units at $45 to $50 for one or two people. (The other two have dining rooms.) *Jipujikuek Kuespem Park* near the junction to Head Bay d'Espoir has camping at $9 per day and likely few people. Harbour Breton does have a *supermarket*.

Getting There & Away

The Bay d'Espoir Bus Service (☎ 709-538-3429 in St Alban's) links Grand Falls to St Alban's. A bus leaves St Alban's on Monday, Wednesday and Friday at 8 am and arrives at Grand Falls at 11 am. The return trip leaves Grand Falls at 4 pm. Hickey's Bus Service (☎ 709-885-2523 in Harbour Breton) does pretty much the same run on the same days from Grand Falls to Harbour Breton.

At Pool's Cove you can board Rencontre East Ferry (☎ 709-891-1050) that makes one trip daily, except Wednesday, to Bay L'Argent on the south side of Fortune Bay. This would save a considerable amount of backtracking for travellers without a car. The cost is $6.50 and includes a stop at Rencontre East; all told the trip takes three hours. At Bay L'Argent, you can hike or hitch to Country Lodge on Hwy 210 to pick up bus transportation either to the Burin Peninsula or to St John's.

BAIE VERTE PENINSULA

Little-visited Baie Verte (Green Bay), north-west of Grand Falls, has a long history of human habitation. The Maritime Archaic Indians originally settled the edges of the peninsula and were followed by the Dorset Inuit who had a camp at or around **Fleur de Lys** from 1000 BC for several hundred years. There is a soapstone outcrop here from which the Inuit gouged the material for household goods such as lamps and for carvings.

Short ferry trips connect several of the islands. Springdale, the largest community in the area, has half a dozen choices for accommodation and camping at *George Huxter Memorial Park (☎ 709-673-4313)* 3km away where sites are $8 per night. There is also *Flatwater Pond Park (☎ 709-532-4472)* with 25 sites in the middle of the

peninsula 15km south of Baie Verte on Hwy 410. Camping is $9 a night here.

At **Baie Verte**, a relatively sizable town at the north-west end of the peninsula, see the Miners' Museum (☎ 709-532-8090) and tunnel; admission is $2. It doubles as the tourist office in town and is open from 9 am to 8 pm daily during summer. Just out of town, open-pit asbestos mining can be seen from an observation point off the main highway. The peninsula also has deposits of copper, gold, silver and zinc though much of it has been mined out. You can also visit some of the many abandoned mines nearby. In the past at little **Tilt Cove**, 5% of the world's nickel was mined.

La Scie is another good place to see an iceberg; boat trips are available.

The only bus service available is oddly enough from Corner Brook. Guy Bailey's Service (☎ 709-532-4642) has one trip per week on Monday. The bus goes to Corner Brook at 9 am, returning at 2 pm. The one-way fare is $25.

Western Newfoundland

DEER LAKE & AROUND

Very little is here for the visitor but it's a convenient jumping-off point for trips up the northern peninsula. A tourist chalet open from 8 am to 9 pm daily sits right on the Trans Canada Hwy. In town the *Driftwood Inn (☎ 709-635-5115, 3 Nicholas Rd)*, a large white, green-trimmed wooden building – an easy walk from Main St – is a good place to stay, although it's not cheap with rooms from $58 for a single. There is also *Deer Lake Municipal Park (☎ 709-635-5885)* which has 40 unserviced sites and showers. It's $9 a night. Most of the restaurants are fast-food chains on the Trans Canada Hwy but there is *Tai Lee Garden*, a simple, cheap Chinese place in the middle of Main St.

The DRL bus stops in Deer Lake at the Irving Big Stop (☎ 709-635-2130) on the

Trans Canada Hwy; straight to/from St John's is $70. If you're coming from the east, the bus gets in at around 5 pm, 10 minutes too late to pick up the Viking Express bus north up the peninsula. In this case you should call Viking in advance and let it know you're coming (see Corner Brook later in this chapter); be forewarned that the bus won't wait long if you're late. If you're coming from Port aux Basques, you could hop off in Corner Brook and line up the bus from there, likely needing an overnight stay.

Between the town of Deer Lake and Corner Brook the road passes through scenic landscape alongside Deer Lake where many locals have summer cottages or trailers. Around **Pasadena Beach** there are some motels and cabins available for visitors.

NORTHERN PENINSULA

From Deer Lake the immense northern peninsula extends 430km northward to Labrador along one of the most extraordinary, eye-catching roads in eastern North America. Called the Viking Trail, Hwy 430 extends between the coast and the Long Range Mountains to two UN World Heritage sites, another National Historic Site, two provincial parks, wonderfully barren far north topography and views over the history-filled Strait of Belle Isle to the coast of remote Labrador. You'll find lots of wildlife, ranging from large mammals to specialised fauna, unbelievably various and abundant – and huge – edible berries, spectacular fjords, excellent salmon fishing, small coastal fishing villages and exceedingly friendly people.

Even for those without a lot of time a trip from Port aux Basques to the northern peninsula, if only as far as Gros Morne, makes a visit to Newfoundland memorable. Many people make this region the focus of their trip to 'The Rock' and never go farther east than Deer Lake. L'Anse-aux-Meadows, a 1000-year-old Viking settlement (by far the oldest European landing site in North America, centuries ahead of Chris Columbus) has become somewhat of a pilgrimage site drawing a small but determined group from all over the USA and, to a lesser extent, Europe.

All of this has led to a growing number of tourists in recent years which has meant an increase in services along the way. Motels, cabins and B&Bs line one end of the peninsula to the other to complement the campgrounds (though they can still fill up in peak summer periods). It can be a wet, cool region with a lot of bugs as well, so if you're tenting be prepared for maybe the odd night in a motel.

It's roughly a five to six-hour drive from Deer Lake to St Anthony but even the price of gasoline is not as exorbitant as it once was.

Bus transportation is possible if a bit spotty along the entire route.

Gros Morne National Park

Gros Morne National Park is a must for its magnificent, preternaturally varied geography which has earned it status as a World Heritage Site, not to mention the moniker 'Galapagos of Geology'. Special features include fjords that rival Scandinavia's, the majestic barren Tablelands, unrivalled mountain hiking trails, sandy beaches and historic little fishing communities. There is plenty of wildlife including caribou and moose, and offshore seals and, occasionally, whales. Part of the UN designation is due to the park's Precambrian, Cambrian and Ordovician rock and the evidence this rock supplies researchers with for the theory of plate tectonics. Another factor was the site's 4500 years of human occupation.

Woody Point, Norris Point and Rocky Harbour are the principal commercial centres with Rocky Harbour being the main community, where there are all the amenities including a laundrette and grocery stores.

In the southern portion of the park, Hwy 431 leads to Woody Point and beyond to the Tablelands and Green Gardens. The village of Woody Point, site of a hostel, makes a good centre for seeing this portion of the park but keep in mind it's more than an hour's drive back to the main visitors centre along winding roads around Bonne Bay.

Information The park has two information centres, a smaller one on Hwy 430 as

you approach Wiltondale and the main one (☎ 709-458-2066) 25km from the entrance on Hwy 430 at the exit to Norris Point. At either centre you need to purchase the entrance permit. It's $3.25 per adult per day, less for seniors and children; the family rate is $6.50. Multi-day passes make it much cheaper. Maps, books and backcountry permits are available at both while the main centre also has an impressive interpretive area that includes a multi-image slide show. Both centres are open daily from 9 am to 10 pm during summer.

Construction is underway on an impressive new **Discovery Centre** in Woody Point. Interactive exhibits and a multi-media theatre will explain the ecology of the park and its World Heritage status. It should be open by the time you read this.

Things to See & Do In the south-west corner of the park are the compelling **Tablelands**, by the road's edge, not far from Woody Point. This is a barren 80km ledge of rock 700m high shoved up from beneath the ocean floor – a glimpse of the earth's insides. You can view this phenomenon from points along Hwy 431 and there's a short trail to the base of the barren mountains.

Heading farther west, **Green Gardens** is a volcanic coast that features sea caves and sea stacks. It's an hour hike from the second trailhead of the Green Garden Trail to the coast. At the end of the highway is **Trout River**, a small, picturesque fishing community. Operating here is Tableland Boat Tours (☎ 709-451-2101) which runs three trips daily up Trout River Pond past the Tablelands.

From the government wharf in Norris Point two-hour boat trips of **Bonne Bay** depart daily at 10 am and 2 pm stopping over in Woody Point for more people to board before cruising the Arms. Tickets cost $20 for adults, less for children. A family rate is $42. Book and purchase tickets for the tour at the Ocean View Motel (☎ 709-458-2730, ☎ 1-800-563-9887) in Rocky Harbour. If you do this trip and the Western Brook Pond boat tour, the operator may give a discount on one or the other. Heritage Schooner Charters

(☎ 709-639-8675) also operates from Government Wharf with its schooner departing at 10 am and 3 pm daily ($40) and heading over to Woody Point for more passengers.

A cheaper way to get a glimpse of Bonne Bay and the Tablelands area would be to get a $10 (less for children; family rates are available) boat/bus combination which allows unlimited travel for one day. Boats travel to and from Norris Point and Woody Point three times from 9 am to 5.30 pm, and buses ply the route to Trout River from Woody Point. Tickets can be purchased at the visitors centres or the Ocean View Motel.

Near Rocky Harbour is a recreation complex with a 25m swimming pool and whirlpool. It has various swim times daily for $3 per adult.

Farther up the coast past Sally's Cove, parts of the wreck of the SS *Ethie* which ran aground in 1919 can be seen on the beach. The storm and subsequent rescue sparked the writing of a song about the incident.

Western Brook Pond is the park's feature fjord with dwarfing cliffs nearly 700m high running vertically from the cool waters. Boat tours of the 15km-long fjord are offered and definitely recommended. The 2½ hour trip takes you past sheer cliffs towering at the water's edge. The trips are very popular and you usually need to make reservations in summer. They can be made at the Ocean View Motel in Rocky Harbour at least a day in advance.

The tours run from June to the end of September with three trips daily at 10 am, 1 pm and 4 pm (and 6 pm if demand warrants it) each taking up to 40 passengers. A ticket costs $27, less for kids. The dock is reached after an easy 3km walk from the road along the Western Brook Pond Trail; keep in mind it takes 40 minutes.

Just north of here in Cow Head are the perennially popular theatrical presentations of the summer-long *Gros Morne Theatre Festival (☎ 709-639-7238, ☎ 1-800-563-1946)*. Performances – nearly every day, except Monday in July and August – may be outdoors or in, and tickets range in price from $5 to $13.

The gentle, safe, sand-duned beach at **Shallow Bay** at the other end of the geographic spectrum seems almost out of place – as if transported from the Caribbean by some bizarre current. The water, though, provides a chilling dose of reality, rarely getting above 15°C.

At **Broom Point** there is a restored fishing camp depicting the inshore fishery of the 1960s. The three Nudge brothers and their families fished here from 1941 to 1975 when they sold the entire camp, including boats, lobster traps and nets, to the national park. Everything has been restored and now staffed with interpretive guides. Broom Point is open daily from 10 am to 6 pm from June to September.

Also keep in mind that the park staff host interpretive programs, guided walks and evening programs throughout summer. The walks are a great way to help understand the fascinating geology of the park.

Hiking & Skiing Gros Morne National Park maintains 23 trails that total 80km and feature seven backcountry camping areas for what arguably could be some of the best trekking in Newfoundland.

The gem of the park's trail system is **James Callahan Gros Morne Trail** to the peak of Gros Morne, the highest point in the area at 806m. The 16km return trek is said to be a seven to eight-hour hike but many people can cover it in less time. The trail is well maintained with steps and boardwalks but is still a tough hike, especially the steep rock gully that must be climbed to the ridgeline of the mountain. This is not a trail for tennis shoes. The views at the top and of 10-Mile Pond, a sheer-sided fjord, make the effort well worth it. There is backcountry camping in Fern Gulch along the trail and a popular backpacking trip is to set up there for a couple of nights and scale the mountain without the packs.

Green Gardens Trail is almost as scenic and challenging. The 18km loop has two trailheads off Hwy 431 with each one descending a valley to the Green Gardens, a volcanic coastline. Plan on seven to 10 hours for the entire loop or book one of the three backcountry camping areas, all of them on the ocean, and turn the hike into an overnight adventure.

Shorter but just as scenic are **Tablelands Trail**, that extends 2km to Winterhouse Brook Canyon for a 4km return hike; **Lookout Trail** near Woody Point, a 5km loop to the site of an old fire tower above the treeline; and **Western Brook Pond Trail**, the most popular trail in the park which is an easy 6km return hike to the western end of the fjord.

Other overnight treks include **Stanley-ville Trail**, a round trip of 4km to the site of an old logging camp where there is backcountry camping. This easy trail begins in the Lomond day-use area off Hwy 431. Western Brook Pond Trail and **Snug Harbour Trail** can be combined for a 7km one-way hike to backcountry camp sites in the famous fjord. Or book your passage on the tour boat and have it drop you off at the head of Western Brook Pond where there are several more backcountry camp sites.

Backcountry camp sites are $10 per person per night and must be booked in advance at the visitors centres. If you plan to do several trails, invest $10 in a copy of *Gros Morne National Park Trail Guide*, a waterproof map of the park with trail descriptions on the backside.

Many of the trails are utilised as cross-country trails but in recent years the park has undertaken an ambitious ski trail construction program and the 55km available now – many designed by Pierre Harvey, Canadian Olympic champion – are impressive. The best place to start is the main visitors centre, with its ski chalet, rentals, loop trails, and lighted night trails.

Organised Tours & Rentals Well organised Gros Morne Adventure Guides (☎ 709-458-2722, ☎ 1-800-685-4624) is found where the road ends in Norris Point. Popular half-day sea kayak tours of Bonne Bay leave three times daily from 9 am to 6 pm and cost $40; a full day runs $90. Multi-day trips or trips to Western Brook Pond can be arranged. There also are day-long or multi-day hiking,

skiing and snowshoeing trips from $65. Reservations are required.

Gros Morne Mountain Bike Outfitters (☎ 709-458-3555) is in Rocky Harbour and rents mountain bikes for $20 per day, along with camping equipment.

Places to Stay & Eat Within the national park are five *campgrounds*, located at Trout River, Lomond, Berry Hill, Green Point and Shallow Bay. The fees range from $11 (for Green Point which does not have showers) to $15.25 a night.

Two hostel possibilities exist, a dizzying, unheard of array for Newfoundland. *Juniper Campground* (☎ 709-458-2917) in Rocky Harbour runs a six-bunk hostel in a large cabin that includes a kitchen and showers. The cost is $10 a night. In Woody Point there is the HI *Woody Point Hostel* (☎ 709-453-7254 ☎ 709-453-2470). It's open from the end of May to October and features a kitchen and 10 beds for $10 a night for members, $12 for nonmembers. It is on School Rd, at the rear of the clinic, just up the hill, first right then first left, from Irving Auto Service which doubles as the bus station, and is open all day.

Also in Woody Point is the *Victorian Manor* (☎ 709-453-2485), a hospitality home with rooms in the nice old house or newer two-bedroom efficiency cabins. In the main house, the four rooms cost $50 and up with a light breakfast included. Laundry and bike/canoe rentals are also offered. In nearby Trout River is the small but cosy and very friendly *Crocker's B&B* (☎ 709-451-5220) next to the gas station with rooms from $30.

Across the bay in Norris Point there are more choices. *Eileen's B&B* (☎ 709-458-2427) has two rooms available from June to September with singles/doubles for $30/35 including a light breakfast.

At Rocky Harbour, you could stay at *Gros Morne Cabins* (☎ 709-58-2020), 22 individual log cabins with kitchens and views over the ocean. Inquire at Endicott's variety store. The price is $69 for a one-bedroom place large enough for up to two adults and two kids. There is also *Ocean View Motel* (☎ 709-458-2730, ☎ 1-800-563-9887) at $60/70 a single or double. *Evergreen B&B* (☎ 709-458-2692) is a pleasant place with laundry facilities and four rooms with shared bath that cost $35/39. Plenty of other B&Bs are here.

Restaurants are found in all villages; grocery stores are in most (not Trout River). For a munch, *Jackie's* in Rocky Harbour has good home-made french fries and fruit pies and an outdoor deck. The *Narrows Head Restaurant*, not far from the Trout River Campground, is good for fresh and affordable seafood. But in Trout River for a splurge head directly for the well regarded *Seaside* (☎ 709-451-3461) with a wide range of moderately priced seafood, all very well done.

Getting There & Around Martin's Bus Service (☎ 709-453-2207 in Woody Point, ☎ 709-634-4710 in Corner Brook) connects Woody Point with Corner Brook via daily runs Monday to Friday. It departs Trout River at 9 am, Woody Point at 9.30 am and Corner Brook for the return trip at 4.30 pm. The one-way fare between Woody Point and Corner Brook is $12. In Woody Point, Martin's departs from Irving Auto Service.

The Viking Express bus (☎ 709-634-4710 in Corner Brook) departs Corner Brook at 4 pm for St Anthony via Deer Lake on Monday, Wednesday and Friday, overnights at St Anthony and then makes a return run the following day. It stops at Norris Point (across Bonne Bay from Woody Point) and at Ocean View Motel in Rocky Harbour on demand for those who want to continue north. Call the bus company in Corner Brook to be sure of pick-up. There is also a Pittman's Bus Service (☎ 709-458-2084 in Rocky Harbour, ☎ 709-634-4710 in Corner Brook) that begins in Rocky Harbour for Corner Brook, departing at 9 am Monday through Friday; no set stop exists so you'll have to call the service to arrange pick-up. In Corner Brook buses depart from the Millbrook Mall (see Corner Brook later in this chapter).

The Arches

Out of the park back northward on Hwy 430, The Arches is worth stopping at for a

stroll down to the beach which is littered with beautiful, smooth, coloured rocks about the size of footballs. The main attractions, though, are the three limestone arches and the remains of maybe three or four more formed some 400 million years ago.

Table Point Ecological Reserve

North of Bellburns along the shore there are protected sections of limestone 470 million years old containing abundant fossils.

River of Ponds Park

On the Pond River which is good for salmon, there is a park with a 40-site campground. The unserviced sites are $9 a night. If nothing else, pull in to see the display of whale bones estimated to be 5000 to 7000 years old. They're huge.

Hawke's Bay

At the turn of the century, there was a whaling station halfway to St Anthony from Deer Lake, Hawke's Bay. There are some excellent salmon waters here and at the salmon ladder, a device to aid the fish in getting upstream.

Just behind the tourist office, open from 10 am to 7 pm daily in summer, is *Torrent River Nature Park (☎ 709-248-5344)*. The park has a campground with 10 serviced sites for $7 to $15 a night as well as showers. Nearby the **Hogan Trail** begins along the Torrent River. Most of the 3km walking trail is on a boardwalk and leads over marsh and through the woods to the salmon ladder. The town has a motel and two B&Bs.

Port au Choix

Busy and interesting Port au Choix is one of the biggest towns between Gros Morne and St Anthony. The principal attraction is **Port au Choix National Historic Site** (☎ 709-861-3522 during the season). Downtown is a Maritime Archaic Indian cemetery dating from 3200 to 4300 years ago. The remains of about 100 individuals as well as tools, weapons and ornaments were discovered here accidentally in 1967. Some of these artefacts are on view in a new visitors centre, situated a few kilo-

metres away through town by road, half-paved, half-gravel; just follow the signs. This site, known as **Phillip's Garden**, deals with the Dorset Inuit people who settled on the Cape Riche Peninsula between 1500 and 2200 years ago. The road continues beyond here to the 1871 **Point Riche lighthouse**. A trail exists from the north side of town; to walk to the lighthouse then loop around via the road to the visitors centre and back would be close to 6km. If you're not up for an ambitious hike, drive to the visitors centre, then take a guided hike into Phillip's Garden. The park's visitors centre (☎ 709-861-3522) is open daily during summer from 9 am to 8 pm and admission into the exhibits is $2. The interior features a reconstructed house along with touch-screen exhibits. The old visitors centre, now known as the Heritage Centre, has some artefacts. New exhibits are planned.

For a little more recent history, just out of town is a plaque outlining some of the tussles between the French and British for the fishing rights in the area which continued from the 1600s until the 1900s. In 1904 yet another treaty was signed in which the French relinquished their rights here in exchange for the privilege in Morocco.

Don't pass up Studio Gargamelle (☎ 709-861-3280), the workshop of artist Ben Ploughman. Outside he has an impressive whale skeleton exhibit, with the bones from an entire whale wired together.

Places to Stay & Eat In Port au Choix the economical choice is *Jeannie's Sunrise B&B (☎ 709-861-3679)* with an ocean view and rooms from $35. The more expensive *Sea Echo Motel (☎ 709-861-3777, ☎ 1-888-861-3777)* recently underwent renovation but look at a few rooms – for the money, they missed a few spots. Singles/doubles are $60 and up. The dining room is quite good, friendly and has good-value lunch specials.

The best meal in town is at *The Anchor Cafe*. Can't miss the place, the front half is the stern of a boat. A wide selection of seafood dinners are around $10 and a big bowl of seafood chowder with bread is $4.

About 50km north of town right beside the provincial picnic park is the private *Three Mile Lake Campground*. It's quiet, wooded and has a beach on the lake. There are 30 unserviced sites at $9 a night.

North from Port au Choix

Close to town, the mountains veer off to the east and don't have the same presence. The landscape becomes more and more barren until it appears pretty much like that found in the far Canadian north – an essentially flat, pond-filled primeval expanse. There is probably no other place in the country where this type of rugged terrain is as accessible.

At Plum Point a gravel road connects with the eastern shore; this is a part of Newfoundland that even travelhardy natives rarely see. At **Main Brook** there is *Tuckamore Lodge* (☎ 709-865-6361, ☎ 1-888-865-6361), an A-frame, B&B cottage with four rooms, a dining room, a fireplace and a sauna. Singles/doubles are $80. Meals are available. Call ahead before driving across the peninsula because the lodge is mainly used as a base for package adventure tours which include trips to see birds, caribou etc. It's also often used by hunters and anglers.

The main town over on this side is **Roddickton** and here, as in Main Brook, there are outfitters for hunting and fishing. *Betty's B&B* (☎ 709-457-2371) has rooms from $35 and a more expensive motel is here as well. There is also some hiking and a trip up Cloud Hill affords good views of the islands offshore.

Back on Hwy 430, **St Barbe** is the site of a ferry to Labrador (see Labrador later in this chapter). From here on up, the coast of Labrador is visible on clear days. *Dockside Motel* (☎ 709-877-2444) is relatively new with 16 rooms that go for $52/62 as well as 10 cabins for slightly more.

Pistolet Bay Provincial Park

With 30 sites in a wild but wooded area 20km from the main road and 40km from the Viking site, *Pistolet Bay Provincial Park* (☎ 709-551-1457) is the place to stay if you're camping. Be prepared for the mosquitoes and blackflies, as they seem to have a real mean streak. There is a comfort station at the park with hot showers and laundry facilities and it's heated. What luxury! Sites are $11 a night.

Also on Pistolet Bay is the privately run *Viking Trailer Park* (☎ 709-454-3541) with serviced sites for camper vehicles. Sites are $10 a night.

Cape Onion

The closest town for milk and bread (and beer) is the fishing village of **Raleigh** while another 8km farther north the road ends at Cape Onion. The cape reveals dramatic coastal scenery of islands, coves and also 'tickles', which in Newfoundland refer to narrow passages of water between two land formations. Also located here is the delightful *Tickle Inn* (☎ 709-452-4321 summer only). This seaside inn, built in 1890, features four rooms, a parlour warmed by a Franklin wood stove and excellent home-cooked meals of local seafood and Newfoundland dishes. Singles/doubles are $45/55 and include a light breakfast. Other meals are by request and boat tours of the coastline or a nearby shipwreck can be arranged.

Saint Lunaire to Straitsview

There are five small, old fishing villages on the way to the historic site of L'Anse-aux-Meadows. You may see kids by the road's edge selling berries collected out on the barrens. In mid-August this will include the queen of all Newfoundland berries, the golden bakeapple sold here for $30 per gallon (4.5L – the people here still use imperial measurements, unlike those in much of the country) and fetching as much as $50 farther south.

L'Anse-aux-Meadows National Historic Park

This is a fascinating place (☎ 709-623-2608) made all the more special by the unobtrusive, low-key approach of the park developers. In an unspoiled, waterside setting are the remains of the settlement – looking pretty much like it did in 1000 AD – created by Vikings from Scandinavia and

Greenland who became the first Europeans to land in North America. Replicas of sod buildings complete with the smoky smell almost transport you back in time.

These guys, led by Leif Eriksson, son of Eric the Red, built their own boats, sailed all over the North Atlantic, landed here, constructed houses which still remain, fed themselves and they were practically all just 20-something years old. Oops, let's not forget they smelted iron out of the bog and forged nails with it – 1000 years ago!

Allow two to three hours to browse through the interpretive centre with its artefacts, see the film and walk around the eight unearthed original wood and sod buildings and the three reconstructions.

Also captivating is the story of Norwegian explorer Helge Ingstad who discovered the site in 1960, ending years of searching. His tale and that of his archaeologist wife is told in the interpretive centre. A short walk behind the replica buildings leads to a small graveyard where lies the body of local inhabitant George Decker who made Ingstad's day by pointing out the mounds in the terrain. Costumed docents walk about, explaining everything; you may even get to sample a Viking meal.

Take time to walk the 3km trail that winds through the barren terrain and along the coast that surrounds the interpretive centre. The park, 43km from St Anthony's, is open from 9 am to 8 pm daily from mid-June to the beginning of September (Labour Day) and until 4.30 pm to October. Admission is $4, less for children, and $10 for a family.

If you're totally captivated by the Viking experience, nearby is Viking Boat Tours (☎ 709-454-3092 in St Anthony), which offers two-hour boat tours on a replica Viking ship. You don't have to row but you can't sail either, the Canadian Coast Guard won't allow it, so you motor around the bay looking at shipwrecks, icebergs and coastal scenery. The cost is $25 per person.

Places to Stay & Eat At the village of Gunner's Cove, 5km from the historic site, is the recommended *Valhalla Lodge* (☎ 709-623-

2018 summer only). The six Scandinavian-themed rooms are $50 with a light breakfast included. Maybe you can stay in the room where E Annie Proulx, Pulitzer Prize-winning author of *The Shipping News* stayed. Even closer and also highly recommended is *Marilyn's Hospitality Home* (☎ 709-623-2811) at Hay Cove, practically across from the entrance to the park. Singles/doubles are $35/40 with a full breakfast. Other meals are by request. The *Northern Delight* restaurant has enormous portions and lots of regional dishes.

There is no camping in the park but just past the entrance is a small roadside park where occasionally cyclists or hitchhikers will pitch a tent. In Straitsview, *Smith's Restaurant* serves meals of cod tongue, salt fish and brewis or scallops for under $3. Cod chowder, coffee and rolls is $6.

St Anthony

You made it! Unfortunately it's a little anticlimactic. With a population of 3500, and as the largest town in the north of the northern peninsula, it's functional and an important supply centre and fish-processing depot, but it's not what you'd call pretty.

At the Viking Mall downtown is a Sobey's grocery store for stocking up if you're taking the boat north. The Ultramar service station on the corner also doubles as a tourist centre with a few pamphlets on a rack.

Grenfell is a big name around here. Sir Wilfred Grenfell was a local legend and, by all accounts, quite a man. Born in England and educated as a doctor, he first came to Newfoundland in 1892 and for the next 40 years built hospitals, nursing stations and organised much needed fishing cooperatives along the coast of Labrador and around St Anthony. The **Grenfell Historic Properties** subsumes a number of local sites pertaining to him. Brand new in 1998 was the Grenfell Interpretation Centre (☎ 709-454-4004) right on Hwy 430 with various panelled displays about his life, as well as Grenfell Handicrafts. It's open from 9 am to 8 pm in summer. Admission is a steep $5, $10 for families. The Grenfell Museum (☎ 709-454-8596) nearby

is his former home and the fine old house with a large wraparound porch outlines his life and work. The museum is open daily from mid-June to the beginning of September from 9 am to 7 pm. Admission is $2. Also near the interpretation centre is the free **Dockhouse Museum**, where Grenfell Mission boats used to be repaired. It's now restored to its original 1920s look.

Follow the main road through town and it ends at **Fishing Point Park**. The towering headland cliffs here are impressive and there are a handful of short trails, with names like Iceberg Alley and Whale Watchers Trail, that head to observation platforms on the edge of the cliffs.

In August, watch for the annual cod filleting contest held in town. Admission is free. These guys can clean fish! And the Administration Building has a stuffed polar bear; this guy showed up on pack ice in 1984 and scared the willies out of locals but died of natural causes in the harbour before he could cause any mischief.

Places to Stay & Eat St Anthony has no shortage of places to stay. Between here and L'Anse-aux-Meadows, 7km from St Anthony, is *Triple Falls RV Park* (☎ 709-454-2599) which has 10 tent sites for $10 each. *Howell's Tourist Home* (☎ 709-454-3402, 76B East St) has four rooms at a good rate of $36/45. Meals are available and it's open all year. A second choice is the *Trailsend Hospitality Home* (☎ 709-454-2024, 1 Cormack St). Rates are $35/45 with a full breakfast.

Alternatively the newer, larger *Vinland Motel* (☎ 709-454-8843) on Hwy 430 in the centre of town is $65/80.

The motels have restaurants but it's almost obligatory to try a cup of chowder at *The Lightkeeper's Cafe*, the former lightkeeper's house at Fishing Point Park. Enjoy dinner while watching icebergs float by. During the summer it opens at 7 am.

Shopping There are three craft outlets in town including Grenfell Handicrafts with parkas embroidered by hand, whale-bone and ivory carvings, and other articles. The Mukluk Factory has sealskin leather goods and some carvings and jewellery. A mukluk is a traditional Inuit soft winter boot made of sealskin or caribou hide and sometimes fur lined. Northern Crafts has a bit of everything.

Getting There & Away In 1998 a road was paved from the St Anthony Airport around Hare Bay to Main Brook, thus opening Main Brook and Roddickton to obviate backtracking. Trouble is, there is still an unpaved (but maintained) segment from Main Brook to Roddickton.

Bus This is the final stop for the Viking Express bus (☎ 709-454-3939). The bus departs St Anthony for Corner Brook at 10 am Sunday, Tuesday and Thursday. To Corner Brook it's $45. From Corner Brook connections can be made for the transisland DRL bus to either Port aux Basques or St John's.

Ferry Coastal Labrador Marine Services runs a passenger and freight-only service – no cars – to Labrador. For information and reservations contact the provincial tourism information office (☎ 1-800-563-6353).

The ferry connects to Cartwright, Happy Valley-Goose Bay and then heads up the coast linking a series of small, remote outports. Other than Goose Bay-Happy Valley, there is no road access to these villages and that is part of their appeal. For car ferries see Getting There & Away under Lewisporte earlier in this chapter.

It's approximately a 12 to 14-day return trip to Nain, the northernmost point, about 1036 nautical miles from St Anthony. (A nautical mile is 6076 feet, a standard mile 5280 feet.) The ferries run from the first week of July to around mid-October not long before the coastal ice meets the Arctic pack ice and everything is sealed up until the summer thaw.

Towards the end of the season, even though November storms are a month away, the weather can play havoc with the schedule and the one-way trip can take twice as long. With high winds and waves close to

15m high, the ship is often harbour-bound for days at a time.

Normally, it's a comfortable ship with four meals a day (you didn't forget 'night lunch' did you?) and a choice not unlike that found in any mainland restaurant but with prices slightly higher. Fares are low and determined by the number of nautical miles travelled. The rate is roughly 25¢ per nautical mile and an additional 12¢ per nautical mile for an economy two-berth cabin (better cabins are available). Children and seniors pay less. To Red Bay it's 64 miles, thus $16, and to Goose Bay it's 570 miles or $142.50. To head to Nain and back with an economy cabin would be $765.

There are 47 possible ports of call along the entire return route and the number of stops partially determines the length of the trip. You can get off at the village of your choice but keep in mind that most of them are not set up for tourists and that there's not a whole lot to do while waiting for the ferry to return. At most ports, the ship usually needs one to two hours to unload and that is enough time for a good look around.

The low prices make the trip a bargain. Because of that, and the chance to visit some of the country's most remote settlements and view fine scenery, the trip has become popular with visitors. Less than half the tickets are for tourists as most are required for local residents and their supplies.

Be prepared when making a reservation to pay a 25% deposit. Most likely a credit card will be necessary. There are three trips a month in July and August, and two in September and October.

Air Flying to St Anthony is technically possible, but the airport is nearly an hour away.

CORNER BROOK

With 22,500 people, this is Newfoundland's second largest town after St John's. Up high beside the waters of Humber Arm, it is fairly attractive despite the often pervasive smell – a reminder that the focus of the town is the huge pulp and paper mill. The Corner Brook area is likely the sunniest re-

gion of the province and the warm, clear skies of summer can be a real treat.

Downtown is Main St by Remembrance Square and up along maple tree-lined Park St towards the Heritage District.

Information

The large tourist office (☎ 709-639-9792) and craft shop can't be missed just off the Trans Canada Hwy near the turn-offs into town. Hours are 8 am to 8 pm during summer.

Captain James Cook Monument

North-west of downtown up on cliffs overlooking the Humber Arm is a National Historic Site commemorating Captain Cook. A map from the tourist office is necessary as the road access is pretty convoluted. Mr Cook certainly got around. He surveyed this entire region in the mid-1760s and his names for many of the islands, ports and waterways such as the Humber Arm and Hawke's Bay remain. His work here was so successful it led to voyages to New Zealand and Australia.

Heritage District

The older section of town dating from 1925 to 1940 surrounds Central St. It's primarily a residential area though there are some shops and a few restaurants.

Humbermouth Historic Train Site

The Humbermouth depot is presently being restored as a provincial historical site. But already on display is rolling stock for the Newfoundland passenger train and a snowplow car, both utilising Newfoundland's narrower gauge.

Arts & Culture Centre

Part of Memorial University, the Arts and Culture Centre (☎ 637-2581) features a 400-seat performing arts facility and The Art Gallery, which displays the works of local artists as well as touring art shows. Culture is fine but many of us head to the centre because it also houses the pool. This is the place to come if you need a shower. There are various swim times during summer and the cost per session is $2.75.

NEWFOUNDLAND & LABRADOR

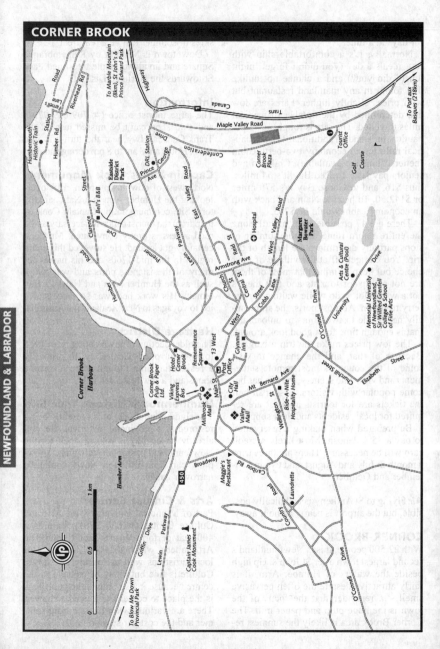

CORNER BROOK

To Marble Mountain (8km), St John's & Prince Edward Park

Trans Canada Highway

Maple Valley Road

Confederation Drive

Corner Brook Plaza

Tourist Office

Golf Course

To Port aux Basques (218km)

Humbermouth Historic Train Station

Humber Rd

Farrell's Lane

Riverhead Rd

Road

Station

Street

Humber Rd

Eastside District Park

Bell's B&B

Clarence Drive

Premier Road

Humber Road

DRL Station

Prince Ave

George St

Valley Road

East Valley Road

Lewin Parkway

West Valley Road

Hospital

Margaret Bowater Park

Armstrong Ave

Reid St

Church St

Central St

Cobb Lane

West St

University Drive

O'Connell Drive

Arts & Cultural Centre (Pool)

Memorial University of Newfoundland, Sir Wilfred Grenfell College & School of Fine Arts

Corner Brook Harbour

Corner Brook Pulp & Paper Ltd

Remembrance Square

Hotel Corner Brook

13 West

Glynmill Inn

Post Office

City Hall

Main St

Mt Bernard Ave

Bide-A-Nite Hospitality Home

Wellington St

Elizabeth Street

Churchill Street

Viking Express Bus

Millbrook Mall

Valley Mall

Humber Arm

Broadway

Maggie's Restaurant

Caribou Rd

450

Country Road

Laundrette

O'Connell Drive

Griffin Drive

Lewin Parkway

Captain James Cook Monument

To Blow Me Down Provincial Park

1 km

0.5

0

NEWFOUNDLAND & LABRADOR

Scene from Acadian Historic Village, near Caraquet, New Brunswick

Acadian Historic Village, New Brunswick

Re-creating Viking village life, Newfoundland

Impromptu music on the Labrador Straits ferry

Sod Viking hut re-creations, L'Anse-aux-Meadows, Newfoundland

Boat scenes near North Rustico, PEI

Pioneer Acadian Village, Mont Carmel, PEI

Parking lot outside North Atlantic Aviation Museum, Gander, Newfoundland

Places to Stay

The closest place to set up a tent is *Prince Edward Park* (☎ 709-637-1580), a five minute drive from the tourist centre. Take the Riverside Drive exit as you approach Corner Brook from the east and follow the signs along, and over, the Humber River. There are 40 unserviced sites in a wooded setting for $9 a night. Farther away but more scenic is *Blow Me Down Provincial Park* (☎ 709-681-230) at the end of Route 450 which leads from town along the Humber Arm. Out here at the tip of the peninsula there are 28 sites, showers and laundry facilities along with hiking trails and some good views of the Bay of Islands. Sites are $11 a night.

Corner Brook has a handful of tourist homes with prices lower than the numerous motel chains. The most affordable is *Bide-A-Nite Hospitality Home* (☎ 709-634-7578, 11 Wellington St) with two rooms for $35/45, breakfast included. The central *Bell's B&B* (☎ 709-634-5736, 2 Ford's Rd) is within walking distance of downtown. It is open all year, has eight rooms that start at $39/49, with continental breakfast. Still cheaper are summertime single dorm rooms at *Memorial University* (☎ 709-637-6477, after 4 pm ☎ 709-637-6200), which usually run around $25.

For more gracious accommodation the *Glynmill Inn* (☎ 709-634-5181) on Cobb Lane in downtown, is recommended. It's a large Tudor-style inn set off by surrounding lawns and gardens and offers a good dining room as well. Rooms and suites range from $62 to $135.

Places to Eat

The *More or Less* store (35 Broadway) is good for hiking and camping foods. Around the corner is the dependable *Maggie's* (26 Caribou Rd) with outstanding Newfie pea soup and a few veggie items.

Corner Brook's mainstay for a splurge has long been the dining room and wine cellar of the Glynmill Inn, but then there's one of the province's most well received new bistros, *13 West* (13 West St), around the corner from Remembrance Square. This creative eatery features an eclectic menu of meat, seafood and pasta. Main courses range from $8 to $21 and rarely miss the mark in quality.

Getting There & Away

Corner Brook is a major hub for bus service throughout Newfoundland. Most – but not all – regional operators use a bus station (☎ 709-634-4710) in the centre of town, adjacent to the Millbrook Mall shopping centre, not far from Main St. Unfortunately, DRL, for points east and west along the Trans Canada Hwy, uses Robertson's Irving station (☎ 709-634-7422) about 3km from the city centre on the highway. It has a bus heading west at 5.55 pm daily, a bus east at 11.25 am. Passage to Port aux Basques is $17, to St John's $75. No city buses link the two bus depots.

Gateway also has a shuttle to Port aux Basques leaving Corner Brook daily at 3.45 pm for $25.

From the main station the Viking Express bus goes up the northern peninsula. A bus leaves Monday, Wednesday and Friday at 4 pm for St Anthony. One way to St Anthony is $45. This will make stops in Rocky Harbour for Gros Morne National Park. Pittman's also departs from here for Rocky Harbour; a bus leaves daily at 4.30 pm.

Martin's Bus Service goes to Woody Point and Trout River in Gros Morne National Park. The bus departs at 4.30 pm Monday to Friday and the ticket is $12. Eddy's Bus Service (☎ 709-634-7777) runs to Stephenville three to four times daily. Its office is at 9 Humber Rd and the one-way fare is $10. Finally, if you need to reach Burgeo on the south coast, Devin's Bus Line (☎ 709-634-7777, ☎ 709-634-8281) provides service with an afternoon bus Monday through Friday. Sunday trips depend on demand. For all trips reservations are necessary.

AROUND CORNER BROOK
Marble Mountain

This major downhill ski centre (☎ 709-634-7616) is in the Humber Valley 8km east of town. The 500m Steady Brook Falls Trail leads from the rear parking lot of Marble Mountain to the cascade that tumbles more

than 30m. Marble Mountain Ski Area Trail is 3.5km one way to the 500m summit of Skill Hill where there are good views.

For more serious walkers, including overnighters, there are numerous hikes in the **Blomidon Mountains** (also spelled 'Blow Me Down'), south of the Bay of Islands along Hwy 450 to Lark Harbour. These mountains were formed about 500 million years ago from brownish peridotite rock pushed up from the earth's mantle when the geographic plates of both North America and Europe bumped together. What makes this special is that Newfoundland is one of the few places in the world where this type of rock is exposed and can be walked over.

Other features are the great views over the bay and islands and a small caribou population. Some of the trails, especially ones up on the barrens, are not well marked at all so bringing topographical maps and proper equipment is recommended. For a general description of the area purchase a copy of *Best Hiking Trails in Western Newfoundland* by Keith Nicol.

One of the easiest as well as most popular trails begins at a parking lot on the left side of Hwy 450 (500m from the bridge which crosses Blow Me Down Brook). The trail can be taken for an hour or so or, for more avid hikers, it continues well into the mountains where you're on your own. At Blow Me Down Park near the end of Hwy 450 there are also well-used marked trails which still provide fine views of the coastline.

South of town there is very good freshwater swimming at Stag Lake and also fairly warm waters at the **Blue Ponds Park** a little farther out. Blue Ponds also has 61 camp sites at $9 a night.

STEPHENVILLE

Formerly a large military base town with the decaying evidence visible from the road, Stephenville with a population of 10,000, now relies mainly on the Abitibi-Price pulp mill. The town sits on St George's Bay between Corner Brook and Port aux Basques and acts as entrance to French Port au Port. Information can be had

from the Chamber of Commerce (☎ 709-643-5854) on Hansen Memorial Hwy.

The Stephenville Festival is a three-week English theatre event, usually held in late July with local and internationally known participants. The festival offers theatre ranging from Shakespeare to modern Newfoundlanders' plays. Call the Arts and Culture Centre (☎ 709-643-4553) for exact dates and tickets.

During lobster season (from April to July), the tasty devils are sold in the streets from trucks and trailers at good prices.

Places to Stay

For campers there is *Indian Head Park* with swimming pool, nature trail and golf course. The wooded campground has 30 sites for $9 a night but no showers. To reach the park turn onto Massachusetts Ave from Hwy 460 and follow it around the airport to the coast.

Harmon House (☎ 709-643-4673, 144 New Mexico Dr) is a B&B not far from the hospital, with singles/doubles at $42/52 with breakfast. Other options are motels of which *Hotel Stephenville (☎ 709-643-5176)* is the cheapest at $54/64.

PORT AU PORT PENINSULA

The large peninsula west from Stephenville is the only French area of the province and has been since the early 1700s when it became known as the French Shore. It was used by the French for fishing in the **Strait of Belle Isle** right up until the early 1900s. **Red Island** was at one time France's most important fishing base in the New World.

Today, the farther west you go stronger the French culture is. At the southwest tip of the Port au Port Peninsula in **Cape St George**. Children still go to French school preserving their dialect which is now distinct from the language spoken in either France or Quebec. Mainland, Lourdes and Black Duck Brook are also very French. In late July or early August each year there is a major French folk festival held in Cape St George with lots of music and other events.

In **Port au Port West**, a small community not far from Stephenville, Our Lady of Mercy Church is worth a look. Begun in

1914, it is the largest wooden building in Newfoundland. During July and August a guide is on hand to show you around and provide some details and stories about the church. On the way there from Stephenville, after going across the small bridge, continue straight on the small road. Don't follow the road around to the left or you'll miss the church like everybody else does. There is also the Lady of Mercy Museum with craft shop, a tearoom and a collection of local artefacts. Hours are 10 am to 8 pm daily during summer and admission is $1.

Along Hwy 463 on the way to Lourdes, you will pass numerous small sheds selling lobsters during the season. At *Piccadilly Head Park* you'll find a rugged stretch of coast, hiking trails and 50 unserviced camp sites.

BARACHOIS POND PROVINCIAL PARK

Located right on the Trans Canada Hwy near the exits to Stephenville is this large provincial park, one of the few in Newfoundland that offers an opportunity for backpacking. From the campground a trail heads 4.5km one way to the top of Erin Mountain, a peak of almost 400m. On top there are excellent views of the surrounding area and backcountry camp sites.

Plan on two hours for the climb up. There are no fees for hiking or camping on the mountain but a night in the park's 150 site campground (☎ 709-551-5155) is $11. The park also has a swimming area, canoe rentals, showers, laundry facilities and a small store.

South-Western Newfoundland

Within the small south-western corner of the province the visitor is offered a remarkable variety of geography and history. It is well worthwhile spending some time exploring it rather than just doing the usual mad dash to or from the ferry. Hilly Port aux Basques, built up and around a jutting, jagged peninsula and offering all the services including a major tourist office, is the centre of the region.

CODROY VALLEY

North of Port aux Basques beyond Cape Ray the broad green, fertile Codroy Valley runs from the coast north-east alongside the Long Range Mountains for about 50km. This is one of the prime farming regions of the province and compared with the generally rugged, rocky landscape looks positively lush. A good spot for a view of the valley (accessible by car) is down near the sea by the town of **Searston.**

Farther along, the road goes up a mountain at **Cape Anguille**; there are views as far as the mainland on a clear day. Back at the inlet, the estuary of the Grand Codroy River is an important wetland area for birds which is impressive at migration times when thousands of geese, black ducks and other species can be viewed.

Despite its long period of settlement and the many quiet farms, the valley does have a nasty side to it. It can be the windiest place in Newfoundland and that's saying something. Along the highway winds can reach 200km/h. They used to have to stop the trains at times to prevent them from blowing off the tracks!

PORT AUX BASQUES

Approaching by ferry from Nova Scotia, the rocky, barren, treeless landscape here – the first glimpse of Newfoundland for most – can look a little forbidding but also appealing in a rough, undeveloped way.

The town itself, at least the older section built on and around the hills to the left of the ferry as it approaches, is very attractive. It has narrow, winding roads edged with traditional wooden houses offering different views and angles at every turn.

Port aux Basques was named by Basque fishers and whalers in the early 16th century who came to work the waters of the Strait of Belle Isle which separates the province from Quebec.

Today, Port aux Basques with a population of 6100, is a principal terminal for the Marine Atlantic ferry. The ferry company is now the largest employer in town, though there are also freight-handling and fish-packing industries.

The town is also sometimes known as Channel-Port-aux-Basques.

Orientation

The town centre is to the south-east of the landing and back the way you came in on the

ferry. To get to this old section of town, cross the bridge after leaving the ferry and turn left.

For the new part of town, turn right along the Trans Canada Hwy. Go past a number of gasoline stations and turn left at the Hotel Port aux Basques on the corner of Grand Bay Rd and High St. This will take you to the shopping mall, the centre of the new district.

Information

The tourist chalet (☎ 709-695-2262) with information on all parts of the province is

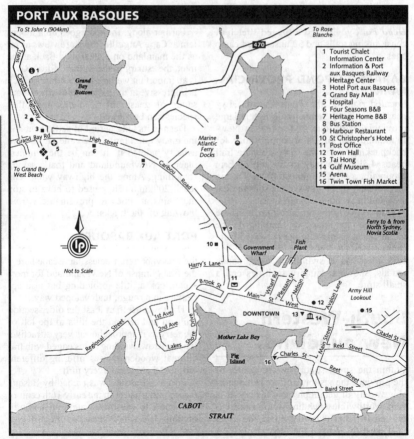

PORT AUX BASQUES

To St John's (904km)

To Rose Blanche

470

Grand Bay Bottom

Trans Canada Highway

Grand Bay Rd

High Street

Caribou Road

Marine Atlantic Ferry Docks

To Grand Bay West Beach

Not to Scale

Harry's Lane

Brook St

1st Ave

2nd Ave

Regional Street

Lakes Shore Drive

Mother Lake Bay

Pig Island

Government Wharf

Fish Plant

Main St

Wharf Rd

Pleasant St

Nelson Ave

West

DOWNTOWN

Avalon Lane

Army Hill Lookout

Main Street

Reid Street

Reet Street

Baird Street

Citadel St

Charles St

CABOT

STRAIT

1	Tourist Chalet Information Center
2	Information & Port aux Basques Railway Heritage Center
3	Hotel Port aux Basques
4	Grand Bay Mall
5	Hospital
6	Four Seasons B&B
7	Heritage Home B&B
8	Bus Station
9	Harbour Restaurant
10	St Christopher's Hotel
11	Post Office
12	Town Hall
13	Tai Hong
14	Gulf Museum
15	Arena
16	Twin Town Fish Market

Ferry to & from North Sydney, Novia Scotia

on the Trans Canada Hwy a few kilometres out of town on the way to St John's. Hours are 6 am to 11 pm daily during summer. Adjacent to the Hotel Port aux Basques is the Railway Heritage Center, the city's information office, open from 9 am to 9 pm daily in summer. Outside are antique railroad cars; tours are $2.

Gulf Museum

In the city centre, at 118 Main St across from the Town Hall, is the two-storey museum (☎ 709-695-2460). Most of the collection is maritime artefacts – many from shipwrecks.

The showpiece of the museum is its astrolabe. This navigational instrument from the 17th century is a striking brass contraption about 17.5cm in diameter made in Portugal in 1628. The design is based on a principal discovered by the ancient Greeks to allow for charting of the heavenly bodies. Variations on it have been used for nautical navigation since 1470.

The astrolabe is in remarkable condition and is one of only about three dozen in the world. It was found by a diver off Isle aux Morts, along the south coast from town, in 1982 and is believed to have been on board either a Portuguese or Basque fishing boat.

Hours are 10 am to 8 pm daily from early July to late August and admission is $2, $4 for families.

Grand Bay West Beach

If you want to hit the beach in Port aux Basques, you head down Grand Bay West Rd and turn onto Klye Lane just before crossing the third bridge. At the end of Klye Lane you'll find a small park overlooking a wide, sandy beach. This is also the start of the Cormack Trail to JT Cheeseman Provincial Park.

Places to Stay

With all the ferry traffic, reservations are a good idea unless you arrive very early in the day. Campers have a good place close to town, close enough to be convenient when arriving late or leaving early. The *JT Cheeseman Provincial Park* (☎ 709-695-7222) 12km along the Trans Canada Hwy

north of town has 102 camp sites for $9 a night. There are no showers but the park features a wide sweeping beach, hiking trails, and boat rentals. Whale bones found on the beach are now displayed in the park.

At the *Heritage Home* (☎ 709-695-3240, 11 Caribou Rd) guesthouse (three rooms) you can stay in bed almost until the ferry, literally across the street, blows the horn. Singles/doubles cost $40/45 with a continental breakfast. Also nearby is *Four Seasons B&B* (☎ 709-695-3826, 82 High St) with four rooms that are $35/45.

St Christopher's Hotel (☎ 709-695-7034, ☎ 1-800-563-4779) with a fine view from its hilltop location on Caribou Rd is a larger, commercial hotel offering more amenities and a dining room. It features a family rate of $59 for one to four people in a room.

The *Gulfside Inn* (☎ 709-695-7091) and *Hotel Port aux Basques* (☎ 709-695-2171) are near the Trans Canada Hwy and offer the same $59 family rate as their competitor.

Places to Eat

The *Harbour Restaurant* on Main St is close to the ferry terminal and has good views of the waterfront if you're waiting for the late boat. The menu is mainly fried chicken or fish and chips. It opens at 7 am with breakfast specials under $3.

For Chinese try *Tai Hong* (116 Main St) with full dinners under $6. If you're heading off for a camp site and want some seafood, there's *Twin Town Fish Market* at the end of Charles St.

The Grand Bay Mall has a no-name – they were still putting up the sign – cheap family *restaurant* with breakfast specials from $1.99.

Getting There & Away

Bus The DRL bus service leaves once a day at 8 am from the ferry dock terminal for the 904km trip to St John's. The trip takes about 14 hours and costs $90 one way. You can stop at any of the towns along the way (and there are plenty of stops). Connections can be made in other towns with other, more local, bus companies

which service destinations other than those on the main route to St John's.

Corner Brook has a number of smaller lines, in particular buses to Gros Morne National Park and the Northern Peninsula. The one-way fare to Corner Brook is $17.

If you're going to Gros Morne, Woody Point or beyond, you might be better off getting a ticket past Corner Brook to Deer Lake because the connections in Corner Brook are poor. The bus from Corner Brook to Deer Lake doesn't leave from the station at which the DRL bus from Port aux Basques arrives, but is inconveniently located across town with no city bus connections. But the Viking bus from Corner Brook stops at the same station in Deer Lake as does the DRL bus. There is a possible problem though. The Viking bus from Corner Brook doesn't always stop at Deer Lake unless the driver knows there are passengers waiting. So, telephone back to Corner Brook (☎ 709-634-4710) to let Viking know that you are coming! In any case, you're looking at an overnight stay, so head for Deer Lake Municipal Park.

Ferry Marine Atlantic (☎ 709-695-4266, ☎ 1-800-341-7981) operates both the ferry routes from Nova Scotia to Newfoundland, one going to Argentia and this one to Port aux Basques.

From the beginning of June to the middle of September there are one to three trips daily on a wildly staggered schedule. Printed schedules are ubiquitous around Nova Scotia and Newfoundland so you should know when boats leave. In midsummer, reservations are recommended and can be made by calling the above number in Port aux Basques or Marine Atlantic's North Sydney office (☎ 702-794-5254), Nova Scotia. Generally one or two days notice is sufficient unless you require a berth in a cabin, in which case the earlier the better. Early morning or late night trips are usually less busy and, if you're walking or cycling, there shouldn't be any trouble. If you'll be arriving in Port Aux Basques or North Sydney on a late, late ferry, you definitely should have a room booked before you arrive or you'll be sorely disappointed.

The fare is $19.50, less for children and seniors, $61 per car, more with a trailer or camper, $9 for a bicycle. The night ferry, which departs at 11.30 pm, saves you the cost of lodging because you can sleep anywhere and everywhere on board. Upon boarding there is a rush to the decks to secure a comfortable, quiet location away from hallways and most traffic. Bring a sleeping bag or blanket and a towel as there are free showers on board. In the cafeteria there is even a microwave oven if you're pinching pennies and want to use your own tea bag. Otherwise the food is reasonably priced.

For those with extra cash, berths and cabins are also available.

Ships take from five to six hours for the summer crossing, longer in winter – up to 7½ hours.

AROUND PORT AUX BASQUES
Cape Ray
Located 14km north of the Marine Ferry Terminal and adjacent to JT Cheeseman Provincial Park is the small community of Cape Ray. The coastal scenery here is engaging and the road leads up to the Cape Ray lighthouse. Outside the lighthouse is a plaque commemorating the first transatlantic cable which was laid in 1856. The lightkeeper's house is now a craft shop and nearby is the site of a Dorset Inuit camp dating to around 400 BC to 400 AD.

Hiking
The Port aux Basques-southern Codroy area offers some interesting hikes, due in part to the Long Range Mountains. The **Cormack Trail** is a long trail under development that some day will stretch from Port aux Basques north to Flat Bay near Stephenville. In Port aux Basques, you can pick up the trail at Grand Bay West Beach where there is a trail map. From there it's an 11km trek along the coast to JT Cheeseman Provincial Park. Signs direct you through Cape Ray and the trail resumes at the lighthouse, reaching the Red Rocks area in 4km.

Table Mountain Trail begins on the Trans Canada Hwy opposite the exit to Cape Ray,

where a Table Mountain Digital Project sign marks a rough dirt road. The 6km trail is actually this rugged road (don't even think about driving up it) that leads to the top of the 518m-high flat-top mountain. On top are the ruins of a radar site, air strip and buildings that the USA put up during WWII. The hike is not hard but plan on three to four hours for the 12km round-trip walk.

Starlite Trail is another access route into the Long Range Mountains. It's 31km north of Port aux Basques on the Trans Canada Hwy near the community of Tompkins and is a one-way hike of 2km to a high point where there are views of the Codroy Valley.

SOUTH COAST

The often ignored Hwy 470, which heads east out of Port aux Basques for about 50km, is a fine short excursion. If you've got an afternoon or a day waiting for a ferry this is an ideal little side trip for those with transportation. Edging along the shoreline the road rises and falls over the rounded, eroded windswept terrain looking as though it's following a glacier that ploughed through yesterday. Visible along the other side of the road are half a dozen evenly spaced fishing towns.

Isle aux Morts (Island of the Dead) came by its name through the many shipwrecks just offshore which have occurred over some 400 years.

Between Burnt Islands and Diamond Cove you pass stunning Barachois Falls plunging out of the hills north of Hwy 470. Look for a small 'Scenic Hike' sign for the start of a boardwalk that winds to almost the base of the falls.

The highlight of the trip is the last village along the road, **Rose Blanche**, an absolutely splendid, traditional-looking village nestled in a little cove with a fine natural harbour – a perfect example of the classic Newfoundland fishing community. To reach the Rose Blanche Lighthouse, turn left at the Town Hall and fire station and follow the side road to the H&P Lounge. Bear left up that imposing gravel road that winds its way up the rocky slopes to the historic structure.

The original stone lighthouse dating from 1873 is unique and at the time of writing was being restored as part of a massive effort to turn the entire small peninsula into a park. It should be gorgeous when completed. Presently there's no access to the lighthouse and a wonderful nearby light meal restaurant – *Hook, Line and Sinker* – accessible only by foot was closed but apparently only temporarily.

For those who long to go that one step further, a trip can be taken by boat (ask around the docks) across the bay to the smaller village of **Petites** which has a population of about 30 families. Here, and visible from the Rose Blanche Lighthouse, is probably the oldest wooden United church in North America (although now the Anglicans have taken over) dating from about 1860. It's a plain and simple church kept in excellent condition and has registers of births, deaths and marriages to pore over for details of local history.

For those without a vehicle, Gateway Bus Lines (☎ 709-695-9700) in Port aux Basques offers tours of the South Coast and Rose Blanche. These aren't scheduled, however, and costs vary wildly depending on current demand.

Outports

'Outport' is the name given to any of the tiny coastal fishing villages accessible only by boat. Some are on one of the major intraprovincial coastal ferry lines, others are not. These little communities represent some of the most remote settlements left in North America. Change is coming at an ever quickening pace, but for the moment these outports harbour the rough Newfoundland life at its most traditional. These villages clinging to the rocky coastlines are perhaps the best place to see the unique culture of the Newfoundland people of European blood born in Canada.

Coastal Labrador Marine Services has runs up the coast of Labrador. But one heads directly to Happy Valley-Goose Bay which is hardly an outport, with soldiers

from a handful of countries stationed there. This ferry takes vehicles and passengers. The other run, from St Anthony, is for passengers only and leapfrogs from one outport to the next. This is the boat to be on. For details see the Labrador, St Anthony and Lewisporte sections in this chapter.

For places to stay on the north coastal trip, ask around beforehand or just take a chance on arrival. You can always stay on the ferry if you're continuing on without a stopover. This can be tiring if you're doing it on the cheap; sleeping on the floor or in a chair can be pretty uncomfortable after a few days, especially if the sea is rough. On a longer trip consider a cabin as the prices actually are quite fair. Ask about stopovers and how long the ticket is good for.

For details and schedules, call the provincial tourism information office (☎ 1-800-563-6353). It also makes reservations.

SOUTH COAST

At the moment you can actually cobble together a number of ferries to bop across the South Coast. Be forewarned however – at the time of writing ferries changed schedules so as to eliminate long waits required in diminutive towns, but this could change overnight (and usually does).

It is possible to depart from Rose Blanche – not Port Aux Basques – and hopscotch to Lapoile and Grand Bruit with only a one-night stopover, instead of the three or four days previously. From Grand Bruit, you can continue on to Burgeo where yet another ferry will link up with Ramea, Grey River, Francois, McCallum, Gaultois and, finally, Hermitage, though from here you'll have to suss out transport back to the main highway and possible bus transport. Up to the minute ferry schedules can be found at the provincial tourist office in Port aux Basques, or contact the Department of Works, Services, and Transportation (☎ 709-635-4100). The provincial tourism office can also help with information.

On Monday, Wednesday, Friday and Saturday, a ferry ($3) leaves Rose Blanche at 3 pm for Lapoile; it continues to Grand

Bruit ($2.75) at 4.45 pm or you could try and overnight here and take another Lapoile-Grand Bruit ferry at 8 am Thursday morning, which then continues on to Burgeo ($4.50) at 9.15 am. The Rose Blanche-Lapoile-Grand Bruit ferry also departs Sunday at 4 pm, leaving you in Grand Bruit waiting, just waiting for that Thursday ferry to Burgeo; obviously this isn't the one you want.

In big – relatively speaking – Burgeo the MV *Marine Voyager* leaves at 2.15 pm Sunday, Monday, Wednesday, Friday and Saturday for Grey River (2½ hours, $4.25), and then continues to very, very tiny Francois (two hours, $3.75) at 5.15 pm (this may be where you have trouble lining up a place to stay); Ramea en route is gorgeous. After an overnight stay, the ferry leaves at 8 am for McCallum (2½ hours, $3.75), finally continuing on to Hermitage (1½ hours, $1.75) via Gaultois.

Once you get to Burgeo you've got other options. The MV *Gallipoli* plies the route to Ramea and Grey River on a fairly complicated schedule. Also, the MV *Terra Nova* does the McCallum-Gaultois-Hermitage run.

Or, if you're dead tired of ferries here, Devin's Bus Line Limited (☎ 709-886-2955 in Burgeo) does have service back to Corner Brook. It leaves daily Monday through Friday at 8 or 9 am. Sunday departures are iffy. Monday, Wednesday, and Friday it is scheduled to wait for the ferry but by the time you read this it could have changed.

It's important to note that reservations are not needed. All but one of these ferries are passenger-only and it's a fairly casual system that is not overly busy.

Places to Stay

Accommodation is easiest to work out in larger Burgeo, but along the way you should have little trouble lining up somewhere to stay, even if it's just with a family. Folks will likely be so shocked to see you they'll be only too glad to take you in. If you're concerned, the phone book or tourist information in Port aux Basques could help you track down numbers before you go.

Some informal boarding houses and suchlike are not registered with the tourism department.

In Grand Bruit there's **Blue Mountain Cabins** (☎ 709-492-2753) with rooms from $55.

Burgeo boasts the **Burgeo Haven B&B** (☎ 709-886-2544, ☎ 1-888-886-7171) with rooms from $40; there is also a motel for more money.

In other outports you'll have to line up local hospitality homes.

Labrador

Labrador is that part of Newfoundland – three times the size of the island – that is adjacent to the Quebec mainland. The Strait of Belle Isle separates Labrador from the Newfoundland Island. This vast, rugged land is one of the last incompletely explored areas in the country and one of the largest, cleanest, natural areas anywhere (at least, cynics and environmentalists sneer, until mineral extraction companies finally kick out the aboriginals and have their say fully).

The geological base of Labrador is the ancient Laurentian Shield – possibly the oldest unchanged region on earth. It's thought the land looks much the same as it did before life on the planet began. Four great caribou herds, including the world's largest with some 750,000 head, migrate across Labrador to their calving grounds each year.

Until recently, small numbers of Inuit, Native Indians and longtime European descendants known as 'liveyers' were the only human residents. They lived in little villages dotted along the rocky coasts as they had done for centuries, eking out an existence fishing and hunting. The interior was virgin wilderness.

Today a new people, with a completely different outlook and lifestyle, has arrived. White southerners have been lured by the overwhelming and nearly untouched natural resources.

And so, not far away from the more or less traditional way of life of the original in-

habitants, lie some of the world's most modern, sophisticated industrial complexes. Most of the development has been far inland, near the border of Quebec. Labrador City and Wabush, with the latest technology, are two towns that produce half of Canada's iron ore. Churchill Falls is the site of an enormous hydroelectric plant that supplies power for north-eastern USA.

Happy Valley-Goose Bay is an older settlement first established as an air force base in WWII. It's now mainly a supply centre, and you can get there from Lewisporte, Newfoundland by ferry. These four centres are home to more than half of Labrador's population of 30,000.

The east coast, accessible by boat from Newfoundland, is also interesting. Tiny villages dot the coast all the way to the far north. As in western Newfoundland, with some planning you can take a unique trip on the supply ferries.

Camping is an option all across Labrador but is mostly done in a van or camper. Tenting is possible but be prepared – although summers can be pleasantly warm, even hot, this is often a cold, wet and windy place. The amount of accommodation has been steadily increasing in all regions and the larger places all have hotels of one sort or another.

As a distinct entity from Newfoundland Island, Labrador has its own flag. The residents, too, consider themselves a breed apart.

LABRADOR STRAITS

Lying 18km across the Strait of Belle Isle and visible from the northern peninsula of Newfoundland, this region of Labrador is the most accessible. It is also the oldest settled area of Labrador. There are about half a dozen small, permanent communities connected by road along the historic coast here. Many of the inhabitants are the descendants of the European fishers who crossed from Newfoundland to fish in the rich strait centuries ago. Attractions include the simple but awesome far north landscape, icebergs, seabirds and whales and the historic Basque site at Red Bay.

The ferry from Newfoundland docks at **Blanc Sablon**, which is in Quebec right at

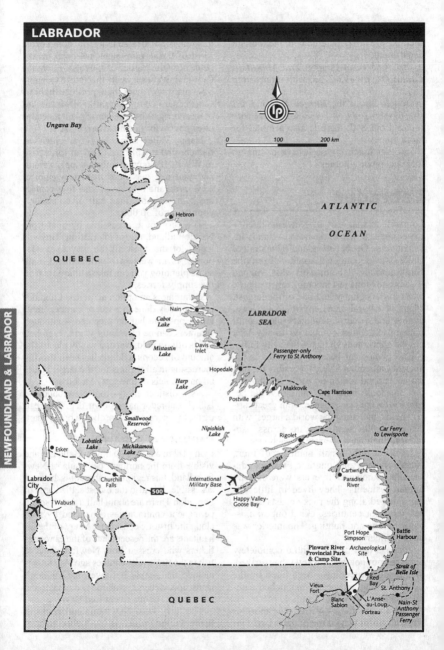

LABRADOR

Ungava Bay

Torngat Mountains

Hebron

QUEBEC

ATLANTIC

OCEAN

Nain

Cabot Lake

Mistastin Lake

Davis Inlet

LABRADOR SEA

Passenger-only Ferry to St Anthony

Scheffervile

Harp Lake

Hopedale

Makkovik

Cape Harrison

Postville

Smallwood Reservoir

Nipishish Lake

Rigolet

Car Ferry to Lewisporte

Esker

Lobstick Lake

Michikamau Lake

Hamilton Inlet

Cartwright

Labrador City

Churchill Falls

500

International Military Base

Paradise River

Wabush

Happy Valley-Goose Bay

Port Hope Simpson

Battle Harbour

Pinware River Provincial Park & Camp Site

Archaeological Site

Strait of Belle Isle

Vieux Fort

Red Bay

St. Anthony

Nain-St Anthony Passenger Ferry

QUEBEC

Blanc Sablon

L'Anse-au-Loup

Forteau

0   100   200 km

the provincial border. There is a motel in Blanc Sablon, and Tilden has an outlet for rental cars. From here the only road runs south along the Quebec coast through four dozen tiny communities and 80km north along the Labrador coast. Also check in local restaurants for the iceberg ice cubes – glacial ice possibly thousands of years old. They are known for their antics when dropped into a drink.

At **L'Anse-au-Clair**, the first community north of Blanc Sablon in Labrador, is the good-value *Beachside Hospitality Home* (☎ *709-931-2662,* ☎ *1-800-563-8999, 9 Lodge Rd)* where singles/doubles are $38/45. Prepared meals are also offered at additional cost. The owner can also organise local tours and boat trips. The ferry to St Barbe is 8km to the south. The *Northern Light Inn* (☎ *709-931-2332,* ☎ *1-800-563-3188)*, a modern motel with a few housekeeping rooms and a dining room, is the only other choice and charges $68/75.

There is also a visitors centre (☎ 709-931-2013) in town located in an old church that doubles up as a museum with a handful of exhibits. It's open daily but afternoons only on Sunday. This is the best place for information along Route 510.

Forteau & Around

Forteau, the largest community along the coast here, is home of the annual Bakeapple Festival in mid-August, a three-day event of music, dance, food and crafts.

There is one small hotel, *Seaview Motel* (☎ *709-931-2840)* in Forteau with four double rooms at $60 each; there is also a dining room. *Grenfell Louis Hall B&B* (☎ *709-931-2916)* has five rooms that go for $35/45. It's an old nursing station located near the trailhead for the Overfall Brook Trail.

On the way to L'Anse-au-Loup along Route 510 is the **Labrador Straits Museum** (☎ 709-931-2067) with exhibits on the early local residents and others which outline the region's traditional way of life, especially the contributions of women. It's open daily from 10 am to 8 pm in summer and doubles as a tourist centre and craft shop. Admission is $2.

L'Anse-Amour

L'Anse-Amour Burial Mound is a Maritime Archaic Indian stone-covered burial site dating from 7500 years ago, the earliest burial mound of its type known in North America. It contains the remains of an Indian youth from earlier people who lived here as long ago as 9000 years.

Continue along the side road, past some impressive rocky bluffs, and you'll end up at the **Point Amour Lighthouse**. In 1995, the lighthouse was renovated as a provincial historic site and features the furnished lightkeeper's house, the tower and a craft shop. The light was first illuminated in 1858 after workers took four years to build the 36m tower. Today you can climb to the top. It's a 127-step climb, however the 360-degree view of the coastline is spectacular. The site is open daily during summer from 10 am to 5.30 pm and is free. Beware – signs warn of WWII-era unexploded ordnance in the area.

Within L'Anse-Amour is *Lighthouse Cove B&B* (☎ *709-927-5690)* at $32/36, dinner upon request. The food is excellent and the couple extremely knowledgeable about the area.

L'Anse-au-Loup

Between here and Red Bay is *Pinware River Provincial Park* (☎ *709-729-2424)* with 15 camp sites for $9 a night and some picnic tables. Don't forget the insect repellent.

The best accommodation deal around is *Barney's Hospitality Home* (☎ *709-927-5634)* with three rooms at $30/35/45 with a light breakfast included and other meals available at additional cost.

From Pinware River Provincial Park to Red Bay is some of the best scenery along Route 510. First you skirt the west side of the river, then cross over on a one-lane iron bridge and skirt the east from high above the rushing whitewater. This stretch of the Pinware is renowned for its salmon fishing and there are three lodges with guiding service in this area. About 10km from Red Bay, you enter a barren, rocky area that is full of blueberries and bakeapples in August.

NEWFOUNDLAND & LABRADOR

Red Bay

Red Bay sits at the end of the road, Route 510, made distinctive by the rusting Quebec freighter in the harbour that ran aground in 1966. The National Historic Site here is the prime attraction of the region. Red Bay Visitor Centre (☎ 709-920-2051) chronicles the discovery in the late 1970s of three Basque whaling galleons from the 1500s on the sea bed just off Red Bay. The ice-cold waters have kept them well preserved, making the area an underwater museum. Subsequent research has found that this was the largest whaling port in the world in the late 16th century, when more than 2000 men resided here.

Some of the excavated land sites can be visited by boat including a cemetery on nearby **Saddle Island** where there is a self-guided interpretive trail.

Inside the visitors centre is one of those Basque whaling vessels pulled from the murky, icy depths; it's the only one in existence. You can also watch an hour-long explanatory video.

The visitors centre is open from 9 am to 6.30 pm Monday through Saturday and noon to 8 pm on Sunday. Admission to the displays and video room is $2. The centre also runs the Saddle Boat tours. Though technically there's a schedule, it's actually pretty much on demand, even for one person. Passage for the short ferry ride is $2.

Accommodation amounts to a few cabins that are rented out at *Whaler's Restaurant* (☎ 709-920-2156), a very pleasant place to have a bowl of seafood chowder. The cabins are $65 single or double.

Hiking

There are a handful of pleasant day-hikes between Forteau and Cape Diable. The first is **Overfall Brook Trail** in the town of Forteau. The 4km trail is a one-way hike along the coast with views of the Point Armour Lighthouse in the distance. It ends at a 30m waterfall. East of the town is **Schooner Cove Trail**, a 3km trek from Route 510 to the cove that was once the site of Archaic Indians thousands of years ago and then a whaling factory.

On the west side of L'Anse-au-Loup is **The Battery Trail**, a 2km or 30 minute hike through a stunted tuckamore forest to the summit of the Battery, where a spectacular view of the Strait of Belle Isle can be enjoyed. Finally near Cape Diable is another marked hiking trail that climbs 2km to a highpoint along a bluff.

Getting There & Away

Air Air Nova, an Air Canada partner, has flights from Deer Lake, Newfoundland, to Blanc Sablon. Also try Provincial Airlines from Corner Brook, Deer Lake or Happy Valley-Goose Bay. Blanc Sablon is also connected to Quebec destinations such as Sept-Îles and Quebec City by Canadian Airlines and partner Inter-Canadien.

Ferry From early May to some time in January the MV *Northern Princess* – a vehicle and passenger ferry – runs from St Barbe (Newfoundland) to Blanc Sablon (Quebec). It is operated by Northern Cruiser Limited (☎ 709-931-2309) out of St Barbe. From the beginning of July to the end of August, when things are at their busiest, the boat runs two or three times a day; at other times service drops to once or twice daily. In peak season, on Tuesday, Thursday and Saturday, the ferry leaves St Barbe at 8 am and 12.30 and 5 pm. On Monday and Wednesday it leaves at 10.15 am and 2.45 pm. Friday times are 11.45 am and 4.15 pm, while Sunday it's 2 and 6.30 pm. Turning around from Blanc-Sablon, Tuesday, Thursday and Saturday the ferry leaves at 8.45 am and 1.15 pm. Monday and Wednesday it leaves at 6.30 and 11 am and 3.30 pm. Friday it leaves at 8 am and 12.30 and 5 pm, while Sunday it leaves at 10.15 am and 2.45 pm. Whew! The rest of the season there are fewer trips.

The two hour trip is $9 per person, $18.50 for a car and more for trailers, vans etc; a bicycle costs $3.50. Reservations are advisable but it's not unknown to arrive in August 15 minutes prior to departure and get a place. The problem then is getting back. Only half the spaces on the ferry for autos are allowed to reserve, and these are

usually gone a week or more ahead of time; thus, you need to get to the ferry office way before it opens to line up and get a number. And keep in mind the time difference – *Blanc Sablon is a half-hour behind Labrador, which is on Newfoundland time!!*

A coastal freight service, the *Nordic Express*, operated by Relais Nordik Inc (☎ 418-968-4707 in Sept-Îles or ☎ 1-800-463-0680 from anywhere in north-western Quebec) runs up the Quebec coast from Sept-Îles on the Gulf of St Lawrence to Blanc Sablon with stops along the way.

The Coastal Labrador Marine Services ferry from St Anthony, Newfoundland up the Labrador coast makes a call at Red Bay as well but it's a passenger-only service. For details see St Anthony earlier in this chapter.

Car The road running up and down the coast from Blanc Sablon is not connected to farther destinations in either Quebec or Labrador. To the south, it continues for 74km into an isolated area of Quebec known as the North Shore. Beyond Blanc Sablon, there are three villages – Middle Bay, St Paul and Vieux Fort – and they all have small stores that sell gasoline but not lodging. The scenery, however, is quite good. Within 19km, you come to Brador River and cross it in front of an impressive waterfall thundering down into a narrow rocky gorge. From there the road climbs steeply into coastal headlands that feature a rocky, barren terrain. Several more waterfalls can be seen in the bluffs above before you reach an incredible viewing point high above the St Paul River. The town of St Paul is on the other side, 12km from the end.

NORTHERN COAST

Beyond Red Bay all the way up to **Ungava Bay** are dozens of small semi-traditional communities and settlements accessible only by sea or air along the rugged, jagged and in some parts unspoiled mountainous coast. This area of Labrador doesn't get a lot of visitors but offers the persistent a look at some of the most remote regions of North America.

Living off the land completely has pretty much disappeared especially now that the fishing industry has all but gone belly up. Between government moratoriums and lack of fish, making a wage from the sea is almost impossible. Some hunting and trapping is still carried on but these days unemployment is high and many people rely on government funds in one way or another. Still, the lifestyle remains unchanged in many ways due simply to the isolation and the small size of the villages. The people are a determined lot – they have to be.

The accommodation situation is a bit of an unknown as most travellers use the ferry as a floating hotel. For those wishing to get off and hang around somewhere until the next boat, it means winging it and asking around town for a spare bed.

The community of **Battle Harbour** dates from the 1770s and was the province's last intact traditional fishing outport until the community moved en masse to nearby Mary's Harbour. The village has been restored; included are buildings 200 years old.

Makkovik, an early fur-trading post, is a traditional fishing and hunting community. Both new and old-style crafts can be bought.

In **Hopedale** a National Historic Site preserves the old wooden Moravian mission from 1782. The site includes a store, residence, some huts and of course, the church. *Hopedale Lodge (☎ 709-933-3811)* has singles/doubles at $78/94 with meals at extra cost.

Nain

This is the last stop on the Coastal Labrador Marine Services ferry and with a population of 1000 is the last town of any size as you go northward. Fishing is the main industry but the potentially massive Diamond Fields nickel mine nearby at Voiseys Bay will obviously affect this community. As in the other smaller settlements, after the fishing season, hunting and trapping continue as they have for centuries. The **Piulimatsivik-Nain Museum** in one of the old mission houses, outlines both Inuit and Moravian history with artefacts relating to both traditions. Admission is free.

NEWFOUNDLAND & LABRADOR

The Moravian Church

The Moravians developed in the mid-1400s as the Church of the Brotherhood. They broke from the Church of Rome and had to flee persecution in their place of origin, the then largely German-speaking provinces of Bohemia and Moravia, in what is now the Czech Republic. A strong evangelical movement, it set up missions in Asia, Africa, the West Indies, and North and South America.

Starting in the late 1700s members began ministering to the Inuit of the New World, doing some good but attempting to diminish the Native people's spirituality and culture at the same time. They were a prominent European group all along the Strait of Belle Isle on both the Newfoundland side and, most notably, on the coast of Labrador. They maintained an extensive mission community here until the 1950s. Many of their former buildings are still in use, some as historical sites.

There is a soapstone craft outlet and Nain has a hotel, the *Atsanik Lodge* (☎ 709-922-2910) with singles/doubles for $80/90. There is often a guesthouse or two here as well.

North of Nain is another Moravian historic site in **Hebron**. Close to the northern tip of Labrador the wild **Torngat Mountains** are popular with climbers because of their altitude (some of the highest peaks east of the Rockies) and their isolation.

Getting There & Away

Coastal Labrador Marine Services' passenger-only (no vehicles) ferry from St Anthony 'bounces' along the Labrador coast from Red Bay, up into Goose Bay and then as far north as the town of Nain. Private vessels can be hired to reach still farther north. See the St Anthony section earlier in this chapter.

CENTRAL LABRADOR

Making up the territorial bulk of Labrador, the central portion is an immense, very sparsely populated and ancient wilderness. Paradoxically, it also has the largest town in Labrador, Happy Valley-Goose Bay, in the south with a population of 7000.

Happy Valley-Goose Bay

Goose Bay was established during WWII as a staging point for planes on their way to Europe and has remained an aviation centre. Today there is a Canadian military base

used by pilots from around both Canada and Europe for testing high-tech planes, in particular controversial low-flying jets which the Innu say disturb their way of life.

The town has all the services including hotels but for the outsider there is not a lot to see or do and it is very isolated. The remote, forested landscape, however, attracts many anglers and hunters and there are numerous fly-in possibilities for camping.

The **Labrador Heritage Museum** (☎ 709-497-8779) outlines some of the history of the area and includes a trapper's traditional shelter, samples of animal furs, some of the minerals found in Labrador, and the ill-fated Wallace-Hubbard expedition into Labrador's interiors. The museum is on the north side of town on the former Canadian Forces base.

At the **Northern Lights Military Museum** (☎ 709-896-5939), 170 Hamilton River Rd, some of the military history of the city is displayed. Also at the Northern Lights building visit the free Trappers Brook Animal Displays, lifelike displays of many of the animals and birds found in the region. Both exhibits are closed on Sunday.

Places to Stay & Eat The city has three fair-sized hotels and a handful of B&Bs. There are also some hospitality homes but these seem to change quickly so try the tourist office lists.

A brand new building houses the cheapest B&B in town – *TMT B&B* (☎ 709-896-4404) – where rooms start at $25. The *Davis' B&B* (☎ 709-896-5077, 14 Cabot Crescent) has two rooms for $40/50 with a light breakfast included.

The *Royal Inn* (☎ 709-896-2456, 5 Royal Ave) with singles/doubles from $57/67 is the most economical hotel. It has some housekeeping units at a higher rate.

Getting There & Away To travel to Happy Valley-Goose Bay there is the choice of air, car or ferry.

Air Goose Bay is well served by air. Provincial Airlines serves Blanc Sablon and Goose Bay from Newfoundland's major towns. Labrador Airways connects to St Anthony and covers all the small communities along the Labrador coast.

Car From Happy Valley-Goose Bay, Hwy 500, which is a gravel road, runs westward through the heart of Labrador to Churchill Falls and then forks. Hwy 500 continues south to Wabush, Labrador City and Fermont, Quebec.

The road makes the entire inland area auto accessible for the first time. Drivers can take vehicles on the ferry from Happy Valley-Goose Bay to Newfoundland allowing for a complete circuit of the region. Potential users should note that this road should only be travelled between June and October and that services are minimal if any exist at all. In fact between Happy Valley-Goose Bay and far western Labrador services are available only at towns. There are no roadside service stations. This makes for some pretty long stretches without a coffee or any other critical requirements. And the roads can be bad. Still, travellers have made it in passenger cars, though to quote one: 'I don't know that I'd do it again'.

The drive from Goose Bay to Labrador City takes about nine hours. The section between Goose Bay and Churchill Falls is rough and slow. The provincial government continues to discuss paving the entire route, but one official Web site estimated finishing the project by 1999 which was either a misquote or egregious optimism. At present epic washouts can close the road down completely, which many local truckers complain about. Government agencies can provide road information but anything they say should be taken with a grain of salt; assume conditions will be worse.

Cars can be rented in Happy Valley-Goose Bay at Avis and Tilden both with desks at the airport but not for travel on Hwy 500 due to its rough conditions.

Ferry The car ferry from Lewisporte makes the trip to Goose Bay direct or with just a stop at Cartwright on the way. See Lewisporte earlier in this chapter for details on this marathon 35 to 38-hour ferry ride. For the passenger-only ferry from St Anthony see Getting There & Away under St Anthony earlier in this chapter.

WESTERN LABRADOR
Accessible from Quebec, everything in this area of Labrador is oversized in the extreme – mega-developments in a mega-landscape which the visitor is able to explore relatively easily.

Remember that there is a one hour time difference between Quebec and Labrador City.

Labrador City/Wabush
These twin mining cities with a collective population of 12,000, just 15km from Quebec, represent modern, industrial Labrador. The largest open-pit iron ore mine in the world is in Labrador City. Since 1958 a modern town has developed around this mine. Another open-pit mine operates in Wabush. You can tour both facilities. All the resource development in this part of the world is colossal in scale as the tours will reveal. Dumptrucks 18m long with 3m-high tyres are almost like absurd works of art.

There is a regional tourist chalet (☎ 709-944-7132) in Labrador City in the Arts and Cultural Centre which will help with information on Churchill Falls and other local

spots as well as answering questions about the cities here.

Height of Land Heritage Centre (☎ 709-944-2284) in a former bank is a museum. Also, paintings by Tom Thompson may be seen in the Labrador City Town Hall.

Most people want to see the land away from town and you don't have to go far to do that. The landscape, a vast expanse of low, rolling, forested mountains interspersed with areas of flat northern tundra, was scraped down by glaciers.

The **Wapusakatto Mountains** are just 5km from town and parts have been developed for skiing. From Wabush 43km on the Trans-Labrador Hwy is **Grand Hermine** also with a beach, tent sites for $12 a night and some fine scenery.

The 15km Menihek hiking trail goes through wooded areas with waterfalls as well as open tundra. Outfitters can take anglers to excellent fishing waters.

Bus tours of the towns or surroundings are available. A real treat is the free lightshow – the aurora borealis, also called the northern lights – about two nights out of every three. Northern Canada is the best place in the world to see them because the magnetic north pole is here. Evidently these otherworldly coloured, waving beams are charged particles from the sun which are trapped in the earth's magnetic field.

Inuit belief is that the shimmering lights are the sky people playing a game of ball. Another is that the lights are unborn children playing. The Ojibway called the lights Waussnodae and believed them to be torches held by their dead grandfathers to light the way along the Path of Souls. The souls of the recently deceased walked this path, the Milky Way, to their final resting place.

Note that in summer, with the extremely long daylight hours, the show may not be visible.

Places to Stay & Eat There are several somewhat pricey hotels and motels, some with dining rooms. In Labrador City on Avalon Drive there's the *Two Seasons Inn* (☎ 709-944-2661, ☎ 1-800-670-7667) with

singles/doubles for $84/89. The *Carol Inn* (☎ 709-944-7736, ☎ 1-888-799-7736, 215 Drake Ave) has 23 housekeeping units where you can do your own cooking at $82, more for suites. Advance booking is recommended for all places. Ask around for guesthouses but don't bet on finding one.

Most of the eight or so restaurants are in Labrador City and include a couple of pizza places and *Ted's Pub*. Fish and sometimes caribou show up on menus.

Churchill Falls

Not quite halfway to Goose Bay is modern Churchill Falls. It is built around one of the largest hydroelectric generating stations in the world which was developed in the early 1970s. The diverted Churchill River falling over a 300m ledge powers the underground turbines and kicks out 550 megawatts, enough to supply almost the entire needs of the New England states. It's quite a piece of engineering. There are tours (☎ 709-925-3335 or ☎ 709-925-3211) offered but they must be booked at least one day in advance.

The town is connected by Hwy 500 to Goose Bay to the east and to Wabush to the west.

Banking, laundry, car repair and gasoline can all be taken care of in Churchill. This is the only place between Goose Bay and Labrador City with any services or supplies, so stock up.

For accommodation there is the central *Churchill Falls Inn* (☎ 709-925-3211, ☎ 1-800-229-3269) with a coffee shop and bar; booking ahead is recommended. Singles and doubles start at $82. Cheaper by half is the *Black Spruce Chalet* (☎ 709-925-3241).

Getting There & Away Transportation here in central and western Labrador, while improving in giant strides, is still an adventure in itself.

Air Several airlines connect with Labrador City – including Canadian Airlines with its regional partner Air Atlantic from Newfoundland – and the rest of Canada. Air Alliance flies in from Quebec City.

Car Hwy 500 from Happy Valley-Goose Bay continues from just west of Churchill Falls south to Wabush and Labrador City and then to Fermont, Quebec. From there it becomes the mainly surfaced (with some fine gravel sections) Hwy 389 and then continues for 581km south through the little-developed northern Manicougan District of Quebec, past Manic 5 with its huge dam to Labrador City. It can be driven in one day, but it's a long day. Some sections are slow due to roughness or the narrow winding road but it is generally smoother and in better shape than the one from Goose Bay to Churchill Falls. Some small bridges are one-way traffic only.

There are motels and campgrounds along the way, for example at Manic 5, and a motel, restaurant and service station at Bassin Manic 5. For those going north from Baie Comeau, road conditions can be checked with the provincial police in that town. For those going south, if you are in any doubt or are wondering about updates or road improvements the police in Labrador can help.

Back at the Hwy 500 fork at Churchill Falls, a northern branch, the No 501, continues to Esker which is halfway between Labrador City and Schefferville where the road ends. Esker is really nothing more than a train station. This road is not maintained by the province.

Tilden and Avis have offices in Wabush but cars may not be driven on Hwy 500.

Train Western Labrador is also accessible by rail. The route begins at Sept-Îles, Quebec (even farther east than Baie Comeau). From there catch the Quebec North Shore and Labrador railway to Labrador City or beyond to Esker and Schefferville back in Quebec.

There are no other train routes in Labrador. With the opening of the road from Happy Valley-Goose Bay to Labrador City/Wabush, the train is accessible to the eastern portion of Labrador.

In Labrador City the Quebec North Shore and Labrador train station (☎ 709-944-8205) is at Airport Rd. The one-way adult fare to Sept-Îles is $49. Through the summer there are three departures weekly – Tuesday, Wednesday, and Friday at noon. The train has a snack car for light lunches.

See the Sept-Îles section in the Quebec chapter for more details of the train and trips around the Labrador City area.

Nova Scotia

In Nova Scotia you're never more than 56km from the sea, a feature which has greatly influenced the character of the province. For generations the rugged coastline, with its countless bays and inlets, has provided shelter for small fishing villages especially along the southern shores.

Inland, much of the province is covered with forest, while low hills roll across the north. The Annapolis Valley, famous for its apples, is gentle, bucolic farm country – resplendent in spring with lovely pink and white blossoms.

The Bay of Fundy region is dominated by the world's highest tides. Along the impressive Northumberland Strait are wide sandy beaches washed by the warmest waters around the province.

The typical Maritime scenes and towns dotted along the coast give way to Halifax-Dartmouth, one of the country's most attractive major metropolitan areas – a modern, cosmopolitan urban centre that retains an historic air.

Visiting rugged and mountainous Cape Breton Island, which shows another side of the varied topography, is the highlight of a trip to Nova Scotia.

The region gets more visitors annually than any of the other Atlantic Provinces and its excellent travel-information network is well geared to tourists. In general, prices are a little higher here than in much of the Atlantic region and many of the lodgings and restaurants are a little more upmarket and sophisticated.

History

When Europeans first arrived in what was to become Nova Scotia, they encountered the Micmac Indians, the dominant people of the Atlantic region.

The French created the first settlement at Port Royal in 1605, calling it Acadia. Despite it changing hands with the English several times in the following 100 years,

HIGHLIGHTS

Entered Confederation: 1 July 1867
Area: 55,491 sq km
Population: 934,587
Provincial Capital: Halifax

- Visit Halifax with its well preserved history, fine dining and lively music scene
- Spend time in Cape Breton Island, reminiscent of the Scottish Highlands, where Gaelic is still spoken
- Forage the fossil-laden shoreline of Parrsboro
- Experience what life was like for the early French settlers at Louisbourg National Historic Site
- Drive the Cabot Trail to see dramatic coastal scenery
- Explore Annapolis Valley with its fascinating Acadian history
- Watch the whales and eat scallops at Digby Neck
- Enjoy the charm of villages such as Lunenburg and Peggy's Cove

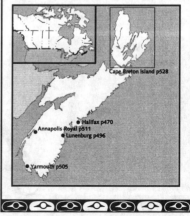

Cape Breton Island p528

Halifax p470
Annapolis Royal p511
Lunenburg p496

Yarmouth p505

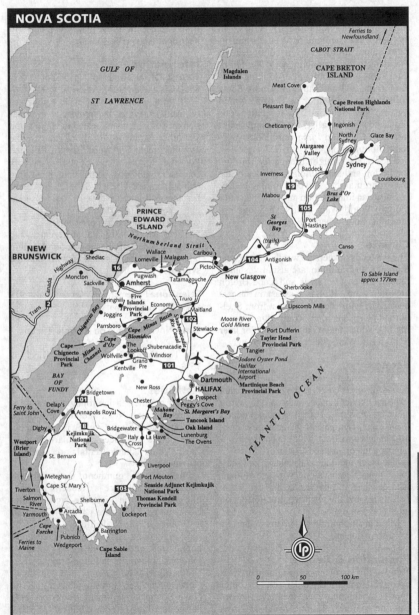

NOVA SCOTIA

Ferries to
Newfoundland

CABOT STRAIT

GULF OF

Magdalen
Islands

**CAPE BRETON
ISLAND**

ST LAWRENCE

Meat Cove

Pleasant Bay

**Cape Breton Highlands
National Park**

Cheticamp

Ingonish

North
Sydney

Glace Bay

Margaree
Valley

Sydney

Inverness

Baddeck

Louisbourg

Mabou

*Bras d'Or
Lake*

**PRINCE
EDWARD
ISLAND**

*St
Georges
Bay*

Port
Hastings

Northumberland Strait

(trails)

Canso

**NEW
BRUNSWICK**

Shediac

Wallace
Lorneville Malagash

Caribou

Pictou

To Sable Island
approx 177km

Highway

Pugwash

Antigonish

Trans Canada

Moncton

Sackville

Amherst

Tatamagouche

New Glasgow

Springhill

Sherbrooke

2

Five
Islands
**Provincial
Park**

Economy

Truro

Lipscomb Mills

Joggins

Maitland

Moose River
Gold Mines

Chignecto Bay

Parrsboro

Cape Minas Basin

Stewiacke

Port Dufferin

**Cape
Blomidon**

Shubenacadie

**Tayler Head
Provincial Park**

Cape
d'Or

The
Lookoff

Windsor

Tangier

Cape
**Chignecto
Provincial
Park**

Wolfville

Grand
Pre

Jodore Oyster Pond

Kentville

*Halifax
International
Airport*

Minas Channel

Dartmouth

*BAY
OF
FUNDY*

Bridgetown

New Ross

HALIFAX

**Martinique Beach
Provincial Park**

*Ferry to
Saint John*

Delap's
Cove

Chester

Prospect

Peggy's Cove

ATLANTIC OCEAN

Annapolis Royal

*Mahone
Bay*

St Margaret's Bay

Tancook Island

Digby

Bridgewater

Oak Island

**Westport
(Brier
Island)**

**Kejimkujik
National
Park**

Italy
Cross

La Have

Lunenburg
The Ovens

St. Bernard

Liverpool

Meteghan

Port Mouton

Cape St. Mary's

Seaside Adjunct Kejimkujik
National Park

Tiverton

Shelburne

Thomas Kendell
Provincial Park

Salmon
River

Arcadia

Lockeport

Yarmouth

*Cape
Forche*

Ferries to
Maine

Pubnico

Wedgeport

Barrington

**Cape Sable
Island**

0   50   100 km

there were really no major British communities until the founding of Halifax in 1749. It was to here the first settlers and pirates came, followed by a contingent of Germans to the Lunenburg area. The Highland Scots landed in familiar-looking Cape Breton in 1773 and thousands more Scots followed to settle Nova Scotia, which means 'New Scotland'. In the late 1700s thousands of Loyalists and a significant number of US and Jamaican blacks swelled the population.

The 1800s brought prosperity through lumbering and shipbuilding, especially for the export markets, and coal mining began.

European immigration mushroomed after the two World Wars and Nova Scotia entered the modern period.

Climate

The sea tends to keep the weather moderate. Summer and autumn are usually sunny, though the eastern areas and Cape Breton are often windy. Rain is heaviest on the east coast. The entire southern coast from Shelburne to Canso is often wrapped in a morning fog, which may take until noon or later to burn off. Winters can be very snowy.

Economy

A visitor may not notice it but manufacturing, mostly resource based, is the most important industry. Agriculture – with dairying, fruit and Christmas trees being the main products – is a significant part of the economy. Fishing remains important, with Lunenburg maintaining a major east coast fleet.

The catch includes cod, lobster and scallops. Nova Scotia, along with Newfoundland, has been hit hardest by the decline in fish stocks and the resulting moratorium on most cod fishing.

Mining, shipbuilding, tourism, and crafts are also major money makers.

Population & People

Many of the Micmac people remain on their original lands in Cape Breton. In other areas, French culture and language live on. But the majority (about 75%) of Nova Scotia's people are of English, Scottish and Irish descent. In a few places you can still hear Scottish Gaelic spoken.

Information

Tourist Offices Tourism Nova Scotia (☎ 1-800-565-0000 in North America, ☎ 902-425-5781 from anywhere else, explore.gov.ns.ca /virtualns) operates the provincial information offices which are located in Halifax and 10 other strategic locations across the province, including Wood Islands, PEI, and Portland, Maine. Nova Scotia's *Doers & Dreamers* guide is better than most free tourist literature. Use it and the toll-free number above to line up advance room reservations. You dial, they do all the work. It's also good to find guided trip operators.

There are 10 designated different scenic routes on older, smaller roads, not the main highways, and each is marked with roadside symbols.

Telephone For emergency service dial ☎ 911 anywhere in the province.

Time Nova Scotia is on Atlantic Time.

Tax The Harmonized Sales Tax (HST) is 15%.

Activities

Aside from the seaside topography and intriguing history, Nova Scotia offers varied outdoor possibilities. Cycling is excellent in parts of the province, particularly around Cape Breton Island. Rentals are available province-wide.

Due to the vast number of waterways, canoeing in the province is excellent. For paddling information visit the Nova Scotia Government Bookstore (☎ 902-424-7580) at 1700 Granville St, Halifax.

Sea-kayaking is becoming increasingly popular and outfitters are found at numerous coastal towns around the province.

For hiking, the national and provincial parks contain easy and strenuous trails. The Nova Scotia Government Bookstore also has good hiking reference books.

Also popular is whale watching along the Digby Neck area and the north shore of Cape Breton. In peak season reserving up to a week in advance might be necessary. Diving is good all around the coast including Halifax Harbour.

Other outdoor pursuits include bird-watching, rockhounding, fossil searching, and freshwater and deep-sea fishing.

Accommodation

Nova Scotia has a wide range of lodgings from backcountry camp sites to fine, historic inns and modern hotels. July and August are by far the busiest months during which time accommodation can be scarce in much of the province. The central and South Shore regions of the province are not as popular as the other areas, however, finding a room each night before dark is always recommended. From October to May many attractions, campgrounds and guesthouses are closed.

Halifax

The Nova Scotia capital Halifax sits by one of the world's largest natural harbours, mid-way along Nova Scotia's south Atlantic shore. With a population of 114,450 and nearly three times that in the surrounding metropolitan area, this is the largest city east of Montreal. The historic central district, never more than a few blocks from the water is, however, pleasingly compact. Modern buildings nestle among heritage structures interspersed with numerous green areas and parks.

The port is the busiest on the east coast partially because it's a year-round harbour – ice forces most others to close in winter. Other major industries are manufacturing, oil refining and food processing. Canada's largest naval base is also here.

Residents are known as Haligonians.

History

The area was first settled by Micmac Indians, and Halifax itself was founded in 1749 as a British stronghold counterbalancing the French fort at Louisbourg on Nova Scotia's south-east tip.

The harbour was used as a British naval base during the American Revolution (1775-83) and the War of 1812. During both World Wars, Halifax was a distribution centre for supply ships heading for Europe, a function which brought many people to the city.

In 1917 a French munitions ship, the *Mont Blanc*, carrying a cargo of TNT collided with another ship in the harbour. The result, known as the Great Explosion, was the world's biggest man-made explosion prior to A-bombs being dropped on Japan in 1945.

The city was the home of Canada's first representative government, first Protestant church and first newspaper.

Orientation

This hilly, park-ridden city lies on a peninsula between the harbour and an inlet called the North West Arm. From Citadel Hill there are views of the town and waterfront – if the city is not lost in one of the frequent fogs.

The downtown area, dating from the earliest settlement, extends from Lower Water St on the waterfront and west up to the Citadel, a star-shaped fort on the hill. Cogswell St to the north and Spring Garden Rd to the south mark the other boundaries of the capital's core. Conveniently, much of what is of interest to visitors is concentrated in this area, making walking the best way to get around.

From this central area the city spreads in three directions. At the extreme east end of the downtown area is the water and the area known as the Historic Properties. This is the original commercial district of town, now restored and containing offices, shops, restaurants and the tourist office.

Up from the Historic Properties there's an interesting mix of historic and contemporary buildings. The streets are wide and there are plenty of trees. At the end of Granville St, Duke St is a small but pleasant pedestrian mall, lined with old buildings in Italianate-style dating from about 1860.

Main streets leading west up from the shoreline are Sackville St and Spring Garden Rd. The latter is lined with shops, including

NOVA SCOTIA

HALIFAX

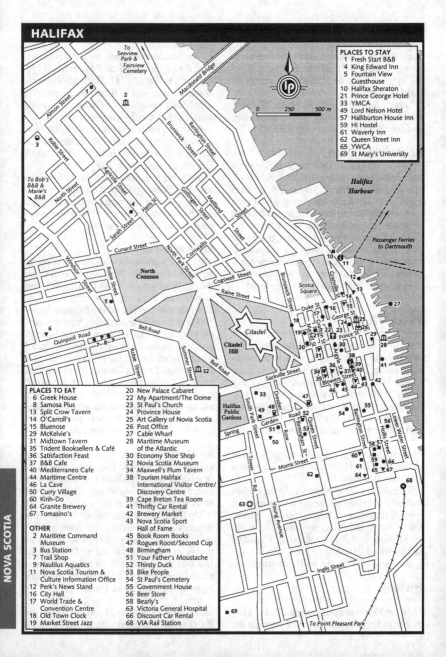

PLACES TO STAY
1 Fresh Start B&B
4 King Edward Inn
5 Fountain View Guesthouse
10 Halifax Sheraton
21 Prince George Hotel
33 YMCA
49 Lord Nelson Hotel
57 Halliburton House Inn
59 HI Hostel
61 Waverly Inn
62 Queen Street Inn
65 YWCA
69 St Mary's University

PLACES TO EAT
6 Greek House
8 Samosa Plus
13 Split Crow Tavern
14 O'Carroll's
15 Bluenose
29 McKelvie's
31 Midtown Tavern
35 Trident Booksellers & Café
36 Satisfaction Feast
37 B&B Cafe
40 Mediterraneo Cafe
44 Maritime Centre
46 La Cave
50 Curry Village
60 Kinh-Do
64 Granite Brewery
67 Tomasino's

OTHER
2 Maritime Command Museum
3 Bus Station
7 Trail Shop
9 Nautilus Aquatics
11 Nova Scotia Tourism & Culture Information Office
12 Perk's News Stand
16 City Hall
17 World Trade & Convention Centre
18 Old Town Clock
19 Market Street Jazz
20 New Palace Cabaret
22 My Apartment/The Dome
23 St Paul's Church
24 Province House
25 Art Gallery of Novia Scotia
26 Post Office
27 Cable Wharf
28 Maritime Museum of the Atlantic
30 Economy Shoe Shop
32 Novia Scotia Museum
34 Maxwell's Plum Tavern
38 Tourism Halifax International Visitor Centre/ Discovery Centre
39 Cape Breton Tea Room
41 Thrifty Car Rental
42 Brewery Market
43 Nova Scotia Sport Hall of Fame
45 Book Room Books
47 Rogues Roost/Second Cup
48 Birmingham
51 Your Father's Moustache
52 Thirsty Duck
53 Bike People
54 St Paul's Cemetery
55 Government House
56 Beer Store
58 Bearly's
66 Victoria General Hospital
66 Discount Car Rental
68 VIA Rail Station

A Christmas Tree for Boston

Few cities have experienced such a sudden and unexpected turning point in their history as Halifax did with the Great Explosion. The day it occurred, 6 December 1917, was bright and clear and WWI was raging somewhere overseas in Europe, not in Canada.

At 8.30 am, out in the harbour, the *Mont Blanc*, a French munitions ship, and the *Imo*, a Belgian relief ship, struck each other due to human error.

Even after the two boats collided the *Mont Blanc* – filled with 300 rounds of ammunition, 10 tonnes of gun cotton, 200 tonnes of TNT, 2100 tonnes of picric acid (used in explosives) and 32 tonnes of highly flammable benzol stacked in barrels on the deck – did not immediately explode. Instead it caught fire and its crew, only too aware of the cargo, took to lifeboats and rowed to Dartmouth. The ship then drifted unattended towards Halifax, drawing bystanders to the waterfront to watch the spectacle.

At 9.05 am the ship exploded in a blinding white flash, the largest man-made explosion before the nuclear age; more than 1900 people were killed and 9000 injured. Almost all of the northern end of Halifax, roughly 130 hectares, was levelled. Most of the buildings and homes that were not destroyed by the explosion burned to the ground because of winter stock piles of coal in the cellars.

All 2830 tonnes of the *Mont Blanc* were shattered into little pieces. The barrel of one of the guns was found 5km away and the anchor shank, which weighed more than a tonne, flew 3km in the other direction; the blast was felt as far away as Sydney on Cape Breton and heard on Prince Edward Island! The misery was compounded when Halifax was hit the following day by a blizzard that dumped 40cm of snow on the city.

Relief efforts were immediate and money poured in from as far away as New Zealand and China; but most Haligonians remember the generosity of the US state of Massachusetts, which donated $750,000 and instantly sent an army of volunteers and doctors to help in the recovery. Halifax was so grateful for the assistance in its hour of despair that the city still sends a Christmas tree to the city of Boston every year as a token of appreciation.

grocery stores, restaurants, pubs and malls. Many of the stores, hotels and other complexes of central Halifax, around the juncture of Barrington and Duke Sts, are connected by a completely indoor system of walking paths known as pedways.

Dartmouth, a twin city, lies east across the harbour and has business and residential districts of its own.

Two bridges span the Halifax Harbour, connecting Halifax to Dartmouth and leading to highways north (for the airport) and east. The Macdonald Bridge, running from the eastern end of North St, is closest to downtown. The toll for cars is 75¢. You can walk and take a bike, but bicycles can not be ridden. Farther north is the MacKay

Bridge, also 75¢. A passenger ferry also links the two downtown areas.

The airport is 40km north-west of town on Hwy 102.

Information

Tourist Offices You won't have any trouble getting information. Outside town is the large, year-round Nova Scotia Visitor Information Centre (☎ 902-873-1223) at the Atlantic Canada Aviation Museum near the airport on Hwy 102. Hours are 9 am to 7 pm (later as necessary) daily. (Note that the airport here is practically halfway across the province!)

Downtown, the Nova Scotia Tourism & Culture information office (☎ 902-424-4247)

is the place to go. On Lower Water St, in the Historic Properties area right down by the water, it's open year-round, daily from 8.30 am to 6 pm in summer, weekdays only from mid-October to May. Information on Halifax and all parts of the province is available here.

Tourism Halifax has its International Visitor Centre (☎ 902-490-5946, ttg.sba.dal.ca /nstour/halifax) in the Discovery Centre building on the corner of Sackville St and Barrington St. It is centrally located and geared to the city. Hours are 8.30 am to 7 pm daily during summer.

Money Major banks can be found along Spring Garden Rd.

Post The post office (☎ 902-494-4000) is at 1680 Bedford Row, near the corner of Prince St.

Foreign Consulates See the Yellow Pages for listings.

Travel Agencies Travel CUTS (☎ 902-494-2054) has an office in the Union Building at Dalhousie University. For discount tickets try United Travels (☎ 902-422-0111) in Scotia Square.

Bookshops The Book Room on the corner of Barrington and Blowers Sts has been around for nearly 160 years.

Medical Services Victoria General Hospital (☎ 902-428-2110) is at 1278 Tower Rd.

Parking Parking in the downtown area can be a real hassle. For a cheap, central place to stash the wheels, go to Citipark with the red signs on Water St near Salter St; there are a couple of other places. Citipark will take campervans and has an all-day ticket for $5 if you arrive before 9.30 am. From 3 pm through the night the flat rate is $3. Parking meters go unenforced on Sunday.

The Historic Properties

The Historic Properties is a group of restored buildings dating from 1800 to 1905.

They were used in the original settlement of Halifax. Many of the buildings here are long two-storey places for easy storing of goods and cargo. Most now house shops and boutiques but there are also restaurants and bars.

Privateer's Warehouse, dating from 1800, is the oldest building in the area. The privateers were government-sanctioned and sponsored pirates who fed off the 'enemy'; the booty was hid here. Among the other vintage buildings are the **Old Red Store** – once used for shipping operations – and a sail loft, now the tourist office.

Simon's Warehouse, built in 1850, was used as an office and warehouse building, then for storing liquor, and still later by a junk and salvage dealer. Along the renovated dock area is the ferry to Dartmouth, which costs $1.55, and some of the 3500 commercial vessels that tie up here each year.

The blue **cable wharf** building along the pier by the ferry terminal is a centre for handicrafts and souvenirs. There are a couple of offices for boat tours, including the McNabs Island ferry.

Often moored at the wharf by Privateer's Warehouse is *Bluenose II*, a replica of Canada's best known boat. The original *Bluenose* schooner was built in 1921 in Lunenburg and never lost a race in 20 years. In tribute, the 10¢ coin bears the schooner's image. The *Bluenose* has become nearly as familiar a Canadian symbol as the maple leaf.

The *Bluenose II* was launched in 1963 and now has a permanent berth at the Historic Properties when not on display at other Canadian ports. Two-hour harbour tours are given on the schooner, but when it's docked you can walk on board to look at this beautiful piece of work for free.

Maritime Museum of the Atlantic

This large museum (☎ 902-424-7490) warrants a peek not only for boat buffs. It's spacious and contains full-scale examples of many regional vessels, with plenty of models, photographs and historical data as well. The lens from a Halifax lighthouse is impressive as are the painted figureheads taken from various ships, many of them wrecks. Also good

is a portion of a boat you can enter which sways realistically as though out on the sea. There is a wildly popular display on the *Titanic* and another on the Great Explosion.

The museum is open from 9.30 am to 5.30 pm Monday to Saturday (until 8 pm on Tuesday) and from 1 to 5.30 pm on Sunday. It's at 1675 Lower Water St, to the south of the Historic Properties, and admission is $4.50, less for children and seniors, or $10 per family. Mid-October to May (and every Tuesday from 5.30 to 8 pm) it's free.

Outside at the dock you can explore the CSS *Acadia*, a retired hydrographic vessel from England. Also docked here is the WWII corvette HMCS *Sackville*, the last of 122 warships of its kind. Adjacent to this is an interpretation centre. Admission to each ship is tied together with the Maritime Museum, or $1 alone.

Atlantic Marine Pavilion Aquarium
Along the wharf near the museum is this aquarium with over 100 varieties of North Atlantic marine life. Lots of exhibits are hands-on at the touch tank. Also on site is a movie theatre; interpreters wander about providing explanations. It's open May through September daily from 10 am to 7 pm. Admission is $5, $3 children, and $10 families.

Brewery Market
Also part of the restored waterfront, this complex is in the Keith's Brewery building

---

A Titanic Legacy

Teary-eyed Leoholics have seen it a dozen times. Video rental shops stock and sell hundreds of copies. When *Titanic* swept through the 1998 Academy Awards like, well, an iceberg, a friendly invasion of tourists headed for Halifax.

Halifax, the base of rescue operations for the tragedy, is home to nearly all the residuals of the fateful voyage. The Maritime Museum of the Atlantic contains a permanent exhibition including one of the only intact deck chairs (get your photo snapped reclining in it); also displayed are a carving from the Grand Salon and memorabilia from Halifax millionaire George Wright, who died in the sinking. The International Visitor Centre features interactive displays on local *Titanic*-related sites and exhibits on the making of the movie, part of which was filmed in Dartmouth.

Three cemeteries contain 150 of the victims, one-third never identified. Of these, 121 rest in nondenominational Fairview Lawn, not far from the MacKay Bridge including, at site No 227, one J Dawson, and it is here that untold numbers of weepy adolescents lay wreaths and make charcoal etchings of the headstone.

However, that J Dawson is not *the* J Dawson but one James Dawson, a lowly seaman. The Catholic Mount Olivet Cemetery contains 19 victims, including the bass player in the band, and the Baron de Hirsch Cemetery has eight unidentified Jewish men interred. A handful of churches where memorials and funerals were held can be visited, as can the Cable Wharf and Karlsen's Wharf, which saw the departure of cable ships to search for victims.

Around Nova Scotia are other sites with memorabilia, including the Yarmouth County Museum, the Hazel Hill Cable Station in Canso (abandoned but standing), the Age of Sail Heritage Centre west of Parrsboro, and the North Highlands Community Museum in Dingwall, Cape Breton. Outside Nova Scotia, the Newfoundland Museum in St John's contains a couple of pieces, and the Cape Race lighthouse still stands. As a sidelight, the St Anthony and Twillingate areas of Newfoundland are suddenly immensely popular for iceberg watching. Or, for a mere US$35,000, you can hop into a oceanographic research submersible and plunge to the ship's resting site.

NOVA SCOTIA

(dating from 1820) at 1489 Hollis St. It now contains boutiques, restaurants and a couple of pubs. A farmers' market is held on the lower level on Saturday from 7 am to 1 pm for much of the year.

Historic Downtown Area

The tourist office has maps for a self-guided walking tour of the Historic Properties, the waterfront boardwalk and the old buildings west up the hill from the water. Most of the buildings which made up the early commercial area are marked with plaques giving a brief history. Using the map, it takes about an hour to do the circuit. Descriptions of some of the best sights follow.

Province House On Hollis St near Prince St, this fine example of Georgian architecture has been the home of Canada's oldest provincial legislature since 1819. There are free guided tours (☎ 902-424-4661) Monday to Friday from 9 am to 5 pm and on weekends from 10 am to 4 pm.

Government House This is between Hollis and Barrington Sts, near the corner of Bishop St. Government House has been the residence of the provincial lieutenant-governor since 1807. It was built by Governor John Wentworth.

St Paul's Cemetery Also known as the Old Burying Ground, the cemetery, first used in 1749, is across the street from Government House on Barrington St.

St Paul's Church St Paul's is on Argyle St near Prince St. It was the first Protestant church in Canada (dating from 1749) and the first church of British origin in the new land. It's open to visitors Monday to Friday from 9 am to 4.30 pm; during summer it's also open Saturday and the hours are extended by a half-hour. A guide is on hand to answer questions. There are some intriguing curiosities here, such as the piece of metal lodged above the door in the north wall, inside the porch. This is a piece of the *Mont Blanc* which exploded 3km away in Halifax Harbour in 1917.

City Hall Built in 1890 at the opposite end of the sunken courtyard from St Paul's Church, City Hall is a gem of Victorian architecture. Visitors can join the mayor for tea Monday to Thursday from 3.30 to 4.30 pm in July and August.

Old Town Clock At the top of George St, at Citadel Hill, stands one of the city's most beloved symbols, the Old Town Clock. The inner workings arrived in Halifax in 1803 after being ordered by Prince Edward, the Duke of Kent, then the Commander.

Citadel National Historic Site

Canada's most visited National Historic Site, the Citadel (☎ 902-426-5080), a huge, oddly angled fort on top of Halifax's big central hill, has always been the city's towering landmark. In 1749, with the founding of Halifax, construction of a citadel began; this version is the fourth, built from 1818 to 1861.

The British realised that the crunch was coming with France over possession of the new land. Halifax was a good location for British purposes as it could be used as a centre for ruling over Nova Scotia and as a military base from which to deal with the French, who had forts of their own in Louisbourg and Quebec City.

It is open daily from 9 am to 6 pm in summer, and from 9 am to 5 pm from early September to the middle of June. Admission is $6 in summer, less for children and seniors, and $14.75 for families; it's free the rest of the year. The excellent guided tours will explain the fort's shape and how, despite appearances, it was not very well designed or constructed. For a freebie, come by for the hourly changing of the full-kilted guard in the ostrich feather hats.

Also in the compound is the Army Museum, with exhibits relating to Atlantic Canada's military history.

Nova Scotia Museum of Natural History

This museum (☎ 902-424-7353) at 1747 Summer St west of the Citadel is considered the headquarters of the provincial system.

History, wildlife, geology, people and industry are all covered. The three-dimensional animal exhibits are excellent – you feel you can reach out and touch the displays. The fish of Nova Scotia exhibit is also well presented. There's a good history section, with an old stagecoach and a working model of a late-1800s sawmill.

From 1 June to 15 October it is open Monday to Saturday from 9.30 am to 5.30 pm (Wednesday to 8 pm) and on Sunday from 1 to 5.30 pm. Through the above months, admission is $3.50 or $8 for a family. The rest of the year it's free but closes at 5 pm each day and is closed Monday.

Maritime Command Museum

This museum (☎ 902-427-0550) is on the Canadian Forces Base (CFB Halifax), off Gottingen St between North and Russell Sts, near Macdonald Bridge. It's in the fine-looking stone building on large grounds protected by numerous cannons. You'll see mementoes like uniforms, medals etc from the military past of the Maritimes. It's open Monday to Friday from 10 am to 3.30 pm. Admission is free.

Art Gallery of Nova Scotia

The provincial Art Gallery (☎ 902-424-7542) is housed in the restored heritage Dominion Building of 1868 (once used as the post office) at 1741 Hollis St across from Province House. Provincial and other Canadian works make up much of the large collection of 5000 pieces. There are both permanent and changing exhibits. Admission is $2.50 (free on Tuesday). During summer the gallery is open Tuesday to Friday from 10 am to 5 pm, until 9 pm on Thursday and noon to 5 pm on Saturday and Sunday. There are tours daily at 2 pm in July and August.

Discovery Centre

The Discovery Centre (☎ 902-492-4422) is a hands-on science centre on the corner of Sackville and Barrington Sts. On the first floor is the Tourism Halifax International Visitors Centre. The museum occupies the next two floors and is mainly geared to kids,

featuring a range of hands-on exhibits in chemistry, physics and even some busker-like floor shows.

The centre is open Monday to Saturday from 10 am to 5 pm, Thursday until 9 pm, and Sunday from 1 to 5 pm. Outside the summer season it is closed on Monday (unless it is a school holiday). Admission is $5 per adult, $3 for children and seniors.

Nova Scotia Sport Hall of Fame

The hall of fame (☎ 902-421-1266) is at 1646 Granville St, Suite 101 in the Centennial Building. It deals with provincial heroes and teams through displays of trophies and photographs. Most fun are the interactive computer exhibits and miniature hockey rink. It's open Monday to Friday from 10.30 am to 4 pm and admission is free.

Halifax Public Gardens

The public gardens may be small – if 17 acres is small – but they're regarded as the finest Victorian city gardens in North America. They're found on the corner of South Park St and Spring Garden Rd. Bands give concerts in the gazebo on Sunday afternoon throughout summer.

Point Pleasant Park

Point Pleasant Park is highly recommended. Some 39km of nature trails, picnic spots, a restaurant, a beach and an old Martello tower – a round defence structure – are all found within this 75-hectare wooded sanctuary. Good views are found all the way around the perimeter. No cars are allowed.

The park is at the far southern end of town, at the tip of the peninsula. The No 9 bus connects the park with the downtown Scotia Centre until 9 pm, or you can drive to the park's edge. Whichever way you come, check out the size of the houses along Young St.

At the city edge of the park is the Port of Halifax, a very busy terminal with containers piled high. Walk out to the lighthouse by the port for great views and a peek at the shipping activity; kids will be tossing in lines hoping for the big catch.

NOVA SCOTIA

An interesting historical aside is that the park still belongs to the British government, which has rented it out on a 999-year lease at the rate of 10¢ per year.

Sir Sandford Fleming Park (the Dingle)

Another highly recommended park is this approximately 30-hectare park on the North West Arm, off Purcell's Cove Rd, in among the yacht clubs and zillionaires' homes. Dedicated to the father of the Standard Time Zones, it's got two moderately extensive trails through four natural habitats and the famed Dingle Tower and lions at the base matching those in Trafalgar Square. It's open dawn to dusk year-round; admission is free.

York Redoubt

The remains of a 200-year-old fort make up this National Historic Site which overlooks the harbour from a bluff just south of the North West Arm (south of the centre). It was designed to protect the city from attack by sea and is built at the narrowest point of the outer harbour. The site was used in various capacities by the military as late as 1956.

Aside from the view, there are mounted guns, a Martello tower and historical information and displays; the underground tunnels are cool enough. The grounds are open all year but the buildings are open only from 15 June to Labour Day, 10 am to dusk.

Seaview Park

At the north end of Barrington St, under the MacKay Bridge to Dartmouth, Seaview affords good views of the Bedford Basin. Footpaths wind through the largely open-style park. The park also has an interesting historic side to it. In the 1840s a black community, known as Africville, was established here. Many of its members were former slaves from the USA. It remained until the 1960s, when the area was demolished and the residents moved south toward central Halifax. A visit after dark is not recommended.

McNabs Island

Out in the harbour and easily seen from York Redoubt, this small island makes a good break from the city. The island offers guided walks, beaches, picnic tables and hiking. There's also a teahouse for basic snacks or seafood. Boats depart from the dock area, and tickets ($11) can be bought from Murphy's on the Water (☎ 902-420-1015) by Cable Wharf Market. McNabs Island Ferry (☎ 902-465-4563) also runs a cheaper boat from Fisherman's Cove across the harbour. To get there, take the ferry to Dartmouth ($1.55), requesting a transfer when getting on board so you can take the No 60 bus to Fisherman's Cove. From here it's $8 return to the island.

Hemlock Ravine

A system of linked walking trails winds through this large wooded estate once called home by Edward, Duke of Kent, Queen Victoria's dad. It includes a view of Bedford Basin, and amid the gardens are some very impressive 30m-tall trees. To reach it by car, drive along the Bedford Hwy (Hwy 2) past Birch Cove then look for the signs.

Beaches

If you're looking for a beach, try Black Rock Beach, in Point Pleasant Park; Crystal Beach, 20km west of town; or Queensland Beach, 35km west of town.

Pier 21 Centre

Pier 21 was to Canada what Ellis Island was to the US. Over 1.5 million immigrants entered and nearly 400,000 Canadian troops exited the country from here. This new National Historic Site is being renovated into a large pavilion with information displays, boutiques, ethnic cafés, and multimedia exhibits detailing the travails of refugees and immigrants hoping to call the country home.

Activities

Kayaking & Canoeing The Trail Shop (☎ 902-423-8736) at 6210 Quinpool Rd has kayaks. Rates are $15 a day and $12 for each additional day. More cost effective is a $35 rate from a Friday morning through

Monday morning. The Dartmouth Recreation Department (☎ 902-464-2228) offers canoe rentals during summer at Graham's Grove waterfront.

Diving There are about 50 wrecks at the mouth of Halifax Harbour and good diving along the coast. For information and equipment rentals, try Nautilus Aquatics (☎ 902-454-4296) at 6162 Quinpool Rd.

Organised Tours

No shortage exists here. The tourist office has a complete list, but some of the more established and interesting ones follow. Most have discounts for seniors, children and/or students.

Double Decker (☎ 902-420-1155) offers 1½-hour city tours in London-style buses which leave from the Historic Properties and Halifax Sheraton three times a day during summer. A ticket costs $15.

Cabana Tours (☎455-8111) has 105-minute city bus trips for $18 but also offers good, longer day trips to various points around the province (such as Peggy's Cove, Lunenburg and Annapolis Valley). The Peggy's Cove trip takes four hours and costs $25. Ask about reductions for doing more than one tour.

Also offering a Peggy's Cove tour is Markland Tours (☎ 902-499-2939). The three hour tour is slightly cheaper at $18 and it picks up at the HI Hostel. Other tours include Annapolis Valley ($75), Lunenburg and Peggy's Cove ($55), and a *Titanic* tour ($21).

The beauteous *Bluenose II* (☎ 1-800-763-1963), perhaps the country's best known boat, takes visitors out on harbour sailing cruises, at least when it's in town or not being worked on. If you're lucky enough to be around when it's operating, don't miss the chance for the too-cheap-to-be-true $20 sailings. The tourist offices will have the schedules.

Murphy's on the Water (☎ 920-420-1015), from Cable Wharf at the Historic Properties, has 19 boat tours throughout the day. The two hour narrated trip aboard the *Harbour Queen* goes past both new and old city landmarks and at $17 is pretty good value. The boat carries 200 people and has both open and closed decks, a snack counter and a bar. From mid-June through August there are three to four runs daily. Out of peak season there are two trips daily, and in winter it closes down completely. Dinner cruises are an option. Murphy's also operates the *Mar II*, a very handsome sailboat, for trips around the harbour. The one hour sailing trips cost $18 with a snack. There's likely to be one with moonlight sailings or some other unique angle which may appeal. Some offer whale watching, but personally I'd be a bit skeptical, as this is not a prime area for that possibility.

Halifax Ghost Walk (☎ 902-469-6716) provides a two hour walk beginning at 8.30 pm through July and August, from the Old Town Clock. The tour features tales of pirates, buried treasure and ghosts from the old city's lore and costs $9.50.

More matter-of-fact walking tours around the historic sections of the city are offered very cheaply by D Tours (☎ 902-455-9977). Its historic downtown walk is at 2 pm Monday to Friday during summer and is $5. The Old Red Store tourist office has a brochure on Alexander Keith's Magical History walking tour, which would get most of the above for free. This office also has a central booking desk for all tour agencies, so it's a logical place to start.

Even sea-kayaking tours are available now. Sea Sun Kayak Expeditions (☎ 902-479-2200) has clinics, rentals ($9 per hour), and tours, as does Sea Horse Coastal Guiding (☎ 902-483-0308).

Special Events

Some of the major events held in Halifax in July and August are:

Canada Day
Canada's birthday on 1 July is celebrated in high style in Halifax with parades, live entertainment, concerts and fireworks.
Nova Scotia Tattoo
This event is held in Halifax during the first week of July (or close to it) every year. It's called the province's 'greatest entertainment extravaganza'.

Halifax Natal Day
   A major event held at the end of July or early August with a parade, street parties, boat races, bridge walk, concerts and a fireworks display.
The DuMaurier Atlantic Jazz Festival
   This festival takes place at the end of July.
Halifax Atlantic Fringe Festival
   This festival in August draws hundreds of performers, from musicians and actors to comics and mimics, for a variety of events that are staged throughout the metro area. Around the same time hundreds of buskers descend en masse for their own festival.

Places to Stay

Camping You can camp right in the city of Dartmouth at the *Shubie Municipal Campground (☎ 902-435-8328)* in Shubie Park, on the shore of Lake Charles. It's on Jaybee Drive near the Shubenacadie Canal, and bus No 55 stops within two blocks of the entrance. (But it doesn't run on Sunday, in which case head to the Micmac Mall via a local trail and pick up the No 10 bus.) Facilities include showers and a laundrette. The fee is $14 a night for unserviced sites.

   Laurie Provincial Park (☎ 902-861-1623) is on Route 2, 6km north of Hwy 102, at the village of Grand Lake on Shubenacadie Grand Lake. It's strictly first come, first served – no reservations are taken. There are 71 sites for $10 a night.

   Going west along Hwy 333 there are several campgrounds within 25km of town. At Glen Margaret are two campgrounds, including the large *Wayside Camping Park (☎ 902-823-2547)*, with both tenting and RV (campervan) areas. Unserviced sites here are $12 a night.

   Woodhaven Park (☎ 902-835-2271) is in Hammond Plains, a small town near Bedford just off Hwy 213, about 15 minutes drive north of Halifax. Sites are $15 a night.

Hostels The HI *Halifax Heritage House Hostel (☎ 902-422-3863, 1253 Barrington St)* is perfectly located in a fine historic house. The hostel is an easy walk to the VIA Rail station or to downtown and the waterfront. There's room for 50 guests and features include cooking facilities, an out-

door patio and a small travel shop. Double and family rooms are available. Prices are $15 for members, $19 for nonmembers, and $25/34 for a single/double for members, or $34/40 if you're not. Check-in is from 8 am to 4 pm, and 4 to 11 pm in summer. From the airport, the Airbus goes to the nearby Westin Hotel. From the bus depot, take the No 7 bus south from the corner of Robie and Almon Sts (you may have to trudge south to Quinpool Rd, a few minutes away) to the corner of Barrington and South Sts. The hostel can be seen from this corner.

   The *YMCA (☎ 902-423-9622, 1565 South Park St)* is in an excellent location, across from the Public Gardens and very near Citadel Hill. Single rooms for men and women are $28 and a room for couples goes for $51. The weekly rate is cheaper. There's a small, cheap cafeteria and you can use facilities like the gym and swimming pool. It's open all year.

   The *YWCA (☎ 902-423-6162, 1239 Barrington St)* for women only is right next door to the HI Hostel between the city centre and the VIA Rail station. There are 30 rooms; singles/doubles cost $26.50/40. Good weekly rates are available.

   Halifax has the highest ratio of educational facilities per capita on the continent. This is good for the traveller, not just in the enjoyment of the erudite citizenry but in being able to take advantage of the abundance of economical rooms offered in dormitories during summer months. All city universities are considering merging into one giant institution.

   At *Dalhousie University* rooms are available from mid-May to mid-August in the Howe and Sherref Hall residences. Contact Room 410 in the Dalhousie Student Union Building *(☎ 902-494-8840, 6136 University Ave)*. Both are on the campus: Howe residence is on the corner of Coburg Rd and LeMarchant St; Sherref Hall is on the corner of South and Oxford Sts. Reservations are required. Singles/doubles/triples cost $34/51/69 including taxes, use of athletic facilities, and breakfast. All other meals are available.

   The *Technical University of Nova Scotia (TUNS; ☎ 902-420-7780)*, also has rooms

from mid-May to the end of August. Prices are $25/40; students $20/34. The *O'Brien Residence* (☎ 902-494-1245, 5217 Morris St) is about a 10 minute walk south of the downtown core. It's on the corner of Barrington St. Free laundry services are included and there is a cafeteria.

Mount St Vincent University rents rooms from May to late August; contact the Conference Officer (☎ 902-457-6364, 166 Bedford Hwy) on the campus. Rates are $25/36. There also are excellent weekly and monthly rates, especially for students. Meals are available and there is a coin laundry. The university is a 15 minute drive west of town on the Bedford Hwy and overlooks the Bedford Basin.

Yet another university with accommodation is *St Mary's University* (☎ 902-420-5845, ☎ 1-888-347-5555, 923 Robie St), which is also cheap and not far from the centre. Singles/doubles/triples are $22/32/61 and there are two-room, self-contained units which are good for families at $79.

B&Bs, Tourist Homes & Hotels Over half of the budget B&Bs and the only two budget hotels in Halifax have closed. And nothing else has filled the void. Still, you should be able to find something, even in summer. Some especially fine options, though more costly, are found in heritage houses and mansions.

Unlike many cities, there are no B&B agencies in Halifax, but everybody does quite well working independently. Throughout summer this popular town does fill up, so don't leave finding a place until too late in the day.

The plain, straightforward *Fountain View Guesthouse* (☎ 902-422-4169, 2138 Robie St) is the bright blue place with white trim, between Compton Ave and Williams St, across from the park and west of Citadel Hill. It's reliable, consistent and open all year. North Common is across the street and the Citadel is within walking distance. The seven rooms, all with TV, go for $24 to $28 a single and $30 a double. Each extra person costs an additional $5. It's popular, so try in the morning after guests have left.

Your only other definite budget option is found along Windsor Street, a good half-hour trudge from downtown to the north-west. Here, *Marie's B&B* (☎ 902-453-4987, 3440 Windsor St) offers three basic rooms (two doubles and a triple) in a simple family home. Because she's basically holding the fort alone for budget digs, she's also always full. Rates are $30/40 single/double. More bad news – she's considering retiring, so before you ring her, call the Nova Scotia toll-free number and ask if she's still open, and you can have a room reserved for you. Bus No 8 runs past.

The spacious, comfortable *Fresh Start B&B* (☎ 902-453-6616, ☎ 1-888-453-6616, 2720 Gottingen St) is in a big, old house. It's tastefully decorated but not prissy. There are five rooms, priced from $55 to $65. Rooms with private bath are more costly. It's open all year and prices drop after the summer season.

The only drawback to this recommended place is the neighbourhood. The B&B's immediate surroundings are fine but much of Gottingen St and its side streets can be quite seedy. Some people will feel uncomfortable walking to and fro, and women alone, especially, should probably not consider doing so after dark. If you're driving, though, don't think twice about it, and there is on-site parking. Also, buses run on Gottingen St.

There's a new option along Windsor St, north-west of Quinpool Rd. *Bobs' Guest House* (☎ 902-454-4374, 2715 Windsor St) has a variety of rooms – the attic suite is cosy – along with nice gardens and a hot tub. The like-named owners are friendly and helpful. Rooms start at around $65. Bus Nos 8, 82 and 17 run along Windsor St.

The *Queen St Inn* (☎ 902-422-9828, 1266 Queen St) near Morris St is in a house dating from about 1860, with six tastefully decorated rooms at $52/58.

The *King Edward Inn* (☎ 902-422-3266, 1-800-565-5464, 2400 Agricola St) is an impressive restored Victorian inn which looks almost out of place standing graciously in its surroundings. There are over 40 well decorated singles/doubles from $60 to $100, with continental breakfast. The Citadel is an easy walk.

The *Lord Nelson Hotel* (☎ 902-423-6331, ☎ 1-800-565-2020, 1515 South Park St) at Spring Garden Rd has 174 rooms with rates beginning at $62 a night.

Top End The following places are in the next bracket up and tend to be larger, more expensive and often in heritage or historical houses or buildings.

For a bit of a splurge, the $80 (and way up) singles/doubles might be a deal at the historic *Waverly Inn* (☎ 902-423-9346, 1266 Barrington St) whose 32 rooms haven't lost a bit of circa-1866 charm. The price includes breakfast and you're quite close to downtown.

Immaculately kept and finished is the *Halliburton House Inn* (☎ 902-420-0658, 5184 Morris St). Built in 1820, it has antiques, a library and a pleasant garden. The 30 rooms start at $110/135 with suites at additional cost.

The central core also has a number of large corporate hotels. The *Prince George* (☎ 902-425-1986, ☎ 1-800-565-1567) for example is ideally situated on the corner of George and Price Sts, close to the Citadel and the waterfront. A double here will set you back $160.

There are also places available out at the airport.

Motels Motels tend to be a little expensive and are clustered along the Bedford Hwy (Hwy 2), north-west of town along the bay called Bedford Basin. They offer good views of the bay and cool breezes; bus Nos 80 and 81 go into town, a 15 minute drive away.

The *Travellers Motel* (☎ 902-835-3394, 1-800-565-3394), open year-round, is right at the city limits. The small, simple cottages (rather than the modern motel units) start at $40 with shower, TV and pool; motel units go from $60.

The *Econo Lodge* (☎ 902-443-0303 or 1-800-561-9961, 560 Bedford Hwy), the big brown place, has 33 fully equipped rooms at $60/70. Breakfast is available and there's a pool.

A third choice is the *Days Inn Halifax* (☎ 902-443-3171, ☎ 1-800-325-2525, 636 Bedford Hwy), which charges $65 a single/double. Breakfast, which costs extra, is served from 7 to 11 am.

Farther out is *Stardust Motel* (☎ 902-835-3316, 1067 Bedford Hwy), which has 51 rooms at $50/60, more for one with a kitchenette.

Places to Eat

Halifax has a good selection of restaurants offering a variety of foods in all price ranges, and generally the quality is high.

For breakfast, try the recommended *Mediterraneo Cafe* just down Barrington St from the International Visitor Centre. It has a full breakfast for under $3, and many pasta dishes such as cannelloni for $3.75.

Spring Garden Rd, between Grafton and South Park Sts, has exploded in recent years with cafés, pubs and restaurants. (Though many travellers find that prices rise in direct proportion to distance away from the harbour.) *Second Cup*, in the Montreal Building on the corner of Queen St, is the largest version of this chain in Canada. It's great for people watching. There are a couple of computers so you can go surfing on the Internet.

The *Midtown Tavern*, on the corner of Prince and Grafton Sts, is a national treasure – a good example of the Canadian workers' tavern. The sociable owner has been offered zillions to develop the corner, but he absolutely balks at it. It's packed with friendly locals at lunch, most of them enjoying a sirloin steak, french fries and coleslaw and washing it down with draught by the glass. Steak and fries is $5 (great steak for the money), and a glass of beer after 4.40 pm is only 99¢.

The longstanding *Bluenose*, on the corner of Duke and Hollis Sts, is another place packed with locals at lunch. Its menu ranges from Greek and Italian to full lobster dinners and there is beer on tap. Lunch specials are under $6, dinners start at $7.

Halifax is blessed with pubs, and many are good for a meal. The upmarket *Granite Brewery* (1222 Barrington St) brews its own beer, which is very good. The food, too, should not be ignored; try the jambalaya. Dinners start at $7.50.

Reconstructed street, Louisbourg, Nova Scotia

Evangeline & Longfellow Church, Nova Scotia

Halifax building aesthetics, Nova Scotia

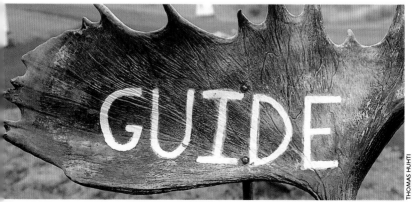

Moose antler, Cape Breton Island, Nova Scotia

Whale skull near North Rustico, PEI

The Big Nickel, Ontario

Folk Art Interiors, Kitsilano, BC

Statue in Calgary, Alberta

Acadian Mural, Pioneer Acadian Village, PEI

The Crab, Vancouver, BC

Several pubs can be found in the mall area of Granville St on the corner of Duke St. Both the *Split Crow* and the *Peddlar's Pub* have outdoor sections and the latter has live music on Saturday afternoon. The Split Crow often has lunch specials like clams and chips for under $4.

Also for lunch or dinner, *Satisfaction Feast (1581 Grafton St)* in the pale blue building is a well established vegetarian restaurant. It's open from 11 am to 9 pm. Dinners start at $8 and sandwiches $4. The spinach-and-cheese curry is definitely worth considering.

For East Indian food, the *Guru (5234 Blowers St)* is good with main dishes starting at $8. The all-you-can-eat lunch buffets are very good value, particularly the vegetarian one, which is $7.95. Much cheaper is the *Samosa Plus (6184 Quinpool Rd)*. Lunch specials are $4, the all-you-can eat vegetarian buffet is $5. One of the most well regarded Indian restaurants in eastern Canada is *Curry Village (5763 Brenton Place)* tucked behind Spring Garden Road. The highly rated East Indian cuisine also has some great southern *madras* as well. Main courses start at $8.

For Vietnamese try the casual *Kinh-Do (1284 Barrington St)*. It offers tasty food, an extensive menu and low prices. There is a daily lunch special for under $5. Around the corner on the other side of the HI hostel is *Tomasino's*, a subterranean Italian eatery with gourmet pizzas and a $7 buffet.

Continuing with the ethnic places there is the small, cosy but much more expensive *Czech Inn (5237 Blowers St)*, a local favourite, with schnitzels, borscht and the like. Mains range in price from $8 to $13. Nearby, the lower-priced *Hungary Hungarian (5215 Blowers St)*, run by the same man, specialises in goulashes.

And there is seafood here, of course. The huge *McKelvie's (☎ 902-421-6161, 1680 Lower Water St)* in an old firehouse is an institution of sorts here. Dinner main courses average $12. Reservations are advisable. Newer and sort of a low-key genteel pub (away from the boisterousness of other Halifax pubs) with superb steak and seafood is

O'Carroll's (1860 Upper Water St). There's good traditional Maritime music here too. Dinners are pricey, with mains *starting* at around $16.

Cogswell St as well as its continuation, Quinpool Rd, are commercial streets with plenty of eating spots. For Greek, the aptly named *Greek House (6253 Quinpool Rd)* has good breakfasts all day along with Greek specials from around $7. The Indian restaurant Samosa Plus is also here.

The somewhat bohemian *Trident Booksellers & Café (1570 Argyle St)*, with the large stained-glass piece in the window, is unbeatable for lingering with a coffee or pot of tea. The various coffees, from espresso to lattes, are good and cheap, and when you've finished with the newspaper, the other half of the café has a fine selection of books, new and used.

La Cave (5244 Blowers St), tucked in the little doorway, is open until 4.30 am on weekends. In the basement, this small bistro offers good desserts; it is perennially voted *the* place to bring a date.

A few natural food stores exist downtown, but none have substantial groceries. Right in the heart of the Maritime Centre is *Super Natural Health Food Store*.

Entertainment

Pubs & Live Music Halifax has the country's highest density of 18 to 25-year-olds, and this has translated into an astonishing number of pubs (55 at last count) and nightlife options, rivalled only by St John's, Newfoundland. Doing the 'pub pinball' is a pastime to the extent that the US Navy – and they know these things – voted it the top liberty call port, along with San Francisco. Local tour operators even give guided tours of the night-time action. For a complete rundown of the music scene grab a copy of *The Coast*, Halifax's offbeat magazine. This publication, offered free at restaurants and pubs, provides a full schedule of music, film and stage performances in the city. The information office in the Old Red Store has an awesome map detailing most of the pubs and clubs in town.

Privateer's Warehouse, in the Historic Properties (near *Bluenose II's* docking area on the waterfront), with two restaurants, also has a busy, inexpensive bar on the lower level. The *Lower Deck* often presents Maritime folk music – good stuff.

On the corner of Grafton and Sackville is *Maxwell's Plum Tavern*, an English-style pub which boasts the largest selection of imported draught beer and single-malt Scotch in Atlantic Canada. Often on the weekends there is live blues or jazz. *Rogues Roost* along Spring Garden Rd has an awfully large selection as well, including its own ales.

More live music, especially bluegrass and blues, can be enjoyed near the HI Hostel at *Bearly's* on Barrington St.

Cape Breton Tea Room, nearly adjacent to the Discovery Centre on Barrington St, is a book and music store heavy on traditional Cape Breton music. It sponsors live ceilidhs on Thursday from 7 to 10 pm.

On Spring Garden Rd there are several bars featuring live music. For the *Thirsty Duck (5470 Spring Garden Rd)*, go through the store and up the stairs. It's got burgers, fish and chips, sandwiches and salads, and draught beer at low prices. Just up the street is *Your Father's Moustache*. Both feature rooftop patios and live music.

My Apartment (1740 Argyle St) has a dance floor with live rock bands nightly; it's part of four establishments under one roof – the *Dome* (dubbed the 'Liquordome'). The tranquil *Birmingham*, at Spring Rd and Park Lane near the Public Gardens, has capacious interiors, along with jazz nightly and an extensive list of imported beers. Another jazz hotspot is *Market St Jazz*, a club near the Prince George Hotel with jazz daily. More jazz in a chummy, agreeable pub can be found at the coolly named *Economy Shoe Shop*, which James Cameron reportedly frequented while filming *Titanic* in Dartmouth.

The large, loud *New Palace Cabaret (1721 Brunswick St)* across from the Citadel has rock and blues bands and lots of grinding nightly till way, way late.

The Harbour Folk Society (☎ 902-425-3655) presents informal concerts on the first Saturday of every month as well as an open mike Wednesday evenings at *The Grad House (6154 University Ave)*.

Performing Arts The Symphony Nova Scotia plays the *Rebecca Cohn Auditorium (☎ 902-421-7311, 1646 Barrington St)*. The *Dalhousie Arts Centre (☎ 902-494-3820)* at the university is a major performance venue for theatre and dance. International artists and bands perform frequently at *Halifax Metro Centre (☎ 902-451-1221, cnr Duke & Brunswick Sts)* across from the Old Town Clock.

The *Neptune Theatre (☎ 902-429-7070, 1593 Argyle St)* is the city's leading theatre venue with a year-round season; it's been in a $25 million two-stage complex since 1997. Halifax also has two dinner theatres: *Graton St Dinner Theatre (☎ 902-452-1961)* and *Historic Feast Company (☎ 902-420-1840)* located in the Historic Properties. There's nothing quite like Shakespeare by the sea and that's exactly what you get from *Shakespeare by the Sea (☎ 902-422-0295)*, four performances by the Bard in Point Pleasant Park during summer. Tickets are $25 to $30.

Cinema Halifax has 39 movie theatres, so you'll find something. For repertory films there is the *Wormwood's Cinema (☎ 902-422-3700, 2015 Gottingen St)*. North-west of the city centre in Bayers Lake Park is a brand-new *IMAX theatre (☎ 902-876-4629)* with hourly shows beginning at noon.

Getting There & Away

Air Air Canada (☎ 902-429-7111) has services to Montreal ($511) and Toronto ($596). Canadian Airlines (☎ 902-427-5500) and Air Canada also both fly to St John's, Newfoundland ($548). Their partners – Inter-Canadien, Air Nova and Air St Pierre – also provide connections throughout Atlantic Canada. One-way stand-by fares via Canada 3000 (☎ 902-873-3555) are Vancouver ($240), Toronto ($95), and St John's ($70).

Bus The principal Nova Scotian bus line is the Acadian line, which connects with the

New Brunswick SMT lines. There are also a couple of smaller, regional lines which service specific regions only. They all use the Acadian bus station (☎ 902-454-9321) at 6040 Almon St, which runs south off Robie St, north-west of the Citadel.

One Acadian line runs through the Annapolis Valley and down to Yarmouth. Others cover the central region, the Northumberland Shore and parts of Cape Breton.

Following are the one-way fares to several destinations. To North Sydney (one express service daily and other milk runs) it's $54, to Yarmouth $41, Moncton $41, Saint John in New Brunswick $59 and Fredericton $64.

DRL Coachlines buses (☎ 902-450-1987) run along the South Shore from Halifax to Yarmouth.

Zinck's bus company runs several services along the Eastern Shore from Halifax to Sherbrooke, stopping at all the small villages along the way. It runs once a day (except Sunday) eastbound and Tuesday to Saturday westbound.

Train The VIA Rail station (☎ 902-429-8421, 1-800-561-3952) is six blocks from the downtown area along Hollis St. It's on Terminal Rd by the big old Halifax Hilton Hotel and is a beautiful example of Canadian train-station architecture. The train is more useful for reaching out-of-province destinations than for getting around Nova Scotia. A train to Moncton, New Brunswick ($48) and eventually Montreal, departs at 1.30 pm daily (except Tuesday) along a route through northern New Brunswick that includes stops at Campbellton, Bathurst, Miramichi, Sackville and Amherst. By booking a week in advance the ticket to Montreal is $108.10; you can reserve up to one month in advance and it's definitely a good idea as only a limited number are sold each day.

Car Byways (☎ 902-429-0092), 2156 Barrington St, charges $30 per day with 250km a day and 14¢ a kilometre beyond. Dollar Rent-Car (☎ 902-429-1892) with a desk at Citadel Inn Hotel, has compacts for $37 a day, 200km a day and 12¢ a kilometre beyond that. Keep in mind that by the time you add tax and insurance costs, the price is more than $50 a day.

Other rental places include Rent-A-Wreck (☎ 902-454-2121), 2823 Robie at Almon St, which offers HI members a discount, and Budget (☎ 902-492-7541), on the corner of Hollis and Sackville Sts in the Ultramar service station. The airport has several rental places.

Getting Around

To/From the Airport From the centre of Halifax the airport is nearly 40km out on Hwy 102, north towards Truro.

There are no city buses to the airport but there is the Airbus (☎ 902-873-2091). It runs between the airport and the downtown centre, with stops at several of the major central hotels such as the Lord Nelson, the Prince George and the Sheraton. It also makes pick-ups at the Holiday Inn and others in Dartmouth. The fares are $12/20 one way/round-trip. The bus makes 18 trips daily with the first run at 6.30 am and the last bus leaving the airport at 11.15 pm. Allow 90 minutes before flight time.

An alternative is Share-A-Cab (☎ 902-429-5555, ☎ 1-800-565-8669). Call at least four hours before flight time and it will find other passengers and pick you up. The price works out about the same as the bus.

Bus Metro Transit (☎ 902-490-6600) runs the good, inexpensive city bus system. Fares are $1.55 or $28 for a 20-ticket booklet. *Perk's News Stand* near the Old Red Store information office sells booklets. Call for route and schedule information or pick up a *Metro Transit Riders' Guide* for free from the Tourism Halifax centres. The No 3 city bus on Robie St goes from the bus station into town. *Fred* is a free city bus running a circuit along South St, Lower Water St, Barrington St, Spring Garden Rd, and South Park back to South St. It runs every 20 minutes from 11 am to 6 pm Monday through Saturday May to mid-October.

Hitchhikers heading north towards Truro will want to pick up bus No 80 or 82 and get

off near Hwy 102 north of Bedford. Those heading west, will want bus No 21 which ends at the village of Timberlea on Hwy 3.

Ferry Ferries run continuously from near the Historic Properties dock. One boat heads across the bay to the city of Dartmouth, the other is a weekday service to Woodside. A ticket is $1.55 one way and the ride makes a nice, short mini-tour of the harbour. Ferries run every 15 minutes at peak times, otherwise every 30 minutes. The last one is at 11.45 pm. On Sunday they run from noon to 5.45 pm but only June through September. Bikes are welcomed.

Bicycle Bicycles can be rented from Bike People (☎ 902-420-0777), 1471 Birmingham St, off Spring Garden Rd. Bikes are $3 per hour, $15 per day.

For any bike information or to join a bicycle tour of the city or Halifax region, call the Velo Bicycle Club (☎ 902-423-4345).

DARTMOUTH

Founded in 1750, one year after Halifax, Dartmouth is Halifax's counterpart just across the harbour. However, the similarities end with the waterfront location of the central area. Dartmouth is a city of 70,000 people spread over a large area and, compared with Halifax, is more residential and the city centre less commercial. The downtown area lacks the history, charm and bustle of Halifax.

Having said that, Dartmouth does make for a cheap afternoon side trip and even a scenic one, thanks to the ferry. The Halifax-Dartmouth ferry, operated by Metro Transit (the bus people), is said to be the oldest saltwater ferry system in North America, dating back to 1752 when it was just a rowboat.

The fact that the city has 23 lakes within its boundaries will suit those seeking accessible water activities. Many of these lakes are good for swimming, seven have supervised beaches, some are stocked with fish and there's in-town boating and canoeing (see Kayaking & Canoeing in the Halifax section for details). Most popular of the

beaches are Birch Cove and Graham's Grove, both on Lake Bannock.

Orientation

Aldernay Gate houses the ferry terminal, the Dartmouth Public Library, city offices, a food court and some shops.

Portland St, running up from the ferry terminal, is the main street. Several years ago it was completely overhauled, with trees planted and the sidewalks widened. Unfortunately there isn't much along it and the stores and businesses seem to be having a tough time. What there is includes several inexpensive restaurants, pizza joints, a couple of antique/junk shops and a bar or two of dubious character.

There are, though, a number of historic sites near the waterfront and the neighbouring downtown area. You can pick up a walking-tour guide at a tourist office in either city. Buildings in old Dartmouth are primarily made of wood, rather than of brick or stone as in Halifax.

Beside the large ferry terminal is Ferry Terminal Park, where a walking path leads along the water and puts you in view of Halifax-Dartmouth Industries, a shipyard, and Dartmouth Cove, the home of Canada's largest coastguard base.

Micmac Mall is the largest shopping centre in the Maritimes.

Information

A small tourist desk is at the ferry complex but has basic brochures only. The main Dartmouth information centre, Dartmouth Tourism (☎ 902-490-7395), oddly enough is in the lower level of Micmac Mall; it too is nothing more than a kiosk with a few brochures.

World Peace Pavilion

Within Ferry Terminal Park is this unusual outdoor exhibit. Metro Youth for Global Unity invited each country in the world to send in a rock or brick to symbolise the earth we all share. More than 65 countries responded and the collection is well worth a look and at times even touching. The rocks

range from a 280-pound piece of the fallen Berlin Wall that Germany sent and a stone from the Great Wall of China to a bit of rubble the USA contributed from a missile silo that was imploded in 1995 in accordance with the Strategic Arms Reduction Treaty.

Shubenacadie Canal

You can also visit the restored Shubenacadie Canal. The canal connects Dartmouth (through a series of waterways, lakes and locks) with the Bay of Fundy, on the other side of the province, built in the mid-1800s along an old Micmac portage route. It's used by canoeists, but parks and various historic sites along it can be reached by road.

For more details on the entire canal and its history and a look at two of the restored locks, visit the **Fairbanks Centre** (☎ 902-462-1826), 54 Locks Rd, at Lake Charles in north Dartmouth. This centre is full of displays pertaining to local history of the canal. It's open from 9 am to 5 pm weekdays, 1 to 5 pm weekends May through September and admission is free. Boat rides and canoe rentals are available. An older visitors centre, around the corner from the shipyards near the ferry landing, still stands but it was shut tight on a last visit.

Dartmouth Regional Museum of Cultural History

The museum (☎ 902-464-2300) is at the junction of Alderney Drive and Wyse Rd, about a 15 minute walk left off the Halifax ferry. It houses an eclectic collection pertaining to the city's natural and human history and includes some Native Indian artefacts and crafts, various tools and fashions and industrial bric-a-brac. The museum is free and during summer is open from 10 am to 4 pm Monday through Saturday, and 11 am to 4 pm. Available literature says it's got a $3 admission but it was free at last check.

Leighton Dillman Park

Beside the museum is this hillside park, part of the original common area of Dartmouth set up in 1788. You can climb to the top of Fairy Hill in the middle where there is a memorial cairn dedicated to the first settlers of the city and a great view of the harbour and Halifax on the other side.

Evergreen House

Built for a judge in 1862, Evergreen House, part of the Heritage Museum, is a fine example of a 19th century house for the well-to-do. Many of the 20 rooms are open to the public and have been furnished in the style of the 1880s. Admission is free and the house is open from 10 am to 7 pm (closed for lunch from 12.30 to 1.30 pm) daily, except Friday and Saturday in summer. The address is 26 Newcastle St.

Quaker Whaler House

At 59 Ochterloney St, near the museum and tourist office and within walking distance of the ferry, is the Quaker Whaler House, the oldest house in the Halifax area, having been built in 1786. The Quakers came to the region as whalers from New England. Guides in costume lead visitors around the house. Hours during summer are 10 am to 7 pm (closed for lunch noon to 1 pm) daily, except Friday and Sunday. Admission is free.

Cole Harbour Heritage Farm Museum

This museum (☎ 902-434-0222) is at 471 Poplar Drive, out of the centre. Built at the end of the 18th century, the farm includes five buildings, including the main house, blacksmith shop, barns and a carriage shop. The museum also includes walking trails and a tearoom. Hours are 10 am to 4 pm daily during summer, except on Sunday when it opens at noon. Admission is free.

Bedford Institute of Oceanography

Just outside Dartmouth is this major government marine research centre (☎ 902-426-2373), Canada's largest. A self-guided walk around the exhibits concerning the fishery and various ocean studies takes a little less than an hour. There is also a video and some aquarium specimens to see. This is the country's leading oceanographic facility and as such has international standing and often

NOVA SCOTIA

carries out research with similar institutes from other countries. The centre is open Monday to Friday only, from 9 am to 4 pm. To get there from Dartmouth by car, take Windmill Rd to the Shannon Park exit, which is near the MacKay Bridge, or take bus No 51 from the Dartmouth ferry terminal.

Black Cultural Centre

Described as the first of its kind in Canada, the centre (☎ 902-434-6223) is a museum and cultural and educational facility all in one. Its principal aim is to preserve and present the history of black people in Nova Scotia. Perhaps surprisingly, Nova Scotia was an early centre for black communities in Canada and a significant depot of the Underground Railway (see Windsor in the Ontario chapter for details). There are various small exhibits, including some African musical instruments and a video. Of more interest may be the scheduled events, lectures, concerts etc, so call for information.

For those more interested in black history in the province, pick up a copy of the *Black Heritage Trail* pamphlet here or at one of the major tourist offices. It lays out various routes around the province, detailing points of note, and provides some little-known historical information.

The centre is open year-round from 9 am to 5 pm Monday to Friday and from 10 am to 4 pm on Saturday. It's in Westphal, just past the eastern border of the city of Dartmouth on Route 7, Cherrybrook Rd. This is about 6 or 7km south-east of central Dartmouth. Admission is $3, less for seniors and students.

Shearwater Aviation Museum

South of town on Pleasant St, at the Canadian Forces Base (CFB Shearwater), the aviation museum (☎ 902-460-1083) details the history of Canadian maritime military aviation. Some aircraft are on display, as well as pictures, uniforms and other salient objects. It's open during summer from 10 am to 5 pm Tuesday through Friday, noon to 4 pm weekends, lesser hours the rest of the season. Admission is free.

The Shearwater International Airshow is held here annually, usually after Labour Day.

Special Events

Festivals include a three-day multicultural festival held in June along the waterfront, featuring ethnic foods and arts; the Maritime Old-Time Fiddlers' Contest in early July; the Tattoo Festival, held along the waterfront in July; and the Dartmouth Natal Day Celebration in early August.

Places to Stay

There are places to stay scattered about on this side of the bay as well. There is camping in the Shubie Beach Park.

Close to the harbour is *Martin House B&B (☎ 902-463-7338, 62 Pleasant St)*, with rooms at $45/50. Less expensive is friendly *Caroline's (☎ 902-469-4665, 134 Victoria Rd)*, not far from the Macdonald Bridge, with three rooms at $35 to $40 including a continental breakfast.

Places to Eat

A couple of places in the old section near the dock are worth noting. More or less opposite the Quaker Whaler House, east of the ferry landing, is a small *tea shop (44 Ochterloney St)* good for an afternoon break.

Opposite the ferry and right, off the corner of Queen St, is the *Alderney Bar & Café*, with new spacious interiors and pub grub from around $6 sandwiches, $8 mains. Next door is *La Perla*, outstanding but prohibitively pricey Northern Italian fare. East of here is Portland St with a string of dives and pizza joints, but also *Nature Things* with natural foods and lunch specials, and a good café, *Café Michele (86 Portland St)* with good lunches, especially pasta dishes, under $5.

Central Nova Scotia

The central part of Nova Scotia, in geographic terms, essentially takes in the corridor of land from the New Brunswick border down to Halifax. For many coming by road

from elsewhere in Canada, this is the introduction to Nova Scotia. But don't turn against the province because of what you see from the Trans Canada Hwy, as it passes through flat, uninteresting terrain on the way to the province's main highway at Truro. Parrsboro is an interesting stop south-west of Amherst and there is some good scenery here along the shores of the Bay of Fundy.

AMHERST

Amherst is the geographic centre of the Maritimes and a travel junction. For anyone heading into Nova Scotia, passing by is a necessity, and Route 104 leads south towards Halifax and then cuts east for Cape Breton Island. Also from Amherst, it's not far to the Northumberland Shore and the north coastal route across the province. Route 16 to the bridge for Prince Edward Island is just across the border in New Brunswick.

There are two tourist offices in Amherst. Just off exit 1 of Route 104 is a huge provincial welcome centre (☎ 902-667-8429) that is open daily during summer from 8 am to 9 pm. The centre features information and a booking service for all of Nova Scotia, an interpretive area and gardens out front. Within town is the Amherst tourist office (☎ 902-667-0696) in a railway car parked on LaPlanche St, from exit 2 off the highway. Hours are noon to 5 pm on Sunday and 9 am to 6 pm the rest of the week during summer.

Amherst is a pleasant town with some fine buildings, and many from the 19th century have been restored. You'll find a number of these along Victoria St, the main street, whose intersection with Church St is the primary one in town. The local tourist centre has a walking tour map. Very good here is the **Amherst Point Migratory Bird Sanctuary** and its walking trails through field and marsh; good for a leg stretch.

Cumberland County Museum (☎ 902-667-2561) is at 150 Church St in the erstwhile home of the Father of Confederation, RB Dickey. The most interesting displays are the articles made by prisoners of war at the Amherst Internment Camp during WWI, which included Leon Trotsky. Hours during summer are 9 am to 5 pm daily, except Sunday when it opens at 2 pm. Admission is $1.

On the east coast there is a good beach at Lorneville on Northumberland Strait.

Places to Stay

Amherst is a great place to stay overnight with moderately priced accommodation. *Brown's Guest Home (☎ 902-667-9769, 158 East Victoria St)* has three rooms and charges $28/30/40 a single/double/triple. *Treen Mansion (☎ 902-667-2146, 113 Spring St)* is a Victorian home built in 1907. There are three rooms at $30/45 including breakfast in the sunroom.

For a motel, consider the *Victorian Motel (☎ 902-667-7211, 150 East Victoria St)*. Rooms are $42/46/50.

Places to Eat

The classic *Hampton Diner* is recommended for good, cheap food and quick, courteous service. It's been open every day from 7 am to 9 pm since 1956! You can't miss it as you come into town from the highway off exit 1. Most sandwiches and hamburgers are $3; two eggs, potatoes and toast is $2.25.

Getting There & Away

Ticket agent and station for Acadian bus lines is the Irving Mainway (☎ 902-667-8435) at 203 S Albion St. There are three buses a day for Halifax at 11.50 am and 3.20 and 9.35 pm; fare is $31.25. SMT will take you north to Moncton daily at 10 am and 3.55 and 6.35 pm for $9.20.

CHIGNECTO

This region south and west of Amherst is named after the bay and the cape at the western tip. This is one of the least visited, least populated areas of the province. The road network is minimal, although the Glooscap Trail tourist route goes through the eastern portion. It's an area with some very interesting geology and ancient history, which attracts dinosaur detectives, fossil followers and rockhounds. The Minas Basin shore has some good scenery and

shoreline cliffs. The tides of the Minas Basin are high even by Fundy standards.

Joggins

A short distance from Amherst on Chignecto Bay is the village of Joggins, known for its seaside cliff full of fossils. It exposes one of the world's best Carboniferous-period fossil collections, consisting of trees, insects, reptiles and others that are 300 million years old. There is a footpath down to the beach and along the 50m-high sandstone cliffs but you're better off first visiting the **Joggins Fossil Centre** (☎ 902-251-2727) on Main St, which is open daily from 9 am to 6.30 pm from June through September. Here you'll see samples including fossilised footprints, and learn more about the site. Admission is $3.50.

Guided tours used to be offered and were fun, but they've not been offered of late. Remember that this is a protected area so do-it-yourselves beware; scavenging is OK, hacking into the cliffs is not. The museum can offer advice if not assistance.

Cape Chignecto Provincial Park

Opened in 1998, this is now the crown jewel of the peninsula and one of the best hiking experiences in Nova Scotia if not the Maritimes. The highlight here is the very challenging yet-to-be-completed 45km Bay of Fundy coastal hiking trail with wilderness – nay, old growth – camp sites. At the time of writing, 23km had been finished, beginning and ending in West Advocate (and they're hacking more every day); 30 primitive camp sites are also available now. Right now the trail from West Advocate to Cape Chignecto is rugged and only for those in shape; rounding the bend from here the views are simply magnificent, with occasional breathtaking drop-offs of 200m in some canyons. For a day hike, you can go halfway to Mill Brook, where a wooden staircase descends to the beach, which you can then hike back along to Red Rocks, near the ranger station. Of course, double-check tide status with rangers before wandering onto a secluded beach here. All told, those in shape should be able to do it in around

two hours. If you plan on camping, reservations are a necessity; call the park office (☎ 902-392-2085). A day pass is $2; camp sites are $14. A private campground is also found 5km from the park, in Advocate Harbour; a B&B is closer to the park entrance.

Cape d'Or

If you make it way down to the end of the peninsula, don't miss Cape d'Or Park at the lighthouse, and walk out to the point for a really spectacular view over the Minas Channel and Bay of Fundy. If you want to spend the night there are two nearby campgrounds and *Lightkeeper's Kitchen & Guest House* (☎ 902-664-2108) near the lighthouse. The Kitchen serves breakfast and lunch and has four rooms available at $30/40.

Diligent River

At Diligent River there is Ward Falls Trail, a 4km-long hike up the river gorge. The trail is well maintained but steep in some places and towards the end passes the 3m cascade.

Parrsboro

Parrsboro is the largest of the small towns along the Minas Basin shore and is a place to stay for a day or two. There are several museums, a fossil-laden shoreline to explore and a half-dozen B&Bs and inns. In the centre of town, beside the Town Hall, is the tourist office, open from 8.30 am to 8.30 pm during summer. Among other things, the office has tide information for visiting rockhounds.

The area is interesting geologically and is known for its semiprecious stones, fossils and dinosaur prints. People scour the many local beaches and rock faces for agates and amethyst and attend the annual Rockhound Roundup, a get-together for rock, mineral and fossil collectors which began in the 1970s and features displays, demonstrations, guided walks and boat tours.

Fundy Geological Museum At the museum (☎ 902-254-3814) you can find out why the Parrsboro beaches have been dubbed 'Nova Scotia's own Jurassic Park'. It features a glittering collection of minerals

and fossils, of course, but also has models, hands-on exhibits and computer-aided displays that explain the fascinating geological history of the area. Naturalists on staff also lead special tours to the nearby beaches.

The museum is on Two Islands Road and is open year-round. During summer the hours are 9.30 am to 5.30 pm daily. Admission is $3.50, less for students and seniors, $8.50 a family, but often the tourist office has coupons that knock $1 off the ticket.

Two Islands Interpretive Site Continue on Two Islands Road away from town and you'll reach the site, dedicated to Wassons Bluff. In 1989, fossilised footprints of one of the oldest dinosaurs in the world were found in the eroding cliffs of the shoreline here. A trail leads to the beach and bluff and during low tide you can continue your dinosaur search out to the Two Islands.

Parrsboro Rock & Mineral Shop This is really the personal museum (☎ 902-254-2981) of Eldon George, who achieved international fame searching the nearby shorelines for gems and fossils. He loves to talk about his collection and has some interesting things on display, like the tooth of a duckbill dinosaur. The museum is on Whiteall Rd and hours during summer are 9 am to 9 pm daily, except Saturday when it's open till 5 pm.

Partridge Island This is not only the most popular shoreline to search for gems (sort of a Mecca for rockhounds) but also a place steeped in history. Among others, Samuel de Champlain landed here in 1607 and took away (what else?) amethyst rocks from the beach. The island is south of town on Whiteall Rd and there is an interpretive display explaining how the powerful Fundy tides break up the layers of rock and expose new gemstones every year. More than likely there will be a dozen people searching the pebbled shoreline or the bluffs for agate, jasper, stilbite etc. Nearby is **Ottawa House Museum**, which preserves Sir Charles Tupper's summer home. Tupper was premier of Nova Scotia and later prime minister of

Canada. Hours are 10 am to 6 pm during summer and admission is $1.

Ship's Company Theatre All the world's a stage or in this case, the entire boat is. The MV *Kipawo*, built in the Saint John Shipyard, was the last of the Minas Basin ferries. Throughout summer a variety of plays are performed here, most of them new works from Maritime writers. The box office (☎ 902-254-3000) is in town.

Places to Stay & Eat There are several B&Bs and one motel in town, none really cheap save for the *Knowlton House B&B* (☎ 902-254-2773, 21 Western Ave), with three rooms from $40/45. For a splurge, the *Maple Inn* (☎ 902-254-3735, 17 Western Ave) nearby drips with character. It has eight various rooms from $55.

The *Harbour View Restaurant* has just what its name claims, along with family fare and seafood.

Five Islands Provincial Park
East of Parrsboro, the park (☎ 902-254-2980) offers camping, a beach and picnicking. Walking trails show the terrain's variety, some leading to the 90m-high cliffs at the edge of the Minas Basin, with views of the islands. Nearby tidal flats are good for clam-digging. The campground has 90 sites, most in a semi-open area with good views of the bay. Sites cost $14.

From here to the Trans Canada Hwy, you'll pass almost a dozen small takeaway stands, all of them offering fried clams. The clams are dug locally and are among the best to be had in the Maritimes, no doubt because of their freshness.

Economy & Around
Closer to Five Islands than the town of Economy, Economy Mountain, at over 200m, affords good views. Some 6km north of Economy on River Phillip Rd, Economy Falls Trail leads 4km into a gorge in the Cobequid Mountains, ending at this stunning 20m cascade. This is one of the best hikes in the area.

Just east of town along Hwy 2 is *That Dutchman's Cheese Farm (☎ 902-647-2751)*, a combination cheese shop, restaurant and interpretive centre. Admission is now a bit steep at $5 but that's credited against any purchases.

SPRINGHILL

Springhill is a small, modest, working-class town known to many Canadians for two things: horrendous coal-mining disasters and as the birthplace of one of the country's most popular singers, Anne Murray. The stories of both are told in museums.

Anne Murray Centre

More or less right in the middle of town, on Main St, is the centre honouring Springhill's best known offspring. It's pretty well just for real buffs, though, with a rather high (relative to most provincial attractions) entrance fee of $5.50, less for seniors and children. For that you learn details of Anne Murray's successful career through pictures, videos, gold records and awards. There's also a gift shop, the only place that sells *From Springhill to the World*, a limited edition album she made just for the centre. The centre is open daily from May to October from 9 am to 5 pm.

Springhill Miners' Museum

Some 3km from the Anne Murray Centre (follow the signs), this site is a story of bravery, toil, guts and tragedy. A visit is worthwhile – interesting, educational and, to many people, emotional. Coal mining began here in 1834 and major accidents occurred in 1891 and again in 1956, claiming a total of 164 lives.

Two years later North America's deepest mine (4.3km) had a 'bump', as cave-ins are called, and 75 miners were killed in what was one of the continent's worst mining accidents. The search for survivors lasted 6½ days and ended when 12 men buried underground were found alive. In 1970 all mining operations here ceased.

The Miners' Museum allows visitors a first-hand look down a mine, as well as displaying equipment, tools and photographs.

The guides, all retired miners, lead the tour with a beautifully warm, human grace.

Admission is just $3 for seeing all the above-ground displays and $4.50 for the complete tour, which includes the guided talk and a trip down a shaft. Go for the latter – when you feel the cold, damp air at the opening, you'll be glad you're not going to work. The museum is open the same hours as the Anne Murray Centre.

TRURO

Truro (pop 13,000), with its central position in the province, is known as the hub of Nova Scotia. The Trans Canada Hwy passes through the north and east of town; Hwy 102 goes south to Halifax. The VIA Rail line goes by and Truro is also a bus transfer point.

The main part of town is around the corner of Prince and Inglis Sts, where some redevelopment has gentrified the streets.

The tourist office (☎ 902-893-2922) is in Victoria Square, a city park since 1860, on the corner of Prince and Commercial Sts. Hours are 8 am to 8 pm daily during the tourist season.

Victoria Park

Located in the heart of the city, this is the gem of Truro. At nearly 1000 acres, Victoria Park is more of a rugged nature reserve than a city park. Cars are banned, leaving most of park to walkers and cyclists. You should at least hike the 2km to view Joe Howe and Waddell Falls, two small cascades set in a rocky gorge. If you feel energetic climb Jacob's Ladder, a stairway of 173 steps.

There is also a pool in the park open daily during summer. The fee for swimming is $2.75. From the train station on Esplanade St, head south on Young St and then east on Brunswick St, where the entrance to the park is signposted.

Colchester Museum

At 29 Young St, in the centre of town, this large museum (☎ 902-895-6284) has exhibits on the region's human history, the founding of Truro and Elizabeth Bishop, a noted poet who grew up in the area. Hours

in summer are 10 am to 5 pm weekdays and 2 to 5 pm on weekends. Admission is $1. The **Little White Schoolhouse Museum** is at 20 Arthur St downtown.

Tidal Bore

The Bay of Fundy is known for having the highest tides in the world, and an offshoot of these is a tidal wave or bore which flows up the feeding rivers when high tide comes in. The advancing tide is often pretty small but, with the right phase of the moon, can be a metre or so in height and runs upstream, giving the impression of the river flowing backwards. The closest viewing place is a lookout on the Salmon River, on Hwy 236, just west of exit 14 off Hwy 102. Better viewing of the bores is at Maitland on Hwy 215 if you are headed that way. Tide schedules are available at the tourist office or call the Dial-A-Tide hotline (☎ 902-426-5494).

Places to Stay

Nova Scotia Agricultural College (☎ *902-893-6671)* offers beds in summer for $30/40 a single/double; call first to verify they're being offered.

Right across from the bus station is the excellent value *Willow Bend Motel (*☎ *902-895-5325,* ☎ *1-888-594-5569, 277 Willow St)*. Rooms in this pleasant motel are $45/55. *Berry's Motel (*☎ *902-895-2823, 73 Robie St)* has similar rates if not slightly cheaper.

For B&Bs, the *Suncatcher B&B (*☎ *902-893-7169, 25 Wile Crest Ave)* is a five minute drive from downtown Truro. Modest but comfortable rooms start at $35. There's a tad more luxury at the *Silver Furs B&B (*☎ *902-893-0570, 397 Prince St)* downtown, with four rooms including a triple suite. Singles/doubles/triples cost $50/75/90.

Wentworth Hostel (☎ *902-548-2379)*, with lots of beds in a big rambling century-old farmhouse, is not quite halfway to Amherst, near Wentworth on Valley Rd. It has kitchen facilities, showers and 75km of mountain-bike trails with a trailhead just outside the door. The hostel is signposted along the Trans Canada Hwy. Open all year, its rates are $11 for members and $14 nonmembers.

Places to Eat

The cross streets of Esplanade St and Inglis Place, the nucleus of downtown, have everything any budget traveller needs: a laundrette, beer store and two Chinese restaurants.

Within the Truro Centre, the train station mall along Esplanade St, there is the *Engine Room*, a lively pub and restaurant where sandwiches are $4.50 to $7 and most dinners are under $8; the similar *Heroe's* is across the street. Nearby is *My Mother's Apron* which serves almost everything from Mexican and Italian to fish and chips with lunch specials for $5. Get subs made to order with all local ingredients at *Old Tyme Deli* back in Truro Centre. There's also a *farmer's market* every Saturday from June to October. But for the cheapest eats anywhere, head to *Ryan's IGA* on Inglis Place. The large supermarket has a good lunch counter where sandwiches are under $2 and hot daily specials, like macaroni and cheese, are under $3. There are a few tables inside and a patio outside overlooking this busy commercial strip.

Getting There & Away

Bus The bus station (☎ 902-895-3833) is at 280 Willow St. It's near the hospital along the motel strip – you'll see the blue-and-white Acadian bus terminal sign. There are up to five buses a day to Halifax ($13) and three a day, with different stops, to Sydney ($42.75). To Saint John, New Brunswick ($49), there's an 8.40 am and 2.15 pm bus daily, with a stop in Amherst; two other buses go to Amherst. There's also one run per day to Antigonish.

Train The train station (☎ 1-800-561-3952) is in town on Esplanade St, near the corner of Inglis Place. Trains into and out of Nova Scotia pass through Truro, so connections can be made for Halifax, various points in New Brunswick and to Montreal. Trains to Halifax ($21) and Moncton depart once daily, except Tuesday. Purchasing tickets five days in advance usually saves a third or more.

MAITLAND & SHUBENACADIE CANAL

To the west of Truro on the Bay of Fundy is the little town of Maitland, at the mouth of the Shubenacadie River. Extending south along the river then through various locks and lakes, the continuous water system eventually leads to the city of Dartmouth and the ocean.

Opened in 1861, the canal is now a National Historic Site with a variety of sites and parks that can be visited along its course, including the Tidal Bore Park. It is also used by boaters and canoeists. Maps available at tourist offices list all the points of interest, walking trails etc. The main interpretive centre is in Dartmouth.

Also in Maitland is **Lawrence House**, a provincial historical site. The grand house was built in 1870 for shipbuilder William Lawrence, who obviously did quite well for himself. From a small room on the second floor Lawrence could watch the progress of his vessels being built in the shipyard at the river's edge. Hours are 9.30 am to 5.30 pm daily, except Sunday when the home doesn't open until 1 pm. Admission is free though a small charge was being considered.

STEWIACKE

At this little town south of Truro, you're halfway between the North Pole and the Equator. The **Mastodon Ridge & Showcase Nova Scotia** (☎ 902-893-4141) is here at exit 11 of Hwy 102. Hand-carved dinosaurs and a fossil discovery centre will entertain kids, but 'bigger' kids will love the lifesize replica of a 9000-year-old mastodon, found nearby. It's open from 9.30 am to 8 pm in summers, and admission is $2.50.

SHUBENACADIE

Not far from Maitland or Truro, off Hwy 215 on the west side of the Shubenacadie River, is a park where the tidal bores can be watched daily. If that's not exciting enough for you then you can raft them. Zodiac rafts powered by outboard motors take six to eight passengers up the river and then ride the tidal bore as it sweeps through, literally a roller coaster in waves one to 3m high.

There is a $2 entry fee just to watch the action at Tidal Bore Park (☎ 902-758-4032) while the two-hour raft trips are $45 per person. Maitland has three other operators, including Tidal Bore Rafting (☎ 902-752-9283) with trips from $65.

Shubenacadie Provincial Wildlife Park (☎ 902-758-2040) is a provincial park housing examples of Nova Scotia's wildlife, including birds, waterfowl, foxes and deer, in large enclosures. It's off Hwy 102 at exit 11, 38km south of Truro, just north of the town of Shubenacadie. It's open daily from 9 am to 7 pm mid-May to mid-October and admission is $3 or $7.50 a family.

South Shore

The South Shore refers to the area south and west of Halifax stretching along the coast to Yarmouth. It contains many fishing villages and several small historic towns. Some of the coastal scenery is good – typically rocky, jagged and foggy. The latter qualities have made the coast here and along the Eastern Shore as much a favourite with modern-day smugglers transporting illegal drugs – if not cigarettes – as it once was to rum runners.

The first one-third of the area, closest to Halifax, is the city's cottage country and is quite busy. The tourist route through here is called the Lighthouse Route and is probably the most visited region of Nova Scotia. Accommodation fills up fast, thanks to all that traffic in high season, so plan to find a place before dark each night.

DRL Coachlines buses service the area from Halifax.

PROSPECT

South-west of Halifax is the quiet and little-visited Prospect, a small but attractive old coastal village. The view from the cemetery at the top of the hill on the approach to town can be impressive, especially if the fog bank is obscuring some of the islands and

shoreline. There is a wharf, rocks to clamber over along the shore and a lighthouse.

PEGGY'S COVE

Canada's best known fishing village lies 43km west of Halifax on Hwy 333. It's a pretty place, with fishing boats, nets, lobster traps, docks and old pastel houses that all seem perfectly placed to please the eye. The 415-million-year-old granite boulders (known to geologists as erratics) littering the surroundings add an odd touch. Even the horror of Swissair Flight 111 in August 1998, which crashed not far offshore, has not dimmed the quintessentially postcard feel, though all those wreaths littering the rocks and at the base of the lighthouse are quite sobering.

The smooth shoreline rock all around the lighthouse just begs to be explored (but do not get too close – every year visitors are swept into the cold waters by unexpected swells). Count on the fog, too. It enshrouds the area at least once every three days and is present most mornings.

Peggy's Cove is one of the most visited in the Atlantic Provinces – and it's close to the capital too, so there are crowds which detract from its appeal. The best time for a visit is before 10 am. Many tour buses arrive in the middle of the day and create what has to be one of the worse traffic jams in the province. To ease that problem, there is a parking area with washrooms on the edge of town. Stop here and walk.

Surprisingly, the village, which dates from 1811, has just 60 residents and most of them are fishers.

See the pictorial in-the-rock monument by local artist DeGarthe outside his art gallery across from the provincial parking lot.

Located down near the lighthouse is *The Sou'wester Restaurant* with its huge gift shop of tacky souvenirs. Lobster dinners are $17 for a one-pounder and an order of fish and chips $7.45. The restaurant is huge but it can still be mobbed at times. The lighthouse is now a small post office which uses its own lighthouse-shaped stamp cancellation mark.

ST MARGARET'S BAY

A little beyond Peggy's Cove, large St Margaret's Bay is an area of small towns, craft shops and small sandy beaches, with a number of motels, campgrounds and cottages. Some visitors prefer to use it as a base for exploring the Halifax/Peggy's Cove region. It's a developed area where many people who work in the city live or have summer places.

Near the head of St Margaret's Bay is the start of the Bowaters Hiking Trail, which can be used for a couple of hours or a full day's walk. At the top of the bay are the beaches. Queensland Beach, the one farthest west, is the largest and busiest and has a snack bar.

Places to Stay

One of the most attractive places to spend a night or two is the *Baybreeze Motel & Cottages* (☎ 902-826-2213, ☎ 1-800-565-2615), nicely laid out by the water in Boutilier's Point. The cottages tend to be rented by the week but the motel units begin at $48 nightly for a double. The cottages are self-contained and some can sleep as many as seven; they start at $110 a night.

CHESTER

Chester, an old village with 1200 residents, overlooks Mahone Bay. Established in 1759, it has had a colourful history as the haunt of pirates and Prohibition bathtub-gin smugglers. It's now a small summer resort, and although there isn't a lot to do in town, a lot of visitors pass through each summer.

The centre of town is along Pleasant St between King and Queen Sts. The *Chester Playhouse* (☎ 902-275-3933), which runs inexpensive comedies, musicals and dramas through July and August, is on Pleasant St. The tourist centre (☎ 902-275-4616) is on Hwy 3 north of town in the old train depot that is being renovated into a museum. Hours are 10 am to 7 pm Wednesday to Sunday during summer.

Tancook Island

Offshore is Tancook Island, which can be reached by a 45 minute ferry ride departing from the Chester wharf five times a day

Monday through Friday and twice on Saturday and Sunday. The fare is $5 round trip; autos are $20. The islands – there is a Big and a Little Tancook – are primarily residential but visitors are welcome to stroll around. Big Tancook has a tourist office, a simple food outlet and *Levy House B&B* (☎ *902-228-2120)*, with rooms from $40. *Carolyn's Cafe* has good seafood. A walking-tour brochure available at the Chester tourist office outlines the paths which lead over much of the island.

The island is known for its plentiful cabbage and sauerkraut. Quite distinctive little cabbage-storage houses can be seen around the island.

Places to Stay

There is *Graves Island Provincial Park* (☎ *902-275-4425)* for camping 3km east of town near East River. The 64 wooded and open camp sites are on the ocean and are $14 a night. The relatively posh *Gray Gables B&B* (☎ *902-275-3983)* sits near the entrance.

Mecklenburgh Inn B&B (☎ *902-275-4638, 78 Queen St)* is a nice-looking place set in an old house built in 1890. Some rooms have private adjacent balconies. Prices are $50/59 with breakfast. For exploring, bicycles and a rowboat are available. It's open from mid-May to mid-October.

Places to Eat

For a casual bite, there's *Julien's Bakery & Cafe* on the corner of Pleasant and Queen Sts. Julien's features fresh baked croissants daily.

Across the street from the Chester Playhouse is *Globetrotter Cafe* for soups, salads and sandwiches in the $4 to $6 range while along the waterfront, across from the Chester Yacht Club, is the venerable *Captain's House* for the nicest and priciest seafood and steak.

MAHONE BAY

A little piece of eye-candy, Mahone Bay, with its islands and history, has become a sort of city escape, with the town of the same name acting as the recreation/accommodation hub. It's a popular destination for a Sunday drive from Halifax, about 100km away, or for an afternoon tea. The town has antique

and craft shops and a decided tourist orientation. You can see fine examples of Victorian gingerbread-house architecture around town, and the cemetery is interesting.

Along Hwy 3 on the east side of town is the tourist cottage (☎ 902-624-6151), which is open from 9 am to 7.30 pm daily during summer. Among the many handouts here is a walking tour brochure of Mahone Bay. At 578 Main St is the **Settlers' Museum & Cultural Centre** (☎ 902-624-6263), which deals mainly with the first German settlers to the area. Displays in two rooms cover the 1850s. Hours are 10 am to 5 pm Tuesday through Saturday. Admission is by donation.

Most tourists come for the famed Wooden Boat Festival in the last week of July.

Kayaking

Sea kayaking is excellent in the island-studded Mahone Bay and located at 618 South Main St, just across from the harbour, is Mahone Bay Adventures (☎ 902-624-6632), a friendly operation with a good reputation. The outfitter will rent singles for $40 a day and doubles for $60 a day. It also has canoes and offers a shuttle service up and down the coast.

For novices, there are half-day introductory lessons for $35, a day-long guided tour for $85 or a two day B&B tour where you kayak from one inn to the next. All equipment, lodging and meals are provided and the cost is $285 per person.

Places to Stay & Eat

There are a dozen upmarket B&Bs here, not uncommon for a trendy area. The local tourist office does a good job of lining folks up with lodgings. For a single, likely the best deal is at the simple but cosy *Dory Inn* (☎ *902-624-6460, 404 Main St)*, with singles/doubles from $45/50. The *Fairmont B&B* (☎ *902-624-8089, 654 Main St)* is central and reasonable for this area. The three rooms offered from May to October are $55/70 for singles/doubles.

Just west of town, featuring a great view of the harbour from its porch, is *Edgewater B&B* (☎ *902-624-9382)*. The three rooms

with shared bath are $45 for a single/double, or $70 for a triple; a full breakfast is included.

Salt Spray Cafe (621 South Main St) has a deck overlooking the harbour. Sandwiches here are about $5 but there is usually a daily special, like lasagne and salad, for under $7. For something a little more upmarket, try *Mimi Ocean Grill* just a little farther on South Main St. Seafood dishes are around $10. The *Old Settler's Place (16 Orchard St)* a block off the waterfront is a steakhouse but just as well known for its fondues.

Getting There & Away
Try Town Transit (☎ 902-543-5522, ☎ 1-877-521-0855) operates a shuttle between Bridgewater, Lunenburg and Mahone Bay. In Mahone Bay it departs from the Government wharf. Fare is $2 between each town; reservations are necessary. DRL Coachlines may stop here when schedules are set.

NEW ROSS
At this small lumbering town in the interior of the province, 26km north-west of Chester, is **Ross Farm Museum** (☎ 902-689-2210), a living agriculture museum of nine buildings set up like a working 19th century farm. Hours during summer are 9.30 am to 5.30 pm daily and admission is $5.

OAK ISLAND
What a story! This is treasure island with no treasure – so far. Said to be the burying place of the treasure of the infamous Captain Kidd or Blackbeard or Captain Morgan – maybe of Inca gold taken by the Spanish or ... the list goes on.

Despite nearly 200 years of digging, it's still up for grabs and has become one of the country's biggest and most captivating ongoing mysteries. Three farmboys stumbled upon a deep shaft in 1795, and since then, six lives and $4 million have been lost on 'the world's longest-running and most costly treasure hunt'. Before you grab your shovel and rush over, you need a permit which you can't get. The search – now using a lot of sophisticated equipment – has recently gone mega-high profile, with a consortium includ-

ing Woods Hole Oceanographic Institute in Massachusetts involved; US$10 million alone has been earmarked for final assaults on the shafts, using the same technology that discovered the *Titanic*.

The island is currently off limits to the public since the digsites are crumbling, but there is a small museum located at the causeway with various historical items and displays.

LUNENBURG
This attractive town of 2800 residents, best known for building the *Bluenose* sailing schooner in 1921, is a UN World Heritage Site. Always a shipbuilding town, this well preserved historic gem is still the linchpin of the provincial fishing industry with one of the major fleets of the north Atlantic seaboard. The largest fish-processing plant in North America is here. From it come Highliner supermarket seafood products.

Nova Scotia, like Newfoundland, has been hard hit by dwindling fish stocks and severely curtailed limits imposed by the federal government. But Lunenburg's burgeoning tourism trade has helped shore up the local economy.

Lunenburg was officially founded in 1753 when the British encouraged Protestants to emigrate from Europe. It soon became the first largely German settlement in the country.

Orientation & Information
The town's main street is Lincoln St, but it's Montague St, running parallel to the harbour, which is of most interest to the visitor. Along it are many of the town's commercial enterprises, including some interesting stores with gifts, crafts, antiques and prints for sale.

The Lunenburg Fisheries Museum is one block closer, along Bluenose Drive, as are the boat tours. Farther east along Montague St are the shipyards and commercial docks for the bigger trawlers. The principal intersection is with King St.

King St contains several banks, including the Royal with a 24 hour banking machine. Pelham St, one street back up the hill from Montague St, also has a number of shops.

LUNENBURG

Back Harbour

Lunenburg Harbour

PLACES TO STAY	OTHER
1 Lunenburg Inn	3 Bus Stop
4 Bluenose Lodge	5 Library
7 Lennox Inn	6 Lunenburg Academy
11 Mariner King	8 Zion Lutheran Church
15 Maplebird House	9 St John's Anglican
23 Campground & View	Church
24 Brook House	10 St Andrew's
	Presbyterian Church
PLACES TO EAT	12 Post Office
2 Knot Pub	13 Jo's Dive Shop
16 Hillcroft Cafe	14 Bailly House
18 Grand Banker	17 Fisheries Museum
19 Dockside	21 Dory Shop
20 Magnolia's Grill	22 Tourist Office

At No 134 is the oldest house in Lunenburg, **Bailly House**, constructed in 1760. Earl Bailly was one of the area's best known seascape painters, despite having had polio and having to wield his brush in his teeth. His brother now lives in the house.

Going up the hill along Lincoln St to Blockhouse Hill Rd is the **Lunenburg Tourist Bureau** (☎ 902-634-8100), open from 9 am to 8 pm daily throughout the season with a great view of the area.

Lunenburg is no Peggy's Cove, but in mid-season tour buses rumble along Bluenose Drive and tourists clog intersections. And thus, the prices – it's almost impossible to find a double anywhere in town for under $50.

Lunenburg Fisheries Museum

The well executed provincial museum is on Bluenose Drive and has one building, and two ships in the water for inspection: a dragger and a fishing schooner. In the building are exhibits on fishing and fish processing,

and a 25 minute film on marine life. There's also an aquarium. It's open daily from 9.30 am to 5.30 pm from June to mid-October and admission is $7. Most people walk away thinking the museum is well worth the admission and if you purchase your ticket in late afternoon, it's good for the next day.

Churches

For a small town the churches are impressive, and there are five of them in the downtown area. St John's Anglican, on the corner of Duke and Cumberland Sts, is a real stunner. The beautiful black-and-white wooden place dates from 1753 and is one of the oldest churches in Canada. Tours are given through summer from 10 am to 5 pm Monday through Saturday and 12.30 to 5.30 pm Sunday. St Andrew's Presbyterian, on Townsend St, is the oldest Presbyterian church in the country.

The Zion Lutheran church on the corner of Fox and Cornwallis Sts has its own claim to fame. In it is one of the original bells from the fort at Louisbourg on Cape Breton Island. When at one time the federal government was considering ordering its return to the National Historic Site, it was removed from the church and hidden at the bottom of Lunenburg's back harbour.

Lunenburg Academy

The Academy, a school, is the huge black-and-white turreted structure on a hill seen rising above the town on your way in from Halifax. Built entirely of wood in 1895, as a prestigious high school, it is one of the rare survivors of the academy system of education. It's now a National Historic Site and the Academy has hit-or-miss tours in summer on Wednesday from 10.30 am to noon. Admission for the half-hour tour is $2.

Activities

The public swimming pool is on Knickle Rd south-west of the centre. The Dory Shop (☎ 902-634-9146), along Bluenose Drive, rents boats by the hour or day – row, sail or motor, depending on your energy level. Jo's Dive Shop (☎ 1-800-JO-DIVE-1) at 296 Lincoln St has everything for the diver including rentals.

Bicycles can be rented and repaired at the Bicycle Barn (☎ 902-634-3426), located at Blue Rocks Road B&B almost 2km from town. The hybrid and mountain bikes are $12 a half-day and $15 a day.

Organised Tours

Walter Flower Charters (☎ 902-527-7175) offers three-hour whale-watching trips departing from the Lunenburg harbour for $35 per person. Star Charters (☎ 902-634-3535) has five trips daily on its two-mast, wooden ketch for $18 a person for a two hour tour ($22 sunset tour).

Special Events

In July, a craft festival is held, and in mid-August the equally popular Folk Harbour Festival (☎ 902-634-3180) is a weekend of traditional music and dance. In late September the town tips a few pints during its Oktoberfest.

Places to Stay

During midsummer making reservations early in the day is strongly recommended. The tourist centre doubles as a booking agency for all the B&Bs and hotels, and late in the day will know who has vacancies.

Camping Right in town beside the tourist office, with great views, there is *Board of Trade Campground (☎ 902-634-8100, ☎ 902-634-3656)* for trailers or tenters. It's an ideal, incredibly convenient place which charges $16 for an unserviced site, $18 for a hook-up. It has 32 sites and does get full, so arrive early. Showers are available.

B&Bs Perhaps the most affordable accommodation in this high rent town is *Brook House (☎ 902-634-3826)* out of town a bit along Blue Rocks Rd, with rooms from $45/55. The *Lennox Inn (☎ 902-634-4043, 69 Fox St)* starts at the same price and is built in an old tavern!

Also reasonably priced is the *Maplebird House (☎ 902-634-3863, 36 Pelham St)*

NOVA SCOTIA

overlooking the harbour. There are three rooms with shared bath that go for $50/60, light breakfast included.

Out on Blue Rocks Rd, 1.3km from town, *Lamb & Lobster B&B (☎ 902-634-4833)* is appropriately named as the owner, William Flower, is a lobster fisherman and a shepherd. In the evening guests may be shown how the family collies round up the sheep. Singles/doubles are $45/55. Nearby on the same road is the hip, laid-back and friendly *Blue Rocks Road B&B (☎ 902-634-8033)*. The eggs are organic, the breakfasts substantial, and the house mutt a treasure. Rooms start at $60. Mountain bikes and hybrids are also for rent.

Inns There are also several more upmarket inns, formed out of the larger, gracious, historic properties around town.

In the middle of town is the *Mariner King (☎ 902-634-8509, 1-800-565-8509, 15 King St)*. It's an attractive old place with a good restaurant and doubles at $65/75, including a light breakfast and in-room tea or coffee.

Bluenose Lodge (☎ 902-634-8851, ☎ 1-800-565-8851, 10 Falkland St) is a big place about 125 years old on the corner of Lincoln St. Singles cost $60 to $70 and doubles are $60 to $75. There's also a family-sized carriage house. In its restaurant the breakfast buffet is good value at $5.

The *Lunenburg Inn (☎ 1-800-565-3963, 26 Dufferin St)* is another large, historic, comfortable hostelry with antique furnishings. Doubles start at $75.

Motels In the motel category, the *Atlantic View Motel (☎ 902-634-4545, 230 Masons Beach Rd)* is on the outskirts of town. Single, double or triple rooms are $50 to $70. There are also cottages available for rent.

Places to Eat

Sampling the fish here is an absolute must. *Dockside (90 Montague St)* is one of the more reasonable places, especially when you consider the large portions you get. A full halibut or haddock dinner, from bread

to dessert is $13. The restaurant also has an outdoor patio. The *Grand Banker* along the waterfront is a pub with half-price seafood happy hours in summer.

Fish or lobster is also available at the *Old Fish Factory*, overlooking the water from the Fisheries Museum building. It offers good, fresh seafood and a nice setting but dinners range from $12 to $20. At lunch, however, there are always specials for under $7. It has menus in German.

Good pub food is on hand downtown at the *Knot Pub (1 Dufferin St)*. There are beer specials most nights before 7 pm and then you can order a large pot of mussels for $5.50 or one of its many sub-$6 sandwich concoctions.

The town has a handful of casually upscale bistros, well worth an extra few dollars. Two local favourites are the *Arbor View Inn (☎ 902-634-3658, 216 Dufferin St)* and the *Hillcroft Café (☎ 902-634-8031, 53 Montague St)*, both as adept with pan-Pacific influenced nouvelle cuisine as with traditional seafood. Reservations are probably a good idea. Both have mains starting at around $13 to $15; the latter has vegetarian options.

Getting There & Away

DRL Coachlines buses pull in at the Blue Nose Mini Mart (☎ 902-634-8845), a convenience store at 35 Lincoln St. Figure on one bus a day either direction and $15 to Halifax. The Try Town Transit also shuttles between Bridgewater, Lunenburg, and Mahone's Bay. The shuttle (☎ 902-543-5522) is $2 for each segment and leaves from the War Memorial. Reservations are necessary.

BRIDGEWATER

Bridgewater is an industrial town on the LaHave River and is the largest centre on the South Shore, with a population of close to 7000.

The **Desbrisay Museum** (☎ 902-543-4033) on 10 hectares of parkland has a small collection of goods relating to the early, mainly German, settlers of Lunenburg County. Hours are 9 am to 5 pm daily during summer, except Sunday when it opens at 1 pm. Admission may no longer be free.

The **Wile Carding Mill** (☎ 902-543-8233) on Victoria Rd (carding is the straightening and untangling of wool fibres in preparation for spinning) is an authentic water mill dating from 1860. Hours are the same as Desbrisay Museum and it's free.

The South Shore Exhibition, held each July, is a major five-day fair with traditional competitions between Canadian and US teams in such events as the ox pull.

Italy Cross International Hostel (☎ 902-543-6984, 606 Somerset Rd) is 17km south. There are eight beds at this organic farm not far from the sea and area parks.

Around **New Germany** are many Christmas tree farms. The trees are shipped from the Bridgewater docks to expectant households along the US seaboard.

THE OVENS

Pleasant, anachronistic Route 332 south from Bridgewater edges along the LaHave River to the sea. It's a pleasant country road reminiscent of the good old Maritime days. At the end of the road is The Ovens (☎ 902-766-4621), a sort of combination nature park and campground, which is popular for its scenery and general easy-going atmosphere.

Gold was found here in 1861 and still can be found on Cunard Beach. Rent a dish at the office and try panning. In a different area, a trail leads along the shore past (and into) numerous caves. The camping is fairly good, with many camp sites right by the shore with fine views over the ocean and a rocky ledge to explore at low tide.

There is also a guided sea cave boat tour (done in inflatable Zodiac boats), a swimming pool, and a comfortable little restaurant which serves up inexpensive fish and chips. Admission into the park is $5 and an unserviced camp site is $18. The gold panning is $6 a day (pan included) and the sea cave tour is $14.

LAHAVE

From Riverport a $1.75 (car and driver), five minute ride by cable ferry takes you across the river to the town of LaHave. Try Town Transit (☎ 902-543-5522 in Bridge-

water) has a shuttle to/from Halifax ($15 one way) and Bridgewater ($5 one way); call for reservations. Risser's (☎ 902-521-0855) also goes to Bridgewater for $5; reservations (same day OK) can be made or schedules sought for either trip at the *LaHave Bakery*, one of the best in eastern Canada, if not the whole country.

Upstairs, the small *LaHave Marine Hostel (☎ 902-688-2908)*, is an HI hostel for cyclists, backpackers or any like-minded soul looking for a cheap place to spend the night. It's open from May to October and the rate is $10/12 for members/nonmembers. Also based at the bakery is LaHave Outfitters, which runs coastal boat excursions.

On the outskirts west of the village is the **Fort Point Museum**, a National Historic Site. It was here in 1632 that the first batch of French settlers soon to be known as Acadians landed from France. A fort, Sainte-Marie-de-Grâce, was built later the same year but very little of it remains today. The site was supplanted by Port Royal on the north coast and never became a major centre. A museum in the former lighthouse keeper's house at the site tells more of this early settlement and its leader, de Raizilly. It's open daily from 10 am to 6 pm June through August, and weekends in September. Admission is free.

Also nearby on Hwy 331 is Crescent Sea Kayak Tours (☎ 902-688-2806). Two-hour tours among the islands are $30 for a single boat and $50 for a double.

LAHAVE ISLANDS

Just south-west of LaHave are the LaHave Islands, a handful of small, pleasant-to-look-at islands connected to the mainland by a long causeway and to each other by one-lane iron bridges. On Bell Island just past the Government Wharf is the **Marine Museum**. The museum is in the St John's Anglican Church and services are occasionally still held among the collection of marine artefacts. Hours are 10 am to 5.30 pm daily in July and August; admission is free.

Near the causeway to the islands along Hwy 331 is **Rissers Provincial Park** (☎ 902-688-2034), which features a very busy

campground and an excellent long, sandy beach, although the water is none too warm. There is also a saltwater marsh with a boardwalk trail. The 90 unserviced sites are each $14 a day.

LIVERPOOL

Situated where the Mersey River meets the ocean, as it does in Britain, Liverpool is another historic English-style town with an economy based on forests and fish. The very helpful **tourist office** (☎ 902-354-5421) on Henry Hensey Drive, just off Main St, in Centennial Park, has a walking-tour pamphlet and excellent brochures of scenic drives. Hours of the centre are 9 am to 8 pm in July and August, 10 am to 5 pm otherwise.

Off Hwy 103 at exit 19 is an old railway station converted into the **Hank Snow Country Music Centre** (☎ 902-354-4675) giving an overview of not just local boy done well Hank Snow but also of Canadian country music in general. It's open daily from 9 am to 6 pm, except Sunday when it opens at noon; admission is $4.

Perkins House (☎ 902-354-4058), built in 1766, is now a museum with articles and furniture from the colonial period. Hours during summer are 9.30 am to 5.30 pm daily, except Sunday when it opens at 1 pm. Admission is free. Next door, the **Queen's County Museum** (☎ 902-354-4058) has some Native Indian artefacts and more materials relating to town history, as well as some writings by early citizens. Hours and admission are the same as Perkins House.

Very new is the enormous and impressive **Sherman Hines Museum of Photography & Art Galleries** (☎ 902-354-2667) at 219 Main St, and the name pretty much says it all. Six – count 'em – galleries run the gamut of media, including the only photographic museum east of Montreal. Amazing that it's free; take advantage of it. Open Monday to Saturday from 10 am to 5.30 pm and in summer also Sunday noon to 5 pm.

At **Fort Point**, marked with a cairn, is the site where Samuel de Champlain landed from France in 1604 and where British privateers were active in the local waters in the early 1800s, protecting the British trade routes from incursions by the USA. The lighthouse here is now open to the clambering public; you can even try to blow the lighthouse hand-pumped foghorn.

There are four sandy **beaches** nearby: Beach Meadows, White Point, Hunt's Point and Summerville. All are within 11km of town, and there are others farther west.

A 12km rail hike/bike trail on an old CNR railway line begins on West St behind the Municipal Offices in Liverpool and ends at Summerville Beach Provincial Park.

Places to Stay & Eat

A simple B&B, the **Geranium House** (☎ 902-354-4484, 87 Milton Rd) has two basic family home rooms from $30/40. It's off Hwy 103 via exit 19. **Lanes Privateer Inn** (☎ 902-354-3456, 33 Bristol Ave) is the 1798 white wooden building with balconies on Hwy 3 by the bridge over the Mersey River, just east of the centre. A double with continental breakfast is $60, and there is a good restaurant which specialises in seafood. It also has canoes and bicycles for rent. Next door the inn runs a B&B with rooms at $45.

Liverpool Pizzeria (155 Main St) has medium pizza for $8 and lasagne with garlic bread for $5. Light lunches and specials like shepherd's pie and cabbage rolls are found at the **Morningside Café** directly opposite the tourist information office; many dinners cost under $6.

SEASIDE ADJUNCT KEJIMKUJIK NATIONAL PARK

The main body of this large national park is in the interior north-west of Liverpool, south-east of Digby, but this undeveloped region of the south coast between Port Joli Bay and Port Mouton (ma-TOON) Bay is part of the same park. The 'Keji Adjunct' (☎ 902-354-2880) protects a beautiful, wild stretch of shoreline and the animals, most particularly the endangered piping plover bird, within it.

Services are nonexistent – no camping or fires are allowed, no toilets or drinking water are available. What you will find is pristine coastline, with two great beaches,

coves, vistas, rock formations and an abundance of birdlife. Officials are working out increased access in the near future but promise it will remain bucolic.

Two trails, one leading in from each end, provide the only access. Both tend to be a little wet. From **South-west Port Mouton**, an 8km track leads to Black Point and the shore. From **St Catherine's River**, a little village, a 3km walk leads to the sea on the western side.

The **Port Joli Basin**, which is adjacent to the above park, also contains other sites of interest to nature lovers. At the end of the natural harbour, near the village of Point Joli, is the **Point Joli Migratory Bird Sanctuary**. Birders will find waterfowl, shorebirds and others in number, especially during migration periods. There are no facilities but visitors can explore on their own. In Port Joli ask for directions to the park.

If you do want to camp, just across Port Joli Harbour is *Thomas Raddall Provincial Park* (☎ *902-683-2664*). The camp sites ($14) are decent enough, with showers and eight walk-in sites, but the 5km-long trail system (bikes welcome on a couple) extends out into the awesome beaches, the real attraction. Plenty of nesting birds and even seals are found here.

LOCKEPORT

At the end of a jutting arm is the little town of Lockeport. The town was founded by New Englanders in the 1700s but became prosperous in the mid-1800s through fishing and, more importantly, as a trading centre with the West Indies. The Locke family between 1836 and 1876 built five of the imposing, nay, ostentatious dwellings on the streets today, using different architectural styles. The short street has been designated an historic site – it's called a 'historic streetscape' – although unfortunately none of the houses are open to visitors.

Before crossing the causeway into town you pass the **Crescent Beach Centre**, the striking building with the steeply pitched roofs. On the first floor is the tourist office (☎ 902-656-3123) open from 10 am to 9 pm

daily during summer. On the second floor is an observation gallery with a 360-degree view of the nearby saltwater marshes and the Lockeport Harbour along with interpretive displays and a viewing scope. From here a boardwalk has been started which should eventually take you all the way into town.

At the other end of Crescent Beach, a long sandy beach that was once featured on the Canadian $50 bill, is the **Little School Museum**. The former one-room school is now filled with local relics, including a replica of a 19th century classroom. Hours are 10 am to 4 pm daily during summer, except Sunday when it opens at noon and admission is free.

In town is *Hillcrest B&B* (☎ *902-656-3300, 35 Crest St*), once run as a hotel in the late 1800s. It has three rooms with shared bath for $40/50. Two other B&Bs are here, as well as two cottage operations which rent by the week only in summer.

The *White Gull Restaurant* offers seafood and an outdoor deck overlooking Lockeport's inner harbour; you can buy fresh fish too. *Locke's Island Inn (18 North St)* has accommodation and its dining room is worth a visit as well for a modestly upscale meal.

SHELBURNE

This is one of the most attractive and interesting towns anywhere on the South Shore. The whole place is pretty much like a museum, with fine buildings and historic sites at every turn – in fact it casually displays Canada's largest concentration of pre-1800 wooden homes. (Disney even filmed *The Scarlet Letter* here.)

This shipbuilding town with a population of 2245 is known as the birthplace of yachts. As well as the prize-winning yachts, though, it produces several other types of boats. Shelburne also boasts a town crier, Perry Wamback, who has won national and international competitions.

Shelburne, like many towns in the Fundy region, was founded by Loyalists, and in 1783 had a population of 10,000, making it the largest community in British North America. The so-called Loyalists were residents of the USA who maintained their allegiance to

Britain during the period of the American Revolution. Life in the USA was not easy for those with loyalty to the British crown, and thousands left for Canada; many of those who came here were from New York aristocracy.

Water St, the main street, has many houses from 100 to 200 years old, and quite a few of the two-storey wooden homes are marked with dates.

Dock St along the harbour features several historic buildings and museums and the tourist office (☎ 902-875-4547), open from 9 am to 7 pm daily during summer.

This is a major port, and boats from Quebec's Gaspé and the Magdalen Islands, from New Brunswick and Prince Edward Island, may be moored here. Recent cutbacks in fishing quotas have resulted in a marked decline in fishing activity. A little farther out are the shipyards where repairs to the regional ferries and other vessels are carried out.

Approximately 7km south-west of Shelburne is **Birchtown**, the first and largest free African-American settlement in North America. By 1784, nearly 1500 freed slaves had moved here after an offer of sanctuary by British generals if they would desert their 'rebel' owners and come to the British side.

Ross-Thompson House
Built in 1784, this house (which has an adjacent store) belonged to well-to-do merchants who arrived from Britain via Cape Cod, and now acts as a small museum. Furniture, paintings, artefacts and original goods from the store can be viewed. The house is surrounded by gardens, as it previously would have been. The Ross-Thompson House (☎ 902-875-3141) and all museums in town are open daily from 9.30 am to 5.30 pm June to mid-October and admission is $2 each or $4 for all three. Sunday till noon they're free.

Shelburne County Museum
Nearby is this Loyalist house dating from 1787, with a collection of Loyalist furnishings, displays on the history of the local fishery and other articles from the town's past. The oldest fire engine in Canada, a wooden

cart from 1740, is quite something. There is also a small collection of Micmac artefacts, including typical porcupine-quill decorative work. The museum (☎ 902-875-3219) is on the corner of Dock St and Maiden Lane.

Dory Shop
Shelburne has long had a reputation for its dories, small boats first used for fishing from a mother schooner and in later years for inshore fishing and as lifeboats. Many were built here from the 1880s until the 1970s. At the museum (☎ 902-875-3219) you can see examples still being made in the workshop upstairs in addition to learning about them.

Organised Tours
Shelburne Harbour Adventure Tours (☎ 902-875-1526) offers three-hour harbour tours for $20. Guided town walking tours depart four times daily from the tourist office; the $6 price includes museum admission.

Places to Stay
Just a few kilometres west of town is a good provincial park, *The Islands (☎ 902-875-4304)*. The 65 unserviced sites are in mature forest and there is swimming nearby. It's quiet during the week but has been known to get rowdy on weekends. A site is $14 a night and the campground has showers.

The *Bear's Den (☎ 902-875-3234, cnr Water & Glasgow Sts)* is a small and economical B&B. You'll pass it on the way into the centre of town. Singles/doubles cost $35/45, including a complete breakfast.

Another affordable B&B in town is *Harbour House (☎ 902-875-2074, 187 Water St)*. The owners are fluent in German and the three bedrooms are $45/55.

Known for its dining room with regional cuisine as well as its charming historic structure, the *Cooper's Inn (☎ 902-875-4656, 36 Dock St)* is worth a splurge. Rooms are $70, luxurious suites $145.

There are also a few motels at the edge of town, including the *Wildwood Motel (☎ 902-875-2964)* along Minto St, with rooms from $50/55 and a complimentary continental breakfast.

Places to Eat

Claudia's Diner on Water St, open every day, is a low-priced restaurant with style and standard fare. The cinnamon rolls are good and a large bowl of lobster chowder is $5.50.

The dining room in the *Coopers Inn* (dating from 1785) is very good. It offers just four dishes and four desserts nightly and does them well. Of course, seafood is on the menu but there's always an alternative. Dinners range from $15 to $17.50. *Charlotte Lane Cafe* offers pasta dishes for $9, or try the Swiss potato roesti which is grated potatoes sautéed and then smothered with cheese and egg for $6.

Getting There & Away

DRL Coachlines connects to Halifax and Yarmouth. Buses stop at the Irving Gas Station, 41 Falls Lane, near the highway. Elliot's Music & Repair (☎ 902-875-1188) in town rents out bicycles for $4 an hour or $20 a day.

BARRINGTON

The small village of Barrington dates back to 1760 when Cape Cod settlers erected their meetinghouse here. The town has four museums, all within walking distance of one another, all open daily and all free. There is also a campground and an historic B&B in town.

The tourist office (☎ 902-637-2625), in the middle of things, has an example of the Cape Island boat, the classic small fishing boat of the North Atlantic, originating on Cape Sable Island and now seen all around eastern Canada. The centre is open from 10 am to 5 pm during summer and usually there is free coffee and doughnuts on hand.

The most interesting museum is the Woollen Mill, restored to represent a small manufacturing mill of the late 1800s. It was the last woollen mill of its age to cease operating and, amazingly, not until 1962. Costumed guides lead you through the entire operation from cleaning the raw wool to spinning it into yarn and then show a video of the mill in operation in the 1950s. It's

open daily from 9.30 am to 5.30 pm, except Sunday when it opens at noon; admission is free. All sites in Barrington follow this schedule and pricing.

The Barrington Meetinghouse reflects the town's early Quaker influence and was used as both church and city hall. There is an old cemetery next door and on the third Sunday of August a community service is still held in the meetinghouse.

The Seal Island Light Museum is a replica of the lighthouse found on Seal Island, 30km out to sea, and is a record of the original and its keepers. Inside it houses the lens from the original lighthouse and other historical sundries while from the top there's a vista of Barrington Bay.

Across the road from the Historical Society Centre, the Western Counties Military Museum has uniforms, medals and other artefacts.

Places to Stay & Eat

Also along Hwy 309 is *Bayberry Campground* (☎ 902-637-2181) with both secluded wooded camp sites and others overlooking the ocean. An unserviced site is $12, more if you want to be by the water.

In town there is *MacMullen House* (☎ 902-637-3892), a B&B that was a hotel in the late 1800s; the barn outside was an oilskin factory. There are three rooms with shared bath for $40/50.

In nearby Barrington Passage is the *Old School House Inn & Cottages* (☎ 902-637-3770), a hotel, restaurant, natural food store and bakery. Good sandwiches and salads are offered, with more substantial meals also available. The six inn rooms with shared bath are $35/45, otherwise there are cottages from $60.

BARRINGTON TO YARMOUTH

From Barrington there is not much of interest until Yarmouth. Cape Sable and West Pubnico were both once Acadian settlements and each has a small general museum. Pubnico remains French and is considered the oldest village in Canada, still lived in by the descendants of its founders.

Yarmouth to Windsor

This region of Nova Scotia stretches from Yarmouth northward and along the south shore of the Bay of Fundy to Windsor and the Minas Basin. It consists, primarily, of two very distinct geographical and cultural regions.

The area between Yarmouth and Digby was one of the first European-settled areas in Canada. This municipality of Clare formed part of Acadia, the French region of the New World colonies. The 'French Shore' and its history are still very much in evidence today.

The best known area, however, is the scenic valley of the Annapolis River, which runs more or less from Digby to Wolfville. It's famous for apples, and in springtime the blossoming valley is at its best.

YARMOUTH

With a population of nearly 8000, Yarmouth is the largest town in western Nova Scotia. It's also a transportation centre of sorts, where ferries from Portland and Bar Harbour in Maine dock. It's an old city and recent town improvements have stressed its historical side.

Whichever way you're going, chances are you'll be passing through, and this is a good place to stop.

There's a huge tourist office (☎ 902-742-5033) down at the ferry docks with both local and provincial information available along with a room reservation service and money exchange counter. There's a walking-tour guide of the city with a map and some historical information. The office is open from 8 am to 7 pm May through October.

Every Saturday throughout summer, a farmers' market and flea market is held at the Centretown Square from 9 am to 3 pm, on the corner of Main and Central Sts.

Yarmouth County Museum

Open every day in summer (on Sunday from noon only), the museum (☎ 902-742-5539) at 22 Collins St, in a grey stone build-ing that was formerly a church, is well worth the price of admission.

Most of the five period rooms are to do with the sea – ship models, a large painting collection etc. Many articles were brought back by sea captains from their travels in Asia, and include ebony elephant carvings from Ceylon and fine ivory work from Japan.

One of the highlights is a runic stone found near town in 1812 and believed to have been carved by Viking Leif Erikson some 1000 years ago. Other evidence has been discovered which suggests that the Vikings were indeed in this area. And even they have a local tie-in to the *Titanic* craze ...

In summer, the museum is open Monday to Saturday from 9 am to 5 pm and on Sunday from 2 to 5 pm; in the off season, hours are shorter and it's closed on Monday. Admission is $2.50 or $5 for a family.

Firefighters' Museum

This museum (☎ 902-742-5525) at 431 Main St has a collection of beautiful fire engines dating from the 1930s. Admission costs $2 or $4 for a family; it's open from 9 am to 9 pm daily, except Sunday when the hours are 10 am to 5 pm.

The Wharves

As a major fishing port, Yarmouth's waterfront is lined with wharves. Beside the ferry terminal is the Public Wharf, where local fishing boats tie up. Many of the small boats of the herring fleet depart from here at around sundown. Also at the Public Wharf, vessels from around the world can sometimes be seen.

Next wharf over is the Killam Brothers Wharf, a waterfront park of sorts and the site of the **Killam Brothers Museum**. The Killam family began trading in 1788 and continued for more than a century on Yarmouth's waterfront. This shipping office was built in the 1830s and used until 1991. Now a museum, inside are the original desks, ledgers and scales that date back to the 19th century. Hours during summer are 9 am to 5 pm Monday to Saturday and admission is free.

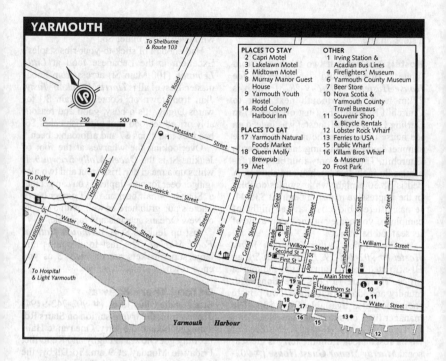

YARMOUTH

To Shelburne & Route 103

Starrs Road

Pleasant Street

Herbert Street

Brunswick Street

To Digby

Water Street

Vancouver St

Main Street

Chester Street

King Street

Porter Street

Grand Street

Parade Street

Collins Street

Willow Street

Alma Street

Second St

First St

John St

Lovitt St

Central St

Brown St

Hawthorn St

Main Street

Cumberland Street

Forest Street

Albert Street

William Street

Water Street

To Hospital & Light Yarmouth

Yarmouth Harbour

0   250   500 m

PLACES TO STAY
2 Capri Motel
3 Lakelawn Motel
5 Midtown Motel
8 Murray Manor Guest House
9 Yarmouth Youth Hostel
14 Rodd Colony Harbour Inn

PLACES TO EAT
17 Yarmouth Natural Foods Market
18 Queen Molly Brewpub
19 Met

OTHER
1 Irving Station & Acadian Bus Lines
4 Firefighters' Museum
6 Yarmouth County Museum
7 Beer Store
10 Nova Scotia & Yarmouth County Travel Bureaus
11 Souvenir Shop & Bicycle Rentals
12 Lobster Rock Wharf
13 Ferries to USA
15 Public Wharf
16 Killam Bros Wharf & Museum
20 Frost Park

Around Yarmouth

The **Yarmouth Light** is 11km from the ferry terminal at the end of Cape Forchu along Hwy 304. Signs from Main St will direct you all the way there. The original light was built in 1860 but torn down in 1964. The new one lacks any charm whatsoever, looking like a giant piece of penny candy. But the drive out is ambitious on the eyes and downright clichéd as you cross Yarmouth Bar where most of the lobster fishermen maintain their boat sheds and traps. At the end there is a small but well detailed interpretive centre with gregarious guides, open from 10 am to 7 pm daily, and walking trails.

More walking trails can be enjoyed at the end of Wedgeport Peninsula, a 15km drive from Yarmouth, via Hwy 3 north and then Hwy 334 south. The **Wedgeport Nature Trail** is a 5.4km network of trails to Wedge Point and features observation platforms,

boardwalks and 12 interpretive displays. The birding can be quite good here.

In the community of Wedgeport, the **Sport Tuna Fishing Museum** (☎ 902-663-4345) traces the pursuit of tuna as a sport; this area bills itself as the capital of this challenge worldwide. It's open daily from 9 am to 6 pm; admission is $2. Leaving from here is Wedgeport Tusket Islands Cruise (☎ 1-800-566-8862), offering tours of the 365 islands around the area, rife with nesting birds and seals. The $40 gets the four hour tour, and a lobster and clams or boxed lunch.

Places to Stay

Camping The nearest campground is *Loomer's Campers Haven* (☎ 902-742-4848), 4km east of the ferry terminal on Hwy 3 in Arcadia. This huge campground (250 sites) is geared primarily for RVers but you can pitch your tent here for $15 to $18

a night. There are showers, a laundrette and a store on site.

Hostels Not one but two to choose from (unheard of!). The old standby is the *Ice House Hostel* (☎ 902-649-2818) which is 22km north of Yarmouth next door to Churchill Mansion Inn (just off Hwy 1) in Darling Lake. This HI hostel was indeed an ice house once when the mansion was the summer home of shipping magnate Aaron Churchill. There are only four beds but facilities do include a kitchen and shower. A bed is $8.50 a night while singles/doubles in the impressive mansion begin at $35/44. It has offered bicyclists a free night of camping if you come out and sample one of its seafood barbecues.

Another option is the *Yarmouth Youth Hostel* (☎ 902-742-5921, 216 Main St), an HI-affiliated hostel right next to the tourist office. There are 13 beds here along with laundry and kitchen facilities. Two private rooms are also available from $35. The manager lives on site. Rates are $13.

B&Bs Just a block from the ferry is the seasonal *Murray Manor Guest House* (☎ 902-742-9625, 225 Main St). There are three rooms and a kitchen that guests may use. With breakfast, singles/doubles are $50/60.

The *Victorian Vogue B&B* (☎ 902-742-6398, 109 Brunswick St) is a sea captain's erstwhile residence. Open year-round, the Victorian charges $38/45 including a full breakfast; one room has a private bath ($60).

Motels The *Midtown Motel* (☎ 902-742-5333, 13 Parade St) is central and rooms begin at $45 for a single or double with a free coffee in the morning; there are triples ($55) and a couple of efficiency units with kitchens too.

Also economical is the *Lakelawn* (☎ 902-742-3588, 641 Main St), where breakfast is available. Singles/doubles are $44/49.

Places to Eat

The cafeteria in the *Met (386 Main St)*, a Woolworth's-style store near Lovitt St, is extremely inexpensive for Canadian basics, with everything under $6.

Had enough of stick-to-your-ribs staples? Excellent is the Lebanese food at *Little Lebanon* (100 Main St) across from Foodmaster. Best of all is *Harris' Quick 'n' Tasty*, 4km from town on Route 3 (Main St) towards Digby. It's a busy, good and reasonably priced seafood spot with fish cakes $6, haddock and chips $7 and affordable beer.

Overlooking the wharves at the foot of Jenkins St is the *Queen Molly Brewpub*. It whips up a mean dry Irish stout and two ales (ginger beer for non-tipplers; you can get it in a 'Shandy' – half beer and half ginger beer). There's pub grub here as well, with a couple of New Orleans specials and rapie pie.

Just up Jenkins St is *Yarmouth Natural Food Market*. The fast-food chains and large supermarkets are on Hwy 3 as you enter town.

Getting There & Away

Bus Acadian bus lines (☎ 902-742-9194) departs from the Irving station on Starrs Rd, a longish hike to the ferry. One run to Halifax only goes now, via Digby and Kentville, Friday to Monday at 9 am. To Digby, the fare is $14; to Halifax it's $41.

DRL Coachlines runs along the South Shore to Halifax. Its buses also stop at the Irving Gas Station on Starrs Rd.

A June-to-October alternative along the South Shore now is Campbell's Shuttle Service (☎ 902-742-6101) which has service to/from Halifax. It arrives in Yarmouth at 7 pm, in time to meet the ferry; it departs the next day at 12.30 pm.

Ferry There are two major ferry routes in and out of Yarmouth, both to the state of Maine in the USA; one connects with Bar Harbor via a high-speed super catamaran and the other with Portland.

The Bay Ferries (☎ 1-888-249-7245) 'Cat' literally skates across the water in 2½ hours to Bar Harbor; the 9500 horsepower engines are truly incredible, as is the computerised ride-control system. The ferry operates from late May through late October.

NOVA SCOTIA

During peak season two trips a day zoom from Yarmouth, at 12.30 and 8 pm; the ferry leaves Bar Harbor at 8 am and 3.30 pm. One-way fares are $34, less for children and seniors; an automobile is $62. For a pricey day cruise, it'd be $48.

The other ferry is operated by Maine's Prince of Fundy Cruises (☎ 902-742-6460 in Yarmouth, ☎ 1-800-341-7540 elsewhere in Canada) and it sails back and forth to Portland, Maine. The trip to Portland is 320km – more expensive than the other ferry – but you could win back the fare in the casino! This is a popular trip and for many is as much a holiday cruise as simple ferry transportation. Quite a few people just go and come back without even bothering to leave ship in port. Like the Bar Harbor boat, this is well appointed and comfortable, but the casino with floor show adds a touch of glamour. There are several other popular packages. There also are many Tuesday, Wednesday, or Thursday special 'one-way rates' for your car (if there is space); this could save you up to 50%.

Sailing time is about 11 hours one way. Note that service is an almost everyday thing, but there are quite a few blackout dates, so check in advance. Through the summer the ferry leaves Yarmouth daily at 10 am and Portland at 9 pm daily. The basic fare is $80, less in the off season. A vehicle is $98. Cabins range from $22 to $95 and you'll likely need to call ahead for them.

Call ahead for either trip, as reservations will probably be required.

In Portland there is a Nova Scotia Tourist Office in the Portland Pier area, across from the old Thomas Block Building.

Getting Around
For car rentals there's Budget (☎ 902-742-9500) at 150 Starrs Rd. For a sub-compact, you're looking at around $50 a day plus 15¢ a kilometre.

The tourist centre has a brochure outlining bike routes in the area. Bikes are available at a souvenir shop behind the tourist office and cost $15 per day.

FRENCH SHORE
From roughly Salmon River for 50km up the coast along St Mary's Bay towards Digby is Old Acadia, also known as the Municipality of Clare. This is where the province's largest, mainly French-speaking Acadian population lives. It's an interesting region where traditional foods and crafts are available, a few historic sites can be seen and, in summer, festivals are held in some of the small villages. Because the towns are small, a visit through the area can be done quite quickly.

Among the crafts offered out of people's houses along the way, the best two are the quilts and the woodcarvings, both of which have earned good reputations.

For campers, there are several campgrounds between Yarmouth and Digby.

Cape St Mary's
A long wide arch of fine sand, the **Mavilette Beach** is marvellous. The marsh behind the beach is good for birdwatching. Across the street, the *Cape View Motel* (☎ 902-645-2258) has both regular motel rooms and some individual cabins. Prices are $52/63 in the units; the self-contained cottages are more costly.

From the restaurant on site the beach looks great at sunset, and the food is good too. The menu is mainly seafood – clams are a local speciality – but also available is rapie pie, an old Acadian dish (for details see Church Point). Main dishes at dinner range from $9 to $13 and a rapie pie is $5.50.

Meteghan
This is a busy fishing port and there is a large commercial wharf where the boats moor. On the main street is **La Vieille Maison**, one of the oldest houses in the region and now set up as a museum depicting Acadian life here during the 18th century. It also doubles as a tourist centre (☎ 902-645-2389) and is open during summer from 9 am to 7 pm daily.

The Wood Studio has carvings and quilts to see or buy. On the way out of town is large *Comear's Farm Market*.

For accommodation try the *Anchor Inn* (☎ 902-645-3390), a B&B in a big old house

at just $25. The *Bluefin Motel* (☎ 902-645-2251) is good from around $45 and has superb views. For a meal there is the *Seashore Restaurant* with seafood but also local specialities or head to the fish market near the quay for grill-your-own.

Church Point (Pointe de l'Église)

Église Sainte Marie towers over the town and most other churches too. Built between 1903 and 1905, it is said to be the tallest and biggest wooden church in North America.

In the corner by the altar is a small museum which contains articles from the church's history, including various vestments and chalices. A guide will show you around and answer any questions. The church museum is open 9.30 am to 5.30 pm daily from July to mid-October and admission is $1.

Nearby is the **Université de Sainte Anne**, the only French university in the province and a centre for Acadian culture.

The oldest of the annual Acadian cultural festivals, Festival Acadien de Clare, is held here during the second week of July.

Places to Stay & Eat For camping there is *Belle Baie Park* (☎ 902-769-3160), just out of town, where the best spots along the shore are saved for overnight tenters. An unserviced site is $15 a night.

Just beyond the church towards Yarmouth, with the Acadian flag outside, *Rapure Acadienne* is the place where all the local establishments get their rapie pie *(paté à la rapure)*. Inside, several women are busy preparing the three varieties: beef, chicken or clam. The result is difficult to describe but it's a type of meat pie topped with grated paste-like potato from which all the starch has been drawn. They are bland, filling and inexpensive and can be bought piping hot. In fact, they are all you can get here. A large rapie pie, enough to feed two people, is $5.

Nearby is *Tides Inn Restaurant*, featuring an extensive menu of seafood dishes such as haddock crepes and seafood casserole au gratin. Dinners range from $8 to $12.

Belliveau Cove

Before stopping to watch the unusually high tides, consider eating at the pleasantly old-fashioned *Roadside Grill*, a comfortable local restaurant/diner with low prices for sandwiches and light foods but also lots of seafood – try the steamed clams, a local speciality, or the rapie pie, both under $6.

St Bernard

Here the grandest of the coast's churches stands – a mammoth granite Gothic-style monument which took 32 years to complete, beginning in 1910.

DIGBY

An old, attractive town with 2500 residents, Digby was built around a hill in the Annapolis Basin, an inlet of the Bay of Fundy. It's famous for its scallop fleet and busy with its terminal for the *Princess of Acadia* ferry, which plies the waters between Digby and Saint John, New Brunswick. The town is also well known for its 'Digby chicks', a type of smoked herring.

The town was founded by United Empire Loyalists in 1783, and since then its life has been based on fishing. Up Mount St from Water St is Trinity Anglican Church and its graveyard. A couple of blocks away, at the south edge of the downtown section, is the old Loyalist cemetery on Warwick St.

From the top of the hill by the high school on King St between Church and Mount Sts, five blocks back from Water St, there is a good view of the area.

From the ferry landing, it is about 5km to Water St in downtown Digby.

Information

On Water St in the centre of town is the local tourist office (☎ 1-888-463-4429, ☎ 902-245-5425), open from 10 am to 5 pm daily during summer and until 8 pm on Thursday and Friday. Along Shore Road from the ferry terminal is the much larger provincial tourist centre (☎ 902-245-2201) with information about Digby and all of Nova Scotia. It is open from 9 am to 8.30 pm during the ferry season.

Admiral Digby Museum

At 95 Montague Row, this small museum displays articles and photographs pertaining to the town's marine history and early settlement. It's open from 9 am to 5 pm daily June through September. Admission is free.

Up the street towards the wharf is the *Lady Vanessa*, an old scallop trawler that you can board and tour around; admission is $1.75.

Places to Stay

No campgrounds are in or near town. Bear River has an extremely basic one, and then there's Smith's Cove, 8km east of Digby via Hwy 101, which has *Smith's Cove Park* (☎ 902-245-4814), a large park on the bay. Rates are $16.

Westway House (☎ 902-245-5071, 6 Carlton St) is a B&B on a quieter street but still within walking distance of things to see. Singles/doubles are $35/42 and one room has a private bath ($43), and outside there is a barbecue to use.

The *Thistle Down Country Inn* (☎ 902-245-4490, ☎ 1-800-565-8081, 98 Montague Row) has a dozen historic rooms. There are chairs out the back on the lawn from where you can watch the harbour. Rooms start at $65/75.

The size of a self-enclosed city-state, the sybaritic *Pines Resort* (☎ 902-245-2511, ☎ 1-800-667-4637) is 2km east of the ferry terminal and caters to every whim. Cottages and hotel rooms start at $140.

Places to Eat

Fundy Restaurant (34 Water St) is pricey but does have two outdoor balconies providing views over the harbour area. Good seafood dinners range from $15 to $20.

Also on Water St is the lively *Red Raven Pub*. The tavern is also a restaurant, featuring an outdoor patio overlooking the wharf with dinner prices from $7 to $13. At night local bands often play. Lastly, consider buying some fresh seafood.

There are several shops by the docks on Prince William St but the *Royal Fundy Fish Market* has the best selection. If you're camping or have cooking facilities at

the motel, even a bag of scallops can make a remarkably delicious dinner. They cost between $11 and $13 a pound. You can also get them pre-cooked. The Digby chicks, the heavily smoked herring for which the town is well known, will last up to two weeks and usually cost $1 each.

Getting There & Away

Bus The bus station is at the Irving service station on the corner of Montague Row (an extension of the main street, Water St) and Warwick St, a short walk from the centre of town. There is one bus Friday through Monday at 10.45 am to Halifax; Thursday to Sunday it runs at 8.35 pm to Yarmouth ($14).

Ferry In summer, Bay Ferries (☎ 902-245-2116, ☎ 1-888-249-7245) runs three ferry trips from Digby to Saint John, New Brunswick, daily, except Sunday when there are just two. Departure times are 5 am and 1.30 and 8.30 pm (no 5 am trip Sunday). The crossing takes a little more than 2½ hours. Prices are a bit steep – $23 per adult passenger and $50 per car, with bicycles $11.25. Reservations are a very good idea for this trip, and arrive at the dock an hour before departure. With two or more people it might be cheaper to drive around.

DIGBY NECK

The long, thin strip of land which protrudes into the Bay of Fundy from just north of town is known as Digby Neck and is visible from much of the French Shore. At the far end are Long and Brier islands, the two sections that have become split from the main arm. Short ferry rides connect them, so a road links Westport (on Brier Island, at the far end) to Digby.

At Tiverton is **Island Museum**, a small museum and tourist information desk. It is open during summer from 9 am to 8 pm if the volunteer staff hold out.

The most interesting sight on Long Island is **Balancing Rock**. The 7m-high stone column is perched precariously on the edge of a ledge just above the pounding surf of St Marys Bay. It is such a striking sight that for

years fishers have used it as a landmark to return to port.

A trail leads to the bay. The round-trip walk is close to 4km along a trail that includes rope railings, boardwalks and an extensive series of steps down a rock bluff to the bay. It's very slippery. At the end there is a viewing platform that puts you within 15m of this balancing act. The trailhead is well posted along Hwy 217, 2km south of the Island Museum.

Brier Island has three lighthouses, with picnic tables and shoreline views and numerous excellent, if rugged, walking trails. Agates can be found along the beaches.

Whale Watching

What draws many people, though, is the sea life off Long and Brier islands. From June to October whale and birdwatching boat cruises run from Tiverton, East Ferry and Westport. Conditions make it a good location for seeing whales; the season is relatively long, beginning in May, building up in June and remaining steady, with a good population of three whale species – finback, minke and humpback – as well as dolphins, porpoises and seals, through August. The whale-watching trips here are the best and most successful of any in Nova Scotia.

There are now over a half-dozen operators who run whale-watching tours with surely more to come. Still, reservations are a good idea and can be made by phone.

In Tiverton, Ocean Explorations (☎ 902-839-2417), doesn't use a boat but rather a Zodiac which, being small, allows for pulsating close encounters and a manageable-sized tour group. Half-day trips are $40, and if the weather is bad, you can still take a $25 1½-hour seal watching trip. Pirate's Cove Whale Cruises (☎ 902-839-2242) uses an 11m vessel and offers at least two cruises daily. The cost of the three hour trip is $35.

In East Ferry, Petite Passage Whale Watch (☎ 902-834-2226) has tours identical in length and rate as Pirate's Cove while in Westport, Brier Island Whales & Seabird Cruises (☎ 902-839-2995, ☎ 1-800-656-3660) has a four hour tour which costs $37

and runs five trips daily in peak season. Westport has a couple of other operators.

Hopeful passengers should take plenty of warm clothing (regardless of how hot a day it seems), sunblock and binoculars, if possible. An antimotion-sickness pill taken before leaving the dock may not be a bad idea, either.

Westport is about 90 minutes from Digby, so leave with plenty of time if you've a boat to catch, and remember there are two ferries. The first leaves East Ferry on the half-hour, and Tiverton on the hour, midnight to 6 am; they are timed so that if you drive directly there is no wait for the second one. Return passage on the ferries is $2 each.

There is no public transportation along Digby Neck so you'll need a car or have to rely on hitching a lift.

Places to Stay & Eat

There are places all along Digby Neck. A new hostel, the **Brier Island Hostel** (☎ 902-839-2273), is run by a friendly Dutchman and his wife, who's from the area. Above a gift shop, there are 18 brand-new beds, including a double, antiseptic washrooms, a full kitchen, a laundrette next door, and even Internet access in the lobby. A bed costs $12.

In scenic Sandy Cove is **Olde Village Inn** (☎ 902-834-2202, ☎ 1-800-834-2206), three classic buildings built in 1830 to 1890 and restored as an inn and restaurant. There are a range of rates but the cheapest doubles start at $65.

In Westport the most economical is the **Westport Inn** (☎ 902-839-2675), with three rooms ($35/45 for singles/doubles). All three daily meals are available.

More upmarket is the **Brier Island Lodge** (☎ 902-839-2300, ☎ 1-800-662-8355). At this much larger place there are 23 rooms, most with an ocean view, and a restaurant open to nonguests. The menu offers a range of fresh seafood – try the fishcakes – but even hamburgers are available. Doubles in the lodge range from $60.

ANNAPOLIS VALLEY

The Evangeline Trail through the valley is really not as scenic as might be expected via

Hwy 1, although it does pass through or by all the major towns and the historic sites. To really see the valley and get into the countryside it is necessary to take the smaller roads parallel to Route 1. From here the farms and orchards, generally hidden from the main roads, come into view.

For those seeking a little work in late summer, there should be some jobs available picking apples. Check in any of the valley towns such as Bridgetown, Lawrencetown and Middleton. Line things up a couple of weeks before picking time, if you can. MacIntosh apples arrive first, at the end of August, but the real season begins around the first week of September.

ANNAPOLIS ROYAL

Known as Canada's oldest settlement, Annapolis Royal is a picture-postcard place and one of the valley's prime attractions

with many historic sites and great places to stay and eat.

The site of Canada's first permanent European settlement, founded by Samuel de Champlain in 1604, is actually out of town at nearby Granville Ferry. As the British and French battled over the years for the valley and land at the mouth of the Annapolis River, the settlement often changed hands. In 1710, the British had a decisive victory and changed the town's name from Port Royal to Annapolis Royal (in honour of Queen Anne).

Despite the town's great age (in Canadian terms) the population is under 800, so it is quite a small community and easy to get around. It's a busy place in summer with most things of interest located on or near the long, curving St George St. There is a waterfront boardwalk behind King's Theatre on St George St, with views over to the village of Granville Ferry.

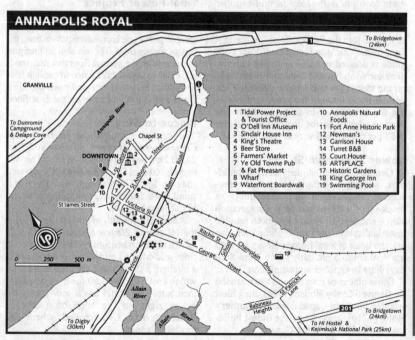

ANNAPOLIS ROYAL

1 Tidal Power Project & Tourist Office
2 O'Dell Inn Museum
3 Sinclair House Inn
4 King's Theatre
5 Beer Store
6 Farmers' Market
7 Ye Old Towne Pub & Fat Pheasant
8 Wharf
9 Waterfront Boardwalk
10 Annapolis Natural Foods
11 Fort Anne Historic Park
12 Newman's
13 Garrison House
14 Turret B&B
15 Court House
16 ARTsPLACE
17 Historic Gardens
18 King George Inn
19 Swimming Pool

GRANVILLE

To Dunromin Campground & Delaps Cove

Annapolis River

Chapel St

DOWNTOWN

St George St

St Anthony St

Chapel Street

Albert Road

To Bridgetown (24km)

St James Street

Victoria St

St George Street

Ritchie St

St George St

School St

Champlain Drive

Allain River

To Digby (30km)

Prince St

Allain River

St Patrick's Lane

Babineau Heights

To Bridgetown (24km)

To HI Hostel & Kejimkujik National Park (25km)

201

0 250 500 m

NOVA SCOTIA

A farmers' market is held every Saturday morning in summer, also Wednesday afternoon in peak season. Daily summer guided walking tours are given by the local historical society.

A Nova Scotia Tourism Information Centre (☎ 902-532-5769) is at the Tidal Power Project site by the Annapolis River Causeway. Hours during summer are 8 am to 8 pm. Pick up a copy of the historic walking-tour pamphlet.

Fort Anne National Historic Site
Right in the centre of town, this park preserves the memory of the early Acadian settlement plus the remains of the 1635 French fort, the mounds and moats intact. A museum has replicas of various period rooms, artefacts, uniforms and weapons; the Acadian room was transferred from an old homestead and the four-panel tapestry is extraordinary. The museum is open from 9 am to 6 pm daily May to mid-October and admission is $2.50.

If you're around on a Sunday or Thursday night, join the fort's special Candlelight Tour of the Garrison Graveyard. Your park guide is dressed in black and sports an undertaker's top hat and cape and everybody on the tour is given a candle lantern. Then you all troop through the graveyard, viewing the headstones in the eerie light and hearing tales of horror and death. The tour is $3 per person and very entertaining.

Lower St George St
St George St contains many historic buildings, with three different centuries represented. The O'Dell Inn Museum – a mock-up of a tavern and former stagecoach stop – and Sinclair House Inn, both provide historic displays, the former of the Victorian era, the latter of local history. Hours for both are 9.30 am to 5 pm daily (from 1 pm Sunday) June to October and admission is $1.

Other places of note around town are the de Gannes-Cosby House (1708), the oldest wooden house in Canada, and the Farmer's Hotel (1710), also one of the oldest buildings in English-speaking Canada.

Historic Gardens
Numerous distinct types of garden, including Acadian and Victorian, are set out in the green 400-hectare grounds. There is an interpretive building, a restaurant, a gift shop and, adjacent, a bird sanctuary. Admission is $3.50. The gardens are not far from the centre of town, on St George St near the corner of Prince Albert Rd, and are open daily from May to October and 8 am to 9 pm in summer.

The Arts
ARTsPLACE (☎ 902-532-7069) at 396 St George St is an artist-run cultural resource centre showcasing local, regional, and national artists' works. It's also got a used bookstore and coffeeshop. Admission is free.

Across from the Fat Pheasant Restaurant is King's Theatre (☎ 1-800-818-8587) in which live music and theatre is performed in summer.

Tidal Power Project
At the Annapolis River Causeway, this project offers visitors the chance to see a hydroelectric prototype harnessing power from the Bay of Fundy tides. There's also an interpretive centre on the second floor that uses models, exhibits and a short video to explain how it works. The site is free and open the same hours as the tourist centre on the first floor.

Places to Stay
The nearest campground is *Dunromin Campsite and Trailer Court* (☎ 902-532-2808) 2km beyond the tourist centre on Annapolis River at Granville Ferry. Unserviced sites go for $13.50 a night and there is a small store, laundrette, swimming pool and kayak rental on site.

About 25km south of Annapolis Royal is the HI *Raven Haven Hostel* (☎ 902-532-7320), in South Milford on Hwy 8. It's open from mid-May to mid-October and there is a kitchen, a shower and six beds in a cabin, which cost $12.50/14.50 for members/non-members. The hostel has a very scenic location right on the edge of a lake in Beachside Park Campground, where you can rent a canoe.

Right in town is the ***Turret B&B*** (☎ *902-532-5770, 372 George St)*, an historic property with three rooms at $45 a single/double. Nearby is the equally stately ***King George Inn*** (☎ *902-532-5286)* with four rooms at $44/49.

At the east end of the town at Aulden Hubley Drive, just off Route 201, is the ***English Oaks B&B*** (☎ *902-532-2066)*. Rooms are from $50 and guests have use of a barbecue and picnic tables.

About 1km east of town on Hwy 201, ***Helen's Cabins*** (☎ *902-532-5207)*, Rural Route 1, has five units for $45 a night for singles or doubles with hot plates included for quick cooking. They are available from May to October.

Places to Eat
Ye Old Towne Pub, on Church St just off St George St, by the wharf, is a busy place for lunch and a brew. Right next door is the *Fat Pheasant*, a little more formal, with dinner from $10 to $20. *Kent's*, on Prince Albert Rd opposite the historic site, has omelettes from $1.99, breakfasts from $3.25, and a full family menu.

Expensive and decorative *Newman's (218 St George St)* has a good reputation for its varied menu, which includes fresh fish, pasta and lamb. It features a dining terrace outside if the weather is good. Dinner ranges from $12 to $22 but its noted scallop linguini is only $8.

Across the river in Granville Ferry are two pricier but good options. The *White Raven* (☎ *902-532-5595)* is a French bistro, and Austrian food is served at the *Dorfgasthaus*.

AROUND ANNAPOLIS ROYAL
Port Royal National Historic Site
Some 15km from Annapolis Royal, this is the actual site of the first European settlement north of Florida. It has a replica, constructed in the original manner, of de Champlain's 1605 fur-trading habitation, destroyed by the English a few years after it was begun. Costumed workers help tell the story of this early settlement. The park (☎ 902-532-2898) is open from 9 am to 6 pm daily during summer and admission is $2.75.

Delaps Cove
On the coast north of town is a series of typical small fishing villages, from Delaps Cove to the west all the way to the Minas Basin.

The Delaps Cove Wilderness Trail, about 24km from Annapolis Royal, is a 15km hiking trail that provides a good cross-section of the provincial coastal scenery. There are streams and waterfalls at various places and an assortment of birds and animals. Just west of Delaps Cove is an interpretive office (where you can get a map) but that's it for amenities. No camping is allowed.

KEJIMKUJIK NATIONAL PARK
This park, located well away from the tourist areas of the seacoast, contains some of the province's most pristine wilderness and best backcountry adventures. Less than 20% of Kejimkujik's 381 sq km is accessible by car, the rest is reached either on foot or by paddle. Canoeing, in particular, is an ideal way to explore this area of glacial lakes and rolling hills and the park is well set up for extended, overnight paddles. Portage routes are well marked, and the main lake, Kejimkujik, features red navigational buoys and many primitive camp sites are on islands.

Kejimkujik is 44km south of Annapolis Royal via Hwy 8. At the main entrance, just south of Maitland Bridge, there is a visitor and interpretive centre (☎ 902-682-2772), where you can reserve primitive sites and purchase maps and books. Hours during summer are 8.30 am to 9 pm and less the rest of the year.

Entry Fees
A daily pass is $3, and for four days it's $9; prices are less for seniors and children. A daily pass for a family is $7, $21 for four days.

Hiking & Canoeing
There are more than 40 primitive camp sites scattered along the trails and among the lakes of Kejimkujik. The main hiking loop is a 60km trek that begins at the east end of Peskowesk Lake and ends at the Big Dam Lake trailhead. Most backpackers take three

to four days to cover it, with September to early October being the prime time for such an adventure. A shorter loop, ideal for an overnight trek, is the 26km Channel Lake Trail that begins and ends at Big Dam Lake.

The park also features more than a dozen lakes connected by a system of portages for flatwater paddling. Extended trips of up to seven days are possible in Kejimkujik with portages ranging from a few metres to 2.4km in length.

You must stay in backcountry sites and book them in advance by calling or stopping at the visitors centre (☎ 902-682-2772). The sites are a hefty $16.25 per night plus a $3.75 reservation fee for each backcountry trip; there's a 14-day maximum, and no more than two nights in any site. A book of topographical maps ($5) may or may not be optional.

Canoes can be rented in the park at Jack's Landing (☎ 902-682-2196) from 8 am to 9 pm daily for $4 per hour, $20 a day and $97 a week. You can also rent them at Loon Lake Outfitters (☎ 902-682-2220, ☎ 902-682-2290) located just north of the park entrance on Hwy 8. Canoes are $15 a day or $75 a week and there also are tents, canoe packs and stoves for rent. Bicycles are available at Jack's Landing for $20 per day.

Places to Stay

Kejimkujik National Park has a huge campground of 360 camp sites at Jeremys Bay, including a handful of walk-in camp sites near the shoreline for those who want to put a little distance between themselves and obnoxious RVers running their generators. The cost is $11 per night.

The *Whitman Inn* (*☎ 902-682-2226*) in Caledonia, five minutes from the park, is a comfortable place to stay for noncampers. It's a restored late 19th/early 20th century house that has an indoor swimming pool, saunas – the works – yet the simplest of the rooms are moderately priced at $50/55. All meals are available. Also keep in mind that the *Raven Haven Hostel* is 19km north of the park off Hwy 8 (see the earlier Annapolis Royal section for details).

BRIDGETOWN

Back along the Annapolis Valley, Bridgetown has many trees and some fine examples of large Maritime houses. A seasonal tourist office is in Jubilee Park, on Granville St. There's also the small **James House Museum**, an 1835 home among the shops along Queen St. In the museum is a tearoom for an afternoon break. Try the rhubarb sparkle. It's open daily from 9 am to 4 pm. Admission is free.

KENTVILLE

Kentville, with a sizable population of 5500, is a functional town which marks the east end of the Annapolis Valley.

The tourist office (☎ 902-678-7170) is in the restored train station on Cornwallis Ave. Summer hours are 7.30 am to 9 pm daily (from 6 am Sunday!).

At the eastern end of town is the **Agriculture Research Station** (☎ 902-678-1093), with a museum related to the area's farming history and particularly to its apples. There is a pleasant walking trail through the old growth woods, one of the few areas in the province with original forest. Hours are 8 am to 4.30 pm year-round and guided tours are offered during summer. Admission is free.

In town, local artefacts, history and an art gallery can be seen at **Old King's Courthouse Museum** (☎ 902-678-6237) at 37 Cornwallis Ave. The courthouse was the seat of justice from 1903 to 1980. Hours are 9.30 am to 4.30 pm year-round and 11.30 am to 4.30 pm on Saturday and Sunday during summer. Admission is free.

Kentville is about a two hour drive from Digby and about one hour from Halifax.

Activities

Frame Break (☎ 902-679-0611) at 102 Webster St rents mountain bikes for $25 a day or $45 for the weekend. It also leads tours into the valley.

Places to Stay & Eat

The *Grand Street Inn* (*☎ 902-679-1991, 160 Main St*), just out of the downtown area towards New Minas, is the very attractive

old grey and pink Queen-Anne revival house. Singles and doubles are $65, which includes a full breakfast as well as use of the swimming pool.

The *Allen's Motel* (☎ *902-678-2683, 384 Park St)* is the most affordable motel with singles, doubles, or triples for $45.

What many other Canadian towns desperately need, Kentville has – a few good pubs. The classic is *King's Arms Pub* on Main St where you can have a drink next to a fireplace or outside on the patio. Steak and kidney pie is only $4.25, a pot of mussels the same price. Happy hour begins at 4.30 pm when pints are $3.25 and half pints under $2.

Nearby *Paddy's* on Aberdeen St doubles as an Irish pub and a small brewery producing such gems as Annapolis Valley Ale and Paddy's Porter. Dinners range from $8 to $11 or just try the Paddy's Irish stew made with Guinness for $4.65.

Getting There & Away

Acadian Bus Lines stops at the tourist office. Only the 11.55 pm bus goes all the way to Yarmouth. Going north the bus leaves for Halifax ($15.50) at 1.05 pm.

NORTH OF KENTVILLE

The area up to Cape Blomidon, on the Bay of Fundy, makes for a fine trip for half a day or longer, with good scenery, a memorable view of much of the valley and a couple of beaches. At Cape Split there is an excellent, dramatic hiking trail high above the Minas Basin and Channel.

Canning

There is the *Farmhouse Inn* (☎ *902-582-7900)* and a small, simple restaurant in tiny Canning, where there are so many large, overhanging trees Main St is dark even on a sunny day.

The Lookoff

From the road's edge at nearly 200m high, this could well be the best view of the soft, rural Annapolis Valley, its rows of fruit trees and farmhouses appearing like miniatures.

Across the street is *Look-off Family Camping Park* (☎ *902-582-3022)* where an unserviced site is $13.

Blomidon

At *Blomidon Provincial Park* (☎ *902-582-7319)* there are camping and hiking trails that skirt dramatic 183m shoreline cliffs. A tent site is $14 a night. As at Kingsport's sandy beach farther south, the water can get quite warm.

Scots Bay

The road continues north to Scots Bay, with a large pebbled beach. From the end of the road, a spectacular 13km hiking trail leads to the cliffs at Cape Split. This is not a loop trail, so you must retrace your steps.

Halls Harbour

On the often foggy coast, Halls Harbour to the west is a classic, scenic little lobster village with a pier and a lobster pound. At the *Halls Harbour Lobster Pound* (☎ *902-679-5299)* they cook live lobsters from noon to 8 pm daily from May to September and sell them at the best prices you'll ever find. All that's sold is the lobster, rolls and butter. There are picnic tables around the dock area.

WOLFVILLE

Wolfville is a quiet, green university town best known as the home of artist Alex Colville. With its art gallery, comfortable inns and impressive historic homes, there is more than a wisp of culture in the air. This is manifested by the summer-long Atlantic Theatre Festival (☎ 1-800-337-6661), with four classics performed virtually every day June through September.

The tourist office (☎ 902-542-7000) is in Willow Park, at the east end of Main St and open from 8 am to 8 pm daily during summer.

Acadia University Art Gallery

The gallery (☎ 902-542-2202, ext 1373) in the Beveridge Arts Centre building, on the corner of Main St and Highland Ave, exhibits mainly the work of other Maritime artists. It also has a collection of the work

(mostly serigraphs) of Alex Colville, some of which is always on display. Hours during summer are noon to 5 pm weekdays and 1 to 4 pm on Saturday and Sunday. Admission is by donation.

Carriage House Gallery

In the middle of Main St, this commercial gallery has the works of local artists for sale, as well as some Colville prints.

Randall House Museum

Set in a house dating from the early 1800s, the museum (☎ 902-542-9775) deals with the early New England planters or colonists who replaced the expelled Acadians and the Loyalists who followed later. It is at 171 Main St and is open from 10 am to 5 pm daily during summer, except on Saturday and Sunday when it opens at 2 pm. Admission is free.

Chimney Swifts

From May to late August, these birds collect to glide and swoop by the hundreds at dusk. There is a full explanation of the phenomenon at Robie Tufts Nature Centre on Front St, which features outdoor displays and a tall chimney where the birds display their acrobatic talents.

Places to Stay

Wolfville has a large number of B&Bs in impressive Victorian homes but unfortunately most of that grandeur comes with a steep rate. Most modest is the good *Blue Shutters B&B* (☎ *902-542-3363, 7 Blomidon Terrace*), an executive-style home within walking distance to downtown. Rooms start at $40, and one room has a private bath.

Also within reason is *Seaview House* (☎ *902-542-1436, 8 Seaview Ave)* just off Main St. This Victorian home has three

---

The Acadians

The story of the Acadians is one of the most interesting, dramatic and tragic in Canada's history. It was played out in what are now five of the country's provinces, as well as the USA, the West Indies and Europe, and although it began in the 1600s it's not over yet.

When the French first settled the area around the Minas Basin southern shore of the Bay of Fundy in 1604 they named the land Acadia. By the next century these settlers thought of themselves as Acadians. To the English, however, they were always to be 'the French'. The rivalry and suspicion between these two powers of the New World began with the first landings and was only to increase in hostility and bitterness.

The population of Acadia continued to grow throughout the 17th and 18th centuries and, with various battles and treaties, changed ruling hands from French to English and back again. Finally, in 1713 with the Treaty of Utrecht, Acadia became English Nova Scotia. The Acadians refused to take an oath of allegiance, though for the most part they weren't much interested in France's point of view either and evidently wanted most of all to be left alone. Things sort of drifted along in this state for a while and the area around Grand Pré became the largest Acadian community. By this time the total regional population was not far off 10,000, with 3500 more people in Louisbourg and still others on Prince Edward Island.

Unfortunately for them, tensions once again heated up between England and France with squabbles and trade-offs taking place all over the east coast. When a new hardline lieutenant-governor Charles Lawrence was appointed in 1754 he quickly became fed up with the Acadians and their supposed neutrality. He didn't trust them and decided to do something about it. He demanded an oath of allegiance and, as the game had always been played, the Acadians said forget it. This time, though, the rules had changed.

In late August 1755, with the crowns of France and England still locked in battle and

rooms for $45 a single/double and is within easy walking distance of the centre of town.

At the other end of the spectrum is *Victoria's Inn (☎ 902-542-5744, ☎ 1-800-556-5744, 416 Main St)*, a very ornate place with rooms in the main lodge or the Carriage House. Doubles are $79; the Carriage House has triples available. It also has a dining room.

Places to Eat

This being a college town you will find a few pizza and sub shops along Main St. There are also a couple of good coffee shops.

Joe's Food Emporium on Main St is a lively place with an outdoor patio and a wide ranging menu. Pasta dinners are $5 to $9, medium pizza $9 to $12 and a quiche and salad $6. There's beer and wine as well. A block away is *Al's Sausage & Deli* where fresh-smoked sausage on a bun is a speciality.

There's lots and lots of similar carnivorous stuff. Everything on the menu is under $5.

For a real splurge *Chez La Vigne (17 Front St)* or *Ivy Cafe (8 Elm St)*, a block off Main, are recommended. The owner/chef of the Chez La Vigne has been voted Canadian chef of the year. Dinners here set you back $12 to $24. Ivy Cafe, owned by a university professor, is slightly more affordable and has good veggie options.

Getting There & Away

Acadian Bus Lines agency is in Nowlan's Canteen (☎ 902-542-5315) on the far west side, but it does make a stop on campus.

GRAND PRÉ

Now a very small English-speaking town, Grand Pré was the site of one of the most tragic but compelling stories in eastern Canada's history, detailed at the National

---

The Acadians

paranoia increasing, what was to become known as the Deportation or the Expulsion began. All told, about 14,000 Acadians were forced out of this area. Villages were burned, the people boarded onto boats.

The sad, bitter departure was the theme for Longfellow's well known, lengthy narrative poem *Evangeline*, titled after its fictional heroine. Many Acadians headed for Louisiana and New Orleans, where the name became anglicised to 'Cajun' (often heard in songs and seen on restaurant menus). The Cajuns, some of whom still speak French, have maintained aspects of their culture to this day. Others went to various Maritime points and north-eastern America, others to Martinique, Santo Domingo or back to Europe, and some even to the Falkland Islands. Nowhere were they greeted warmly with open arms. Some hid out and remained in Acadia. In later years many of those deported people returned.

Today, most of the French people in Canada's Atlantic Provinces are the descendants of the expelled Acadians and they're still holding tight to their heritage.

In Nova Scotia the Cheticamp area in Cape Breton and the French Shore north of Yarmouth are small strongholds. A pocket in western Prince Edward Island and the Port au Port Peninsula in Newfoundland are others. New Brunswick has a large French population stretching up the east coast past the Acadian Peninsula at Caraquet and all around the border with Quebec.

There has recently been an upsurge in Acadian pride and awareness; in most of these areas you'll see the Acadian flag flying and museums dealing with the past and the continuing Acadian culture. There is another major National Historic Site dealing with the Acadians and their expulsion near St Joseph, New Brunswick, not far from the Nova Scotia border – a visit is recommended. Festivals held in some of these areas provide an opportunity to see traditional dress, sample foods and hear some of the wonderful fiddle-based music.

Historic Site north of the main highway and town, 5km east of Wolfville.

Grand Pré National Historic Site

Grand Pré means 'great meadow' and refers to the farmland created when the Acadians built dikes along the shoreline, as they had done in north-west France for generations. There are 1200 hectares below sea level. It's a beautiful area and one you wouldn't want to leave, especially after the work that made it home. The park is a memorial to the Acadians, who had a settlement here from 1675 to 1755 and then were given the boot by the British.

It consists of an information centre, church, gardens, space and views, and free tours of the site are offered. The worthwhile gift shop has a selection of books on the Acadians, among other things.

A new stone church, built in the Acadian style, sits in the middle of the site as a monument to the original inhabitants. Inside, the history of those people is depicted in a series of colourful paintings done in 1987 by New Brunswick painter Claude Picard.

Walk down through the gardens to the old blacksmith's shed, where there are views of the surrounding gorgeous, fertile farmlands, the air an aromatic mix of sea breeze and worked fields.

In the gardens are a bust of Henry Wadsworth Longfellow, honoured for his poem which chronicles the Acadian's saga, and a statue of Evangeline, who was born here and is now a romantic symbol of her people.

The park (☎ 902-542-3631) is open daily from 9 am to 6 pm from mid-May to October and admission is $2.50, $7 for a family. Acadian Days, an annual festival held sometime towards the end of July, consists of music, storytelling, and arts and crafts.

WINDSOR

Windsor is a small town on the Avon River, halfway between the North Pole and the Equator. At one time it was the only British stronghold in this district of French power and Acadian farmers.

Hwy 1 becomes Water St in town and the main intersection is with Gerrish St. Just off exit 6 of Hwy 101 is the helpful tourist centre (☎ 902-798-2690), open from 9 am to 7 pm during summer.

Nearby, off King St, there's an old blockhouse and earthen mounds still intact amid portions of the British fort at **Fort Edward National Historic Site** (☎ 902-542-3631) dating from 1750. It was used as one of the assembly stations during the expulsions of the Acadians and is one of the oldest blockhouses in Canada. The fort is open from 10 am to 5 pm daily June to October and admission is free.

Another site is **Haliburton House**, once the home of Judge Thomas Chandler Haliburton, one of the founders of written American humor. He created the Sam Slick character in Mark Twain-style stories. Although these aren't read much now, many Haliburton expressions, such as 'quick as a wink' and 'city slicker', are often still used. Haliburton's large estate is open from 9.30 am to 5.30 pm daily from mid-July to mid-September, except on Sunday when it opens at 1 pm. Admission is free. It's on Clifton Ave, which runs off Grey St, itself leading from Gerrish St just north of Lake Pesaquid, in the eastern section of town.

Shand House, part of the provincial museum system, is a small museum on Water St evoking the life of a well-to-do family at the start of the 20th century. It's on Ferry Hill and has the same hours and admission as Haliburton House.

Windsor calls itself the birthplace of ice hockey, though this has created a heated debate with Kingston, Ontario which makes the same claim. They say the boys of King's College School began playing the game on Long Pond around 1800. In 1836, Haliburton even referred to 'playing ball on ice' in his book *The Clockmaker*. These titbits and more (the first pucks were slices of a thick pine branch and the Micmac Indians supplied hand-made hockey sticks to the North American market well into the 1930s) can be gathered at the **Windsor Hockey Heritage Society** (☎ 902-798-1800). The souvenir

shop/museum is a storefront at 128 Gerrish St and is only the first step towards a more permanent centre. Hours are 9 am to 5 pm daily and admission is free.

A bit more wacky are the Brobdingnagian pumpkins at **Howard Dill Enterprises** (☎ 902-798-2728) at 400 College Rd. A four-time world record holder (he grew one 450kg!), Dill's patch is a must near autumn. It's open August to October and is free.

New for this edition is the *Evangeline Express* (☎ 902-798-5667), a refurbished train service running from here to Wolfville and back. There are two trips daily: one at 11 am and one at 3.30 pm. They last four and three hours, respectively. It stops at Grand Pré but the ticket doesn't include admission. A round-trip ticket costs $16.

Tides
The tides in the bay and Avon River near Windsor are impressive – falling and rising up to 12m. At Poplar Grove, off Hwy 14 East, you can view a tidal bore. Ask at the tourist office for good times and locations because it varies a lot.

Port Williams, near Wolfville, is also a good place to see the difference between high and low tides.

Places to Stay & Eat
The *Clockmaker's Inn* (☎ 902-798-5265, 1399 King St) is one of the most recognisable homes in town and its rates of $40/45 are worth it. There's also bicycles for guests. Two motels are here; the *Downeast* (☎ 1-800-395-8117) at the junction of Hwys 1 and 14 has clean rooms from $45, while *Muddy Waters* is near the Hockey Society on Gerrish St and has good coffee as well as inexpensive quiches, pasta and bruschetta.

Getting There & Away
Acadian bus lines from Halifax to Windsor continues on to Yarmouth, making numerous stops through the Annapolis Valley. In Windsor the bus stops at Irving Mainway (☎ 902-798-2126) out on Hwy 1, closer to Falmouth. The one-way fare to Yarmouth is $34, to Halifax $8.

Northumberland Shore

This is the north coastal district of the province, from the New Brunswick border to Cape Breton Island.

The Northumberland Strait is situated between this shore and Prince Edward Island and has some of the warmest waters north of the US Carolinas. Hwy 6, also called the Sunrise Trail tourist route, runs along this strip of small towns, beaches and Scottish history.

On Hwy 104 right at the New Brunswick border is a large tourist office with maps and overviews of the driving trails around Nova Scotia.

The Northumberland shoreline is busy, and as accommodation is not plentiful, places to stay fill quickly. It's strongly recommended that you find a place by lunchtime in July and August.

PUGWASH
This small port, with good beaches nearby, has an average water temperature along this coast slightly over 20°C in summer. Pugwash's two claims to fame are the large salt mine, which produces boatloads of salt to be shipped from the town docks, and the colourful Gathering of the Clans festival, which takes place each year on 1 July. Street names in town are written in Scottish Gaelic as well as in English.

There are several craftspeople in town and their wares are sold along the main street or on Saturday when they set up tables at the **Pugwash Train Station**. Built in 1889, this is one of the two oldest stations in Nova Scotia and today serves as a tourist centre and library. Outside is the *Caboose Cafe* with inexpensive meals – many mains under $8 – and live music.

WALLACE
Wallace is not a major tourist attraction but there is an interesting town titbit. The sandstone from the quarry just out of town has been used to build many fine buildings,

including the Parliament Buildings in Ottawa and Province House in Nova Scotia.

Wallace does have a thriving lobster fishery and the delicacy can be purchased from several places in town. There is also a couple of B&Bs here, a historical museum, and Grant's, a classic general store from another era.

MALAGASH

The Jost Winery (☎ 902-257-2636) off Route 6 is one of only two vineyards in Nova Scotia. Run by a German family, the winery began operation in 1970 and now, with 13 hectares, produces several varieties, with the Riesling style perhaps the best known. Free tours are offered at noon and 3 pm Monday through Saturday and 3 pm on Sunday during summer. There is a store on the premises with a tasting bar and a deli. The winery also rents bicycles at $5 an hour and $13 for three hours for touring the Malagash area.

Malagash was the site of the first rock salt mine in Canada, which operated from 1918 to 1949 and produced more than two million tons of salt. The **Malagash Museum** (☎ 902-257-2897) preserves that mining history with equipment and artefacts from the mine as well as a movie made during its peak production year in 1941. Hours are 10 am to 5 pm daily during summer and admission is $2.

TATAMAGOUCHE

Despite having a population of just 726 (and one road – the highway), Tatamagouche is somewhat of a visitor centre.

Not to be missed is the quirky **Fraser Culture Centre** (☎ 902-657-3285), a museum-cum-art gallery. The showpiece is the room dedicated to Anna Swan who, at 2.4m tall and weighing 187kg, was known as the giantess of Nova Scotia and went on to achieve some celebrity. Born in one of the surrounding villages in 1896, she parlayed her size into a lucrative career with Barnum & Bailey's circus and even ended up meeting Queen Elizabeth II in London, where Anna was married. Clothes, newspaper clippings and photographs tell the big story.

The centre also has some historical pieces and several gallery rooms displaying the work of local artists. The tourist office is here, in another of the many rooms. Hours are 8.30 am to 7.30 pm daily during summer and admission is by donation.

A few doors down is the less idiosyncratic **Sunrise Trail Museum** (☎ 902-657-3007) of local history, with emphasis on the shipbuilding industry, once of major importance here. The Acadian French settled this area in the 1700s and a display tells of them and their expulsion. Hours are 9 am to 5 pm during summer and admission is $1.

In Tatamagouche, Oktoberfest is held at the end of September or beginning of October.

Places to Stay & Eat

For camping *Nelson Memorial Park* (☎ 902-657-2730) is just west of Tatamagouche and has 76 camp sites, showers and a beach. Tent sites are $12 a night. Keep in mind that the *Wentworth Hostel* (☎ 902-548-2379) is only 27km south of town via Route 246 (see Truro earlier in this chapter).

Two miles out of town via Pine St and Truro Rd is the *Mountain Breeze Farm B&B* (☎ 902-657-3193), with rooms for $40/45 a single/double or triple, including a sauna with whirlpool, and a full breakfast. German is spoken.

The *Train Station Inn* (☎ 902-657-3222) is in the – you guessed it – old train station on Main St. It features three rooms in the station that range from $50 to $68 for a single or double and two cabooses outside that have been converted into suites. They sleep two to four people and are $98 a night.

The *Villager Inn & Restaurant* has daily specials, some seafood and quite good chowders. Most dinners are under $10. For breakfast there is the *Marthon Bakery* which opens at 7 am. The *Mill Dining Room* of the Balmoral Motel has German cuisine; dinners start at $10.

AROUND TATAMAGOUCHE

South down Route 311, **Balmoral Grist Mill Museum** (☎ 902-657-3016) has one of the province's oldest grist mills, which opened

in 1874. Grinding demonstrations held from 10 am to noon and 2 to 4 pm daily during summer show the flour (oatmeal, barley, wheat) milling process from start to finish and the completed products are even offered for sale. It's open from 1 to 5.30 pm on Sunday and 9.30 am to 5.30 pm the rest of the week. Admission is free.

Another provincial historic site is outside the village of Denmark. The **Sutherland Steam Mill** (☎ 902-657-3365) was built in 1894 and was run continuously by family members until 1953. The sawmill is no longer a commercial entity but the machinery and steam engine are still operational and on the first Saturday of the month (check this first) they cut lumber. Hours, season and admission is the same as Balmoral Mills.

This part of the province has a bit of a German colony, and at the *Bavarian Garden Restaurant* in Denmark, various made-on-the-premises German foods are offered. It's open every day in July and August but only on weekends in May, June and September. The Pork Shop next door sells a wide variety of German sausage, kassler, hams etc.

PICTOU

Pictou (pronounced 'pik toe'), one of the most attractive and engaging towns along the North Shore, is where the Highland Scots first landed in 1773, to be followed by thousands in the settling of 'New Scotland'. In town, among the many older structures, are several buildings and historic sites relating to the early Scottish pioneers. Pick up a walking-tour brochure at the large tourist office (☎ 902-485-6123) at the rotary (roundabout) north-west of the town centre. Hours are 8 am to 9 pm daily in peak season.

Water St is the main street and reflects the architectural style of the early Scottish builders. Above it Church, High and Faulkland Sts are lined with some of the old, capacious houses for which the town is noted.

Pictou, with its stone buildings and scenic waterfront, is a haven for artists. Throughout town there are numerous art studios and craft shops, with most of them cluttered along Water and Front Sts.

The ferry to Prince Edward Island leaves from just north of town at Caribou. For details see the Charlottetown Getting There & Away section in the Prince Edward Island chapter.

Hector Heritage Quay

Part of the waterfront has been redeveloped to preserve both history and access. At the boatyard a full-size replica of the first ship to bring the Scottish settlers, the three-masted *Hector*, is being constructed. Begun in 1993, it will take about a decade to complete. Guides tell the story of the crossing and settlement.

Other features are the interpretive centre (☎ 902-485-4371), with varied displays and dioramas depicting the life of the Scottish immigrants, a blacksmith shop and a collection of shipbuilding artefacts. Hours are 9 am to 8 pm Monday through Friday, noon to 6 pm Saturday and 10 am to 6 pm Sunday. Admission into the interpretive centre and shipyard is $3 or $8 per family.

From the pier nearby bicycles can be rented for $8 for four hours or $20 per day. A **water taxi** also makes three runs per day to and from New Glasgow.

deCoste Entertainment Centre

This impressive performing arts centre on Water St is the site of a range of live performances, from plays and comedies to the leading Scottish and Celtic musicians in Canada. For the current event or tickets call or stop at the box office (☎ 902-485-8848).

Grohmann Knives

The small family-run business (☎ 902-485-4224) at 116 Water St has a well deserved reputation for the very fine outdoor and kitchen knives it produces. One of them, a classic belt knife available in many countries, is in the Museum of Modern Art in New York.

Many of the production stages are done by hand, as they were when the operation began in the mid-1950s, and can be seen on the free tours around the plant offered on demand (minimum four people) Monday

to Friday from 9 am to 3 pm May to September.

On display is the folding knife Rudolph Grohmann handcrafted in 1912 for his apprenticeship as a knifemaker. It would put any Swiss Army knife to shame as it features 108 tools and requires a half-hour to fully open.

Northumberland Fisheries Museum

On Front St in the old train station, the museum tells the story of the area's fishing. It had been damaged by fire at the time of writing and may be closed. It's normally open from 9.30 am to 5.30 pm Monday through Saturday and 1 to 5.30 pm Sunday during summer and admission is $2.

Hector National Exhibit Centre & McCulloch House Museum

Away from the town centre but still within walking distance on Haliburton Rd, a continuation westward of High St, this centre (☎ 902-485-4563) presents a variety of ever-changing shows. Always on display are the quilts, pewter items and embroidery produced by the Pictou County Art & Crafts Association. The centre has the same hours as the Fisheries Museum. Admission is $1.

Just up the hill from here is the McCulloch House Museum (☎ 902-485-1150). Built in 1806 for Thomas McCulloch, a minister and important educator, this home now displays articles pertaining to his career as well as items relating to other early Scottish settlers. It is open the same hours as the centre and admission is free.

Beaches

There are a couple of very good beaches outside Pictou. The most popular is Melmerby Beach ('the Merb'), which is actually north of New Glasgow but draws visitors from far and wide. It's a long, wide sandy beach; there is a basic hamburger stand but no shade.

A better choice is Caribou Beach, which is equally sandy with gradually deepening water but is more scenic, with picnic tables along a small ridge above the beach and

trees for when the sun gets too intense. It is much closer to town, north of Pictou near the Prince Edward Island ferry terminal. Both beaches are free and the water along this strip of ocean is as warm as any in Nova Scotia.

Special Events

The Lobster Carnival, a three-day event at the beginning of July, marks the end of the lobster season. The Hector Festival in mid-August is four days of celebration of the area's Scottish heritage, including concerts.

Places to Stay

Pictou has about a dozen possibilities for spending the night. Bear in mind that, while not crowded, the town has a steady stream of people passing through and most accommodation is full (or close to it) throughout summer.

Of the many B&Bs, the most economical and central is near the waterfront. The *WH Davies House B&B* (☎ 902-485-4864, 90 Front St) is in yet another grand old home. There are three rooms that begin at $35/40. Some $5 cheaper is the *Linden Arms B&B* (☎ 902-485-6565, 62 Martha St), a five minute walk from town.

The *Willow House Inn* (☎ 902-485-5740, 3 Willow St) is another B&B in a large historic house dating from 1840 and once belonging to the mayor. It features 10 rooms starting at $50.

Away from the downtown area, near the tourist office by the traffic rotary, is *The Lionstone Inn* (☎ 902-485-4157). It has some newish motel units as well as a number of older individual cabins with their own kitchens. Singles are $55 and spartan cottages start at $50.

People mostly come here to splurge though. The most recent four-star addition in town is the *Customs House Inn* (☎ 902-485-4546, 38 Depot St) with a view of the harbour. All rooms have private bath and rates start at $60. Housed in the former American consulate is the *Consulate Inn* (☎ 902-485-4554, ☎ 1-800-424-8283, 157 Water St) with a wide variety of rooms and

suites, all with private bath, starting at $54. It's boasts a well regarded dining room.

Places to Eat

Right in the centre at 11 Water St is the *Stone House Café & Pizzeria*, where the food isn't great but the selection is wide. There is a nice outside patio and local entertainment is often on tap in the evenings. Dinners range from $10 to $13.

At 41 Water St is the casual *Pirate's Pier*, with very well priced seafood and daily specials under $10.

Relics is a friendly Scottish pub located in the Old Custom House Art and Craft Gallery. It features a menu of seafood, salads and sandwiches that start at $3. Also on the waterfront is *Saltwater Cafe* on Caladh with a higher priced menu. The restaurant has a deck overlooking the harbour and often live entertainment featuring traditional Maritime music.

Though out of the way and virtually impossible to reach without a car, one of the best known restaurants in the area is the *Lobster Bar*, across the bay from Pictou in Pictou Landing, where there is a Native Indian reserve and not a lot more. Driving involves a rather circuitous route over one of the bridges towards New Glasgow – get the map distributed at the Pictou tourist office.

It's a casual (take the kids), busy and not badly priced seafood house specialising in lobster. A full lobster meal costs about $20. They've been serving up fish, clams and all the rest since the late 1950s and have fed former US president Jimmy Carter as well as former Canadian prime minister Brian Mulroney and his wife Mila.

NEW GLASGOW

With a population of 10,000, New Glasgow is the largest town along the Northumberland Shore. It originally was, and remains, a small industrial centre. There is little to see in town, but it can be useful as a stopping point as it's close if you're coming or going to the ferry for Prince Edward Island.

Provost St, the main retail and shopping avenue, has a couple of restaurants. Temper-ance St, parallel to Provost St and up the hill from the river, is attractive, with lots of trees, some large older houses, a couple of churches and **Carmichael-Stewart House**. The latter, at 86 Temperance St, is an historic building with a small free museum illustrating the town's history in shipbuilding and coal mining. Hours are 9 am to 4.30 pm Monday through Friday and 1 to 4.30 pm on Saturday.

Fraser's Mountain, not far from town, offers excellent views of the entire region. Drive east through town on Archimedes St and turn right on George St. Continue up the hill, veering left around the church, and keep going straight to the summit.

Nova Scotia Museum of Industry

The most compelling attraction is actually in neighbouring Stellarton; take exit 24 of Hwy 104. This impressive provincial museum (☎ 902-755-5425) features almost 14,000 artefacts and numerous hands-on exhibits. There are several galleries that display everything from the Samson, the earliest standard gauge locomotive to operate in North America, and the first car to drive the streets of Halifax to Stellarton's glassworks industry that produced millions of soda bottles. The museum itself is located on the site of the Albion coal mine.

Hours are 9 am to 5 pm daily during summer and admission is $5 for adults or $13 for a family. There is a tea shop in the museum with a pleasant outdoor patio.

Places to Stay

For spending the night, the *Wynward Inn* (☎ 902-752-4527, 71 Stellarton Rd), a B&B since 1930, makes a fine choice. Actually an attractive old house, it's central and has a nice balcony. Rates start at $38 for singles/doubles, including a light breakfast.

There are motels on the highway outside town with most of them charging $55 a single.

ANTIGONISH

If you are coming from New Brunswick or Prince Edward Island, this is where you should spend the night. Pleasant Antigonish

(pronounced 'An-tee-guh-NISH') is also a good stop between Sydney and Halifax. It has good places to stay and the beach is nearby. It's a university town with no industry.

Information

The tourist office (☎ 902-863-4921) is just off the highway at the west entrance to Antigonish, coming from New Glasgow at exit 32. It's open from 9 am to 8 pm.

Heritage Museum

Located in the classic Antigonish Depot that was built in 1908 by the Intercolonial Railway, the museum (☎ 902-863-6160) features displays pertaining to the early days of Antigonish. The most interesting exhibit is the 1864 hand-hauled fire engine the town once used to put out blazes. The depot is at 20 East Main St and hours are 10 am to 5 pm Monday through Saturday in July and August. Admission is free.

St Francis Xavier University

The attractive campus of this 125-year-old university is behind the cathedral near the centre of town. It's a pleasant place to walk.

County Courthouse

In 1984 this 129-year-old building was designated a National Historic Site. Restored in 1970, it still serves as the county's judicial centre. The design (by Alexander Macdonald) is typical of many of the province's courthouses from the mid-19th century.

Special Events

Antigonish is known for its annual Highland Games, held in mid-July. These Scottish games have been going on since 1861. You'll see pipe bands, drum regiments, dancers and athletes from far and wide. The events last a week.

Festival Antigonish is a summer theatre festival, with all performances held at one of the university auditoriums.

Places to Stay

Whidden's Campground & Trailer Court (☎ 902-836-3736), right in town on the corner of Main and Hawthorne Sts, is an unusual accommodation complex. It's a very large place and offers a real blend of choices. Tent camping is $17.50 for a night, full serviced sites $20 a night, $10 if you show up on foot or a bike. There are also motel apartments with kitchens (from $60) and mobile homes with complete facilities ($68 a double plus $5 for each additional person). The grounds have a swimming pool and a laundrette for all guests to use.

For rooms at the central *University* from mid-May to mid-August, call the Residence Manager (☎ 902-867-3970). It has a dining room, laundrette and pool. Singles/doubles are $19/38 including a full breakfast and use of the university facilities. After 4 pm, go to the Security Office.

Most of the inexpensive B&Bs have closed, though the tourist office may have new openings. Cheapest now is *Bekkers* (☎ 902-863-3194), a couple of miles out of town, with rooms from $45.

Most motels in town have singles that begin at $50. Head east for more affordable accommodation. The *Chestnut Corner B&B* (☎ 902-386-2301), off Hwy 4 at Afton Station, is $35/40. *Porter's* (☎ 902-386-2196), 16km east in Pomquet, has four rooms ($35/45) in an old farmhouse and a full breakfast.

Places to Eat

The *Sunshine Café (332 Main St)* is a sort of café with a bistro complex. Creative light main courses are under $9, full dinners $14, and vegetarians aren't ignored. You find excellent value for your money. Up the street is *Sunflower Health Food Store*.

Wong's is friendly and provides the local Chinese option, with full dinners in the $10 to $12 range. *Frescoes*, just off Main St on College St is recommended for Greek dinners that range from $13 and pasta dishes.

West out of town along the Trans Canada Hwy is the more costly *Lobster Treat* restaurant for the widest selection of seafood.

Getting There & Away

Bus The Acadian Bus Lines terminal (☎ 902-863-6900) is on the Trans Canada Hwy at the

turn-off for James St into town, on the west side of the city, and is within walking distance of the downtown area. Buses include those to Halifax (one to four a day, $29.75) and to Sydney (one morning and two afternoon trips, $27.26).

AROUND ANTIGONISH
Monastery
East of town in the small village of Monastery, the old monastery is now home to the Augustine Order of monks. It was originally a Trappist monastery established by French monks in 1825. Visitors are welcome to tour the chapel and the grounds.

Beaches
There are some good sandy beaches on the coast east or north from town. For the eastern ones, take Bay St out of town.

Driving Tours
There are several driving tours of the area, each no more than 80km – a descriptive pamphlet is available from the tourist office. They try to take in some good scenery and points of historical note. One recommended 'off-the-track' route goes north along the coast to Cape George on Hwy 337. Right out of town by the Antigonish Museum, a hiking/biking tail goes to natural reserve **Antigonish Landing**. At Crystal Cliffs there are huge cormorant roosts. Also along here is superb day hiking along the **Fairmont Ridge Trail**, a 12km system ranging from leisurely 30-minute strolls around meadows and ponds to very challenging, rough scrambles through bear country. Shoreline Adventures (☎ 902-863-5958) has kayak tours and rentals (from $8 per hour) at Harbour Center.

Eastern Shore

The 'Eastern Shore' designation refers to the area east from Dartmouth to Cape Canso, at the extreme eastern tip of the mainland. It's one of the least visited regions of the province; there are no large towns and the main road is slow, narrow and almost as convoluted as the rugged shoreline it follows. Marine Drive, the designated tourist route, is the only route through the area. There are some campgrounds and good beaches along the coast but the water on this edge of the province is prohibitively cold.

MARTINIQUE BEACH PROVINCIAL PARK
Martinique, 4.8km south of the village of Musquodoboit Harbour, is the longest beach in the province and a good place for a break.

The beach has resulted in a number of interesting places to spend a night in and around Musquodoboit Harbour. Within town there is **Camelot Inn** (☎ 902-889-2198), a five-room inn overlooking a river that is fished for salmon. The inn features a restaurant on the 1st floor along with a fireplace lounge for guests. Singles are $34 to $45, and doubles are $56.

East of town is **Seaview Fishermen's Home** (☎ 902-889-2561), reached by departing Hwy 7 and heading south 13km for Pleasant Point. The home, built in 1861, is surrounded by great coastal scenery that includes a lighthouse and a fisherman's wharf, where you can purchase lobster straight from the boat during the season. Rooms are $45/50.

JEDORE OYSTER POND
Quite the name for a town. See the small **Fisherman's Life Museum** – it's a model of a typical 1900s fishing family's house, now with costumed guides and eternal tea-time. It's open 9.30 am to 5.30 pm daily during summer, except Sunday when it opens at 1 pm. Admission is free. Also here on the water is the **Golden Coast Restaurant**, a place to buy fresh seafood to take away or to enjoy a seafood dinner. Dinners range from $8 to $15 and its seafood chowder, with chunks of lobster, scallops and haddock, is excellent.

SHIP HARBOUR
Off the shore here you'll see the buoys and nets of the local aquaculture industry. This is North America's largest mussel-farming centre. Fish-farming of every description is

poised to become ever more significant as the natural stocks show the effects of centuries of indiscriminate hauling.

MUSQUODOBOIT VALLEY

A side trip away from the coast follows the course of the Musquodoboit River into the forested interior and along the valley's farming regions to the village of Upper Musquodoboit.

Along the road that heads south to Tangier on the coast there is **Moose River Gold Mines**. Prospecting in the area began in 1876 and Moose River Gold Mines reached their peak production between 1890 and 1909. In an attempt to reopen them in 1936, three men, including a Toronto barrister and a prominent Toronto doctor, became trapped 43m below after a cave-in. The rescue effort took 10 days and captivated the hearts of millions of people across Canada, the USA and Britain due to daily live reports of the Canadian Radio Broadcasting Company (later the CBC). These broadcasts represented the first 'media event' in North America and for the most part changed the course of radio in Canada. Today the site is a provincial park with interpretive displays and mining equipment. Nearby is the **Moose River Gold Mines Museum** which has displays on the mines and the famous rescue. Hours are 10 am to 5 pm daily during summer, except Sunday when it opens at 1 pm. Admission is free. Note that at the end the road is unpaved and can get dicey after lots of rain.

TANGIER

Visiting **Willy Krauch's Smokehouse** (☎ 902-772-2188), a short distance from the main road in Tangier, is worthwhile. Begun by Willy, a Dane, and now run by his sons, it's a small operation with a big reputation. They smoke Atlantic salmon, mackerel and eel, but the ultimate is the Cape Breton smoked trout. You can keep it without refrigeration or it can be mailed, as it has been to Queen Elizabeth at Buckingham Palace. The shed is open every day until 6 pm.

Also in town is Coastal Adventures Sea Kayaking (☎ 902-772-2774), for lessons,

rentals and guided trips. Its day clinic is an introduction to kayaking and includes a tour to offshore islands. The cost is $85. Half-day rentals are $30, full day $40. It also has canoes and double kayaks.

TAYLOR HEAD PROVINCIAL PARK

Just east of the village of Spry Harbour, this day-use park has a very fine, sandy beach fronting a protected bay. The water, though, doesn't seem to warm up much. In recent years, the park has developed an extensive trail system along the shoreline of the point. The Headland Trail is the longest at 8km and follows the rugged coastline to scenic views at Taylor Head. The trail is a three to four-hour walk. Shorter is the Bob Bluff Trail, a 3km return trip to views off the bluff at the end. Park entry is free.

LISCOMB PARK GAME SANCTUARY

North of Sheet Harbour lies this large preserve, 518 sq km in area. There's lots of wildlife and some good canoeing, swimming, fishing and hiking.

PORT DUFFERIN

Tiny Port Dufferin, population 157, is mentioned for the *Marquis of Dufferin Seaside Inn* (☎ 902-654-2696, ☎ 1-800-561-2696), a highly regarded retreat featuring coastal views, breezes and tranquillity. Rooms are in a new motel-like strip alongside the original house. Singles/doubles are $50/55 and include a continental breakfast; off-season rates are excellent. The dining room in the restored house of 1859 serves outstanding Maritime-style seafood meals such as fish casserole, haddock baked with eggs and shrimp. Dinners range from $11 to $16.

Port Dufferin is approximately a two hour drive from Halifax, Antigonish or the Halifax international airport.

LISCOMB MILLS

In a green wooded area where the Liscomb River meets the sea is one of the provincial government's luxury resort lodges, *Liscomb Lodge* (☎ 902-779-2307). It has all

the amenities, and prices to match; singles/doubles begin at $105/115. But you may want to have a look as the river here rushes through a maze of large boulders, making for a scenic setting.

SHERBROOKE

Inland towards Antigonish, the pleasant little town of Sherbrooke is overshadowed by its historic site, which is about the same size.

Sherbrooke Village (☎ 902-522-2400) recreates life 125 years ago through buildings, demonstrations and costumed workers. It's called a living museum and all of the houses, stores and various workshops are the original ones. The green, quiet setting helps to evoke a real sense of stepping back in time. The site is open daily from 9.30 am to 5.30 pm from 15 May to 15 October and admission is $6 per adult or $18 per family.

The local tourist office is also at Sherbrooke Village, open the same hours as the village.

About 500m away is the **Sherbrooke Village Sawmill**, the former town mill, which is in working order and has a guide to answer questions. Across the street and a nice walk through the woods along a stream is a cabin in which the workers at the mill would have lived.

Sherbrooke itself, although not the major centre it was at the start of the 20th century, is one of the biggest towns in the area, so stop here for tourist information, groceries and gasoline.

Places to Stay & Eat

At *Riverside Campground* (☎ 902-522-2913), a five minute walk from Sherbrooke Village, a site costs $12 and there's a pool.

St Mary's River Lodge (☎ 902-522-2177), adjacent to the village, is $44/54 with shared bath facilities, and breakfast is available. A couple of other B&Bs in town are the same price; outside of town along the highway there's a motel.

PORT BICKERTON

East of Sherbrooke along Hwy 7, then 29km south, is the **Nova Scotia Lighthouse Centre** (☎ 902-364-2000), part of a park with good walking trails. The small centre gives an overview of all Nova Scotia's lighthouses, great for lighthouse aficionados. It's open daily from 10 am to 8 pm and admission is $2.

CANSO

With a population of just 1300, this town at the edge of the mainland is probably the largest on the whole eastern shoreline. Since the first attempted settlement in 1518, Canso has seen it all: Native Indian battles, British and French landings and captures, pirates, fishing fleets and the ever-present difficulties of life ruled by the sea.

A museum, **Whitman House** (☎ 902-366-2170), on the corner of Main and Union Sts, has reminders of parts of this history and offers a good view from the roof. The museum also doubles as the tourist office and is open from 9 am to 6 pm daily during summer. Admission is free.

An interpretive centre on the waterfront tells the story of the **Grassy Island National Historic Site**, which lies just offshore and can be visited by boat. In 1720, the British built a small fort here to offer some protection from the French, who had their headquarters in Louisbourg. The island, however, was extremely vulnerable to military attacks and was totally destroyed in 1744. Among the ruins today there's a self-guiding hiking trail with eight interpretive stops explaining the history of the area.

The visitors centre (☎ 902-366-2170) is open from 10 am to 6 pm during summer. The boat to Grassy Island departs from the centre twice a day – usually 11 am and 4 pm – in July and August, and only once a day in June and September. Admission to the site is $2.75.

Cape Breton Island

Cape Breton, the large island adjunct at the north-east end of Nova Scotia, is justly renowned for its rugged splendour. It's the roughest, highest, coolest, most remote area of the province. The coast is rocky and rugged, the interior a blend of mountains,

CAPE BRETON ISLAND

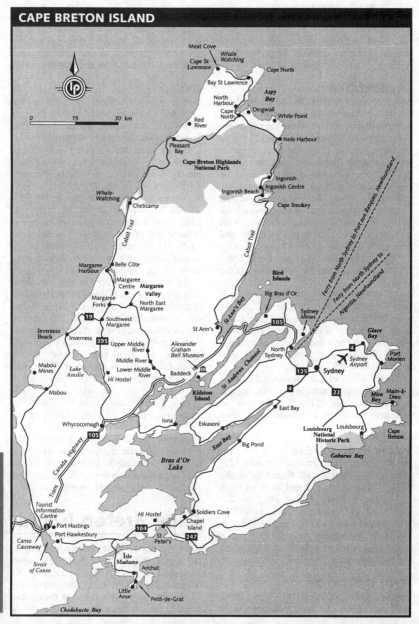

Meat Cove
Whale Watching
Cape St Lawrence
Cape North
Bay St Lawrence
Aspy Bay
North Harbour
Cape North
Dingwall
White Point
Red River
Pleasant Bay
Neils Harbour
Cape Breton Highlands National Park
Whale-Watching
Cheticamp
Ingonish
Ingonish Centre
Ingonish Beach
Cape Smokey
Cabot Trail
Margaree Harbour
Belle Côte
Bird Islands
Margaree Centre
Margaree Valley
Big Bras d'Or
Margaree Forks
North East Margaree
19
Southwest Margaree
St Ann's Bay
Sydney Mines
Glace Bay
Inverness Beach
Inverness
395
Upper Middle River
St Ann's
105
North Sydney
Port Morien
Mabou Mines
Lake Ainslie
Middle River
Lower Middle River
Alexander Graham Bell Museum
Sydney Airport
Sydney
Mabou
HI Hostel
Baddeck
St Andrews Channel
125
4
Mira Bay
Main-à-Dieu
Kidston Island
22
Whycocomagh
Iona
Eskasoni
East Bay
East Bay
Louisbourg National Historic Park
Louisbourg
105
Big Pond
Cape Breton
Bras d'Or Lake
Gabarus Bay
Trans Canada Highway
Tourist Information Centre
HI Hostel
Soldiers Cove
Port Hastings
Port Hawkesbury
104
Chapel Island
Canso Causeway
St Peter's
247
Strait of Canso
Île Madame
Arichat
Little Anse
Petit-de-Grat
Chedabucto Bay

Ferry from North Sydney to Port aux Basques, Newfoundland
Ferry from North Sydney to Argentia, Newfoundland

0   15   30 km

valleys, rivers and lakes. The nearly 300km-long highway, the Cabot Trail, around the Cape Breton Highlands National Park is one of Canada's grandest and best known roads, winding and climbing to 500m between mountain and sea.

The island offers more than natural beauty – it has a long and captivating human history encompassing the Native people, the British, the French and, especially, the Scottish, who were attracted to this part of the province because of its strong resemblance to the Scottish Highlands.

Except for the struggling former coal and steel industrial centres of Sydney and Glace Bay, most towns are small enough to be considered villages. People in some areas still speak French; in others even Scottish Gaelic can be heard. Life is hard here and unemployment is very high. Fishing, and mining with its steel plant spin-off, have for generations been the backbones of the local economy, but have all declined sharply. While fish stocks may rebound, there is no such hope for mining and steel.

For the visitor it is a very appealing, relatively undeveloped area, with the excellent national park in the highlands and a top historic site in Louisbourg. For a taste of the rich culture, there is now the Celtic Colours International Festival, usually held the second week of October; it's a smorgasbord of nearly three dozen performances spread all over the island – Celtic fiddlers to the world's biggest square dance.

North Sydney is the terminal for ferries to Newfoundland.

The Cabot Trail, understandably the most popular area, can be busy, even a little crowded in July and August, but it isn't difficult to get away if solitude is what you seek. The words most often used to describe the weather are windy, wet, foggy and cool. Summer days, however, can be warm and sunny. The sketchy public transportation system makes getting around Cape Breton difficult without a vehicle. Acadian Bus Lines runs from Halifax or New Glasgow and Antigonish to Sydney, stopping at popular Baddeck along the way. Transoverland

Ltd runs a bus route from Baddeck to Chéticamp through the Margaree Valley.

Information

A big and busy tourist office sits on the east side of the causeway in Port Hastings and is open from 8.30 am to 8.30 pm daily. From here you can pick up information on all parts of Cape Breton or book rooms with a courtesy phone. If you need to make ferry reservations for a trip to Newfoundland, do it at least a few days before your planned departure.

NORTH COAST

From the Canso Causeway, Hwy 19, known as the Ceilidh (pronounced 'KAY-lee') Trail, goes up the northern side of the island to the highlands. The first part of the route is not very interesting but it still beats the Trans Canada Hwy (No 105), which goes straight up the middle.

At **Mabou**, things pick up. It's a green, hilly region with valleys following numerous rivers and sheltering traditional towns. This is one of the areas on Cape Breton where Scottish Gaelic is still spoken and actually taught in the schools. Right in the centre of little Mabou is An Drochaid – or, 'The Bridge' – in an old general store. This acts as a centre for crafts, genealogy, and local music. Aside from information there are books, tapes and various items relating to its Scottish heritage. On 1 July a Scottish picnic is held, with music and dancing.

New for this edition is the HI *Mabou River Hostel* (☎ 902-945-2356, ☎ 1-888-627-9744, 19 Mabou Ridge Rd), well marked 100m off Hwy 19. This hostel has 25 beds, with some family rooms available. There's a large kitchen. Rooms are $18/20 members/nonmembers and include breakfast. After October it's open on a reservation-only basis. Tents also pop up on a sweeping beach next to a small harbour just south of Port Hope off Shore Road. In Mabou, start the day at *Shining Waters Bakery & Eatery*. The homemade bread is a steal at around $2 a loaf, while a full breakfast featuring thick slices of it is $3.75. The *Mull Café* on Hwy 19 has an

eclectic menu of salads, sandwiches, and vegetarian dishes with mains beginning around $5 at lunch, $7.50 for dinner.

At the coast, off the main road, around Mabou Mines, the **Mabou Highlands** offer some good walking trails. To get there, head for Mabou Harbour and then swing off on the gravel road marked 'Mabou Mines'. You'll quickly return to the coast to pass a handful of houses and then follow a rough track as it climbs into the highlands. Within 3km, you pass two posted trailheads, though the signs are easy to miss.

Between Mabou and Inverness on Hwy 19, the thirsty may wish to stop at **Glenora Falls**, where North America's only single-malt Scotch whisky is made, at the *Glenora Inn & Distillery* (☎ 902-258-2662). Tours of the whisky operation take place daily during summer on the hour from 9 am to 5 pm and cost $5. You can have something to eat or even spend the night but the room rates are steep at $87 a double.

INVERNESS

This is the first town of any size on the northern shore. There are miles of sandy beach with some nice secluded spots and few people and, surprisingly, the water temperature is not too bad, reaching 19°C to 21°C, which is about as warm as it gets anywhere around the Atlantic Provinces – cool but definitely swimmable. Pilot whales can sometimes be seen off the coast.

Places to Stay & Eat

The *Gables Motel* (☎ 902-258-2314) right on Hwy 19 is slightly less expensive than other town B&Bs and inns, with singles/doubles for $42, and at the north end of town try the comfortable *Cayly Café*, located next door to a laundrette. More expensive is the *Casual Gourmet* on Beach Rd No 2 – you'll find steaks and seafood but also low-fat, vegetarian, and even vegan dishes. Most dinner mains are around $10.

MARGAREE VALLEY

North-east of Lake Ainslie, in a series of river valleys, is a postcard-perfect, relatively gentle region known collectively as the Margaree Valley. With a half-dozen different towns named Margaree this or Margaree that, it's an oasis of sorts in the midst of the more rugged, wild and unpopulated highlands.

In North East Margaree is the **Salmon Museum** (☎ 902-248-2848), with information on the river, its fish and the human artifices they must avoid. An aquarium contains both salmon and trout. It is open daily from 9 am to 5 pm and admission is $1.

This is also a good spot for local ceilidhs; check the local paper *Oran* for schedules.

Places to Stay

For a small, low-key resort valley, there is a fair number of places to stay and eat. Best known is the *Normaway Inn* (☎ 902-248-2987, ☎ 1-800-565-9463), a three-star luxury country inn operating since 1928, known for its dining room as well as its accommodation. Rates range from $75 to $100 a double with the morning meal included; with no meals involved the rates actually are quite good; or, check in after 4 pm and if there are any rooms available, $25 comes off the room rate. This isn't usually the case in high season but is often possible in May and September. Barn dances and live traditional music are the norm here.

Getting back to reality there's *Brown's Brunaich na H'Aibhne B&B* (☎ 902-248-2935, ☎ 1-800-575-2935), in Margaree Centre. Rates start at $33 a single and $40 a double or triple. Margaree Harbour has a plethora of affordable B&Bs, including the *Harbour View Inn* (☎ 902-235-2314), with rooms from $35 and an A-frame chalet from $60. Just south of Margaree Harbour on Hwy 219 is *Whale Cove Summer Village* (☎ 902-235-2202) with its own private beach on a small cove. The resort has 30 cabins with daily rates from $62.

Places to Eat

In Margaree Harbour, out of the valley on the coast, the *Schooner Village Tea House* serves light meals and inexpensive fish chowders. It also consistently hosts traditional

music, especially Scottish Gaelic singing at 8 pm on Tuesday.

BELLE CÔTE

From Belle Côte, where the Cabot Trail meets the coastline, northward to the Cape Breton Highlands National Park, another strong culture adds a different interest to the island. The people here are predominantly French, the descendants of the Acadians who settled the area – and the area north of Yarmouth – in the 1750s after being expelled from the mainland by the British during the Seven Years' War.

The strength of this culture in Cape Breton is remarkable because of its small size and isolation from other French-speaking people. Almost everyone, it seems, speaks English, although an accent is sometimes detectable. Among themselves, they switch to French, keeping the language very much alive. Aside from the language, the French food, music and dance are worth sampling.

At Belle Côte look for the **Theatre of Scarecrow**, by the highway beside Ethel's Takeout restaurant. It's a humorous, quasi-macabre outdoor collection of life-sized stuffed figures. Watch out after midnight.

CHETICAMP

Just before the Cape Breton Highlands National Park, busy Cheticamp (population 3000) is the centre of the local Acadian community and the gateway to the nearby national park. From Cheticamp the Cabot Trail becomes more scenic, with superlative vistas and lots of hills and turns as you climb to the highest point just before Pleasant Bay.

The church, St Pierre, dominates the town, as is so often the case in French centres. It dates from 1883 and has the characteristic silver spire.

From Government Wharf, across and down from the church, whale-watching cruises are run. The three-hour boat excursions by Whale Cruisers (☎ 902-224-3376, ☎ 1-800-813-3376) are pretty good value. It runs three trips daily from May until the end of September at 9 am, 1 pm and 5 or 6 pm.

The cost is $28.75. Another offering whale trips at the same cost is Seaside Whale & Nature Cruises (☎ 1-800-959-4253), while Acadian Whale Cruise (☎ 902-224-1088) is only $24. The most common species in the area is the pilot whale, also called the pothead, but fin whales and minkes are sometimes seen, as are bald eagles and a couple of species of seabirds. At the tourist office on Government Wharf they keep a chart of the whales spotted each day during summer.

Over on Ile de Cheticamp, Plage Saint Pierre is a good sandy beach with picnic tables and camping. The island is connected by road to the mainland at the south end of town.

The Acadians have a tradition of handicrafts, but in this area one product, hooked rugs, has long been seen as of particular beauty and value. Many of the local women continue this craft; their wares are displayed and sold in numerous outlets in and around town. A good rug costs $200 to $300 and up, so they aren't cheap but they are distinctive and attractive. Each is made of wool, and to complete the intricate work takes about 12 hours per 30 sq cm.

Les Trois Pignons

At the north end of town, this cultural centre and museum (☎ 902-224-2642) shows, among other things, the rugs and tapestries of many local people, including those of Elizabeth Lefort, who has achieved an international reputation. Her detailed representational rugs and portraits in wool hang in the White House, the Vatican and Buckingham Palace. It's open from 8 am to 6 pm. Admission is $3.50.

Musée Acadienne

In the middle of town don't miss the Acadian museum, which has a limited but fascinating display of artefacts, furniture and some older rugs.

Perhaps the highlight of the Acadian museum is its restaurant, with a large menu of mainly standard items, the low prices and freshness separating them from what's offered in run-of-the-mill places. The best dishes are the three or four traditional

Acadian ones, all of which are excellent. The soup and meat pie make a great lunch. Fish cakes may be sampled (here, as in Newfoundland, fish means cod; other types are called by name). The desserts, which are all freshly made, include gingerbread and a variety of fruit pies. Everything is good and cheap (dinners under $9); the women who run the place and do the cooking and baking wear traditional dress.

The museum and restaurant (☎ 902-224-2170) are open daily from 8 am to 9 pm from the middle of May to the end of October.

Places to Stay

Throughout July and August accommodation is tight, so calling ahead or arriving early in the afternoon is advisable.

As mentioned, there is *camping* on Île de Cheticamp at Plage Saint Pierre (☎ 902-224-2624), where a site is $13.

In the heart of town on Main St, *Albert's Motel* (☎ 902-224-2077) has clean $50 doubles. Just before the park, if there are three or more of you *Les Cabines du Portage* (☎ 902-224-2822) would be good, with two-bed motel units and housekeeping cabins (includes kitchen), at $60 a single or double plus $5 for each extra person. There are also three bigger, two-bedroom cabins for $70. Weekly rates are offered for all the cabins. The *Cheticamp Motel* (☎ 902-224-2711), on Main St just beyond the south edge of town, is well kept and friendly and has a dining room for breakfast. Singles/doubles are $45/50.

There is a growing number of bed and breakfasts in town, including *Auberge déjeuner de soleil B&B* (☎ 902-224-1373), not far from the post office at Belle March Rd, with seven rooms (two with private bath) from $40/45.

Brand new for this edition and still very spiffy are the spacious chalets at *Pilot Whale* (☎ 902-224-1040), each with wood flooring, covered veranda, and private beach access. Each has a kitchen and some have two bedrooms. Rates start at $110. Call ahead as they're often full.

Places to Eat

One of the main catches here is crab, which turns up on several menus, including *Harbour Restaurant*, which has a view and outdoor patio to complement the food. Lobster is also offered throughout summer. Dishes range from $13 to $16 though some pasta dishes are less. Very highly rated but more expensive again is the dining room at *Laurie's Motel*, which has been operating since 1938.

On the more affordable end is *Wabo's Pizza* next to Government Wharf with large pizzas that start at $15 and subs for under $5. Right next door is *La Chaloupe*, a small café with a menu of fish, clams and scallops and a pub upstairs. Both places have outdoor seating overlooking the boat traffic. *Le Gabriel* – can't miss it for the lighthouse entrance – is a family-style place with some Acadian dishes; it also has square dances Tuesday and fiddling Saturday afternoon.

For entertainment, the *Doryman Beverage Room* on the north side of town appears a bit rough but every Thursday at 8 pm is open microphone night, and local musicians perform.

Getting There & Away

Cheticamp is connected to Baddeck by bus with Transoverland Ltd (☎ 902-248-2051). The buses also run from Baddeck to Sydney. The schedule for now is a departure at 7.30 am Monday, Wednesday and Friday; this can vary a lot. Route 19 Shuttle Service (☎ 902-224-3567) also runs a shuttle to Halifax's QEII Health Centre at 7 am. There is, unfortunately, no bus service through or around the park.

CAPE BRETON HIGHLANDS NATIONAL PARK

The park protects and features some of the grandest terrain not just of the impressive highlands but of all the Maritimes.

Summer conditions tend to be rather rainy, foggy and windy even while remaining fairly warm. The driest month is generally July, with June and September the runners-up. Maximum temperatures during

midsummer usually don't exceed 25°C and minimums are around 15°C.

At either of the entrances, Cheticamp or Ingonish, there are information centres that are open daily during the season from 8 am to 6 pm for maps (including topographical ones), hiking brochures and advice. Cheticamp's has a bookstore. You can also purchase a motor-vehicle entry permit at either. A one-day pass is $3.50, four days $10.50, less for seniors and children; family passes are $8 for one day, $24 for four.

The Cabot Trail, one of the best known roads in the country, gets its reputation from the 106km park segment of its Cape Breton loop. The drive is at its best along the northern shore and then down to Pleasant Bay. The road winds right along the shoreline between mountains, across barren plains and valleys up to **French Mountain**, the highest point (459m). Along the way are lookout points, the best of which is at the summit. If possible, save the trip for a sunny day when you can see down the coastline. From French Mountain the road zigzags through switchbacks and descends to Pleasant Bay, just outside the park. If you're driving, make sure your brakes are good and can afford to burn off a little lining. Despite the effort required, the park is a popular cycling destination. However, it is not suggested that it be used as your inaugural trip.

There are eight campgrounds in the park, some for tenters only; the park motto is 'We always have room' but don't be surprised if it's tight on peak season weekends. The campgrounds tend to be small, with space for 10 to 20 people. Camping is $14 for a tent site ($16 for a fireplace site), $15 for serviced sites. After four days, discounts kick in. In the campgrounds, pick a site and set up. A warden will come around, probably in the evening, to collect the money.

Coming from Cheticamp there are a few park highlights to watch for; it all starts with whales and bald eagles along the coastline. The tops of **Mackenzie Mountain** and **French Mountain** afford great views of the interior; the latter has numerous interpretive geological displays.

In the small town of **Pleasant Bay**, the *Rusty Anchor* is a lively restaurant with lots of seafood prepared local-style. Better still, you can sit on the patio and use the binoculars to watch for the regularly seen pilot whales just offshore. Seafood dinners cost from $10 to $14. Nearby is the *Celtic Vision Café*, believe it or not, an Internet joint in the middle of the Cabot Trail!

Pleasant Bay also has whale tours. Pleasant Bay Whale & Seal Tour (☎ 902-224-1315) has three cruises at 9.30 am, and 1 and 5 pm from mid-June to mid-September for $20 per adult.

Towards Ingonish, the **Grand Anse Valley** contains virgin forest; the short **Lone Shieling Trail** leads through 300-year-old maple trees to a replica of a Scottish Highland crofter's hut, a reminder of the area's first settlers.

From the village of **Cape North** out of the park, the extreme northern portion (also called Cape North) of Cape Breton can – nay, should – be visited. In Cape North village there is a private campground in case the park is full. *Hide-Away Campground* (☎ 902-383-2116) on Shore Road off Cabot Trail offers both wooded sites and open ones that put you on the edge of the bluff in full view of that rugged coastline you just drove along. Sites are $13 for tents and $15 for electricity, and there is even a small oyster bar in the campground. Kayaks and canoes are available from here or a place nearby. At the junction of the Cabot Trail with the turnoff you'll find the **North Highlands Community Museum** open daily from 10 am to 6 pm (free) and the great *Morrison's*, a casual café with super seafood and pasta specialities, with mains from $7. *The Octagon* (☎ 1-800-872-6084) is a performance arts venue nearby featuring regular Celtic and traditional Cape Breton music.

Just north of here, at Cabot's Landing Provincial Park on Aspey's Bay, is the location where John Cabot is believed to have landed in 1497. Every 24 June a re-enactment is held on the beach at Sugarloaf Mountain. At **Bay St Lawrence** whale-watching boat tours are organised through both Captain Cox's (☎ 902-383-2981) and Captain Ken's

(☎ 902-383-2379); both leave at 10.30 am and 1.30 and 4.30 pm and cost $25. While waiting for the boat, there's a diminutive little schoolhouse museum. Bay St Lawrence also has a private campground and a couple of inexpensive B&Bs, including the *Highlands by the Sea* (☎ *902-383-2537*), with rooms from $38/45. There's a super view and impeccable efficiencies from $88 at *Burton's Sunset Oasis Motel* (☎ *902-383-2666*).

The road to Bay St Lawrence ends at Meat Cove where there is *Meat Cove Campground* (☎ *902-383-2379*). Sites are $15 a night and many say these are some of the most scenic sites in Cape Breton; you can actually watch whales from your site. From Meat Cove the trails head west to the Cape St Lawrence lighthouse and Lowland Cove.

From Cape North, a side trip is recommended to **Neils Harbour**, an attractive little fishing village. In fact, it's one of the nicest you're likely to see in Nova Scotia. Down at the wharf you can buy fish and lobster, or try the to-die-for chowder at the inexpensive and wildly popular *Chowder House*, by the water at the lighthouse.

At the eastern entrance to the park are **Ingonish** and **Ingonish Beach**, two small towns with accommodation and basic supplies. There are several campgrounds, both government and private ones, as well as motels and a park information office. SeaQuarium (☎ 902-285-2103) runs whale tours from North Bay and has three tours daily for a cheap $20.

The beach at Ingonish Beach is a wonderful place, with a long, wide strip of sand tucked in a bay surrounded by green hills. The water can get pleasantly warm here after a few sunny days. Tired of sun? Ingonish Ferry, just south, has the Screaming Eagle, a chair lift up the mountain – supposedly the steepest in Atlantic Canada. A bar and lounge await you at the top. The trip costs $5. Nearby is Seavisions (☎ 902-285-2628), with whale tours from $30 with three sailings daily.

Hiking

For as big and rugged as Cape Breton Highlands National Park is, the hiking is surprisingly limited with (legitimate) multi-day trails now nonexistent since the Lake of Islands trail closed. The park has 25 trails and only one of them leads to backcountry camp sites. Fishing Cove Trail is an 8km one-way walk that descends 330m to camp sites on the mouth of rugged Fishing Cove River.

The backcountry camp sites are $14 a night and you generally must book them in advance at one of the two visitors centres, which adds an additional $5 fee.

Most of the other trails are shorter and close to the road. If the day is clear, many trails take you to ridge tops for impressive views of the coast. The best is probably Skyline Trail, a 7km loop that puts you on the edge of a headland cliff right above the water. This trail is posted along Cabot Trail just beyond Corey Brook Campground. Other trails with ocean views from mountaintops include Aspy, Glasgow Lake and Franey Mountain Trail.

Cycling

The riding is tough but the views are spectacular when cycling through the park or other coastal roads in the area. Despite the heavy numbers of tourists and steep hills, considerable biking takes place here. If you need to rent try Sea Spray Cycle Center (☎ 902-383-2732) in Dingwall. Sea Spray is an especially good outfitter that also has maps with suggested coastal routes for self-guided tours. It also has organised tours. Expect to pay about $25 a day.

Kayaking

The highlands are the attraction but there is still ocean right there too. The national park maintains no official water trails but a half-dozen kayak outfitters operate tours or rent supplies for do-it-yourself kayaking, including Cape Breton Sea Coast Adventures (☎ 902-929-2800) in Ingonish Beach, which has half-day/full-day instructional tours for $49/89, a dusk tour ($25) for those with skills, or a mix-and-match tour with whale watching.

Organised Tours

Gaboteux Tours (☎ 902-224-2940) offers a full-day (eight hours) tour leaving at 8.30 am

from Cheticamp for $55, not including lunch. Northeast Highlands Tours (☎ 902-285-2605) has a 3½ hour tour from Ingonish Beach's Keltic Lodge to Bay St Lawrence twice daily for $30.

Places to Stay & Eat

Some 8km north of the park entrance, near Ingonish, is *Driftwood Lodge* (☎ 902-285-2558), run by a great host, Mrs Wanda Tacreiter. Rooms in the older building are cheapest and start at $25 for a single with shared bath. Doubles are $50 and $55 and she even has two-bedroom apartments with balconies overlooking the ocean for $65/70. Breakfast is served and a German-Polish lunch and dinner are available.

Also in Ingonish, the *Sea Breeze Cottages & Motel* (☎ 902-285-2879) has a dozen cottages of varying sizes and amenities, some completely self-contained. The six motel units are rented at $52 a double, the one-bedroom cottages begin at $66.

The other 'Ingonishes' also have places, like *Knotty Pine Cottages & Tourist Home* (☎ 902-285-2058) in Ingonish Ferry, with 10 basic cottages with varying levels of amenities starting at $45 for a single/double. There are also three rooms in the house from $38. Ingonish Beach has probably the most luxurious lodge in the area, the very expensive *Keltic Lodge* (☎ 902-285-2880, ☎ 1-800-565-0444), up on a hillside with commanding views. Rooms start at – this is not a misprint – $174 for a single.

For a place to eat, *Coastal Waters Restaurant* in Ingonish is a sitdown place with sandwiches, hamburgers and seafood dinners and breakfast specials from $2.99. Even better, if the weather is nice, is *Muddy Rudder Seafood Shack*. The small eatery features steamed lobster, mussels, crabs and clams and has a handful of tables outside. It's located on Cabot Trail just before you cross Ingonish River and you can stop at the beer store in Ingonish on the way.

CAPE SMOKEY

From Ingonish south and up to Cape Smokey there is some fine scenery. At the peak on Cape Smokey, at a small roadside park with picnic tables, there are very good sea and coastal views. Also in the park is the trailhead for the Cape Smokey Trail, a round trip of 11km where you descend 150m along the coast past several viewing points.

ST ANN'S

The **Gaelic College of Celtic Arts & Crafts** is at the end of St Ann's Bay. Founded in 1938 and the only one of its kind in North America, the college offers programs in the Scottish Gaelic language, bagpipe playing, Highland dancing, weaving and kilt-making and other things Scottish to students of all ages from across the land. Drop in any time during summer and the chances are you'll hear a student sing a traditional ballad in Scottish Gaelic or another play a Highland violin piece; miniconcerts and recitals are performed throughout the day. You can stroll around the grounds, see the museum with its historical notes and tartans or browse the giftshop for books, music tapes or kilts. There is also a *cafeteria* serving light meals or tea.

A Scottish festival, the Gaelic Mod, is held at the end of August each year, with events daily.

BIG BRAS D'OR

After crossing the long bridge over an inlet to Bras d'Or Lake on the way towards Sydney, a secondary road branches off and leads to the coast and the village of Big Bras d'Or. Offshore are the cliff-edged **Bird Islands**, Hertford and Ciboux. The islands are home to large colonies of razorbills, puffins, kittiwakes, terns and several other species. Boat tours run from town from May to September. The islands are about 1.6km from shore and take about 40 minutes to reach. The entire boat trip takes 2½ hours. Nesting time is June and July, so these are the prime months for a visit, but plenty of birds can be seen any time from May to September. Bald eagles can also be seen, as they nest in the vicinity as well. Binoculars are handy, but not necessary (they can be rented) as the tour boats go to within 20m or so of the islands.

The boat tours depart from *Mountain View By The Sea* (☎ 902-674-2384), where there are housekeeping cabins for rent, B&B rooms and a campground. The tour is $28 per adult and to camp is $13 a night.

NORTH SYDNEY

Nondescript North Sydney is important as the Marine Atlantic terminal for ferries to either Port aux Basques or Argentia, Newfoundland. For details see under those destinations.

There isn't much in town but it makes a convenient place to put up if you're using the ferry. The best place for tourist information is in the kiosk (☎ 902-539-9876) right at the ferry landing.

The main street in town is Commercial St, where you'll find the stores and places to eat. For drivers, there is public parking behind the Town Hall, on Commercial St near the corner of Blowers St. On the waterfront off Commercial St, right in the centre of town at the foot of Caledonia St, is a boardwalk leading to the Ballast Grounds harbour area. The small **North Sydney Heritage Museum** is here, with a collection of historical marine detritus. It's open daily from 10 am to 6 pm.

Places to Stay & Eat

If you're coming in on a late ferry, you will likely need advance room reservations, or spend a fitful night in your car. The *Arm of Gold Campground* (☎ 902-736-6516, ☎ 902-736-6671), mainly for trailers, is closest to the ferry, at just 3.2km away. A site is $13.95 a night.

With a view over the water, *Alexandra Shebib's B&B* (☎ 902-794-4876, 88 Queen St) is 2km west of the ferry terminal. This is a nice place, open all year for $40/50.

Other than this there are several motels in the vicinity at about twice the above rate; a couple of cheaper motels are fairly dumpy and not worth the money. One to try is the *Clansman Motel* (☎ 902-794-7226, ☎ 1-800-565-2668), on Peppett St, off exit 2 on Hwy 125. Rooms are $65/75.

There are only a few basic restaurants in town. If it's breakfast you're looking for, head to *Robena's Bakery and Restaurant* on

Commercial St. Full breakfast is $3.50 and includes big slices of home-made bread. *Rollie's* near the wharf has good seafood, while the *North Star Inn* beside the terminal dining room has a commanding view of the harbour.

Getting There & Away

Bus There is no real bus depot in North Sydney; the depot proper is in Sydney. However, the Acadian line bus between Sydney and Halifax can be picked up at the North Star Inn, beside the ferry terminal, twice a day. There is also a local bus which runs back and forth between Sydney and North Sydney for $3.25. It, too, can be caught at the ferry dock, or at some points along Queen St. See Getting There & Away under Sydney for information on the Transoverland buses to Baddeck.

Ferry For detailed information on ferry crossings, see the St John's and Port aux Basques sections in the Newfoundland chapter. Reservations may be required and are recommended in midsummer; call Marine Atlantic (☎ 902-794-5254, ☎ 1-800-341-7981) in North Sydney. The ferry terminal is central, at the end of Commercial St at Blowers St. The Trans Canada Hwy (Route 105) leads straight into or out of the ferry terminal.

SYDNEY MINES

Long known simply as the Mines, this small coastal town north-east of North Sydney was a depressed and dirty mining centre from as early as the 1700s. Working these now closed mines was no picnic but it was work. Most of the shafts were out under the sea – one ran 6.4km from shore below the ocean floor.

SYDNEY

Sydney is the third largest town in the province, the only real city on Cape Breton and the embattled core of the island's collapsed industrial centre. This is a very old town which, as the heart of a coal-mining district, has seen its share of grief and hardship. Long a drab, rather grim place with a hard-drinking, warm and friendly population, the city has managed without much spare money to modestly upgrade the downtown

districts. Heritage buildings have been preserved and there are a number of hotels and restaurants for visitors. Tourism may help to offset the 1999 coal mine closing which was the largest employer in town.

The main street downtown is Charlotte St, which has many stores and restaurants though a large mall has since popped up near the exit off Hwy 125. There isn't a lot to do, but with the ferry to the north and Louisbourg to the south, many people do pass by.

A caveat – Sydney's parking sentinels are thought to be omniscient. They will ticket you.

There is a tourist office (☎ 902-539-9876, ☎ 1-800-565-9464) inside the Civic Centre on the waterfront, but it's more of a chamber of commerce. It's open from 8.30 am to 4 pm.

Northend

Just north of the city centre on Charlotte St, the Esplanade (which runs parallel to the river) and the adjoining streets is the old historic part of town, with a half-dozen buildings from the 1700s and many built during the 19th century. All sites below are open from 9.30 am to 5.30 pm Monday through Saturday, from 1 to 5.30 pm Sunday; admission is free.

On the Esplanade across from Government Wharf you can visit the oldest Roman Catholic Church, now a museum, in Cape Breton. Dating from 1828, **St Patrick's Church Museum** features the stone church with its three-foot thick walls and a variety of interesting artefacts inside, including the town's whipping post from the mid-19th century.

Cossit House on Charlotte St dates from 1787 and is the oldest house in Sydney. It's now a museum with period furnishings. Just down the road is the **Jost House**, also built in 1787 and now a museum housing a marine exhibit.

At the Lyceum, the former cultural centre, 225 George St, is the **Centre for Heritage & Science**. The museum features the human and natural history of this region and houses an art gallery.

Action Week is an annual event held in the first week of August. Festivities include music, sports and various other goings-on.

Places to Stay

Kings Rd leading in from Hwy 125 along the Sydney River, has the lion's share of motel/hotel options, from cheap to expensive. The *City Lodge (☎ 902-567-3311, ☎ 1-800-580-2489, 100 Kings Rd)* has singles/doubles from $40/50, along with laundry, a pub and restaurant. Most of the rest are chains.

Quite central is *Park Place (☎562-3518, 169 Park St)*, a late 19th/early 20th century B&B with rooms at $40/50, including a triple. Other good B&Bs are centrally located.

The *University College of Cape Breton (☎ 902-563-1791)* on the highway to Glace Bay has rooms from 1 May to 21 August for $27/38.

Places to Eat

Charlotte St has an impressive selection of restaurants that offer cuisine from around the world. Along with the usual Chinese restaurants and a handful of pizza-and-pasta shops, there's *Sit & Gid's Lebanese Restaurant* where a felafel sandwich can be enjoyed for $5 or a serving of hummus and pita bread for $4. *Ike's Delicatessen Joe's Warehouse*, also on Charlotte St, has a varied menu featuring steak and a large salad bar, and an outdoor patio with views of the water.

If it's Sunday, about the only thing open will be *Jasper's*, with several locations around town, including a central one on the corner of George and Dorchester Sts. This is an inexpensive 24 hour family restaurant where nothing on the large menu is more than $13 and most dinners are under $8.

Getting There & Away

Bus The Acadian bus line's depot (☎ 902-564-5533) is away from the centre a bit (walkable if necessary), across the street from the big Sydney Shopping Centre Mall on Terminal Drive. There are two buses a day to Halifax at 8.30 am and 4.30 pm. A ticket is $54. They may go to the ferry terminal in

NOVA SCOTIA

North Sydney if necessary and make many other stops along the way.

For Charlottetown, Prince Edward Island, the fare is $84 and a change of buses is required in Moncton.

Transoverland Ltd (☎ 902-248-2051 in Cheticamp) runs buses to Baddeck, via St Anne's, and from there north through the Margaree Valley and up the coast to Cheticamp. Buses depart Monday, Wednesday and Friday at 3 pm and the fare is $11.

A couple of private shuttles make the run down to Halifax or over to North Sydney; ask at the tourist office.

GLACE BAY

As part of the Sydney area's industrial region, the difficulties of Cape Bretoners are reflected here. The district has a long, bitter history of work – when there is any – with low pay and poor conditions and, regularly, one of the highest unemployment rates in the country.

Glace Bay's coal-mining tradition is over, the mines are now shut and the population has decreased.

The **Miners' Museum** (☎ 902-849-4522), less than 2km east from the town centre in Quarry Point, at 42 Birkley St off South St, provides a look at the history of local coal mining. There are equipment displays and a re-created village depicting a miner's life at the beginning of the 20th century. The highlight, though, is an hour-long underground tour led by a retired miner, that includes walking in the tunnel. It's $6.50 for the complete tour, less if you forgo (but don't) the mine visit. The museum is open all year and daily during summer from 10 am to 6 pm.

The **Marconi National Historic Site** marks the place where, in 1902, Italian Guglielmo Marconi sent the first wireless message across the Atlantic, to Cornwall, England. There is a model of the original transmitting station, and other information on the developments in communications that followed. The site is on Timmerman St at the area of Glace Bay referred to as Table Head and is open daily from 10 am to 6 pm during summer. Admission is free.

MAIN-À-DIEU

Known as the Marconi Trail, the coastal road south of Glace Bay leads to the town of Louisbourg and its top-rate historic site, along the way passing a handful of small villages. One of them is Main-à-Dieu, which features a thriving lobster fleet and the most scenic harbour along this stretch.

At the north end of Main-à-Dieu is the **Fishermen's Museum**, two rooms packed with model ships and displays tracing the local history of this fishing village. It is open daily from noon to 5 pm in summer and is located at the base of a scenic overlook of the village. Departing from the overlook is Moke Head Trail. It's a picturesque round trip of 4km to Moke Head and the views of Scatterie Island, where 30 families once lived.

At the south end of town is the unique **Boardwalk Park**, where boardwalks connect a beach, observation decks, a pond and even a walk-through lobster trap. Based near Main-à-Dieu is Island Seafari (☎ 902-733-2309), which offers guided kayak trips, including a three hour paddle of the harbour.

The main, more direct route running south of Sydney has a half-dozen campgrounds along it.

LOUISBOURG

At the edge of the ocean with an excellent harbour sits Louisbourg (population 1400), the largest of the region's fishing towns and now famous for its adjacent historic fort. There are a couple of other things to see in the village as well.

The **Sydney & Louisbourg Railway Museum** (☎ 902-733-2720), which includes the tourist office, is at the entrance to the town. The museum has displays pertaining to the railway, which ran up to Sydney from 1895 until 1968, shuffling fish one way and coal the other. Hours are 8 am to 8 pm daily during summer and admission is free.

On the waterfront, behind the fire station, is the **Louisbourg Playhouse** (☎ 902-733-2996). The theatre was originally built at the Fortress of Louisbourg in 1993 for the

Walt Disney movie *Indian Warrior*. The playhouse is now a permanent performing arts centre for Louisbourg and hosts a variety of plays during the year.

South of town are the ruins of Canada's oldest lighthouse with an interpretive display and walking trails.

Places to Stay & Eat

You'll find accommodation steeper in price and often filled during the height of the summer season. *Louisbourg Trailer & Campsite (☎ 902-733-3631)* is right on the waterfront and has most sites for RVers but there are a few tent sites for $8 a night.

A couple of B&Bs have rooms at $35, including *The Manse (☎ 902-733-3155, 10 Strathcona St)*, overlooking the harbour. No motels are dirt-cheap but the *Fortress Inn (☎ 902-733-2844, ☎ 1-888-367-5353)* is centrally located and very good, with rooms from $50. Most luxurious is the *Louisbourg Harbour Inn (☎ 902-733-3222, ☎ 1-888-888-8466, 9 Warren St)*, an old sea captain's home overlooking the harbour with rooms and suites from $85.

Reasonably priced places include the *The Picnic Basket* for home-made bread and soups and deli sandwiches. *Fortress View Restaurant* offers the usual fish and chips menu as well as $4 hamburgers while the *Grubstake* is the place for a good seafood dinner which ranges from $9 to $20.

Getting There & Away

Louisbourg Shuttle Service (☎ 902-564-6200) departs from Cape Breton Tours, 24 King's Rd in Sydney, 8.45 am (returning at 4 pm) and charges $25 a round trip.

LOUISBOURG HISTORIC NATIONAL PARK

This excellent, historic site (☎ 902-733-2280) is about 50km south of Sydney on the south-east tip of Cape Breton Island and is well worth the trek.

After the Treaty of Utrecht in 1713, the French lost their bases in Newfoundland. This left them Prince Edward Island, Saint Pierre and Miquelon islands, and Cape Breton Island, which became the conduit for exporting cod to France and, later, a new military base. Louisbourg, a massive walled fort and village complex, was worked on continually from 1719 to about 1745. It looked daunting but was poorly designed, and the British took it in 46 days during 1745 when it was barely finished. It would change hands twice more. In 1760, after Wolfe (the British general who led the Louisbourg onslaught) took Quebec City, the walls of Louisbourg were destroyed and the city burned to the ground.

In 1961, with the closing of many Cape Breton coal mines, the federal government began a make-work project – the largest historical reconstruction in Canada. Today the site depicts in remarkable detail what French life was like here in the 1700s. All the workers, in period dress, have taken on the lives of typical fort inhabitants. Ask them anything – what the winters were like, what that tool is for, who they had an affair with – and they'll tell you. (And Anglophones are 'harassed' as spies by the French guards at the gates!) Three restaurants serve food typical of the time. Definitely go to the bakery and buy a 1kg loaf of soldiers' bread. It's delicious; one piece with cheese makes a full meal.

You'll need a lot of time to see the park properly – plan on spending at least half a day at the site. The best times to visit are in the morning, when there's more going on and fewer tourists, and during June or September. Take in the movie in the interpretive centre first. Free guided tours around the site are offered through the day; cannons are fired four times daily.

The weather here is very changeable and usually bad. Take a sweater and raincoat even if it's sunny when you start out, and be prepared for lots of walking. As well as the fort area itself, there are hiking trails around the grounds.

The park is open daily from 9.30 am to 5 pm in June and September and 9 am to 7 pm in July and August. Admission seems steep at $11 or $24.50 for the family but the fort is well worth it. (Prices drop in off-season.)

NOVA SCOTIA

AROUND BRAS D'OR LAKE
Baddeck

An old resort town in a pastoral setting, Baddeck is on the north shore of the lake, halfway between Sydney and the Canso Causeway.

It's small but is a visitors centre of sorts as nearly everyone travelling Cape Breton spends some time here. It's attractive and the Alexander Graham Bell Museum is well done.

Chebucto St is the main thoroughfare. On Water St, along the waterfront, Government Wharf is lined with pleasure craft, sailing boats and tour boats offering cruises around Bras d'Or Lake. One of them, Amoeba Sailing Tours (☎ 902-295-1426), offers four tours daily on its tall-mast sailboat for $16 per person.

An excellent tourist office (☎ 902-295-1911) sits on the corner of Chebucto St and Shore Rd and is open daily during summer from 9 am to 8.30 pm.

Alexander Graham Bell National Historic Site Alexander Graham Bell, the inventor of the telephone, had a summer place in Baddeck. This large museum (☎ 902-295-2069) is in a national historic park overlooking the saltwater Bras d'Or Lake that covers all aspects of this incredible man's inventions and innovations. Written explanations, models, photographs and objects detail his varied works. On display are medical and electrical devices, telegraphs, telephones, kites and seaplanes. You'll need at least two hours if you want to view all three exhibit halls. Hours are from 9 am to 8 pm July and August, until 7 pm in June and September and 5 pm the rest of the year. Admission is $3.75.

Kidston Island This micro-island lies just offshore and serves as a park for Baddeck, where you'll find a fine swimming beach, some nature trails and a lighthouse. The original lighthouse was built in 1875 and then moved across the ice to Shenacadie, which was experiencing more shipwrecks than Baddeck. The present lighthouse was built in 1915 but lost its lantern when the Coast Guard tried to remove it.

The Baddeck Lions Club operates a pontoon boat at Government Wharf to make the short – and free – run to the island every 20 minutes during summer from 10 am to 6 pm on weekdays and noon to 6 pm on weekends. Another way to reach the island is to rent a kayak at the wharf from Harvey's (☎ 902-298-3318). The rate is $10 an hour or $40 for the day.

Places to Stay Everything you can walk to here is pricey. *Bras d'Or Lakes Campground* (☎ 902-295-2329) is 5km west of town on Hwy 105 and has sites from $16. About two miles west of here is a *KOA campground*.

The *Tree Seat B&B* (☎ 902-295-1996) located left of the Bell museum entrance is a simple B&B that has four rooms – one with a private bath – from $35 and a nice lake view.

Then there's the *Restawyle Tourist Home* (☎ 902-295-3253) just south of town on Shore Rd. The B&B has four rooms, including a double for $40; you may be able to get a break if you're solo.

For what one could call a 'historic motel', *Telegraph House* (☎ 902-295-1100), right in the centre of town, is very attractive in grey with white shutters, but a double with breakfast is $52 to $85 depending on the room.

Any number of B&Bs oozing charm or creature comforts exist. Best known is the *Duffus House Inn* (☎ 902-295-2172, 108 Water St), a complex with 10 rooms including three suites. Prices have jumped up to $75/85 a single/double.

Places to Eat A Baddeck eatery that offers some inexpensive possibilities while maintaining high standards, is the *Highwheeler Café/Deli/Bakery*, with a mouth-watering selection of sandwiches, salads and bakery items. Deli sandwiches are $5.

The *Village Kitchen*, just off the main street, is a spot for an eggs-and-toast breakfast for $3 or in the evening the 'Steak & Stein' for $10. The *Bell Buoy* has pricey popular seafood but for an upscale meal, the

Lynwood Inn (23 Shore Rd) has a very well regarded dining room.

Lobster suppers, with a one-pounder and everything else you can eat from the buffet, are available in the old *Legion Hall*, on Ross St. At $25, they don't compare with the value of the real Prince Edward Island lobster suppers but the food is good and plentiful. It's open daily from 11.30 am to 1.30 pm and 4 to 9 pm June to October.

For homegrown produce, there's the *farmer's market* every Saturday from 1 to 3 pm in the Baddeck Arena.

Getting There & Around Acadia buses serve Baddeck along its Halifax to Sydney run. A bus arrives daily at 8.35 am and then continues on to New Glasgow, Truro and Halifax. To New Glasgow the fare is $28.25. Also from Baddeck, Transoverland Ltd buses run north through the Margaree Valley and then up the coast to Cheticamp. Buses out of town depart from the Irving service station near the Hwy 105 junction.

For seeing the immediate area, there's Island Eco-Adventures (☎ 902-295-3303) which rents mountain bikes by the hour or the day. It's located diagonally opposite the tourist office on Chebucto Rd.

Lake Ainslie

Just north of the Trans Canada Hwy, via Hwy 395, and 40km from Baddeck, is this large lake that attracts a healthy population of bald eagles, ospreys and loons. You can spend an afternoon following the 53km drive around Lake Ainslie, stopping at **Mac-Donald House Museum** (☎ 902-258-3317) on Hwy 395 along the east side. The 150-year-old farmhouse is maintained by the Lake Ainslie Historical Society and features furnished rooms and a barn full of farming machinery and tools. Hours are 9 am to 5 pm daily during summer and admission is $3.

Nearby is *Glenmore International Hostel* (☎ 902-258-3622). The HI hostel is reached by turning onto Twin Rock Valley Rd from Hwy 395 and heading east for 2km. If coming from the Trans Canada Hwy, the road is reached immediately after you cross the sec-ond bridge. The small hostel is pretty basic: four beds on the first floor, seven more in a loft, kitchen facilities but no showers. Rates are $10 for members and $12 for nonmembers. The managers can help arrange sailing tours of Bras d'Or Lake or overnight tours of Cape Breton National Park.

Iona

This is a small village south of Baddeck, on the south side of the peninsula, by Barra Strait in Bras d'Or Lake (on Hwy 223). Iona (pop 130) is a bit out of the way but may appeal for that reason. The **Highland Village Museum** depicts the life of the Highland Scots at home, and here as pioneers. The 10 historic buildings include an example of the smokey peat-heated homes of the Scottish Highlanders in the early 1800s, the first pioneer houses in the new land, and the later houses in which new skills and materials were employed. Summer hours are 9 am to 5 pm Monday through Saturday and 10 am to 6 pm Sunday. Admission is $5 for adults or $10 for a family.

A Highland festival held on the first Saturday in August features the Celtic-based music of the island. Special events are scheduled throughout summer, and something to watch for are the traditional suppers.

A short ferry ride connects with roads for the south side of Bras d'Or Lake.

SOUTH OF BRAS D'OR LAKE

This is a little-visited, sparsely inhabited area of small villages, lakes and hills. It's a farming and forestry region where many of the roads have not been paved.

Big Pond

On the south shore of East Bay, Big Pond has *Rita's Tea Room*, run by the hometown Cape Breton singer Rita MacNeil in a converted one-room schoolhouse. Adorning the walls are her music awards and records. Every July the Big Pond Concert, a sizable annual Cape Breton music event, is held.

Bald eagles can frequently be seen along the Bras d'Or Lake shoreline, particularly in the Big Pond area. Big Pond Eagle Tours

NOVA SCOTIA

(☎ 902-828-3052) offers two-hour walking tours with local naturalists sighting and identifying a variety of birds, particularly eagles. The daily tours are $15.

St Peter's

This town (pop 731) is on a narrow strip separating the Atlantic Ocean and Bras d'Or Lake along Hwy 4 and is the birthplace of noted photographer Wallace MacAskill. It was MacAskill's photo of the *Bluenose* that was used for the design of Canada's 10¢ piece. The home of his birth on Main St is now the **Wallace MacAskill Museum** and features 26 of his hand-tinted photographs. Hours are 10 am to 6 pm daily during summer and admission is free.

Also in town is **St Peter's Canal**. Built in the 1850s, the canal includes a 91m, double-gate lock to assist vessels to move between the different water levels of the lake and the ocean. There is an outdoor exhibit explaining the lock and the history of the canal as well as a museum nearby.

The French Corner

The extreme southern corner of Cape Breton, like the Cheticamp area, is largely French. The region all around Île Madame was settled by Acadians, who had first tried to make Martinique in the West Indies home after the Expulsion but later returned to Nova Scotia. **Arichat**, on the ocean, is the largest town and boasts a restaurant and a traditional-style wooden Acadian inn called

L'Auberge Acadienne (☎ 902-226-2200), whose dining room offers some Acadian dishes. Rooms at the inn begin at $50 for singles or doubles. The **LeNoir Forge Museum** (☎ 902-226-2800) on Route 320 is a restored 18th century French blacksmith shop, open from May to September. Admission is free.

Just down the road, **Petit-de-Grat** holds an Acadian festival every August, with music, food etc. This small town is the oldest on Île Madame and was a busy trading port during Prohibition, but now it's a fishing centre.

East of Arichat on Hwy 320 is the *Acadian Campsite (☎ 902-226-2447)* with 48 sites, showers and laundry facilities. A site is $12 a night. From Little Anse, a trail leads to a lighthouse.

SABLE ISLAND

Lying south of Cape Breton, about 177km from the mainland, this is the 'graveyard of the Atlantic'. Countless ships from the 1500s to the present have gone down around the island, with its rough seas and hidden sandbars. The island, 32km long by 1.5km wide, is little more than a sandbar itself, with no trees or even shrubs. There are about a dozen inhabitants, a small herd of tough, wild ponies and lots of cranberries – though as of 1998 the government was having much trouble trying to maintain a human presence. The people maintain the two lighthouses, a meteorological station and a few other installations. Where the ponies came from is a source of endless debate.

Prince Edward Island

Known as 'the island' or PEI, Prince Edward Island is a pastoral, peaceful, wonderfully Irish-green expanse of quiet beauty. Mainlanders are seen on roadsides all over the island trying to capture the landscape on film: a few black and white cows here, some purple lupins there, perhaps a wave of sea in the distance. The pace of life here is slow. Laws against billboards further add to the old-country flavour of the island. Indeed, in some ways it has changed little from the descriptions in the internationally known novel *Anne of Green Gables*, written here by Lucy Maud Montgomery early in the 20th century.

This is not an exciting place; there is not a lot to do, particularly after dark, and if you get a week of rain, you'll be more than a little restless. But for a really lazy holiday, take the chance.

Prince Edward Island is the smallest and most densely populated province. You'd never guess this, however, as it's rural and the towns aren't big at all, though countless little-used roads crisscross every segment of land.

In March 1993, the province became the first in Canadian history to elect a woman premier. Catherine Callbeck led the Liberals to victory with a convincing 31 of 32 seats. In 1997, after much debate and protests among the islanders themselves, PEI was linked to New Brunswick and the mainland by the controversial Confederation Bridge, the world's longest at almost 13km.

As in all of the Atlantic Provinces, the visiting season is short. This is perhaps noticed here more than anywhere, with many attractions, tour operations and guesthouses open only during the two midsummer months. Keep in mind, however, that on Labour Day weekend room prices are heavily discounted, sometimes as much as 50%, the crowds are gone and often you enjoy a touch of Indian summer.

HIGHLIGHTS

Entered Confederation: 1 July 1873
Area: 5657 sq km
Population: 136,388
Provincial Capital: Charlottetown

- Spend time in Charlottetown, the birthplace of Canadian confederation

- Take in a ceilidh with traditional music and dance

- See the House of Green Gables near Cavendish, the setting for the story *Anne of Green Gables* by Lucy Maud Montgomery

- Enjoy a summer's day on one of the north-coast beaches

- Dine out on casual, delicious lobster suppers, often held in church halls throughout the province

- Drive along the quiet, relaxed roads as they wind their way through bucolic landscapes

- Stimulate the artist deep inside as you saunter through the picturesque village of Victoria

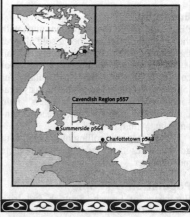

History

Aboriginal peoples have been here for about 11,000 years, before the land was separated from the mainland. The Micmacs, a branch of the Algonquin nations, arrived at about the time of Christ.

Jacques Cartier of France in 1534 was the first European to record seeing the island. Settlement didn't begin for another 200 years with a small French colony which grew somewhat with the British expulsion of the Acadians, mainly from Nova Scotia, in the late 1750s.

After the Treaty of Paris in 1763, the island became British and was renamed the Island of Saint John. In the early 1800s there was a marked rise in population with immigrants from the British Isles. The island became self-governing in 1769 and switched names in honour of one of the sons of King Edward III.

The island joined Confederation in 1873, deciding to forgo its independence for the economic benefits. The population has remained stable since the 1930s.

Climate

Conveniently, July and August are the driest months of a fairly damp year. Because of warm ocean currents, the province has a milder climate than most of Canada and the sea gets warm enough for swimming.

Economy

PEI is primarily a farming community, with the main crop, potatoes, being sold all over the country. The rich, distinctively red soil is the secret, the locals say. Fishing, of course, is also important, particularly for lobsters, oysters and herring. The tasty, reasonably priced lobster suppers held throughout the province have become synonymous with the island.

The quiet, gently rolling hills edged with good beaches have made tourism a reliable moneymaker.

Population & People

Europeans of French, Scottish and Irish background make up nearly 90% of the population. The Native inhabitants at the time of colonisation, the Micmacs, now represent about 4% of the island's people.

Information

Tourist Offices The head office of the Tourism Industry Association of PEI (☎ 1-888-734-7529 free from anywhere in North America, or ☎ 902-629-2400 elsewhere, www.peiplay.com, tourpei@gov.pe.ca) can be contacted at PO Box 940, Charlottetown, C1A 7M5. There are about a dozen offices around the island with main ones in the capital and one in an ersatz 'traditional' PEI village complex at the foot of Confederation Bridge.

Telephone In the event of emergency dial ☎ 0, for which no money is required.

Time PEI is on Atlantic Time.

Tax The provincial sales tax is 10%, added to the 7% GST.

Activities

If your idea of being active is flipping the pages of a book while lolling on a beach or maybe cracking the claws of a steaming lobster, you've found your spot. You could drag yourself aboard a boat for a little deep sea fishing or if you're really feeling energetic cycle through the quiet, flat countryside. There are also a number of small museums and historic sites to look over.

Or you may just bask in having stepped out of the rat race.

Accommodation & Food

The province has a reservation hotline (☎ 1-888-268-6667 in Canada) which handles all accommodation.

The island is covered with campgrounds – 13 provincial parks, one national park and numerous private campgrounds.

Most provincial parks range from $15 for an unserviced site to $20 for fully serviced ones. They accept reservations, generally beginning after 1 April, and following certain restrictions.

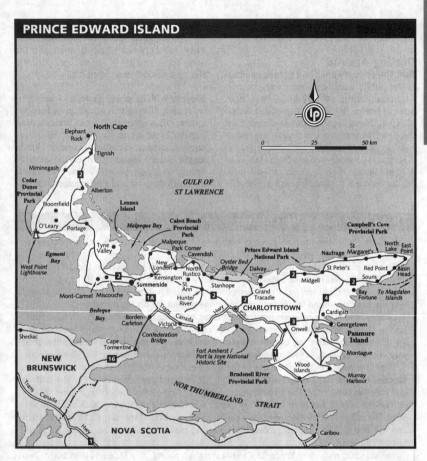

PRINCE EDWARD ISLAND

North Cape
Elephant
Rock
Tignish
Miminegash
Cedar
Dunes
Provincial
Park
Bloomfield
Alberton
Lennox
Island
O'Leary
Portage
Malpeque Bay
Cabot Beach
Provincial
Park
Malpeque
Park Corner
Cavendish
Prince Edward Island
National Park
Campbell's Cove
Provincial Park
St
Naufrage
Margaret's
North
Lake
East
Point
*GULF OF
ST LAWRENCE*
Tyne
Valley
New
London
North
Rustico
*Egmont
Bay*
West Point
Lighthouse
Kensington
Summerside
St.
Ann
Hunter
River
Miscouche
Mont-Carmel
Oyster Bed
Bridge
Dalvay
St Peter's
Red Point
Souris
Basin
Head
Midgell
Stanhope
Grand
Tracadie
To Magdalen
Islands
Bay
Fortune
*Bedeque
Bay*
Borden-
Carleton
Victoria
Trans
Canada
CHARLOTTETOWN
Cardigan
Georgetown
Orwell
Panmure
Island
Shediac
Cape
Tormentine
*Confederation
Bridge*
Fort Amherst /
Port la Joye National
Historic Site
Montague
**NEW
BRUNSWICK**
Wood
Islands
Murray
Harbour
*Brudenell River
Provincial Park*
NORTHUMBERLAND STRAIT
Trans Canada
NOVA SCOTIA
Caribou

0   25   50 km

Across the province there are few hotels, but fortunately the entire island has an abundance of good guesthouses. The quality is generally high and the prices excellent. PEI guesthouses and tourist homes offer some of the best accommodation deals in Canada. A double room averages about $40 and rarely goes above $50, and sometimes that includes breakfast. Many places are rented by the week. Much accommodation is in beautiful old wooden homes in the east-coast style. Tourist offices have a –

mostly – complete list of these places and will make reservations for you.

There are nearly 40 outlets around the island for buying fresh seafood – good if you're camping and can cook your own food. Some guesthouses offer cooking facilities or use of barbecues.

Also look for the famous lobster suppers held in church basements or community halls or restaurants – these are usually buffet style and good value. Perhaps not as much fun, the restaurants offering lobster suppers at least do

so on a regular basis and are reliable, whereas the others are sometimes hit and miss.

Getting Around

Bus You're pretty much out of luck on intra-island public transport. One spotty shuttle, Maritime Shuttle (☎ 902-882-3190), does operate between Tignish, Summerside and Halifax, Nova Scotia, but it doesn't go through Charlottetown; it departs Tignish at 6 am weekdays and stops in Summerside at 7.30 am. It generally returns from Halifax at 4.30 pm, unless there's not enough demand. Visitors can use the handy beach bus shuttle offered by Abgeweit Tours (☎ 902-894-9966) and Beach Shuttle (☎ 902-566-3243). They run between Charlottetown and the north coast beaches of the national park and charge around $16 a round-trip.

Bicycle With its winding country roads, gently rolling hills and short distances between towns, PEI is probably one of Canada's most popular destinations for cyclists. Hills here rarely exceed a 30 degree incline or 1km in length and the highest point on the island at Springton is only 142m. You can rent wheels in Charlottetown and put together a multi-

---

That Crazy Mixed-Up Lobster

Unfortunately for this mottled green or bluish or blackish prehistoric wonder, somebody realised it tasted bloody good.

This has meant that we've learned a lot about it, although the facts on this 100-million-year-old crustacean read like a joke book: it tastes with its feet, listens with its legs (of which there are 10) and has teeth in its stomach (which is found just behind the head). The kidney is in the head, the brain in the neck and the bones (shell) are on the outside.

Lobster is widely associated with the east coast of Canada but perhaps Prince Edward Island, with its famous lobster suppers, is most closely linked with this symbol of gourmet dining. It's now hard to believe but there wasn't much interest in the delicate meat until a good way into this century. In fact, islanders used to use lobster as fertiliser for the island's farms.

There are two fishing seasons, one in the spring ending in late June and one in the winter. Wooden or metal traps baited with herring bits are dropped overboard to rest on the bottom and checked soon after. The trap's ingenious cage design allows the lobster's claws to narrow on the way in, but once inside they spread apart again and crawling back out is impossible. The older wooden traps are available for purchase around the island at about $5 each and will one day be museum pieces. Huge holding tanks allow fresh, live lobster to be offered throughout the year.

The standard restaurant lobster in Canada weighs a pound, or a little less than 500g. Two and three pounders are often available but bigger ones are not often seen. Along the Quebec coast of the St Lawrence around Rivière-du-Loup, you may see five and six pounders (2.5kg) for sale but tell me who's going to pick one of those suckers up and put it in a pot of hot water?

Most people are satisfied with the regular portion as it seems to be a rich food. The meat is lean, however, and is permitted on low-cholesterol diets (but hold the butter).

Lobster can be baked, broiled or barbecued, but the best method is boiling. They should be cooked in boiling, salted fresh water for 12 to 15 minutes for the first pound, adding four minutes for every extra pound (500g). When done, the lobster has the characteristic orange-red shell, not unlike that of some bathers at Cavendish beach. Most meaty is the tail, followed by the larger claws. Though most people quickly discard it, the green mushy liver, known as tomalley, is considered a delicacy and one of the choicest parts to savour.

day tour of the island. For route suggestions ask at the bike shops or obtain a copy of *Prince Edward Island Cycling Guide* that is sold for $12 at Bookmark in the Charlottetown city centre or Coles Book Store in the Charlottetown Mall. The grandaddy of trails in the Maritimes might eventually be the Confederation Trail, a 350km stone dust multi-use trail stretching from Tignish to Elmira along abandoned railway lines. Well over 230km have been completed, including lengthy sections from Tignish to Kensington and Mount Souris to the eastern peninsula. Signs and some shelters are up.

See the Charlottetown Getting Around and Cavendish sections later in this chapter for bike rental information.

Hitching Thumbing around the island is common, accepted and often done by residents. The island is relatively free of violence and you can generally hitch without expecting trouble. Your safety cannot be guaranteed, however, and hitching is not recommended without some reservations. Caution is advised.

Charlottetown

Charlottetown (population 45,000) is an old, quiet country town that also happens to be the historic provincial capital. It is Canada's smallest capital, with a downtown area so compact that everything is within walking distance. The slow-paced, tree-lined colonial and Victorian streets make Charlottetown the perfect urban centre for this gentle and bucolic island. In July and August the streets are busy with visitors but things are rather quiet out of season.

History

When the first Europeans arrived here in the early 1700s, they found the area settled by the Micmac Indians. Nevertheless, they established Charlottetown as a district capital of their own in 1763, named after Charlotte, Queen of Great Britain and Ireland (1744-1818).

In 1864, discussions to unite Canada were first held here. An agreement was finally reached in 1867, when the Dominion of Canada was born; Charlottetown became known as the birthplace of Canada. Though times are much less heady these days, many of the townspeople are employed by various levels of government. Indeed, one out of four people across the island works directly for the government.

Orientation

University Ave is the city's main street; it ends at Grafton St and the large war memorial statue depicting three soldiers. Behind it, the entire block is taken up with the Provincial Archives, Province House National Historic Site and the large Confederation Centre of the Arts complex.

A block west along Grafton St is Queen St, parallel to University Ave. This is the other main street of Charlottetown and of more interest to visitors.

Off Queen St, south behind the Confederation Arts Building, is Richmond St. For one block east of Queen St, this is off limits to traffic during summer and becomes a pedestrian mall called Victoria Row. Along it are street vendors, restaurants, crafts shops and galleries.

Four blocks south is the city harbour. From Richmond St south on and around Queen St to the waterfront is old Charlottetown. A number of buildings have been renovated and are now used as government offices, restaurants or shops. Many have plaques giving a bit of their history and the date of construction; some are over 100 years old. Great George St running downhill from Richmond St at Province House is particularly attractive.

At the foot of Great George St, south of Water St, is Peake's Wharf and Confederation Landing, a park. This redeveloped waterfront area now has restaurants, souvenir shops and is often the focal point of the city festivals. The main tourist centre is nearby.

West of town is the large Victoria Park, with Queen Elizabeth Drive running along its edge and the bay.

CHARLOTTETOWN

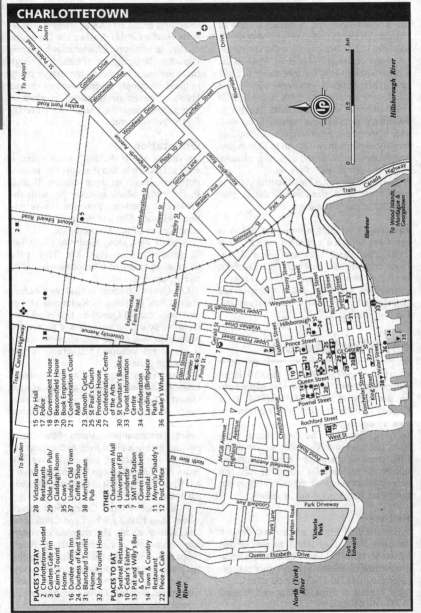

PLACES TO STAY
2 Charlottetown Hostel
3 Garden Gate Inn
6 Cairn's Tourist
   Home
16 Dundee Arms Inn
24 Duchess of Kent Inn
31 Blanchard Tourist
   Home
32 Aloha Tourist Home

PLACES TO EAT
9 Seatreat Restaurant
10 Cedar's Eatery
13 Pat and Willy's Bar
   & Grill
14 Town & Country
   Restaurant
22 Piece A Cake

28 Victoria Row
   Restaurants
29 Olde Dublin Pub/
   Claddagh Room
35 Cows
37 Linda's Old Town
   Coffee Shop
38 Merchantman
   Pub

OTHER
1 Charlottetown Mall
4 University of PEI
5 Laundrette
7 SMT Bus Station
8 Queen Elizabeth
   Hospital
11 Myron's/Shaddy's
12 Post Office

15 City Hall
17 Police
18 Government House
19 Beaconsfield House
20 Book Emporium
21 Confederation Court
   Mall
23 Smooth Cycles
25 St Paul's Church
26 Province House
27 Confederation Centre
   of the Arts
30 St Dunstan's Basilica
33 Tourist Information
   Centre
34 Confederation
   Landing (Birthplace
   Park)
36 Peake's Wharf

Information

Tourist Offices The tourist office (☎ 902-368-4444) for Charlottetown and the main office for the whole island is in the Stone Cottage near Confederation Landing (sometimes called Confederation Birthplace Park) at the foot of Hillsborough St just off Water St. It's open daily from 8 am to 8 pm during the summer season. Inside are courtesy phones to make local reservations.

There's a tourist information office (☎ 902-566-5548) at City Hall, on the corner of Queen and Kent Sts. It's open from 8 am to 5 pm daily in summer and specialises in Charlottetown.

Money Several of the big banks can be found in Confederation Plaza.

Post The central post office is at 135 Kent St.

Bookshops The Book Emporium at 169 Queen St has a selection of books on PEI and Anne of Green Gables.

Medical Services The Queen Elizabeth Hospital (☎ 902-894-2111, ☎ 902-566-6111) is on Riverside Drive just out of the centre.

Confederation Centre of the Arts

The architectural style of this large modern structure at the south-east corner of Queen and Grafton Sts is at odds with the rest of town, which has made it controversial since construction began in 1960. It houses a museum, an art gallery, a library and a theatre. The art gallery and museum charge $3 admission in July and August but are free for the rest of the year and are always free on Sunday. The gallery features shows from the collection of works by Canadian artists. Free tours of the centre (☎ 902-628-1864) are given all year Monday through Saturday. It is open daily through summer from 10 am to 8 pm, lesser hours thereafter.

Province House

Next door to the arts centre, this neoclassical, three-storey, sandstone building is both a national historic site (☎ 902-566-7626) and the base of the current Provincial Legislature. The Confederation Room on the 2nd floor is known as the 'birthplace of Canada', for it was here in 1864 that the 23 representatives of the New World British colonies began working out the details for forming the Dominion of Canada.

This room and a couple of others have been restored to what they looked like in 1864. Inside or perhaps out at the entrance, you may also see costumed workers, each representing one of the original founders. Once daily in summer, there is a 'fathers of confederation' re-enactment. Check here or at the tourist office for current times of the presentation.

The current Legislative Chamber is also on this floor, and the summer breeze wafting in through open windows to this small, comfortable room lends an intimate informal atmosphere which is quite unlike that of the legislatures in Canada's larger provinces. Various rooms can also be seen on the 1st floor. Province House is open daily from 9 am to 6 pm during summer and admission is free.

St Dunstan's Basilica

This large basilica is south of Province House, on the corner of Great George and Richmond Sts. Built in 1898, the town's Catholic church is surprisingly ornate inside, painted in an unusual style, with a lot of green trim which blends well with the green and blue tints in the marble. Masses are held daily from June to the beginning of September.

St Paul's Church

On Church St east of Province House, this red, sandstone building dating from 1747 is the oldest Protestant church on the island.

Beaconsfield House

This beautiful yellow Victorian mansion (☎ 902-368-6603) at 2 Kent St was built in 1877. It is now the headquarters of the PEI Heritage Foundation. There are 11 historically furnished rooms along with a gift shop and a bookstore specialising in books about PEI. During summer guided tours are given

and afternoon tea is served on the large veranda. The house is open from 9 am to 5 pm daily, except Monday, from mid-June to Labour Day and shorter hours the rest of the year. Admission is $2.50.

Government House

Across Kent St is Victoria Park and Government House, another beautiful old mansion. This one has been used as the official residence of PEI's lieutenant-governor since 1835. No visitors are allowed.

Organised Tours

Abegweit Sightseeing Tours (☎ 902-894-9966), 157 Nassau St, Charlottetown, offers double-decker bus trips around the island. There are three trips: the north shore, the south shore and Charlottetown itself.

The north shore trip takes about six hours and costs $50 all-inclusive. The city tour takes just an hour and costs $8. The south shore trip makes a stop at Fort Amherst National Historic Park and is also $50.

If you just want to go to the beach for the day, you can take the North Shore Tour bus. It will pick you up on the way back. The cost is $15 return to Dalvay/Stanhope and $16 return to Cavendish Beach.

Peake's Wharf Boat Cruises (☎ 902-566-4458) departs from the marina at the wharf and has a 70 minute harbour tour or 6.30 pm sunset cruise for $12 and a three hour tour to see the seals off Government Island for $18.

Finally, walking tours of the historic Charlottetown area commence at City Hall (☎ 902-566-5548) at 10 am, 1 and 3 pm. Alternatively, the good self-guided tour brochure available at the tourist office covers the waterfront area and Peake's Wharf. See Getting Around for Smooth Cycles' city bike tour.

Special Events

All across the province, look for the local ceilidhs – mini-festivals at which there is always some music (usually of the traditional Celtic-based variety) and dancing. There is usually one a week. Some of the major events held in PEI from June to September are:

Jazz & Blues Festival
Bigger every year, this early-May festival has major Canadian performers.

Charlottetown Festival
This festival is held each year from mid-June to mid-September. It's a theatrical event with drama and musicals. Each year *Anne of Green Gables*, which is called 'Canada's favourite musical', is performed. Tickets to any of the plays are available at the Arts Centre and are $24 to $32 for evening performances of 'Anne' and $16 to $30 for matinee shows. The festival also includes free outdoor performances, a children's theatre and dance programs.

Blue Grass Music Festival
This is a new tradition which seems to be developing; this festival is held annually in July. It's a two-day camping event held at a park or campground. Tickets are not costly.

Provincial Exhibition
This event, held in the first week or two of August, features tractor pulls, a carnival with rides, harness racing, entertainment and games of chance along with the traditional horse and livestock shows.

National Milton Acorn Festival
This is a unique event worth considering. Sometimes known as Canada's People's Poet, Acorn was born and raised on PEI. The festival, held in the third week of August, includes poetry readings and music.

Festival of the Fathers
Held along the historic waterfront in late August, this festival celebrates the Charlottetown Conference for the confederation with street musicians, dances, traditional food and a 10-tavern pub crawl.

Places to Stay

Camping Just 500m outside Charlottetown there's the *Southport Trailer Park* (☎ 902-569-2287, 20 Stratford Rd) overlooking the Hillsborough River. The nightly rate is $21.50, less if you're tenting or staying a week or longer. This is the only campground near town.

Hostels The good, friendly HI *Charlottetown Hostel* (☎ 902-894-9696, 153 Mount Edward Rd) is about 3km from the downtown area and close to the university. The barn-shaped building has room for 54 people and there's a kitchen with a microwave available for light cooking. Rates are $14

Milton Acorn

Born in Charlottetown in 1923, Milton Acorn was to become somewhat the bad boy of Canadian literature. Despite living and working as a poet, he did not fit the usual academic mould and was always known for voicing his firmly held left-wing opinions. He supported a range of radical causes and his poems often reflected his political biases as well as his unwavering support of the working person. Spending much of his life in Montreal, Toronto and Vancouver, he became known as the People's Poet, being honoured as such by fellow poets. He died in his home town in 1986.

Dig up my Heart: Selected Poems 1952-1983 is the most complete and representative collection of Acorn's poetry, offering a good sample of his subject matter and style. Many prefer his numerous nature poems and reflective poems, some of which have a wonderful, easy lyricism.

for members, $16.50 for nonmembers. The hostel is open from the beginning of June through Labour Day weekend and will have a list of all the hostels on the island.

The *University of PEI* (☎ 902-566-0442) has rooms from mid-May to the end of August. Reservations are a good idea. Rates begin at $28/42, more if you want breakfast in the university cafeteria or a two-bedroom apartment.

Tourist Homes Very central, the unassuming *Aloha Tourist Home* (☎ 902-892-9944, 234 Sydney St) is in a large old house and has four rooms to rent. Singles/doubles are $30/40. There is a large kitchen that visitors can use. There isn't much privacy at the shared bathroom off the kitchen but the owner, Maynard MacMillan, is an affable, helpful host. Cyclists can stash their bikes in the garage and off-season rates are discounted 25%.

Also central is the *Blanchard Tourist Home* (☎ 902-894-9756, 163 Dorchester St)

with three rooms at $18/30; it's spartan but it's OK.

In behind the mall and provincial beer store, is the spotless and friendly *Cairn's Tourist Home* (☎ 902-368-3552, 18 Pond St), in a modern house on a residential street. The home has three rooms available for $24/26.

Morais' Guest Home (☎ 902-892-2267, 67 Newland Crescent), near the tourist office, will pick you up from the airport or bus depot. The owner speaks English and French. Singles/doubles here go for $33/40 including a light breakfast.

Some of the least expensive choices are on the eastern side of downtown, close to the racetrack. You might check along Edward St or York Lane. Houses here are smaller and less gracious than many but the area is still conveniently walkable to the city centre.

B&Bs In this category are many places much like the tourist homes but offering the morning meal. As a rule, they tend to be outside the city centre and in newer houses but there are also several more central, upmarket places established in fine heritage homes and decorated with antiques and collectables.

The *Duchess of Kent* (☎ 902-566-5826, ☎ 1-800-665-5826, 218 Kent St), in a heritage house from 1875 with period furnishings, is central. The seven rooms of varying features range in price from $70 to $85 a double, including the morning meal. Washrooms are shared, but there are so many that this is no hardship.

Some of the larger historic places have been converted to inns. One such is the *Dundee Arms Inn* (☎ 902-892-2496, 200 Pownal St) in an impressive, restored late 19th/early 20th century mansion complete with antiques, dining room and pub. A double here ranges from $100 to $144 with a continental breakfast included. Newer units more akin to a motel are cheaper.

Motels There are motels along Hwy 1 west of Charlottetown towards Borden-Carleton; across from the airport north of town along Brackley Point Rd are a couple of very cheap and OK motels. Also on this commercial

strip are restaurants and service stations. Motels here usually cost at least $55 a double. The ones farther from town tend to be more modest in appearance, amenities and price. Those in town provide more comforts and the price goes up accordingly.

Close to town on the south side is the *Garden Gate Inn* (☎ 902-892-3411, ☎ 1-800-465-5556). It's small and well off the highway but, like many of the motels, expensive at $65/70.

Some 3km from town on the Trans Canada Hwy is the *Queen's Arms Motel* (☎ 902-368-1110) with a heated pool. Rooms cost about $48 for a single, $98 for a housekeeping unit.

Farther out, near the Hwy 2 junction, the brown *Banbridge Inn* (☎ 902-368-2223, ☎ 1-800-355-2223) offers doubles for $99 and rooms with kitchens for $130. There is a laundrette.

Places to Eat

There are lots of eateries here for a small city, but they're a bit costly. With the ocean minutes away, a fresh seafood dinner is still not too outrageous and the low prices elsewhere around the island make up for costs here.

Cedar's Eatery (81 University Ave), open every day and right in the middle of town, is a fine little place. At the chunky wooden tables the speciality is Lebanese food, ranging from felafels to more expensive kebabs. But there is also standard Canadian fare: soups, salads, sandwiches and steaks. Dinners range from $6 to $14. Cedar's stays open late, one of the few places that does. Also good for Lebanese and Canadian fare is *Shaddy's* (44 University Ave); it also has some vegetarian options. Here, main courses start at $9 but also come in 'small' sizes.

For breakfast, a simple meal or snack, the cheap and unpretentious *Town & Country Restaurant* (219 Queen St), fits the bill with its basic Canadian menu. Also small and cheap but with a certain charm is *Linda's Old Town Coffee Shop* (32 Queen St). It opens at 7 am and a full breakfast is $3.50 or so. A natural foods store is adjacent.

The most affordable seafood is at *Seatreat* on the corner of University Ave and Euston St. The restaurant features a basket of steamed mussels for $5, salmon or haddock dinners for $9, a bowl of fish chowder for $3.50 and, of course, lobster dinners.

For Mexican, there's *Pat & Willy's Bar & Grill* with an entrance near the corner of Kent St and Queen St. Dinners range from $8 to $11.

The upstairs *Olde Dublin Pub* (131 Sydney St) has pub meals from $7, an agreeable outside deck and live entertainment at night. The *Claddagh Room* downstairs has pricey but good seafood and the like; mains start at around $15. If you're enamoured of upscale pubs, the excellent *Merchantman Pub* at South and Water Sts is a casually upmarket place, at least in prices, similar to those of the Claddagh Room.

Behind the Confederation Centre of the Arts is the gentrified Victoria Row, a section of Richmond St that is closed off to vehicle traffic in summer and lined with cafés with outdoor seating. *Island Rock Cafe* boasts Atlantic Canada's largest beer bottle collection (it's hard to doubt it) as well as a menu that ranges from fettucine primavera to Thai chicken skewers. This can be a lively pub at night with dinners from $9 to $17. A couple of doors down is *Black Forest Cafe* if you want to finish your evening with a slice of double chocolate tort.

In Confederation Court Mall, on the corner of Kent and Queen Sts, the 2nd floor has a collection of cheap *fast-food outlets* offering pizza, chicken, burgers etc with a common eating area.

In the splurge category, the dining room of the *Dundee Arms Inn* (200 Pownal St) offers fine eating in a traditional setting with top-notch service. Next door to the Confederation Court Mall is *Piece A Cake*, a recommended casual bistro with salads, pastas, and creative mains with detectable Asian overtones. There's also live music on the quiet side most evenings. Main courses start below $8. Down at the edge of Confederation Landing on Charlottetown's waterfront is *Mackinnon's*, where you can buy fresh mussels, clams and oysters, as well as live or cooked lobster.

Cows, an island institution, has a location on Queen St near Grafton St, in the mall complex. It is not a large place but it turns out good home-made ice cream. A second location is at Peake's Wharf. There are also outlets, open in summer only, in Cavendish and North River. People across Canada can be seen sporting the colourful, humorous Cows T-shirts.

Entertainment

For a complete rundown on the plays, dinner theatre, and what band is playing where in Charlottetown, get hold of *The Buzz*, the free entertainment guide for PEI.

Myron's (151 Kent St) off University Ave is a popular spot with different types of music featured each night. *Island Rock Cafe* often has live jazz and blues.

Live Irish and Maritime music can also be enjoyed at the *Olde Dublin Pub (131 Sydney St)* with its outdoor deck. Another pub with consistent live music – though perhaps not always of the traditional bent – is *Peake's Quay* at Peake's Wharf.

Nearly every Friday night mid-May through late October the *Irish Hall (☎ 902-566-3272, 582 North River Rd)* has a ceilidh with traditional Irish, Scottish, and PEI music and dance – and great fun. Admission is $6.

Getting There & Away

Air Charlottetown has a small airport, north of the city west off Hwy 2, about 6km from the centre. Air Canada and Canadian Airlines – actually their subsidiary link airlines – connect PEI with the major Canadian cities and some New England USA points like Boston, usually through Halifax. Air Canada's flight from Toronto is daily and nonstop. Examples of one-way fares with one-month notice: Toronto ($674); St John's, Newfoundland ($634); and Moncton, New Brunswick ($292). Round-trip fares are only $30 to $50 more.

Bus SMT Bus Lines (☎ 902-628-6432) uses the Confederation Bridge to connect with Moncton, New Brunswick. There are two trips daily, except for Friday and Sunday when there are three. For Moncton, a ticket is $33. The SMT depot is at 330 University Ave.

If you're headed to Halifax or any point along the way, private van shuttles pop up now and again offering departures. The Visitor Information Centre or HI hostel will have current options. An example is Murphy's Off-Island Shuttle (☎ 902-626-6550) which has daily shuttles at 8 am to Moncton ($24) and departures at 7 am Friday through Sunday to Halifax ($90). Other destinations include Fredericton ($45), Saint John ($40), Amherst ($17), Truro ($45), and even Bangor, Maine ($75).

Beach Shuttle (☎ 902-566-3243) and Abgeweit Tours (see Organised Tours earlier in this chapter) operate shuttles to the areas north of Charlottetown. Beach Shuttle leaves four times daily from 8.50 am through 5.10 pm from the Visitor Information Centre on Water St and then twice daily makes stops at the HI hostel and Dundee Arms Inn, then on to the Sunset Campground and Cavendish Visitor Centre at the junction of Hwys 6 and 13. A round-trip is $15.

Train There is no passenger train service to, from or on the island.

Ferry The remaining ferry service to PEI links Wood Islands (in the eastern section of PEI province) to Caribou, Nova Scotia. It is anticipated that this ferry will continue operating even though the bridge is completed. This 22km trip takes 1½ hours and costs $10 per person return, $46 return per car and $15 per bicycle. In summer there are eight runs in each direction daily. This route is busy – during peak season you may have a one or two-ferry wait. Seasonal, it generally runs the first week of May to late December. There's a cafeteria on board. The head office is in Charlottetown, at 54 Queen St, or call ☎ 1-888-249-7245 for information. Reservations are not taken.

Car & Motorcycle Well, it's finally open – The Bridge (see boxed text 'Bridge Over Troubled Waters'). Whatever one's take on it, the bridge is an absolute flip-out to drive

Bridge Over Troubled Waters

Almost nothing in the history of Prince Edward Island has islanders so divided as the massive and controversial Confederation Bridge project. Either they love it or they hate it; there is nobody in between.

Opened in 1997, the bridge connects Cape Jourimain, New Brunswick, with Borden-Carleton, Prince Edward Island. It's the narrowest point of the strait, yet the bridge is still nearly 13km long, allowing Canadians to claim they have the longest bridge in the world. There is a longer one in Denmark, but an island in the middle technically makes it two bridges.

At a cost of $900 million, the project included 44 spans. Each span is almost a city block long and is made from 8000 tons of steel-reinforced concrete that had to be lifted into place. Each towers 20 storeys above the water. Driving at posted speeds – and, with the wind behind you, any faster is truly frightening – it takes 12 minutes to cross.

With the bridge completed, Prince Edward Island is now part of mainland Canada, and that's the source of all the ballyhoo. Those who rail against the bridge say it carries hordes of tourists, who in turn bring crime, litter and a growth of chain restaurants and tacky tourist attractions. Friends of the Island, an anti-bridge coalition, even went to court to stop construction, claiming the bridge causes ice build-up in the strait that will harm lobster and scallop stocks.

Pro-bridge forces say the link is necessary because travel to and from the island was always a nightmare for locals. During summer most of a day would be killed waiting for a ferry, and in winter boats would often get stuck for hours in the ice pack. With the bridge, PEI companies are able to compete more effectively with their mainland competition. And as for kitsch – where there are tourists there is kitsch, and it preceded the bridge by decades, albeit in less damaging doses than is feared.

There is no argument that once the toll gates opened, PEI had entered a new era of uncertainty and transition. At least for the present, changes haven't been too palpable – no brazen packs of hoodlums roam streets, the tourists are as tacky as anywhere but no worse than before, and you still see contented moo-cows chewing cud pretty much everywhere. The only serious problem has been the traffic accidents caused by literally hundreds of cars trying to pull over on the approaches to take photographs (an off-ramp is actually going to be built, just for shutterbugs). In 1998 two knuckleheaded Air Force helicopter pilots performed a below-the-spans daredevil stunt because, well, it was *there* one supposes.

Perhaps most symbolically, PEI radio stations still broadcast incessant reminders of the Wood Islands-Caribou, NS, ferry schedule.

across. Traffic can access the bridge 24 hours per day, seven days per week; sadly the 1.1m-high guardrails steal away any panorama you'd hoped for. There are two lanes and two breakdown lanes, with emergency callboxes every 750m. The fare is $35.50 for car and driver and is only collected when you leave PEI. (Note that the ferry costs $46 if you're trying to scrimp; but if you're heading into or out of Nova Scotia that $11 isn't worth the extra driving.) Bicycles and pedestrians are banned and must use a free, demand-driven shuttle service; it may be prudent to call the head office (☎ 1-888-437-6565) and let it be known you're going to arrive on a bike.

Charlottetown is about 60km from Borden-Carleton, at the PEI end of the bridge, and the drive takes about 40 minutes.

Car Rental A car, for better or worse, is the best and sometimes only means of seeing

much of the island. There are several outlets in the capital. The supply of cars is limited and with the local bus system shut down, getting a car is not easy. They can all be booked up for a week, so try to reserve well ahead through an office of one of the major chains in whatever city you're in prior to your PEI visit.

Avis Rent-A-Car (☎ 902-892-3706) is on the corner of University Ave and Euston St. Its least expensive compacts cost $34 per day, with 200km free.

There is also a Rent-A-Wreck (☎ 902-566-9955) at 57A St Peters with undoubtedly cheaper rates. But this office has moved several times in the past few years and never seems to have a person on duty when you call.

Getting Around
To/From the Airport As there is no airport bus in town, the only transportation is by cab which costs about $6.

Bicycle Smooth Cycles (☎ 902-566-5530) on the corner of Prince and Kent Sts rents hybrid bicycles for $22 a day or $75 a week. There's a popular $28 Tuesday tour of Charlottetown atop a bike, leaving at 1.30 pm. MacQueen's Bicycles (☎ 902-368-2453), 430 Queen St, has road bikes for around $22 a day and $88 a week. Both shops rent panniers and helmets while MacQueen's also arranges bike tours.

AROUND CHARLOTTETOWN
Fort Amherst/Port la Joye
National Historic Site
Very close to Rocky Point is the site of the old French capital and more recently Fort Amherst (☎ 902-672-6350), built by the British in 1758 after they had taken over the island. There isn't really anything left to see other than foundations but the interpretive centre features exhibits and an audiovisual show. There are views of the city and three lighthouses and a beach within the park area. The centre is open from mid-June to Labour Day from 10 am to 6 pm daily and admission is $2.25.

AROUND THE ISLAND
The island is small and, with a car, easy to get around. In one day it's possible to drive from Charlottetown up to the beaches for a swim, along the north coast all the way up to North Cape, then back along the western shoreline, over to Summerside and down to Borden-Carleton to the bridge. And you're not even rushing!

There are about 12 provincial tourist offices around the island, including one at the Wood Islands ferry terminal, one at the foot of the big bridge, and one in Charlottetown. Any one of them can arrange accommodation anywhere on the island within an hour.

Three equal-sized counties make up the island: Prince in the west, Queen's in the middle and King's to the east. Each county has a scenic road network mapped out by the tourist bureau. Though far from the only options, these routes do take in the better known attractions and the historical and geographical points of note.

North of Charlottetown

The area north of the capital in Queen's County is where all the action is on Prince Edward Island (refer to the Cavendish Region map). The national park is here, with its camping and beaches, and most of the island's main attractions are in this area. To feed and house the vacationers, many of the province's lodging and dining establishments are found not far from the north coast. The description here covers areas from east to west outside the park, and then, again in the same direction, areas within the park boundaries.

GRAND TRACADIE
Little more than a crossroads at the southeastern edge of the national park and not far from its entrance on Route 6, this is a 'must stop' for *Beulah's Bake Shop*, a tiny shed beside the house and kitchen where all the cooking is done. The strawberry and

raspberry pies are unbelievable and are cheap to boot. There are other things too, including bread and a variety of buns. Campers at Stanhope, stock up here.

STANHOPE

There is really nothing in this town, but near the park entrance are a couple of restaurants. You can also get a bite at the golf course.

Stanhope is one of the major accommodation centres, with dozens of places renting cottages, often by the week or longer. Weekly rates vary but most are between $350 and $450. The daily rate for most of the housekeeping units is around $50.

Campbell's Tourist Home (☎ 902-672-2421) in Stanhope is a B&B with a double for $50 and a weekly rate of $400. Decidedly more posh is the circa-1817 historic inn *Stanhope by the Sea* (☎ 902-672-2047, ☎ 1-888-999-5155) overlooking Covehead Bay, with doubles from $80. There is a private beach here and the dining is excellent.

From Stanhope to Cavendish there are about 10 privately operated campgrounds. (See also details of places to stay within Prince Edward Island National Park later in this chapter.)

NORTH RUSTICO

There is a post office and a government liquor store here as well as two supermarkets and a bank.

This is the home of *Fisherman's Wharf Lobster Suppers*, probably the best known, busiest restaurant in the province. It's huge but in peak season it still gets crowded, with lines from 6 to 8 pm. This fun, casual, holiday-style restaurant offers good-value dinners. For $25 (or more, depending on which size you choose) you are served a 500g lobster and can help yourself to an impressive salad bar, unlimited amounts of chowder, good local mussels, rolls and a variety of desserts. If you get really lucky, along the back wall are tables with a view of the ocean.

At the wharf in North Rustico is *Aiden Doiron's* where you can get fresh seafood ranging from lobsters and mussels to scallops, salmon and mackerel. If there are two

of you, consider feasting on a four or five-pounder lobster (2.5kg), available live or cooked.

At Doiron's and in **Rusticoville** fishing charters can be arranged down at the quay. Boats often hold six to 10 people, who catch cod, mackerel and several other species during the three-hour trips. Most charters are $20 to $25 per person.

Outside South Rustico on the small Route 242 is the quirkiest of island attractions, **Jumpin' Jack's Old Country Store Museum**. It's in the middle of nowhere and doesn't charge admission. The museum is a junk collector's dream – an old two-storey house jammed with dust-covered articles of every description and function collected from far and wide for who knows how many years. It's open from 10 am to 6 pm Tuesday through Saturday and 1 to 6 pm on Sunday in July and August.

North Rustico also has a lot of accommodation, including many tourist homes where it's possible to get something for less than a week fairly easily. A double room in someone's home can be had for $40 to $45.

North Rustico Harbour is a tiny fishing community with a lighthouse which you can drive to from North Rustico or walk to from the beach once you're in the national park. Located here is *Blue Mussel Cafe*. This pleasant dockside café has an outdoor deck overlooking the harbour, excellent chowder and a seafood menu that includes lobster dinners for $16 and two pounds (1kg) of mussels, steamed in wine and garlic, for $7.

The Rustico area is the base for one of the province's largest fishing fleets. Prince Edward Island's fishing industry is inshore (as opposed to offshore), meaning that the boats head out and return home the same day.

CAVENDISH

At the junction of routes 6 and 13, this little town is the area's commercial heart. You're in the centre of town when you see the service station, Cavendish Arms Pub, the church and the cemetery.

Also situated at the junction, as part of the police station and city offices, there's

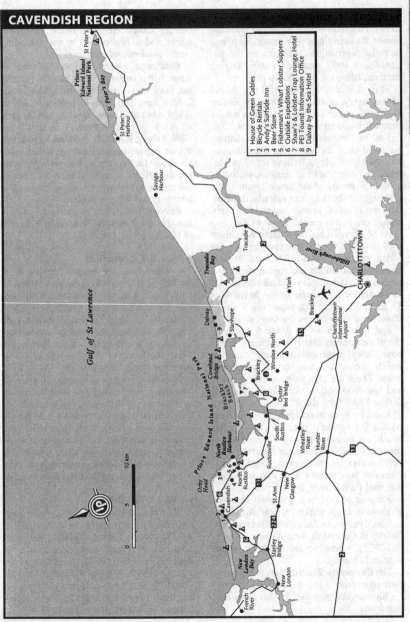

CAVENDISH REGION

1 House of Green Gables
2 Bicycle Rentals
3 Andy's Surfside Inn
4 Beer Store
5 Fisherman's Wharf Lobster Suppers
6 Outside Expeditions
7 Shaw's & Lobster Trap Lounge Hotel
8 PEI Tourist Information Office
9 Dalvay by the Sea Hotel

Gulf of St Lawrence

Prince Edward Island National Park

0   5   10 km

Prince Edward Island National Park

St Peter's

St Peter's Bay

St Peter's Harbour

Savage Harbour

Tracadie Bay

Tracadie

York

Dalvay

Stanhope

Brackley

Winsloe North

Covehead Bridge

Brackley Beach

Orby Head

North Rustico Harbour

Cavendish

North Rustico

South Rustico

Rusticoville

Oyster Bed Bridge

Wheatley River

Hunter River

Brackley

CHARLOTTETOWN

Charlottetown International Airport

Hillsborough River

New London Bay

French River

New London

Stanley Bridge

New Glasgow

St Ann

224

13

2

6

15

the **Cavendish Visitor Centre** (☎ 902-963-2391). This outlet has a wealth of information on the area along with a courtesy phone to make reservations, exhibits on the national park and a small craft shop. During summer, hours are 9 am to 10 pm.

This is also the home of Lucy Maud Montgomery, author of *Anne of Green Gables*. For more information on this see the Prince Edward Island National Park section.

East of Cavendish is a large amusement park and close by are a wax museum, go-kart tracks, a Ripley's Believe It or Not Museum and other tacky diversions, including a life-size model of the Space Shuttle. The growing number of these manufactured attractions in recent years is sad and definitely an eyesore in this scenic region of PEI.

At Stanley Bridge the **Marine Aquarium** (☎ 902-892-2203) has live samples of some of the native fish and a few seals. It isn't large, so to broaden the appeal there is a pinned butterfly display and a collection of 700 mounted bird specimens. Admission is $5 and hours during summer are 9 am to dusk. Save it for one of the rainy days.

Just west of town on Route 6 is one of the more popular family attractions, **Rainbow Valley**, a recreational water complex which includes a variety of slides and boats. There are also animals, picnic areas and fast-food outlets. Admission is a stiff $10 or $8.50 for kids.

Tourist homes, motels and cottages, some within the national park or close to the beach, can be found around Cavendish. Remember that this is the busiest and most expensive area for accommodation. See also Places to Stay under Prince Edward Island National Park later in this chapter.

Just east of town is a restaurant complex all done in cedar shakes. It contains a few fast-food places, including one for breakfast. Nearby is Cavendish Rent-A-Bike (☎ 902-963-2075), where bicycles are $5 to $6 an hour or $18 a day.

The *Cavendish Tourist Mart* is a grocery store open from 8 am to 10 pm daily, good for all essential supplies. It also features a laundrette.

To the west of town, near the park entrance, **Cavendish Boardwalk** has some stores and a few places to eat, including pizza, chicken and 'sub' outlets.

Fiddles 'n' Vittles, 3km west of town on Route 6, has been described as a fun place to eat; the food is good and there are half-price kids' dishes. The menu includes a variety of seafood but also steak, chicken and burgers, all at low or moderate prices. Similar is the *Galley* along Route 13 in Marco Polo Land. It's an expansive, well run operation that's also good for families with three huge meals per day offered at reasonable prices. Sunday features a morning and evening buffet. The takeaway dairy bar is popular.

Another popular daily evening buffet is found at the *Friendly Fisherman* 1km east of Cavendish on Route 6.

Around Cavendish

Two *lobster-supper houses* are nearby in the village of New Glasgow, and in St Ann on Route 224. Both offer a lobster plus all-you-can-eat chowder, mussels, salads, breads and desserts. You may even get some live music to help the food go down. Neither is quite the operation of the one in North Rustico and the selection is not as large, but the price is lower.

The one in St Ann is an original and still operates the St Anne's Church basement, as it has done for the past few decades. It's busy, casual and friendly and full of people from all over Canada, the USA and Europe. Lobster dinners are $21 and offered daily, except Sunday, from 4 to 9 pm; there's also a luncheon special from noon to 2 pm. The one in New Glasgow is offered on Sunday.

NEW LONDON

Aside from the *New London Lobster Supper*, which runs from 11 am to 9 pm daily, New London is known for being the birthplace of Lucy Maud Montgomery, author of *Anne of Green Gables*. The house where she was born in 1874 is now a museum (☎ 902-886-2099) and contains some personal belongings. Hours are 9 am to 7 pm during summer and admission is $2.

Not far away in the village of Park Corner is a house which was once owned by Montgomery's uncle when she was a girl. This was one of her favourite places and she was married in the parlour in 1911. The home is called the **Anne of Green Gables Museum** (☎ 902-886-2884) and contains such items as her writing desk and autographed first-edition books. There is also a tearoom and craft shop here. The museum is at Silver Birch and opens from 9 am to 6 pm June to October, later during the height of the tourist season. Admission is $2.50.

A stone's throw from here up the hill is the **Lucy Maud Montgomery Heritage Museum** (☎ 902-886-2807) in the home of Lucy Maud's grandfather. The site has a list of Anne paraphernalia and there's a path leading to the famed Lake of Shining Waters. It's open daily from 9 am to 6 pm June through September. Take a guided tour; there's a guarantee that if you're not absolutely fascinated, you don't pay the $2.50 admission.

PRINCE EDWARD ISLAND NATIONAL PARK

Just 24km north of Charlottetown, this is one of Canada's smallest national parks but has 45km of varied coastline, including some of the country's best sand beaches.

Sand dunes and red sandstone cliffs give way to wide beaches (widest at Cavendish) and the warmest waters around the province. The Gulf Stream does a little loop around the island, causing water temperatures to be higher than those found even farther south along the east coast. This is not quite tepid bath water but temperatures do get up to around a comfortable 20°C.

A day pass to the park costs $3 per person or $6.50 per family; after Labour Day it's free. You can also get a combination pass for the park and Green Gables. The park maintains an information desk and the exhibits in the Cavendish Visitor Centre (see Cavendish earlier in this chapter). There is also the Brackley Visitor Centre (☎ 902-672-7474) which is passed on the way to Brackley Beach on Hwy 15. It's open from 9 am to 6 pm daily during summer and until 9 pm

from July to mid-August. Failing that, the Dalvay Administration Office (☎ 902-672-6350) is off Route 6 near the Dalvay by the Sea Hotel; it's open year-round from 8.15 am through 4.30 pm weekdays.

Things to See & Do
House of Green Gables This is in the park near Cavendish and is, apart from the national park itself, the most popular attraction in the province.

The house is known as the place where Anne, the heroine of many of Montgomery's books, lived. The surrounding property was the setting of the 1908 novel *Anne of Green Gables* – a perennial favourite not only in Canada but around the world, having been translated into nearly 20 languages. The warm-hearted book tells the story of a young orphan, Anne, and her childhood tribulations in late 19th/early 20th century Prince Edward Island in a way that makes it a universal tale.

Everything relating to either the story or the author anywhere on the island has now pretty well become part of the Green Gables industry, not in a negative way.

At House of Green Gables, actually a rather attractive place, the over-popularisation reaches its zenith, with bus loads of visitors arriving at the door continuously and when you park you might have to deftly sidestep a golf ball whizzing by your head from the – natch, Green Gables Golf Course – links adjoining the site. Visiting first thing in the morning is highly recommended. Admission is $5, $12 for a family and the home is worth a visit.

There are many farm demonstrations and period programs throughout summer; a new interpretive centre (☎ 902-672-6350) has audiovisual displays. Parks Canada now runs the operation and it certainly appears lots (and lots) more is on the planning table. The house is open from 9 am to 8 pm in high season, till 5 pm otherwise, early May through late October.

The quieter trails from the house through the green, gentle creek-crossed woods are worthwhile. 'Lover's Lane', particularly, has maintained its idealistic childhood ambience.

A Yen for Anne

Although Prince Edward Island is generally little known internationally, up to 10,000 of the island's annual visitors are now from Japan. This makes it easily one of the country's top destinations for the Japanese traveller. There is even a direct Tokyo-Charlottetown flight.

The attraction is partly because Charlottetown has become the twin city of Ashibetsu, a rural city situated in northern Japan. Student exchanges have taken place, as well as a number of tourist related activities.

The main draw, however, is the Japanese fascination with *Anne of Green Gables*. The book has been on Japanese school curriculums since the 1950s, and Anne's story has found a spot in the national psyche, especially among women, who identify strongly with Anne's character.

Many Japanese also now come to PEI to marry. Weddings in Japan can be prohibitively costly and are often difficult to prepare. Here couples enjoy the quiet countryside and, in some cases, the Christian church and ceremony to which many young people are attracted. Quite a few couples are married at Silver Birch in Park Corner, where Anne's author LM Montgomery herself was married. Arrangements are handled by the local tourism ministry.

Not far away, near the United Church in Cavendish, you can visit the site of the house where Montgomery lived with her grandparents and where she wrote *Anne of Green Gables*. The farmhouse no longer stands, just the stone foundations and surrounding gardens. Admission here is $2. From here you can walk the short path to the post office to get a 'Green Gables' postmark.

Other Anne-related sites include the cemetery in Cavendish (where Montgomery is buried), the museum at Silver Bush in Park Corner on Route 20 (where Montgomery spent much time when it was owned by her uncle), another house nearby in Park Corner owned by her grandfather, and the museum in the Confederation Centre in Charlottetown (which contains some original manuscripts).

All tour operators have an Anne-themed tour (they'd be nuts not to), including Cavendish Tours (☎ 902-963-3002), which has a three hour tour for $35 and is good as its schedule follows the arrival of the Beach Shuttle from Charlottetown. Another much longer tour is $60 and starts in Charlottetown.

Beaches There are several long stretches of beach in the park and they are all good. **Cavendish Beach**, edged with large sand dunes at the west end of the park, is the widest of them all. It is easily the most popular beach and gets relatively busy in peak season. This does not mean crowded, though.

Between Rustico and Cavendish is some of the park's most impressive terrain. At Cape Turner there is a good look-out area but don't miss **Orby Head** with its trails leading along the high red cliffs with great seaside views. There are other stopping-off points along this stretch of coastal road.

Brackley Beach, in the middle of the park, is also well attended, the others less so. Long, wide Brackley Beach backed by sand dunes is popular with locals, young people and visitors. There is a snack bar and change rooms by the boardwalk to the beach. Lifeguards are on hand but watch out for riptides. Between here and Stanhope Beach near Covehead Bridge are some deep-sea fishing charter boats, including *Salty Seas* and *Richard's* (☎ 902-672-2316), both of which have three 3½ hour trips daily from around $20.

Stanhope Beach opposite the campground of the same name has no cliffs or dunes and the landscape is flat and the beach wide. At the entrance to the beach is a snack bar and change rooms with showers. A boardwalk leads to the beach which has lifeguards on duty through the day.

Dalvay Beach is the easternmost beach and a couple of short hiking trails begin in the area. Two called Farmlands and Bubbling Springs Trails are quite good, with a small graveyard, some remnants of old stone dikes

and a spring for a cool drink found along the way. They can be combined for a 4km walk.

An appealing landmark is the **Dalvay by the Sea Hotel** (☎ 902-672-2048) built in 1895 and looking like something out of a novel by F Scott Fitzgerald. For a splurge this Victorian seaside lodge offers a varied menu – lobster bisqué to coq au vin. Reservations are required. If you're thinking of spending the night, the price of a double room (from $180 and up) includes dinner and breakfast.

All the north coast beaches tend to have red jellyfish. They are known locally as bloodsuckers but they aren't. Most are much smaller than a closed fist and, while unpleasant, are not really dangerous, although brushing against one can irritate the skin. There is virtually no shade to be had at any of the beaches, so for your own protection consider using an umbrella, a shirt, and lots of sunscreen lotion.

Parks Canada in 1998 opened another rather incredible section of the national park, this one along a peninsula north and west of St Peter's. Do check this place out for the rare parabolic dunes – found only here and in one spot along Germany's North Sea coastline; 3% of the planet's piping plovers are found here too. Still being developed, at present there are 922 acres and 7km of great trails. Backcountry camp sites were being proposed at the time of writing. An interpretive centre is now open with few exhibits but well informed rangers.

Hiking The park has around 40km of trails, most easy, some rated moderate (though this is a slight exaggeration). The main trail, the 8km Homestead, starts near the Cavendish Campground and is moderate only in length.

Kayaking Outside Expeditions (☎ 1-800-207-3899) is a Charlottetown-based outfitter that offers kayaking trips in the national park from June to October. The three-hour introductory trips, that begin with a lesson in kayaking techniques, are held three times daily at 9 am, 1 pm and near sunset. The cost, which includes all equipment, is $45. In Cavendish, phone ☎ 902-963-2391.

Places to Stay
Camping The national park has three campgrounds and, as you might expect, all are in heavy demand during summer. Rates range from $13 for a bare-bones site to $21 for a three-way hookup. Reservations (☎ 1-800-213-7275) are now taken at all three. They're taken for late August through September only at *Cavendish Campground*, 3km west of the town of Cavendish and with showers, a kitchen shelter and laundry facilities. Being near the centre of things, this campground tends to be the most popular and is often filled by noon.

Stanhope Campground across the road from Stanhope Beach has similar facilities but features a more wooded setting and a well stocked store. The relatively isolated *Rustico Island Campground* is near the end of the road to Brackley Beach. It has a kitchen shelter and showers have just been installed. Sites are cheapest here.

Winter camping is available near Dalvay Activity Centre.

Outside the park and occasionally adjacent to it are many private campgrounds. *Marco Polo Land* (☎ 902-963-2352) near Cavendish has a range of amenities over its 100 acres, including two swimming pools. An unserviced site is $21.50. At the other end of the national park, near Grand Tracadie on Route 6, the much smaller *Ann's Whispering Pines* (☎ 902-672-2632) has unserviced sites for $18.50. Both take reservations.

Other Accommodation Tourist homes, motels and B&Bs are found along the length of the national park. The prices are steep compared to what you pay elsewhere and the closer to the beach the accommodation is, the steeper it gets. Phoning for a reservation, even if only a few days in advance, helps considerably in obtaining a bed at night.

For these reasons, serious consideration should be given to visiting the national park after Labour Day if your schedule will allow it. The crowds are gone, the weather often provides those delightful Indian summer days and every B&B and motel is practically begging you to stay there. By Sunday of that

holiday weekend room prices are crashing. Two-bedroom cottages that were $100 in July can now be obtained for $60, B&Bs that were asking $65 a few weeks earlier are teasing you with $30 doubles.

One of the best places to stay during the tourist season is *Andy's Surfside Inn* (☎ 902-963-2405) inside the national park on the way to Orby Head from North Rustico. This large rambling house overlooking Doyle's Cove has been an inn since the 1930s and offers eight rooms at $35/50. A light breakfast is included and the kitchen is open to those who want to bring home a few live lobsters. The view from the porches is simply stunning.

Parkview Farm Tourist Home & Cottage (☎ 902-963-2027, ☎ 1-800-237-9890) is 2km east of Cavendish and has rooms for $35/45 and cottages on the farm that sleep four people for $110.

Not far from the ocean in Brackley Beach is the *Linden Lane Guest House* (☎ 902-672-3091) with three rooms from $40; the owners speak French and German and welcome cyclists.

The most affordable motel is *Tortuga Motel* (☎ 902-621-2020) at Oyster Bed Bridge, intersection of Hwys 6 and 7. The motel is pretty basic and a little far from the beaches if you don't have a car, but rooms begin at $45, less than what every other motel is charging.

For luxury, the two top options have been mentioned previously – Stanhope by the Sea and Dalvay by the Sea.

Places To Eat
Besides all the lobster suppers, the *Café St Jean* at Oyster Bed Bridge is a consistent, creative bistro with a Cajun and regional flair. Mains are below $10. This place has constant live traditional music and it stocks more regional music CDs than most music stores.

Entertainment
Things are very sedate compared to, say, Halifax, but you've got a few options. The only pub for miles it seems is the *Lobster Trap Lounge* adjoining Shaw's Hotel near Rustico Island Beach; it's fairly rollicking.

Regularly scheduled shindigs alternate from Shaw's Hotel to the Café St Jean at Oyster Bed Bridge, Rustic Dreams in Rusticoville, and the North Winds Motel in Brackley Beach. Admission is usually $2 to $4. The North Rustico Legion has wild ceilidhs on Wednesday and Saturday nights; admission is $5 to $10.

Getting Around
The **Cavendish Red Trolley** runs from the Marco Polo Land campground at the top of every hour from 10 am to 6 pm; it stops at Cavendish Country Inn, the Cavendish Visitor Centre, Cavendish Beach, and Green Gables. For $2 you can use the ticket all day.

West of Charlottetown

LADY SLIPPER DRIVE
The western third of the island is made up of Prince County. Lady Slipper Drive is 288km long and is the marked tourist route around this portion of the island.

The northern section of Prince County is, like so much of the province, pretty farm country. The southernmost area, along Egmont and Bedeque bays, retains some evidence of its Acadian French history.

VICTORIA
Straddling Queens and Prince counties is this picturesque fishing village just off Hwy 1 and 35km west of Charlottetown. Victoria is something of a haven for artists and features a number of studios and art galleries as well as Island Chocolates, a shop that produces excellent Belgian chocolates. The community centre becomes the *Victoria Playhouse* (☎ 1-800-925-2025) during summer.

You can purchase cooked lobster on the wharf then enjoy them at a table overlooking the beach at Victoria Provincial Park. Or enjoy home-made soups, quiches or salads at *Landmark Cafe*. Those interested in spending a night or two can check into the *Victoria Village Inn* (☎ 902-658-2483), a

19th century home that has three rooms beginning at $65 a double; the Actor's Retreat Café on the first floor is excellent. Outside town on the Trans Canada Hwy is the *Simple Comforts B&B* (☎ *902-658-2951)* which also bills itself as a 'bicycle hostel'. Indeed it has a 13-bed hostel where you can bed down for $10 along with double rooms. The B&B has rooms from $35.

SUMMERSIDE

The second largest city in the province, Summerside has a population of 10,000. At one time residents of the capital would move to this side of the island in the hot months. The closure of the large military base here has caused a major economic setback.

The approach along Hwy 1A is much like that to Charlottetown, lined with motels, hamburger joints and a few campgrounds. But centrally, it's a quiet village with quaint old homes on streets trimmed with big trees. The one main street, Water St, has most of the commercial establishments.

The Lady Slipper Visitor Information Centre (☎ 902-888-8364) is on Hwy 1A 2km east of Summerside and is open from 9 am to 8 pm daily during summer. The walking-tour pamphlet of historic Summerside details some of the town's finer buildings from 1850.

For a week in mid-July each year there's the Lobster Carnival, with nightly feasts, contests, games and music. At the end of the month there is a hydroplane regatta.

International Fox Museum & Hall of Fame

The controversial story of island fox farming is told at 260 Fitzroy St (☎ 902-436-2400), one block from Water St. In 1890 a local successfully bred two wild silver foxes captured on the island, the first time wild fur-bearing animals had been bred in captivity. The principles learned are now used around the world. Through the 1920s, fortunes were made in Summerside through shipbuilding and fur farming. For a time, the latter was PEI's most important economic activity.

From June to September, the museum, created in Holman Homestead, a beautiful historic house with a lovely garden, is open from 9 am to 6 pm and is free. Holman himself was a fox breeder, and there are still fox farms on the island today.

The College of Piping & Celtic Performing Arts

The school (☎ 902-436-5377), 619 Water St, provides visitors with nearly continuous entertainment through the day – bagpipes, singing, dancing. Drop in any time Monday to Friday from 11 am to 5 pm. There are also exhibits and a lunch room for light meals. A ticket is $7 for the special Thursday night Scottish Ceilidh shows (outdoors – bring a sweater). Watch for the International Highland Gathering at the end of June at the college.

EPTEK National Exhibition Centre & PEI Sports Hall of Fame

One of 22 national exhibition centres in the country, EPTEK (☎ 902-888-8373) features a small, changing art and history exhibit. A section on provincial sports figures is permanent. The centre, on the waterfront near Spinnaker's Landing, is open from 10 am to 4 pm Tuesday through Friday and 1 to 4.30 pm Saturday and Sunday. Admission is $2.

Spinnaker's Landing

This is the boardwalk area along Summerside's waterfront, which includes the usual over-priced gift shops and the Whale's Tail Pub. But also here is The Boat Shed Interpretive Centre that has displays on the town's history and the traditional boat-building methods once employed here. Next door is the city's Lighthouse Lookout, which houses a visitors centre on the first floor and observation platform at the top. Both the lighthouse and the Boat Shed are free and hours are 9.30 am to 9.30 pm daily during summer. The tourist centre offers an hour-long walking tour of the city at 2 and 6 pm daily during summer. A ticket is $2 but includes entrance to the EPTEK Centre. Bicycles are also rented here for $25 per day.

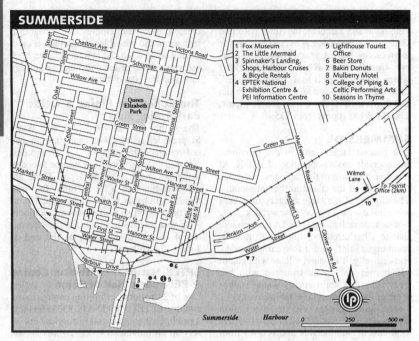

SUMMERSIDE

1 Fox Museum
2 The Little Mermaid
3 Spinnaker's Landing,
   Shops, Harbour Cruises
   & Bicycle Rentals
4 EPTEK National
   Exhibition Centre &
   PEI Information Centre
5 Lighthouse Tourist
   Office
6 Beer Store
7 Bakin Donuts
8 Mulberry Motel
9 College of Piping &
   Celtic Performing Arts
10 Seasons In Thyme

Spinnaker's Landing also contains a small outdoor stage area for free live music in summer.

Places to Stay

Summerside has a handful of moderately priced motels, a rarity in PEI.

For campers, there is **Linkletter Provincial Park** (☎ 902-888-8366), on Route 11, 8km west of Summerside. There's a beach and a store for basic supplies. Rates start at $15.

In town, the **Warn House** (☎ 902-436-5242, ☎ 1-888-436-7512, 330 Central St) sits on two central acres. Four suites all have private bath and start at $55.

Two farm B&Bs are next to each other just before Hwy 1A crosses the Wilmont River. **The Island Way Farm** (☎ 902-436-7405, ☎ 1-800-361-3435) has four rooms – two perfect for up to four people – from $55. Another one nearby is similarly priced.

Both include breakfast and maintain a riding stable for guests.

Motels are relatively cheap here. The **Cairns** (☎ 902-436-5841, 721 Water St) on the east side of town charges $38 and up for a double. A little cheaper, but a little farther out, is **Glade Motor Inn** (☎ 902-436-5564) on Hwy 1A just before crossing the Wilmont River with doubles for $45, cottages for more. **Mulberry Motel** (☎ 902-436-2520, 6 Water St) is more upmarket and offers housekeeping (kitchen) facilities with some of the rooms. Doubles range from $60. A coffee shop serves breakfast.

Places to Eat

The best place for breakfast is **Bakin Donuts**, on Water St heading towards the city centre. The muffins are huge and good value at 60¢ each, and two full breakfast specials are offered daily for under $4. **The Little Mermaid**

(240 Harbour Drive) on the waterfront has fine views of the harbour and is recommended. At prices of $6 to $9, it offers standard fare of mainly fried foods, such as burgers, but there are also fish dishes, and the home-made french fries are great. Fresh fish, mussels and lobster can be purchased too.

An excellent creative eatery is *Seasons in Thyme (644 Water St)*. Regional and international cuisine is rather pricey but worthwhile – you can even take a cooking course.

Getting There & Away

Maritime Shuttle (☎ 902-882-3190) runs from Tignish, PEI, to Halifax, stopping in Summerside along Water St. Schedules vary wildly season to season but presently do run daily; to Tignish would be around $9.50.

AROUND SUMMERSIDE
Miscouche

As you head west of Summerside along Route 2, the **Acadian Museum** (☎ 902-432-2880) in Miscouche has a small collection of early Acadian memorabilia relating the engrossing history of the Acadians before and after the mass expulsion from Nova Scotia by the British in 1720. An audiovisual exhibit provides more information. A visit to learn something of this tragic story is worthwhile.

Most of the descendants of these early French settlers live in this section of the province. Six thousand still speak French as a first language. Admission to the museum is $3 and in summer it's open daily from 9.30 am to 7 pm, less other times. Sunday evenings the museum hosts soirées ($4) with Acadian music; you can actually meet the musicians at performances Tuesday through Thursday. (See the Nova Scotia and New Brunswick chapters for more information on the Acadians.)

Mémé Jane's (8 Lady Slipper Drive South) is a restaurant with a few Acadian dishes on the menu as well as burgers, sandwiches, salads and daily specials.

Mont Carmel

A little farther west from Miscouche and then south down to the coast on Route 11 is the little village of Mont Carmel, home to the **Pioneer Acadian Village** (☎ 902-854-2227). This is a replica of an early 19th century settlement. The village has a school, store and church, among other things. A highlight is the restaurant in the grounds, *L'Étoile de Mer*, which offers a couple of traditional Acadian dishes, such as chicken fricot and paté à la rapure. Admission to the village is $3.50 and it's open daily from 9 am to 7 pm mid-June to mid-September.

Malpeque Bay

North of Summerside, this bay produces the world-famous oysters of the same name. About 10 million of them are harvested each year from the controlled 'farms' of the bay.

Cabot Beach Provincial Park (☎ 902-836-8945) north of Malpeque village is one of the larger parks on the island. There is camping ($15), a beach and lots of picnic areas.

AROUND PRINCE COUNTY

Tyne Valley is worth a visit. There are also a few craft places to visit, including a pottery. Also here, the *Doctor's Inn (☎ 902-831-3057)* is a fine country B&B whose superlative dining room is able to take full advantage of its surrounding organic garden. Rooms are $55 for a double and dinner is by reservation only. The inn also sells its organically grown vegetables and potatoes.

Just north of Tyne Valley along Hwy 12 is **Green Park Provincial Park** (☎ 902-831-2370), which includes a beach, campground ($15) and the Green Park Shipbuilding Museum. PEI's 19th century shipbuilding industry at one time included almost 200 small shipyards where crews of 20 men were building boats in six months or less. On the grounds there's an interpretive centre, a re-created shipyard with a partially constructed 200-ton brigantine in it and Yeo House, the renovated home of a wealthy shipowner in the 1860s. Hours are 9 am to 5 pm daily during summer and admission is $2.50.

A band of about 50 Micmac families live on **Lennox Island**, in Malpeque Bay. The scenery is good, and inside the Band Council Complex are paintings and artefacts

dealing with the history of the people who were the first in Canada to be converted to Christianity. St Ann's Church, dating from 1875, can be visited, along with an Indian craft shop. The island is connected by road from the west side of the bay, near the village of East Bideford, north of Tyne Valley.

The inland town of **O'Leary**, right in the middle of Prince County, is a small commercial hub which sees few tourists. There is, however, the **PEI Potato Museum** (☎ 902-859-2039) on Parkview Drive in Centennial Park. Everything you ever wanted to know about the lowly tuber is carefully explained. You walk away with such gems of knowledge as man began cultivating the potato in Peru 4500 years ago and that french fries alone take up 85% of all potatoes grown in North America. There also are several other historic buildings in the park and a kitchen that sells potato dogs – baked potatoes with hot dogs in them and covered with cheese. Hours are 9 am to 5 pm daily, except Sunday when the centre opens at 2 pm. Admission is $2.50 and, surprisingly, is worth it.

To the north in Bloomfield is **MacAusland's Woollen Mill** (☎ 902-859-3005), the only woollen mill remaining on the island and Atlantic Canada's only producer of virgin wool blankets. Tours of the mill are offered and pure woollen goods can be bought.

If you're near **Tignish** at meal time, drop in at the Royal Canadian Legion. It's cheap, and you're bound to find conversation. The Parish of St Simon and St Jude Church has an impressive pipe organ built in Montreal and installed here in 1882. It employs 1118 pipes.

Equally interesting is the convent behind the church that was built in 1868 and now is *Tignish Heritage Inn* (☎ 902-882-2491). The huge brick building has 14 rooms, most with private baths, that are $65 for singles/doubles. Near the village of Norway is **Elephant Rock**, a large erosion formation at the seashore. To find it, head north of the town on Hwy 14 and then follow signs that will lead you on a dirt road to the coast.

Lovely if windblown **North Cape** is a promontory with a lighthouse. A wind turbine station has been set up to study the efficacy of wind-powered generators. The interpretive centre provides information and features an aquarium. Hours are 9 am to 8 pm daily and admission is $2. Upstairs there is a rather pricey restaurant. Even more interesting is the rock reef at North Cape which can be explored at low tide – look for sea life in the pools and watch for coastal birds and even seals.

About midway down the coast on the western shore along Route 14 is the village of Miminegash, in one of the more remote sections of the province. Right on Hwy 14 is the **Irish Moss Interpretive Centre** (☎ 902-882-4313). It was begun by local women whose families have long been involved in the collecting or harvesting of the moss, a type of seaweed.

Almost half the world's supply of Irish moss comes from PEI. If you're dying to savour seaweed, there is the *Seaweed Pie Cafe* at the centre which has a standard lunch menu but also serves a special pie. The moss is in the middle layer of cream. Hours during summer are 10 am to 7 pm daily, except Sunday when the centre is open from noon to 8 pm. Admission is $1.

Cedar Dunes Provincial Park (☎ 902-859-8785), at the southern tip of Prince County, has a lighthouse, restaurant and beach and a campground ($15). The lighthouse, dating from 1875, has been restored, and there is now a museum outlining its history. Overnight guests can stay at the inn, *West Point Lighthouse* (☎ 902-859-3605, ☎ 1-800-764-6854), part of the former lightkeeper's premises, but rooms range from $75 to $120 a night.

East of Charlottetown

THE KING'S BYWAY

The 374km circular sightseeing route around King's County (the eastern third of the province) is called the King's Byway. It's a lightly populated, rural region of farms and fishing communities. Much of

this section of the province is peopled by ancestors of Scottish settlers rather than by the French of the western side or the Irish of the central district. The ferry to Nova Scotia is on the south coast, while the ferry to the Magdalen Islands is at Souris, on the east coast. Plenty of B&Bs and tourist homes are found along the roadways.

ORWELL

Just out of town is the **Orwell Corner Historic Village** (☎ 902-651-2013), a restored and preserved 19th century community. Originally settled by Scottish immigrants in 1766, the village includes a farm, blacksmith's, post office and store among other buildings still in their original settings. During summer it's open daily from 9 am to 5 pm, less other times, and costs $3. Concerts are held on Wednesday evening.

Nearby is the **Sir Andrew MacPhail Homestead** (☎ 902-651-2789). The national historic site preserves the farm that MacPhail and his brother used to start the island's seed potato industry and now features a restaurant in the wrap-around porch of the home. The site is open daily from 10 am to 9 pm in July and August, less other times. Admission is free.

WOOD ISLANDS

Down on the south coast, 'Woods' is where you'll find the PEI-Nova Scotia ferry terminal, and as such it's a somewhat busy visitors centre. There are two tourist offices here with the one for PEI open from 9 am to 9 pm daily during summer. The other is for Nova Scotia. The mainland is 22km (75 minutes) across the Northumberland Strait. Nearby the ferry terminal is the free day-use **Wood Islands Provincial Park** with a nice lighthouse. In town there are about half a dozen places to eat.

MURRAY HARBOUR & MURRAY RIVER

Little visited and tucked out of the way, Murray Harbour is a fishing town with its own canning plant. You'll whiz past the **Log Cabin Museum** (☎ 902-962-2201) here,

home to 3000 articles of the past century. Admission is $2.

Nearby in Murray River, Captain Garry's Seal Cruises (☎ 902-962-2494) departs three times daily from the town wharf to view PEI's largest seal colony, Bird Island and a mussel farm. The cost is $13.50. Outside Expeditions (☎ 1-800-207-3899) also leads day-long kayak tours ($95) from the harbour.

BRUDENELL RIVER PROVINCIAL PARK & AROUND

The campground in the park (☎ 902-652-8966) is just a bare field, but there's a lodge and a golf course for those not roughing it. At **Panmure Island Provincial Park** (☎ 902-838-0668), just south down the coast, there is a good beach, swimming and picnicking as well as a campground with laundry facilities. Unserviced sites at either park are $15.

Montague features the King's Byway Visitor Centre (☎ 902-838-2977), which has racks of brochures and information as well as a vacancy board that will list openings in motels and B&Bs for the region. There is also an extensive set of displays and exhibits on PEI and a small video theatre. Hours are 9 am to 7 pm daily. From the Montague marina *Cruise Manada* (☎ 902-838-3444) offers tours of PEI's largest seal colony for $17. An extensive set of B&Bs, motels and tourist homes is in this modest town, as is the *Page Mistress Bookstore & Café*.

Cardigan, an old shipbuilding port north of the park, has a lobster-supper house right down by the harbour; it's open from 5 to 9 pm daily from June to October and includes chowder, salad bar and desserts as well as the lobster. The cost is $24. Cardigan Sailing Charters (☎ 902-583-2020) operates a schooner tour; it's steep at around $50 per person.

BAY FORTUNE

The dining room at *The Inn at Bay Fortune* (☎ *902-687-3745*) is considered to be one of the finest in the province. Main courses could be goat-cheese stuffed chicken in a walnut crust or mustard-crusted Atlantic swordfish. Dinners range

from \$19 to \$26. There are also 11 comfortable guest rooms from \$125 to \$185 a night. This inn was once the home of Broadway playwright Elmer Harris.

The **Fortune River** flowing near Hwy 2 which cuts across the island is a good place for canoeing.

SOURIS

With a population of 1500, Souris feels like a real town after you've passed through so many small villages. First settled by the Acadian French in the early 1700s, it was named Souris, meaning 'mouse', due to several plagues. The name has been anglicised and the last 's' is pronounced. The town is an important fishing and processing port and is also important for the ferry (☎ 902-986-3278) which departs for the Magdalen Islands of Quebec, five hours and 134km north in the Gulf of St Lawrence. See under Magdalen Islands in the Quebec chapter for more information on the ferry.

Main St, a strip with buildings from the 1920s and 1930s as well as some older distinctive architecture, is pleasantly slow, with cars stopping to let pedestrians cross. The shops, the newspaper office and a few simple restaurants are found here.

St Mary's Roman Catholic Church, built of island sandstone in 1901, is off Main St on Pacquet St and is the dominant structure in town. However, the Town Hall on Main St, the Georgian-style Beacon House and several other buildings are worth a look on the way by.

Ocean Spray Lobster Cruises (☎ 902-357-2632) offers two evening scenic tours daily on lobster boats for \$15.

There is a tourist office at **Souris Beach Provincial Park**, a day-use facility with a wide sweeping beach at the south-west corner of town.

Places to Stay

Souris gets quite busy due to the ferry traffic. There is a hostel, *A Place To Stay Inn* (☎ 902-686-4626, ☎ 1-800-655-7829, 9 Longworth St), located right behind landmark St Mary's Church. This absolutely superb facility includes dorm rooms for \$18 a night (\$2 more for bedding) as well as 12 guest rooms at \$45 for a double, rates for the latter including a continental breakfast. It has full kitchen and laundry facilities, a lounge and TV room and mountain bikes for rent at \$4 per hour or \$20 per day, and many more extras. Transport is tough – there isn't any, but you might be able to line up something if you call ahead.

Church Street Tourist Home (☎ 902-687-3065, 8 Church St), 10 minutes from the ferry, is simple but good. Doubles are \$35 and you can use the kitchen. Another B&B, the *Matthew House Inn* (☎ 902-687-3461, 15 Breakwater St), is gorgeous but very highly priced – \$145 for a single/double.

The good *Hilltop Motel* (☎ 902-687-3315, add 1- if calling from Quebec) gets full with ferry traffic even when the ferry arrives from Quebec at four or five in the morning. Call from the Magdalen Islands for a reservation before leaving or someone will probably beat you to the available bed. The motel has a restaurant that is good for breakfast. It's on the east side of town. Rates are \$68 a double.

RED POINT PROVINCIAL PARK

Three miles east of Souris the white sands begin. Red Point is a small park with a sandy beach and some pleasant shaded tent sites. The beaches around here are known for the squeaking sound they make when you walk on them.

BASIN HEAD

Not even really a village, Basin Head is at the ocean's edge and is the site of **Basin Head Fisheries Museum** (☎ 902-357-2966). This provincial museum traces the history of the island's fishing industry with an interpretive centre, boat sheds with vessels on display and Smith Fish Cannery, which now houses a coastal ecology exhibit including salt water aquariums. At one time you used to be able to jump off the bridge at the beach and be swept out to a sandbar by tidal wash, but it's frowned upon officially now. Hours are 10 am to 7 pm daily

during summer, less other times, and admission is $3. Canoes are rented here for $10 per hour.

EAST POINT

At East Point, the north-east tip of the island, cliffs are topped by a lighthouse, which can be climbed as part of a little tour for $2.50. The assistant's old house nearby has a restored radio room and a gift shop. It's expected that in a few years the whole thing will have to be moved (as the lighthouse has been moved previously) because of the creeping erosion of the shoreline. The lighthouse is open from 10 am to 6 pm daily from 1 June to the end of September.

The north shore area of King's County all the way along towards Cavendish is more heavily wooded than much of the island but that doesn't mean the end of farms and potatoes altogether. There is a lot of fishing done along the coast here – you could try a charter in search of tuna. Inland there are a couple of trout streams worth investigating.

The people of the north-eastern area have a fairly strong, intriguing accent not unlike that heard in Newfoundland.

NORTH LAKE

This is one of the four fishing centres found along the north coast of King's County. Although small, the dock area with its lobster traps, storage sheds and boats is always good for a poke around. With autumn comes tuna season and quite a busy sportfishing period, drawing anglers from abroad. Some of the world's largest bluefin tuna have been caught in these waters. Indeed the world-record catch, a 680kg behemoth, was reeled in off North Lake in 1979.

CAMPBELL'S COVE PROVINCIAL PARK

Quiet and relaxing through the day, this small park, the best one in the county, fills up by evening in July and August. As always shade is at a premium, with about half the camp sites offering some sun relief. Most campers are tenters as there are no electric hook-ups. Facilities are minimal so bring all necessary supplies. Rates are $15.

The beach, with cliffs at each end, is excellent for beachcombing.

ST MARGARET'S

At the big church in St Margaret's, lobster suppers are held daily from 4 to 9 pm and are $21.95. Aside from the deep-sea fishing, there are some good trout streams along the road, and one of them, the **Naufrage River**, is just west of town. At the village of **Naufrage**, on the coast, there is another lighthouse and some colourful fishing boats around the wharf area.

ST PETER'S

The nets for commercial mussel farming can be seen stretched around St Peter's Bay. In town don't miss *Wilma's Bake Shop* for bread, muffins and cinnamon buns. A new section of the national park has opened nearby.

MIDGELL

On Hwy 2 south of St Peter's Bay is the Midgell Centre (☎ 902-961-2963). Set up principally for the guests of the Christian centre, visitors are welcome to stay overnight at the hostel. There are 60 beds at $14 each. Light cooking is possible and there are showers and a lounge. It's open to visitors from 1 June to 1 September.

New Brunswick

NEW BRUNSWICK

New Brunswick is, along with Nova Scotia and Prince Edward Island, one of Canada's three Maritime Provinces. It was also one of the four original members of the Dominion of Canada established in 1867. The province's essential characteristic is that it remains largely forested. Yet, for most visitors, it is the areas apart from the vast woodlands that have the most appeal.

From the Quebec border the gentle, pastoral farming region of the Saint John River Valley leads to the Bay of Fundy with its cliffs, coves and tidal flats caused by the world's highest tides. The eastern shore offers warm, sandy beaches and some of the finest salmon-fishing rivers anywhere flow out of the forested interior. The wooded highlands of the north contain one of the highest mountains in eastern Canada.

Saint John, the largest city, and Fredericton, the capital, both have intriguing Loyalist histories.

History

What is now New Brunswick was originally the land of the Micmacs, and, in the southern areas, the Maliseet (Malecite) and Passamaquoddy Native peoples.

The French first attempted settlement in the 1600s. The Acadians, as they came to be known, farmed the area around the Bay of Fundy using a system of dikes. In 1775 they were scattered by the English whose numbers rose by some 14,000 with the arrival of the Loyalists after the American Revolution. They settled the Saint John and St Croix river valleys and established Saint John. Through the 1800s, lumbering and shipbuilding boomed and by the start of the 20th century other industries, including fishing, were developed. That era of prosperity was ended by the Depression.

It has only been since the 1970s that New Brunswick has improved in infrastructure and further diversified its economy. Low costs combined with relatively inexpensive

HIGHLIGHTS

Entered Confederation: 1 July 1867
Area: 73,437 sq km
Population: 752,999
Provincial Capital: Fredericton

- Explore the Saint John River which eases its way through the province-long valley

- Hike through huge, undeveloped Mt Carleton Provincial Park

- Take a trip back in time by visiting two pioneer villages: British Loyalist King's Landing near Fredericton, and French Acadian Historic Village near Caraquet

- Be amazed by the world's highest tides along the Bay of Fundy

- Visit the Fundy Isles, a peaceful ocean retreat

- Fish for salmon in rivers such as the fabled Miramichi

- Gargle your way through a tour of the famous Moosehead Brewery in Saint John

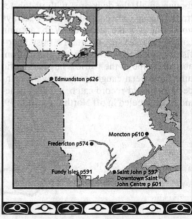

Edmundston p626

Moncton p610

Fredericton p574

Fundy Isles p591

Saint John p 597
Downtown Saint John Centre p 601

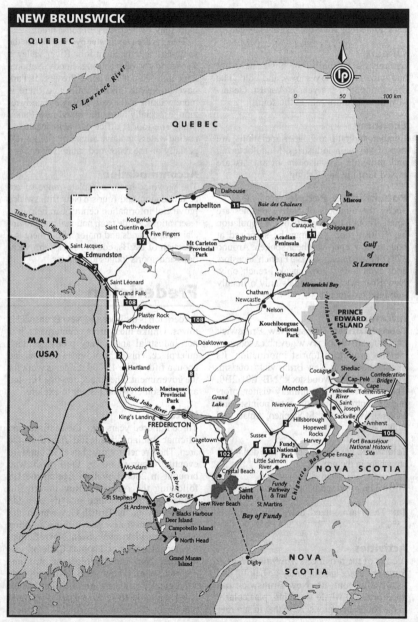

NEW BRUNSWICK

QUEBEC

QUEBEC

St Lawrence River

Île Miscou

Dalhousie

Campbellton **11**

Baie des Chaleurs

Kedgwick
Saint Quentin
Five Fingers **17**

Grande-Anse
Caraquet **11**
Shippagan

Bathurst

Acadian Peninsula

Mt Carleton Provincial Park

Tracadie

Trans Canada Highway

Saint Jacques
Edmundston **2**

Neguac

Gulf of St Lawrence

Saint Léonard

Grand Falls **108**
Plaster Rock
Perth-Andover **108**

Chatham
Newcastle
Nelson

Miramichi Bay

Northumberland Strait

Kouchibouguac National Park

PRINCE EDWARD ISLAND

MAINE (USA)

2

Hartland

Doaktown

8

Cocagne
Shediac
Cap-Pelé

Confederation Bridge
Cape Tormentine

Woodstock

Mactaquac Provincial Park

Saint John River

Grand Lake

Moncton
Petitcodiac River
Saint Joseph
Sackville
Amherst **104**

King's Landing

FREDERICTON

Riverview

Hillsborough
Hopewell Rocks
Harvey

Fort Beauséjour National Historic Site

McAdam **3**

Magaguadavic River

Gagetown **102** **7**

Sussex

1

Fundy National Park **111**

Little Salmon River

Cape Enrage

Chignecto Bay

NOVA SCOTIA

St Stephen
St Andrews

St George
Blacks Harbour
Deer Island
Campobello Island

Crystal Beach

New River Beach

Saint John

St Martins

Fundy Parkway & Trail

Bay of Fundy

Digby

NOVA SCOTIA

North Head

Grand Manan Island

0   50   100 km

and bilingual labour have resulted in winning back some jobs from the rest of Canada.

Climate

Summers are usually not blisteringly hot and winters are very snowy and cold. The driest month of the year is August. Generally, there is more rain in the south.

Economy

Lumber, and pulp and paper operations, are two of the main industries. Manufacturing and minerals are also important, as are mixed farming and fishing.

Population & People

Today the numbers of Native peoples are small. Though the majority of the population has British roots you may be surprised at how much French you hear spoken. Around 37% of the population have French ancestors and, even today, 16% speak French only. New Brunswick is Canada's only officially bilingual province.

Information

Tourist Offices Tourism New Brunswick (☎ 1-800-561-0123, www.gov.nb.ca/tourism) handles provincial tourist information. Its mailing address is New Brunswick Tourism, PO Box 12345, Woodstock, NB E0J 2B0. The province has five primary visitor information centres at strategic entry points: Saint Jacques, Woodstock, St Stephen, Aulac, and Campbellton.

Telephone For emergency service dial ☎ 911 anywhere in the province.

Time The province is on Atlantic Time.

Tax The Harmonized Sales Tax (HST) is 15%.

Activities

A copy of the province's *Adventures Left & Right* or *Craft Directory* may be helpful and lists useful contacts. New Brunswick has good bird and whale watching, particularly in the southern regions. Note that in summer booking up to a week in advance for whale tours may be necessary in some areas.

There is the Dorchester cycling loop in the south-east and the Saint John River Valley is also good for bike touring. Fundy National Park and Mount Carleton Provincial Park have numerous hiking trails and there is more walking in the eastern Bay of Fundy region, especially along the brand new Fundy Trail. The tourist office can help locate canoeing waters and give advice on fishing, especially on the renowned salmon rivers.

Accommodation

The province has a complete range of accommodation, and Tourism New Brunswick's provincial information centres can help with reservations. Aside from national and provincial campgrounds and major hotels there is a selection of B&Bs, country inns, farm vacations and sports lodges and cabins.

Fredericton

Fredericton is the queen of New Brunswick's towns. Unlike most of its counterparts, it is non-industrial and a very pretty, genteel, quiet place. This is the province's capital and about a fifth of the 45,000 residents work for the government. The small, tree-lined central area has some visible history to explore.

History

Three hundred years ago, the Maliseet and Micmac Indians lived and fished in the area. The French followed in 1732 but were eventually burned out by the British, who brought in 2000 Loyalists fleeing the US following the American Revolution. But Fredericton really came into its own the next year when the British Government decided to form a new province by splitting New Brunswick away from Nova Scotia. Lieutenant-governor Thomas Carleton visited then Ste Anne's Point and was impressed with how the village was strategically situated on the Saint John River, suitable to receive large ships and practically in the centre of the new

province. In 1785, he not only made it the province capital and base for a British Garrison but renamed it 'Frederick'stown' in honour of Sir Frederick, Duke of York and the second son of King George III.

Long ago the town produced Canada's first English-speaking poet, Loyalist Jonathan Odell. Later, Lord Beaverbrook, who was to rise to international prominence as a newspaper publisher, was born here.

Orientation

The centre of the city – or at least the part which concerns travellers – is on a small, rounded peninsula which juts into the south side of the Saint John River. The Westmorland St Bridge connects the downtown area with the north shore residential areas. From the downtown side some fine big houses and a couple of church spires are visible across the river.

Farther east along the river, the Princess Margaret Bridge, as part of the Trans Canada Hwy, links the two segments of the highway as it swings around the eastern edge of the city and over the river en route to and from Moncton. Not far beyond the bridge are the green woods and farmlands typical of the Saint John River Valley.

Coming into town from the west along the Trans Canada Hwy, take exit 292B (Regent St) which will take you straight down to the heart of town.

In town, King St and the parallel Queen St are the main streets, just a block up from the river. Northumberland and Saint John Sts are the west and east edges of the small downtown area. The park on the corner of Queen and Regent Sts, called Officers' Square, is pretty much the centre of things.

Information

Tourist Offices The Visitors Centre (☎ 506-460-2129, www.city.fredericton.nb.ca) is in City Hall at 397 Queen St. It's open Monday to Friday year-round from 8 am to 4.30 pm and until 8 pm during summer.

There's a tourist bureau (☎ 506-460-2191) on the Trans Canada Hwy near Hanwell Rd, exit 289. It's open daily from mid-May to early October, from 9 am until 8 pm June through August, lesser times thereafter.

If you're driving in, the visitors centres should be your first stop if for no other reason than they will give you a pass to park free at all municipal parking meters and carparks.

Post The post office, open Monday to Friday from 8 am to 5.15 pm, is at 570 Queen St.

Historic Walking Tour

A roughly six-square-block area of central Fredericton contains most of the city's attractions and is also the most architecturally appealing portion of the city. A walking tour around some of the following places plus other historical sites is outlined on the map of Fredericton, available at the tourist office. In a rush? Then just concentrate on The Green (a park) and Waterloo Row, where the architecture is most dynamic, and many Loyalist sites are found.

Officers' Square

This is the city's central park – on Queen St between Carleton and Regent Sts. The square was once the military parade ground and still sits among military buildings.

At 11 am and 7 pm Monday to Friday, from mid-July to the third week in August, you can see the full-uniform Changing of the Guard ceremony.

Also in the park during summer is the Outdoor Summer Theatre, which performs daily at 12.15 pm on weekdays and 2 pm weekends. This free theatre-in-the-square is performed by a local group known as the Calithumpians, whose skits of history are laced with a good dose of humour.

On Tuesday and Thursday evenings in summer at 7.30 pm, free band concerts attract crowds. There might be a marching, military or pipe band, and sometimes classical music is played too. In the park is a statue of Lord Beaverbrook, the press baron and the province's most illustrious son.

On the west side of the square are the former Officers' Barracks, built between 1839 and 1851. The older section, closest to the water, has thicker walls of masonry and

NEW BRUNSWICK

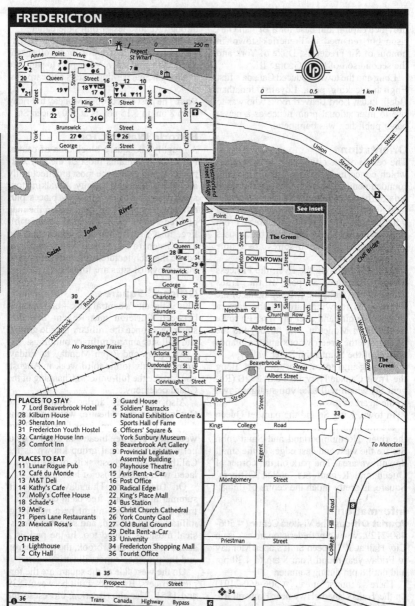

FREDERICTON

Regent St Wharf

To Newcastle

To Moncton

See Inset

DOWNTOWN

The Green

The Green

No Passenger Trains

To Edmundston & Woodstock

Trans Canada Highway Bypass

PLACES TO STAY
7 Lord Beaverbrook Hotel
28 Kilburn House
30 Sheraton Inn
31 Fredericton Youth Hostel
32 Carriage House Inn
35 Comfort Inn

PLACES TO EAT
11 Lunar Rogue Pub
12 Café du Monde
13 M&T Deli
14 Kathy's Cafe
17 Molly's Coffee House
18 Schade's
19 Mei's
21 Pipers Lane Restaurants
23 Mexicali Rosa's

OTHER
1 Lighthouse
2 City Hall

3 Guard House
4 Soldiers' Barracks
5 National Exhibition Centre &
   Sports Hall of Fame
6 Officers' Square &
   York Sunbury Museum
8 Beaverbrook Art Gallery
9 Provincial Legislative
   Assembly Building
10 Playhouse Theatre
15 Avis Rent-a-Car
16 Post Office
20 Radical Edge
22 King's Place Mall
24 Bus Station
25 Christ Church Cathedral
26 York County Gaol
29 Delta Rent-a-Car
33 University
34 Fredericton Shopping Mall
36 Tourist Office

hand-hewn timbers. The other, newer end is made of sawn timber.

York-Sunbury Historical Museum

This museum (☎ 506-455-6041) is in the old officers' quarters, a building typical of those designed by the Royal Architects during the colonial period. The museum has a collection of items from the city's past spread out in 12 rooms: military pieces used by local regiments and by British and German armies from the Boer and both World Wars; furniture from a Loyalist sitting room and Victorian bedroom; Native Indian and Acadian artefacts and archaeological finds. The highlight of the museum is a stuffed 19kg frog. It was the pet of a local innkeeper.

Opening hours 1 May to Labour Day are Monday through Saturday from 10 am to 6 pm but till 9 pm Monday and Friday. In winter it's only open Monday, Wednesday and Friday from 11 am to 3 pm. Admission is $2, less for students, and $4 for a family.

Soldiers' Barracks

On the corner of Carleton and Queen Sts in the Military Compound you can see where the common soldier lived in the 1820s and also the Guard House (dating from 1828) where the naughty ones were sent. The Guard House now contains military memorabilia. A well written, interesting history of it is available and admission is free.

School Days Museum

Also located in the Military Compound is the School Days Museum (☎ 506-459-3738) on the first floor of the Justice Building Annex. The New Brunswick Society of Retired Teachers began this classroom museum featuring desks, textbooks and teaching aids from another era. Hours are 10 am to noon and 1 to 4 pm daily during summer and admission is free.

Around the corner is Gallery Connexion (☎ 506-454-1433), a nonprofit, artist-run centre showing contemporary and experimental art. During summer the centre is open from noon to 4 pm Tuesday through Friday, and 2 to 4 pm on Sunday.

New Brunswick Legislative Assembly Building

Built in 1882, this government building (☎ 506-453-2527) stands on Queen St near Saint John St, east of Officers' Square.

When the Legislative Assembly is not in session, guides will show you around, pointing out things of particular merit, like the wooden Speaker's Chair and the spiral staircase. Hours are 9 am to 6 pm weekdays and 10 am to 5 pm weekends 1 June through 31 August with the free tours leaving every half-hour. But from 1 September through 30 May the weekday hours are 9 am to 4 pm. When the assembly is in session, visitors are welcome to listen to the proceedings.

NEW BRUNSWICK

Fredericton's Famous Frog

Move over Lord Beaverbrook. Without question, Fredericton's most beloved character is not the legendary publisher but a 19kg frog. The famous frog made its first appearance in 1885, when it literally leaped into the small boat of local innkeeper Fred Coleman while he was rowing on Killarney Lake.

At the time the frog weighed a mere 3.6kg but Coleman kept it at the inn by feeding it a steady (very steady) diet of buttermilk, cornmeal, whisky and june bugs. Little wonder it became the world's largest frog. With the leisurely life of a gourmand, this was one frog that definitely didn't want to return to being a prince.

Today the Coleman frog is forever enshrined in a glass case at the York-Sunbury Museum while in the gift shop Coleman frog T-shirts are the best selling items.

Regent St Wharf

Down at the river with an entrance off Queen St beside the Beaverbrook Hotel is the small wharf with a lighthouse and pier. The lighthouse contains a museum and the open top level affords views down the river. Admission is $2. At ground level (no admission charge) there is a snack bar and gift shop. The lighthouse is open daily in summer but it's only open on weekends from noon in the off-peak season. Boats and bikes can be rented here in season.

Beaverbrook Art Gallery

Another of Lord Beaverbrook's gifts to the town is this gallery (☎ 506-458-8545), opposite the Legislative Assembly Building on Queen St. There's a collection of British paintings including works by Gainsborough, Turner and Constable. There's also a Dali as well as Canadian and provincial works. The gallery is open weekdays from 9 am to 6 pm, weekends 10 am to 6 pm 1 June to 30 September; lesser times the rest of the year (closed Monday). Admission is $3 per adult and $6 per family.

Christ Church Cathedral

Built in 1853, this is a fine early example of the 19th century revival of decorated Gothic architecture. The cathedral is interesting because it's very compact – short for the height, yet with balance and proportion that make the interior seem both normal and spacious.

There is some good stained glass, especially around the altar, where the walls are painted above the choir. Free tours are offered daily mid-June to Labour Day. The church is just off Queen St at Church St, by the river, east of town.

Old Burial Ground

An easy walk from downtown is the Loyalist cemetery (dating from 1784) on Brunswick St on the corner of Carleton St. The Loyalists came from the 13 colonies after the American Revolution and were instrumental in settling this area. Many of the earliest Loyalists to arrive are buried here

and it's interesting to browse around the grounds, open from 8 am to 9 pm daily.

New Brunswick Sports Hall of Fame

On the corner of Carleton St at 503 Queen St in town, this building (☎ 506-453-3747) dates from 1881 and has been used as a post office, customs house and library. It now houses the New Brunswick Sports Hall of Fame with titbits about achievements of local sportspeople, ranging from NHL hockey players to jockey great Ron Turcotte. Hours for the Sports Hall of Fame during summer are 10 am to 6 pm daily, weekdays noon to 4 pm the rest of the year. There is no admission fee.

Boyce Farmers' Market

The farmer's market is on George St between Regent and Saint John Sts. It's open Saturday from 6 am to 1 pm. On Saturday there are nearly 150 stalls selling fresh fruit, vegetables, meat and cheese, and also handicrafts, home-made desserts and flowers. There is a restaurant here, too, open for breakfast and brunch.

Conserver House

Near the corner of Brunswick St, at 180 Saint John St, is this house (☎ 506-458-8747) dating from 1890, now used as a model and information centre for energy conservation. Tours and advice are free. The house is open Monday to Friday from 9 am to 5 pm.

Parks

In addition to the riverfront park and several smaller city parks, you can visit the following two. **Odell Park**, south-west of the downtown centre off Smythe St, covers 175 hectares and contains some primeval provincial forest. There are picnic tables, a kids' zoo and walking paths. **Killarney Lake Park** is about 5km from town over the Westmorland St Bridge. A spring-fed lake is used for swimming and fishing.

Tula Farm

A 20 minute drive west of Fredericton on the Trans Canada Hwy leads to the impressive

Tula sustainable agriculture education centre (☎ 506-459-1851). At the 29-acre project on Keswick Ridge overlooking the Saint John River Valley, visitors can witness ecologically sound farming practices along a self-guided interpretive trail. Wearing boots or other suitable footwear is suggested. From the Mactaquac/Keswick Ridge turn-off from the Trans Canada Hwy, cross the dam and take the first right onto Route 105. Take a second left onto McKeen Drive and look for the large 'Tula Farm' sign.

Activities

Rent a canoe for drifting along the river. In town, they're available at Fredericton Lighthouse (☎ 506-459-2515) at Regent St Wharf, which has boats for $5 an hour or $24 a day.

The Small Craft Aquatic Centre (☎ 506-460-2260) has canoes, kayaks and rowing skulls for rent. The centre also offers guided canoe tours from one hour to three-day river ecology trips and instruction in either canoeing or kayaking. Two-hour paddles depart daily during summer at 2 pm and are $25 for the first person, $20 for the second.

There are free swimming pools at Henry Park and Queen Square. There is a small admission fee to use the swimming pools at the YM-YWCA, 28 Saunders St.

Organised Tours

The first thing to do is head to the information office to pick up the excellent *Tourrific Tours* guide from the city. There are literally dozens of tours of all sorts available, free or otherwise.

Throughout July and August, a member of the Calithumpian actors' group wearing a historic costume leads a good free hour-long walking tour around town, beginning at City Hall, Monday through Friday 10 am and 2, 4, and 7 pm; weekends there is no 2 pm tour. Ultra-popular are the Haunted Hikes, given by the same, suddenly ghoulish thespians Tuesday and Thursday at 9.15 pm for $10.

To see Fredericton from the water, the *Carleton* (☎ 506-454-2628) has riverfront cruises on the Saint John River; a one hour tour costs $5. They depart weekdays at noon

and 1 pm. The tour boat is basically a houseboat and is docked at Regent St Wharf.

Special Events

Fredericton is a hotspot of the old craft of pewtersmithing. Examples can be seen any time of year at Aitkens Pewter, downtown at 81 Regent St, or you can arrange tours of the main plant there. Other craftspeople in the town do pottery and woodcarving. Some of the major events and festivals celebrated in the province between July and September are listed here.

NB Highland Games Festival
This two-day Scottish festival with music, dancing and contests is held each summer in late July.

Canadian National New Brunswick Day Canoe Race
This race is held annually in early August in the Mactaquac Headpond.

New Brunswick Summer Music Festival
Four days of classical music held at Memorial Hall at the University of New Brunswick campus in late August.

Handicraft Show
This free provincial handicraft show is held at Mactaquac Park on the weekend before Labour Day. All types of handicrafts are exhibited and sold.

The Fredericton Exhibition
This annual six-day affair starts on Labour Day. It's held at the exhibition grounds, on the corner of Smythe and Saunders Sts. The exhibition includes a farm show, a carnival, harness racing and stage shows.

Harvest Jazz & Blues Festival
This event transforms the downtown area into the 'New Orleans of the North' in early September when jazz, blues and Dixieland performers arrive from across North America.

Places to Stay

Camping The best place nearby is *Mactaquac Provincial Park* (☎ 506-363-4747), 20km west off the Trans Canada Hwy on Hwy 105, on the north side of the river. There are 334 sites and a tent site costs $14. Also within the campground is a swimming beach, grocery store and a kitchen shelter. *Lake George Family Campground* (☎ 506-366-2933), 12km south of the Trans Canada

NEW BRUNSWICK

Hwy, via Route 635 and Route 636, on Lake George, has tent sites at $15, full-hook-ups $17. The campground has a nice beach area as well as laundry facilities and a small store.

The closest campground to Fredericton is *Hartt Island Campground* (☎ *506-450-6057*) 10km west of the city on the Trans Canada. This is more like an amusement park as there are water slides, mini-golf course, batting cages, something called 'Bankshot Basketball', and, oh yeah, camp sites. Tent sites are $15, full-service sites $22 a night.

Hostels HI-affiliated *Fredericton International Hostel at Rosary Hall* (☎ *506-450-4417, 621 Churchill Row*) is set up in a capacious older residence hall oozing with character. In summer it's fully a hostel, but even in other seasons when students return the management keeps rooms open for hostellers. Beds for now are $16/18 for members/nonmembers but could rise; travellers were shocked to find that this often got them their own room on most nights. More expensive doubles or family rooms are available for $38 and sleep up to four. A private kitchen and laundry facilities are available, as are many other extras the solicitous managers keep coming up with. It's close to a 24 hour market.

You shouldn't need it then, but the *University of New Brunswick* (☎ *506-453-4891*) rents single and double rooms in the dorms, available from mid-May to mid-August. For tourists singles/doubles are $29/41, and for students the price drops to $18/30. Facilities include a pool. The campus is within walking distance of the downtown area in a south-east direction.

Hotels & Tourist Homes There isn't a vast selection of budget places in town – most are outside of the city limits – but the ones that exist are good. Cheapest in the city limits is *Kilburn House* (☎ *506-455-7078, 80 Northumberland St)*, with two rooms starting from $45.

The *Carriage House Inn* (☎ *506-452-9924, ☎ 1-800-267-6068, 230 University Ave)* is central but more expensive at $55/59

and breakfast is served in the solarium of this nice late 19th/early 20th century home.

Moving upmarket, the venerable *Lord Beaverbrook* (☎ *506-455-3371, 659 Queen St)* is relatively moderate for a place of its class at $79/89. It has 165 rooms with all the amenities used mainly by business people and government officials. Fredericton's most impressive hotel is the *Sheraton Inn* (☎ *506-457-7000, 225 Woodstock)* near Wilmont Park. Overlooking the Saint John River, this 223-room hotel often has room specials during summer for $85 a night, otherwise it's $92. The Sheraton's dining room is generally considered to be the finest in town.

Motels Motels are your cheapest option in town, an uncommon occurrence, and most of these are on the fringes of downtown.

On the west side of town on Rural Route 6, which is the Trans Canada Hwy West, there are several places. The *Roadside Motel* (☎ *506-450-2080*) is along this strip with singles/doubles at $42/45. Some rooms, however, are too close to the highway for a good night's sleep. On the east side of town across the river on Rural Route 8 (also known as Hwy 2 or the Trans Canada Hwy for Moncton) is the plain *Norfolk Motel* (☎ *506-472-3278, ☎ 1-800-686-8555)* where rooms are only $34/38. Across the river in North Fredericton *Fort Nashwaak Motel* (☎ *506-472-4411, 15 Riverside Drive)* has good views, singles/doubles for $38/48 and housekeeping units or individual cabins at $55 a double.

The *Comfort Inn* (☎ *506-453-0800, 255 Prospect St)* is one block north of the Trans Canada Hwy towards town off Regent St and rooms start at $69. There are a few places to eat within walking distance.

Places to Eat

There has been a small explosion of outdoor cafés and restaurants featuring outdoor decks in Fredericton. The best place to head for supper and fresh air is Pipers Lane, a courtyard of sorts between King and Queen Sts, west of York St. Surrounding this open area are almost a dozen restaurants, coffee shops, five pubs, ice-cream parlours, and

even a microbrewery, half of them with outdoor seating.

Also located in Pipers Lane is **Dimitri's**, good for an inexpensive Greek lunch or dinner of souvlakia, pita, brochettes, moussaka and the like. A plate of moussaka is $8.95 and you can enjoy it on the restaurant's rooftop patio.

More outdoor dining can be enjoyed at **Mexicali Rosa's** (546 King St) and at the **Lunar Rogue Pub** (625 King St), a 'maritime pub' which has British ales on tap and a nice selection of sandwiches and burgers from $4 to $6. The Rogue also features live Maritime (and other) music Thursday through Saturday and is popular on local pub crawls.

The **M&T Deli** (62 Regent St) is a small but comfortable and casual delicatessen with an interesting noticeboard. It serves all the standards, including smoked meat from Ben's, the famous deli in Montreal. Various sandwiches, salads and quiches are served at the stools for about $4.25 and up. It's not open on Sunday.

For lighter fare and good coffee, **Molly's Coffee House** (554 Queen St) has from-scratch baking and a few vegetarian options, all from under $6. For a café au lait and more substantial fare head to **Café du Monde**, a quaint little restaurant on Queen St, directly opposite Officers' Square. The restaurant adorns its walls with art and its menu with an interesting selection of salads, soups and vegetarian sandwiches and dishes. Dinners range from $9 to $14.

Mei's (73 Carleton St) is the best Chinese restaurant in the city and is even open on Sunday until 10 pm. It offers some Sichuan and even Taiwan-style dishes and has some combination plates (egg roll, fried rice and main course) for $6.50. Most full dinners cost from $11 to $14.

Schade's (536 Queen St) has German and Central European cuisine, with main courses starting at around $10. One new eatery focusing on ethnic cuisines is **Kathy's Cafe** (74 Regent Promenade), with prices slightly lower.

In the enclosed King's Place shopping mall on the corner of Brunswick and York

Sts is **Crispins** which has cheap cafeteria-style lunches.

Away from the centre near the Trans Canada Hwy, the Fredericton Mall on Prospect St West off Regent St South has **Sobey's** grocery store and a liquor outlet.

Entertainment

Sports freaks have their choice of sports bars in Fredericton, including the **Upper Deck Sports Bar** in Piper's Lane. There's cheap beer, lots of billiards and live music on the weekends. **Lunar Rogue Pub** (625 King St) presents live music on Thursday, Friday and Saturday. **Dolan's Pub** in Piper's Lane also has live Celtic music.

Fredericton's got its own craft brewery now. **Picaroon's** is in Piper's Lane and has weekday tours at 7 pm, and Saturday at 3 pm. It has its own outdoor *biergarten*.

The University of New Brunswick often has concerts and folk performers. Cheap films are also shown at the university in the **Tilley Hall Auditorium**.

Live stage performances can be enjoyed at the **Playhouse Theatre** (☎ 506-453-4697, 686 Queen St). Most performances begin at 8 pm, Tuesday through Sunday in summer.

Getting There & Away

Air Fredericton is a small city, but as the provincial capital it does get a fair bit of air traffic. Many flights in and out are stopovers between various other points. Air Canada (☎ 506-458-8561) serves the city and has one nonstop flight daily from Toronto for $553.

Bus The SMT bus station (☎ 506-458-6000) is on the corner of Regent and Brunswick Sts. Schedules and fares to some destinations include: Moncton at 11.15 am and 6 pm daily ($28.46); Campbellton and then Quebec City at 11.30 am ($31.05) as well as 2.50 and 8.15 pm via Edmundston; Halifax, the same times as Moncton ($69); and Amherst, which is also the same times as Moncton ($36). It also goes to Summerside and Charlottetown, PEI, the same times as Moncton ($57.21). West to Bangor, Maine is daily at 11.20 am ($33.25).

Car For car rentals, Avis (☎ 506-454-2847) is at 81 Regent St and has cars for $37 per day, plus 200km free, then 20¢ per kilometre. Delta (☎ 506-458-8899) at 304 King St is slightly cheaper at $36 a day with 100km free, then 14¢ per kilometre. There is also a good weekend package available.

Getting Around
To/From the Airport The airport is 16km south-east of town. A taxi to the airport costs around $20.

Bus The city has a good system, Fredericton Transit (☎ 506-454-6287), and the $1.25 fares include free transfers.

The university is a 15 minute walk from the downtown area; if you want to take the bus, take No 16S south on Regent St. It runs about every 20 minutes.

For hitching on the Trans Canada Hwy you want the Fredericton Mall bus, which is No 16S or 11S.

For heading back into the city from these places catch the No 16N.

Bicycle Rentals are available at Radical Edge (☎ 506-459-3478) at 386 Queen St; it costs $5 per hour or $20 per day. You can also rent bikes at the Regent St Wharf (☎ 506-459-2515) for $5 an hour or $25 a day and then load them on the cruise ship to be dropped along the Saint John River. There are bike paths on either side of the river that will return you to the downtown area. A one-way fare is $2, bicycles are an extra $1. The tourist office or Radical Edge can give you help on myriad trails around the area; you can pick up the multi-coloured free *Trail Guide* brochure.

AROUND FREDERICTON
Gagetown
A 45 minute drive from Fredericton is Gagetown, a charming little village located on the banks of Gagetown Creek just down from its confluence with the Saint John and Jemseg rivers. Founded shortly after the 1758 Moncton expedition drove the French settlers from the lower Saint John River Valley, Gagetown is one of the oldest English settlements in the area. Today the town is something of an artist's haven and supports almost a dozen galleries, pottery shops and **Loomcrofters**, the renowned weaving studio housed in a former British trunk house built in 1761. The studio (☎ 506-488-2400) is open during summer from 10 am to 5 pm Monday through Saturday, from 2 pm Sunday, and inside you can watch looms weaving material that is sold as tartans, scarves, stoles and ties among other items.

Gagetown also serves as the gateway to what is commonly referred to as Ferry Land. Six small ferries, all of them free, operate in the lower Saint John River system and make for an interesting tour of this rural area. One of them operates at the south end of Gagetown, crossing the Saint John River from 6 am to midnight daily.

There are some good restaurants and places to stay that make spending a day here well worth it. *Loaves & Calico* (☎ 506-488-3018) is an excellent café. Most dinners are about $9 and can only be topped by a slice of the restaurant's home-made pie. More upmarket is *Steamer's Stop Inn* (☎ 506-488-2903), a large colonial-style home overlooking the river. The seven rooms are $65 for a double and include a full breakfast. Dinners range from $15 to $22. Just south of Gagetown on Hwy 102 in Queenstown is *Broadview B&B* (☎ 506-488-2266), offering rooms on a working farm for $35/45. There is also a restaurant here with the biggest portions in the valley. The roast beef dinner, which includes home-made soup, vegetables, juice, dessert and an endless supply of hot rolls, is $11.

A great way to see Ferry Land would be by bicycle. You can rent them at Steamers Stop Inn or from Ferry Land Adventures (☎ 506-488-3263). Make sure not to confuse this historic village with Gagetown, the largest military base in the country which is located nearby in Oromocto.

Sussex
Sussex is a small country town in the middle of some pastoral and productive dairy lands. Fortunately all the local cows aren't

the size of the one seen on the outskirts of town.

On Hwy 2 at the exit into the centre is **Kings County Tourist Office** run by volunteer seniors and open from 9 am to 8 pm daily during summer. In town one of the streets, Queen St, has been somewhat remodelled and is reminiscent of earlier decades. It's off Main St opposite the VIA Rail station. Here you'll find the licensed *Broadway Cafe*, a little sanctuary from the standard small-town greasy spoons, offering good, inexpensive lunch specials in a comfortable and casual atmosphere complete with an outdoor garden terrace. It's also open for breakfast and until 9 pm Friday and Saturday. A breakfast bargain can be obtained at *Main Street Diner Cafe (600 Main St)*. It opens at 7 am and two eggs and toast is $2.20, a full breakfast with ham and home-fries $3.

In town there is *Blue Bird Motel (☎ 506-433-2557)*, across the street from the King County Tourism Office, with singles/doubles for $50/55. Just to the east on Hwy 2 is *Pine Cone Motel (☎ 506-433-3958)*, good at $45/50 and it has a campground.

The surrounding King's County has 17 appealing old wooden covered bridges often situated so prettily they look like pictures from a calendar. One, the 1908 Salmon River Bridge, is just five minutes north of the tourism office on Hwy 890. Five more are a short drive from Hwy 1 on the way to Saint John. If you have a spare afternoon, pick up the covered bridge map from the tourism office (you're going to need it) and then tour the countryside looking for a dozen or so.

Mactaquac Provincial Park

Some 22km west of Fredericton is New Brunswick's biggest provincial park (☎ 458-363-4747). It runs along the 100km-long pond formed by the Mactaquac Power Dam. The park offers swimming, fishing, picnic sites, camping and boat rentals. There's also a golf course where you can rent all equipment. The campground is huge at 300 sites but also busy and through much of the summer it will be full on the weekends. There is a $3 vehicle fee just to enter

the park while camping is $14 a night for tents and $16 for sites with electricity.

Mactaquac Power Dam

The Mactaquac Dam across the park is responsible for creating the small lake and therefore the park's location. Its 400,000 kilowatt output is the largest in the Maritime Provinces. Free tours, lasting about 45 minutes, include a look at the turbines and an explanation of how they work. The generating station (☎ 506-363-3071) is open seven days a week from 9 am to 4 pm.

Woolastock Wildlife Park

Just a few kilometres west of the Mactaquac Park, Woolastock Wildlife Park (☎ 506-363-5410) is open daily from 9 am to 9 pm. The 1200-acre park has a collection of Canadian animals, many typical of this region. That said, the concentration is on waterpark, rather than waterfowl. There are also some water slides, picnic areas and camping spots. If you camp, you get a discount on the ticket to the wildlife section. It's $17 for a tent site, $19 for electricity. Admission into the park is a steep $16 for an adult and $44 for the family; hourly rates are available.

King's Landing Historical Settlement

The settlement (☎ 506-363-5090) is 37km west of Fredericton, on the way to Woodstock. Take exit 259 off the Trans Canada Hwy. Here you can get a glimpse of (and taste) pioneer life in the Maritimes. A community of 100 costumed staff inhabits 11 houses, a school, church, store and sawmill typical of those used a century ago. The *King's Head Inn* serves traditional food and beverages.

The settlement is open all year. From July through to Labour Day in September the opening hours are from 10 am to 5 pm daily. The rest of the year, it closes an hour earlier at 5 pm. Admission is $9 per adult and $24 for a family. A good tip to consider is that the ticket for King's Landing entitles you to free entrance to the Acadian Historic Village near the town of Caraquet.

Saint Croix Waterway Recreation Area

This area of 336 sq km is south-west of Fredericton near the Maine (USA) border. The town of McAdam is pretty much the commercial centre of this little developed territory of woods and lakes. In McAdam itself, check the Canadian Pacific train station dating from 1900. It's one of the finest in Canada and was made a National Historic Site in 1983.

Some 16km from McAdam is **Spednic Provincial Park**, with rustic camping and access to some of the Chiputneticook chain of lakes. The Saint Croix River is good for whitewater canoeing. Other canoe routes connect lakes, and about 100km of hiking trails wind through the area. There's another campground at Wauklehegan.

Fundy Shore

Almost the entire southern edge of New Brunswick is presided over by the ever-present, constantly rising and falling, always impressive waters of the Bay of Fundy.

The fascinating shoreline, the resort town of St Andrews, the quiet Fundy Isles, the city of Saint John and the Fundy National Park make this easily one of the most appealing and varied regions of New Brunswick.

ST STEPHEN

Right at the US border across the river from Calais in Maine, St Stephen is a busy entry point for US visitors coming east. It's a small, old town that forms the northern link of what is known as the Quoddy Loop – a circular tour around south-eastern New Brunswick and north-western Maine around Passamaquoddy Bay. From St Stephen the loop route goes to St Andrews, St George and then goes on to Deer Island and lastly to Campobello Island which is connected by bridge to Maine. It's a popular trip taking anywhere from a day to a week, and includes some fine seaside scenery, interesting history and a number of pleasant, easy-going resort-style towns.

In St Stephen the Festival of International Cooperation is held in August with concerts, parades and street fairs.

St Stephen also has quite a reputation as a chocolate mecca due to being the home of **Ganong's** (a family chocolate business since 1873), whose products are known all around eastern Canada. Some say the chocolate bar was invented by the Ganong brothers and they are credited for developing the heart-shaped box of chocolates now seen everywhere on Valentine's Day. The old factory on the main street of town, Milltown Blvd, is just a store now with not much to see but plenty to buy ranging from boxed chocolates to bars such as Pal O'Mine, a very sweet little number. The modern factory is away from the centre towards St Andrews and is not open to visitors except during the annual Chocolate Fest which occurs in August. The Ganong's Store is open daily during summer and until 8 pm on weekdays. Plans are being tossed around for a chocolate museum complex.

Around the bay, a little north and west of St Stephen, on the border is **Salmon Falls Park**. This delightful little spot overlooks the rapids in the Saint Croix River and a fish ladder that assists spawning salmon to continue upstream. A gravel path connects the park to **Generating Station Park**, site of a former cotton mill. Both overlook Milltown Generating Station, one of the continent's oldest hydroelectric plants, operated by Power NB. Due to insurance constraints, tours are no longer given.

Nearby at 443 Milltown Blvd, 2.8km from the border-crossing, is the **Charlotte County Museum**. There are displays on shipbuilding and lumbering as well as other local industries and the town's ties to the USA. The museum (☎ 506-466-3295), an impressive mansion built in 1864, is open from 9.30 am to 4.30 pm Monday through Saturday during summer.

Near the corner of Prince William and King Sts, next to the Loyalist Burial Grounds, is a large tourist office for all of New Brunswick that is open daily until 8 pm and includes currency exchange. Head

The Tides of Funnel-Shaped Fundy

The tides of the Bay of Fundy are the highest in the world. This constant ebb and flow is a prime factor in the life of the bay, the appearance of the shoreline and even how residents set shipping and fishing schedules.

The explanation for these record tides is in the length, depth and gradual funnel shape of the bay. As the high tide builds up, the water flowing into the narrowing bay has to rise on the edges. It is pushed still higher by the shallowing sea bed. A compounding factor is called resonance. This refers to the sloshing or rocking back and forth from one end to the other of all the water in the bay as if in a giant bath tub. When this mass swell is on the way out of the bay and meets a more powerful incoming tide head on, the volume of water increases substantially.

The eastern end of the Bay of Fundy and around the Minas Basin is where the contrasts between the high and ebb tide are most pronounced with tides of 10 to 15m twice daily about 12½ hours apart. The highest tide ever recorded anywhere was 16.6m, the height of a four-storey building, at Burncoat Head near the village of Noel, Nova Scotia. Other places around the world with noteworthy (that is, over 10m high) tides are the Bristol Channel in England, the Bay of St Malo in France and Turnagain Arm in Alaska.

All tides, large and small, are caused by the rise and fall of the oceans due to the gravitational pull of the sun and the moon. Consequently, the distance of the moon and its position to the earth relative to the sun determine tidal size. When the moon is full or new the gravitational forces of the sun and moon are working in concert, not at cross purposes, and the tides at these two times of the month are higher than average. When one of these periods coincides with the time (perigee, once every 27½ days) when the moon is at its closest to earth the tides are at their most dramatic.

Throughout the centuries various methods have been used around the bay to tap the tides as an energy source. Simple but successful grist mills spurned dreams of grandiose generating stations feeding the eastern seaboard. There is still no commercial electricity production but there is an experimental and working tidal power plant which can be visited at Annapolis Royal, Nova Scotia.

The times and heights of the tides change around the bay but local schedules are available at many tourist offices in the region.

Extremely Boring

A feature related to the tides is the tidal bore, a daily occurrence in some of the rivers flowing into the Bay of Fundy, most notably the Saint John River running through Saint John, the Petitcodiac River in Moncton and the Salmon River in Truro, Nova Scotia.

As the tide advances up a narrowing bay it starts to build up on itself, forming a wave. The height of this oncoming rush can vary from just a few centimetres to about 1m. The power behind it forces the water up what is normally a river draining to the sea. This wave flowing upstream is called a tidal bore.

The size and height of the bore is determined by the tide, itself regulated by the moon. In the areas where the bore can be most interesting it is not difficult to get hold of a bore schedule. As with the tides, there are two bores a day, roughly 12 hours apart. While this is an interesting occurrence, especially in theory, the bores are not often overwhelming experiences to observe.

NEW BRUNSWICK

straight up King St towards Fredericton for 8km and you'll come to Maxwell's Crossing, where you'll find a good covered bridge; get specific directions (and a map) from the tourist office.

Along King St towards the turn-off for Fredericton or St Andrews you pass a number of motels. The *Busy Bee Motel and Cabins* (☎ 506-466-2938) is the least expensive with some rooms for $30.

For a place to eat on King St try the non-smoking *McNay's White House* where breakfasts of two eggs, home-fries, toast and coffee are $3 and large subs are under $5. The Ganong store complex has a couple of restaurants, including the meat-and-potatoes *St Jerome Grille*, specialising in barbecue chicken and ribs.

ST ANDREWS-BY-THE-SEA

As its name suggests, this is a summer resort of some tradition and gentility. Together with a fine climate and picturesque beauty, St Andrews has a long, charming and often visible history – it's one of the oldest towns in the province and for a long period was on equal terms with Saint John.

History

The original group of Native Indians were the Passamaquoddies, very few of whom still live in the area.

White settlement began in 1783 after the American Revolution. Many British pioneers, wanting to remain loyal, deserted their new towns and set up home in the British territory around the fort in Castine, Maine.

The new British-American border was changed and these people once again found themselves on American soil. The tip of the bay across the water was scouted and agreed upon as being a place of equal beauty. So the pioneers loaded up ships and headed out, some even dragging their houses on rafts behind them, and St Andrews was founded in 1784.

Prosperity came first with shipbuilding and, when that was dying, continued with tourism. Oceanic research is now also a prominent industry. In the early part of the century, the Canadian Pacific Railway owned and ran the Algonquin Hotel, which more or less started St Andrews as a retreat. Soon moneyed Canadians and US citizens were building luxurious summer cottages alongside the 19th century mansions of the lumber and shipbuilding barons. Nearly 100 of the beautiful houses first built or brought here from Maine are still used and maintained in excellent condition.

Orientation & Information

Water St, the main street, is lined with restaurants, souvenir and craft shops and some places to stay. King St is the main cross-street; one block from Water St, Queen St is also important. There is an information office (☎ 506-466-4858) near the junction of Hwys 1 and 127 that is open from 10 am to 6 pm daily in summer. A second centre (☎ 506-529-3556, stachamb@nbnet.nb.ca) is in town at 89 Reed Ave, next to the arena, and is open daily from 8 am to 8 pm.

Walking Tour

There are more than 200 houses over a century old in town, many marked with plaques. Pick up the walking guide from the tourist office – it includes a map and brief description of 34 particularly interesting places.

Heritage Discovery Tours (☎ 506-529-4011) provides historical walking or van-assisted tours daily at 10 am from the Algonquin Resort and 2 pm from the Market Wharf; the cost is $15 per person plus $2 if a van is used. A family rate is $40, $5 for a van.

Algonquin Hotel

Also worth a look is the classic 1899 resort hotel with its veranda, gardens, tennis courts and pool. Inside, off the lobby, are a couple of places for a drink, be it tea or gin.

Opposite the hotel you may want to take a peek at the English-style thatched-roof cottage called Pansy Patch with its surrounding garden. Sometimes called 'the most photographed house in New Brunswick', Pansy Patch (☎ 506-529-3834, ☎ 1-888-726-7972) is now a rather high-priced B&B with rooms that begin at $105.

Kingsbrae Garden

Opened in 1998, this site (☎ 506-529-3335) displays some 2000 varieties of trees, shrubs, and plants over its 27 acres with a cedar maze, ponds and streams, a functional windmill, and a woodland trail devoted to New Brunswick trees. The gardens will change annually. The site also has a café. It's open from 9 am to 8 pm mid-May through October. Admission is $6, less for children and seniors.

Blockhouse Historic Site

The restored wooden guardhouse (☎ 506-529-4270) is the only one left of several that were built here for protection in the War of 1812 and it almost didn't survive the 20th century. In 1993 arsonists set fire to the historical structure, resulting in the floors and ceiling being rebuilt out of white pine. The original hand-hewn walls survived and are the darker timber inside. The blockhouse is open daily during summer. Admission is free, and there are some good views through the gun holes on the 2nd floor. The park is at the north-west end of Water St. If the tide is out, there is a path that extends from the blockhouse out across the tidal flats.

Huntsman Aquarium Museum

Out past the Blockhouse and then the Fisheries & Oceans Biological Station is the Huntsman Marine Science Centre (☎ 506-529-1202) with research facilities and labs. It's part of the Federal Fisheries Research Centre – St Andrews' most important business. Some of Canada's leading marine biologists work here.

The Huntsman lab also maintains its Aquarium Museum that features displays of most specimens found in local waters, including seals. There is a good seaweed display and one pool where the various creatures can be touched, even picked up, which is great for kids. The high point of the day at the museum is feeding of the centre's harbour seals in a large tank, usually done at 11 am and 4 pm. The centre, west of town on Brandy Cove Rd, is open daily from 10 am to 4.30 pm May to October and until 6 pm in July and August; Monday and Tuesday in

September and October it opens at noon. Admission is $4.50 for adults, $3 for children.

Ross Memorial Museum

The Ross Memorial Museum (☎ 506-529-1824) is in a neoclassical house of some size on the corner of King and Montague Sts, downtown. It features the furniture, metal objects and decorative arts collections of its former owners, Mr and Mrs Ross, who lived in the house until 1945. It's open from 10 am to 4.30 pm Monday through Saturday in summer, but closed Monday in the off-season. Admission is by donation.

Sheriff Andrew House

On the corner of King and Queen Sts is this restored middle-class home (☎ 506-529-5080) dating from 1820 and now redecorated in period style and attended by costumed guides. The back garden is also typical of this past era. It's open from 9.30 am to 4.30 pm daily, except on Sunday when hours are 1 to 4.30 pm. Admission is free.

Sunbury Shores Arts & Nature Centre

This is a nonprofit educational and cultural centre (☎ 506-529-3386) offering instruction in painting, weaving, pottery and other crafts in summer, as well as natural science courses. Various changing exhibits run through summer. It is based in Centennial House, an old general store at 139 Water St. Hours are 9 am to 5 pm daily May to September, weekdays the same hours and Saturday noon to 5 pm the rest of the year.

The centre also maintains a nearby conservation area with a walking trail, located off Water St past the Blockhouse.

Science-by-the-Sea Kiosk

This roadside exhibit showcases the scientific and historical wealth of the St Andrews area and directs you to local points of interest. It's located at Indian Point, not far from Passamaquoddy Park, and includes a telescope from which you can view much of the bay including Minister's Island.

NEW BRUNSWICK

Minister's Island Historic Site

Minister's Island was bought and used as a summer retreat by William Cornelius van Horne, builder of the Canadian Pacific Railway across the country and the company's first president and later chairman of the board. The island, his cottage of 50 rooms and the unusual bathhouse with its tidal swimming pool can now be visited.

Minister's Island is accessible at low tide, even by car, when you can drive on the hard-packed sea floor. A few hours later this route is under 3m of water. You can only visit the island on a guided tour through Friends of Minister's Island (☎ 506-529-5081). The two-hour tours are offered once or twice a day, depending on the tides, and the times are listed in the tourism office. Meet at the end of Bar Rd, off Hwy 127 to Saint John, where a guide then leads the caravan across the tidal flats. The cost is $5 per adult, half-price for children, and you have to have your own vehicle.

Atlantic Salmon Conservation Centre

North of town about 6km, in the village of Chamcook, the Salmon Centre (☎ 506-529-4581) tells the story of Atlantic salmon, prized by anglers and gourmets. Displays, including live fish, show the fish's history and life cycle. In recent years many additions have been opened – there's now a conservation hall of fame, waterfalls and streams right in the complex, multimedia rooms, and bucolic trails outside. The centre is open daily from 10 am to 6 pm May to September and admission is $4.50, less for children.

Dochet's Island

In the Saint Croix River, 8km from town on Hwy 127, is Dochet's Island with a National Historic Site marking the place where in 1604 French explorer Samuel de Champlain spent his first winter in North America. The island itself is inaccessible without a boat, but looking at it from the shore makes an excuse for a good, quick sunset drive. There is also a plaque on the Maine shoreline across from the island.

Organised Tours

Whale Watching Two companies run whale-watching trips from the town wharf. Because the waters best for whale watching are farther out in the bay, it's better to take this tour from either Deer Island or Campobello if you happen to be visiting those places, where you'll spend more time actually watching the whales. In St Andrews, Fundy Tide Runners (☎ 506-529-4481) uses a 24-foot Zodiac boat to zip you around on the bay. A pair of two-hour tours are offered daily and the cost is $43 per person. Quoddy Link Marine (☎ 506-529-2600) has a more conventional catamaran and charges $43 for its three hour tour.

Harbour Tours The tallship *Cory* (☎ 506-529-8116) sails about Passamaquoddy Bay three times daily. Tours cost $49 adults, less for seniors and children. Dutch, French, and German are spoken.

Kayaking Eastern Outdoor Tours (☎ 506-529-4662) is a St Andrews-based outfitter that offers a variety of paddle trips, including three-hour ($29) and full-day kayak tours ($65). It also has rentals of kayaks, canoes, and mountain bikes, the latter going for $25 per day.

Places to Stay

St Andrews has plentiful accommodation with quite a range in type and price including many guesthouses and B&Bs. Motels can be found on Reed Ave and Mowat Drive.

Camping At the far east end of town on Indian Point is *Passamaquoddy Park* (☎560-529-3439) run by the Kiwanis Club, for tents and trailers. A tent site is $16 a night, electricity $20.

Near St Andrews are two provincial parks with beaches. *Oak Bay* (☎ 506-466-4999) is 8km east of St Stephen, north of St Andrews. There is a protected bay where the water warms up nicely for ocean swimming and an interesting shoreline to explore at low tide. There is also *Island View Camping* (☎ 506-529-3787), on Hwy 127 from St Stephen,

where tent sites have a nice overview of the St Croix River. Both parks are $15 a night for a tent, $19 for electricity.

Tourist Home One could call it a Victorian tourist home with a hostel complex; even the proprietor dubs it 'Chateau Alternatato'. The *Salty Towers (☎ 506-529-4585, 340 Water St)* is unlike anything in St Andrews, if not Canada. Run by a local naturalist, it's a sprawling 1840s structure turned into an offbeat, very casual place for wanderers to call home – you'll also find local students on the premises. The 16 rooms – of every conceivable size and fashion, so take a look at lots – start at $28 and include three doubles with private bath and two efficiencies also with private kitchen (both $54). This is not for those looking for gingerbread Victorian quaint.

B&Bs & Hotels The central *Heritage Guesthouse (☎ 506-529-3875, 100 Queen St)* is a modest but very appealing place that has been serving guests for many years. It is about average at $50. Breakfasts are offered. Slightly higher is *A Seascape B&B (☎ 506-529-3872, 190 Parr St)* in an 1860s Cape Cod home.

The *Shiretown Inn (☎ 506-529-8877, 218 Water St)*, run by Best Western, has been a hotel since 1881 and now is a blend of the old with modern conveniences and a dining room. It's right in the middle of town and is a little pricier with singles/doubles from $55/68.

The classic Canadian Pacific-run *Algonquin Resort Hotel (☎ 506-529-8823, ☎ 1-800-441-1414)* has rooms that start at $125 (you pay for the charm and the amenities). A walk through the lobby or maybe a drink on the porch will give nonguests a sense of the atmosphere. Actually exceeding this posh place is the *Kingsbrae Arms Relais & Chateau (☎ 506-529-1897, 219 Kings St)*, Canada's first inn to nail down a five-star rating. In summer rooms *start* at $200 – $300 for a suite – but all reports have been glowing.

The more affordable motels lie on the edge of town. Practically next door to each other are *Blue Moon Motel (☎ 506-529-3245)* and *Greenside Motel (☎ 506-529-3039)* on Hwy 127 East (also known as Mowat Dr). Both have singles/doubles for $45/55.

Places to Eat

Market Square downtown hosts a Thursday morning *farmer's market*. For cheap eats, the *Waterfront Takeout (cnr King & Water Sts)* has fish and chips from $5.50 and sandwiches from $3.50.

Right in the middle of town with a pleasant patio overlooking the boats in the harbour, the *Smuggler's Wharf* has a bit of everything but a lot of seafood. The stuffed sole ($9.95) is worth trying.

For a burger and a dose of Elvis, there's *Chef Cafe (180 Water St)* with its 1950s décor and classic jukebox. The place is open 24 hours during summer and the big selection of hamburgers starts at $6.

Not far away is the cheery *Sunrise Bistro (153 Water St)* with healthy mains including pastas; best of all are the late opening hours. Breakfasts are copious. Sandwiches start at $4 and mains are around $8.

Perhaps the best meals are at the cosy *L'Europe*, a German-style white stucco place on King St which is open for dinner only and prices start at $17. Lobster is the main dish at the *Lighthouse Restaurant* and at lunch you can enjoy a grilled lobster and cheese sandwich for $7.50. Dinners start at $10.

Getting There & Around

SMT Bus Lines connects St Andrews and the surrounding area to Saint John with one bus trip daily. The bus departs HMS Transportation at 260 Water St at 4.10 pm for the 1½ hour trip to Saint John. It goes the other way toward Maine daily at 2.35 pm. A one-way ticket is $14.

HMS Transportation (☎ 506-529-3101) also rents cars.

ST GEORGE

St George, 40km east of St Stephen on the Magaguadavic River, is a small town with 1500 residents. The river gorge and falls between the highway and the centre of town

Whale Watching Galore

Whales, the great mammals of the depths, first rediscovered by nonhunters in California then later up the coast in British Columbia, have now become major attractions around Atlantic Canada. Tours out to sea to photograph the awesome creatures depart from ports in places ranging from Quebec's Gulf of St Lawrence to Newfoundland's east coast. From most accounts, the trips are generally successful and well worth the uniformly reasonable cost, averaging $30 to $40 for a couple of hours.

Some of the best areas for such a trip are around the Bay of Fundy islands in New Brunswick or from the tip of Digby Neck in Nova Scotia. Also in Nova Scotia, the north shore of Cape Breton up around the national park is good. Over in Newfoundland, Notre Dame Bay is 'fruitful', with some tours based out of Twillingate. Whales can even be seen up and down the coast out of St John's from where more tours originate.

In the St Lawrence River, Quebec, boat tours operate in the Saguenay River area. Although finback (one of the world's largest at 20m), minke (8m) and the huge blue whale are seen here, the principal species is the beluga, whose numbers, although precarious, have stabilised at about 600 whales. Regulations now suggest that no boat approach belugas too closely as these whales have enough problems to deal with.

Around the Grand Manan region the most commonly seen whales are the fin (or finback), the humpback (12m), the right (12m, and less commonly seen), and the minke. In addition porpoises and dolphins are plentiful. In this area the best whale watching begins in early August and lasts until September.

From Westport at the tip of Digby Neck the season seems to begin a little earlier with good sightings reported in late June, although by mid-July there are good numbers of all species.

The humpback, one of the larger whales of the east coast, is the one to put on the best show, breaching and diving with tail clearly visible above the surface.

Up around Cape Breton and in Newfoundland the smaller pilot or pothead whales, also sometimes known as blackwhales, are common and they're sometimes even seen from shore. Finbacks frequent these waters as well. Operators in these regions run trips in July and August.

Regardless of the weather or time of year take plenty of clothing, perhaps something for seasickness, and lots of film.

Research continues to determine if whale watching itself is detrimental to the always vulnerable whale populations.

make a local beauty spot where salmon can be seen jumping a ladder in summer.

St George is known for its granite and its water. They began mining granite from the gorge in 1872 and created a thriving industry that lasted more than 60 years. Black granite and 'St George Red' were the most sought after blocks and today there is St George granite found in the Parliament Buildings of Ottawa and the American Museum of History in New York City.

The town water, from deep artesian wells, is also said to be the best in the country. You can see the granite and sample the water at a monument in the centre of town next to the post office. One of the buildings located along the Magaguadavic River also serves as the town's tourist office.

Organised Tours

All local tour operators are found adjacent to the tourist office on Route 770, along

NEW BRUNSWICK

Whale Watching Galore

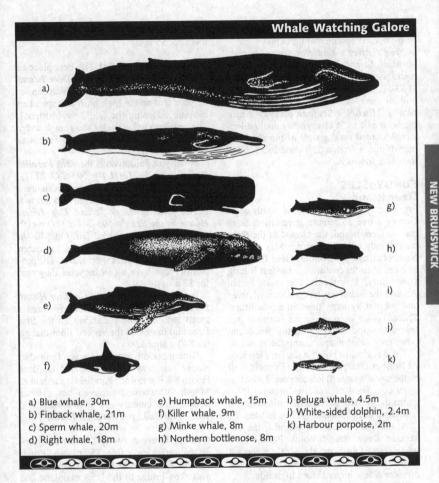

a) Blue whale, 30m
b) Finback whale, 21m
c) Sperm whale, 20m
d) Right whale, 18m
e) Humpback whale, 15m
f) Killer whale, 9m
g) Minke whale, 8m
h) Northern bottlenose, 8m
i) Beluga whale, 4.5m
j) White-sided dolphin, 2.4m
k) Harbour porpoise, 2m

the Magaguadavic River. The Outdoor Adventure Company (☎ 506-755-6415, ☎ 1-800-667-2010) specialises in a wildlife kayak tour ($49, up to four hours) but offers canoeing, biking, and lobster bakes as well; it works in concert with the Granite Town Hotel. Piskahegan River Company (☎ 506-755-6269, ☎ 1-800-640-8944) has kayak and canoe tours starting at $59 for a half-day. Two-hour pontoon boat tours are offered by Natural Canal River Cruises

(☎ 506-755-0920); they cost $18, less for children.

Places to Stay & Eat

The most popular place to stay in town is *Granite Town Hotel* (☎ 506-755-6415), a nice hotel but a bit pricey at $69/79. About 15 minutes west of town is the *Fundy Lodge Motel* (☎ 506-755-2963). It has a pretty location on the water; the rooms are entirely lined with pine, inside and out. It's not really

cheap either at $66 a double but includes a help-yourself continental breakfast.

Fred's River's End Restaurant is right on Main St and features the usual dinner menu with a lot of seafood. Breakfasts start at $3.50, sandwiches and hamburgers at $3 and dinners at $11. If you're camping nearby, *Mitchell's Seafood* on Hwy 1 near the west exit to St George has cooked lobster. Mounted on the wall of the shed is a pair of claws from a 25-pound lobster that look like footballs.

FUNDY ISLES
Deer Island

From Letete on the mainland south of St George a free 25 minute government ferry runs to Deer Island, the closest of the three main Fundy Isles. Ferries run May through November every half-hour. Deer Island is, as it has been for centuries, a modest fishing community. Lobster is the main catch. Around the island are half a dozen wharves and the net systems used in aquaculture. There is not a lot to see on the island as it is primarily wooded and residential. Roads run down each side towards Campobello Island.

There is a tourist booth at the ferry landing. At **Northern Harbour** is a huge (it could well be the world's largest) lobster pound which at times contains 400kg of live lobster. All together the lobster pounds on the islands could hold three million pounds of live lobster.

At the other end of the island is the 16-hectare **Deer Island Point Park** where whales and Old Sow, the world's second largest natural tidal whirlpool, can be seen offshore a few hours before high tide.

Deer Island has been proposed as the location for a new West Isles Nature and Marine Park, but any movement on this appears years away.

Whale-Watching Tours Whale watching is good here, given the island's location. Cline Marine Charters (☎ 506-747-0144), departing from Richardson on Deer Island, offers whale-watching tours at 9.30 am and 12.15 and 3.15 pm daily. The three-hour tours cost $40 per person. From Lord's

Cove Lambert's (☎ 506-747-2426) has tours for $5 less.

Places to Stay & Eat The best place to spend a night on the island is *Deer Island Point Park* (☎ 506-747-2423). You can set up your tent on the high bluff and spend an evening watching the Old Sow whirlpool. The campground includes showers, laundry facilities and even a small store. Tent sites are $13 a night.

Nearby in Fairhaven is the *45th Parallel Restaurant & Motel* (☎ 506-747-2231), which has singles for $40 and a restaurant that opens at 11 am. Fairhaven also has two B&Bs and the *Deer Island Log Guest House by the Sea* (☎ 506-747-2221) which is a fine place and priced fairly at $40/48. The accommodation is a quaint log cabin and includes continental breakfast. The proprietors also have a few bicycles they rent for $8 a day.

In Lambert's Cove is the *Gardner House B&B* (☎ 506-747-2462) which features a small but charming restaurant on the first floor and rooms on the second floor that go for $40 a single.

Dining options are pretty much limited to places one stays in, especially Gardner House B&B and 45th Parallel Restaurant & Motel. Otherwise Fairhaven has a diner housed in a century old schoolhouse and you'll find a takeaway place at Lord's Cove.

Getting There & Away Two privately operated ferries leave from Deer Island Point: one for Campobello Island which is connected by bridge to the USA mainland and one to Eastport, Maine.

The ferry to Campobello costs $13 to $18 for a car and driver and $2 per passenger. It's basically a floating dock strapped to an old fishing boat. It's a very scenic 45 minute trip past numerous islands and Eastport, an attractive seaside town where you may see freighters moored. During summer there are seven trips a day between 9.15 am and 7 pm.

For Eastport the ferry leaves every hour on the hour and is $10 for car and driver, $2 for each passenger. Either ferry can be used

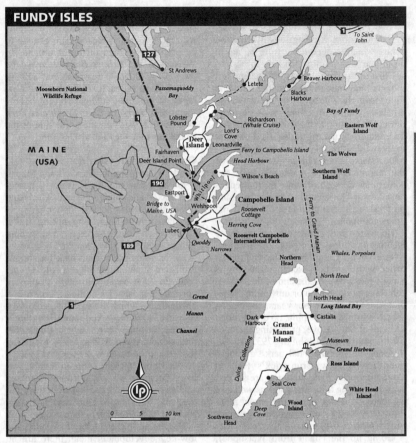

FUNDY ISLES

To Saint John

St Andrews

Moosehorn National Wildlife Refuge

Passamaquoddy Bay

Letete

Beaver Harbour

Blacks Harbour

Bay of Fundy

Lobster Pound

Richardson (Whale Cruise)

Eastern Wolf Island

Lord's Cove

MAINE (USA)

Deer Island

Leonardville

Ferry to Campobello Island

The Wolves

Fairhaven

Deer Island Point

Head Harbour

Southern Wolf Island

Wilson's Beach

Eastport

Welshpool

Campobello Island

Roosevelt Cottage

Bridge to Maine, USA

Lubec

Herring Cove

Roosevelt Campobello International Park

Ferry to Grand Manan

Whales, Porpoises

Quoddy Narrows

Northern Head

North Head

Grand

Manan

Channel

North Head

Long Island Bay

Dark Harbour

Castalia

Grand Manan Island

Dulce Collecting

Museum

Grand Harbour

Ross Island

Seal Cove

Wood Island

White Head Island

Deep Cove

Southwest Head

0   5   10 km

NEW BRUNSWICK

as part of the circular Quoddy Loop tour around Passamaquoddy Bay through both Canada and the USA.

Campobello Island

Campobello is a gently scenic, tranquil island that has long been enjoyed by the wealthy as a summer retreat. Due to its accessibility and proximity to New England, the island has always felt as much a part of the USA as it does a part of Canada. Like many moneyed families, the Roosevelts

bought property in this peaceful coastal area at the end of the 1800s and it is for this that the island is best known. Today you can see the 34-room 'cottage' where Franklin D Roosevelt grew up (between 1905 and 1921) and which he visited periodically throughout his time as US president (1933-45).

The ferry from Deer Island arrives at Welshpool, which is halfway up the 16km-long island. The southern half is almost all park and the southernmost region of this green area is taken up by the 1200-hectare

Roosevelt Campobello International Park
(☎ 506-752-2922). This is the site of Roosevelt house and a reception-information centre which is open daily from 10 am to 6 pm late May to mid-October.

Most of the park, however, has been left in its natural state to preserve the flora and fauna which Roosevelt appreciated so much. A couple of gravel roads meander through it leading to the shoreline, beaches and numerous nature trails. It's a surprisingly wild, little-visited area of Campobello Island. Deer and coyote are among the mammals in the park, and seals can sometimes be seen offshore on the ledges near Lower Duck Pond. Among the many birds along the shoreline are eagles, ospreys and loons.

Below the park at the southern tip of the island, a bridge connects with Lubec, Maine. On the Campobello side is a tourist office with currency exchange. Nearby is Snug Cove where, at the end of the American Revolution, the notorious traitor Benedict Arnold lived for four years. His wife, a socialite from Philadelphia, no doubt found life dull at Snug Cove, prompting the couple to move to Saint John in 1793.

Along the international park's northern boundary is New Brunswick's **Herring Cove Provincial Park**. Here too are several seaside walking trails and paths as well as a campground and a picnic area on an arching 1.6km-long beach. It makes a fine, picturesque place for lunch.

Going up the island from Welshpool, **Wilson's Beach** has a large pier where fish can be bought, and a sardine-processing plant with an adjacent store. There are various services and shops here in the island's biggest community.

Head Harbour with its lighthouse at the northern tip of the island is the second busiest visitor spot. Whales can often be seen from here and many people put in some time sitting on the rocky shoreline with a pair of binoculars enjoying the sea breezes.

Campobello Whale Watch Company (☎ 506-752-2359) in Welshpool has two-hour tours for $32 per person.

Places to Stay There are a few places to stay in Welshpool as well as some cabins for rent at Wilson's Beach. Things tend to be pricier here than on the mainland. In Welshpool, the *Friar's Bay Motor Lodge* (☎ *506-752-2056*) is reasonable at $30/39.

In Wilson's Beach, *Pollock Cove Cottages* (☎ *506-752-2300*) has 10 cabins starting at $60. *Herring Cove Provincial Park* (☎ *506-752-7010*) on the north side of the island has tent sites for $14 a night.

Grand Manan Island

South of Campobello Island, Grand Manan is the largest of the Fundy Isles – a peaceful, relaxed and engaging island. The island offers spectacular coastal topography, excellent birdwatching, fine hiking trails, sandy beaches and a series of small fishing villages along its 30km length.

On one side are ancient rock formations estimated to be billions of years old. On the other side, due to an underwater volcano, are volcanic deposits 16 million years old, a phenomenon which draws many geologists.

In 1831, James Audubon first documented the many birds which frequented the island. About 312 species, including puffins and Arctic terns, live or pass by each year, so birdwatchers come in numbers as well. Offshore it's not uncommon to see whales feeding on the abundant herring and mackerel. Whale species include the humpback, finback (rorqual), minke and pothead.

Despite all this, the relative isolation and low-key development mean there are no crowds and little obvious commercialisation, making it a good place for cyclists. It is small enough to do as a daytrip with your own bike; they can also be rented on the island, if you wish to leave your car off-island.

One thing of possible interest to sample on the island is the dulce – alternately dulse – an edible seaweed, for which Grand Manan Island is renowned. It's a very popular snack food around the Maritime provinces and most of it (and the best, say connoisseurs) comes from this island. Dulce is sold around the island mostly from people's homes. Watch for signs.

North Head The ferry terminal is at North Head. There are more business establishments in this village than elsewhere on the island but it is still small enough to walk through.

There are a few craft and tourist-oriented stores along the main drag but of most interest is the **Whale & Sea Bird Research Station** (☎ 506-662-3804) open daily from 10 am to 4 pm June through September, with a lot of good information on the marine life of the surrounding waters. Exhibits include skeletons and photographs and there are some books on whales and the island in general.

Sea-Land Adventures (☎ 506-662-9804) offers full-day schooner tours with a marine biologist and three-course lunch for $75 per person, half-price children under 12.

Island Coast Boat Tour (☎ 506-662-8181) also runs trips from the North Head Fisherman's Wharf, offering four-hour whale-watching tours in a 12m vessel daily at 7.30 am and 12 pm July through September. The cost is $40. A little bit different are the tours from Sea-View Adventures (☎ 506-662-3211) which offer not only whales, porpoises etc on the surface, but divers also film bottom-life for those onboard; kids can also get their hands on sealife. All for $45 per person, less for children.

North End Some of the most popular of the numerous short walking trails around the island are in this area. The 'Hole in the Wall' is an unusual rock formation. It does have trails to it, but most unfortunately pass through private land now operated as Hole in the Wall Park, also a campground. (Locals will offer up ways to circumvent private land however to get to the formation.) If you want to go through the park, a day-pass is $4.

Highly recommended is the somewhat pulse-quickening (especially in the fog) trail and suspension bridge out to the lighthouse at Swallow Tail on a narrow cliff-edged promontory. Farther up-island, the rock formations (reaching 80m high at Seven Days Work) and the lighthouse at Northern Head are also fine walks with seaside vistas. From either of the lighthouses whales may be seen, most easily on calm days when they break the surface most conspicuously.

Grand Harbour At Grand Harbour is the Grand Manan Museum (☎ 506-662-3542) which doubles as the tourist office. It's open daily from mid-June to 30 September but closed Sunday after Labour Day. Recently expanded, it has a marine section, displays on the island's geology, antiques and reminders of the Loyalist days, but the highlight is the stuffed-bird collection with examples of species seen on the island.

US writer Willa Cather worked here for many years and some of her personal belongings, including a typewriter, are still here. There is also a good book selection, including one on trails around the island. Bird checklists are available too. Admission is $4.

Dark Harbour This, the only village on the west side of the island, is the centre of the dulce industry. The seaweed is hand-picked at low tide along the shores of the island. It is then dried in the sun and is ready to eat.

Ross Island Uninhabited Ross Island can be visited at low tide. Or rather you can walk there at low tide, spend about four hours exploring the place, and then return before the tide gets too high. The island was the site of the first settlement on Grand Manan, established when Loyalists arrived from the USA in 1784.

Seal Cove In this small community is Sea Watch Tours (☎ 506-662-8552). It has been around for 25 years and knows the waters. Most of the trips are long (up to six hours), so take lunch, an antimotion sickness pill and a warm sweater. Peak whale watching begins in early August and continues through September. Tours cost $44, less for children.

Down at the docks the tasty island-smoked herring can be bought at Helshiron Sundries, a small all-purpose store. Smoked fish is also available at a couple of other places around the island. You could try MG Fisheries in Grand Harbour.

Anchorage Park in Seal Cove is good for birdwatching – wild turkeys and pheasant are common.

Southwest Head The walk to the lighthouse and beyond along the edge of the 180m cliffs here should not be missed.

Hiking The island now features more than 18 marked and maintained foot paths that cover 70km of some of the finest hiking in New Brunswick. The most extensive system of trails are found at the north end of the island and several can be linked for an overnight trek. Begin with the 10.4km Seven Days Work Trail, reached from the Long Eddy Lighthouse off Whistle Road north of the ferry terminal. This route ends at Whistle Beach where you pick up the Northwestern Coastal Trail that extends 11.6km along the west side to Money Cove. At Money Cove you can either return to North Head along the Money Cove Trail or continue south to Dark Harbour on the Dark Harbour North Trail. Such a trip would be a walk of 29km to 33km.

Note that trails may change with property decisions by landowners; know before you go. For more information obtain a copy of the brochure *Heritage Trails and Foot Paths on Grand Manan*.

Places to Stay There are over two dozen places to stay and the prices tend to be high if you want your own bathroom, even after Labour Day. They're not glitzy but are comfortable; many of the cabins have a really unpretentious country feel to them. Cheapest digs are found in Seal Cove.

The *Cross Tree Guesthouse* (☎ 506-662-8263) in Seal Cove has just three rooms and charges $30/40 or $45 for two people with two beds. Dinner is available at extra cost. Also in Seal Cove is *McLaughlin's Wharf Inn* (☎ 506-662-8760) in a distinctive old post office; rooms here are $59/69 and there's a restaurant.

North Head has the only motel, the *Surfside* (☎ 506-662-8156) with rooms from $60. You'll also find one or two pricey inns,

including the *Shorecrest Lodge* (☎ 506-662-3216) with cosy rooms from $89 in high season. There's also a dining room. The *Swallowtail Inn* (☎ 506-662-1900) is in an erstwhile lighthouse keeper's residence, with commanding views. Rooms are $65 to $100.

For camping the only place is the good *Anchorage Provincial Park* (☎ 506-662-7022), a large campground with 100 sites. Most people are tenters and, if you arrive early, there are some nice tent sites with trees edged into the woods. There is a kitchen shelter for rainy days, a playground and a long sandy beach. The park is near Seal Cove and it's $21.50 for a tent and $24 for sites with electricity. Alternately, near the ferry dock there's *Hole-in-the-Wall Park* (☎ 506-662-3152), with sites on the cliff edge ($23) or back off a bit ($20); for the acrophobic, inland sites are $17. Power hook-ups are available.

Places to Eat North Head village has the widest selection with a couple of takeout places, two or three regular restaurants and a finer dining room in the *Shorecrest Lodge*. The *Griff-Inn* is good for breakfasts and light lunches. The *North Head Bakery* is outstanding as well.

There are two more places in Grand Harbour halfway up the island, including *Fundy House Takeout* which serves pizza as well as clams and chips.

In Seal Cove the small *Clarkbury Grill*, a cheerful and casual eatery with sandwiches, burgers, beef, pasta and seafood; mains range from $5.50 to $15. It also has a grilled Cheez Whiz and cherry sandwich, purportedly a local favourite.

Getting There & Away The ferry (☎ 506-662-3724 in North Head or ☎ 506-456-3842) operated by Coastal Transport Ltd is from Blacks Harbour, south of St George on the mainland to North Head on Grand Manan Island. Actually, there are two ferries – one old and one new. The *Grand Manan V* is larger and quicker, knocking half an hour off the two hour trip. Both ferries have

snack bars, outdoor decks, and inside chairs. Seeing a whale is not uncommon.

In summer, there are six trips Monday through Saturday and five on Sunday, but there are still usually lines if you have a car, and there is no reservation system. For walk-ons, bicycles etc there is no problem. From September to the end of June the number of trips drops markedly. Actually the trip is free on the way over to Grand Manan. You just board the boat in Blacks Harbor and go. A ticket is needed to return to the mainland. There are advance-ticket sales at North Head but only for the first trip of the day; if you don't have a ticket, get there real, real early for the 7.30 am boat.

For either boat the return fare is $8.70 per adult, less for children and $26 for a car. For campervans and trailers you pay according to their length.

Getting Around Lori's Island Tour (☎ 506-662-9889) has an island tour *or* half-day guided hike; they leave Thursday and Saturday afternoons and Friday mornings. For $25 you also get Grand Manan Museum admission and a snack.

Bike and kayak rentals, kayak tours – including a sunset dinner cruise – and more are offered by Adventure High Sea Kayaking (☎ 506-662-3563) in North Head.

White Head Island
White Head Island, connected by a no-charge car ferry from Ingalls Head, is the only other inhabited island in the archipelago. A few families on the island make a living fishing. There are six to 10 20-minute ferry services daily. The island has a good long sandy beach, another lighthouse to visit and some plant and animal life not found on Grand Manan. Note that the last ferry back leaves at 4 pm on weekends, 7 pm weekdays.

Machias Seal Island
Sixteen kilometres south-west of Grand Manan is the small island bird sanctuary of Machias Seal Island. Unlike at many other sanctuaries, visitors are permitted on shore here accompanied by a wildlife officer, but the number is limited to 25 people per day. The feathered residents include terns, puffins, razorbacks and several others in lesser numbers. Sea Watch Tours (see Seal Cove earlier in this chapter) also offers trips to this island, if the seas aren't rough.

BLACKS HARBOR
The jump-off spot for Grand Manan Island is Blacks Harbor. Sardine lovers will note that this seaport is also home of Connor Brothers, one of the world's largest producers of those delectable little fish-in-a-can. Its trademark brand is Brunswick Sardines and the company runs a factory outlet store in town. Load up!

NEW RIVER PROVINCIAL PARK
Between St Stephen and Saint John, about 35km from the latter, is gorgeous New River Provincial Park. The park is noted for having the best beaches along the Fundy Shore, a wide stretch of sand, bordered on one side by the rugged coastline of Barnaby Head. The park *campground (☎ 506-755-4042)* is across the road and features 87 sites, both rustic and serviced, in a wooded setting.

You can spend your day hiking Barnaby Head along a 5km network of trails. The Chittick's Beach Trail leads you through coastal forest and past four coves, where you can check the catch in a herring weir or examine tidal pools for marine life. Extending from this loop is the 2.5km Barnaby Head Trail that hugs the shoreline most of the way and at one point puts you on the edge of a 15m cliff above the Bay of Fundy.

Camping at the park is $17.50 for tents and $21 for sites with electricity. It's $4 per vehicle to drive into the day-use area and beach or you can walk in for free.

SAINT JOHN
Historic Saint John (whose name is always spelled out in full, never abbreviated, to avoid confusion with St John's, Newfoundland) is the province's largest city and leading industrial centre. Sitting at the mouth of the Saint John River, on the bay, it is also a major year-round port.

NEW BRUNSWICK

As well as a refurbished downtown area, Saint John has a proud past. Known as the 'Loyalist City', it is the oldest incorporated city in the country. Evidence of this Loyalist background is plentiful. The town museum, dating from 1842, is Canada's oldest.

History

The Maliseet Indians were here when the British and French began squabbling about furs. Samuel de Champlain had landed in 1604, and soon a fort was built. However, the area remained pretty much a wilderness until 1755, when about 4000 British people loyal to the homeland and fleeing the revolutionary America arrived.

They built up and incorporated the city in 1785. It soon became a prosperous shipbuilding centre. Though now using iron and steel rather than wood, shipbuilding is still a major industry in town. The dry dock is one of the world's largest.

Fog very often blankets the city, particularly in the mornings. This helps to keep the area cool, even when the rest of the province is sweating it out in midsummer.

Orientation

Saint John sits on the waterfront at the mouth of the Saint John River. The downtown area, Saint John Centre, lies on a square peninsula jutting into the bay east of the river.

King Square, a small and pleasant park, marks the nucleus of town. Its pathways are placed to duplicate the pattern of the Union Jack. Streets on the east side of the park are designated that way eg King St East.

Going west from the square are the principal downtown streets – which include Charlotte, Germain, Canterbury and Prince William – running south off King St. Modern Brunswick Square, a major city shopping mall, is on the corner of King and Germain Sts. One block farther west at Water St is the Saint John Harbour. Here is the redeveloped waterfront area and Market Square with shops, restaurants and the Trade & Convention Centre. Across the street east from Market Square is City Hall.

A Touch of Tinsel in Saint John

No one will ever confuse Saint John for Hollywood, but it is uncanny how this east coast Canadian city is connected to that Tinsel Town on the US west coast. Louis B Mayer, founder of Metro-Goldwyn-Mayer (MGM) studios, immigrated to Saint John with his parents as a boy and eventually became one of Hollywood's most powerful men. His mother is buried in Saint John's Shaarie Zedek cemetery, whose chapel was donated by Mayer.

Actor Walter Pidgeon, one of Hollywood's leading men in the 1940s and known to most Baby Boomers as Grandpa in the television show *The Real McCoys*, was born here in 1898. So was Donald Sutherland, who had leading roles in such hits as *M.A.S.H.* and *JFK*.

Saint John was also the filming location of the movie *Children of a Lesser God* during the summer and autumn of 1985 and many of the residents played extra roles in it. The film starred William Hurt and Marlee Matlin, who went on to win an Oscar for Best Actress for her performance.

Provincially, the province has formed Film New Brunswick, a consortium of government agencies designed to promote film-makers from around Canada if not North America to relocate here. Given New Brunswick's francophone population, it's already become a haven for Montreal film-makers looking for a French-speaking population and, as a bonus, living in the original place of inhabitation by Acadians.

South from King Square a few blocks is Queen Square, laid out in the same fashion. The district below the square is known as the South End. On Courtenay Bay, to the east, are the dry dock and the shipbuilding yards.

West over the Harbour Bridge (25¢ toll) is Saint John West, of equal size to the downtown area but (excepting a few sites) of less interest to the visitor. Many of the street names in this section of the city are

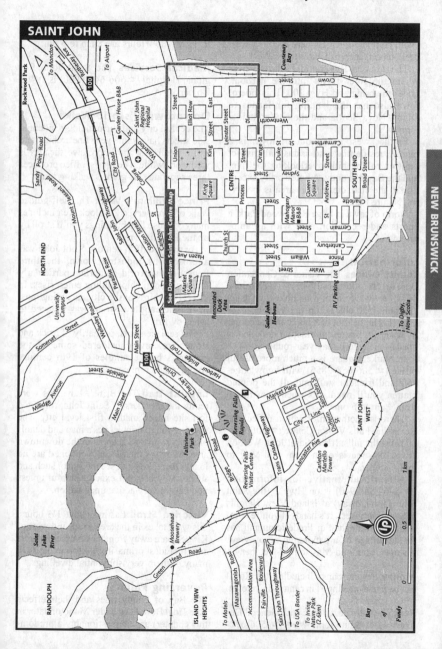

SAINT JOHN

NEW BRUNSWICK

identical to those of Saint John proper. To avoid confusion, streets here end in a west designation, such as Charlotte St West.

The famous Reversing Falls are here where the river flows into the harbour, under the bridge on Hwy 100. This side of town also has the landing for ferries to Digby, Nova Scotia and the city container terminals.

Farther west going out of town is a mostly residential and industrial district built on rolling hills overlooking the river and the Bay of Fundy. A noteworthy exception to the character of this area is the Irving Nature Park.

North of town is large Rockwood Park, a sports and recreation area with a campground.

Information

Tourist Offices The Visitor & Convention Bureau (☎ 506-658-2990, ☎ 1-888-364-4444, www.city.saint-john.nb.ca, visitsj@ city.saint-john.nb.ca), on the 11th floor of City Hall at the foot of King St on the corner of Water St, has an information desk and is open Monday to Friday year-round.

In Market Square is a much more useful office (☎ 506-658-2855) with knowledgeable and friendly staff and all the printed matter you'll need. It's open year-round from 9 am to 6 pm.

There is another information office, the Reversing Falls Visitor Centre (☎ 506-658-2937) at the falls. It's in Saint John West on Hwy 100, and is open from mid-May to mid-October.

A fourth alternative for information (☎ 506-658-2940) is on Hwy 1 (the Saint John Throughway) at Island View Heights in Saint John West. It's handy if you're coming from St Stephen or Fredericton and has the advantage of a panoramic ocean view. It's open from mid-May to mid-October.

Money Several banks including the Royal can be found on King St in central downtown.

Post The main post office with General Delivery is in Saint John West (☎ 506-672-

6704) at 41 Church Ave West, Postal Station B, E2M 4P0. Hours are 8 am to 5 pm.

Medical Services The Saint John Regional Hospital (☎ 506-648-6000) is at 400 University Ave.

Downtown Historic Walks

The central city and surrounding residential side streets have some very fine architecture and a stroll past the impressive façades is well worthwhile. The tourist office produces three separate self-guided walking tours:

Prince William's Walk This self-guided walk of a preserved 20-block area includes many of those fine buildings you'll stroll by on the Loyalist Trail.

By the mid-19th century Saint John was a prosperous industrial town, the third largest in the world, important particularly for its wooden shipbuilding enterprises. In 1877, two-thirds of the city, including most of the mercantile district, was reduced to ashes by fire.

The replacements, primarily of brick and stone, are now considered some of the country's best examples of 19th century commercial architecture.

Loyalist Trail The British Loyalists were really the founders of Saint John, turning a fort site into Canada's first legal city. The walking-tour pamphlet has a map and details of the best historical spots in the downtown area. Many of the places mentioned are no longer there; you just see the site of such and such – which is not exactly helpful unless you have a very active imagination.

Victorian Stroll Lasting about 1½ hours, this walk takes in the area south and west of King Square away from the commercial area and includes primarily Victorian houses, many of them very substantial dwellings.

Reversing Falls

The Bay of Fundy tides and their effects (see Tidal Bore Park under Moncton later in this chapter) are unquestionably a predom-

inant regional characteristic. The falls here are part of that and are one of the best known sites in the province. However, 're-versing falls' is a bit of a misnomer. When the high Bay of Fundy tides rise, the current in the river reverses, causing the water to flow upstream. When the tides go down, the water flows in the normal way.

To really see and appreciate this phe-nomenon you need to do two things – skip the touristy observation deck and free up about three or four hours. From one of the tourism centres pick up a *Reversing Falls Tide Table* brochure and then arrive about three hours after low or high tide. Pack along an easy chair, sandwiches and some of that bottled refreshment with the moose-head on it they brew just up the road. This is going to take a while.

Head to Fallsview Park, reached on the east side of the bridge, at the end of Fallsview Rd off Douglas Rd. This park puts you right above the river's narrowest gorge but, unfortunately, also right across from a pulp mill. Plug your nose. Given enough time (and enough beer), what you'll see is the river rush through in one direction, be-come calm during slack tide and then begin flowing in the other direction. Seen in its en-tirety, this is a remarkable display of na-ture's power. At high tide, this spot is a wild scene of rapids, whitewater and huge whirlpools with both waterfowl and harbour seals playing in the wicked current.

For a little more exciting look at the rapids check Reversing Falls Jet Boat Rides (☎ 506-634-8987) at Fallsview Park, near the Reversing Falls information centre. The 20 minute rides to and through the white-water depart daily. The cost of getting soaked is $20 per person but rain gear and life jackets are provided.

Loyalist House
On the corner of Union and Germain Sts, the Loyalist House (☎ 506-652-3590) dat-ing from 1810 is the city's oldest unchanged building. The Georgian-style place is now a museum depicting the Loyalist period and contains some fine carpentry. This attrac-

tion is open from 10 am to 7 pm weekdays, till 5 pm Saturday and 1 to 5 pm Sunday in July and August, 10 am to 5 pm weekdays in June and September, and by appointment through the winter. Admission is $3.

Loyalist Burial Ground
This interesting site is just off King Square, in a park-style setting in the centre of town. Here you can see tombstones dating from as early as 1784.

Chubb Building
On the corner of Prince William and Princess Sts is the Chubb Building erected in the late 1800s. Chubb, the owner, had likenesses of all his children and half the town's politicians placed on the façade in

Tea with the Mayor

Most politicians are only seen for a few weeks before the election and then disap-pear until the ballot boxes are hauled out again. Not Shirley McAlary. Upon becoming mayor of Saint John, she changed the rules forever. Every Wednesday during July and August she serves tea at the Loyalist House on Union St from 2 to 3:30 pm. Literally.

'Milk or sugar' McAlary dutifully asks a group of tourists stunned to learn that the mayor of this large city is actually there, handing them a tea cup and offering a plate of sweets. The tradition is now car-ried on in other cities of Atlantic Canada but most observers agree that McAlary has taken political tea to new heights, arriving in a period costume reflecting the 185-year history of this Loyalist home and even (gasp!) serving the tea herself. 'Sometimes I serve as many as 150 cups in an after-noon,' the mayor says.

Whether she runs again is anybody's guess but whoever takes over the office, one thing is for sure – they'll be serving tea on Wednesday. 'It would be political sui-cide if they didn't,' says one city council member, quietly sipping his tea.

little rosettes. Chubb himself is immortalised as a grinning gargoyle.

Old Courthouse
The County Court of 1829, which overlooks King Square on the corner of Sydney and King Sts, is noted for its spiralling stone staircase, rising three storeys without any support.

Old City Market
On Market St between Germain and Charlotte Sts is the colourful, interesting market which has been held here in the same building since 1876. Outside the door on Charlotte St, see the plaque outlining some of the market's history. The heavy old roof beams show shipbuilding influences in their design.

Inside, the atmosphere is friendly but busy. Apart from the fresh produce stalls, most active on weekends when local farmers come in, there are several good eating spots, a deli and some antique stores. Good bread is sold, and dulce and cooked lobster are available.

An underground walkway leads to Brunswick Square. Market hours are 7.30 am to 6 pm Monday to Thursday, until 7 pm on Friday and to 5 pm on Saturday.

Market Square
At the foot (western end) of King St is the redeveloped waterfront area known as Market Square. It offers views over the working dockyards and container terminals along the river.

In the adjacent complex is a major hotel, a convention centre, and shopping and restaurant hub. The indoor mall is actually pleasant to be in. There are about 15 restaurants in here with the better ones featuring patios along the outside wall in summer. There is also a library, art gallery, craft shop and some benches for just sitting. An enclosed walkway connects with City Hall across the street. Along the way you'll come to the Canada Games Aquatic Centre (☎ 506-658-4715), one of the nicer recreational facilities open to the public.

Barbour's General Store & Little Red Schoolhouse
This is a renovated old general store at Market Square. Inside it's packed with the kind of merchandise sold 100 years ago, including old stoves, drugs, hardware and candy. Most items are not for sale. Beside it, the Little Red Schoolhouse is a tiny museum. They're open daily from 9 am to 7 pm in midsummer, till 6 pm otherwise, mid-May to mid-October. Guided tours depart from here twice daily.

Partridge Island National/ Provincial Historic Site
Out in the bay, Partridge Island was once a quarantine station for the Irish who were arriving after fleeing the homeland's potato famine. There are the remnants of some houses and a few old gun placements on the island.

Unfortunately, tours had all been suspended and access was limited as we went to press.

City Hall
On King St near Prince William St in the modern section of town is the new City Hall. On the top floor is an observation deck with a good view (on fog-free days!) of the city and harbour. Go to the 15th floor and then climb the steps to the 16th floor where you'll find the 'deck', an unused office, open from 8.30 am to 4.30 pm Monday to Friday.

New Brunswick Museum
Relocated in 1998 to Market Square, this is an eclectic, worthy place (☎ 506-643-2300) with an odd collection of things – some interesting, some not. There's a very good section on marine wildlife, with some aquariums and information on lobsters (you may as well know about what you'll probably be eating) and an outstanding section on whales. There's a collection of stuffed animals and birds, mostly from New Brunswick. The displays on the marine history of Saint John are good, with many excellent models of old sailing ships.

The upper floor of the museum is an art gallery which includes local contemporary

work and a hands-on work area for kids. Museum hours are from 9 am to 9 pm weekdays, 10 am to 6 pm Saturday, and noon to 5 pm Sunday. Admission is $6, students $3.25, and families $13.

Carleton Martello Tower

In Saint John West, the national historic site Carleton Martello Tower (☎ 506-636-4011) is just off Lancaster Ave, which leads to the Digby ferry terminal. It's on Fundy Drive. Look for the signs at street intersections. A Martello tower is a circular two-storey stone coastal fortification. They were first built in England and Ireland at the beginning of the 19th century. In North America the British built 16 of them during the early 1800s. Inside you can explore the restored powder magazine, barracks and the upper two levels that were added during WWII for the defence of the Saint John Harbour. Guides will show you around and provide background information. Go when there's no fog because the promontory sits on one of the highest points in the city and the view is outstanding. The tower is open from 9 am

to 5 pm daily from 1 June to 30 September. Admission is $2.50, family rate $6.50.

Moosehead Brewery

Moosehead Brewery used to claim it was the country's oldest independent beer maker, dating back to 1867, the year of Confederation. Now it also bills itself as the largest Canadian-owned brewery. This is due to the 1995 purchase of Labatt by a Belgium conglomerate and the fact that Carlton & United Breweries of Australia (producers of Foster's Lager) and Miller Brewing of the USA own a hefty slice of Molson. This Oland family pride and their defiance of repeated takeover bids is felt throughout a tour of the Moosehead plant at 89 Main St West, just up the road from the Reversing Falls centre.

The tours are offered at 9.30 am and 2 pm daily mid-June through August and are free but so popular it's wise to book them a day in advance at any tourist centre or by calling the Moosehead Country Store (☎ 506-635-7000). They begin with a movie and end with beer tasting. The country store, open

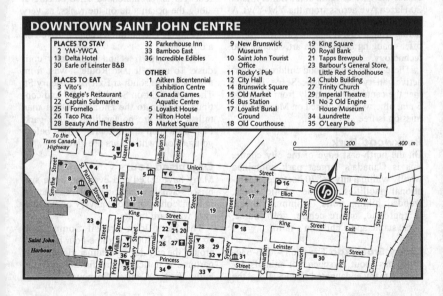

DOWNTOWN SAINT JOHN CENTRE

PLACES TO STAY
2 YM-YWCA
13 Delta Hotel
30 Earle of Leinster B&B

PLACES TO EAT
3 Vito's
6 Reggie's Restaurant
22 Captain Submarine
25 Il Fornello
26 Taco Pica
28 Beauty And The Beastro

32 Parkerhouse Inn
33 Bamboo East
36 Incredible Edibles

OTHER
1 Aitken Bicentennial Exhibition Centre
4 Canada Games Aquatic Centre
5 Loyalist House
7 Hilton Hotel
8 Market Square

9 New Brunswick Museum
10 Saint John Tourist Office
11 Rocky's Pub
12 City Hall
14 Brunswick Square
15 Old Market
16 Bus Station
17 Loyalist Burial Ground
18 Old Courthouse

19 King Square
20 Royal Bank
21 Tapps Brewpub
23 Barbour's General Store, Little Red Schoolhouse
24 Chubb Building
27 Trinity Church
29 Imperial Theatre
31 No 2 Old Engine House Museum
34 Laundrette
35 O'Leary Pub

Monday through Saturday, has great logo attire for all you mooseheads.

Telephone Pioneers' Museum

This museum (☎ 506-694-6388) in the lobby of 1 Brunswick Square is small but good. It's open Monday to Friday from 10 am to 4 pm mid-June to mid-September and is free. To find it, enter the mall off Germain St opposite Reggie's Restaurant.

No 2 Old Engine House Museum

The city's newest museum is this partially restored 1840 firehouse, located at 24 Sydney St, overlooking King Square. Inside are old alarm systems, firefighting artefacts and, most interesting, historical photos that retell the story of the Great Saint John Fire of 1877. Hours are 9.30 am to 5 pm Monday through Saturday, 1 to 5 pm Sunday in July and August, other months visits are by appointment only. Admission is free.

Aitken Bicentennial Exhibition Centre

The centre (☎ 506-633-4870), which includes the City of Saint John Gallery, is at 20 Hazen Ave across from the YM-YWCA in an attractive rounded sandstone building dating from 1904. It has six galleries which offer changing displays on art, science and technology.

There is also a very good children's interactive gallery called ScienceScape. In summer the centre is open daily from 10 am to 5 pm, otherwise it's closed on Monday. Admission is free.

Rockwood Park

On the north-east edge of the city centre, this is Canada's largest park contained wholly within a city at 870 hectares. Recreational facilities include picnic spots, wooded hiking trails, swimming areas, campground, nature centre, golf course, horse stable and a children's farm.

Cherry Brook Zoo The zoo (☎ 506-634-1440) has about 35 species of animals, including many endangered species. It's at the far northern edge of Rockwood Park in the north of the city and is open every day from 10 am to dusk. Admission costs $6, students $4.50 and families $15.

Lakewood Beach

On Route 111 south-east of town (15 minutes by car) there is swimming and a sandy beach at Lakewood Reservoir Park. Route 111 is called Loch Lomond Rd in town.

Irving Nature Park

For those with vehicles and an appreciation of nature, the park is a must (well worth the 20 minute drive south-west from the centre) for its rugged, unspoiled coastal topography. It is also a remarkable place for bird-watching, with hundreds of species regularly reported. Seals may be seen offshore, too.

Though the park is said to be on Taylors Island, this is not an island at all but rather a 245-hectare mountainous peninsula protruding into the Bay of Fundy. Four trails of varying lengths lead around beaches, cliffs, woods, mudflats, marsh and rocks. Good footwear is recommended. Also be careful along the ocean side on the rocks, as very large waves can occasionally catch the unsuspecting. The perimeter can be driven on a dirt road.

The park is free and open daily until dusk. To reach it take Route 1 west from town and turn south at Exit 107, Bleury St. Then turn right on Sand Cove Rd and continue for 2km to the entrance. Other than toilets, there are no facilities at the park. Pick up a map at the tourist office before going. Worthwhile tours are given.

Organised Tours

Many have asked and even more are surprised – whale watching is not an attraction in Saint John, save for the very occasional, very wayward minke.

The Saint John Transit Commission (☎ 506-658-4700) has three-hour bus tours around the city during summer months. Departures and tickets are from Reversing Falls Visitor Centre, Barbour's General

Store at Market Square, and Rockwood Park Campground. Two tours daily depart. At 9.30 am the bus leaves Reversing Falls, and takes 15 minutes to get to each of the other two stops. The trip is reversed from 12.30 to 1 pm. In September and October there are autumn foliage tours up the valley with lunch included. The Saint John Valley of New Brunswick is one of the best places in Canada for seeing the leaves changing colour. The cost of the bus tour is $14.

Also from Barbour's, in July and August, guided walking tours are offered around the historic portions of downtown. They are free and depart daily at 10 am and 2 pm.

Retreat Charters (☎ 506-757-0130) offers tours of the Saint John River; a two hour tour costs $30.

Special Events

Loyalist Days, an eight-day event held annually during the second week of July, celebrates the city's Loyalist background. Featured are a re-creation of the first arrival, period costumes, parades, arts and crafts, music recitals, lots of food and fireworks on the last night of the festival.

Each August the city hosts the very popular, highly regarded Festival by the Sea. For 10 days (the dates change) this performing arts event presents hundreds of singers, dancers and other performers from across Canada in concerts and shows put on throughout the city night and day. Many of the performances staged in parks and along the harbour front are free.

The Grand Ole Atlantic National Exhibition is held annually at the end of August in Exhibition Park and includes stage shows, livestock judging, harness racing and a large midway (fairground).

Places to Stay

Camping Just north of Rothesay Ave, north of the downtown area, is huge *Rockwood Park* (☎ 506-652-4050) with its small lakes, picnic area, golf course and part of the University of New Brunswick's campus. It's an excellent place to camp, with pleasant camp sites and a view of the city. It could not be

more convenient – close to the downtown area and the main roads out of the city.

The rate for tenters is $14 and $16 for those who need electricity, less for longer stays and the ticket office is also a mini-tourist centre.

Hostels HI-affiliated, the *YM-YWCA* (☎ 506-634-7720, 19-25 Hazen Ave) features single rooms that are clean but a little threadbare. (There is no dormitory.) Still you can't beat the price, $30 a night and $25 for students or those with a hostel card. Renters have full use of the facility which includes a swimming pool, a common room, an exercise room, and a snack bar with cheap food. There are 30 rooms; you get your own room key and the lobby is always open. The *University of New Brunswick* Saint John campus (☎ 506-648-5768) off Sandy Point Rd has offered $29/41 for singles/doubles in summer, $10 less if you're a student – bus No 15 gets you there from downtown.

B&Bs A short walk from King Square in a late 19th/early 20th century three-storey building there's the *Earle of Leinster B&B* (☎ 506-652-3275, 96 Leinster St) with seven rooms, all with a private bath. Rates begin at $39 and climb to $68 but include laundry facilities and a VCR with videos and popcorn. Calling ahead is a good idea as the place tends to fill up in summer.

A little farther away but still within easy walking distance of King Square is *Garden House B&B* (☎ 506-646-9093, 28 Garden St), near the Wall Street exit of Hwy 1. The 19th century Victorian home has three rooms, two with a shared bath, that are $38/48. There are laundry facilities.

Just out of the centre is *Mahogany Manor* (☎ 506-636-8000, 220 Germain St) with three rooms from $55. It's not far from Queen Square.

In Saint John West, the *Five Chimneys B&B* (☎ 506-635-1888, 238 Charlotte St West) is within walking distance of Reversing Falls and the Digby ferry, but is a minor hassle to get to by bus. It has rooms for $50/55.

NEW BRUNSWICK

Manawagonish Rd has long been an important accommodation street in Saint John. Along this road are guesthouses, B&Bs, cabins and motels charging varying but mostly reasonable prices. The hassle is that it is a long way west of the downtown area beyond Saint John West, parallel to and north of Hwys 1 and 100. City buses do come and go into town from Manawagonish Rd but even in a car it's a 20 minute trip. One place to try is the *Manawagonish B&B* (☎ 506-672-5843, 941 Manawagonish Rd) with rooms from $40/45.

Hotels & Inns There are actually few hotels in Saint John and they tend to be in the middle or upper-price brackets. The *Hotel Courtenay Bay* (☎ 506-657-3610, ☎ 1-800-563-2489, 350 Haymarket Square) with 125 rooms is central, and not badly priced with rooms ranging from $62 to $93.

A couple of historic inns are worth investigating. The *Dufferin Inn* (☎ 506-635-5968, 357 Dufferin Row) has rooms for $50 to $100 for a double, but it's more popular for its consistently outstanding dining room's fixed-price dinners. This is also not far from the Digby ferry, in Saint John West.

With a commanding if not stunning view, the *Inn on the Cove* (☎ 506-672-7799, 1371 Sand Cove Road) is west of Saint John at exit 107A of Hwy 1 (you'll need directions). Its seven rooms start at $75 – one a jacuzzi suite. This is also well known for dining, as the owners produce a television cookery show. It's adjacent to Irving Nature Park, so you can waltz right out the door and onto trails.

Motels There are many motels along Manawagonish Rd and they tend to be less expensive than average. At times other than June to September prices tend to fall even further.

Fundy Ayre Motel (☎ 506-672-1125, 1711 Manawagonish Rd) is small with only nine units, but they go for $55 a single or double with one bed. The rooms are tucked away off the road so they are quiet, and the very fine views of the Bay of Fundy and Taylors Island are a bonus.

Second choice is the *Island View* (☎ 506-672-1381, ☎ 1-888-674-6717, 1726 Manawagonish Rd) across the street. It also has kitchenettes as well as a heated swimming pool. Singles/doubles are $48/53.

Slightly closer to town is *Fairport Motel* (☎ 506-672-9700, 1360 Manawagonish Rd), which has rooms for $45/50 and a pleasant little restaurant.

On the east side of town is a strip of motels along Rothesay Ave on Hwy 100, which leads out to Moncton. It's north-east of the city centre but a little closer to it than Manawagonish Rd. Most of the places out this way are more expensive.

Places to Eat

Saint John is not as limited as it once was when it comes time to tie on the bib.

For cheap eats there's *Reggie's Restaurant* (69 Germain St), which has been around for more than a quarter of a century. Near the Loyalist House, this is a classic downtown no-nonsense diner which specialises in smoked meat from Ben's, a famous Montreal deli. Also on the menu are chowders at $3.50 or less, dinners for under $6 and most sandwiches for under $3. It opens at 6 am for breakfast when you can have Reggie's Favorite – three sausages, an egg, home fries, toast, coffee and hot mustard, for $3.40. There also are cheap eats at *Captain Submarine* along King St next to a brewpub; it doesn't compare with Reggie's but it is open 24 hours.

Incredible Edibles (42 Princess St) in the Brodie Building is a nice spot for a bit of a splurge. It offers pastas, curries, omelettes and seafood. Specialities are the local desserts such as blueberry cobbler – a tasty fruit-based dessert with a crispy cake crust, usually topped with milk or cream. Most of the fresh pasta dinners start at $10 and often there are specials for under $10 but dinner for two, however, is unlikely to be under $50.

If you're in the market to lay out that kind of bistro cash, then *Beauty and the Beastro* (cnr Charlotte St & King Square South) is among the most consistent in Canada. It's noted for lamb but it also has luscious duck,

fresh pasta, and Indian-tinged dishes. Main courses range from $12 to $20.

Not too far away is *Il Fornello (33 Canterbury)*. The Italian restaurant has a pleasant open setting where you would feel comfortable just sipping wine and watching the traffic go by. Speciality of the house is thin-crust pizza that starts at $7.50.

A longtime Italian restaurant is *Vito's (cnr Hazen Ave & Union St)*. Spaghetti dinners start at $5, or try another pasta dish like Tortelline a la Vitos – tortelline stuffed with green peppers and mushrooms for $7.75. A large pizza starts at $13.

Perhaps the best ethnic cuisine in Saint John is the fusion of Guatemalan and Mexican at *Taco Pica (96 Germain St)*, a respected cooperative restaurant. Mains range from $8 to $15; an economical introduction to the cuisine is the *pepian*, a simple but spicy beef stew that is as good as you'll find in any Guatemalan household.

The *Old City Market* is a good place to be when hunger strikes. Aside from the produce there are numerous small restaurants or takeout counters and a delightful solarium eating area along King St. The *Lord's Fish Market* is good for fish, clams and scallops with chips or huge lobster rolls. *The Pasta Place* sells plates of pasta salad, *Jeremiah's* is a deli and sandwich bar, and *Slocum & Ferris* has a good salad bar and great sausage on the grill (try the Hungarian garlic).

On the corner of the market is *Billy's Seafood Company Fish Market and Oyster Bar*. The place is both a fish market and a quaint little restaurant with a three-stool bar inside. Billy's Fish Chowder is excellent at $5.25 a bowl, while the dinners start at $11.

Market Square has a number of restaurants, four of them with pleasant outdoor patios side-by-side overlooking the beach volleyball area of the wharf. *Grannan's*, not exactly budget, has a good selection of seafood with steaks too. Dinners range from $12 to $20, and if you're hungry for lobster there's the Lobster Feast – a cup of lobster stew, bucket of clams and two lobsters for $37. *Keystone Kelly's* is less expensive and more casual with various finger foods at $9

to $13 for a meal, while big glasses of beer and even bigger television screens can be had at *Don Cherry's Grapevine Restaurant*.

The *Bamboo East (136 Princess St)* offers Chinese food. The weekday lunch buffet is $6.95 and runs from noon to 2 pm; the weekend dinner buffet is $9.95 from 5 to 8 pm.

For an exceptional evening of dining, make reservations at *Parkerhouse Inn (☎ 506-652-5054, 71 Sydney St)* near King Square, and ask for a table in the circular solarium. This stunning 1891 Victorian mansion has a fine restaurant on the 1st floor where patrons enjoy their candle-lit meals in small rooms of two or three tables. Dinners start at $16 and include such dishes as poached salmon and scallops Cinzano. Upstairs is a nine-room inn with rates that begin at $65 a night.

Entertainment

For an outdoor bar with a little bounce to it, try the *Sand & Slip*, on the wharf across from Market Square. This place overlooks the beach volleyball area where there are usually tournament games going on, however, if there isn't just ask your waiter for a volleyball and kick off the shoes.

Practically across the street in Market Square and reached from a stairway is *Rocky's Pub (59 St Patrick St)*, a sports bar with a lively clientele, daily drinks specials, reasonably priced food and 19 TV screens.

On King St between Germaine and Charlotte Sts is *Tapps Brewpub* with decent India pale ale and a *weissbier* made on the premises. It also has sandwich-style pub grub and lots of live music during the week.

Most of the action at night is around the corner of Princess and Prince William Sts. *Gargoyles* is right on the corner and has them hopping to DJ music.

O'Leary's (46 Princess) is a good old fashioned Irish pub with plenty of British and Irish brews as well as live music on Thursday, Friday and Saturday evening. On Wednesday it's open mike night. Take a stab, you could be a star.

The *Imperial Theatre (King Square)* is the new performing arts centre that opened

in 1994 after having been restored to its late 19th/early 20th century splendour. Performances range from classical music to live theatre. Call the box office hotline (☎ 506-674-4100) for both the schedule and ticket information.

Horse racing can be enjoyed every Wednesday evening and Saturday afternoon during summer at *Exhibition Park Raceway (☎ 506-633-2020)* on McAllister Drive off Hwy 100 on the east side of the city.

Getting There & Away

Air Air Canada (☎ 506-632-1500) to Montreal costs $519. Canadian (☎ 506-657-3860) flies to St John's, Newfoundland for $624, Toronto for $429.

Bus SMT Bus Lines (☎ 506-648-3500) is the provincial carrier. The station is at 300 Union St on the corner of Carmarthen St, a five minute walk from the town centre. SMT Bus Lines connects with Orleans Express lines in Rivière-du-Loup, Quebec for Quebec destinations. For cities in Nova Scotia, SMT connects with Acadian Bus Lines.

To Fredericton there are two trips daily at 9.30 am and 6.15 pm, costing $17. That same bus is used for connections for passengers carrying on to Quebec City, for which the fare is $63. The bus to Moncton leaves at 8.30 am and 3.30 pm and the fare is $23; you'll have to go here to get to Charlottetown, for which the fare would be $52 all the way through. The same schedule holds for buses to Halifax ($63).

Always ask staff at the station which bus is quicker – for farther destinations you could save yourself lots and lots of stops.

Buses also run to Moncton where VIA trains can be caught for Quebec or Nova Scotia. Combination road-and-rail tickets can be purchased at the SMT bus terminal but first you have to reserve with VIA (☎ 1-800-561-3952), then deal with the bus. To Quebec City daily, except Tuesday, the bus/train fare is around $120, depending on when you purchase the ticket.

Ferry The Bay Ferries' (☎ 506-649-7777, ☎ 1-888-249-7245) *Princess of Acadia* sails between Saint John and Digby, Nova Scotia, across the bay. Depending on where you're going, this can save a lot of driving around the Bay of Fundy through Moncton and then Amherst, Nova Scotia, but the ferry is not cheap. In comparison with the other ferry routes around the region, and for the distance covered, the price is inexplicably high.

This route is heavily used by tourists which could be one explanation. For peak season of late June through mid-September fares are $24.50 per person one way and $50 per car. Bicycles are $11.25. There is a very slightly reduced return passenger-only fare if you want to make a day cruise out of a trip there and back. Also, prices go down outside the summer season which is from the middle of June to the first week of September.

Crossing time is about three hours. In summer there are three services daily from Digby: 5 am, 1 and 8.45 pm, except for Sunday when there is no 5 am crossing. From Saint John, times are Monday through Saturday 12.45 and 9 am and 4.45 pm, no 12.45 am trip Sunday. Arrive early or call ahead for reservations, as the ferry is very busy in July and August. Even with a reservation, arrive an hour before the ferry sails or your space may be given away. Walk-ons and cyclists should be OK. There's a restaurant and a bar on board.

Car There are several choices for rentals. Delta (☎ 506-634-1125), 378 Rothesay Ave, is open seven days a week, and charges $35 (including insurance) with 200km free, then 15¢ per kilometre. There is also a weekly price of $175 with 1400km free.

Avis (☎ 506-634-7750) is located conveniently right behind the market building at 17 North Market St. For a middle-sized car, the rates are pretty much the same as the above. Ask about the weekend special which is quite good value. Drivers should note that west of the town centre, Hwy 1 crosses over the Saint John River. There's a toll bridge where you pay 25¢. Farther out

westward, connections can be made with Hwy 7 (northward) for Fredericton.

Getting Around

To/From the Airport The airport is east of town out along Hwy 111. There is an airport shuttle (☎ 506-648-0666) costing $9 that leaves approximately 1½ hours before all flights, from top hotels like the Hilton on Market Square and the Delta Brunswick on Brunswick Square. For a share taxi call Vets (☎ 506-658-2020); it should cost around $20. City bus No 22 goes to the airport, and terminates in King Square.

Bus Saint John Transit (☎ 506-658-4700) has 30 routes around the city. Major departure points for many buses are King Square in the city centre, Simms Corner at Bridge Rd, and Main in West Saint John. The bus fare is $1.45.

AROUND SAINT JOHN

North out of the city is a green rural area interspersed with deeply indented bays, rivers and islands, eventually leading to Grand Lake and Fredericton. The Saint John River flows south through here to its mouth at the Bay of Fundy and the ferries connecting roads in the area are all free. The **Kingston Peninsula**, not far from Saint John, has scenery typical of the river valley landscapes and is particularly beautiful in autumn with the leaves changing colour. **Crystal Beach** is a popular spot for camping and swimming. If you're driving to Fredericton, don't take dull Hwy 7. Go along Hwy 102, which winds along by the river through small communities.

ST MARTINS

A rather uninteresting hour drive east of Saint John will take you to the worthy destination of St Martins, one of the province's historic towns, situated on the Bay of Fundy. It's a small, pretty, out of the way place that was once the centre of the wooden shipbuilding trade. Or it was out of the way. With the opening of the Fundy Parkway/Trail, this place will be a hotspot in years to come. Expect development.

On entering the town you'll see a quintessentially Maritime, picturesque scene: **Old Pejepscot Wharf** edged with beached fishing boats waiting for the tide, two wooden covered bridges and a lighthouse. (If on the other hand, the tide is in, the boats will likely be out, working.) The **Quaco Museum** depicts the shipbuilding period. But keep going over one of the bridges and around the corner where a vast expanse of beach opens up. At the far end there are a couple of caves cut into the shoreline cliffs to explore. At the parking lot is a snack bar, right by the beach.

Places to Stay & Eat

Back in town there is the *Fundy Breeze Lodge* (☎ 506-833-4723) for spending the night or having a meal in the restaurant. Doubles are $50. There are also three more expensive inns. Camping is found just out of town at *Seaside Tent & Trailer Park* (☎ 506-833-4413), where a tent site is $16. Most lodgings have dining rooms, and in town you'll find a diner and a family restaurant.

FUNDY TRAIL PARKWAY

The cliff-edged coastal region between St Martins and Fundy National Park and inland towards Sussex is a rugged and gorgeous undeveloped section of the province which is the only remaining coastal wilderness between Florida and Labrador. Late 1998 saw the culmination of years of effort by local environmentalists, when this jewel in New Brunswick's crown was opened to the public.

Plans are to have the drivable parkway and its adjoining littoral hiking/biking trail stretch all the way to Fundy National Park, an ambitious stretch of nearly 40km. Eventually, a triangular hiking region will link St Martins, Sussex, and Alma at the edge of the national park.

Currently, the trails are open from just outside St Martin's to Big Salmon River, a lovely, lovely (and easy) stretch of 12km; no camping is allowed along here. At the time of writing, trail hacks had blazed the trail 8km beyond here. After this, you'd better be prepared for wilderness, rocky scree, and even a rope ladder or two.

NEW BRUNSWICK

At Big Salmon River is an interpretive centre with exhibits and a fascinating 10 minute video presentation. This is a good first stop for information on current progress and conditions.

FUNDY NATIONAL PARK

Fundy National Park (☎ 506-887-6000) is one of the country's most popular parks. Aside from the world's highest tides, the park on the Bay of Fundy has an extensive network of hiking trails. Irregularly eroded sandstone cliffs and the wide beach at low tide make a walk along the shore interesting. There's lots of small marine life to observe and debris to pick over.

The park is home to much wildlife, including black bears, moose, beavers and peregrine falcons. The ocean is pretty bracing here, so there is a saltwater swimming pool (not far from the eastern entrance to the park) where you can have a dip. If you are camping in the park the pool is free, otherwise admission is $3.25, less for children.

You can reach the park, 129km east of Saint John and about halfway to Moncton, by following Hwy 114. Entering from the north you first reach Wolfe Lake Centre, open daily from 10 am to 6 pm 25 June through 7 September. At the south entrance is the park's visitors centre, and it is open from 8 am to 10 pm weekdays, daily mid-June through early September, much less other times. Both have bookstores and information counters where you can purchase your motor entry permit. It's $3.50 per person for the day or $10.50 for four days; family rates are $7 for one day, $21 for four.

Hiking & Biking

The park features 104km of walking trails throughout its backcountry where it's possible to enjoy a short stroll down to the ocean or a three-day backpack. The most popular backpacking route is the Fundy Circuit, a three to four-day trek of 50km through the heart of the park. Begin at the visitors centre to reserve a series of wilderness camp sites ($2.50 per person per night; you should reserve if possible) along the

route. From there the trail begins by heading north along the Upper Salmon River.

Another overnight trek is to hike Goose River Trail, an old cart track that extends from Point Wolfe 7.9km to the mouth of the river, where there is backcountry camping. Enjoyable day hikes include Coppermine Trail, a 4.4km loop to an old mine site, as well as Third Vault Falls Trail, a challenging one-way hike of 3.7km to the park's tallest falls. Note that several of the park's trails require river fordings, so be prepared.

Mountain biking is allowed on six trails: Goose River, Marven Lake, Black Hole, Bennett Brook (partially), East Branch, and Maple Grove.

From the park, Dobson Trail, another long-distance trek, leads north to the town of Riverview near Moncton.

On a lighter note, Fundy has a popular night-time guided three hour walk with a ranger for $12, including a snack; it's great, if spooky, fun.

Kayaking

FreshAir Adventure (☎ 506-887-2249, ☎ 1-800-545-0020) based out of Alma offers myriad kayaking tours in and around Fundy. Two-hour estuary and harbour tours cost $25; bay tours cost $35. It also offers half-day, full-day and multi-day trips.

Places to Stay & Eat

The park has four campgrounds with individual sites and a fifth for groups; there are also 15 wilderness sites. Reservations can be made via the park's hotline (☎ 1-800-213-7275). In the interior are *Chignecto* with serviced sites ($16 to $18) and tent sites ($11) and *Wolfe Lake* with tent sites ($11). Along the coast are the very popular *Point Wolfe* with tent sites ($11) and *Headquarters* with serviced sites ($18) and tent sites ($11). Expect sea breezes and cooler temperatures at the coastal campgrounds. Wolfe Lake has no showers.

In addition to the camping possibilities, there's *Jeunesse Fundy HI Hostel (☎ 506-887-2216)*, a convenient facility just off Chemin Point Wolfe Rd close to the golf

course. The hostel has a kitchen, lounge area and beds that run $9 for members and $12 for nonmembers. There are also motel-style rooms and chalets at the *Caledonia Highlands Inn* (☎ 506-887-2930) within the park. The chalets have cooking facilities but tend to be a little pricey; $75 for singles or doubles. *Fundy Park Chalets* (☎ 506-887-2808) are similar but are $65 for the unit that will hold up to four people.

At the small town of **Alma**, just east of the park on Hwy 114, there is the *Alpine Motor Inn* (☎ 506-887-2052) for $45/60 along with usual tourist services: food market, liquor store, bank and laundrette. At *Kelly's Bake Shop* a sticky bun is a must. One is enough for breakfast and possibly lunch. *Collins Seafood* will sell you live or cooked lobsters to take back to your camp site.

CAPE ENRAGE

Heading east to Moncton take the smaller road, Hwy 915, as it detours closer to the coast and offers some fine views. At Cape Enrage, out on the cliffs at the end of the peninsula, the power of the elements is often strongly and stimulatingly in evidence.

For a different view of those cliffs, give Cape Enrage Adventures (☎ 506-887-2273, or ☎ 506-865-6081 in Moncton) a call. While refurbishing the local lighthouse, some local high-schoolers also established a not-for-profit outdoor workshop, offering regular rock-climbing, rappelling, kayak, canoe, and hiking tours; they'll even customise a two-day tour. The cost is $40 for a three hour rappelling outing, $50 in a kayak. The café in the old lighthouse keeper's house is very good.

SHEPODY NATIONAL WILDLIFE AREA

South of the town of Riverside-Albert and the village of Harvey at Marys Point on the Bay of Fundy is this gathering place for literally hundreds of thousands of shore birds. From mid-July to mid-August the beach is almost obliterated by huge numbers of birds, primarily sandpipers. Along the dikes and marsh there is a nature trail.

South-East New Brunswick

The corner of New Brunswick leading to Nova Scotia and Prince Edward Island is most interesting for its various geographic or topographic attributes. The regional centre is Moncton whose two principal attractions are places where nature appears to defy gravity. Outside the city are some fine, sandy beaches and, on the Petitcodiac River, The Rocks are the impressive result of seaside erosion.

MONCTON

Moncton, with a population of 57,000, is the third city of the province and a major transportation and distribution centre for the Atlantic Provinces. It's near the Confederation Bridge to Prince Edward Island, and the train to Nova Scotia passes through it. The city's experiencing considerable economic growth and development. And due to a couple of odd attractions – Magnetic Hill and a tidal bore – it's worth a brief stop on your way by.

The first Europeans to settle in the area were Germans from Pennsylvania. There's a fairly large French population and many people speak both of Canada's official languages. The Université de Moncton is the only French university outside Quebec.

Orientation

The small downtown area extends north and south off Main St. The river lies just to the south and the Trans Canada Hwy runs east-west north of town. Between Duke and Foundry Sts along Main St, the sidewalks have been gentrified and many of the old buildings contain restaurants and nightspots. Unfortunately, development means fast-food chains are taking root and mega-malls creep toward the city centre. In Moncton alone, there are 16 Tim Horton doughnut shops!

Lengthy Mountain Rd leading in and out to the west side of town from the Trans Canada Hwy is also a main street for service stations, chain restaurants, fast-food joints and the same franchises seen in most

Canadian cities. There are also some motels along here.

Information

The main tourist information centre (☎ 506-853-3590) is in the City Hall at 655 Main St across from the Blue Cross Centre. Hours for the office are 8.30 am to 6.30 pm daily 1 June to Labour Day.

If coming in on the Trans Canada Hwy, there is a seasonal tourist office (☎ 506-853-3540) at the Wharf Village Shoppes at Mag-

netic Hill, open from 8.30 am to 6.30 pm late-May through Thanksgiving weekend.

There's another office (☎ 506-387-2053) south across the Gunningsville Bridge along Hillsborough Rd in Riverview.

Magnetic Hill

This is the best known attraction (☎ 506-384-0303) in the area. Gravity here seems to work in reverse – start at the bottom of the hill in a car or on a bike and you'll drift upward. Go as many times as you like, and maybe you'll

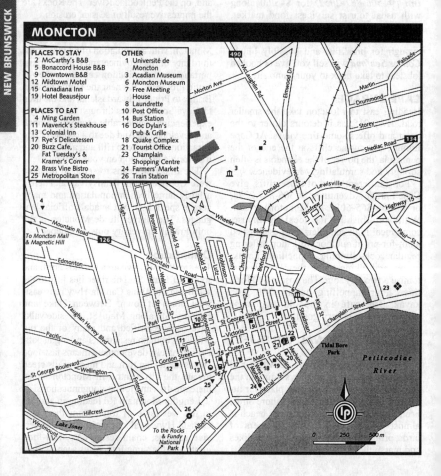

MONCTON

PLACES TO STAY
2 McCarthy's B&B
5 Bonaccord House B&B
9 Downtown B&B
12 Midtown Motel
15 Canadiana Inn
19 Hotel Beauséjour

PLACES TO EAT
4 Ming Garden
11 Maverick's Steakhouse
13 Colonial Inn
17 Rye's Delicatessen
20 Buzz Cafe,
   Fat Tuesday's &
   Kramer's Corner
22 Brass Vine Bistro
25 Metropolitan Store

OTHER
1 Université de
   Moncton
3 Acadian Museum
6 Moncton Museum
7 Free Meeting
   House
8 Laundrette
10 Post Office
14 Bus Station
16 Doc Dylan's
   Pub & Grille
18 Quake Complex
21 Tourist Office
23 Champlain
   Shopping Centre
24 Farmers' Market
26 Train Station

figure it out. The hill is on the corner of Mountain Rd (Hwy 126) and the Trans Canada Hwy. There is a $2 per car fee, worth it if there are several of you in the vehicle.

In recent years the hill has become the centre of a variety of attractions which now include a small zoo next door ($6 adult, $15 family), a water park with slides of various sorts ($19.50 adult, $59 family), restaurants, stores, and even a golf course. A mini-train links the different diversions. The hill itself is open from 8 am to 8 pm, but unfortunately schedules vary from place to place otherwise.

Tidal Bore Park
The tidal bore is a twice-daily incoming wave caused by the tides of the Petitcodiac River, which are in turn related to the tides in the Bay of Fundy – known as the world's highest tides. The bore rushes upstream and sometimes raises the water level in the river by 6m in a few minutes. The wave itself varies in height from a few centimetres to over 30cm.

A good place to watch for it is in Tidal Bore Park at the east end of Main St where a large clock displays the time of the next bore. The pleasant park is filled with old men sitting on the benches until close to bore time when the water's edge gets really crowded with expectant visitors. Don't anticipate anything spectacular though – mostly the wave is not at all impressive, but the troop of street performers usually on hand help makes this an entertaining event. The bore is best in spring and autumn, if it's raining or if the moon is right.

Moncton Museum
At 20 Mountain Rd near Belleview St, the museum (☎ 506-856-4383) outlines local history from the time of the Micmac Indians and early settlers to the present. Displays show the influence of shipbuilding and the railway on the area and an old-style street has been recreated. The museum's free and open daily in summer from 10 am to 8 pm, but has shorter hours the rest of the year. Next door is the oldest building in town, the **Free Meeting House** dating from 1821, used by numerous religious congregations over the years.

Free 90-minute guided walking tours of the city commence at the museum from Tuesday to Friday at 9.30 am throughout summer.

Acadian Museum
On the university campus in the Clement Cormier Building, this museum (☎ 506-858-4088) has displays offering a brief history and chronicles aspects of the day-to-day life of these people who were the first European settlers in the Atlantic region, driven out of Nova Scotia to New Brunswick and abroad by British troops. The museum's free and open daily from 10 am to 5 pm during summer, except on Saturday and Sunday when it opens at 1 pm. It has shorter hours the rest of the year. Admission is $2.

Thomas Williams' House
Built in 1883, this 12-room Victorian Gothic-style house remained in the family as a home until 1983 when it was bequeathed to the city as a heritage house. Much of the fine original work remains intact both inside and out, and the furnishings add to the overall effect. The tearoom on the veranda is fun.

The house is open daily from 9 am to 5 pm in July and August, except on Sunday when it opens at 1 pm. In May, June and September it's open only Monday, Wednesday and Friday. It's at 103 Park St in the downtown area and admission is free.

Farmers' Market
On Saturday, from 7 am to 1 pm, a produce market is set up on Robinson St south of Main St year-round and on Wednesday as well during the harvest season from mid-August to Thanksgiving.

Special Events
In early May there's the Acadian Art Festival, and in July a bluegrass and old-time fiddle-music festival.

Places to Stay
Camping The nearest campground to the city is *Magnetic Hill Campground* (☎ 506-384-0191), just off the Mountain Rd exit (exit 488) of the Trans Canada Hwy. It's pretty

much a grassy clearing but there is showers and a laundrette. A tent site is $16. Three others are not too distant from the city limits.

Hostels The *Université de Moncton (contact Housing Services on ☎ 506-858-4008)* rents rooms during summer in two of the residences. There are shared washrooms and a cafeteria. The cost is $25/35 or $18/30 for students and seniors. Contact the tourist information centre at City Hall to see if Atlantic Baptist University also has rooms – a possibility.

Tourist Homes The lack of hotels is partially offset by quite a few guesthouses and B&Bs. During summer, these are often full by the end of the day.

McCarthy's B&B (☎ 506-383-9152, 82 Peter St), with three rooms, is good and inexpensive at $30/40. Note that it is open only from May to October. Peter St is just under 2km north of the downtown centre.

Within walking distance (but a fair jaunt of seven or so blocks) is the *Bonaccord House B&B (☎ 506-388-1535, 250 Bonaccord St)*. It's the appealing yellow-and-white house on the corner of John St with a porch, and the four rooms are $40/50.

Centrally located is the *Downtown B&B (☎ 506-855-7108, 101 Alma St)*, open all year with three rooms at $50 a single/double.

Hotels In a central location near Main St is the yellow, wooden *Canadiana Inn (☎ 506-382-1054, 46 Archibald St)*. It's a beautiful place – as if you've stepped back in time – with wood everywhere and hanging lamps and, indeed, it's more than 100 years old. There are 17 rooms beginning at $65, $75 in peak summer.

The *Hotel Beauséjour (☎ 506-854-4344, ☎ 1-800-441-1414)* on Main St is the largest and most expensive place in town and is primarily for business clientele. Rooms here begin at $82, up to $159 nearer the upper end in summer.

Motels There's no shortage of motels, and a fair range of prices. Not far from town is

the good *Beacon Light Motel (☎ 506-384-1734, ☎ 1-800-668-3548, 1062 Mountain Rd)*, reached by taking Hwy 126. Doubles cost $55/65 and there are some kitchenette rooms available. Mountain Rd has a couple of other places as well.

On Hwy 2 near Magnetic Hill are numerous motels. The *Atlantic (☎ 506-858-1988)* is no-frills with rooms for $35/40. There are also some motels found to the east.

The only motel in the centre of town within walking distance to either the bus or train station is the *Midtown Motel (☎ 506-388-5000, 61 Weldon St)*, which is in a quiet location. It's pricier at $65 and also has some kitchenette rooms.

There are several other *motels* strung out along Rural Route 1, towards and in River Glade.

Places to Eat
The *Colonial Inn* on Highfield St off Main St has a 24 hour basic restaurant. *Crackers (700 Main St)* is a nice place for sandwiches, salads, ribs or Italian food. The large Caesar salad at $5 makes a good lunch and there is a wide selection of tempting desserts. At night it becomes a sort of club and is open very late on weekends.

Rye's Delicatessen (785 Main St) near Westmorland St has great bagels and nightly specials that might be fettucine on Tuesday and steamed mussels on Friday. It also has a happy hour that begins at 4 pm and features pints for under $3.

Robinson St just north of Main is a small pedestrian area that features a couple of espresso shops. *Cafe Robinson* is a cosy spot to have coffee or a filled croissant. A large café au lait is $2.25 and there are tables outside. Good coffee and lightning-speed Internet access are found at the *Buzz Cafe (728 Main St, www.buzzcafe.com)*. This whole stretch of Main St is casually gentrified and you'll find many pubs. *Fat Tuesday's* is rocking with live music and has lots of Cajun. East of here, a once cheap Lebanese eatery has now become *Brass Vine Bistro* offering upscale Lebanese cuisine and a wine bar.

The food counter at the *Metropolitan* store at the Highfield Mall on Main St has the lowest prices in town with meals at about $5. Nearby the *Traveller's Café* in the bus station has cheap breakfasts with two eggs, toast and coffee for $3 and the good-value lunches are under $7.

A culinary institution in these parts is *Cy's*, or at least was – it was bulldozed during our last visit to make way for a new mega-hotel; this well known seafood joint might reopen inside this new complex on Main St. Near the Midtown Motel is *Maverick's*, for serious carnivores only. Hand-carved steaks start at around $15 here. The wine list is fairly extensive.

Mountain Rd has numerous eating spots, including almost a dozen Chinese restaurants, three alone near the corner of McSweeney Ave. One is *Ming Garden* which claims to have a 101-item buffet (no, I didn't count them). The all-you-can-eat affair is $8 for dinner Monday through Thursday, $7 during lunch. Also along this stretch of Mountain Rd is every chain restaurant imaginable.

Entertainment

Look for a free copy of *Action* magazine giving a lengthy rundown on Moncton's somewhat surprisingly vibrant nightlife. Be careful – lots of wet T-shirt or home-made bikini contests are to be found. Central Main St has several bars catering to the young with live bands and dancing. *Spanky's* has live rock. The *Quake Complex* houses a couple of separate clubs. It's loud, it's danceable, and might even be packed with gyrating bodies.

More live music can be enjoyed at *Doc Dylan's Pub & Grille (cnr Main & Foundry Sts)*. The pub features live music on the weekends. For just a wine or scotch, your best bet is *Kramer's Corner* in the 700 block of Main St.

The *Coliseum* is home to major shows, concerts and sporting events.

The impressive Capitol Theatre, a 1920s vaudeville house, has been restored and is now the city's *Performing Arts Centre (811 Main St)*. Call the theatre box office (☎ 506-856-4379) for a schedule of performances,

which includes both Theatre New Brunswick and Symphony New Brunswick on a regular basis throughout the year.

Getting There & Away

Bus The station for SMT Bus Lines (☎ 506-859-2170) is at 961 Main St between town and the train station on the corner of Bonaccord St. Some schedules with one-way ticket prices are: Fredericton, 11.55 am and 5.40 pm daily ($28.50); Saint John, 11.30 am and 6 pm daily ($22.15); Halifax, 11 am, 2.15 and 8.30 pm daily ($38); and Prince Edward Island, 11.15 am and 2.20 pm daily, except Wednesday, and an extra trip at 8.30 pm Friday and Sunday ($32.75).

Train The VIA train station (☎ 506-857-9830) is south-west of the downtown area near Cameron St 200m off Main St. Look for it behind the building at 1234 Main St or behind Sobey's grocery store at the Highfield Mall. It's only open from 9.30 am to 7 pm on weekdays and 10 am to 7 pm on weekends. Regular one-way fares are $47 to Halifax and $135 to Montreal. If you purchase your ticket a week in advance you save considerably. There is no train service to Saint John. The *Ocean* goes through northern New Brunswick, including Campbellton and Quebec, on its way to Montreal daily at 5.55 pm, except Tuesday. The train to Halifax departs daily at 11.25 am, except Tuesday.

Getting Around

Codiac Transit (☎ 506-857-2008) is the local bus system running daily, except Sunday; it has no service nights Monday through Wednesday and Saturday. Gary's (☎ 506-855-2394) at 239 Weldon St has bicycles for rent for $25 per day and up.

AROUND MONCTON
Covered Bridges

Within 100km of Moncton, 27 of the province's historic covered bridges can be seen. Two driving trips south of Moncton, called the Scenic Trail and the Covered Bridge Trail, take in many of these bridges.

Dobson Trail

Just south of Moncton in Riverview, this 60km hiking trail leads you through the Albert County hills and maple forests down to Fundy National Park. The entire trail is a three-day, one-way hike to where it connects with the Laverty Falls Trails in the national park.

To reach the northern trailhead, take the causeway across the Petitcodiac River to Riverview and then turn east on Hwy 114. Turn south on Pine Glen Rd and in 3km you reach the trailhead marked by a white sign on one side of the road and a small parking area on the other. The first section of the trail is the 9.4km trek to Beaver Pond where you'll find areas to make camp and a hut.

For information get in touch with the Trailmaster, Edwin Melanson (☎ 506-855-5089), in Riverview.

Hillsborough

Hillsborough, about 20km south-east of Moncton, is a small town overlooking the Petitcodiac River. From here the Salem-Hillsborough Railroad (☎ 506-734-3195) has a restored steam engine which pulls antique coaches beside the river to Salem 8km away. It takes an hour for the return trip. The fare is $7.50, less for kids. The train runs at 1.30 and 3 pm every Sunday in July and August and on a few weekends in September. Hillsborough also can provide spelunking adventures from Baymount Adventures (☎ 506-734-2660) for $40 per person.

Hopewell Rocks Provincial Park

Continuing south-east from Hillsborough, you'll encounter the park at Hopewell Cape, the point at which the river meets the Fundy waters in Shepody Bay. The 'rocks' are unusual erosion formations known as 'flowerpots'. The shore is lined with these irregular geological forms, as well as caves and tunnels, all of which have been created by erosion from the great tides. It's also lined with tourists.

An exploratory walk along the beach at low tide is well worthwhile – check the tide

tables at any tourist office. You can't hit the beach at high tide but the rock towers are visible from the trails above. In either event, morning is best for shutterbugs. Camping is not allowed. Admission is $4.

Baymount Adventures (☎ 506-734-2660) offers two-hour kayak tours of the area for $30 per person.

Saint Joseph

Here, 24km south-east of Moncton, is the very worthy Monument Lefebvre National Historic Site (☎ 506-758-9783), which tells the enthralling but difficult history of the Acadians, the early French settlers of the Bay of Fundy region, most of whom were expelled by the British in 1755. The exhibits, including paintings, crafts and life-size models, are well done and, unlike those at many such history-based sites, also devote some attention to the subjects' lives through the years to the present.

Saint Joseph is in the Memramcook Valley, the only area near the Bay of Fundy where some Acadians live on what was the land of their forebears before the mass banishments.

The site is open daily from 9 am to 5 pm June to mid-October and entry is $2, less for seniors and children, $5 for families. It's between Moncton and Dorchester off Route 106.

This site is actually on the grounds of the *Memramcook Valley Learning & Vacation Resort* (☎ 506-758-2511), a spa housed in the former Université Saint-Joseph. All the amenities of a spa are here, down to golf course, massage, gourmet Acadian restaurant, and displays of local Acadian history. Rates start at around $60 in summer for a single/double.

SACKVILLE

Sackville is a small university town that's in the right place for a pit stop. There is a tourist office (☎ 506-364-0431) on York St just up from Main St. Hours are 8 am to 8 pm daily during summer and usually there is free coffee and doughnuts.

In the centre of town is **Mount Allison University** and the park on campus is good

for stretching the legs. Among the facilities open to the public is the Owens Art Gallery and the pool and athletic centre. The gallery is open daily from 10 am to 5 pm, except on Saturday and Sunday when it opens at 1 pm. On the edge of town, off East Main St, is the **Sackville Waterfowl Park** on a major bird migration route. Boardwalks have been built over portions of it and there is another trail and some interpretive signs.

Also in the Sackville area is the **Tintamarre National Wildlife Reserve**. The Wildlife Service office (☎ 506-364-5044), 63 E Main St, has a few displays on the reserve and information for those wishing to see more.

South of town towards Nova Scotia on the Trans Canada Hwy you go right past the **Radio Canada International Transmitter Station** (☎ 506-536-2690). You definitely won't be sorry if you take in one of the free, chatty guided tours between 10 am and 6 pm in July and August. It's great fun and highly educational.

If you stay the night, consider a show at *Live Bait Theatre*, Sackville's professional stage company which often performs comedies. Call the box office (☎ 506-536-2248) for tickets and schedule.

Places to Stay & Eat

Mt Allison University (☎ 506-364-2247) right in the centre of town opens rooms to overnight guests from May to August and charges $28/48, $8 less for students. It also serves inexpensive meals.

There's a good B&B called the *Different Drummer* (☎ 506-536-1291, 146 West Main St). It's a fine old Victorian house; each of the four rooms is furnished with antiques and has a bath. Breakfasts include home-made muffins and bread. Singles/doubles cost $49/55. The favourite among locals is *Mel's Tea Room* on Bridge St which has the charm of an 1950s diner with the jukebox and prices to match. More expensive is the regional cuisine at *Marshland's Inn*, also with more expensive lodging.

FORT BEAUSÉJOUR NATIONAL HISTORIC SITE

Right by the Nova Scotia border at the shoreline, the park (☎ 506-536-0720) preserves the remains of a French fort built in 1751 to hold the British back. It didn't work. Later it was used as a stronghold during the American Revolution and the War of 1812. There are some pretty good displays within the fort and some evocative pictures set in the surroundings. Hours for the interpretive centre are 9 am to 5 pm daily June through mid-October and admission is $2.50.

SHEDIAC

Just 22km north-east of Moncton on the coast, Shediac is a popular summer resort town with a population descended mainly from the Acadian French. The beaches here are blessed with warm waters due to sand bars and shallow water. Most popular are Parlee Beach (east of Shediac) and Pointe du Chêne, with water temperatures of around 20°C all summer. The waters of the Northumberland Strait are possibly the warmest north of the Carolinas in the USA.

There are other beaches on the small coastal roads and north and south of Shediac, and lots of camping places.

The area also is a lobster centre of some repute and Shediac is home to the annual lobster festival in July. You can enjoy it even on pizza!

The tourist office (☎ 506-532-7788) is at the west end of Main St, just before you cross the causeway across the Scoudouc River into town. It's open daily from 8 am till 10 pm July and August, less otherwise. Free email access is here. Right outside – by the giant lobster – are boat shuttles ($10) and tours ($20) to and around Shediac Island Nature Park. Kayak tours and rentals ($13 per hour) are also available.

At night the many lights and decorative seagulls add a festive touch. **Pascal Poirer House**, built in 1835 is the oldest house in town and is now open as a small museum. The home was the birthplace of Poirer, a noted writer and the first Acadian senator, and was moved to Shediac from Grande Digue. Hours

are 1 to 9 pm Tuesday through Sunday from June through August. Admission is free.

Places to Stay & Eat

The best bet for camping is *Parlee Beach Park* (☎ 506-532-1500), a grassy campground beside the provincial beach where a tent site is $15 per person. Reservations should be made for holiday weekends, but for any weekend, arrive as early as possible on Friday.

Even the tourist homes and B&Bs are pricey here though there are many fine choices. The big white *Hotel Shediac* (☎ 506-532-4405) is a central, mid-range place dating from 1853. Singles/doubles range from $45 to $65 depending on the season. A less expensive option is the *Neptune Motel* (☎ 506-532-4299) at $40 to $60. There are also a couple of places with cabins rented by the week.

East of town is a strip of eateries and takeaways. You'll find clams and lobsters, cooked or fresh, dead or alive. *Fisherman's Paradise* packs them in with fair (but that doesn't mean cheap) prices. The *House of Lobster* is more upmarket with the boiled lobster dinner at $25 and other seafood dinners starting at $16.

Lobsters can be bought at various outlets and at the wharves. The largest is *Shediac Lobster Shop* passed after just crossing the Scoudouc River on Main St. This being a tourist town, expect to pay anywhere from $6 to $8 a pound.

Any number of inns and B&Bs have highly rated dining rooms.

CAP-PELÉ

East of Shediac there are a series of less used beaches such as the one at Cap-Pelé where there is also a water slide. Farther south at Murray Corner is a provincial park with more sandy beaches.

North & East New Brunswick

North of Fredericton and Moncton lie the province's vast forests. Nearly all the towns are along the east coast or in the west by the Saint John River along the US border. The interior of northern New Brunswick is nearly inaccessible rocky, river-filled timberland.

Inland, highways in this area can be quite monotonous with thick forest lining both sides of the very straight roads. In the eastern section the coastal roads are where pretty well everything of interest lies. Kouchibouguac National Park protects a variety of littoral environments and their natural flora and fauna.

The Acadian Peninsula with its little-touristed islands and French population based around Caraquet is one of the most appealing regions with the Baie des Chaleurs shoreline. The peninsula also has a major historic attraction. Campbellton and Dalhousie at the edge of the northern uplands are access points to the province of Quebec.

KOUCHIBOUGUAC NATIONAL PARK

The highlights of this park (pronounced 'KOO-she-boo-gwak') are the beaches, lagoons and offshore sand dunes stretching for 25km. The sands are good for beach combing, birdwatching and clam digging. Seals are often seen offshore. For swimming, the water is warm but much of it is too shallow for adults.

The park also has populations of moose, deer, black bears as well as some smaller mammals. Other features are the birdlife around the salt marsh and a bog where there is an observation platform.

The park is 100km north of Moncton with an entrance just off Hwy 11. The visitors centre (☎ 506-876-2443) is open daily from mid-May to mid-October from 8 am to 8 pm and features interpretive displays and a small theatre as well as an information counter and gift shop. Entry fee into the park is $3.50 per adult, $10.50 for four days, or $7 for a family, $35 for a four-day family pass.

Check with the centre for the variety of programs offered at the park, including a three hour tour in a large Voyageur canoe

where you paddle to offshore sand bars to view birds and possibly seals. The tours are offered four times a week and are $25 per adult, $15 for children.

Cycling Kouchibouguac features hiking trails and canoe routes but what really sets it apart from other national parks is the 32km network of bikeways – crushed gravel paths that wind through the heart of the park's backcountry. From Ryan's day-use area, where bikes can be rented, it's possible to cycle a 23km loop and never be on the park road for any of it. Bicycles are $4.60 an hour and $26 a day. Ryan Rental Center (☎ 506-876-3733) also rents out canoes and kayaks for around $25 a day.

Camping Kouchibouguac has two drive-in campgrounds and three primitive camping areas totalling 359 sites. The camping season is from May to October and the park is very busy throughout July and August, particularly on weekends. Reservations are taken for half of the sites; call ☎ 1-800-213-7275. Otherwise, you'll have to get on a very lengthy 'roll call' waiting list – which can take up to four days to clear.

South Kouchibouguac is the largest campground, located 12km inside the park near the beaches and featuring 311 sites along with showers and a kitchen shelter. The rate is $16.25 to $22 a night during summer. *Cote-a-Fabien* is on the north side of Kouchibouguac River, away from the bike trails and beaches, and does not have showers. A site here is $14 a night.

If the park is full, a good alternative is the *Daigles Park (☎ 506-876-4540)* a private campground 2km outside the park in Saint Louis-de-Kent. An unserviced site is $12 a night. There are many others.

The three primitive campgrounds in the park have only vault toilets and a pump for water and are $10 a night for two people. *Sipu* is located midway along the park's longest trail, the 14km Kouchibouguac River Trail. *Petit Large* is on a bike path and *Pointe-a-Maxime* is along the shore and can be reached only by canoe.

MIRAMICHI BAY

North of the national park, in and around Miramichi Bay, are more beaches. Folks here, like those farther south and in north Prince Edward Island and Nova Scotia where the same claim is made, say the waters are the warmest north of either Virginia or the Carolinas in the USA. In any case, the water at all these places is quite suitable for swimming, having been warmed by spin-off currents of the Gulf Stream.

MIRAMICHI CITY

In late 1995, six communities including Chatham and Newcastle were amalgamated to form Miramichi City.

Chatham

This portion of the new city was a prosperous town when it was the centre of the wooden shipbuilding industry, but the development of steel ships put an end to that and the Canadian Forces base closed in the early 1990s. The revamped downtown area along Water St by the Miramichi River is pleasant enough in a quiet way.

Approaching town on Hwy 11, you pass a tourist centre (☎ 506-778-8444) that is open daily from 8 am to 9 pm May to September. Two blocks away from the waterfront the WS Logge Cultural Centre (☎ 506-773-7645), in a restored Victorian house at 222 Wellington St, is primarily a locally oriented art gallery.

At 149 Wellington St on the corner of University Ave, the Natural History Museum (☎ 506-773-7305) has a small idiosyncratic collection and free admission. It's open from mid-June to mid-August.

In **Douglastown**, halfway between the Chatham bridge and the Newcastle area is the Rankin House Museum (☎ 506-773-3448), three floors of artefacts relating to early life in New Brunswick. The Rankin House also doubles up as a tourist centre and anchors the Lower Town Walk, a posted route past other historical buildings along Douglastown's waterfront.

North of Douglastown in Bartibog on Hwy 11 is **MacDonald Farm Historic Site** (☎778-6085). Overlooking the Miramichi

River, the 1820 farm is typical of Scotland. Also on site is a barn, net shed and spring house while costumed guides continue the traditional activities of cooking over an open hearth, soap making and so on. Hours are 9.30 am to 4.30 pm and admission is $2.50.

Newcastle

Though the site of another huge paper mill, Newcastle is pleasant – a good place to break up the trip north or south. Around the attractive town square are some fine old wooden buildings and shops. Here in the central square park is a statue to Lord Beaverbrook, one of the most powerful press barons in British history and a statesman and philanthropist of no small reputation. Beaverbrook spent most of his growing years in Newcastle. Beaverbrook House (☎ 506-622-4721), his boyhood home at 225 Mary St, is now a museum. Among the many gifts he lavished on the province are the 17th century English benches and the Italian gazebo in the square here. His ashes lie under the statue presented as a memorial to him by the town. Beaverbrook House is open weekdays from 10 am to 4 pm.

A riverfront boardwalk park across the river in **Nelson**, the Ritchie Wharf has playgrounds for kids, cafés, a lighthouse with information centre and summer boat tours to Beaubears Island. The island has been a Micmac camp site, a refugee camp for Acadians during the expulsion and a shipbuilding site. Tours leave every two hours when enough people are present and cost $10.

Also in Nelson is the Murray House Museum (☎622-9100). Hours are 9 am to 7 pm daily during summer.

Each summer the Miramichi Folk Song Festival, begun in the 1960s and the oldest one in North America, is held. Through traditional song, the local history and culture are preserved. The largest Irish festival in the province is held in July.

Places to Stay South of town off Hwy 8 is another of Lord Beaverbrook's gifts – a provincial park called The Enclosure. The campground in the park is now privately run as **Enclosure Campground** (☎ 506-627-4071) and is a pleasant place to pitch a tent. There is no fee for using the park's day-use area.

Across the river in Nelson is the large **Governor's Mansion** (☎ 506-622-3036), without a doubt the most intriguing hostel and inn in New Brunswick. The huge house, with three floors of antiques, model ships and history, was built in 1865 and was the home of J Leonard O'Brien, the first Irish lieutenant governor of the province. On the grounds is an Ogham stone that dates back to the 4th century and exhibits early writing of the Celts. Numerous bedrooms on the second and third floor are $25 to $50 a night. A full breakfast is a few dollars more. At the time of writing this was the only hostel option, as the Beaubear Mansion was closed for renovations, with no timetable for reopening. Ask at the lighthouse information centre at Ritchie Wharf.

Getting There & Away The SMT bus station (☎ 506-622-0462) is at 60 Pleasant St in Newcastle; it also stops in Chatham on the highway at an Irving station. One bus a day arrives from Saint John at 2.15 pm and makes the return at 2.35 pm. From Chatham you can make connections to other destinations, including the Acadian Peninsula.

MIRAMICHI RIVER

South-west of Miramichi City, the South-west Miramichi River extends beyond Doaktown, about halfway to Fredericton. The river runs 800km and the waters are crystal clear. The area, in particular the main river, is renowned for Atlantic salmon fishing. Together with the Restigouche and Saint John rivers, it has gained the province an international reputation among serious anglers. Even Prince Charles has fished the Miramichi! Both residents and visitors need licences and there are special regulations for nonresidents.

Doaktown has become more or less the unofficial fishing centre for the region. In town is the Atlantic Salmon Museum (☎ 506-365-7787), which is actually pretty interest-

ing and includes pools of live salmon ('king of the freshwater game fish') on the 1.5-hectare grounds. Hours are 9 am to 5 pm daily June through September.

One of Canada's best fly-fishing shops is here, WW Doak & Sons. It sells about 60,000 flies a year, many tied on the premises. Other points of interest include the Glendella Mansion (a rather unexpected sight) and Doak Historic Park, concerning local history and with a preserved house from the 19th century and costumed interpreters for the farm section.

Hours for the historic park (☎ 506-365-4363) are 9.30 am to 4.30 pm Monday through Saturday, 1 to 4.30 pm Sunday during summer and admission is free. Near town is an 1870s covered bridge, one of the province's oldest.

ACADIAN PENINSULA

The large peninsula, which extends from Chatham and Bathurst out to two islands at the edge of the Baie des Chaleurs, is a predominantly French area which was first settled by the Acadians who were the unhappy victims of the colonial battles between Britain and France in the 1700s. The descendants of Canada's earliest French settlers proudly fly the Acadian flag around the region and many of the traditions live on in music, food and the language which is different to that spoken in Quebec.

For visitors, by far the most interesting section and best scenery is around Caraquet.

Getting There & Away

Transportation around this part of the province is very limited although there is some service. A couple of individuals run vans around the Acadian Peninsula from Monday to Friday.

The Gloucester Coach Lines (☎ 506-395-5812) runs between Tracadie and Bathurst via Shippagan and Caraquet once each way every weekday. In Caraquet, the bus stops at the Irving service station on Boulevard Saint Pierre Ouest; to Bathurst it generally heads out between 8 and 9 am. In Bathurst, a bus departs the SMT station at 1.15 pm

Monday through Friday for the return trip around the peninsula. A ticket from Bathurst to Caraquet is $10.

The Tracadie Coach Lines (☎ 506-395-5639) has a bus that leaves the Irving service station in Tracadie at noon Monday through Friday, reaching Newcastle/Chatham at 2.30 pm. The fare is $15.

The drivers for both of these coach lines can be reached at these numbers only in the evenings and on weekends – the rest of the time they are out driving the routes.

Tracadie

From Neguac, north-east of Chatham, the road passes by a mixture of old houses and modern bungalows. It's not a wealthy area and there isn't much to see as the road is too far inland for coastal views. In Tracadie is Le Musee Historique de Tracadie (☎ 506-395-1500) on the second floor of the huge Academie Ste-Famille building on Main St. This unusual museum, the only one of its kind in Canada, offers a glimpse of leprosy in the 19th century through photos and artefacts. Hours during summer are 9 am to 6 pm daily, except on the weekends when it opens at noon. Admission is $2.

Notice the Quebec-style double silver-spired Saint Jean Baptiste church. Just across the river at the north side of town is a tourist office.

Shippagan

At the tip of the mainland, Shippagan has the Aquarium and Marine Centre (☎ 506-336-3013), the highlight of which is the aquarium. Examples of many of the species, including seals, found in the Gulf of St Lawrence region are displayed. There is also a freshwater exhibit and displays showing all the electronic equipment used by today's fishing industry.

The centre is open from 10 am to 6 pm daily during summer. Admission is $6 for adults and $12 for a family.

Adjacent to the centre is a marina with a restaurant and the tourist office in a small lighthouse. The tourist office is open the same hours as the Marine Centre.

A causeway connects Île Lamèque, a boggy island where the collection and shipping of peat competes in importance with fishing. Île Miscou, reached over a new bridge and with quiet stretches of beach, sees few tourists. At the tip is a lighthouse and the island is rife with piping plover. Many people fall in love with this diminutive island and its rich Acadian culture.

Caraquet

The oldest of the Acadian villages, Caraquet was founded in 1757 and is now the main centre of the peninsula's French community. It has one of the oldest churches in the province, Sainte Anne du Bocage, 7km from the village 'centre'. Down at the dock area on Boulevard Saint Pierre Est is a big fish market with fresh, salted, and frozen seafood for sale. Note that there can be tremendous, smelly traffic jams around the church.

Acadian Museum In the middle of town, with views over the bay from the balcony, is this museum (☎ 506-727-1713) with a neatly laid out collection of artefacts donated by local residents. Articles include household objects, tools, photographs and a fine wood stove in the corner. Most impressive is the desk/bed which you can work at all day and then fold down into a bed when exhaustion strikes. It belonged to a superior at the Caraquet Convent in 1880.

The museum is open daily in summer from 10 am to 8 pm, except on Sunday when it opens at 1 pm. Admission is $3.

Other Attractions Behind the museum is the Théâtre Populaire d'Acadie (☎ 506-727-0290), which puts on shows during midsummer. The tourist office (☎ 506-727-1705) is nearby. At the wharf below here are whale-watching tours in rigid-hull Hurricane boats for $50 and kayak rentals and tours. In August there is an Acadian Festival with a variety of events.

A few kilometres east out of town near Caraquet Park is the Sainte Anne du Bocage religious shrine.

Places to Stay Back a bit from the street at 143 Boulevard Saint Pierre Ouest is the *Hotel Paulin* (☎ 506-727-9981) by the water. It's open all year with singles/doubles from $40 to $60, and there is a restaurant for lunches and dinners.

Out close to the shrine is *Maison Touristique Dugas* (☎ 506-727-3195, 683 Boulevard Saint Pierre Ouest) with rooms beginning at $25/30 and camp sites for $8 to $10 a night. Also for camping there is a provincial park (☎ 506-727-3474) close to the shrine; sites are $15.

West of Caraquet in Bertrand is *La Pantrie* restaurant with Acadian cuisine with fixed-price dinners for around $7 to $16 taxes included.

Acadian Historic Village

The Acadian Historic Village (Village Historique Acadien), 14km west of Caraquet, is a major historic museum (☎ 506-727-2600) set up like a village of old, with 26 buildings and workers in period costumes reflecting life from 1780 to 1880. The museum depicts daily life in a typically post-expulsion Acadian village and makes for an intriguing comparison to the obviously prosperous British King's Landing historic village outside Fredericton.

A good two hours is required to see the site, and you'll want to eat. For that there are three choices: two *cafeterias* or a *restaurant* at the Dugas House, the latter serving Acadian dishes.

The museum is open from 10 am to 6 pm daily in summer. It's on Hwy 11 towards Grande-Anse. Tickets are $9 or $23 for the family. After Labour Day, when most of the custom guides have departed, tickets are steeply discounted. The village has a program ($25) for kids which allows them a costume and seven hours of supervised historical 'activities'.

The previously mentioned Gloucester Coach Lines van from Bathurst goes right by the door.

Grande-Anse

This small town boasts the popular Pope's Museum (☎ 506-732-3003), which houses

images of 264 popes from St Peter to the present one, as well as various religious articles. There is also a detailed model of the Basilica and St Peter's Square in Rome. Open summers from 10 am to 6 pm, admission is $5, $10 for a family.

GRANDE-ANSE TO BATHURST

All along the route from Grande-Anse to Bathurst the rugged, shoreline cliffs are scenic and include views across the bay to the mountains of the Gaspé Peninsula. There are some beaches (the one at Maisonnette is good), picnic sites and, at **Pokeshaw Provincial Park**, coastal erosion including a sea stack to see, along with thousands of seabirds.

Near **Janeville** there is a restored grindstone mill which can be visited. For camping there's *Chapman's Tent & Trailer Park* (☎ 506-546-2883), 14km east of Bathurst on Hwy 11, which is highly recommended for its open sites overlooking the beach and ocean. An unserviced site is $10 a night.

BATHURST

Bathurst is yet another industrial town, but based on extremely rich zinc mines to buttress lumber. With about 15,000 people, the town is split into three sections: South, East and West Bathurst by the Nepisiguit River and the Bathurst Basin. The principal street is Main St in South Bathurst and this is where a couple of restaurants can be found.

St Peter Ave has the range of food-chain places and service stations as well as the War Museum (☎ 506-546-3135), displaying weapons, uniforms and photos and a reproduction of a WWI trench. Hours are 11 am to 9 pm daily during summer and admission is free.

On the coast north-east of the harbour at the edge of the city is the **Daly Point Reserve**, a mix of woods and salt marshes with several trails that can be followed for observing birds. An observation tower provides views to the Gaspé Peninsula.

Some 20km north of town towards Dalhousie in **Petit-Rocher** is the New Brunswick Mining & Mineral Interpretation Centre (☎ 506-783-8714). This mining museum has various exhibits, including a deep shaft to descend, and features the local zinc-mining industry. The site is open daily from 10 am to 6 pm June through August and a tour takes about 45 minutes. It's on Route 134 and admission is $4.50.

Places to Stay & Eat

At Salmon Beach, just east of Bathurst is *Carey's By The Sea* (☎ 506-546-6801), a small resort with a great restaurant run by Johnny and Tomi Carey. Tomi is the author of six cookbooks and the pair host a cooking show, *Carey's Magic Kitchen*, that is taped in the restaurant. The cottages are extremely comfortable and begin at $30 for a double while another, which can sleep four people, is $40. Dinner at the restaurant ranges from $10 to $19 but is well worth it. The frozen drinks (try the Moonlight Margarita) are the only civilised way to begin a meal.

Getting There & Away

You can walk to the old downtown section at the end of Nepisiguit Bay from the VIA Rail station (☎ 506-546-2659) which is at 690 Thornton Ave on the corner of Queen St. The station is open only when there is a train – 7 to 11.30 am daily, except Wednesday, and 4 to 9 pm daily except Tuesday. SMT Bus Lines (☎ 506-548-0900) is at 15 St Peter Ave on the corner of Main St. A bus departs north at 3.45 pm daily for Campbellton and south at 1 pm daily for Moncton.

DALHOUSIE

Dalhousie is a small, agreeable town on the north-east coast of New Brunswick on the Baie des Chaleurs opposite Quebec. William St and the parallel Adelaide St near the dock are the two main streets. On the corner of Adelaide St at 437 George St is the **Restigouche Regional Museum** (☎ 506-684-7490) with local artefacts and history. Hours are 9 am to 9 pm weekdays, till 5 pm weekends June through August and admission is free. On Route 134 towards Campbellton is Eel River Sandbar, among the longest in the world.

NEW BRUNSWICK

The cruise boat *Chaleur Phantom* (☎ 506-684-4722) departs from the town wharf at the foot of Renfrew St on a nature cruise ($15) at 9 am in the bay and a scenic cruise ($10) at 2 and 7 pm along the Restigouche River. The cruises spot birds, seals and possibly whales.

Places to Stay

Two kilometres east from the ferry dock at the end of Victoria St is *Inch Arran Park* (☎ *506-684-7363)*, right on the water with camp sites, a swimming pool, the tourist office, the beach and fine views across the bay. An unserviced site is $14 a night and there is a laundrette across the street. A *Best Western* is near the museum.

Getting There & Away

You can take a car ferry from across the bay to Miguasha, Quebec. The ferry (☎ 506-684-5107) leaves every hour on the hour from 9 am to 9 pm and cuts about 70km off the driving trip around the bay. The ferry takes about 20 minutes and costs $12 for a car and driver and $1 for each passenger. It runs from the end of June to some time in September.

CAMPBELLTON

Campbellton, on the Quebec border, is in the midst of a scenic area at the edge of the Restigouche Highlands. The Baie des Chaleurs is on one side and rolling hills encase the town on the remaining sides. Across the border is Matapédia and Hwy 132 leading to Mont Joli, 148km into Quebec.

The last naval battle of the Seven Years' War was fought in the waters just off the coast here in 1760.

Main streets in this town of about 10,000 residents are Water St and Roseberry St, around which the commercial centre is clustered. Campbellton is truly a bilingual town with store cashiers saying everything in both French and English.

Nearby, **Sugarloaf Mountain**, rising nearly 400m above sea level and dominating the skyline, is the principal attraction and provides excellent views of the town and part of the Restigouche River. It looks remarkably like its namesake in Rio. From the base, it's a half-hour walk to the top; another trail leads around the bottom.

There's camping in Sugarloaf Provincial Park and skiing in winter. A large provincial tourist centre (☎ 506-789-2367) is located on Water St near the town square in which a focal point is a huge statue of a salmon surrounded by man-made waterfalls.

About 10km west of town towards Matapédia is **Morrisey Rock**, another place for a good view of the scenic river area.

Places to Stay

There are 65 semi-serviced sites in a pleasant wooded setting at *Sugarloaf Provincial Park* (☎ *506-789-2366)* on Route 270, off Hwy 11. A site is $15 a night.

There is the distinctive HI *Campbellton Lighthouse Hostel* (☎ *506-759-7044, 1 Ritchie St)* along the Restigouche River just up from the information centre. It's open from early June to September. There are only 20 beds in this converted lighthouse, so calling ahead to check availability is advisable. The rate is $10 for members, $15 for nonmembers and $5 if you just want to pitch your tent outside.

Auberge Wandlyn Maritime Inn (☎ *506-753-7606, ☎ 1-800-561-0000, 26 Duke St)* is a good choice if you'd like to be right in the centre of town. Singles begin at $60.

Between here and Dalhousie on Hwy 134 are a couple of *motels* with attractive seaside locations. Others are found on Hwy 134 West.

Sanfar Cottages (☎ *506-753-4287)* is west of town at Tide Head on Route 134. There are 12 cabins here, at $43 for two people, and a light breakfast is included.

Places to Eat

In the centre of town along Roseberry St is the usual assortment of chain and family restaurants – one open 24 hours – and for a cheap breakfast, *Art's Dog Cart*. This funky little place has only stools and counters but Art will cook you a full breakfast, including coffee, for $2.50. *Miss Saigon* has very friendly owners and good Vietnamese-Chinese food. For a casually upscale meal,

Something Else (65 Water St) has eclectic regional cuisine and is a good bet.

Getting There & Away

The SMT bus stop is at the Pik-Quik variety store on Water St near Prince William St. The VIA Rail station is conveniently central on Roseberry St. There is one train daily, except Tuesday, going south to Moncton and Halifax and one daily, except Tuesday, heading the other way to Montreal.

MT CARLETON PROVINCIAL PARK

This 17,427-hectare park is the largest and wildest in the province, offering visitors mountains, valleys and rivers in a wilderness setting. The main feature of the park is a series of peaks and ridges, including Mt Carleton, which at 820m is one of the highest peaks in Atlantic Canada. This range is actually an extension of the Appalachian Mountains from the USA and development is underway to extend the 3200km Appalachian Trail, which begins in the state of Georgia, from Maine into New Brunswick (see under Matapédia in the Quebec chapter).

Access to Mt Carleton Provincial Park is via Hwy 180 from **Saint Quentin**, a town that's south-west of Campbellton along the Restigouche River. The park is roughly 130km south of Campbellton and 43km from Saint Quentin, the last place to purchase gasoline, food and beer. Saint Quentin, the capital of the maple syrup industry, has an awesome rodeo and western festival in July.

At the entrance is a visitors centre (☎ 506-235-0793) for maps, information and park-entry permits. The centre is open 7 am to 10 pm daily in summer and the motor-vehicle permits are $4 a day.

Hiking

Day hiking is the best way to explore Mt Carleton. The park has a 60km network of trails, most of them loops winding to a handful of rocky knobs that are the peaks.

The easiest peak to climb is **Mount Bailey Trail**, a 7.5km loop to the 563m hillock that begins near the day-use area. Most hikers can walk the route in two to three hours.

The highest peak is reached from the **Mount Carleton Trail**, a 10km route that skirts over the 820m knob, where there is a firetower. Along the way is a backcountry camp site located near three beaver ponds and in full view of the mountain. Plan on three to four hours for the trek and pack your parka. The wind above the treeline can be brutal at times.

The most scenic hike is **Sagamook Trail**, a 6km loop to the 777m peak with superlative vistas of Nictau Lake and the highlands area to the north of it. Plan on three hours for this trek.

Mountain biking isn't on any maps, but there are endless logging truck-free roads for explorations.

Places to Stay & Eat

Armstrong Brook Campground is on the north side of Nictau Lake with toilets, showers, kitchen shelter but no serviced sites. It's $10 a night to camp here. There are two more walk-in areas, and one backcountry spot of four sites.

AROUND MT CARLETON

To the north toward Campbellton, pinhead-sized **Kedgwick** has the Forestry Museum, open from 9 am to 6 pm with admission of $5; it also doubles as a campground ($8). Also here is the only remaining regional railway station, now a small museum; this also has a vegetarian *restaurant* open for lunch only.

Saint John River Valley

The Saint John River, which has been likened to the Rhine, begins in Maine, USA, on the north-western corner of New Brunswick and flows south for over 700km before entering the Bay of Fundy at Saint John.

It winds along the western border of the province past forests and beautiful lush farmland, through Fredericton between tree-lined banks, and then around rolling

hills to the bay. The valley is particularly picturesque and gentle from just north of Saint John to near Woodstock.

There are bridges and ferries across the river at various points. The Trans Canada, Hwy 2, follows the river up to Edmundston and then crosses into Quebec.

Because of its soft, eye-pleasing landscape and because the main highway connecting the Atlantic Provinces with central Canada runs along the river, not surprisingly, it is a busy route in summer. So much so that accommodation can be difficult to find in July and August – use the tourist office's toll-free reservation service to book ahead. In the off-peak season there is no problem at all.

There is a choice of two routes, the quicker Trans Canada Hwy mostly on the west side of the river, or Hwy 105 on the east. The slower route is not any more scenic but does go right through many of the smaller villages.

WOODSTOCK

A small town set in a rich farming area, Woodstock acts as a tourist crossroad. The Trans Canada Hwy goes through town, as does the road to Maine, USA. Hwy 95 to Bangor, Maine, and then Hwy 2 is an alternative and shorter route to Montreal than going north through Edmundston and then along the St Lawrence River. Main St through Woodstock has some fine, old large Maritime houses.

There is a bluegrass music festival held in town in summer.

Places to Stay

Down Home B&B (☎ 506-328-1819, 698 *Main St)* is in a 19th century Victorian home with three rooms, one with a private bath. Rates are $55/60.

Fifteen kilometres from the centre via Route 105 but with a quiet, country location is the *Chalet Swiss B&B* (☎ 506-328-6751). The house looks as though it might have been lifted from the Alps. A double is $45 and includes breakfast. Among the motels there's *Motel Haven* (☎ 506-272-2100) on Route 2, with rooms at $34.

HARTLAND

Hartland is an attractive little town with a nice setting and it does have the granddaddy of New Brunswick's many wooden covered bridges. There are 74 of these bridges dotted around the province on secondary roads; the tourist office has a complete listing if you're interested. The bridges were covered to protect the timber beams used in the construction. With such protection from rain and sun, a bridge lasts about 80 years. They are generally high and wide because cartloads of hay pulled by horses had to pass through.

Halfway between here and Grand Falls is a provincial park at Kilburn.

Places to Stay & Eat

The *Ja-Se-Le Motel* (☎ 506-375-4419, ☎ 1-800-565-6433), north of town, is the only local motel. It has a pretty good restaurant serving mainly German food, but you can get the standard Canadian fare. Rooms are $45/52. Of the B&Bs, try *Campbell's B&B* (☎ 506-375-4775), overlooking the Saint John River and just 3km from the famous covered bridge on Hwy 105. Rooms range from $30 to $45.

GRAND FALLS

A town with 7000 residents, Grand Falls consists essentially of one main street and the falls that make it an interesting short stop.

In a park in the middle of town, the falls drop about 25m and have carved out a 1.5km-long gorge with walls as high as 70m. At the site is the Malabeam Reception Centre that doubles as a tourist office (☎ 506-473-4538). Hours during summer are 9 am to 9 pm. Among the displays inside is a scale model of the gorge showing the extensive trail system that follows the edge of it. Entrance to the park and centre are free but there is a $2 admission for a 253-step stairway that leads down into the gorge. You can also take a 45 minute boat ride to get up close; they run up to eight times per day when water levels are high and cost $10.

The falls are best in spring or after a heavy rain. In summer, much of the water is diverted for generating hydroelectricity. The

dam for this also takes away from the rugged beauty the site once would have had. The area at the bottom of the gorge reached by the staircase is more scenic than the falls themselves and permits a glimpse of how the pre-development days would have looked.

The town celebrates its primary resource, the potato, in a festival each year around 1 July.

Places to Stay & Eat
The *Maple Tourist Home* (☎ *506-473-1763, 142 Main St)* is a B&B with doubles for $50/55. Along the highway to the north of town are several *motels* and *camping*.

For something to eat there are a couple of quick places down the main street, Broadway. At *Grits Bar & Grill (cnr Broadway & Main Sts)* most dinners are under $8 and there always seems to be a beer special going on. *LaBouffe Restaurant*, also on Broadway, serves café latte and filled croissants.

AROUND GRAND FALLS
East of Grand Falls around the farming community of New Denmark is the largest Danish population in North America. In the middle of July there's a festival celebrating all things Danish. In town, there is a small museum while the *Valhalla Restaurant* serves Danish food all year.

Hwy 108, the Plaster Rock Hwy, cuts across the province to the east coast. The highway slices through forest for nearly its entirety. Animals aren't much used to traffic here, so take care. There are some camping spots along the way.

SAINT LÉONARD
As the name suggests, Saint Léonard is primarily a French town, like many in this region. Some are old Acadian settlements although the Acadian descendants are more concentrated in the north-east of the province.

In Saint Léonard is the Madawaska Weavers group, formed in 1939 and still using hand looms to make fabric for items such as ponchos and scarves. Visit the centre at Main and Saint-Jean Sts.

From here, Hwy 17 runs north-east through the dense forests of northern New Brunswick.

EDMUNDSTON
If you're coming from Quebec there's a good chance this will be the first town in the Maritimes you get a look at, as the border is only about 20km away. From here it is a three hour drive to Fredericton. Maine is just across the river and there is an international bridge on Dupont St at the south end of town not far from City Hall.

Edmundston is an industrial pulp and paper centre with numerous mills in and around town. It's split pretty well in half by the Madawaska River and the old central district on the west side of the river is built around some low hills which give it some character.

The population of about 13,000 is 85% French-speaking. Nearly all of them, like most of New Brunswick's French, also speak English.

The main intersection downtown is that of Church St and Canada Rd. Within a few blocks of this corner are many of the shops, a couple of restaurants, City Hall plus an indoor shopping mall. Victoria St, between the highway and this central section, is also a busy commercial street.

Clustered around exit 18 from the highway is the tourist office, a shopping mall, some fast-food restaurants and nearby a motel.

The local citizens have a whimsical notion of Edmundston as the capital of a fictitious country known as Madawaska whose inhabitants are known as Brayons. Evidently this traditional community-uniting concept has historical origins in a period during the late 1700s when the region existed in a sort of political vacuum between the border-bickering of the US and British governments.

Information
The local tourist office (☎ 506-739-8191) is south of the museum building on Boulevard Hébert.

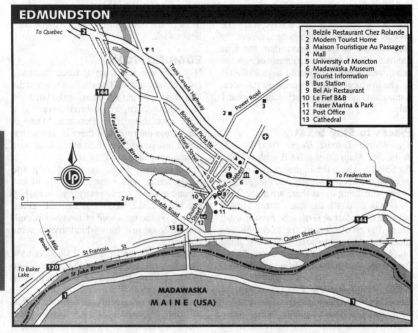

EDMUNDSTON

To Quebec

Trans Canada Highway

Madawaska River

Boulevard Pichette

Victoria Street

Power Road

To Fredericton

Canada Road

Church Street

Two Mile Brook

St Francois St

St John River

To Baker Lake

Queen Street

MADAWASKA
M A I N E (USA)

1 Belzile Restaurant Chez Rolande
2 Modern Tourist Home
3 Maison Touristique Au Passager
4 Mall
5 University of Moncton
6 Madawaska Museum
7 Tourist Information
8 Bus Station
9 Bel Air Restaurant
10 Le Fief B&B
11 Fraser Marina & Park
12 Post Office
13 Cathedral

0   1   2 km

NEW BRUNSWICK

Madawaska Museum
At 195 Boulevard Hébert on the corner of
Boulevard Pichette is the Madawaska Museum (☎ 506-737-5064) which outlines the
human history of the area from the time of
the original Maliseet (Malecite) Indians
through colonial times to the present. The
museum also has displays on local industries such as the timber trade. It's open daily
from 9 am to 8 pm in summer, but has reduced hours the rest of the year. Admission
is free.

Petit Témis Interprovincial Linear Park
This unique park stretches from Edmundston
to Cabano in Quebec and features a 62km bicycle trail that winds along the Madawaska
River and Temiscouata Lake. A rather pleasant afternoon can be enjoyed cycling just a
portion of it; the best place to start is at

Fraser Marina just off Victoria St on the east
side of the river in Edmundston. At the marina there's a foot bridge to the west side of
the river, a boat launch and two bike rental
shops. Outdoor Adventures (☎ 506-739-
6800) rents canoes, kayaks, and bicycles.

Special Events
Each year on the nine days preceding the
first Monday in August is the 'Foires' Festival, which celebrates the physically
nonexistent republic of Madawaska. There
are cultural, social and sporting activities as
well as some good traditional Brayon cooking to sample.

Places to Stay
The *University of Moncton* (☎ 506-737-
5016) is just north of the museum and in
summer has rooms from $20; at times you
get your own washroom (a steal).

On Power Rd, in the north-west section of the city just off Hwy 2, are a couple of cheap tourist homes: the *Modern Tourist Home* (☎ *506-735-7926, 224 Power Rd)*, which charges $25, and the *Maison Touristique Au Passager* (☎ *506-735-5781)* just up the street, which charges a whopping $30.

Le Fief B&B (☎ *506-735-0400, 87 Church St)* is a little more expensive but centrally located, open all year, and excellent. The four rooms tend to fill up in midsummer. The rate is a whopping $79 in summer, much less off-season.

There are also plenty of motels around town. *La Roma* (☎ *506-735-3305)*, about 1.5km south of town, charges $41/43 and there are larger family rooms available.

Places to Eat
The central downtown area has very few restaurants. The *Bel Air (cnr Victoria St & Boulevard Hébert)*, with the sign that can't be missed, has been here since the 1950s and is open 24 hours. It has become a city landmark. The extensive menu offers Italian, Chinese, seafood or basic Canadian fare. Chinese dinners are under $7, most other dinners are under $10 and the portions are pretty filling. Adjoining the Bel Air is *Steak & Seafood Paradise*, more upmarket with dinners starting at $10. There are also a couple of *Chinese restaurants* along Victoria St.

The locals flock to *Belzile Restaurant Chez Rolande (815 Victoria St)*, a 10 minute drive from the centre, for sandwiches, burgers etc and a couple of French Canadian specialities such as *poutine* (fries topped with melted cheese curds and gravy) and its 'famous' sugar pies. Hamburger plates or fish and chips are under $5.

Getting There & Away
Bus The SMT terminal (☎ 506-739-8309) is across the street from the Bel Air restaurant, at 169 Victoria St near the corner of Boulevard Hébert at the bridge.

You can catch buses here for Quebec City and points east such as Saint John, Moncton or Halifax, although a transfer may be necessary for the longer trips. For trips to Maine (Bangor), New York, Boston or other USA destinations, departures are from Saint John.

To Moncton and Amherst there are two services daily on SMT Bus Lines from which a transfer can be made to continue onto Halifax. One-way fares are Halifax $105 and Moncton $65. For Moncton, ask for the express bus.

There are three buses daily to Quebec City, which includes transferring to the Orleans Express bus line at Rivière-Du-Loup. Orleans is the company which covers eastern Quebec. The one-way fare is $47.

SAINT JACQUES
Seven kilometres north of Edmundston, about halfway to the Quebec border, is the small community of Saint Jacques which has a couple of places of interest. Les Jardins de la Republique Provincial Park (☎ 506-735-4871) offers good *camping* and has picnic sites along the river. Admission costs $2.25 and camp sites cost $15. Next to it, somewhat inexplicably, is an auto museum.

Also here is the wonderful New Brunswick Botanical Gardens (☎ 506-739-6335), put together by a group from the well known Montreal Botanical Gardens in Quebec. With both natural and cultivated sections running along the edge of the Madawaska River, it makes a refreshing, tranquil respite from the highway if you've had a long drive. The garden is open daily from 9 am till dusk early June to the middle of October and there is a snack bar. Admission is $4.75 or $11.25 per family.

There are a couple of motels here, a few kilometres from the commercial strip around Edmundston. One, *Motel Guy* (☎ *506-735-4253)*, is on the Trans Canada Hwy and charges $45.

Manitoba

Manitoba, Canada's fifth province, probably gets its name from the Algonkian Indian languages – in Lake Manitoba there is a strait where the water hits the limestone edges, making an odd echoing sound; the Native Indians associated this sound with the 'great spirit' ('manito') and named the spot 'Manito Waba', which means Manito Strait. Manito Waba became Manitoba.

The province is the first of the three prairie provinces as you head westward. The southern half is low and flat; the western edge is best for farming. The Canadian Shield, which covers about half the country, cuts across northern Manitoba, making this rocky, hilly forested lake land.

Winnipeg, the capital, has had a long and interesting history which greatly influenced the development of the west in general. The city has a variety of things to see and do, and many are within walking distance of each other along architecturally diverse streets.

Winnipeg is a major cultural centre and offers plenty of choice in accommodation and eating out. Neighbouring St Boniface is the largest western French community in Canada

Scattered across the province are large parks, ideal for exploring the terrain. Way up on Hudson Bay, Churchill with its intriguing wildlife is one of the destinations most alluring to visitors.

Manufacturing is the most significant economic sector. Wheat is the major agricultural product, with various other grains and cattle following closely behind. In the northern Shield area there are rich deposits of gold, copper, nickel and zinc.

History

The Assiniboine and Cree First Nations were the principal groups inhabiting the region upon the arrival of Europeans. The Chipewayen of the northern sections and around Hudson Bay soon became involved with the fur traders. The Ojibway, found

HIGHLIGHTS

Entered Confederation: 15 July 1870
Area: 650,090 sq km
Population: 1,138,872
Provincial Capital: Winnipeg

- Enjoy Winnipeg's museums and take in the Folk Festival in early July

- Take part in the cultural life of western Canada's largest French community

- Visit the far-north natural attractions of Churchill, which include polar bears, caribou and beluga whales

- Drive past fields of nodding sunflowers in the south-eastern part of the province

- Explore some of the 3000 sq km of Riding Mountain National Park with its multitude of forests, lakes, rivers and meadows

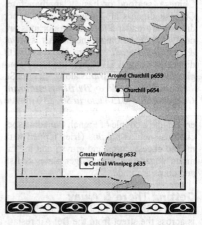

Around Churchill p659
Churchill p654
Greater Winnipeg p632
Central Winnipeg p635

mainly across Ontario, also moved as far west as the great lakes of Manitoba.

Unlike in much of the country, early European exploration and settlement occurred not in the more hospitable south but along

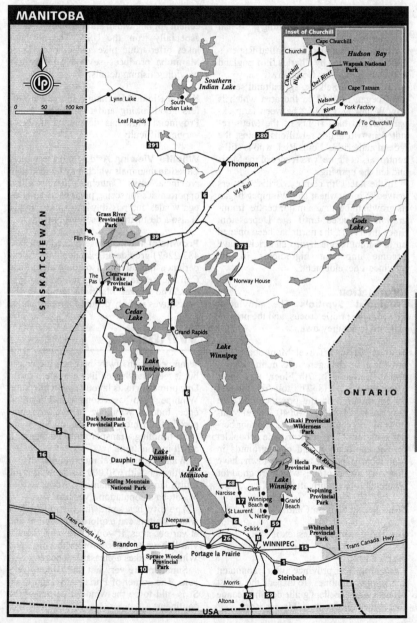

MANITOBA

Inset of Churchill
Cape Churchill
Churchill
Hudson Bay
Churchill River
Owl River
Wapusk National Park
Nelson River
Cape Tatnam
York Factory
To Churchill

Southern Indian Lake
Lynn Lake
South Indian Lake
Leaf Rapids
391
280
Gillam
Thompson
6
VIA Rail
373
Gods Lake
Grass River Provincial Park
Flin Flon
39
Norway House
The Pas
Clearwater Lake Provincial Park
10
Cedar Lake
6
Grand Rapids
Lake Winnipegosis
Lake Winnipeg
ONTARIO

SASKATCHEWAN

Duck Mountain Provincial Park
5
16
Dauphin
Lake Dauphin
Lake Manitoba
Atikaki Provincial Wilderness Park
Bloodvein River
Hecla Provincial Park
Lake Winnipeg
Nopiming Provincial Park
Riding Mountain National Park
68
Narcisse
Gimli
17
Winnipeg Beach
Grand Beach
St Laurent
Netley
1
Trans Canada Hwy
16
Neepawa
6
Selkirk
59
Whiteshell Provincial Park
Brandon
1
26
8
WINNIPEG
Trans Canada Hwy
15
Portage la Prairie
1
Spruce Woods Provincial Park
10
Steinbach
Morris
75
59
Altona
USA

0   50   100 km

MANITOBA

the cold, remote coasts of Hudson Bay. By the early 17th century fur-trading posts had been set-up.

Much of Manitoba, first called Rupert's Land, was granted by Charles II of England to the Hudson's Bay Company.

Led by Lord Selkirk, agricultural settlement began in 1812 in the area which is now Winnipeg. Conflict between farm expansion and land rights of the Métis resulted in two major rebellions against the federal authorities. Louis Riel, who is still a controversial figure, was leader of the Métis and led the uprisings.

In the late 19th century, British settlers arrived to grow wheat and Winnipeg began its growth to become a major centre. Immigration increased until the Depression. Since the 1950s, the north has been opened up and mining and hydro-electricity have become important ingredients in the province's development.

Information

Provincial Symbols The provincial flower is the prairie crocus, and the provincial bird is the grey owl.

Tourist Offices Travel Manitoba is the provincial tourist agency. Its main office is at 155 Carleton St, 7th Floor, Winnipeg, Manitoba R3C 3H8. The toll free number for information on the province and free material is ☎ 1-800-665-0040. Travel Manitoba offices can also be found at major border crossings. The staff provide a booklet on accommodation and campgrounds in Manitoba. Winnipeg and other towns have their own tourist offices which are good for obtaining local information.

Time Manitoba is on Central Time.

Tax The provincial sales tax is 7%.

Activities

Canoeing The province offers abundant canoeing possibilities. To this end the tourist office has an excellent guide detailing canoe routes including some wilderness trips.

Fishing The province is renowned for excellent angling which attracts many visitors, especially from the USA. The northern lakes offer trout, pike and others. Travel Manitoba produces several publications providing fishing details.

Hiking Riding Mountain National Park offers good hiking and riding. Whiteshell Provincial Park has developed trails of varying difficulty.

Wildlife Viewing Aside from the typical Canadian mammals which may be spotted in provincial parks, Churchill offers excellent opportunities for seeing polar bears and beluga whales and possibly caribou. Churchill is also a destination for serious birders.

Provincial Parks These parks (☎ 1-888-482-2267) provide an excellent way to experience the land and outdoor activities. Call the central camping reservation system. The Travel Manitoba guide to the parks gives activity details for major parks.

Winnipeg

Winnipeg sits halfway between the coasts but it feels very much like a western town. Due primarily to its layout and architecture, Winnipeg also has a somewhat US ambience. Indeed, Winnipeg is regularly compared to Chicago – its mid-western, grain-handling, transportation counterpart, albeit in miniature.

Winnipeg does feel much bigger than it is, although with 650,000 residents, it is the fourth largest Canadian city. About half of Manitoba's population lives here.

The city has some fascinating history which visitors can explore in museums and at various sites. If you're crossing Canada you'll have to pass through the city, and Winnipeg makes a pleasant stopover.

Summers are very hot and winters very cold. The corner of Portage Ave and Main St is said to be the windiest corner of the continent.

History

The Cree Indian people called the area 'Winnipee', meaning 'muddy water'. They shared the land now occupied by Winnipeg with the Assiniboines, before de la Véren-drye, the first European trader, arrived in 1738. In the early 19th century the area was the centre of fur-trading rivalry between the Hudson's Bay Company and the North West Company.

In 1812 Lord Selkirk led Scottish and Irish immigrants to the area to create the first permanent colonial settlement. Later, Fort Garry was built. Louis Riel, a native son and one of Canada's most controversial figures, led the Métis in voicing concerns over their way of life. He is considered the father of Manitoba. The railway arrived in Winnipeg in 1881.

The 1970s saw urban redevelopment upgrade the provincial capital. In the 1980s, the main street, Portage Ave, underwent a massive change, with the building of a mega-mall complex taking over several blocks. The wide downtown streets, edged with a balance of new and old buildings, give a sense of permanence as well as of development and change.

Orientation

As you approach Winnipeg from the east, the trees start to disappear. With about 50km to go, the flat prairie land that stretches to the Rockies appears. Near town is a sign marking the longitudinal centre of Canada.

Once in Winnipeg, Main St is the main north-south street. Portage (pronounced 'Port-idge') Ave, the major east-west artery, is also the main shopping street, leading westward towards the airport and eventually to the westbound Trans Canada Hwy. The downtown core spreads out evenly from their junction. Most of the hotels and restaurants and many of the historic sites are within a 10-block square around this point. The railway station is central, on the corner of Main St and Broadway Ave. The Legislative Building and other government buildings are on Broadway Ave, too.

The corner of Portage Ave and Main St has many office buildings and examples of newer architecture. Portage Place, a rede-velopment project of stores and offices, runs from Carlton St all the way to Vaughan St and has transformed much of the north side of Portage Ave. Enclosed walkways (known as skywalks) over Portage Ave connect Portage Place to major department stores on the south side. Many of the downtown side streets are one-way streets, which alternate in direction as a rule.

To the north-east of the city core is the old warehouse area known as the Exchange District. Nearby, north up Main St, the Centennial Centre is an arts and cultural complex.

The small Chinatown is also in this area.

North of Rupert St on Main St is an area of cheap bars and dingy hotels. Farther north on Main St, you'll find some evidence of the many ethnic groups, primarily Jews and Ukrainians, who once lived here in greater numbers.

South of the downtown area, across the Assiniboine River on Osborne St, is Osborne Village, a popular area containing boutiques, stores and restaurants. Back across the bridge in the downtown area, the art gallery is on the corner of Memorial Blvd and Portage Ave and the bus station is nearby.

South of Osborne Village, along Corydon Ave for a few blocks, between Cockburn St N and Daly St N, is a small Italian district which has become the centre of a little café and restaurant scene. It's particularly good for a stroll in summer, when many of the places have outdoor patios along the street.

Information

Tourist Offices The main tourist office (☎ 204-945-3777, ☎ 1-800-665-0040) is the Travel Manitoba Idea Centre in the Johnstone Building at The Forks, the historic site and market by the riverside, not far from the train station. The office is open daily in summer until 9 pm.

Travel Manitoba operates another office (☎ 204-945-5813) in the Legislative Building on Broadway Ave. During summer it's open daily from 8 am to 7 pm. Winter hours are 8 am to 4.30 pm, Monday to Friday.

Tourism Winnipeg (☎ 204-943-1970, ☎ 1-800-665-0204) can also be found at The

GREATER WINNIPEG

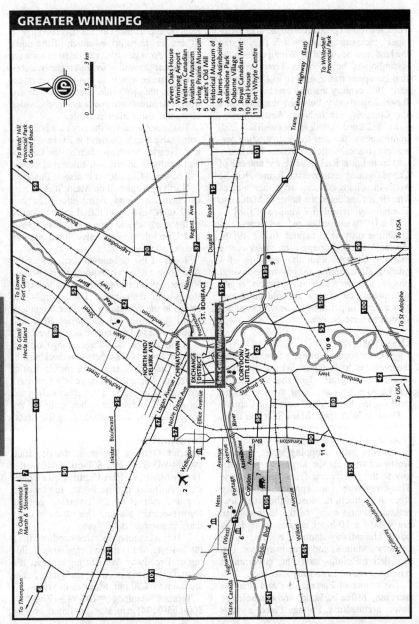

1 Seven Oaks House
2 Winnipeg Airport
3 Western Canadian Aviation Museum
4 Living Prairie Museum
5 Grant's Old Mill
6 Historical Museum of St James-Assiniboine
7 Assiniboine Park
8 Osborne Village
9 Royal Canadian Mint
10 Riel House
11 Fort Whyte Centre

To Birds' Hill Provincial Park & Grand Beach

To Whiteshell Provincial Park

Trans Canada Highway (East)

0   1.5   3 km

To Lower Fort Garry

To Gimli & Hecla Island

To Oak Hammock Marsh & Stonewall

To Thompson

To USA

To St Adolphe

To USA

Regent Ave

Dugald Road

Naim Ave

Lagimodiere Boulevard

Red River

Main Street

McPhillips Street

Inkster Boulevard

Logan Avenue

Notre Dame Ave

Ellice Avenue

Portage Avenue

Ness Avenue

Roblin Blvd

Assiniboine River

Corydon Avenue

Wilkes Avenue

Kenaston Blvd

Pembina Hwy

Wellington

McGillivray Boulevard

Trans Canada Highway (West)

Henderson Hwy

Stafford St

NORTH END/ SELKIRK AVE

CHINATOWN

EXCHANGE DISTRICT

ST. BONIFACE

CORYDON/ LITTLE ITALY

See Central Winnipeg map

MANITOBA

Forks, on the 3rd floor of the Johnston Terminal, and is open Monday to Friday from 8.30 am to 4.30 pm.

There's also a Tourism Winnipeg Information Centre on the main floor of the airport. It's open daily from 8 am to 9.45 pm.

Money The Custom House Currency Exchange (☎ 204-987-6000), 245 Portage Ave, has better rates and longer hours than the banks.

Post & Communications The main post office is at 266 Graham Ave. The general delivery window is open on Saturday morning as well as during the regular weekday hours. There is a postal outlet in McKnight's Pharmacy, 120 Donald St, near Broadway.

Travel Agencies Travel CUTS (☎ 204-269-9530) has an office in the University Centre at the University of Manitoba on Portage Ave.

Bookshops For an assortment of travel books and maps and everything else check McNally Robinson on the ground floor of Portage Place with a patio on the north side of the mall.

Medical Services The Health Sciences Centre (☎ 204-787-3167) is at 820 Sherbrooke St.

Museum of Man & Nature

This excellent museum (☎ 204-956-2830) at 190 Rupert St beside the Centennial Concert Hall, has exhibits of history, culture, wildlife and geology. The dioramas of Native Indian life and animals are realistic, incorporating sights, sounds and even smells. Take a look at the grizzly claw necklace given to artist Paul Kane in 1848 by Assiniboine chief Mah-Min. Plains Indians wore them as proof of their bravery – to get one you either had to kill four grizzlies or a Sioux Indian who was already wearing one!

There is an excellent re-creation of a 1920s town, with 'sod' house, barber shop, drug store and old cinema (complete with Chaplin movies). In another section, you can climb aboard a full-sized replica of the *Nonsuch*, the 17th century ketch that took the first load of Hudson's Bay Company furs to England.

The museum is worth an afternoon's visit. Admission costs $5. A combined ticket to the museum, planetarium and science centre is $11. It's open every day from 10 am until 6 pm in summer (until 9 pm Thursday). From September to June it's open from 10 am until 4 pm on weekdays and until 5 pm on weekends. It's closed on Monday.

Planetarium

The planetarium (☎ 204-943-3139), housed within the museum, has good programs on space, the solar system and different aspects of the universe. There are also laser rock shows, fashion shows and other performances which utilise the unique equipment. The usual programs are $4; the laser rock shows are more expensive. Ring for information.

Science Centre

In the museum basement is a 'hands-on' science gallery with participatory displays designed to help reveal how our senses perceive the world. The staff put on demonstrations on a range of scientific topics. Admission is $4, less for children.

Ukrainian Centre

The Ukrainian Centre (☎ 204-942-0218) at 184 Alexander Ave, near the Museum of Man & Nature, contains a gallery and museum. Set up to preserve and present the culture of the Ukraine, the museum has costumes, textiles, ceramics as well as painted Easter eggs *(pysankas)*. The gallery displays both old and contemporary works. A specialised library holds 60,000 volumes relating to this important Canadian immigrant group.

The centre is open Tuesday to Saturday from 10 am to 4 pm, and on Sunday from 2 to 5 pm. Admission is $2.

Holy Trinity Ukrainian Orthodox Cathedral

Within this church with bulbous Byzantine domes is the provincial branch of the Ukrainian Museum of Canada (☎ 204-582-7345).

Examples of traditional arts and crafts are displayed. The cathedral is at 1175 Main St. Call for opening times, as they vary seasonally and by day of the week.

The Forks

This very successful redevelopment project has made The Forks the busiest people place in Winnipeg. The fetching location at the forks of the Red and Assiniboine rivers, behind the VIA Rail station off Main St near Broadway Ave, has in one way or another been the site of much of Manitoba's history.

Parks Canada staff on hand at the Travel Manitoba Idea Centre (☎ 204-983-6757) in the Johnstone Terminal can provide information on what's gone on through the years at this national historic site. Walking tours are offered summer Saturdays or pick up a self-guided walking tour pamphlet.

Native Indians first used the area some 6000 years ago. The early explorers and fur traders stopped here, forts were built and destroyed, and Métis and Scottish pioneers later settled The Forks. Behind the Children's Museum, the Orientation Circle has a history exhibit. The Riverwalk is a path with historic notes written on plaques in English, French and Cree. Parts of the trail also provide views of the city along the way.

The site, though, is essentially a riverside park/recreation area, with shops, restaurants, bars and events all centred around overhauled late 19th/early 20th century stables, warehouses and factories.

The Market Building is buzzing with produce stalls, craft shops, galleries and cafés. It's a fine place for a coffee and a cinnamon bun (a local speciality) with a newspaper. The Johnston Terminal is similar but features shops and restaurants.

Canoes can be rented at the site; a paddle along the historic river, perhaps past the Basilica over in St Boniface, is not a bad way to spend a couple of hours. A water bus runs back and forth across the river, too, or to Osborne Village with a stop at the dock behind the Legislature. Full-scale boat tours of the river depart from the nearby Provencher Bridge area. In winter there is skating on the river or you can walk over the ice to the impressive-looking St Boniface Basilica façade. Cross-country ski trails are groomed along the river. Take a break and warm up beside the fire in the Pavilion.

City buses connect the downtown area to the site near the Market Building, but it is quite walkable. The No 99 or No 38 bus runs from here up to Broadway Ave and around by the Art Gallery and Portage Ave.

Manitoba Children's Museum

Here's a museum (☎ 204-956-5437) set up just for kids, especially those between the ages of three and 11 years. Located at The Forks, the museum has a whole range of hands-on exhibits that encourage play and learning at the same time. Included are a fully functional television studio, an exhibit on exploring computer technology, a tree that preschoolers can climb to spot life-sized animals and birds, and a refurbished 1950s diesel engine. The museum is open daily from 10 am to 5 pm (from 11 am weekends, until 8 pm Thursday and Friday) and admission is $4.75.

Legislative Building

The Legislative Building (☎ 204-945-5813) on Broadway Ave on the corner of Osborne St, is one of the world's great examples of the neoclassical architectural style. It was built using rare limestone and is now one of the most valuable buildings in North America. 'Golden Boy', a bronze statue perched jauntily at the top of the building, is covered in 23½-carat gold and has become a city symbol. His torch lights up at night. Inside are two massive bronze bison either side of the staircase. There are good, free tours throughout the day and the building has a cheap and pleasant cafeteria.

Behind the Legislative Building, a park with a monument to Louis Riel, the Métis leader, runs beside the river. At night this is an area for gay cruising.

Macdonald House (Dalnavert)

Near the Legislature, this beautiful Victorian house at 61 Carlton St is also called

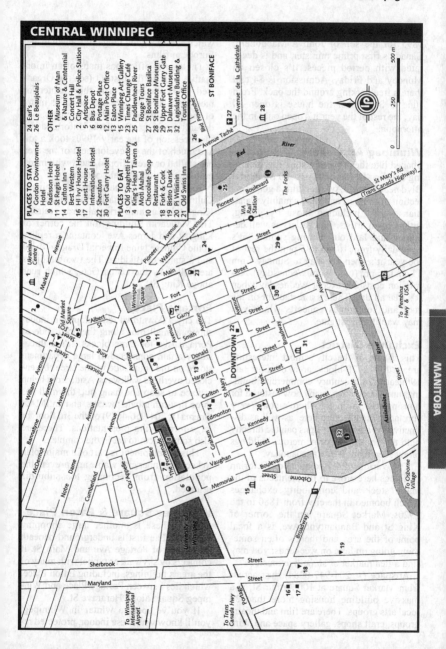

CENTRAL WINNIPEG

PLACES TO STAY
7 Gordon Downtowner Hotel
9 Radisson Hotel
11 St Regis Hotel
14 Carlton Inn - Best Western
16 HI Ivy House Hostel
17 Guest House International Hostel
22 Sheraton
30 Fort Garry Hotel

PLACES TO EAT
3 Old Spaghetti Factory
4 King's Head Tavern & Moti Mahal
10 Chocolate Shop Restaurant
18 Fork & Cork
19 Bistro Dansk
20 Pj Wiissinin
21 Old Swiss Inn

24 Earl's
26 Le Beaujolais

OTHER
1 Museum of Man & Nature & Centennial Concert Hall
2 City Hall & Police Station
5 Artspace
6 Bus Depot
8 Portage Place
12 Main Post Office
13 Eaton Place
15 Winnipeg Art Gallery
23 Times Change Café
25 Paddlewheel River Rouge Tours
27 St Boniface Basilica
28 St Boniface Museum
29 Upper Fort Garry Gate
31 Dalnavert Museum
32 Legislative Building & Tourist Office

ST BONIFACE

Red River

The Forks

St Mary's Rd
(Trans Canada Highway)

To Pembina Hwy & USA

DOWNTOWN

University of Winnipeg

To Osborne Village

To Winnipeg International Airport

To Trans Canada Hwy

MANITOBA

Dalnavert (☎ 204-943-2835). It was built in 1895 for the son of John A Macdonald, Canada's first prime minister, and is decorated with period pieces. It's closed on Monday and Friday. Admission is $4 and there's free parking around the back. From June to September the house is open all day; the rest of the year it's open only in the afternoon.

Winnipeg Art Gallery

Shaped like the prow of a ship, this gleaming building (☎786-6641) at 300 Memorial Blvd near Portage Ave, contains a good collection of Inuit art and shows mainly Canadian works, including those by young, little-known artists. The gallery is well designed and laid out. During summer it's open daily from 10 am to 5 pm; the rest of the year it's open Tuesday to Sunday from 11 am to 5 pm (until 9 pm Wednesday). Admission costs $4, except Wednesday when it's free all day. There's a restaurant on the roof and sometimes concerts which you may want to investigate.

Exchange District

This is one of the city's most interesting areas. It's a 20-block area of fine late 19th/early 20th century commercial buildings and warehouses, many now restored for housing and business. There's some very substantial architecture here, as well as distinctive old advertising signs painted directly onto the brick walls of numerous buildings rarely seen in most of Canada today.

The various Edwardian and Victorian buildings here arose to fill the needs of the many stock and commodity exchanges which boomed in the city from 1880 to the 1920s. Market Square, on the corner of King St and Bannantyne Ave, is a focal point of the area and there's often something going on here on weekends; you may find a flea market or some live music.

Artspace (☎ 204-947-0984), just across from Market Square at 100 Arthur St, is a massive building housing more than 20 local arts groups. There are film and theatre groups, craft shops, gallery space and Win-

nipeg's Cinémathéque (☎ 204-925-3457), which shows a good range of Canadian and European films.

The tourist office has maps of an informative walk in the district (see the Organised Tours section later in this chapter for more details). The area also contains many of the city's theatres and some clubs, so it doesn't close up after dark. Unfortunately, the recession of the early 1990s took a toll and much of the redevelopment of the area has stalled or even slipped back, with many buildings sitting partially vacant.

Just north in Chinatown, the Chinese Cultural Building/Dynasty Building, at 180 King St, has a small oriental garden retreat. The Mandarin Building, on the corner of King St and James Ave, contains a replica of the Chinese Nine Imperial Dragon Mural and a statue of Buddha. The two buildings are linked by the China Gate, which runs above King St.

Portage Place

The city's downtown redevelopment indoor shopping mall runs along the north side of Portage Ave for three blocks. It's a three-storey affair, connected to large department stores on the south side of the street by enclosed overhead walkways. Aside from being a place to shop and hang out, the mall has three first-run movie theatres, and an IMAX cinema (☎ 204-956-4629) on the 3rd floor for large-format film presentations. There are also some places to eat in the complex.

This development is part of a major plan to keep the inner city viable and prevent the population from becoming too suburbia oriented.

Winnipeg Square & Eaton Place

Each of these is another large shopping complex. The first is underground beneath the corner of Portage Ave and Main St. It connects by skywalk or tunnel with many of the area's buildings, including Eaton Place, which lies between Portage Place and Winnipeg Square along Hargrave St.

If you've spent a winter in Winnipeg, you'll know why these indoor, protected re-

tail centres are so commonplace. There are food fairs in both, as well as several restaurants covering a variety of price ranges.

Winnipeg Commodity Exchange

Canada's largest and oldest commodity futures market (☎ 204-925-5000) is here, with a visitors gallery which overlooks the trading area. It's on the 5th floor of the Commodity Exchange Tower, 360 Main St. You can see grains and other crops being traded and prices fluctuating with the Chicago markets. Don't forget to find out how pork bellies are doing. Guides can explain some of this very different world to you at no charge. The exchange is open Monday to Friday from 9.30 am to 1.15 pm.

Upper Fort Garry Gate

In the small park on Main St, near Broadway Ave and across from the train station, is the old stone gate and some remaining wall (restored in 1982) of Fort Garry. Since 1738, four different forts have stood on this spot, or nearby. The gate dates from 1835 and was part of the Hudson's Bay Company's fort system. There are also some photographs and written descriptions.

St Boniface

Primarily a residential district, St Boniface, across the Red River on Boulevard Provencher, is one of the oldest French communities in Canada. There's not much to see, but the imposing façade of the St Boniface Basilica, dating from 1908, is worth a look. The rest of the church was destroyed by fire in 1968. Churches were built and rebuilt on this site from as early as 1818. In front, facing the river, is a cemetery used by the local French from the early 19th century to the present. Louis Riel, the Métis leader, was born in St Boniface and is buried here.

Next door, at 494 Rue Taché, is the St Boniface Museum (☎ 204-237-4500), in what was the nunnery around 1850. This is the oldest building in Winnipeg and evidently is the largest oak-log construction on the continent. It contains artefacts and relics pertaining to Riel and to other French, Métis and

Native Indian settlers as well as to the Grey Nuns, who lived and worked here after arriving by birch-bark canoe from Montreal, a trip of nearly 3000km. There is also some information on Jean Baptiste Lagimodière, one of the best-known of the voyageurs (early French fur traders/explorers) who canoed between here and Montreal. There is a diorama of a Métis hunter's camp, with an example of the famous Red River Cart, which could be floated across rivers by repositioning the wheels. Also in the museum are some articles that were saved from the destroyed basilica.

Admission is $2. In summer, it's open from 9 am to 9 pm Monday to Friday, from 9 am to 5 pm on Saturday, and from 10 am to 9 pm on Sunday and holidays. In winter it closes at 5 pm every day.

The tourist office has a booklet on the area of St Boniface which includes a map and self-guided walking tour. To get there from downtown, take the bus east along Portage Ave across the bridge and then walk along the river to the church and museum. From The Forks it's a short, pleasant walk to St Boniface.

Taché Promenade follows the Red River along Rue Taché, past much of St Boniface's history. A few plaques indicate the major points of interest and provide some details about the Grey Nuns.

Gabrielle Roy House, 375 Rue Deschambault, was built in 1905 by Léon Roy, the father of Gabrielle, a well known Canadian fiction writer who used the house as the setting for some of her works. Outside the house there is a small plaque but nothing much to see unless you're a literary fan.

At 340 Boulevard Provencher is the **Centre Culturel Franco-Manitobain** (☎ 204-233-8972). The centre is open daily and is responsible for organising, creating and promoting a variety of French cultural events around the city. There's a bar, and a restaurant serves French Canadian food at lunch.

Royal Canadian Mint

The real money is made south-east of town at 520 Lagimodière Boulevard, on the corner of the Trans Canada Hwy (☎ 204-257-3359).

This ultramodern, glass, pyramid-shaped building contains some of the most modern minting machinery in the world. The mint produces Canada's coinage as well as coins for many other countries, especially Asian. Admission is $2 and includes a tour offered every half-hour from 9 am to 5 pm Monday to Friday showing the procedures used in cranking out two billion coins a year. On Saturday (noon to 5 pm) there are no guides. It's open May to September; call for winter hours and tours.

Western Canadian Aviation Museum

One of the country's largest aviation museums, the WCAM (☎ 204-786-5503) is in a hangar at 958 Ferry Rd, opposite the Winnipeg international airport. It has a good collection of 25 planes. The museum is open Monday to Saturday from 10 am to 4 pm, and on Sunday afternoon. Admission is $3. From the 'Flight Deck', traffic at the airport can be observed. About five minutes west by car is the **Air Force Base Heritage Park** with about 10 aircraft mounted outside. It's on Ness Ave at the end of Sharpe Blvd.

Police Museum

At the Winnipeg Police Academy (☎ 204-986-3976), 130 Allard Ave, a small museum features uniforms, 'wanted' posters, a Harley Davidson and a jail cell from 1911. It's free, but call about opening hours.

Riel House National Historic Park

At 330 River Rd, in a residential area known as St Vital, quite a distance south of downtown, Riel House (☎ 204-257-1783) details Louis Riel's life here in the 1880s.

The restored and furnished traditional French Canadian-style log farmhouse, built in 1881, belonged to Riel's parents. He was brought here to lie in state after his execution in Saskatchewan in 1885. A staff interpreter offers information on the Riels and on the Métis in general.

To get there, take the No 16 bus from Portage Ave going west; after passing through Osborne Village, it will take you nearly to the door. The site looks out of place beside the modern bungalows which surround it. Opening hours are 10 am to 6 pm, Mid-May to Labour Day and weekends only in September (it's closed for the rest of the year). Admission is by donation, but phone to be sure it is open before making the trip.

Seven Oaks House

The oldest habitable house in the province, Seven Oaks House (☎ 204-339-7429) was built (without nails) in 1851. It's about 4km north of Portage Ave and Main St, at 115 Rupertsland Ave, and is open daily from the last weekend in May to Labour Day.

Historical Museum of St James-Assiniboine

This small museum (☎ 204-888-8706), 3180 Portage Ave, has a collection of Native Indian, Métis and pioneer artefacts from the area at the turn of the century. It's open from 10 am to 5 pm daily, but is closed on weekends after Labour Day until the following spring. Admission is by donation. There's a 100-year-old log house on site with authentic furnishings.

Ross House

Ross House (☎ 204-943-3958), the first post office in the west, is an example of Red River log construction. It's open from mid-May to Labour Day, Wednesday to Sunday from 11 am to 6 pm, and is free. It can be found in Joe Zuken Heritage Park, on the west side of Mead St between Sutherland and Euclid Sts.

North Point Douglas & Selkirk Ave

This section of the city, the North End, is one of the most historic areas west of Montreal. Many of the houses are over 100 years old, and plaques and monuments commemorate various historical events.

It's north up Main St, just north and east of the junction of Hwy 42, which leads over the river and north out of town. Selkirk Ave has long been the commercial centre of the city's north end and the first home of a range of immigrant groups. See Organised

Louis Riel, Hero of the Métis

The Métis are people of mixed Native Indian and French blood, almost always the result of unions between white men and Native Indian women. Many Métis can trace their ancestors to the time of western exploration and fur trading, when the French voyageurs travelled the country, living like (and often with) the Native Indians.

The term is also used more loosely to include English-Indian mixed bloods, in order to avoid the term half-breed.

As time passed and their numbers grew, many Métis began to use the St Boniface/Winnipeg area as a settlement base, living a life which was part European, part traditionally Native Indian. This unique juxtaposition soon became an identity, and those born into it began to think of themselves as a distinct people with their own needs. The ensuing rebellions against the political authorities were the almost inevitable product of this consciousness.

Born in St Boniface in 1844, Louis Riel led the Métis in an antigovernment uprising in 1869, partly to protest the decision to open up what they saw as their lands to new settlers and partly to prevent possible assimilation. When complaints went unheeded, he and his men took Upper Fort Garry. Government troops soon reversed that and, to the Canadian government, Riel became a bad guy. Land was allotted to the Métis, however, and the province of Manitoba was created. As part of the turning twists of Riel's fate, he was then elected to the House of Commons, but was forbidden to serve.

There is some question about what transpired in the next few years. Riel may have spent time in asylums. In any case, he took refuge in Montana for several years from the stress of personal persecution and political machinations. Later he returned to lead the again protesting Métis in their 1885 struggle in Saskatchewan, where they had fled seeking greater autonomy. They again lost the battle. Riel surrendered and, after a dramatic trial, was called a traitor and hanged. The act triggered French anger and resentment towards the British that has not yet been forgotten. Riel's body was returned to his mother's house in Winnipeg and then buried in St Boniface. Ironically, Riel is now considered the father of the province.

Important sites relating to the Métis and Riel can be seen in Winnipeg, St Boniface and in and around Saskatoon.

Louis Riel

Tours later in this chapter for details of free walking tours of the area.

Assiniboine Park

Assiniboine is the largest city park and is open from 7 am until dark. The grounds hold an English garden, a 40-hectare zoo with animals from around the world and an art gallery/restaurant in the historic Pavilion building. See the statue of Winnie the Bear, a bear purchased in White River, Ontario by a soldier from Winnipeg on his way to England to serve in WW I. The bear ended up at the London Zoo and is said to have been the inspiration for AA Milne's *Winnie the Pooh*.

Other features are the conservatory (with some tropical vegetation) and, nearby, the Leo Mol Sculpture Garden and collection. The sculpture garden displays a very good range of work by the internationally regarded Mol. There are also numerous playing fields. At the beginning of July, watch

MANITOBA

for the free evening outdoor Shakespearean performances.

The park is south of the Assiniboine River and just south-west off Portage Ave, about 7km west of the downtown area. Entrances are off Corydon Ave West (at Shaftsbury) or at the west end of Wellington Crescent.

Assiniboine Forest

South of the Assiniboine Park, between Shaftsbury and Chalfont Aves, this largely undeveloped forest area is even larger than the park itself. In the middle is a pond with an observation area for birdwatching, and deer may be seen along the winding trails.

Grant's Old Mill

Grant's is a reconstruction of an 1829 water mill (☎ 204-837-5761), which is thought to be the first use of hydropower in the province. There's not really very much to see, although grist (grain) is ground every day and offered for sale. The mill is open daily from May to Labour Day. It's on the corner of Booth Drive and Portage Ave West, near Sturgeon Creek.

Living Prairie Museum

At 2795 Ness Ave, north of Grant's Mill, the Living Prairie Museum (☎ 204-832-0167) is really a park, or rather a preserve, where a 12-hectare area of now very scarce, original, unploughed tall prairie grass is protected and studied.

Within this small area, 200 native plants can be found, as well as a variety of animal and birdlife. The interpretive centre at the site is open daily through the summer, and naturalists are on hand. Walking trails and guided walks are offered. Admission is free.

Fort Whyte Centre

The centre (☎ 204-989-8355), at 1961 McCreary Rd in a conservation area with a marsh, lake and woods, is an environmental education facility with walking trails, exhibits, demonstrations and slide shows on local wildlife. A freshwater aquarium depicts the province's different aquatic life. It's not a bad place to get a glimpse of some of the features of rural, undeveloped Manitoba as well as some of the province's fauna. Trails lead through replicas of various provincial wetland areas, where birds, waterfowl and even the odd mammal such as deer may be viewed. Admission is $4 for adults, $3 for students and seniors. It's open daily and is about a 20 minute drive from downtown.

Other Parks

There are numerous parks in and around the city, some quite large. Aside from the ones mentioned, Little Mountain Park has hiking trails and examples of local forest and prairie vegetation. It's 2km east of Sturgeon Rd off Oak Point Hwy.

Activities

Swimming The city Parks & Recreation Dept (☎ 204-986-3700) operates several pools. One of the country's largest is the Pan-Am Pool (☎ 204-986-5890) at 25 Poseidon Bay built for the Pan-American games, another is Sherbrook Pool at 381 Sherbrook St.

Other In summer the larger city parks are good for walking and cycling. In winter there is skating on the rivers, with perhaps the best spot on the Red River near The Forks, in front of the St Boniface Basilica.

Organised Tours

One hour walking tours of the Exchange District depart Pantages Playhouse Theatre once daily in July and August. Tours cost $5.50 per adult; call (☎ 204-986-6937) for times.

Free walking tours (☎ 204-586-2720) of Selkirk Ave are offered in summer at 10 am and 2 pm Tuesday to Saturday. Tours leave from the Amphitheatre on Selkirk Ave, four blocks west of Main St. (See North Point Douglas earlier in this chapter.)

Art Walk (☎ 204-786-6641) offers guided walks of the city's art scene – traditional, Native and contemporary, taking about four hours, including a lunch break. It's a deal at $5.

Gray Line together with Paddlewheel River Rouge (☎ 204-944-8000) have five

boat and bus tours ranging in length and price. The basic downtown double-decker bus tour lasting 3½ hours is $17.

The lower-priced boat tours depart from a wharf down by The Forks Historic Site, at the foot of the Provencher Bridge on the corner of Water Ave and Gilroy St. The ticket office is also here. There are straight along-the-river cruises ($10.75 for a two hour cruise), or more costly evening dinner-dance cruises ($11.75 plus cost of meals, which start at $12.50, and the cruise lasts for three hours), on a replica paddlewheeler. Another travels down to Lower Fort Garry. The MS *River Rouge* also has dinner cruises, dance cruises and Sunday afternoon cruises.

Special Events

The following are some of the major festivals:

Le Festival du Voyageur
This mid-February, 10-day event commemorates the early French voyageurs or fur traders with concerts, a huge winter street party, a Governor's Ball with period costumes, arts and crafts displays and lots of outdoor activities.

The Red River Exhibition
Held in late June at the Winnipeg Arena, this festival is a week-long carnival, with an amusement park and lots of games, rides and exhibits.

Gay Pride Day
Watch for the big parade held at the end of June.

Winnipeg Folk Festival
This annual festival (☎ 204-231-0096) is probably the country's biggest and best known. It takes place for three days in summer, usually early July, with more than 200 concerts plus a craft and international food village. The festival is held at Birds Hill Park, 20km north of downtown.

Black-O-Rama
Held in mid-July, this is an annual summer festival of music, dance and poetry of West Indian origin.

Winnipeg Fringe Festival
This is a nine-day event held in the Exchange District in late July, featuring international fringe theatre, comedy, mime, music and cabaret.

Folklorama
This is the city's big, popular festival of nations. The tourist office will have up-to-date details on this August event which celebrates the city's surprising number of ethnic groups through two weeks of music, dance, and food in pavilions throughout downtown Winnipeg.

Places to Stay

Camping There are a few places to camp around town but most are a long way out, off the main highways or up at the beach areas around Lake Winnipeg.

Jones Campground (☎ 204-864-2721) is 13km west on Hwy 1. Unserviced sites are $12. *Conestoga Campsites (☎ 257-7363, 1341 St Anne's Rd, St Vital)* is a little closer to town, south-east of Winnipeg. Sites are $12. Both campgrounds are open from May to mid-October.

Hostels The HI *Ivey House Hostel (☎ 204-772-3022, 210 Maryland St)* is good and central. It's in an old turreted house near the corner of Broadway Ave and Sherbrook St, not far from the bus station. The hostel sleeps 40 and has kitchen and laundry facilities. During summer it's open from 8 am to midnight and in winter from 8 to 10 am, and 4 pm to midnight. The rates are $15 for members, $17 for nonmembers. Nearby, at 194 Sherbrook St, is the hostelling regional office (for memberships etc).

From the airport, catch the No 15 bus to the corner of Sargent and Maryland Sts. From there, take bus No 29 to the corner of Broadway Ave and Maryland St. From the train station, walk west along Broadway Ave, or take the No 29 bus to the corner of Broadway Ave and Sherbrook St and walk a block west.

Just a few doors away in a similar large, three-storey house dating from 1912 is the comfortable Backpackers *Guest House International (☎ 204-772-1272 or ☎ 1-800-743-4423, 168 Maryland St)*, run by Bill Macdonald. It, too, can accommodate about 40 people in a variety of rooms, including four for couples. There's a kitchen, laundry facilities and Internet access. *X-Files* aficionados should know that the woman who played Fox Mulder's sister once stayed here. She may or may not have been abducted from a second floor bedroom. Dorm beds are $15 and double bed private rooms $35 (no membership required) and it's open all day in summer. Both hostels can be full (or close to it) in July and August, so calling ahead is not a bad idea. Notification prior to

arrival is necessary at Backpackers from November to March because winter months are slow and Bill is not always at home.

An interesting alternative to consider is *Sonja Roeder House* (☎ 204-233-6169, 271 Archibald St) in St Boniface just south of the corner of Boulevard Provencher. The place provides accommodation and meals to adult, immigrant or overseas students but takes in travellers, too. A bed and morning meal is $17 or you can opt for the full-meal plan at excellent rates. All bedrooms have attached washroom and there is parking.

The *University of Manitoba* rents rooms from mid-May to mid-August. Rooms are around $21 per person per night. For information, contact the conference coordinator (☎ 204-474-9942) at 26 MacLean Crescent, Pembina Hall.

B&Bs The provincial B&B Association (☎ 204-661-0300) is based in Winnipeg, and many of its members are also here. In addition there are independent operators in the city and around the province – the tourist office has a fairly extensive list. Prices aren't bad at all, with most in the range of $35/45 for singles/doubles. Breakfast may vary from a light breakfast to a complete hot meal.

Butterfly (☎ 204-783-6664, 226 Walnut St) is in a pleasant old tree-lined residential area near Portage and Broadway Aves. Prices are $42/52.

More upmarket is *West Gate Manor* (☎ 204-772-9788, 71 West Gate) in the historic well-to-do area of Armstrong Point. It's about a 20 minute walk south-east of the Art Gallery or bus station to this quiet neighbourhood. The tasteful, well decorated rooms are $45 a single, $55 a double.

Over in St Boniface, the French area of town, there are good values. The Victorian furnished *Masson's* (☎ 204-237-9230, 181 Rue Masson) is a 15 minute walk to The Forks. There are three rooms with rates at single $35, double $40 to $50 with full breakfast. A second choice is *Gites de la Cathedrale* (☎ 204-233-7792, 581 Rue Langevin), across from Provencher Park.

The small single is just $25 and doubles are $45 with a good breakfast.

Hotels – Budget For grit seekers, there are several skid row specials in the downtown area. In this very basic category not recommended for women is the *Winnipeg Hotel* (☎ 204-942-7762), a few blocks up Main St towards Portage Ave from the railway station. Rooms cost around $25.

Many of the cheapies are clustered around the Exchange District near the intersection of Notre Dame Ave and Albert St. Two are the *Royal Albert Hotel* (☎ 204-943-8750) and the *Oxford Hotel* (☎ 204-942-6712), but neither is particularly savoury. The downstairs bars are the primary feature. Rooms start at about $30; rooms with a bath cost more.

Hotels – Mid-Range Winnipeg is well served by moderately priced hotels with clean, safe rooms in a conveniently central location.

The *Gordon Downtowner Motor Hotel* (☎ 204-943-5581, 330 Kennedy St) is very central, just a few blocks from Portage Ave. It has a restaurant, a couple of bars and free parking. Rates are $50/54.

Similar is the *St Regis* (☎ 204-942-0171, 285 Smith St), just south of Portage Ave, with rooms at $45/55.

The always reliable, *Carlton Inn-Best Western* (☎ 204-942-0881, 220 Carlton St) has rooms from $62/67.

Hotels – Top End The attractive *Hotel Fort Garry* (☎ 204-942-8251, 222 Broadway Ave), built in 1913, is the city's classic old hostelry. It's close to the train station, whose passengers it was meant to serve. Prices fluctuate wildly (up to $140) but look for the regular specials when doubles go for as little as $69. The fabulous buffet breakfasts can make this a real luxury bargain.

Others in this category include the *Radisson* (☎ 204-956-0410, 288 Portage Ave), with rooms for $160/170 and the *Sheraton* (☎ 204-942-5300, 161 Donald St), at about the same rates.

Motels Portage Ave west out of the centre has a handful of places. Closest to downtown is the recommended *Assiniboine Garden Inn* (☎ 204-888-4806, 1975 Portage Ave), on the park, with singles or doubles for $50 and a dining room offering food at good prices.

Reasonable is the simple but friendly *Boulevard Motel* (☎ 204-837-5891, 3120 Portage Ave), 9km from the centre, at $40/44. *Down's Motor Inn* (☎ 204-837-5831, 3740 Portage Ave) charges from $40.

Pembina Hwy (Hwy 42) going south out of town also has several motels. The *Capri* (☎ 204-269-6990, 1819 Pembina Hwy), about 6km out, charges from $42 plus tax for a single in one of the small, quiet cabins at the back and there is a swimming pool. Some of the units have cooking facilities. *Comfort Inn* (☎ 204-269-7390, 3109 Pembina Hwy) is farther out but immaculate, for $75/80.

Places to Eat

The cheapest place to eat in town is the *cafeteria* in the Administration Building, in the cluster of government offices between Main and King Sts on William Ave. Different lunches are served each day. The cafeteria is on the 2nd floor and opens from 8.30 am to 4.30 pm Monday to Friday. Non-employees shouldn't have any problems getting in unless you look like you've slept in the woods for a week. The *Golden Boy Cafeteria* in the Legislative Building is similar and is definitely open to the public.

Downtown on a Sunday most things are closed, but *Salisbury House* (354 Portage Ave) is open early and closes late every day. There's another one, in the bus station. This local chain began in 1931 and has remained successful serving cheap, plain food in a cafeteria-style setting. They're good places for breakfast but their reputation has been built on their hamburgers, which are known as 'nips'.

The *Chocolate Shop Restaurant* (268 Portage Ave) is a likeable place for lunch, dinner, coffee and sweets or for the popular teacup and tarot card readings. It's moderately priced.

The *Old Swiss Inn* (207 Edmonton St) offers steaks, veal and seafood. The food is good, priced from $16.

Pi Wiisiinin (208 Edmonton St) is a mid-priced Native Indian eatery with Canadian standards interspersed with bannock, venison, buffalo, wild rice and other traditional fare.

Earl's (191 Main St) is the 'in' place. It's a big bar/restaurant with a popular patio, near the railway station. The menu offers a bit of everything at moderate prices. While certainly OK, the food's not great; it's more the place, the people and the drinks that make it work.

West along Portage Ave away from the centre at No 1405 is *Rae and Jerry's*, a Winnipeg institution. This large, 1950s-style (dark with lots of red) steak and roast beef house has been serving up its classic panache for many years. Main dishes are about $20.

Down in the Exchange District there are a few eating spots. The *King's Head Tavern* (120 King St) is a busy British-style pub. One section of it contains the *Moti Mahal*, serving East Indian food. There's the colourful *Old Spaghetti Factory* (219 Bannantyne Ave), always reliable and cheap (under $15 at dinner) for standard Italian.

The Chinese Dynasty Building has *Heritage Gardens* (180 King St) out the front. Slightly beyond is the city's tiny Chinatown, on Rupert, Pacific and Alexander Aves. The restaurants are mainly on King St. *Little Saigon* (33 William St) serves rice or vermicelli dishes in the $6 to $9 range and the ginger chicken is quite good. It's closed Sunday. The moderately priced *Foon Hai* (329 William Ave) has both Cantonese and Sichuan dishes and is open late every day.

The *Forks Historic Site* is a pleasant place for a bite, and along with the food stalls and the small cafés of the Market Building, there is *Branigan's*, for a more substantial meal. Weekend brunches are offered. There also is a lounge which is open late. In the nearby Johnston Terminal, *Right On Q Billiards Café* is a good place for coffee, desserts and perhaps a game of pool.

MANITOBA

There are several worthwhile places in the area around Sherbrook St and Broadway Ave.

Bistro Dansk (63 Sherbrook St) is a perennial Danish favourite, with well prepared food, good lunches under $10 and pricier dinner specials. It's open from 11 am to 3 pm and 5 to 9.30 pm daily (closed Sunday).

Down near the corner of Broadway Ave, the *Fork & Cork (218 Sherbrook St)* is a more expensive but congenial spot for a dinner out. The speciality is fondue ($14 to $18, try the bouillon fondue) but there are other items, too. There are plenty of good restaurants with a range of prices in Osborne Village and along Corydon Ave, in the Italian area; both are south of the downtown area. *Carlos & Murphy's (129 Osborne St)* is a well established Mexican place with an outdoor patio, a big menu and moderate prices ($8 to $10). *Baked Expectations (161 Osborne St)* is primarily for sweets. The *Toad in the Hole (112 Osborne St)* is a popular pub.

Sofia's Caffé (635 Corydon Ave), with Italian food (around $20), has a wonderful little summer courtyard outback. *Bar Italia*, on the corner of Cockburn St, draws a funky mixed crowd to sip cappuccino.

Over in St Boniface, *Le Café Jardin (340 Boulevard Provencher)*, in the cultural centre, is a small place which offers low-priced French Canadian lunches. Elegant, French and expensive, *Le Beaujolais (131 Boulevard Provencher)* is one of the best restaurants in the province. The menu offers red meats, fowl and seafood.

Pembina Hwy leading south out of town has numerous restaurants, including many of the familiar franchises.

Many of the better downtown hotels have Sunday brunches at noon, which are good value.

Entertainment

To find out what's going on in the city, the *Winnipeg Free Press* has complete bar and entertainment listings on Thursday, or look for the free entertainment weekly *Interchange*.

Casinos Winnipeg pioneered permanent legal gambling houses in Canada. The somewhat swish, upmarket *Crystal Casino (☎ 204-957-2600, 7th floor, Hotel Fort Garry, 222 Broadway Ave)* features many of the classic games such as roulette, blackjack, baccarat and, of course, the slot machines. As we went to press, the casino was due to move to McPhillips Station (see below). The casino is open from 10 am to 3 am Monday to Saturday and from noon Sunday. There is a dress code meaning no jeans, T-shirts etc. Ask about the free chips given to non-Manitoba residents.

Because the casino has proven so lucrative for the provincial government, it has built two more casinos, or rather video terminal and slot-machine palaces, around town where you can call upon Lady Luck.

The *McPhillips Station (☎ 204-957-3900, 484 McPhillips St)*, with an old-west train station motif, is in the city's north end. Aside from the many, varied slot machines, this casual, no-dress-code, no-alcohol monument to the one-armed bandit features a McDonald's. *Club Regent*, with a sort of Caribbean Island-paradise theme, is in the eastern suburb of Transcona.

Both have the same hours as Crystal and are busy. The government allocates money to gambling-addiction programs.

Bars & Music The main nightlife areas are Osborne Village, Corydon and The Forks. The *Pyramid (176 Fort St)* presents new and/or young alternative rock bands, as does the *Albert (48 Albert St)*. Cover charge varies but is generally low. *Wise Guys (65 Rorie St)* is a casual place for a simple meal and local bands.

Close to the railway station, the inexpensive *Times Change Café (cnr Main St & St Mary Ave)* is good for jazz and blues. Live shows are on Friday, Saturday and Sunday nights. More blues can be heard at the *Windsor Hotel (187 Garry St)*.

Blue Note Café (875 Portage Ave) is a local institution. with good, varied live music nightly. Rock legend Neil Young got his start here, so it has good credentials.

In Osborne Village, *Die Maschine (108 Osborne St)* is a popular dance bar. The *Rogue's Gallery (432 Assiniboine Ave)* is a gay-friendly coffeehouse often with singer/songwriters.

The *Red Cactus (685 Corydon Ave)* is a cool place for a drink. The bar on the 30th floor of the *Royal Crown building (83 Garry St)* has great views ($5 minimum) and there is a revolving restaurant one floor up.

The *MS River Rouge*, departing from The Forks, has nightly cruises with pop bands through the summer months.

The *West End Cultural Centre (☎ 204-783-6918, 586 Ellice Ave)* often has cheap folk or classical concerts in a relaxed, casual atmosphere. The *Centre Culturel Franco-Manitobain (☎ 204-233-8972)* presents all kinds of interesting shows, concerts and productions. It's in St Boniface; call for information. Some performances require a knowledge of French, some transcend language and still others use French and English.

Performing Arts Though not well known, Winnipeg is, on a per capita basis, one of the top performing arts capitals of North America.

The *Royal Winnipeg Ballet (☎ 204-956-0183 or ☎ 1-800-667-4792, cnr Graham Ave & Edmonton St)* has an excellent international reputation, and offers student rates on tickets.

The Winnipeg Symphony Orchestra plays at the *Centennial Concert Hall (☎ 204-956-1360, 555 Main St)* from November to May. The Manitoba Opera (☎ 204-942-7479) presents three or four operas every year in Winnipeg.

The *Manitoba Theatre Centre (☎ 204-942-6537)* presents a wide range of live theatre. Plays, dance, mime and more are presented at the *Gas Station Theatre (☎ 204-284-9477, 445 River Ave)* in the centre of Osborne Village.

Cinema *Cinema 3 (☎ 204-783-1097, cnr Ellice Ave & Sherbrook St)* is a good, low-priced repertory cinema. *Cinémathéque (☎ 204-925-3457, Artspace, 100 Arthur St)*

has an ever-changing selection of good Canadian and international films.

Spectator Sports

In summer and autumn, the Winnipeg Blue Bombers play professional football in the Canadian Football League (CFL). Games are played at the Winnipeg Stadium (cnr Portage Ave & King Edward St), west of the downtown core. The Winnipeg Goldeneyes play Northern League baseball at the stadium during July and August. For information on stadium events call ☎ 204-982-5400.

Shopping

Factory Outlets Bargain hunters rejoice; Winnipeg has a surprising array of factory retail outlets. Canada's only Ralph Lauren factory store is here. Other such outlets include Canada West Boot for cowboy boots, and Danier Leather factory for fashion wear.

For cheap camping equipment, and a stupendous range of army surplus in the basement, have a rummage in United Army Surplus Sales on the corner of Portage Ave and Memorial Blvd.

Native People's Art Winnipeg is a focal point for Native people's art, as is Churchill in the far north of the province. To see or perhaps purchase some quality contemporary work (mainly Inuit) try these stores/galleries: Northern Images, in Portage Place; Upstairs Gallery, 266 Edmonton St and Concourse Aboriginal Gallery, 224 Notre Dame St.

Getting There & Away

Air The international airport is about 20 minutes north-west of the city centre. Several airlines serve Winnipeg, both for local trips and for destinations in the USA.

Canadian Airlines (☎ 204-632-1250) flies to Sault Sainte Marie at least three times daily. Air Canada (☎ 204-943-9361) also serves Winnipeg.

Canadian Airlines flies to Churchill three times a week but it's not cheap. If you want to go, book at least two weeks in advance for the best deal. For more information about Churchill, see the relevant section later.

MANITOBA

MANITOBA

Bus The station for both Greyhound and Grey Goose lines is the Mall Centre Bus Depot, 487 Portage Ave, open from 6.30 am to midnight. There are left-luggage lockers and a restaurant in the station.

Greyhound (☎ 204-982-8747) covers all Ontario destinations (or at least to the required connecting point) and many western cities. There are three buses daily eastbound for Thunder Bay ($92) and beyond, four buses a day for Regina ($59) and two for Saskatoon. Be sure to ask which buses are express and which are the mail runs, because on a trip to Saskatoon, for example, the difference can be three hours.

The Greyhound desk also handles the small Beaver Bus Line, which serves Fort Garry, Selkirk and other points north of town. There's at least one bus an hour.

Grey Goose buses (☎ 204-784-4500) go to Thunder Bay, Fort Francis and many small Manitoba towns including Thompson. It also connects Riding Mountain National Park.

Train The VIA Rail station (☎ 1-800-561-8630) is central where Broadway Ave meets Main St. In summer there's a tourist information booth in the station. The western route goes to Edmonton and Jasper and then down to Vancouver. The eastern route goes north over Lake Superior en route to Sudbury and the major cities of Ontario. There is no train to Regina or Calgary.

For Edmonton the fare is $189 with departures on Sunday, Wednesday and Friday. There are also three trains a week to Sudbury ($220). For Churchill see that section later.

Car Auto Express (☎ 204-944-0660) at 409 Selkirk Ave, with used cars for local use only, is the cheapest at about $20 a day. Executive car rentals (☎ 204-478-7283) at 104 Pembina Hwy is good value with rates from $30 per day with 150km free, or $189 for the week with 1200km free.

Budget (☎ 204-989-8505) is on the corner of Sherbrook St and Ellice Ave.

Hitching For hitching west out of town, take the express St Charles bus along Portage Ave. After 6 pm, take the Portage Ave-St Charles bus.

For hitching east on Hwy 1, catch the Osborne Hwy 1 bus or the Southdale bus on Osborne St South, on the corner of Broadway Ave.

Getting Around
To/From the Airport Very conveniently and economically, the Sargent No 15 city bus runs between the airport and Vaughan St on the corner of Portage Ave every 20 minutes.

A taxi from the airport to the centre of town is about $14. There is an airport limo, which runs from 9 am to nearly 1 am to and from the better hotels, but it costs more than a cab.

Bus All city buses cost $1.50, exact change. For transit information, call (☎ 204-986-5700, 24 hours a day). Routes are extensive but you need a transfer, which is obtained from the driver, if you're changing buses.

Bicycle There are bicycle routes through town and some out of town. Ask at the tourist office for details. The hostels rent bicycles.

AROUND WINNIPEG
Birds Hill Provincial Park
A reader has raved about this park, just 20km north-east of downtown. Highlights are miles of forested hiking trails, a bike path, a beach, deer and wild turkeys. It's about 30 minutes by car, off Hwy 59.

Lower Fort Garry
Lower Fort Garry (☎ 204-785-6050), 32km north of Winnipeg on the banks of the Red River, is a restored Hudson's Bay Company fort dating from 1830. It's the only stone fort from the fur-trading days that is still intact.

Although the fort was a failure as a fur-trading post, it remained in use as a police training centre, a penitentiary, a 'lunatic asylum', a Hudson's Bay Company residence and, later, a country club.

The buildings are historically furnished and the grounds are busy with costumed workers who'll answer questions. Go early

in the day to avoid the crowds, and see the film at the entrance for the historical background – you should allow one or two hours for a visit. Admission is $5. It's open from 10 am to 6 pm daily from mid-May to Labour Day. During the rest of September it's open on weekends only. There's a restaurant and a picnic area.

To get there, take the Beaver Line bus from the main station and tell the driver you're going to the fort – the fare is about $8 return.

Selkirk

Beyond the fort, halfway to Lake Winnipeg, is Selkirk, 'Catfish Capital of the World'. The lunkers that are taken out of the Red River here would certainly turn heads in the southern USA, where the fish is considered prime eating. The Marine Museum of Manitoba (☎ 204-482-7761) is also here, with six high-and-dry ships, including a restored steamer and an icebreaker.

Oak Hammock Marsh

Southern Manitoba has several important, very large marshes. These critical wetlands are home to thousands of waterfowl and other birds and act as way stations along major migration routes for thousands more.

Oak Hammock Marsh is a swamp area north of the city, about 8km east of Stonewall, and 15km west of Selkirk. It's noted as one of the best bird sanctuaries on the continent; over 280 species can be seen. You can amble about on viewing boardwalks or take out a canoe, and there is an information centre with interpretive displays. It's open daily all year. Most people consider the bird viewing here better than at Netley Marsh.

East of Winnipeg

Dugald, not far east of Winnipeg along Route 15, is the home of the **Dugald Costume Museum** (☎ 204-853-2166), a collection of 35,000 items of dress and accessories dating from 1765 to the present. The various garments are displayed on soft mannequins in realistic settings. One section offers a view of hundreds of accessories and workroom restoration activities. The costume

museum is open weekdays from 10 am to 5 pm, weekends noon to 5 pm June to August. Call for times otherwise. Admission is $4 and there's a tea room and gift shop.

Also here is a restored pioneer home dating from 1886, furnished as it would originally have been.

South of Winnipeg

South and slightly west of Winnipeg and bordered by North Dakota is an area known as the **Pembina Valley**. The Red River flows northward through this prime farming region.

Morris is the site of a major annual rodeo, second in size only to Calgary's. It takes place for five days at the beginning of August.

This is also sunflower country, and a festival to mark this is held in **Altona** on the last weekend in July. The Mennonites of the area supply some very fine home-made foods for the occasion.

Three kilometres east of the village of Tolstoi, near the Minnesota border on Hwy 209, is the **Tall Grass Prairie Preserve** (☎ 204-945-7775). The Manitoba Naturalists' Society oversees the protection of the 2000-hectare area of increasingly rare original prairie ecosystem. Walking trails, accessible year-round, provide access through one of the best remaining examples of this grassland.

Eastern Manitoba

The border region of Manitoba continues with the same rugged woodland terrain as is found in neighbouring Ontario. Toward Winnipeg this begins to give way to the flatter expanse more typical of the southern prairies. In the north-east, the sparsely populated timberlands continue through a series of gigantic government parks. The southern area of this side of the province is primarily farmland.

MENNONITE HERITAGE VILLAGE

South-east of Winnipeg, about an hour's drive down through sunflower country, is the town of Steinbach. Two kilometres north of

MANITOBA

the town on Hwy 12 is this museum complex featuring the Mennonites, a religious utopian group originating in Europe which reached Manitoba via Pennsylvania and Ontario. An information centre gives some of the history of the movement.

Most of the site is a re-created late 19th century Mennonite village with some century-old buildings. Various special events are held through the summer.

There's a *restaurant* on the grounds, which serves good, fresh traditional Mennonite food. The village is open from 1 May to 30 September. For more information on the Mennonites, see Kitchener in the Ontario chapter.

LA BROQUERIE

Just out of Steinbach, this little village with a population descended from French and Belgian pioneers celebrates its Gaelic roots on 24 June (Fête Franco-Manitobaine de la St Jean Baptiste).

WHITESHELL PROVINCIAL PARK

Due east of Winnipeg and lying along the Ontario border is this 2590 sq km park. Though some parts are heavily commercialised (particularly around Falcon Lake), other areas, especially northward, are less developed. The park contains 200 lakes, and all kinds of outdoor activities are available, summer and winter. There are some good hiking trails – some short and others as long as 60km – as well as numerous canoe routes (rentals available) including the popular tunnel route. The park headquarters (☎ 204-369-5232, ☎ 1-800-214-6497), in the village of Rennie on Hwy 44 in the south-west corner of the park, has information on hiking etc, although recommendations are offered at all access points.

The park has 17 *campgrounds*, and there are moderately priced *lodges* which are rented by the day or week – a quarter of the province's fishing lodges are found within the park. More expensive, well equipped *resorts* can be found at several locations. *Caddy Lake campground* is good for tenters. Summer weekends are busy.

Near the park headquarters in Rennie, the Alf Hole Goose Sanctuary is worth a visit, particularly during spring and autumn migrations. There is a visitors centre, and an observation deck overlooking the small lake where geese spend summer.

At Bannock Point, not far north of Betula Lake, are centuries-old Native Indian petroforms – rock formations in the shapes of fish, snakes and birds.

ATIKAKI PROVINCIAL WILDERNESS PARK

Heading north, the province quickly becomes rather wild. This wilderness park (☎ 204-277-5212) is best visited by canoe with loops from three days to several weeks long. Along the Bloodvein River, there are remnants of Native Indian cliff paintings thought to date back 6000 years. Pigeon River serves up whitewater.

There are no roads into the park; canoe access can be gained from Wallace Lake reached by rough road and then portaging. Outfitters in Bisset offer fly-ins. There is no organised campground.

NOPOMING PROVINCIAL PARK

More accessible but still offering a taste of the true northern wilderness is quiet Nopoming Provincial Park (☎ 204-534-7204), north of much busier Whiteshell. This park has three *campgrounds* and at least a sketchy road system. One reader has recommended Tulibee Campground, and another, the Ancient Mountains walk. There are also some woodland caribou, though you are unlikely to see them in summer months.

Lake Winnipeg

Canada's fifth largest lake, with its southern tip lying about 50km north of Winnipeg, is far and away the dominant geographic feature of the province. It begins just beyond suburban Winnipeg and ends in virtually untouched northern wilderness.

The easily accessible southern region is where Manitobans play in summer. The two

prime recreational features are the fine, sandy beaches, and the numerous parks and wetlands ideal for wildlife observation, most notably birdwatching. For the later, Oak Hammock Marsh (listed under the Around Winnipeg section earlier in this chapter as it is very close to the city) is most recommended.

The eastern shoreline is lined with beaches, including the unofficial centre of summer fun, **Grand Beach** which is very popular and a good place to relax. There's an excellent sandy beach and dunes as high as 8m. The lagoon formed behind the dunes is home to hundreds of species of birds. The good *Grand Beach Provincial Park* (☎ 204-754-2212) campground is one of the busiest in the province. Patricia Beach, closer to Winnipeg, is for day use only. Most of the commercial services and motel and cabin accommodation are available just south of the park, in **Grand Marais**. Many are rented by the week. *Parkview Cabins (☎ 202-783-1980)* charges $50 on a daily basis with kitchenette.

After you're sunburnt, a couple of **industrial tours** north and east of the beach district can be made. At Pine Falls, the Generating Station (☎ 204-474-3233) is open for tours through the summer. Call for the schedule. Also here, the Pine Falls Paper Company (☎ 204-367-5219) offers guided trips around the mill.

The other side of the lake is less accessible to visitors, as much of the land is privately owned; many people have cottages in the area. However, there are some good, popular public beaches, such as **Winnipeg Beach**. This is the resort centre for the west side of the lake. A provincial park protects the best strip of sandy beach for public use and there is good windsurfing out in the bay. In and around Winnipeg Beach there's an abundance of campgrounds, motels, restaurants and all other services.

At the southern end of the lake, is **Netley Marsh**, formed where the Red River drains into the southern end of Lake Winnipeg. This is one of the major waterfowl nesting areas on the continent, and hunters and watchers bring their conflicting points of view to enjoy the 18 species of duck and the flocks of geese. Autumn is a particularly good time, as the birds collect in number, but this is also hunting season. The Breezy Point Observation Tower, within the Netley Creek Provincial Recreation Park, allows for views over a section of the marsh. Still, this is primarily a boating and tourist-oriented area and for birding, Oak Hammond (see above) is better. Netley is 16km north of Selkirk.

Interlake

The region north of Winnipeg, wedged between massive Lake Winnipeg to the east and Lake Manitoba to the west, is known as the Interlake. The southern region of this area has been detailed in the Around Winnipeg section. In the northern Interlake region, to the east of Lake Winnipegosis, the population thins markedly, the cottage communities disappear and the real north begins.

GIMLI

Ninety kilometres north of Winnipeg, on the western shores of Lake Winnipeg and marked by the Viking statue, this fishing and farming community is made up largely of the descendants of Icelandic pioneers. Once known as the Republic of New Iceland, the area was settled by Icelanders around 1880. The **Gimli Historical Museum** outlines the history with some artefacts of the local settlement, as well as items suggesting the influence of the Ukrainians, a major early immigrant group in the western provinces. Every summer, around the beginning of August, **Islendingadagurinn** (the Icelandic Festival) is held, with three days of games, contests, parades and folk music.

The attractively redeveloped central waterfront is based along the wide, sandy beach characteristic of the lake's southwestern shore.

Gimli has a couple of standard hotels and motels.

MANITOBA

HECLA PROVINCIAL PARK

Farther north (Gimli is halfway from Winnipeg) is Hecla Provincial Park (☎ 204-378-2261), comprised of several islands jutting into and almost across Lake Winnipeg. A causeway leads to Hecla Island, the principal island, with its villages and amenities. Hecla Village was the site of an Icelandic settlement in 1876. A museum and short walking trail detail some of the historical highlights. At *Solmundson Gesta Hus* (☎ *204-279-2088)* double B&B goes for $60. At the northern tip of the island is Gull Harbour with the *campground* and where all supplies can be purchased.

The island is well populated with moose, although deer and smaller mammals are also commonly seen. The Grassy Narrows Marsh teems with waterfowl including pelicans. Numerous hiking trails wind through the woods and along shorelines.

To the north, adjacent **Grindstone** is a less developed park.

SNAKE PITS

Snake lovers, you're in luck. Here in Manitoba is the world's largest population of red-sided garter snakes, concentrated in wiggling mega-dens of up to 10,000 of the little funsters. Researchers, pet dealers and those with a taste for the macabre come from distant continents to view the snake pits, which are about 6km north of Narcisse, off Hwy 17 due west of Gimli.

In fact, the pressure of attention on them has resulted in a drastic decline in the numbers of snake dens and harvesting is now regulated.

The mating ritual, when tens of thousands emerge from their limestone sinkhole lairs to form masses of entwined tangles, takes place around the last week of April and the first two weeks of May, or when the weather has warmed enough to perk up the slitherers. The greatest intensity of activity occurs when the snow has melted and the first hot, sunny days of spring have arrived. Autumn is the other time of the year when viewing is good. Early in September, after a fancy-free summer, the snakes return to

their dens, but remain at the doors until the cold autumn weather forces them to crawl inside for the winter. The snakes are not dangerous and can be picked up – no screaming please – but may not be removed from the site.

The **Narcisse Wildlife Management Area** protects one area of the snake pits and provides a walking trail and parking lot 6km north of Narcisse – just follow Hwy 17. It's just under a two hour drive from Winnipeg. Bring the camera and the kids, and make a day of it by visiting nearby **Komarno**, where there's a statue of the world's largest mosquito. Packing a lunch (or at least a snack) and something to drink is not a bad idea, as there isn't much around, although well water is available.

Other locations for snake pits are around Chatfield and Inwood.

PEGUIS & FISHER RIVER

North of Narcisse, Hwy 17 leads to two fairly isolated Native Indian Reserves: Peguis and Fisher River. This is an undeveloped area, with few services and little in the way of tourist development. The **Peguis Powwow** is a five-day event featuring games, song, crafts and various activities, to which the Cree and Ojibway of the reserves invite the public. Call the Manitoba Association of Friendship Centres (☎ 204-943-8082) for exact dates and more information. There is some camping in the area, and Hecla Provincial Park is just over 40km to the east.

LAKE MANITOBA SHORELINE

Much less developed than Lake Winnipeg but with a series of small towns and some cottage communities, Lake Manitoba also has some fine, sandy beaches, particularly at Twin Lakes (in the south), around the town of Lundar and at Silver Bay (west of Ashern). St Laurent, a predominantly French and Métis community, is a regional supply town.

The area between the lakes is important for beef cattle, and some of the farms take in overnight guests.

NORTHERN WOODS & WATER ROUTE

This is a series of roads linked as one which connects Winnipeg with British Columbia, running across northern portions of Saskatchewan and Alberta. Most of the roads are surfaced, though there are stretches of gravel. There are no cities, but many small communities, nine provincial parks and numerous campgrounds along the way. You'll find lots of lakes and woods up here, as well as fishing areas and wildlife. Nights are cool.

From Winnipeg, the route heads to The Pas (in the north-west of the province), continues to Prince Albert, Saskatchewan then into Alberta ending at Dawson Creek, British Columbia. The road is marked on signs as 'NWWR'.

Northern Manitoba

Two-thirds of the province still lies north of The Pas, above the two big lakes at the 53rd parallel. Northern Manitoba is rugged, resource-based, lake-filled timberland which slowly evolves into the treeless tundra of the far north. Flin Flon, The Pas and Thompson are important towns. Way up on Hudson Bay is Churchill, remote but one of the province's top draws.

THE PAS

Once an important meeting site for Native Indians and British and French fur traders, The Pas is now a district centre and acts as a 'gateway to the north'. Although lumber is important, this is a rich agricultural area as well. During summer, days are long and sunny.

The small **Sam Waller Museum** at 306 Fischer Ave is an eclectic collection of indigenous wildlife, curios, coins and more. It's open Wednesday to Sunday from 1 to 5 pm.

Christ Church (☎ 204-623-2119), on Edwards Ave, was founded by Henry Budd, the first Native Indian ordained by the Anglican Church. On one wall, the Lord's Prayer and the 10 commandments can be seen written in Cree. Call and someone will arrange to let you visit.

Also of interest is Opaskwayak Indian Days, an annual festival in mid-August put on by the local Cree Nation who live across the Saskatchewan River from town. Included are traditional contests and games and a 30km canoe race. Call The Pas Friendship Centre (☎ 204-623-6459) for exact dates.

Within Clearwater Lake Provincial Park, deep crevices and huge chunks of rock fallen from cliffs can be seen along the Caves Trail. It's called Clearwater for a reason – the bottom can be seen from over 10m.

Places to Stay

Clearwater Lake Provincial Park, 24km north, has *camping*. There are about half-a-dozen motels or hotels in town, and finding a vacancy shouldn't be a problem. The *Wescana Inn* (☎ *204-623-5446)*, across the road from the bus station, is clean and comfortable and has singles/doubles for $63/69.

Getting There & Away

The Pas is connected to Winnipeg by air, Grey Goose buses and VIA Rail. Driving takes about eight hours if you take Route 327 and Hwy 6. The bus takes a longer route. VIA Rail continues on to Thompson and Churchill.

FLIN FLON

Farther north, right on the Saskatchewan border, Flin Flon is a copper and zinc-mining centre. The unusual name is taken, it's said, from the protagonist of a novel some prospectors found up here in 1915. A goofy statue of the character, Josiah Flintabbatey Flonatin, greets visitors at the edge of town.

Also here, on Hwy 10 as the town is entered, is a tourist office and campground run by the Chamber of Commerce (☎ 204-687-4518). At the tourist office, have a look at the examples of birch-bark biting. This is an old Cree women's craft which has almost disappeared. Using their teeth, they etch patterns, often of animals, into the bark. You can sometimes see examples of this art in some of the better Native Indian craft outlets around Saskatchewan.

MANITOBA

The town of about 10,000 residents is built on the rocky Canadian Shield, meaning you'll be going up and down hills as you make your way around town.

The Hudson Bay Mining & Smelting Company surface mine in town can be toured from June to August. Copper, zinc, gold and silver are mined.

The city is surrounded by typical northern rocky, wooded lakeland. There are canoe and camping outfitters in town and the huge Grass River Provincial Park (☎ 204-472-3331) is not far east. The fishing is excellent. The Grass River system is ideal for canoeing with about 150 lakes strung along the river. Woodland caribou, moose and deer are among the animals resident within the park. The river has been used for centuries by Native Indians and, later, European explorers and traders.

About halfway between Flin Flon and Grass River, south of town, is **Bakers Narrows Provincial Recreation Park**. It offers camping and canoeing and, with its beach and tranquillity, is also good for a relaxing day.

Flin Flon has a couple of older hotels in the centre, on Main St, and a couple of motels around the edges. The basic **Royal Hotel** (*☎ 204-687-3437, 93 Main St*) has rooms for $35/45. The **Victoria Inn** (*☎ 204-687-7555*) is more expensive and has a full range of facilities.

Buses run to The Pas and Winnipeg.

THOMPSON

The last town northwards connected by surfaced road, Thompson (population 15,000) is a nickel-mining centre. There is virtually nothing but wilderness on the long road up here, whether you've come from The Pas or along Lake Winnipeg. And just out of town in any direction, civilisation disappears quickly. If driving, make sure you have the necessary supplies, water and fuel, as services are few to nil, especially on Hwy 6

The Mighty Canadian Shield

The 'Shield' is one of Canada's most dominant physical characteristics. It surrounds Hudson Bay on the east, south and west in a vast U pattern, with a shield-like shape around the perimeter. In the north, it runs from the Atlantic Ocean on the coast of Labrador 3000km west past Lake Winnipeg north-west to Lake Athabasca, to Great Slave Lake, Great Bear Lake and on to the Arctic Ocean. From the Hudson Bay areas, it stretches south from Lake Superior to the St Lawrence River around Kingston.

And just what is it? A mass of ancient, stable rock, the first region of the continent raised permanently above the sea. The predominantly igneous, fossil-free, stratified rock from the archaeozoic period is among the world's oldest. The entire region was scraped and gouged by glaciers, resulting in an almost uniformly flat to undulating rocky surface very sparsely and intermittently covered with soil. Rarely across its expanse does it rise more than 500m above sea level. Many of the dips, dents, cracks and pits in the surface are filled with water – lakes, rivers and ponds of every shape and size. In several sections, as much as 40% of the surface is freshwater.

The southern sections tend to be forested and, in Manitoba, these boreal woodlands extend as far north as Churchill. Farther north the trees begin to diminish, and eventually disappear altogether, leaving lichen and mosses as the principal vegetation.

The southern areas, bordering as they do much of the heavily populated regions of the country, have become part of the Canadian mental landscape. Synonymous with outdoor living, camping, cottages, hiking, fishing and wildlife, this generally inhospitable but wildly beautiful land is part of the quintessential Canada.

north of Lake Winnipeg. The minimum eight hour trip is pretty tedious but one worthwhile stop is **Pisew Falls**. Also south of Thompson, Paint Lake Provincial Park has a lodge, good campground, beaches and fine northern scenery.

You can visit the Inco nickel mine but the tour does not descend underground, instead showing the surface operations. The Heritage North Museum, in an impressive log building, has exhibits and artefacts relating to natural history, the fur trade and early white settlement. The Thompson Folk Festival is held annually on the weekend closest to the summer solstice, usually around 22 June.

VIA Rail, en route to Churchill, serves the city, as does Grey Goose Bus Lines ($73). If you're going on to Churchill you can park at City Hall, which is free and more secure than leaving the car at the train station away from the centre.

McReedy Campground, less than 2km from town north on Hwy 6, offers vehicle storage and a free shuttle to the train. *Anna's B&B* (☎ 204-677-5075, 204 Wolf St) is a good place to stay, and will pick up guests from the airport or station. English and Dutch are spoken and a single goes for $35.

Calm Air (☎ 1-800-839-2256) flies to Churchill from here four times a week but not weekends. A return flight is $285 if you book 14 days in advance.

GILLAM

Situated about halfway to Churchill on the train line, Gillam exists because of its major hydropower development along the Nelson River. A gravel road now runs from Thompson and Grey Goose provides transportation.

CHURCHILL

Other than Winnipeg, this is the province's most interesting draw, especially for international travellers. It is one of Canada's few northern outposts that is relatively accessible, made so by the train line running all the way up from Winnipeg.

Despite its forbidding, remote location and extremes of weather – July and August are the only months without snow –

Churchill has always been of importance. The area is one of the oldest, in terms of European exploration, in the country. The first Hudson's Bay Company outpost was set up here in 1717 (and was named after Lord Churchill, Governor of the HBC and later the first Duke of Marlborough). Much of the exploration and settlement of the west came via this route. Explorers, traders and the military have all been here and it was once one of the largest grain-handling ports in the world. The railway was completed in 1929, giving the prairies an ocean port that is closer to Europe than Montreal. After some years of decline, grain handling is again increasing under new management. A communications satellite launching and monitoring station, built at a cost of $250 million about 20km east of town, on the site of the former Churchill Research Range, was, unfortunately, a bust after one launch.

The population of about 1000 is relying more on tourism and bills itself as the 'Polar Bear Capital of the World'. It sits right in the middle of a polar bear migration route, which means the great white bears often wander into the township. During September and October, visitors are taken out on the frozen tundra in large motorised buggies to see the huge, very dangerous bears.

The raggedy township itself, with its port and grain elevator to the west of the train station, sits at the juncture of the Churchill River and Hudson Bay. It feels small and naked in comparison to the vastness all around and the immense Arctic sky above. Facilities are minimal; there are no luxury hotels, no pavements, no traffic lights and no trees.

All the lodgings and information offices are within walking distance of the train station. Overlooking Hudson Bay at the north end of town, the large Town Centre Complex houses everything from a high school and library to recreational facilities, which include a swimming pool and a movie theatre.

Information

There is a tourist information office on Kelsey Blvd, opposite the train station. Up towards the Town Centre Complex, in the

same building as the Royal Bank, Parks Canada (☎ 204-675-8863) operates a visitors centre and a small, general museum. It's open 1 to 9 pm daily from June to November. Films (admission charged) on Churchill and the polar bears are shown. There are also some displays of furs and articles relating to the Hudson's Bay Company. The company was so widespread in area and influence that it's been said the initials HBC stand for 'Here Before Christ'. The knowledgeable park staff will answer questions and sometimes perform live shows (appalling but quite funny) about the history of the region.

Natural Attractions

The area around Churchill is wild and starkly beautiful. The coastline is heaped with huge quartzite boulders worn smooth by the retreating glaciers, and in summer the tundra is covered in red, orange and vi-

olet wildflowers. There is an incredible variety of wildlife to see, from polar bears to beluga whales, and during winter it's one of the best places in the world for watching the aurora borealis (northern lights). Other wildlife in the Churchill area includes seals, beaver, caribou, grey wolves, lemmings and Arctic foxes. Apart from all that, the air itself is so unbelievably clean it'll make the hairs in your nostrils stand up and sing.

Polar Bears Towards the end of September and into October the polar bears of the region start to make their way from their inland summer retreats to coastal areas where the ice first freezes. After a summer diet of berries and grasses they're keen to get onto the ice to hunt for seals again. As many as 150 polar bears pass close to Churchill.

The township is an attraction for the animals (food and fun), but it's also thought

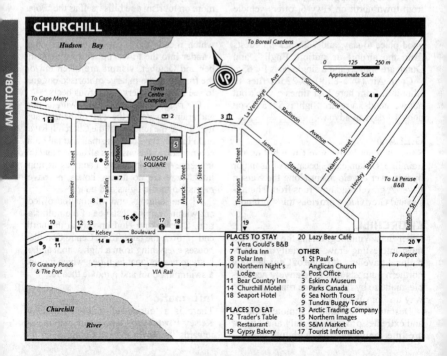

CHURCHILL

PLACES TO STAY
4 Vera Gould's B&B
7 Tundra Inn
8 Polar Inn
10 Northern Night's Lodge
11 Bear Country Inn
14 Churchill Motel
18 Seaport Hotel

PLACES TO EAT
12 Trader's Table Restaurant
19 Gypsy Bakery

20 Lazy Bear Café

OTHER
1 St Paul's Anglican Church
2 Post Office
3 Eskimo Museum
5 Parks Canada
6 Sea North Tours
9 Tundra Buggy Tours
13 Arctic Trading Company
15 Northern Images
16 S&M Market
17 Tourist Information

To Boreal Gardens
To Cape Merry
To La Peruse B&B
To Granary Ponds & The Port
To Airport
VIA Rail
Hudson Bay
Churchill River

that the older bears force the younger ones to move inland and that this could be why they sometimes lumber into town. Local police and government authorities maintain a 24 hour vigil from September to November to protect bears and humans from each other. An alert system has been set up (if you see one, ☎ BEAR) and if bears do come into town they're trapped and carted off to the out-of-town polar bear 'jail' and later released onto the ice.

To be certain of seeing polar bears at close range safely, a tundra buggy tour (booked well in advance) in September to early November is the only sure option. See under Organised Tours.

Beluga Whales During summer, from around mid-June until the end of August, up to 3000 beluga whales move into the Churchill River. It's thought that the whales are drawn by the warmer water temperatures. They spend summer feeding on large schools of capelin, calving, mating and checking out *Homo sapiens.*

Adult belugas are glossy white and about 3m to 5m long. Though they're easily spotted from the shore of Hudson Bay, a boat

---

Fluffy White Killers

Most of the world's population of polar bears, thought to be between 21,000 and 28,000 strong, live in the Arctic regions of Canada. Since becoming protected in the early 1970s numbers have been steadily increasing, particularly along the coasts of Manitoba and Ontario, and in 1983 polar bears moved from being an endangered species to being classified as 'vulnerable'.

Their continued survival is dependant on a protected habitat and, perhaps more than anything else, an abundant and healthy population of seals – their primary food source and the reason they have become supremely adapted to life in the Arctic. Their streamlined heads and long necks even resemble the shape of seals. Their huge rounded bodies, thick fur and heavy layers of fat help to conserve heat as well as keep them buoyant in the water. The undersides of their enormous paws, which are bigger than a man's face, are covered in hair so that they don't slip and slide (and look silly) on the ice.

Though the average male weighs around 600kg, polar bears can run incredibly fast across rough ice, leap over tall hurdles and clamber up steep ice cliffs. They're also able to gently lower themselves backwards into the sea, swim underwater or on the surface with only their noses showing, and then come barrelling out again at top speed.

The bears of Manitoba spend winter on the pack-ice of Hudson Bay hunting seals. Their sense of smell is so good they can detect dinner under three feet of ice and snow. Mating takes place on the ice during April and May. When the sea ice melts they head inland for the summer where they laze about nibbling on berries and grasses and patiently waiting for the ice to re-form. Towards the end of September they begin to make their way to coastal areas where the ice first freezes. Pregnant females stay behind to look for sites to build maternity dens where the cubs are born – tiny, blind and helpless – in December or January. In March the small family (there are usually two cubs) moves onto the ice in search of seal pups.

The main migration route followed by the bears of Northern Manitoba runs along the coast between Nelson River, about 200km south of Churchill, and Cape Churchill, about 25km east of Churchill. Up to 300 bears have been sighted on the Cape during the migration season (September to November).

Though bear numbers are increasing, their survival is far from assured. Threats include oil exploration, oil spills and general pollution of the oceans. Despite living in the remote Arctic, polar bears have been found to carry excessively high levels of insecticides in their tissue.

trip is the best way to see them. The whales come right up to the boat and a special microphone dropped over the side allows passengers to hear their extraordinary song. Early whalers who heard them through the hulls of their ships called them sea canaries. Belugas were heavily hunted right up until 1968; now only Inuit hunters are allowed to take a small number.

Birds From the end of May to mid-June, it's possible to see up to 200 species of birds in and around Churchill. Even a casual observer is likely to see about 100 species in the space of a week. The rare Ross's gull (its breast turns pale pink in the mating season) nests in Churchill. More common visitors include Pacific and red-throated loons, Smiths' longspurs, Arctic terns, yellow warblers and snow geese. From late June to mid-August it's also possible to see up to 40 species of rare tundra butterflies.

Cape Merry, the Granary Ponds by the port, Bird Cove and Akudlik Marsh, 4km south of Churchill, are all excellent birdwatching spots.

Visitor Tips Churchill is not a cheap place to visit but is well worthwhile. For most people, a three-day stay suffices. Those with a special interest generally remain for five days. Taking at least one of the tours is recommended to get the most out of a trip. Many visitors get off the morning train, dump their gear and head out on one of the tours without pause. As the return train leaves at night you can have an active last day, too.

As wildlife is the principal attraction bring a camera, lots of film and binoculars, if possible. Mosquitoes and black flies are ferocious in July and August, so be prepared to do battle. Repellent-saturated jackets and head-nets can be bought but are often sold out. The United Army Surplus store in Winnipeg has them and is cheaper – the nets are a good investment.

Average temperatures are -2.3°C in May, 6.1°C in June, 12°C in July, 11.5°C in August, 5.7°C in September and -1°C in October. You don't want to know about the rest of the year – lets just say that -50°C is normal. Even though temperatures can get to the high 20s in July, it is advisable to bring warm clothing – sweaters and reasonable footwear – for any visit. By early September, the snow is flying.

The prime bear season (September to November) is very busy, so reserve transportation, lodging and sightseeing trips in advance. Rooms in particular should be booked months ahead. Summer (June, July and August) is also fairly busy. At this time, to be safe, call B&Bs a week or so ahead.

Eskimo Museum
The museum, on La Verendrye Ave, has an excellent collection of Inuit artefacts and carvings, including kayaks from as early as 1700 BC. There are also northern fauna displays and various articles and books for sale. It's open Monday to Saturday, but only in the afternoon on Monday. Admission is by donation.

Thanadelthur's Cairn
With the establishment of the Hudson's Bay Company outpost here, Lord Churchill got to be the Duke of Marlborough. The Chipewyan woman who arranged a peace treaty between the warring tribes of the region, which made the post possible, got this small cairn behind the Anglican church in 1967.

National Historic Sites
Fort Prince of Wales This is one of four National Historic Sites in the Churchill area administered by Parks Canada. The partially restored stone fort, built on the peninsula head opposite Cape Merry, was originally built to protect the fur-trading business of the Hudson's Bay Company from possible rivals. It took 40 years to build but was surrendered to the French without a shot being fired because it was never seriously manned. From July to September, guides are on hand to tell the fort's story. The fort is included on many of the boat tours.

Sloop's Cove Private operators run trips to Sloop's Cove, 4km upriver from the fort.

The cove was used by European boats out on whaling excursions and on trading trips with the local Inuit. Names of some of the early Hudson's Bay Company people, including that of Samuel Hearn, the local 18th century governor, can be seen carved into the seaside rocks.

Cape Merry The third site, Cape Merry, is on the headland north-west of Churchill. It's a 2km walk west of town along a gravel road. Here you can see the remains of a stone battery built in 1746. In summer it's a good spot for whale watching and along the way you'll see dozens of species of birds. But don't forget the repellent. And be aware of the bear situation. Guides are on hand and it is free.

York Factory Much farther afield (250km south-east of Churchill), York Factory was a fur-trading post that operated for over 250 years. In the 18th and 19th centuries it was one of the Hudson's Bay Company's most significant trading posts. The remaining wooden building, built around 1832, has no foundations so it can 'ride' the permafrost. Also at the site are other ruins, some recovered artefacts and a cemetery. Situated deep in polar and black-bear country, and with limited facilities and unpredictable weather conditions, York Factory is accessible only by air or (for the very determined and experienced) by canoe.

Bird Cove

Bird Cove, about 15km east of town and accessible by vehicle (tours are available), is one of the best spots for viewing birdlife. Along the way (and with a short hike), you can see the wreck of the *Ithaca*, a freighter which went down in a storm in 1961 at the western edge of the cove. Visitors are advised to take care when walking on the beach because the tides rise and fall very quickly. The decks of the freighter are rusted through and are not safe to walk on.

Boreal Gardens

About 1.5km east of town on Shore Rd, the gardens and greenhouses here produce some food for local consumption. Free tours are offered on Sunday afternoons from 2 to 4 pm during July and August.

Northern Studies Centre

Housed on the site of the old rocket range 25km east of town, the centre (☎ 204-675-2307) offers a variety of Arctic studies courses and is a base for researchers from around the world.

Wapuska National Park

In 1996, 11,000 sq km remote Wapuska was created 45km south-east of town along the shores of Hudson Bay. This massive wetland area protects polar bear breeding dens and habitat for hundreds of thousands of birds. Public access and level of tourism to be permitted is still being determined. For current details visit the Churchill Parks Canada office (☎ 204-675-8863).

Other Attractions

The simple graveyard at the western edge of town with some far north-related epitaphs is worth a stroll. Getting work in the hotels and restaurants is possible. The Legion Hall is good for a quiet drink with the locals, the bar at the Seaport Hotel fairly ... well, let's say colourful. There's a beach behind the Town Complex; stick a toe in the Arctic Ocean.

Organised Tours

There are about a dozen tour operators, most based in town, but others work out of Winnipeg. It's worth calling to see if things are busy and whether reservations are required. Options include tours for viewing whales, birds, icebergs, historical sites, flowers or bears. In winter you can even go on dog-sled trips. Despite some specialisation, any operator can arrange any kind of trip – this is a small place.

The polar bear tours are the biggest attraction but remember that likely the only time you will see bears on the tundra is from mid-September to early November. The buggies used are shortened buses of varying sizes, generally carrying 20 or so passengers. They have lots of big windows

MANITOBA

and ride on huge, deeply treaded tyres which protect the delicate tundra.

Tundra Buggy Tours (☎ 204-675-2121, ☎ 1-800-544-5049), 124 Kelsey Blvd, is the main operator. Its eight hour trip is $165 with lunch. Some trips include an overnight stay in a Tundra Buggy Lodge. In summer, without the bears, prices drop to $75 for a four hour trip. Caribou, foxes and birds may be seen.

A much smaller but good company is Great White Bear Tours (☎ 204-675-2781, ☎ 1-800-765-8344) which has the same types of trips at about the same price.

Sea North Tours (☎ 204-675-2195) run by residents Mike and Doreen Macri specialises in boat and sea-life tours. A 2½ hour boat tour, which includes Fort Prince of Wales and most likely dozens of whales at close range (no guarantee) costs around $50. They can also arrange scuba diving tours with the whales!

Also recommended is Churchill Wilderness Encounter (☎ 204-675-2248) run by Bonnie Chartier who uses her extensive knowledge of local flora, birdlife and history on mini-bus tours which vary with the season and the clients' interests. A trip is about $35 but varies with the destination.

A variety of walking tours are offered from May to October by Adventure Walking Tours (☎ 204-675-2147) in Churchill. The small-group walks range from just an hour to a full day and can take in four distinct eco-zones – marine, sub-Arctic forest, tundra and boreal forest.

From May to November, Steve Miller of Hudson Bay Helicopters (☎ 204-675-2576) offers half-hour ($100) or one hour ($200) flights with a four-person minimum. The latter comes with a bear sighting or refund guarantee. Vistas over the tundra, boreal forest and hundreds of beluga whales swimming in the river make for an interesting trip.

For booking Churchill tours and packages out of Winnipeg, try Frontiers North (☎ 204-949-2050) and the Great Canadian Travel Company (☎ 204-949-0199). The Winnipeg tourist office can also help with a listing of hotels and tour operators in Churchill.

Special Events
The hardy may like to participate in the July Dip in the Bay event, part of which requires relay team members to jump into the not-so-balmy Arctic waters.

Places to Stay
There are about 10 places to stay, all within walking distance. Accommodation costs mostly around $75/85 for singles/doubles. Reservations are recommended.

Best bargain is *Vera Gould's B&B* (☎ 204-675-2544, 87 Hearne St). A single in this modern bungalow is $30 ($40 in bear season) with a very full breakfast (which often includes pancakes with Quebec maple syrup or toast with home-made jams). She has room for six people in three rooms (twin rates are twice the single).

Comfortable *La Peruse* (☎ 204-675-2254, 100 Button St), run by Vera's daughter Anne and husband, has two rooms with shared bathroom. From here to the train station is about the longest walk in town (15 minutes). From June to September rooms are $36/60. During prime polar bear season (October to the first week of November) rates rise to $45/70. You may find another B&B or two around town as well.

For hotels, *Bear Country Inn* (☎ 204-675-8299, 126 Kelsey Blvd) is recommended for its friendly, casual atmosphere and reasonable prices ($68/78, $10 more at bear time) with toast and coffee.

More expensive and with a few more amenities, including video editing machines, is the *Polar Inn* (☎ 204-675-8878, 15 Franklin St). Rooms are $77/84, more at peak time. The rooms for four people are good value. It also operates a lodge (big dollars) across the Churchill River (boat and helicopter access). Bears can be seen right outside this heavily screened former brothel!

The straightforward *Churchill Motel* (☎ 204-675-8853, cnr Kelsey Blvd & Franklin St) has rooms at $75/85 all year.

A hotel to watch for is the one resident Brian Ladoon is building more or less by hand one stone at a time down by the shore

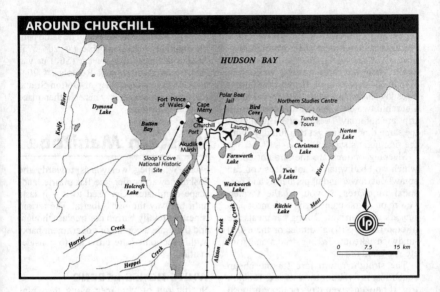

AROUND CHURCHILL

HUDSON BAY

Knife River
Dymond Lake
Button Bay
Fort Prince of Wales
Cape Merry
Polar Bear Jail
Bird Cove
Northern Studies Centre
Churchill
Port
Launch Rd
Tundra Tours
Norton Lake
Akudlik Marsh
Sloop's Cove National Historic Site
Farnworth Lake
Christmas Lake
Holcroft Lake
Warkworth Lake
Twin Lakes
Mast River
Ritchie Lake
Churchill River
Creek
Harriet Creek
Heppel Creek
Alston Creek
Warkworth Creek

0   7.5   15 km

MANITOBA

on La Verendrye Ave. Go have a look at his attractive random rubble construction dream due open by century's end.

Note the hotels add sales tax. Many of the hotel rooms are monopolised by temporary professional workers doing government or research work; others are taken by bush pilots, photographers and the like.

Places to Eat

Gypsy's Bakery, east along Kelsey Blvd, is a good place for breakfast or lunch. The bakery serves very good soups, sandwiches and home-made pastries. It's open daily until 8 pm.

The attractive, log *Lazy Bear Café (cnr Kelsey Blvd & Button St)* at the eastern edge of town serves a good chilli in a bowl of bread ($6) and often offers wild meat – caribou, musk ox – at dinner.

The *Trader's Table*, at the other end of Kelsey Blvd, is the most pleasant restaurant for dinner. You'll find steak, Arctic char (the local fish) and desserts featuring locally grown berries on the menu. An evening meal costs around $24.

Most of the hotels have dining rooms. The *Churchill Motel* has low-cost standards and the cheapest char in town while the more upmarket dining room at the *Northern Nights Lodge* is varied and good. There's a cheap *cafeteria* in the Town Centre Complex and the *S&M Supermarket* sells a pretty decent range of fresh fruit and vegetables.

Shopping

Various outlets sell contemporary Inuit arts and crafts. The Arctic Trading Company has interesting souvenirs such as carvings and Inuit-style boots called *mukluks*. Northern Images has books and expensive carvings. The Eskimo Museum also has some articles for sale.

Getting There & Away

Air There is no road to Churchill; access is by plane or train. Canadian Airlines (☎ 204-632-1250 in Winnipeg) has three flights a week from Winnipeg. The regular return airfare is $1090, but savings of hundreds of dollars are offered on flights booked one or – even better – two weeks in advance. Calm

Air (☎ 1-800-839-2256) flies between Winnipeg and Churchill about four times a week. In summer there are extra flights.

Train There are three trains a week from Winnipeg, departing at 10 pm on Sunday, Tuesday and Thursday. They arrive in Churchill two days later at 8.30 am. Return trips are Saturday, Tuesday and Thursday at the same time so you get two full days with the first night's stay.

Sleeping options are the straight coach which isn't bad when its not full as you can sprawl out, lower and upper berths and personal roomettes. If you do the former, you're on a first-name basis with most passengers upon arrival. Dining car meals are offered ($8 to $10) at dinner or there is a sandwich takeout. Taking drinks and fruit etc is a good idea.

The straight return fare for the cheap coach seat is $410 for the 1½-day, 1600km trip. If booked seven days or more prior to departure, the fare drops to $250. It's worth calling VIA a few times as quoted fares can vary *a lot* depending who you talk to. When you get a good price, book. Booking just seven days ahead shouldn't be a problem, as this train is rarely full, but be careful in midsummer and more so in polar bear season.

It's not a great idea to leave your car at the train station or on the streets of Winnipeg as break-ins are common. A reasonable place is the multi-levelled lot downtown on Edmonton St near St Mary Ave.

An option is to drive or bus to Thompson, The Pas or Gillam and take the train from there. This is quicker as the train travels excruciatingly slowly (see under Thompson earlier in this chapter).

In Churchill, the station (☎ 1-800-561-8630) is only open for arrivals and departures.

Getting Around
The two B&Bs listed offer free use of clunker bicycles (perfectly adequate) or the Polar Motel has mountain bike rentals by the hour or $22 per day.

Churchill Taxi (☎ 204-675-2345) will take you in and around town. The same people operate Polar U Drive (☎ 204-675-2727) on Franklin St for car ($60) or van ($80) rentals. Tamarack Rentals (☎ 204-675-2192) on the corner of Button St and Kelsey Blvd also has vans. Neither place charges mileage.

Western Manitoba

From Winnipeg westwards towards the Saskatchewan border, the flat prairie landscape dominates. Get used to it – it lasts until halfway through Alberta! The terrain is neither totally barren nor treeless though, and there are a couple of government parks in this section of the province to consider visiting.

WHITE HORSE LEGEND
Not far out of Winnipeg along the Trans Canada Hwy, where Hwy 26 runs north off the highway, is a statue of a white horse. Native Indian legend has it that a Cree rode this way on his white horse with his new bride, hotly pursued by his failed rival in love, a Sioux. Eventually overtaking the couple, the scorned man killed both bride and groom. The young woman's spirit entered the horse, which continued to roam the prairie for years, a living reminder of the tragic couple.

PORTAGE LA PRAIRIE
Portage is a farm centre. Look for the crop identification markers by the highway indicating wheat, flax, mustard, etc. Other common crops include barley, sunflowers and rapeseed (often known as canola these days, for sociological reasons). The latter two are grown for their oils, used in cooking and prepared-food production.

The Trans Canada has the tourist office. The main street in Portage is Saskatchewan Ave, East and West.

At the western end there are a couple of places to eat (beware the strong smelling water), some motels and the Greyhound

Bus Depot on Royal St, but disembarking really can't be recommended.

There is a museum on the site of **Fort La Reine**, originally built by explorer de la Vérendrye in 1738.

Also at the fort is Pioneer Village Museum, which depicts life in a simple 19th century village. Exhibits include a replica of the famous Red River Cart, essentially the truck the pioneers used to travel from Quebec to Manitoba's Red River Valley. It was an ox-drawn cart made entirely of wood. Because of the dust of the trails, the axles were not oiled, and it is said that the creaking and squeaking of a caravan of carts could be heard for miles. The site is open daily from May to September.

Portage Campground (☎ 204-267-2191), 15km east of Portage, is a deal at $13 for a tent. It's quiet, green and has a pool.

North of town, along the southern shores of Lake Manitoba, is another of the province's essential wetlands. Eight kilometres long, **Delta Marsh** is internationally known and is one of the most significant waterfowl staging marshes in North America. Public access to much of it is limited by research and wildlife management controls, but there is camping at the eastern edge, just north of the town of St Amboise.

The Trans Canada Hwy splits into two segments 11km west of Portage. The Yellowhead Route runs north along the southern edge of Riding Mountain National Park and on to Edmonton, Alberta. The southern portion, the original, heads due west to Brandon and on to Calgary, Alberta.

SPRUCE WOODS PROVINCIAL PARK

Thirty kilometres south of the highway, this 27,000 hectare park (☎ 1-888-482-2267) features an area of desert-like sand dunes as high as 30m, which support the northern prairie skink (Manitoba's only lizard), the western hognose snake and two species of cacti not found elsewhere in the province. Walking trails lead to some of the more interesting sections of the park, including the dunes known as Spirit Sands and beyond to underground-fed pools. Alternatively, horse-drawn covered wagons (additional charge) can be taken to these attractions or for one to three-night family-oriented camp-outs. Other areas such as the *Kiche Manitou campground* ($14/tent) offer woods and lakes. Weekends are busy; call ahead. There is also backcountry camping via hiking. Canoes can be rented. A three-day park pass is $5.

BRANDON

The second largest city in the province, with a population of 40,000, has little to attract the visitor, although it is considered a good place to live. Primarily a commercial centre, it's 4km south of the highway.

Agriculture Canada, a federal government department, operates a research centre investigating everything from cattle breeding to barley pasture weed control. In one form or another, this experimental farm has been operating since 1886. There's also a university and large rail yard. The Assiniboine River flowing through town keeps it a fairly green-looking place.

The main street, Rosser Ave, has a few places to eat and the Greyhound Bus Depot, on the corner of Rosser and Sixth St. The *YWCA (☎ 204-727-5014, 148 11th St)* offers cheap accommodation and meals to both sexes. The least costly motels are on 1st St leading into town from the highway.

The tourist information booth is on the Trans Canada Hwy among more motels and restaurants including huge *Harry's Ukrainian Kitchen*.

At the airport the **Commonwealth Air Training Museum** tells the story of the thousands of recruits from around the British Commonwealth who trained as pilots, navigators etc in Canada from 1939 to 1945 before heading over to Europe. There are 13 original training planes housed in the old Brandon hangar. Small training centres such as this one dotted the prairies.

Other displays include photographs, aircraft engines and other artefacts and memorabilia. It's open daily in summer with a small admission charge.

The **Brandon Folk Music & Art Festival** takes place around the beginning of August.

AROUND BRANDON
Royal Canadian Artillery Museum

South-east of Brandon on Hwy 340, there is a Canadian military base, in Shilo. For those with a special interest, this museum has a vast indoor-outdoor collection of uniforms, guns, ammunition, vehicles and more, dating from 1796. It's open daily through the summer, but afternoons only on weekends and holidays. The rest of the year it's closed weekends and Monday.

Grand Valley Provincial Recreation Park

Ten kilometres west of Brandon is this privately operated park, campground, picnic area and Thunder Mountain water slide complex. Perhaps of more interest, is its provincial heritage **Stott Site**, a Native Indian bison kill area dating back some 1200 years. Displays offer information on how it

---

When the Bison Reigned Supreme

In the days before the European arrival in the west, huge herds of bison roamed from what is now Manitoba to the Rocky Mountains, from Texas to the shores of Great Slave Lake. On the wide, open, grassy plains of the prairies, herds could number in the hundreds of thousands.

The name buffalo is very commonly, if not nearly always, used in relation to the North American bison, but this is incorrect. A buffalo is a type of heavy oxen found across Africa and Asia.

The bison is a large, shaggy form of wild cattle. An old bull can weigh as much as 900kg and full-grown females average over 500kg. To the western Indians, the bison were stores with legs, but were also beings with spirits, to be respected. Bison were the principle source of food. The hides and hair made clothes, tents and bedding. Horns were used in crafts and rituals, the bones as knives. Nothing went to waste – even the 'chips' (dried excrement) were burned as fuel.

Aside from eating the fresh meat, much was prepared and preserved during the summer for the long winters. It could be cut into strips, pounded with herbs and dried in the sun to create a type of jerky. Native groups from more northern areas added currants and berries and boiled fat to the dried meat to form pemmican, a nutritious mix which kept many a fur trader and explorer alive.

Bison would be hunted in a number of ways. Sneaking up on them, often disguised as an animal, and then firing arrows, was one simple method. Later, they were chased on horseback. (The horse, icon of the west, was unknown in North America before the arrival of the Spanish. Until then, Native Indians roamed the prairies on foot, aided only by domesticated dogs, who pulled materials and supplies.)

When possible, hunters made use of the lay of the land, such as at Head-Smashed-In, Alberta, or the Stott Site in Grand Valley Provincial Recreation Park. Animals would be herded and rushed over cliffs. While effective for the Indians' needs, none of these methods appreciably diminished the bison's numbers.

Through the late 19th century, Europeans with rifles and horses slaughtered the immense herds to near extinction, often for nothing more than amusement. For the Plains Indians, the demise of the bison led to starvation and meant the end of their way of life. In Canada, the largest remaining wild herd is found at Wood Buffalo National Park (see the Northwest Territories chapter). Smaller groups and individual specimens can be seen at various parks and zoos around the country.

was used, and a Native Indian encampment has been re-created. There are also some live bison to send one's imagination to a time when the prairies saw herds of thousands. When they moved, the earth literally shook.

West to the Border

From Brandon west, derricks may be seen pumping oil. Remember that during summer, clocks move back one hour at the Saskatchewan border because Saskatchewan, unlike the rest of the country, does not use daylight-savings time.

Neepawa

North of Brandon, Neepawa was the childhood home of well known writer Margaret Laurence. Her home, at 312 First Ave, has been set up as a type of Laurence museum and mini cultural centre with writers workshops, book sales etc.

RIDING MOUNTAIN NATIONAL PARK

Also north of Brandon, 300km north-west of Winnipeg, Riding Mountain is the major attraction of western Manitoba. Covering nearly 3000 sq km, it is a huge island of a park rising from the surrounding plains. Much of it is highland, set on a forested escarpment that runs from North Dakota to Saskatchewan. Within the park are deciduous forests, lakes, rivers and meadows.

Around **Clear Lake** is the developed area, but most of the park is wilderness. Pleasant **Wasagaming**, on the south shore of Clear Lake, is a casual, low-key resort town featuring log construction with all amenities including a beach and the main campground. Bicycles can be rented in town. The park information centre (☎ 1-800-707-8480) is also here and takes camping reservations. Grey Goose Bus connects the park to Winnipeg and Dauphin. It runs from Winnipeg to Wasagaming once daily, except Saturday, through the summer.

The park has over 400km of walking, cycling and horseback riding trails providing access to various sections of interest. One trail leads to a cabin used by Grey Owl. At **Lake Audy**, about 40km from Wasagaming, is a fenced herd of 30 bison but you shouldn't cycle through the area. Elk, moose and bear are plentiful and not uncommonly seen from a road.

Canoeing is good and rentals are available at Wasagaming but Clear Lake, with winds and motorboats, is not recommended.

The park is patrolled by rangers on horseback, and a couple of companies run horseback tours. Trips range from an afternoon's outing to three-day camping treks. Try High Mountain Outfitters (☎ 204-967-2077) in Kelwood. Note that the eastern section of the park is the highest, so the views are best.

For camping, there are also several small, basic *campgrounds* as well as backcountry opportunities. At Shawenequanape Kipichewin, an Ojibway village 9km from Wasagaming, there are tent sites, teepees and cultural demonstrations. The Lake Audy campground is ugly. Motels and cabins can be found in and around Wasagaming. *Manigaming Resort (☎ 204-848-2459)* has doubles from $50.

Also of note is the First Nation Celebration, held in early June, which provides an opportunity to see traditional Native Indian dance, costume, games and crafts.

DAUPHIN

North of the park up Hwy 10, nondescript Dauphin is one of many Ukrainian centres found all across the prairie provinces. South-west of town 13km is Selo Ukraina (Ukrainian Village), the location of the country's **National Ukrainian Festival**, held at the beginning of August each year. Dancing, traditional costumes and lots of food are part of the festivities. Farther north, **Duck Mountain Park** is wilder, less busy and has better fishing than Riding Mountain.

Saskatchewan

Saskatchewan is a Cree Indian word which refers to the Saskatchewan River and means 'river that turns around when it runs'.

Prior to the arrival of Europeans, first the fur traders and explorers, then the farmsteading settlers, the region was primarily Cree territory. They were a semi-nomadic people whose life was inextricably linked with the herds of bison which roamed the vast plains.

Tourism is not a major industry in Saskatchewan but many people do pass through. Each of the two major cities has some interesting things to consider on a stopover, and there are several good historical parks around the province which give a glimpse into the Native Indian way of life. Prince Albert National Park is accessible Canadian timberland. The southern region has some intriguing landscapes and desert-like topography.

Many people find the scenery monotonous; the south of the province is mercilessly flat, often without a tree in sight. But such wide-open space is a scene much of the world cannot even imagine. And the sight of golden, ripening wheat rippling to the horizon in all directions can be beautiful. The sunsets, sunrises, cloud formations and night skies are all fantastic. There's a lot of space. You might hear people out this way say 'the Rocky Mountains are nice but they get in the way of the view'.

The northern half of Saskatchewan has over 100,000 lakes and few roads. Between this area and the bald, open prairie of the south is a transition zone stretching across the province, covering the lower middle section of Saskatchewan in rolling hills and cultivated farmland. This range, called the parklands, contains some large government parks and both the North and South Saskatchewan rivers. Dozens of canoe routes have been mapped within these two regions and there are canoe outfitters at many of the parks and towns.

HIGHLIGHTS

Entered Confederation: 1 September 1905
Area: 651,903 sq km
Population: 1,024,387
Provincial Capital: Regina

- Experience the seemingly endless skies and uncluttered space of the vast Canadian prairies

- Visit Wanuskewin Heritage Park to gain an appreciation of Native Indian culture and history

- Jangle along to the Kinsmen Big Valley Jamboree in Qu'Appelle Valley in July

- Canoe and hike in Prince Albert National Park, once the home of famous naturalist Grey Owl

- Discover Moose Jaws' underground secret

- Enjoy outdoor theatre along the river in Saskatoon

- Explore Cypress Hills, a camping retreat and the location of Fort Walsh, an historic RCMP base

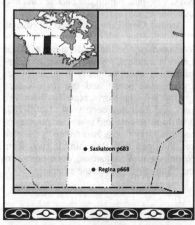

Saskatoon p683

Regina p668

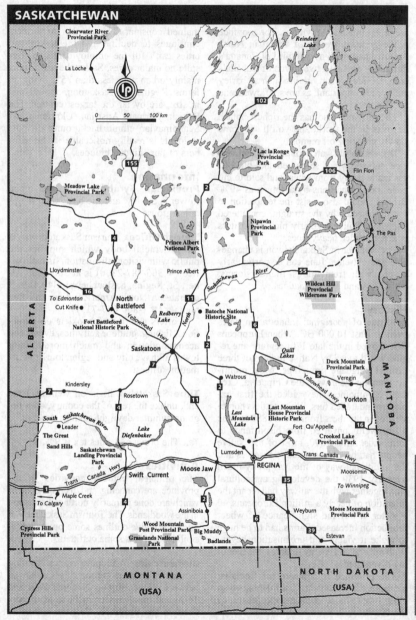

SASKATCHEWAN

0   50   100 km

Clearwater River
Provincial Park

La Loche

Reindeer
Lake

102

Lac la Ronge
Provincial
Park

155

106   Flin Flon

Meadow Lake
Provincial Park

2

The Pas

Nipawin
Provincial
Park

4

Prince Albert
National Park

Lloydminster

Prince Albert   Saskatchewan   River   55

Wildcat Hill
Provincial
Wilderness Park

To Edmonton

Cut Knife

North
Battleford

Redberry
Lake

11

Batoche National
Historic Site

North

6

Fort Battleford
National Historic Park

Yellowhead   Hwy

Saskatoon

7

Duck Mountain
Provincial Park

5

Quill
Lakes

2

Veregin

Kindersley

7

Rosetown

Watrous

2

Yellowhead   Hwy   Yorkton

16

South   Saskatchewan River

Leader

The Great

Sand Hills

Lake
Diefenbaker

11

Last
Mountain
Lake

Last Mountain
House Provincial
Historic Park

Fort Qu'Appelle

Crooked Lake
Provincial Park

Saskatchewan
Landing Provincial
Park

Swift Current

Trans   Canada   Hwy

Moose Jaw

Lumsden

REGINA

1   Trans Canada   Hwy

Moosomin

To Winnipeg

35

Maple Creek

4

2

Assiniboia

39

Weyburn

Moose Mountain
Provincial Park

To Calgary

Cypress Hills
Provincial Park

Wood Mountain
Post Provincial Park

Grasslands National
Park

Big Muddy
Badlands

6

39

Estevan

MONTANA

(USA)

NORTH DAKOTA

(USA)

SASKATCHEWAN

Economically, Saskatchewan and wheat are pretty much synonymous. The province is the greatest grower of wheat in North America and, with over a third of Canada's farmland, produces two-thirds of Canada's crop. Besides wheat, grains such as barley and rye are important, as are sunflowers and beef cattle.

The province also has the richest potash deposits in the world and you'll see some slowly cranking oil pumps.

Drivers should watch for the Mohawk service stations, which sell an ethanol-blended gas made partly from wheat and said to cut undesirable emissions by as much as 40%. Drivers should also resist the temptation to speed presented by the straight, uncluttered highways. Police regularly pick-off visitors who are handed heavy fines.

The weather in Saskatchewan is changeable and extreme. June can be particularly severe with tremendous thunderstorms, hailstorms and even tornadoes.

History
Evidence of aboriginal inhabitation dates from at least 10,000 BC. When Europeans first arrived in the late 17th century, the region was divided by Native Indians of three distinct language groupings. Most prominent among them were the Chippewa, Cree and Assiniboine. They aided the first explorers and traded furs. White settlers homesteaded in numbers from about 1880 and the plains were converted from bison range to farmlands. After 1890, most of the Native people had been designated to reserves and the traditional way of life was pretty much over. By 1930 the developing agricultural area together with the railway had meant the migration of nearly a million Europeans.

After WWII the significance of wheat production increased. Farms had to be huge to make it viable and urbanisation began. With mineral and energy reserves, the economy diversified.

The province is home to the Socialist movement in Canada and has maintained its allegiance to those ideals more or less since the 1930s.

In recent years, the population has remained constant. The number of farmers continues to decline and the towns and cities can't fill the employment gap. Despite no major cities, Saskatchewan is now mainly urban with less than 25% living on farms. Regina and Saskatoon, about equal in size, are by far the largest centres. The British, German, Austrian, Ukrainian and Scandinavian ethnic background of most residents is readily noticeable in the numbers of fair-skinned blondes.

Information
Provincial Symbols The provincial flower is the lily, and the bird is the sharp-tailed grouse.

Tourist Offices Tourism Saskatchewan is the provincial body which supplies the public with visitor information. Its main office (☎ 306-787-2300) is at 500-1900 Albert St, Regina, Saskatchewan S4P 4L9. It operates a North America-wide, toll-free number (☎ 1-800-667-7191).

It offers a series of booklets on attractions, fishing, outdoor activities, events and accommodation and much more. Major towns all have city and region tourist information offices.

Time Saskatchewan is on Central Time and, unlike the rest of the country, does not go on summer daylight-savings time.

Tax The provincial sales tax is 9%.

Activities
The principal outdoor activities in the province are canoeing and fishing, both of which are done primarily north of Saskatoon in the woodlands. The Tourism Saskatchewan Vacation Guide outlines some outdoor possibilities and lists some outfitters.

Birdwatching Whooping cranes, battling extinction, migrate through Saskatchewan between Wood Buffalo National Park and Texas and are often seen in the southern portions of the province. Call the Canadian

Wildlife Service in Saskatoon (☎ 306-975-5595) for sighting information. Last Mountain Lake north of Regina, Chaplin Lake, west of Moose Jaw and Galway Bay west of Kyle are major waterfowl migration observation points.

Canoeing Tourism Saskatchewan has a general leaflet suggesting canoe possibilities or detailed booklets on mapped canoe routes from novice to advanced. Prince Albert National Park has designated routes. In Saskatoon, consult the Meewasin Valley Authority (☎ 306-665-6887) for details on canoeing the South Saskatchewan River.

Fishing With 100,000 lakes there are a few fish bound to be hungry. Walleye, pike and trout are prime species. The province produces its own *Fishing and Hunting Guide* available at tourist offices.

Provincial Parks The parks provide a good chance to see another side of the province. Much of Saskatchewan's intriguing landscapes are situated below the level of the plains. For camping reservations call ☎ 1-800-667-2757.

Regina

Regina (population 184,000) is Saskatchewan's capital. It is the largest city and acts as the commercial, financial and industrial centre of the province, but it's still a relatively small, quiet town that pretty much closes down after dark.

Wascana Creek and its parkland run through town, providing a change from the golden grain fields stretching in all directions.

Two interesting facts about the city: Regina is the sunniest capital in Canada and, oddly, every single tree you see here was planted by hand. It's for good reason that this part of the world is known as the bald prairie.

History
The Cree Indians originally lived in this area, butchering bison and leaving the remains along the creek. It became known as Wascana, a Cree word meaning 'pile of bones'. Later, European settlers were prompted to dub the settlement Pile O'Bones. In 1882 the city was made capital of the Northwest Territories and its name was changed to Regina in honour of Queen Victoria. The Northwest Mounted Police used the city as a base from the 1880s, and in 1905 it became the capital of the newly formed Saskatchewan.

In 1933, the Cooperative Commonwealth Federation (CCF), a socialist party, held its first national meeting in Regina and called for the end of capitalism. In 1944 it became the first socialist party to form a Canadian provincial government. The CCF merged with the New Democratic Party (NDP) in 1961 to form Canada's left-wing party.

Orientation
The city's two main streets are Victoria Ave, running east-west, and Albert St, going north-south. Both streets are lined with fast-food restaurants and service stations. East of the downtown area, Victoria St becomes Hwy 1 East (the Trans Canada Hwy) for Winnipeg. South of the downtown area, Albert St leads to both Hwy 6 (southbound) and Hwy 1 West. Albert St north leads into Hwy 11 for Saskatoon.

The downtown core is bounded by Albert St to the west, 13th Ave to the south, Osler St to the east and the railway tracks to the north. Victoria Park sits in the middle of the downtown area. Scarth St and 12th Ave, which edge the park, are important shopping streets.

Scarth St, between 11th and 12th Avenues, has been converted into a small, pleasant pedestrian mall with trees and benches. On the north-east corner is the old city hall, which houses a theatre, shops and a museum. With its pyramid shapes, the Continental Bank building on the south corner is distinctive. The large Cornwall Centre, a major shopping mall, is opposite the Scarth St mall on 11th Ave.

Wascana Centre, a 1000-hectare park, is the dominant feature of the city and, aside from its own natural appeal, contains many

SASKATCHEWAN

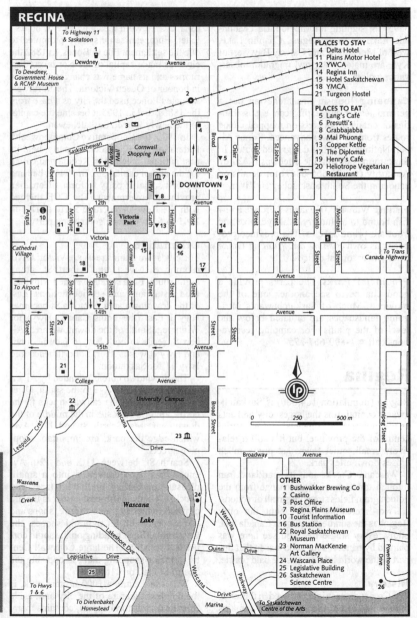

REGINA

To Highway 11
& Saskatoon

To Dewdney,
Government House
& RCMP Museum

Dewdney   Avenue

Saskatchewan   Drive

Cornwall
Shopping Mall

11th   Avenue

DOWNTOWN

12th   Avenue

Albert

Angus

Cathedral
Village

To Airport

Victoria   Avenue

Cornwall

13th   Avenue

14th

15th   Avenue

College   Avenue

University Campus

0   250   500 m

Wascana   Drive

Broadway   Avenue

Wascana
Creek

Wascana
Lake

Lakeshore Dr

Legislative   Drive

To Hwys
1 & 6

To Diefenbaker
Homestead

Quinn   Drive

Marina

To Saskatchewan
Centre of the Arts

PLACES TO STAY
4 Delta Hotel
11 Plains Motor Hotel
12 YWCA
14 Regina Inn
15 Hotel Saskatchewan
18 YWCA
21 Turgeon Hostel

PLACES TO EAT
5 Lang's Café
6 Presutti's
8 Grabbajabba
9 Mai Phuong
13 Copper Kettle
17 The Diplomat
19 Henry's Café
20 Heliotrope Vegetarian
     Restaurant

OTHER
1 Bushwakker Brewing Co
2 Casino
3 Post Office
7 Regina Plains Museum
10 Tourist Information
16 Bus Station
22 Royal Saskatchewan
     Museum
23 Norman MacKenzie
     Art Gallery
24 Wascana Place
25 Legislative Building
26 Saskatchewan
     Science Centre

SASKATCHEWAN

of Regina's primary attractions. It lies four blocks south of the corner of Victoria Ave and Albert St.

The airport is a 15 minute drive southwest of downtown. The bus station is on Hamilton St, just south of Victoria Ave. The black-and-white eyeball street signs around town with adjoining names and arrows lead to the city's principal attractions.

Information

Tourist Offices The Saskatchewan Tourism Authority (☎ 306-787-2300, ☎ 1-800-667-7191), at 500 Albert St, at 12th Ave, has information on the entire province as well as city information. The office is open from 8 am to 5 pm Monday to Friday, and the phone line remains open on weekends. Tourism Regina (☎ 306-789-5099) has an office 6km east of downtown on Hwy 1 East just by the CKCK Television building. In summer it's open from 8 am to 7 pm Monday to Friday and on weekends and holidays from 10 am to 6 pm. From September to May, it's closed weekends.

Money A centrally located bank is the Toronto-Dominion at 1914 Hamilton St.

Post & Communications Regina's main post office is at 2200 Saskatchewan Drive, a few blocks west of Broad St.

Travel Agencies Travel CUTS (☎ 306-586-0011) is at University Centre on the campus.

Bookshops Smith Books is a good all-purpose store and Travellers Shop, 2014 14th St, has travel guides and maps.

Medical Services The Regina General Hospital (☎ 306-766-4444) is central at 1440 14th St.

Dangers & Annoyances The area on and around Osler St gets pretty tacky at night, even though the police station is there. Be careful generally downtown after dark – this is a small city but it can be unsafe.

Walking Tours

The tourist office has free booklets detailing eight different self-guided walks around town.

Views

SGI Building From the cafeteria on the 18th floor of this insurance company building at 2260 11th Ave, near the corner of Lorne St, the city and ever-present surrounding prairie can be seen. The cafeteria, which serves inexpensive food, is open Monday to Friday from 7.30 am to 4 pm, however, you don't need to buy anything to have a peek out the windows.

Sask Power Building This central office building (☎ 306-566-2553) has an outdoor, covered observation deck providing great views of the city. The **Gallery on the Roof**, a corridor just off the elevator, displays the work of provincial artists. There is also an inexpensive cafeteria here. It's all on the 13th floor of the Power Building, 2025 Victoria Ave, and is free. It's open daily from 8 am to 9 pm (afternoons only on weekends and holidays).

Wascana Centre

Regina is blessed with many parks, nearly all of them adjoining Wascana Creek, which meanders diagonally through the southern portion of the city. Wascana Centre park, the largest of these, is about eight times the size of the city centre. The park begins five blocks south of 12th Ave. Take Hamilton, Lorne or Broad Sts south; the park extends to the south-east.

The predominant feature is the artificial Wascana Lake. But as well as the lake, the picnic areas and sports fields, the green park contains many of the city's points of interest.

It's hard to imagine, but originally there was nothing here but a small creek called Pile O'Bones, surrounded by treeless prairie.

Wascana Place (☎ 306-522-3661), the headquarters of the park, is on Wascana Drive, west of Broad St, east of Wascana Lake and north of the marina. There's not really much of interest here, but there is an

information office, a good view from the 4th level of the building and bike rentals.

A little ferry, which is cheap, runs to Willow Island on the lake, a good site for picnics. Catch it off Wascana Drive by the north end of the lake. Boats can be rented beside the Wascana Pool building off College Ave. There is no swimming in the lake but the pool is open to all. There are flower gardens in the section north of the Legislative Building.

A waterfowl park off Lakeshore Drive, east of the Saskatchewan Centre of the Arts, has 60 species of birds and helpful identification displays. A boardwalk leads into the marsh, and naturalists are on duty through the week. The waterfowl park is open from 9 am to 9 pm from 1 May to 1 November.

The tourist office has a map of the Wascana Centre and a booklet detailing six walks through the park. At the Wascana Marina, there is the very good *Park Place* restaurant with a patio overlooking the lake. Free Sunday afternoon concerts are given through the summer at the Bandshell.

The University of Regina is on the northeast side of the park.

Saskatchewan Science Centre

In the park is the Saskatchewan Science Centre (☎ 306-791-7914), with its series of exhibits, hands-on participatory displays and demonstrations on the planet, its place in the solar system, physical laws and life.

The Science Centre is in the interesting, overhauled old Regina Power Plant (see the bank of old dials and meters in the lobby), on the north shore of the lake, east of Broad St near the corner of Wascana Drive and Winnipeg St. A bus up Broad St from downtown will get you to within a two-block walk of the door. The centre also houses a snack bar, a restaurant and a nifty little store.

A large-format IMAX movie theatre (☎ 306-522-4629) and the Kalium Observatory are other features of the centre, and have their own programs. Stargazing nights, held two or three times a month at the observatory, are worthwhile and cost just a couple of dollars.

Entry to the Science Centre is $5.50 per adult, with lower senior and family rates. IMAX shows are $7 each, or you can buy a money-saving combination ticket. In summer the centre is open daily from 10 am to 9 pm. During the winter it's open from 9 am to 4 pm Monday to Friday and from noon to 6 pm on weekends.

Provincial Legislature

Just off Albert St, on the park's west side, this beautiful building was built in 1919 in loose English Renaissance style at a cost of $3 million. Inside, 34 kinds of marble were used. The building is open all day, every day, and there are free tours given on the hour (except at lunchtime) from June to Labour Day. While at the Legislature, take a look at the Native Heritage Foundation Gallery, in the east wing on the main floor. The gallery exhibits and promotes Native Indian art and is open daily.

Royal Saskatchewan Museum

Also in the park, the museum is just south of the corner of College Ave and Albert St (☎ 306-787-2815). Upstairs there are realistic displays of North American wildlife, particularly animals native to Saskatchewan, with good explanations accompanying the exhibits. Downstairs the displays outline the biology of insects, birds, fish and animals and attempt to explain their behaviour. Space is also given to palaeontology (fossils) and archaeology.

The First Nations Gallery presents thousands of years of Saskatchewan's Native Indian history. There are often films on a variety of topics.

The museum is open daily from the beginning of May to the beginning of September; call for the off-season schedule. Admission is free and a visit will take about one hour.

Norman MacKenzie Art Gallery

Next door to the museum is the Norman MacKenzie Art Gallery (☎ 306-522-4242), which specialises in Canadian painting, much of it by local artists. Exhibits change

and may be historical or contemporary. The collection also contains works from US and European artists and good touring exhibitions are staged. The gallery is free and is open daily from 11 am to 6 pm (until 10 pm Wednesday and Thursday).

The art gallery is the venue for dramatic performances of *The Trial of Louis Riel*, which are held during August (see the Entertainment section later for details).

Diefenbaker Homestead

Although not in its original location, but on Lakeshore Drive west of Broad St in the park, this house is the boyhood home of former prime minister John Diefenbaker and is furnished with pioneer articles, some from the politician's family. It's open daily from the end of May to Labour Day, and is free.

Regina Plains Museum

There is life away from the park. The Regina Plains Museum (☎ 306-780-9435) is on the 4th floor of the old City Hall, on the corner of Scarth St and 11th Ave. Staff will guide you around, lovingly telling stories about items from Saskatchewan's past. The museum deals with the various people in the city and province's life: the Native Indians, Métis and European settlers.

Through the summer, the small museum is open weekdays from 10 am to 4 pm. The rest of the year it's Saturday to Wednesday. Admission is $2, less for seniors.

Government House

Government House (☎ 306-787-5717) is the restored home of the lieutenant-governor of the Northwest Territories and Saskatchewan from 1891 to 1945. Saskatchewan's current lieutenant-governor works (but doesn't live) in this house.

The Northwest territorial government was set up in 1870 to oversee the huge tract of land which was passing from the control of the fur-trading companies.

You can imagine what a sight this building must have been in the dusty village of Regina in the 1890s.

Government House contains furnishings from the turn of the century, and interpreters are on hand to show visitors around.

The site is north-west of the centre, at 4607 Dewdney Ave, slightly west of Lewvan Drive. It's open Tuesday to Sunday from 1 to 4 pm. Admission is free.

RCMP Centennial Museum & Depot

This museum (☎ 306-780-5838) details the history of the Royal Canadian Mounted Police from 1874, when they first headed west to keep the peace. It was in this part of the country that their slogan 'we always get our man' became legend. On display are uniforms, articles, replicas and stories of some of the famous and/or notorious exploits of the force.

The training facilities and barracks, known as the depot, can also be seen. Mounties still police many of Canada's western and more remote towns and communities, as well as having various federal responsibilities, such as being part of the national security forces. Tours run almost hourly until 3.30 pm, Monday to Friday. In addition, a daily drill takes place each weekday at 1 pm.

Open daily, the museum is on Dewdney Ave West, beyond Government House, near the corner of McCarthy Rd. From downtown, city bus No 8 goes to the museum.

Also at the depot you can see the popular Sunset Ceremony, a formal drill spectacle of drumming and marching surrounding the flag-lowering. It's a bit slow – call it a long hour – but the uniforms are colourfully impressive, and hey, the Mounties are one of Canada's best known symbols! The ceremony, like everything here, is free, but is held on Tuesday only, at 6.45 pm, in July and August. Ask at the tourist office or call for confirmation. Additional ceremonies take place at the Pile O'Bones Sunday event (see Special Events later for details) and on 1 August at the Legislature.

Sports Museum & Hall of Fame

Situated in the former Land Titles building, a heritage site, this small provincial museum

The Royal Canadian Mounted Police

The 'Mounties', for better or worse, are one of Canada's two most enduring and clichéd symbols (the other is the beaver). No doubt the traditional scarlet uniforms are striking, particularly when worn by a handsome young man atop a fine chestnut steed. Alas, the opportunities for appreciating this sight are somewhat rare now, as the garb of lore is pretty much exclusively ceremonial and the horses have been largely replaced by gasoline-driven horsepower.

Still, this emblem of the west, much like the US cowboy, does have its origins in reality. Originally formed as the Northwest Mounted Police in 1873, the force was charged with bringing peace and order to the developing west, then known as the Northwest Territories. Its headquarters were set up in 1882 at a tiny settlement beside Pile O'Bones Creek, later to become Regina. Perhaps the best known police force in the world, they developed a reputation for always 'getting their man'. What with the Native Indians caught in the middle of the rapidly changing west, the ever increasing numbers of arriving pioneers and the coming of the railway, they had their hands full, and generally earned the respect of most. Canada did largely manage to avoid the full-scale Indian wars that plagued the westward expansion in the USA.

Now involved in counterintelligence and thwarting international smuggling, terrorism and narcotics trade, the Mounties' actions are more controversial if less visible.

Traditionally attired Mounties can be seen in Regina at the RCMP Museum and, often, around the Parliament Buildings in Ottawa. Contrary to some international perceptions (and suggested by many a postcard), they are not seen on horseback in front of Niagara Falls, thief in hand, with beavers industriously gnawing away in the background.

(☎ 306-780-9232) is at 2205 Victoria Ave, across from Victoria Park. It honours local athletes and teams, with a tribute to Gordie Howe, a local boy made good as one of the greatest players in hockey history. The museum is open daily (in the afternoons on weekends) and is free.

Historical Telephones
SaskTel, the provincial telephone company, has an historical display area on the main floor of their building at 2121 Saskatchewan Drive. It's free and is open all day, Monday to Friday.

Fire Hall
Displays of old firefighting equipment can be seen in this modern, working fire station (☎ 306-777-7830) at 1205 Ross Ave. It's open to the public on weekdays and is free.

Antique Mall
For a mooch around on a rainy day or a Sunday when things are pretty quiet, try the

Antique Mall, a grouping of 25 or so antique booths and dealers. It's open all year at 1175 Rose St, at Sixth St. Note that on Sunday, even this isn't up and running until after noon.

Farmers' Market
A smallish farmers' market is set up two days a week through the summer along Scarth St on the east side of Victoria Park. Produce and baked goods (including jams and pies) as well as some crafts are offered for sale. Hours are 11 am to 4 pm on Wednesday and 8 am to 1 pm Saturday.

Other Attractions
The tourist office can give you information about swimming at public pools. There's one in Wascana Centre, just south of College Ave.

The Devonian Pathway is 11km of paved bike routes through four city parks. It begins and ends at Rotary Park, off the Albert St bridge. Bicycle rentals are available at

Lobster traps abound along the harbour near North Rustico, PEI.

Polar bear traps, Churchill, Manitoba

Grain silos in Denholm, Saskatchewan

Writing-on-Stone Provincial Park, Alberta

Wascana Place in Wascana Park by the hour or $20 per day.

The Saskatchewan Wheat Pool (☎ 306-569-4411) can help you plan a visit to a grain elevator or a livestock saleyard.

Special Events

Some of the festivals held here from April through to November are:

Saskatchewan Indian Federated College Powwow
The powwow in the Agridome of the Exhibition Grounds in April features dancers from around North America, as well as traditional Native Indian crafts and foods.

Mosaic
This three-day multicultural event with ethnic foods, music and entertainment is held in early June.

Buffalo Days
This six-day celebration is a big annual event held towards the end of July or beginning of August. Stores put up special décor and some workers wear pioneer garb. A talent stage is set up to offer free entertainment and the days are filled with competitions, pancake breakfasts, a beard-growing contest and parades, peaking with a big concert/barbecue in Wascana Park on what is known as Pile O'Bones Sunday. The amusement park features rides, music shows, a casino and various displays and exhibits. A fireworks display wraps up the festival.

Regina Folk Festival
This three-day festival, based in Victoria Park but with concerts elsewhere around town, has been held in August recently but check, it may be earlier. Call ☎ 306-757-7684.

Agribition
This is a five-day agricultural and livestock show held at the end of November.

Places to Stay

Camping As you approach Regina from the east on Hwy 1, there is *King's Acres* (☎ 306-522-1619) geared mainly to trailers and recreational vehicles but with some tent sites. It's just 6km from town near the tourist office, so it's convenient rather than rustic.

There's much better camping to be had in the Qu'Appelle Valley, about an hour's drive north-east of Regina. Try *Echo Valley Provincial Park* (☎ 306-332-3215), 8km

west of Fort Qu'Appelle or *Katepwa Campground* (☎ 306-332-4264), 26km north of Indian Head on Hwy 56, at Katepwa Beach.

Hostels The very good HI *Turgeon Hostel* (☎ 306-791-8165, 2310 McIntyre St) is in a fine old house once belonging to William Turgeon, an Acadian Frenchman who was Attorney General in 1907. The hostel is quite central – McIntyre St is a residential street near Wascana Centre. The rates are $13 for members, $18 for nonmembers. It has 50 beds, as well as cooking and laundry facilities, and stays open until midnight.

The men-only *YMCA* (☎ 306-757-9622, 2400 13th Ave) rents small, quiet rooms for $19. There is a cheap cafeteria and a pool you can use. Note that in summer it is not unusual for all the rooms to be booked out.

The *YWCA* (☎ 306-525-2141, 1940 McIntyre St), for women only, is spiffier and quite expensive at $35 for the single rooms, no doubles. There is a kitchen and a steam room.

B&Bs *B & J's* (☎ 306-522-4575, 2066 Ottawa St) east of downtown three blocks from Osler St, is comfortable and recommended. In the two-storey house on a residential street near 13th Ave there are four rooms at $25/35, breakfast included.

Daybreak Bed & Breakfast (☎ 306-586-0211, 316 Habkirk Drive) is a 12 minute drive south-west of town. There are two rooms and prices are also around $25/35. Free transport both to and from the airport is offered.

Hotels The last of the basics that can be considered even half-decent is the *Empire* (☎ 306-522-2544, 1718 McIntyre St) on the corner of Saskatchewan Drive. It's an easy walk north-west of the central downtown area. The clean, simple rooms have no toilet or bath but do have a sink. Rooms are $30, but they can't be recommended for women alone. Any other cheap hotels around town are pretty grim.

A good budget hotel suitable for anyone is the central *Plains Motor Hotel* (☎ 306-757-8661, 1965 Albert St) on the corner of

Canadian Means Quality

Since it's all you're looking at, a word about the golden grain is in order.

Wheat, brought to the New World by European settlers, was largely responsible for the development of the Canadian prairies. It is the primary crop across Manitoba, Saskatchewan and Alberta but by far the bulk of it is grown in Saskatchewan.

So productive are the fields here that Canada is the world's sixth largest producer after Russia, China, the USA, India and France.

The majority of wheat is produced for the export market. Russia, despite its own massive wheat production, is one of Canada's most important clients. Canadian wheat is sought after for its quality and high protein content.

Because of the cold climate the principal variety grown is hard red spring wheat, a bread wheat which is planted in spring and then harvested in August and September. The other main type is durum wheat, its characteristics making it especially suitable for the production of pasta.

In late summer, when the ripened wheat is golden brown, it is not uncommon to see the huge self-powered combines cutting and threshing through the fields at any hour of the night or day, often in teams. At night in particular, with the bright light beams skimming across the fields from the droning machines, it's quite a memorable sight.

The Canadian Wheat Board markets the crop. This organisation represents the farmers, the consumers and the government in buying, selling, setting quotas and regulating export. Needless to say, the board's actions are hotly debated.

Farmers are paid when they deliver their bushels to the grain elevators, where the entire crop is pooled and then sold by the board. Once that is accomplished the wheat is carried to ports by train and loaded onto freighters for destinations far and wide.

Wheat Castles of the New World

The unique, striking, columnar red, green or grey grain elevators seen along rail lines across the province are the classic symbol of midwestern Canada. These vertical wheat warehouses have been called the 'castles of the New World' and to this day are the artificial structure most visible across the plains.

Very simple in design and material and built solely for function they have been described as Canada's most distinctive architectural form. Western painters, photographers and writers have taken them as objects of art, meditation and iconography.

Across much of the province they have represented the economic life of the town and district and indeed have topped in size, if not in importance, that other traditional landmark, the church.

The first grain elevators were built in the 1880s. While Canada was becoming the 'breadbasket of the world' at the start of the 20th century, the number of elevators mushroomed, reaching a peak of nearly 5800 in 1938. Through consolidation and changing conditions that number is down to just 700. Their destruction concerns many individuals and groups who hope to prevent (not just lament) their disappearance.

Formerly made all of wood, they are now built from materials such as steel and cement. The classic shape, about 10m square and 20m high, is being experimented with as well, in an attempt to improve efficiency.

The stark beauty of elevators catching the light or looming out of the horizon is certainly an unmistakable part of the prairie landscape.

Victoria Ave. Rooms cost $39/43 plus tax and each room has its own bath and colour TV. There is a restaurant and free parking. The neon tower atop the hotel sign indicates the weather forecast – blue means clear, green means precipitation and orange means unsettled weather. If the lights are running up, the temperature will rise, and vice versa.

Moving upmarket, the *Travelodge* (☎ 306-565-0455, 1110 Victoria Ave E) is good and has nearly 200 modern rooms. Rates are $57/70. Other hotels in the downtown area are costlier.

The *Sands Hotel & Resort* (☎ 306-569-1666, 1818 Victoria Ave) – though no one can figure out the resort bit – has singles and doubles from $70.

The central *Delta* (☎ 306-525-5255, 1919 Saskatchewan Drive) features a three-storey indoor water slide, a swimming pool and whirlpools. Prices start at $89 for a double bed and go way up, but there are weekend specials.

The business-oriented *Hotel Saskatch-ewan* (☎ 306-522-7691, cnr Scarth St & Victoria Ave) costs from $130, with weekend specials for $87.

Motels The east side of town along Victoria St has the cheapies. The *North Star* (☎ 306-352-0723), 6km east of town, is the last motel on the north side of the highway. It's basic in the extreme and in need of work but the rooms are clean and the bed good. It's quiet, as it is set back from the road – behind a bunch of old trucks and junk! Rooms cost $29/32 with dubious air-conditioning and a wonky TV. Women alone should give it a miss.

Much better is the *Sunrise* (☎ 306-757-5447), down Victoria toward the centre near the overpass on Hwy 1 East, just out of town. Rooms with TV and air-conditioning cost from $45.

The *Coachman Inn Motel* (☎ 306-522-8525, 835 Victoria Ave) is good and closer to town. Rooms vary from $40 to $45 plus tax and cots are available for extra people.

Albert St south of town toward the Trans Canada has the larger, newer, pricier motels.

Places to Eat

Most choices listed here are in the central area, many of which are closed on Sunday. However, the Saturday newspaper is full of ads for Sunday brunch buffets around town, and most of the eateries around the outskirts remain open on Sunday.

A basic friendly place for breakfast is the *Town & Country* (1825 Rose St), open from 8 am daily, closed Sunday.

The *Copper Kettle* (1953 Scarth St), opposite Victoria Park, is open daily from 7 am to 1 am and offers pizzas, Greek dishes, cheap breakfasts and a $6 lunch buffet.

The *Elephant & Castle* is a British-style pub in the Cornwall Centre, which you enter on the corner of 11th Ave and Scarth St. Part of the restaurant façade is from the bank building built on the site in 1911. Also in this shopping mall is a cheap food fair, found on the 2nd level. Minutes away in the pedestrian section of Scarth St, *Grabbajabba* at No 1881 is a good place for coffee and dessert.

Upstairs at the 1928 Market Mall, a restored building on Lorne St near the corner of 11th Ave, is the huge Italian restaurant *Presutti's*, a casual place with an outdoor patio and wood-burning oven. Pizzas, pastas and the like are specialities ($8 to $13).

For Chinese food, there's *Lang's Café* (1745 Broad St). It's open for lunch and closes late. The décor is plastic but the food is cheap and not bad and there are a few Thai and vegetarian dishes. A Vietnamese place, *Mai Phuong* (1837 Broad St), has a $5 lunch buffet.

The small but appreciated Cathedral Village, the city's fledgling alternative area, is found along 13th Ave, west of Albert St. Past a health food store and a couple of bookshops get to the *13th Ave Coffee House* (3136 13th Ave). It's open every day for good coffee, excellent sandwiches ($4), soups and sweets. There is also a *Great Canadian Bagel* café beside the Safeway supermarket.

Slightly south of the centre are a few places to consider. *Henry's Café (2320 14th Ave)*, open until 5.30 pm (4 pm Sunday), serves very good pasta meals with salad for $7 or sandwich plates. Try the baked chicken

primavera. There's a range of coffees and desserts, an outdoor patio and an adjacent gift shop. Nearby is the *Heliotrope Vegetarian Restaurant (cnr 14th Ave & McIntyre St)*, also with outdoor tables. It's closed Monday.

For a steak, there is the well established *Diplomat (2032 Broad St)*. It's open from 11 am to 2 pm and again from 4 pm to midnight (except Sunday).

The reputation at the *Park Place (☎ 306-522-9999)* restaurant at the Wascana Marina, in the park near Broad St, is such that reservations are suggested for both lunch and dinner. Lunch is mainly well presented salads and sandwiches although you could try a buffalo burger. Dinners choices ($14) include an interesting international slant. The patio overlooks the lake making the city seem miles away. It's open every day but call for hours.

Entertainment

Music & Pubs *The Plains (1965 Albert St)*, in the Plains Hotel, has live bands (often blues on weekends) and there is a late Saturday afternoon jam.

The *Pump Country Roadhouse (641 Victoria Ave)* has live country Wednesday through Saturday.

On the eastern edge of town, *Brewsters (1832 Victoria Ave E)* brews its own beer. Closer to downtown, and not far from the RCMP Museum, is the *Bushwakker Brewing Co (2206 Dewdney Ave)*, which runs between Albert and Broad Sts. On offer are several of their own brews, including an oatmeal stout.

The fine, defunct old train station at 1880 Saskatchewan Drive houses *Casino Regina (☎ 1-800-555-3189)*, open daily until 4 am.

Also browse *Prairie Dog*, the free local entertainment monthly.

Performing Arts *The Trial of Louis Riel*, held in the *MacKenzie Art Gallery (☎ 306-522-4242, 3475 Albert St)*, is a theatrical dramatisation of the 1885 court battle fought over this leader of the Métis. One of Canada's most famous historical figures, Riel led two uprisings against the government. The re-creation of the trial highlights issues that are still important, as well as demonstrating the animosity between the country's French and British settlers.

It's worth catching, if your timing is right, and has become one of the longest-running shows in the country. There are shows three nights a week in July and August. Tickets ($11) are available at the tourist office or at the door.

Applause Dinner Theatre (☎ 306-791-6868, 1975 Broad St) is a popular dinner theatre which doesn't cost an arm and a leg ($38). Two-act musical comedies are presented with dinner (it's in the Holiday Inn).

The *Saskatchewan Centre of the Arts (☎ 306-525-9999, Wascana Centre, 200 Lakeshore Drive)* is a venue for concerts and performances ranging through folk, musicals and rock to opera and the symphony orchestra.

Cinema There's a *repertory cinema (☎ 306-777-6104, 2311 12th Ave)* in the lower level of the Central Library.

Spectator Sports

In summer and autumn, the Saskatchewan Roughriders (☎ 306-569-2323) plays professional football at Taylor Field as part of the Canadian Football League (CFL).

Curling is a major winter sport on the prairies, and the Curlodrome at Exhibition Park holds major competitions (known as bonspiels) through the snowy months.

Getting There & Away

Air Air Canada (☎ 306-525-4711) has flights east and west. There's no office but any travel agency can organise tickets. Standard one-way fares include $201 to Vancouver and $325 to Thunder Bay. Canadian Airlines also serves Regina. Athabaska Airways flies to Saskatoon, Prince Albert and some of the smaller northern towns.

Bus The bus station is downtown on Hamilton St, just south of Victoria Ave. There are left-luggage lockers and a quick-lunch counter. Four bus companies operate out of the station. Greyhound (☎ 306-787-3360)

has four trips daily, west to Calgary and Vancouver and east to Winnipeg and Toronto.

The Saskatchewan Transportation Company (☎ 306-787-3340) covers many small towns in the province and runs to Saskatoon and Prince Albert. There are three trips a day to Saskatoon ($27). The 240km trip takes three hours.

The other two bus lines service several farming communities.

The hostel has cheap bus tickets available to members for trips around the province.

Train There is no train service in or out of the city.

Car Thrifty (☎ 306-525-1000) is central, in the Holiday Inn at 1975 Broad St, on the corner of 12th Ave. Other companies are Discount (☎ 306-569-1222) which will pick you up and Budget. They all have offices at the airport.

Hitching For hitching east, take the No 4 bus from downtown, going west grab the No 79, Albert Park.

Getting Around
To/From the Airport The airport is about a 15 minute drive from downtown, and the only way to get there is taxi, which costs about $9.

Bus Regina Transit (☎ 306-777-7433) operates the bus routes around the city. Buses run from 6 am to midnight Monday to Saturday and from 1.30 to 8.30 pm on Sunday. Call for route information.

Bicycle Rentals are available at Wascana Place in the park (☎ 306-522-3661) by the hour or $20 per day. The Devonian Pathway is a system of 11km of paved bike routes through four city parks.

AROUND REGINA
Lumsden
North-west of Regina, Lumsden sits nestled and protected in a convoluted, lumpy, hilly little valley on the main road (Route

11) to Saskatoon. The Franciscan Monks here run the St Michael's retreat. The Heritage Museum outlines the history of the Qu'Appelle Valley.

Qu'Appelle Valley
The Qu'Appelle Valley runs east-west from the town of Fort Qu'Appelle, north-east of Regina, and makes a good contrast to the prairies. Following the Qu'Appelle River and interspersed with lakes, this valley is one of the green and pretty playgrounds of Saskatchewan.

There are several provincial parks and historic sites along the glacially formed valley. North of Lumsden, in Craven, the **Last Mountain House Provincial Historic Park**, is a fur-trading post dating from 1869 to 1871. Staff, displays and reconstructed buildings tell the story of the site. It's open from the beginning of July to the beginning of September each afternoon from Friday to Monday.

The **Kinsmen Big Valley Jamboree**, held annually in the middle of July, is one of the province's big country-music festivals, drawing acts from around Canada and the USA. Beer gardens, free camping and booths selling all manner of western garb are part of the three-day event.

In August, the **Craven Valley Stampede** is worth catching. Chuck-wagon races, roping contests and country and western music are some of the features. There isn't much in Craven, but as it is only 37km north-west of Regina, you can find accommodation in the city.

Fort Qu'Appelle
Fort Qu'Appelle, a town of 2000 people, lies north-east of Regina, by the Qu'Appelle River. The museum, on the corner of Bay Ave and Third St, has a collection of Native Indian artefacts, pioneer articles and some things from the old Hudson's Bay Company post (from 1864), which is adjacent to the museum. It's open every day through the summer. At Qu'Appelle Crafts, 310 Broadway, Native Indian crafts produced for the commercial market can be

seen or purchased. Each year in early or mid-August a large **Native Indian pow-wow**, takes place at the Standing Buffalo Reserve, 9km west of town. Dance competitors come from far and wide. Phone ☎ 306-332-4685 for exact dates.

Also west of town is the **Echo Valley Provincial Park** (☎ 306-332-3215) with a *campground*, swimming and trails around the valley.

East Saskatchewan

VEREGIN
Veregin lies near the Manitoba border, north of Yorkton, 265km north-east of Regina.

In town is the **Doukhobour Heritage Village**, a series of mainly reconstructed buildings and homes which reveal aspects of the settlers' lives at the beginning of the 1900s.

Houses and the Prayer Home are decorated in typically traditional fashion and include some attractive textiles. The museum contains many other artefacts, as well as photographs. Bread baked in the old-style brick ovens can sometimes be purchased.

The village is open daily from mid-May to mid-September, on weekdays only through the winter. Admission is $3.

There is also a statue of author Leo Tolstoy, commemorated for his assistance in the Doukhobours' emigration.

YORKTON
The onion-domed churches of this retail and distribution centre reflect the area's Ukrainian heritage. There's a branch of the provincial museum system here which depicts the struggles of the various immigrant groups of the province.

St Mary's Church is worth seeing, particularly the painted dome.

Every May the town hosts the Yorkton Short Film and Video Festival – the oldest continuously running short-film festival in North America.

Broadway St has motels, inns and a couple of standard restaurants. The *Gladstone* is the best place to eat.

Veregin and the Doukhobours

Veregin is a small, essentially unknown town, more or less in the middle of nowhere, but it has a rather unexpected, intriguing history. The town and its surrounding area were settled between 1898 and 1899 by the Doukhobours, a determined and somewhat extraordinary religious sect from Russia.

At the turn of the 20th century, with help from writer Leo Tolstoy, a good many of these people left their homeland and the persecution there to come to Saskatchewan in search of religious freedom and seclusion. Here, under the leadership of Peter Veregin, they created a small but successful community.

Bliss was not to last, however, and soon the Doukhobours were in trouble with their neighbours and government again. They resisted all mainstream authority, be it church or state. Partially based on fact, but somewhat exaggerated, are the well known tales of nude demonstrations and arson which have, rightly or wrongly, come to be closely associated with the group.

After about 20 years here, many of the Doukhobours moved to British Columbia, where there's still a community. In the 1950s some of them returned to Russia, or headed to new lands once again, this time settling in Paraguay.

Within an hour's drive are **Good Spirit Provincial Park** with beaches and sand dunes and the larger **Duck Mountain Provincial Park**, on the border of Manitoba.

Dauphin is two hours away.

CROOKED LAKE PROVINCIAL PARK
Due south of Yorkton, 30km north of the Trans Canada, Crooked Lake Park (☎ 306-728-7480), can make a pleasant overnight stop. The park is along the eastern stretches of the Qu'Appelle Valley and Qu'Appelle River.

MOOSE MOUNTAIN PROVINCIAL PARK

Farther off the highway, west from Manitoba along the Trans Canada Hwy and south down Hwy 9, Moose Mountain (☎ 306-577-2600) is another place to consider camping the night or stopping for a break from the unchanging pancake landscape. The park provides an oasis of woods on the highest plateau in this area of the province. It is a fairly developed area, however, with golf courses, water slides and the like available around the park's main gate. The central and western portions of the park are quieter, and walking trails can be found in these parts.

Twenty-six kilometres south-east of the park is **Cannington Manor Historic Park**. The park records an English settlement here between the years 1882 and 1900. The park is open daily from 10 am to 6 pm.

There are a couple of motels in nearby Kenosee.

Southern Saskatchewan

Running across the southern section of the province is the Red Coat Trail, a highway route from Winnipeg, Manitoba to Lethbridge, Alberta. The trail is named after the Mounties and roughly parallels the route they took in coming to tame the west.

Tourist offices have a pamphlet which highlights the historical and geographical points of interest along the way. Here, as in much of the province, the towns themselves don't have much to interest visitors but the government parks do have areas of geographic, historic or cultural significance.

ESTEVAN

Near the US border, Estevan (population 10,800) is one of the largest towns in southern Saskatchewan. It's a town with energy – it has the world's largest deposits of lignite coal, three electrical generating stations and some natural gas pockets and is surrounded by oilfields.

Local attractions include the sandstone rock formations at **La Roche Percée**, once a site of Native Indian religious observance, and the **Estevan Brick Wildlife Display**, which has samples (stuffed and live) of most local species, including bison and antelope.

Ask at the tourist office about rockhounding or visiting the dam and coal mines. There are about half a dozen standard motels.

South of town, in North Portal, Chicago gangster Al Capone used to hang out in the Cadillac Hotel – this was a huge booze-smuggling area during the Prohibition days (1920-33) in the USA.

WEYBURN

From Weyburn, a farming supply centre with nearly 10,000 residents, the so-called CANAM International Hwy leads northward to Regina and beyond, and southward through North and South Dakota and Wyoming. A promotional pamphlet lists the attractions of a trip along the designated route.

There isn't a lot in Weyburn, but there is a park with camping facilities and tourist information, and the **Soo Line Historical Museum** which has some Native Indian artefacts and articles from the pioneer days.

Weyburn is the birthplace of Canadian author WO Mitchell and the setting for his best known book, about a boy growing up, *Who Has Seen The Wind*.

BIG MUDDY BADLANDS

Off Hwy 34 south of Regina and Moose Jaw, near the US border, this vast, hot area of sandstone formations, hills and valleys was once used by stagecoach robbers, cattle-rustlers and all the other bad-guy types you see in western movies. In fact, the outlaw Butch Cassidy used to ride here.

Food, accommodation and camping is available in the small town of **Bengough**. There is another *campground* in Big Beaver, and guided tours of the badlands are available. Conspicuous Castle Butte, nearby, is a prominent landmark.

Farther east, two provincial parks may be of interest. At **St Victor's** there are prehistoric

SASKATCHEWAN

Native Indian petroglyphs (carvings in rock). **Wood Mountain Post Historic Park** has more recent history, with displays on the North West Mounted Police and the Sioux people. Wood Mountain was where Chief Sitting Bull brought his Sioux warriors after their victory against Custer at the famous 1876 Battle of Little Bighorn (in what is now Montana, USA). There are some reconstructed buildings and tours are given. Note that the park is open from 1 June to mid-August but is closed Tuesday and Wednesday.

MOOSE JAW

Moose Jaw is a small, fairly typical-looking farm-supply town but with some industry and several unexpected attractions. Situated halfway between the former railway towns of Winnipeg and Calgary, Moose Jaw was selected as a major Canadian Pacific Railway terminal in the late 19th century. Theories on the origins of the once-heard, never-forgotten name are numerous and nebulous; 'moosegaw' is a Cree word meaning 'warm breezes', so this possibility has some credence. A series of parks are strung along the Moose Jaw River in the Wakamow Valley just south of the centre.

Information

The Chamber of Commerce (☎ 306-692-6414), closed weekends, is situated at 88 Saskatchewan St E. It also operates a booth (☎ 306-693-8097) (open daily in summer) out on the Trans Canada Hwy, beside the statue of the moose. Out of province cars can park free at meters.

Things to See & Do

The **Mineral Spa** in the downtown Temple Gardens Resort Hotel draws a lot of visitors. The heated mineral pool is the main attraction (from $7) but there is a lengthy list of pampering services offered.

Highly recommended is the stranger-than-fiction **Tunnels of Little Chicago** (☎ 306-693-5261) tour under the streets complete with fascinating history lesson. The $7 ticket is well worth it and includes a museum-like exhibit at the office, 108

Main St. There is a very good value combination spa-tunnel ticket offered.

The downtown area has a number of heritage buildings from the town's boom days in the 1920s; the tourist office produces a pamphlet for a self-guided historical walking tour along Main St and nearby. About 30 painted murals with an historical theme can be seen on buildings in the core area. The Mural Centre, with more information on the project, is at 445 Main St.

There are four **Western Development Museums** around the province, each specialising in an aspect of provincial history. The one in Moose Jaw concentrates on the development of transportation in the west, with old carts, cars and trains. Admission costs $5.

The **Burrowing Owl Interpretive Area** at the Exhibition Grounds offers a glimpse of these little known endangered birds.

Curiosity-seekers might enjoy the **Sukanen Ship & Pioneer Village Museum**, 13km out of town, with plenty of pioneer relics and remains and the ship built here for sailing on the sea. The odd collection also contains old cars and tractors. It's open in summer only.

The town also hosts a major **international band** (pipe, brass, marching, etc) and **choral festival** in May. There is an armed forces base in Moose Jaw, which is home to the famous Snowbirds, an aerial acrobatic squadron which performs at air shows across the continent. The **Saskatchewan Air Show**, largest on the prairies, is held here each July.

Places to Stay

For camping, the *Besant Trans Canada Campground* (☎ 306-756-2700) is a 20 minute drive west on the Trans Canada Hwy. There are both tent and trailer sections within the park, and a small pond for a swim. The *Prairie Oasis Campground* (☎ 306-692-4894, cnr Ninth Ave North-East & Hwy 1) is a family-oriented recreation centre (water slides etc) with mobile homes (for up to six people) which can be rented for $70 a night.

There are about 10 motels and hotels and a B&B. The inexpensive *Dreamland Motel* (☎ 306-692-1878, 1035 Athabaska St E) is central.

Getting There & Away
The downtown Greyhound station (☎ 306-692-2345) is on High St, one block east of Main St. There are numerous trips daily to Regina and one for Saskatoon.

CHAPLIN LAKE
West of Moose Jaw stop at the Interpretive Site here beside the mounds of snow-like sodium sulphate produced by Chaplin Lake. The salty lake supports brine shrimp (sea monkeys!) which attract thousands of shorebirds, many of them endangered. For birdwatchers, a dusty road encircles the lake and tours are offered. Farther west on the Trans Canada, watch for the American white pelicans at Reed Lake beside Morse.

GRASSLANDS NATIONAL PARK
Not yet completed, this park preserves noteworthy flora & fauna as well as remarkable geological and historical features. It's a two-section park lying between Val Marie and Killdear, south of Swift Current and west of Assiniboia. The eastern block consists of the Killdeer Badlands west of Wood Mountain Post Provincial Park. Information on this section of the park can be found at the Rodeo Ranch Museum, in Wood Mountain.

The western section of the park lies along the Frenchmen River Valley south-east from the town of Val Marie, at the junction of Hwys 4 and 18. Information and the latest details on the park are available at the Park Service Office and visitors centre (☎ 306-298-2257) in Val Marie. Basic wilderness camping is permitted. As yet, there are no facilities in the park.

Surrounded by ranchland, the park protects a section of original, natural, short-grass prairie land. Features include the badlands, 70-Mile Butte which is the second highest point in the province, cliffs and coulees (gulches, usually dry), a prairie-dog town and some historic Native Indian sites.

SWIFT CURRENT
Though a fairly large town, Swift Current has little for the visitor. Still, a bed or a meal can be found without difficulty. Country music fans may want to check out the **Canadian Country Music Hall of Fame** (☎ 306-773-7854), off the Trans Canada Hwy, or the fiddle championships which are held in September. The **Mennonite Heritage Village** reveals something of this Christian sect or you can tour through the religious Hutterite community outside of town.

SASKATCHEWAN LANDING PROVINCIAL PARK
Straight north up Hwy 4 from Swift Current, the section of the Saskatchewan River here was used as a crossing point by the early European explorers and, later, the white settlers. Goodwin House, built by the North West Mounted Police, is the visitors centre with historical details and information on Native Indian sites within the park. There is also camping and hiking.

GREAT SAND HILLS
Just west of Swift Current (or north of Gull Lake and Maple Creek) is a semidesert area with dunes and near-arid vegetation. The best viewing area is about 10km south of the little village of **Sceptre**, in the north-western section of the hills near the town of Leader. Antelope and mule deer may be seen. There are farm B&Bs in the area. The tourist office in Swift Current has accommodation information and Sand Hills maps and Sceptre has a Sand Hills museum.

EASTEND
Quiet Eastend, south-west of Swift Current on Hwy 13, is surrounded by badlands which early in the morning or at dusk offer panoramas of pinks and golds, textures and shadows. Pick-up the Guide to the Valley of Hidden Secrets for a driving tour of the nearby geographical highlights. Jones Peak is good at sunset. Nearby, Sioux chief Crazy Horse once camped.

In 1994 excavations unearthed the first *Tyrannosaurus Rex* skeleton found in Saskatchewan. It proved to be one of the most complete found anywhere. Visit the **Fossil Research Station**, with working lab, open all

year. Frenchman Valley Tours (☎ 306-295-3606) offers area tours in July and August.

There's a *campground* and a *motel* right in town, and a small museum.

CYPRESS HILLS INTERPROVINCIAL PARK

Straddling the provincial border, the park (☎ 306-662-4411) typifies this pretty region of small lakes, streams and green hills up to 1400m high which offers a pleasant geographical respite from the prairies.

The west block sector is larger and more natural. There's camping here, notably on the Alberta side, around the lakes where tenting costs $13, but it gets crowded in summer. A dirt road links this area to **Fort Walsh**, a national historic site. The fort, built in the late 1870s as a North West Mounted Police base, is a remnant of the district's rich but sad history. The hills, always a sanctuary for animals, were at one time also a welcoming retreat for the Plains Indians. Information at the old fort tells the story of the time when 'a man's life was worth a horse and a horse was worth a pint of whisky'. Bicycles can be rented.

The centre block sector has the more modern facilities.

MAPLE CREEK

At the northern edge of Cypress Hills, Maple Creek is worth a look for its old western main street. Many of the storefronts in this ranching district town are heritage vintage. The **Old Timer's Museum**, 218 Jasper St, is the oldest in the province. It has artefacts on the RCMP and some on the Native Indian and pioneer communities.

If you're around in late summer (usually September), ask about the weekend-long **Cowboy Poetry Gathering**. Begun in 1989, the poetry event attracts storytellers and singers who carry on the tradition of cowboy (and cowgirl) narrative. You can also see the work of artisans such as saddlemakers and silversmiths. On Saturday night there's a big western dance.

There are a couple of motels in and around town, and there is the *Willow Bend Trailer Court*, a campground geared to those with campervans.

Saskatoon

Saskatoon (population 200,000) is a small, slow-paced city sitting smack in the middle of the Canadian prairies. The clean, wide streets, low skyline and flat surroundings give the city a western flavour. The South Saskatchewan River meanders through the centre banked by parkland which provides a welcome touch of greenery and shade.

The largest employer in town is the university, and Saskatoon has pretty much become the provincial cultural centre, with an active arts community. As the second city of the province, however, Saskatoon is also a farm-trading centre, acting as a transportation, communication and commercial hub. In addition, the city has a major agricultural research centre, called Innovation Place.

There isn't a lot here for the visitor, and after a short look-see you'll have a feel for the place. But it's an attractive little city with a few things of interest, and the Wanuskewin Heritage Park makes it an even better and more convenient crossroads for the traveller.

Just off the main thoroughfares, residential streets are lined with small, neat, square houses. Seven bridges link the city across the river.

History

In 1883, 35 members of the Temperance Colonisation Colony from Ontario founded a settlement on these Cree lands. The town stayed (though the ban on alcohol didn't), taking its name from the Cree word 'misaskwatomin', for one of the indigenous berries still enjoyed today in pies and jams. In 1890 the railway hit town and growth continued until the Depression. The city has had its ups and downs since then, but is now well established and diversified beyond its agricultural roots. Uranium mines and some of the world's largest potash deposits are found nearby.

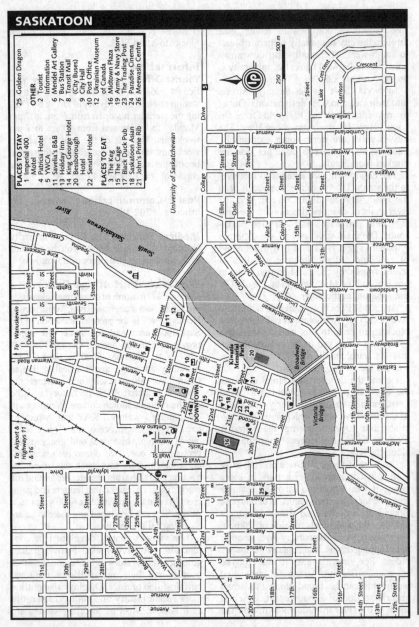

SASKATOON

PLACES TO STAY
1 Imperial 400 Motel
4 Patricia Hotel
5 YWCA
13 Savelia's B&B
14 Holiday Inn
King George Hotel
20 Bessborough Hotel
22 Senator Hotel

PLACES TO EAT
3 The Keg
15 The Cage
17 Black Duck Pub
18 Saskatoon Asian
21 John's Prime Rib

25 Golden Dragon

OTHER
2 Tourist Information
6 Mendel Art Gallery
7 Bus Station
8 Transit Mall (City Buses)
9 City Hall
10 Post Office
12 Ukrainian Museum of Canada
16 Midtown Plaza
19 Army & Navy Store
23 The Trading Post
24 Paradise Cinema
26 Meewasin Centre

SASKATCHEWAN

Orientation

The South Saskatchewan River cuts through the city diagonally from north-east to south-west. The small main downtown area lies on the west bank; the university is on the opposite side.

Idylwyld Drive divides the city's streets into their east and west designations. Out of town in each direction, Idylwyld Drive becomes Hwy 16, the Yellowhead Hwy. The city is split into north-south sections by 22nd St, and the streets on either side are marked accordingly.

The downtown core extends to the river to the south, 1st Ave to the west, 25th St to the north, and Spadina Crescent and the river again (it changes direction) to the east.

Streets run east-west, avenues north-south. The main street is 2nd Ave. Another important street is 21st St E with its blend of new and old architecture and lots of stores, framed by the Bessborough Hotel at one end and the Midtown Plaza, the old CN train station, at the other.

At 23rd St E, between 3rd Ave N and 2nd Ave N, is the Greyhound Bus Depot, in a block open only to bus traffic. Most bus routes can be picked up here. Note though that the transit mall, a few blocks farther west, is the city bus terminal.

Behind the Bessborough Hotel is one of the city's large parks, Kiwanis Memorial Park, running beside the river. At each end of the attractive park, which is used by cyclists and joggers during the summer months, Spadina Crescent continues on along the river.

Just west of Idylwyld Drive on 20th St W is an old commercial area, now in some decay. It was formerly a largely Ukrainian area, and there are some remnants of this past, along with a determined Chinese segment found on the side streets running off 20th St.

Faring better is Broadway Ave, another old shopping district and actually the town's oldest. For several years it has enjoyed some gentrification. A range of stores and restaurants can be found along this small historic section of Broadway St, which is south of the river from downtown, over the Broadway Bridge. The area of interest runs from the bridge south about half a dozen blocks to Main St E.

Information

Tourist Offices The Tourism Saskatoon office (☎ 306-242-1206) is in the old CP train station at No 6 305 Idylwyld Drive N. During the summer it's open from 9 am to 7 pm Monday to Friday and from 10 am to 7 pm weekends. The rest of the year, it's closed weekends. There is a seasonal information booth open daily from May to August on the corner of Ave C N and 47th St W.

Post & Communications The main post office is at 202 4th Ave N.

Medical Services The Royal University Hospital (☎ 306-665-1000) is on the grounds of the university, just north of downtown.

Wanuskewin Heritage Park

Just over 17km north of downtown, alongside the South Saskatchewan River, Wanuskewin Heritage Park is the premier attraction in the Saskatoon area and for some, the entire province. The 100-hectare site (☎ 306-931-6767 or ☎ 1-800-665-4600) around the remarkably attractive and scenically diverse Opamihaw Valley presents and interprets the area's rich archaeology, prehistory and the Northern Plains Indian culture. Wanuskewin (pronounced wah-nus-KAY-win, which is Cree for 'seeking peace of mind') is a fascinating cultural, historical and geographical centre all in one. Two dozen prehistoric archaeological sites have been unearthed, attracting attention from researchers around the world. They've learned that hunters and gatherers lived in the area at least 6000 years ago. Active digs can be visited and there is an archaeological lab on site.

The visitors centre, developed in conjunction with provincial Native Indian groups, tells the story of the regional Native peoples and their way of life on the once buffalo-filled prairies. Displays also outline more recent history and Native Indian life as it is now. Most of the site workers are

Native Indian. During summer there are daily dance performances at 2 pm.

Best of all is the land itself, left untouched to reveal why so many people over so many years found it a sacred place. Virtually invisible from the surrounding prairie, four trails lead the visitor down and around the valley amid wildflowers, songbirds and such park highlights as the old buffalo trail, a buffalo jump, the mysterious medicine wheel and tipi rings. The site harbours a rich concentration of flora and fauna, including a small herd of deer.

From June to September visitors can camp out in the park in a traditional tipi (bring insect repellent). An overnight stay, including breakfast and admission to the park, costs just $23 for hostel members. Full price is $39 for adults and $20 for children. There are also full-day packages which might include learning how to build and raise a tipi, listening to traditional stories, guided walks along Wanuskewin's ancient trails, cooking Native Indian foods and making crafts such as dream catchers.

If visiting for the day, a suggestion is to arrive early in the morning – the earlier the better. There will be few people, if any, and a walk around the trail system at this time is sure to be quiet and peaceful – the way the Native people would have found it. Also, if it is midsummer, the air will be fresh and cool and the odds of seeing some of the wildlife markedly increased. When it gets busy after lunch, the visitors centre can be viewed.

For the trails, wear flat comfortable shoes and in high summer take a juice or water bottle because it can get extremely hot. To see the site thoroughly – walk the trails, watch a performance, take a break for lunch – allow yourself around six hours.

The *restaurant* provides an opportunity to try Native Indian foods such as buffalo, wild rice and Saskatoon berry desserts. The buff stew with bannock, an unleavened bread, is inexpensive and good.

Getting to the site presents some difficulties for those without a car. The city has considered a weekend bus run to the park. Call the park or city bus information for the latest news. The Lawson Heights No 18 bus gets you to within about 8km. If you're staying at the Patricia Hotel, mention to the managers that you'd like to go to Wanuskewin and they may be able to arrange transportation, especially if there's a bunch of you.

Taxis by the meter cost about $22 one way, although you may be able to negotiate a cheaper rate. Cycling is another option, but this is not really cheap either – $20 for the full day. Bikes (with lock) can be rented at the Ramada Renaissance Hotel and Sheraton Cavalier. Riding steadily at a good clip – the trip takes almost exactly an hour one way. The ride makes a good introduction to the park – an oasis surrounded by vast, open prairie.

Follow Warman Rd out of the centre (just keep going and going) and then look for signs with the park symbol (a buffalo in a circle). These signs are also seen if you're driving north out of the city along Idylwyld Drive, which becomes Hwy 11. For those with more time and a map, the pleasant Meewasin cycling trail can be used for part of the trip.

The site is open daily from 9 am to 9 pm from the end of May to Labour Day, and from 9 am to 5 pm Wednesday to Sunday the rest of the year. Admission is $6 for adults, less for seniors and children, and there is a family rate.

Western Development Museum

You open the door of this museum (☎ 306-931-1910) and suddenly you're looking down Main St, circa 1910. It looks like a movie set, with stores, workshops, a hotel, a printing shop and other establishments. The general store is good. Don't miss the model of men playing chess. There are all manner of goods, tins, relics and supplies on display, as well as old wagons, cars and farm machinery.

The museum is at 2610 Lorne Ave, quite a way south of town. To get there, take a No 1 Exhibition bus from Second Ave downtown. When leaving the museum, get on the bus going the same way as when you arrived. It loops around, then goes back a different way. The museum is open daily. Admission costs $5, less for seniors and kids; it may be worth

showing a HI hostel card too. There's a café at the site. Call to check opening hours.

Ukrainian Museum of Canada

This museum (☎ 306-244-3800), at 910 Spadina Crescent E, preserves and presents a Ukrainian heritage through articles donated by Ukrainian immigrants.

The highlight is the collection of fantastic textiles used in formal and everyday dress and for other household purposes. In style, colour and design, they rival South American textiles.

Also interesting is the exhibit on symbolic, festival or special-occasion breads (such as wedding breads). Other items are the painted eggs (pysanka) and a brief history of the pioneers' arrival.

The museum is open Monday to Saturday (closed Monday in winter) from 10 am to 5 pm and on Sunday and holidays from 1 to 5 pm. Admission is $2.

There are branches of this museum in other Canadian cities, such as Winnipeg and Edmonton, but this is the main one.

Ukraine Museum

A small museum (☎ 306-244-4212) at 202 Ave M S, this one has examples of Ukrainian crafts and dress, and through the exhibits portrays aspects of Ukrainian culture from prehistoric times to the mid-20th century. It's open daily. Admission is $5.

The adjacent Byzantine-style Ukrainian cathedral can be visited; ask at the museum.

Marr Residence

Just a block from the river, at 326 11th St E, sits the oldest building (☎ 306-665-6887) in Saskatoon still in its original location. Built in 1884, it was used as a hospital the following year, during the North West Rebellion. Admission is free; call for hours.

Meewasin Valley & Centre

The pretty, green Meewasin Valley follows the South Saskatchewan River down the middle of the city. (Meewasin is a Cree word meaning 'beautiful valley'.) From behind the Bessborough Hotel, the valley park runs in both directions and on both sides of the river for a total of 17km.

There are pleasant views of the river. The Meewasin Valley Trail is good for walking and cycling, and picnic tables are scattered among the trees, where black-and-white magpies flit. Bridges span the river at several places and the trail follows the banks on both sides. Many of the city's attractions and events are along the river. The university lies along the east shore.

The Meewasin Centre (☎ 306-665-6888), 402 3rd Ave S, is at the bottom of 3rd Ave S, on the corner of 19th St E. It's really a museum about the river and the city's history, with some good displays.

Although it's hard to imagine, the river is melted glacier ice from the Rockies far to the west near Lethbridge, Alberta. It flows north from Saskatoon, joining the Assiniboine River on its way to Winnipeg. The Meewasin Centre is open daily, and has good maps of the trail with its various parks. Admission is free.

Mendel Art Gallery & Conservatory

These are at 950 Spadina Crescent E, a short walk along the river from the downtown area. The gallery (☎ 306-975-7610) has three rooms of changing exhibits, usually featuring Canadian works. One of the three galleries shows historical works, while the other two display contemporary art. The small conservatory has a few palms, among other plants. Admission is free and the centre is open daily from 9 am to 9 pm in summer, shorter hours in winter. There is a coffee shop and gift store on the premises.

University of Saskatchewan

There are a few things to look at on the campus (☎ 306-966-4343), which is on a huge tract of land along the river. There's a small biology museum, an observatory for stargazing (open Saturday evening after dusk), two art galleries and other small faculty museums. The Natural Sciences Museum has some life-size replicas of dinosaurs. For opening hours and information on free tours

of the campus and many of the points of interest, call during office hours.

Also on campus is the **Diefenbaker Centre**, detailing aspects of former prime minister's Diefenbaker's life. It also has other historical and craft displays. The centre is open daily, but afternoons only on weekends and holidays. His grave site is next to the centre.

The **Little Stone School**, dating from 1887, is the oldest public building in the city. It can be visited Saturday and Sunday afternoons. A costumed interpreter provides information. It's free, as are all the university sights.

If you're going to stroll around the campus, pick up a copy of the architectural pamphlet *Building the University*, which offers details of the various structures and their dates of construction.

Forestry Farm Park & Zoo
This park (☎ 306-975-3382) is 8km northeast of the downtown area, across the river and along Attridge Drive and then Forest Drive.

The zoo inside the park is home to around 300 animals, mostly those found in Saskatchewan and other parts of Canada: wolves, lynx, caribou and bison. There are also gardens, picnic sites, a restaurant and a fishing lake. In winter the park has a ski trail. The park is over University Bridge; for specific details of how to get there, ask at the tourist office or call the park, but there are signs to follow along Attridge Drive. There is a vehicle charge of $2 and tickets for the zoo are $4. It's open 365 days a year, until 9 pm through the summer months.

Beaver Creek Conservation Area
About 13km south of the Meewasin Valley (from the Freeway Bridge) is the Beaver Creek Conservation Area, a large park protecting some of the river valley and its wildlife. Walking trails run through the area and the information centre provides geographical and historical background. The park contains some of the little remaining uncultivated prairie in the province. Beaver Creek is open daily from May to August and admission is free.

Saskatchewan Railway Museum
The province's railway history is here (☎ 306-382-9855), spread over 2.5 hectares. There are engines, cabooses, even transplanted railway buildings. Smaller artefacts have also been collected from around Saskatchewan. It's open Wednesday to Sunday from 1 to 6 pm. Admission is $2. The site is 4km southwest of town via Hwys 7 and 60. Call for detailed instructions.

Berry Barn
On a working farm 11km south-west of town, the Berry Barn (☎ 306-978-9797) sells a range of foods made with the Saskatoon berry. Light meals are offered at tables overlooking the Saskatchewan River. There's also a substantial gift shop upstairs. In season, you can go into the fields and pick your own berries. Call for hours (they vary), information on the harvesting time and directions.

Activities
There are numerous city-operated swimming pools around town; the tourist office will help locate a convenient one. In winter there is a skating rink on the parkland beside the Bessborough Hotel.

Organised Tours
Shearwater Boat Cruises (☎ 306-934-7642) at 2301 Clarence Ave has frequent one-hour trips along the river departing from behind the Bessborough Hotel for $8. It also offers longer, gentle rafting trips. Cruises run from May to October.

Canoeski Discovery (☎ 306-653-5693) can arrange long or short guided canoe and cross country ski trips. Borealis Outdoor Adventures (☎ 306-343-6399) runs weekend and longer bicycle trips around the province.

Guided walks of the university and some of its attractions are offered on Monday and Friday from June to August; call ☎ 306-966-8384 for information.

SASKATCHEWAN

Special Events

Some of the major events held from June through to September are:

Shakespeare on the Saskatchewan
This is a successful and popular summer-long theatre program, held in a tent near the river by the Mendal Art Gallery. Each year, one play by the Bard is presented for the season. Performances are in the evening and advance tickets are advised; call ☎ 306-652-9100 for bookings.

Saskatchewan Jazz Festival
This festival (☎ 306-652-1421) is held at the end of June or beginning of July and takes place at various locations around town. Most of the concerts and performances are free. Emphasis is on conventional jazz, but bands range from Dixieland to free form.

Louis Riel Day
This is a one-day event held in the first week of July, with various outdoor activities and contests taking place by the Bessborough Hotel.

The Exhibition
This is an eight-day event in mid-July, with livestock competitions, exhibits, concerts, rides and parades.

International Fringe Festival
At the end of July, look for this week-long festival, showcasing varied, experimental and inexpensive theatre, including drama, mime, comedy and dance.

Folkfest
This three-day festival (☎ 306-931-0100) takes place in mid-August. The fee of $10 gets you into 25 multicultural pavilions set up around the city presenting food, crafts, music and dances. A free shuttle bus does the circuit around the various pavilions.

Places to Stay

Camping Quite close to the centre is the *Gordon Howe Campsite* (☎ 306-975-3328), on Ave P south of 11th St, operated by the City Parks Department. It's fairly green and although geared to campervans, there are tent sites for $10. It's open from April to September and is often full on weekends. There is a small store for basic supplies.

Just a five minute drive north-west of town on Hwy 16 there's *Saskatoon 16 West RV Park* (☎ 306-931-8905), which is open from April through October and sites are $18 for tents.

Hostels Some rooms at the neat and central *Patricia Hotel* (☎ 306-242-8861), on 2nd Ave between 24th and 25th Sts, have been converted to hostel dormitories with bunk beds. A bed costs $14 with a membership card or $19 without. Unfortunately, the hostel rooms are above the very noisy bar. Don't figure on sleeping before 2 am. Most of the ordinary hotel rooms have the same problem. The bar is quite inexpensive, as is the restaurant in the basement.

The *YWCA* (☎ 306-244-0944, cnr 25th St E & 5th Ave N) rents rooms year-round to women ($38 a single). Look for the blue sign near Third Ave. It has a pool and a small kitchen.

There is accommodation available at the *University of Saskatchewan* (☎ 306-966-8600), a 25 minute walk north-east of town along the river, from the beginning of May to the end of August. A shared room is $22; a single room is $28 including tax, but there is a three-day minimum.

B&Bs *Brighton House* (☎ 306-664-3278, 1308 5th Ave N), 2.3km north of downtown and near the river, is the top choice. It's friendly, immaculate and provides a very good breakfast. There's even a garden hot tub, bicycles and, for a small fee, transport can be arranged. The No 8 bus up 7th Ave goes very close. Rates are $45/55 and rooms come with telephone.

Closer to downtown is central *Savelia's* (☎ 306-653-4646, 330 6th Ave N), just south of 25th St. There are three rooms with shared bathroom at $30/40 a single/double. A full breakfast is included. A drawback is that it operates on the whims of the casual owner.

For a real taste of prairie hospitality you can stay on a 40-hectare farm complete with cows, pigs, sheep and goats. *Chaplin's Farm* (☎ 306-931-3353) is about 11km south-east of Saskatoon and has rooms for $35/50. Call for reservations and directions.

The Country Vacation Association (☎ 306-931-3353) has a full list of B&Bs in the area.

Hotels The *Patricia Hotel* (☎ 306-242-8861, 345 2nd Ave N), between 24th and

25th Sts, is the best and cleanest of the cheap places. In fact, this is one of the best budget hotels in the country – central, friendly and well run. It offers good value, with rooms at $34/43 with tax (some with private bathroom) but get one of the front rooms or the bar noise will really bother you. See also under Hostels earlier in this section. The sports bar and restaurant on the premises are both good and inexpensive.

The *Senator* (✆ 306-244-6141, cnr 3rd Ave S & 21st St E) is right in the centre of town. It's old but has been renovated with fine rooms at $43/48. It has a beautiful pub-style bar (although some patrons are a little too regular) and a very good dining room and rooftop eating area. The large *King George* (✆ 306-244-6133, 157 2nd Ave N), one block from the bus station, costs $42 to $46. There's a laundrette in the basement.

Moving up the scale, the *Westgate Inn* (✆ 306-382-3722, 2501 22nd St W) has rooms with one double bed at $50 for one or two people.

At the classic *Delta Bessborough* (✆ 306-244-5521, 601 Spadina Crescent E), a city landmark, rates range from $80 to $130. It's the large, chateau-like place at the bottom of 21st St, by the river.

There are also several expensive hotels out around the airport.

Motels The *Travelodge* (✆242-8881, 106 Circle Drive W), near the airport on the corner of Idylwyld Drive, is like the others in the chain. The motel section has rooms from $64. Also near the airport is *Comfort Inn* (✆ 306-934-1122, 2155 Northridge Drive), with rooms at $69/75.

The *Circle Drive Suites* (✆ 306-665-8121, 102 Cardinal Crescent), on the corner of Airport Drive, is clean and some of the rooms offer simple kitchens. For those who want to sleep during the day and travel at night, it also offers a day rate of $45 for a room from 8 am to 5 pm.

There is a motel strip on Idylwyld Drive close to downtown. The *Imperial 400* (✆ 306-244-2901) at No 610 charges $67. *Colonial Square Motel* (✆ 306-343-1676, 1301 8th

St E) near the university has rooms for $64 to $75.

Places to Eat

The *Cage* (120 2nd Ave N) is a basic, all-purpose restaurant but it has a varied menu and the décor and furniture are a cut above the usual. Breakfasts are good value and will hold you long past lunch. It's open 24 hours every day.

Next door is the *Gotta Hava Java*, a good place for a caffeine fix, salad or piece of cake.

An excellent meal and suitable for any budget, can be had at the upstairs *Saskatoon Asian* (136 2nd Ave S). The menu offers mainly Vietnamese dishes, but there are also some Thai-influenced items and Chinese plates to round out the options. It's open every day from lunch to 10 pm.

The *Black Duck* (154 2nd Ave S) is a pub which has a student special of dinner and half-pint on Monday and Tuesday evenings.

The *Keg* (301 Ontario Ave N), on the corner of 24th St, is a medium-priced place serving good steaks. There's an outdoor patio and a popular bar adjoining the restaurant.

More formal and pricier, *John's Prime Rib* (401 21st St E), on the corner of 4th Ave S, is also good for steak with main courses about $23.

Seafood Sam's (819 2nd Ave N) is a wacky sports bar featuring seafood, Chinese dishes and Sam – restaurateur and hockey fan. Main dishes are about $15 at dinner and it's open daily.

Broadway Ave is worth strolling at feeding time with its variety of eateries and a couple of coffee shops. *Nino's* at No 801 is a casual Greek/Italian place with a popular patio and meals from $10 to $15. The *Broadway Café* at No 818 is a busy 1950s-style burger and sandwich joint.

The upmarket *Taj Mahal* (✆ 306-978-2227, 1013 Broadway Ave) is the best Indian restaurant in town. Reservations are recommended and it's closed Monday. Meat dishes are around $12, the vegetarian ones a bit less.

There's a small Chinatown in the tacky, once mainly Ukrainian area around 20th St W and Ave C, a few blocks from Idylwyld

Drive. The large *Golden Dragon (334 Ave C South)* has been around for years.

Around the outskirts, and for those with wheels, 8th St E and 22nd St W both offer abundant choices. For a choice of prime rib of beef, steak or seafood, and a good atmosphere, try the *Granary (2806 8th St E)*, with meals for around $20.

Toward Wanuskewin, *Taunte Maria's Mennonite Restaurant (cnr Faithful Ave & 51st St)*, off Idylwyld Drive N a block or so, offers perogies, vereniki and basic healthy farm food for any meal of the day. The soups are excellent. It's closed Sunday.

Entertainment

Bars & Live Music *Bud's (817 Broadway Ave)* has live rhythm and blues nightly and a Saturday afternoon jam. *Amigo's (632 10th St E)* features alternative local and regional bands. The *Sutherland Bar (810 Central Ave)*, popular with students, plays classic recorded rock Thursday to Saturday nights.

There's a mini-nightlife area around the corner of 24th St and Pacific Ave near Ontario Ave. About half-a-dozen places can be found here in old warehouses. *Cowpokes Bar (303 Pacific Ave)* has country music and dance lessons every Tuesday night.

For jazz, check out the *Bassment (245 3rd Ave S)*. It brings in some good acts and it's not expensive.

The Saskatoon Brewing Company sells beer made on the premises in the casual *Maguire's Irish Pub (2105 8th St E)* at Grosvenor Mall.

Performing Arts The Saskatoon Symphony plays at the *Centennial Auditorium* (☎ 306-938-7800, 35 22nd St E) and other venues regularly from September to May. Large-scale theatrical productions and dance performances are also held here.

Saskatoon is also home to a French theatre company and a dance troupe.

La Troupe du Jour performs an international repertoire throughout the province and La Ribambelle specialises in French Canadian folk dancing.

Spectator Sports

The Saskatoon Blades plays Western League (which includes four Canadian provinces and two US states) junior hockey from September to March at Saskatchewan Place.

Shopping

A store that might be worth checking out is the large old Army & Navy, on the corner of 21st St E and 3rd Ave S. This is one of Canada's oldest discount department stores and is a real classic, with three floors of cheap goods.

Another place to have a peek at is the Trading Post, 226 2nd Ave S. It specialises in crafts and souvenirs, with an emphasis on Native Indian goods. There is some junk, but also some good stuff, including fine, wool Cowichan-style sweaters, Inuit prints and sculpture, jewellery, woodcarvings and British Columbian jade.

Getting There & Away

Air The airport is 8km from the centre, in the north-east of the city, off Idylwyld Drive. Air Canada (☎ 306-652-4181) and Canadian Airlines (☎ 306-665-7688) both fly in and out of Saskatoon. It's about a two hour flight to either Winnipeg, Calgary or Edmonton. Athabaska Airways (☎ 306-665-2700) serves Prince Albert and various small northern towns from Saskatoon and Regina.

Bus The big Greyhound Bus Depot (☎ 306-933-8000), for various destinations all over Saskatchewan, is on the corner of 23rd St E and Ontario Ave. The station has a cafeteria and small store. The washrooms even have showers, which people with tickets can use.

Services include: Regina, daily at 8 am, 1.15pm and 5.30 pm ($26); Winnipeg, two a day, one in the morning and one in the evening ($83); and Edmonton, four a day, including one late at night ($62). There are also three buses a day to Prince Albert and one to Watrous.

Train You won't be too happy with this station's location – it's way out, a long way west from downtown on Chappell Drive. The taxi fare is about $11, but a city bus runs

to town at a quarter to and quarter past each hour, from Elevator Rd (behind the curling rink, which is across from the station). It doesn't run very late at night, however. For train information call ☎ 1-800-561-8630.

You'll be even less happy with the Saskatoon timetable. Trains run to Edmonton ($88) and on to Jasper and Vancouver three times a week, on Monday, Thursday and Saturday at 2.40 am. To Winnipeg ($127) and on to Toronto, trains also run three times a week, but on Monday, Wednesday and Saturday at 2.45 am.

There is no longer a train service to Regina.

Car For rentals, Budget (☎ 306-244-7925) is at 234 1st Ave S. There are other local and well known companies around town and at the airport. Two are Dollar and Thrifty.

Getting Around

To/From the Airport A taxi to the airport is about $11. Alternatively, catch the No 1 bus from the Transit Terminal, a section of 23rd St E between 3rd Ave N and 2nd Ave N blocked off to all traffic but the buses. Tell the driver you're going to the airport because you'll need to transfer to a No 21 en route. There is a bus every half-hour through the day.

Bus All routes and schedules can be accessed through city bus information (☎ 360-975-3100), although most things of interest to the visitor are within walking distance of the centre of town. Many of the bus routes begin at the Transit Terminal. There are signs for all the bus routes, benches to sit on and lots of people milling about waiting. One of the drivers will be able to help you with any destination questions. City fares are $1.50.

For the train station, which bus you catch will depend on the time of day, so ask. None goes right into the station, but they do go within two blocks or so (see Train under Getting There & Away for details).

Bicycle Bicycles can be rented at the Radisson Hotel (☎ 306-665-3322) for $20

for the entire day – it doesn't close so you don't have to worry about getting back. A second choice is the Sheraton Cavalier Hotel, 612 Spadina Crescent.

AROUND SASKATOON
Little Manitou Lake Spa

Six kilometres north of the town of Watrous, about 120km south-east of Saskatoon, Little Manitou Lake contains mineral water denser than that of the Dead Sea. It was called Lake of Healing Waters by the Plains Indians and in the 1930s and 40s became a popular Canadian resort. Today it has the ambience of a place past its prime but you can still swim in the very buoyant, pungent-smelling lake for free. The upscale *Manitou Springs Resort & Mineral Spa (☎ 306-946-2233)* is working to revive the reputation as well as its clients health. It's open year-round offering pools of heated mineral water, massage therapy and adjacent hotel. Spa costs start at $6.50, and day or longer passes are available.

Near the resort are several modest *inns*, a *B&B*, two *campgrounds* and the beach.

Watrous has a *bakery*, a couple of *restaurants* and two *motels*. Saskatoon is connected by bus.

Redberry Lake

Redberry Lake, about an hour's drive northwest of Saskatoon, is a prime birdwatching location. The lake and its islands are all protected as a federal bird sanctuary. Of most interest are the large, white pelicans and the small, scarcer piping plover, but there are many others. Birdwatching tours can be taken and boats and canoes or windsurfers can be rented. The town of **Hafford** has all the conveniences.

Thirteen kilometres east of town on Hwy 40 is the Stuart Houston Ecology Centre in a park, admission charged. Interpretive displays on the white pelicans and closed-circuit TV of their nesting sites can be seen, and then guided boat tours can be taken out on the lake. Note that tours don't get close to the birds for much of the summer so as not to disturb their nesting. The centre is open daily.

SASKATCHEWAN

Batoche National Historic Site

North-east of Saskatoon, 80km up Hwy 11 and then along Route 225 off Hwy 312 from the town of Rosthern, is the site of the 1885 Battle of Batoche, fought between the government and the Métis (led by Louis Riel).

The visitors centre tells the story of the battle, and includes an audiovisual display on the Métis from the 1860s to the present. Also here are the few remains of the village of Batoche, including the church and some of the trenches dug for military purposes. The site is open from 9 am to 5 pm every day from mid-May to mid-October. Admission is $4.

Batoche was the centre of a Métis settlement and its provisional government in the late 19th century; many of these people had left Manitoba after running into difficulties over land there.

Batoche is about halfway between Saskatoon and Prince Albert. Driving through this area you'll see the remains of 19th-century wooden farmhouses.

North of Batoche

Just north of Batoche on Hwy 11, **Duck Lake** is worth a brief stop. Throughout the town, which has been revamped with antique street lamps and brick sidewalks, painted murals tell some of the area's cultural and historical stories. One outlines the tale of a Cree, Almighty Voice, and how he and a white policeman ended up dying over the killing of a cow. The Duck Lake Regional Interpretive Centre, at the north end of town off Hwy 11, has an artefact collection relating to the pioneers, Native Indians and Métis of the region.

Twenty-six kilometres farther west, **Fort Carlton Historic Park** provides more information on the fur trade, the treaties signed with the Plains Indians and the Riel rebellion.

Northern Saskatchewan

The area north of Saskatoon seems like the northern portion of the province and it's re-ferred to that way, but really this is central Saskatchewan. Geographically, Prince Albert National Park isn't even halfway to the northern border, so technically north begins somewhere beyond that point.

From Saskatoon, the Yellowhead Hwy, a branch of the Trans Canada, which comes from Winnipeg, runs north-west through North Battleford on its way to Edmonton and British Columbia. Pick up the Yellowhead map and pamphlet, which has some historical background, from the tourist office.

Between Saskatoon and Prince Albert is a farm belt which runs the width of the province. Prince Albert seems a long way north, and indeed, the growing season is short. At Prince Albert the land begins to change, and Prince Albert National Park just north of town marks the start of the vast boreal (northern) forest which takes up the northern half of Saskatchewan.

Saskatchewan has over 100,000 lakes, and a good percentage of these are in the wilderness regions north of Prince Albert. This rugged region of the province is much like the north of the country everywhere from Newfoundland westward. It forms part of the rough, rocky Canadian Shield.

The national park and several others in the region are about as far north as most visitors (or residents) get.

Ask at a provincial tourist office for the booklet titled *Heart of Canada's Old Northwest*, which provides a more detailed look at the region north and west of Saskatoon, including historical information and sites and other things to see and do.

PRINCE ALBERT

Prince Albert (population 35,000) is the most northerly town of any size in the province. Forests lie to the north, the flat grain fields to the south. It also sits right in the middle between Alberta and Manitoba. Known as PA, it acts as the jumping-off point for trips into the huge Prince Albert National Park. In 1776 a fur-trading post was built here among the Cree. The town was founded in 1866 by a churchman who came to set up a mission, and was named after Queen Victoria's husband.

The Tourism and Convention Bureau (☎ 306-953-4385) is south of the centre at 3700 2nd Ave W.

There are a couple of quite minor attractions. The **Historical Museum** (☎ 306-764-2992), in the old fire station at the end of Central Ave, has displays on the city's past. The museum tea room overlooks the North Saskatchewan River, which flows through town to be joined, not far east, by the South Saskatchewan River.

Prince Albert is the location of a major three-part prison. (The locals could have opted for a university but they chose a penitentiary instead.) The **Rotary Museum of Police & Corrections**, beside the tourist office at 3700 2nd Ave W, outlines related history.

In mid-August, Prince Albert hosts a large powwow at the Exhibition Grounds and in mid-September there's a Métis Fall Festival. Check with the tourist office for exact dates.

Places to Stay

There's camping at *Whispering Pines Campground* (☎ 306-763-3863), 5km northeast of town just off Hwy 2.

Hamilton Hall (☎ 306-764-1893, 565 20th St W) is a B&B in a fine house from 1913 with antique-furnished rooms at $40/45.

The *Marlboro Inn* (☎ 306-763-2643, ☎ 1-800-661-7666, 67 13th St E) is right downtown, with rooms at $65. The budget *Twilite Motel* (☎ 306-764-1491) on Hwy 2 south, behind the OK Economy store, is $34/37.

Places to Eat

Amy's on Second (2990 2nd Ave W) on the corner of 30th St West, south of the centre, is known far and wide for excellent food or just a good coffee. Specialities might include grilled pickerel or steaming hot wild-rice soup. There's a cosy open fire and local art on the walls. Lunch, including cheesecake and coffee, costs around $16.

Freckles Deli (30 13th St W) is a good place for breakfast. *Venice House* (1498 Central Ave) serves cheap lunches and dinners (pasta, steak, ribs). *Choices Choices Buffet* (195 17th St W) has a bargain all-you-

can-eat spread including Chinese, Mexican, Italian, salad and more.

Getting There & Away

The bus station (☎ 306-953-2955) is central on the corner of 1st Ave E and 15th St E. There's one bus a day for Saskatoon ($16) and one a day (the Lac La Ronge bus) to Waskeiu ($11) in the national park.

AROUND PRINCE ALBERT

East of town, 18km out on Hwy 55, the **Weyerhaeuser Pulp & Paper Mill** (☎ 306-953-5194) can be visited. The free two hour tour showing the pulping, bleaching, drying and more is definitely an industrial tour, not a stroll in the park. Wear suitable clothes and footwear and be prepared for some noise.

In 1988, De Beers, the diamond company from South Africa, staked a claim on some land 40km or so from Prince Albert. Since then, with obvious respect for De Beers' expertise, millions of hectares nearby have been staked for diamond searching and processing of ore has begun at some of the sites.

The area north of town is known as the lake district, a relatively undeveloped area of woods, bush, lakes and cottages. Aside from those found within the national park, other mega-lakes of the region are **Candle Lake** with a provincial park and Montreal Lake.

PRINCE ALBERT NATIONAL PARK

The national park (☎ 306-663-4522) is a huge, primarily wilderness tract of softly rolling terrain where the prairie of the south turns to the woodland of the north. Among the geographic features are huge cool lakes, spruce bogs and forested uplands. There are trails of greatly varying lengths and good canoe routes providing access to much of the park. There's fishing, a range of camping possibilities and, in winter, cross-country ski trails.

Other highlights are **Lavallee Lake** (with the second largest white-pelican colony in the country), the herd of wild bison in the south-western grassland portion of the park and the cabin occupied for seven years by the controversial conservationist **Grey Owl**.

Grey Owl at Home in the Wilderness

Naturalist Grey Owl was somewhat of a legend through the 1930s for his writings and lectures on conservation and for his love of the wilderness. He toured widely across North America and the United Kingdom, encouraging preservation and appreciation of the environment.

His first book, *The Men of the Last Frontier*, was published in 1931. *Tales of an Empty Cabin*, published in 1936, is possibly the best known work, but in between there were several others.

Upon his death, in 1938 in Prince Albert, it was discovered that his identity and lifestyle as a Native Indian had been assumed and that in fact he was Archibald Stansfield Belaney of Hastings, England. This only enhanced his reputation. He had emigrated to Canada, become a trapper and guide, married an Iroquois woman and been adopted as a brother by the Ojibway tribe.

His wife, Anahereo, who died in 1986, was awarded the Order of Canada for her work in conservation. Her ashes are buried by the graves of Grey Owl and their only daughter, beside the cabin where they lived and worked in Prince Albert National Park. Much of his research was done in the park.

The small, simple, one-room cabin on Ajawaan Lake has become a pilgrimage site of sorts. From the cabin (known as Beaver Lodge), the couple worked to restore the nearly obliterated beaver population. It sits right on a beaver lodge by the lake's edge.

It is still a fairly inaccessible spot, which can be reached one of two ways. First is the Grey Owl Trail, a 20km hike along Kingsmere Lake. Alternatively, you can canoe from the end of the road, on Kingsmere River upstream to Kingsmere Lake. From there, paddle across the lake to the northern end, where there is a choice of either a 3km walking trail or a 1km portage to Ajawaan Lake, from where you can paddle to the cabin.

The park's southern border is about 50km north of Prince Albert. The eye-pleasing resort village of **Waskesiu**, on the huge lake of the same name acts as the park focal point. Here you'll find the park's interesting information centre, lodgings (from simple to luxurious), restaurants, groceries, gasoline, and a sandy beach with swimming. The bus from Prince Albert stops at the Chamber of Commerce building.

There are many *campgrounds* (☎ 1-888-333-7267 for reservations) in the park, one about a 20 minute walk from where the bus stops. This main one and another for RVs are popular and fill up on any midsummer weekend, especially holiday weekends. It's best to arrive as early as possible on a Friday or reserve. Other camping areas are geared to tenters. The smaller campgrounds are simple and quiet, or there is back country camping for canoeists and hikers.

Among the 10 or so accommodation possibilities in town, *Skyline Motel* (☎ 306-663-5373) is among the lowest priced at $35 to $55.

Bicycles can be rented in town and some of the many trails begin close by.

Of the many hiking trails only a couple begin in or near the village. The trail-head for the Grey Owl Cabin hike (about 20km) begins 32.5km away but can be reached by road.

The three marinas within the park, all contactable on ☎ 306-663-5994, rent canoes. Unfortunately, none of these is in Wakesiu making it a difficult proposition without your own transport. In addition, Waskesiu Lake is way too big and rough for most paddlers – you need to transport the canoe to one of the smaller lakes. The office can recommend good three-day ventures.

Park entry passes are issued for one day ($4), a week or the season.

LAC LA RONGE PROVINCIAL PARK

La Ronge (☎ 1-800-772-4064), which completely surrounds enormous, island-filled

Lac la Ronge, is Saskatchewan's largest provincial park. Aside from the main lake, often called among the most attractive in the province, it contains about 100 more, and a portion of the Churchill River known for its falls and rapids. Boat tours take visitors along the river and to some of the more impressive sights, or you can rent a canoe and paddle one of the many established routes. *Campgrounds* can be found along the western side of the lake and at the northern edge, at Otter Lake.

On the west side of the park is the village of **La Ronge**, a small resort centre. Free tours are given of the La Ronge Wild Rice Corporation, which processes the rice gathered by local producers. It's open weekdays from mid-August to mid-October. If you are not familiar with Canadian wild rice, don't miss giving it a taste. Long used by Native peoples, it is black-hulled and has a mild, nutty flavour. Also here, the Mistasinihk Place Interpretive Centre, on La Ronge Ave, has displays on the life, crafts and history of the people of the north. It's not open on weekends.

Among the four or five motels is the *Drifters Motel (☎ 306-425-2224)*, on Hwy 2 on the way into town. Beyond these areas is untouched wilderness.

THE BATTLEFORDS

The Battlefords refers to two towns linked by bridge across the North Saskatchewan River and the adjacent district. There is more varied landscape around the Battlefords, about 140km north-west of Saskatoon off the Yellowhead Hwy, than in much of this region of Saskatchewan.

In North Battleford, the interesting **Western Development Museum** deals with agricultural history. The **Fort Battlefield National Historic Site** is 5km from town. The North West Mounted Police built the fort in 1876 to help settle the area and police the Native Indians, traders and white settlers. Inside the walls are five buildings you can visit to see police and Native Indian artefacts, tools and memorabilia. The barracks contain an information display and there are guides in costume around the park. The site is open daily from about mid-May to mid-October. Admission is $4.

Good camping can be found at **Battlefords Provincial Park**, north of North Battleford.

From the Battleford area, Hwy 16, the Yellowhead, runs north-west to Lloydminster (on the border) and then on to Edmonton, Alberta.

A short stop can be made at **Cut Knife**, 50km west of Battleford on Hwy 40, which was the site of a battle between the government authorities and the Native people in early summer 1885. About 15km north of town through the Poundmaker Reserve, plaques mark the site of Chief Poundmaker's grave and outline the story of the skirmish. In Cut Knife itself, you can't miss the huge eight tonne tomahawk. A small *campground* is adjacent.

MEADOW LAKE PROVINCIAL PARK

About 200km north-west beyond the Battlefords, Meadow Lake (☎ 306-236-7680) running along a chain of lakes by the Alberta border, is similar to Prince Albert National Park. Nature trails and a series of longer hiking trails allow for wildlife viewing. Aside from *campgrounds*, visitors can stay in simple, privately operated rental *cabins*.

The park is north of Meadow Lake off Hwy 55, and is part of the Northern Woods & Water Route, a road system that begins in Manitoba and ends in British Columbia.

SASKATCHEWAN

Alberta

Not so long ago Alberta was a vast, sparsely inhabited wilderness. Today it has two of the largest cities in Canada – Edmonton and Calgary. Its huge wheat farms, cattle ranches and rich deposits of minerals and fossil fuels are the basis of its wealth. For the visitor, Alberta's main attractions are its wildlife, historic sites, diverse scenery and the wide range of recreational pursuits it offers. Banff and Jasper national parks in the Rocky Mountains attract visitors from around the world for their beauty, wilderness and winter sports.

Alberta, the most westerly of the prairie provinces, is bordered in the north by the Northwest Territories, in the east by Saskatchewan, in the south by Montana and in the west by British Columbia. The east is a continuation of the Canadian prairies. The northern area is filled with rivers, lakes and forests; it's a rugged and largely inaccessible region, especially in the north-east. The south-western edge of the province rises from foothills into the Rocky Mountains, while much of the rest of the south is dry and flat with badlands (barren, convoluted arid land) in some areas.

Although Edmonton is the most northerly of Alberta's major cities it is geographically in the centre of the province. The rivalry between Edmonton and Calgary, a three hour drive south, is palpable. The former is set among the northern woodlands and, besides being the somewhat staid provincial capital, holds the dubious distinction of being home to the world's largest mall. The latter exalts in its western heritage, exploiting the image of cowboys at every chance. It is a city of new wealth created by its many oil and mineral companies and exemplified by the charmless suburbs stretching over the arid hills.

History

From 9500 to 5500 BC, Alberta – particularly the southern portion – was occupied by the Plains Indians. For millennia they lived a nomadic life, walking great distances

HIGHLIGHTS

Entered Confederation: 1 September 1905
Area: 661,185 sq km
Population: 2,914,918
Provincial Capital: Edmonton

- Enjoy the scenery and fun of the Rocky Mountains

- See elks roaming the streets of Banff and Jasper

- Have your breath taken away by the awesome splendour of mountain lakes like Moraine and Peyto

- Follow the dinosaur trail around Drumheller and Dinosaur Provincial Park

- Take in all the action of the Calgary Stampede, one of the country's best known events maintaining the western tradition

- Feel the wind on your face and listen for the ghostly thundering hooves at Head-Smashed-In Buffalo Jump

- Commune with a moose at Elk Island National Park

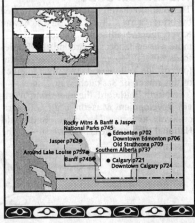

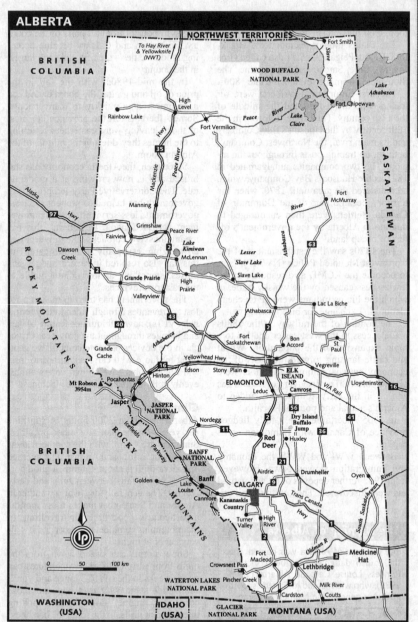

ALBERTA

NORTHWEST TERRITORIES

BRITISH COLUMBIA

To Hay River & Yellowknife (NWT)

Fort Smith

Slave River

WOOD BUFFALO NATIONAL PARK

Rainbow Lake

High Level

Peace River

Fort Vermilion

Lake Claire

Fort Chipewyan

Lake Athabasca

Mackenzie Hwy

Manning

Grimshaw

Peace River

Fort McMurray

Alaska Hwy

97

Fairview

Dawson Creek

Lake Kimiwan

McLennan

Lesser Slave Lake

Athabasca River

63

ROCKY

Grande Prairie

Valleyview

High Prairie

Slave Lake

Lac La Biche

SASKATCHEWAN

43

Athabasca River

Athabasca

Fort Saskatchewan

Bon Accord

St Paul

40

Grande Cache

Yellowhead Hwy

Hinton

Edson

Stony Plain

16

ELK ISLAND NP

EDMONTON

Vegreville

VIA Rail

Lloydminster

16

MOUNTAINS

Pocahontas

Mt Robson 3954m

Jasper

JASPER NATIONAL PARK

Leduc

Camrose

Nordegg

11

2

56

Dry Island Buffalo Jump

Huxley

36

41

BRITISH COLUMBIA

ROCKY

Icefields Parkway

BANFF NATIONAL PARK

Golden

Lake Louise

Banff

Canmore

Kananaskis Country

Red Deer

21

Airdrie

Drumheller

Oyen

9

CALGARY

Trans Canada Hwy

South Saskatchewan River

Turner Valley

High River

1

MOUNTAINS

Crowsnest Pass

Pincher Creek

Fort Macleod

Oldman R

2

Lethbridge

5

Milk River

Coutts

Medicine Hat

3

Cardston

WATERTON LAKES NATIONAL PARK

WASHINGTON (USA)

IDAHO (USA)

GLACIER NATIONAL PARK

MONTANA (USA)

0   50   100 km

hunting the vast herds of bison they used for food, clothing and shelter.

The Plains Indians included the Blackfoot, Blood, Peigan, Atsina (also called Gros Ventre), Cree, Sarcee and Assiniboine. The Sioux came from the south in the late 1800s.

The first Europeans in Alberta were fur traders who arrived around the middle of the 17th century. They were followed in the 18th century by the Hudson's Bay Company and its main rival, the Northwest Company; both set up trading posts throughout the region. The two companies amalgamated in 1821 as the Hudson's Bay Company, which administered the area until 1870, when the territory became part of the Dominion of Canada. Settlers were then encouraged to migrate to Alberta by the government's offers of cheap land.

The 1870s saw the establishment of the Northwest Mounted Police (NWMP), later to become the RCMP, as a response to the lawlessness caused by the whisky trade, in which the Plains Indians were given cheap alcohol in exchange for bison hides.

The coming of the railway in the 1880s made access to the west easier and led to a rapid expansion of the population. Wheat and cattle farming formed the basis of the economy but coal mining and timber were also important. The discovery of natural gas and oil in the early 20th century added to Alberta's actual and potential wealth.

In 1905 Alberta became a fully fledged province of Canada with Edmonton as its capital.

Between WWI and WWII the economy and immigration slowed down. However, from 1947 further deposits of oil and natural gas were discovered. Then, with the oil crisis of the early 1970s, people and money began to pour in from all parts of the country. Edmonton and Calgary became booming, modern cities – the fifth and sixth largest in the country.

In the mid-1980s, with the fall in the price of oil and grains, the boom ended and hard times came quickly to many people. Some Albertans left the province but most of those leaving were easterners returning to the homes they'd left in the middle of the Alberta boom.

Since then, the Alberta economy has stabilised and is now growing at a moderate rate. The Conservative Party-led provincial government has helped to pioneer the less-government, less-services, less-tax movement across Canada. In Alberta, this has meant massive cutbacks and government downsizing, especially in health care. But this has also resulted in record budget surpluses, something almost unimaginable to the eastern provinces.

The government has tried to make up for lost tax revenues through video lottery terminals (VLTs), now a ubiquitous feature of bars and lounges throughout the province. Critics claim the devices promote compulsive gambling by those who can least afford to lose, and referendums have shown voters almost evenly split for and against the machines.

Climate

Alberta has about 2000 hours of sunshine per year – more than any other province. Summers are warm, with the southern areas getting hot in July and August. The average annual rainfall is about 450mm, a good portion of which falls between June and early August. The generally dry, warm weather in August and September makes these months a particularly good time for travelling. In the mountains summers are short and it's always cool at night.

Snow storms can sweep down from the north from early October. Temperatures can go for weeks in the sub 0°C range and you'll soon understand why cars have all those cords for engine block heaters poking through their grills. In the south the harshness

---

The Naming of Alberta

The province of Alberta was named after the fourth daughter of Queen Victoria, Princess Louise Caroline Alberta (1848-1939), who was married to Canada's fourth governor general, the Marquis of Lorne.

They Call the Wind Chinook

The chinook is a warm and dry, south-westerly, winter wind which blows off the eastern slopes of the Rocky Mountains. These winds can change the snowy streets of Calgary, for example, to slush and puddles within hours. The name is derived from the Chinook Indians who lived along the north-west Pacific coast, mainly in what is now Washington state. In the days of the fur trade a language developed which mixed Chinook and other Native Indian words with French and English and was known as Chinook jargon.

of winter is reduced by the chinooks – warm, dry winds from the west which can quickly raise temperatures by as much as 20°C.

Information

Provincial Symbols Alberta's provincial flower is the wild rose, while the lodgepole pine is the province's official tree. The great horned owl is Alberta's provincial bird, and the big horned sheep is its official mammal.

Tourist Offices Tourist offices are run by the Alberta Tourism Partnership Corporation, a blend of private associations, independent operators and government agencies operating under the moniker Travel Alberta. The main office is in Edmonton. It can supply general information as well as contact information for the provincial regional and local tourism offices.

Travel Alberta
(☎ 780-427-4321 in Edmonton, ☎ 1-800-661-8888 in North America for information) Box 2500, Edmonton, Alberta T5J 2Z4

Time Alberta is on Mountain Standard Time.

Tax There is no provincial consumer sales tax. There is, however, a 5% tax levied on accommodation.

Activities

With its mountains, rivers, lakes and forested wilderness areas, Alberta provides plenty of opportunities for independent or guided outdoor recreational activities. Tourism Alberta's free brochure, *Accommodation & Visitors' Guide*, lists companies offering fishing, horse riding, cycling, canoeing, whitewater rafting, hiking, rock climbing and mountaineering. It's available from any visitor information centre. In addition, there are a range of good, detailed books on specific activities and locations available at bookshops.

National & Provincial Parks Alberta has five national parks, three of which are in the Rocky Mountains: Banff, Jasper and Waterton Lakes. Wood Buffalo National Park, the largest and least accessible, is in the far north-east, while Elk Island National Park, the smallest, is just east of Edmonton. Camping in the parks operates on a first-come, first-served basis and sites cost between $6 and $18, depending on facilities. For more information on the national parks see the Facts about Canada chapter and the specific sections in this chapter.

Hiking & Cycling There are lots of hiking and cycling trails in the national and provincial parks and in other recreation areas such as Kananaskis Country. Two of the more spectacular cycling routes are the Icefields Parkway between Banff and Jasper, and the Bow Valley Parkway between Banff and Lake Louise. Edmonton and Calgary have trails within their city boundaries for hiking and cycling.

Canoeing & Kayaking Some of the more popular places for canoeing are the lakes and rivers in Banff, Jasper, Waterton Lakes and Wood Buffalo national parks as well as Writing-on-Stone Provincial Park. In Jasper National Park there is whitewater kayaking and rafting on the Athabasca, Maligne and Sunwapta rivers. There is no shortage of operators in any of these places – see the individual listings for details.

ALBERTA

The two major universities offer canoeing information and rentals in their respective areas:

Campus Outdoor Centre
(☎ 780-492-2767) P154 Van Vliet Centre, University of Alberta, Edmonton T6G 2H9
Outdoor Program Centre
(☎ 403-220-5038) University of Calgary, 2500 University Drive NW, Calgary T2N 1N4

To find out more about whitewater rivers contact the Alberta Whitewater Association (☎ 780-453-8585), Percy Page Centre, 11759 Groat Rd, Edmonton T5M 3K6.

Skiing The best downhill skiing areas are Nakiska in Kananaskis Country; Mt Norquay, Sunshine Village and Lake Louise in Banff National Park; and Marmot Basin in Jasper National Park. Many of the hiking trails in the national and provincial parks become cross-country ski trails in winter.

Rock Climbing & Mountaineering The Rocky Mountains provide plenty of challenges for the climber, from beginners to advanced. Mt Rundle near Lake Louise is a popular destination. Organisations based in Banff, Calgary, Canmore and Jasper offer instruction and guided climbing. Contact Yamnuska Inc (☎ 403-678-4164, yamnuska@telusplanet.net), 1316 Railway Ave, Canmore T1W 1P6.

Accommodation

Campers should get a copy of *Alberta Campground Guide*, a free booklet available at visitor information centres. It gives an alphabetical listing of places and their campgrounds, both government and private. In national parks sites cost from $6 to $18, in provincial parks from $9 to $18, and in private campgrounds from $10 to $25, depending on facilities. Also available is the *Alberta Accommodation & Visitors' Guide* which lists hotels and motels in the province. Both guides are published annually.

Hostelling International (HI) has 18 hostels in Alberta. For information about HI hostels in northern Alberta contact Hostelling Association Northern Alberta (☎ 780-432-7798, NAB@HostellingIntl.ca), 10926 88th Ave, Edmonton T6G 0Z1. For southern Alberta contact Hostelling International Southern Alberta (☎ 403-283-5551, SAB@HostellingIntl.ca), 203 1414 Kensington Rd NW, Calgary T2N 3P9.

Edmonton

Edmonton, Canada's fifth largest city, sits astride the banks of the North Saskatchewan River. The city was founded on the abundant resources of the surrounding area and these remain the basis of the economy. As an early aviation centre, Edmonton was once known as 'The Gateway to the North' but that title changed to 'Oil Capital of Canada' in the 1970s, when the entire province boomed and shrugged off its cowboy image. The city experienced explosive growth; the downtown area was totally modernised. Calgary has the head offices and oil and gas management but Edmonton has the technicians, the scientists and the wells (some 7000 within a 160km radius).

Since those heady days the fluctuating fortunes of the oil and gas industries have meant a series of minor ups and downs for the city. The 1990s have brought more diversity, stability and a manageable, ongoing prosperity. The city continues to develop, albeit at a modest pace.

Visitors are attracted to Edmonton due to its proximity to Jasper and other national parks, its transportation links to the far north and its range of attractions and shopping. The city has an average of over six hours of sun per day. Summers are short, generally dry and warm, with daytime temperatures averaging 22°C. In January, the coldest month, the average daytime high is -11°C. Ouch!

History

Until the arrival of European explorers and fur traders in the late 18th century the area had been populated by the Cree and Blackfoot nations for over 5000 years.

In 1795 the Hudson's Bay Company built Fort Edmonton, which grew as a fur trading centre until about 1870, when the Canadian government bought the land from the company and opened up the area for pioneers. By 1891 the railway had arrived from Calgary and in 1892 Edmonton was officially incorporated as a town, then, in 1904, as a city. In 1905, with the creation of Alberta, Edmonton – then numbering 8000 residents – became the capital.

With the discovery of gold in the Yukon in 1897, Edmonton was the last outpost of civilisation for many gold seekers heading north to the Klondike. In 1938, North America's first mosque was built here. WWII brought a large influx of people, many to work on the Alaska Hwy. Though the province's population is mainly of British descent, many residents have German backgrounds. Ukrainians, too, have had a large hand in the development of the region and for this reason the city is sometimes humorously referred to as Edmonchuk.

It was in the late 1940s and 50s that real development in Edmonton began, when wells started hitting oil with great regularity. The rise in oil prices in the early 1970s gave a further boost to development and brought a dramatic change to the city skyline.

These rapid changes have caused some ongoing problems. Many of the city's 25,000 Native Indians have little education or job training and the changes made life harder for them. However, the establishment of educational programs has meant more Native Indians are completing high school and going on to trade school or college.

Greater Edmonton now has a population of nearly 800,000 and ethnic diversity remains. The steep prices of the 1970s and early 80s have levelled off and the cultural life of the city has grown dramatically. The rivalry with Calgary continues unabated.

Orientation

From Edmonton the Rocky Mountains are about 300km to the west, the lake country and Alaska Hwy are to the north, Lloydminster in Saskatchewan is 250km to the east and Calgary 300km to the south. The North Saskatchewan River, which starts in the Columbia Icefield in the Rocky Mountains, drifts through the centre of town.

Numbered avenues run east and west, while numbered streets run north and south. Odd-numbered street addresses are on the eastern side of the street and on the southern side of the avenue.

North of the River Edmonton's main thoroughfare, Jasper Ave (101st Ave), is very long and has mainly stores and restaurants. The major commercial street is 124th St. Both Jasper Ave and 102nd Ave go west from downtown through the West End, a wealthy district of fine homes. They then lead on through subdivisions and strip malls to Stony Plain Rd, a commercial strip which becomes the Yellowhead Hwy to Jasper.

Six kilometres north of the centre, the Yellowhead Trail (Hwy 16) is an industrial beltway that joins the Yellowhead Hwy east to Saskatoon and west to Jasper. Note that this road is especially scenically challenged. If you're just passing through, you're better off opting for the much more interesting 101st Ave route through the centre.

Though the city is spread out, the downtown centre with the Greyhound bus station, VIA Rail station, restaurants and hotels is quite small. The central area is bounded by 104th Ave to the north and 100th Ave to the south. The western edge is marked by 109th St, the eastern side by 95th St. The area is easily walkable and tends to be pretty quiet in the evenings and on weekends.

The main intersection is Jasper Ave and 101st St. On 99th St, two blocks north of Jasper Ave, is the civic centre. Opposite is Sir Winston Churchill Square, one block north of which is City Hall with its glass pyramid. To the east are the art gallery and law courts.

Another block north to 104th Ave is VIA Rail station below the CN Tower. To the west, covering four blocks between 105th and 109th Sts, is the City Centre Campus of the Grant MacEwan Community College. With its concrete towers, this is one of the city's more striking architectural complexes.

ALBERTA

EDMONTON

PLACES TO STAY
14 This Is It B&B
17 Rainbow Valley Campground
18 Derrick Motel

OTHER
1 Edmonton Space &
   Science Centre
2 Edmonton Municipal Airport;
   Aviation Museum
3 Skyreach Centre
4 St Josephat's Ukrainian
   Catholic Cathedral
5 Royal Alexandra Hospital
6 Ukrainian Museum of Canada
7 Ukrainian Canadian Archives
8 Muttart Conservatory
9 Provincial Museum
10 Government House
11 University of Alberta
12 Rutherford House
13 Jubilee Auditorium
15 Valley Zoo
16 Fort Edmonton Park

0   1   2 km

To Visitor Information Centre, Edmonton
International Airport & Calgary

The downtown area consists of many mirrored, 1970s design, high-rise buildings. The southern end of 100th St is the office and banking section. This is also the theatre and shopping district, with the Eaton and Edmonton centres housing all types of stores.

Both above and below the downtown streets is a maze of pedestrian walkways (called pedways) which connect shopping malls, hotels, restaurants and the VIA Rail station.

The eastward redevelopment of the city centre during the 1970s and 80s stopped at 97th St and for a few blocks east some of the streets are sleazy, especially 96th St. The bars and hotels here aren't recommended. Along the eastern side of 97th St are pawnshops and cash-for-goods stores. Also in this area is the small, down-on-its-heels Chinatown, north of Jasper Ave and 97th St, and the Farmer's Market at 102nd Ave and 97th St. The old part of downtown extends northwards as far as 103A Ave.

A few blocks west of Sir Winston Churchill Square are a number of hotels in all price ranges, and the Greyhound bus station. West of the centre, 124th St between 102nd and 109th Aves is a small, expensive shopping district, with a few fashion boutiques, art galleries and a bistro or two.

South of the River Across the river, 82nd Ave (also called Whyte Ave) is the main street. The historic district known as Old Strathcona runs for several blocks east and west of 104th St. This lively mini-downtown area has a good selection of stores and restaurants, and contains many restored buildings dating from when the village was distinct from Edmonton itself. The area is definitely the 'hip focus' of the city.

At the western end of 82nd Ave is the sprawling campus serving the 30,000-odd students of the University of Alberta. Following the river south-west is Fort Edmonton, where the town began. Most of the southern side is residential.

Heading south, 104th St joins the Calgary Trail (Hwy 2), which leads to the international airport, Red Deer and Calgary.

Information

Tourist Offices Edmonton Tourism has two offices. The downtown one (☎ 780-426-4715) is in the Shaw Conference Centre at 9797 Jasper Ave NW. It is open Monday to Friday from 9 am to 4 pm.

The main office (☎ 780-496-8400 or ☎ 1-800-463-4667, fax 780-496-8413) is in Gateway Park south of town, 2404 Calgary Trail northbound, at the Leduc £1 oil derrick. It's open daily in summer from 8 am to 9 pm; the rest of the year it's open Monday to Friday from 8.30 am to 4.30 pm and weekends from 9 am to 5 pm.

For information on other parts of Alberta, contact Travel Alberta (☎ 780-427-4321 or ☎ 1-800-661-8888) on the 3rd floor in the Commerce Place building at 10155 102nd St.

Money Major banks have branches on Jasper Ave. American Express (☎ 780-421-0608), 10180 101st St, is open Monday to Friday from 8.30 am to 5.30 pm. Currencies International (☎ 780-484-3868) changes most foreign currencies and is at shop No 2698 deep inside the West Edmonton Mall.

Post & Communications The main post office (☎ 780-944-3271), 9808 103A Ave, on the corner of 99th St (Hull St), is open Monday to Friday from 8 am to 5.45 pm.

Planet Inc Cyber Cafe (☎ 780-433-9730), 10442 82nd Ave, in Old Strathcona, is open 24 hours and charges $6 an hour for Internet access.

Foreign Consulates Refer to the Facts for the Visitor chapter for complete listings of foreign consulates. Many countries, including Britain, are represented in Edmonton; contact details can be found under Consulates in the Yellow Pages.

Travel Agencies For cheap air fares check out The Travel Shop (☎ 780-439-3096), 10926 88th Ave, and Travel CUTS (☎ 780-488-8487), 10127A 124th St. Travel CUTS has another office in the student union building at the University of Alberta.

Bookshops The Travel Shop (☎ 780-439-3809), 10926 88th Ave, is run by HI Canada and has a wide range of travel books, maps and travel goods. Audrey's Books (☎ 780-423-3487), 10702 Jasper Ave, on the corner of 107th St, has two floors of books including Canadiana, travel guides and maps. Similar is Greenwood's Bookshoppe (☎ 780-439-2005), 10355 82nd Ave, in Old Strathcona. Map Town (☎ 780-429-2600) at 10344 105th Ave is an excellent source of maps and atlases.

Orlando Books (☎ 780-432-7633), 10123 82nd Ave, has a good selection of gay and lesbian titles and holds readings on Friday nights.

Libraries The Stanley A Milner Public Library (☎ 780-496-7000), 7 Sir Winston Churchill Square, has a large collection of books and periodicals and limited free Internet access.

Laundry Whyte Ave Laundry (☎ 780-439-0285), 9904 82nd Ave, at the eastern edge of Old Strathcona, has coin washers and dryers and a fine selection of abandoned magazines.

Medical Services The Royal Alexandra Hospital (☎ 780-477-4111) is at 10240 Kingsway Ave.

Emergency Within Edmonton, dial ☎ 911 for police, medical and fire emergencies.

Parking Parking is a problem in downtown Edmonton but you can get free parking permits and a map of parking lots from the tourist offices from June to August.

Parks
On each side of the North Saskatchewan River is parkland, appearing to be one long park, though actually a series of small parks joined together. You can walk, jog or cycle all day along the system using the many trails and bridges. In some, like **Whitemud Park**, south-west of downtown, and **Strathcona Science Provincial Park**, north-east of town, the paths become cross-country ski trails in winter.

Whitemud Park also has a hang-gliding area. To get to the park, from the southern side of town head south on 99th St and then turn right (west) along Whitemud Drive.

The 61 hectare **Hawrelak Park**, Edmonton's largest, is south-west of downtown on the southern banks of the river off Groat Rd. It has a lake used for boating and fishing in summer and for ice-skating in winter. The annual Edmonton Heritage Festival is held here in early August.

Throughout the parkland are dozens of picnic spots. Many of the city's other sights are in this green belt area.

Provincial Museum
This excellent museum (☎ 780-453-9100), 12845 102nd Ave, west of downtown, is set in attractive grounds overlooking the river. The natural history section describes the forces that have shaped Alberta and its life forms. It has a large display of fossils and minerals.

The section devoted to aboriginal people reopened in expanded quarters in 1997 after a much-needed renovation. The exhibits documenting the lives of the Plains Indians are definitely in the must-see category.

The museum also has frequent cultural shows and dance performances, and free film programs. It is open daily from 9 am to 5 pm and admission is $6.50/3 for adults/children. From downtown, take bus No 1, 100, 111 or 120 west along Jasper Ave.

Government House
The large and impressive former residence (☎ 780-452-7980) of provincial lieutenant-governors beside the museum is now used for government conferences. It can be visited on Sunday from 1 to 5 pm; admission is free.

Rutherford House
This provincial historic site (☎ 780-427-3995) at 11153 Saskatchewan Drive, by the university, was built by Alexander Rutherford, the first premier of Alberta. Completed in 1911, the mansion symbolises the

Rocky Mountain Lake near Jasper, Alberta

Moose and men at Maligne Lake, Alberta

The Athabasca Glacier, Icefields Parkway, Alberta

CHRIS WYNESS

Library Square, Vancouver, BC

CHRIS WYNESS

Main Entrance, Marine Building, Vancouver, BC

CHRIS WYNESS

Stamps Landing, False Creek, Vancouver, BC

end of the pioneer architectural style. The building has been restored and costumed volunteers re-enact their concept of life in 1915. It's open daily in summer from 10 am to 6 pm and Tuesday to Sunday from noon to 5 pm the rest of the year. Admission is $2. The Light Rail Transit (LRT) serves the university from downtown.

Alberta Legislature

The Alberta Legislature (☎ 780-427-7362), on the corner of 97th Ave and 108th St, is on the site of the original Fort Edmonton. A beautiful Edwardian building erected from 1912, it is surrounded by fountains and manicured lawns overlooking the river. Its dome has remained one of the permanent landmarks of Edmonton. There are free 30-minute tours offered on a schedule a bureaucrat would love: from June to August tours are available weekdays between 8.30 am and 5 pm, on weekends between 9 am and 5 pm. Call for the schedule at other times of the year.

Fort Edmonton Park

On the southern side of the river, Fort Edmonton Park (☎ 780-496-8787) has a reconstruction of the old Hudson's Bay Company fort and the surrounding town circa 1885. The fort contains the entire post of 1846, which was built to promote the fur trade (not as a military fort). While lacking the flavour of the era, the careful construction is excellent.

Outside the fort is a street re-creating downtown Edmonton between 1871 and 1891, when the railway arrived. It's quite interesting, with good explanations of the buildings, though hard to visualise as the early Jasper Ave. Along the wooden sidewalks are examples of the various merchants and their goods. A newspaper office and a schoolhouse are represented. Check all the cabinets, bottles and vials in the chemist. Rides on the steam train and street car are included in the admission price of $6.75/3.25 for adults/children.

The park is open daily from 10 am to 6 pm in July and August. There are reduced hours (and admission fees) in May, June

and September. Call for details, as well as for the occasional special events during the rest of the year when the park is normally closed. Bus Nos 104 and 105 reach the park from downtown.

Beside the fort is the **John Janzen Nature Centre** (☎ 780-496-2939), where you'll find a few examples of both living and dead local animals, insects and reptiles. Best of the lot is the demonstration beehive, while outside there are some good interpretative trails. In July and August the centre is open weekdays from 9 am to 6 pm and on weekends from 11 am to 6 pm. The rest of the year it is open weekdays from 9 am to 4 pm and on weekends from 1 to 4 pm. Admission is free.

Valley Zoo

North-east of Fort Edmonton Park, this zoo (☎ 780-496-6911) in Laurier Park, at the southern end of Buena Vista Rd, has about 500 animals and birds, but it's mainly a children's zoo with models of storybook characters. It's open daily from 9.30 am to 8 pm in July and August and admission is $4.95/2.50. Hours and admissions are reduced during the rest of the year.

Muttart Conservatory

South of the river off James Macdonald Bridge, the Muttart Conservatory (☎ 780-496-8755), 9626 96A St, comprises four glass pyramids sheltering the plants from the seemingly endless winters. Each pyramid highlights a different type of climate: arid, tropical, temperate and another for changing exhibitions (Easter lily fans take note!). The conservatory is open daily for hours that vary radically through the year, so call for details. Admission is $4.25/2. It's on bus routes Nos 8 and 112.

Edmonton Art Gallery

At 2 Sir Winston Churchill Square, the Edmonton Art Gallery (☎ 780-422-6223) displays mainly historical and modern Canadian paintings. There are regular special exhibitions. The gallery is open Monday to Wednesday from 10.30 am to 5 pm, Thursday and Friday until 8 pm and weekends and

ALBERTA

DOWNTOWN EDMONTON

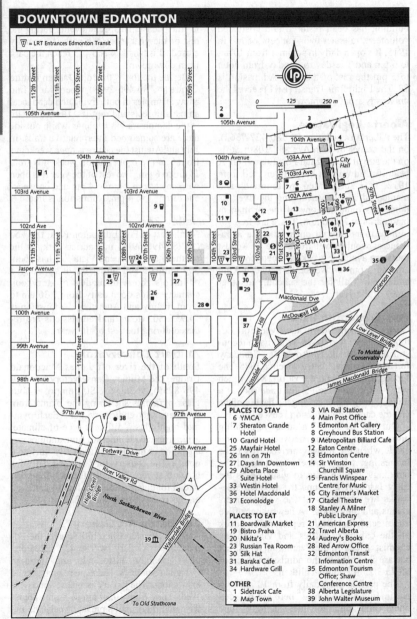

⟅T⟆ = LRT Entrances Edmonton Transit

112th Street
111th Street
110th Street
109th Street
105th Street

105th Avenue
105th Avenue

104th Avenue
104th Avenue

103rd Avenue
103rd Avenue

102nd Ave
102nd Avenue

Jasper Avenue

100th Avenue

99th Avenue

98th Avenue

97th Ave
97th Avenue
96th Avenue

Fortway Drive

River Valley Rd

High Level Bridge

North Saskatchewan River

Walterdale Bridge

To Old Strathcona

103A Ave
103rd Ave
102A Ave
101A Ave

City Hall

Macdonald Dve

McDougall Hill

Bellamy Hill

Rosedale Hill

Grierson Hill

Low Level Bridge

To Muttart Conservatory

James Macdonald Bridge

97th Street
96th St

0   125   250 m

PLACES TO STAY
6 YMCA
7 Sheraton Grande Hotel
10 Grand Hotel
25 Mayfair Hotel
26 Inn on 7th
27 Days Inn Downtown
29 Alberta Place Suite Hotel
33 Westin Hotel
36 Hotel Macdonald
37 Econolodge

PLACES TO EAT
11 Boardwalk Market
19 Bistro Praha
20 Nikita's
23 Russian Tea Room
30 Silk Hat
31 Baraka Cafe
34 Hardware Grill

OTHER
1 Sidetrack Cafe
2 Map Town
3 VIA Rail Station
4 Main Post Office
5 Edmonton Art Gallery
8 Greyhound Bus Station
9 Metropolitan Billiard Cafe
12 Eaton Centre
13 Edmonton Centre
14 Sir Winston Churchill Square
15 Francis Winspear Centre for Music
16 City Farmer's Market
17 Citadel Theatre
18 Stanley A Milner Public Library
21 American Express
22 Travel Alberta
24 Audrey's Books
28 Red Arrow Office
32 Edmonton Transit Information Centre
35 Edmonton Tourism Office; Shaw Conference Centre
38 Alberta Legislature
39 John Walter Museum

holidays from 11 am to 5 pm. Admission is $3/1.50.

Alberta Aviation Museum

The aviation museum (☎ 780-453-1078), 11410 Kingsway Ave, at the municipal airport north of downtown, has an extensive collection of models, photos, displays, films and biographies of important figures in Canadian aviation as well as 23 restored aircraft. It is open daily from 10 am to 4 pm (from noon Sunday) and admission is $5/3.

Edmonton Space & Science Centre

The suitably futuristic-looking Edmonton Space & Science Centre (☎ 780-451-3344) is in the western part of town at 11211 142nd St in Coronation Park. The **planetarium**, the largest in Canada, presents multimedia programs on the solar system and universe. Not surprisingly, there's an IMAX theatre as well. Rock-music laser shows are offered frequently in the **Margaret Ziedler Star Theatre**.

The centre has galleries and exhibits on all things spatial. Don't miss the **Bruderheim meteorite**, which fell near Edmonton in 1960. It's 4.6 billion years old, which makes it about as old as the solar system. There's also a small gift shop and a cafeteria.

The planetarium and IMAX schedules vary widely. The centre is open daily from 10 am to 10 pm in July and August, closing on Monday the rest of the year. Admission is $7/5 (add $5/3 for the IMAX theatre).

From downtown take bus No 125 to Westmount St next to Coronation Park.

John Walter Museum

This site (☎ 780-496-7275), 10627 93rd Ave, comprises four historic buildings, including the first home (1875) south of the river and Edmonton's first telegraph station. It's open on Sunday in summer from 1 to 5 pm, closing at 4 pm the rest of the year. Admission is free.

St Josephat's Ukrainian Catholic Cathedral

This imposing church (☎ 780-422-3181), 10825 97th St, on the corner of 108th Ave,

has good examples of colourful Ukrainian decorative art.

Ukrainian Museum of Canada

The Ukrainian Museum of Canada (☎ 780-483-5932), 10611 110th Ave, has a small collection of costumes, Easter eggs, dolls and fine tapestries. It's open weekdays from 9 am to 4 pm from May to August. Close by, the **Ukrainian Canadian Archives & Museum of Alberta** (☎ 780-424-7580), 9543 110th Ave, has more of those delightful Easter eggs as well as other artefacts of Ukrainian culture. It's open Tuesday to Friday from 10 am to 5 pm and on Saturday from noon to 5 pm. Admission to both museums is free.

City Farmers' Market

This food market is in downtown Edmonton on the corner of 102nd Ave and 97th St at the edge of Chinatown. It's open daily, but is best on Saturday, until 3 pm.

Old Strathcona

This charming area south of the river along 82nd Ave was once the town of Strathcona. It amalgamated with Edmonton in 1912. Though now absorbed into the city, the area is rich in historical buildings dating from 1891. There are about 75 houses built before 1926 in the residential district and about 40 buildings of note in the former commercial core. This is now one of the most vibrant areas of town with numerous cafés, restaurants, bookshops and buskers. It is a perfect antidote for those dazed by the mall.

From 105th St east, 82nd Ave has been spruced up with brick sidewalks and old-style lamp posts. Within walking distance are several small attractions. Whatever the weather, it's worth prowling the streets of Edmonton's most interesting area.

Model & Toy Museum The intricate, miniature world displayed in this museum (☎ 780-433-4512) at 8603 104th St, in a residential area, makes for a fun half-hour. Primarily made of cut and folded paper, 400

detailed models, including the Kofuku-ji Pagoda of Japan, the Sydney Opera House, aeroplanes and ships, are on display. A $2 donation is requested and the tangle of opening hours usually includes every afternoon.

C&E Railway Museum The 1891 Strathcona train station (☎ 780-433-9739) contains artefacts and memorabilia from the early rail era. It's open Wednesday to Sun-

day from 10 am to 4 pm from June through August. Admission is by donation. The museum is at 10447 86th Ave.

Telephone Historical Centre Anyone with a hang-up for phones should enjoy this small museum (☎ 780-441-2077) at 10437 83rd Ave. The wall exhibit on switching technologies is a behind the scenes eye-opener. The museum is open Tuesday to

---

The Mall That Ate ...

Sprawled over 48 hectares, the **West Edmonton Mall** bills itself as 'the world's largest shopping and entertainment centre'. Big it certainly is, how entertaining is another matter. From its roots as a humble suburban shopping mall, 'West Ed' has metasticised into a commercial monster that has sucked zillions of dollars out of the rest of Edmonton's retail life.

If you are drawn by the spectacle of the world's largest shopping mall, be forewarned that all is not what it seems. For there's less diversity than the claim of 'over 800 stores and services' implies. The collection of stores will be familiar to North American mall rats everywhere; the numbers padded by counting numerous outlets of the same store scattered throughout the labyrinth. Fans of Orange Julius, the ubiquitous purveyor of a treacly orange drink, will be cheered that West Ed has three. Meanwhile, those in search of a good book had best bring one, because the lone bookshop is primarily concerned with the needs of buyers of gaudy calendars.

Much of the recent construction at the mall – like Canadian airports, the West Edmonton Mall is never complete – has been for entertainment rather than retail attractions. The frost-bitten denizens of the Canadian Plains have flocked to West Ed's artificial climate where a growing number of diversions awaits those looking for more in life beyond browsing the 29 moderately priced shoe stores. Again, hype often outpaces substance. 'Bourbon Street' has all the allure of a watered down Hurricane cocktail and features the non-New Orleans-native Hard Rock Cafe and Hooters.

Elsewhere, there's a slew of attractions ready to prove that West Ed isn't just the mall that ate Edmonton, but is also the mall ready to eat your wallet. Among them (prices given are admission for adults/children): Deep Sea Adventure, a submarine ride ($12/5); The Ice Palace skating rink ($4.50/2.50); Galaxyland Amusement Park, a carnival where the workers all have complete sets of teeth ($22.95/16.95); and World Waterpark, a huge enclosed beach and waterslide area where you'll never need sunscreen ($22.95/16.95).

If this spendthrift spree leaves you tuckered out, West Ed also has the Fantasyland Hotel (☎ 780-444-3000 or ☎ 1-800-737-3783) complete with theme suites such as the evocatively named 'Truck Room', where you can bed down in the back of a pick-up under the romantic glow of a stop light. Rooms start at $139 a night.

West Ed (☎ 780-444-5330 or ☎ 1-800-661-8890) is open daily. Hours for the main retail area are 10 am to 9 pm weekdays, 10 am to 6 pm Saturday and noon to 6 pm Sunday. The entertainment attractions keep different hours which vary throughout the year, while the restaurants and clubs keep longer hours at night. The complex is bounded by 87th Ave and 170th St. From downtown, take bus No 1, 2, 100, 111 or 112.

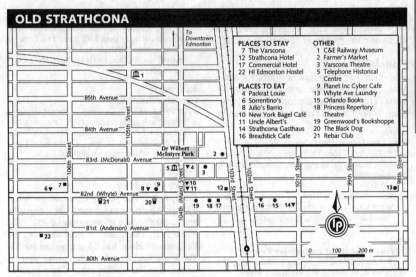

OLD STRATHCONA

To Downtown Edmonton

PLACES TO STAY
7 The Varscona
12 Strathcona Hotel
17 Commercial Hotel
22 HI Edmonton Hostel

PLACES TO EAT
4 Packrat Louie
6 Sorrentino's
8 Julio's Barrio
10 New York Bagel Café
11 Uncle Albert's
14 Strathcona Gasthaus
16 Breadstick Cafe

OTHER
1 C&E Railway Museum
2 Farmer's Market
3 Varscona Theatre
5 Telephone Historical Centre
9 Planet Inc Cyber Cafe
13 Whyte Ave Laundry
15 Orlando Books
18 Princess Repertory Theatre
19 Greenwood's Bookshoppe
20 The Black Dog
21 Rebar Club

Friday from 10 am to 3 pm and Saturday from noon to 4 pm; admission is $3/2.

Farmer's Market Everything from organic food to vintage clothing is offered by vendors every Saturday from 8 am to 3 pm. In July and August, the market (☎ 780-439-1844), at 10310 83rd Ave, also operates on Tuesday and Thursday afternoons.

Activities

For information on park and recreation facilities like outdoor swimming pools, skating and skiing areas, and bicycle paths, call Edmonton Parks & Recreation (☎ 780-496-4999). See also the Parks entry earlier in this chapter.

The Kinsmen Sports Centre (☎ 780-496-7300), 9100 Walterdale Hill, has public swimming and other programs. It's open Monday to Friday from 5.30 am to 10 pm, weekends from 7 am to 10 pm. Admission is $5. Mill Woods Recreation Centre (☎ 780-496-2900), 7207 28th Ave, has a wave pool, saunas, ball courts and other facilities. It's open weekdays from 5.30 am to 9 pm, on Sat-

urday from 6 am to 9 pm and Sunday from 8 am to 9 pm. A swim in the wave pool costs $5. The Commonwealth Stadium Sports & Fitness Centre (☎ 780-944-7400), located at 11000 Stadium Rd, has a gym and racquetball courts.

Edmonton has an extensive network of bicycle routes and the best area to cycle is along the river. *Cycle Edmonton* is an excellent free map showing these routes and is available from the tourist offices.

You can go horse riding in Whitemud Park; contact the Whitemud Equine Centre (☎ 780-435-3597), 12505 Keillor Rd, for details. You can also go hot-air ballooning – every day if the weather is fine – with Windship Aviation (☎ 780-438-0111), 5615 103rd St.

Organised Tours

Royal Tours (☎ 780-435-6069), 3105 112A St, offers several bus tours of Edmonton. The four hour historical tour of the city costs $31/14.75. Tours generally operate daily, except Monday, from May to September and include pick-up from many hotels.

Nite Tours (☎ 780-453-2134) does night trips around the city, featuring pubs and clubs or comedy shows. Tickets cost $20.

Special Events

Edmonton has many festivals throughout the year, attracting people from throughout Alberta. The following are some of the larger ones. Note that exact dates change annually.

June

Jazz City International Music Festival
(☎ 780-432-7166) There are concerts all over town, many outside and free, during this week-long event.

The Works
(☎ 780-426-2122) This is a major visual arts celebration and exhibition featuring events around town, including in city parks.

July

International Street Performers Festival
(☎ 780-425-5162) Amazing buskers bring the streets alive during this multi-day event.

Klondike Days
(☎ 780-479-3500) Edmonton's biggest festival is held late in July and celebrates a less than honourable period in the city's history. In the gold-rush days, unscrupulous entrepreneurs lured gold seekers to the city with false tales of a trail from Edmonton to Dawson City in the Yukon. Many died trying to find the trail; others gave up and returned to settle in Edmonton. Festival events include locals in period costume, road-side stages alive with singers and dancers, parades through the streets and nightly concerts at Northlands Coliseum. A Klondike village, with old-time stores and a gambling saloon, is set up in Northlands Park and the Citadel Theatre stages corny melodramas. The street festivities last five days; the Northlands Park exhibition continues for another five days.

August

Edmonton Heritage Festival
(☎ 780-488-3378) This three day Hawrelak Park festival celebrates the city's ethnic diversity.

Folk Music Festival
(☎ 780-429-1899) Gallagher Park just east of Muttart Conservatory is the site for blues, jazz, country and western, bluegrass and traditional folk music.

Fringe Theatre Event
(☎ 780-448-9000) Well worth catching, this event has a 10 day program of live alternative theatre, with over 800 performances of 150 productions in 14 theatres, in the parks and on the streets. Many performances are free and no ticket costs more than $10; there's no booking – you choose a theatre and stand in line. The festival takes place in Old Strathcona around the middle of August.

November

Canadian Finals Rodeo
(☎ 780-471-7210) Canada's major indoor rodeo boasts the biggest money prizes for roping, riding and all those other steer-wrestling treats. The main event at Skyreach Centre is held concurrently with a huge agricultural show.

Places to Stay

Camping Several camping areas, some run by the Alberta government, are close to town. *Ardrossan Campground (☎ 780-922-3293)*, 18km east of Edmonton on the Yellowhead Hwy, has 24 camp sites for $8. There are firepits, but nothing else, and no water. Similar is *Bretona Campground (☎ 780-922-3293)*, 18km south-east of Edmonton near Sherwood Park on Hwy 14 at the junction of Hwy 21, with 28 camp sites.

The privately owned *Half Moon Lake Resort (☎ 780-922-3045, 21524 Township Rd 520, Sherwood Park)* charges $15 for a tent site and has every convenience including showers and laundry. The resort is large and you can swim in the lake. It's 29km southeast of Edmonton; follow 82nd Ave east to Wye Rd, then head south. Within the city is the city-run *Rainbow Valley Campground (☎ 780-434-5531)*, off Whitemud Drive in Whitemud Park. It has a laundry and showers, and tent sites for $14.

Hostels *HI Edmonton Hostel (☎ 780-988-6836, fax 780-988-8698, eihostel@Hostel lingIntl.ca, 10647 81st Ave)* is delightfully located in a modern building in Old Strathcona that was formerly a convent. The 104 bed facility has kitchens, a laundry, library, mountain bike rentals and more. Rates in the two to eight-bed rooms are $15/20 for members/nonmembers. From downtown take bus No 7 or 9 south.

The central *YMCA (☎ 780-421-9622, fax 780-428-9469, 10030 102A Ave)*, opposite

the Edmonton Centre and next to the Hilton Hotel, is close to the Greyhound bus station and VIA Rail station and takes in men and women. Singles/doubles cost from $33/50 and there are cheaper weekly rates. Dormitory accommodation is $17 with a maximum of three nights. It has a TV room, gym facilities including a pool, and a cheap cafeteria open from 6 am.

University of Alberta, in south-western Edmonton, rents out rooms from May to August. It has good facilities and cheap cafeterias. Rates are $25/34 for a single/double, with weekly and monthly rates available. Contact Guest Services (☎ 780-492-4281, fax 780-492-7032), 44 Lister Hall, on the corner of 87th Ave and 116th St. Also part of the university, *St Joseph's College* (☎ 780-492-7681 ext 235, 11325 89th Ave), on the corner of 114th St, has singles for $24 from May to August.

B&Bs The Bed & Breakfast Association of Greater Edmonton (☎ 780-464-3515) maintains a list of member establishments and can make bookings.

Chez Suzanne (☎ 780-483-1845, 18603 68th Ave), not far from the West Edmonton Mall, has singles/doubles from $50/60. The hosts offer tourist advice and can accommodate families. More upmarket is *This Is It* (☎ 780-439-8481, 11013 87th Ave), west of central Old Strathcona. The large, well restored home charges $80/88 with full breakfast and offers numerous amenities.

Hotels – Budget Edmonton is not blessed with a great selection of cheap central hotels. Downtown, the *Grand Hotel* (☎ 780-422-6365 or ☎ 1-888-422-6365, 10266 103rd Ave), opposite the bus terminal, is friendly and clean. For singles/doubles with bath you'll pay $40/45; rooms without bath are $29/35. All rooms have cable TV. There's a bar and a restaurant with cheap breakfasts.

In Old Strathcona, the *Strathcona Hotel* (☎ 780-439-1992, 10302 82nd Ave), on the corner of 103rd St, has almost barren rooms for $17.30/26.35. It's a great timbered building dating from 1891 and is registered

as an Alberta Historic Resource. Nearby, the bare-bones *Commercial Hotel* (☎ 780-439-3981, 10329 82nd Ave) has live music in the bar downstairs and rooms for $25/28.

Hotels – Mid-Range The good value *Mayfair Hotel* (☎ 780-423-1650 or ☎ 1-800-463-7666, 10815 Jasper Ave) has apartments as well as rooms available. A continental breakfast is included in the room price of $45. The *Econolodge* (☎ 780-428-6442 or ☎ 1-800-613-7043, 10209 100th Ave) also offers a free breakfast and parking with its rooms, costing from $49/54 for singles/doubles. *Days Inn Downtown* (☎ 780-423-1925 or ☎ 1-800-267-2191, 10041 106th St) is very central, with well equipped rooms for $56/59.

At *Alberta Place Suite Hotel* (☎ 780-423-1565 or ☎ 1-800-661-3982, 10049 103rd St) all the rooms have a kitchen. Large rooms begin at $75 and include a continental breakfast. The hotel has a sundeck, exercise room, laundry and indoor parking.

Hotels – Top End Edmonton's oldest and most elegant hotel is the regal *Hotel Macdonald* (☎ 780-424-5181 or ☎ 1-800-441-1414, 10065 100th St). The main part of the hotel dates from 1915 and commands a prime spot overlooking the river. Still run by the Canadian Pacific Railway, it has rooms from $129, which is a pretty good deal.

Downtown is the *Westin Hotel* (☎ 780-426-3636 or ☎ 1-800-228-3000, 10135 100th St) on the corner of 101A Ave. It's a modern convention hotel with singles/doubles for $190/200, although there are often specials. Also in the charmless modern category, the *Sheraton Grande* (☎ 780-428-7111 or ☎ 1-800-263-9030, 10235 101st St) has rooms from $119. Pedways connect the hotel with the Edmonton Centre and Eaton Centre.

The Varscona (☎ 780-434-6111 or ☎ 1-888-515-3355, 10620 82nd Ave) is a new addition to Old Strathcona. Prices for amenity laden rooms start at $99.

Motels The bulk of the city's mid-range accommodation is in motels. Most motels have plug-ins (electric sockets for engine

heaters) for your car – very useful on winter mornings.

There are two areas near town where most of the motels are located. One is along Stony Plain Rd and the Yellowhead Hwy, west of downtown in the suburban sprawl of the West Edmonton Mall environs. The other is along the Calgary Trail south of the city, with mostly reasonably priced motels.

Royal Scot Motel (☎ 780-447-3088, *20904 Stony Plain Rd)* is about 1.5km west of Edmonton. It has singles/doubles from $36/40. Among the many chain motels in this area, *Sandman Hotel* (☎ 780-483-1385 or ☎ 1-800-726-3626, 17635 Stony Plain Rd) makes up for a complete lack of charm with a large indoor pool that will keep the kids wet and wild for hours. Rooms start at $65/70.

South of town try *Derrick Motel* (☎ 780-434-1402, 3925 Calgary Trail North), which has rooms for $40/44. Kitchenettes and waterbeds are available. *Chateau Motel* (☎ 780-988-6661, 1414 Calgary Trail South-West) has a friendly owner and offers free local calls and coffee. Room rates start at $36/39.

Out at the international airport, *Nisku Place Motel* (☎ 780-955-3078 or ☎ 1-800-637-2561) is good and has an airport shuttle. Rates start at $39/49 and you can request a room with a spa to bubble away your jet lag.

Places to Eat – Budget

The *cafeteria* in the Alberta Legislature serves plain, decent food at the best prices in town. It's open Monday to Friday from 7 am to 4 pm, with lunch from 11.30 am to 1.30 pm.

The *Silk Hat* (☎ 780-425-1920, 10251 Jasper Ave) dates from 1940. It still has the small wall jukeboxes at the booths and movie posters on the walls and is the local hang-out. Three pancakes go for $4 and lunch specials are $4.95. The shakes are made with real ice cream. Up the street, *Baraka Cafe* (☎ 780-423-1819, 10088 Jasper Ave), on the corner of 101st St, is a good coffee bar with various bakery treats.

The *Boardwalk Market*, on the corner of 103rd St and 102nd Ave, a renovated old building also containing offices and stores, has a food court with all kinds of food, including Chinese and East Indian.

In Old Strathcona there are quite a few good eating places on and around 82nd Ave. *Uncle Albert's*, on the corner of 104th St and 82nd Ave, is popular. It has pancakes for $5 and fish and chips from $6.25. The *New York Bagel Café (8209 104th St)*, next to Uncle Albert's, is a laid-back and cosy spot that serves excellent cappuccinos and light foods. The *Breadstick Cafe* (☎ 780-448-5998, 10159 82nd Ave) is one of the best 24 hour restaurants in town, with fresh breads, sandwiches and salads.

Out west in mall country, *Hap's Hungry House* (☎ 780-483-2288, 16060 Stony Plain Rd) is an unadorned diner loved by locals for its great breakfasts ($6 and you won't be hungry any more) and its lack of chain affiliation.

Places to Eat – Mid-Range

Where 101A Ave and 100A St meet, right in the centre of town, there's a group of restaurants around a small pedestrian-only zone. Most have outdoor sections. The *Bistro Praha* (☎ 780-424-4218, 10168 100A St) is a European-style spot with salads for $4 and main meals like schnitzel for about $14. During non-meal hours it's pleasant for a good coffee with a cake or pastry and a flip through a newspaper. Down a couple of doors, *Nikita's Martini Bar* (☎ 780-414-0606, 10162 100A St) has innovative snacks, sandwiches and pastas from $6 and is generally a cool place to hang out.

Also downtown, the *Russian Tea Room* (☎ 780-426-0000, 10312 Jasper Ave) is a dainty little place known for its teas, coffees, sandwiches ($4 to $6) and cakes ($4). It's open daily.

Old Strathcona teems with moderately priced restaurants. For German food try the alpine-like *Strathcona Gasthaus* (☎ 780-433-5307, 8120 101st St), just south of 82nd Ave. Central European staples like *ziguener schnitzel* cost about $12 and on many nights there's live accordion music. *Julio's Barrio* (☎ 780-431-0774, 10450 82nd Ave) is a popular Mexican place filled with noisy groups

slurping tequila and tossing down classics like grilled tacos for around $10. *Packrat Louie* (☎ 780-433-0123, 10335 83rd Ave) is a casually elegant place with creative Italian dishes like basil pesto pizza for $10.

West of the centre, *Szechuan Restaurant* (☎ 780-484-8883, 10080 178th St), just south of Stony Plain Rd, is run by recent Chinese immigrants who didn't leave their cooking skills at home. Excellent main courses average $8.

Places to Eat – Top End

Downtown, *Hardware Grill* (☎ 780-423-0969, 9698 Jasper Ave) is widely regarded as the finest restaurant in town. The dining room sits quietly behind huge windows in a restored historic building. The menu changes regularly and features dishes with native Canadian food, such as seafood, game, berries and whole grains. The salmon cooked on a cedar plank ($25) is a perennial favourite.

In Old Strathcona, *Sorrentino's* (☎ 780-439-7700, 10401 82nd Ave) is one of many Edmonton eateries run by a famous local family of restaurateurs. Like the others, this outlet features a bustling open kitchen turning out unusual Italian dishes as well as char-grilled steaks to appreciative diners in the always crowded and stylish dining room. Fresh pastas such as *penne Mediterranie* and mains like *pollo portofino* average $11 to $17.

Entertainment

See and *Vue* are free local art and entertainment papers found around town; the latter is the most complete. For daily listings see the entertainment section of the *Edmonton Journal* newspaper.

Theatre & Nightlife Edmonton offers a wide selection of live theatre. The *Citadel Theatre* (☎ 780-425-1820, 9828 101A Ave), Edmonton's foremost playhouse, is actually a complex of theatres featuring mainstream drama, comedy, experimental productions, concerts, lectures and films. Its season is from September to May. Depending on the production, theatre tickets cost from around

$20 to $50. The *Varscona Theatre* (☎ 780-433-3399, 10329 83rd Ave) stages edgier, more fringe productions.

The *Jubilee Auditorium* (☎ 780-433-7741, 11455 87th Ave) is the venue for the Edmonton Opera (☎ 780-429-1000) and special performances. The Edmonton Symphony Orchestra (☎ 780-428-1414) plays in the new *Francis Winspear Centre for Music* on Sir Winston Churchill Square. Tickets cost from $35.

Jubilations Dinner Theatre (☎ 780-484-2424, West Edmonton Mall) presents musical standards with vim and vigour. Just down the mall, *Yuk Yuk's* (☎ 780-481-9857) on Bourbon St has stand-up comedy from Tuesday to Saturday.

There are lots of venues around town catering to different musical tastes. In Old Strathcona, *Blues on Whyte* (☎ 780-439-3981, 10329 82nd Ave) in the Commercial Hotel features live blues music, as does the *Sidetrack Cafe* (☎ 780-421-1326, 10333 112th St), west of downtown, which also has local rock groups. The *Yardbird Suite* (☎ 780-432-0428, 10203 86th Ave) is the jazz bar in town. Admission varies but is only $2 on Tuesday.

Two popular bars among the many in Old Strathcona are *Rebar Club* (☎ 780-433-3600, 10551 82nd Ave) and *The Black Dog* (☎ 780-439-1082, 10425 82nd Ave). The former is a hard-edged joint with techno, punk, ska and house music, while the latter is a mellow Irish pub with ancient wooden furniture, well poured pints and occasional live rock.

Visitors often enjoy a night at the *Cook County Saloon* (☎ 780-432-2665, 8010 103rd St), on the corner of 80th Ave, where you get a real taste of the west with country music and line dancing. The *Metropolitan Billiard Cafe* (☎ 780-990-0704, 10250 106th St) attracts a young college crowd with pool tables, rock music and video games.

Cinema The *Princess Repertory Theatre* (☎ 780-433-5785, 10337 82nd Ave), near 104th St, is Edmonton's main outlet for good, varying films. It charges nonmembers $5 or $7, depending on the film. On

Saturday it shows matinees, mostly for kids. The cinema itself is an historic site – it was the first marble-fronted building west of Winnipeg and at one time showed first-runs of Mary Pickford films.

Spectator Sports

If you're here during the ice hockey season from October to April, try to see a home game of the National Hockey League's Edmonton Oilers (☎ 780-451-8000). Matches are played at the Skyreach Centre, 7428 118th Ave, on the corner of 73rd St. Tickets are $15 to $60. Alternatively, you could see the Edmonton Eskimos play Canadian League football, from July to October, at the Commonwealth Stadium (☎ 780-448-3757), 11000 Stadium Rd. Tickets are $18 to $28. The Edmonton Trappers play the Pacific Coast Baseball League play their home games at Telus Park (☎ 780-429-2934), 10233 96th Ave, from April to August. Admission is $6.50 to $9.50.

Getting There & Away

Air Edmonton international airport is about 30km south of the city along the Calgary Trail, about a 45 minute drive from the centre of town. This large airport is perpetually under construction and handles scheduled flights. Passengers have to pay a mandatory fee of $10. Although airport management tries to obscure this fact, Calgary has a much more extensive air service.

Edmonton municipal airport, 3km north of downtown off 97th St near 118th Ave, is generally used by private planes.

The major carriers are Air Canada (☎ 780-890-8111) and Canadian Airlines (☎ 780-421-1414). Both have frequent services to major cities such as Vancouver, Calgary and Toronto. With their small commuter partners, they also serve many smaller communities in Alberta and British Columbia.

The discount carrier West Jet (☎ 780-890-8040) has flights to several cities in western Canada, usually at prices that beat the two majors. Charter carriers Canada 3000 (☎ 780-890-4590) and Royal Airlines (☎ 1-800-361-6674) have infrequent but cheap flights to other cities in Canada, the

USA and, during summer, Europe. NWT Air (☎ 780-423-1222) serves Yellowknife in the Northwest Territories (NWT).

Connections to the USA are limited to Delta Air Lines (☎ 780-890-4410) to Salt Lake City, Northwest Airlines (☎ 1-800-225-2525) to Minneapolis-St Paul and Horizon Air (☎ 1-800-547-9308) to Seattle.

Bus The large Greyhound bus station (☎ 780-421-4211), 10324 103rd St on the corner of 103rd Ave close to the VIA Rail station, is central. It's open from 5.30 am to midnight and has left-luggage lockers ($2) and a fast-food restaurant. Greyhound goes east to Winnipeg (two hours, $139) and west to Vancouver (17 hours, $119) twice a day. There are four daily trips to Jasper (five hours, $47) and two to Prince George (10 hours, $90). A web of services goes north as far as Hay River (16 hours, $130) and Whitehorse (29 hours, $230). There are 10 express buses each day to Calgary via Red Deer (four hours, $38).

Another bus line serving Calgary is Red Arrow (☎ 780-425-0820), with its office in the Howard Johnson Hotel, 10010 104th St. It has six buses a day leaving from outside the hotel; the one-way fare is $40. The deluxe buses have free soft drinks, power ports for laptop computers and other niceties.

Train Entry to the VIA Rail station (☎ 1-800-835-3037 for arrival/departure information, ☎ 1-800-561-8630 for fares and reservations), 10004 104th Ave, on the corner of 100th St, is through the CN Tower entrance and down the stairs. There's a small shop and left-luggage lockers ($1).

The legendary *Canadian* travels three times a week eastwards to Saskatoon, Winnipeg and Toronto and westwards to Jasper, Kamloops and Vancouver. At Jasper, you can connect to Prince George and Prince Rupert. VIA Rail services and fares are constantly in flux, so confirm details in advance.

Car All the major car rental firms have offices at the airport and around town. See the Getting Around chapter for their national

reservations numbers. Local car rental companies include:

Discount Car & Truck Rentals
(☎ 1-800-263-2355) 12912 97th St & 6053 103rd St
Rent-A-Wreck
(☎ 780-448-1234) 11225 107th Ave

Getting Around
To/From the Airport City buses don't go as far south as the international airport. The cheapest option is Sky Shuttle Airport Service (☎ 780-465-8515 or ☎ 1-888-438-2342), which runs vans on three routes serving hotels located in downtown, in the west end and the university area. Rates are $11/5.50 for adults/children. The downtown route operates at least every 30 minutes and takes 40 minutes.

Taxicabs charge a flat $29 to downtown and about $38 to the west end.

Bus & LRT Edmonton Transit System (ETS) operates city buses and the short tram system, the Light Rail Transit (LRT). The LRT has 10 stops running north-east from the university, east along Jasper Ave, north along 99th St and then north-east all the way to 139th Ave in Clareview. Between Clareview station and Stadium station the LRT travels above ground; from Churchill station to Grandin station it runs underground.

A single one-way fare is $1.60/1 for adults/children on the LRT or buses. You can transfer from one to the other but you must get a transfer receipt when you pay your fare and use it within 90 minutes. You can also buy a day pass for $4.75. On weekdays from 9 am to 3 pm and on Saturday from 9 am to 6 pm, travel between the five subway LRT stations between Churchill and Grandin is free.

There is an information centre (open weekdays from 9.30 am to 5 pm) at Central station on the corner of Jasper Ave and 100A St. Telephone information (☎ 780-496-1611) is available weekdays from 6.30 am to 10.30 pm, Saturday from 7 am to 6 pm and Sunday from 9 am to 5.30 pm. Blue

bus routes provide basic services and generally operate at 30 minute intervals throughout the day. Red bus routes only operate during the peak morning and evening rush hours on weekdays. The LRT line operates from about 6 am to 10 pm daily. There is a limited late-night bus service.

Taxi Two taxi companies are Yellow Cab (☎ 780-462-3456) and Alberta Co-Op Taxi (☎ 780-425-8310). The fare from downtown to the West Edmonton Mall is about $14. The drop is $2, then it's 10¢ for every 105m.

Bicycle River Valley Cycle & Snowboards (☎ 780-465-3863), 9124 82nd Ave, rents out bikes for $7 an hour or $21 per day. HI Edmonton Hostel also rents out bikes (see Places to Stay earlier for details).

AROUND EDMONTON
Alberta Railway Museum
This museum (☎ 780-472-6229) has a collection of over 50 steam and diesel locomotives and rolling stock depicting the railways from 1877 to 1950. On certain weekends, volunteers fire up some of the old engines and you can ride along for $2. It's open daily from 10 am to 6 pm from mid-May to early September. Admission is $4/2.50 for adults/children. To get there, drive north on 97th St (Hwy 28) to Namao, turn east onto Hwy 37 for 7km, then south on 34th St for about 2km.

Elk Island National Park
In the northern Beaver Hills, 45km east of Edmonton on the Yellowhead Hwy, is this 194 sq km tract of original aspen forest preserved in 1906 as a wildlife sanctuary. For those interested in Canadian fauna, the park is a must for its high concentration of animals. There are free-roaming herds of elk and plains bison and a small herd of threatened wood bison. Bison can often be seen from the road and almost certainly along the walking trails.

About 35 other mammals also inhabit the park and many can be sighted on early morning or evening hikes. Beavers are abundant

at these times in the many boggy areas. Autumn is a particularly good time for wildlife viewing, as much of the vegetation has thinned out. Although dangerous up close, moose are always popular and can be found in large numbers.

The park is a popular weekend spot with camping, hiking, cycling and canoeing in summer and cross-country skiing and snow-shoeing in winter. It can be reached in under an hour from Edmonton and makes a good day trip. The information office (☎ 780-922-5790) near the entrance off Yellowhead Hwy (Hwy 16) distributes an excellent free guide to the park's features and wildlife. Read the guide to bison viewing as these animals can be very aggressive. The park's interpretative centre (☎ 780-992-6392) schedules a variety of special programs and walks during the summer.

Some of the park's facilities close from early October to May. Admission is $4/2 for adults/children. Tent *camp sites* cost $14 a night. For detailed information contact the superintendent (☎ 780-992-2950), Elk Island National Park, RR 1, Site 4, Fort Saskatchewan T8L 2N7.

Ukrainian Cultural Heritage Village

This historic park (☎ 780-662-3640), 50km east of Edmonton on Hwy 16, pays homage to the 250,000 Ukrainian immigrants who came to Canada in the late 19th and early 20th centuries. Many settled in central Alberta, where the landscape reminded them of the snowy steppes of home. There is a restored pioneer home and other exhibitions of the first settlers in the area. Among the dozen or so other structures relocated to the park is an impressive Ukrainian Greek Orthodox church. It's open daily from 10 am to 6 pm from mid-May to early September and weekdays only from 10 am to 4 pm the rest of the year. During the peak season, admission is $6.50/3 for adults/children (half-price the rest of the year).

Vegreville

The Ukrainian community in this town (120km east of Edmonton on Hwy 16) has constructed the **world's biggest** *pysanka*, or painted Easter egg. Built of aluminum, 9m tall and 5.5m wide, the egg sits just off the highway on the eastern side of town. The Ukrainian Pysanka Festival takes place in early July. The Vegreville Chamber of Commerce can be contacted on ☎ 780-632-2771.

Red Deer

Halfway to Calgary, this town of 60,000 is in the centre of grain and cattle country. The compact downtown area has a sprinkling of structures dating from the pioneer days. An international folk festival is held every early July and an international air show every August. The Red Deer Convention and Visitors Bureau can be contacted on ☎ 403-346-0180 or ☎ 1-800-215-8946.

Travellers to either Calgary or Edmonton may find Red Deer a useful stopping-off point. During either Calgary's stampede or Edmonton's Klondike Days it might be worth considering Red Deer as a base. Either city is about 1½ hours away on Hwy 2. Accommodation will not be as tight or as expensive. One option is the *Rest E-Z Inn* (☎ 403-343-8444, 37557 Hwy 2) at the South Red Deer exit, which has simple rooms from $50.

Edmonton to Jasper

Jasper is 370km from Edmonton along the Yellowhead Hwy. On the way there are commercial and government campgrounds as well as numerous motels, lodges and guest ranches.

About 30km west of Edmonton is **Stony Plain**, where the Multicultural Heritage Centre (☎ 780-963-2777), 5411 51st St, has displays on different pioneer groups and their crafts. It's based in the area's first high school, which dates from 1925, and is open daily from 10 am to 4 pm, on Sunday until 6.30 pm.

For about 100 years, since prayers at **Lac Sainte Anne** by the Roman Catholic Mission to end a drought were answered, it has been believed that the waters of this lake have God-given curative powers. Here, 50km west of Edmonton (about 25km north off the Yellowhead Hwy on Hwy 765), an annual

Map Maker, Bible Reader and Tireless Trekker

From 1784 to 1812 David Thompson led four major expeditions for fur trading companies that mapped much of the Canadian Rockies and the surrounding region. He is credited with discovering the source of the Columbia River in British Columbia, helped map the border with the USA and found the Athabasca Pass near Jasper, which for 40 years was the only route used by traders across the Rockies.

An energetic leader who covered about 130,000km by canoe, foot and horse, his daring exploits were not matched by an unbridled lifestyle. He extolled the virtues of soap in his meticulous journals, he refused to use alcohol for trade with the Native peoples he met and he enjoyed reading the bible to the crustier members of his parties around the evening campfire.

His relations with Native Americans were generally good, he understood the value of their knowledge and readily adopted their advice for survival on his lengthy treks. His wife was part Cree and he came to understand the native beliefs in the spirituality that was inherent in the land.

Thompson died at the age of 86 in 1857 and 59 years later material from his 77 notebooks was published in a volume simply titled *Narrative*. This caused a minor sensation as Canadians and Americans began to realise the scope of his accomplishments. At the same time modern map making techniques revealed the remarkable accuracy of the maps he had carefully drawn on his journeys 100 years before.

As you travel in Alberta, you'll often run into Thompson's name. In the town of Rocky Mountain House, 80km west of Red Deer, there is a national historic park (☎ 403-845-2412) of the same name. It preserves the site of fur trading posts that were used at different times from 1799 to 1875 and which early in the 19th century were a base for Thompson's explorations. The park site is open year-round, but the excellent visitors centre is only open from 10 am to 6 pm daily May to September. The park is 5km west of the modern town on Hwy 11A. The 180km stretch of Hwy 11 from Rocky Mountain House west to the Icefields Parkway in the Rockies has been named the David Thompson Highway.

One of the best books on Thompson is *Sources of the River* by Jack Nisbet. It places his accomplishments in the context of the times, both historical and modern.

pilgrimage takes place in July drawing about 10,000 people from around the province and across North America. It's a five-day event.

Hinton is the home of the Athabasca fire lookout tower. West of Hwy 40, some 14km north of the Yellowhead Hwy, there is a Nordic ski centre along the access road that is reputedly one of the best cross-country ski centres in North America. It has nighttime skiing and a luge run. For more information, contact the Alberta Forest Service (☎ 780-865-2400), Hinton Ranger Station, 227 Kelly Rd, Hinton T7V 1H2.

Hinton is also the starting point for a 250km driving tour through the **Coal Branch**,

a scenic range of rolling foothills dotted with abandoned mines south of the town. The well marked tourist information centre (☎ 780-865-2777) is on Gregg Ave, parallel to the Yellowhead Hwy. It's open daily from 8 am to 7 pm from June to August, but weekdays only from 8 am to 4 pm the rest of the year.

Northern Alberta

The land north of Edmonton is a vast, sparsely populated region of farms, forests, wilderness areas, lakes, open prairies and oilfields. The Cree, Slavey and Dene were the

first peoples to inhabit the region and many of them still depend on fishing, hunting and trapping. The north-east has virtually no roads and is dominated by Wood Buffalo National Park, the Athabasca River and Lake Athabasca. From its headwaters in British Columbia, the mighty Peace River makes its way to Lake Athabasca in the north-east of the province. The north-west is more accessible, with a network of highways connecting Alberta with northern British Columbia and the Northwest Territories.

PEACE RIVER & AROUND

From Edmonton, Hwy 43 heads north-west to connect with Hwy 34 and then Hwy 2 to Dawson Creek (a distance of 590km), the official starting point of the Alaska Hwy. Numerous campgrounds and several provincial parks line the route. The scenery is generally flat or gently undulating with dairy and cereal farms, and with grain silos in nearly every town. **Grande Prairie**, a large sprawling community, is an administrative, commercial and agricultural centre. Most of the accommodation is centred on 100th St and 100th Ave. The Chamber of Commerce (☎ 780-532-5482) is at 10011 103rd Ave.

Hwy 2, heading north directly out of Edmonton, is a more interesting route as it follows the southern shore of **Lesser Slave Lake** part of the way. Just north of McLennan, **Lake Kimiwan** and its surrounding marshland is a special place for birdwatchers. It's in the middle of three migratory routes and nearly 300,000 birds pass through each year. The provincial park has an interpretative centre, next to Hwy 2, which is open from May to September, and a boardwalk that takes you through the bird habitats. For information call ☎ 780-324-2004.

The Peace River is so called because the warring Cree and Beaver Indians made peace along its banks. The town of **Peace River** sits at the confluence of the Heart, Peace and Smoky rivers. The visitor information centre (☎ 780-624-2044), in a log building off Hwy 2, is open daily from 8.30 am to 4.30 pm from June to September. The town has several *motels* and two *campgrounds*. Greyhound buses

leave daily for the Yukon and Northwest Territories. West out of town, Hwy 2 leads to the Mackenzie Hwy.

MACKENZIE HIGHWAY

The small town of **Grimshaw** is the official starting point (though you might bypass it if you come via Peace River) of the Mackenzie Hwy (Hwy 35) north to the Northwest Territories. The relatively flat and straight road is paved for the most part, though there are stretches of loose gravel or earth where the road is being reconstructed.

The mainly agricultural landscape between Grimshaw and Manning gives way to endless stretches of spruce and pine forest. Come prepared, as this is frontier territory and services become fewer (and more expensive) as the road cuts northwards through the wilderness. A good basic rule is to fill your tank any time you see a gas station from here north.

High Level, the last settlement of any size before the border, is a centre for the timber industry and workers often stay in the motels in town during the week. Between High Level and Enterprise in the Northwest Territories the only service station is at Indian Cabins.

LAKE DISTRICT

From St Paul, over 200km north-east of Edmonton, to the Northwest Territories border lies Alberta's immense lake district. Fishing is popular (even in winter when there is ice-fishing) but many of the lakes, especially farther north, have no road access and you have to fly in. St Paul, gateway to the lake district, is a trading centre. Its claim to fame is the only **flying-saucer landing pad** in the world. It's still waiting for its first customer. The region around St Paul has lots of provincial parks and campgrounds.

Hwy 63 is the main route into Alberta's north-eastern wilderness interior. The highway, with a few small settlements and campgrounds along the way, leads to **Fort McMurray**, which is 439km north of Edmonton. Originally a fur trading outpost, it is now home to one of the world's largest oilfields.

The Fort McMurray Oil Sands Interpretative Centre (☎ 780-743-7167), at the junction of Hwy 63 and MacKenzie Blvd, tells the story of how crude is extracted from the vast tracts of sand. It's open daily from 10 am to 4 pm (until 6 pm from mid-May to September). Admission is $3/2 for adults/children. You can join tours of the enormous production facilities by making a reservation on ☎ 780-791-4336 or ☎ 1-800-565-3947.

The Fort McMurray Visitor's Bureau (☎ 780-791-4336 or ☎ 1-800-565-3947) is at 400 Sakitawaw Trail.

WOOD BUFFALO NATIONAL PARK

Established in 1922 and nearly 28,000 sq km in size, Wood Buffalo is Canada's largest national park and one of the world's largest parks. Bigger than Switzerland, this wilderness World Heritage Site lies two-thirds in Alberta and one-third in the Northwest Territories. Vegetation ranges from boreal forest to plains, bogs and marshes. This is a good place to get a glimpse of the hardships the early fur traders overcame.

The park is home to the world's largest free-roaming bison herd – about 3000 – and is the only nesting ground of the rare whooping crane. Though few in number and endangered, the crane population has been stabilised, thanks to conservation efforts. Moose, caribou, bears and wolves abound as well as many smaller animals, and more than one million ducks, geese and swans pass by in autumn and spring on their migratory routes. At nearby Fort Smith rare white pelicans nest by the Slave River rapids. Other major features include the Peace-Athabasca Delta, Salt Plains and underground caves and sinkholes.

Most of the scenic areas in the park are not visible from the roads, which are not themselves always open. On the shores of Lake Athabasca, **Fort Chipewyan** is the oldest continuing European settlement in Alberta.

Fort Smith (☎ 867-872-2515) and Fort Chipewyan each has a visitors centre, or contact the Park Superintendent (☎ 867-872-7900), Box 750, Fort Smith, Northwest Territories X0E 0P0. The road to Fort Chipewyan is only passable in winter. Also note that bugs can be a serious problem so come prepared for battle. For additional details on the park, see the Fort Smith and Wood Buffalo National Park sections in the Northwest Territories chapter.

Activities

You can go swimming at **Pine Lake**, hike on the marked trails or explore the deltas of the **Athabasca** and **Peace rivers** by canoe. The park staff run field trips, overnight camping trips and buffalo-watching hikes. In winter there are cross-country ski trails.

Places to Stay

There are few comforts in Wood Buffalo National Park. The small *Pine Lake Campground* (☎ 867-872-2349 in Fort Smith), 56km south of Fort Smith in the most developed area of the park, has 36 sites for $10, pump water and a beach. In addition there are two small *campgrounds* just outside the park's border: the one 17km northeast of Fort Chipewyan at Dore Lake is operated by the Alberta Forestry Service, while the other is near Fort Smith. Within the park there are numerous designated basic camp sites for individual campers which offer some primitive facilities such as an outhouse and sometimes a firepit. The more adventurous may set off on their own and camp anywhere they find agreeable.

Getting There & Away

Canadian Airlines (☎ 1-800-661-1505) operates regional services to Fort Smith from Edmonton.

The park is accessible by road but not from Alberta. By road, travel up the Mackenzie Hwy north-west of Edmonton to the Northwest Territories where Hwy 1 and then Hwy 2 lead to Hay River on the southern shore of Great Slave Lake. South of Hay River, Hwy 5 heads east to Fort Smith; two roads lead off from the highway south into the park. Greyhound (☎ 867-874-6966 or ☎ 1-800-661-8747) runs buses from Alberta to Hay River. From there, Frontier Coachlines (☎ 867-874-2566) serves Fort Smith.

Calgary

Calgary protrudes conspicuously from the flat plains of southern central Alberta. Farms are minutes away, and the rising foothills of the Rockies are just visible to the west, yet the streets of the city centre by the Bow River, headquarter of the oil industry, are lined with office towers. Calgary is young and modern, having re-created itself from regional town to major Canadian city in the last 25 years. With a population fast reaching 800,000, Calgary has surpassed Edmonton in size. It is an economic centre with a university, professional sport franchises and an increasingly diverse cultural life. It is now also second only to Toronto as the home for major Canadian corporations.

The residents generally are educated and well paid and work in high-tech, energy and resource based industries. It's also said there are more single people here than anywhere else in Canada. Perhaps that is why tanning salons and fitness centres are so prevalent. The previously popular cowboy boots and hats have become vestiges of the recent past.

Calgary's climate is dry and sunny. It gets hot in summer but remains amazingly cool in the shade. In winter the warm chinook winds periodically blow off the mountains, drastically raising temperatures – at least temporarily.

One of Alberta's greatest assets, Banff National Park, is just 120km west. Edmonton is 294km north.

History

The name Calgary, meaning 'clear, running water' in Gaelic, comes from Calgary Bay on the Isle of Mull in Scotland. The area was initially home to the Blackfoot but they were joined in the 18th century by the Sarcee and the Stoney. In the 1800s there was war between them and trouble with European trappers and traders, so the Northwest Mounted Police were sent to cool things down.

The NWMP established Fort Calgary in 1875. The Canadian Pacific railway came this far in 1883. Settlers were offered free land and the population jumped to 4000 by 1891. Soon, cattle herders from the USA were pushing north, looking for better grazing. Calgary became a major meat-packing centre and cowboy metropolis. Slowly, with moderate growth, it became a transportation and distribution point and is still the leading cattle centre in Canada. But since the late 1960s the city has had to deal with some dramatic changes, exploding from a fair-sized cow town to a brand-new city of steel and glass.

The reason for Calgary's changeable fortunes is simple: oil. Oil had been discovered as far back as 1914, but it wasn't until the late 1960s that the black gold was found in vast quantities across Alberta. This discovery, coupled with the energy crisis of the 1970s, which bumped prices up sharply, saw the industry boom. The city took off, becoming the headquarters of 450 oil companies and home to more US citizens than any place outside of the USA.

After a brief, breath catching period, the cultural side of the city began to develop as well. However, during the 1980s the bottom fell out of the oil market and, with 70% of the workforce relying on it, times quickly became tough. But Calgary's fortunes and reputation were boosted when it hosted the Winter Olympics in 1988. By 1993 there was an upturn in the fortunes of the oil and gas industries. The city now has a broader economic base and is poised to be one of Canada's major cities in the 21st century.

Orientation

Calgary lies on flat ground. It began at the confluence of the Bow and Elbow rivers and has spread equally in all directions; the city is the country's second largest in area. The downtown core is still bounded by the Bow River to the north. The Elbow River cuts through the southern portions of the city.

The street-numbering system is a jumble and one of the oddest. For example, if you are on a stretch of street with a 2nd St crossing at one end and a 3rd St at the other, the street numbers begin at 300 at the 2nd St end and climb to the high 300s at the 3rd St

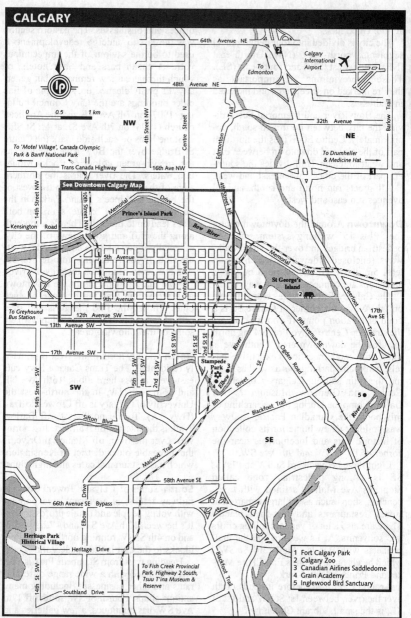

CALGARY

0   0.5   1 km

NW

To 'Motel Village', Canada Olympic
Park & Banff National Park

Trans Canada Highway

See Downtown Calgary Map

Kensington   Road

Prince's Island Park

Memorial   Drive

Bow River

64th   Avenue NE

48th   Avenue NE

32th   Avenue

16th Ave NW

To
Edmonton

Calgary
International
Airport

NE

To Drumheller
& Medicine Hat

5th   Avenue

7th   Avenue

9th   Avenue

12th   Avenue SW

To Greyhound
Bus Station

13th   Avenue SW

17th   Avenue SW

Memorial   Drive

St George's
Island

1

2

17th
Ave SE

SW

Sifton   Blvd

Stampede
Park

3

9th   Avenue SE

Ogden   Road

Blackfoot   Trail

5

SE

Bow   River

Macleod   Trail

58th   Avenue SE

66th   Avenue SE   Bypass

Heritage Park
Historical Village

Heritage   Drive

To Fish Creek Provincial
Park, Highway 2 South,
Tsuu T'ina Museum &
Reserve

Southland   Drive

1 Fort Calgary Park
2 Calgary Zoo
3 Canadian Airlines Saddledome
4 Grain Academy
5 Inglewood Bird Sanctuary

end, where crossing that street, they begin at 400. Good luck.

The city is divided into four geographical segments: north-west (NW), north-east (NE), south-west (SW) and south-east (SE). These abbreviations are important as they're marked on street signs and included in addresses.

The Bow River and Memorial Drive divide the city between north and south, approximately. Centre St divides the northern part of the city and downtown between east and west; Macleod Trail divides the southern part of the city between east and west.

All streets run north and south, and all avenues run east and west.

Downtown Around the downtown centre the 'Plus 15' walking system refers to pedestrian bridges and over-the-street walkways (enclosed sidewalks) which are at least 5m above ground. Various buildings and shops are connected in this way.

The Calgary Tower, in the centre of town on 9th Ave on the corner of Centre St, is a good orientation point. If you look across the street up Centre St, you're looking north towards the downtown area. Ninth Ave is lined with modern offices, expensive hotels, banks and parking lots as well as hosting the train station, Calgary Convention Centre and Glenbow Museum & Art Gallery complex. During the researching of this book, the Canadian Pacific Railway was building a new home for its collection of historic cars and locomotives near the corner of 1st St SW and 9th Ave SW.

Eighth Ave between 3rd St SW and 1st St SE is a long pedestrian zone called Stephens Ave Mall. It's lined with trees, benches, shops such as the large department stores, restaurants and fast-food places. There are also a lot of vendors selling crafts and souvenirs. At its western end the mall connects with Barclay Mall (3rd St SW), which heads north towards Eau Claire Market and Prince's Island Park.

Around Centre St, before it heads north over the river, between 1st St SW and 1st St SE, is the small, vibrant Chinatown.

The western downtown area has mainly offices and businesses. The eastern section was the last to undergo redevelopment. It used to be the saviour of the impecunious with its cheap bars and tatty hotels, of which there are a few remnants, but generally it's pretty cleaned up. A couple of fine older buildings are the City Council building (1907) on 7th Ave SE and the Anglican church (1904) on 7th Ave SE at 1st St SE.

Stone lions on each side mark the Centre St Bridge over the Bow River, which has the greyish-green colour of Rocky Mountain waters. The river marks the northern edge of the downtown area. To the west of the bridge is Prince's Island Park. On the northern side of the bridge, stairs on both sides lead up to the cliff. There's a footpath along the cliff and good views of the city, especially if you take the stairs on the western side. If you're driving, turn left on 8th Ave NW, then head back towards the river.

Note that most places in the downtown area are within walking distance of each other. Those who find the glass and steel central core a little sterile should investigate some of the following areas.

North The city north of the river is primarily residential. The Trans Canada Hwy cuts east-west across here along 16th Ave NE and 16th Ave NW. In the north-west the University of Calgary is off Crowchild Trail (Hwy 1A). To the north-east, off Barlow Trail, is the international airport. Just northwest over the river, off Memorial Drive, is the agreeable older district of Kensington, which has restaurants, cafés and nightclubs.

South South of Calgary Tower, over the railway tracks, is a vibrant area popular with young people and single professionals. It's between 10th Ave SW and 17th Ave SW and on 4th St SW running north-south. Five blocks to the east is Stampede Park.

Heading west from Stampede Park is 17th Ave SW, lined with a wide range of restaurants and other businesses, including many antique shops. Fourth St SW, south off 17th Ave SW, has boutiques, a few galleries and

yet more eating places and nightspots. These two streets are particularly good for strolling and browsing.

Farther south is Macleod Trail (Hwy 2), which eventually heads to the USA. The most exclusive section of Calgary is east of Macleod Trail around the Bow River.

Information

Tourist Offices The visitor service centre (☎ 403-263-8510 or ☎ 1-800-661-1678, fax 403-262-3809, destination@visitor.calgary .ab.ca) is on the ground floor of Calgary Tower at the junction of 9th Ave SW and Centre St. Run by the Calgary Convention & Visitors Bureau, it has maps of the city and pamphlets on things to do and will help you to find accommodation. It's open daily from 8 am to 5 pm (until 8 pm from June to August). There are information booths at both the arrivals and departures levels of the airport.

The City of Calgary Planning Department (☎ 403-268-5333), on the 4th floor at 800 Macleod Trail SE, has walking tour maps for the city, some of which highlight various historic buildings.

Money There are numerous banks on Stephens Ave Mall, many of which open on Saturday. Most large branches will exchange foreign currency. American Express (☎ 403-261-5085) is at 421 7th Ave SW.

Post & Communications The main post office (☎ 403-292-5512), 220 4th Ave SE, is open Monday to Friday from 8 am to 5.45 pm. Wired – The Cyber Cafe (☎ 403-244-7070), 1032 17th Ave SW, has full Internet access and is open daily from 9 am to 10 pm.

Foreign Consulates Many countries are represented diplomatically in Calgary. Check in the Yellow Pages under Consulates.

Bookshops The Hostel Shop (☎ 403-283-8311), 1414 Kensington Rd NW, is open daily. It has travel and outdoor activity guides and maps, as well as travel goods. Map Town (☎ 403-266-2241), 400 5th Ave

SW, has travel guides and a wide range of maps. The Book Store (☎ 403-237-8344), 315 8th Ave SW, is a good general purpose bookshop. Orlando Books (☎ 403-263-5256), 1412 Centre St S, has a good selection of gay and lesbian books.

Libraries The WR Castell Central Library (☎ 403-260-2600), 616 Macleod Trail SE, is open Monday to Thursday from 10 am to 9 pm and Friday and Saturday from 10 am to 5 pm. It has very limited free Internet access.

Laundry Avenue Coin Laundry (☎ 403-229-4269), 333 17th Ave SE, is in a modern apartment tower.

Medical Services Budget cuts meant that Calgary General Hospital was literally blown up in 1998, leaving central Calgary without major medical services. The closest hospital is Foothills Hospital (☎ 403-670-1110), 1403 29th St NW.

Emergency Within Calgary, dial ☎ 911 for police, medical and fire emergencies.

Calgary Tower

This building (☎ 403-266-7171), 101 9th Ave SW, at the foot of Centre St, is a landmark and symbol of the city. The 191m tower houses a revolving restaurant, an observation gallery and, at the top, a cocktail lounge. The observation gallery is open daily from 8 am to 11 pm. Admission to the elevators (58 seconds to the top) is $5.50/2.50 for adults/children.

Glenbow Museum & Art Gallery

Glenbow Museum & Art Gallery (☎ 403-268-4100) is excellent. The collections are varied and the displays effectively laid out. The complex shows part of human history through artefacts and art.

The 2nd floor contains frequently changing exhibitions of international, national and local art; there is always some Inuit art and a painter's work on show.

The 3rd floor has historical displays, mainly to do with the Canadian west. There

ALBERTA

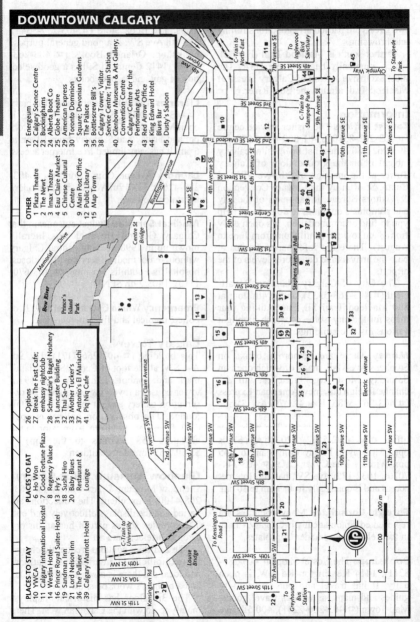

DOWNTOWN CALGARY

PLACES TO STAY
10 YWCA
11 Calgary International Hostel
14 Westin Hotel
16 Prince Royal Suites Hotel
19 Sandman Inn
21 Lord Nelson Inn
36 The Palliser
39 Calgary Marriott Hotel

PLACES TO EAT
6 Ho Won
7 Good Fortune Plaza
8 Regency Palace
13 Hy's
18 Sushi Hiro
20 Baby Blues
   Restaurant &
   Lounge
26 Options
27 Break The Fast Cafe;
   embassy nightclub
28 Schwartzie's Bagel Noshery
31 Lancaster Building
32 Thai Sa-On
33 Mother Tucker's
37 Antonio's El Mariachi
41 Piq Niq Cafe

OTHER
1 Plaza Theatre
2 The Newt
3 Imax Theatre
4 Eau Claire Market
5 Chinese Cultural
   Centre
9 Main Post Office
12 Public Library
15 Map Town
17 Energeum
22 Calgary Science Centre
23 Buckinghams
24 Alberta Boot Co
25 Globe Theatre
29 American Express
30 Toronto Dominion
   Square; Devonian Gardens
34 The Palace
35 Bottlescrew Bill's
38 Calgary Tower; Visitor
   Service Centre; Train Station
40 Glenbow Museum & Art Gallery;
   Convention Centre
42 Calgary Centre for the
   Performing Arts
43 Red Arrow Office
44 King Edward Hotel
   Blues Bar
45 Dusty's Saloon

is a superb collection of Native Indian dress and jewellery. Woodcarving from coast to coast is also represented. There's a section with Inuit tools and a kayak, the traditional one-person boat, as well as a huge collection on pioneer days that includes old wagons, tractors, CP Railway relics, saddles and cowboy tools and implements. Another area presents an interesting collection from the 1920s and 30s. Articles include old washing machines, a car, slot machines, bathing suits and a 1930 brassiere.

On the 4th floor is the military and arms collection. There are figures dressed in Japanese samurai armour, and armoured knights of Britain's Middle Ages. The WWI and WWII posters are interesting and the newspaper headlines make it all come alive.

The museum is open daily from 9 am to 5 pm, closing on Monday from November to April. Connected to the convention centre, it is on the corner of 9th Ave SE and 1st St SE. Admission is $8/6.

Devonian Gardens

The Devonian Gardens (☎ 403-268-5207) are situated 15m above street level on the 4th floor of Toronto Dominion Square, a complex on Stephens Ave Mall between 2nd and 3rd Sts SW.

This place makes a pleasant sanctuary from the concrete of downtown Calgary. Built entirely indoors, it's a one hectare park with more than 20,000 plants and the freshness of a greenhouse. More than 1km of pathways skirts fountains, pools, benches and a sculpture court. There's a small stage for regular entertainment, often during weekday lunch hours, and a special display area for art exhibitions. The gardens are open daily from 9 am to 9 pm; entry is free. Outside regular business hours, elevators must be used to reach the gardens.

Energeum

The Energeum (☎ 403-297-4293), on the main floor of the Energy Resources building at 640 5th Ave SW, outlines the development and uses of Alberta's energy resources. Models and charts depict the formation, discovery

and exploitation of coal, oil and natural gas, and include a good explanation of the province's valuable yet problematic oil sands. Some interactive computers supply further details, as does a film. A gorgeous pink 1958 Buick, the kind of gas guzzler that made the oil companies rich, is on display. The Energeum is open Monday to Friday from 10.30 am to 4.30 pm (plus Sunday from June to August) and admission is free.

Calgary Science Centre

The entertaining and educational Calgary Science Centre (☎ 403-221-3700), 701 11th St SW, is just west of downtown in Mewata Park at the junction of 7th Ave SW. A series of hands-on exhibits reveal natural phenomenon. The main attraction, though, is the **Centennial Planetarium** with its ever-changing one hour show about all things stellar.

Weekend nights are given over to laser rock-music shows. Also on the premises is a small observatory with telescopes focused on the moon, the planets and star clusters. This is open on clear nights. There's also a new display area, **Discovery Dome**, which has overwhelming multimedia entertainment. The **Pleiades Theatre** (☎ 403-221-3707) puts on holiday variety shows and mystery plays four times a year.

The centre is open daily from 10 am to 8 pm from June to August and Tuesday to Sunday from 10 am to 5 pm the rest of the year. Dome shows take place at night and on weekends. Admission is $9/6.

Chinese Cultural Centre Museum

This centre (☎ 403-262-5071), blocking 2nd Ave at 197 1st St SW, was built in 1993 by skilled Chinese artisans. It hosts changing cultural exhibitions and has a collection of replica terracotta soldiers from China. You can watch people playing chess in the main hall. The small museum is open daily from 11 am to 5 pm; admission is $2/1.

Prince's Island Park

This is a pretty park on an island in the Bow River north of the downtown area,

connected to both sides of the river by pedestrian bridges. It's a cool, quiet spot with lots of trees and flowers, picnic tables and jogging and cycling paths. This is a good antidote to a hot summer's day in Calgary. As the signs say, the water in the Bow River is dangerous for swimming – it moves fast and is cold. The bridge to the island from downtown is at the northern end of 3rd St SW.

Heritage Park Historical Village

This is an area of 26 hectares portraying life in a town of the Canadian west before 1914 and on a good day offers views of the Rockies. The park (☎ 403-259-1900), 1900 Heritage Drive at the junction of 14th St SW, south-west of downtown, sits on a peninsula in the Glenmore Reservoir formed by the Elbow River.

The reconstructed frontier village includes a Hudson's Bay Company fort, a working grain mill, an 1896 church and many stores full of artefacts and antiques. The well laid-out grounds have a ranch house, a teepee, a trapper's cabin and other housing. The old schoolhouse with its desks and slates is interesting. There is an excellent collection of horse-drawn buggies in section E, which includes stagecoaches, traps and surreys, and the chemist and general store are particularly good. Also, be sure to see the two storey outhouse, for which the phrase 'look out below!' has special meaning.

The park actually covers more than just pioneer days, encompassing development into the early 1920s. There are old cars, a railway exhibit of old coaches and a working steam engine as well as a paddlewheel boat that cruises the reservoir.

Around the site are several eating places and you can buy fresh bread from the bakery. The park is open daily from 9 am to 5 pm from mid-May to early September, after which it is open weekends only until mid-October. Admission is $10/6; tack on an extra $6 for a train and boat ride. To reach the park, take the C-Train to Heritage station and transfer to the No 20 bus.

Fort Calgary

This is not really a fort but a 16 hectare park (☎ 403-290-1875) at 750 9th Ave SE, just east of downtown, where Calgary's original settlement began. Here in 1875, where the Bow meets the Elbow River, the first detachment of the Northwest Mounted Police arrived. They built a fort and called the developing settlement the 'Elbow'. Later it became Fort Calgary and remained a police post until 1914, when it was sold to the Grand Trunk Railway. All that remains of the fort are a few foundations. Plaques give some of the history.

In the park is an interpretative centre, the remains of the fort and two of Calgary's earliest houses. Other historic buildings are being moved to the site. The interpretative centre tells the story of Calgary's development; there are displays and a video show on the Northwest Mounted Police every 30 minutes in the theatre, and a re-created store and carpentry shop. The centre is open daily from 9 am to 5 pm from May to October; admission is $5/2.50.

The fort site is pleasant and has good views. You can follow paths down to the river and walk across the footbridge to St Patrick's Island and on to Calgary Zoo. The park is open daily and entry is free.

To the east, across the Elbow River, is **Hunt House**, probably the oldest building on its original site in the Calgary area. It was built by the Hudson's Bay Company in 1876 for one of its employees. Next door, the larger **Deane House** was built in 1906 for the commanding officer of Fort Calgary.

Calgary Zoo

The zoo (☎ 403-232-9300), one of Canada's largest and best and Calgary's most popular attraction, is east of downtown on St George's Island and the northern bank of the Bow River. It brings together 1200 species of mammals, birds, amphibians and reptiles, many in enclosures simulating the animals' natural habitats. Underwater viewing areas allow you to see polar bears, seals and other creatures as they behave beneath the water, while blacked out rooms enable you to see

nocturnal animals. There is a new area where African animals are shown in realistic tropical settings. Call ahead to check on feeding times. Hundreds of tropical birds are kept in greenhouses full of the plants of warmer climes. Picnic areas dot the zoo and island and there is a café at the site.

The **Botanical Garden** in the zoo has changing garden displays, a tropical rainforest and a good butterfly enclosure. The three hectare **Prehistoric Dinosaur Park**, an extension of the zoo, contains fossil displays and life-size replicas of dinosaurs in natural settings.

The zoo is open daily from 9 am with closing times dictated by the season. Admission is $9.50/4.75; Tuesday, Wednesday and Thursday are half-price days. During winter, when neither you nor the animals will care to linger outdoors, there are additional discounts. The zoo is easily reached by the C-Train east to the Zoo stop.

Inglewood Bird Sanctuary

This 32 hectare sanctuary (☎ 403-269-6688) is south-east of downtown at the end of 9th Ave, on a forested section of the Bow River flats. The area is home to at least 260 species and is a resting spot for those on the migratory trail. Trails lead through the sanctuary, which is open daily from 9 am to 5 pm, and until 8 pm Friday to Sunday from June to August. Admission is free. Bus No 411 goes within a few blocks of the sanctuary on weekdays only, or take bus No 1 from downtown which stops a bit farther away.

Calgary Stockyards

The stockyards (☎ 403-234-7429), 100 2635 Portland St SE, are one of the centres for western livestock dealing. There are cattle auctions (☎ 403-934-3344) on weekdays. Take bus No 24 from downtown.

Grain Academy

Operated by the Alberta Wheat Pool, the academy (☎ 403-263-4594) tells the story of the province's grain through film, models, tools and guides. The entire grain han-

dling system is outlined. The academy is open weekdays from 10 am to 4 pm year-round, plus Saturday from noon to 4 pm from April to September. Admission is free. It's at the main entrance to Stampede Park, off 4th St SE. Take the C-Train south to the Victoria Park/Stampede stop.

Museum of the Regiments

The Museum of the Regiments (☎ 403-974-2850) is at the Canadian Forces base, Currie Barracks, 4520 Crowchild Trail SW between 33rd Ave SW and 50th Ave SW. It pays homage to Calgary's home regiments: Lord Strathcona's Horse, Princess Patricia's Light Infantry, the Calgary Highlanders and the King's Own Calgary regiment. There are displays about the foreign wars to where the regiments have been called to battle.

The museum is open daily, except Wednesday, from 10 am to 4 pm; admission is free. Take bus No 18, 108, 111 or 112 from downtown.

Fish Creek Provincial Park

On the south-western edge of Calgary, this huge tract of land protects more than 10km of Fish Creek, which flows into the Bow River. It acts as a shelter for many animals and birds and is the largest urban park in Canada. Park interpreters present slide shows and walking tours to explain some of the local ecology.

For details, contact the administration office (☎ 403-297-5293). There are numerous access points to the park; from downtown, bus No 3 reaches it via Elbow Drive.

Calaway Park

This large amusement park (☎ 403-240-3822), 10km west of town on the Trans Canada Hwy (Hwy 1) at the Springbank Rd exit, features more than 24 rides, a cinema with a 180° screen, restaurants and entertainment events. The park is open daily from 10 am to 8 pm from mid-June to August, and weekends only for a month preceding and following that period. Admission is $17.50/12 for adults/children under six.

Canada Olympic Park

Calgary hosted the 15th Winter Olympics in 1988, a first for Canada. Some of the locations and facilities were already in place, others were specially built, but they all remain in use.

A 15 minute drive west of town on the Trans Canada Hwy to the Bowfort Rd exit, the Canada Olympic Park (☎ 403-247-5452) is interesting to visit. You can see the 70m and 90m ski jumps – from the top you realise how crazy those guys are – and the concrete bobsled and luge runs. You can ride the Bobsleigh Bullet on the actual track from November to March for $39. Some of the facilities are now used as an Olympic training centre.

The **Olympic Hall of Fame** has three floors of exhibits honouring athletic achievements, and simulators that re-create the sensation of bobsledding and skiing. You can look around the park yourself for $5 or take a 'grand tour' that includes a bus around the grounds and admission to the Hall of Fame for $10/5 for adults/children. The park is open daily from 10 am to 10 pm, opening and closing one hour earlier from June to August.

The adjacent downhill ski area is open to the public in winter. But the real Olympics alpine skiing took place 55km west of town in Kananaskis Country (see that section later in this chapter).

Bow River

The Bow River begins as clean, clear, barely melted ice in Bow Lake in the Rockies not far from Banff, and flows swiftly through Calgary. From Calgary it slows and warms and eventually reaches Medicine Hat near the Saskatchewan border. There it melds with other meandering rivers, changes name and eventually slips into Hudson Bay.

The Bow River in its middle section – the 60km from Calgary east to Carseland – is considered one of the best trout-fishing rivers in North America and the best dry fly-fishing river in the world. The fish, mainly brown and rainbow trout, are numerous and big. And the river will just float you along with no effort required. It sounds good even

for those who don't fish. Swimming is out, though: the water here is far too cold.

A good access point is just at the southern edge of Calgary's city limits under the Hwy 22X bridge. There are numerous fishing guide services in town as well as sporting goods stores for fishing tackle and information. One place that combines the two is Country Pleasures (☎ 403-271-1016), 10816 Macleod Trail S.

Tsuu T'ina Museum & Reserve

The Sarcee Indian Nation has a community about 30 minutes south-west of town at the end of Anderson Rd. There is a small museum (☎ 403-238-2677) which can be visited for free or more in-depth tours are offered around the reserve. Guides will talk about the peoples' past, culture and current status. There are some historical sites and bison grazing. The tours must be arranged in advance. The museum is open weekdays from 8 am to 4 pm. Take the C-Train to the Anderson stop and then take a taxi.

Aero Space Museum of Calgary

Visitors with a keen interest in planes and aviation history may enjoy this collection (☎ 403-250-3752), 64 McTavish Place NE, of civil and combat aircraft and engines. Members carry out a lot of restoration and are working on several major projects. The museum is open daily from 10 am to 5 pm. Admission is $6/2 for adults/children. Take bus No 57 from the C-Train Whitehorn stop.

Activities

Calgary has 180km of bicycle and hiking trails, many in the parks and nature areas. An excellent map, *Calgary Pathway and Bikeway*, is available from tourist information centres.

Two leisure centres run by Calgary Parks & Recreation have giant wave pools, year-round skating, racquetcourts, hot tubs, climbing walls and more. They are: Village Square Leisure Centre (☎ 403-280-9714), 2623 56th St NE, and Southland Leisure Centre (☎ 403-251-3505), 2000 Southland Drive SW, near the corner of 19th St SW. Downtown, the Eau

Claire YMCA (☎ 403-269-6701), 101 3rd St SW, has the latest in keep-fit facilities. Admission is $8 outside of peak hours.

Horse riding, including lessons, is available at Fish Creek Provincial Park with Happy Trails (☎ 403-251-3344) riding stable. A one hour trail ride costs $18.

Organised Tours

The cheapest tour of the town is to take the No 10 bus from along 6th Ave. For $1.60 this bus goes on a 2½ hour circular route past old and new areas, taking in the highest point of the city with views to the foothills, the university and some wealthy districts in the north-west.

Brewster Gray Line (☎ 403-221-8250), 808 Centre St S, runs traditional bus tours of Calgary and various Rocky Mountain locations from Calgary. The tour of Calgary takes about four hours, covers about 50km and costs $43. It includes Fort Calgary, Canada Olympic Park and the downtown area, with admission prices included in the ticket. A history of the city is given. Its 'Beautiful Banff' tour takes nine hours and costs $80 in summer and $60 at other times.

Two small tour companies have a delightfully informal approach. Hammerhead Tours (☎ 403-260-0940) operates two $55 trips, one east to the Drumheller Badlands and Tyrrell Museum and another south to Head-Smashed-In Buffalo Jump. Both are full day trips with a small group in a van, and take in various attractions along the way. The tour picks up at several locations around town including the Calgary International Hostel and the Calgary Tower. The office is at 4714 14th St NW and trips are run from May to November. HI members are offered 15% discounts.

Working in conjunction with the Calgary International Hostel is True North Tours (☎ 403-912-0115 or ☎ 1-888-464-4842). It operates the Rocky Mountain Express, a six day trip through some of the highlights of the mountains with accommodation in various hostels along the way. The price is $199 plus the hostel rates. Vans are used, and the optional group meals can really keep costs

down. There is also a three day trip with shorter hikes. Reservations should be made about two or three weeks in advance. Trips run from the beginning of June through mid-October.

Whitewater rafting on either the Kananaskis or Red Deer rivers is available through Rainbow Riders Adventure Tours (☎ 403-850-3686). The cost is $45 for about 2½ hours. Calgary Helicopters (☎ 403-291-0017), 575 Palmer Rd NE, offers tours of the city for $85 per person and of the Rocky Mountains for $325.

Special Events

The following are some of Calgary's major festivals:

July

Calgary Stampede
(☎ 403-269-9822 or ☎ 1-800-661-1767 for information and tickets) Dating from 1912, this is a wild, 10 day festival that starts with a huge parade in the second week of July each year. Most organised events take place in Stampede Park south-east of the downtown area, but many of the streets are full of activity too. Stampede Park comes alive with concerts, shows, exhibitions, dancing and eating, attracting over 100,000 people each day. There is also an amusement area with rides, a gambling hall and lots of contests. Highlights are the chuck-wagon race and the rodeo, which is said to be the biggest and roughest in North America. Events include rides on bucking broncos and bulls, and calf-roping and branding. At night the Stampede Stage Show takes over, with singers, bands, clowns and dancers. Tickets for the main events go early and range in price from about $17 to $45. The town and nearby countryside are packed for the duration of the celebrations, so it's a good idea to book well ahead for somewhere to stay, or arrive early. For more information write to Calgary Exhibition & Stampede, Box 1060, Station M, Calgary T2P 2K8.

Calgary Folk Festival
(☎ 403-261-4060) During this festival in late July there are free weekday lunchtime performances in Stephens Ave Mall, Century Park Garden and Olympic Plaza. In the evenings there are performances in venues around town including Kensington Delicafé and King Edward Hotel. The main events take place on Prince's Island. Both three day and one day

passes are available. The festival includes local, national and international artists.

August

International Native Arts Festival

This takes place in mid-August and includes traditional dancing, music and arts and crafts by the indigenous peoples of North America and other places around the world.

Places to Stay

The prices quoted in this section are normal for summer; some rise during the Stampede, while others fall during winter. The visitor service centre will make free bookings (see Tourist Offices earlier).

Camping There are several campgrounds near the city for both RVs and tents. *Whispering Spruce Campground* (☎ *403-226-0097*) is in Balzac along Hwy 2 about 15 minutes north of the city. It's convenient and large enough to always have space, but maintenance and cleaning are virtually nonexistent. It's open from mid-April to mid-October and has tent sites for $15. *Mountain View Campground* (☎ *403-293-6640*), on a farm 3km east of Calgary on the Trans Canada Hwy, is open all year. It has showers, laundry, a barbecue, even a small zoo, and tent sites for $16. *Calaway Park* (☎ *403-249-7372*), 10km west of Calgary on the Trans Canada Hwy, has full facilities, including showers and laundry, and tent sites for $15.

The quietest place is south of Calgary, 5km east of Okotoks on Railway St. *Okotoks Wilderness Campground* (☎ *403-938-6036*) has sites for $20 and there are showers and hiking trails. To get there go 33km south on Hwy 2 and take the Okotoks turn-off, then turn left at the lights and travel for about 1km; the campground is just past the car wash.

Hostels The popular HI *Calgary International Hostel* (☎ *403-269-8239, fax 403-266-6227, chostel@HostellingIntl.ca, 520 7th Ave SE*), just east of downtown not far from Fort Calgary, is open 24 hours. It is a large hostel complete with laundry, kitchen and snack bar but still often gets full in summer, especially

for men. Reservations are recommended. The hostel organises a lot of events and activities and offers a variety of cost-saving ideas. There is Internet access. Rates are $15 for members, $19 for nonmembers.

The central *YWCA* (☎ *403-263-1550, 320 5th Ave SE*) is for women only. The single rooms are $35/45 without/with bath, doubles are $45/50. The rooms are clean, you can use the pool or gym and there's a cafeteria which is open every day.

The *University of Calgary* rents out rooms in the residences from early May to the end of August. For details and information contact the University Housing Office (☎ 403-220-3202), Room 18, Dining Centre, University of Calgary, 2500 University Drive NW, Calgary T2N 1N4. Dormitory accommodation (meaning a small simple room) starts at $27. There are also two sizes of apartments with kitchens. The smaller ones are $40/25 unshared/shared, the larger are $52/34. There are good facilities on campus, including a gym and a cheap cafeteria. The university, which is north-west of the centre off Crowchild Trail, is serviced by the C-Train.

B&Bs The visitor service centre keeps a list of B&Bs and makes bookings. An association which checks and lists houses offering B&B in the city is the Bed & Breakfast Association of Calgary (☎ 403-543-3900, fax 403-543-3901). The *Alberta Accommodation & Visitors' Guide* lists about 30 B&Bs in Calgary. Rates start at $30/50 for singles/doubles. A central and inexpensive B&B is the *Tumble Inn* (☎ *403-228-6167, 1507 6th St SW*). A room is $40/50 with full breakfast.

Hotels Central Calgary doesn't have an abundance of lodgings in any price range. Many places in the central area are modern convention hotels linked to the Plus 15 walkways. On weekends, when business travellers are away, many of these places drop their rates.

The *Lord Nelson Inn* (☎ *403-269-8262 or* ☎ *1-800-661-6017, 1020 8th Ave SW*) is central and has full facilities, including a

fridge in each room. Rooms are $65/70 for singles/doubles. *Prince Royal Suites Hotel* (☎ 403-263-0520 or ☎ 1-800-661-1592, 618 5th Ave SW) is a modern all-suite hotel. Rooms have a kitchenette and prices start at $135. On weekends you can get substantial discounts. You can also rent by the week or month.

The *Sandman Hotel* (☎ 403-237-8626 or ☎ 1-800-726-3626, 1-888 7th Ave SW) is a good, standard mid-range hotel with rooms for $68/72. It has full facilities including gym, swimming pool, a 24 hour Denny's coffee shop and bar.

Among the large chain hotels with extensive meeting facilities, the *Calgary Marriott Hotel* (☎ 403-266-7331 or ☎ 1-800-661-7776, 110 9th Ave SE) is a vast high-rise with rooms from $149. The *Westin Hotel* (☎ 403-266-1611 or ☎ 1-800-937-8461, 320 4th Ave SW) has more than 500 large and luxurious rooms as well as a complete business centre. Rates start at $175, with significant weekend discounts. When Queen Elizabeth drops by Calgary, she stays at *The Palliser* (☎ 403-262-1234 or ☎ 1-800-441-1414, 133 9th Ave SW), a grand Canadian Pacific Railway hotel dating from 1914. The 336 rooms vary greatly in size and rates start at $165. There is a large new swimming pool.

Motels Much of the good moderately priced accommodation is found outside the city centre in motels. Calgary has dozens of them in all parts of the city, but there are some areas of heavy concentration, making it easy to shop around.

One of these is south of the city along Macleod Trail, a commercial strip with service stations, fast-food restaurants, motels and furniture shops.

Cedar Ridge Motel (☎ 403-258-1064, 9030 Macleod Trail South) is reasonably priced. Singles/doubles cost $50/60. *Flamingo Motor Hotel* (☎ 403-252-4401, 7505 Macleod Trail South), near the corner of 75th Ave SW, is marked by a large pink flamingo. Rooms cost from $59/65 with a laundry, pool and a sauna. The woodsy grounds are pleasant and there are restaurants nearby.

The *Travelodge Calgary Macleod Trail* (☎ 403-253-7070 or ☎ 1-800-578-7878, 9206 Macleod Trail South), near 90th Ave SE, is a two storey building containing a pool, spa and sauna. Rooms cost $70/80.

'Motel Village', as it's been dubbed, is a motel area in the north-western section of the city on and just off 16th Ave (the Trans Canada Hwy). South-east of the University of Calgary, 16th Ave meets Crowchild Trail; linking the two on a diagonal, forming a triangle, is Banff Trail (also called Hwy 1A). The area is thick with independent and chain lodgings and, although it is a fair way from downtown, Motel Village is well linked by C-Train service to the Banff Trail stop.

One of the cheapest motels is *Savory Lodge* (☎ 403-220-1229, 2373 Banff Trail NW). It has 30 rooms, most of them for $40/45 a single/double; those with kitchenettes cost $5 extra. There's a restaurant and a pub. The *Holiday Motel* (☎ 403-288-5431, 4540 16th Ave NW) offers free local calls and basic rooms for $49/55. *Budget Host Motor Inn* (☎ 403-288-7115 or ☎ 1-800-661-3772, 4420 16th Ave NW) is simple but fine and has free coffee. Rooms are $64 and there's no extra charge for kids under 12. The *Travellers Inn* (☎ 403-247-1388, 4611 16th Ave NW) is a small, older place with simple rooms from $49/55.

Among the chains, *Econolodge* (☎ 403-289-2561 or ☎ 1-800-553-2666, 2440 16th Ave NW) has a Latin American look. Some of its 55 rooms have kitchenettes but there's no extra charge for these. Rooms cost from $58/68. The *Holiday Inn Express* (☎ 403-289-6600 or ☎ 1-800-465-4329, 2227 Banff Trail NW) is a new property with well equipped and comfortable rooms. There's a pool, spa and sauna and free newspapers after you dry off.

Out near the airport and north-east of downtown, there's *Best Western Airport* (☎ 403-250-5015 or ☎ 1-800-528-1234, 1947 18th Ave NE), which is a straightforward place with decent rooms, a restaurant, bar, pool and rates from $59/69. It has a free airport shuttle. In the airport itself, and connected to the terminals, *Calgary Airport*

Hotel (☎ *403-291-2600 or* ☎ *1-800-441-1414, 2001 Airport Road NE)* is almost luxurious and features a health club among other amenities. The suitably soundproofed rooms start at $160. Should jet lag get you down, there's a masseuse on call.

Places to Eat

Steaks still figure prominently in the 'Old West' image of Calgary, but the growing number of ethnic groups is reflected in the variety of restaurants.

Downtown The name *Piq Niq Cafe* (☎ *403-263-1650, 811 1st St SE)* says it all about this café with gourmet aspirations. There are creative breakfasts and lunches and at night you can turn the tables with the create-your-own-pasta bar. On weekends there is live jazz in the funky bar downstairs. Also good for breakfast, *Break the Fast Cafe* (☎ *403-265-5071, 516 9th Ave SW)* has tasty omelettes and pancakes from $6 as well as Ukrainian-style lunch specials. On nice days you can read the paper on the rooftop deck.

For lunch or dinner, check out the 2nd floor of the nearby *Lancaster building (304 Stephens Ave Mall)*, on the corner of 2nd St SW. There are 17 food kiosks serving cheap Chinese, Mexican, Indian and other foods. Curry dishes or tacos are around $4.50. You get street views, too. Also in the Lancaster building, but downstairs, is the agreeable *Unicorn Pub* (☎ *403-233-2666)* with an Anglo-Irish flavour. It's a busy, friendly place which serves moderately priced and typically Brit fare like fish and chips for $6.50 and steak and kidney pie for $7.50. On many nights there is live music.

Also near Stephens Ave Mall, *Schwartzie's Bagel Noshery* (☎ *403-296-1353, 509 8th Ave SW)* is part of a local chain good for coffee and a wide range of bagels and toppings for under $5. Nearby, *Options* (☎ *403-265-9483, 513 8th Ave SW)* has an organic bakery, juice bar and many vegetarian choices for breakfast, lunch and early dinner.

There are good pizzas for $8 to $18 at *Baby Blues Restaurant & Lounge* (☎ *403-234-9282, 937 7th Ave SW)*. Try the pizza

with spinach. Live music is also featured at night. Antonio is cooking away in the kitchen at *Antonio's El Mariachi* (☎ *403-264-2233, 109 8th Ave SW)*. The place is always bustling with folks downing tacos and margaritas in equal proportions. On weekends there's live music.

Alberta in general, and Calgary in particular, has long had a reputation for steak – this is the heart of cattle country after all. For a downtown dinner featuring beef – prime rib or steak – try *Quincy's (609 7th Ave SW)*. It offers an attractive wood-lined dining room and moderate prices. Main courses are $15 to $20 and include seafood. Top of the line in the cow department, *Hy's* (☎ *403-263-2222, 316 4th Ave SW)* has changed little from when it opened in 1955. It's a classic plush steakhouse where the carpets are as dark and thick as the prime Alberta beef. Actually, one thing has changed – the prices. Expect to pay $30 or more per person before you even look at the bar tab.

A less expensive way to sample the local cattle is with a city lunch speciality known as beef dip. This consists of thinly sliced roast beef served plain in a long bun, usually with fries and a bowl of 'sauce' to dip the meat into. In the better places this dip is nothing but juice from the roast – it should not be like gravy. Prices are about $5 to $7. The Unicorn Pub (see earlier in this section) serves a fine one.

Sushi Hiro (☎ *403-233-0605, 727 5th Ave SW)*, near the corner of 7th St SW, is a well regarded Japanese restaurant. Expect to pay about $20 per person for well prepared sushi.

There is a small Chinatown on 2nd and 3rd Aves at Centre St. Now largely based in a number of new shopping complexes, the area is particularly lively on Sunday around noon, when lots of fresh pastries are on offer. *Diamond Bakery* (☎ *403-269-1888)*, downstairs in the Good Fortune Plaza on 3rd Ave SE, is a tiny place offering tasty Chinese and western treats and sweets from around 75 cents. The small, old *Ho Won* (☎ *403-266-2234, 115 2nd Ave SE)* offers dim sum lunches for around $6. This kind of traditional spot is

giving way to newer, larger eateries such as the cavernous, but pleasant *Regency Palace* (☎ 403-777-2288, 328 Centre St SE) in the Dragon City building. Dim sum begins at $2.50 per item but there is an extensive menu of complete dishes. The rudimentary *Pho Pasteur Saigon* (☎ 403-233-0477, 207 1st St SE) is famous for its 18 kinds of beef noodle soup. Toss on the plate of vegetation that comes with it, add some sauce and you have a great meal for under $4.

South of Downtown *Thai Sa-On* (☎ 403-264-3526, 351 10th Ave SW) is a good Thai restaurant with lunchtime specials for $5 and main dishes at dinner from $8. It's closed on Sunday. Nearby at *Mother Tucker's* (☎ 403-262-5541, 347 10th Ave SW) you can get huge sandwiches and salads for $6.50 to $8 and seafood dishes for $13 to $18. This is a very popular place and has music at night.

Farther south, 17th Ave SW and 4th St SW, running west and south respectively of where they meet, are lined with pubs, cafés and restaurants. *Nellie's Kitchen* (☎ 403-244-4616, 738 17th Ave SW), near 7th St SW, is a small, pleasant café with fantastic breakfasts for about $2.50 to $6 and has a patio out the back. It has another location at 2306 4th St SW.

Bread Line (☎ 403-245-1888, 2118 4th St SW) has excellent baked goods, sandwiches, fresh juices and even simple Internet access ($2 for 20 minutes). With a busy patio and always packed dining room, *Fiore Cantina Italiana* (☎ 403-244-6603, 638 17th Ave SW) is a hub of activity in a lively neighbourhood. The long list of fresh pastas averages $8. The beers are as carefully brewed as the food is cooked at *Mission Bridge Brewing Company* (☎ 403-228-0100, 2417 4th St SW). This open and airy microbrewery is known for innovative casual food, like gourmet burgers for $8.

Other Areas North of the river off Memorial Drive within walking distance of downtown is Kensington, a district based on Kensington Rd and 10th St NW. It's an old city neighbourhood with plenty of restaurants and is well worth checking out. There are several coffee bars and patios in the area to linger over a drink or meal.

Outside the central area, the commercial strips along Macleod Trail south and the Trans Canada Hwy east-west across the north of the city have many familiar food chains.

The well known *Peters' Drive-In* (☎ 403-277-2747), on the corner of 16th Ave NE and 2nd St NE, makes milkshakes worth stopping for even if you're just driving right through town. The banana shake is excellent.

Entertainment

For complete entertainment guides pick up a copy of *ffwd*, the city's largest entertainment weekly, or the music-oriented *The Calgary Straight*. Both are available for free around town. The Friday edition of the *Calgary Herald* has a pull-out called *What's Up* that does a good job of outlining the pleasures of the weekend and beyond. *Outlook* is a gay-oriented weekly newspaper distributed throughout the province.

Theatre The city has several live theatre venues. The *Calgary Centre for the Performing Arts* (☎ 403-294-7455), known as The Centre, is on Stephens Ave Mall on the corner of 1st St SE. It has performances by Alberta Theatre Projects (☎ 403-294-7475). The *Loose Moose Theatre* (☎ 403-233-9100, 1229 9th Ave SE), in Inglewood just east of the downtown area, puts on comedy and drama – old and new. *Pumphouse Theatre* (☎ 403-263-0079, 2140 9th Ave SW) has experimental plays.

The Alberta Ballet performs at the *Jubilee Auditorium* (☎ 403-299-8888, 1415 14 Ave SW). Tickets often go fast and cost from $20.

Music The Calgary Philharmonic Orchestra plays at the *Jack Singer Concert Hall* (☎ 403-571-0849, 205 8th Ave SE) at the Arts Centre. Tickets average $35. It also stages a series of free community concerts at various locations around the city. Big-name concerts

are held at *Canadian Airlines Saddledome*, in Stampede Park, and Jubilee Auditorium.

Nightlife Many of the places to eat listed above have live music at night. This is especially true of places on Stephens Ave Mall. On 11th Ave SW, between 4th and 6th Sts SW (known as Electric Avenue), there is a concentration of pubs and clubs catering to the young.

Downtown, the *King Edward Hotel* (☎ 403-262-1680), on the corner of 9th Ave SE and 4th St SE, is the city's prime blues bar. It's been around as long as some of the ancient musicians. For jazz, *Chaos* (☎ 403-228-9997, 718 17th Ave SW) is considered the best bet. *Dusty's Saloon* (☎ 403-263-5343, 1088 Olympic Way SE) is famous for having the largest country and western dance floor in Calgary. It's the place to go for some cowpoke shuffle, and on Tuesday and Wednesday nights two-step lessons are held. Yee-haw!

The Palace (☎ 403-263-9980, 219 8th Ave SW) is a great venue for dances, live comedy, concerts and classic films. *Buckingham's* (☎ 403-233-7550, 805 9th Ave SW) has live rock and good bar chow like burgers and fries. There are good drinks specials at *embassy* (☎ 403-213-3970, 516C 9th Ave SW), a groovy place with disco, soul, house and jazz.

North across the river in Kensington, *The Newt* (☎ 403-283-1132, 107 10A St NW) is a hip bar with a vast selection of martinis, and live music that runs the gamut from folk to Latin to classic rock.

Bottlescrew Bill's (☎ 403-263-7900), on the corner of 1st St SW and 10th Ave SW, has a vast selection of brews from around the world. There is an extensive wine-by-the-glass selection as well. The *Rose & Crown* (☎ 403-244-7757, 1503 4th St SW) is a huge British style pub with an excellent beer selection and an outdoor patio.

Cinema The repertory *Plaza Theatre* (☎ 403-283-3636, 1113 Kensington Rd NW) has two different shows each night plus midnight performances on Friday and Saturday. It presents off-beat US and foreign films. The

Globe Theatre (☎ 403-262-3308, 617 8th Ave SW) has an interesting schedule of foreign and revival movies.

Calgary's *IMAX Theatre* (☎ 403-263-4629, 132 200 Barclay Parade SW) is in the Eau Claire Market just south of the Bow River. Next door is the *Cineplex Odeon* multiplex theatre.

Spectator Sports

The Calgary Flames (☎ 403-777-000 for tickets), arch rival of the Edmonton Oilers, plays ice hockey from October to April at the Canadian Airlines Saddledome in Stampede Park. Tickets cost from $12 to $50. The Calgary Stampeders (☎ 403-289-0258) of the Canadian Football League plays from July to September at McMahon Stadium, 1817 Crowchild Trail NW in north-west Calgary. Tickets range from $20 to $41.

Shopping

Many visitors are taken by the western apparel seen around town, especially that worn at Stampede time or in country music bars. The Alberta Boot Co (☎ 403-263-4623) is the only western boot manufacturer in the province. You can visit its factory and store at 614 10th Ave SW. For cowboy hats, shirts, skirts, vests, spurs and other western gear, check Riley and McCormick (☎ 403-266-8811), 220 8th Ave SW.

Getting There & Away

Air Calgary international airport (☎ 403-735-1372) is about 15km north-east of the centre off Barlow Trail, a 25 minute drive away. It is in a permanent state of construction. The baggage claim area is notable for its vast area of taxidermied local wildlife.

Air Canada (☎ 403-265-9555), 333 5th Ave SW, and Canadian Airlines (☎ 403-235-1161), 407 2nd St SW, fly to cities throughout Canada, the USA and beyond.

Discount carrier WestJet (☎ 403-250-5839) serves Alberta and British Columbia. Charter carrier Canada 3000 (☎ 403-509-3000) has infrequent, but cheap, flights to major tourist destinations throughout North America.

Most of the major US airlines serve Calgary from their hubs in the USA. They are: America West (☎ 1-800-235-9292), American Airlines (☎ 1-800-433-7300), Delta Air Lines (☎ 1-800-221-1212), Northwest Airlines (☎ 1-800-225-2525) and United Airlines (☎ 1-800-241-6522).

To Europe, Air Canada has nonstop services to Frankfurt and London, and Canadian Airlines also serves London. British Airways (☎ 1-800-247-9297) flies to London, and Lufthansa (☎ 1-800-563-5954) goes to Frankfurt.

Bus The Greyhound bus station (☎ 403-265-9111), 850 16th St SW on the corner of 9th Ave SW, is away from the centre. It's walkable but most people opt for the free city shuttle bus from the C-Train 10th St SW stop which goes to the door. It has a small shop, cafeteria and left-luggage lockers ($2) and is open daily from 5 am to 1 am.

Five buses daily serve Vancouver (15 hours, $105), Regina (11 hours, $87) and Banff (two hours, $19). There are also daily services to Winnipeg (20 hours, $138), Kamloops (nine hours, $77) and Saskatoon (nine hours, $71). Ten express buses a day serve Edmonton via Red Deer (four hours, $38).

Red Arrow Express (☎ 403-531-0350) has six luxury buses a day to Edmonton from its Calgary terminal at 205 9th Ave SE. The one-way fare is $40.

From mid-May to October, Alberta Adventure tours (☎ 1-877-364-7533) runs the Summer Hostel Shuttle linking the Calgary HI hostel with those in Banff, Lake Louise and many of the small seasonal hostels north towards Jasper. The fares vary by distance; Calgary to Banff is $23. The shuttles also carry bikes for an extra fee. Usually there is one trip each day in each direction, check with the company or the hostels for details.

Train You can travel by train from Calgary to Vancouver via Banff on the privately owned *Rocky Mountaineer* (see The Rocky Mountaineer section in the Getting Around chapter), but it isn't cheap. To Vancouver the one-way fare costs from $625 double occu-

pancy, including some food and an overnight stop in a hotel in Kamloops. The service, which is like a cruise ship on rails, runs from May to mid-October. For information contact a travel agent or Rocky Mountaineer Rail Tours (☎ 1-800-665-7245).

The train station is conveniently located in the Calgary Tower, on the corner of 9th Ave and Centre St.

Getting Around

To/From the Airport The Airporter Bus (☎ 403-531-3907) runs from 5.30 am to 11.30 pm between all the major downtown hotels and the airport, and charges $10. A bus departs every 20 minutes from the Westin Hotel at 320 4th Ave SW.

A cheaper alternative is the C-Train, which connects with the No 57 bus to/from the airport at the Whitehorn stop north-east of the centre. This takes about one hour to/from downtown on weekdays. Unfortunately, for some unfathomable reason, the No 57 bus runs a bizarre and erratic schedule on weekends, making this service very inconvenient.

A taxi to the airport costs about $23.

Bus & LRT Calgary Transit (☎ 403-262-1000) operates the bus and Light Rapid Transit (LRT) rail system. Its office at 240 7th Ave SW has route maps, information and tickets and is open Monday to Friday from 8.30 am to 5 pm. Maps are also available at the visitor service centre.

The Calgary LRT train is known as the C-Train. One fare entitles you to transfer to other buses or the C-Train. The C-Train is free in the downtown area along 7th Ave between 10th St SW and 3rd St SE. If you're going farther or need a transfer, buy your ticket from a machine on the C-Train platform. Most of the bus lines run at 15 to 30 minute intervals daily. There is no late night service.

The single fare for the C-Train and buses is $1.60/1 for adults/children. A book of 10 tickets costs $13.50/8.50 and a day pass $5/3. Transfers are free and are good for 90 minutes. When going from the C-Train to a bus, present your ticket to the driver. When

going from a bus to the C-Train or another bus, you must request a transfer from the driver when you pay your initial fare.

Car All the major car rental firms are represented at the airport and downtown. They include: Avis (☎ 403-269-6166), Budget (☎ 403-226-1550), Discount Car Rentals (☎ 403-299-1224), Hertz (☎ 403-221-1300), National/Tilden (☎ 403-263-6386), Rent-A-Wreck (☎ 403-237-6880) and Thrifty (☎ 403-262-4400).

Taxi For a cab, call Alberta South Co-Op Taxi Lines (☎ 403-531-8294) or Yellow Cab (☎ 403-974-1111). It costs $2.10 for the first 220m and 20¢ for every 220m thereafter.

Bicycle Budget (☎ 403-226-1550), 140 6th Ave SE, rents out bikes for $6/18 per hour/day. The Bike Shop (☎ 403-264-0735), 801 11th Ave SW, has a large selection of bikes in all price ranges.

AROUND CALGARY
Western Heritage Centre
In the fast-growing bedroom community of Cochrane, 45km north-west of Calgary on Hwy 1A, Western Heritage Centre (☎ 403-932-3514) is a new museum dedicated to the lives of the cowboys and the culture of the ranches that are the legacy of southern Alberta.

The museum is in a rugged valley that manages to have a view that excludes the rapidly proliferating suburbs. Displays explain types of horses as well as the workings of various barnyard animals. This is the place to come to find out about the vital role of the rumen, a cow organ which is like a stomach. One of the most unusual exhibits is a virtual reality vet which lets you try to remove a hairball from a computerised calf. It's not easy and you'll find yourself making a lot of veal before you get it right.

The museum can also be reached from the Trans Canada Highway (Hwy 1) on the way to Banff by exiting at Hwy 22 and driving 35.5km north. It is open daily from 9 am to 8 pm from June to August, and Tuesday to Sunday from 9 am to 5 pm the rest of the year. Admission is $7.50/5.50 for adults/children.

Dry Island Buffalo Jump
This isolated provincial park begins on a dramatic bluff overlooking the Red River Valley near the town of Huxley, about 170km north-east of Calgary. The initial view is like that of a mini-Grand Canyon, whose multihued walls have been exposed by 63 million years of geological history. Among the many fossils that have been found here are those of the enormous and carnivorous tyrannosaurus rex.

Some 2000 years ago, Native tribes drove bison over the edge of the 45m bluffs. Today the park site is seldom crowded and almost eerie when the wind howls down the river valley. To reach the park, which has no entrance gate or office, take the well marked part-gravel road that runs 19km east of Hwy 21 just north of Huxley.

Southern Alberta

Southern Alberta is cattle ranching country, although wheat is important, too. Here you can visit the badlands with their unusual rock formations and vestiges of prehistoric beasts around Drumheller and Dinosaur Provincial Park, or see Head-Smashed-In Buffalo Jump, where the Blackfoot used to hunt the herds of buffalo. In the south-eastern corner rising out of the prairies is Cypress Hills Provincial Park. In Writing-on-Stone Provincial Park you can see hoodoos and ancient petroglyphs. To the west are the spectacular Alberta Rockies, which you may see beckoning on clear days.

DRUMHELLER
Little known Drumheller is slowly getting the attention it warrants. A small city in a strange setting 122m below prairie level, Drumheller is about 150km north-east of Calgary in Red Deer River Valley dinosaur country. The city has caught on to the tourism potential of dinosaurs, and there are

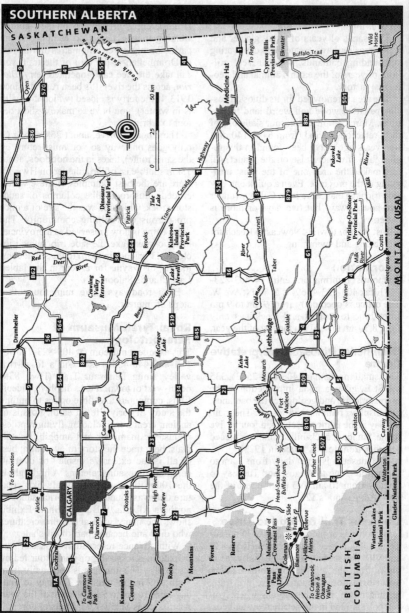

SOUTHERN ALBERTA

statues and symbols of the extinct critters all over town.

Thousands of years of wind, glacier and water erosion have created the captivating surrounding badlands, which reveal millions of years of the earth's animal and geological history.

The area is renowned for its dinosaur fossils, petrified wood and weird land formations. More complete dinosaur skeletons of the Cretaceous period (from 64 to 140 million years ago) have been found in this region than anywhere else on the planet. All this makes the area one of the most intriguing in the province. Even a quick one-day side trip is manageable from Calgary (under two hours away) but two days or more is better.

Just west of town is Newcastle Beach for picnicking and swimming.

Information

The tourist information centre (☎ 403-823-1331, fax 403-823-4469) is at 60 1st Ave W. The office is open daily from 9 am to 9 pm from June to August and weekdays only from 8.30 am to 4.30 pm the rest of the year.

Drumheller Dinosaur Interpretative Centre

This small museum (☎ 403-823-2593), 335 1st St E, gives a good introduction to the prehistoric life and geology of the badlands, and displays remains and fossils. The main display is the **Edmontosaurus**, a four to five tonne, 9m long, duck-billed dinosaur pieced together from fossils found in 1923.

The museum is open daily from 9 am to 9 pm from June to August and Tuesday to Sunday from 10 am to 5 pm the rest of the year. Admission is $2.

Dinosaur Trail & Hoodoo Drive

Drumheller is at the beginning of Dinosaur Trail, a 48km loop that includes Hwys 837 and 838. The scenery along the trail takes in views from the top of **Horsethief Canyon** and **Horseshoe Canyon**. There are trails leading down into the canyons where you can poke around in the petrified oyster beds.

In **Midland Provincial Park**, north-west of Drumheller, you can go on self-guided walking tours. There's no camping in the park. Twenty-seven kilometres north-west of Drumheller, at the turn of the trail, you can take the free cable-operated ferry, *Bleriot*, across the river. It's been running since 1913. If the ferry is closed (which it usually is in winter), you have to make a short detour to a bridge.

The Hoodoo Drive, about 25km long (it only goes one way so you must return by the same route), takes in the **hoodoos**, about 18km south-east of Drumheller on Hwy 10. Here are the best examples of these weird, eroded, mushroom-like columns of sandstone rock. This area was the site of a once prosperous coal-mining community. The Atlas Mine is now preserved as a provincial historic site. Take the side trip (which includes 11 bridges in 6km) to the small community of Wayne for a beer at the fabled Last Chance Saloon.

Both roadways have numerous other stops of interest.

Royal Tyrell Museum of Palaeontology

This excellent museum (☎ 403-823-7707 or ☎ 1-888-440-4240) is set in a fossil-rich valley along Dinosaur Trail (Hwy 838) north-west of town. It uses displays, videos, films, computers and fibre optics to outline the study of early life on earth. Fossils of ancient creatures, including flying reptiles, prehistoric mammals and amphibious animals, help trace the story of evolution; best of all is the extensive display of over 30 complete dinosaur skeletons. A highlight is the 100-million-year-old whale-like creature that was found in the oil-rich sands of northern Alberta. A Burgess Shale Exhibit shows the many wild and weird creatures who died and became part of oil-shale.

With advance reservations you can participate in a fossil dig or join a tour led by a scientist. The museum is open daily from 9 am to 9 pm in summer, Tuesday to Sunday from 10 am to 5 pm the rest of the year. Admission is $6.50/3 for adults/children.

Passion Play

Each year during the first weekend in July the classic story of Jesus is told in the old world setting of Drumheller's outskirts. The half-dozen or so outdoor performances are always sold out, so call the tourist information centre in advance.

Places to Stay & Eat

A few kilometres south of Drumheller, the small communities of Rosedale and Wayne have small municipal *campgrounds* with minimal facilities for $5 a night. About 6km north of town, the *campground* at Nacmine is good and also charges $5. About 23km farther out, the *Bleriot Ferry Campground* (☎ *403-823-1749)* has pump water and sites for $7. In town, the *River Grove Campground & Cabins* (☎ *403-823-6655, 25 Poplar St)* on the northern side of the river is open year-round, has most facilities, including showers, and charges $17 for a basic site. Cabins are $45 a night. A little farther north, *Dinosaur Trailer Park* (☎ *403-823-3291)*, near the corner of Dinosaur Trail and Hwy 9, has tent sites for $14 and showers.

In an old hotel, the rather shabby *Alexandra Hostel* (☎ *403-823-6337, 30 N Railway Ave)* holds 55 people and has showers, laundry and kitchen. It charges $20 a night. Bikes can be rented for $15 a day.

Drumheller has several hotels on and around Railway Ave, but one of the better value places is the *Badlands Motel* (☎ *403-823-5155)* just north of town on the Dinosaur Trail. It has comfy rooms from $52. There are many B&Bs in and around town at $60 a double. Check with the tourist information centre for availability. Behind the McDonald's at the junction of Hwys 9 and 10, the new *Super 8 Motel* (☎ *403-823-8887 or* ☎ *1-888-823-8882, 680 2nd St SE)* has a nice pool with a water slide for cooling off on the hot summer days. Comfortable singles/doubles cost $72/92.

For breakfast try the *Diana Restaurant (388 Centre St)*. The *Bridge Restaurant*, near the bridge, serves good Greek food; try the chicken with feta cheese. *Sizzling House (160 Centre St)* has surprisingly good Chinese food for under $10. Lastly, there is a *cafeteria* at the Tyrell museum.

Shopping

The Fossil Shop, 61 Bridge St, immediately north of the bridge, is worth visiting for a look around and perhaps a purchase of a 75-million-year-old souvenir. There are all kinds of bones and dinosaur fragments to examine and the staff are very knowledgeable. Some of these ancient treasures aren't even all that expensive.

Getting There & Away

The Greyhound bus station is on the corner of Centre St and 3rd Ave. Buses run to Calgary three times a week and return the same days. See Organised Tours in the Calgary section for inexpensive trips to Drumheller.

HIGHWAY 22

This two lane road traverses the rolling foothills of the eastern Rockies. South of the Trans Canada Hwy (Hwy 1), Hwy 22 bisects vast ranchlands spread across the picturesque terrain. The 113km stretch between Longview and Hwy 3 west of Fort Macleod is especially scenic as it winds through the desolate heart of cowboy country.

Bar U Ranch National Historic Site

Near the village of Longview off Hwy 22, the Bar U (☎ 403-395-2212) marks the significance of ranching to the development of the west. There is a visitors centre, and guided tours around the range are offered daily. Many of the ranch's original buildings have been restored. Inquire about special events and demonstrations. Admission is $4.

CROWSNEST PASS

Farther west of Fort Macleod the Crowsnest Hwy (Hwy 3) heads through the prairies and into the Rocky Mountains to Crowsnest Pass (1396m) and the BC border. At the beginning of the 20th century this was a rich coal-producing region, which gave rise to a series of small mining towns. In 1903 one of these, Frank, was almost completely buried when part of nearby Turtle Mountain

collapsed and killed around 70 people. This and other mining disasters, plus a fall in demand for coal, eventually led to the demise of the coal industry, although a mine at Bellevue operated until 1961.

The **Frank Slide Interpretive Centre** (☎ 403-562-7388) overlooks the Crowsnest Valley 1.5km off the Crowsnest Hwy and 27km east of the provincial border. As well as displays on the cause and effects of the slide, it has exhibits on the coming of the railway and late 19th-early 20th century life and mining technology. It's open daily from 9 am to 8 pm from June to August and from 10 am to 4 pm the rest of the year. Admission is $4/2 for adults/children.

Coleman near the BC border is an example of the many communities in this area that once relied entirely on coal mining.

HEAD-SMASHED-IN BUFFALO JUMP

About 18km west of Fort Macleod, Head-Smashed-In Buffalo Jump (☎ 403-553-2731), on Spring Point Rd 16km off Hwy 2, is a World Heritage Site and the most significant attraction of southern Alberta. It's the oldest, biggest and best preserved bison-jump site in North America. For thousands of years Blackfoot used it to stampede bison over the edge of the cliff here. They then used the meat, hide, bone, horns and nearly everything else for their supplies and materials. Head-Smashed-In was one of a series of communal-kill sites and was last used for this purpose in the early 19th century. According to legend, a young brave wanted to view a killing from beneath the cliff but became trapped and was crushed by the falling bison, hence the name Head-Smashed-In.

The excellent interpretative centre, which is built into the hillside, provides explanations of the site and how the Blackfoot's work was achieved. There are nearly 2km of outdoor trails. A 10 minute film, a dramatised re-enactment of the buffalo hunt, is shown regularly during the day and sometimes Native people give lectures on the lives of their ancestors. The centre is open daily from 9 am to 7 pm from June to August and from 9 am to 5 pm the rest of the year. Admission is $6.50/3 for adults/children. Allow an hour for the trails and 1½ hours for the indoor displays. A snack bar serves bison, chicken and sandwiches. The site gets quite busy by late morning so arriving early is advisable; also you may see deer and more birds on the trails before the sun gets too hot. See Organised Tours in the Calgary section for tours to here.

FORT MACLEOD

On Oldman River about 50km west of Lethbridge, and two hours south of Calgary, is the town of Fort Macleod. The historic centre has many restored buildings.

Fort Macleod Museum (☎ 403-553-4703), 219 25th St, is a replica of the Northwest Mounted Police fort of 1874, the first in the region. Faux Mounties wearing traditional red uniforms ride around the fort four times a day in July and August. Inside there is a small local history collection. Admission is $4.50/2.50 for adults/children.

Fort Macleod is the home town of popular singer-songwriter Joni Mitchell.

LETHBRIDGE

Lethbridge on the Crowsnest Hwy is the largest town in southern Alberta, the third largest in the province and a centre for the local agricultural communities. The main streets are 5th and 6th Sts South and 3rd Ave South. One of the city's landmarks, High Level Bridge, is the world's longest and highest trestle railway bridge. Easily visible from Hwy 3, it spans the Oldman River Valley. The parkland along the Oldman contains 62km of walking and cycling trails. When you walk around town you'll see some people dressed in early 19th century clothing. These are Hutterites, members of a Protestant sect who live on collective farms and eschew many aspects of modern society.

Information

There are two visitor information centres (☎ 403-320-1222 or ☎ 1-800-661-1222) in Lethbridge. One is on Brewery Hill at the western end of 1st Ave South. The other is

at 2805 Scenic Drive South at the junction of Mayor Magrath Drive South. The latter is open daily from 9 am to 5 pm, and until 8 pm from June to August.

The main post office (☎ 403-320-7133) is at 704 4th Ave South on the corner of 7th St South. If you're interested in learning about Native Indian culture contact the Sik-Ooh-Kotok Friendship Society (☎ 403-328-2414 or ☎ 403-327-0087).

Things to See
The **Nikka Yuko Japanese Gardens** (☎ 403-328-3511), on the corner of 7th Ave South and Mayor Magrath Drive South, were built to symbolise Japanese-Canadian friendship. These authentic gardens consist of ponds, rocks and shrubs. The buildings and bridges were built in Japan and re-assembled here on the 1.6 hectare site. Young women in traditional Japanese costume greet you at the entrance and recite their oft-repeated descriptions. The gardens are open daily from 9 am to 8 pm from mid-May to early October; admission is $4/2 for adults/children.

On the western side of the city along Scenic Drive and beside Oldman River is **Indian Battle Park**, named after a famous battle between the Blackfoot and the Cree, the last battle in North America between Native Indians.

Within the park is **Fort Whoop-Up** (☎ 403-329-0444), a replica of Alberta's first and most notorious illegal whisky trading post. Around 25 of these outposts were set up in the province between 1869 and 1874 for the purpose of trading whisky, guns, ammunition and blankets for buffalo hides and furs from the Native Indians. Their existence led directly to the formation of the Northwest Mounted Police, who arrived in 1874 at Fort Macleod to bring law and order to the Canadian west.

You can tour the fort by a small train and there is an interpretive centre. Fort Whoop-Up is open Monday to Saturday from 10 am to 6 pm and on Sunday from noon to 5 pm during summer. It closes at 4 pm and all day Monday the rest of the year.

Admission is $2.50/1 for adults/children, and the train costs an extra $1/50¢.

Also in Indian Battle Park is the small **Sir Alexander Galt Museum** (☎ 403-320-3898), at the western end of 5th Ave South, displaying artefacts from Lethbridge history. It's open daily from 10 am to 4 pm and admission is free. Nearby, under the High Level Bridge, is the **Helen Schuler Coulee Centre and Nature Reserve** (☎ 403-320-3064), with a small exhibition centre and nature trails among the woods and coulees along the river. It's free, is quiet and cool and offers a range of flora and fauna. The trails are open from 7 am to 11 pm.

The **Alberta Birds of Prey Centre** (☎ 403-345-4262), about 10km east of Lethbridge off the Crowsnest Hwy in Coaldale, is the largest rehabilitation centre for injured predatory birds, such as owls, hawks and bald eagles. The admission fee of $4.75/4 helps wildlife conservation. Call for visiting times.

Places to Stay & Eat
The closest campgrounds to downtown are *Bridgeview Campground* (☎ 403-381-2357, 910 4th Ave South), off the Crowsnest Hwy north-west of town, and *Henderson Lake Campground* (☎ 403-328-5452) in Henderson Park off Parkside Drive (7th Ave South). Both have showers and laundries and charge $18 for a tent site.

The *YWCA* (☎ 403-329-0088, 604 8th St South) is for women only, has a laundry and gym and charges $22/40 for a single/double.

The *University of Lethbridge*, south-west of downtown over Oldman River, offers accommodation between May and August. Fully appointed apartments in Aperture Park cost from $18 for shared accommodation, with higher rates of around $50 for private rooms and $54 for family rooms. For details contact Housing Services (☎ 403-329-2244), University of Lethbridge, C420, 4401 University Drive, Lethbridge T1K 3M4.

Motels line Mayor Magrath Drive. *Parkside Inn* (☎ 403-328-2366 or ☎ 1-800-240-1471, 1009 Mayor Magrath Drive S) has simple singles/doubles from $45/50. The *Pepper Tree Inn* (☎ 403-328-4436, 1142

Mayor Magrath Drive S) is friendly and has well equipped rooms with fridges and VCRs from $50/60.

The moderately priced *Treat's Eatery (1104 Mayor Magrath Drive S)* is hugely popular with locals for its pasta platters and large sandwiches. The *Tumbleweed Cafe (707 9th Ave N)* is a good escape from franchise hell with its home-made soups, breads, sandwiches and vegetarian specials. You can stock up for the road at the *Safeway supermarket (2750 Fairway Plaza Rd)* off Mayor Magrath Drive South.

Getting There & Around
The Greyhound bus station (☎ 403-327-1551), 411 5th St S, has services to Regina and Calgary. For detailed information about local bus services call the Transit Infoline (☎ 403-320-3885).

CARDSTON
Cardston, 70km south-west of Lethbridge at the junction of Hwys 5 and 2, is a centre for the Mormons. The town, adjacent to the Blood Indian Reservation, gets its name from Charles Ora Card, who founded it in 1887. The huge, renovated, box-shaped **Alberta Temple** (☎ 403-653-4060), 348 3rd St W, was built in 1923. Although only Mormons can enter the temple, visitors can roam the grounds. The **Remington-Alberta Carriage Centre** (☎ 403-653-5139), south of Lee Creek off Main St, records the history of 19th and early 20th century horse-drawn transportation. It places the carriages in the context of the times and shows the vital role they played in society. The collection has 200 carriages, wagons and sleighs. The centre includes a museum, carriage factory, blacksmith and stable. It's open daily from 9 am to 8 pm in summer, closing at 5 pm the rest of the year. Admission is $5.50/3 for adults/children.

WRITING-ON-STONE PROVINCIAL PARK
This park (☎ 403-647-2364) is south-east of Lethbridge and close to the US border; the Sweetgrass Hills of northern Montana are visible to the south. To get to the park take Hwy 501 east of Hwy 4 from the town of Milk River, a distance of 42km. The park is named for the carvings and paintings made by the Plains Indians over 3000 years ago on the sandstone cliffs along the banks of Milk River. This is North America's largest collection of rock art.

You can see some of these **petroglyphs and pictographs** for yourself if you follow the 2km hoodoo trail along the north of the valley. But the best art is found in a restricted area (to protect it from vandalism) which you can only visit on a guided tour (free) with the park ranger. In the valley is a police outpost dating from 1887 which has been restored to its original condition.

The river is used for canoeing and swimming (there's even a small beach beside it) and in winter there's cross-country skiing. The park also provides a wide variety of habitats for wildlife, which includes more than 160 species of birds, 30 kinds of mammals, four kinds of amphibians and three kinds of reptiles, not to mention the fish in the river. The park is always open; the tours leave weekdays at 2 pm and on weekends at 10 am and 2 pm from mid-May to September. You can pick up free tickets from the naturalist's office one hour before tour time.

The *campground* by the river has sites for $13 with running water and is very popular on weekends.

On the way to the park from Lethbridge, dinosaur enthusiasts may want to stop at **Devil's Coulee** near Warner, where dinosaur nests and eggs were uncovered in 1987. There is an interpretative display and an active dig.

DINOSAUR PROVINCIAL PARK
This isn't Jurassic Park but, as a World Heritage Site, it's the next best thing. The 6 sq km Dinosaur Provincial Park (☎ 403-378-4344) is a 76.5-million-year-old dinosaur graveyard and is a must if you're passing by. It's roughly halfway between Calgary and Medicine Hat some 48km north-east of Brooks. From the Trans Canada Hwy (Hwy 1), take Hwy 36 or secondary road 873 to Hwy 544.

The badlands of the park are now a dry, convoluted lunar landscape, but at one time the area was a tropical rainforest on the shores of an inland sea where dinosaurs thrived. More than 300 complete skeletons have been found, and many now reside in museums around the world.

Entrance to the park is free and there are five interpretive hiking trails and a driving loop. Access to one-third of the park is restricted but there are guided walks through these strange, eroded landscapes and an interpretative two hour bus tour for $5. These popular excursions operate from late May to October and should be booked at the field station early on the day of departure.

The **Tyrell Museum Field Station** (☎ 403-378-4342) has four display areas where nearly complete skeletons have been uncovered, dusted off and encased in glass. Archaeologists are on hand to answer questions during summer. It's open daily from 8.15 am to 9 pm in summer and on weekdays only from 8.15 am to 4.30 pm the rest of the year. Admission is $2.

A full day can easily be spent exploring the park. Wildlife can be seen, wildflowers are abundant and good photographs are easily taken; the hoodoos especially make an excellent subject. Take plenty of water in summer (walking in the valley can be as hot as hell), a hat, sunscreen and insect repellent.

There are two good *campgrounds* in the park by a creek which makes a small, green oasis in this stark place. A tent site costs $11 and a laundry and hot showers are available. These sites fill up regularly, so you should phone (☎ 403-378-3700) for reservations. Motel accommodation is available in Brooks.

KINBROOK ISLAND PROVINCIAL PARK

This is a good camping spot on the way to or from Calgary. It's off the Trans Canada Hwy (Hwy 1), 13km south of Brooks, then 2km east off the secondary road 873 beside **Lake Newell**. This artificial lake is home to many species of waterfowl, including Canada geese, blue herons, cormorants and pelicans. You can swim and fish, or simply

escape the very flat, totally treeless stretch of highway between here and Medicine Hat. The *campground* (☎ 403-362-2962/4525) has 167 sites, running water, a store and many recreational programs. Sites cost $11.

MEDICINE HAT

This city, on the banks of the South Saskatchewan River and at the junction of the Trans Canada and Crowsnest highways, was formed in 1883, when the Canadian Pacific Railway, drilling for water, hit natural gas. Enough gas was subsequently found to prompt Rudyard Kipling to label it 'the city with all hell for a basement'. Even today the downtown street lamps are lit by gas.

The visitor information centre (☎ 403-527-6422 or ☎ 1-800-481-2822), 8 Gehring Rd SW, south of downtown off the westbound side of the Trans Canada Hwy, is open daily from 8 am to 9 pm in summer and from 9 am to 5 pm the rest of the year. The Greyhound bus station (☎ 403-527-4418), downtown at 557 2nd St SE, is open daily. It has left-luggage lockers and a cafeteria.

Most of the accommodation is along the Trans Canada Hwy. The *Super 8 Motel* (☎ 403-528-8888 or ☎ 1-800-800-8000, 1280 Trans Canada Hwy SE) has a pool and decent singles/doubles from $49/58. Nearby, *Rustler's (901 8th St SW)* is an atmospheric old-west place with huge breakfasts for under $5 and equally good chow the rest of the day.

From the visitor information centre or from the highway you can see the 'world's tallest tepee', a tribute to Native Indians. It's actually made of metal and was used ceremonially at the 1988 Winter Olympics in Calgary. There is a small cultural display and a trail around a Native Indian archaeological site by the teepee. Medicine Hat is also notable for its parks and walking trails, some of which line the South Saskatchewan River, and the fine, old red-brick buildings of downtown. If you miss Calgary's Stampede, there's one held here during the last weekend in July at the Exhibition & Stampede Grounds (☎ 403-527-1234), 5km south-east of downtown off 21st Ave SE.

ALBERTA

CYPRESS HILLS PROVINCIAL PARK

This park, an oasis of forest surrounded by seemingly endless prairie, straddles the Saskatchewan border off Hwy 41 south of the Trans Canada Hwy (Hwy 1). See the Saskatchewan chapter for details.

The Alberta Rockies

Much of the Rocky Mountains area of Alberta, running along the British Columbia border, is contained and protected within two huge, adjacent national parks, Banff to the south and Jasper to the north. The Icefields Parkway links the two, though there is no real boundary. Adjoining the southern boundary of Banff National Park is Kananaskis Country, an outdoor recreational area. To the south on the US border is the less visited Waterton Lakes National Park.

The entire area is one of spectacular beauty with some of the best scenery, climbing, hiking and skiing in the world. The national parks offer jagged, snow-capped mountains, peaceful valleys, rushing rivers, natural hot springs and alpine forests. The opaque emerald-green or milky-turquoise colour of many Rocky Mountains lakes will have you doubting your eyes. The parks also have both modern conveniences and backcountry trails to choose from, and wildlife abounds, particularly in Jasper National Park.

Banff National Park was Canada's first national park and is the best known and most popular. It covers an area of 6641 sq km and contains 25 mountains of 3000m or more in height. The skiing and climbing are world-famous. Jasper National Park is larger, wilder and less explored but, like Banff, offers excellent hiking trails. Waterton Lakes National Park, the smallest of the three, contains wildlife, scenery and activities to match its northern neighbours.

To preserve the region, the Canada Parks Service controls the impact of visitors by designating specific park areas for campgrounds, picnic sites, service centres and town sites. The *Backcountry Visitors' Guide*

has a section on how to minimise your effect on the parks' environment.

The small town sites of Banff, Lake Louise, Jasper, Canmore and Waterton act as focal points for orientation, supplies and information. In Banff National Park, accommodation during summer is expensive and hard to find. It's worth booking ahead or staying in one of the towns outside the park, such as Canmore in Alberta or Field, Golden, Radium Hot Springs, Windermere or Invermere in British Columbia, and making day trips.

Information

On entering Banff and Jasper national parks you will be given an excellent booklet with information and maps about all the parks, as well as Kootenay and Yoho national parks in BC.

Fees There is a fee to enter the parks. Passes are sold to individuals, no matter how they arrive in the park. Rates for adults/seniors/children are $5/4/2.50 for one day; the passes are good until 4 pm the following day. A Great Western Annual Pass is also available, entitling the bearer to unlimited admission to all 11 national parks in western Canada for one year. Rates are $35/27/18 and you can upgrade your day pass to one of these. For more information, call ☎ 1-800-748-7275.

There are also backcountry hiking and wilderness camping fees of $6 per night with a maximum charge of $30. Passes are available from all the park visitors centres. Note that there may be a limit on the number of backcountry passes to some popular areas. Check with the relevant park visitors centre for details.

Precautions In the backcountry you should boil all water for at least 10 minutes before drinking it, due to the risk of catching 'beaver fever', or giardiasis. This is caused by an intestinal parasite spread by animal waste.

If you're heading into wilderness regions, read the pamphlet *You are in Bear Country*, which gives advice on how to steer clear of bears and what to do if this becomes un-

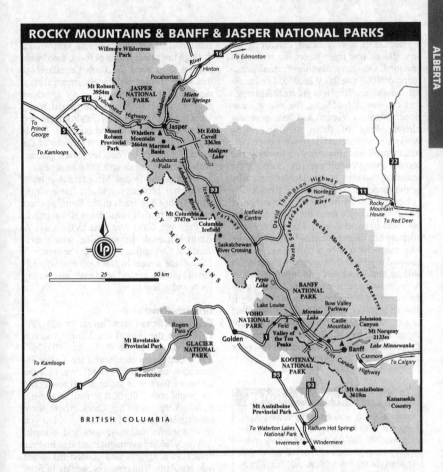

ROCKY MOUNTAINS & BANFF & JASPER NATIONAL PARKS

avoidable. You can get a copy from the visitor information centres.

The trails heavily used by horse trips are a real mess; long-distance hikers will want to avoid them. Ask at the park-warden offices or the visitor information centres about which trails are used most by the horses.

Tenters should note that pretty well all the campgrounds in and around the Rockies are covered in pebbles or stones, so a sleeping pad or foam mattress is essential. Also, you can expect to bend or snap a few tent pegs.

BANFF

Banff, 138km west of Calgary, is Canada's No 1 resort town in both winter and summer and as such is really the centre of the Rockies. The town is neat and pleasant, and its surroundings unbeatable. It makes a good rest spot after travelling or camping in the backcountry. On the other hand, if you're keen to get exploring it's a fine base for a range of day trips and hikes. Stores sell or rent out skiing, hiking and camping equipment and supplies.

Despite attracting several million visitors a year, Banff is very small, consisting essentially of one main street, so it can get crowded. On many days the normal population of 7000 swells by 25,000. The heaviest months are July and August. Although this can cause problems, the many vacationers create a relaxed and festive atmosphere. Many of those smiling young workers in and around town were once visitors themselves, now enjoying low pay and squalid living conditions (the housing for seasonal workers is regularly decried by health inspectors) to live in the Rockies.

Constrained by its place inside the park, Banff has recently been the scene of major conflicts over its future. The federal government has decreed that only those people who can demonstrate a valid need will be allowed to live in the town, those that don't will be taken to court and made to move. Also, moves are afoot to begin buying up the commercial part of town and tearing it down for government buildings. Needless to say, these plans from Ottawa are not popular with locals. With Banff's popularity continuing to grow, the debate will only intensify.

The Ultimate Mountain Man

Entering Banff, you'll see the town's signs adorned with the image of a rugged looking man. It's Bill Peyto, a legendary character who explored much of the wilderness around Banff. From his arrival from England in 1886, his exploits in the high peaks were matched by his hijinks around town. His cabin featured a set bear trap to thwart burglars, he brought a wild lynx into a bar, then sat back with a drink while chaos reigned, and more. Generally regarded as the hardiest of the hardy breed who first settled high in the Rockies, he died in 1943 at age 75. In his honour, one of the region's most beautiful lakes is named for him as well as a glacier and, perhaps most appropriately, a bar in Banff, Wild Bills.

Orientation

Banff Ave, the main street, runs north-south through the whole length of town, then heads north-east to meet the Trans Canada Hwy. The street is lined with hotels, stores, restaurants and souvenir shops, many of which cater to the heavy Japanese tourist trade. Over the bridge at Banff Ave's southern end is the Parks Administration building. This is a good place for a view and a photo of the town. Behind the building are flower gardens with a stream, ponds and a few benches.

South of the bridge Mountain Ave leads to Sulphur Mountain and the hot springs, while Spray Ave leads to the Banff Springs Hotel, the town's most famous landmark. To the west, Cave Ave goes to the Cave & Basin National Historic Site, which contains the first springs found in the area.

The side streets in town are mainly residential but the central ones also have eating spots and a few shops.

Information

Tourist Offices Parks Canada (☎ 403-762-1550) and the Banff/Lake Louise Tourism Bureau (☎ 403-762-8421, fax 403-762-8545) both have counters in the visitor information centre at 224 Banff Ave, near the corner of Wolf St in the centre of town (add the postal code T0L 0C0 to mail inquiries). Before doing any hiking, check in here; there are detailed maps and the staff will tell you about specific trail conditions and hazards. Anybody hiking overnight must sign in. Free naturalist programs and guided hikes are held regularly. The centre is open daily from 8 am to 8 pm from June to September and from 9 am to 5 pm the rest of the year.

Money You can change money at the Foreign Currency Exchange (☎ 403-762-4698) in the Clock Tower Village Mall, 112 Banff Ave. It is open daily from 9 am to 9 pm.

Post & Communications The main post office (☎ 403-762-2586), 204 Buffalo St, on the corner of Bear St at the southern end of downtown, is open Monday to Friday from 9 am to 5.30 pm. Back Alley Net Surf (☎ 403-

760-0854), in the Bear St Mall at 220 Bear St, is one of several Internet cafés around town. It charges $3 for 15 minutes.

Bookshops & Libraries The Book & Art Den (☎ 403-762-3919), 94 Banff Ave, is an excellent bookshop in new and comfortable quarters. It has all manner of guides and books on the mountains, hiking, canoeing and history of the area.

The modern public library (☎ 403-762-2661) is at 101 Bear St opposite the post office. It charges $1 for 15 minutes of limited Internet access.

Laundry Johnny O's Emporium (☎ 403-762-5111), open daily at 223 Bear St, makes doing the chore a little more agreeable as it has a TV lounge, restaurant and pinball games.

Medical Services Mineral Springs Hospital (☎ 403-762-2222) is on Bow Ave near the corner of Wolf St.

Emergency For problems in the backcountry, the Banff Warden Office (☎ 403-762-1470, in emergencies ☎ 403-762-4506) is open 24 hours year-round. In town, for police emergencies dial ☎ 762-2226; for medical and fire emergencies dial ☎ 762-2000.

Dangers & Annoyances The police are very strict in Banff and after 1 am cars are often checked for drunk drivers and drugs. The fines are heavy. Drinking on the street or even carrying an open beer can or bottle is illegal. Don't leave valuables in cars day or night.

As for all those photogenic elk you may see wandering the streets, remember they are wild animals and will charge if they feel threatened. Every year people are attacked and it's advisable to stay 100m away particularly during the autumn rutting and spring calving seasons.

Work Employment is usually easy to come by in and around Banff in the hotels, bars, restaurants and ski areas. However, working without a permit has become more difficult for non-Canadians and many establishments are asking for proper documentation. If you want to be absolutely sure of being able to earn some money, inquiring at home for the correct visa is advisable.

Some employers offer accommodation, but don't expect great wages. At some of the hotels accommodation may be included or offered at modest rates. Look for classified advertisements in the local newspaper *Crag & Canyon* and for signs in the windows around town.

Museums

Banff Park Museum The park museum (☎ 403-762-1558), 93 Banff Ave, by the Bow River Bridge at the southern end of town, is in an old wooden building dating from 1903. The museum has been declared a National Historic Site and contains a collection of animals, birds and plants found in Banff National Park. Included are two small stuffed grizzlies and a black bear so you can study the difference. There's also an 1841 graffiti-carved tree. The museum is open daily from 10 am to 6 pm in summer (from 1 to 5 pm the rest of the year) and admission is $2.25/1.25 for adults/children. At 11 am and 3 pm daily there is a free half-hour tour.

Whyte Museum of the Canadian Rockies The Whyte Museum complex (☎ 403-762-2291), 111 Bear St, between Buffalo and Caribou Sts, contains an art gallery and a vast collection of photographs telling the history of the area. The archives also contain manuscripts, oral history tapes and maps. On the property are four log cabins and two Banff heritage homes, one dating from 1907 and the other from 1931. There are guided tours, including one of the heritage homes, Tuesday to Sunday. The museum foundation presents films, lectures and concerts regularly. This must-see site is open daily from 10 am to 6 pm. Admission is $3/2.

Luxton Buffalo Nations Museum This museum (☎ 403-762-2388), 1 Birch Ave, in the fort-like wooden building to the right as you head south over the bridge is worth a

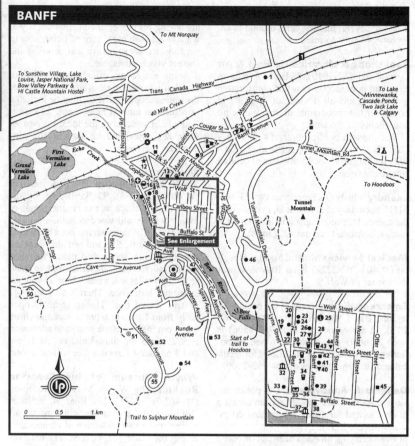

BANFF

To Mt Norquay

To Sunshine Village, Lake
Louise, Jasper National Park,
Bow Valley Parkway &
HI Castle Mountain Hostel

Trans Canada Highway

1

40 Mile Creek

Marmot Cres

Cougar St

6·5 4

Banff Avenue

8

Echo Creek

Squirrel St

Elk St

10

11

3

To Lake
Minnewanka,
Cascade Ponds,
Two Jack Lake
& Calgary

First
Vermilion
Lake

Grand
Vermilion
Lake

Tunnel Mountain Rd

2

Gopher St

Marten St

Moose St

9

12

13

14

15

16

17

18

Wolf St

Caribou Street

Buffalo St

Bow Ave

Birch Ave

See Enlargement

Grizzly St

St Julien Rd

Tunnel Mountain Drive

Tunnel
Mountain

To Hoodoos

Marsh Loop

Cave   Avenue

Birch Ave

49

47

48

46

Ave

Glen Avenue

Bow

River

Bow
Falls

50

Spray Avenue

Kootenay Ave

Park

Mountain Avenue

51

52

Rundle
Avenue

53

Start of
trail to
Hoodoos

54

55

0   0.5   1 km

Trail to Sulphur Mountain

Enlargement:

Wolf   Street

20

23

24

26

i 25

28

19

21

27

44

43

22

30

29

Caribou Street

31

42

41

40

32

34

Lynx Street

Bear Street

Banff Avenue

Beaver Street

Muskrat Street

Otter Street

33

39

35·36

Buffalo Street

45

37

38

visit. It deals mainly with the Native Indians of the Northern Plains and the Rockies but also covers indigenous groups from all over Alberta. The museum has life-sized displays, models and re-creations depicting aspects of their traditional cultures. Note the woven porcupine quills, the old photographs and the human scalp as well as the stuffed animals. The museum is open daily from 9 am to 7 pm in summer and Wednesday to Sunday from 12.30 to 5.30 pm the rest of the year. Admission is $5.50/2.25.

Natural History Museum This private museum (☎ 403-762-4652) on the 2nd floor of the Clock Tower Village Mall at 112 Banff Ave has displays on early life forms, including Canadian dinosaurs. It features a model of the notorious Sasquatch, the abominable snowman of the Rockies. This character is said to be about 3m tall and to have been sighted more than 500 times. Of course, many of those who claim sightings also claim to have been abducted by aliens. The museum is open daily from

BANFF

PLACES TO STAY		
2	Tunnel Mountain Village	
	Campground	
3	Banff Hostel	
5	Spruce Grove Motel	
7	Irwin's Mountain Inn	
8	Red Carpet Inn	
9	Traveller's Inn	
11	C Riva's Place	
13	Holiday Lodge	
42	Mt Royal Hotel	
45	Tan-Y-Bryn	
47	YWCA	
52	Rimrock Resort Hotel	
53	Banff Springs Hotel	

PLACES TO EAT	
4	Bumper's Beef House
6	The Pines
19	Melissa's Restaurant
27	Evelyn's Coffee Bar
38	Grizzly House

30	Coyote's
40	Welch's Chocolate Shop
44	Aardvark Pizza & Sub

OTHER	
1	Banff Warden Office
10	Train Station
12	Police Station
14	Safeway Supermarket
15	Mineral Springs Hospital
16	Brewster Bus Station
17	Canoe Dock
18	Park n' Pedal
20	Johnny O's Emporium
21	Canadian Mountain Holidays
22	Banff Adventures Unlimited
23	Mountain Magic
24	Bear St Mall
25	Visitor Information Centre
26	Sundance Mall
29	Wild Bill's
31	Outabounds

32	Whyte Museum of the
	Canadian Rockies
33	Public Library
34	Barbary Coast
35	Main Post Office
36	Harmony Drug
37	Banff Park Museum
38	Book & Art Den
39	Clock Tower Village Mall
41	Trail Riders Store
43	Rose & Crown
46	Banff Centre
48	Parks Administration
	Building
49	Luxton Buffalo Nations
	Museum
50	Cave & Basin National
	Historic Site
51	Middle Springs
54	Sulpher Mountain Gondola
	Terminal
55	Upper Hot Springs

10 am to 10 pm in summer; admission is free.

Banff Centre

The Banff Centre (☎ 403-762-6300) on St Julien Rd, east of downtown, contains one of Canada's best known art schools with facilities for dance, theatre, music and the visual arts. Exhibits, concerts and various other events are presented regularly. Throughout summer during the Festival of the Arts, students, together with internationally recognised artists, present works in workshops and performances. Events are held most days and some are free. The visitor information centre has a complete schedule.

Harmony Drug

In this working drugstore (☎ 403-762-5711), 111 Banff Ave, take a look at the photos dating from about 1915, all around the ceiling. Some were taken by Byron Harmon, who once owned the drugstore and ran a photography business. Many of the business's early photos are for sale around town and reproduced in books or as postcards.

Sulphur Mountain Gondola

The Sulphur Mountain gondola (☎ 403-762-2523) runs to the summit and provides spectacular views over the surrounding mountains, Bow River and Banff town site from an altitude of 2285m. You can walk up in about 1¼ hours if you don't pause to look at the scenery, and will be rewarded with a free lift down; tickets are only needed going up.

The lower terminal is just over 3km south of Banff on Mountain Ave, near the Upper Hot Springs. To get there, you can hitch fairly easily or take the Brewster bus from town. The walking path starts under the gondola cables. The gondola runs daily from 7.30 am to 9 pm in summer and from 1 to 5 pm in winter. Tickets are $14/7 for adults/children.

Cave & Basin National Historic Site

This is the birthplace of Banff. The discovery of hot sulphur springs in a cave here led to the creation of Banff National Park. The swimming pool and complex (☎ 403-762-1557), south-west of town at the end of Cave Ave, has been rebuilt to the original style of 1914 but there is no bathing at the

site. Visitors can see (and smell) the cave and sulphurous waters as well as view exhibits and a film. It's open daily from 9 am to 6 pm from June to early September and from 9.30 am to 5 pm the rest of the year. Admission is $2.25/1.25.

The attractive grounds can be strolled around for no charge and both natural and artificially made pools can be seen. It's a good place for picnics as there are tables, a fine view and a snack bar. Several pleasant short **walks** begin here: the 400m Discovery Trail, the 2.7km Marsh Loop and the 3.7km Sundance Trail.

Upper Hot Springs

There is a soothing hot pool and steam room at the Upper Hot Springs spa (☎ 403-762-1515), 3km south of town near Sulphur Mountain. You can also get a massage. Admission to the pool is $5 and you can rent bathing suits ($1.50) and towels ($1). In summer the busy hot springs are open daily from 9 am to 11 pm and from 10 am to 10 pm the rest of the year.

Lake Minnewanka

Lake Minnewanka, the largest reservoir in the national park, is 11km east of Banff town site. It is a scenic recreational area surrounded by forests and mountains with hiking, swimming, sailing, boating and fishing available. Lake Minnewanka Boat Tours (☎ 403-762-3473) has a 1½ hour cruise on the lake to Devil's Gap for $20.

Activities

Hiking There are many good short hikes and day walks around the Banff area. The visitor information centre has *Drives & Walks*, which describes trails in and around Banff. For longer, more remote hiking, the excellent brochure *Backcountry Visitors' Guide* has a simple map showing trails in the whole park. Some good walks begin more or less right in town, like those to Tunnel Mountain and the hoodoos; others begin a little farther out.

You can take a pleasant, quiet stroll by **Bow River** just three blocks west of Banff Ave beside Bow Ave. The trail runs from the corner of Wolf St, along the river under the Bow River Bridge and ends shortly after on Buffalo St. If you cross the bridge, you can continue south-west through the woods along a trail to **Bow Falls** – it's not far.

For a good short climb to break in your legs and to view the town and area, walk up stubby **Tunnel Mountain** east of the downtown area. There's a trail leading up from St Julien Rd; you can drive here, but it's not a long walk from downtown to the start of the path. From the southern end of Buffalo St a trail between Bow River and Tunnel Mountain heads north and east to the **hoodoos**.

Just west of downtown off Mt Norquay Rd is the 2km **Fenland Trail** loop which goes through marsh and forest and connects the town with First Vermilion Lake.

If you follow Banff Ave north and north-east from town towards Lake Minnewanka for about 5km you come to **Cascade Ponds**, just past the Trans Canada Hwy. There you can follow the trail north to join the **Bankhead Interpretative Trail** or climb up beside the waterfall for good views.

One good hike that's not difficult is the **Johnston Canyon Trail**. The canyon is 25km north-west of Banff on the Bow Valley Parkway (Hwy 1A) that branches off from, and later rejoins, the Trans Canada Hwy en route to Lake Louise. The 12km trail passes many waterfalls, including two large ones, and leads to some underground-fed crystal-clear, blue-green pools known as the Ink Pots. Here in the meadow is an ideal picnic spot. The first 2.7km of the trail is along catwalks and is busy as it winds through the woods by the falls; it is well worthwhile as a short walk on its own. Along the Bow Valley Parkway watch for impressive **Castle Mountain** in the distance; it's a huge piece of rock which catches the late-afternoon light. From Castle Mountain you can follow the **Rockbound Lake Trail**, which is 18km return, takes about six to seven hours and has some strenuous patches. The trailhead is opposite Castle Mountain Hostel.

Sunshine Village is a quiet and beautiful place that's well worth visiting for its scenic lakes and long and short trails. On one trail

you can walk across the boundary into British Columbia. A popular trail is the overnight trip to nearby **Egypt Lake**. From Sunshine Village it's a long, steady climb with great scenery over **Healy Pass**, including views to Mt Assiniboine (3618m) in British Columbia. You'll see lots of butterflies and flowers in the alpine meadows.

Another popular trip is to **Sunshine Meadows**, a 5km hike from the Sunshine Village parking lot. White Mountain Adventures (☎ 403-678-4099) runs buses to the meadows from Banff ($35) or the parking lot ($17). You can take hikes to the higher lakes and fish for cut-throat trout. At the lakes is a basic hut that sleeps about 10 people, but you should register in Banff before you go because it may be booked out. There's tenting around the hut, so a place inside is not essential. **Mt Norquay** offers good hiking trails.

Swimming & Fishing Johnson Lake, north-east of town off Lake Minnewanka Rd, is ideal for whiling away an afternoon and is the only swimmable lake in the park. The shallow water gets warm enough for a dip, there are picnic tables by the shore and you can even cast a line here and there by following one of the lakeside paths. On the far side there's a rope hanging from a tree, which you can use to swing out over the water just like Huckleberry Finn. See also the Lake Minnewanka entry earlier.

People wishing to fish should get a permit at the visitors centre. Permits cost $6 and are good for one week.

Canoeing & Rafting You can go canoeing on **Two Jack Lake** north-east of Banff, the **Vermilion Lakes** (which have lots of wildlife) west of town, **Echo Creek**, **40 Mile Creek** and **Bow River**. Rocky Mountain Raft Tours (☎ 403-762-3632) rents out canoes for $13/39 per hour/day from Canoe Dock by the river on the corner of Bow Ave and Wolf St. It also has a one hour rafting tour on the Bow River from Bow Falls to the hoodoos for $24.

Numerous companies offer whitewater rafting. Wet 'N Wild (☎ 1-800-668-9119) has exciting trips down the Kicking Horse River

from Golden (in BC). Half-day trips are $52, full-day trips are $74 with lunch and transport from Banff. Kootenay River Runners (☎ 403-762-5385 or ☎ 1-800-599-4399) has half-day ($49) and full-day trips ($75) on the Kootenay River. For a more sedate journey, Manachaban River Tours (☎ 403-678-6535) has two-hour float trips on the Bow River ($39).

Cycling You can cycle on the highways and on some of the trails in the park. Contact the visitor information centre for trail conditions and permits. Excursions for a few hours, a day or several days with overnight stops at campgrounds, hostels or lodges are possible. Cycling is not allowed off the trails. Two good, short cycling routes close to Banff are along **Vermilion Lakes Drive** and **Tunnel Mountain Drive**. For a longer trip the scenic, 24km **Bow Valley Parkway** connecting Banff and Lake Louise is very popular.

For bicycle rentals see the Getting Around section later.

Horse Riding In Banff the most popular routes are south of Bow River on the trail beside **Spray River**, the **Marsh Loop**, the **Sundance Trail**, the trail alongside **Cave Ave** and the one to **Middle Springs**. Holidays on Horseback, operated by Warner Guiding & Outfitting (☎ 403-762-4551) in the Trail Riders Store at 132 Banff Ave, offers horse-riding trips from one hour to one week in length. Rates start at $20 per hour.

Climbing Quite a few companies offer climbing courses and organised tours into the mountains. Mountain Magic (☎ 403-762-2591), 224 Bear St, has classes for $15 per person for groups of four, and outdoor classes from $60. Experienced climbers can use the indoor climbing wall free of charge.

Banff Alpine Guides (☎ 403-678-6091) offers climbing instruction and guided climbs from $250 a day but you really need your own group.

In Canmore, Yamnuska (☎ 403-678-4164), 1316 Railway Ave, offers a lengthy list of mountaineering adventures for all skill levels around Banff and throughout the Canadian

Rockies. A basic week-long course in mountaineering costs $990. Also in Canmore, the Alpine Club of Canada (☎ 403-678-3200) can provide information and/or a guide.

Skiing Three of the finest ski centres in Canada are in Banff and Lake Louise. They have runs for skiers of all abilities and run shuttle buses from Banff. The least expensive, most convenient ski holiday is a package which includes accommodation, lift passes and various extras. The three areas (general information ☎ 403-762-4561) have multiday tickets good for each. Three-day lift tickets cost $152, with each additional day costing roughly $50.

Mt Norquay, 9km north of Banff along Mt Norquay Rd, has difficult runs and moguls and offers night skiing. The season is from early December to April. A day pass is $35. For information and snow reports contact Mt Norquay (☎ 403-762-4421, ski report ☎ 403-221-8259), PO Box 1258, Banff T0L 0C0.

Sunshine Village, 22km north-west of Banff, has tonnes of natural snow, which means the ski season lasts about seven months from mid-November to late May. It has 82 runs, 55% intermediate and one which is 8km long. A day pass is $50. For information contact Sunshine Village (☎ 403-762-6500, ski report ☎ 403-762-6543), PO Box 1510, Banff T0L 0C0.

For details on the Lake Louise ski area, see the Lake Louise section later in this chapter.

Ski Rental There are numerous rental shops in Banff, and Banff/Lake Louise Tourism maintains a list. Prices for a complete package of skis, boots and other equipment average about $20 a day. Protective clothing, snowboarding and cross-country skiing equipment are also widely available. Mountain Magic (☎ 403-762-2591), 224 Bear St, rents out ski packages for $15 to $27 a day and snowboarding packages for $30 a day. Rude Boy's (☎ 403-762-8480), on the lower level of the Sundance Mall on Banff Ave, is the best place for snowboard rental (packages are $29) and sales and it sells some pretty salacious T-shirts.

Heli-Skiing Canadian Mountain Holidays (CMH; ☎ 403-762-7100 or ☎ 1-800-661-0252), 217 Bear St, specialises in four to 10-day heli-skiing trips to some of the best and most remote areas in the western mountain ranges. These superb trips are in the $5000 range. RK Heli-Ski (in Banff ☎ 403-762-3771, otherwise ☎ 1-800-661-6060) has one-day trips from $510 as well as longer packages. Both companies use ski areas in BC.

Organised Tours

Brewster Gray Line (☎ 403-762-6767) has a three hour tour of Banff for $40. The bus goes to the hoodoos, Bow Falls, Tunnel Mountain Drive, Buffalo Paddock and Sulphur Mountain.

Brewster also runs tours to Lake Louise, the Columbia Icefield and Jasper. The tour to Lake Louise goes via the Vermilion Lakes and Bow Valley Parkway, stopping at Johnston Canyon and Castle Mountain. The return trip takes four hours and costs $45, or $36 one way. The tour to the Columbia Icefield in Jasper National Park takes approximately 9½ hours one way and costs $81. To Jasper takes 9½ hours, stopping at Lake Louise, then along the Icefields Parkway, stopping at the Columbia Icefield with time allowed for a ride on the Athabasca Glacier (not included in the price). The one-way fare is $81; a return trip costs $112 and you must spend the night in Jasper, with an extra charge for accommodation. All these rates are about 25% cheaper outside the peak season.

True North Tours (☎ 403-912-0407 or ☎ 1-888-464-4842) runs good three and six-day low-cost adventure bus trips between Calgary, Banff and Jasper. For details see Organised Tours in the Calgary section. Bookings can also be arranged through the HI hostel in Banff. In midsummer, two to three weeks advance registration is advised.

Helicopter tours offering spectacular views of the park are also available. Some popular sights are Mt Assiniboine, the Goat and Sundance mountain ranges, Hidden Glacier and the Three Sisters. Alpine Helicopters (☎ 403-678-4802) is one of several

ALBERTA

companies based in Canmore. Rates start at $110 for a 25 minute flight.

Places to Stay

Accommodation is fairly costly and, in summer, hard to find. The old adage of arriving early to find accommodation really holds true and booking ahead is strongly recommended. The numerous hotels and motels can be expensive during the summer high season. If you're not camping or hostelling, B&Bs and private tourist homes can be a reasonable alternative, as well as being good sources of local information.

Banff/Lake Louise Tourism tracks vacancies on a daily basis at the visitor information centre.

Some people stay in Canmore or Golden (in BC) just outside the park, where the rates are lower, and then enter the park on a day-trip basis.

Camping There are many campgrounds in the area around Banff. Most are only open between May or June and September. They are all busy in July and August, and availability is on a first-come, first-served basis, so check in by noon or you may be turned away. Campgrounds with showers always fill up first.

Tunnel Mountain Village is not bad. Tunnel Mountain is close to town and has three sites with showers, two for RVs only and one for tents at $16 per site. At night you may hear coyotes howling. At Two Jack Lake there are two campgrounds. *Two Jack Lakeside*, 12km north-east of Banff on Lake Minnewanka Rd, is open from July to early September and charges $16 per site. About 1km north, *Two Jack Lake Main* has 381 sites at $13 each. Both campgrounds have running water but no showers. Along the Bow Valley Parkway there is a *campground* at Johnston Canyon, about 26km west of Banff, charging $16 with showers. It's wooded and secluded, though trains whistle by at night. *Castle Mountain*, 2km north of Castle Junction, charges $13 per site.

There are those who unfold sleeping bags anywhere in the woods surrounding Banff,

including just up the road towards Sulphur Mountain. If you do this *don't ever* light a fire or use the food bag for a pillow. Who knows what animal is on the prowl?

Hostels The HI *Banff Hostel* (☎ 403-762-4122, fax 403-762-3441, banff@Hostelling Intl.ca) on Tunnel Mountain Rd, 3km from the downtown area, has 154 beds in small rooms, a cafeteria, laundry and a common room with a fireplace. Rates are $19/23 for members/nonmembers. This hostel handles reservations and inquiries for all the other HI hostels in the region (except Lake Louise), including the seasonal ones along the Icefields Parkway. The HI *Castle Mountain Hostel* on the Bow Valley Parkway holds up to 36 people, has pit toilets, hot showers and volleyball courts. Rates are $12/16.

The *YWCA* (☎ 403-762-3560, 102 Spray Ave) is central, its facilities have been upgraded and it has been dubbed the 'Y Mountain Lodge'. It takes both men and women, can hold up to 60 people and has a cafeteria and cooking facilities. Dorm beds are $19 and rooms are $49/52 without/with bath.

B&Bs & Tourist Homes Banff/Lake Louise Tourism in the visitor information centre has a list of B&Bs and tourist-home accommodation. It can be contacted at 224 Banff Ave, PO Box 1298, Banff, Alberta T0L 0C0. Some places rent out rooms in houses or small separate cabins.

The prices for B&Bs and tourist homes vary depending on size and facilities, your duration of stay and the season, but are generally in the $25 to $80 range for a single or double. Banff has quite a few such places but you should check around first. Some prefer at least a week's stay and some prefer not to take young people.

C Riva's Place (☎ 403-762-3431, 328 Elk St) has one room ($60) and one cabin ($80) with accommodation for up to eight people. *Tan-Y-Bryn* (☎ 403-762-3696, 118 Otter St) has room for 20 people in eight rooms. The cost is $30 to $50 all year.

Marten St has several tourist homes. *Holiday Lodge (☎ 403-762-3648, 311 Marten St)* is one of the nicest in town. Rooms cost from \$55 to \$85.

Hotels & Motels Banff has no cheap hotels or motels. There are about 20 places lining Banff Ave north of Elk St; they are generally fairly large and cater to tour groups as well as having numerous facilities like saunas and hot tubs. There are many places geared for skiers which offer kitchens and can be good value for groups of four or more.

The cheapest motel in town is *Spruce Grove Motel (☎ 403-762-2112, 545 Banff Ave)*, with standard rooms with satellite TV from \$40/70 in the low/high season. *Red Carpet Inn (☎ 403-762-4184 or ☎ 1-800-563-4609, 425 Banff Ave)* is close to town and charges \$55/110. It has a licensed restaurant and spa and is usually full in summer. Close by, *Irwin's Mountain Inn (☎ 403-762-4566 or ☎ 1-800-661-1721, 429 Banff Ave)* has covered parking and a sauna and charges \$60/120.

The *Traveller's Inn (☎ 403-762-4401 or ☎ 1-800-661-0227, 401 Banff Ave)* is close to the centre and has friendly staff. The rooms feature large balconies and the hotel has heated underground parking. Rates are from \$85/175. *Rimrock Resort Hotel (☎ 403-762-3356 or ☎ 1-800-661-1587)* is 4km out of town on Sulphur Mountain Road next to the Upper Hot Springs. This large resort has excellent mountain views and large, luxurious rooms from \$135/225.

The historic *Banff Springs Hotel (☎ 403-762-2211 or ☎ 1-800-441-1414)* is on Spray Ave, 2km south of downtown. Since it was completed in the 1920s, this 800 room baronial palace has posed for thousands of postcards and millions of snapshots. Within its thick granite walls are myriad public spaces, bars and restaurants. Even if you're not staying here, it's a fascinating place to wander around. In summer high season rooms start at \$390 and are often booked well in advance. At other times however, you might find deals closer to \$100 a night.

Places to Eat

Like any resort town, Banff has plenty of restaurants. However, there are those that cater only to tourists who aren't likely to return, and there are those sought out even by discriminating locals. We've listed the latter below.

Places to Eat – Budget

For reasonably priced meals try *Café Alpenglow* in the HI Banff Hostel, which even attracts longtime residents for its 'awesome' breakfasts from \$4.

Evelyn's Coffee Bar (☎ 403-762-0352), in the Town Centre Mall on Banff Ave, is the best local coffee place and has good sandwiches and an excellent bakery. On the upper level of the Sundance Mall, the *Fossil Face Café (☎ 403-760-8219)* serves healthy and organic soups, salads, sandwiches, hot dishes and desserts. A lunch is \$6 and it's a nice place to sit and write a postcard.

Shiki Japanese Restaurant (☎ 403-762-0527, 10 Banff Ave), in the Clock Tower Village Mall, serves large and warming ramen soups for \$7 in an unadorned setting.

For those of you who would rather be eating chocolate, go to *Welch's Chocolate Shop (126 Banff Ave)*, a local institution. It's great for energy on the trails and, besides, you're burning off calories, right? *Aardvark Pizza & Sub (☎ 403-762-5500, 304A Caribou St)* has the best delivered pizza in town. You can get a medium pizza oozing with cheese for \$10. *Safeway (☎ 403-723-3929, 318 Marten St)*, just off Banff Ave, is the best supermarket. It has numerous prepared foods good for picnics, or for preparing at your accommodation.

Places to Eat – Mid-Range

Melissa's Restaurant (☎ 403-762-5511, 217 Lynx St), near the corner of Caribou St, looks sort of like a wood cabin inside and sort of like an English cottage outside. The menu includes pizza, burgers, steaks and seafood with main dishes between \$8 to \$20. It has a bar and is open daily from 7 am to 10 pm. The breakfasts are popular.

Every local we talked to raved about *Coyote's* (☎ 403-762-3963, 206 Caribou St). It's easy to see why, with inventive south-western cuisine served in a hip and lively setting. Main courses average about $15 and the menu changes continually. If you want to see the chefs in action, sit at the counter. It serves breakfast, lunch and dinner, when it's a good idea to book.

Cilantro (☎ 403-760-3008), on Tunnel Mountain Rd near the hostel, is in a log cabin and specialises in fresh food prepared with seasonal ingredients. Salads, sandwiches and pastas are all popular. The gourmet pizzas are a treat and cost from $12.

Places to Eat – Top End
Grizzly House (☎ 403-762-4055, 207 Banff Ave) is open until midnight and is another local institution. It's rather dark and the booths are secluded, which contributes to the romantic atmosphere. The menu centres on fondue, and you and your partner can dip away to your heart's content. Prices average about $25 before wine from the vast cellar.

Bumper's Beef House (☎ 403-762-2622, 603 Banff Ave), north of downtown behind a service station, serves good prime rib, barbecued ribs and steaks for around $18. There's a very good salad bar and the atmosphere is very relaxed.

The Pines (☎ 403-760-6690, 537 Banff Ave), in Rundlestone Lodge, is probably the finest restaurant in town. Fresh Canadian ingredients such as salmon and venison are artistically crafted in dishes that average $17 to $25 for mains. This is another place where it's best to book.

Entertainment
Banff is the social and cultural focus of the Rockies. You can find current listings in the weekly *Banff Crag & Canyon* newspaper or the monthly *Wild Life*.

The *Banff Centre* (☎ 403-762-6300) on St Julien Rd presents movies, theatre and concerts throughout the year, but especially from June to late August during the Festival of the Arts, when it puts on over 80 performances.

The *Rose & Crown* (☎ 403-762-2121, 202 Banff Ave), on the corner of Caribou St, is a British-style pub and restaurant which has live rock music and one room where you can play darts and pool. *Barbary Coast* (119 Banff Ave), upstairs, is a friendly local place with live rock and jazz. *Outabounds* (☎ 403-762-8434, downstairs, 137 Banff Ave), downstairs, is a hot dance bar (don't look up or you'll see a Hard Rock Cafe, ack!).

Wild Bill's Legendary Saloon (☎ 403-762-0333, 201 Banff Ave) is dedicated to the memory of legendary Bill Peyto (see the boxed text 'The Ultimate Mountain Man'). On any night it's crammed full with folks hoping to re-create some of its namesake's wilder exploits.

Many of the larger hotels and motels provide live entertainment.

Getting There & Away
Bus Greyhound (☎ 403-762-6767) buses run from the Brewster bus station, 100 Gopher St, near the police station. There are five buses a day to Calgary (two hours, $19). There are also services to Kamloops (7½ hours, $62) and Vancouver (14 hours, $98). Many of these buses also serve Lake Louise ($10) and Canmore ($7); check with Greyhound for times.

Brewster Transportation (☎ 403-762-6767) has one express bus a day to Jasper (4½ hours, $51) from April to October. It also has buses to Lake Louise ($10).

Bigfoot's Backpacker Adventure Tours (☎ 1-888-244-6673) has economical tours and transportation to Kamloops and Vancouver with stops along the way. The fare is $99 and you can book at the Banff Hostel.

Train It's really a crime that VIA Rail no longer serves Banff, as the line goes right through town. However, the privately owned *Rocky Mountaineer* travels via Banff between Calgary and Vancouver. The basic one-way fare from Banff to Vancouver is $565 double occupancy, which includes some meals and an overnight stop in a hotel in Kamloops. The service runs between mid-May and early October. There are seven trips

a month in June, July and August. For information contact a travel agent or Rocky Mountaineer Rail Tours (☎ 1-800-665-7245).

The train station is the ochre building at the northern end of Lynx St past the police station.

Car The major car rental companies have offices in Banff. Their addresses are:

Avis
 (☎ 403-762-3222 or ☎ 1-800-879-2847) Cascade Plaza, Wolf St
Budget
 (☎ 403-762-4565 or ☎ 1-800-268-8900) 204 Wolf St
Hertz
 (☎ 403-762-2027 or ☎ 1-800-263-0600) Banff Springs Hotel, Spray Ave
National/Tilden
 (☎ 403-762-2688 or ☎ 1-800-227-7368) Lynx St, on the corner of Caribou Ave

During summer all the cars may be reserved in advance. Reserving a car from Calgary airport, where the fleets are huge, may yield better a deal than waiting to pick up a car when you reach Banff.

Getting Around

To/From the Airport For Calgary airport, Brewster Transportation (☎ 403-762-6767) runs a limited schedule of buses each day for $36. The most frequent service is provided by Banff Airporter (☎ 403-762-3330 or ☎ 1-888-449-2901), which makes eight runs each way daily (two hours, $30).

Bus Banff Transportation operates the 'Happy Bus', a fake trolleybus, on two routes through town. One goes along Spray and Banff Aves between the Banff Springs Hotel and the RV parking lot north of town; the other goes from the Luxton Museum along Banff Ave, Wolf St, Otter St and Tunnel Mountain Rd to the hostel and Tunnel Mountain Village campgrounds. The fare is $1 and trams operate every 30 minutes from May to September. There is a reduced service in April and from October to December and no service from January to March.

Brewster has an hourly daytime service to Sulphur Mountain ($11) from mid-May to early October.

Bicycle There's no shortage of bike rental places in Banff. Park n' Pedal (☎ 403-762-3191), 229 Wolf St, rents out many types of bikes. Most cost $6/24 per hour/day. Banff Adventures Unlimited (☎ 403-762-4554), 209 Bear St, rents out mountain bikes for $7/24 and high performance bikes from $10/30.

LAKE LOUISE

About 57km north-west of Banff is Lake Louise, known as the jewel of the Rockies. Before you get to the lake is the uninspiring village of Lake Louise, which is really nothing more than the Samson Mall shopping centre and a service station. Though small, the convenient strip of shops has everything from groceries, restaurants and liquor to a place to buy film. Get what you need and carry on to the lake itself, 5km away by road. There's no transport; if you're walking, it takes about 45 minutes on the footpath.

Lake Louise itself is a much visited and stunning lake sitting in a small glacial valley, surrounded by treed, snowcapped mountains. Visit early in the morning, when it's less crowded, and your chances of seeing the classic reflection in the water are better. One of the Rockies' best known and original hotels, the Chateau Lake Louise, is situated grandly at the northern end of the lake. There are also some very fine nearby walks and hikes. A proposed convention centre for the hotel has stirred controversy because it will be built on a grizzly bear habitat.

The Bow Valley Parkway is a slightly slower but much more scenic drive than the Trans Canada Hwy between Banff and Lake Louise.

Information

The visitor information centre (☎ 403-522-3833, fax 403-522-1212) in the village is open daily from 8 am to 8 pm from June to September, from 9 am to 5 pm other times.

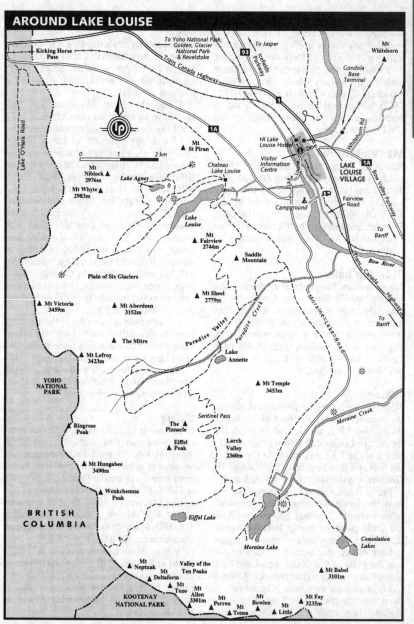

AROUND LAKE LOUISE

To Yoho National Park,
Golden, Glacier
National Park
& Revelstoke

To Jasper

Kicking Horse
Pass

Trans Canada Highway

93

Icefields
Parkway

1

Mt
Whitehorn

Gondola
Base
Terminal

Whitehorn Rd

Lake O'Hara Road

1A

Mt
St Piran

HI Lake
Louise Hostel

Lake Louise
Drive

Visitor
Information
Centre

LAKE
LOUISE
VILLAGE

1A

Bow Valley Parkway

0   1   2 km

Mt
Niblock
2976m

Lake Agnes

Chateau
Lake Louise

Mt Whyte
2983m

Lake
Louise

Mt
Fairview
2744m

Saddle
Mountain

Campground

Fairview
Road

To
Banff

Bow River

Plain of Six Glaciers

Mt Sheol
2779m

Mt Victoria
3459m

Mt Aberdeen
3152m

Paradise Valley

Paradise Creek

Lake
Annette

Trans Canada Highway

To
Banff

Moraine Lake Road

The Mitre

Mt Lefroy
3423m

YOHO
NATIONAL
PARK

Mt Temple
3453m

Moraine Creek

Ringrose
Peak

The
Pinnacle

Sentinel Pass

Eiffel
Peak

Larch
Valley
2360m

Mt Hungabee
3490m

Wenkchemna
Peak

BRITISH
COLUMBIA

Eiffel Lake

Consolation
Lakes

Moraine Lake

Mt
Neptuak

Valley of the
Ten Peaks

Mt Babel
3101m

Mt
Deltaform

Mt
Tuzo

Mt
Allen
3301m

Mt
Perren

Mt
Tonsa

Mt
Bowlen

Mt
Little

Mt Fay
3235m

KOOTENAY
NATIONAL
PARK

It has information both from Parks Canada and Banff/Lake Louise Tourism. It also has an exhibition on the geological and natural history of the Rocky Mountains. Next door in Samson Mall are camping equipment rentals and a laundry which offers showers. Woodruff & Blum bookshop (☎ 403-522-3842) has general guides to the Canadian Rockies, as well as hiking, cycling and climbing guides and maps.

Mt Whitehorn

East of the village along Lake Louise Drive is Mt Whitehorn. A gondola (☎ 403-522-3555) takes you to the top, from where there are hiking trails and views of Lake Louise and Victoria Glacier. The gondola ride costs $9 return and there's a buffet restaurant and snack bar. Mt Whitehorn is an important ski centre in winter.

Moraine Lake

Lesser known Moraine Lake, about 15km (mostly uphill) from Lake Louise, is for many the more impressive of the two. Surrounded by peaks and a deep teal in colour, it is stunning. There is an attractive lodge, gift shop and numerous trails at the lake. There is no bus but, with all the traffic, hitching isn't too bad.

Hiking

Note that trails may be snowbound beyond the 'normal' winter season and it snowed during one LP research visit in July! The main Lake Louise trail follows the northern banks of the lake westwards to the end of the lake and then beyond to the **Plain of Six Glaciers**. On the way, there is a teahouse.

For a more rigorous venture take the switchbacks up to **Mirror Lake**. There's another teahouse here and good views from the **Little Beehive** or **Big Beehive** mountains. From there you can climb still higher to **Lake Agnes**, then around the long way to join the Plain of Six Glaciers trail and back along Lake Louise to the chateau. Alternatively, a popular two hour hike takes you from the Chateau Lake Louise to Lake Agnes. These trails can be followed for a

couple of hours or turned into a good day's walk.

For a shorter stroll, there's a less-used path on the southern banks of Lake Louise beginning by the boathouse and ascending through spruce forest; it offers excellent views of the lake and the hotel.

The roughly 20km hike through the **Valley of the 10 Peaks** between Moraine Lake and Lake Louise is highly recommended.

Take a quick detour to **Larch Valley**, where there's a stream and superb scenery. Before Larch Valley a trail heads west past **Eiffel Lake** into Yoho National Park. Better still, hike to Moraine Lake from Lake Louise via **Paradise Creek** and **Sentinel Pass**. This is a full day's hike with some steep parts but is an excellent route with great scenery. You can do it the other way round, which is an easier hike. Getting up through Sentinel Pass is a long, scree-filled trek but well worth it. At the top, 2600m high, it's cool and breezy. Once at Moraine Lake you can hitchhike back to Lake Louise along Moraine Lake Rd.

It is common to see pikas (plump, furry animals also called conies) and the larger, more timid marmot along these trails. You often hear ice rumbling on the slopes, too.

There are other trails in the area as well. The Parks Canada brochure *Drives & Walks* lists and describes them.

Skiing

Lake Louise has a large ski area that operates in conjunction with the two Banff areas. It has 50 runs and thousands of hectares of open bowls. It could well be the most scenic ski area in Canada. A day pass is $49. For information call or write to Lake Louise Ski Area (☎ 403-522-3555, snow report ☎ 403-244-6665), Box 5, Lake Louise T0L 1E0. Many of the hiking trails become cross-country ski trails in winter.

Wilson Mountain Sports (☎ 403-522-3636) in Samson Mall rents out a full range of winter sports gear. See the Banff section earlier in this chapter for details on ski passes good for all three areas, as well as heli-ski operators.

Climbing

Rock climbing on the **Back of the Lake**, a backwater crag, is popular. Access is easy and there are lots of different routes with interesting names like Wicked Gravity and Chocolate Bunnies from Hell. Other places to climb, of varying degrees of difficulty, include **Mt Fairview**, **Mt Bell** and **Eiffel Peak**. Check with Parks Canada for more details.

Places to Stay

Camping The two campgrounds in Lake Louise (☎ 403-522-3980) are run by Parks Canada and both are on the Trans Canada Hwy. The *tenting campground*, off Moraine Lake Rd, is open year-round with sites for $14; the *RV campground* is open from mid-May to October with sites for $18. Both have flush toilets but no showers.

Hostel The HI *Lake Louise International Hostel (☎ 403-522-2200 or ☎ 403-522-2253, llouise@HostellingIntl.ca)*, on Village Rd north of Samson Mall, has eased a little pressure on accommodation. There's room for 150 people and it has a kitchen, showers and laundry. Dorm beds cost $20/24 for members/nonmembers. It also has private rooms and a large mountaineering library.

Hotels Hotels mean serious dollars. *Paradise Lodge & Bungalows (☎ 403-522-3595)* is a cute and good choice, just a short walk from Lake Louise. Rates are from $77/130 in the low/high seasons. *Lake Louise Inn (☎ 403-522-3791 or ☎ 1-800-661-9237, 210 Village Rd)* has numerous facilities, including a gym and a hot tub. The 230 rooms start from $77/120.

The *Chateau Lake Louise (☎ 403-522-3511 or ☎ 1-800-441-1414)*, on the lake, does not have quite the same classic charm of its sibling, the Banff Springs Hotel. However, it has a more scenic location and things are definitely quieter here, especially at night after the tour buses have gone. There are a number of programs for outdoor activities through the year. The wide assortment of rooms start at $150 a night in the high summer season. Look for deals at other times.

Places to Eat

Aside from Samson Mall, there are several places to eat at all price levels in the *Chateau Lake Louise*. The Sunday brunch in the Poppy Room is a Bow Valley institution. Be sure to reserve. *Lake Louise Station (☎ 403-522-2600)* is a restaurant in the historic train station of 1884. It's open daily for lunch and dinner and is 1km from the mall on Sentinel Rd. It has a broad-based menu that averages $12 a person.

Getting There & Around

The bus terminal (☎ 403-522-3876) is at Samson Mall. See the Banff section earlier for bus service details. A taxi to the lake is about $8 one way.

ICEFIELDS PARKWAY

This 230km road (Hwy 93), opened in 1940 and linking Lake Louise with Jasper, is one of the most spectacular stretches of asphalt in Canada. The highway follows a lake-lined valley between two chains of the Eastern Main Ranges which make up the Continental Divide. The watershed rivers from the Continental Divide flow eastwards towards the Atlantic Ocean and westwards towards the Pacific. The mountains here are the highest, most rugged and maybe the most scenic in all the Rockies. To best appreciate this if you're on the bus, sit on the left-hand side going from Lake Louise to Jasper. The highway is good but slow, as animals such as goats, big horned sheep and elk are often beside or even on it.

You can drive the route in a couple of hours but stopping at the many viewpoints, picnic spots and sights, or hiking on one of the many trails, can take a full day or longer. Visitor information centres have trail details. Cycling the Icefields Parkway is very popular. Because of the terrain it's easier to go from Lake Louise to Jasper than vice versa.

The tabloid-sized *Official Visitors' Guide*, which Parks Canada hands out at all the entrances to the mountain national parks, has excellent maps detailing sights along the route. Parks Canada also has a

Glaciers are Cool but Icefields are Awesome

The Columbia Icefield contains about 30 glaciers and is up to 350m thick. This remnant of the last Ice Age covers 325 sq km on the plateau between Mt Columbia (3747m) and Mt Athabasca (3491m) off the parkway connecting Banff to Jasper. This mother of rivers straddling the Great Divide is the largest icefield in the Rockies and feeds the North Saskatchewan, Columbia, Athabasca, Mackenzie and Fraser river systems with its meltwaters. They flow to three oceans.

The mountainous sides of this vast bowl of ice are some of the highest in the Rocky Mountains with nine peaks over 3000m. One of its largest glaciers, the Athabasca, runs almost down to the road and can be visited on foot or by specially designed bus-like vehicles. The water you see at the toe of the glacier fell as snow on the icefield about 175 years ago.

useful brochure, *The Icefields Parkway*, which has further details about the route.

As is so often the case, the best time to see **Peyto Lake**, one of the world's most beautiful glacial lakes, is early in the morning. Farther north, around **Waterfowl Lake**, moose are plentiful.

Athabasca Glacier

About halfway between Lake Louise and Jasper is the Athabasca Glacier, a tongue of the vast **Columbia Icefield**. The icefield itself covers 325 sq km and parts of it are over 300m thick. Its meltwaters flow into the Mackenzie, North Saskatchewan and Columbia rivers.

The new Columbia Icefield Visitor Information Centre (☎ 780-852-6288), open from 9 am to 6 pm from May to mid-October, is across the highway from the glacier. There are numerous well designed displays that explain glaciers. One of the best is a time-lapse film showing a glacier in action altering the ground beneath it. The Parks Canada desk offers trail details, ecology information and backcountry trek planning. In addition to the obligatory gift shop, the centre has several restaurants that share two unfortunate qualities: they're pricey but the food is not tasty.

Should you feel compelled to bed down in glacier country, the centre also has a hotel (in season ☎ 780-852-6550, other times ☎ 403-762-6735) where rooms start from $90 to $165, depending on the time of year.

You can walk to the toe of the glacier from the information centre, but it's better to save yourself from slogging across the moonscape of gravel by driving the short distance.

For a further look, Athabasca Glacier Icewalks (☎ 780-852-6288 or ☎ 1-800-565-7547), with an office in the information centre, is recommended. It has a three hour trip for $28 and a five hour trip to various destinations in the snowfields for $32.

You'll find it impossible to miss the hype and hard-sell for the 'snocoach' ice tours offered by Brewster (☎ 403-762-6735). The 90-minute tours drive out on the ice and reach the vast areas of the glacier that can't be seen from the road. They cost $23.

Athabasca Glacier to Jasper

Other points of interest are **Sunwapta Falls** and **Athabasca Falls**, closer to Jasper. Both are worth a stop, though you may be appalled by the bonehead decision to put an ugly utility road bridge over the most scenic part of Athabasca Falls.

Places to Stay

The Icefields Parkway is lined with a good batch of rustic HI hostels charging $11 or $12 for members, $15 or $16 for nonmembers. Most are quite close to the highway in scenic locations; they're small and without showers but there's usually a 'refreshing' stream nearby. Contact the HI Banff International Hostel (☎ 403-762-4122, fax 403-

762-3441, banff@HostellingIntl.ca) for details on these hostels.

Choices include the excellent *Mosquito Creek Hostel*, on the Icefields Parkway about 27km north of Lake Louise, with cooking facilities and a sauna. It has 38 beds in four cabins and is open year-round. The *Rampart Creek Hostel*, 11km north of the Saskatchewan River Crossing, also has a sauna and closes for part of the winter. The *Hilda Creek Hostel* (☎ 780-762-4122), 8.5km south of the Columbia Icefield Visitor Information Centre, has 21 beds and a kitchen.

The following two HI hostels are also on the Icefields Parkway and can be contacted through the HI Jasper International Hostel (☎ 780-852-3215, fax 780-852-5560, jihos tel@HostellingIntl.ca). They have the same facilities as those listed earlier. *Beauty Creek Hostel* is 87km south of Jasper and *Athabasca Falls Hostel* is 32km south of Jasper.

You can also find campgrounds and moderately priced motels along the way.

JASPER

Jasper, 369km west of Edmonton, is Banff's northern counterpart. It's smaller, with fewer things to see and do and its setting is less grand, but some people prefer its quieter streets and less tourist-oriented attitude.

It's a good connecting point, with the Yellowhead Hwy and VIA Rail running east to Edmonton and west to Prince George, and the Icefields Parkway going south to Lake Louise. The town is a good supply centre for trips around Jasper National Park, which is teeming with wildlife and has excellent backcountry trails of various lengths.

Some of the most apparent wildlife in Jasper are the elk who hang out downtown during the autumn rutting and spring calving seasons. Besides leaving millions of nut-sized pellets of poo on almost every surface, they occasionally charge tourists, and emit a haunting cry like that of a child in agony.

Orientation
The main street, Connaught Drive, has virtually everything including the bus terminal, train station, banks, restaurants and souvenir shops. Outside the toy-like train station is a 21m totem pole carved by a Haida artisan from British Columbia's Queen Charlotte Islands. Nearby is an old CN steam engine. On Patricia St, parallel to Connaught Drive, traffic runs one way north of Hazel Ave. No, it's not just you – the street numbers throughout town, when posted at all, are difficult to follow.

Off the main street, the town comprises small wooden houses, many with flower gardens befitting this alpine setting.

Information
Tourist Offices Right in the centre of town at 500 Connaught Drive is the visitor information centre (☎ 780-852-6176), easily one of Canada's most eye-pleasing tourist offices. It's a stone building covered in flowers and plants. The large lawn out the front is a popular meeting place and often has people and backpacks lying all over the place.

The centre has information on trails in the park and will offer suggestions to fit your specifications. It has two good publications on hiking in the area, *Day Hikes in Jasper National Park* and *Backcountry Visitors' Guide*, and a list of tourist homes in town. In summer the centre is open daily from 8 am to 7 pm, in winter from 9 am to 5 pm.

Jasper Tourism & Congress (☎ 780-852-3858, fax 780-852-4932, jaspercc@incen tre.net), 632 Connaught Drive, has information on the town and is open weekdays from 9 am to 4 pm.

Post & Communications The main post office (☎ 780-852-3041), 502 Patricia St, near the corner of Elm Ave, is open Monday to Friday from 9 am to 5 pm. The Jasper Municipal Library (☎ 780-852-3652), 500 Robson St, has Internet access for $5 an hour. For a small fee you can also use its fax machine and copier. It's open Monday to Thursday from noon to 9 pm, Friday from noon to 5 pm and Saturday from 10 am to 3 pm.

ALBERTA

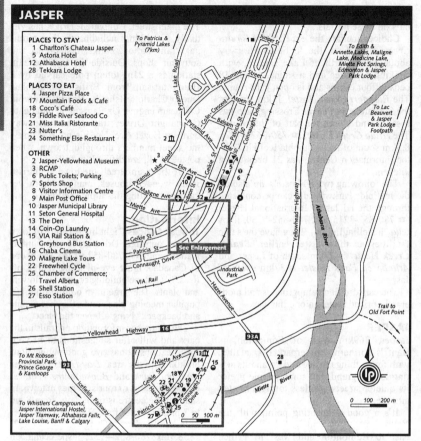

JASPER

PLACES TO STAY
1 Charlton's Chateau Jasper
5 Astoria Hotel
12 Athabasca Hotel
28 Tekkara Lodge

PLACES TO EAT
4 Jasper Pizza Place
17 Mountain Foods & Cafe
18 Coco's Café
19 Fiddle River Seafood Co
21 Miss Italia Ristorante
23 Nutter's
24 Something Else Restaurant

OTHER
2 Jasper-Yellowhead Museum
3 RCMP
6 Public Toilets; Parking
7 Sports Shop
8 Visitor Information Centre
9 Main Post Office
10 Jasper Municipal Library
11 Seton General Hospital
13 The Den
14 Coin-Op Laundry
15 VIA Rail Station & Greyhound Bus Station
16 Chaba Cinema
20 Maligne Lake Tours
22 Freewheel Cycle
25 Chamber of Commerce; Travel Alberta
26 Shell Station
27 Esso Station

To Patricia & Pyramid Lakes (7km)

To Edith & Annette Lakes, Maligne Lake, Miette Hot Springs, Edmonton & Jasper Park Lodge

To Lac Beauvert & Jasper Park Lodge Footpath

See Enlargement

Yellowhead – Highway

Athabasca River

Trail to Old Fort Point

Yellowhead Highway 16

93A

To Mt Robson Provincial Park, Prince George & Kamloops 93

To Whistlers Campground, Jasper International Hostel, Jasper Tramway, Athabasca Falls, Lake Louise, Banff & Calgary

Icefields Parkway

Industrial Park

Hazel Avenue

Miette River

0   100   200 m

0   50   100 m

Laundry Clean yourself and your clothes at Coin-Op Laundry (☎ 780-852-3852), 607 Patricia St. It has showers for $2 and is open from 8 am to 11 pm.

Medical Services Seton General Hospital (☎ 780-852-3344) is at 518 Robson St.

Jasper-Yellowhead Museum

The small historical society museum (☎ 780-852-3013), 400 Pyramid Lake Rd, has some interesting displays on the town's varied de-

velopment, making it a good half-hour stop. The story of the two sisters, the first women guides in the mountains who were hired by Brewster in the 1920s, is an intriguing little background titbit. It's open daily from 10 am to 9 pm in summer and from 10 am to 5 pm the rest of the year (closing Monday to Wednesday in winter). Admission is by donation.

The Den

The wildlife museum downstairs at the Whistlers Inn on the corner of Connaught

Drive and Miette Ave has a collection of stuffed animals in natural-like settings representing Jasper National Park's wildlife. It's open daily from 9 am to 10 pm and admission is $3.25.

Jasper Tramway

The lower terminal of Jasper Tramway (☎ 780-852-3093) is about 7km south of Jasper along Whistlers Mountain Rd off the Icefields Parkway. The busy gondola goes up Whistlers Mountain in seven minutes and offers panoramic views 75km south to the Columbia Icefield and 100km west to Mt Robson in British Columbia. The upper terminal is at an altitude of 2285m and there's a restaurant and hiking trails. It's a 45 minute walk to the summit over the tree line where it can be very cool. The tramway is open during daylight hours daily from April to October. Tickets are $16/8.50 for adults/children.

Patricia & Pyramid Lakes

These lakes, about 7km north-west of town along Pyramid Lake Rd, are small and relatively quiet. They have hiking and horse-riding trails, picnic sites, fishing and beaches; you can rent canoes, kayaks and windsurfers. In winter there's cross-country skiing and ice skating. It's not uncommon to see deer, coyotes or bears nearby.

Lakes Annette & Edith

Off the Yellowhead Hwy, 3km north-east of town along Lodge Rd, Lake Annette and Lake Edith are at about 1000m altitude and can be warm enough for a quick swim. There are beaches, hiking and bike trails, picnic areas and boat rentals in the wooded parks around the lakes.

Jasper to Maligne Lake

About 11km east of Jasper on the way to Maligne (pronounced 'ma-LEEN') Lake you pass **Maligne Canyon**, a limestone gorge about 50m deep, with waterfalls and interesting rock formations. You can walk from the teahouse along the floor of the canyon. A farther 21km brings you to **Medicine Lake**, whose level rises and falls due to

the underground drainage system; sometimes the lake disappears completely.

Maligne Lake, 48km south-east of Jasper at the end of Maligne Lake Rd, is the largest of the glacier-fed lakes in the Rockies and the second largest in the world. The lake is promoted as one of the most scenic of mountain lakes but this is perhaps unwarranted. It's a very commercial, busy destination and the classic view with the island is some kilometres out in the lake, accessible only by boat. You can, however, go horse riding nearby for a good view, or hire a canoe for $10 an hour from Maligne Tours (☎ 780-852-3370). Alternatively, take the 20km, 1½ hour boat tour to Spirit Island with Maligne Tours for $31 ($55 with bus transfers to/from Jasper). Make a reservation in Jasper at the Maligne Lake Tours office, 626 Connaught Drive, open daily from 8.30 am to 9 pm in summer. There are also some fine hiking trails in the lake's vicinity and excellent cross-country skiing in the highlands around the lake from November to May.

Miette Hot Springs

A good spot for a bathe is Miette Hot Springs (☎ 780-866-3939), 61km north-east of Jasper off the Yellowhead Hwy (Hwy 16) near the park boundary. Miette has the warmest mineral waters in the Canadian Rockies. The modern spa has three pools. It's open daily from 8.30 am to 10.30 pm in summer and costs $4; you can hire bathing suits for $1.50 and towels for $1.

Activities

Hiking Hikers are generally fewer in Jasper than in Banff and wildlife is more plentiful. If the weather has been wet you may want to avoid the lower trails where horse trips are run; they make the path a mud bath. Topographic maps are available for all routes. As well as the hikes around the lakes mentioned earlier there are many others. The leaflet *Day Hikers' Guide to Jasper National Park* has descriptions of most of the walks. If you're hiking overnight you must obtain a backcountry permit from Parks Canada in the visitor information centre.

These cost $6 a night up to a maximum of $30. For detailed information and reservations for routes that have capacity restrictions, call ☎ 780-852-6177.

Off the Icefields Parkway, about 10km south-east of Jasper, is the small **Valley of the Five Lakes**. The 8km loop around the lakes is mostly flat and makes a pleasant two to three hour stroll. Alternatively, you can take the trail that heads off north from the loop to **Old Fort Point** about 2km from Jasper. The **Mt Edith Cavell** and **Miette Hot Springs** areas also have good day hikes. There are quite a few two and three-day hikes in the park. One is the 45km **Skyline Trail**, which starts at the north-western end of Maligne Lake and finishes on Maligne Lake Rd about 13km from Jasper. Approximately 26km of the trail is at or above the tree line and has great scenery. The trail has plenty of wildlife too; watch out for grizzlies.

There are also four, seven and 10-day hikes that you can do.

Cycling As in Banff National Park you can cycle on the highways and on most of the trails in the park. Cycling is not allowed off the trails. Journeys of a few hours, a day or several days with overnight stops at campgrounds, hostels or lodges are all possible. For more information get a copy of *Trail Bicycling Guide, Jasper National Park* from the visitor information centre.

A good cycling route close to town is along **Maligne Lake Rd** to Maligne Canyon or farther to Medicine Lake. A popular, scenic but fairly tough trail ride is through the Valley of the Five Lakes to Old Fort Point, a distance of about 23.5km. For bicycle rentals see the Getting Around entry later in the Jasper section.

Climbing Jasper Climbing School & Mountaineering Service (☎ 780-852-3964), PO Box 452, Jasper T0E 1E0, has beginner to advanced climbing courses, ranging from three hours to five days. Courses run from May to September; in winter you can waterfall ice-climb or ski mountaineer. The three hour rappelling adventure for beginners is $25.

One-day guided climbing tours go to Mt Morro, Messner Ridge, Mt Athabasca, Mt Andromeda and Mt Edith Cavell. The cost depends on the size of the group but is from $100 per person.

Horse Riding Pyramid Riding Stables (☎ 780-852-3562) has one/two/three-hour rides for $24/39/54 through the stunning hills above Jasper. To reach the stables, follow Pyramid Lake Rd 4km uphill from the town centre and watch for the signs.

Whitewater Rafting Calm to turbulent rafting can be found on the **Maligne River**, **Sunwapta River** and the **Athabasca River** near Athabasca Falls. Numerous companies offer trips of varying lengths. Maligne River Adventures (☎ 780-852-3370) has a 13km trip on the fast, rough Maligne River for $50 per person; you can book a ticket at Maligne Lake Tours, 626 Connaught Drive. Whitewater Rafting Ltd (☎ 780-852-4386 or ☎ 780-852-7238), with an office at the Esso station, 702 Connaught Drive, has 3½-hour trips to Athabasca Falls and four-hour rides on the Maligne or Sunwapta rivers. Prices start from $40.

Skiing Jasper National Park's only skiing area is **Marmot Basin** (☎ 780-852-3816), which lies 19km south-west of town off Hwy 93A. It has good downhill runs for both beginners and experts, plenty of scenic cross-country trails, seven lifts and a new chalet. Call for a snow report. A day pass costs $42.

Near Maligne Lake, the **Moose Lake Loop** (8km) and the trail in the **Bald Hills** (11km) are easy introductions to the 200km of cross-country skiing in the park. The skiing season runs from December to May.

Organised Tours

There are three main companies in town which book tickets for the various tours and activities. Jasper Travel Agency (☎ 780-852-4400), in the VIA Rail station, coordinates and sells tickets for tours, river trips, sightseeing and adventures. Maligne Lake Tours (☎ 780-852-3370), 626 Connaught

Drive, does the same. The third is Jasper Adventure Centre (☎ 780-852-5595) at 604 Connaught Drive in the Chaba Cinema.

Brewster Gray Line (☎ 780-852-3332) has a three hour drive to some of the local sights, including Jasper Tramway, Whistlers Mountain, Pyramid and Patricia lakes and Maligne Canyon. The trip costs $38. Its Maligne Lake cruise takes five hours and costs $56. It also has Icefields Parkway tours to Lake Louise for $74 one way, taking 7½ hours. Prices are lower in spring and autumn.

Places to Stay
In general, prices here are lower than in Banff.

Camping Jasper National Park has 10 campgrounds operated by Parks Canada (☎ 780-852-6176). They are generally open from May to September, although a few stay open until the first snowfall (which may not be that much later). Closest to town is *Whistlers Campground*, about 3km south off the Icefields Parkway on Whistlers Rd. It's quite good, with electricity, showers and flush toilets, but, though it has 781 sites, it does get crowded. In summer, films and talks are presented nightly. Sites cost from $15 to $22.

About 2km farther south on the Icefields Parkway, *Wapiti Campground* beside the Athabasca River is the only campground in the park open during winter. It has sites for $14 to $18. Two other campgrounds reasonably close to town are *Wabasso Campground*, 17km south on Hwy 93A, with sites for $13, and *Snaring River Campground*, 17km north on the Yellowhead Hwy, with sites for $10.

Hostels The HI *Jasper International Hostel* (☎ 780-852-3215, fax 780-852-5560, ji hostel@HostellingIntl.ca) is 6.3km south of Jasper on Skytram Rd towards the Jasper Tramway; the last 2km are uphill. The hostel has a barbecue, a laundry and a large kitchen. Ask about the shuttle bus into town. Rates are $15/20 for members/nonmembers.

The HI *Mt Edith Cavell Hostel* is south of Jasper on Mt Edith Cavell Rd, 13km

from the junction with Hwy 93A. It's open from May to October and charges $9/14. The HI *Maligne Canyon Hostel*, 11.5km east of town on Maligne Canyon Rd, has 24 beds in two cabins and charges $9/14.

Tourist Homes The visitor information centre and Jasper Tourism & Congress both have lists of over 100 tourist homes that are usually centrally located and open all year. Bizarre national park regulations forbid breakfast being served but some places may offer you a muffin with a cup of tea. (That's why you won't find any B&Bs in Jasper.)

Jasper Tourism & Congress will send you its list of rooms so you can make reservations. Or you could check the streets close to the centre where almost every house has a sign offering rooms. In summer many of these places fill up early, so it's a good idea to book ahead. Rates average $40/50 for a single/double and may be lower in the off season.

Hotels, Motels & Bungalows The prices listed are summer rates, but at other times you can get significant discounts. In town, the newly renovated *Athabasca Hotel* (☎ 780-852-3386 or ☎ 1-800-563-9859, 510 Patricia St) has basic singles/doubles from $75/80. The *Astoria Hotel* (☎ 780-852-3351 or ☎ 1-800-661-7343, 404 Connaught Drive) has doubles from $130. Both hotels have a pub and restaurant.

Charlton's Chateau Jasper (☎ 780-852-5644 or ☎ 1-800-661-9323, 96 Geikie St), on the corner of Juniper St, is a quiet and refined motel with large rooms and a gourmet restaurant. Rooms go for $275 in summer and less than half that in winter. The deluxe *Jasper Park Lodge* (☎ 780-852-3301 or ☎ 1-800-441-1414), with small cabins beside Lac Beauvert north-east of town, is Jasper's answer to the Banff Springs Hotel. Here the charm is contained in a massive log cabin-style building and the resort has every possible amenity, including a world-class golf course. Rates start at $275.

Numerous motels line Connaught Drive on the approaches to Jasper. Outside of

town, there are several places offering bungalows (usually wooden cabins) that are only open in summer.

Patricia Lake Bungalows (☎ *780-852-3560)*, on Patricia Lake Rd about 5km north of town, has rates from $65. A little farther north along the road *Pyramid Lake Resort Bungalows* (☎ *780-852-4900)* is open year-round and has rooms from $120. It's beside the lake and has a licensed dining room. *Tekkara Lodge* (☎ *780-852-3058)* is 1km south of Jasper off Hwy 93A at the confluence of the Miette and Athabasca rivers. You can stay in the lodge or in one of the cabins. Rooms cost from $75 and it is open from May to September.

Other Accommodation *Blue Lake Adventure Lodge* (☎ *780-865-4741 or* ☎ *1-800-582-3305)* is about an hour's drive north-east of Jasper, 25km north of Hinton. Situated in Switzer Provincial Park, the lodge has cabins, chalet rooms and camping. Summer and winter sports equipment can be rented and various adventure courses are offered. Meals are available. The cost for two adults in a cabin is $58, or $79 for four.

Places to Eat

Many of the hotels and lodges have their own dining rooms.

Coco's Café (☎ *780-852-4550, 608 Patricia St)* is comfortable and good for $3 breakfasts such as muesli or muffins. At lunch there are sandwiches and burritos. *Papa George's* (☎ *780-852-3351)*, in the Astoria Hotel, has classic breakfasts for $6. *Mountain Foods & Cafe* (☎ *780-852-4050, 606 Connaught Drive)* is open all day and serves vegetarian foods, burgers, and breads from its own bakery. Follow the scent of garlic to *Miss Italia Ristorante* (☎ *780-852-4002, 610 Patricia St)* on the 2nd floor. It has great pasta specials from $10. The friendly *Something Else Restaurant* (☎ *780-852-3850, 621 Patricia St)* has spicy Greek dishes from around $12 plus pastas and pizzas.

Locals love *Jasper Pizza Place* (☎ *780-852-3225, 402 Connaught Drive)*, which has a rooftop patio and excellent pizza for $9 to $13. The best seafood in town can be found at *Fiddle River Seafood Co* (☎ *780-852-3032, 620 Connaught Drive)*, which has a fine view from its 2nd floor location. The salmon and trout average about $16 and couldn't be any fresher.

For a wide selection of bulk and natural foods check *Nutter's* (622 Patricia St). The best supermarket is *Robinson's IGA (218 Connaught Drive)*.

Entertainment

Jasper gets quiet – except for the cries of rutting elk – pretty early. Save your night-time energy for an early morning hike.

The *Atha-B Pub* in the Athabasca Hotel regularly has live rock bands and dancing. The *De'd Dog Bar & Grill* in the Astoria Hotel is famous for its imported draught beers. You can also play pool and darts with the colourful locals who like to hang out here.

Chaba Cinema (☎ *780-852-4749, 604 Connaught Drive)*, opposite the VIA Rail station, shows first-run movies.

Getting There & Away

Bus The Greyhound bus station (☎ 780-852-3332) is in the VIA Rail station on Connaught Drive. Four daily buses serve Edmonton (five hours, $47). There is a twice-daily service to Prince George (five hours, $47), Kamloops (six hours, $49) and Vancouver (12 hours, $92).

Brewster Transportation (☎ 780-852-3332), at the same station, has one daily express bus to Lake Louise ($44) and Banff (4½ hours, $51).

Train Jasper lies on the route of VIA Rail's (☎ 780-852-4102 or ☎ 1-800-561-8630) tri-weekly service linking Vancouver and Toronto. In addition, there is a tri-weekly service to Prince George, where after an overnight stay the train continues to Prince Rupert. Basic fares are usually a bit more than the bus, although the train is more comfortable, if slower. With the gutting of rail funding by the Canadian government, these trains are geared mostly towards sightseeing

tourists. Call or check at the VIA Rail station for exact schedule and fare details.

The private *Rocky Mountaineer* tour train runs between Jasper and Vancouver via Kamloops. It operates from May to mid-October and the number of trips varies each month. The one-way fare to Vancouver is $565 double occupancy with some meals and an overnight stay in Kamloops included. See the Vancouver and Banff Getting There & Away sections for further details.

Car Car rental in Jasper is available through the following:

Avis
  (☎ 780-852-3970) Petro Canada station, 300 Connaught Drive
Budget
  (☎ 780-852-3222) Shell station, 638 Connaught Drive
Hertz
  (☎ 780-852-3888) VIA Rail station, 607 Connaught Drive
National/Tilden
  (☎ 780-852-4972) VIA Rail station

Rates average $50 a day plus an irritating mileage charge.

Getting Around
Jasper doesn't have a public transport system. For a taxi, call Heritage Taxi ☎ 780-852-5558.

Freewheel Cycle (☎ 780-852-3898), 618 Patricia St, rents out mountain bikes for $18 a day. Sports Shop (☎ 780-852-3654), 416 Connaught Drive beside the CIBC bank, has similar rates.

KANANASKIS COUNTRY
Adjacent to the south-eastern corner of Banff National Park and 90km west of Calgary, Kananaskis Country is an outdoor recreational area. The 4000 sq km region offers facilities for skiing, climbing, cycling, hiking, horse riding, boating, camping and picnicking. Kananaskis Country is most notable for the downhill skiing at **Nakiska** on Mt Allan (☎ 403-591-7777, snow report ☎ 403-244-6665), off Hwy 40, where the alpine skiing

events of the 1988 Winter Olympics were held. Cross-country skiing is also good, with trails throughout Kananaskis Country.

Canmore
Unhindered by the growth limits imposed on Banff, 26km west, fast growing Canmore is a popular alternative to the resorts inside the national parks. Just off the Trans Canada Hwy (Hwy 1) and squeezed between Banff National Park and Kananaskis Country, Canmore has a pleasant downtown that has not yet been buried under tourism.

Tourism Canmore/Kananaskis (☎ 403-678-1296, canmore4@telusplanet.net) has a small office downtown at 801 8th St. It has accommodation lists and is open weekdays from 9 am to 5 pm. There is a good possibility it will move to flashier quarters in 1999. Travel Alberta has a well marked provincial tourist office (☎ 1-800-661-8888) just off the Trans Canada Hwy. It's open daily from 8 am to 9 pm from June to August and from 9 am to 5 pm the rest of the year.

Places to Stay & Eat The Alpine of Canada operates a hostel, the *Canmore Clubhouse* (☎ 403-678-3200, fax 403-678-3224), which has a laundry and offers classes in mountaineering. Beds cost $15/21 for club members/nonmembers. It also maintains several backcountry huts. The hostel is about 5km from town on Indian Flats Rd, a 45 minute walk. The downtown *Bow Valley Motel* (☎ 403-678-5085 or ☎ 1-800-665-8189, 610 8th St) has basic rooms for $85/90 for singles/doubles in the high season and half that at other times.

Grizzly Paw Pub (☎ 403-678-2739, 622 8th St) is a noted microbrewery which also has good soups, burgers and very popular nachos ($7). You'll love the creamy head on the Rutting Elk Red, its most popular beer.

WATERTON LAKES NATIONAL PARK
This 25 sq km national park and World Heritage Site in the far south-western corner of Alberta, 130km from Lethbridge, was opened in 1895. The land rises from the

One Park, Two Nations

Waterton Lakes National Park is joined with Glacier National Park in the USA to form the Waterton-Glacier International Peace Park. Although the name evokes images of bi-national harmony, in reality each park is operated separately and entry to one does not entitle you to entry to the other. And there's always those annoying border formalities to deal with as well.

Glacier National Park was created in 1910 and comprises over one million acres (over 400,000 hectares) that perfectly complement the Canadian park. The park is open year-round, however most services are only open from mid-May to September. Entry to the park costs US$5 per person or US$10 per car. From Waterton Lakes, take Hwy 6 22km south to the US border where the road becomes US Hwy 17. Follow this 23km south to US Hwy 89 and continue a farther 21km south to the park entrance at St Mary, Montana. The road into the park here is sometimes closed in winter. The main services for the park are on the south-western side at West Glacier, Montana.

For more information on Glacier National Park (☎ 405-888-7800, fax 406-888-7808), contact the US National Park service, PO Box 128, West Glacier, MT 59936. For campground reservations, call ☎ 1-800-365-2267; for hotel reservations in the park, call ☎ 403-236-3400 from Canada and ☎ 602-207-6000 from the USA.

---

prairie into rugged, beautiful alpine terrain with many lakes, waterfalls and valleys. Spotting wildlife is common and there are more than 800 species of wildflowers. Ask about the cougar situation. Waterton Lake, a central feature, is the deepest lake in the Rockies. The park gets considerably fewer visitors than Banff and Jasper, and the town of Waterton is smaller and much more low-key than Banff.

The Waterton Visitor Centre (☎ 403-859-2224, fax 403-859-2650) at the park entrance on Prince of Wales Road, is open daily from 8 am to 8.30 pm from mid-May to mid-September, closing at 6 pm for the first month. Admission is $4/2 for adults/children. Backcountry campers must obtain a permit from the visitors centre.

There are 255km of hiking trails, some of which are also good for cycling and horse riding, while in winter many become cross-country skiing trails. Among the many hikes, the 8.7km Crypt Lake Trail is considered one of the best in Canada. The route is both challenging and exhilarating, and you take a boat (☎ 403-859-2362, $9) to the trailhead. Details are available at the visitors centre.

Waterton Shoreline Sightseeing Cruises (☎ 403-859-2362 in summer, ☎ 403-859-

2180 in winter) operates cruises on Upper Waterton Lake with boats holding up to 200 passengers. A limited operation begins in May with no stops in the USA; the full schedule operates in July and August with most cruises stopping at Goat Haunt in Montana. The fare is $18/8 for adults/children. There are also cruise/hike trips offered.

The **Akamina Parkway** provides a scenic 16km route west from Waterton along the Cameron Valley to Cameron Lake, while the 15km **Red Rock Parkway** follows the Blakiston Valley to Red Rock Canyon and has excellent wildlife viewing.

Places to Stay

The park has three Parks Canada campgrounds. The *Waterton Townsite Campground*, on Hwy 5 at the southern end of town, is the largest with full facilities and sites for $15 to $21. There are also a few privately owned campgrounds just outside the park.

The HI *Waterton International Hostel* (☎ 403-859-2150 or ☎ 1-888-985-6343, fax 403-859-2229, ecolodge@compusmart.ad .ca) shares facilities with the much more expensive *Lodge at Waterton Lakes*. This means the place is well equipped, with a spa

centre, private washrooms, a playground and more. Beds in the 22 bed dorm cost $20/24 for members/nonmembers. Summer rates in the lodge begin at $135. Note that you'll have to specify the hostel when you use the contact information above. The property is 2½ blocks from the lake on Clematis Ave.

Northland Lodge (☎ 403-859-2353) is on Evergreen Ave and open from mid-May to September. The nine rooms cost from $50. The ***El Cortez Motel*** (☎ 403-859-2366) on Mountview Rd has comfortable rooms from $65/75 for singles/doubles.

The town's showpiece accommodation is the venerable railway ***Prince of Wales Hotel*** (☎ 403-859-2231 in season, ☎ 602-207-6000 other times). Its location on the lake is stunning and the views alone make the rooms worth the prices, which start at $136. Designated a national historic site, the hotel is open from mid-May to September.

British Columbia

British Columbia, known simply as BC, contains some of the most varied and spectacular scenery in the world. The Rocky Mountains are in the east and the northern interior is full of mountain ranges, forests, lakes and wilderness. The southern interior has a small desert, while the lush Pacific coastal area has rainforests and countless inlets and islands. In short, the range of landscapes provides habitats for wildlife and opportunities for outdoor activities to suit every taste.

The general atmosphere in BC, particularly on the south-west coast, is slightly different than that of the rest of Canada.

The culture, more lifestyle-conscious than in the east, partially reflects the influence of California.

These factors combine to make tourism – in a province with many lucrative industries – the second largest moneymaker.

As in California, much of the early settlement was due to gold fever around the 1850s. The bulk of the population is of British ancestry, although Vancouver has a large Asian community.

BC is Canada's most westerly province. It's bordered in the north by the Yukon and the Northwest Territories; in the east by Alberta; in the south by the three US states of Montana, Idaho and Washington; in the north-west by Alaska; and in the west by the Pacific Ocean.

Victoria, the province's capital, is at the southern tip of Vancouver Island, which lies south-west of the mainland. Vancouver, the province's business centre and by far BC's largest city, sits alongside the ocean near the mouth of the Fraser River.

The bulk of the province is mountainous lying inside the Western Cordillera, which runs roughly north-west to south-east. Within the cordillera there are three major mountain ranges – the Rocky Mountains to the east, the Cassiar (north) and Columbia (south) mountains in the centre and the Coast Mountains to the west.

HIGHLIGHTS

Entered Confederation: 20 July 1871
Area: 948,596 sq km
Population: 4,009,922
Provincial Capital: Victoria

- Walk the streets and parks of Vancouver where the wilderness meets the metropolis

- Feel the spray on your face on the wild west coast of Vancouver Island

- Drive the Sunshine Coast-Vancouver Island circle tour

- Hit the slopes at Whistler, a world-class ski resort

- Soak in one of the regional hot springs

- Taste the fruit in the sunny Okanagan Valley

- Hear the rumble of an avalanche on Rogers Pass

- Smell the smells at the North Pacific Cannery Village near Prince Rupert

- Gaze at the haunting totem poles on the Queen Charlotte Islands

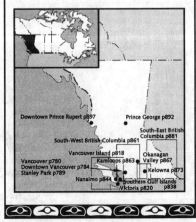

Downtown Prince Rupert p897 — Prince George p892 — South-East British Columbia p881 — South-West British Columbia p861 — Vancouver Island p818 — Kamloops p863 — Okanagan Valley p867 — Vancouver p780 — Downtown Vancouver p784 — Stanley Park p789 — Kelowna p873 — Nanaimo p844 — Southern Gulf Islands p838 — Victoria p820

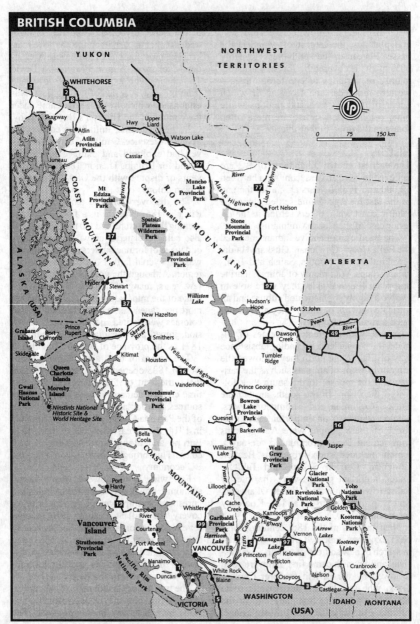

BRITISH COLUMBIA

The province contains scores of fresh-water lakes and fast-flowing rivers plus several plateaus, the largest of which is the Fraser Plateau in the south-west. Roughly 60% of BC is covered by forest, consisting mainly of varieties of coniferous trees – western red cedar and Douglas fir which occur in the moist coastal regions while pine, hemlock and spruce are more often found in the drier, higher interior.

History

The earliest known inhabitants of BC are believed to have arrived from Asia between 12,000 and 10,000 years ago, after the end of the last Ice Age. Some settled along the Pacific coast while others settled in the interior east of the Coast Mountains.

The Pacific coast Native Indians included the Bella Coola, Cowichan, Gitskan, Haida, Kwakiutl, Niska, Nootka, Salish and Tsimshian groups. With plenty of animal, marine and plant life available, they were able to evolve a highly sophisticated culture and an intricate network of trade. They also developed a rigid class system.

Inland, with its greater extremes of climate, the people led a nomadic, subsistence way of life. To the north they followed the migratory herds of animals such as the caribou and the moose; to the south they followed the bison. In the south, around the Fraser, Columbia and Thompson rivers, salmon was also an important resource. Most of these people were Athapaskans (now called Dene, pronounced 'de-nay'), which included such groups as Beaver, Chilcotin, Carrier, Sekani and Tahltan. Other important groups were the interior Salish (divided into the Lillooet, Okanagan, Shuswap and Thompson) and the Kootenay (or Kootenai).

Near the end of the 18th century, European explorers appeared off the west coast in search of new sources of wealth. The Russians and Spanish came first and were soon followed by the British explorer Captain Cook, who was looking for a water route across North America from the Pacific to the Atlantic – the legendary Northwest Passage.

He was unable to find it, but his account of the riches to be had from furs brought traders eager to cash in on the lucrative market. The most famous of these were Alexander Mackenzie, Simon Fraser and David Thompson, who explored routes overland from the east. A series of trading posts was established which, by the 1820s, came under the control of the Hudson's Bay Company.

In the meantime, initially to counter the Spanish presence, Captain George Vancouver had explored and claimed Vancouver Island for Britain. Then in 1849, following years of dispute with the USA, it became a crown colony.

The discovery of gold along the Fraser River in 1858 brought in a flood of people seeking their fortune and led to mainland BC also being declared a crown colony. A second wave of fortune hunters came when gold was discovered farther north in the Cariboo region. Although the gold rush only lasted a few years, many of those who came in the wake of the miners remained behind to form more permanent settlements. In 1866 the two colonies were united and, after much discussion, joined the Canadian Confederation in 1871 as the province of British Columbia.

The arrival of the trans-continental railway in 1885 opened up BC to the east; and the settlement of the prairies around this time created demand for the province's resources, particularly timber. The building of the Panama Canal, which was completed in 1914, meant easier access to markets in Europe and along North America's east coast. This brought about a boom for the BC economy.

Following WWI, however, there was an economic downturn which led to industrial unrest and unemployment. After a brief recovery, the Wall St crash of 1929 brought severe depression and hardship. Prosperity only returned with the advent of WWII and was sustained after the war with the discovery of new resources and the development of a manufacturing base.

The two major Canadian political parties, the Liberals and the Conservatives, have made little headway in this province. The

Social Credit Party, ostensibly the party of small business, was in power for much of the 1970s and 1980s. In 1991 its main opposition, the New Democrat Party (NDP), which advocates a form of limited socialism, came to power.

At the beginning of the 1990s, BC experienced an economic boom led by Vancouver, which enjoyed its links to then-booming Asia as well as a large influx of moneyed immigrants fleeing Hong Kong ahead of the handover to China. However, what goes up must come down and these economic ties to Asia were both a blessing and a curse. The crash of the Asian economies in the late 1990s sent a chill through Vancouver and devastated the lumber industries, which counted on Asian exports. This, coupled with the collapse of fishing stocks, resulted in a recession stretching from the metropolitan south-west to the rural towns of the far north.

Climate

BC's climate is varied, influenced as it is by latitude, distance from the moderating effects of the Pacific Ocean and by the mountainous terrain. On the coast it is mild with warm, mostly dry summers and cool, very wet winters. The interior is much drier, particularly in the south along the Okanagan Valley; summers are hot and winters cold. In the mountains, summers are short, tend to wetness and the nights are cool. Winter snowfalls are heavy.

Unless you're coming for winter activities like skiing, the best time to visit is from around early June to early October. During this period there is less rain, temperatures are warm, daylight hours are long and the transport routes are open.

Information

Tourism BC is the name of the body which operates the province's impressive and comprehensive tourism infrastructure and also produces a mountain of literature covering just about everything the visitor needs to know. It oversees a broad network of well signposted tourist offices – called Visitor

Butt Out!

As of 1 January 2000, smoking in public buildings (bars and restaurants) is illegal in British Columbia.

The provincial government banned smoking in public places in Greater Victoria from 1 January 1999, as a precursor to implementing a province-wide ban a year later.

Fines range from $100 for a first offence to many thousands of dollars for multiple offences, so be warned!

Info Centres – throughout BC, many of which operate as an arm of, or in conjunction with, the local Chamber of Commerce. Some are open year-round (mainly those in towns) but the majority are seasonal, only opening their doors between April or May and the first weekend in September.

For information on travel and accommodation reservations in BC contact Tourism BC (☎ 250-387-1642, ☎ 1-800-663-6000 in North America, ☎ 250-663-6000 in Vancouver), PO Box 9830, Stn Prov Govt, Victoria V8W 9W5.

Tax The provincial sales tax is 7%. There also is a provincial Room Tax that varies from 8 to 10%.

Activities

For general and detailed information about activities contact local tourist offices.

Canoeing With the Pacific Ocean to the west and so many inlets, lakes and rivers there are plenty of opportunities to go canoeing on BC's waters. Some of the more popular spots are Bowron Lakes and Wells Gray provincial parks, and Slocan and Okanagan lakes; and for ocean canoeing around Vancouver, the Gulf Islands and the Queen Charlotte Islands. There are dozens of destinations for whitewater canoeing.

Cycling You can either go cycling on your own or in organised group tours. Many

places in BC have bicycles for rent. In Vancouver one of the most popular spots for cycling is around the 10km seawall in Stanley Park. Around BC other favourite areas are the Rocky and Kootenay mountains for mountain-biking, the Fraser River Valley, the Gulf Islands, and along Vancouver Island's east coast. For detailed information and maps contact Cycling BC (☎ 604-737-3034), 1367 West Broadway, Vancouver V6H 4H9.

Fishing Fishing, both the saltwater and freshwater variety, is one of BC's major tourist attractions. Particularly popular are the waters around Vancouver Island (where several places claim the title 'salmon capital of the world') and the Queen Charlotte Islands; the Fraser, Thompson, Nass, Skeena, Kettle, Peace and Liard rivers; and the lakes of the High Country, Cariboo, Chilcotin and Okanagan Similkameen regions. Commercial operators offer boat rentals or charters or there are all-inclusive packages which include transport and accommodation. For further information contact BC Tourism.

Fishing is controlled by law and you will have to obtain a licence. This is a simple procedure; they are widely available from sporting good stores and outfitters. There are short-period licences and annual permits.

The Endangered BC Salmon

As does the rest of the Pacific Northwest, BC confronts the issue of wild salmon depopulation in its rivers. The problems that have put the salmon in danger in BC are much the same as in Oregon and Washington: decades of over-fishing, pollution of streams and rivers, the practice of clear-cutting forests and hydroelectric dams that stop migrating fish. However, BC salmon – and the governmental bodies and environmentalists who work to protect the salmon population spawned in BC rivers – face one unique adversary: Alaska.

While the states of Oregon and Washington, the province of BC, and most of the region's Indian tribes (who often have treaty rights to fish for salmon) have largely worked together to preserve the salmon population by restricting catches and improving watersheds, the government and fishing industry in Alaska have been almost totally uncooperative. Alaska has refused to adopt the fishing restrictions advocated by the other governments in the region, continuing to fish the waters of the Gulf of Alaska with what seems like environmental abandon.

This is a particular problem for BC. Adult salmon – which will later enter Canadian waters to spawn – spend most of their lives in the waters of the Northern Pacific, where Alaskan trawler boats harvest fish in great numbers. Alaskan fishers take a huge bite out of the BC fish population before the fish enter Canadian jurisdiction and protection. The animosity between Canadian and Alaskan fishers is often very intense, highlighted by the 1996 stand-off at Prince Rupert, when BC fishers blockaded an Alaska ferry in the Prince Rupert harbour for over a week.

Salmon numbers continue to dwindle in BC. In 1998 the federal government completely banned fishing for Coho salmon, in response to evidence pointing to the species' imminent extinction. For instance, in the Skeena and Thompson Rivers, Coho stocks are down to 1% of what they were just a few decades ago. (Other species of salmon are still harvested in BC, though in greatly restricted numbers.)

Most Canadian anglers, charter and commercial fishers and Native groups grudgingly accept the government-enforced ban. However, their anger is reserved for the Alaskans, who continue to harvest Coho and other salmon by the thousands as those fish swim through US waters on their way towards Canadian rivers.

Hang-Gliding British Columbia's rugged mountains offer some of the best terrain for hang-gliding to be found anywhere. Back-country roads take you to launch sites throughout the province. Mt Seven, south-east of Golden, has been the site of several world and Canadian hang-gliding records. Some of the best sites for hang-gliding are the south-east of Vancouver Island, Salt Spring Island, the Fraser Valley, the Kamloops area, the Okanagan Valley, the Kootenay Mountains, and in the north around Dawson Creek.

Hiking Almost any kind of hiking experience is possible in BC: from short walks of a few hours along well marked, easily accessible trails to treks of one or two weeks in remote terrain where you have to take your own food and equipment and be flown in by helicopter. There are well over 2000km of maintained trails in the national and provincial parks giving you access to many of the province's most outstanding scenic features.

Close to Vancouver there are many good walks: in the Coast Mountains, Garibaldi Provincial Park and around Whistler to the north; and in the Cascade Mountains to the east. From Manning Provincial Park the Pacific Crest Trail goes all the way to Mexico! On Vancouver Island the trails in the Pacific Rim National Park as well as Strathcona Provincial Park offer opportunities to see both marine and land wildlife.

In the south-east of the province there is a host of walks (varying in degree of difficulty) in the provincial and national parks in and around the Rocky, Columbia and Cariboo mountains. Finally, to the north, for the adventurous, there is Tweedsmuir Provincial Park and in the far north Spatsizi Plateau and Kwadachi wilderness parks.

Many of these areas are also very good for rock climbing or mountaineering.

Sailing Sailing is another popular form of recreation and, though the best time is from mid-April to mid-October, in the sheltered waters of BC's Pacific coast it's possible almost year-round. Coastal marine parks provide safe all-weather anchorage and offer boat hire. Inland, some of the more favoured places include Harrison, Okanagan, Arrow and Kootenay lakes in the south, and Williston Lake in the north.

Scuba Diving The rich and varied marine life in the waters along BC's 7000km Pacific coast make scuba diving a very rewarding activity. The best time to go is winter when the plankton has decreased and visibility often exceeds 20m. The water temperature drops to about 7°C to 10°C in winter while in summer it reaches 15°C. At depths of more than 15m, though, visibility is good throughout the year and temperatures rarely rise above 10°C.

The best places to dive are in the waters off the Pacific Rim National Park on Vancouver Island's west coast; in Georgia Strait between Vancouver Island's east coast and the mainland's Sunshine Coast north of Vancouver; and in Queen Charlotte Strait off Vancouver Island's north-east coast.

Skiing BC's climate and mountainous terrain provide great conditions for downhill and cross-country (Nordic) skiing in the many skiing resorts and provincial and national parks. Most of the downhill ski resorts are equipped with chair lifts which serve vertical rises that range between 400m and 700m plus a few around the 1100m mark. The cross-country resorts offer about 1500km of prepared trails with thousands more kilometres of unmarked trails. Many of the ski resorts have hotel accommodation either on the mountain or nearby. It's also possible to go heli-skiing in the remoter parts of the province. Pick up a copy of Tourism BC's brochure *British Columbia Skiing* which lists the scores of major downhill and cross-country skiing centres in the province. Most of these centres are in the south, from Vancouver Island eastward through to the Rocky Mountains.

Whistler attracts skiers from around the world, while the area around Golden is popular with heli-skiers. Other ski areas can pretty much be found anywhere there are

people, mountains and snow. Numerous resorts are listed throughout this chapter.

Surfing In Pacific Rim National Park on Vancouver Island, Long Beach reputedly has the best surfing in BC. The waves come rolling in right off the tempestuous North Pacific.

Whale Watching Killer (orca) whales inhabit the waters off the west coast around Vancouver Island. Tours run south from Victoria and north from Telegraph Cove. Pacific grey whales migrate between Baja California and Alaska, travelling north in spring and south in the autumn. They may be seen anywhere around the island but best are trips from Ucluelet or Tofino.

Whitewater Rafting BC's topography means that there are many rivers throughout the province suitable for this increasingly popular sport. Check with the local Visitor Info Centre for details of where to go and which companies to use. You don't need to be experienced. Commercial rafting is regulated by the provincial government and operators are allowed only on rivers that have been checked by experts, guides must meet certain qualifications and companies must provide equipment that meets government requirements. Trips can last from three hours up to a couple of weeks. Wilderness rafting averages about $200 per day for everything, while half-day trips start from about $45.

The more favoured rivers are the Fraser, Thompson and Chilliwack close to Vancouver; to the east in the High Country near Kamloops the Adams and Clearwater rivers; in the Rockies the Kootenay, Kicking Horse and Illecillewaet rivers; the Chilko and Chilcotin rivers in the Cariboo region west of Williams Lake; and in the north the Skeena, Spatsizi, Stikine, Alsek and Tatshenshini rivers.

National & Provincial Parks BC has six national parks and more than 340 provincial parks covering 9% of the province, an area nearly twice the size of Switzerland. *Road Map & Parks Guide*, produced by Tourism BC and available free at Visitor Info Centres, lists them all with their location and facilities. More information is available from the tourist offices nearest the various parks.

Four of the national parks are close to each other in the south-east – Yoho, Kootenay, Glacier and Mt Revelstoke. Yoho and Kootenay adjoin Alberta's Banff National Park in the Rocky Mountains while Glacier and Mt Revelstoke are to the east in the Columbia Mountains.

Pacific Rim National Park stretches along Vancouver Island's west coast and is divided in two by Barkley Sound and includes the Broken Group Islands. Gwaii Haanas National Park Reserve, inaccessible by road, is in the Queen Charlotte Islands.

Provincial parks occur throughout BC. They vary enormously in size from, for example, the 6568 sq km of Spatsizi Plateau Wilderness Park in the north-west to the one hectare of Ballingall Islets between southern Vancouver Island and the mainland. Most of them can be reached on sealed or gravel roads in conventional vehicles, while for some you will need a 4WD vehicle. Some parks have no road access at all and you'll have to hike in. You can take a ferry to a few of them.

Some of the national and provincial parks are open all year, but the majority are closed during winter and only open from April or May to September or October. Many have vehicle (RV) and tent camp sites, picnic areas and toilets and offer activities such as hiking, swimming, boating and fishing. At most of them a camping fee, between $6 and $17, is charged during the peak visiting season. Near the more popular parks there are motels and privately run campgrounds.

Some places considered historically significant have also been set aside as parks. Examples of these are Barkerville east of Quesnel, Fort Rodd Hill near Victoria and Fort Steele in the south-east near Cranbrook.

Much of the forests of the province can be used for recreation and camping at no cost. Because these areas are not well publicised they are generally not busy and camping spots may be found when others in

the area are fully booked. Most tourist information centres around the province will have copies of the good maps available for the local forest district.

Accommodation

There is a fee for camping in nearly all provincial and national parks during the summer season, generally they range from $9 to $20 per night. BC Parks has introduced a reservation service (☎ 1-800-689-9025, in Vancouver only ☎ 250-689-9025) for camping at the most popular provincial parks. The non-refundable service fee is $6.42 a night up to a maximum charge of $19.26. The service operates from March to mid-September and reservations may be made up to three months in advance.

Hostelling International has 16 hostels in BC. For information contact Hostelling International, BC Region (☎ 604-684-7111, fax 604-684-7181, www.hihostels.bc.ca), Suite 402, 134 Abbott St, Vancouver, V6B 2K4. There are also scores of independent hostels.

The Tourism BC publication *Accommodations*, published annually, is an encyclopaedic listing of places to stay including motels, hotels and hostels and campgrounds – both public and private. There is also a listing of regional B&B agencies. Tourism BC will also make reservations at the properties listed, call ☎ 250-387-1642, ☎ 1-800-663-6000 in North America, ☎ 250-663-6000 in Vancouver.

Vancouver

Easily one of the most spectacularly scenic cities in Canada – if not the world – Vancouver lies nestled between the sea and mountains in the extreme south-western corner of BC. The natural world intrudes on the city's busy urban life at every turn: Vancouver's impressive high-rise centre is dwarfed only by the snow-clad mountains rising immediately north of the city; inlets of the Pacific reach far inland, isolating parts of the city on thumb-like peninsulas; and sandy beaches dot the shoreline. Parks

are numerous and large. One, Stanley Park, an extension of downtown, equals the size of the downtown business area.

But Vancouver has a lot more to offer than its postcard good looks. Certainly one of the most cosmopolitan cities in North America, Vancouver is still a city of new immigrants – wander the streets and you'll hear the languages of a dozen nations (the city is now the most Asian in North America). The recent influx of young people from other parts of Canada also adds spice to the cultural mix. Vancouver, and BC in general, has one of the most dynamic economies in Canada, and the city attracts young professionals and artists from the eastern provinces who come here to enjoy the city's recreation and easy-going sophistication. Yet for all the bustle of these newcomers, the city also provides an old-fashioned cultural refinement which reflects Vancouver's British heritage. With almost two million people in the metropolitan area, Vancouver is Canada's third largest city (behind Toronto and Montreal). It also has the lowest median age of any large Canadian city.

Vancouver is Canada's second largest English-speaking city, making this a national centre for the arts, business, fashion, sports and politics. The city is one of Canada's film making centres; there's more New Age awareness, progressive politics and recognition of alternative lifestyles (including a large gay and lesbian population) here than anywhere else in Canada. If this list of attributes reminds you of somewhere else, you're right. Easterners often refer to Vancouver as the California of Canada.

The port, the busiest on North America's west coast, operates year-round in the beautiful natural harbour of Burrard Inlet, and it handles nearly all of Canada's trade with Japan and Asia. The frequent take-offs and landings of float planes are reminders of the vast wilderness just to the north.

History

The Vancouver area was first inhabited by the Salish Indians. The first European to see the region was the Spanish explorer Don Jos, Maria Narváez in 1791.

As a condition of confederation with the rest of Canada, Ottawa promised BC in 1870 that it would build a transcontinental railroad. However, if the Canadian Pacific Railway (CPR) was to link east and west, then BC would need a mainland coastal terminus since the new province's population centre and capital, Victoria, was on an island. Railroad engineers set their sites on the sheltered Burrard Inlet, then a sparse ragtag of saloons, forests, lumber mills and farms. The first train arrived from Montreal in 1886, stopping at a thrown-together, brand-new settlement barely more than a siding, called Vancouver. A year later, the first ship docked from China, and Vancouver began its boom as a trading centre and transportation hub. In 1890, just four years after it was founded, Vancouver had already outpaced Victoria in population.

On June 13, 1886, a fire almost completely destroyed the city in less than an hour, killing 21 people. Reconstruction began immediately and by 1889 the town was rebuilt in brick.

The building of the Panama Canal, which was completed in 1914, meant easier access to markets in Europe and along North America's east coast. This brought about a boom for the BC economy and for its main trade centre, Vancouver. As big business grew, so did big unions. Workers in great numbers organised into labour unions in the 1910s, protesting working conditions and pay rates. A number of strikes targeted key industries like lumber mills and shipping, and in several instances Vancouver saw armed confrontations between union members and soldiers.

However, one issue where the unions, the government and business were in accord was with non-white workers – the growing Chinese and Japanese population was a problem that only punitive legislation and violence could solve.

Large numbers of Chinese had moved to the province, and were instrumental in building the CPR; they later established their own community just east of downtown, Chinatown. Japanese settlers came slightly later, establishing truck farms and becoming the area's principal commercial fishermen.

That these were hard working people seeking opportunity, like the Europeans who were also flooding the province, seemingly didn't matter to whites. On several occasions in the city's early history, Vancouver's Chinatown and Little Tokyo were the scene of white mob violence, and in the 1920s BC passed legislation effectively closing its borders to non-white immigration.

WWI and the Wall Street crash of 1929 brought severe economic depression and hardship to Canada. Vancouver, with its comparatively mild climate – at least for Canada – became a kind of magnet for young Canadian men who were hungry, desperate and out of work. But Vancouver had no work to offer, and held no easy answers for the problems of mass unemployment, and soon the streets were filled with street demonstrations, occupation of public buildings and rioting.

The war years were also hard times for non-white immigrants. During WWI, anti-German riots took hold of the streets of Vancouver, and businesses with German owners were burned. In 1941 Japanese Canadians were removed from their land and their fishing boats, and were interned by the government on farms and work camps in inland BC and Alberta, Saskatchewan and Manitoba.

Prosperity only returned with the advent of WWII, when both shipbuilding and armaments manufacturing bolstered the region's traditional economic base of resource exploitation.

WWII catapulted the city into the modern era, and from then on it changed rapidly. The western end became the high-rise apartment centre it now is. In 1974 Granville Street became a mall. Redevelopment included housing as well as office buildings and this set the basis for the modern, livable city Vancouver is today.

In 1986 the city hosted Expo '86, a very successful world's fair. A few prominent structures remain, while the rest of the area where it took place is now being redeveloped.

During the mid-1990s Vancouver saw a wave of immigration that has had a signifi-

cant economic and social impact. In advance of China's takeover of Hong Kong in 1997, tens of thousands of wealthy Hong Kong Chinese emigrated to the Vancouver area. Unlike previous waves of emigrants, the Chinese that came to Vancouver were from the Hong Kong business classes. As a result Vancouver real estate prices shot through the roof, with cost-of-living figures suddenly rivalling those of Paris, London and Tokyo. New suburbs shot up, particularly around Richmond, which are now essentially single-race enclaves of ethnic Chinese.

In the late 1990s problems with Asian economies and the generally poor state of the BC economy slowed the meteoric economic development seen earlier in the decade.

Climate

It rarely snows in Vancouver and it's not often oppressively hot. The only drawback is the rain, particularly in winter when it rarely stops and the cloud cover obliterates the view of the surrounding mountains. Even in summer a rainy spell can last for weeks. But when the sun shines and the mountains reappear, most people here seem to forget all the soakings they've endured.

Orientation

Greater Vancouver is built on a series of peninsulas bounded on the north by Burrard Inlet and on the south by Fraser River and Boundary Bay. The Coast Mountains rise directly behind the city to the north, while to the west the Georgia Strait is cluttered with islands. The many bays, inlets and river branches, as well as the Pacific coastline, are major features of the city. Much of the city's recent growth has pushed suburbs far up the Fraser River to the east.

Hwy 99, the continuation of I-5 from Washington State, enters the city on Oak St, which unfortunately doesn't have a bridge to downtown. If you're heading to downtown, you'll need to detour west to Granville St or east to Cambie St, which have bridges. The Trans Canada Hwy (Hwy 1), bypasses Vancouver proper to the east; from it, Hastings St leads to downtown.

Downtown Vancouver's city centre is itself on a peninsula, cut off from the southern portion of the city by False Creek and from the northern mainland by Burrard Inlet. The tip of this peninsula is preserved as Stanley Park, one of Vancouver's greatest treasures. Three bridges – Burrard, Granville and Cambie – link the southern part of the city, known confusingly as the West Side, with downtown. Only one bridge, the high-flying Lions Gate Bridge, links downtown to the northern suburbs, resulting in traffic nightmares.

Pacific Centre, a three-block complex of offices, restaurants, shops and theatres, beginning on the corner of Robson and Howe Sts, is pretty much the centre of downtown. Robson St and Georgia St, two blocks north, are the two principal north-west to south-east streets. Robson St is lined with boutiques and restaurants. Davie St, between Burrard St and Stanley Park, is a secondary commercial and shopping street. Only Georgia St, which becomes the Stanley Park Causeway, continues through Stanley Park to Lions Gate Bridge.

The main north-east to south-west streets are, from west to east: Burrard, Howe, Granville and Seymour. North of Georgia St, bordered by Howe and Burrard Sts, is the main office, banking and financial district. At the water's edge, at the foot of Howe St, is the impressive Canada Place, the convention centre, with its jagged white 'sails.' Much of Granville St, from Nelson St north to West Hastings St, is closed to cars. It's not a true mall as trucks and buses are still permitted and it has never worked very well as a central showcase.

The high-density area to the west of the downtown shopping area is known as the West End – *not* to be confused with West Vancouver on the North Shore, or the West Side, south of downtown.

Three downtown districts are worth noting. Yaletown, on Hamilton and Mainland Sts between Davie and Nelson Sts, is currently the 'hot' part of town with old warehouses being converted into hip bars, restaurants and loft apartments. Gastown, along Water St, north of West Hastings St between Richards and Columbia Sts, is the historic centre of old

BRITISH COLUMBIA

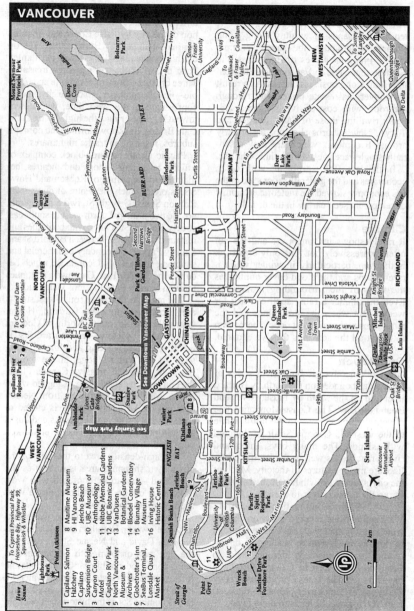

VANCOUVER

1 Capilano Salmon Hatchery
2 Capilano
3 Canyon Court Motel
4 Capilano RV Park
5 North Vancouver Museum & Archives
6 Globetrotter's Inn
7 SeaBus Terminal, Lonsdale Quay Market
8 Maritime Museum
9 HI Vancouver Jericho Beach
10 UBC Museum of Anthropology
11 Nitobe Memorial Gardens
12 UBC Botanical Gardens
13 VanDusen Botanical Gardens
14 Bloedel Conservatory
15 Burnaby Village Museum
16 Irving House Historic Centre

Vancouver, with many restored Victorian buildings. Bustling Chinatown is just to the south-east, in the area around Pender St between Carrall St and Gore Ave.

Neighbourhoods To the south of the West End and downtown, over False Creek, lies most of Vancouver – this vast area is primarily residential. Heading west after crossing Burrard Bridge or Granville Bridge is Kitsilano, filled with students, young professionals and now-successful ex-hippies. Between Kitsilano and Sea Island – where the Vancouver international airport is located – are some of the city's most exclusive areas, such as Shaughnessy Heights. Farther south is the rapidly growing municipality of Richmond, built on a portion of the Fraser River Delta. Still farther south is the port of Tsawwassen, where you can catch a ferry to Vancouver Island and the Gulf Islands.

East of downtown running south from Powell St, Commercial Drive was once the centre of Vancouver's Italian community. It's now the focal point for a developing alternative and student-oriented neighbourhood.

Burnaby, east of Vancouver proper, is another residential area and contains Simon Fraser University. South-east of Burnaby is the city of New Westminster, once the capital of BC and now an industrial area along the Fraser River. Across the river from New Westminster on the southern side is Surrey.

Over Lions Gate Bridge and Second Narrows Bridge lie West Vancouver and North Vancouver (which comprise the North Shore), both essentially upper middle-class residential areas. The shore of Burrard Inlet in North Vancouver is lined with commercial docks. To the north are two provincial parks, Lynn Canyon Park and Mt Seymour Provincial Park. To the north-east, along Capilano Rd, are Capilano Canyon, the Lions Peaks (from which Lions Gate Bridge takes its name), Grouse Mountain and the Coast Mountains. Farther west and north lie Cypress Provincial Park, Horseshoe Bay (from where you can take a ferry to Vancouver Island) and the Sunshine Coast (which is also reached by ferry from Horseshoe Bay).

Street Savvy Generally, the avenues in Greater Vancouver run east to west while the streets run north to south. Some of the streets in the downtown area – as well as many of the avenues in the Greater Vancouver area – are given east or west directionals. So Hastings St, for example, is divided into West Hastings St and East Hastings St. As a general rule the dividing cross street is Main St. However, for address numbering purposes, the downtown east-west streets begin numbering at Carrall St near Chinatown (and with Ontario St on Vancouver's West Side). North-south streets begin numbering at Waterfront Rd, along Burrard Inlet. As a reference in downtown addresses, Robson St begins the 800 block. Don't be confused on the West Side, in Kitsilano, when numbered avenues don't predict the street addresses. For instance, West 1st Ave is, for numbering purposes, the 1600 block.

Vancouver doesn't really have a freeway system to carry trunk traffic through the city, and congestion on the surface streets can be extreme. The Lions Gate Bridge, between Stanley Park and West Vancouver, should especially be avoided during rush hour. Only three lanes wide, the bridge's centre lane changes direction during the day to accommodate traffic flow. Little better is Granville St, the main thoroughfare south to the airport and beyond. Not much more than a residential street, it is often a sclerotic mess.

Information

Tourist Office The Visitor Info Centre, Plaza Level, Waterfront Centre, 200 Burrard St, is open in summer from 8 am to 6 pm daily, and the rest of the year 8.30 am to 5 pm weekdays, 9 am to 5 pm Saturday. Though usually busy, the staff are friendly and helpful but don't forget to take a number!

The staff will help you with bookings for accommodation, tours, transport and activities. For information call ☎ 604-683-2000, fax 604-682-6839; for bookings call ☎ 604-683-2772, ☎ 1-800-663-6000. At the Info Centre get a free copy of *The Vancouver Book*, the official visitors' guide, which has

information on shopping, accommodation, entertainment, local transport, etc. Also useful is the monthly booklet *Where Vancouver* and *Visitor's Choice*, both available around town, often at hotels.

On the corner of Georgia and Granville Sts (at Eatons department store) is a kiosk with downtown information open from 10 am to 6 pm Tuesday to Friday in summer.

Consulates Many countries have diplomatic representation in Vancouver. See the Yellow Pages under Consulates & Other Foreign Government Representatives.

Money The major national banks, such as Toronto Dominion, Bank of Montreal, Canada Trust and CBIC, have branches throughout the city; some are open on Saturday. ATM machines are liberally sprinkled throughout all the shopping and business districts.

Thomas Cook Exchange has a number of offices in Vancouver, including one (☎ 604-687-6111) in the Pacific Centre Shopping Mall at 701 Granville St and another at suite 130, 999 Canada Place. American Express (☎ 604-669-2813) is at 666 Burrard St. Both are open on Saturday. A walk along Robson St reveals a number of exchange bureaus open until very late at night. The Vancouver international airport provides banking and moneychanging facilities, too.

Post & Communication The main post office (☎ 604-662-5725), 349 W Georgia St, between Homer and Hamilton Sts, is open from 8 am to 5.30 pm weekdays. It has no separate poste restante (general delivery) counter; you just join the queue, show some identification and the person behind the counter will look for your mail. Electric Zoo (☎ 604-801-5788), 679 Denman St, has an Internet café and various other computer services.

Travel Agencies Travel CUTS, the student travel organisation, has four offices in Vancouver: one (☎ 604-681-9136) at 567 Seymour St; another (☎ 604-687-6033) at

1516 Duranleau St, Granville Island; and one each at the University of British Columbia (☎ 604-822-6890) and Simon Fraser University (☎ 604-291-1204).

Bookshops Duthie's Books (☎ 604-684-4496), 919 Robson St, on the corner of Hornby St, has a range of books, including a travel and a Canadiana section. It has several other branches, including one (☎ 604-689-1802) at 650 W Georgia St on the corner of Granville St, and one at UBC. Duthie's also operates Manhattan Books & Magazines (☎ 604-681-9074), 1089 Robson St, with an excellent selection of foreign (mainly French) language books, magazines and newspapers.

World Wide Books & Maps (☎ 604-687-3320), 552 Seymour St, has an extensive selection of travel guides and maps.

Book Warehouse (☎ 604-872-5711), 632 W Broadway, with branches throughout the city, has good quality books, many at bargain prices. It's open from 10 am to 10 pm daily and has free coffee. The Granville Book Company (☎ 604-687-2213) at 850 Granville St is particularly strong in fiction, sci-fi and computer books.

Another good bookstore is Blackberry Books (☎ 604-685-6188), 1663 Duranleau St, Granville Island. It's open from 9 am to 6 pm daily.

In Kitsilano, the Travel Bug (☎ 604-737-1122) at 2667 W Broadway has travel guides and maps, plus language tapes and travel accessories, as does Wanderlust (☎ 604-739-2182) at 1929 W 4th Ave.

Banyen Books (☎ 604-732-7912), 2671 W Broadway, is a well established and pretty amazing New Age bookstore. Vancouver Kidsbooks (☎ 604-738-5335), 3083 W Broadway, is a huge store carrying a vast selection of children's books, plus great puppets, games and plush stuffed animals.

Library The huge, architecturally controversial Vancouver Public Library (☎ 604-331-3603) is at 350 W Georgia St. Looking somewhat like the Roman Coliseum, the airy, striking building is open from 10 am to

8 pm Monday to Thursday, and 10 am to 5 pm Friday and Saturday. There is Internet access for $5 for 55 minutes.

Media The two daily newspapers are the tabloid *Province* and the broadsheet *Vancouver Sun*.

The best source for arts and entertainment is *The Georgia Straight*, a newsweekly that's available free in coffee shops, music stores and many other locations.

Another entertainment-oriented weekly paper is the *WestEnder*. The local gay newspapers are *Xtra West* and *Angles*, both free.

Laundry Downtown, do the laundry at Davie Laundromat (☎ 604-682-2717), 1061 Davie St.

Medical Services The Vancouver Hospital & Health Sciences Centre (☎ 604-875-4111) is at 855 W 12th Ave. For a walk-in clinic downtown, go to Carepoint Medical Centre (☎ 604-681-5338), 1175 Denman St, which is open daily.

Emergency For police, fire or a medical emergency, call ☎ 911.

Dangers & Annoyances The area around Hastings and Main Sts is quite seedy with many forms of vice right out in the open. It should be considered dangerous day and night.

Downtown

Downtown Vancouver is bordered on two sides by water, and on a third by the enormous Stanley Park. This constriction has forced the city upward. While none of the business towers are startlingly high, the cumulative effect of so many skyscrapers makes Vancouver seem very modern and somewhat forbidding. Another anomaly of downtown Vancouver is that the vast majority of the high-rises in the West End, the area near Stanley Park, are residential towers erected after WWII. A *lot* of people live right downtown, and this has kept small markets and other neighbourhood facilities in operation. Downtown has a real lived-in quality unusual in a city of this size.

For travellers, the centre of downtown is **Robson St**, especially if you like shopping. A collage of tourist shops, fashion boutiques, coffee shops and restaurants, Robson St is the best place in the city for people watching. Locals, international tourists and recent immigrants all throng here, giving the street the feeling of a mini United Nations. Shops and restaurants stay open very late at night, often till midnight in summer.

Walking Tour Start a walking tour of downtown at Robson and Howe Sts, at a small plaza called **Robson Square**. The Vancouver Art Gallery, a handsome late 19th/early 20th century stone building that was once a courthouse, is to the north; across the street is an artificial waterfall that forms the wall of the provincial courthouse. To the east is Eatons, the department store, which serves as anchor for the three-block-long underground shopping arcade, Pacific Centre.

Stroll west on Robson St. Part of the fun of browsing here is that the shops are really eclectic: you can find everything here from Giorgio Armani suits to hologram portraits of Elvis to fancy condoms. At Burrard St you can detour north to the tourist office, and have a glimpse of Canada Place – the convention centre and cruise-ship terminal with its famous white sails – reaching far out into the bay. Farther west on Robson St is the Robson Public Market, 1610 Robson St at Cardero St, a lively food market that's also a good place to buy ethnic takeout food.

At Denman St you can either continue on to Stanley Park, just to the west, or turn south and follow Denman St past numerous neighbourhood-oriented cafés, shops and inexpensive restaurants. Denman St ends at aptly named Beach Ave. Here, you get a view over English Bay to the West Side, which is the residential and commercial area flanking the University of British Columbia. A seawall and sandy beachfront extend in both directions. Follow Beach Ave east until Burrard or Hornby Sts. At the base of both streets you can catch a water taxi –

BRITISH COLUMBIA

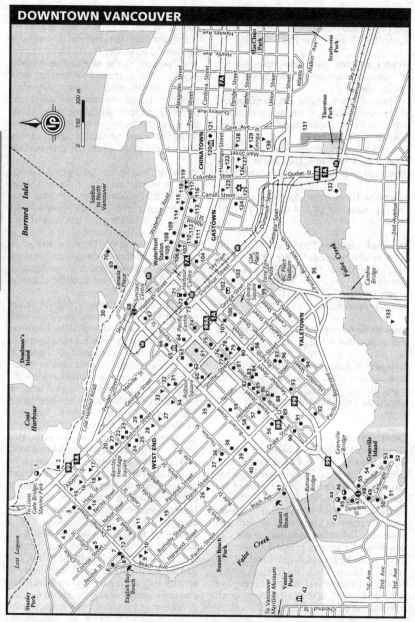

DOWNTOWN VANCOUVER

DOWNTOWN VANCOUVER

PLACES TO STAY

2 Westin Bayshore
4 Buchan Hotel
5 Shato Inn Hotel
6 Sylvia Hotel
11 Oceanside Hotel
20 Riviera Motor Inn
22 Greenbriar Hotel
23 Tropicana Motor Inn
24 Barclay Hotel
25 Listel Vancouver
29 Blue Horizon Hotel
35 YMCA
40 HI Vancouver Downtown
52 Granville Island Hotel
58 Burrard Motor Inn
59 Sheraton Wall Centre Hotel
60 Wedgewood Hotel
63 Hotel Vancouver
64 Hotel Georgia
67 Days Inn Vancouver
    Downtown
69 Pan Pacific Hotel
74 Four Seasons Hotel
83 Global Village Backpackers
84 Hotel Dakota; BaBalu
    Lounge; Fred's Uptown
    Tavern
85 Bosman's Motor Hotel
87 Holiday Inn Vancouver
    Downtown
88 Howard Johnson Hotel;
    The Gate
89 Gateway Hotel
90 Travelodge Vancouver
    Centre
98 Dufferin Hotel
99 YWCA
101 Kingston Hotel
104 New Backpackers Hostel
110 Dominion Hotel
111 Cambie International
     Hostel

PLACES TO EAT

8 Raincity Grill
9 Bombay Curry House
10 Liliget Feast House
12 Brass Monkey
15 Musashi
16 De Dutch Pannekoek
    House
17 Capers
18 Robson Public Market
19 Romano's Macaroni Grill
21 Greenhut Vietnamese
    Cuisine

26 Hamburger Mary's
27 Bread Garden
28 Kitto Japanese House
32 Cafe Il Nido
33 Joe Fortes
34 Pezzo; Thai House
    Restaurant
37 Kisha Poppo
43 Bridges Restaurant & Pub
51 Isadora's Cooperative
    Restaurant
54 Kamei Royale Ocean
    Japanese Restaurant
77 Kitto Japanese House
79 Notte's Bon Ton
86 Goulash House Restaurant
    & Pastry House
106 Mick's
107 Water Street Cafe
112 La Ventana Restaurant
115 Brother's Restaurant
116 The Irish Heather
118 Jewel of India
119 Incendio
122 Buddhist Vegetarian
123 The Only Seafood
     Restaurant
126 New Town Bakery &
     Restaurant
127 Kam's Garden Restaurant
128 Gold Pavillion Bakery &
     Restaurant
129 Gain Wah
130 Phnom Penh
133 Monk McQueens

OTHER

1 Harbour Ferries cruises
3 Electric Zoo
7 Carepoint Medical Centre
13 Denman Place Discount
    Cinema
14 Denman Station Cabaret
30 Seaplane Base
31 Manhattan Books &
    Magazines
36 Stone Table Coffee House
38 Davie Laundromat
39 Celebrities Club
41 Vancouver Aquatic
    Centre
42 Vancouver Museum, HR
    MacMillan Planetarium &
    Pacific Space Centre
44 False Creek Ferries
45 Granville Island Public
    Market

46 Aquabus
47 Blackberry Books
48 Granville Island
    Information Centre
49 Granville Island Brewery
50 Waterfront Theatre
53 Emily Carr College of Art
    & Design
55 Arts Club Theatre &
    Backstage Lounge
56 Odyssey
57 Pacific Cinémathèque
61 Vancouver Art Gallery
62 Duthie Books
65 Canadian Craft Museum
66 American Express
68 Vancouver Tourist Info
    Centre
70 CN IMAX Theatre
71 Picadilly Pub
72 Travel Cuts
73 Railway Club
75 Eatons
76 Granville Cineplex
    Odeon Cinema
78 Granville Book Company
80 Arts Club Revue Theatre
81 Paradise Cinema
82 Royal Hotel
91 Yale
92 MaRS
93 DV8
94 Yaletown Brewing Co
95 The Rage; Yuk Yuk's
96 Starfish Room
97 Richard's on Richards
100 Ford Centre for the
     Performing Arts
102 Main Post Office
103 Queen Elizabeth Theatre
     & Vancouver Playhouse
105 Steamworks
     Brewing Co
108 Steam Clock
109 Hill's Indian Crafts
113 Sonar Dance Club
114 Purple Onion
117 Gassy Jack Statue
120 Vancouver Police
     Centennial Museum
121 Firehall Arts Centre
124 World's Narrowes
     Office Building
125 Dr Sun Yat-Sen Classical
     Chinese Garden
131 Pacific Central Station
132 Science World

BRITISH COLUMBIA

actually a mini passenger ferry – across False Creek to the Granville Island Public Market, or to the museums, beaches and green spaces at Vanier Park. Return to Robson St along either Howe or Granville Sts, the latter partly a pedestrian mall with colourful, if rather seedy, street life.

To put downtown Vancouver in perspective, take the elevator up 169m to **The Lookout!** (☎ 604-689-0421) for a 360-degree view of the city. The Lookout! is atop Harbour Centre at 555 W Hastings at Seymour St. Tickets to the top cost $8/7 adults/seniors and $5 students, and they're good all day; open from 9 am to 9 pm.

Vancouver Art Gallery The city's art gallery (☎ 604-682-5621) at 750 Hornby St is right at the centre of things across from Robson Square. It has a large collection of work by Emily Carr, who was born in Victoria in 1917; as one of the most prominent of Canadian painters who dominated Canadian art from the 1940s to 60s, she was also among the first to portray BC and its landscapes. Group of Seven artists are well represented in the permanent collection. The museum also hosts various travelling shows, and has an especially good gift shop with local crafts. The Gallery Cafe, which overlooks the Sculpture Garden, is a great place for coffee and a snack.

The gallery is open from 10 am to 6 pm Monday to Friday, Thursday till 9 pm, 10 am to 5 pm Saturday, and noon to 5 pm Sunday. It's closed Monday and Tuesday from mid-October to Easter weekend. Admission costs $7.50/5 adults/seniors, $3.50 students and children get in free; it's pay what you want between 5 and 9 pm Thursday.

Canadian Craft Museum This pleasant museum (☎ 604-687-8266), 639 Hornby St, is dedicated to the role of crafts in human culture. Dominating the permanent collection are both contemporary and historical works from Canada; touring shows and special collections frequently have a more international focus. As you might expect, the gift shop here is wonderful, and a great place to find a truly unique handmade gift. The museum is open from 10 am to 5 pm Monday to Saturday (Thursday till 9 pm), and noon to 5 pm Sunday; closed Tuesday in winter. Admission is $4/2 adults/seniors and students.

Canada Place & Waterfront Station
Canada Place, built to coincide with Expo '86, juts into the harbour at the foot of Howe St. The building's stridently modern design invites comparisons. Does it resemble an ocean liner with tent-like sails, the white exoskeleton of a very large and spiny insect, or just the Sydney Opera House? In any case, Canada Place has become a major city landmark. The complex contains the World Trade Centre, the Vancouver Trade and Convention Centre and the Pan Pacific Hotel, and is also a terminal for cruise ships. Also here is the CN IMAX Theatre (☎ 604-682-4629). At the northern end are the promenade shops and a food court, plus good views across Burrard Inlet.

Just a block away from Canada Place is Waterfront Station, the grand old CPR station. The deteriorating building was restored and now serves as the terminus for an entirely different kind of transportation – the SeaBus. Catch the SeaBus, an aquatic bus, across to North Vancouver (with excellent views of the city and the busy Port of Vancouver). Also at Waterfront Station, you can hop on the SkyTrain, a computerised commuter train that runs on an elevated track to the eastern suburbs, with stops at the sports stadiums and Science World on its way.

Gastown Vancouver's Victorian-era business district is called Gastown, the name taken from 'Gassy' Jack Deighton, an English sailor who forsook the sea to open a bar servicing the developing timber mills in 1867. When a village sprang up around his establishment it was called Gassy's Town. (A statue of Gassy Jack has been erected in Maple St Square, where Cordova and Water Sts meet.)

After the centre of Vancouver moved elsewhere, the whole Gastown area gradually became a skid row, but in the 1970s it

was restored and renovated, simply pushing Vancouver's seedier characters a little farther south to Hastings St. The old Victorian buildings now house restaurants, bars, boutiques and galleries; some of the city's best nightlife is here. The brick streets have been lined with old lamps. Street vendors and buskers, or entertainers, add to the holiday feel of the area. The historic flavour is only a little marred by the parking structure several stories high on Water St.

At the western end of Water St is the world's first clock run by steam. The clock stands on a steam tap that vents steam lines that were formerly used to heat local businesses. Although the clock looks old, it was built in 1977. You can see the steam works through the side glass panels and will hear it toot every 15 minutes.

The Gastown area today is bounded by Columbia and Richards Sts, with Water St the main thoroughfare.

Vancouver Police Centennial Museum You don't need to be a local to enjoy this unusual museum (☎ 604-665-3346), 240 E Cordova St. Housed in the city's former morgue and coroner's court, the atmosphere is suitably macabre to tell the story of Vancouver's most famous crimes and criminals. Weapons, counterfeit money, forensic autopsy tools and a century's worth of drug paraphernalia help illustrate the story of law enforcement in Vancouver.

Chinatown About 36,000 people of Chinese descent live in the area around W Pender St, roughly bordered by Abbott St and Gore Ave; thousands of others come here to shop, making this one of the largest Chinatowns in North America.

For the most part, this is a real Chinese market and business district; nearly all signs are in Chinese and English is rarely spoken. The colours, smells, signs and occasional old Chinese-style balcony can make you believe for a second that you're in Hong Kong. Throughout the day the streets are full of people going in and out of stores that have hanging ducks, bales of strange dried fish, exotic fruits and Asian remedies. There are restaurants and bakeries as well; this is obviously a good place to come for dim sum.

For years the area has contended with the run-down blights of Hastings and Main Sts and this is finally taking a toll. Now that the Hong Kong Chinese have colonised Richmond, a suburb of Vancouver, the centre of Chinese Canadian business and culture has at least in part relocated there. But there's still plenty of vitality here.

Called the Sam Kee, the **World's Narrowest Office Building** at 8 W Pender St near the corner of Carrall St has made it into Ripley's *Believe It or Not!* and the *Guinness Book of World Records*. It's easy to miss not only due to its narrowness but because it looks like the front of the larger building behind, to which it is attached.

Dr Sun Yat-Sen Classical Chinese Garden This is the only full-scale classical Chinese garden (☎ 604-662-3207) found outside China. Its design is subtle but exquisite in execution and effect. Modelled after the Ming Dynasty gardens, best represented in the city of Suzhou, it makes a real sanctuary in the centre of the city. The Taoist principles of Yin and Yang are incorporated in numerous ways throughout the garden.

The guided tours are included in the admission and are well worthwhile. If possible, go during the week when it won't be too busy. Admission is $5.25/3.75 adults/seniors and students, and $12 families. In summer, the park is open from 10 am to 7.30 pm; the rest of the year, the park closes at dusk. It's at 578 Carrall St behind the Chinese Cultural Centre in Chinatown. The adjacent park, built by local artisans using Chinese materials, is similar in design and has free entry.

Science World Another vestige from Expo '86 is the geodesic dome at 1455 Quebec St near Main St Station, on the fringe of downtown, just south of Chinatown. The gleaming dome now houses Science World (☎ 604-268-6363), a science, technology and natural history centre with interactive exhibits. Aimed primarily at children,

hands-on experiments help explain scientific and physical phenomena; kids also love the laser theatre. Also in the dome is the Alcan OMNIMAX Theatre, with one of the world's largest domed screens.

Science World is open from 10 am to 5 pm weekdays and 10 am to 6 pm weekends and holidays. Admission to the museum is $10.50/7 for adults/children. Admission to the OMNIMAX Theatre is $9. Combination tickets are $13.50/9.50.

Yaletown Once the city's downtown warehouse district, Yaletown has been 'lofticised'; this former eyesore is now home to some of Vancouver's trendiest addresses. Beside trendy restaurants and watering holes, this is also the place to come for art galleries and interior-decorating and furniture shopping. On a nice day, this is a great place to wander and window-shop. The centre of Yaletown is at Hamilton and Mainland Sts, between Nelson and Davie Sts.

BC Place Stadium & GM Place These two large sports arenas shore up the eastern edge of downtown. Both are unmistakable. **BC Place Stadium** (☎ 604-669-2300 for general information, ☎ 604-661-7373 for events), 777 Pacific Blvd S, is covered by a translucent dome-shaped roof. The roof is 'air-supported,' which means it is inflated by huge fans (no, not sports fans), and kept in place by crisscrossed steel wires, hence its quilted appearance. Concerts, trade shows, sports events and other large-scale gatherings are held during the year in this 60,000-capacity stadium, which is also the home ground of the BC Lions of the Canadian Football League (CFL).

Adjacent, **GM Place** (☎ 604-899-7889) makes the area the major focus for the city's professional sports. It is home to the Vancouver Canucks of the National Hockey League (NHL) as well as the Vancouver Grizzlies of the National Basketball Association (NBA).

To get to the stadium, catch either bus No 15 or No 17, or take the SkyTrain to Stadium Station.

Stanley Park Vancouver's largest and much-beloved green space, Stanley Park is a 1000-acre forest of cedar flanked by beaches that extend north and west of downtown. Hiking, cycling and jogging trails meander through the woods. The seawall walk winds more than 9.5km (6 miles) along the park's shoreline and is one of the world's great urban walks. The three park beaches – Second Beach, Third Beach and English Bay Beach – are popular in summer for sunbathers and swimmers; additionally, there is an outdoor swimming pool at Second Beach and the Variety Kids Water Park at Lumbermen's Arch. From various points there are nice views of downtown Vancouver, the North Shore and out to sea toward the islands.

Near **Brockton Point**, on the east side of the park, there is a good collection of totem poles. Off the southern side near the yacht club is **Deadman's Island**, once used, it's said, by a northern Native Indian tribe as a camp for women captured in raids. Later it became a burial ground for Chinese people and Native Indians. It is now used as a naval reserve. For children, there's the Variety Kids Farmyard and a miniature railway.

Lions Gate Bridge extends from the northern tip, and the road – Stanley Park Causeway (or Lions Gate Bridge Rd) – through the park to the bridge is usually busy. Just to the west of Lions Gate Bridge is **Prospect Point**, a popular point for views of the First Narrows and passing ships.

Vancouver Aquarium One of the city's premier destinations is the Vancouver Aquarium (☎ 604-268-9900), Canada's largest, with 8000 sea creatures. The most popular attraction here is watching the dolphins and killer whale (orca) engage in 'natural' activities; due to pressure from animal-rights activists, the dolphins and whale no longer 'perform'. There is also a special, albeit controversial, tank for beluga whales. Other exhibits include octopuses, crocodiles, eels, piranhas and a wide variety of local sea life and freshwater fish. The Asian Tropical Seas exhibit is also a standout, as

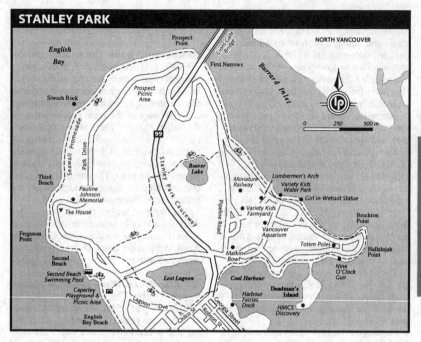

STANLEY PARK

is the Amazon Gallery, a re-creation of a tropical rainforest, complete with crocodiles, toucans, piranhas and tree frogs. The aquarium is also Canada's largest marine-mammal rescue and rehabilitation centre. A new area devoted to BC's Pacific Coast was due to open as we went to press.

The Vancouver Aquarium is open from 9.30 am to 8 pm daily July to early September, and 10 am to 5.30 pm the rest of the year. Admission is $11.95/7.95 for adults/children. The aquarium is located on the eastern edge of Stanley Park; from downtown follow Georgia St into the park; you'll need to pay for parking if you drive.

The West Side

Don't let the name confuse you – Vancouver's West Side is in fact the long-established residential neighbourhoods and bustling commercial centres south of downtown

across False Creek. The Cambie, Granville and Burrard bridges lead to the West Side; the main arterials are 4th Ave and Broadway, both of which lead west to Pacific Spirit Regional Park and the University of British Columbia (UBC) at the tip of the peninsula. Note that the easiest form of transport from downtown to some of the following sites is by water taxi from the base of Burrard and Hornby Sts.

Granville Island On the southern side of False Creek, under the Granville Bridge, this little, formerly industrial island has been redeveloped into a busy blend of businesses, restaurants, galleries and theatres. The centre of activity is the **Granville Island Public Market**, a food lover's dream made manifest. Dozens of greengrocers, fishmongers, butchers, bakers, cheese shops and other food merchants squeeze into the bustling market,

making this a great place to experience the natural bounty of BC. There are also coffee shops and counters with takeout food. The market fronts onto False Creek, and – in all but antediluvian downpours – the waterfront plaza behind the market is filled with harried shoppers, frolicking children, buskers and swarms of pigeons and gulls.

Granville Island is also an artisan's mecca: a number of craftspeople have studios and shops, there are several commercial art galleries and the Emily Carr College of Art & Design (☎ 604-844-3800), 1299 Johnston St, has frequent exhibits in its galleries. A number of ship chandlers and recreational-equipment shops are also on Granville Island. At night, the focus shifts from shopping to the performing arts. A number of theatre companies and live music clubs open their doors; there are no shortages of places to eat and drink.

The Granville Island Information Centre (☎ 604-666-5784), 1592 Johnston St, across from the Arts Club Theatre, is open from 9 am to 6 pm daily and has displays on the area's history.

Parking can be very tight on Granville Island. Unless you must drive, consider taking bus No 4, 7, 8, 10, 16 or 50 from downtown, or take the water taxi. Much of the island's activity is shut down on Monday, though the market remains open Monday in summer.

Vanier Park Vanier Park, on English Bay south of False Creek and below the Burrard Bridge, is home to a number of museums, a fine beach and a stand of lovely old maple trees. Also in the park are a swimming pool, tennis courts, and other sporting grounds. The park is a popular area and when the weather's fine you'll see people strolling, jogging, cycling, walking their dogs or simply sitting and watching the ships moving between English Bay and False Creek.

In addition to the sights listed below, Vanier Park is also home to the Vancouver Archives, Academy of Music, Canadian Coast Guard and Burrard Civic Marina. To reach Vanier Park from downtown, take the

No 22 bus, or take the water taxi from downtown or Granville Island.

Vancouver Museum This museum (☎ 604-736-4431), 1100 Chestnut St, specialises in the history of Vancouver and south-western BC. On display are historic photos and artefacts, including an exhibit on the archaeology and ethnology of the area, concentrating on the Salish Indians. There are several examples of most Native Indian crafts (check the totem pole in front of the museum). The basketry is impressive, especially those made of cedar and pine roots. The part of the museum documenting the European exploration and settlement of Vancouver is also good.

The museum is open from 10 am to 5 pm daily from May to September, and 10 am to 5 pm Tuesday to Sunday from October to April. Admission costs $8/5.50 adults/students and seniors.

HR MacMillan Planetarium & Pacific Space Centre The planetarium (☎ 604-738-7827), part of the Vancouver Museum complex, has regularly changing, entertaining and educational shows which are projected onto a dome 20m across. You should make reservations for these popular shows.

The centre now has a new virtual reality simulator called Virtual Voyages. You can find yourself stalking dinosaurs or probing the ocean depths depending on which program is on offer.

Adult admission is $12/9.50. There are also music-laser shows for $7.50 at 8.30 pm Sunday to Thursday and at 9.30 pm Friday and Saturday. The planetarium is closed on Monday during winter, but open daily in summer. On Friday, Saturday and Sunday afternoons when the sky is clear, the Gordon Southam Observatory (☎ 604-738-2855) is also open to the public and is free.

Vancouver Maritime Museum This museum (☎ 604-257-8300), 1905 Ogden Ave at the foot of Cypress St, is a five minute walk from the Vancouver Museum. There are two parts to the museum: the museum itself which has lots of wooden models and some

BRITISH COLUMBIA

old rowing boats plus good displays on the city's rich maritime heritage – and the *St Roch*. This 1928 Royal Canadian Mounted Police (RCMP) Arctic patrol sailing ship was the first vessel to navigate the legendary Northwest Passage in both directions. There are interesting guided tours on the ship every half-hour or so. The site is open from 10 am to 5 pm daily; closed Monday in winter. Admission is $6/3 adults/children.

Kitsilano The southern shore of English Bay, roughly from Burrard St to UBC, is the neighbourhood of Kitsilano. During the 1960s and 70s, Kitsilano was considered a hippie enclave and a centre of counter-culture sympathies and lifestyles. However, everyone and everything grows up, and the hippies are now lawyers and the neighbourhood has gone genteel. Old single-family homes are now unaffordable to the students who once gave the area its élan, and many old homes are now broken up into flats; new apartment buildings straggle and rise upwards, hoping for glimpses of downtown across the bay.

Kitsilano – usually referred to locally simply as Kits – is still a fun area to explore, particularly along W 4th Ave and W Broadway, the primary commercial streets, which are lined with unusual shops, bookstores and ethnic restaurants. The old counter-culture atmosphere is still here; you'll still find organic food stores and vegetarian restaurants, but chances are good that they are now next door to European clothing boutiques and spendy Italian trattorias.

One thing that hasn't changed in Kitsilano are the beaches. Kits faces onto English Bay, and the sandy strands that flank the water are very popular gathering spots in summer. **Kitsilano Beach**, near Vanier Park, and **Jericho Beach**, farther west on W 4th Ave at Jericho Beach Park, are two of the most popular places to gather and sun-worship.

University of British Columbia Often just called UBC, the University of British Columbia (☎ 604-822-2211) is at the most westerly point of Vancouver, Point Grey, on the spit jutting out into Georgia Strait. The huge campus serving 32,000 students is spread over 400 hectares, much of which is still forest, particularly Pacific Spirit Regional Park. Besides the pleasant grounds and the bustle of students, UBC offers a number of excellent gardens and a world-class museum of anthropology. The UBC Aquatic Centre (☎ 604-822-4521), off University Blvd, has pools, saunas and exercise areas open to the public. Bus Nos 4, 10 and 14 run to the university every 10 minutes or so from downtown; the journey takes about 30 minutes.

UBC Museum of Anthropology This excellent museum (☎ 604-822-5087), 6393 NW Marine Drive, focuses on exhibits of art and artefacts from cultures around the world. Asia, Africa and the Pacific are all well represented but the emphasis is on the work of BC's coastal Indians. This is reckoned to be the best collection of totem poles and wood carvings in the world. Be sure to step outside to see **Totem Park**, with re-created longhouses and totem poles gazing out to sea. The museum is open from 11 am to 5 pm daily in summer (till 9 pm Tuesday). It's closed Monday during the school year. Admission is $6/3.50 adults/seniors and students; it's free on Tuesday between 5 and 9 pm.

Nitobe Memorial Gardens These beautiful Japanese-style gardens (☎ 604-822-3825) are near the museum. Designed by a leading Japanese landscape architect, they're a perfect display of this symbolic art form. Get a free brochure at the gate when you buy a ticket. The gardens are open from 10 am to 6 pm daily in summer, and 11 am to 3 pm weekdays the rest of the year. Admission is $2.50/1.50 adults/seniors and students; free admission in winter.

UBC Botanical Gardens A real gem, these gardens cover 28 hectares near the corner of W 16th Ave and SW Marine Drive. There are several thematic plantings, including gardens with plants specific to regions of the world and to particular environments (for instance, the Asian and Alpine gardens), Canada's

largest collection of rhododendrons, and a 16th century apothecary garden. Even off season, these gardens will please – the aptly named Winter Garden features plants that bloom in wintertime. It's open from 10 am to 6 pm daily (till 2.30 pm in winter). Admission is $4.50/2.25 adults/seniors and students; free admission in winter.

Wreck Beach Along NW Marine Drive, heading south past the Rose Garden and the Museum of Anthropology, are markers for trails into the woods. Follow one of the trails marked No 4, 5 or 6 down the steep steps to Wreck Beach, a pleasant though rather busy nude beach. Kitsilano's counter-culture heritage is still in evidence here.

Queen Elizabeth Park This 53-acre park is between Cambie and Ontario Sts and near 33rd Ave; this is also the highest point in Vancouver. Up the hill on the way to the Bloedel Conservatory there are great views of the city in nearly every direction. The park features a mix of sports fields, manicured lawns and formal botanical gardens. The well designed sunken garden surrounded by small cliffs has some fantastic plants, one with leaves a metre across. Next to the parking lot is an unusual, Asian-looking garden consisting of many pools and fountains. Catch bus No 15 heading south-east on Robson St to get there.

Bloedel Conservatory Crowning the hill at Queen Elizabeth Park is this domed conservatory (☎ 604-257-8570). This 'garden under glass' has three climate zones, including desert and rainforest; beside the 500 species of plants, 50 species of free-flying tropical birds live in the conservatory. It's open from 9 am to 8 pm weekdays, 10 am to 9 pm weekends. Admission is $3.25/2 adults/children.

VanDusen Botanical Gardens This 55-acre park (☎ 604-878-9274) at 5251 Oak St between 33rd and 37th Aves, is not far from Queen Elizabeth Park. The gardens are one of Vancouver's highlights and contain a large collection of ornamental plants from around the world. Be sure to find your way

through the Elizabethan Hedge Maze. The gardens are open from 10 am to 9 pm daily in summer. The admission price is $5/2.50 adults/students. Take bus No 17 south on Burrard St from downtown.

Richmond

South of the North Arm Fraser River is Richmond, a suburb that has become closely identified with the recent influx of Hong Kong Chinese; in fact, the area is often referred to as Asia West. But don't expect to find the bustling, slightly seedy and peculiar charm of a Chinatown – everything here is very upscale, very sanitised and very suburban. It's what modern BC would be like if the Chinese, and not the British, had colonised the area. Which is why a detour to Richmond is more interesting than you might expect.

For the real Richmond experience, drive along No 3rd Rd, and stop at one of the many large shopping malls; there are four of them in a row. Yaohan Centre or Parker Place are both good destinations. Here you'll find brand-new gleaming shopping centres filled almost exclusively with Chinese stores, Chinese products and Chinese shoppers. Needless to say, you'll find excellent Chinese food here at very reasonable prices. As you drive through the neighbourhoods, you'll also notice the vast new homes favoured by the Hong Kong immigrants.

To reach No 3rd Rd in Richmond, take bus No 401, 403, 406 or 407 from Howe St in downtown Vancouver.

Richmond Nature Park, a 200-acre park (☎ 604-273-7015), 11851 Westminster Hwy, is dedicated to environmental education. The park features boardwalks through various ecosystems (a marsh, forest and a pond), with interpretative displays and signage. The Nature House Centre continues the theme with interactive exhibits designed with kids in mind. Free admission; open dawn to dusk.

Steveston In the south-west corner of Richmond is the old fishing village of Steveston, Canada's largest commercial fishing port. Steveston was settled largely by Japanese immigrants in the early 20th

century, however, during WWII nearly all the Japanese Canadians were sent to internment camps far inland, and their boats and homes were sold at auctions.

The old part of town that fronts onto Fraser River is quite charming, and has a number of good restaurants and pubs. There's lots of activity in the harbour, and the sights and smells of the fishing fleets make for a good escape from the rush of downtown Vancouver. Walk along Government Wharf where fisherfolk hawk their fresh catch directly from the boat.

If you're interested in the history of Steveston, stop by the **Steveston Museum** (☎ 604-271-6868), 3811 Moncton Rd, which tells the story of the town's fishing past and the internment of the Japanese; free admission. There's more history at the **Gulf of Georgia Cannery National Historic Site** (☎ 604-664-9009) at Bayview St and 4th Ave, a museum of the region's maritime past housed in an old fish cannery. The cannery tours are especially revealing of why you don't want to be a fish. It's open from 10 am to 5 pm daily in July and August; closed Tuesday and Wednesday other times.

To reach Steveston via public transport, take bus No 401, 406 or 407 south from Howe St.

East Vancouver

East of Main Street was traditionally the working-class and non-British section of Vancouver; Commercial Drive was once known as 'Little Italy.' The close-in east side is still where most non-Chinese immigrants make their homes. Farther east are the suburbs of Burnaby, Coquitlam and New Westminster. While these mostly residential communities aren't tourist destinations, there are a few interesting sites.

Commercial Drive In the early 20th century, this street was the centre of Vancouver's Italian community, and soon developed a reputation for good food and street life. Nowadays, Commercial Drive is still about cultural diversity, but of a broader sort. Portuguese, Latin American and South-East Asian restaurants and markets abound between 1st and 12th Aves. This is also a counterculture area as well, with rainbow flags hanging in shop windows, and earnest political conversations echoing in vegetarian cafés and third-world-solidarity coffee shops. The **Vancouver East Side Cultural Centre** (☎ 604-254-9578), 1895 Venables St, just off Commercial Drive, is a church converted into an avant-garde performance space which captures perfectly the area's left-of-centre politics and artistic tastes.

Simon Fraser University Simon Fraser, established in 1965, sits atop Burnaby Mountain in Burnaby, about 20km east of downtown. A showcase of modern architecture, the university was designed by noted Canadian architect Arthur Erickson; the design, incorporating unusual use of space and perspective, was – and remains – controversial. There are huge courtyard-like quadrants and many fountains, including one on a roof. Some areas of the complex are reminiscent of Mayan ruin sites in Mexico. The university's **Museum of Archaeology & Ethnology** (☎ 604-291-3325) features a collection of coastal Indian artefacts and has a cheap cafeteria. The museum is open from 10 am to 4 pm weekdays, and admission is by donation.

For information on tours around the university, call ☎ 604-291-3111. To get there, catch bus No 10 or 14 on E Hastings St then change near Boundary Rd to bus No 135, which will take you to the university.

Burnaby Village Museum This museum (☎ 604-293-6501) at 6501 Deer Lake Ave, beside Deer Lake, is in Burnaby's Century Park, near Deer Lake Park and close to the Trans Canada Hwy. It's a replica village that attempts to preserve both the artefacts and atmosphere of a south-western BC town in the years 1890 to 1925. There's an old schoolhouse, printing shop, drugstore and other establishments; a large, working steam-train model is next to the village. The restored carousel with 36 wooden horses is a highlight. Friendly, informed workers are in period dress. It's open from 10 am to 4.30 pm daily during summer, shorter hours

during the rest of the year. Admission is $6.20/4.35 adults/students and seniors. Catch bus No 120 on E Hastings St.

New Westminster The oldest town in western Canada, New Westminster was established in 1859, and briefly served as BC's capital city; nowadays New Westminster has been absorbed into greater Vancouver. This was once the area's primary seaport, and the districts along the Fraser River have retained their period charm. The waterfront esplanade has been overhauled and, together with the Westminster Quay Public Market, has become a casual people-watching kind of place with restaurants and bars as well as shops. The small downtown area is here, too, just north of the New Westminster SkyTrain stop.

Irving House Historic Centre Built in 1865, this 14-room home (☎ 604-521-7656), 302 Royal Ave, is one of the oldest structures in BC, and now functions as a museum of frontier life and furnishings. The original owner was a riverboat captain on the Fraser River. Adjacent is the **New Westminster Museum**, which tells the story of this historic township. It's open from 11 am to 5 pm Tuesday to Sunday in summer; 1 to 5 pm weekends only in winter. Admission is by donation.

The North Shore

North and West Vancouver, divided roughly by the Capilano River, together make up the North Shore. There are three principal ways to experience this side of the inlet. You can take the SeaBus for city views, stroll Lonsdale Quay and spend a few hours eating and sightseeing around lower North Vancouver. Or, with a vehicle, tour along Marine Drive through West Vancouver, possibly all the way to Horseshoe Bay stopping at parks and enjoying the harbour alongside some of Vancouver's wealthy neighbourhoods. Lastly, you can visit one of the provincial parks for some fine vistas and real hiking.

North Vancouver The **Lonsdale Quay Market** (☎ 604-985-6261) is the centre of the North Shore SeaBus terminal complex which includes a water's edge park, offices and apartments. The 1st floor is devoted to fresh and cooked food; the 2nd floor is mainly speciality shops but has a restaurant with good views. As you leave the ferry, there's an information booth to offer guidance on the North Shore's attractions. The local bus terminal is here as well. The market is open from 9.30 am to 6.30 pm daily (till 9 pm Friday). To get there catch the SeaBus from the downtown terminal at Waterfront Station.

North Vancouver Museum & Archives The small museum (☎ 604-987-5618), 333 Chesterfield Ave, offers rather good changing exhibits on a wide range of subjects such as transport, antiques and Native Indian crafts. It's open from noon to 5 pm Wednesday to Sunday (till 9 pm Thursday). Admission is by donation.

Capilano Suspension Bridge This bridge (☎ 604-985-7474), 3735 Capilano Rd, in Capilano River Regional Park spans the Capilano River for almost 140m at a height of 70m. It's pretty impressive; however, the suspension bridge is *very* popular, and the crowds can be oppressive. You decide if you want to pay the steep admission just to walk across a bridge. It's open from 8 am till 9 pm daily in summer. Admission is $8.95/7.50/6 adults/seniors/students, and $2.75 children (six to 12).

To get to the park, from downtown take bus No 246, marked 'Highlands', going west on W Georgia St or bus No 236 from Lonsdale Quay to Edgemont Village; you then change to bus No 232. (This bus also goes to Capilano Salmon Hatchery and Cleveland Dam; in summer bus No 236 goes all the way to Grouse Mountain.) If you're driving, head north over Lions Gate Bridge to Marine Drive in North Vancouver, then turn left (north) onto Capilano Rd.

Capilano Salmon Hatchery The hatchery is a fish farm (☎ 604-666-1790) run by the government to help stop the depletion of valuable salmon stocks. Although you can't see the holding pools, there are exhibits

with good explanations of the whole process. Salmon in various stages of growth are on display in tanks, and you can see how they are channelled from the river into the hatchery when they head upstream to spawn. Admission is free. It's in Capilano River Regional Park, off Capilano Rd not far north of the suspension bridge.

Cleveland Dam The dam (☎ 604-224-5739) blocks Capilano Lake, which supplies much of Vancouver's drinking water. You'll get good views of the Lions, two peaks of the Coast Mountains. There are picnic areas and trails and it's free. The dam is slightly farther north of the salmon hatchery up Capilano Rd, which becomes Nancy Greene Way.

Grouse Mountain Just out Vancouver's backdoor, Grouse Mountain (☎ 604-984-0661), 6400 Nancy Greene Way (the northern extension of Capilano Rd), is the city's most convenient ski area; several runs are lit for night skiing. Grouse Mountain is famous for its Swiss-built **Superskyride** cable car which operates daily from 9 am to 10 pm. The lift remains open all year, and Grouse Mountain has a full schedule of summer activities. From the top – 1100m – you can see all of Vancouver, the coast, part of Vancouver Island and northward over the mountains. You can rent mountain bikes at the lift-top lodge or strike out on a hiking trail. If you're not feeling athletic, there is a chain-saw sculpture tour and a small movie theatre with a complimentary film at the lodge. There are restaurants at the top and bottom of the mountain.

If you take the Superskyride, make sure it's a clear day. If it's raining, foggy or at all hazy with low clouds, forget it – by the time you reach the top you won't see a thing. Go in late afternoon; then you can see the city by day and by night. The Superskyride is an expensive ride at $15.95/13.95 for adults/seniors, $9.95/5.95 youths/children, and $39.95 families.

Lynn Canyon Park Set in thick woods, this park gives a good glimpse of the temperate rainforest vegetation found in the coastal

Pacific Northwest. There are many hiking trails, and you can find your own picnic and swimming spots. Over Lynn Canyon is the **Lynn Canyon Suspension Bridge**; although not as big as Capilano, it's much the same but it's free. The **Lynn Canyon Park Ecology Centre** (☎ 604-987-5922), 3663 Park Rd, has displays, films and slide shows about the biology of the area. It's open from 10 am to 5 pm daily.

To get to the park take bus No 228 or 229 from Lonsdale Quay. If you're driving go over Second Narrows Bridge, take Lynn Valley Rd then go right (east) on Peters Rd, where you'll see signs that lead you into the park.

Mt Seymour Provincial Park This park (☎ 604-924-2200), 13km north-east of downtown, is a quick escape from the city. There is a road most of the way up and a chair lift goes to the peak. The park has several hiking trails and the views of Vancouver's surroundings are beautiful. Some areas are very rugged, so visitors going on overnight trips should register with park rangers. There's also skiing here in winter.

There are parking lots for RVs but no real tent campgrounds. You can, however, pitch a tent along the many alpine trails. From Lonsdale Quay take bus No 229 or 239 to Phibbs Exchange then bus No 215. If you're driving, head over the Second Narrows Bridge and turn right (east) off the Trans Canada Hwy onto Mt Seymour Parkway.

West Vancouver West of the Capilano River and north of Burrard Inlet are the communities of West Vancouver, one of the wealthiest municipalities in Canada. Marine Drive passes by the Park Royal Shopping Centre (Canada's first mall, and still a good place to shop) into **Ambleside** with its waterside park on Burrard Inlet. Farther west is **Dundarave**, a commercial strip with a number of restaurants and cafés, some with balconies overlooking the water, amid the shops. Antique shopping is good in this area. Northward up the hill and on the other side of the Upper Levels Hwy are expensive houses with

BRITISH COLUMBIA

good views over the harbour. Marine Drive follows the coast to Horseshoe Bay.

Lighthouse Park Here in a stand of original coastal forest are some of the largest trees in the Vancouver area; you'll also see the unusual arbutus, a wide-leaf evergreen with orange peeling bark. There are 13km of hiking trails; the most popular one leads to the **Point Atkinson Lighthouse**, which commands the inlet from its rocky perch. The park is about 9.5km to the left (west) on Marine Drive after crossing Lions Gate Bridge. Catch bus No 250 going west on West Georgia St.

Horseshoe Bay North of Vancouver, the small coastal community of Horseshoe Bay marks the end of Marine Drive and West Vancouver. It's a pretty spot, with great views across the bay and up the fjord to distant glaciered peaks. There are a number of good places to eat and shop here.

Horseshoe Bay is one of BC's busiest ferry terminals; ferries leave here for Nanaimo on Vancouver Island and Langdale on the Sunshine Coast.

Just beyond Horseshoe Bay, on Marine Drive, is **Whytecliff Park**, a great little park right on the water. Trails lead to vistas and a gazebo, from where you can watch the boat traffic wend its way in and out of Burrard Inlet. This is a favourite spot for scuba diving.

Activities

Hiking There are tons of hiking opportunities in the many provincial mountain parks just north of Vancouver (see The North Shore earlier in this Vancouver section for more options).

Cypress Provincial Park is the closest, just 8km north of West Vancouver off Hwy 99. It has eight hiking trails, including the Baden-Powell, Yew Lake and Howe Sound Crest trails. Mt Seymour Provincial Park, 13km north-east of downtown, has 10 trails varying in difficulty and length. At both parks you should be prepared for continually changing mountain weather conditions. On clear days both parks offer magnificent views.

There's hiking in **Garibaldi Provincial Park**, north of Vancouver (for details see North of Vancouver later in this chapter). **Golden Ears Provincial Park** is 48km northeast of Vancouver. Take Hwy 7 as far as Haney, then turn left (north) and follow the 13km road to Alouette Lake. The park has 11 hiking trails, plus camp sites and picnic areas.

Skiing Vancouver has some great downhill and cross-country skiing just minutes from downtown; each of the following ski areas allows snowboarding. **Grouse Mountain** (☎ 604-984-0661), off Capilano Rd in North Vancouver, is the nearest to the city and is notable for its night skiing, when most of the downhill runs are illuminated and open till 10 pm. The day pass for an adult is $30. From downtown, take the SeaBus to Lonsdale Quay, then bus No 236 to the Grouse Mountain Skyride.

Other nearby ski resorts include Cypress Bowl (also with night skiing) and Hollyburn (☎ 604-926-5612 for either resort, snow report ☎ 604-419-7669) both in **Cypress Provincial Park** on Vancouver's North Shore. Cypress Bowl has downhill but is best known for its cross-country trails. Also in the North Shore, **Mt Seymour** (☎ 604-986-2261) in North Vancouver is a semi-wilderness provincial park only 13km from downtown. The park contains downhill runs, groomed cross-country trails and a tobogganing slope. It also has night skiing.

For information on downhill skiing at Whistler and Blackcomb, and cross-country skiing at Garibaldi Provincial Park, see North of Vancouver later in this chapter.

Cycling A good way to get around Vancouver and its numerous parks and beach areas is by bicycle. Some areas with designated bicycle paths are the 9.5km seawall promenade in Stanley Park; the route from Granville Island, through Vanier Park to Kitsilano Beach; and if you want to keep going west you could take Point Grey Rd to Jericho Beach Park then follow the shoreline to Spanish Banks Beach. See Getting Around at the end of this Vancouver section for details on bicycle rental.

Swimming You can swim at a number of city beaches: Second and Third beaches in Stanley Park, English Bay and Sunset Beaches downtown, or at Kitsilano and Jericho Beaches on the southern side of English Bay. Kitsilano Beach is the largest and most popular and where the beach-culture scene peaks – on a hot summer day as many as 10,000 people hit the sands. The prime spot to see and be seen is around the lifeguard section; other areas attract those who prefer a little more material used in the construction of their bathing suits. At one portion of the beach you might catch one of the professional or semi-professional volleyball tournaments which occur regularly throughout the summer months. Wreck Beach (see University of British Columbia earlier in this Vancouver section) is Vancouver's nude beach.

The Vancouver Aquatic Centre (☎ 604-665-3424), 1050 Beach Ave near Sunset Beach, has an indoor heated swimming pool, whirlpool, diving tank, gym and sauna. There's another aquatic centre at UBC and one (☎ 604-926-8585) in West Vancouver at 776 22nd St. Kitsilano Beach has an outdoor heated saltwater pool (☎ 604-731-0011). Admission to these heated pools is usually $4.

Canoeing, Kayaking & Windsurfing If you've got the energy for canoeing or kayaking, the Fraser River and the Chilliwack River (east of Vancouver) offer plenty of opportunities for the beginner to the experienced. On Granville Island you can hire canoes. Ecomarine Ocean Kayak Centre (☎ 604-689-7575), 1668 Duranleau St, hires out solo kayaks for $19 for two hours or $39 a day. It has another outlet at the Jericho Sailing Centre at Jericho Beach in Kitsilano near the HI Vancouver Jericho Beach hostel. Ecomarine also offers educational tours of the islands in Georgia Strait and in Clayoquot Sound on the west coast of Vancouver Island.

In North Vancouver, on Indian Arm, Deep Cove Canoe & Kayak (☎ 604-929-2268), 2156 Banbury Rd, has rentals and will teach you how to use a canoe. At Deer Lake, east of town in Burnaby, you can rent solo canoes for $12 an hour from Deer Lake Boat Rentals (☎ 604-255-0081).

Windsure Windsurfing School (☎ 604-224-0615), 1300 Discovery St at the Jericho Sailing Centre, gives windsurfing lessons and also rents boards.

Scuba Diving Scuba diving is popular north-west of the city off Lighthouse Park and at Porteau Cove 26km north of Horseshoe Bay, both in Howe Sound; and on Indian Arm at the eastern end of Burrard Inlet. A number of outfitters offer equipment, training and trips, including the Diving Locker (☎ 604-736-2681), 2745 W 4th Ave, in Kitsilano.

Organised Tours

The Gray Line Bus Company (☎ 604-879-3363) offers a wide selection of traditional bus sightseeing tours ranging from city tours to 10-day tours of the Canadian Rockies. Most begin at the Hotel Vancouver, but all major hotels sell tickets and offer pickup. The Deluxe Grand City Tour is a 3½ hour tour taking in most of Vancouver's tourist sites, and costs $39/28 adults/children; the tour is available in five different languages. A less structured tour is the Decker and Trolley Tour. For a $23 ticket, you can hop on and off buses at over 20 designated stops, and the ticket is good for two consecutive days. For $96 you can go on a day trip to Victoria and Butchart Gardens.

Another bus tour option is operated by the Vancouver Trolley Co (☎ 604-801-5515). The ticket costs $20 and allows you a full day of transport between 17 different stops.

West Coast Sightseeing (☎ 604-451-1600) runs the usual city bus tours, but it also has a four hour Native Culture Tour that visits various Vancouver museums and sights relating to the First Nations people. The cost is $41/25 for adults/children.

The major long-distance tour operator in western Canada is Brewster Tours (☎ 1-800-661-1152), which runs many trips from Vancouver, including circle tours of Vancouver Island and multi-day tours to the Canadian Rockies.

BRITISH COLUMBIA

Pacific Coach Lines (☎ 604-662-7575) at Pacific Central Station operates a number of one-day excursions for about the same price as a normal bus ticket. Destinations include Vancouver Island and the Sunshine Coast.

Harbour Ferries (☎ 604-688-7246) offers 1½-hour cruises for $16, as well as longer more costly evening dinner sailings around False Creek, English Bay and Burrard Inlet. Boats leave from its office at the north foot of Denman St by Stanley Park.

Harbour Air Seaplanes (☎ 604-688-1277) offers air tours aboard float planes from its water terminal at the base of Burrard St (one block north of Canada Place). The least expensive flight ($72) tours the Vancouver area for 20 minutes; longer mail-run flights up the Sunshine Coast are available.

There are free daily walking tours, sponsored by the Gastown Business Improvement Society (☎ 604-683-5650), of the historic district during summer. The walks begin at 2 pm in front of the Gassy Jack Statue on Maple St Square.

Special Events
Following is a list of some of the major events in Vancouver during the year. *The Vancouver Book*, available from the Visitor Info Centre, has an up-to-date list of current events.

January
Polar Bear Swim
This popular, chilly affair has been taking place at English Bay Beach annually on 1 January since 1819. If you can't handle the water, watching is allowed. Call ☎ 604-605-2304 for information.

February
Chinese New Year
Chinatown provides the setting for one of Vancouver's most colourful events, with dancers, music, fireworks and food. Based on the Chinese calendar, the celebration begins in early February or at the end of January and lasts for two weeks. Call ☎ 604-687-6021 for information.

June
Canadian International Dragon Boat Festival
This annual event takes place in False Creek over three days in late June. It attracts nearly 2000 competitors from around the world and about 150,000 spectators. As well as the boat races, there's music, theatre and international cuisine. Call ☎ 604-688-2382 for information.

July
Vancouver Folk Music Festival
Held in mid-July, the Folk Music Festival is three days of music, including concerts and workshops, from some of the best North American folk musicians. It attracts about 30,000 visitors and most of the action takes place at Jericho Beach Park. For ticket information call ☎ 604-879-2931.

August
Abbotsford International Air Show
Known as Canada's National Air Show, this three-day event, held in early August, has everything that flies, from fighters to the Concorde. It's held 65km south-east of Vancouver in Abbotsford near the US border. Call ☎ 604-859-9651 for information.

Gay Pride Day
Also in early August, watch for its festive parade drawing 15,000 people along Denman St.

Pacific National Exhibition
Known as the PNE (☎ 604-253-2311), this big fair, the second largest in Canada, features a little bit of everything – sports, competitions, international exhibits, concerts and shows, as well as amusement park rides. It starts off each year with a two hour parade. The exhibition lasts about two weeks, from late August to Labour Day. The PNE usually takes place in Exhibition Park on E Hastings St near the Second Narrows Bridge but is due to move. Catch bus No 14 or 16 from downtown.

September
Vancouver Fringe Festival – This popular theatre event presents drama, musical theatre, comedy and dance from around the world. It takes place over a fortnight from early to mid-September in various theatres around Main St, between E 6th and E 17th Aves in the Mt Pleasant area (just east of False Creek). Call ☎ 604-873-3646 for information.

Places to Stay
Vancouver is unusual in that a great many inexpensive and moderately priced hotels and motels remain in the otherwise high-rent downtown area – in addition to the landmark luxury and business hotels com-

monly associated with city centres. Unless you prefer staying on a motel strip some distance from the city centre, there's no reason not to stay right in the centre of things.

Summer is very busy in Vancouver, and you should make reservations weeks, even months, in advance if you have your heart set on a specific hotel. The Vancouver Visitor Info Centre (☎ 1-800-663-6000) offers a free accommodation reservation service, which can be indispensable if you are trying to find a room at the last minute.

Camping There are no public campgrounds in the Vancouver area and, except for one, the RV parks right in Vancouver do not allow tenting. In North Vancouver, the *Capilano RV Park (☎ 604-987-4722, 295 Tomahawk Ave)* has everything, including a jacuzzi and tent sites from $22. Exit onto Capilano Rd south off Hwy 1.

Other campgrounds are south of the city, on or near Hwy 99, which runs to the US border. South of the Middle Arm of the Fraser River, *Richmond RV Park (☎ 604-270-7878, 6200 River Rd, Richmond)*, near Hollybridge Way is one of the closest to town. It's open from April to October and has sites from $16 for two people. *Park-Canada RV Inns (☎ 604-943-5811, 4799 Hwy 17, Delta)* is north-east of the Tsawwassen ferry terminal. It has free showers and sites from $14.

Hostels Travellers have an ever-increasing array of hostel choices, including some real dodgy old hotels trying to cash in on the increase in traffic; these didn't make it into this guide. Most of the good hostels are pretty much full throughout summer and quite busy the rest of the year.

The HI *Vancouver Downtown (☎ 604-684-4565, fax 604-684-4540, van-downtown@hihostels.bc.ca, 1114 Burnaby St)*, on the corner of Thurlow St, is in a former nunnery and health-care centre. There are 212 beds with no more than four in any one room. Family rooms are available. Prices are $19 members, $23 nonmembers. Facilities include a patio, library and games

room. This very convenient hostel is walkable from anywhere in the downtown area and is open 24 hours.

The new *Global Village Backpackers (☎ 604-682-8226, ☎ 1-888-844-7875, 1018 Granville St)* is a welcome addition. Considerable renovations have made this central, large (250 beds) facility an appealing, comfortable, well appointed hostel. Features include rooftop patio, private bar and informative travel desk. Rates are $20 for quad room dorms and $45 to $50 for a double room.

The central *Cambie International Hostel (☎ 604-684-6466, ☎ 1-877-395-5335, info@cambiehostels.com, 300 Cambie St)* at Cordova St has dorm beds in two or four-bunk rooms costing $20 for students or HI members, and $27 to anyone else. Bedding is provided, and bathrooms are down the hall; there's also bicycle storage and laundry facilities. A bakery, café and a fun saloon on the ground floor make it a convenient and potentially noisy place to spend the night.

The *New Backpackers Hostel (☎ 604-688-0112, 347 W Pender St)*, centrally located in the big hotel building, is bare bones and tatty. Despite this, the $10 dorm beds go quickly and you may have to wait for a shower. Single/double rooms are $25/35.

Although the HI *Vancouver Jericho Beach (☎ 604-224-3208, fax 604-224-4852, van-jericho@hihostels.bc.ca, 1515 Discovery St, Kitsilano)* is away from the centre of town, its location is great. The hostel is close to the beach in Jericho Beach Park on English Bay, about 20 minutes from downtown by bus. It's open 24 hours, although there is a 'quiet time' between 11 pm and 7 am. With 288 beds, it's the largest in Canada and has complete facilities. The rates are $16 for members, $20 for nonmembers. From downtown take bus No 4 south on Granville St.

Over in North Vancouver, the *Globetrotter's Inn (☎ 604-988-2082, globies@hotmail.com, 170 W Esplanade)* is small and quiet; it's only a two minute walk to the SeaBus at Lonsdale Quay and close to all amenities. It has a kitchen and laundry and

a range of rooms. Rates are $17.50 for dorm and $45 double.

The *YMCA (☎ 604-681-0221, 955 Burrard St)* is right downtown, on the corner of Barclay St. Depending on whether you'd like a TV, singles are $36 or $39, doubles are $44 or $46 (tax included). Women and couples are allowed and quite a few travellers stay here. The only drawback is the constant unlocking of doors. There are gym and pool facilities and a small inexpensive restaurant serving good-value breakfasts and sandwiches.

The *YWCA (☎ 604-895-5830, ☎ 1-800-663-1424 in Canada, 733 Beatty St)* between Georgia and Robson Sts near the BC Place Stadium, is really like a hotel and accommodates men, women, couples or families. There are 155 rooms in various configurations ranging from singles with bathrooms down the hall ($51) to family rooms ($94) and one with five single beds ($141). Doubles start at $62 and go to $98 with a private bathroom. Each room has a fridge but there are also communal kitchens as well as TV lounges and a laundry. Fitness facilities are offered but are off the premises. The stadium SkyTrain stop is a five minute walk.

Universities The *University of British Columbia* rents rooms from about the first week in May to the end of August. Singles/doubles with shared bathroom are $22/44 or you can get self-contained apartments for $84 to $95. Contact the Conference Centre (☎ 604-822-1010), Gage Towers, 5961 Student Union Blvd, UBC Campus, Vancouver, BC V6T 2C9. The pleasant campus has a cafeteria, some cafés, coin laundry, pub and sports facilities.

In East Vancouver, *Simon Fraser University* rents out rooms from May to August. They're all fully furnished and bathrooms are shared; singles without bedding (bring your own sleeping bag) cost $19, with bedding $31, doubles with bedding $51. The university also has four-bedroom townhouse units for $115.

Contact Housing & Conference Services (☎ 604-291-4503), Room 212, McTaggart-Cowan Hall, Burnaby, BC V5A 1S6.

B&Bs Vancouver B&Bs are usually not cheap, averaging $75 to $105 a double with shared bathroom. Because B&Bs come and go rather quickly, it's good to use a reservation service to book a room. Each of the following have rooms in all price ranges. Old English B&B Registry (☎ 604-986-5069) can be contacted at 1226 Silverwood Crescent, North Vancouver, BC V7L 1L3. Town & Country B&B (☎ 604-731-5942) is at PO Box 74542, Vancouver, BC V6K 1K2.

Although not a booking agency, contact the Western Canada B&B Innkeepers Association (☎ 604-255-9199), PO Box 74534, Vancouver, BC V6K 4P4, for member listings in Vancouver and across the province.

The historic neighbourhoods of Kitsilano, Kerrisdale and Shaughnessy are where you'd expect to find nice B&Bs. Contact the booking agencies listed above, or if you want to call and reserve on your own, try one of the following. *Windsor Guest House (☎ 604-872-3060, 325 W 11th Ave)* is an 1895 home in Kitsilano with two rooms, one with private bathroom ($75); $65 without private bath.

Walnut House B&B (☎ 604-739-6941, 1350 Walnut St) is another heritage home in Kitsilano's best location. Near the beach and Vanier Park, it has three rooms with private bathrooms; $100/110 for a single/double. For a more modern alternative, try *Treehouse B&B (☎ 604-266-2962, 2490 W 49th Ave)*, with contemporary décor, jacuzzi tubs, private baths and three guest rooms at $110.

An inexpensive and popular place on the West Side is *Paul's Guest House (☎ 604-872-4753, 345 W 14th Ave)*, two blocks east of Cambie St between Alberta and Yukon Sts in a quiet residential area. Paul speaks 11 languages – that should cover most guests! It's very clean and friendly and there's a laundry service. Singles are $50 and doubles $60 to $80 from May to September dropping to $40 to $50 the rest of the year. If this place is full, Paul has another guesthouse just down the street.

Hotels – Budget Be aware that Vancouver has many inexpensive hotels right downtown, especially along Granville, Pender

and Hastings Sts. While some are well kept and offer good value, many serve the downtrodden and those on very low incomes or government assistance, whose numbers are greater here than in any other Canadian city.

The best low-cost hotel in town is the *Kingston Hotel* (☎ 604-684-9024, ☎ 1-888-713-3304, 757 Richards St). It was the city's first B&B hotel and still offers the morning meal (although it's just enough to get the eyes open). Singles range from $45 to $65, doubles from $50 to $80. Extras offered are a sauna, laundry and an overnight parking subsidy. The *Dufferin Hotel* (☎ 604-683-4251, 900 Seymour St), with prices beginning at $65/70 a single/double, is a good choice and gets the Kingston's overflow. There's a dining room and free parking.

In Gastown, the old but renovated *Dominion Hotel* (☎ 604-681-6666, 210 Abbot St) dates from 1899. The rooms go for $65 with shared bathroom or $75 with private bathroom.

Hotels – Mid-Range One of the city's best deals is the *Bosman's Motor Hotel* (☎ 604-682-3171, ☎ 1-888-267-6267, 1060 Howe St). It is extremely central, has free parking, and is everything most people will ever need in a moderately priced lodging with rooms from $99 to $109 (each room has two queen-size beds).

A moderately priced motel, the *Burrard Motor Inn* (☎ 604-681-2331, ☎ 1-800-663-0366, 1100 Burrard St) is convenient and a favourite of families and budget travellers with rooms at $85/95 a single/double. The well loved and slightly faded *Sylvia Hotel* (☎ 604-681-9321, 1154 Gilford St) has a marvellous location on English Bay close to Stanley Park. The old ivy-covered hotel is where the politically alternative stay when they come to town. Don't resist, it's a nice place – $65/110, kitchen suites from $120. For good-value suites in a former apartment building, you can't beat *Oceanside Apartment Hotel* (☎ 604-682-5641, 1847 Pendrell St) with single rooms starting at $90.

You can't get much closer to Stanley Park than *The Buchan Hotel* (☎ 604-685-5354, ☎ 1-800-668-6654, 1906 Haro St), a nicely appointed older hotel with rooms at $90/100 a single/double; forego a private toilet, and rooms drop to $65/75. The *Shato Inn Hotel* (☎ 604-681-8920, 1825 Comox St), off Denman St a couple of blocks from Stanley Park and English Bay Beach, also has some rooms with cooking facilities. Rooms are $85/90; $20 extra for the kitchen.

Robson St, west of the busy shopping district, has some good lodging deals in a prime area. The *Barclay Hotel* (☎ 604-688-8850, 1348 Robson St) has air-con, TV and a licensed lounge; $75/95. *Riviera Motor Inn* (☎ 604-685-1301, ☎ 1-888-699-5222, 1431 Robson St) has apartments with fully equipped kitchens, beginning at $78. From some of the apartments you get a good view of the North Shore.

Along Robson St, you get more amenities for a little more money. *Blue Horizon Hotel* (☎ 604-688-4461, ☎ 1-800-663-1333, 1225 Robson St) with rooms at $145, has great views, balconies and an indoor pool. The *Greenbriar Hotel* (☎ 604-683-4558, 1393 Robson St) is a former apartment building that's been transformed into a suite hotel. It's nicer than it looks from the outside, as each room ($149 to $169) has a full kitchen and sitting area in addition to the bedroom. The *Tropicana Motor Inn* (☎ 604-687-5724, 1361 Robson St) is another high-rise option in this area with similar amenities, and a pool and sauna; double rooms start at $139.

Over by the Granville Bridge, the *Travelodge Vancouver Centre* (☎ 604-682-2767, ☎ 1-800-665-2080, 1304 Howe St) has basic but fine rooms, and there's a heated outdoor pool; $95/105. A couple of blocks in from the waterfront is the *Holiday Inn Vancouver Downtown* (☎ 604-684-2151, ☎ 1-800-663-9151, 1110 Howe St), a class act for a chain hotel, with large rooms, pool, health club and some kitchens; double rooms cost $169 to $189.

Days Inn Vancouver Downtown (☎ 604-681-4335, ☎ 1-800-329-7466, 921 W Pender St) has a great location near the harbour, free parking and small but nicely furnished rooms starting at $125/135 a single/double.

One of the older, more elegant hotels with wooden panelling and chandeliers is the *Hotel Georgia* (☎ 604-682-5566, ☎ 1-800-663-1111, 801 W Georgia St). For this class of hotel, rooms are good value at $145 to $180/175 to $210 a single/double.

In the burgeoning entertainment district along Granville St downtown, the porn shops are in decline and entrepreneurs are turning faded hotels into hip places to stay where you don't pay a lot to be surrounded in style. The *Hotel Dakota* (☎ 604-605-4333, ☎ 1-888-605-5333, 645 Nelson St) at Granville St has comfy rooms with thick duvet covered beds that cost from $69/99 a single/double. The ground floor is home to the hot and trendy BaBalu Lounge, a salsa movie come to life. The former Hotel Linden has become a *Howard Johnson Hotel* (☎ 604-688-8701, ☎ 1-888-654-6336, 1176 Granville St). It has rooms aimed at business travellers and a breakfast room right out of a small European pension. Rooms start at $55/99 in the low/high season. The *Gateway Hotel* (☎ 604-685-1111, ☎ 1-888-835-0078, 1221 Granville St) has 117 well equipped rooms that average $79/139 in the low/high season.

Hotels – Top End Downtown Vancouver has a number of elegant older hotels, as well as brand-new hotel towers with luxury-class accommodation.

Despite the rising skyline, the *Hotel Vancouver* (☎ 604-684-3131, ☎ 1-800-441-1414, 900 W Georgia St) remains a city landmark recognisable by its green copper roof. This Canadian Pacific hotel is one of the largest and most famous in Vancouver, offering all the comforts known to the modern hospitality industry. A recent complete remodel brought this vintage doyenne even more up to date. Rooms begin at $220/245 a single/double.

If you want a more personalised experience, try the *Wedgewood Hotel* (☎ 604-689-7777, ☎ 1-800-663-0666, 845 Hornby St), another fantastic vintage boutique hotel with luxury-class rooms beginning at $200 a double. The list of amenities is exhaustive and the hotel has many repeat customers.

There are a couple of opulent choices along Robson St, the best of which is *Listel Vancouver* (☎ 604-684-8461, ☎ 1-800-663-5491, 1300 Robson St). Rooms are modern, large and very well appointed ($180/200 a single/double), and the hotel restaurant is very good.

On the shores of Burrard Inlet, by the harbour, are two other notable hotels. The *Pan Pacific Hotel* (☎ 604-662-8111, ☎ 1-800-663-1515 in Canada, ☎ 1-800-937-1515 in USA) is in the white-winged Canada Place. You pay a lot for the location, with rooms at $400/430, but the views are superb and the service extraordinary. The *Westin Bayshore* (☎ 604-682-3377, ☎ 1-800-228-3000, 1601 W Georgia St) offers the same superlatives from a location right on the waterfront and closer to Stanley Park; rooms cost $260 to $285 double.

An even more stylish alternative is the *Sheraton Wall Centre Hotel* (☎ 604-331-1000, ☎ 1-800-663-9255, 1088 Burrard St), a modern high-rise in the centre of the city with a distinctly arty and modernistic atmosphere. Rooms begin at $190/210.

Vancouver's highest-rated hotel, the *Four Seasons Hotel* (☎ 604-689-9333, ☎ 1-800-268-6282, 791 W Georgia St), is above the Pacific Centre shopping complex. To get to the reception area, take the escalator to the left of the Buddha statue. Room prices vary widely, and start from $320. Expect every luxury here.

Hotels – Kitsilano & the West Side *Shaughnessy Village* (☎ 604-736-5511, 1125 W 12th Ave) is a high-rise complex incorporating a B&B, hotel, resort, apartment building and fun centre all rolled into one. The least expensive rooms, tiny ship-like studio cabins, cost $78/87 a single/double with breakfast and come packed with every amenity. In the dead of winter the price plummets to $40/50. Ask for one of the limited parking spots when you book the room.

There aren't many mid-range choices in Kitsilano. The *Holiday Inn Vancouver Centre* (☎ 604-879-0511, ☎ 1-800-663-9151, 711 W Broadway), with rooms at

$159/179, is a large complex with a pool and two restaurants. **Ramada Vancouver Centre** (☎ 604-872-8661, ☎ 1-800-663-5403, 898 W Broadway) has rooms with balconies for $155.

In one of the city's top locations, the **Granville Island Hotel** (☎ 604-683-7373, 1253 Johnston St, Granville Island) is a modernistic structure right on the waterfront with great downtown views. The hotel is near the island's famed market, arts and crafts galleries, and theatres; you'll be just seconds away from the water taxis to downtown. Suite-style rooms are $199/209 a single/double.

Hotels – Near the Airport There are a number of hotels in Richmond that service the Vancouver international airport. Each has free airport shuttle vans. One of the least expensive places to stay out here is **Holiday Inn Express** (☎ 604-223-9971, ☎ 1-800-465-4329, 9351 Bridgeport Rd) with basic clean rooms at $69/79. The **Stay 'N Save Motor Inn** (☎ 604-273-3311, ☎ 1-800-663-0298, 10551 St Edwards Drive) has the usual high standards of comfort from this economical chain. Rooms start at $89/99.

For a touch more luxury, try the **Delta Vancouver Airport Hotel & Marina** (☎ 604-278-1241, 3500 Cessna Drive) which has business-class rooms from $145 to $205.

Motels – East Vancouver The closest motel strip to downtown is along E Hastings St around Exhibition Park and east into Burnaby. This is a convenient area, close to Second Narrows Bridge leading over Burrard Inlet to North Vancouver. The **Best Western Exhibition Park** (☎ 604-294-4751, ☎ 1-800-528-1234, 3475 E Hastings St) on the corner of Cassiar St has rooms from $80.

The second motel area is along Kingsway, a major road which branches off Main St south of 7th Ave. One of the closest motels to town is the **Biltmore Hotel** (☎ 604-872-5252, ☎ 1-800-663-5713, 395 Kingsway). It has aircon, TV, licensed restaurant and coffee shop. Rooms start at $89. A bit farther out, the **2400 Motel** (☎ 604-434-2464, ☎ 1-888-833-2400, 2400 Kingsway) is a great deal with rooms starting at $65.

Motels – North Shore Another motel area is on the North Shore, over Lions Gate Bridge. Look along Marine Drive and north up Capilano Rd. There are also a couple of spots on the Esplanade, which runs east-west along the North Shore, past the SeaBus terminal. The **Canyon Court Motel** (☎ 604-988-3181, ☎ 1-888-988-3181, 1748 Capilano Rd, North Vancouver), close to Lions Gate Bridge, has rooms costing around $100 for a single or double. There's a laundry, free coffee, swimming pool and at extra cost, kitchens.

One of the nicer places to stay is the **Grouse Inn** (☎ 604-988-7101, ☎ 1-800-779-7888, 1633 Capilano Rd), with kitchen suites and a guest laundry. Rooms start at $98 double.

Places to Eat

When it comes to restaurants, Vancouver is one of the most cosmopolitan cities in North America, and that's good news for food lovers. You can journey gastronomically from country to country by wandering down the streets, some of which are groaning with choices. You aren't confined by budget either, because all types of food are available in all price categories. Add the Northwest's natural bounty of farm, garden and sea, and you've got the makings of a cuisine capital.

The restaurants below are listed by neighbourhood and within each section listed in order of ascending price.

Granville St There are plenty of cheap greasy-spoon cafés and restaurants along Granville St, with a few that stand out. **Kitto Japanese House** (☎ 604-687-6622, 833 Granville St) is sometimes described as the McDonald's of Japanese food, but be that as it may the food is good, fast and inexpensive; there's a second restaurant at 833 Bute St. The six combination dinners cost $8, while other items start at around $6.

A European-style cake shop and tearoom, *Notte's Bon Ton* (☎ 604-681-3058, 874 Granville St) can't be beat for delicious pastries and cakes.

Goulash House Restaurant & Pastry Shop (☎ 604-688-0206, 1065 Granville St) is in an unfortunate part of the city but worth the walk past the adult video stores and seedy hotels just for the delicious food at great prices. Try the stuffed cabbage rolls ($8.50), beef goulash ($11), or vegetable ragout with chicken schnitzel ($12.50).

Robson St Heading north toward Denman St, *Pezzo* (☎ 604-669-9300, 1100 Robson St) is a lively place for gourmet pizza by the slice ($3.50), or spaghetti ($5) and lasagne ($6), both of which come with a salad. Head up the stairs to *Thai House Restaurant* (☎ 604-683-3383, 1116 Robson St) where most dishes are around $10 and the lunch special is $7.

Bread Garden Bakery & Cafe (☎ 604-688-3213, 812 Bute St), just around the corner off Robson St, serves things like quiche or wraps ($4.50) and chicken pot pie ($5). The restaurant, which is open 24 hours, even has a takeout window designed for skateboarders.

Farther down the street you'll find the *Robson Public Market* (☎ 604-682-2733, 1610 Robson St) with fresh fruit and vegetables, cheese, bread and other ingredients for a picnic. Upstairs there is a small food court with a selection of takeout food. Across the street, *Capers* (☎ 604-687-5299, 1675 Robson St) is a combination wholefoods market, deli and bakery with an emphasis on 'organic' and fresh.

De Dutch Pannekoek House (☎ 604-687-7065, 1725 Robson St) specialises in Dutch pancakes and is a good place for a filling breakfast or lunch. Also, try the omelettes ($6 to $12) or the sandwiches ($7). Open daily from 8 am to 3.30 pm. There are several around the city.

Even though the address is 780 Thurlow St, *Cafe il Nido* (☎ 604-685-6436) can be accessed by way of a ramp beside Manhattan Books & Magazines on Robson St. The food here is highly recommended and most dishes are in the $15 range.

For Vietnamese food at very good prices, *Greenhut Vietnamese Cuisine* (☎ 604-688-3688, 1429 Robson St) has curries for $11, brochettes for $12, dinner-for-two plates for $27 and lunch specials starting at $6.

For steaks, oysters, grilled fish and other stalwarts of the traditional Northwest cooking, go to *Joe Fortes* (☎ 604-669-1940, 777 Thurlow St), just off Robson St, where most mains, such as the swordfish or the crusted tuna, are between $20 and $25.

Denman St Close to Stanley Park, this is another lively, pleasant street to stroll along, offering lots of eating options. *Musashi Japanese Restaurant* (☎ 604-687-0634, 780 Denman St), between Robson and Alberni Sts, is cosy, casual and cheap with dishes for $6 or combination dinners for $15. Closed Monday.

With lots of hanging lamps, knick-knacks on the walls and a large fireplace at one end, the *Brass Monkey* (☎ 604-685-7626, 1072 Denman St) is like being in someone's living room. The small menu offers pasta ($12), seafood ($16) and roast beef ($18).

The elegant *Raincity Grill* (☎ 604-685-7337, 1193 Denman St) has a menu that changes with the seasons and offers vegetarian choices for about $15, while the other selections range from $18 to $25.

Davie St While the *Bombay Curry House* (☎ 604-688-9930, 1726 Davie St) might look like a plain café inside, the meals are hard to beat when it comes to prices, such as the tandoori chicken leg or the 'seesh kababs' for $5. For good hamburgers, great milkshakes and interesting clientele, *Hamburger Mary's* (☎ 604-687-1293, 1202 Davie St) is worth a visit, especially on a warm night when you can sit outside and watch life go by. Most hamburgers are around $7 and pasta is $8. Open daily from 7 am to 3 am.

Set in a beautiful Queen Anne stone mansion built in the early 1900s, *Romano's Macaroni Grill* (☎ 604-689-4334, 1523 Davie St) has a bag of tricks to bring in the

business – including opera singers, cooking exhibitions and pay-what-you-drink jugs of wine. Oh yes, there's food here too, including pizza ($10), chicken ($12), pasta ($12) and meat dishes ($15).

The Japanese restaurant *Kisha Poppo* (☎ *604-681-0488, 1143 Davie St)* specialises in all-you-can-eat dining. For lunch (daily from 11.30 am to 3 pm) there are 30 items ($11 weekdays, $12 weekends), and for dinner (daily from 5 to 10 pm) there are 40 items ($17 weekdays, $18 weekends).

Pacific Northwest dining doesn't get much better, or more authentic, than *Liliget Feast House* (☎ *604-681-7044, 1724 Davie St)*. The Native Indian cuisine and unique setting make this a real cultural experience, with dishes like venison steak ($22), arctic caribou tenderloin ($30) or one of the 'feast' dishes for two ($40).

Gastown For fabulous Indian cuisine, the *Jewel of India* (☎ *604-687-5665, 52 Alexander St)* has main courses for around $9 and the tandoori dishes, the house speciality, are around $11, while the lunch specials are around $7. There is live sitar music on Friday and Saturday evenings. Check the breeding ground of new and inventive pizza (from $8 to $20) at *Incendio* (☎ *604-688-8694, 103 Columbia St)* or try the excellent pasta ($10).

Another restaurant worth mentioning, which is just on the outskirts of Gastown, is *The Only Seafood Restaurant* (☎ *604-681-6546, 20 East Hastings St)*, near Carrall St. A Vancouver tradition since 1912, this restaurant still serves up great fresh seafood at reasonable prices. Don't be put off by the shabby interior or the rough neighbourhood. The clam chowder with bread is $3.25; items like salmon, cod and halibut are between $8 and $10. Open daily from 11 am to 8 pm.

A good bet for a good meal is the *Water Street Cafe* (☎ *604-689-2832, 300 Water St)*, housed in one of the few buildings to escape the Great Fire of 1886, where you'll get pasta for $13 and other mains for around $18.

For a touch of the neo-Gothic, *Mick's Restaurant & Rhythm Bar* (☎ *604-684-2883, 332 Water St)* has sandwiches ($8),

pasta ($8 to $12), and other mains like beef stroganoff ($10) and New York steak ($18). Downstairs in the music lounge on Friday, Saturday and Monday nights you can hear Latin, techno and jazz.

La Ventana Restaurant (☎ *604-682-8667, 162 Water St)* specialises in Spanish cuisine in surroundings that make you feel like you're dining in Barcelona. Tapas range from $6 to $13, paellas from $13 to $18 and other main dishes are around $18. At *Brother's Restaurant* (☎ *604-683-9124, 1 Water St)* the décor has a monastic theme complete with Gregorian chants emanating from the front door. The 'Brothers' serve items like the Monastery burger ($8), pasta ($10), seafood and poultry ($12).

The Irish Heather (☎ *604-688-9779, 217 Carrall St)* not only pours the best Guinness in town but serves up some good food such as sandwiches (around $6), beef in Guinness ($13) and, of course, Irish stew ($14).

Chinatown The *Kam's Garden Restaurant* (☎ *604-669-5488, 509 Main St)* specialises in wonton and barbecue dishes, with a bowl of wonton soup going for $4, or the dinner-for-one combination for $8. Across the street the *Gold Pavilion Bakery & Restaurant* (☎ *604-688-6708, 518 Main St)* has daily specials like spareribs with black bean sauce on rice, or black pepper chicken on rice, for $4, or one of the filled buns for 80¢.

On East Pender St, down from Main St, try the *Buddhist Vegetarian Restaurant* (☎ *604-683-8816, 137 East Pender St)* where you get chow mein dishes for $8, one-person set dinners for $8.50 or deluxe vegetarian dishes for $12. Right across the street, *New Town Bakery & Restaurant* (☎ *604-681-1828, 158 East Pender St)* has specials ($5), a buffet lunch ($7) or dinner ($8) – and for children you pay 55¢ per year of the child's age.

Along Keefer St, the heart of Chinatown, you'll find lots of restaurants, including *The Gain Wah* (☎ *604-684-1740, 218 Keefer St)* with 16 different varieties of congee (a rice or noodle soup loaded with goodies) starting at $4.

For Cambodian cuisine, go to **Phnom Penh** (☎ 604-682-5777, 244 East Georgia St), just off Main St, where you can expect to pay around $12 for most dishes.

Granville Island With the public market so close at hand, you would rightly expect Granville Island to feature fresh and tempting food. **Isadora's Cooperative Restaurant** (☎ 604-681-8816, 1540 Old Bridge St) has a healthy cooking bent, with many delicious vegetarian dishes.

Kamei Royale Ocean (☎ 604-602-0005, 1333 Johnston St) is one of the city's best sushi bars and Japanese restaurants with mains at around $18. On a warm summer evening, there's no place quite like **Bridges** (☎ 604-687-4400, 1696 Duranleau St) with its large outdoor deck and great views. The food isn't bad either, mostly pub fare on the patio, or more serious Northwest cuisine in the upstairs dining room where you'll pay around $14 for most mains.

West 4th Ave The **India Grill** (☎ 604-734-5777, 1835 West 4th Ave) has good curries and vegetarian dishes for $9, while up the street the **Surat Sweet Restaurant** (☎ 604-733-7363, 1938 West 4th Ave) has vegetarian-only Gujarati Indian cooking with most dishes costing about $6.

For spicy Chinese, **Won More Szechuan Cuisine** (☎ 604-737-2889, 1944 West 4th Ave) charges around $8 for most items, and the lunch special is $6.

A relic of Kitsilano's hippie past, the 24-hour **Naam** (☎ 604-738-7151, 2724 West 4th Ave) is a vegetarian health-food restaurant serving stir-fries ($9), burger platters ($9) and pizza ($10). There is live guitar music nightly.

The **Topanga Cafe** (☎ 604-733-3713, 2904 West 4th Ave) serves up Californian-Mexican dishes that are a good value such as the enchilada and burrito combo for $15, or have one of the standard dinners for $10.

For a great cultural experience, the **Nyala Restaurant** (☎ 604-731-7899, 2930 West 4th Ave) serves Ethiopian food to be eaten without the use of cutlery – you use bread instead. Prices range from $9 for vegetarian dishes to $13 for most meat dishes. Every Saturday night there's African or Caribbean music and dancing.

West Broadway **Szechwan Chongqing Seafood Restaurant** (☎ 604-734-2668, 1668 West Broadway) was recently voted by readers of the *Vancouver Sun* as the favourite Chinese restaurant in Vancouver. Not only do the staff serve up searing-hot delicacies, they also deliver. Most dishes are around $10.

Rasputin (☎ 604-879-6675, 457 West Broadway) brings fine Russian dining to Vancouver with dishes like cabbage rolls ($14), chicken Kiev ($19), and the evocatively named Rasputin's Feast ($25).

Commercial Drive The **Cafe Deux Soleil** (☎ 604-254-1195, 2096 Commercial Drive) is a very funky and child-friendly restaurant, offering 'kid food' selections for $2.25, and a play area on the small stage where bands play on the weekend. For adults the food includes veggie chilli ($5), a soup and sandwich special ($7), and pasta and stir-fries ($8).

The **Old Europe Restaurant** (☎ 604-255-9424, 1608 Commercial Drive) is like a café you might find down a side street in Budapest. The goulash and borscht is $4.50, veal stew with dumplings is $7.50, and Wiener schnitzel is $9.

El Cocal (☎ 604-255-4580, 1037 Commercial Drive) specialises in Salvadoran and Brazilian food, with more familiar Mexican dishes thrown in for good measure, with items like feijoada (pork stew) and mukeka de peixe (fish stew) for around $10.

Nick's Spaghetti House (☎ 604-254-5633, 631 Commercial Drive) has been here forever serving up large portions of the old favourites such as spaghetti and meat balls ($12), lasagne ($13), or the rack of ribs with spaghetti ($20).

Punjabi Market The section of the city running south along Main St from East 48th to East 51st Aves is the Indian section, complete with street signs in Punjabi. There are

two restaurants along here that are great value for excellent food.

Zeenaz Restaurant *(☎ 604-324-9344, 6460 Main St)* offers an all-you-can-eat buffet with a selection of about eight items which change daily; for lunch (noon to 3 pm) it's $9, and for dinner (3 to 9 pm) it's $11. You can also select items off the regular menu for around $12, but with a smorgasbord as good as this one, why bother. Closed Tuesday. Not to be outdone, the ***All India Sweets & Restaurant*** *(☎ 604-327-0891, 6505 Main St)* has a 40-item all-you-can-eat vegetarian buffet for $6. And, as the name implies, the speciality is the Indian sweets.

North Vancouver Lonsdale Quay Market has lots of places to munch at or to buy food to take out. The British-style ***Cheshire Cheese Inn*** *(☎ 604-987-3322)* on level 2 sells traditional British food like steak and kidney pie and shepherd's pie as well as chicken, ribs and steak for around $10. Located on the 3rd floor of the market, the *Q Cafe* *(☎ 604-986-6111)* has great views of the city, and on a nice day you can sit out on the patio. Breakfast selections are around $9, lunch starts at around $6 for sandwiches and burgers, while the dinner menu offers mains for around $17. Open daily.

The ***Thai House Restaurant*** *(☎ 604-987-9911, 180 West Esplanade)*, just above the quay, has to be one of the more lovely premises you'll find. It's almost like being in Thailand. Most of the dishes are around $10, however, the all-you-can-eat lunch buffet on the weekend is a great deal at $7.50.

Sailor Hagar's Brew Pub *(☎ 604-984-7669, 235 West 1st St)*, a couple of blocks up and over from the quay, not only produces some excellent beer, but also makes pretty good food. Items such as sandwiches, burgers, pizza, and fish and chips go for about $8.

The next best thing to a dinner cruise is having dinner on the ***Seven Seas Seafood Restaurant*** *(☎ 604-987-3344)* at the foot of Lonsdale Ave to the east of the quay, where dinner comes with great views of the city.

This floating restaurant, built in 1941, was originally a ferry travelling between North Vancouver and Vancouver before the Second Narrows Bridge was completed in 1957. Since then it has been a restaurant serving up, among other things, a remarkable seafood smorgasbord for $35. There is also a full selection of items on the regular menu for around $20. Only open for dinner from 5 to 10.30 pm.

Entertainment

Vancouver has a lot going on at night; remember that this is the largest and just about the only city on the entire Canadian west coast.

The best source of information on entertainment in Vancouver is *The Georgia Straight*, which comes out every Thursday. The weekly *WestEnder* and the monthly *Playboard* give reviews and dates of events in the visual and performing arts. *Xtra West* has listings for the gay scene. All are free and you can pick them up around town. The daily newspapers, *Vancouver Sun* and *Province* also have complete entertainment listings, including theatre, dance and concerts.

Tickets for most major events are available from TicketMaster (☎ 604-280-4444).

Coffeehouses Vancouver is, like other cities in the Northwest, awash in good coffee. If you're just looking for a cup of joe and a muffin, then try the following: Canadian giants ***Grabbajabba*** and ***Second Cup***, Seattle latte magnates ***Starbucks***, and local roasters-made-good, ***Blenz***, all have multiple outlets throughout the city.

However, if you're looking for a little poetry, folk music or performance art with your coffee, or just an alcohol-free place to meet people, check the following. ***Stone Table Coffee House*** *(☎ 604-255-3538, 1155 Thurlow St)* has live music on weekends. ***Café deux Soleils*** *(☎ 604-254-1195, 2096 Commercial Drive)* is a New Age café with an interesting clientele and some live music. ***Myles of Beans*** *(☎ 604-524-3700, 7010 Kingsway)*, east of the city, has live music nightly.

Performing Arts *Ballet British Columbia* (☎ 604-732-5003) is Vancouver's top dance troupe; it performs at the Queen Elizabeth Theatre (see Theatre, below). The season runs from September to June. The *Vancouver Opera* (☎ 604-682-2871) also stages its five productions at the Queen Elizabeth Theatre. *Vancouver Symphony Orchestra* (☎ 604-876-3434) performs at the Orpheum Theatre, on Granville St at Smithe St.

Theatre For same-day, half-price theatre tickets, check the little booth on the ground level in Robson Galleria, 1025 Robson St. It's open from noon to 1 pm and 4.30 to 6 pm Monday to Saturday. Otherwise you can call TicketMaster (☎ 604-280-3311, ☎ 604-873-3311) for normal-priced tickets to almost all theatrical events in the city.

Theatre, from mainstream to fringe, is flourishing in Vancouver. Across the street from the main post office, on Hamilton St, the *Queen Elizabeth Theatre* (☎ 604-280-4444) puts on major international productions; the *Vancouver Playhouse* is part of the same complex. The *Ford Centre for the Performing Arts* (☎ 604-602-0616, 777 Homer St) specialises in grand Broadway musicals.

The *Metro Theatre* (☎ 604-266-7191, 1370 SW Marine Drive) and *Firehall Arts Centre* (☎ 604-689-0926, 280 E Cordova St) put on plays by Canadian and foreign playwrights. The *Arts Club Theatre* (☎ 604-687-1644) has more experimental productions with three locations in town – two on Johnston St on Granville Island, and the other at 1181 Seymour St on the corner of Smithe St. Also on Granville Island, the *Waterfront Theatre* (☎ 604-685-6217, 1410 Cartwright St) is the venue for a number of local theatre companies.

Several fringe theatres worth checking are the *Vancouver East Cultural Centre* (☎ 604-254-9578, 1895 Venables St), near Commercial Drive, and *Vancouver Little Theatre* (☎ 604-876-4165, 3102 Main St) at 15th Ave. Vancouver's *TheatreSports League* (☎ 604-687-1644), the famed improv troupe, plays at the Arts Club Theatre on Johnston St, Granville Island.

Live Music Downtown around Richards and Seymour Sts, and in Yaletown around Davie and Hamilton Sts, it's bustling at night. The *Railway Club* (☎ 604-681-1625, 579 Dunsmuir St) is a pub-like place with live music seven nights a week and good-quality, original jazz on Saturday afternoon. *Richard's on Richards* (☎ 604-687-6794, 1036 Richards St) is a popular, dressy singles bar with a hefty but varying entry charge. The *Starfish Room* (☎ 604-682-4171, 1005 Homer St) is one of the city's top venues for live local and international bands.

Nearby, Granville St is interesting after dark with lots of street activity. The *Yale* (☎ 604-681-9253, 1300 Granville St) is one of the best blues bars in the country. One of the best clubs in town, *The Gate* (☎ 604-608-4283, 1176 Granville St) both looks and sounds great; bands are the best of the locals and sometimes it gets touring big names.

There is a fair bit of nightlife in the Gastown area. The *Purple Onion* (☎ 604-602-9442, 15 Water St) offers live jazz in the lounge, and salsa, Latin and funk in the cabaret.

The *Picadilly Pub* (☎ 604-682-3221, 620 W Pender St) has live rhythm and blues on Friday night. There's live, mostly traditional jazz at the *Hot Jazz Club* (☎ 604-873-4131, 2120 Main St).

Call the Jazz Hotline (☎ 604-872-5200) for information on what's going on in the jazz clubs.

Dance Clubs If you want to dance – whatever your sexual orientation – head to the gay clubs. If that doesn't suit you, the *Big Bam Boo* (☎ 604-733-2220, 1236 W Broadway) is one of the best nightclubs on the West Side, with pool and sushi on the main floor, and disco downstairs. *MaRs* (☎ 604-663-7707, 1320 Richards St) is the hottest, high-tech place to dance downtown, with amazing light effects and a huge fibre-optic screen above the dance floor. Cutting-edge music and a deafening sound system make *The Rage* (☎ 604-685-5585, 750 Pacific Blvd S) the favourite for the musically progressive. The *Sonar Dance Bar* (☎ 604-

683-6695, 66 Water St) attracts a good mixed crowd.

Every city's gay scene is different, and much of Vancouver's is drag-oriented. The places to dance and dish are the ***Dufferin Hotel*** *(☎ 604-683-4251, 900 Seymour St)* and ***Royal Hotel*** *(☎ 604-685-5335, 1025 Granville St)*; the latter is the city's only gay bar with live music. The biggest gay bar in Vancouver is ***Celebrities*** *(☎ 604-689-3180, 1022 Davie St)* with DJ dancing and crowds every night of the week. ***Denman Station Cabaret*** *(☎ 604-669-3448, 860 Denman St)* is a lot of fun, with dancing, darts, drag acts and other entertainers, and theme parties; catch the Electrolush Lounge on Thursday. ***The Lotus*** *(☎ 604-685-7777, downstairs, 455 Abbot St)* is Vancouver's only dance club for women and their friends; women only on Friday. ***Odyssey*** *(☎ 604-689-5256, 1251 Howe St)* is the wildest gay dance club; with go-go boys, shower-room viewing and theme nights, you won't be bored.

Bars & Brewpubs Until Expo '86, BC had very strict liquor laws that basically restricted bars to private clubs, restaurants and hotels. Needless to say, that wasn't the kind of atmosphere that would produce a great bar culture. Thus, the classic 'great old bar' really doesn't exist in Vancouver. Most of the fun or hip places to drink are dance clubs or spin-offs of restaurants.

However, there are a few nice places to recommend. ***Fred's Uptown Tavern*** *(☎ 604-331-7979, Hotel Dakota, 1006 Granville St)* is a comfortable, pub-like place to meet friends. ***DV8*** *(☎ 604-682-4388, 515 Davie St)* is a hip lounge that's open late.

The craze for locally brewed beer has swept Vancouver like other Pacific Northwest cities. However, there aren't as many brewpubs as you might expect in a city this size. One of the best here is ***Steamworks Brewing Company*** *(☎ 604-689-2739, 375 Water St)* in Gastown, with pool tables, great views over the North Shore, and two levels of seating. Note that the beer is much better than the food (a common brew-pub problem). ***Yaletown Brewing Co*** *(☎ 604-681-2719,*

1111 Mainland St) is upscale and attracts a singles-bar kind of crowd. Famed microbrewery ***Granville Island Brewery*** *(☎ 604-687-2739, 1441 Cartwright St)*, on the island, offers tours and tastings daily from 10 am to 4 pm.

Cinemas Downtown's principle first-run multiplex theatres are the ***Granville Cineplex Odeon*** *(☎ 604-684-4000, 855 Granville St)* and ***Fifth Avenue Cinemas*** *(☎ 604-734-7469, 2110 Burrard St)*.

The ***Paradise*** *(☎ 604-681-1732, 919 Granville St)* shows commercial films at half-price every day and the ***Denman Place Discount Cinema*** *(☎ 604-663-2201, 1737 Comox St)* shows three films for $3 on Tuesday.

Vancouver also has a number of low-cost repertory theatres which show a mix of independent, vintage and foreign films. You may need to buy a cheap membership. Try the ***Hollywood Theatre*** *(☎ 604-738-3211, 3123 W Broadway)*; and the ***Ridge Theatre*** *(☎ 604-738-6311, 3131 Arbutus St)* that is in the shopping centre on the corner of 16th Ave. The schedule at ***Pacific Cinémathèque*** *(☎ 604-688-3456, 1131 Howe St)* is so varied that it's best to think of it as an ongoing film festival.

Comedy Clubs ***Yuk Yuks*** *(☎ 604-687-5233, 750 Pacific Blvd S)* is the city's primary spot for stand-up comedy. For laughs and competitive improvisational acting, you can't beat ***TheatreSports League*** *(☎ 604-738-7013)*. They perform late-night shows at the Arts Club Theatre, 1585 Johnston St, Granville Island.

Spectator Sports

The BC Lions (☎ 604-589-7627) plays Canadian League professional football from July to September in BC Place Stadium. The Vancouver Canadians (☎ 604-872-5232), the local baseball team, plays its home games at Nat Bailey Stadium, 4601 Ontario St, next to Queen Elizabeth Park. A combination of bad attendance and an ageing stadium means it may leave in 2000. The Grizzlies (☎ 604-589-7627) of the National Basketball Association

BRITISH COLUMBIA

plays at GM Place as does the Vancouver Canucks (☎ 604-254-5141).

Shopping

Downtown Vancouver's central district has some of the city's most dynamic shopping areas. Robson St – more than just the busiest shopping street in Vancouver – is also a major hangout and people-watching area. You can buy everything from couture to condoms, from Italian newspapers to fresh crab; there are lots of tourist shops here as well. If you don't find what you were shopping for, you'll certainly not be bored. The other major focus for downtown shopping is Pacific Centre, which runs from Robson to Pender Sts between Granville and Howe Sts. Most of the stores are national and international chains; the major department-store anchor is Eatons, and the Hudson's Bay Company – The Bay – is just a block south.

Hill's Indian Crafts (☎ 604-685-4249), 165 Water St, has a good selection of carvings, prints, masks and excellent Cowichan sweaters. The Inuit Gallery (☎ 604-688-7323), 345 Water St, sells Inuit sculptures, drawings and tapestries and Northwest Coast Native Indian masks, carvings and jewellery. Images for a Canadian Heritage (☎ 604-685-7046), 164 Water St, and the Marion Scott Gallery (☎ 604-685-1934), 481 Howe St, also feature Native Indian art.

If you like furniture, home furnishings and interior decorating, Yaletown is a good place to check. The old warehouse-district-gone-lofts is loaded with stylish design shops.

West Side Next to Robson St, there's nowhere else in Vancouver more fun to shop than Granville Island.

The famous public market (☎ 604-666-5784) is a warehouse-like structure loaded with fresh fish, vegetables, butcher shops, cheese stands, bakeries and everything else you might need to put together a meal. It's an amazing place to visit, even if you aren't in the market for a whole salmon or a head of Savoy cabbage. Merchants also sell fancy jams, syrups and other preserved foods that make good gifts; the fishmongers

can pack fish for air shipment. As well as the market, Granville Island has many arts and crafts galleries, a good bookstore and chandlers devoted to sailing and kayaking.

Both Broadway and W 4th Ave are lined with shops, many reflecting both the area's old hippie past and its *trés* hip and upscale present. However, for a concentrated shot of shopping, go to South Granville, across the Granville Bridge from downtown, between W 4th Ave to W 16th Ave. In many ways a microcosm of Vancouver, you'll find high-end boutiques, Asian groceries, art galleries and antique stores.

There are a number of good places selling camping and outdoor equipment, guidebooks and maps, mainly in the Kitsilano area. Mountain Equipment Co-operative (☎ 604-872-7858), 130 W Broadway, sells all kinds of outdoor equipment at reasonable rates. It is hugely popular and attracts customers from all over the west.

Getting There & Away

Air Vancouver international airport (YVR) is about 10km south of the city on Sea Island – between Vancouver and the municipality of Richmond. Vancouver is the largest airport on the Canadian west coast. It is a major hub of domestic and international flights. Besides frequent service to other cities in Canada, there are regular flights to Seattle, Portland, San Francisco and Los Angeles. Regional flights serve Victoria and most other BC cities with a commercial airport.

The airport is under construction – surprise! This is funded by a departure tax that ranges from $5 to $20 depending on your destination. People flying to the USA go through US customs and immigration *before* they board their flights. In the process, they encounter a miserable new feature of YVR that forces US-bound passengers to walk through an overpriced gift shop before customs. The aisles are narrow and the demands are heavy for you to part with your spare Canadian dollars here. It's an outrageous bit of crass commercialisation and very inconvenient as well. On top of the extortionate departure tax, it's almost a legalised mugging.

If you arrive on an international flight be warned that afternoons can be horribly crowded. Note that some of the Canadian immigration desks have two officers, others one. Thus some of the very long lines move twice as fast as others. Once in the main part of the terminal, there are exchange services and ATMs.

The two major Canadian airlines – Air Canada and Canadian Airlines – dominate service at YVR. Both have commuter subsidiaries that fly to the smaller towns in the region.

Many major airlines serving Vancouver include the following (addresses of downtown ticket offices are given where applicable):

Air Canada/Air BC
  (☎ 604-688-5515) 1040 W Georgia St
Air China
  (☎ 604-685-0921) 1040 W Georgia St
Air India
  (☎ 604-879-0271) 601 W Broadway
American Airlines
  (☎ 1-800-433-7300)
British Airways
  (☎ 1-800-247-9297)
Canada 3000
  (☎ 604-609-3000) 1201 W Pender St
Canadian Airlines
  (☎ 604-279-6611) 1030 W Georgia St
Cathay Pacific
  (☎ 604-899-8520) 550 W 6th St
Japan Airlines
  (☎ 604-606-7715) 777 Hornby St
Lufthansa Airlines
  (☎ 1-800-563-5954) 1030 W Georgia St
Northwest Airlines
  (☎ 1-800-225-2525)
Singapore Airlines
  (☎ 604-689-1233) 1030 W Georgia St
United Airlines
  (☎ 1-800-241-6522)
WestJet Airlines
  (☎ 1-800-538-5696)

Bus The bus station is part of the train station, Pacific Central Station, 1150 Station St (see Train, below).

Greyhound buses (☎ 604-482-8747) link Vancouver with Seattle and other cities in the USA, as well as cities in eastern Canada. Greyhound does not have service to Victoria.

The following are sample tours and travel times to major western Canada destinations:

Banff, 14 hours, $98
Calgary, 15 hours, $105
Jasper, 12 hours, $92
Kamloops, five hours, $46
Kelowna, six hours, $51
Prince George, 12½ hours, $90
Whitehorse, 45 hours, $300

Pacific Coach Lines (☎ 604-662-8074) has eight buses daily to Victoria, leaving the bus station every hour at 10 minutes to the hour from 5.50 am to 8.45 pm. The one-way fare is $25 including ferry; the journey takes about three hours.

Maverick Coach Lines (☎ 604-662-8051) operates eight buses daily to Nanaimo on Vancouver Island for $19 one way (including ferry); the trip takes 3½ hours. It also has bus services to Powell River, Squamish, Whistler and Pemberton.

If you're heading for the USA, Quick Coach Lines (☎ 604-940-4428) operates a daily bus shuttle to downtown Seattle for $44 one way; the bus also makes stops at Seattle's Sea-Tac airport and Bellingham airport. Buses leave from most major hotels in downtown Vancouver.

If you want a funky journey to Banff or Calgary, Bigfoot Adventure Tours (☎ 604-278-8224, ☎ 1-888-244-6673) runs two-day trips from Vancouver with an overnight hostel stay along the way. The cost is $99 (excluding hostel and food costs) and the vans leave three times a week during summer, less frequently other times.

An even longer adventure is provided by Moose Run Adventure Tours (☎ 604-461-7402, ☎ 1-888-388-4881, info@mooserun .com) which runs 10-day trips through western Canada that include Whistler, Jasper, Banff, and Kelowna. There's plenty of time for fun like hiking, rafting and skiing. You can pause at any stop and rejoin the next bus one week later. The cost is $350.

Train Vancouver is the western terminus for Canada's VIA Rail. The magnificent Pacific

BRITISH COLUMBIA

Central Station is off Main St, at 1150 Station St, between National and Terminal Aves. There is a small park in front of the station. For 24-hour information on fares and reservations call ☎ 1-800-561-8630. The ticket office is open daily. Left luggage is open from 8 am to 10 pm.

On VIA's only route from Vancouver *The Canadian* departs a paltry three times a week and serves a route that includes Kamloops, Jasper and Edmonton in Alberta before ending in Toronto.

Amtrak (☎ 604-585-4848, ☎ 1-800-872-7245) connects Vancouver to Bellingham and Seattle with one train daily that takes four hours. In addition, Amtrak runs three buses a day from Vancouver to Seattle to connect with other main-line departures; $26 one way.

BC has its own railway system, BC Rail (☎ 604-631-3500, ☎ 1-800-663-8238), which operates the *Cariboo Prospector* with service from North Vancouver to Squamish, Whistler, Lillooet, 100 Mile House, Williams Lake, Quesnel and Prince George, where it connects with VIA Rail. One train leaves daily with service as far as Whistler and Lillooet; one-way fare to Whistler is $30, Prince George $194. Three days a week – Sunday, Wednesday and Friday – the train continues on to Prince George. Reservations are advised.

Trains leave from North Vancouver at the BC Rail Station, 1311 W 1st St, at the southern end of Pemberton Ave. To reach the station take bus No 239 west from the SeaBus terminal at Lonsdale Quay.

The privately owned *Rocky Mountaineer* train travels through some of the country's most scenic landscapes from BC to Banff and Calgary (VIA Rail no longer provides service along this route). This isn't a service for people just trying to get from place to place, rather it's a cruise ship on land. Tickets come with accommodation (there's an obligatory overnight stay in Kamloops) and meals. The cheapest off-season fare from Vancouver to Banff or Jasper is $475; a basic four-day package costs $975.

The service runs between mid-May and early October. There are seven trips a month in summer. For detailed information, contact a travel agent or Rocky Mountaineer Railtours (☎ 604-606-7245, ☎ 1-800-665-7245).

Car If you're coming from the USA (Washington State), you'll be on I-5 until the border town of Blaine. At the border is the Peace Arch Provincial and State Park. The first town in BC is White Rock. Hwy 99 veers west, then north to Vancouver. Close to the city, it passes over two arms of the Fraser River and eventually turns into Granville St, one of the main thoroughfares of downtown Vancouver.

If you're coming from the eastern part of the province, you'll almost certainly be on the Trans Canada Hwy (Hwy 1), which takes the Port Mann Bridge over the Fraser River and snakes through the eastern end of the city, eventually meeting with Hastings St before going over the Second Narrows Bridge to North Vancouver.

If you're coming from Horseshoe Bay in the north, the Trans Canada Hwy heads through West Vancouver and North Vancouver before going over the Second Narrows Bridge. In West Vancouver you can follow the exit for Hwy 99 that will take you over Lions Gate Bridge into Stanley Park.

Car Rental There are many car-rental companies in Vancouver; the larger ones have several offices around town and some also have offices at the international airport. Some have discount coupons which are available at various outlets, including the Visitor Info Centres. Check the Yellow Pages for a thorough listing of car-rental companies. Following is a small selection with their downtown addresses; all have service at YVR as well.

Avis
   (☎ 604-606-2872) 757 Hornby St
Budget
   (☎ 604-668-7000) 1705 Burrard St
Hertz
   (☎ 604-606-4711) 28 Seymour St
Lo-Cost
   (☎ 604-689-9664) 1105 Granville St

National/Tilden
   (☎ 604-685-6111) 1130 W Georgia St
Rent-A-Wreck
   (☎ 604-688-0001) Sheraton Wall Centre, 1083 Hornby St
Thrifty
   (☎ 604-606-1666) Landmark Hotel, 1400 Robson St

Ferry BC Ferries (☎ 1-888-223-3779) operates the ferry routes between the mainland and Vancouver Island. The main route is from Tsawwassen to Swartz Bay, which is just north of Sidney. There are between eight and 15 ferries in each direction depending on the day and season. Sunday afternoon, Friday evening and holidays are the busiest times and if you have a car there is often a one or two-ferry wait. To avoid long delays it's worth planning to cross at other times if you can.

Ferries also operate to Nanaimo from Tsawwassen and Horseshoe Bay. The one-way fare on all routes is $7.50 per adult, $2.50 for a bicycle and $24 per car (driver not included).

To get to Tsawwassen from downtown Vancouver, catch the SkyTrain to Scotts Rd Station and there catch the No 640. The fare either way is $3; $1.50 on weekends. From Swartz Bay you can take bus No 70 into Victoria. To get to Horseshoe Bay from Vancouver take bus No 250 or 257 northbound on W Georgia St downtown.

Getting Around
For BC Transit information call ☎ 604-521-0400 or obtain one of the two publications it produces on getting around the city. One is the *Transit Guide*, a map of Greater Vancouver showing bus, train and ferry routes. It costs $1.50 and can be bought at newsstands and bookstores. *Discover Vancouver on Transit* lists many of the city's attractions and how to get there (and includes Victoria). It's free and is available at the Visitor Info Centre.

To/From the Airport There are two ways of getting between the airport and downtown by bus – a city bus or the Vancouver

Airporter. The Vancouver Airporter (☎ 604-244-9888) buses run to/from the Pacific Central Station and all major central hotels for $9 ($15 return with no time limit). Tickets can be purchased from the driver. Buses leave the airport every 30 minutes from 6.15 am to 12.15 am. The length of the journey varies with traffic and your ultimate destination. If Granville St is jammed – not unlikely – and your hotel is last on the route it can take 90 minutes or more.

To get to the airport by city bus, take No 8 south on Granville St to 70th Ave. From there transfer to bus No 100 to the airport. From the airport, do the reverse. The total travel time is one hour and the fare is $3; $1.50 at night and on weekends. You need to have exact change.

A taxi between downtown Vancouver and the airport takes about 25 minutes and costs around $30.

Bus, SkyTrain & SeaBus BC Transit (☎ 604-521-0400) offers three modes of public transportation: regular buses, the SkyTrain automated light-rail system and SeaBus ferries to North Vancouver.

The transport system is divided into three zones: the inner zone covers central Vancouver; the next zone includes the suburbs of Richmond, Burnaby, New Westminster, North Vancouver, West Vancouver and Sea Island; the outer zone covers Ladner, Tsawwassen, Delta, Surrey, White Rock, Langley, Port Moody and Coquitlam.

On weekdays before 6.30 pm you pay a flat fare of $1.50/2.25/3 for one/two/three zones of travel. At night and on weekends all travel is $1.50. You can get a free transfer good for 90 minutes from the driver when you pay your fare. Day passes good for unlimited travel cost $6, but you can't buy them on buses and not all newsagents carry them.

The wheelchair-accessible SkyTrain connects downtown Vancouver with Burnaby, New Westminster and Whalley in Surrey. The trains are fully automated and travel mostly above ground along a specially designed track. The trains are scheduled to connect with buses. They leave from Waterfront

BRITISH COLUMBIA

Station downtown; other handy downtown stops are at Granville St and the Stadium stop, near GM Place.

The SeaBus passenger-only catamarans zip back and forth across Burrard Inlet between Waterfront Station downtown and Lonsdale Quay in North Vancouver. They leave every 15 minutes on weekdays, every half-hour at other times. The trip lasts only 12 minutes but gives good views of the harbour and city skyline, although on nice days you'll wish they had an open deck. Try to avoid rush hours when many commuters crowd aboard.

Car If you're driving, you'll notice the city doesn't have any expressways – everyone must travel through the city. Congestion is a big problem, especially along Lions Gate Bridge (probably best avoided altogether), and Second Narrows Bridge. Hardly any downtown streets have left-hand turn signals, and traffic can back up for blocks during rush hours, especially with people trying to get onto Georgia St from the south. On a wet or snowy day it's worse so try to avoid rush hours. It's also costly to park and/or very difficult to find a parking spot in the inner city. You're better off parking the car out a bit and catching a bus or SkyTrain into the centre; it'll probably be quicker and better for your blood pressure, too.

Taxi Unless you're staying at a big hotel, the best bet is to phone for a cab; trying to hail one in the streets can be difficult. Three of the companies are Black Top (☎ 604-731-1111), MacLure's (☎ 604-731-9211, ☎ 604-683-6666) and Yellow Cab (☎ 604-899-8666).

Bicycle Cycling is a good way to get around town, though riding on the sidewalk is illegal. Bikes are now allowed on the SeaBus. Get a copy of the Bicycling Association of BC's cycling map of the city, which you can get at the Visitor Info Centres or bike shops. To rent a bike, contact:

Bayshore Bicycles
  (☎ 604-688-2453) 745 Denman St
Kitzco Beachwear & Rentals
  (☎ 604-684-6269) 1168 Denman St

Spokes Bicycle Rental & Espresso Bar
  (☎ 604-688-5141) 1798 W Georgia St

There are many others so check the Yellow Pages. Rates start at $6 an hour, $15 for four hours or $20 a day.

Mini-Ferries Two companies operate mini passenger ferry shuttles across False Creek. From 10 am to 8 pm daily False Creek Ferries (☎ 604-684-7781) runs between the Vancouver Aquatic Centre near Sunset Beach, Granville Island, the Vancouver Maritime Museum at Kitsilano Point and Stamp's Landing near the Cambie Bridge. Aquabus (☎ 604-689-5858) travels between the Arts Club Theatre on Granville Island and Hornby St via Stamp's Landing and the Concord-Yaletown dock near BC Place. Basic fares are $1.75.

Water Taxi If your destination is directly accessible by water, you might want to consider making an entrance on a water taxi. Burrard Water Taxi (☎ 604-293-1160) offers a 24 hour water-taxi service to the greater Vancouver maritime region.

NORTH OF VANCOUVER
Sea to Sky Hwy to Whistler

If you feel like getting out of the city, there are few more scenic routes than the 105km Sea to Sky Highway (Hwy 99) from Horseshoe Bay and Whistler. The mountain scenery here rivals the Canadian Rockies. If you're driving, allow plenty of time – the road is narrow, hilly and winding; besides you'll be enjoying the views. The publication *99 North*, available from tourist offices along the route, is a comprehensive guide to the wealth of activities at numerous points along the way.

After leaving Horseshoe Bay, Hwy 99 spectacularly edges along Howe Sound. At **Brittania Beach** the BC Museum of Mining (☎ 604-896-2233) covers the time early in the 20th century when this area had the largest copper mine in the British Empire. It's open from 10 am to 4 pm mid-May through mid-October and costs $8.50/6 adults/children and

includes a mine tour. A bit farther along, **Shannon Falls** tumble over a 335m cliff just off the road.

Some 48km from Horseshoe Bay, **Squamish** is noted for its rock climbing. The granite cliffs here are some of the world's longest unbroken rock faces; pull over and watch for climbers hanging from the rock like colourful spiders. Thousands of bald eagles winter around town. The Visitor Info Centre (☎ 604-892-9244), 37950 Cleveland Ave, is open from 9 am to 5 pm daily. The casual and friendly *Squamish Hostel (☎ 604-892-9240, hostel@mountain-inter.net, 38490 Buckley Ave)* organises rock-climbing and rafting trips and has beds for $15. It's an easy walk from the centre. Just south of town, the West Coast Railway Heritage Park (☎ 604-898-9336) is filled with equipment from the days when the railroad was the only means of transport. Open from 10 am to 5 pm daily from May to October, the park costs $4.50/3.50 for adults/children.

Just north-east of Squamish is **Garibaldi Provincial Park** (☎ 604-898-3678), a 195 sq km mountain wilderness. Most of the park is undeveloped and is known mostly for its hiking areas – Diamond Head, Garibaldi Lake, Cheakamus Lake, Singing Pass and Wedgemount Lake – covered by more than 67km of developed trails. The trails become cross-country ski runs in winter.

Whistler & Around

Whistler is one of the top ski resorts in North America, and has plenty of recreation options even if you are visiting in summer. Don't assume you can't ski if it's high summer in Vancouver as Whistler has runs that remain open nearly year-round. In summer, you can also go hiking, cycling, canoeing, take the cable car up the mountain or visit an aquatic park.

The Visitor Info Centre (☎ 604-932-5528, fax 604-932-3755) covers the area in addition to the ski resort. Located at the south end of town at Hwy 99 and Lake Placid Rd, it is open from 9 am to 5 pm daily.

Whistler Village Built almost entirely from scratch, starting in the 1980s, the resorts, hotels and shopping precincts of Whistler were designed to look and feel much older. The massive hotels look like castles and even shopping centres are built of venerable-looking quarried stone. The commercial centre of Whistler is a European-like pedestrian village with winding streets, brightly lit shops, fine restaurants and boisterous après-ski brewpubs. Whistler Village has a sort of contrived feel about it – it is very new – but the skiers, shoppers and hikers who gather are having fun and they lend the place a light, relaxing atmosphere.

Skiing Whistler ski district has three centres, Whistler Village itself, **Blackcomb** (at the base of one of the two lifts) and **Whistler Creek**. The latter is the least expensive, while the village has the most action and socialising – with the larger hotels it is also more costly. Together the three areas make up Canada's largest ski resort.

Blackcomb Mountain has the largest downhill ski area in North America, offering 8500m of continuous skiing. Whistler Mountain is a close second with 8060km. The usually reliable snow, the vertical drop and mild Pacific air combine to provide some of the most pleasant skiing to be found anywhere, from novice slopes to glacier skiing. The latter is available pretty much all year, providing the country's only summer skiing. Heli-skiing companies based in Whistler Village offer services to more than a hundred other runs on glaciers near the resort. Snowboarders consider Whistler Mountain, with banked runs and rocky bluffs, to be a boarder's dream come true. There are cross-country trails as well.

For information about either ski slope, or for any of the facilities (including lodgings) in Whistler, contact the central reservation desk (☎ 604-932-4222, ☎ 604-664-5625 in Vancouver, ☎ 1-800-944-7853). For a snow report, call ☎ 604-932-4191.

A one-day lift ticket costs $60; four days $220. There are reduced prices outside the peak winter season.

Places to Stay By far the easiest way to make reservations is to use the central reservation service (☎ 604-932-3141, ☎ 604-687-1032 in Vancouver, ☎ 1-800-944-7853). They can book you rooms at nearly any of the area's two dozen inns and lodges. In winter, expect rooms to begin at $100 a night, and to go up quickly from there. There is some off-season discounts, though not as many as you might expect – Whistler also does a brisk trade in conventions.

Most rooms in Whistler are rather spendy, though there are some budget options. HI *Whistler Hostel (☎ 604-932-5492, ☎ 604-932-4687, whistler@hihostels.bc.ca)* is in a beautiful setting on Alta Lake (on West Rd) about 4km by foot from Whistler Village. Dorm-style accommodation is $18.50/23.50 for members/nonmembers. With room for just 35 people, it's a good idea to book ahead especially during ski season. It's a 45 minute walk from the village or there are three buses per day. The *Shoestring Lodge (☎ 604-932-3338, fax 604-932-8347, 7124 Nancy Greene Drive)*, a 15 minute walk from the village, has dorm beds from $20; private rooms start at $65. Nesters Rd, about 1.5km north of the village, has several moderately priced pension-style B&Bs.

Places to Eat There are over 90 restaurants in Whistler, most of them concentrated in the large pedestrian district in Whistler Village. You'll have no trouble finding something good to eat. Like everything else in Whistler, dining is quite expensive, though there are a number of inexpensive options. For Thai food, go to *Thai One On (☎ 604-932-4822, 4557 Blackcomb Way)*. For family dining, try *Blacks (☎ 604-932-6408, 4270 Mountain Square)*.

If you want to splurge, then Whistler has some excellent restaurants. Well loved, the *Rim Rock Cafe (☎ 604-932-5565, 2101 Whistler Rd)* is one of the top dining rooms, though without undue pretension. Fresh seafood is the speciality.

Getting There & Away Maverick Coach Lines (☎ 604-255-1171 in Vancouver, ☎ 604-932-5031 in Whistler) has six buses daily (2½ hours) to Whistler from Pacific Central Station in Vancouver. The fare is $18/34 one way/return.

Perimeter's Whistler Express (☎ 604-266-5386 in Vancouver, ☎ 604-905-0041 in Whistler) runs buses daily from Vancouver international airport (three hours). The fare is $47 one-way in winter, $41 in summer.

There's one train daily (2½ hours) from Vancouver to Whistler on BC Rail (☎ 604-984-5246, ☎ 1-800-663-8238); one-way fare is $31.

Sunshine Coast

The name refers to the coastal area north of Horseshoe Bay to Lund, 24km north of Powell River. It's a narrow strip of land separated from the mainland by the Coast Mountains. The scenery is excellent: hills, mountains, forests, inlets, harbours and beaches. Slow and winding Hwy 101, edging along the coast, is broken at two separate points where you'll need to take a ferry – from Horseshoe Bay to Langdale and from Earls Cove to Saltery Bay. The highway ends completely at Lund. At Powell River there is a ferry over to Comox on Vancouver Island. For information about the ferries, call BC Ferries (☎ 1-888-223-3779) or pick up a copy of its schedules from one of the Visitor Info Centres.

The region remains quiet but is increasingly busy with both commuters and visitors. For the latter, it can be part of an interesting circuit from Vancouver, around Vancouver Island and back. BC Ferries offers a circular ferry ticket known as the Sunshine Coast CirclePac which includes all four ferries around the loop – to Vancouver Island via Horseshoe Bay or Tsawwassen, then across to Powell River, and then down the Sunshine Coast with ferries at Egmont and Gibbons – at a good reduction from full fare. The normal fare is $22/79.75 for adults/cars, CirclePac fares are $18.70/67.80. Maverick Coach Lines (☎ 604-681-3526) has bus service between Vancouver and Powell River, with the two ferries included. The fare is $32.

Sechelt and Powell River are the commercial and activity centres of the coast. Aside from the good hiking, camping and fishing in the area, these towns are bases for some of the world's best diving, although it's not for novices and local guides should be used.

In **Powell River**, the Visitor Info Centre (☎ 604-485-4701) is at 4690 Marine Ave. The Beach Gardens Resort Hotel (☎ 604-485-6267), 7074 Westminster Ave, rents boats and diving equipment and runs charters out to diving spots such as the submarine cave formations in Okeover Inlet near Lund. From Powell River there is a 65km canoeing circuit which takes five to seven days. North of Lund, **Desolation Sound Provincial Marine Park** has abundant wildlife, diving, canoeing and wilderness camping.

Places to Stay & Eat Accommodation around Powell River include hotels, motels and campgrounds. The *Beach Gardens Resort Hotel* (☎ *604-485-6267,* ☎ *1-800-663-7070, 7074 Westminster St*) is one of the more upscale places to stay along the Sunshine Coast, with an indoor pool, fitness centre, a good restaurant and easy access to recreation. Rooms begin at $90/99 a single/double. Less expensive is *Inn at Westview* (☎ *604-485-6281, 7050 Alberni St*) with basic rooms at $46/50. If you're heading north to Desolation Sound Marine Park, try the European-style pension lodging at *Cedar Lodge B&B Resort* (☎ *604-483-4414),* 27km north of Powell River off Hwy 99. There are six units, starting at $45/50.

One of the most interesting hostels in western Canada is the HI *Fiddlehead Farm* (☎ *604-483-3018, let phone ring 10 times, Box 421, Powell River, V8A 5C2),* which is about 20km up Powell Lake from town and is accessible only by boat. A fine retreat for a few days of hiking and canoeing, all meals at the hostel are included in the prices of $32 per night in the house, $25 for camping. If you're feeling like a spot of work, you can stay in the house for $22 and do two hours of farm chores. Make arrangements at least one week in advance so the owners can schedule your boat transportation.

Vancouver Island

The attractions of Vancouver Island, the largest island off the west coast of the Americas, range from its rugged wilderness to the grand rooms of its provincial legislature.

The island is 450km long and has a population of over 500,000 people, most of whom live along the south-eastern coast.

The geography is scenically varied. A mountain range runs down the centre of the island, its snow-capped peaks setting off the woods and many lakes and streams. The coast can be either rocky and tempestuous or sandy and calm.

South of the island, across the Strait of Juan de Fuca, the sea is backed by the substantial Mt Olympus (2428m) in Washington State's Olympic National Park.

Across Georgia Strait, which runs along the island's eastern shore, the mainland's Coast Mountains form the skyline. The open west coast is fully exposed to the Pacific. The waters around the island are filled with marine life, much of which is commonly seen and some, like the salmon, eaten. Crab is a BC culinary delicacy and the world's largest octopuses are found here.

Vancouver Island also has a diverse birdlife, with over 440 different species. The bald eagle is widespread and can be seen near rivers and lakes; the golden eagle is an endangered species but can still be seen along the coast.

The central north-south mountain chain divides the island into distinct halves. The sparsely populated west coast is rugged, hilly, forested and cut by deep inlets. The more gentle eastern side is suitable for farming. The island's industries – forestry, mining and fishing – and nearly all of the principal towns are found along this side of the ridge. Up the east coast the resort towns and villages have plenty of campgrounds, motels, hotels and guesthouses. However, don't imagine the entire east coast to be urban sprawl. It's still quite undeveloped in places, especially north of Campbell River.

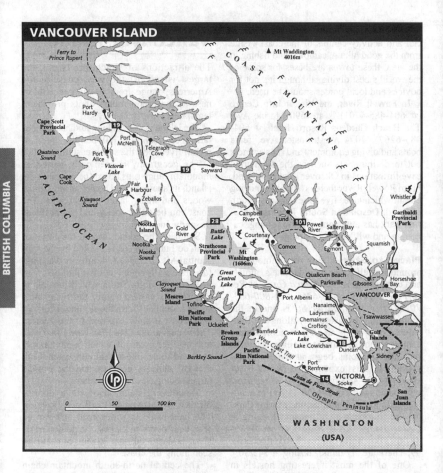

VANCOUVER ISLAND

Evidence of Vancouver Island's history of logging is everywhere in defoliated hillsides. However, the collapse of lumber prices in the late 1990s has decimated logging towns like Gold River and caused much misery in the lives of long-term residents. So too, the collapse of fishing stocks has hit communities like little Alert Bay hard and there have been a rash of suicide attempts and other tragedies.

The tourist industry is fast becoming a primary income-producer for the island, but this is little consolation to the towns that supported themselves by exploiting their natural resources and now have few left to exploit for tourists.

The island has the mildest climate in the country. It's particularly moderate at the southern end, where the northerly arm of Washington State protects it from the ocean. There is substantially less rain in Victoria than in Vancouver. August and September, when the sky is usually blue, are excellent months during which to visit.

Vancouver Island is a popular tourist destination and Victoria especially can get crowded in midsummer. For those seeking quieter spots, a little effort will be rewarded.

VICTORIA

Victoria, the second largest city in British Columbia and the provincial capital, lies at the south-eastern end of Vancouver Island, 90km south-west of Vancouver. Although bounded on three sides by water, Victoria is sheltered from the Pacific Ocean by the Olympic Peninsula across the Strait of Juan de Fuca in Washington State.

With the mildest climate in Canada, architecturally compelling buildings, an interesting history and its famed gardens and parks, it's not surprising that two million tourists visit Victoria annually. This quiet, traditional seat of civilisation was once described by Rudyard Kipling as 'Brighton Pavilion with the Himalayas for a backdrop.'

Many people come here expecting to find a kind of Olde English theme park; certainly that is the city's reputation and the point of much of the hype generated by the tourist industry. In reality, much of Victoria feels like any other city in western Canada.

Nowadays, it's not clear any longer what's authentically British and what's laid on for the tourists, but Victoria remains a charming city on a lovely bay. If the crowds thronging the narrow streets get to you, take a whale-watching cruise, or spend a couple of hours in the city's excellent museums.

Although it is the provincial capital and home to an important university and naval base, Victoria is not an industrial city. About 30% of its 300,000 or so residents work in tourist and service-oriented businesses, while another 20% work in the public sector. The island is also a major retirement centre, with retirees making up around 20% of the population. Along with Vancouver, it is one of the faster-growing cities in Canada and has a population of 300,000.

History

Victoria's first residents were the Salish Indians, who fished and hunted on the protected bay. The felicitous site of future Victoria was not colonised until 1843, when James Douglas, acting for the Hudson's Bay Company (HBC), founded Fort Victoria as a fur-trading post.

The history of BC departs from that of Washington and Oregon when the British and US governments in 1846 fixed the US-Canadian border at the 49th parallel. The HBC, which heretofore had controlled the entire Pacific Northwest from its headquarters at Fort Vancouver, near present day Portland, re-established its head of operations at Fort Victoria. In order to better protect its interests and citizens, the British government, in 1849, established Vancouver Island as a crown colony, just in case the Americans got more expansionist-minded. In 1866 Vancouver Island merged with the mainland to form British Columbia.

As a colony, BC had little local control, and was largely governed by edict from London. If BC and its population were to have greater self-determination, the growing colony had two choices: join the prosperous USA to the south, with which it shared much history and many commercial ties, or join the new Dominion of Canada far to the east.

Joining the USA made a lot of sense to many in BC, as there were already strong regional ties. The political debate raged in the colony's drawing rooms and in Victoria's pugnacious newspapers. After Ottawa promised to build a railroad to link eastern and western Canada in 1870, delegates from BC voted to join Canada in 1871 with Victoria as capital of the new province.

For Victoria, without a land link to the rest of Canada or the USA, industrial growth was not an issue and the city didn't experience the same boom-and-bust cycles that many of the manufacturing and mercantile cities of the west did. The city's beautiful location was an early attraction – the fabulous Empress Hotel opened in 1908, and the tourist trade began in earnest.

Victoria and BC generally prospered after WWII. With its solid base of government employment, the city has avoided the

BRITISH COLUMBIA

VICTORIA

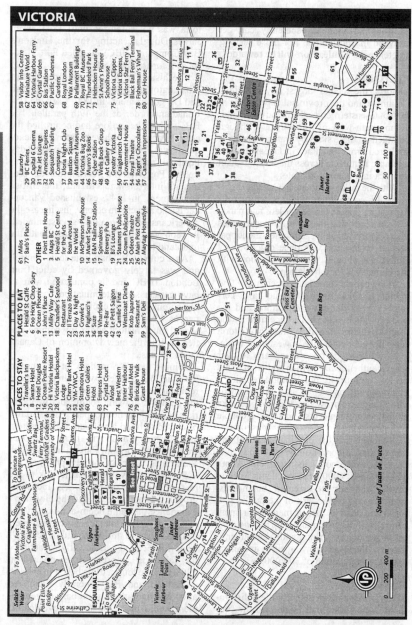

PLACES TO STAY
2 Traveller's Inn
8 Swans Hotel
12 Hotel Douglas
16 Ocean Pointe Resort
20 HI Victoria Hostel
28 Victoria Backpackers Lodge
52 Cherry Bank Hotel
53 YM-YWCA
55 Strathcona Hotel
60 Empress Hotel
63 Green Gables Hotel
72 Crystal Court Motel
74 Best Western Inner Harbour
76 Admiral Motel
79 Birdcage Walk Guest House

PLACES TO EAT
4 Herald St Caffé
6 Foo Hong Chop Suey
9 Ocean Phoenix
13 Milky Way Cafe
18 Chandler's Seafood Restaurant
22 Il Terrazo Ristorante
23 Day & Night
33 Growlie's
34 Pagliacci's
38 Wharfside Eatery
40 Re-Bar
42 Le Petit Saigon
43 Camille's Fine Westcoast Dining
45 Koto Japanese Restaurant
59 Sam's Deli
61 Milos
77 Barb's Place

OTHER
3 Point Ellice House
5 Maps BC
7 Herald St Centre for the Arts
14 Bean Around the World
17 McPherson Playhouse
15 S&N Railliner Station
36 Brewery Pub
19 BJ's Lounge
21 Steamers Public House
24 Crown Publications
25 Odeon Theatre
27 Maytag Homestyle Laundry
29 BC Ferries
30 Capital 6 Cinema
31 The Jet Lounge
32 American Express
35 Sasquatch Trading Company
37 Utonia Night Club
39 Bastion Square
44 Maritime Museum
46 Victoria Bug Zoo
47 Munro's Books
48 Cyber Station
49 Arts Council of Greater Victoria
50 Craigdarroch Castle
51 Government House
54 Royal Theatre
56 Roger's Chocolates
57 Canadian Impressions
58 Visitor Info Centre
62 Miniature World
64 Victoria Harbour Ferry
65 Crystal Garden
66 Bus Station
67 Pacific Undersea Gardens
68 Royal London Wax Museum
69 Parliament Buildings
70 Royal BC Museum
71 Thunderbird Park
73 Helmcken House & St Anne's Pioneer Schoolhouse
75 Victoria Clipper; Victoria Express; Victoria Star Ferry & Black Ball Ferry Terminal
78 Fisherman's Wharf
80 Carr House

problems of over-reliance on natural resources for its economic base.

Today, there are still more British-born residents in Victoria than anywhere else in Canada, and they have entrenched their style rather than forgotten it. Rising numbers of immigrants and visitors from around the world are imparting an increasingly cosmopolitan air.

Orientation

The city lies at the south-eastern tip of Vancouver Island, actually closer to the USA than to the Canadian mainland. The downtown area is simply laid out and really not very large. Bounded on two sides by water, the central area of the city has very few high-rise buildings, and is easy and pleasant to explore on foot; you'll have little trouble getting your bearings.

The focal point is the Inner Harbour, a section of Victoria Harbour surrounded by several of the city's most important structures. The Empress Hotel faces out over its lawns to the waterfront. Across the way are the enormous provincial Parliament Buildings. In between the two is the Royal BC Museum. To the east of the museum is Thunderbird Park, with its totem poles, and south of this is Beacon Hill Park, the city's largest. Surrounding the park and extending down to the ocean are well kept residential houses, many with attractive lawns and gardens.

Along Wharf St, north of the Empress Hotel, is the central Visitor Info Centre, overlooking the Inner Harbour. Following Wharf St north along the water will take you through Old Town, the restored original area of Victoria, to Bastion Square, the city's old central square and the site of old Fort Victoria. Parallel to Wharf St and a couple of blocks east is Government St, a principal shopping street and tourist hub, also lined with historic buildings. One block east is Douglas St, downtown's main thoroughfare and busy commercial centre.

The northern boundary of the downtown area is marked by Fisgard St, between Government and Store Sts, which has a small Chinatown with Oriental-style street lamps and buildings, Chinese characters on the street signs and, of course, restaurants. The area is remarkably neat and clean and very colourful, due mainly to the brightly painted façades of the buildings. Fan Tan Alley, in the middle of Chinatown, has a few small shops and connects Fisgard St with Pandora Ave. In the 1860s when this alley – Canada's first Chinatown – was in its heyday and much bigger, it was lined with opium dens and gambling houses. It's a lot quieter now with no evidence of those early vice-filled days. To keep it that way, the alley is locked at night.

Beyond Downtown Following Fort St east up the hill and then along Oak Bay Ave will lead you through the 'tweed curtain' to the wealthier, very British area of Oak Bay. The Info Centre has detailed information on walks to take in this attractive and traditional district.

Both Douglas and Blanshard Sts lead north out of the city, the former to the Trans Canada Hwy (Hwy 1) and Nanaimo, the latter to Hwy 17 (Patricia Bay Hwy), Sidney and the Swartz Bay ferry terminal. To the north-west of downtown is Gorge Rd, an area of heavy motel concentration. It forms part of Hwy 1A, which cuts across Douglas St, runs along the northern side of the gorge and meets up farther west with Craigflower Rd and the Trans Canada Hwy.

Victoria international airport is in Sidney, about 19km north of Victoria on Hwy 17. The bus station is at 700 Douglas St, on the corner of Belleville St and opposite Crystal Garden.

Information

Tourist Offices The Visitor Info Centre (☎ 250-953-2033, fax 250-382-6539), 812 Wharf St, is by the water at the Inner Harbour, diagonally opposite the Empress Hotel. It has dozens of pamphlets, maps and information on shopping, sightseeing, transportation, where to stay and where to eat. The Info Centre also operates a room reservation service. It's open from 9 am to 9 pm daily (Sunday till 7 pm). There is also an office 2km south of the Swartz Bay ferry

terminal on Patricia Bay Hwy, and another in Sidney.

If you'd like to find out more about Victoria before you arrive, contact Tourism Victoria (☎ 250-414-6999, fax 250-361-9733), 4th floor, 31 Bastion Square, Victoria, BC V8W 1J1.

Money The major banks have branches along Douglas St. The Toronto Dominion Bank, 1070-1080 Douglas St, has regular banking hours, plus it's open on Saturday from 9.30 am to 4.30 pm. You can change money at Money Mart, 1720 Douglas St, opposite the Bay department store, and at Currency Exchange, 724 Douglas St, opposite the Budget car-rental office; its hours are 7 am to 9.30 pm daily. You can also change money at American Express (☎ 250-385-8731), 1203 Douglas St. US currency is accepted in many establishments but usually at a worse exchange rate than found at money exchange offices or banks.

Post & Communications The main post office (☎ 250-935-1351) is at 714 Yates St. It's closed Sunday. Cyber Station (☎ 250-386-4687), 1113 Blanshard St, has Internet access and computer use for $5.50 for 30 minutes.

Travel Agency Travel CUTS (☎ 250-721-6916, ☎ 1-800-663-6000) is located in the University of Victoria Student Union Building.

Bookshops The city's best bookstore is Munro's Books (☎ 250-382-2464), 1108 Government St. Munro's is in a beautiful old building originally built for the Royal Bank and restored in 1984. It is now classified as a heritage building; the atmosphere inside is almost ecclesiastical and is worth a look even if you aren't in the market for a book.

Crown Publications (☎ 250-386-4636), 546 Yates St, sells maps, federal and provincial publications on Canadiana, as well as books on Native Indian culture, nature and travel guides. Maps BC (☎ 250-387-1441),

3rd floor, 1802 Douglas St, is a government office with maps and atlases of the province.

There are also a number of second-hand bookstores along Fort St, including Wells Book Group (☎ 250-360-2929), 832 Fort St, which has vintage and rare books as well as cheap paperbacks.

Media The daily paper is the *Times Colonist*. Arts and entertainment news is featured in the weekly *Monday Magazine*.

Laundry The Maytag Homestyle Laundry (☎ 250-386-1799), 1309 Cook St, has self-service machines, drop-off service and dry cleaning.

Medical Services If your medical needs aren't grave, avoid the emergency room and head to Mayfair Medical Treatment Centre (☎ 250-360-2282), 3147 Douglas St, in the Mayfair Shopping Mall. It's open daily and you don't need an appointment. The Royal Jubilee Hospital (☎ 250-595-9200, ☎ 250-595-9212 in an emergency) is at 1900 Fort St.

Useful Organisations Greenpeace (☎ 250-388-4325), 2007 Fernwood St, has details of environmental issues and helps organise information nights.

Dangers & Annoyances At night, Broad St between Yates and Johnson Sts is often occupied by prostitutes and drunks. Some drunks also hang out on the corner of Yates and Douglas Sts.

Inner Harbour
Royal British Columbia Museum This excellent museum (☎ 250-387-3701), 675 Belleville St, is a must-see, even for people who normally avoid such places. The wide variety of displays is artistically arranged, beautifully lit and accompanied by informative, succinct explanations. There are good sections on geology, vegetation, wildlife and ethnology. Many of the models and exhibits are incredibly realistic.

In the areas devoted to the BC Native Indians, see the detailed models of villages, the

1914 documentary film *In the Land of the War Canoes* on the Kwakiutl people, and the rock on which a man 'fell from the sky'. Also look at the Haida craftwork in argillite, a dense black carbon shale. The pipes represent some of the best Native Indian art anywhere.

There's a town made up of 19th and early 20th century buildings and goods, including a Model T Ford. Chaplin movies are shown in the old movie theatre. The museum also has an interesting collection of artefacts from the 1920s to the 1970s. Outside there is a garden of BC's native wildflowers.

Admission is $8/5.85/2.15 for adults/seniors/students, or $16 for a family. The museum provides free tours and is open from 9 am to 5 pm daily.

Helmcken House This house (☎ 250-361-0021) in Eliot Square beside the Royal BC Museum is the oldest in BC to have remained unchanged. The rooms are preserved much the way they would have appeared in the early 1850s. John Helmcken, a doctor and politician, was very active in the local community. The house contains period furniture and examples of decorations and implements. Staff members are friendly and helpful. It's open from 10 am to 5 pm daily May to October and noon to 4 pm other times. Admission is $4/2 for adults/children.

St Anne's Pioneer Schoolhouse Also in Eliot Square, this schoolhouse, operated as part of the Royal BC Museum, is one of the oldest buildings in Victoria still in use. Built sometime between 1840 and 1860, it was moved to its present site in 1974 from the grounds of St Anne's Academy.

Thunderbird Park This small but interesting park beside the Royal BC Museum has a collection of both plain and painted wooden totem poles, some of which are labelled. In the Thunderbird Park Carving Studio you can watch Native Indian artists at work and talk to them too. The studio is run on a volunteer basis with help from the Royal BC Museum.

Parliament Buildings The multi-turreted Parliament Buildings (☎ 250-387-6121), 501 Belleville St facing the Inner Harbour, were designed by Francis Rattenbury and finished in 1898. On top of the main dome is a figure of Captain George Vancouver, the first British navigator to circle Vancouver Island. Rattenbury also designed the Empress Hotel and the Parthenon-like Royal London Wax Museum, which was once a Canadian Pacific railway ticket office. The buildings are open from 8.30 am to 5 pm daily and free 30-minute guided tours are offered every day in summer.

The paintings in the lower rotunda depict scenes from Canadian history. Around the upper rotunda are paintings of four of BC's main industries. The Legislative Chamber is where all the BC laws are made (there is no Senate in the provincial parliament). You can view the debates from the public gallery when the session is in. In the Legislative Library is the dagger used to kill Captain Cook in Hawaii, while on the lawn are a statue of Queen Victoria and a sequoia tree from California planted in the 1860s. The buildings are lit spectacularly at night, by more than 3000 light-bulbs.

Pacific Undersea Gardens A sort of natural aquarium, the gardens (☎ 250-382-5717) are found on the Inner Harbour at 490 Belleville St. Visitors descend beneath the water's surface to view a range of corralled sea creatures such as octopuses, eels, crabs etc. Children especially find it intriguing. Admission is $7/6.25 for adults/seniors, $5 for students (aged 12 to 17) and $3.50 for children.

Royal London Wax Museum This museum (☎ 250-388-4461), 470 Belleville St, in front of the Parliament Buildings, contains more than 200 wax models of historical and contemporary figures. Kids love the dungeon. It's open from 9.30 am to 5 pm daily and admission is $7.50/3 for adults/children.

Miniature World At Miniature World (☎ 250-385-9731), 649 Humboldt St, beside the Empress Hotel, you'll find many

layouts depicting (in exact detail) various themes, such as the world of Dickens. The highlight is a large model train representing the development of the Canadian Pacific Railway from 1885 to 1915. It is open from 9 am to 5 pm daily and admission is $8/6 for adults/children.

Crystal Garden This site (☎ 250-381-1277), 713 Douglas St, is one of the more popular commercial attractions. The principal draw is the colourful tropical-like garden complete with 65 varieties of international endangered animals and birds as well as free-flying butterflies. Designed by Francis Rattenbury, it was fashioned after London's Crystal Palace and built in 1925. Once a focal point for the social elite, it was restored in 1977 as a visitor attraction, but remains a venue for splashy events.

It's open from 10 am to 9 pm daily in July and August; the rest of the year it closes at 5.30 pm. Admission is $7/4 for adults/children.

Old Town & Government St
The original Victoria was centred along Wharf St and Bastion Square. This was where the first fur-trading ships moored. Wharf St was once busy with miners, merchants and all those fortune seekers heading for the Klondike.

Bastion Square, along Wharf St between Yates and Fort Sts, was where Fort Victoria was situated and held the courthouse, jail, gallows and brothel. The whole area has been restored and redeveloped. The square is pleasant for strolling around and people watching.

Farther north along Wharf St you'll come to **Market Square**, a former warehouse on the corner of Johnson St, dating from the 1890s. Renovated in 1975, this compact, attractive area now has two floors of over 40 shops and restaurants, built around a courtyard shaded by trees.

Busy Government St is an especially attractive street, with many fine shops and handsome Victorian buildings. It's especially lovely at night, when the structures are lit.

Maritime Museum This collection of artefacts, models, photographs and naval memorabilia provides a fascinating look at the maritime traditions at the heart of Victoria's history. A large new area was scheduled to open as we went to press. The open-cage elevator inside the front door is a gem. The museum (☎ 250-385-4222), 28 Bastion Square near Government St, is open from 9 am to 4.30 pm daily and admission is $5/2 for adults/children.

Victoria Bug Zoo At the Victoria Bug Zoo (☎ 250-384-2847), 1107 Wharf St, there are displays you'll either love or want to step on. You'll see everything from fist-sized beetles to the perpetually pregnant Australian stick insect. The leaf-cutter ants going about their business inside the metres of Plexiglas tubes are mesmerising. Open from 9.30 am to 6 pm daily, admission to the zoo costs $6/4 for adults/children. Ask about the sleep-over option.

Victoria Eaton Centre This shopping centre incorporates the façades of some of the original buildings. The centre occupies two blocks between Government and Douglas Sts, and between View and Broughton Sts.

Fisherman's Wharf
Just west of the Inner Harbour, around Laurel Point, is Fisherman's Wharf. It's a busy spot, with fishing boats and pleasure craft coming and going. You can sometimes buy fresh seafood from the boats or the little shed. Take a look at the mix of houseboats moored at one end of the dock.

South of Downtown
Scenic Marine Drive Starting either from Fisherman's Wharf or Beacon Hill Park, the Scenic Marine Drive, with great views over the sea, skirts the coast along Dallas Rd and Beach Drive. The road heads north past some of Victoria's wealthiest neighbourhoods.

You'll see several parks and beaches along the way, though access to the shore for much of the way is restricted because of private housing right on the coastline.

Beacon Hill Park

Just south-east of the downtown area, along Douglas St, this 153-acre park is Victoria's largest. The park is an oasis of trees, flowers, ponds and pathways. (You don't see trees of this size anywhere but on the west coast.) The southern edge overlooks the ocean and offers good views of the coastline. At the lookout above Dallas Rd is a marker indicating the direction of places such as Seattle, and noting the elevations of mountains. At the south-western corner of the park, the path along the water meets the **'Mile 0' marker**, the Pacific terminus of the Trans Canada Hwy. To reach the park, take bus No 5 from downtown.

Carr House

South of the Inner Harbour, a short walk leads to the birthplace of Emily Carr, one of Canada's best known painters. The Carr House (☎ 250-383-5843) at 207 Government St shows something of her background and displays some of her work, both in painting and literature. It's open from 10 am to 5 pm daily from mid-May to mid-October. Admission is $4.50/3.50 for adults/children. Note that the Victoria Art Gallery usually has an Emily Carr exhibit.

Rockland Area

Just east of downtown Victoria, Rockland, which lies between Fort St and Fairfield Rd, and extends east to Moss St, is a wealthy neighbourhood filled with handsome old homes and a number of civic buildings.

Art Gallery of Greater Victoria The gallery (☎ 250-384-4101) is in a Victorian mansion at 1040 Moss St, 1.5km east of the downtown area, just off Fort St. It's best known for its excellent Asian art, including the Japanese and Chinese collections. It

The Life and Times of Emily Carr

Emily Carr was born in Victoria in 1871. After her parents died when she was young, she was discouraged from pursuing her love of painting because it was 'unladylike.' Eventually, she was forced to forsake her avocation entirely and work as a teacher.

Her career as an artist took a pivotal turn when, in 1898, she accompanied a churchman to his mission at Ucluelet on Vancouver Island. The life and arts of the Native Indian village had a profound effect on Carr. Inspired by what she saw she began using both the landscape and the Native Indians as her subject matter. However, she felt that the power of both nature and Native culture were missing from her painting. A trip to Paris at age 39 gave her new insights and her work took on a unique use of colour, brush stroke and subject matter.

Back home her new paintings were not taken seriously. At the age of 42, after a disastrous exhibition of paintings that scandalised the staid values of the time, she became a social outcast. To make ends meet she became a landlady in central Victoria. It wasn't until the late 1920s, when her scorned paintings were shown in eastern Canada, that she began getting the respect she deserved. Carr returned to painting with renewed energy and until the latter 1930s she painted some of her best known works.

As her health failed she wrote several books about her life. Her book *Klee Wyck* is a collection of stories recalling her life among the Native Indians. Its title means 'The Laughing One'.

Carr's house in Victoria is open to the public, and her paintings can be viewed at the Art Gallery of Greater Victoria and other galleries across Canada.

Emily Carr

also has artworks from other parts of the world and Emily Carr's work is usually displayed. Take bus No 10, 11 or 14 from the downtown area. It's open from 10 am to 5 pm Monday to Saturday, from 10 am to 9 pm Thursday and 1 to 5 pm Sunday. Admission is $5/3 for adults/students and seniors, and children are free.

Government House This house is the official residence (☎ 250-387-2080) of the province's lieutenant-governor. The impressive grounds are open to the public. The building is not far from the Art Gallery of Greater Victoria, away from the downtown area, at 1401 Rockland Ave. Take bus No 1 from downtown.

Craigdarroch Castle Near Government House, but off Fort St, this rather impressive home (☎ 250-592-5323), 1050 Joan Crescent, was built in the mid-1880s by Robert Dunsmuir, a coal millionaire. The castle-like house has been completely restored and is now a museum. It's open from 9 am to 7 pm daily in summer and 10 am to 4.30 pm the rest of the year. Admission is $7.50/5 for adults/students. To get there take bus No 11 or 14.

North-West of Downtown & Esquimalt

Point Ellice House This beautifully kept house (☎ 250-380-6506), built in 1861, was sold in 1868 to Peter O'Reilly, a member of government and a very successful businessman. It's open from 10 am to 5 pm daily May to mid-September and admission is $4/2 for adults/children. It's north-west of the downtown area at 2616 Pleasant St, off Bay St, at Point Ellice Bridge. Take bus No 14 from downtown.

English Village This gimmicky but effective re-creation of some English Tudor-style buildings is on Lampson St, across Victoria Harbour from downtown Victoria. The highlights are the replicas of Shakespeare's birthplace and the thatched cottage of his wife, Anne Hathaway. The cottage (☎ 250-

388-4353) at 429 Lampson St and the rest of the 'village' are furnished with 16th century antiques. It is open from 9 am to 8 pm daily from May to October and 10 am to 4 pm other times. Admission is $7.50/4.50 for adults/children. Take bus No 24 from the downtown area.

Craigflower Farmhouse & Schoolhouse The farmhouse (☎ 250-383-4627) was built by Kenneth McKenzie in 1856. It was the central home in the first farming community on Vancouver Island and its construction heralded Victoria's change from a fur-trading settlement to a permanent one. Admission also includes a visit to the historic schoolhouse. The farmhouse is open from noon to 4 pm daily and admission is $5. It's north-west of town, on the corner of Craigflower and Admirals Rds, near Gorge Rd (Hwy 1A). To get there catch bus No 14 from downtown.

Fort Rodd Hill National Historic Park

This scenic 45-acre park (☎ 250-478-5849) overlooking Esquimalt Harbour contains some historical points of interest. The gun batteries were maintained until 1956. There are information signs around the park, as well as guides. The park is open from 10 am to 5.30 pm daily from March to November, 9 am to 4.30 pm other times. Admission is $3/1.50 for adults/children.

Also in the park is **Fisgard Lighthouse**, western Canada's first, which still works and has been in continuous use since 1860.

The park is at 603 Fort Rodd Hill Rd, off Ocean Blvd, about 12km north-west of downtown, on the western side of Esquimalt Harbour. To get there catch bus No 50 which takes you to within 1km of the park.

Butchart Gardens

These gardens, 21km north-west of Victoria, are probably the most publicised of all Victoria's sights. Located on the site of a former limestone quarry, these 50-acre gardens were created by the family of a local cement manufacturer, beginning in 1904.

The Butchart Gardens is comprised of smaller individual gardens, including a rose garden, Italian garden and a sunken garden with water features. No doubt the gardens are beautiful and extensive, but admission is costly at $11.50/5.75 for adults/children.

You can walk through in about 1½ hours, but plant lovers will want to linger much longer. In the evenings from June to September the gardens are illuminated. There are also concerts and puppet shows around dusk. On Saturday nights during July and August there is a spectacular fireworks display set to music at no extra charge.

The gardens (☎ 250-652-4422), 800 Benvenuto Ave, in Brentwood Bay, are open daily from 9 am till dusk year-round. If you're driving, follow Hwy 17 north toward Sidney. City bus Nos 74 and 75 go within 1km during the week and 3km on Sunday.

Western Shore

West of Victoria, Hwy 14 takes you from the city's manicured parks and gardens to the pristine wilderness of Vancouver Island's west coast. The highway runs through Sooke then along the coast overlooking the Strait of Juan de Fuca to Port Renfrew, at the southern end of the West Coast Trail (see Pacific Rim National Park later in this chapter). There are parks and beaches along the way for walking, beachcombing and picnicking.

Before you reach Sooke follow the signs from Milnes Landing to the **Sooke Potholes** where you can go swimming, picnicking and hiking. Sooke's Visitor Info Centre (☎ 250-642-6351) and local museum are housed in the same building at 2070 Phillip's Rd. Victoria's bus network extends to Sooke – take bus No 50 to the Western Exchange then change to No 61.

Farther along Hwy 14, the windswept **French Beach** and **China Beach** provincial parks have swimming, camping and walking trails.

At **Port Renfrew**, often the destination for a day trip from town, the main attraction is **Botanical Beach**, a sandstone shelf, which at low tide is dotted with tidal pools containing all manner of small marine life: starfish, anemones etc. To return to Victoria without retracing your tracks, take the logging road across the island to Lake Cowichan, from where better roads connect to Duncan and Hwy 1. For those without transportation, the West Coast Trail Express (☎ 250-477-8700, ☎ 250-995-7189), 3954 Bow St (also listed under PBM Transport in the phone book), runs buses from Victoria to Port Renfrew twice a day. Use it for an interesting day trip to the west coast beaches along the Strait of Juan de Fuca or to begin the hiking trail to Bamfield (for details see West Coast Trail under Pacific Rim National Park later in this chapter).

Activities

Whale Watching Scores of excursion operators offer trips out into the Georgia Strait to watch orcas, or killer whales. Other wildlife you may see on these trips are bald eagles, seals and sea lions, and many kinds of seabirds.

Going on a whale-watching trip is as easy as walking to the waterfront and signing up for the next excursion. Whale-watching trips cost between $75 and $80 adults, $50 to $55 children, for a three hour excursion. For information or reservations, contact Ocean Explorations (☎ 250-383-6722, ☎ 1-888-422-6722), 146 Kingston St, at the Coast Victoria Harbourside Hotel near Fisherman's Wharf; Prince of Whales (☎ 250-383-4884), 812 Wharf St (just below the Visitor Info Centre office); or Cuda Marine (☎ 250-995-2832) on the Wharf St pier.

Swimming One of the best swimming places is the **Sooke Potholes**, about an hour's drive west of Victoria on Hwy 14, by the town of Sooke, on the southern shore. Watch for signs at Milnes Landing. You can find your own swimming hole but the water ain't balmy. There's good picnicking and some walking trails too. Don't get caught drinking alcohol because the fines are heavy for drinking in a public area.

Also popular is **Thetis Lake Park**, not too far north-west of town (about 20 minutes

driving), off the Trans Canada Hwy. It's very busy at the main beach but if you hike around the lake you'll find a quiet spot.

Scuba Diving The Georgia Strait provides opportunities for world-class diving. The undersea life is tremendously varied and has been featured in *National Geographic*. Several excellent shore dive sites are found near Victoria, including Saanich Inlet, Saxe Point Park, the Ogden Point Breakwater, 10-Mile Point and Willis Point for deep diving. Race Rocks, 18km south-west of Victoria Harbour, offers superb scenery both above and below the water. Diving charters and dive shops in Victoria provide equipment sales, service, rentals and instruction.

Fishing The waters around Victoria are renowned for deep-sea fishing with salmon being the top prize. The Visitor Info Centre can supply information and you should also check the Yellow Pages. There are freshwater lakes and streams within an hour or two of Victoria as well as up-island that are good for trout and/or salmon fishing. Saanich Inlet has one of the highest concentrations of salmon in the world.

Scores of charter companies offer deep-sea fishing trips of varying lengths. Most supply all equipment, bait and even coffee. For a complete list of outfitters, contact the Info Centre. As an example of prices, Duffy's Salmon Charters (☎ 250-642-5789) has minimum four-hour trips for $225 but four adults can go for that price.

Other Activities Windsurfing is popular, especially in Cadboro Bay near the university, and at Willows Beach in Oak Bay. Rentals are available at both for around $17; some places offer lessons, too. Oak Bay is also a popular canoeing spot. Ocean River Sports (☎ 250-381-4233), 1437 Store St, rents canoes and kayaks, sells equipment and runs courses. Sports Rent (☎ 250-385-7368), 611 Discovery St, hires canoes for $25 per day and kayaks for $45 per day.

A few people offer horseback trips in the nearby highlands and lake areas. Some include overnight camping. Ask at the Visitor Info Centre. Lakeshore Trailrides (☎ 250-479-6853), 482 Sparton Rd, has one-hour rides for $25.

Organised Tours

There is no shortage of companies offering all sorts of tours. The Visitor Info Centre has details on many of the options.

Gray Line Bus Company (☎ 250-388-5248), 700 Douglas St, offers a variety of tours here, as it does in so many North American cities. Its city tour on double deckers costs $16.50 for 1½ hours and takes in some of the major historical and scenic sights. You can buy tickets in front of the Empress Hotel, the same place from where buses depart.

Heritage Tours (☎ 250-474-4332), 713 Bexhill St, offers more personalised city tours in limousines seating six people for $75 for 1¼ hours, or $90 for two hours. The rate is per car, not per person. When friends and relatives come to visit, locals prefer Enchanted Tours of Victoria (☎ 250-475-3396). It has commentary and itineraries less canned than others and charges from $22.50.

Tallyho Sightseeing (☎ 250-383-5067) gives 45-minute city tours in a horse-drawn carriage. The standard tour costs $30 for two people, and leaves from the corner of Belleville and Menzies Sts.

Ask about the free walking tours at the Visitor Info Centre or buy a copy of the booklet *Victoria on Foot* (Terrapin, Victoria, 1989), by Barrie Lee, which gives details of walking tours around the Old Town.

Seagull Expeditions (☎ 250-360-0893, ☎ 1-800-580-3890), unit 213, 951 Topaz St, runs good, low cost backpacker tours up-island to Pacific Rim National Park. Stops en route allow visits to geographic and activity highlights with overnight camping (equipment supplied) or hostelling. Most trips leave from Victoria but there's one from Vancouver. The basic three-day tour is $99 and there are one-day and five-day trips too. Food and accommodation costs are extra but very reasonable. Another trip goes

to Strathcona Park for fine hiking. Pick-up can also be made in Nanaimo. Trips run from April to the end of September.

Midnight Sun (☎ 250-480-9409, ☎ 1-800-255-5057), 843 Yates St, also runs reliable small-group van trips to Pacific Rim and Strathcona Park. The three-day trips go from April to September and cost $155, less for hostellers. Costs include camping and some meals. It also has a 12-day camping trip through the Rockies. On all trips a range of activities is possible.

Special Events

May
Victoria Day Festival

Held during the fourth week of May to celebrate Queen Victoria's birthday, it features a parade, performances by the town's ethnic groups, stage shows and many sporting events. Call ☎ 250-382-3111 for information. A 10-day harbour festival is held concurrently and the Swiftsure Lightship Classic, a sailing race, ends the event. Call ☎ 250-592-2441 for information. The last weekend can get pretty wild – a real street party.

June
Jazz Festival

In late June the Victoria Jazz Society (☎ 250-388-4423) puts on its annual jazz festival at various locations around town.

June/July
Folkfest

Held at the end of June and the beginning of July, this celebrates Canada's cultural diversity. Dance and musical performances take place at Centennial Square.

June/August
Victoria International Festival

This festival, offering classical music performed by Canadian and foreign musicians, lasts through the summer till mid-August. For information contact the McPherson Playhouse (☎ 250-386-6121).

August
First Peoples' Festival

This takes place in mid-August beside the Royal BC Museum and along the Inner Harbour. It lasts three days and includes traditional craftwork, dancing, a potlatch and war-canoe rides. For more information call ☎ 250-383-2663.

August/September
Fringe Theatre Festival

Featuring more than 50 performances in various locations around town, the festival includes drama, comedy, acrobatics, jugglers and street performers. It takes place in late August and early September. For further details call ☎ 250-384-3211.

September
Classic Boat Festival

During this Inner Harbour festival, held on the first weekend in September each year, vintage wooden boats powered by sail or engine compete in various categories. Free entertainment is provided on the quayside for the spectators. For information call ☎ 250-385-7766.

October
Salmon Run

Observe the fish and take part in events and educational displays marking the annual salmon migration at Goldstream Provincial Park (☎ 250-391-2300), north of town.

Places to Stay

Lodging in Victoria can be very expensive, and in summer, hard to find. Reserve as soon as you know your travel plans. In the downtown area there are several older hotels that have been renovated and are good value; to stay in the prime locations on the Inner Harbour will take a bite out of your budget. If you're looking for inexpensive lodgings, you'll need to stay at one of the hostels, or else head out of the downtown area to one of the motel strips in the suburbs. Prices for accommodation are very seasonal; if you travel outside of the main summer season, you'll save considerably on rooms.

If you're having trouble finding a room, the Info Centre's reservation service (☎ 250-382-2127, ☎ 1-800-663-3883) can help you find one.

Camping Closest to town is *Fort Victoria RV Park* (☎ 250-479-8112, *340 Island Hwy*), off Island Hwy 1A, 6.5km north-west from the city centre. Take bus No 14 or 15 from the downtown area; there's a bus stop at the gate. The park caters mainly to RVs. It does have a few tent sites but there are no trees,

BRITISH COLUMBIA

and open fires are not allowed. It charges $26 per site.

A little farther out, *Thetis Lake Camp-ground* (☎ 250-478-3845, 1938 Trans Canada Hwy) on Rural Route 6 is about a 15 minute drive north-west of the city centre. All facilities are available, there's a store, and you can swim in the nearby lake. A site for two people is $15 including tax; electricity is $2 extra. The campground is open all year.

The best campground is *Goldstream Provincial Park* (☎ 250-391-2300) on the Trans Canada Hwy about 20km north-west of Victoria. A tent site costs $15.50 for one to four people and you can go swimming, fishing or hiking. Take bus No 50 from Douglas St. South of Goldstream Provincial Park, about 3.5km off the Trans Canada Hwy at 2960 Irwin Rd, on Rural Route 6, is *Paradise Campground* (☎ 250-478-6960). It's part of a nature sanctuary and is open from early June to September. It has full facilities, canoe and kayak rentals and charges $18 for two people.

The Visitor Info Centre can tell you of other campgrounds not too far from town.

Hostels The HI *Victoria Hostel* (☎ 250-385-4511, fax 250-385-3232, victoria@hihostels.bc.ca, 516 Yates St) is in the old part of town just up from Wharf St. It has room for over 100 people, with family rooms, a large common area, kitchen, laundry and a good notice board. Memberships are available. A bed costs $16 for members and $20 for nonmembers. In peak season it's advisable to check in before 4 pm.

Also central is the new *Ocean Island Backpacker's Inn* (☎ 250-385-1788, ☎ 1-877-706-2326, ocean_island@hotmail, 791 Pandora Ave), on the corner of Blanchard St, which was being developed as we went to press. The former apartment building can't be missed – look for the flat trees growing up the walls. This large hostel with room for 130 has four to six-bed dorms at $17 to $20 and doubles at $40. There is Internet access and 24 hour check-in.

The *Selkirk Guest House International* (☎ 250-389-1213, ☎ 1-800-974-6638, 934 *Selkirk Ave)* in Esquimalt over the Johnson St Bridge, charges $18 for a dorm bed and has private rooms from $40. Travellers with kids can be accommodated. Features include a garden complete with hot tub on the shore of The Gorge. The No 14 bus from Douglas St gets you within two blocks.

Victoria Backpackers Lodge (☎ 250-386-4471, 1418 Fernwood Rd) has dormitory beds for $13, and private singles/doubles for $30/35. The hostel has no curfew and is close to the shops and restaurants of Fernwood Village. Buses east along Fort St will take you there; the No 10 bus goes right past the door.

Nearby on a residential street is small *The Cat's Meow* (☎ 250-595-8878, 1316 Grant St) where dorms are $17.50 and private rooms $40 to $53, all with breakfast. Call before arriving. Daphne, the owner, can help with advice on tours and things to see around town.

Also in the neighbourhood is *Renouf House* (☎ 250-595-4774, renouf@isl andet .com, 2010 Stanley Ave), which has beds in a co-ed dorm room for $20 (bunk and breakfast) in addition to several private B&B rooms.

The *Hannah Lodge Hostel* (☎ 250-598-7323, fax 250-598-7324, 1729 Oak Bay Ave), offers two to six-bed bunk rooms in a four-storey renovated heritage home for $18 to $20. Amenities include a self-service kitchen and an outdoor deck and BBQ. The hostel is wheelchair-accessible. Take bus No 1 or 2 from downtown.

The *YM-YWCA* (☎ 250-386-7511, 880 Courtney St) are both in the same building, but the residence is only for women. A dorm bunk with bedding costs $19. Private single rooms, when available, cost $37. There's also a cafeteria and a heated swimming pool.

The *University of Victoria* rents rooms from the start of May to the end of August. Singles/doubles are $38/50, including breakfast and free parking. Contact Housing & Conference Services (☎ 250-721-8396) at the University of Victoria, PO Box 1700, Victoria, BC V8W 2Y2. Catch bus No 14 on

Douglas St to the campus; it takes about 20 minutes.

B&Bs There are several B&B associations that approve members, list them and make reservations at one central office. Prices are between $45 and $75 for singles and between $55 and $120 for most doubles, though some go up to as much as $190.

A couple of associations to try are All Seasons B&B Agency (☎ 250-655-7173), PO Box 5511, Station B, Victoria, BC V8R 6S4; and Victoria Vacationer B&B (☎ 250-382-9469), 1143 Leonard St, Victoria, BC V8V 2S3. Many B&Bs advertise independently and have pamphlets at the Visitor Info Centre. A few of them are listed here.

North-east of the centre, *Renouf House* (☎ 250-595-4774, 2010 Stanley Ave) is a 1912 heritage home. It can cater to people with special diets and has home-baked bread. Private rooms with a shared bathroom start at $35/55 a single/double, rooms with a private bathroom start at $50/70. It's a friendly, casual and comfortable place which also offers kayaking (one of the owners makes kayaks). *Marion's B&B* (☎ 250-592-3070, 1730 Taylor St), about a 10 minute bus ride from downtown, is recommended. Rooms are $35/55, the good breakfasts are enormous and the owners are friendly and helpful.

Convenient to sights on the Inner Harbour, *Birdcage Walk Guest House* (☎ 250-389-0804, 505 Government St) offers five guest rooms with private bathrooms in a historic home; rooms cost $89/99.

Hotels – Inner Harbour The most appealing and most expensive hotels are those along the Inner Harbour, with views of the bay and downtown. From here, it's a short walk to downtown and the shopping precincts.

While these prices certainly press the upper limits of the middle range, they're about the best you'll find in this much sought-after area. The best deal here is the *Admiral Motel* (☎ 250-388-6267, 257 Belleville St). With singles/doubles at $115/135, this attractive motel with larger-than-average rooms is a great choice. Hidden in a grove of trees, the

High Tea at the Empress

English-style high tea at the Empress Hotel is so mandatory an experience for most visitors as to be a cliché. While high tea isn't usually considered a meal in itself, this extravagance of clotted cream, berries, scones and biscuits will surely ruin your appetite for an evening meal. The tearooms at the Empress are lovely and have actually taken over much of the lobby so they can fit in more people. High tea isn't cheap – you'll spend $29 per person for the honour. Reservations are a good idea in all but the dead of winter.

Best Western Inner Harbour (☎ 250-384-5122, ☎ 1-800-528-1234, 412 Quebec St) has balconies and nicely decorated rooms starting at $119 for a single or a double. Just a block in from the harbour and from the Parliament Buildings, the *Royal Scot Inn* (☎ 250-388-5463, ☎ 1-800-663-7515, 425 Quebec St) offers studio, one and two-bedroom suites starting at $119; if you need a little extra room, this is a good choice.

The *Empress Hotel* (☎ 250-348-8111, ☎ 1-800-441-1414, 721 Government St) is practically synonymous with Victoria. Staying here on honeymoon is a tradition throughout the Northwest; many well heeled travellers wouldn't think of staying anywhere else. This grand doyenne is nearly a century old, but she's never looked better. The hotel looks out over the Inner Harbour and, along with the Parliament Buildings, is the focal point of Victoria. Even if you're not staying here, the Empress Hotel is worth a visit; many visitors come here for the famous and very commercialised afternoon tea service. Singles/doubles are priced from $225/255.

Hotels – Downtown & Old Town There are a few reasonable places right in the downtown area. *Hotel Douglas* (☎ 250-383-4157, ☎ 1-800-332-9981, 1450 Douglas St), centrally located on the corner of Pandora Ave, has rooms starting at $65/70 a single/double.

At the **Strathcona Hotel** (☎ 250-383-7137, ☎ 1-800-663-7476, 919 Douglas St), a couple of blocks east of the Inner Harbour, rooms start at $74/84.

Crystal Court Motel (☎ 250-384-0551, 701 Belleville St), on the corner of Douglas St, is across the road from the Bus Depot and Crystal Garden. Rooms are $70/73 a single/double, and a kitchen costs just $2 more. It's clean and the rooms have a TV, radio and telephone.

In the middle range, the attractive **Green Gables Hotel** (☎ 250-385-6787, ☎ 1-800-661-4115, 850 Blanshard St) is close to the Inner Harbour and has an indoor pool, as well as a sauna and restaurant; single rooms cost $105 to $120, double rooms cost $159. Nicely refurbished, **Swans Hotel** (☎ 250-361-3310, ☎ 1-800-668-7926, 506 Pandora Ave) is a gem of a building in the Old Town area, right on the waterfront. All rooms are suites, with great contemporary art and luxury touches; single rooms cost $135 to $165, double rooms start at $165.

Hotels – Around Downtown Victoria is a very compact city, and the following hotels and motels are just a few minutes from the downtown sights, but much cheaper than those right in the centre.

Opened in 1897, the **Cherry Bank Hotel** (☎ 250-385-5380, ☎ 1-800-998-6688, 825 Burdett Ave) is east of the downtown area opposite the law courts. It's simple but reasonable value at $50/58 a single/double with a shared bathroom, or $66/73 with a private bathroom. Prices include breakfast but rooms have no TV or telephone.

Just north of downtown along Douglas St is an area of inexpensive motels. **Traveller's Inn** (☎ 250-370-1000, ☎ 1-888-753-3774, 710 Queens Ave) at Douglas St is one of the best, with clean, large and simple rooms for $59/69. The **Doric Motel** (☎ 250-386-2481, 3025 Douglas St) is a five minute drive north of the downtown area. It has TV, laundry and free coffee. Rooms cost $64/69.

Another good area for motels – not far north-west of the downtown area – is along Gorge Rd, which forms a section of Island

Hwy 1A. From Gorge Rd it's about a five minute drive to town. At the **Capri Motel** (☎ 250-384-0521, 21 Gorge Rd E) rooms cost $60/70. The **Traveller's Inn on Gorge** (☎ 250-388-9901, 120 Gorge Rd E) has a sauna, heated pool and coin laundry. Rooms cost $50/52; kitchenettes are $10 extra.

Slightly more expensive and back on the Douglas St motel strip, **Paul's Motor Inn** (☎ 250-382-9231, 1900 Douglas St) has a 24 hour restaurant; rooms start at $88/93. **Horizon West** (☎ 250-382-2111, ☎ 1-800-830-2111, 1961 Douglas St) has rooms at $73/83; farther out, **Blue Ridge Inn** (☎ 250-388-4345, 3110 Douglas St) has rooms at $75/85.

The **Stay 'N Save Motor Inn** (☎ 250-475-7500, ☎ 1-800-663-0298, 3233 Maple St) has one of its friendly and comfortable motels here, about 10 minutes from downtown. Rooms cost from $74/84.

At the high end, across the Inner Harbour from downtown and the Parliament Buildings, and with tremendous views of both is the **Ocean Pointe Resort** (☎ 250-360-2999, ☎ 1-800-667-4677, 45 Songees Rd). It combines luxury-class rooms with the facilities of a spa. On-site amenities include an indoor pool, hydrotherapy services, racquetball and squash courts, tennis courts and sauna; rooms are top-notch and start at $169 for a single or double.

Places to Eat
Though a small city, Victoria has a varied array of restaurants, due in part to its many visitors, and prices are generally good. As befits a tourist town, especially one with British roots, there are numerous cafés and teashops. Some dining rooms offer good lunch specials but are fairly pricey in the evening. The pubs in town are also good for reasonably priced meals.

Budget A good place to shop around for a decent, inexpensive meal is in Chinatown (Fisgard St between Douglas St and the harbour), or in the Market Square shopping centre at Johnson and Wharf Sts, where there are a number of casual eateries and food booths. One of the best places for breakfast in this

area is the *Milky Way Cafe* (☎ 250-360-1113, 126-160 Johnson St). *Foo Hong Chop Suey* (☎ 250-386-9553, 564 Fisgard St) is small and basic yet has good, simple Cantonese food. The *Ocean Phoenix* (☎ 250-360-2818, 509 Fisgard St), closed Monday, offers a small, neat dining room, an extensive menu and good food. Try the Cantonese lunch specials.

Modest and casual *Day & Night* (☎ 250-382-5553, 622 Yates St) is good for any meal, with good-value plain food, including one of the cheapest breakfasts in town. Sandwiches and pasta dishes start from $4.

Sam's Deli (☎ 250-382-8424, 805 Government St), under the maroon awnings on the corner of Wharf St and diagonally opposite the main Visitor Info Centre, is a perfect spot to have an espresso and write a postcard. There are a dozen tables outside on the sidewalk and more inside, where the walls are covered in 1920s and 1930s posters. It serves good-value soups, salads and sandwiches for less than $5.

It's worth joining the crowds at colourful *John's Place* (☎ 250-389-0799, 723 Pandora Ave) for the large portions at breakfast or lunch. *Growlie's* (☎ 250-383-2654, 615 Yates St) takes coffee shop standards and makes them sublime. The BLT for $5.95 is the best one on the planet.

The fish and chips are excellent in Victoria and there are several outlets for them. *Barb's Place* (☎ 250-384-6515, 310 St Lawrence St) at Fisherman's Wharf is a wooden shack on the dock serving fish and chips in newspaper. Fresh crabs can be bought from the boats nearby.

Brady's (☎ 250-382-3695, 20 W Burnside Rd) by the corner of Harriet Rd is also a good spot for fish and chips.

Mount Royal Bagel Factory (☎ 250-380-3588, 1115 N Park St) – the entrance is on Grant St – in the Fernwood Village area, has fresh Montreal-style bagels. The cinnamon ones are so good, you don't need to toast them.

Mid-Range An excellent, popular place for good light meals, drinks and a friendly

welcome is *Suze* (☎ 250-383-2829, 515 Yates St). The menu involves Pacific Northwest takes on pizza, pasta and fresh seafood dishes; the lounge, with exposed brick and a vintage 7.5m-long mahogany bar, is one of the cosiest yet hippest places in Victoria.

Perhaps the most happening place in town is the *Re-Bar* (☎ 250-360-2401, 50 Bastion Square), with its eclectic contemporary international menu and funky décor to match. It's busy all day for breakfasts, coffees, desserts, salads and main dishes, which are mostly vegetarian and all well prepared.

If the weather's good and dining on a outdoor deck is appealing, then the *Wharfside Eatery* (☎ 250-360-1808, 1208 Wharf St) is your best bet. While fresh seafood is the speciality, the menu also offers wood-fired pizzas. Bustling and popular, *Il Terrazo Ristorante* (☎ 250-361-0028, 555 Johnson St) is the best place in Victoria for Italian pastas, grilled meats and tempting pizzas. The atmosphere is nice, and there is courtyard dining in good weather. Victoria has a number of good Greek restaurants, but *Milos* (☎ 250-382-5544, 716 Burdett St) has the reputation for the best roast lamb; stay late for the belly dancers.

Both a brewpub and a great place for lunch or light dinner, *Swan's Brew Pub* (☎ 250-361-3310, 506 Pandora Ave) has good burgers and sandwiches, and one of the most appealing, art-filled barrooms in the city.

Pagliacci's (☎ 250-386-1662, 1011 Broad St) between Fort and Broughton Sts is a moderately priced Italian restaurant, with big portions of pasta and pizza. At night this is a busy place, partly for the food, partly for the live music. *Herald St Caffé* (☎ 250-381-1441, 546 Herald St) is a small Italian restaurant serving delicious pastas for around $12 to $15. It also has vegetarian dishes, great desserts and a wine bar that gets busy after 10 pm.

Le Petit Saigon (☎ 250-386-1412, 1010 Langely St) is recommended for Vietnamese meals. The menu includes meat, fish and vegetarian dishes.

Top End *Chandler's Seafood Restaurant* (☎ 250-385-3474), near the Victoria Regent

Hotel and the corner of Yates and Wharf Sts, is an established dining room specialising in ocean fare. Locals call it 'amazing.' Overlooking the Inner Harbour, the *Harbour House Restaurant (☎ 250-386-1244, 607 Oswego St)* is formal and elegant and has the best steaks in town.

Koto Japanese Restaurant (☎ 250-382-1514, 510 Fort St), just up from Wharf St, serves mainly seafood and has a sushi and salad bar; main courses cost $16 to $26. There's a detailed, colourful display in the window of the kinds of dishes available in the restaurant. *Camille's Fine Westcoast Dining (☎ 250-381-3433, 45 Bastion Square)* has the reputation of being Victoria's most inventive restaurant, with fusion cooking bringing the best of Northwest ingredients into contact with eclectic, international cuisine.

Entertainment

Monday Magazine, the weekly entertainment paper available free around town, has extensive coverage of what's going on.

Performing Arts The *Victoria Symphony Orchestra (☎ 250-846-9771)* performs from August through May at the Royal Theatre, 805 Broughton St. The *Pacific Opera Victoria (☎ 250-385-0222)* offers three performances a year at McPherson Playhouse.

Theatre Victoria has a number of live theatres that provide venues for plays, concerts, comedies, ballets and operas. The *McPherson Playhouse (☎ 250-386-6121, 3 Centennial Square)* on the corner of Pandora Ave and Government St, regularly puts on plays and comedies. The box office is open from 9.30 am to 5.30 pm Monday to Saturday. The elegant *Royal Theatre (☎ 250-386-6121, 805 Broughton St)* between Blanshard and Quadra Sts, hosts a range of performances, including ballet, symphony, dance and concerts. Other theatres worth checking are the *Belfry (☎ 250-385-6815, 1291 Gladstone Ave)* north-east of the downtown area, and the *Phoenix Theatre (☎ 250-721-8000)* on the University of Victoria campus. More experimental theatre is staged by Dark

Horse Theatre at the *Herald St Centre for the Arts (☎ 250-475-4444, 520 Herald St)*.

Live Music Victoria's best live-jazz venue is *Millennium Jazz Club (☎ 250-360-9098, 1601 Store St)* beneath Swan's Pub.

Pagliacci's is popular not only for its food but also for its jazz. For information about jazz around town, call the Jazz Hotline at ☎ 250-658-5255.

In the same building as the Strathcona Hotel, 919 Douglas St, there are several clubs that feature live music and shows including *Legends (☎ 250-383-7137)*, a long-standing rock and blues night-club. *Steamers Public House (☎ 250-381-4340, 570 Yates St)* just below Government St, is a good blues bar and has Sunday afternoon sessions.

Pubs Often heralded as Canada's first brewpub, *Spinnakers Brewery Pub (☎ 250-386-2739, 308 Catherine St)* has a nice mix of locals and visitors. In good weather there's deck seating with views over the Inner Harbour. *Swan's Brew Pub (☎ 250-361-3310, 1601 Store St)* is half the main floor of a popular refurbished hotel. Besides the good beers, the owner has an extensive modern art collection in the pub. Two places with good beer selection are *Garrick's Head (69 Bastion Square)* and the *Sticky Wicket Pub (Strathcona Hotel, 919 Douglas St)*, which has volleyball on the roof in summer.

Coffeehouses Besides a good cup of coffee, at *Bean Around the World (☎ 250-386-7115, 533 Fisgard St)* you can also join one of the discussion groups; 'What is Reality?' was the topic at one of their philosophy nights. *Java Coffee-house (☎ 250-381-2326, 537 Johnson St)* is a classic coffeehouse, with more standard entertainment, like live music and poetry readings. There are about a zillion other places; one on almost every corner.

Dance Clubs One of the most popular dance clubs is *The Planet (☎ 250-385-5333, 15 Bastion Square)*, on the corner of Wharf St, above Rebecca's restaurant. *BJ's Lounge*

(☎ 250-388-0505, downstairs, 642 Johnson St) is a gay dance club. **Uforia Night Club** (☎ 250-381-2331, 1208 Wharf St) gets a young crowd. **The Jet Lounge** (☎ 250-920-7343, 751 View St) has hip-hop, rhythm and blues, top-40 covers etc.

Cinema The **Odeon Theatre** (☎ 250-383-0513, 780 Yates St) and the **Capital 6** (☎ 250-384-6811, 805 Yates St) are the main downtown cinemas.

Shopping

There are a number of craft shops along Douglas and Government Sts selling Native Indian art and craftwork such as sweaters, moccasins, carvings and prints. Be prepared as the good stuff is expensive.

Canadian Impressions (☎ 250-383-2641), 811 Government St, has some quality items and Native Indian crafts. The small Indian print greeting cards make good, inexpensive presents and some are even signed by the artist. Canadian Impressions has another shop at the airport.

Sasquatch Trading Company (☎ 250-386-9033), 1233 Government St, has a good selection of Cowichan sweaters. These hand-spun, hand-knitted sweaters average between $140 and $200 but are warm and should last a decade or more. No dyes are used.

On Fort St, between Cook and Quadra Sts, there are a number of antique and bric-a-brac shops.

For chocolate lovers, Roger's Chocolates, 913 Government St, dating from 1885, offers a treat to both nose and tongue. Try one (or more) of the Victoria creams – chocolate-covered discs in more than 20 flavours. Everything on sale here is made on the premises.

Getting There & Away

Air If you're flying to Victoria, you'll arrive at Victoria international airport in Sidney, about 19km north of Victoria on Hwy 17.

Two airlines with offices in Victoria are Air Canada (☎ 250-360-9074), 20 Centennial Square, and Canadian Airlines (☎ 250-382-6111), 901 Gordon St. Air Canada and Canadian Airlines connect the airports of Vancouver and Victoria. The normal, one-way, pre-tax economy fare is $214 return, but weekend return specials can lower this to around $120 return. A number of smaller regional airlines offer service between Victoria and Vancouver; consult a travel agent for information.

If you're flying to Vancouver and beyond, the cost of a ticket from Victoria is just a few dollars more than one from Vancouver itself, so it's not worth paying the ferry price to catch a flight directly from Vancouver.

You can also catch a seaplane to Victoria harbour from Vancouver harbour with Harbour Air (☎ 250-384-2215, ☎ 1-800-665-0212). The 35 minute flight costs $79 one way.

Horizon Air (☎ 206-762-3646 in Seattle; ☎ 1-800-547-9308) has service between Victoria and Seattle, Port Angeles, and Bellingham. North Vancouver Air (☎ 1-800-228-6608) links Vancouver, Victoria and Tofino.

Bus Although Greyhound has no service on the island or to the mainland it does have an office (☎ 250-385-5248) in the bus station at 700 Douglas St where you can get information and purchase tickets.

Pacific Coach Lines (PCL; ☎ 250-385-4411) and Island Coach Lines (☎ 250-385-4411) also operate out of the same station. PCL runs buses to Victoria from Vancouver, some of the southern BC mainland and to Seattle. A bus leaves for Vancouver every hour between 6 am and 9 pm; the one-way fare, which includes the cost of the ferry, is $25. It's the same price to Vancouver international airport; it connects with the airport shuttle bus at Delta Pacific Resort. The bus to Seattle, via Sidney and Anacortes, leaves at 10 am and gets there at 5 pm.

Island Coach Lines, sometimes referred to as Laidlaw Lines, covers Vancouver Island. There are eight buses a day to Nanaimo and northern Vancouver Island.

The bus station has left-luggage lockers for $2.50.

Car For rentals, shop around as prices can vary. A couple of the cheapest places are ADA Rent A Used Car (☎ 250-474-3455), 892 Goldstream Ave, and Rent-A-Wreck (☎ 250-384-5343), 2634 Douglas St.

All major rental companies are represented in and around the downtown area (as well as at the airport).

Three on Douglas St are Avis (☎ 250-386-8468) 843 Douglas St, Budget (☎ 250-388-5525), 757 Douglas St, and National/Tilden (☎ 250-381-1115), 767 Douglas St.

Train The Esquimalt & Nanaimo Railiner (or E&N Railiner), operated by VIA Rail (☎ 250-383-4324, ☎ 1-800-561-8630), connects Victoria with Nanaimo, Parksville and Courtenay. There is one train in each direction per day – northbound from Victoria at 8.15 am, southbound from Courtenay at 1.15 pm.

The journey, through some beautiful scenery, takes about 3½ hours. The *Malahat*, as the train is known, is very popular so book ahead. Some one-way fares from Victoria are to Nanaimo $19, Parksville $24 and Courtenay $36. Seven-day advance purchases are much cheaper.

For the full schedule, get a copy of the E&N Railiner pamphlet from the station, a travel agency or the Visitor Info Centre. The station, 405 Pandora Ave, is close to town, right at Johnson St Bridge, near the corner of Johnson and Wharf Sts. It's open from 7.30 am to noon and 1 to 3 pm.

Ferry BC Ferries (☎ 250-386-3431, ☎ 1-888-223-3779), 1112 Fort St, on the corner of Cook St, runs frequent trips from Swartz Bay to Tsawwassen on the mainland. The 39km crossing takes about 1¾ hours. There are between 10 and 15 sailings per day; the schedule varies according to the season. The high-season passenger fare is $9, while a car costs $30 or $32 weekends and holidays. Bus No 70 from the downtown area to the ferry terminal costs $2.25.

BC Ferries also operates between Swartz Bay and five of the southern Gulf Islands: Galiano, Mayne, Saturna, Salt Spring and Pender. There are about three or four services a day.

The passenger-only *Victoria Clipper* and *Victoria Clipper II*, run by Clipper Navigation (☎ 250-382-8100), 430 Belleville St, sail between Seattle and Victoria. The journey lasts about 2¾ hours and the fare one way is $75; it's a little cheaper the rest of the year. For those with cars, the *Princess Marguerite III* operates between Ogden Point, Victoria, and Seattle. A car and driver costs $64.

The ferry MV *Coho*, operated by Black Ball Transport (☎ 250-386-2202), 430 Belleville St, is much cheaper. It sails between the Inner Harbour and Port Angeles just across the Strait of Juan de Fuca. It costs US$6.75 per person or US$27.25 with a car. It's a 1½ hour trip, and there are four a day in each direction during summer months.

The passenger-only, summer-only *Victoria Express* (☎ 250-361-9144), 430 Belleville St, also goes to Port Angeles. The trip takes one hour and the return fare is US$25. The *Victoria Star*, operated by Victoria Cruises (☎ 1-800-443-4552) based in Bellingham, Washington, goes back and forth once a day. The passenger-only ferry leaves from 430 Belleville St.

Lastly, Washington State Ferries (☎ 250-656-1531, ☎ 250-381-1551 in Victoria), 2499 Ocean Ave in Sidney, has a ferry service from Swartz Bay through the San Juan Islands to Anacortes on the Washington mainland. It's a very scenic trip and you can make stopovers on the islands; vehicle fare one way is US$32 in high season. The trip takes 3¼ hours.

Getting Around
To/From the Airport Victoria International Airporter (☎ 250-386-2525), links the airport to 60 downtown area hotels. It leaves every half-hour from downtown and the airport between 4.30 am and 1 am and costs $13.

City bus No 70 passes within 1.5km of the airport, while a taxi to the airport from the downtown area costs about $35 to $40.

Bus For local transit information call BC Transit (☎ 250-382-6161) or get a copy of BC Transit's guide from the Visitor Info

Centre listing bus routes and fares. The city buses cover a wide area and run quite frequently. The normal one-way fare is $1.50; it's $2.25 if you wish to travel out to suburbs such as Callwood or Sidney. Have the exact change ready. You can get an all-day pass for $5 for as many rides as you want, starting as early as you like. These all-day passes are not sold on buses but are available from various outlets around town such as convenience stores. The system runs until about midnight.

Bus No 70 goes to the ferry terminal in Swartz Bay; bus No 2 goes to Oak Bay. The Oak Bay Explorer double-decker bus costs just $1 and takes a 90 minute run between the Empress Hotel and Oak Bay. You can stay on or get off along the way.

Taxi Two of several companies are Victoria Taxi (☎ 250-383-7111) and Blue Bird Cabs (☎ 250-384-1155). You can also hire three-wheeled bicycle taxis called pedicabs – a more leisurely way of getting around.

Bicycle Downtown you can hire bikes from Cycle Victoria (☎ 250-885-2453), 950 Wharf St at the Victoria Marine Adventure Centre. Bikes are also available at Sports Rent (☎ 250-385-7368), 611 Discovery St, and at the HI Hostel.

Ferry Victoria Harbour Ferry runs an enjoyable, albeit short, ferry trip of about half an hour return from the Inner Harbour to Songhees Park (in front of the Ocean Pointe Resort), Fisherman's Wharf and Westbay Marina. The boat takes just a dozen people per trip and costs $3 one way.

SOUTHERN GULF ISLANDS

Lying north of Victoria, and off Tsawwassen on the mainland, this string of nearly 200 islands in the Georgia Strait is the continuation of Washington State's San Juan Islands.

With a few important exceptions, most of the islands are small and nearly all of them virtually uninhabited, but this island-littered channel is a boater's dream. Vessels of all descriptions cruise in and out of bays, harbours and marinas much of the year. The fishing is varied and excellent and several species of prized salmon can be caught in season. BC Ferries connects with some of the larger islands, so you don't need your own boat to visit them. Lodging is tight, so reservations are mandatory, especially in high season. Pick up a copy of the free newspaper *The Gulf Islander* which details island happenings and lodging options.

Most of the restaurants on the Gulf Islands are associated with lodges, resorts and B&Bs. Campers may want to make sure they have cooking supplies, as casual restaurants can be hard to find.

Due to the mild climate, abundant flora and fauna, relative isolation and natural beauty, the islands are one of Canada's escapist-dream destinations. Indeed, many of the inhabitants are retired people, artists or counterculture types of one sort or another. In fact, some of the 'farmers' are taking their new product to Amsterdam where they compete in contests, much the way brewers compete for international medals.

Cycling the quiet island roads is a very popular pastime.

Getting There & Away Ferry service to the islands is good, though potentially very confusing. Pick up one of the ferry schedules (available at most Info Centres) and give yourself a few minutes to figure out the system. In general, there are more ferries in the morning than in the afternoon, so make sure you know when and how you're getting back if you're planning a day trip. Generally, here's what the service consists of.

Ferries connect to the Southern Gulf Islands from both Tsawwassen on the mainland and Swartz Bay near Sidney on Vancouver Island. Tsawwassen-departing ferries go to Saturna, Mayne, Galiano, Pender and Salt Spring Islands. A one-way passenger fare is $8.50, or $34.50 for a car. Ferries from Swartz Bay go to all the above islands, except Mayne. One-way fare is $5 for a passenger, or $18 for a vehicle. For all these runs, reservations for cars are strongly advised in high season.

BRITISH COLUMBIA

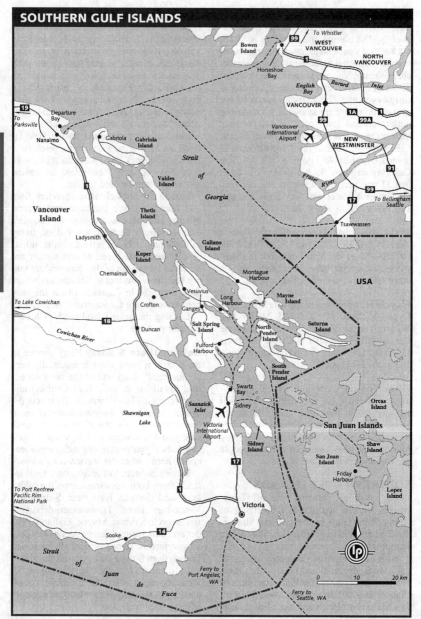

SOUTHERN GULF ISLANDS

In addition to the ferries between the mainland and Vancouver Island, there are also inter-island ferries. Fares on these are $2.50 for passengers, $6 for a car.

Salt Spring Island

Salt Spring Island is the largest island in both size and population; its usual population of more than 8500 swells to three times that size in summer. Artists, entertainers and craftspeople have chosen to live here. As a consequence, there are craft fairs and art galleries with national reputations.

The island has a long, interesting Native Indian history, followed by settlement not by white people but by pioneering African-Americans from the US. Seeking escape from prejudice and social tensions in the States, a small group of settlers formed a community at Vesuvius Bay. Unfortunately, the Native Indians didn't care for them any more than they cared for the British in the area. Still, the blacks stuck it out, began farms and set up schools. Later, immigrants came from Britain and Ireland.

There are three ferry terminals: Long Harbour serves Vancouver, Swartz Bay and the other Southern Gulf Islands; and Fulford Harbour and Vesuvius Bay are for ferries plying back and forth to Vancouver Island, the former to Swartz Bay, the latter to Crofton.

Ganges, not far from the Long Harbour landing, is the principal village. It has the most accommodation and has a summer arts and crafts fair, a few tourist-oriented shops and a Saturday morning market. Artists welcome visitors to their studios – the Visitor Info Centre (☎ 250-537-5252), 121 Lower Ganges Rd, has a list. **Mouat Provincial Park** is nearby and has 15 camp sites. Salt Spring Island Bus (☎ 250-537-2311) runs between Ganges and the ferry terminals.

South of Ganges, **Mt Maxwell Provincial Park** offers excellent views, fishing and picnic areas. In **Ruckle Provincial Park**, a former homestead 10km east of the Fulford Harbour ferry terminal, you can enjoy hiking through forests and along the shoreline, plus fishing and wilderness camping.

Places to Stay The campground at *Ruckle Provincial Park* (☎ 250-391-2300) on Beaver Point Rd has 70 primitive camp sites for $9.50. There are a few more camp sites ($8) near Cusheon Lake at the *Salt Spring Island Hostel* (☎ 250-537-4149, hostel@saltspring.com, 640 Cusheon Lake Rd), which also has dorm beds in either a cedar lodge or teepee for $14/18 for members/nonmembers. The hostel is a short walk from the lake or ocean beach.

There are quite a few B&Bs on the island; the operators of most will pick you up at the ferry terminal. The breakfast is particularly good at the pastoral *Old Farmhouse B&B* (☎ 250-537-4113, 1077 North End Rd), near St Mary Lake, a restored century-old farmhouse with four guest rooms ($125 to $150), all with private bathrooms and balconies.

Head to Ganges if you're looking for a motel. The *Seabreeze Inn* (☎ 250-537-4145, 101 Bittancourt Rd) has quiet rooms overlooking Ganges Harbour and a few kitchenettes; rooms cost $74/94 a single/double. A number of cottages along St Mary Lake go for roughly the same price as a motel room. The *Cottage Resort* (☎ 250-537-2214, 175 Suffolk Rd) features a sandy swimming beach, free canoes and rowboats, and small lakefront cottages with a few kitchenettes; cottages rent for $75 to $105, depending on the size.

The health-oriented *Salty Springs Spa & Seaside Resort* (☎ 250-537-4111, 1460 North Beach Rd) in Vesuvius Bay features upscale seaside chalets (some with kitchens) with fireplaces for $159/189 a single/double. Rooms lack a TV or phone, as guests are expected to be busily rejuvenating themselves with massage and mud baths.

North & South Pender Islands

These two islands are joined by a small bridge. There are arts-and-crafts studios to visit and a golf course. For beaches, try **Hamilton** in Browning Harbour on North Pender and **Mortimer Spit** on South Pender (just after crossing the bridge). You might see some of the more-or-less tame deer around the islands. You can hike and camp at **Prior Centennial Provincial Park** on North Pender,

close to **Medicine Beach** at Bedwell Harbour. On South Pender there are good views from the summit of the 255m **Mt Norman**.

Places to Stay Accommodation is mainly in B&Bs and cottages. *Corbett House B&B* (☎ *250-629-6305, 4309 Corbett Rd*), 1.5km from the ferry terminal, is a cosy heritage farmhouse with congenial hosts; rooms go for $70/85 a single/double. *Inn on Pender Island* (☎ *250-629-3353, ☎ 1-800-550-0172, 4709 Canal Rd*), a small inn in the woods, is popular with cyclists. This is one of the least expensive places to stay on the islands, with an on-site restaurant, and rooms with private entrances and coffee-makers for $60/70. *Cliffside Inn On-the-Sea* (☎ *250-629-6691, 4230 Armadale Rd*) is an oceanfront B&B with great views (especially from the cliff-side hot tub over the bay). All rooms have private bathrooms.

Saturna Island
At Saturna Point, by the ferry terminal in Lyall Harbour, there's a store and pub. **Winter Cove Marine Park** has a good sandy beach from where you can go swimming, fishing, boating and hiking. At the top of **Mt Warburton Pike** is a wildlife reserve with feral goats and fine views. There are also good views of the Washington Cascades from the road on the island's leeward side. Just north of Saturna Island is **Cabbage Island Marine Park**, with swimming, fishing and wilderness camping.

Accommodation on Saturna Island is limited to only a few B&Bs, so be sure to book in advance. *Breezy Bay B&B* (☎ *250-539-2937, 131 Payne Rd*) on a farm less than 1.5km from the ferry terminal has singles/doubles for $55/65. All four rooms at the English-style *Stone House Farm B&B* (☎ *250-539-2683, 207 Narvaez Bay Rd*) feature private bathrooms and balconies, and have views of the waterfront and Mt Baker; $95/100.

Mayne Island
The ferry between Tsawwassen and Swartz Bay squeezes through Active Pass, which

separates Mayne and Galiano Islands. Village Bay, on the southern side of Mayne Island, is the ferry terminal, although there are docking facilities for boaters at other points. There are some late 19th century buildings at **Miners Bay**, including the museum, which was formerly the jail.

Places to Stay *Mayne Inn Hotel* (☎ *250-539-3122, 494 Arbutus Drive*) is a small waterfront hotel; all rooms have a view. It's a pleasant and inexpensive place to stay, with rooms starting at $50/60 a single/double.

Fernhill Lodge (☎ *250-539-2544, 610 Fernhill Rd*) is a secluded hilltop B&B about 5km from the ferry dock. The inn is loaded with character, with seven rooms in period theme, a herb garden and a sauna; rooms start at $75/90. *Oceanwood Country Inn* (☎ *250-539-5074, 630 Dinner Bay Rd*) is both pastoral and upscale. All rooms have private bathrooms and views of Navy Channel, some rooms have whirlpool tubs and private balconies. Rooms start at $120/130, tea service and breakfast included. The restaurant at the Oceanwood is one of the best restaurants in the Gulf Islands, with four-course Northwest-cuisine dinners.

Galiano Island
Despite its relatively large size, Galiano Island has fewer than 1000 residents on its long, narrow landmass. About 75% of the island is forest and bush. There's a Visitor Info Centre (☎ 250-539-2233) at the ferry terminal in Sturdies Bay. Again, local artists and artisans invite visitors to their studios.

You can hike almost the length of the east coast and climb either **Mt Sutil** at 323m or **Mt Galiano** at 342m, from both of which you can see the Olympic Mountains about 90km away. If you're willing to tackle the hills, you can go cycling, while Porlia Pass and Active Pass are popular places for diving and fishing. The coast is lined with cliffs and small bays, and canoeing along the western shoreline is possible in the calmer waters. On the north-eastern tip of the island is the rugged **Dionisio Point Provincial Park** with swimming, fishing, hiking and wilderness camping.

Places to Stay You can camp at *Montague Harbour Marine Park* (☎ 250-391-2300), about 9.5km from Sturdies Bay ferry terminal for $12; sites are primitive and reservations are available. Around the island there are B&Bs and several places with cottage rentals. *Sutil Lodge* (☎ 250-539-2930) dates from the 1920s and is on the beach at Montague Harbour. It has singles/doubles from $60/75 and offers free use of canoes.

Bodega Resort (☎ 250-539-2677, 120 Monasty Rd) is a favourite family destination for its horseback-riding trails and trout-fishing pond. The two-storey log cottages have three bedrooms and kitchens and start at $40/60.

SOUTHEASTERN VANCOUVER ISLAND

For information on provincial parks in this region, contact BC Parks (☎ 250-391-2300), 2930 Trans Canada Hwy, Victoria, V9E 1K3.

Duncan & Cowichan Valley

About 60km north of Victoria along the Trans Canada Hwy is the small town of Duncan. It marks the beginning of the Cowichan Valley which runs westward and contains large Cowichan Lake. This is the land of the Cowichan people, who comprise BC's largest Native Indian group. Despite some problems they still maintain aspects of their unique culture.

A good day trip from Victoria, for those with wheels, is to head up to Chemainus, back to Duncan, then over to Lake Cowichan, across to Port Renfrew and down the west coast back to town. It's a lot of driving but if you're in no hurry and can stop a lot it makes an interesting, full day. For information, ask at the Visitor Info Centres. The well used logging road from Lake Cowichan to Port Renfrew is gravelled and in good shape; with a basic map, you shouldn't have any difficulty.

The Visitor Info Centre (☎ 250-746-4636) in Duncan, on the corner of the Trans Canada Hwy and Coronation St, is open from 9 am to 5 pm daily in summer. In Lake Cowichan the Visitor Info Centre (☎ 250-749-4324) is open from 9 am to 5 pm Sunday to Thursday, and 8.30 am to 8 pm Friday and Saturday.

There really isn't much to see in Duncan (although the old part of town is worth a look around) or the township of Lake Cowichan, but the valley and lake are good for camping, hiking, swimming, fishing and canoeing. The turnoff for Lake Cowichan is about 4km north of Duncan, left (east) of the Trans Canada Hwy; from the turnoff the lake is another 22km.

Since 1985, Duncan, the 'City of Totems', has developed a project with the Cowichans to have totem poles carved and displayed in the town area. There are now more than 20 examples of this west-coast art form.

Native Heritage Centre If coming to Duncan from the south on Hwy 1, take the first left turn after crossing the bridge, onto Cowichan Way. The centre (☎ 250-746-8119), 200 Cowichan Way, has exhibits of Cowichan craftwork and carvings; you can often watch carvers and weavers at work. There's a gift shop and restaurant serving Native Indian food. It's open from 9.30 am to 5.30 pm daily in summer, and 10 am to 4 pm the rest of the year. The admission price is $7.25/6/3.25 adults/seniors and students/children, and includes a 20 minute movie about the centre and Cowichan People.

BC Forest Museum This is about 3km north of Duncan, offering both indoor and outdoor features on its 40 hectares. There's a stand of original forest of Douglas firs, 55m tall, that were present before Captain Cook arrived in 1778. Included in the price is a ride around the site in a small steam train. You can visit a bird sanctuary or view a replica of an old logging camp and logging equipment. There are also indoor displays and movies of old logging operations. The museum (☎ 250-748-9389) is open from 9.30 am to 6 pm daily in summer and admission is $7/6/4 adults/seniors and students/children.

Activities There are many hiking trails around Cowichan River and Cowichan Lake. One is the **Cowichan River Footpath**. It's about 18km long with a good variety of

scenery along the way. You can either do it in a day or camp en route. The path goes to Skutz Falls; from there you can head back to Duncan or keep going up the river. Maps of the trail are available at sporting stores. The lake gets warm enough to swim in. You can also go fishing and canoeing in the lake and river.

Places to Stay *Lakeview Park Municipal Campground* (☎ *250-749-3350)* is on the southern shore of Cowichan Lake about 3km west of town on South Shore Rd. It has showers, toilets and free firewood. It charges $15 a car, less without one. Farther west along the lake there is a campground at *Gordon Bay Provincial Park*, about 13km from Hwy 18 on South Shore Rd, with 130 sites for trailers and tents, showers and flush toilets. The fee is $14.50 and reservations are accepted.

Hotels and motels pop up along the Trans Canada Hwy in Duncan and in the small townships along the river and lake. Two of the cheapest are *Duncan Motel* (☎ *250-748-2177, 2552 Alexander St)*, which has some kitchenettes and singles/doubles for $34/39; and *Falcon Nest Motel* (☎ *250-748-8188)*, which has a heated outdoor pool and rooms for $44/50. The park-like *Best Western Cowichan Valley Inn* (☎ *250-748-2722, 6474 Trans Canada Hwy)* is convenient to the BC Forest Museum and Native Heritage Centre, and has a pool, restaurant and pub; rooms cost $79/85.

Places to Eat In Duncan most of the eating places are along the Trans Canada Hwy but there are a few small places in the old part of town. *Good Rock Café* (☎ *250-748-4252, cnr Government & Jubilee Sts)* is a 1950s-style diner, complete with jukebox (and old 45s hanging from the ceiling). It's good for breakfasts and has Friday-night East Indian buffets.

Getting There & Away Island Coach Line buses travel between Duncan and Victoria for $9 including tax, one way. The 70 minute train trip between Duncan and Victoria on the E&N Railiner costs $11 including tax; there is one a day in each direction.

Carmanah Walbran Provincial Park

Take logging roads from Lake Cowichan to reach this majestic wilderness park adjacent to the West Coast Trail, which was created after years of bitter fighting over logging rights. The park protects a rich rainforest containing some of the world's tallest trees including a giant Sitka spruce 94.5m high. There are some basic tent sites, drinking water, about 5km of marked trails and an information office.

Trails extend beyond the park north into the Carmanah Valley with wilderness camping. The rough trails can often be very muddy. The road from Lake Cowichan takes 2½ hours and watch for trucks! Along the way is Nitinaht Lake, the 'confused sea', renowned for windsurfing, and another road leading to the Ditidaht First Nation visitors centre. It offers tours around the region. The Info Centre in Duncan has some information on the park.

Duncan to Nanaimo

About 16km north of Duncan on Hwy 1A is the small town of **Crofton**, from where you can catch ferries to Vesuvius Bay in the north of Salt Spring Island (see Southern Gulf Islands earlier in this chapter).

Chemainus

Chemainus, 10km north of Crofton, had a novel and interesting way of putting itself on the tourist map. In 1983 the town sawmill shut down, and to counter the inevitable slow death, an artist was commissioned to paint a large outdoor mural relating to the town's history. People took notice, more murals were painted and now there are over 30 of them. A bustling and prosperous community developed and the sawmill reopened.

The brightly painted Chemainus Theatre has been restored and is the most striking building in town. There are now lots of craft shops and restaurants, all making a short visit a worthwhile proposition. The Visitor

Info Centre (☎ 250-246-3944) is in an old railway carriage on Mill St.

Off the coast of Chemainus are **Thetis Island** and **Kuper Island**. Kuper Island is a Native Indian reserve for which you need permission from the chief to visit.

The ferries for these islands leave from Oak St and the ticket office is opposite the Harbourside Cafe; the fare is $4 and $10.75 for a car. The ferry to each island takes about 30 minutes from Chemainus. Thetis Island is primarily geared to boaters and has two marinas. There is a pub, however, at Quinn's Marina. Turn left when you get off the ferry then left again into Harbour Drive where you see the anchor sign. There's one restaurant, the Pump House, which you can see to the left as the ferry pulls in. At Pilkey Point there are sandstone formations along the beach.

Places to Stay Once an old mill-workers' dorm, the *Chemainus Hostel (☎ 250-246-2809, 9694 Chemainus Rd)* features separate sleeping areas for men and women, a laundry room and secure bike storage; beds go for $15. The *Fuller Lake Chemainus Motel (☎ 250-246-3282, 9300 Trans Canada Hwy)* has a few pleasant rooms and some kitchenettes for $45/55 a single/double.

Chemainus is largely a town of B&Bs. *Hummingbird House B&B (☎ 250-245-8412, 11120 Chemainus Rd)* has two rooms in a modern oceanfront home, both with private bathrooms for $45/60. Rooms are more nostalgic at the Victorian *Bird Song Cottage (☎ 250-246-9910, 9909 Maple St)* and cost $70/85.

Ladysmith

A small town about 26km north of Duncan on the Trans Canada Hwy, Ladysmith sits on the 49th parallel, which on the mainland divides Canada from the USA. Originally built as a coal-shipping port by the industrialist James Dunsmuir, the town was named after the South African town of the same name.

The Visitor Info Centre (☎ 250-245-8544) and the **Black Nugget Museum**, on Gatacre Ave, are in the same building, constructed in 1896 as a hotel. Many of the late 19th/early 20th century buildings have been restored. The warmest seawaters north of San Francisco are said to flow at **Transfer Beach Park**; it's right in town and you can camp there. About 13km north of town, a 15 minute drive off the highway, on Yellow Point Rd (follow the signs), pub aficionados will find the *Crow & Gate (☎ 250-722-3731)*, the oldest British-style pub in the province. The atmosphere is very authentic and the steak-and-kidney pie and the Cornish pasties are really good, and worth the detour.

Petroglyph Provincial Park

About 3km south of Nanaimo on the Trans Canada Hwy, this small green park features some ancient Native Indian carvings in sandstone. Most of them are now barely visible having been overgrown with moss and plants. As well as the original petroglyphs there are castings from which you can make rubbings.

NANAIMO & AROUND

Nanaimo is Vancouver Island's second major city, with a rapidly increasing population of 70,000. Long considered drab and still bad-mouthed by residents of Victoria, Nanaimo gets an unfair rap. It has a diverse cross section of people, a busy little downtown and a major people-oriented waterfront redevelopment.

A number of Native Indian bands once shared the area, which was called *Sne-Ny-Mos*, a Salish word meaning 'meeting place'. Coal was discovered in 1852 and for the next 100 years coal mining was the main industry in the town. Coal has declined in importance, but the city is now the centre of a forest-products industry as well as being a major deep-sea fishing port and a terminal for BC Ferries. Tourism continues to gain importance and the city has become a retirement centre as well.

Orientation & Information

Nanaimo, about 110km north of Victoria, is a convenient stopover and a departure point to Vancouver, the islands just off Nanaimo Harbour and spots up-island.

The entire waterfront area off Front St along the harbour has been redone with a seaside walkway, docks, shops, restaurants, coffee bars and pubs. Behind the harbour lies the central core. Most of the restaurants and shops are on Commercial and Chapel Sts and Terminal Ave, which run more or less parallel to the harbour. To the south, Nicol St, the southern extension of Terminal Ave, leads to the Trans Canada Hwy. To the north, Terminal Ave forks – the right fork becomes Stewart Ave and leads to the BC Ferries terminal in Departure Bay; the left fork becomes Hwy 19A, which heads north up-island to Courtney, Campbell River and Port Hardy. Sealand Market at the Departure Bay ferry terminal has a couple of restaurants, a pub, tourist-oriented shops and the Oceanarium, a commercial attraction featuring underwater viewing of sea creatures. The entire town is by-passed by the new Nanaimo Parkway which carries Hwy 19 around the west side. It has an excellent hiking and biking trail well away from traffic.

There are quite a few parks in and around Nanaimo. The waterfront promenade, which takes in a number of the downtown ones, begins at the seaplane terminal and heads north to **Georgia Park**, where there are a few totem poles, a display of Native Indian canoes, including a large war canoe and a fine view of Nanaimo Harbour. It then continues to Swy-A-Lana Lagoon (good for children to splash in) and **Mafeo-Sutton Park**, from where ferries leave to Newcastle Island.

The Visitor Info Centre (☎ 250-756-0106, fax 250-756-0075, ☎ 1-800-663-7337), 2290 Bower Rd, is 1km off Hwy 19 at Northfield Rd. Watch for the many large signs. Located in a 60-year-old mansion, the centre has local and regional information and is open from 8

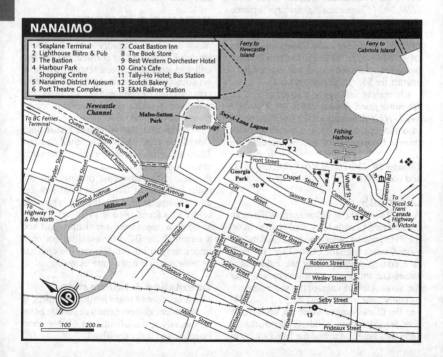

NANAIMO

1 Seaplane Terminal
2 Lighthouse Bistro & Pub
3 The Bastion
4 Harbour Park Shopping Centre
5 Nanaimo District Museum
6 Port Theatre Complex
7 Coast Bastion Inn
8 The Book Store
9 Best Western Dorchester Hotel
10 Gina's Cafe
11 Tally-Ho Hotel; Bus Station
12 Scotch Bakery
13 E&N Railiner Station

am to 7 pm daily May to September, 9 am to 5 pm weekdays and 10 am to 4 pm the rest of the year. There's a walking guide, *Step Into History*, of the town's historic area around the harbour, although note that many of the original buildings downtown have been destroyed and are now marked only by plaques. Throughout summer there is an information office open daily located in the Bastion historical site on the waterfront.

The Old City Quarter, a small section of downtown around Bastion, Fitzwilliam, Selby and Wesley Sts, is being rejuvenated. The impressive new Port Theatre (☎ 250-754-8550) performing arts complex dominates downtown on the corner of The Bastion and Front St. It includes the new Vancouver Island Regional Library (☎ 250-753-1154).

The main post office is located near the Harbour Park Shopping Centre which is on the corner of Front St and Terminal Ave. There's a funky and eccentric bookstore, The Book Store (☎ 250-753-3011), at 76 Bastion St. It has everything a real reader could want, including a 2nd floor devoted mainly to children's books. Nanaimo Regional General Hospital (☎ 250-754-2121) is at 1200 Dufferin Crescent, north-west of the downtown area.

Nanaimo District Museum
The small museum (☎ 250-753-1821) at 100 Cameron Rd displays items of significance in the growth of Nanaimo. Included are Native Indian, Hudson's Bay Company and coal-mining artefacts. It's open from 10 am to 6 pm daily. Admission is $2.

The Bastion
The Bastion on Front St, on the corner of Bastion St, is the highlight of Nanaimo's old buildings. Built by the Hudson's Bay Company in 1853 for protection from Native Indians, it was never used but for the odd firing of a cannon to quell a disturbance. It's now a museum and tourist office and is open from 9 to 11.30 am and noon to 5 pm daily. Admission is free. The cannons are fired over the water at noon Wednesday to Sunday.

Newcastle Island Provincial Marine Park
Just offshore of the downtown area is Newcastle Island, which offers cycling, hiking and beaches. It's also a good place for a picnic or overnight camping. Cars are not allowed. The island was once dotted with mineshafts and sandstone quarries but later became a quiet resort. In summer a small ferry travels between the island and the mainland every hour.

Gabriola Island
Farther out into the strait is Gabriola Island, the most northerly of the Southern Gulf Islands. A fine day can be had exploring, but you'll need a bicycle or car. It has several beaches and three provincial parks offering swimming, shoreline walking and tidal pool examination. At **Malaspina Galleries** are some unusual sandstone caves carved out by the wind and tides. There is a ferry from Nanaimo (see the Getting There & Away section later for details).

Activities
Off the coast, **scuba diving** is possible among the northern Gulf Islands in excellent dive sites like Dodd Narrows, Gabriola Passage, Porlier Pass and Northumberland Channel. Three nearby spots where you can go **hiking** or **canoeing** are Nanaimo Lakes, Nanaimo River and Green Mountain. Hikes from **Colliery Dam Park** lead to Harewood and Overton Lakes. Kayaks can be rented at the Kayak Shack beside the Sealand Market.

Nanaimo also has three good spots for **birdwatching**: Buttertubs Marsh Sanctuary, Morrell Sanctuary (take Comox Rd west off Terminal Ave to both) and Piper's Lagoon Park off Hammond Bay north of the city.

Special Events
The top annual event is the Nanaimo Bathtub Race to Vancouver, held each mid-July as part of Nanaimo's Marine Festival. Hundreds of fibreglass tubs start out, about 100 sinking in the first five minutes. Winners complete the 48km passage of the Georgia Strait's wild waters to reach the beaches at

BRITISH COLUMBIA

Vancouver. For details call ☎ 250-753-7223.

Places to Stay

Camping The best place is just off the coast at *Newcastle Island Provincial Marine Park* with 18 tent sites at $9.50; no reservations. Farther out is the much larger *Gabriola Island* where there are private campgrounds. Convenient to the ferry, *Gabriola Campground* (☎ 250-247-2079) has 28 beachside camp sites at $14.

North of town are several campgrounds. *Jingle Pot Campsite & RV Park* (☎ 250-758-1614, 4012 Jingle Pot Rd) is 8km north of Nanaimo off Hwy 19. It has showers, laundry and tent sites for $12. The closest to town is *Beban Park Campground* (☎ 250-756-5200, 2300 Bowen Rd) about 1.5km west of Hwy 19, which has sites for $12. *Brannen Lake Campsites* (☎ 250-756-0404, 4228 Briggs Rd) is on a working farm; sites are $14.

Hostels The homy *Nanaimo International Hostel* (☎ 250-753-1188, gmurray@island.net, 65 Nicol St) is two blocks south of the Harbour Park Shopping Centre. Beds are $15; tenting sites are $8. Check in between 4 and 11 pm.

Linked with the Cambie in Vancouver is the downtown *Cambie International Hostel, Nanaimo* (☎ 250-754-5323, ☎ 1-877-395-5335, nanaimo@cambiehostels.com, 63 Victoria Crescent). It has room for about 50 people in small dorms and charges $25, $5 less with student or hostel card.

Hotels Many of the motels are on the highway north and south of the city. On the south end of town the *Diplomat Motel* (☎ 250-753-3261, 333 Nicol St) has single/double rooms for $42. On the north end of town close to the Departure Bay ferry terminal, is the *Colonial Motel* (☎ 250-754-4415, 950 North Terminal Ave), with rooms (some with kitchenettes) from $39/45.

South of town, *Buccaneer Motel* (☎ 250-753-1246, 1577 Stewart Ave) is just three blocks from the ferry terminal. It's diver friendly and has comfortable rooms from

$45/50 a single/double. Some have ocean views. The *Tally-Ho Hotel* (☎ 250-753-2241, ☎ 1-800-663-7322, 1 Terminal Ave), near the ferry terminal, has an outdoor pool and rooms starting at $65 for a single or a double.

Downtown the *Best Western Dorchester Hotel* (☎ 250-754-6835, ☎ 1-800-661-2449, 70 Church St) is a refurbished historic hotel featuring rooms and suites with harbour views starting at $85.

The *Coast Bastion Inn* (☎ 250-753-6601, ☎ 1-800-663-1144, 11 Bastion St) is another pleasant downtown waterfront hotel; rooms have views of the harbour and start at $89/99.

About 5km north of town, the *Long Lake Inn Resort* (☎ 250-758-1144, ☎ 1-800-565-1144, 4700 N Island Hwy) is a large vacation resort featuring a swimming beach, marina and canoe rentals. The balconied rooms all front onto Long Lake and cost $109 to $168 a single or double.

Places to Eat

A stroll along Commercial St from the corner of Terminal Ave will turn up a number of places.

The *Scotch Bakery* (☎ 250-753-3521, 87 Commercial St) has great baked goods, including Nanaimo bars, a classic Canadian sweet known across the country. Down at the Harbour, *Lighthouse Bistro & Pub* (☎ 250-753-3212, 50 Anchor Way) is a casual place with great views and pasta, seafood and burgers ($7).

For lunch or dinner, *Gina's Cafe* (☎ 250-753-5411, 47 Skinner St) is recommended for its inexpensive Mexican food, atmosphere and view.

Another fine place for an evening meal is the pleasantly casual *Dinghy Dock Marine Pub* (☎ 250-753-2373) at the waterfront over on Protection Island, an eight minute trip from downtown on a small ferryboat. Seafood and various barbecue meals are offered for about $10. The outdoor patio has views across the harbour to Nanaimo and after dinner you can stroll the small, quiet residential island. Get the ferry from the

docks at the south end of Government Wharf across from the museum.

Getting There & Away

Bus & Train Island Coach Lines (☎ 250-753-4371) connects Nanaimo with points north and south; the one-way fare to Victoria is $17. The station is at the Tally-Ho Hotel at 1 Terminal Ave north of the centre near Comox Rd. The E&N Railiner passes through once a day in each direction; the one-way fare to Victoria is $19. There's no ticket office at the station, 321 Selby St; call ☎ 1-800-561-8630 for information. Tickets can be purchased from the conductor.

Ferry The 39km ferry trip to Horseshoe Bay takes about 1½ hours. There are about 12 to 15 services in each direction daily, depending on the season. As we went to press, BC Ferries (☎ 1-888-223-3779) was planning to introduce new high-speed ferries that will shorten the journey by a promised 30 minutes. Peak-season tickets are $9 per person, and $30 for a vehicle on weekdays, $2 more on weekends. The terminal is in Departure Bay at the northern end of Stewart Ave. The ferry between Nanaimo and Tsawwassen, the *Mid-Island Express*, goes four times a day in each direction and takes two hours and is the same price. This ferry terminal is at Duke Point. For more information, call BC Ferries at ☎ 250-381-3431.

Getting Around

Bus For information about local buses call ☎ 250-390-4531 or get a transit guide at the tourist office. All buses pass through the Harbour Park Shopping Centre at Front St and Terminal Ave. Bus No 2 goes to the Stewart Ave ferry terminal.

Ferry Ferries to Newcastle Island leave from Mafeo-Sutton Park and cost $4 return. It's the same price to Protection Island. The ferry to Gabriola Island leaves from near the Harbour Park Shopping Centre and takes cars for $10.75, but only charges $4 if you're walking and bikes are free. After 2 pm you're stuck on the island until the next

morning when the ferry returns. The ferry trip takes about 20 minutes.

PARKSVILLE & QUALICUM BEACH

These towns and the coast towards Comox are known for their long stretches of beach. Though still not fabulous, the beach at Parksville is busier, wider and sandier than at other places and you can stop by the road, tone up the tan and have a quick swim in the nippy water.

Just south of Parksville is Hwy 4, the road to Port Alberni and the west coast. You can also connect with Hwy 4 from Qualicum Beach via Hwy 4A. At Coombs check the goats grazing on the roof of the general store! From Parksville to Port Alberni is some very fine scenery, with several provincial parks where you can stop awhile.

Places to Stay

Beaches at Parksville and Rathtrevor (just south of Parksville) are developed with a large number of oceanfront resorts. Facilities vary in style and character from modern condos to funky beach cottages, so it's worth shopping around if you'll be here for a while. There's slightly less development at Qualicum Beach, though a big luxury resort currently under construction will soon change that.

Camping The popular *Rathtrevor Beach Provincial Park*, 3km south-east of Parksville, has a large campground with 175 forested sites, flush toilets, free hot showers, playground and an RV dump station. Sites cost $9.50 to $15.50, and reservations are accepted.

Hotels In Parksville, the *Sandcastle Inn* (☎ 250-248-2334, ☎ 1-800-335-7263, 374 Island Hwy W) features clean, well kept motel rooms with ocean views and some kitchenettes starting at $59 for a single or a double. The *Ocean Crest Motel* (☎ 250-752-5518, ☎ 1-888-234-5661, 3292 W Island Hwy) situated in Qualicum has similar amenities and rooms starting at $55/60 a single/double.

BRITISH COLUMBIA

The **Old Dutch Inn** (☎ 250-752-6914, ☎ 1-800-661-0199, 2690 W Island Hwy) is nicer, with an indoor pool, hot tub and rooms for $80/85.

Beach Resorts Rooms at the **Best Western Bayside Inn Resort** (☎ 250-248-8333, ☎ 1-800-663-4232 in Canada, 240 Dogwood St) on Parksville Beach have both ocean and mountain views and start at $79, and there's an indoor pool and hot tub, fitness centre, volleyball net and scuba shop. Another oceanfront resort, the **Tigh Na Mara Resort Hotel** (☎ 250-248-2072, ☎ 1-800-663-7373, 1095 E Island Hwy), 1.5km south of town, has forested log cabins and condos with kitchens and fireplaces starting at $94 for a single or a double, plus a fitness room, indoor pool, watercraft rentals and restaurant.

Around Parksville & Qualicum Beach

About 13km south-west of Parksville at the end of Errington Rd is **Englishman River Falls Provincial Park** – a pleasant side trip with its 30 minute walking trail through the woods past waterfalls and emerald pools. There is also swimming and camping. **Little Qualicum Falls Provincial Park**, 13km southwest of Parksville on Hwy 4, is another good park. Both areas are heavily forested. About 32km south-west of here, **Mt Arrowsmith** has skiing in winter, hiking trails in summer.

Horne Lake Provincial Park

North of Qualicum Beach, 16km off Hwy 19, spelunking (caving) enthusiasts can explore the limestone caves. There are three undeveloped but explorable caves, and tours of varying lengths and difficulty occur daily in July and August, on weekends in June and September. They range from inexpensive half-hour introductions to challenging five-hour $60 trips with full equipment and training in Riverbend Cave, the most spectacular, with a total of 383m of mapped passages. Don't drink much at breakfast because there is no toilet until you're back in daylight. Alternatively, equipment can be rented to explore the lesser two caves, Main and Lower

Main, independently. Bring some very warm clothing and a good pair of shoes. For reservations call ☎ 250-248-7829. The park also has a good campground on the lake. The road to the park is an active logging road, so be careful of the trucks.

PORT ALBERNI & AROUND

Halfway across the island is this town built on forestry and fishing. Over 300 commercial fishing boats work out of the area, most catching salmon. At Harbour Quay, at the bottom of Argyle St, there's an observation tower, the Forestry Visitor Centre (☎ 250-724-7890), open from 10 am to 8 pm daily in summer, and some restaurants. Visitors can tour both the paper mill and the sawmill; inquire at the forestry centre.

The Alberni Valley Chamber of Commerce (☎ 250-724-6535, fax 250-724-6560) operates a useful and friendly information centre at the junction of Hwy 4 and Alberni Hwy at the entrance to town. Open from 8 am to 8 pm daily June to September; 9 am to 5 pm weekdays and 10 am to 2 pm weekends other times.

Perhaps the most noteworthy features of Port Alberni are the MVs *Lady Rose* and *Frances Barkley*, which sail out of Harbour Quay to the west coast of the island. They're operated by Alberni Marine Transportation (☎ 250-723-8313). Those planning to canoe or kayak around the Broken Group Islands can take their boats onboard, though the trip is more popular as a scenic cruise. The ferry company is one place that rents canoes and kayaks (see the Getting There & Away section, below, for more information).

In MacMillan Provincial Park **Cathedral Grove**, right by the road at the western end of Cameron Lake, is a must half-hour stop. Regarded by Native Indians as a sacred place, it is a grove of virgin forest with huge Douglas firs and red cedars, some dating back 800 years. A series of trails lead through the delicate, ancient ecosystem of towering trees. It is very popular and on many days the roadside parking can be horrendous.

At **Stamp Falls Provincial Park**, 14.5km north of Port Alberni, salmon can sometimes

be seen jumping on their way up the river and there are petroglyphs at nearby **Sproat Lake**.

Hikers also come to Port Alberni to reach Della Falls, North America's highest waterfall (see Strathcona Provincial Park later in this chapter) by an alternative route – canoeing the length of Great Central Lake from Port Alberni and taking the trail up from there.

Places to Stay
Stamp Falls Provincial Park, 14.5km west of Port Alberni on Beaver Creek Rd, is a small wooded campground near a waterfall, with primitive sites for $9.50.

The *Port Alberni International Hostel (☎ 250-723-0938, ☎ 250-723-2484, 4908 Burde St)* is a simple place with beds for $15. The modest *Esta Villa Motel (☎ 250-724-1261, ☎ 1-800-724-0844, 4014 Johnston Rd)* is one of the cheapest motels in Port Alberni, with single/double rooms at $55/59. The *Alberni Inn (☎ 250-723-9403, ☎ 1-800-815-8007, 3805 Redford St)* is a bit nicer, and has a few rooms with full-size kitchens; rooms cost $61/65.

Getting There & Away
Bus Island Coach Lines (☎ 250-723-6924), 4541 Margaret St, runs twice daily to Tofino and Ucluelet from Port Alberni. Western Bus Lines (☎ 250-723-3341), 4521 10th Ave, has one bus Monday, Wednesday and Friday mid-May to September to Bamfield for $17. It also picks passengers up at the main Island Coach Lines bus station.

Boat Freighters operated by Alberni Marine Transportation (☎ 250-723-8313), take mail, cargo and passengers between Port Alberni and Bamfield at the end of the West Coast Trail, the Broken Group Islands and Ucluelet. Fares to Bamfield are $20 one way, to Ucluelet $23. One-day return trips allow passengers some free time at Bamfield and Ucluelet for exploring.

The freighters depart for Bamfield on Tuesday, Thursday and Saturday all year, and for Ucluelet and the Broken Group Islands on Monday, Wednesday and Friday

from 1 June to 30 September. In midsummer there are Sunday cruises to Bamfield only. Regardless of the weather, take a sweater and/or raincoat.

PACIFIC RIM NATIONAL PARK
A rough, rugged, inhospitable yet beautiful coastal area, the park is a long, thin strip of land divided into three distinct units – Long Beach, Broken Group Islands and the West Coast Trail. Each is separated by land and water and is reached by a different route.

Whale-watching trips can be a highlight of a visit to the west coast. From mid-February to June, Pacific grey whales migrate up the coast from Mexico to the Arctic Ocean; the peak time to catch them heading north is mid-April. In late autumn they head back south. Other attractions are the rainforest and undeveloped beach. With the forests of huge cedar and fir meeting the edge of the beach, and the huge waves rolling in off the Pacific, it really does feel like you are standing at the far edge of the continent.

Hundreds of thousands of geese and ducks fly overhead in spring and autumn. Also, the pools left behind by the tides are often filled with interesting life forms: starfish, anemones, sponges, fish, snails and many other small creatures.

For general information about the park, contact Pacific Rim National Park, PO Box 280, Ucluelet, BC V0R 3A0, or call ☎ 250-726-7721 or ☎ 250-726-4212.

Getting There & Away
Specific information regarding transportation to and from the various park units is included in the appropriate sections. However, getting there and away is by no means straightforward, so an overview of the logistics involved is helpful.

Easiest to reach is the Long Beach Unit, accessed by Hwy 4 from Port Alberni. Port Alberni is also the terminus for the only public transportation to the northerly park units (see Getting There & Away under Port Alberni & Around earlier in this chapter), with buses to Ucluelet, Tofino and Bamfield.

BRITISH COLUMBIA

Ucluelet, at the southern end of Long Beach, is served by passenger-carrying cargo ships from Port Alberni. Freighters from Port Alberni also carry passengers (and their canoes or kayaks) to the Broken Island Unit, and to Bamfield, at the northern end of the redoubtable West Coast Trail. You can also drive a long gravel road from Port Alberni to Bamfield. Port Renfrew, at the southern edge of the West Coast Trail, is accessed by gravel road from Lake Cowichan, or by Hwy 14 from Victoria. In summer, both Port Renfrew and Bamfield are served by hiker-oriented minibuses.

Long Beach

The most northerly third of the park, Long Beach is exactly that – about 20km of wide, log-strewn surf and windswept, sandy beach. At other parts, the waves pound into a craggy, rocky shoreline. At each end of Long Beach is a small fishing and tourist village – Tofino in the north, Ucluelet in the south. This area is the easiest to get to in the park, and the closest to all services. Hwy 4 leads from Port Alberni through the magnificent scenery (some heavily logged areas notwithstanding) of the Mackenzie Ranges at the southern edge of Clayoquot (pronounced clak-wot) Sound into this section of the park.

In summer there are interpretative programs and guided walks run by the Wickaninnish Centre next to the beach.

Visitors will find plenty of campgrounds, motels and resorts in either Tofino and Ucluelet; budget accommodation is scarce in either place. Ucluelet has the greatest selection of modest mid-priced motels; Tofino is home to BC's most extravagant beach resorts. Travellers should be sure to make reservations well in advance regardless of how much they plan to pay.

Note that the weather is generally poor here. Most days are cold, windy and rainy. A warm, sunny day about 1km or so from the coast can disappear into mist and fog at Long Beach. A sweater or raincoat is protection not only against the weather but also against the mosquitoes.

Hiking There are eight short hiking trails in the park in the Long Beach Unit; the Park Information Office (☎ 250-726-4212) has a description of them. The South Beach Trail leads to an area good for watching, and hearing, the huge waves. Half Moon Bay Trail leads to a calm, sandy bay. Radar Hill is good for views and has trails leading down to some small, secluded beaches. The Rainforest and Schooner Cove trails are good, accessible forest walks.

Surfing Long Beach reputedly has the best surfing in BC. Wetsuits and drysuits are absolutely necessary given the frigid water. Surfboards can be rented but ask about etiquette as there have been run-ins between locals and visitors over which waves are whose.

Other Activities Another activity is looking for and maybe watching some of the local marine life. Seals, sea lions and porpoises are common, killer and Pacific grey whales a possibility depending on the time of year. Good viewing spots are Schooner Cove, Quistis Point, Radar Hill with its telescope and Combers Beach near Sea Lion Rocks.

Tofino

At the northern end of Long Beach, just outside the park boundary, is the village of Tofino, the centre of the coast's tourism and one of the major destinations on Vancouver Island. Once a simple fishing village, the winter population of about 1200 swells to at least twice that through the summer. It's a busy, resort-like place with a bit of an undercurrent of tension resulting from the friction between environmentalists and those involved in the resource industries. All in all it makes an interesting town for a few days of activities.

The Visitor Info Centre (☎ 250-725-3414, fax 250-725-3296), 380 Campbell St, is open from 9 am to 7 pm daily May to September. The Friends of Clayoquot Sound (☎ 250-725-4218) has an office at 331 Neill St. The Forest Information Centre (☎ 250-725-3295), 316 Main St, is open from 10 am to 6 pm daily.

Things to See & Do The **Whale Centre** (☎ 250-725-2132), 411 Campbell St, has a small museum and whale exhibit; it's open from 9 am to 6 pm daily in summer. The **Eagle Aerie Gallery** (☎ 250-725-3120) on Campbell St houses the works of Roy Henry Vickers, an internationally established Native Indian artist based in Tofino.

Whale-watching, fishing and rainforest trips can be arranged in town. For around $40 several companies offer boat trips to see Pacific grey whales. Best time is March to May when they migrate through the area, but many linger through summer. Clayoquot Whaler will take you out and also fill you in on the history and Native Indian culture of the area. For information and tickets call Clayoquot Sound Charters (☎ 250-725-2888, ☎ 1-800-665-9425), 320 Main St. The Whale Centre will also take you to see the whales and other wildlife.

A good trip is to **Hot Springs Cove** where a 20 minute hike will lead you to the hot springs (the only ones on Vancouver Island) overlooking the ocean. There are several pools, which become progressively cooler down the hillside to the sea. You can hire a boat or seaplane to the cove; contact Remote Passages or the Whale Centre. Overnight camping is possible.

Highly recommended is a trip to **Meares Island**, a 15 minute cruise past the Harbour Islands. This is a magical place of virgin rainforest with trees of mind-boggling age and stature – one is over 1000 years old and nearly 19m in diameter. Species include cedar, yew and varieties of spruce.

To organise a trip to Meares Island, call Dutch before 10 am or in the evenings at ☎ 250-725-3793. His small boat, *Salty Dog*, makes the trip several times a day for $15 return, departing from the dock at the foot of Fourth St. Make arrangements with him for how long you want to stay. Weigh West Marine Resort (☎ 250-725-3277), 634 Campbell St, also offers the same deal but can't match Dutch for character.

There are several rugged but well marked trails on the island; the basic loop takes about 2½ hours. Before going on to the island find out about the condition of the trails; except for the boardwalked area at the beginning, mud can be a problem.

Tofino Sea Kayaking Co (☎ 250-725-4222), also at 320 Main St, offers paddling tours to the nearby islands; tours start at $50 for four hours. For fishing, you can try Springtime Charters (☎ 250-725-2351), 586 Campbell St.

Places to Stay Tofino is very often booked up in summer, so don't get caught looking after dark or you'll be on the park bench – if it's not taken. Expensive resort hotels and oceanfront housekeeping cottages represent the bulk of the market here, and you can count on spending at least $100 a night. There are only a few hostels and cheap hotels here, so budget travellers should make reservations for these places far in advance. As we went to press a much needed new hostel was being developed. It is to be an HI affiliate with about 50 beds.

There is one place to camp in the park itself, *Green Point Campground* (☎ 250-726-4245, ☎ 1-800-689-9025), near Tofino. It has bathrooms with hot water and flush toilets and costs $18. Arrive early in the morning to get a place or have reservations made by calling the above number. It has a few walk-in sites that are often vacant even at the end of the day when the 'No Vacancy' sign is up.

About 3km south on Mackenzie Beach there are several private campgrounds with both tent and RV sites, and some beachfront cottages. *Bella Pacifica Resort & Campground* (☎ 250-725-3400) has full facilities and good beach sites starting at $21. The much smaller *Mackenzie Beach Resort* (☎ 250-725-3439, 1101 Pacific Rim Hwy) charges $28 and has one and two-bedroom beach cottages starting at $119. *Crystal Cove Beach Resort* (☎ 250-725-4213, 1165 Cedarwood Place) has sites starting at $22 and log cottages beginning at $160. There is cheaper tent camping on Indian Island off Grice Bay, south of Tofino.

In town, the *Backpackers' Hostel* (☎ 250-725-9439, 241 Campbell St) has room for 18 people in dorm beds for $15 and double

BRITISH COLUMBIA

rooms for $30, with lower off-season rates. It's pretty basic and cramped but it fills a need.

There are two other hostel-style places located on nearby islands. The closest, within view of town, is *L'Auberge on the Island* (☎ 250-726-7968) with rooms at $35/55 a single/double. Camping is cheaper. Instead of the former marine telephone you can now call the above cell phone number in the evening. Louise, the owner, will boat shuttle you across. A couple of the rooms are open all year. You can use the kitchen so bring groceries although some basics like rice are supplied.

Alternatively, try the comfortable, quiet *Vargas Island Inn and Hostel* (☎ 250-725-3309). Here lodge rooms begin at $60 including meals but hostel accommodation is offered at $40 per person. Both also include transportation, which is a 20 minute boat ride from town.

Cheapest of the motels is *Dolphin Motel* (☎ 250-725-3377, 1190 Pacific Rim Hwy), about 3km south of town with singles/doubles beginning at $45/49.

Downtown overlooking the bay, *Schooner Motel* (☎ 250-725-3478, 311-312 Campbell St) has a few moderately priced rooms (some with kitchens) starting at $65/69.

The *Best Western Tin Wis Resort* (☎ 250-725-4445, ☎ 1-800-661-9995, 1119 Pacific Rim Hwy) on Templar Channel has beach access and convention facilities. Rooms cost $125 to $180 for a single or a double.

Among the many resorts south of Tofino, the *Middle Beach Lodge* (☎ 250-725-2900, Pacific Rim Hwy) has rustic oceanfront lodge rooms, suites and cabins (some with fireplaces and kitchens) on a wilderness headland near a sandy beach. There are two lodges – one for families and the other for adults only – and a restaurant; doubles cost $100 to $200.

About 5km south of Tofino at Chesterman Beach, a multi-million dollar reconstruction of the *Wickaninnish Inn* (☎ 250-725-3100, ☎ 1-800-333-4604, Osprey Lane) is perched on a rugged promontory above the sea. This completely new mega-resort and restaurant is a reincarnation of the landmark lodge put out of commission by the creation of Pacific Rim National Park in 1977. The inn's grand rooms feature views of the pounding surf, while guest rooms have push-button gas fireplaces, two-person hot tubs and private balconies; rooms start at $200/220 a single/double.

Places to Eat Most restaurants are associated with the lodges and resorts in the area, and are open to nonguests; it's a good idea to call ahead for reservations in high season.

There are also some good places to eat in the town. The *Common Loaf Bake Shop* (☎ 250-725-3915, 180 1st St) is recommended. It has just a few tables but a large selection of excellent, delicious home-made muffins, cookies, breads and cakes. In the morning try the warm cinnamon buns. The *Alley Way Café* (☎ 250-725-3105), tucked in the yard behind the corner of 1st St and Campbell St, has a range of all-day breakfasts, Mexican-style dishes and various vegetarian meals all under $8.

Pointe Restaurant at the Wickaninnish Inn, surrounded on all sides with churning surf, is the fine dining option in the Tofino area.

Entertainment The pub downstairs in *Maquinna Lodge* (☎ 250-725-3261, 120 First St) is the only place in town for a beer and is a real happening place on Friday and Saturday nights with lots of dancing.

Ucluelet

Ucluelet (the name is a Nootka word meaning 'people with a safe landing place') is not as attractive as Tofino and is not exactly a visitor mecca. It's more a town for the 1700 locals working in fishing and logging. The Visitor Info Centre (☎ 250-726-4641, fax 250-726-4611), 227 Main St, is open from 9 am to 6 pm daily in summer.

You might like to walk to the lighthouse at **Amphitrite Point**, at the foot of Peninsula Rd, or take one of the trails at **Terrace Beach** north of town. South of town, **Big Beach** is a quiet, rocky bit of shoreline with tidal

pools. Subtidal Adventures (☎ 250-726-7336), on the right as you head into town just after Ucluelet Campground, is an outfitter which offers trips to see Pacific grey whales in March and April only; trips start at $40 for two hours. It also runs tours around the Broken Group Islands, will drop off people wishing to camp on an island and has scuba-diving cruises. Majestic West Coast Wilderness Adventures (☎ 250-726-2868) offers one and four-day kayaking trips starting at $45 for 2½ hours.

Places to Stay The *Ucluelet Campground (☎ 250-726-4355, 260 Seaplane Base Rd)*, overlooking the harbour, with hot showers and flush toilets, has sites starting at $16. Ucluelet has quite a stable of reasonably priced motels, mostly on Peninsula Rd, and a couple of simple cheap ones. *Ucluelet Hotel (☎ 250-726-4324, 250 Main St)* has doubles without bath at $25. Accommodation can also be cheap at the *Canadian Princess Resort (☎ 250-726-7771, ☎ 1-800-663-7090)*, a survey ship moored in Ucluelet Harbour. A berth in a stateroom with a shared bathroom starts at $45/55 a single/double. Fancier rooms are available at the resort's main lodge on shore; they cost up to $155 a double.

Just around the harbour from Long Beach, the *Pacific Rim Motel (☎ 250-726-7728, 1755 Peninsula Rd)* has rooms for $60/65. The *West Coast Motel (☎ 250-726-7732, 247 Hemlock St)* has rooms and suites (some with kitchenettes) overlooking the harbour, plus an indoor pool and gym; rooms start at $69 for a single or a double.

Places To Eat Most restaurants are located in hotels and lodges. For a light meal try *Blueberries Café & Cappuccino Bar (☎ 250-726-7707, 1627D Peninsula Rd)*, with sandwiches and pasta under $10. For something meaty, try *Mountain Boy Chicken & Ribs (☎ 250-726-2221, 1627C Peninsula Rd)*, with barbecued beef ribs for $12. For fine dining, take a drive to the *Wickaninnish Inn (☎ 250-726-7706)*, 10km north of Ucluelet, midway between Tofino and Ucluelet.

Broken Group Islands

The middle section of Pacific Rim National Park, called the Broken Group Islands, is made up of about 100 islands at the entrance to **Barkley Sound**, famous for its variety of rockfish.

This area is popular with canoeists, is good for wildlife and offers some of the best scuba diving in Canada. You can view wrecks in the shallow waters and observe the abundant marine life found around all the islands. The waters can be dangerous and you should prepare for a trip using *Marine Chart 3670*, available from the Canadian Hydrographic Service, Chart Sales, Institute of Ocean Sciences, 9860 Saanich Rd, PO Box 6000, Sidney, BC V8L 4B2.

The only way to reach this section is by boat from Bamfield, Ucluelet or Port Alberni. There are some primitive *campgrounds* on the islands.

West Coast Trail

The third and most southerly section of the park is called the West Coast Trail, one of Canada's best known and toughest hiking paths. The 77km trail runs between Port Renfrew and Bamfield. Either end can be reached by road, but to reach one from the other you've got to walk – and that's a challenge along this rugged, often rain-soaked trail. It is *not* for novices although some people walk for just a day or two at the north end.

Bamfield, the village at the northern head of the West Coast Trail, has a Marine Biological Station, a lifesaving station and not much else. The West Coast Trail Information Centre (☎ 250-728-3234) is 5km south-east of Bamfield on Pachena Bay. At the southern end of the trail is **Port Renfrew**, which can be reached by dirt road from Lake Cowichan or by the mostly paved Hwy 14 along the coast from Victoria. There is a seasonal trail information centre (☎ 250-647-5434) in the village. To reach the start of the trail from Port Renfrew you must charter a boat to take you across the narrow San Juan River. Because of the difficult terrain, getting out of the bay here is, well, let's say, one of the less enjoyable segments of the trail northbound.

To protect the environment and to keep hiker traffic to manageable limits, a quota system restricts the number of hikers using the trail. Only 52 people are permitted to begin the trail each day, 26 in each direction. Of those, six in each direction are on a first-come, first-served basis, the others have all been prebooked. Prebooking costs $85, the trail fee without the reservation is $60. You may well not get a place by turning up at the trailhead and so should put your name on the waiting list; however, you may have to wait several days. For an information package and reservation registration call ☎ 1-800-663-6000 or write to the Pacific Rim National Park Reserve, Box 280, Ucluelet, BC V0R 3A0. Reservations are taken after 1 March for the upcoming summer, and, on the first day of reservations, July is pretty much booked up. The main season is May to September. You can go two weeks earlier and later at half-price but these times are not recommended as the weather can be even more brutal. July and August are the driest and best months.

The trail is clogged with trees, and the camping areas are wherever you can find them. Passing cliffs, beaches and rainforests, the trail takes between five and eight days to travel. You've got to take all your food. The southernmost part is the roughest and most difficult, but you get to see some spectacular scenery and have a chance to test your stamina. Some people prefer to do this last when the pack is lighter and the legs stronger, others want to get it out of the way and then 'cruise' to the other end. Near the centre of the trail you pass close to the old-growth forest of Carmanah Valley. There are two small ferries to take along the way, totalling $15, which are operated by Native Indians. The trail was historically used as a lifesaving route for shipwreck survivors and you should carry tide charts.

Places to Stay

There are only a few places to stay in Bamfield, including two campgrounds. The nearest is 8km east of Bamfield and is run by the Ohiaht people. The other, *Sea Beam Fishing Resort & Campground* (☎ 250-728-3286), is 19km north of Bamfield. Camp sites cost $15, rooms cost $15/30 a single/double.

One of the cheapest places to stay is the *Bamfield Lodge* (☎ 250-728-3419, Cape Beale Trail), a no-frills retreat house and marine-education centre with a few rustic cottages and lodge rooms with optional meals starting at $35/60 a single/double. It also organises fishing, whale-watching and diving excursions.

There's also a number of waterfront lodges near Bamfield. Good ones to try are the *McKay Bay Lodge* (☎ 250-728-3323), with a hot tub and nine rooms for $85 to $95, and the secluded *Woods End Landing Cottages* (☎ 250-728-3383, 168 Wild Duck Rd), which has six private cottages with log beds; cabins rent for $95 to $185.

Accommodation is again rather limited in the remote town of Port Renfrew. You can camp along the beach and there are also a couple of B&Bs. There is also a small store, but supplies are limited. The *Arbutus Beach Lodge* (☎ 250-647-5458, 5 Queesto Drive) has four rooms on the beach with private bathrooms for $59/74. If Port Renfrew happens to be all booked up, you'll find no shortage of B&Bs in the tiny burg of Sooke, 68km south.

Getting There & Away Bamfield can be reached by boat from Ucluelet and Port Alberni; the one-way fare on the MVs *Lady Rose* or *Frances Barkley* from Port Alberni is $18. There is also a 100km gravel road from Port Alberni to Bamfield. Western Bus Lines (☎ 250-728-3491, ☎ 250-723-3341 in Port Alberni) operates the Pachena Bay Express, which connects Pachena Bay and Bamfield with Port Alberni on Monday, Wednesday and Friday. From Victoria, West Coast Trail Express (☎ 250-380-0580) runs a daily 11-person shuttle van to Bamfield and Pachena Bay for $48. PBM Transport (☎ 250-475-2010) runs buses between Victoria and Port Renfrew.

To save hikers a lot of logistical hassles there is a boat service, West Coast Express Charters (☎ 250-647-5409) which links

Bamfield to Port Renfrew three times a week. The Pacheenaht Indian Band (☎ 250-647-5521) runs a similar service but by road.

DENMAN & HORNBY ISLANDS

Farther up the east coast are two lesser known Gulf Islands – Denman and Hornby. There's good birdwatching on Hornby Island. The ferry for Denman Island leaves from Buckley Bay, about 20km south of Courtenay, and takes 10 minutes. For Hornby Island you take another ferry from Gravely Bay on Denman Island. The fare for each is $3.50 per person, or $9.25 with a car.

Each island has provincial parks, hiking, swimming, fishing, scuba diving and beaches, but only *Fillongley Provincial Park* on Denman Island allows camping; there are 10 primitive sites fronting Lambert Channel for $9.50.

On Hornby Island there's private camping for tents and RVs near the beach at the small, family-oriented *Bradsdadland Country Camp Resort* (☎ 250-335-0757, 1980 Shingle Split Rd); sites cost $16 to $19, plus $1 for each utility hook-up. Also near the beach, *Outer Island B&B* (☎ 250-335-2379, ☎ 1-800-364-1331, 4785 DePape Rd) has four rooms in an old farmhouse with both shared and private bathrooms, a small cabin and an outdoor swimming pool; single/double rooms start at $99/109. The *Sea Breeze Lodge* (☎ 250-335-2321) at Tralee Point has 12 modest cottages overlooking the ocean for $635 to $700 a week, meals included. It's one of the few places to eat on Hornby Island, and it's open to nonguests with advance notice. The two other dinner options are *Thatch* (near the ferry) and *Pizza Galore*.

COURTENAY & COMOX

Basically commercial centres for the local farming, logging and fishing industries, these two towns are also important supply hubs for Mt Washington, 32km west of Courtenay, and Forbidden Plateau just outside Strathcona Provincial Park, two major summer and winter recreation areas. Courtenay is the larger of these two essentially joined towns. The Visitor Info Centre

(☎ 250-334-3234), 2040 Cliffe Ave, in Courtenay, serves both towns and is open from 8 am to 8 pm daily.

In Courtenay there is a small museum (☎ 250-334-3234), 360 Cliffe Ave, and not far out is the Puntledge River Fish Hatchery which farms salmon.

At the Canadian Air Force base in Comox an international air show takes place each August in even-numbered years.

There is good hiking in the area, from afternoon walks to some overnight climbs. **Miracle Beach Provincial Park** (☎ 250-755-2483), 22km north of Courtenay, has hiking trails, a campground and a long, sandy beach. **Comox Glacier** is a good two-day hike, as is **Mt Albert Edward** in the Forbidden Plateau area, which offers excellent views. Ask at the Visitor Info Centre for more information. You must register if you're going on an overnighter.

Places to Stay

About 6km out of Courtenay is the *North Comox Lake Mini-Hostel* (☎ 250-338-1914, 4787 Lake Trail Rd), which charges $12. Meals are available; call to arrange a pick-up at the bus or train station. It's open all year and in summer there is extra sleeping space in a teepee. Near Comox are several places renting cottages by the beach.

Also outside Courtenay, the elaborate English-style gardens and waterfront views make the *Greystone Manor B&B* (☎ 250-338-1422, 4014 Haas Rd) a pleasant place to stay. Rooms have private bathrooms and start at $55/60 for a single/double.

In town the *Sleepy Hollow Inn* (☎ 250-334-4476, ☎ 1-800-811-5955, 1190 Cliffe Ave) has one and two-bedroom motel units with kitchenettes, an indoor pool and exercise room starting at $45/50. There's also the recently renovated *Travelodge Courtenay* (☎ 250-334-4491, ☎ 1-800-795-9486, 2605 Island Hwy) with rooms for $59/65. At the top end, the *Coast Westerly* (☎ 250-338-7741, ☎ 1-800-668-7797, 1590 Cliffe Ave) has the full amenities of a convention-style hotel; balconied rooms overlooking the Courtenay River start at $93/98.

NORTH VANCOUVER ISLAND

Travelling north of Campbell River, Hwy 19 heads inland and much of the urbanisation that characterises the eastern coastline to the south disappears.

It's a less-populated, less-visited, rugged area with lots of good opportunities for outdoor activities. Aside from Strathcona and Cape Scott Provincial Parks, the Telegraph Cove-Port McNeil area is of most interest with its whale watching and Native Indian sites. Many of the travellers you meet will be heading north to Port Hardy to catch the ferry to Prince Rupert (see Port Hardy later in this chapter for details).

Campbell River

Campbell River is a major centre for salmon fishing, and marks the beginning of the northern part of Vancouver Island. It is also the main departure point for Strathcona Provincial Park.

The Visitor Info Centre (☎ 250-287-4636, fax 250-286-6490), 1235 Shoppers Row, is open from 10 am to 8 pm daily. In the same building is the Campbell River Museum, open from 10 am to 4 pm daily.

There isn't much to see or do in town itself. Most visitors come here to fish for one or more of the five salmon species – Coho, Chinook, sockeye, humpback (or pink) and chum. But there is now another option. Campbell River Snorkel Tours offers fascinating guided river trips to watch the migrating salmon. Get details at the tourist office. Off the coast in **Discovery Passage**, scuba diving is excellent at such dive sites as Row & Be Damned, Whisky Point, Copper Cliffs and Steep Island. On **Quadra Island**, just offshore, you can see marine and birdlife or the ancient petroglyphs of the Kwakiutl people at Cape Mudge in the south. Some petroglyphs are in the Kwakiutl Museum along with tribal costumes, ceremonial masks and potlatch artefacts. The island also has hiking trails including one up Chinese Mountain. **Cortes Island**, east of Quadra Island, has plenty of deserted beaches and lots of wildlife. It's about an hour, and two ferries, from Campbell River.

Places to Stay About 10km west of Campbell River on Hwy 28 there's a huge riverside campground at *Elk Falls Provincial Park*, with 122 sites and flush toilets for $9.50. *Loveland Bay Provincial Park*, 19km north-east at Campbell Lake, and *Morton Lake Provincial Park*, 19km north off Hwy 19, are both small and secluded and have primitive sites for $6.

Numerous motels line the highway south of the downtown area. The *Rustic Motel* (☎ 250-286-6295, ☎ 1-800-567-2007, 2140 N Island Hwy) is good value for quiet rooms with kitchenettes, suites and cabins starting at $50/60 for singles/doubles. The renovated *Best Western Austrian Chalet* (☎ 250-923-4231, ☎ 1-800-667-7207, 462 S Island Hwy), right on the waterfront, has an indoor pool and features loft chalets with some kitchenettes for $84/94.

On Quadra Island there is a backpacker's hostel, *A Travellers Rural Retreat* (☎ 250-287-9232) at Quathiaski Cove. Call ahead. Quiet Cortes Island has the *Amigo's Hostel* (☎ 250-935-6403) on Manzanita Rd, about a 20 minute drive from the ferry; rides can be arranged. Cost is $15. The hosts can tell you how to spend some time around the laid-back, off-the-track island.

Quadra Island features several small waterfront resorts with rooms ranging from $60 to $80. If you're after a secluded fishing lodge, look no further than the *April Point Lodge & Fishing Resort* (☎ 250-285-2222) on April Point Rd, where there's a number of oceanfront guesthouses and lodge rooms with great views, hot tubs and fireplaces for $99 to $395. While it's more upscale than your typical fishing lodge, it's earnest enough to offer fishing charters and guides.

The *Tsa-Kwa-Luten Lodge* (☎ 250-285-2042, ☎ 1-800-665-7745) on Lighthouse Rd close to the beach, is a theme lodge run by Native Indians. Don't expect to be put up in traditional tribal homes – Native Indian art, architecture and food prevail as a theme, and the rooms in the 'longhouse' feature modern waterfront hotel units, the cabins have kitchens, and there's a fitness room and sauna; rates are $80/90 a single/double.

Getting There & Around Island Coach Lines (☎ 250-287-7151), on the corner of 13th Ave and Cedar St, runs one bus north daily to Port Hardy ($41 one way) and four buses south to Victoria. For information about local buses call ☎ 250-287-7433.

Ferries leave regularly from Discovery Crescent across from Tyee Plaza for Quathiaski Cove on Quadra Island; the return fare is $3.50. Another ferry departs Heriot Bay on Quadra Island for Whaletown on Cortes Island; the return fare is $4.50. Ask about the van service to Cortes four times a week from the Island Coach Lines depot.

Strathcona Provincial Park

This is the largest park (☎ 250-755-2483) on the island and is basically a wilderness area. To simplify, the three main areas of interest each have different access points. Campbell River acts as the main access point, with Hwy 28 between Campbell River and Gold River cutting across the most developed portion of the park providing access to campgrounds and some well marked trails. The Mt Washington area, just out of the park, and Forbidden Plateau are reached by different roads out of Courtenay.

At **Forbidden Plateau**, to the east of the park, are a series of high-altitude hiking trails, as well as trout fishing in the lakes on the plateau. In winter it's a major ski area, the island's original. In summer the chair lift runs 11 am to 6 pm Wednesday to Sunday to give hikers a head start into the alpine areas. A ticket is $10 return. At **Mt Washington Ski Resort** (☎ 250-338-1515) it's much the same thing. Here the lift operates summer weekends only and is $12. The Paradise Meadows hike leading to the plateau is popular. This major ski resort has five lifts and 41 major marked runs, plus 35km of cross-country ski trails.

In the Buttle Lake district, two well known hikes are the **Elk River Trail** and the **Flower Ridge Trail**. Both lead to very fine alpine scenery. Like other developed trails, these two are suitable for all age groups. This area also has a number of short trails and nature walks. Other less-developed trails demand more preparation and lead to remote areas.

In the south part of the park the **Della Falls Trail**, for example, is a tough two or three-day walk but is great for scenery and ends at the highest falls (440m) in North America. You need a good map. Other fine walks are those in the **Beauty Lake** area and one crossing the **Big Interior Massif** up to Nine Peaks. From the highest peaks, such as Golden Hinde (at 2200m the highest on the island), Colonel Foster and others in the 650m range, you can see the ocean to the west and Georgia Strait to the east. One thing you won't have to look at is a grizzly bear as there aren't any on Vancouver Island.

Places to Stay The park has two serviced campgrounds with running water and pit toilets. *Buttle Lake* near the northern entrance to the park is the nicer, the other is at *Ralph River*, at the southern end of the lake on its eastern shore. Camp sites are $12 and $9.50, respectively. Wilderness camping is free.

Strathcona Park Lodge (☎ 250-286-8206), a resort outside the park on Hwy 28 on Upper Campbell Lake, has a range of accommodation. There are lakefront cottages and apartments priced from $40 to $125. You can camp near the beach for $16 with the use of facilities. Camping equipment can also be rented. Alternatively, you can bed down in hostel-style rooms for $16 with use of a communal kitchen. Van transportation from Campbell River can be arranged by the lodge.

You can rent canoes, kayaks and bicycles, or go rock climbing, windsurfing, hiking, sailing and swimming. Or you can take organised day trips if you wish. The lodge has an education centre which offers courses in various outdoor activities.

Gold River

In the centre of the island, west of Strathcona Provincial Park, Gold River, accessed by Hwy 28, is the last stop on surfaced roads. The little town is a caving capital and is the headquarters of BC's Speleological Association. Visitors can join spelunking trips to **Upana Caves** and also to **Quatsino**

Cave, the deepest vertical cave in North America. Kayakers can try their luck on the whitewater section of the river known as the **Big Drop**. For more information, ask at the Visitor Info Centre (☎ 250-283-2418, fax 250-283-7500) in Village Square Plaza.

Summer cruises go to **Friendly Cove**, where Captain Cook first met the west coast Native Indians in 1778.

The working freighter, *Uchuk III* (☎ 250-283-2325), a converted WWII mine-sweeper, makes year-round trips to some of the remote villages and settlements in **Nootka Sound** and **Kyuquot Sound**. Passengers can go on a choice of two one-day trips or on an overnight trip.

The *Ridgeview Motel (☎ 250-283-2277, ☎ 1-800-989-3393, 395 Donner Court)* is pretty much the only motel around here, though it's a sizable one, with single/double rooms for $75/85.

Port McNeill

Here you can go scuba diving, book fishing charters or go on killer-whale tours. Port McNeill is also the departure point for Cormorant and Malcolm Islands. The regional offices of three major logging companies help sustain this town of over 2700. The Visitor Info Centre (☎ 250-956-3131, fax 250-956-4633) is next to the ferry terminal. There are several campgrounds, including one near the terminal, and hotels.

Telegraph Cove East off Hwy 19, about 8km south of Port McNeill and about a five hour drive to Nanaimo, this small community is one of the best of the west coast's so-called boardwalk villages – villages in which most of the buildings are built over the water on wooden pilings. Formerly a sawmill village, it has good fishing, but the **killer whales** are its main attraction. Johnston Straight, between Sayward and Alert Bay, is one of the very best places in Canada to see them. The boat tour to Robson Bight, an ecological reserve south of Telegraph Cove, is recommended. The tour, run by Stubbs Island Charters (☎ 250-928-3185/17, ☎ 1-800-665-3066 in BC), might seem a bit pricey at $65, but you are out for five hours and it includes lunch. It's a good idea to book ahead and take warm clothing. Trips run from June to October.

Sea Orca Expeditions (☎ 1-800-668-6722) offers three-hour whale trips in Zodiacs (recommended) or longer, more expensive sailing trips. Either way, dress warmly.

Places to Stay Point McNeill has a few private campgrounds and modest motels. Don't head up this way without a reservation. *Pacific Hostelry (☎ 250-974-2026)* in Alert Bay is an associate-HI hostel, open year-round and has room for only 12 people, so call ahead. It costs $14 for members, $16 for nonmembers. The *Dalewood Inn (☎ 250-*

Having a Whale of a Time

Using sonar to track the fish, over a dozen pods of killer whales (each pod containing about 20 members) come to Johnstone Strait in summer to feed on the migrating salmon. Many of the whales swim in Robson Bight, along one of its beaches, rubbing their sides and stomachs on the pebbles and rocks that have been smoothed and rounded by the action of the water. No-one knows quite why they do this, but the whales obviously get a lot of pleasure from it and maybe that's reason enough. Who would want to tangle with a pleasure-seeking killer whale?

The Johnstone Strait killer whales feature in David Attenborough's documentary *Wolves of the Sea*.

Killer whale

956-3304, 1703 Broughton Blvd) is a basic place with rooms for $56/60 a single/double. The **Haida-Way Motor Inn** (☎ 250-956-3373, 1817 Campbell Way) downtown is another to try, with rooms for $63/78.

Getting There & Away Ferries, taking 45 minutes and costing $5.50 return, run to Alert Bay on the 5km-long Cormorant Island, a blend of old fishing settlement and Native Indian culture. The Nimpkish Reserve is here. The U'Mista Cultural Centre shows examples of Kwakiutl art, mainly masks, and the ceremonial Kwakiutl Bighouse can be seen. Like some other places in BC, Alert Bay claims to have the world's tallest totem pole, here measuring 52m. There are also a few minor historical sites including the Alert Bay Museum. Gator Gardens Ecological Park, with its giant cedars, mosses and wildlife, is also worth a look.

Port Hardy

This small town at the northern end of Vancouver Island is best known as the departure point for the ferry trip aboard the *Queen of the North* through the famed Inside Passage to Prince Rupert. The terminal is 3km south of town across Hardy Bay at Bear Cove, which is one of two sites where evidence of the earliest human occupation of the central and northern coastal areas of BC – around 8000 to 10,000 years ago – was found. (The other site is Nanamu, now a canning town on the eastern shore of Fitzhugh Sound.)

The Visitor Info Centre (☎ 250-949-7622, fax 250-949-6653) at 7250 Market St is open from 9 am to 8 pm daily in summer; much shorter hours the rest of the year. There's a coin laundry up the hill on the same side.

There's little in the town itself except a small museum at 1110 Market St, open from 10 am to 5 pm Monday to Saturday, but the area around Port Hardy has good salmon fishing and scuba diving. North Island Diving & Water Sports (☎ 250-949-2664) on the corner of Market and Hastings Sts, rents and sells equipment and runs courses. You can also rent canoes and kayaks at the end of the jetty.

Places to Stay In and around town there are campgrounds, hotels, motels and about 20 B&Bs. Several of the campgrounds are near the ferry terminal. One of the closest campgrounds is **Wildwoods Campsite** (☎ 250-949-6753) on the ferry terminal road, with sites for $15. Others are **Sunny Sanctuary Campground** (☎ 250-949-8111, 8080 Goodspeed Rd) and **Quatse River Campground** (☎ 250-949-2395, 5050 Hardy Bay Rd).

Kay's B&B (☎ 250-949-6776, 7605 Camarvon Rd) is close to town and costs $42/57. One of the cheaper hotel options is the **North Shore Inn** (☎ 250-949-8500, 7370 Market St), across Hardy Bay from the ferry terminal, with rooms starting at $70/79 a single/double. Another nice hotel is the **Glen Lyon Inn** (☎ 250-949-7115, 6435 Hardy Bay Rd), with river-view rooms that overlook the marina.

The town fills up the night before a ferry is due to depart so it's worth booking ahead.

Getting There & Around Island Coach Lines (☎ 250-949-7532) on the corner of Market and Hastings Sts has one bus a day to Victoria for $78. North Island Transportation, operating out of the same office, runs a shuttle bus to/from the ferry terminal for $5 one way. The bus will pick you up and drop you off wherever you're staying.

BC Ferries (☎ 1-888-223-3779) sails the *Queen of the North* up the Inside Passage to Prince Rupert on daylight sailings (15 hours) from mid-May to mid-October. The voyages are quite spectacular for scenery and wildlife. Reservations for vehicles are an excellent idea. The fare is $104/52 for adults/children and $214 for a car. 'Discovery Coast' ferries serve Bella Coola on the BC mainland from Port Hardy from June to September. Again the sights are great and from Bella Coola you can take rugged Hwy 20 456km to Williams Lake and Hwy 97. The fare is $112/56 for adults/children and $225 for a car.

Cape Scott Provincial Park

About 60km west of Port Hardy over an active logging gravel road, this remote park offers challenging hiking, wilderness camping

The Inside Passage to Prince Rupert

BC Ferries runs the 15 hour, 440km trip along the coast, around islands and past some of the province's best scenery. The classic *Queen of the North* ferry leaves every other day at 7:30 am (check in by 6:30 am, if you have already booked a place) and arrives in Prince Rupert at 10:30 pm. (In winter the ferry leaves just once a week.)

There's a short stop at Bella Bella, about one-third of the way up, which is mostly for the locals but also to drop off kayakers. The one-way fare per person is $104/52 adults/children, $214 for a car and $356 for RVs up to 6m long. Outside the summer peak period (late May to the end of September) the fares can be half as much.

If you're taking a vehicle in summer you should reserve well in advance. Call BC Ferries in Victoria (☎ 250-386-3431) or from any place else in BC (☎ 888-223-3779). However, it's possible to go standby and to do so put your name on the waiting list as early as possible and be at the ferry terminal by 5:30 am at the latest on the day of departure. Binoculars are useful as you're often close to land and the wildlife viewing is good: the possibilities include bald eagles, porpoises, sea lions and humpback and killer whales.

Once in Prince Rupert you can continue on Alaska State Ferries farther north to Juneau and Skagway; catch BC Ferries to the Queen Charlotte Islands; or go by land into the BC interior and up to the Yukon and Alaska.

and exploring along pristine beaches for those wishing to get away from it all. Most accessible is the undisturbed expanse of sandy beach at San Josef Bay under an hour's walk along a well maintained trail.

Beyond this, things get serious. The eight hour 24km slog to wild Cape Scott, an old Danish settlement at the park's far end, weeds out the Sunday strollers. Just submit totally to the 'goddess of mud' and rewards will come to you. Nels Bight Beach, at six hours and with camping, is one of them. Wildlife is abundant.

Note that the west coast of this northern tip of the island is known for strong winds, high tides and heavy rain. You'll need to take all supplies and equipment if you're camping. Also, it's suggested water be purified.

South-West British Columbia

The heavily populated area immediately surrounding Vancouver is known as the Lower Mainland. Most people see the region as something to get through on the way to somewhere else. We won't quibble with this, but there are a few places to break up the trip and once into the Fraser Canyon, BC's legendary topography takes over.

At the small town of Hope, 150km from Vancouver, the road east splits. The Trans Canada Hwy follows the Goldrush Trail (the route the old wagon trail took to the Cariboo gold rush) north up the Fraser River Valley towards Cache Creek. As the road follows the river, which winds and twists through the canyon, there are many points of interest and viewing areas. The farther north you go, the drier the land becomes and the fewer trees there are, until around Cache Creek the landscape resembles that of a cowboy movie.

North-east of Hope the Coquihalla Hwy heads to Kamloops. It's a wide, straight express route with a $10 toll. Service stations are few, so leave with a full tank. The scenery along the way is pleasant and there are plenty of places to stop and view it. Farther west, between Chilliwack and Vancouver, the road is uninterestingly flat and straight; it's more or less an expressway right into the city. There's no point trying to hitch along this stretch, as

S-W BRITISH COLUMBIA

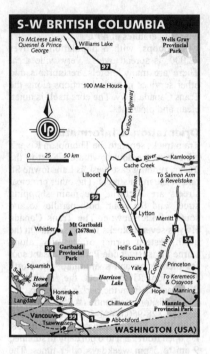

To McLeese Lake,
Quesnel & Prince
George

Williams Lake

Wells Gray
Provincial
Park

97

100 Mile House

Cariboo Highway

0   25   50 km

River — Kamloops
Cache Creek

Lilloet

To Salmon Arm
& Revelstoke

Thompson

12

99   Fraser

Lytton
Merritt

Mt Garibaldi
(2678m)

River

1   5

Whistler

99   Garibaldi
Provincial
Park

Hell's Gate

5A

Spuzzum

Coquihalla Hwy

Squamish

Yale   Princeton

Harrison
Lake

To Keremeos
& Osoyoos

Howe
Sound

Horseshoe
Bay

Hope   Manning

Langdale

Chilliwack   Manning
Provincial Park

Vancouver   99

Tsawwassen   1   Abbotsford

WASHINGTON (USA)

it's illegal for cars to stop. Note that this entire area is a hotbed of police speed traps.

The Crowsnest Hwy (Hwy 3) east of Hope heads first southward through Manning Provincial Park and then into the Okanagan Valley – the dry, beautiful fruit-growing region of BC. The green hills of the Hope area fade to brown as the road heads towards Osoyoos.

HOPE

There's not much in Hope itself but it's a good access point for the Fraser River Canyon and southern BC. Several lakes and more than a dozen provincial parks are close by. If you have a bit of time, the **Othello Tunnels**, 15 minutes by car from Hope, is worth the trip. Situated in the Coquihalla Canyon Recreation Area and running alongside the river of the same name, a series of tunnels were cut for a railway line between

1911 and 1919. It's an interesting hour stroll along the gorge and unique enough to have been used in several movies including *First Blood*, which you may recall was the first 'Rambo' movie. Obviously, the scenery is better than the film.

South-east of town, a 15 minute drive on the Crowsnest Hwy, are the remains of the infamous 'Hope slide'. In 1965 four people were killed when a small earthquake caused part of a mountain to crumble.

The Visitor Info Centre (☎ 604-869-2021, fax 604-869-2160), 919 Water Ave near the river, is a good place from which to collect information. There's plenty of *camping* in the area and both long and short hiking trails. *Motels* can be found on the Old Princeton to Hope Rd as well as downtown, with singles or doubles starting from $40.

FRASER RIVER CANYON

One of the province's principal rivers, the swift flowing historic Fraser, pours out of central BC into the ocean at Vancouver. The Thompson River, a major tributary, joins it at Lytton. A trip along Highway 1 by the steep-sided canyon offers some of the more impressive scenery of the province.

There are several provincial parks along the canyon. **Emory Creek Provincial Park**, just north of Hope, has camping, fishing and hiking. A good picnic stop is **Alexander Bridge Provincial Park** 1km north of Spuzzum. The open grate suspension bridge, built in 1926, spans the Fraser River and is free to cross.

Whitewater rafting down the Fraser and its tributaries' fast-flowing rapids is popular and a number of companies offer trips. The Visitor Info Centres in Hope and **Lytton** (☎ 250-455-2523, fax 250-455-6669), 400 Fraser St, have info on the scores of trips available. Those with motorised rafts allow more time for watching the ever-changing scenery, while paddle rafts where you have to work are more exciting. Either way you'll get soaked. In Yale, Fraser Rafting Expeditions (☎ 604-863-2336, ☎ 1-800-363-7238) on Hwy 1 is a major operator.

About 25km north of Yale is the **Hell's Gate Airtram**, a widely advertised cable-car

system that goes down to the rushing Fraser River daily. Look it over before buying the hype and $9 ticket.

Lytton is a pleasant town sitting where the clear Thompson waters meet the cloudy Fraser River. Northward, Hwy 1 goes to Cache Creek.

MANNING PROVINCIAL PARK
This 66,000-hectare park (☎ 250-840-8836, fax 250-840-8700) in the Cascade Mountains, close to the border with the USA, is about 30km south-east of Hope on Hwy 3. The park is noted for wildlife which includes more than 200 species of birds plus mammal species such as marmots, black bear, mule deer and coyote. In summer there's swimming, fishing, canoeing, hiking and wilderness camping. In winter there's downhill and cross-country skiing (with nearly 80km of trails), and snowmobiling. The **Pacific Crest Hiking Trail** begins in this park and goes south all the way to Mexico. See you, good luck!

The park has four fully serviced *campgrounds* with sites for $9.50 and $15.50, or at *Manning Park Resort (☎ 250-840-8836)* on the highway you could try one of the cabins which start at $99/104 a single/double.

KAMLOOPS
Sitting at the point where the North Thompson, South Thompson and Thompson rivers meet, Kamloops has always been a service and transport crossroads. In fact the town was once called 'Kahmoloops', a Shuswap word meaning 'meeting of waters'. The Trans Canada Hwy cuts east-west through town, the Yellowhead Hwy (Hwy 5) heads north, Hwy 5A heads south and the Coquihalla Hwy heads south-west to Vancouver. With this strategic location, the city has grown rapidly since the late 1960s and is the major service and industrial centre in the district.

The city is not all business, though. It is surrounded by some 200 lakes, making it a good watersports area. The dry, rolling hills make interesting scenery and excellent ranching territory. Summers can be extremely hot with temperatures of 40°C.

Kamloops, with a population of over 72,000, is spread over a very wide area. There are many motels, restaurants and other services in both directions along the Trans Canada Hwy. The core itself is quiet, clean and pleasant.

Orientation & Information
Train tracks separate the Thompson River's edge from the downtown area. Next to the tracks, running east-west, is Lansdowne St, one of the main streets. The other principal streets are Victoria, the main shopping street, and Seymour, both parallel to and south of Lansdowne. The Trans Canada Hwy is several blocks farther south. On the north-western corner of the city, along Lorne St, is Riverside Park, a pleasant spot for picnicking and swimming. The North Thompson River meets the Thompson River across from the park's shoreline.

The Visitor Info Centre (☎ 250-374-3377, fax 250-828-9500, ☎ 1-800-662-1994) is at 1290 West Trans Canada Hwy at exit 368. It's open from 9 am to 6 pm daily in summer, 9 am to 5 pm weekdays other times. The main post office (☎ 250-374-2444) is at 301 Seymour St near the corner of 3rd Ave. The Royal Inland Hospital (☎ 250-374-5111) is at 311 Columbia St. McCleaners coin laundry (☎ 250-372-9655) is at 437 Seymour St.

Things to See & Do
The **Kamloops Museum** (☎ 250-828-3576) is at 207 Seymour St on the corner of 2nd Ave. On display are pioneer implements and Salish tools and ornaments. It's open Monday to Friday from 9 am to 8 pm, weekend afternoons and admission is by donation. **Kamloops Art Gallery** (☎ 250-828-3543) in the library at 465 Victoria St, charges $3/2 for adults/children.

Secwepemc Native Heritage Park (☎ 250-828-9781), 355 Yellowhead Hwy north of the centre, is the most interesting site in town. It has re-created traditional winter and summer houses and has an indoor museum which outlines the history and the culture of

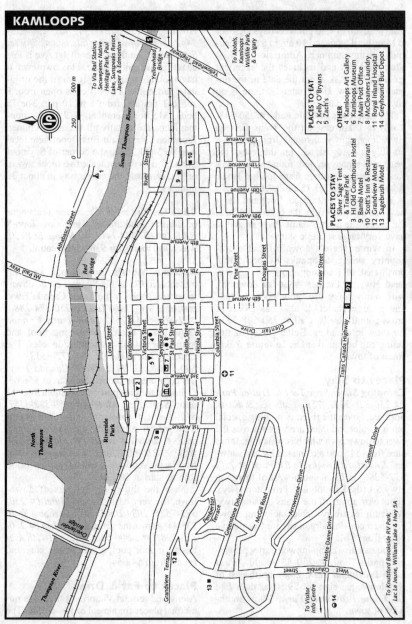

KAMLOOPS

PLACES TO STAY
1   Silver Sage Tent
    & Trailer Park
9   Bambi Motel
10 HI Old Courthouse Hostel
12 Scott's Inn & Restaurant
    Grandview Motel
13 Sagebrush Motel

PLACES TO EAT
2   Kelly O'Bryans
5   Zach's

OTHER
4   Kamloops Art Gallery
6   Kamloops Museum
7   Main Post Office
8   McCleaners Laundry
11 Royal Inland Hospital
14 Greyhound Bus Depot

To Via Rail Station,
Secwepemc Native
Heritage Park, Paul
Lake, Sunpeaks Resort,
Jasper & Edmonton

To Motels,
Kamloops
Wildlife Park,
& Calgary

0   250   500 m

South Thompson River

North Thompson River

Thompson River

Yellowhead Bridge

Yellowhead Highway

River Street

Athabasca Street

Red Bridge

Mt Paul Way

Riverside Park

Overlander Bridge

Lorne Street

Landsowne Street

Victoria Street

Seymour Street

St Paul Street

Battle Street

Nicola Street

Columbia Street

Pine Street

Douglas Street

Fraser Street

12th Avenue

11th Avenue

10th Avenue

9th Avenue

8th Avenue

7th Avenue

6th Avenue

5th Avenue

3rd Avenue

2nd Avenue

1st Avenue

Clantair Drive

Trans Canada Highway

Summit Drive

Arrowtone Drive

McGill Road

Greenstone Drive

Pemberton Terrace

Notre Dame Drive

Grandview Terrace

West Columbia Street

To Knutsford Brookside RV Park,
Lac Le Jeune, Williams Lake & Hwy 5A

To Visitor
Info Centre

BRITISH COLUMBIA

the European-named Shuswap People. Open from 8.30 am to 4.30 pm weekdays October to May, until 8 pm and 10 am to 6 pm weekends during summer. Admission is $6/4 adults/children and includes the excellent guided tours. Ask about the date of the annual Pow Wow. Unfortunately, there is no city bus to the park.

The **Kamloops Wildlife Park** (☎ 250-573-3242) is 18km east on the Trans Canada Hwy. Open daily year-round (from 8 am to 8 pm July and August, to 5 pm the rest of the year), it has many animals found in Canada's west as well as critters from foreign lands. Admission is $6.75/3.75 adults/children.

You can fish for salmon, trout and steelhead; as a general rule, the bigger the lake, the bigger the trout. **Adams River** is said to have very large sockeye salmon.

In winter there's downhill and cross-country skiing. **Sunpeaks Resort**, 53km north-east of Kamloops, off the Yellowhead Hwy, is the best spot for downhill, with many long, dry, powder-snow runs and a large chalet. It also has 24km of cross-country trails. Call ☎ 250-578-7232 for snow information. Better cross-country skiing can be found at **Lac Le Jeune**, 25km south of town.

Places to Stay

Camping *Silver Sage Tent & Trailer Park* (☎ 250-828-2077, 771 Athabasca St East), north-east over the river, is nothing special but it's quiet and there are views across the river to downtown which is walkable. It has sites from $15 and a coin laundry and showers. *Knutsford Brookside RV Park* (☎ 250-372-5380) is 12km south-west of town, on Hwy 5A (the Kamloops to Princeton Hwy), about 6km south off the Trans Canada Hwy. All facilities are available, including showers and a coin laundry; a site for two people costs from $14.

You can also camp in two nearby provincial parks (both ☎ 250-851-3000). *Paul Lake Provincial Park*, 24km north-east of Kamloops, has sites for $9.50, as does *Lac Le Jeune Provincial Park*, 37km south-west of town.

Hostel The spacious HI *Old Courthouse Hostel* (☎ 250-828-7991, fax 250-828-2442, kamloops@hihostels.bc.ca, 7 West Seymour St) on the corner of 1st Ave is in a beautiful old building close to downtown. It has a lounge and dining room in the original courtrooms. The office is open from 8 am to 1 pm and from 5 to 10 pm. The 76 beds, $15 for members, $19.50 for non-members, are usually all taken in summer. From the Greyhound Bus Depot take local bus No 3 ($1.25) to the corner of Seymour St and 3rd Ave, then walk two blocks west, or you can walk the entire way in about 30 minutes.

B&Bs The Visitor Info Centre has a catalogue of B&Bs in and around Kamloops. *Joyce's B&B* (☎ 250-374-1417, 49 Nicola St West), which has rooms for $38/45, is central.

Hotels & Motels The two main areas for motels is in Columbia St, west of the downtown area, and on the Trans Canada Hwy, east of town. *Thrift Inn* (☎ 250-374-2488, ☎ 1-800-661-7769, 2459 Trans Canada Hwy) has a heated swimming pool and rooms for $40/42 for singles/doubles. The *Courtesy Inn Motel* (☎ 250-372-8533, ☎ 1-800-372-8533, 1773 Trans Canada Hwy) has comfortable rooms that start at $56/65.

One of the cheapest on Columbia St is the basic *Sagebrush Motel* (☎ 250-372-3151, 660 West Columbia St), which has rooms from $45/50. Among the many others in this area, *Grandview Motel* (☎ 250-372-1312, ☎ 1-800-210-6088, 463 Grandview Terrace) has large outdoor gardens and a pool. Rooms start at $60/70.

Near the thumping delights of downtown, the very basic *Bambi Motel* (☎ 250-372-7626, 1084 Battle St) has rooms from $38/44. Across the street, *Scott's Inn* (☎ 250-372-2281, ☎ 1-800-665-3343, 551 11th Ave) has an indoor pool, a welcoming café and rooms from $48/54.

Places to Eat & Drink

Along and around Victoria St there are numerous places for a meal or just coffee. The

Plaza Café in the Plaza Hotel serves good breakfasts and has soup-sandwich-and-dessert lunch specials for $5.50. *Zach's (cnr 4th & Victoria Sts)* is a mellow coffee house that bakes its own bagels. It's open from 6 am to 3 pm.

Kelly O'Bryans (244 Victoria St) is a merry Irish pub with cheap burgers and well poured pints.

Getting There & Away

Bus At the Greyhound Bus Depot (☎ 250-374-1212), 725 Notre Dame Drive south-west of the downtown area off West Columbia St, there's a cafeteria and left-luggage lockers. There are regular buses daily to Vancouver, Calgary, Jasper, Edmonton, Prince George and Kelowna.

Train The VIA Rail station (☎ 1-800-561-8630) is 11km north of town off the Yellowhead Hwy and is only open 30 minutes prior to departures. There are three trips weekly either east to Jasper, Edmonton and beyond or south to Vancouver. For Prince George you must transfer in Jasper.

The privately operated *Rocky Mountaineer* tour train stops here overnight on its various trips. (See the Getting There & Away section in Vancouver for details).

Getting Around

For information about local bus routes call Kamloops Transit Service (☎ 250-376-1216). A one-way fare is $1.25. For a taxi call Yellow Cabs (☎ 250-374-3333).

WELLS GRAY PROVINCIAL PARK

In the Cariboo Mountains about halfway between Kamloops and Jasper, off the Yellowhead Hwy (Hwy 5), is this huge, undeveloped, and relatively little-visited, 541,000-hectare wilderness park. In **Clearwater**, the Visitor Info Centre (☎ 250-674-2646, ☎ 250-674-3693) on the corner of the Yellowhead Hwy and Clearwater Valley Rd has lots of useful information and maps on the park.

You can hike along more than 20 trails of varying lengths, go mountain biking, canoe-

ing on the lakes and rivers, whitewater rafting on Clearwater River, mountain climbing, downhill or cross-country skiing, and horse riding. Canoeing often provides the only access to hiking trails and only experienced, fully equipped mountaineers should attempt climbing or venture onto the snow-fields and glaciers. Wildlife is plentiful. Of the many scenic waterfalls in the park **Helmcken Falls**, where the Murtle River plunges 137m, is the most spectacular.

Places to Stay

Wells Gray has five designated *campgrounds* (Saphats Creek, Pyramid, Clearwater Lake, Hemp Creek and Mahood Lake) with sites costing $9.50, plus plenty of wilderness camping along the shores of the larger lakes.

Getting There & Away

There are three access points to the park. From Clearwater to the south, the Clearwater Valley Rd enters the park at Hemp Creek; from Blue River a 24km gravel road and 2.5km track lead to Murtle Lake in the south-east; and from 100 Mile House off Hwy 97 it's 88km on paved road to Mahood Lake in the south-west.

MT ROBSON PROVINCIAL PARK

Skirting the Fraser River, the Yellowhead Hwy and the railway run along the valley of this 217,000-hectare park which adjoins Alberta's Jasper National Park. At the western end of the park, Mt Robson (3954m) is the highest point in the Canadian Rockies and, when the clouds are not hugging it, is visible from the highway. At the base of the mountain the visitors centre (☎ 250-566-4325, fax 250-566-9777) has information on the park and runs interpretative programs during summer. Like Wells Gray, the park offers the full range of activities as well as many picnic areas and lookout points. In August and September you can see salmon spawning on the river at Rearguard Falls.

Watch for roadside markers detailing the work of the interned Japanese labourers

who built this stretch of the Yellowhead Hwy during WWII. Adjoining the western end of the park is the tiny **Mt Terry Fox Provincial Park**, named after the runner who lost a leg to cancer, then attempted to run across the country to raise money for cancer research.

Places to Stay

Mt Robson Provincial Park has three *campgrounds*: two are near the visitors centre at Robson Meadows and Robson River with sites for $14.50; the third is at Lucerne on the southern shore of the Yellowhead Lake 10km west of the Alberta border, with sites for $9.50. There is also wilderness camping in the park and commercial facilities at its western edge.

KAMLOOPS TO WILLIAMS LAKE

West of Kamloops, the Trans Canada Hwy heads to **Cache Creek**, north of which Hwy 97 (the Cariboo Hwy) follows the Goldrush Trail to Barkerville east of Quesnel. The dry, scrub-covered hills around the cross roads of Cache Creek give way to endless forest as you head north from Clinton. From 100 Mile House (named after the roadhouse located at this distance from the start of the original Cariboo Wagon Rd) you can travel to Mahood Lake in Wells Gray Provincial Park.

Charmless **Williams Lake** is a transport and industrial centre best known for the Williams Lake Stampede which takes place at the beginning of July. It's BC's answer to the Calgary Stampede and is a wild time lasting four days. It includes athletics and other sports as well as the rodeo. Accommodation prices go up a little while it's on. The Visitor Info Centre (☎ 250-392-5025, fax 250-392-4214), 1148 S Broadway on Hwy 97, is open from 9 am to 5 pm daily in summer and 9 am to 4 pm weekdays other times.

North of Williams Lake is **McLeese Lake**, a small lakeside resort with log cabins. Bighorn sheep can be seen along Highway 20 west towards huge, undeveloped Tweedsmuir Provincial Park (☎ 250-398-4414).

Okanagan Valley

The Okanagan, a beautiful and unique area of Canada, is a series of valleys running about 180km north-south in south-central BC. To the east are the Monashee Mountains, to the west the Cascade Mountains. The valleys were carved out by glaciers and are linked by a series of lakes, the largest of which is Okanagan Lake. The varied and interesting landscape makes the entire region very scenic.

The northern end is gentle green farmland that climbs to woods of evergreens. The farther south you get, the drier the terrain becomes. Near Osoyoos, close to the US border, cactuses grow on desert slopes that get only 250mm of rain a year. And everywhere are rolling, scrubby hills, narrow blue lakes and clear sky.

The Okanagan is a significant retirement centre. This, in some measure, is responsible for the large growth of the area's major towns which are increasingly popular with seniors from not only BC but also from across the prairies and as far as Ontario. The entire region is also a vacation mecca for those searching for some hot summer sun which is so unreliable in the mountains or on the coast. Through July and August expect all types of accommodation to be tight.

Okanagan Lake is said to contain a monster similar to that of Loch Ness but known as Ogopogo. The Native Indians first reported it and would offer the creature sacrificial animals before venturing on the lake. Claimed occasional sightings have proved especially unverifiable.

Fruit Orchards & Vineyards

The hot, dry summers attract many visitors, but the climate, in combination with the fertile soil and heavy irrigation, has made the region the country's top fruit-growing area as well. There are about 100 sq km of orchards in the Okanagan.

During April and May the entire valley is enlivened with blossoms from thousands of fruit trees. In late summer and autumn the

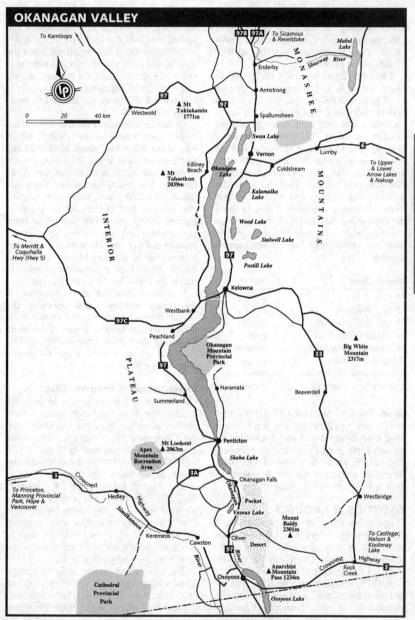

orchards drip with delicious fresh fruit. Stands dotting the roads sell the best and cheapest produce in Canada. Grapes, grown on 12 sq km of vineyards, are the last fruit of summer to ripen.

So-called agri-tourism with visits to farms, orchards and wineries has become very popular. *Tours of Abundance* is a widely distributed free guide to the many orchard visits and wine tastings offered through the valley. The drive north along Hwy 97 from Osoyoos is an almost endless succession of orchards, farms, fruitstands and the like. If you want to drive fast, fly to Germany and try the autobahn since the slow-moving tourists and retirees on this route will give you plenty of time to smell the apples, peaches, and, yes, the roses.

If you wish to tie your trip to a specific fruit, the approximate harvest times are as follows:

harvest times	fruit
25 June-25 July	cherries
15 July-10 August	apricots
20 July-10 September	peaches
20 August-1 September	pears
28 August-30 September	tomatoes
1 August-20 October	apples
1 September-20 September	prunes
9 September-18 October	grapes

Work There's work fruit picking; it's hard and the pay isn't great, but you don't always need a work permit and you'll meet lots of young people. Arrive early and shop around. The season starts first around Osoyoos, where the weather is warmer. Many towns have agricultural employment offices.

OSOYOOS & AROUND
Osoyoos is a big resort in a small town. It sits at the edge of dark-blue Lake Osoyoos in an area of stark, dry rolling hills at the southern end of the Okanagan Valley. The skies are sunny and the waters warm.

In 1975, in cooperation with the provincial government, the locals adopted a theme to beautify the town. Because of the cli-

mate, topography and agriculture, a Spanish motif was chosen and some businesses and houses maintain this look. With its hot, dry weather, the Osoyoos region produces the earliest and most varied fruit and vegetable crops in Canada. Look for roadside stands selling cherries, apricots, peaches, apples and other fruit. There are also many vineyards in the area.

On the eastern side of the lake lies a small desert, known as a 'pocket desert', which runs about 50km northward to Skaha Lake and is about 20km across at its widest point.

Averaging less than 200mm of rain a year, the area has much specialised flora and fauna, including the calliope hummingbird (the smallest bird in Canada), rattlesnakes, painted turtles, numerous species of mice and coyotes and various cactuses, desert brushes and grasses. The area is actually an extension of the northern Mexican desert and the life found here is remarkably similar to that at the 600m level two borders south.

In a province where all the superlatives describing scenery work overtime the stretch between Osoyoos and Penticton on a clear day has to rank as one of the more deserving. And it's not too shabby leading west out of town toward the Okanagan Highlands either.

Orientation & Information
Osoyoos is at the crossroads of Hwy 97 heading north to Penticton (past several provincial parks where you can camp) and the Crowsnest Hwy running east to the Kootenay region and west to Hope.

The US border, cutting through Lake Osoyoos, is just 5km to the south.

The Visitor Info Centre (☎ 250-495-7142, fax 250-495-6161) is slightly northwest of town, on the corner where the Crowsnest Hwy branches off westward from Hwy 97, next to the Husky gas station. It is open from 9 am to 5 pm daily in summer, weekdays only other times.

The Greyhound station is in Chucker's Convenience Store (☎ 250-495-7252) at 6615 Lakeshore Dr (Hwy 3) east of town at the east end of the motel strip. There are

buses to/from Vancouver, Calgary and north up the valley.

Things to See & Do

The climate makes **Lake Osoyoos** the warmest in the country. That together with the sandy beaches means great swimming.

The small **Osoyoos Museum** (☎ 250-495-2582) in Gyro Community Park has displays on natural history, the Inkameep people, orchards and irrigation. It's open from 10 am to 3.30 pm daily from June to September and admission is $2.

The **pocket desert**, off Black Sage Rd, is on the Inkameep people's reserve but you can visit by first asking permission from their office there. If you follow Black Sage Rd north from there to Oliver you'll pass several **wineries**. From Oliver, rough Camp McKinney Rd goes east to the **Mt Baldy** ski area (☎ 250-498-2262) which has cross-country trails and 11 downhill runs with a vertical drop of 420m. East of Osoyoos, on the Crows-nest Hwy, the **Anarchist Mountain Lookout** at 700m, offers a superb view of the town, valley, desert, lake and US border. You need a car or a ride to reach it.

West of town 8km on the south side of Hwy 3 look for the **spotted lake**, a weird natural phenomenon. Farther west is **Cathedral Provincial Park**, a 33 sq km mountain wilderness area characterised by unusual rock formations. Mule deer, mountain goat and California bighorn sheep may be seen. The park is accessed by a gravel road off the Crowsnest Hwy (Hwy 3) 3km west of Keremeos. Surrounded by orchards **Keremeos** is noted for its fruit and wines. More fruit stands dot the highway as it passes through the town and valley.

Places to Stay

Camping *Haynes Point Provincial Park* (☎ 250-494-0321) jutting into the lake 2km south of downtown has the most sought-after sites. In fact, short of using a shotgun you're not likely to get in until next year. However, the park is part of the new reservations system (☎ 1-800-689-9025) so you might be able to nab a $14.50 spot if you plan early.

A good alternative and where there are usually some spaces is *Inkameep Campground* (☎ 250-495-7279) on the Indian Reserve 4km east of town off Hwy 3 at 45th St and 1km north. Tenting is $16. There are RV sites as well as a beach. It's open May to September.

More developed *Cabana Beach Campground* (☎ 250-495-7705, 2231 East Lakeshore Drive) on Rural Route 1, 3km south-east of town, has small cabins, as well as tent and trailer space. For two people, tenting costs from $16 to $22.

Motels There are pricey central beachside motels along motel row on Main St. *Sunbeach Motel* (☎ 250-495-7766, 7304 62nd Ave) on Hwy 3 has barbecues, boat docks and patios. Rooms start at $58. West of town, *Plaza Royale Motor Inn* (☎ 250-495-2633, 8010 Valiant Lane) at the junction of Hwys 3 and 97 has standard rooms from $55.

Places to Eat

The *Oysoyoos Burger House* (6910 Main St) – actually 62nd Ave – has cheap soups, sandwiches and burgers. *Finny's* (☎ 250-495-2224, 8311 78th St) is a local favourite with a fine assortment of salads, burgers ($6), steaks and more on a large menu.

PENTICTON

Penticton, the southernmost of the three Okanagan sister cities, sits directly between Okanagan Lake and Skaha Lake which are connected by the Okanagan River. The sun shines for an average of 600 hours in July and August – about 10 hours a day – and that's more than it shines in Honolulu! It's not surprising, then, that the number-one industry is tourism.

To the Salish, Pen-Tak-Tin means 'place to stay forever', an idea that many people took to heart. Between 1975 and 1985 the population rose from 13,000 to 25,000 and is now over 31,000. Penticton became a townsite in 1892, when several nearby mine claims were being developed. Fruit companies started buying up land in early 1900, the industries grew and by the 1930s Penticton's

BRITISH COLUMBIA

location and climate were gaining a reputation. It soon became a vacation destination. The downtown core is undergoing something of a revival, particularly along the small Front St. Okanagan beach is very close by, making this a good spot to cool your heels for a day or two.

Orientation

The downtown area lies just south of Okanagan Lake. Most of the land alongside the lake is park. Lakeshore Drive runs west beside it from the downtown area to Riverside Drive and Hwy 97. The main street is fittingly Main St, running north-south; at the southern end it continues straight on to South Main St, and to the right it forks off to become Skaha Lake Rd, which then turns into Hwy 97.

The downtown area extends for about 10 blocks southward from the lake. Martin St to the west and parallel to Main St is also important. Running west-east, Westminster, Nanaimo and Wade Aves are the principal thoroughfares. Most of the restaurants and bars are in this area.

Information

The Visitor Info Centre (☎ 250-492-4103, fax 250-492-6119, ☎ 1-800-663-5052), next to the convention centre at 888 Westminster Ave W, is open from 8 am to 8 pm daily in summer, 9 am to 5 pm the rest of the year. There is a postal outlet at Gallop's Flowers, 187 Westminster Ave W. Penticton Regional Hospital (☎ 250-492-4000) is south of downtown at 550 Carmi Ave. The Bookshop on Main St has a huge collection of second-hand books.

Things to See & Do

Close to the downtown area, **Okanagan Beach** is about 1300m long. It's sandy and the water temperature is about 22°C. You can visit the SS *Sicamous*, an old stern-wheeler, which sits dry-docked at the western end of the beach. This section of the Okanagan Lake has some of the best wind-surfing conditions in the Okanagan Valley. Pier Water Sports (☎ 250-492-6826) on Okanagan Lake next to the Lakeside Re-

sort, rents windsurfing boards and catamarans from $12 and $25 per hour.

Parasail Penticton (☎ 250-492-2242) offers rides on both lakes. You start on the beach and a speedboat pulls you up 50m into the air. It costs $40 for a 10 minute ride, but people say the feeling and the views are worth the money. At the southern end of town **Skaha Beach** is about 1.5km long and has sand, trees and picnic areas and there's windsurfing here too.

Coyote Cruises (☎ 250-492-2115) at 215 Riverside Drive rents inner tubes that you can float on all the way down to Skaha Lake. It takes nearly two hours and then it will bus you back, all for $10.

The **SS** *Sicamous* (☎ 250-492-0403), 1099 Lakeshore Drive W, carried passengers and freight on Lake Okanagan from 1914 to 1936. It's been restored and can be visited 9 am to 10 pm daily in summer and 9 am to 4 pm weekdays other times. Admission is $3/1 for adults/children.

The **Penticton Museum** (☎ 250-490-2451) at the library complex, 785 Main St, is an excellent small-town museum. Displays are varied, well presented and pleasingly eclectic. Admission is by donation and it's open from 10 am to 5 pm, closed Sunday.

Of the many area **wineries**, Hillside Cellars (☎ 250-493-4424), 1350 Naramata Rd, north-east of downtown is the closest. Open from 9 am to 9 pm daily. Nearby is Lake Breeze Vineyards (☎ 250-496-5659), 930 Sammet Rd, in Naramata. It's open from 10 am to 6 pm daily.

On 2.25 sq km of dry land overlooking Skaha Lake, **Okanagan Game Farm** (☎ 250-497-5405) has about 650 animals of 130 species, including Canadian and foreign animals. It's 8km south of Penticton, on Hwy 97, and is open all year from 8 am to dusk. Admission is $10, or $7 for students.

Special Events

The city's premier event is the Peach Festival, a week-long event that has taken place around the beginning of August since 1948. There are sports activities, novelty events, music and dance, nightly entertainment, and

a major parade held on Saturday. At about the same time is the Annual BC Square Dance Jamboree. It goes on for six nights from 8 to 11 pm, and about 3500 dancers take part. There's an enormous dance floor in Kings Park. There are also street dances, dances held at both lakes – in the water! – pancake breakfasts and other activities.

At the end of August athletes are put through their paces in the Ironman Canada Triathlon. In early October for 11 days the Okanagan Wine Festival, centred in Penticton, takes place throughout the valley.

Places to Stay

Camping There are many tent and trailer parks, especially south of town, around Skaha Lake. Many are just off Hwy 97. Most are about $15 to $22 for two people in a tent. This is in no way wilderness camping, but is a cheap place to stay. The beach closes at midnight and stays that way until 6 am.

Hostel The excellent HI *Penticton Hostel* (☎ 250-492-3992, fax 250-492-8755, penticton@hihostels.bc.ca, 464 Ellis St) is right downtown just south of the Greyhound Bus Depot. Facilities include private rooms, kitchen, laundry, patio, bike rental and discounts in town. It also has details about finding fruit-picking work. The office is open daily from 7 am to 12.30 pm, and from 4 pm to midnight. Rates in a dorm are $15/19 for members/nonmembers.

B&Bs The Visitor Info Centre has a list of local B&Bs. One that's been going a long time is *Apex Alpine Guest Ranch* (☎ 250-492-2454) in Green Mountain Rd, 22km west of Penticton. Rooms cost $50. It's near the ski resort and offers horseback riding and hiking. Close to downtown, *The Rose Bed & Breakfast* (☎ 250-492-6743, 230 Farrell St) has reasonable rates at $45/60.

Motels Penticton is chock full of motels with Lakeshore Drive/Riverside Drive and South Main St/Skaha Lake Rd being the two main areas. The *Club Paradise Motel*

(☎ 250-493-8400, 1000 Lakeshore Drive) is a motel fronting Okanagan Lake. It has free coffee with singles and doubles costing from $50 to $70. Also fronting the lake but closer to the downtown area is the restful *Slumber Lodge Penticton* (☎ 250-492-4008, ☎ 1-800-663-2831, 274 Lakeshore Drive) where rooms start at $60/70. The *Penticton Lakeside Resort* (☎ 250-493-8221, ☎ 1-800-663-9400, 21 Lakeshore Drive W) is a large high-rise on the lake with extensive facilities. Rooms start at $134 in season, $89 other times.

At the southern end of town *Valley Star Motel* (☎ 250-492-7205, 3455 Skaha Lake Rd) has pleasant rooms from $50/55. *Log Cabin Motel* (☎ 250-492-3155, 3287 Skaha Lake Rd) has very nice grounds, a pool and nice rooms from $65/71.

Places to Eat

Nearly all the downtown restaurants are on or near Main St, and the revival of the downtown core has brought an increase in choice.

The *Elite* (340 Main St), with the 1950s Las Vegas-type sign outside, serves standard fare. Eggs with hash browns and toast cost $4.50 and it has lunchtime specials for $4. *La Casa Ouzeria* (☎ 250-492-9144, 2406 Skaha Lake Rd) is an old local favourite with Greek and Italian standards from $8. *Pacific Brimm* (☎ 250-490-8720, 2210 Main St), in the Lougheed strip mall, has coffees, cakes and free Internet access.

Entertainment

Element (535 Main St) is a hot dance club. There's usually a cover charge of around $5. *The Blue Mule* (218 Martin St) near the corner of Westminster Ave, has country music and dancing. The *Barking Parrot* in the Penticton Lakeside Resort gets a local crowd who lounge around at the outdoor tables.

Getting There & Away

The Greyhound Bus Depot (☎ 250-493-4101), 307 Ellis St, on the corner of Nanaimo Ave one block east of Main St, has a cafeteria and left-luggage lockers. Buses depart daily for Vancouver (seven hours),

Kelowna (1¼ hours), Vernon (one hour) and Calgary (12 hours).

Getting Around

For local bus information contact Penticton Transit (☎ 250-492-5602), or visit the Visitor Info Centre and pick up a copy of the leaflet *Rider's Guide*, which lists routes and fares. The one-way fare is $1.25, $3.25 for a day-pass. The lake-to-lake shuttle bus runs along both waterfronts back and forth every day until 7.30 pm. Also, bus No 202 from the corner of Wade Ave and Martin St goes down South Main St to Skaha Lake. There are no buses on Sunday or holidays, except for the summer lake shuttle.

AROUND PENTICTON
Vaseaux Wildlife Centre

Just south of Okanagan Falls watch for the small sign at the north end of Vaseaux Lake. There is excellent birdwatching here as well as bighorn sheep and the northern Pacific rattlesnake.

Summerland

Summerland is a small lakeside resort town north of Penticton. From **Giant's Head Mountain**, an extinct volcano south of the downtown area, there are great views of Okanagan Lake. In town there are some fine 19th century heritage buildings.

Summerland Trout Hatchery You can tour the hatchery (☎ 250-494-3346), 13405 Lakeshore Drive, from 8.30 to 11.30 am and from 1.30 to 4.30 pm all year for free. This is one of three BC hatcheries used to stock lakes; here they concentrate on rainbow, eastern brook and Kokanee trout.

Agricultural Research Station This centre, 11km north of Penticton on Hwy 97, was designed for the study of fruit trees, their growth, diseases and production. There is an ornamental garden displaying a variety of plants and trees, as well as picnic grounds. The grounds are open from 8 am to 8 pm daily April to October, to 5.30 pm the rest of the year.

Apex Mountain Ski Resort

Apex Mountain Ski Resort (☎ 250-292-8111, ☎ 1-800-387-2739), 37km west of Penticton, off Green Mountain Rd, has more than 50 downhill runs which cater for all levels of ability, plus cross-country trails. Lift tickets cost $35 and there are numerous packages with Penticton motels.

KELOWNA

Kelowna sits halfway down Okanagan Lake, midway between Vernon and Penticton encircled by the rounded, scrubby hills typical of the valley. Closer to town they become greener, with terraced orchards lining their slopes and, unusually, the greenest area is the town itself, with its many parks and gardens. Beneath skies that are almost always clear, sandy beaches rim the dark blue water of the lake.

The city's name is a Salish word meaning 'grizzly bear'. A number of oblate missionaries arrived in 1858. One of them, Father Pandosy, established a mission and planted the area's first apple trees. He has become Canada's lesser known equivalent of the USA's Johnny Appleseed. It was the success of his work that led to the first full-scale planting of apples in 1890.

In 1892 the townsite of Kelowna was drawn up and today with 89,000 people, it is the Okanagan's major city. There are nearly 2000 hours of sunshine here each year. Summer days are usually dry and hot, the nights pleasantly cool and winters are not harsh. The combination of excellent weather and the lake makes Kelowna not only an ideal agricultural area but a very popular tourist destination. The numbers of visitors lend the town a distinct resort feel.

Orientation

The large City Park on the lake's edge forms the western boundary of town. Starting from the big white modern sculpture 'Sails' and the model of Ogopogo, the mythical lake monster, at the edge of City Park, Bernard Ave runs east and is the city's main drag. Other important thoroughfares are Water, Pandosy and Ellis Sts, all running

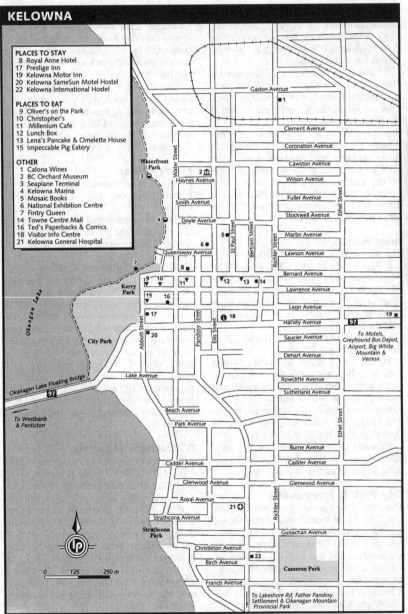

KELOWNA

PLACES TO STAY
8   Royal Anne Hotel
17 Prestige Inn
19 Kelowna Motor Inn
20 Kelowna SameSun Motel Hostel
22 Kelowna International Hostel

PLACES TO EAT
9   Oliver's on the Park
10 Christopher's
11 Millenium Cafe
12 Lunch Box
13 Lena's Pancake & Omelette House
15 Impeccable Pig Eatery

OTHER
1   Calona Wines
2   BC Orchard Museum
3   Seaplane Terminal
4   Kelowna Marina
5   Mosaic Books
6   National Exhibition Centre
7   Fintry Queen
14 Towne Centre Mall
16 Ted's Paperbacks & Comics
18 Visitor Info Centre
21 Kelowna General Hospital

BRITISH COLUMBIA

Gaston Avenue
Clement Avenue
Coronation Avenue
Cawston Avenue
Wilson Avenue
Fuller Avenue
Stockwell Avenue
Martin Avenue
Lawson Avenue
Bernard Avenue
Lawrence Avenue
Leon Avenue
Harvey Avenue
Saucier Avenue
Dehart Avenue
Rowcliffe Avenue
Sutherland Avenue
Burne Avenue
Cadder Avenue
Glenwood Avenue
Guisachan Avenue

Waterfront Park
Haynes Avenue
Smith Avenue
Doyle Avenue
Queensway Avenue

Water Street
St Paul Street
Bertram Street
Richter Street
Ethel Street

Kerry Park

Okanagan Lake

City Park

Okanagan Lake Floating Bridge
97

To Westbank
& Penticton

Lake Avenue
Beach Avenue
Park Avenue
Cadder Avenue
Glenwood Avenue
Royal Avenue
Strathcona Avenue

Strathcona
Park

Christleton Avenue
Birch Avenue
Francis Avenue

Cameron Park

Abbott Street
Pandosy Street
Ellis Street

97
To Motels,
Greyhound Bus Depot,
Airport, Big White
Mountain &
Vernon

To Lakeshore Rd, Father Pandosy
Settlement & Okanagan Mountain
Provincial Park

0   125   250 m

LP

north-south. South of town Pandosy St becomes Lakeshore Rd. Hwy 97, called Harvey Ave in town, is the southern edge of the downtown area; it heads westward over the bridge towards Penticton.

Eastward, along roughly a 15km stretch, Harvey Ave is a slightly restrained commercial strip lined with service stations, junk-food restaurants, motels and the rest of the usual suspects.

At the northern end of Pandosy St, where it meets Queensway Ave, is the town clock tower, standing in a fountain that marks the civic centre. There are an amazing 65 parks in the city area, including seven with beaches along the shore of the lake. Several other parks are south-west of town, on the other side of the bridge.

Information

The Visitor Info Centre (☎ 250-861-1515, fax 250-861-3624, ☎ 1-800-663-4345), 544 Harvey Ave (Hwy 97), near the corner of Ellis St, is open from 8 am to 7 pm daily in summer, 10 am to 4 pm weekdays other times. It has extensive local and regional information.

Most of the banks are on Bernard Ave, between Water and Ellis Sts.

Mosaic Books (☎ 250-763-4418), 1420 St Paul St, sells maps (including topographic ones), atlases, travel and activity guides and has a section on Native Indian history and culture. Ted's Paperbacks & Comics (☎ 250-763-1258), 269 Leon Ave, one block up from City Park, is a used-book store.

Kelowna General Hospital (☎ 250-862-4000) is south of Harvey Ave, at 2268 Pandosy St, on the corner of Royal Ave.

City Park & Promenade

The central downtown park is excellent, with 'Hot Sands Beach', lots of shade trees, and water just slightly cooler than the summer air at 23°C. There are flower gardens and tennis courts and with the view across the lake it's no wonder would-be fruit pickers are sitting around picking only guitars. It has now been joined by the equally bucolic Waterfront Park, just to the north.

The beach runs from the marina to **Okanagan Lake Bridge** west of City Park. This is Canada's longest floating bridge; it's supported by 12 pontoons and has a lift span in the middle so boats up to 18m high can pass through.

From Bernard Ave, the lakeside promenade extends north past the marina, lock and artificial lagoon to a condominium complex, a blend of Canadian and Spanish architectural styles. The promenade is good for a stroll or jog in the evenings.

Fintry Queen

At the foot of Bernard Ave, behind the model of Ogopogo, the old ferry boat *Fintry Queen* (☎ 250-763-2780) is moored in the lake. Now converted into a restaurant, it also provides lake cruises from June to September. The two hour cruise costs $9.

National Exhibition Centre

Housing the **Kelowna Centennial Museum** (☎ 250-763-2417), this is part of the civic centre complex at 470 Queensway Ave on the corner of Pandosy St. The museum features a reconstructed Salish underground winter home. Other exhibits include models of some of the town's first buildings and stores, stocked with goods and relics and a small permanent art collection, mainly of the works of BC artists. Admission to both is free. The centre is open from 10 am to 5 pm Monday to Saturday (closed Monday in winter).

BC Orchard Museum

Also downtown, Orchard Museum (☎ 250-763-0433), 1304 Ellis St, is located in an old packinghouse and recounts the conversion of the Okanagan Valley from ranchland to orchards. The exhibits show just about everything you can do with fruit, from seeds to jam. Open from 10 am to 5 pm Monday to Saturday (closed Monday in winter), admission is by donation.

Tucked away in the same building is the **Wine Museum** (☎ 250-868-0441) which is primarily a marketing front for the high-quality BC wines.

Father Pandosy Settlement

This is the major historic site in the area. On the spot where this oblate priest set up his mission in 1859 are some of the original buildings. The church, school, barn, one house and a few sheds from what was the first white settlement in the Okanagan have been restored.

The site is small, well out of the centre and there's not a lot to see, but it's free. To get there, go south along Lakeshore Rd, then east on Casorso Rd to Benvoulin Rd. It's open from 8 am to sundown, April to October.

Beaches

As well as the beach in town, there are several beaches south of Okanagan Lake Bridge along Lakeshore Rd. The Okanagan Shuswap Nudist Society has information on local buff beaches. Write to it at Box 5149, Station A, Kelowna, V1Y 7V8.

Activities

There is excellent hiking around town with over a dozen places to explore. The Info Centre has an excellent brochure *Heritage Walking Tour.* Well worth asking about is the **Kettle Valley Railway Trail**, an 8km loop around the Myra Canyon through tunnels, over old trestles and with great views. Access to it is by rough logging road or try cycling. The 10.5 sq km **Okanagan Mountain Provincial Park**, south of Kelowna off Lakeshore Rd, is a popular spot for hikers and horse riders. Many of the trails date from the days of the fur trade.

Fishing is possible on Okanagan Lake and many of the 200 lakes near Kelowna. You'll need a $16 licence from sporting goods stores and gas stations. From Kelowna Marina you can take fishing trips or cruises. Windsurfers leave from the old seaplane terminal near the corner of Water St and Cawston Ave.

About 8.5km north-west of Kelowna, **Bear Creek Provincial Park** also has windsurfing as well as fishing, swimming, hiking and wilderness camping.

For skiers there's **Big White Ski Resort** (☎ 250-765-3101, ☎ 1-800-663-2772, snow report ☎ 250-765-7669), 55km east of Kelowna, off Hwy 33. It's covered in deep dry powder and is the highest ski area in the province. Adult lift tickets cost $44 for the 840 hectares of ski runs and there is night skiing. There are numerous inns and lodges at the resort which can be reserved through the central office.

Kelowna Land & Orchard Co (☎ 250-763-1091), 3002 Dunster Rd, is one of many local places with orchard tours. It also has fruit products and baked goods available. Admission which includes a tour on a wagon costs $5 for adults, children under 12 are free.

Wineries Wine tours are one attraction you might not want to miss. Most of BC's multiplying wineries are in the Okanagan. Several vintners in and near Kelowna offer tours and free samples.

Calona Wines (☎ 250-762-9144), 1125 Richter St, right in Kelowna, is one of BC's largest producers and was the first in the Okanagan; it started in 1932. Open from 10 am to 5 pm daily. In Westbank, about 13km south-west of Kelowna, is Mission Hill Winery (☎ 250-768-7611). It's at 1730 Mission Hill Rd, off Boucherie Rd, and has tours, tastings and sales 10 am to 5 pm daily (until 7 pm in summer). Cedarcreek Estate Winery (☎ 250-764-8866), 5445 Lakeshore Rd, is open from 9.30 am to 5.30 pm. There are many more wineries listed in *Tours of Abundance* available from the Info Centre.

Places to Stay

In common with the rest of the Okanagan Valley, accommodation here can be difficult to find in summer; book ahead or arrive early in the day.

Camping Camping is the cheapest way to stay in the area, though you'll be a fair way from town. The best place is *Bear Creek Provincial Park (☎ 250-494-6500)*, 9km west of Kelowna off Hwy 97 near Summerland, where a site is $15.50.

There are numerous privately owned places around Kelowna, especially in Westbank and south along Lakeshore Rd. The grounds are usually crowded and the sites

close together. To get to Westbank, head west along Hwy 97 over Okanagan Lake Bridge then turn off at Boucherie Rd. Follow this for quite a while and you'll hit the so-called resort area. This area is quite far from town – you'll need a car. Sites cost between $15 and $25.

Closer to town, *Willow Creek Family Campground* (☎ 250-762-6302, 3316 Lakeshore Rd) has its own beach, a fire pit and is near shops and restaurants. Sites cost $16.

Hostels The *Kelowna International Hostel* (☎ 250-763-6024, fax 250-763-6068, kelowna_hostel@silk.net, 2343 Pandosy St) on the corner of Christleton Ave is a short walk from the beach. The enthusiastic new owners have spiffed the place up and will pick you up at the bus station if you call ahead. It has a kitchen, large deck and parking. Beds cost $14 and private rooms are available.

The HI *Kelowna SameSun Motel Hostel* (☎/fax 250-763-9814, samesun@silk.net, 245 Harvey Ave) is very centrally located on Hwy 97. Housed in an old motel, there are volleyball courts, a barbecue and bike and canoe rentals. Beds are $15/19 for members/nonmembers and private rooms are $39/49 a single/double.

At Big White Mountain ski resort, *Bumps* (☎ 250-765-2100, fax 250-765-3035, bumps@ bc.sympatico.ca) on Porcupine Rd off Hwy 33 across from the Greystoke Inn is recommended. The two-part hostel is close to nightlife and charges $20 per person. Visitors usually prefer the converted ski lodge. There is a low-cost shuttle bus to the mountain from Kelowna in the busy ski season.

SameSun operates another hostel, the *Alpine Centre* (☎ 250-765-7050, 7660 Porcupine Rd). Rates are from $15 and there are ski packages.

Note that while there are plenty of eateries and pubs at the resort, there is no bank machine.

B&Bs Contact Okanagan B&B Association (☎ 250-764-2124), PO Box 5135, Station A, Kelowna, V1Y 8T9, for a list of valley

B&Bs, or ask at the Travel Info Centre. Prices begin at $45/55 a single/double.

Hotels & Motels *Royal Anne Hotel* (☎ 250-860-7200, 348 Bernard Ave) has good rooms from $60/70 and a popular bar. The more upmarket *Prestige Inn* (☎ 250-860-7900, 1675 Abbott St) has a pool and sauna with prices from $100/110 a single/double.

Most of the motels are along Hwy 97, north of the downtown area. There are some good choices not far past the Hwy 33 junction. *Western Budget Motel* (☎ 250-763-2484, 2679 Hwy 97 North) is the cheapest, with singles/doubles from $39/42 and it accepts pets. *Town & Country Motel* (☎ 250-860-7121, ☎ 1-800-665-2610, 2629 Hwy 97 North), near the junction with Hwy 33, has rooms from $69/75 and has a pool and sauna.

The *Stay 'N Save* (☎ 250-862-8888, ☎ 1-800-663-0298, 1140 Harvey Ave) is a well run place on Hwy 97 with comfortable rooms from $84. Nearby, the *Kelowna Motor Inn* (☎ 250-762-2533, ☎ 1-800-667-6133, 1070 Harvey Ave) has an indoor pool and rooms from $65/69.

Places to Eat

Many of the eateries are in Bernard Ave. *Lena's Pancake & Omelette House* at No 533 is open every day and has all types of pancakes and omelettes from $4.75, and cheaper breakfast specials. At the *Lunch Box* (☎ 250-862-8621, 509 Bernard Ave), near the corner of Ellis St, you can sit outside with its excellent salads for $3, sandwiches for $4.50 or pies such as chicken and asparagus for $3.50. The *Millennium Cafe* (☎ 250-868-2085, 371 Bernard Ave) has a varied menu with many vegetarian and vegan specialities. It also has a good Balti (Indian) menu with mains around $10.

The *Impeccable Pig Eatery* (☎ 250-762-0442, 1627 Abbott St) has famous pork sandwiches and vegetarian fare at lunch. *Oliver's on the Park* (☎ 250-862-5122, 1585 Abbott St) has a long menu of Cajun and Italian stir-fries that all average about $12. It has an outdoor area and good lake and park views. More expensive *Christopher's* (☎ 250-861-

3464, 242 Lawrence St) is the best place for steak or seafood. If you need a fast-food fix head for Harvey Ave south and east of downtown where you'll find all the usual suspects.

Entertainment

The Sunshine Theatre Company (☎ 250-763-4025) puts on a range of productions during winter at the *Kelowna Community Theatre (cnr Water St & Doyle Ave)*. On Friday and Saturday nights during summer there are free concerts downtown in *Kerry Park*. Every summer Sunday afternoon there are free music concerts in *City Park*.

The Royal Anne Hotel contains a popular pub, *Sergeant O'Flaherty's*. It's frequented by all types – visitors, workers and locals – and entry is from the rear of the hotel in Queensway Ave. Locals describe the place as 'delightful, raucous, fun-filled and vibrant' and there's often impromptu dancing.

Getting There & Away

Air The airport is about 20km north of town, on Hwy 97. Air Canada (☎ 250-861-8441) and Canadian Airlines (☎ 250-763-6620) have daily flights to Vancouver, Calgary and Edmonton. Discount carrier WestJet (☎ 250-491-5600) has flights to those cities plus Victoria. Horizon Airlines (☎ 1-800-547-9308) flies non-stop to Seattle. Regional airlines link the city to smaller cities around BC.

Bus The Greyhound Bus Depot (☎ 250-860-3835) is north of the downtown area, at 2366 Leckie Rd, off Hwy 97. To get there, take city bus No 110 from the corner of Bernard Ave and Ellis St. It runs roughly every half-hour from 6.30 am to 9.30 pm.

Daily there are buses up and down the Okanagan Valley as well as Kamloops (three hours, $23), Prince George (11 hours, $84), Calgary (10 hours, $75) and Vancouver (six hours, $51).

Getting Around

To/From the Airport The Kelowna Airporter bus (☎ 250-765-0182) charges $8; the Vernon Airporter bus (☎ 250-542-7574)

charges $15. The one-way fare in a taxi is about $26.

Bus For information about local buses call Kelowna Regional Transit Systems (☎ 250-860-8121) or pick up a copy of *Kelowna Regional Rider's Guide* from the Visitor Info Centre; there are three zones and the one-way fare in the central zone is $1. A day pass for all three zones costs $3.50. Bus services are centred downtown on Queensway St between Pandosy and Ellis Sts.

Car Kelowna has all the major rental companies. Among them are:

Budget
   (☎ 250-712-3380) 1328 Water St
Rent-A-Wreck
   (☎ 250-763-6632) 2702 Hwy 97 North
Thrifty Car Rentals
   (☎ 250-765-2800) 1980 Springfield Rd

Taxi Kelowna has several taxi companies; try Kelowna Cabs (☎ 250-762-4444/2222).

VERNON & AROUND

Vernon, the most northerly of the Okanagan's 'Big Three', lies in a scenic valley encircled by three lakes: the Okanagan, Kalamalka and Swan. The town developed because of its location. First there were the fur traders, then the gold prospectors streaming up the valley to the Cariboo district. Later, cattle was brought in, and in 1891 the railway made it. But it was in 1908, with the introduction of large-scale irrigation, that the town took on an importance that was more than transitory. Soon the area was covered in orchards and farms.

Vernon's population of 32,000 is surprisingly cosmopolitan, with good numbers of Germans, Chinese and Native Indians. The Native Indians have a reserve to the west of town. Vernon itself doesn't have many attractions but accommodation is cheaper than in Kelowna or Penticton.

Orientation

Surrounded by rolling hills, downtown Vernon is a clean, neat, quiet place. Main St,

also called 30th Ave, is lined with trees and benches. To the north of 30th Ave, 32nd Ave is an important thoroughfare, as is 25th Ave to the south. At 25th Ave, Hwy 6 leading south-east to Nelson and Nakusp, meets Hwy 97, which runs north-south, becoming 32nd St in Vernon and bisecting the city. On 32nd St, north of 30th Ave, is a commercial strip with service stations, motels and fast-food outlets. The other major north-south street is 27th St, which eventually joins Hwy 97 north of town.

On 27th St is the provincial courthouse, the city's most impressive structure. All the downtown sights are within easy walking distance of each other.

Information

The Visitor Info Centre (☎ 250-542-1415, fax 250-542-3256) is about 5km north of town at 6326 Hwy 97 N near the south-eastern shore of Swan Lake – a bit of a hike to get to if you don't have your own transport. It's open from 8.30 am to 6 pm daily.

The main post office (☎ 250-545-8239), 3101 32nd Ave, is on the corner of 31st St opposite the civic centre. Bookland (☎ 250-545-1885), 3401 30th Ave, between 33rd and 34th Sts, has topographical maps of the region plus travel guides and books on activities in the Okanagan and BC.

The Vernon Jubilee Hospital (☎ 250-545-2211) is at 2101 32nd St.

Polson Park

Polson Park, off 25th Ave and next to 32nd St, is very pleasant, with lots of flowers and shade and the small Vernon Creek running through it. If it's hot this is a good rest spot. The Japanese and Chinese influence is evident in the gardens and open cabana-like structures dotting the park, at one end of which is a floral clock.

Provincial Courthouse

Built entirely of local granite, the courthouse (☎ 250-549-5422) sits majestically at the eastern end of the downtown area, on the corner of 30th Ave and 27th St. In front of it across the road is a rather bizarre garden.

Vernon Museum and Archives

This museum (☎ 250-542-3142) is in the civic centre, 3009 32nd Ave, at 31st St behind the glockenspiel-like clock tower. On display are historical artefacts from the area, including old carriages and clothes. It has a good antique telephone collection and lots of photos of the area and the locals. It's open from 10 am to 5 pm Monday to Saturday and is free. There's an art gallery, too.

O'Keefe Historic Ranch

Twelve kilometres north of Vernon, this old ranch (☎ 250-542-7868) on Hwy 97 was home to the O'Keefe family from 1867 to 1977. Among other things you'll see the original log cabin, a general store and St Ann's, the oldest Roman Catholic church in the province. It's a good introduction to life in the valley before it was taken over by fruit. The ranch is open from 9 am to 5 pm daily May to October. Admission is $6/4.50 for adults/children.

Beaches & Cruises

On blue-green Kalamalka Lake, about 4km south of town, is **Kalamalka Beach** with a campground nearby. To get there take Kalamalka Rd south off Hwy 6. There's also **Kin Beach** on Okanagan Lake, which is about 7km west of downtown. Head west along 25th Ave which becomes Okanagan Landing Rd, then turn right onto Tronson Rd which leads to the beach. It has a campground as well. Cruise Okanagan (☎ 250-549-1669) runs popular boat trips around the lake.

Provincial Parks

The 8.9 sq km **Kalamalka Lake Provincial Park**, south of town and on the eastern side of Kalamalka Lake, provides swimming, fishing, hiking and picnic areas. **Ellison Provincial Park**, 25km south-west of Vernon on Okanagan Lake, is the only freshwater marine park in western Canada. Scuba diving is a popular activity here.

Silver Star Provincial Park is 22km north-east of Vernon. Take 48th Ave off Hwy 97. The park offers good walking in summer, with views possible all the way west to the

Coast Mountains. In winter there are 50km of cross-country skiing on **Silver Star Mountain** (☎ 250-542-0224, ☎ 1-800-663-4431, snow report ☎ 250-542-1745). There also are downhill ski runs, a lodge and hotels.

Places to Stay

Camping By far the best campground is *Ellison Provincial Park* (☎ 250-494-6500), but it has only 54 camp sites and is often full, so call ahead. A site costs $12.

There are lots of privately owned campgrounds, some close to town at Okanagan and Kalamalka lakes. These, too, get crowded. One of the closest campgrounds to town is *Swan Lake RV Park* (☎ 250-545-2300, 7255 Old Kamloops Rd), 5km north of Vernon, which has tent sites from $16. Head west along 43rd Ave then turn right (north) onto Old Kamloops Rd. Two kilometres south of town, *Dutch's Tent & Trailer Court* (☎ 250-545-1023, 15408 Kalamalka Rd) has sites from $16.

Hostel *Lodged Inn* (☎ 250-549-3742, fax 250-549-3748, ☎ 1-888-737-4927, lodge dinn@bc.sympatico.ca, 3201 Pleasant Valley Rd) is close to downtown. It charges $15 a night.

B&Bs Vernon has lots of B&Bs, many located on the surrounding hills. For information contact the Visitor Info Centre. Close to downtown is *Tuck Inn* (☎ 250-545-3252, 3101 Pleasant Valley Rd), a large, white Victorian house with doubles for $65 including full breakfast. Nearby is *Pleasant Valley B&B* (☎ 250-545-9504, 4008 Pleasant Valley) at $55 a double. Up in the hills, *Melford Creek Country Inn & Spa* (☎ 250-558-7910, 7810 Melford Rd), 1km off Silver Star Rd, has a huge indoor spa area and pool. Rooms start at $79.

Hotels & Motels The reliable, downtown *Travelodge* (☎ 250-545-2161, ☎ 1-800-578-7878, 3000 28th Ave) has standard rooms and is fairly priced at $54/64. Farther north, at the *Best Western Vernon Lodge* (☎ 250-545-3385, ☎ 1-800-663-4422, 3914 32nd St) on

the corner of 39th Ave, singles/doubles cost from $90/95. The hotel has an indoor tropical garden, disco and nightclub.

There are many, many motels in and around Vernon especially along 32nd St (Hwy 97). The *Schell Motel* (☎ 250-545-1351, 2810 35th St) on the corner of 30th Ave has a heated pool and sauna. Rooms cost $50/56, or $8 extra with a kitchen. The *Comfort Inn* (☎ 250-542-4434, ☎ 1-800-228-5150, 4204 32nd St) has free calls and an indoor pool and whirlpool. Rooms start at $64/74.

Places to Eat

For a small town, Vernon has lots of eateries – particularly little coffee shops and sandwich places.

Downstairs, near the corner of 34th St, is *Jackie's Coffee Shop (3313 30th Ave)*, popular with the locals and good for breakfast. A popular lunch place downtown is *Johnny Appleseed (3018 30th Ave)*, with great soups, sandwiches, veggie specials and its own bakery.

Little Tex Cafe & Bistro (3302B 29th St) has fantastic salsa, and excellent quesidillas from $8. It's small and quaint. *Merona Restaurant (2905 29th St)* has good Greek food, weekend belly dancers and huge platters from $10. One of the favourites with locals is *Eclectic Med* (☎ 250-558-4646, 3117 32nd St), which lives up to its name with foods from around the world. The Thai beef rolls are $6; the Moroccan lamb $15.

Entertainment

The *Wildhouse Saloon (cnr 30th Ave & 29th St)*, next to Kelly O'Bryan's, features live country or country rock nightly Wednesday to Saturday from 8 pm to 2 am. North of the centre, *Squires Pub (6301 Stickle Rd)* is a laid-back joint with a fireplace and 25¢ chicken wings that actually have meat on the bone.

Getting There & Away

The Greyhound Bus Depot (☎ 250-545-0527) is at 3102 30th St at 31st Ave. Service radiates in all directions of BC.

Getting Around

For information about local buses contact Vernon Regional Transit System (☎ 250-545-7221), 4210 24th Ave, or get a copy of the leaflet *Vernon Regional Rider's Guide*, which gives details of fares and routes, from the Visitor Info Centre. For Kalamalka Lake catch bus No 1 south on 33rd St; for Okanagan Lake take bus No 7 west on 30th Ave. The one-way fare is $1 and a day pass costs $2.50.

For a taxi, you should try Vernon Taxi (☎ 250-545-3337).

NORTH OF VERNON

At Sicamous there's a major highway junction where Hwy 97A meets the Trans Canada Hwy (Hwy 1). From there the Trans Canada Hwy heads west past Shuswap Lake to Salmon Arm and Kamloops; west the highway goes to Revelstoke then through Mt Revelstoke, Glacier and Yoho national parks to Lake Louise in Alberta.

The Shuswap Region

The district around **Shuswap** and **Mara** lakes is picturesque, with green, wooded hills and farms. The grazing cattle and lush, cultivated land make a pleasant change of scenery no matter which direction you're coming from. There are many provincial parks in the region, three with camping: Shuswap Lake, Herald and Yard Creek.

Salmon Arm, at the northern end of the Okanagan Valley on the southern tip of one of Shuswap Lake's 'arms', is mainly a resort town, although timber and fruit-growing are also important. If you're here in October head north to Adams River in **Roderick Haig-Brown Provincial Park** (☎ 250-851-3000) where you'll see between 25,000 and 2.5 million sockeye salmon migrating upriver to spawn. Haig-Brown, a Canadian naturalist and angler, has many books in print.

One way to explore the Shuswap and Mara lakes is by houseboat, which can be hired from **Sicamous**, the self-styled 'houseboat capital of Canada'. You can also rent them from Salmon Arm. The Sicamous Chamber of Commerce (☎ 250-836-3313, fax 250-836-4368), 110 Finlayson St, has area information.

The HI *Squilax General Store and Hostel* (☎ 250-675-2977) about 10km east of Chase on Shuswap Lake makes a rural hub for exploring the area. If you've ever wanted to explore the rear of a train here's your chance as accommodation is in old cabooses. Beds cost $14/18 for members/nonmembers, and $4 more for a private room. You can also get a caboose to yourself for $33.

South-East British Columbia

The south-eastern part of BC is dominated by the Rocky, Selkirk, Purcell, Monashee, and Columbia mountain ranges. National and provincial parks found throughout the area preserve and make accessible much of the varied terrain. Wedged between the parallel mountain chains is an incredibly scenic series of lakes, rivers and thinly populated valleys.

The Purcell Mountain region below Golden, west from the Rockies and including Kimberley, is known as the East Kootenays. The West Kootenays run in and around the Selkirk Mountains west of Creston to Grand Forks and include Nelson, Nakusp and the Kootenay, Slocan and Arrow lakes. This, in particular, is a gorgeous area of mountains and valleys generally overlooked by visitors and definitely worth considering for a few days of exploration, especially along Hwys 3A and 6. It's an outstanding region for outdoor activities: camping, hiking and climbing in summer, and some of North America's best skiing in winter.

Several ferries across lakes and rivers connect highways throughout the region. They generally run from about 6 am to midnight and are mostly free. The south-eastern corner of BC is on Mountain Standard Time, while most of the rest of the province is on Pacific Standard Time, a difference of an hour.

REVELSTOKE & AROUND

This small town with a population of 8000, on the Trans Canada Hwy (Hwy 1) 70km east of Sicamous, is picturesque, with quiet

residential streets lined with neat wooden houses and tidy gardens. It's surrounded by mountains (not often seen) at the western edge of Mt Revelstoke National Park and is about halfway between the Okanagan Valley and the Rocky Mountains. Revelstoke is also a busy railway centre.

The main street is 1st St and MacKenzie is the major cross street. Grizzly Plaza, between MacKenzie and Orton Aves, is a pedestrian precinct. The Visitor Info Centre (☎ 250-837-5345, fax 250-837-4223) is in the Chamber of Commerce at 206 Campbell Ave. It's open from 8.30 am to 4.30 pm daily; in summer it has a well marked location at the east end of town on the Trans Canada Hwy. Parks Canada (☎ 250-837-7500) has information about Mt Revelstoke and Glacier national parks at its regional offices at 301 3rd St. It's open from 8 am to 4.30 pm weekdays. In the same building, the Friends of Mt Revelstoke & Glacier (☎ 250-837-2010) has books and maps of the parks. The main post office is next door.

BRITISH COLUMBIA

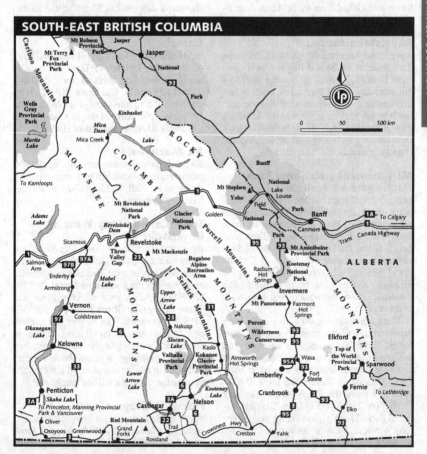

SOUTH-EAST BRITISH COLUMBIA

Most of the things to see are not in the town itself but around the Revelstoke area, so you'll need transport.

Railway Museum
The railway museum (☎ 250-837-6060) in a beautiful building downtown right off Victoria Road has steam locomotives and well thought out displays on the CPR which was instrumental in linking Canada (see boxed text 'Iron Link an Engineering Marvel'). Open from 9 am to 8 pm daily in July and August, 9 am to 5 pm weekdays other times and closed January to April. Admission is $5/2 for adults/children.

Revelstoke Museum
Revelstoke Museum (☎ 250-837-3067) on the corner of 1st St and Boyle Ave is open from 10 am to 5 pm daily in summer, 1 to 4 pm weekdays other times. It's worth a few minutes and admission is by donation. It holds a permanent collection of furniture plus odds and ends of historical interest from the area including mining, logging and railway artefacts.

Mt Revelstoke National Park
This is a relatively small national park, just east of Revelstoke, in the Selkirk Mountains which are known for jagged, rugged peaks and steep valleys. The view of these from Mount Revelstoke is excellent. Access is along the 26km Summit Rd (1.5km east of Revelstoke, off the Trans Canada Hwy) which leads through cedars, alpine meadows and near-tundra to Balsam Lake within 1.5km of the peak. From here walk to the top.

There are several good hiking trails from the summit, with backcountry camping permitted. No other camping is allowed. You are required to have a free backcountry camping permit which is available from Parks Canada in Revelstoke (☎ 250-837-7500) or from the Rogers Pass Visitor's Centre (☎ 250-814-5233) in Glacier National Park. There's good skiing in the very long winters. Much of the summer is rainy so check that tent for leaks.

Admission to Mt Revelstoke and Glacier national parks (the two are administered jointly) is $4/2 for adults/children per day.

Canyon Hot Springs
These springs (☎ 250-837-2420) are a great spot for a quick visit, 35km east along the Trans Canada Hwy between Revelstoke and Glacier national parks. The site consists of a hot pool (40°C) and a larger, cooler swimming pool. The site is open from 9 am to 9 pm daily May to September. Admission is $5/3.50 and that includes a locker and shower; a day pass is $7.50/5.50. You can rent a bathing suit and towel.

Dams
BC Hydro (☎ 250-837-6515) runs free tours of the 175m **Revelstoke Dam** on the Columbia River, 4km north of town, off Hwy 23 and adjacent to Columbia View Provincial Park. It also runs tours of the **Mica Dam**, 149km north of Revelstoke, in a bend of the Columbia River, at the end of Hwy 23.

Mt Mackenzie
Five kilometres south-east of Revelstoke, this is a major downhill and cross-country skiing area. Call ☎ 250-837-5268 for detailed information.

Trans Canada Hwy West of Revelstoke
Between Revelstoke and Sicamous are many roadside attractions of the kitsch kind once popular several decades ago. Prime examples are the **Enchanted Forest** (☎ 250-837-9477), 32km west of Revelstoke and **Three Valley Gap Ghost Town** (☎ 250-837-2109), 19km west. The former has numerous fairies and other figures scattered around a forest while the latter combines historical buildings, a stage show, a motel and more in a large complex. At either place your fudge cravings will be amply met.

Places to Stay
South of Revelstoke, on Hwy 23, you can camp at *Blanket Creek Provincial Park* (☎825-3500) for $9.50. It has running water

but no showers. Nearby **Martha Creek Provincial Park** has similar facilities.

There are many private campgrounds east and west of Revelstoke along the Trans Canada Hwy. **Canyon Hot Springs** (☎ 250-837-2420), 35km east, has full facilities including showers, toilets and a grocery store. Sites cost $18, cabins from $82.

Budgeters should call the **Smokey Bear Hostel** (☎ 250-837-9573) for directions to this casual place close to outdoor activities which costs $15 a person. In town, **Daniel's Guest House** (☎ 250-837-5530, 313 1st St E) is a 100-year-old three-storey house with dorm rooms at $15 and private rooms ($30) available as well. The immaculate HI **Revelstoke Traveller's Hostel and Guest House** (☎ 250-837-4050, fax 250-837-5600, 400 2nd St W) has free Internet access, bike rentals, several kitchens and much more. It's $15 a night in dorms or $23/30 a single/double. It has a ski package in winter for only $19.

The **Cat Powder Ski Lodge** (☎ 250-837-5151, ☎ 1-800-991-4455, 1601 3rd St W) has ski and fishing packages and a restaurant. Rooms start at $48/53.

Getting There & Away

The Greyhound Bus Depot (☎ 250-837-5874) is west of town at 1899 Fraser Drive, just off the Trans Canada Hwy.

GLACIER NATIONAL PARK

In the Columbia Mountains, about halfway between Revelstoke and Golden, lies this 1350 sq km park containing more than 430 glaciers. If you think the other mountain parks have been wet then you'll like this place. It only rains here twice a week – once for three days and then again for four. It's the same in winter; it snows nearly every day. The annual snowfall can be as much as 23m. Because of the sheer mountain slopes, this is one of the world's most active avalanche areas. For this reason skiing, caving and mountaineering are closely regulated; you must register with the park warden. Around Rogers Pass you'll notice the many snowsheds protecting the highway. With the nar-

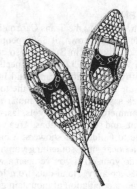

Snowshoes are handy in Glacier National Park.

row road twisting up to 1330m, this is a dangerous area, sometimes called Death Strip – an unexpected avalanche can wipe a car right off the road. Still, the area is carefully controlled, and sometimes snows are brought tumbling down with artillery before they fall by themselves.

At the east side of the park is the dividing line between Pacific Standard and Mountain Standard time zones.

At Rogers Pass there's an information centre (☎ 250-814-5233), open daily from 8 am to 8 pm in summer; 7 am to 5 pm other times. The centre has films on the park and in summer organises guided walks. Displays document the railway's efforts to conquer the pass and vice-versa. There's a 24 hour cafeteria and a service station next door.

Not far from here are the park's only two campgrounds: **Illecillewaet River** and **Loop Brook** both have running water and flush toilets and charge $14 a night per site.

To stop and use any of the facilities in this and Mt Revelstoke National Park you need a day-pass costing $4/2 for adults/ children. Information on both parks is available from Parks Canada in Revelstoke (☎ 250-837-7500) or the visitors centre. **Footloose in the Columbias** is an excellent free guide from Parks Canada to hiking in both parks.

BRITISH COLUMBIA

GOLDEN

As you travel along the Trans Canada Hwy from Alberta, this town of 3800 people is the first of any size in BC. It's also at the junction with Hwy 95 which connects the town with Radium Hot Springs and Invermere to the south. Despite what the tourist brochures say, Golden is not much more than a commercial strip of motels, fast-food restaurants and service stations. Area workers come to Golden for showers, a bite to eat and a booze-up – something you might want to do yourself if you've been a while in the backcountry. Hand-outs from locals also attract a population of mountain goats.

The Visitor Info Centre (☎ 250-344-7125, fax 250-344-6688, ☎ 1-800-622-4653), 500 10th Ave, is open from 9 am to 7 pm daily in July and August; 9.30 am to 4 pm weekdays other times. This and the centre of town are 2km south of the highway. *Golden Municipal Campground (☎ 250-344-5412, 1407 South 9th St)* has most facilities including showers (but no laundry) and sites costing $11. *Station Avenue Backpackers Hostel (☎ 250-344-5071, 518 Station Ave)* is a casual place that charges $15 a person. One of scores of neighbouring motels, the *Golden Super 8 Motel (☎ 250-344-0888, ☎ 1-800-800-8000, 1047 Trans Canada Hwy)* serves free breakfast and has nice rooms from $50.

Golden is the centre for whitewater rafting trips on the turbulent Kicking Horse River. These trips are among the roughest with lots of class-three and four rapids. One of many operators, Wet 'n' Wild (☎ 250-344-6546, ☎ 1-800-668-9119) has exciting half ($52) and full day trips and more importantly, quality staff on board.

Wildlife-observing float tours of the major Columbia Valley wetlands are offered by Kinbasket Adventures (☎ 250-344-6012) for $30/15 for adults/children.

Heli-Skiing & Hiking

South of Golden, in the Purcell Mountains, is the world's centre for helicopter skiing – in districts such as the Gothics, Caribous and, perhaps best known, the Bugaboos. The last named is a region of 1500 sq km of rugged, remote mountains accessible only by helicopter during the winter months. This dangerous, thrilling sport attracts rich visitors from around the world each winter and spring.

The skiing is superb but a portion of the appeal is the danger. Avalanches are not uncommon, tumbling snows claim lives on a regular, though not frequent, basis – just often enough to give the run down that extra kick.

Canadian Mountain Holidays (CMH; ☎ 403-762-7100, ☎ 1-800-661-0252), 217 Bear St in Banff, AB, specialises in four to 10-day heli-skiing trips to some of the best and most remote areas in the BC mountain ranges. These superb trips are in the $5000 range. RK Heli-Ski (☎ 403-762-3771, ☎ 1-800-661-6060) has one-day trips from $510 as well as longer packages. In Golden, Purcell Heli-Skiing (☎ 250-344-5410, ☎ 1-877-435-4754) has many programs including three days of heli-skiing from $1800.

During summer months you can visit some of the area lodges and enjoy hiking. Mountaineers, too, come from around the world to test their skills on the sheer rock faces and granite pinnacles in Bugaboo Glacier Provincial Park (☎ 250-422-4200).

YOHO NATIONAL PARK

Yoho National Park in the BC Rockies, adjacent to the Alberta border and Banff National Park to the east and Kootenay National Park to the south, offers mountain peaks, river valleys, glacial lakes and beautiful meadows – a bit of everything. Yoho is not as busy as Banff and has campground vacancies when Banff is full. A possible drawback is the often wet or cloudy days. Still, Yoho is more accessible and the weather better (not saying much) than at Glacier. The name is a Cree word expressing astonishment or wonder. The rushing Kicking Horse River flows through the park.

Field

Very small Field, lying in the middle of the park, is the first town in BC as you head west along the Trans-Canada Hwy (which follows the Kicking Horse River). Many of

Iron Link – an Engineering Marvel

British Columbia had an almost separate existence from the rest of Canada until 1885 when the Canadian Pacific Railway across the Rockies was completed. These rails for the first time linked the disparate territories of the west and east and were instrumental in cementing the unity of the nation.

Running the rails through the Rockies was an enormous challenge that was accomplished by the labour of thousands of immigrant workers who endured harsh conditions to complete the dangerous work. Hundreds were killed by disease and accident. Among the challenges they faced were the horrific avalanches of Rogers Pass which swept away men and trains like toys. Eventually huge tunnels and snow sheds were laboriously constructed to protect the trains.

East of Field, the gradients were so steep that any braking problem caused trains to run away down the hill where they would eventually fly off the tracks with terrible loss of life. To solve this problem, two huge spiralling tunnels were built inside the granite mountains so that the grades were cut in half to a much more manageable 2.2%. These remain in use and are an internationally recognised engineering marvel.

Along with the trains, Canadian Pacific built grand hotels in Calgary, Banff, Lake Louise, Vancouver and elsewhere to encourage tourists and business travellers to ride the line and explore the region. The line was completed on 7 November 1885 and carried passengers for over 100 years until government stinginess cut VIA Rail trains. Today it is still traversed by Canadian Pacific Railway freight trains and the very occasional Rocky Mountaineer Railtours cruise train. West from Calgary, much of the route is paralleled by the Trans Canada Hwy (Hwy 1).

There are three excellent places to learn about the history of this rail line in BC.

A lookout from the Trans Canada Hwy 8km east of Field gives a good vantage of the lower of the two spiral tunnels. It has good explanatory displays.

A museum area inside the Rogers Pass Visitor's Centre in Glacier National Park shows the hazards of avalanches. The free publication *Snow War* details the railway's efforts to beat the winter. See Glacier National Park in this chapter for details.

The railway museum in Revelstoke documents the history of the entire Canadian Pacific Railway line through the mountains. See Revelstoke in this chapter for details

The railway played a pivotal role in unifying Canada.

its buildings date from the early days of the railways.

The park information centre (☎ 250-343-6783) is open from 9 am to 7 pm in summer, to 4 pm the rest of the year. BC Tourism and Alberta Tourism both have desks here in summer.

The free *Backcountry Guide* is an excellent resource for exploring the park.

In town, the Siding General Store, open daily, is good for supplies and booze if you're going to stay in the park. It also has a pleasant little café with home-made food.

Lake O'Hara

Nestled high in the mountains this somewhat exclusive beauty spot more than lives up to its exalted reputation. It's definitely worth the

sizable hassle to reach for the excellent series of walking trails in what is in effect a miniaturisation of the Rockies. Compact wooded hillsides, alpine meadows, snow-covered passes, mountain vistas and glaciers are all concentrated around the stunning lake. Day and half-day hikes, most fairly rigorous, make it all accessible. A simple day trip is well worthwhile, but overnighting makes hiking more trails possible. The very fine Alpine circuit trail (12km) offers a bit of everything.

To reach the lake, you can either walk 13km from the parking area or take a bus ($12) which runs daily from 19 June to 30 September. The bus leaves from the Lake O'Hara parking lot, 15km east of Field on the Trans Canada Hwy. Places on the bus are very limited as are permits for the very popular backcountry *camping* ($6). You may reserve for both up to three months in advance of your visit by calling ☎ 250-343-6433 from 8 am to 4 pm weekdays 20 March to 30 September. The reservation fee is $10 and given the popularity of Lake O'Hara, reservations are basically mandatory. However, if you don't have advance reservations, six day-use places and three to five camp sites are obtainable by showing up in person at the park information centre in Field the day *before* you want to go. In high season there's often a line long before the doors open at 9 am. The area around Lake O'Hara is usually snow-covered or very muddy until mid-July.

Hiking & Other Activities

Near Field is the turn-off for **Takakkaw Falls** – at 254m, one of the highest waterfalls in Canada. From here, **Iceline**, a 20km hiking loop, passes many glaciers.

The beautiful green **Emerald Lake**, 10km off the Trans Canada Hwy, has a flat circular walking trail with other trails radiating from it and the water in the lake is just warm enough for a quick swim in late summer.

The **Burgess Shale World Heritage Site** protects the amazing Cambrian age fossil beds on Mt Stephen and Mt Field. These 515 million-year-old fossils preserve the remains of marine creatures that are some of the earliest forms of life on earth. The Royal Tyrrell

Museum in Drumheller, AB, has a major display on these finds. The only way to see this area is by guided hikes. Call ☎ 250-343-6006, ☎ 1-800-343-3006 for information on these strenuous jaunts.

Also east of Field by the Trans Canada Hwy are the famous spiral tunnels, the feats of engineering that enable Canadian Pacific trains to navigate the challenging Kicking Horse Pass.

Places to Stay

Yoho has five campgrounds. Only the *Kicking Horse* campground at $17 has showers. This makes it the most popular. *Chancellor Peak* ($12) has the river and good views. Other campgrounds are the very wooded *Hoodoo Creek* ($14), quiet *Monarch* ($12) and *Takakkaw Falls* ($12). The last named, a five minute walk from parking, is especially beautiful and tents only.

Field has several B&Bs and a lodge; the Info Centre has details. The HI *Whiskey Jack Hostel (☎ 403-762-4122, fax 403-762-3441)*, 15km off the Trans Canada Hwy on Yoho Valley Rd just before the Takakkaw Falls campground, is open June to September and has 27 beds. Nearby and recommended is the pleasantly rustic *Cathedral Mountain Lodge & Chalets (☎ 250-343-6442)* at the base of Cathedral Mountain, from $110 a single or double.

Getting There & Away

Greyhound buses stop at Field.

KOOTENAY NATIONAL PARK

Kootenay National Park is solely in BC but is adjacent to Banff National Park and runs south from Yoho National Park. Hwy 93 (the Banff-Windermere Parkway) runs down the centre and is really the only road in the park. From the northern entrance at Vermillion Pass to Radium Hot Springs at the park's southern end there are campgrounds, points of interest, hiking trails and views of the valley along the Kootenay River.

Kootenay has a more moderate climate than the other Rocky Mountain parks and in the southern regions especially, summers can

be hot and dry. It's the only national park in Canada to contain both glaciers and cactuses.

The Kootenay Park Information Centre (☎ 250-347-9505, out of season ☎ 250-347-9615), 3km from Radium at the hot springs pools, is the main Parks Canada facility. It's open from 9 am to 5 pm (until 7 pm in summer) daily mid-May to September. The Vermillion Crossing Visitor Centre (no phone), 8km south of the pass, is open from 11 am to 6 pm daily April to mid-October.

Stop at **Marble Canyon** for the 30 minute walk – it is a real adrenaline-rush. The trail follows the rushing Tokumm Creek, criss-crossing it frequently on small wooden bridges with longer and longer drops below as you head up to the waterfall. Some 2km farther south there is a short, easy trail through forest to ochre pools known as the **Paint Pots**. For years, first the Kootenay people and then European settlers collected this orange and red-coloured earth to use as a colouring agent.

At the southern edge of the park where Hwy 93 joins Hwy 95, is **Radium Hot Springs**, with an odd blend of new and old, garish and tasteful architecture. The Visitor Info Centre (☎ 250-347-9331, fax 250-347-9127), 7585 Main St W, is open May to October. The hot springs, 3km north of the town, are always worth a visit, though they can be busy in summer when they're open daily from 9 am to 9 pm. Admission varies by season.

Places to Stay

The **Marble Canyon Campground**, across the road from the information centre, is good, but basic with no electricity or showers; it does have toilets and cold running water and costs $13. **McLeod Meadows Campground**, in the park's south, is similar. **Redstreak Campground**, near the West Gate Information Centre, is fully serviced including showers and costs from $16.

If you're looking for a roof over your head, Radium Hot Springs has lots of motels, many in alpine style. Typical is the **Motel Tyrol** (☎ 250-347-9402, ☎ 1-888-881-1188) on Hwy 93, which has a heated pool, sauna and balconies. Rooms start at $49.

MT ASSINIBOINE PROVINCIAL PARK

Between Kootenay and Banff national parks is this lesser known, 39 sq km provincial park, part of the Rockies World Heritage designated area. The craggy summits of Mt Assiniboine (3618m), often referred to as Canada's Matterhorn, and its near neighbours are a magnet for climbers. The park also offers hiking and all the usual activities.

From Hwy 93 two hiking trails start from near the highway at Vermillion Crossing in Kootenay National Park. From Banff National Park in Alberta a gravel road takes you close to the park through the ski resort of Sunshine Village. Another road leads from Spray Reservoir south of Canmore to the trailhead near Shark Mountain. The trails all meet at Lake Magog where there is the park headquarters (☎ 250-422-4200), a **campground**, some **cabins** and the commercially operated **Mt Assiniboine Lodge** (☎ 403-678-2883 in Banff). There's wilderness camping in other parts of the park.

RADIUM HOT SPRINGS TO CRANBROOK

South from Radium Hot Springs, Hwy 93/95 follows the Columbia River between the Purcell and Rocky mountains until the road splits shortly before Wasa. From there Hwy 95 heads south-west to Kimberley and Cranbrook, while Hwy 93 goes south-east to Fort Steele.

Invermere, 14km south of Radium, is a small, local resort town, on the shores of Windermere Lake. The Visitor Info Centre (☎ 250-342-6316, fax 250-342-3261) on the corner of 5A St and 7th Ave is open daily May to September.

Mt Panorama, in the Purcell Mountains 18km south-west of Invermere, is BC's second highest vertical rise ski resort (after Whistler/Blackcomb). Mt Panorama (☎ 250-342-6941) has a spectacular setting and almost two-thirds of the downhill runs are ranked intermediate. **Fairmont Hot Springs** is another resort town with the hot springs as its focus. A single swim costs $5. It gets very crowded on weekends and public holidays

and caters to families. At Skookumchuk, shortly before Wasa, a gravel road provides access eastward to **Top of the World Provincial Park** (☎ 250-422-4200), where there are hiking trails and wilderness camping.

At 1113m, **Kimberley** is one of the highest cities in Canada and the best place to stop for sustenance in the East Kootenays. Before 1973, Kimberley looked like what it is – a small mountain mining town – but was revamped to look like a Bavarian alpine village. Most of the downtown section, the Platzl, was transformed and with enough detail to make it interesting. A huge **cuckoo clock** and several good restaurants are in this area. Accommodation can also be found here or around the outskirts. A restored mining train toodles 2.5km around town. The Julyfest in Kimberley is a week of dancing, parades and lots of beer. The Visitor Info Centre (☎ 250-427-3666, fax 250-427-5378), 350 Ross St, is open year-round.

To the north-west, **Purcell Wilderness Conservancy** has hiking trails, fishing and wilderness camping; access is by a gravel road off Hwy 95A.

The heritage park of **Fort Steele** (☎ 250-426-7352), 20km south-east of Wasa on Hwy 93, is a re-creation of an East Kootenay town in the late 1800s. Fort Steele was the first Northwest Mounted Police (later to become the RCMP) outpost in western Canada and arose as a commercial, social and administrative centre when major silver and lead discoveries were made in 1892. It was named after Sam Steele who was the first commander of the fort. Its fortunes turned when, in 1898, the BC Southern Railway bypassed it in favour of Cranbrook. Fort Steele has more than 60 restored and reconstructed homes and buildings. The Fort is open from 9.30 am to dusk daily. Admission in summer is $5.50/3.25 for adults/children.

CRANBROOK & AROUND

Sitting at the base of the Rocky Mountains, Cranbrook, with a population of 17,000, is about 30km south-east of Kimberley on the Crowsnest Hwy. The Visitor Info Centre (☎ 250-426-5914, fax 250-426-3873), 2279 Cranbrook St North, is open year-round. There's not a lot to see in the town itself, but it is located where you can enjoy many outdoor activities on the nearby lakes and mountains.

The municipal *campground* (☎ 250-426-2162, cnr 14th Ave & 1st St South) is central, with full facilities, and charges $15. More pleasant surroundings (without showers) can be found at Jim Smith Lake (☎ 250-422-4200) and Moyie Lake provincial parks south-west of town. Many motels line the highway at the northern end of town, and there are a few hotels downtown. *Almo Court Motel* (☎ 250-426-3213, 316 2nd St), close to downtown, has well equipped rooms from $36/39 for singles/doubles.

Fernie, sitting between the high peaks of Sisters Mountain and Mount Fernie, had a devastating fire in 1908 which resulted in a brick and stone building code. These fine late 19th/early 20th century buildings give the town an appearance unique in the East Kootenays. The HI *Raging Elk Hostel* (☎ 250-423-6811, fax 250-423-6812, raginelk@elkvalley .net) is central and has ski packages. Beds cost $16/20 for members/nonmembers.

Near the US border, **Creston** is the centre of a green, fruit-growing district. Just off Canyon, the main street, at 11th Ave, take a look at the murals depicting the region's character. West of town along the highway, the wetlands of the Creston Valley Wildlife Centre are excellent for birding. Farther out is the Kootenay Pass Summit with a provincial park and campground. Grizzlies and caribou frequent the area.

NELSON & AROUND

Nelson, 43km north-west of Castlegar, at the junction of Hwy 6 and Hwy 3A, is beautifully situated on the shore of Kootenay Lake surrounded by the Selkirk Mountains. The very picturesque town of 9600, nestled in the hillside, with over 350 carefully preserved and restored late 19th/early 20th century buildings, is the perfect base for exploring the region. Its friendly, laid-back character and location make it the heart of the Koote-

nays. The large, active artists' colony adds a cultural and alternative flavour.

Baker and Vernon Sts are the two main downtown thoroughfares. Baker St has many shops and restaurants, while Vernon St has government buildings including city hall, the courthouse and the post office. In summer the Visitor Info Centre (☎ 250-352-3433, fax 250-352-6355), 225 Hall St, is open from 8.30 am to 7 pm weekdays, 10 am to 6 pm weekends from May to October (closed weekends the rest of the year). The post office is at 514 Vernon St. The Greyhound Bus Depot (☎ 250-352-3939), 1112 Lakeside Drive, is in the Chacko Mika Mall.

In town there's a walking trail through **Lakeside Park**, or, using the *Heritage Walking Tour* leaflet from the Visitor Info Centre, you can take a look around the town's historical buildings. From the top of **Gyro Park** there are good views. **Streetcar No 23**, one of the town's originals, has been restored and now follows a track beside the lake from the bridge near Lakeside Park to the wharf at the bottom of Hall St.

Excellent outdoor possibilities abound. Practically in town is the climb to **Pulpit Rock** affording fine views. There is swimming, hiking, fishing and camping at **Kokanee Creek Provincial Park** (☎ 250-825-3500 for all parks in the region) north of town, and an **old growth forest** off the Kokanee Creek Road. A free ferry runs between Balfour and Kootenay Bay across scenic Kootenay Lake and the road then travels south along the lake. At **Ainsworth Hot Springs** on Hwy 31 not only is there the usual pool to soak in but also hot-water-filled caves. Good exploratory tours are offered at **Cody Caves** 4km farther north. Hiking and backcountry camping is superb in lake-filled **Kokanee Glacier Provincial Park**. The two hour hike to Kokanee Lake is wonderful and can be continued to the glacier.

In quiet and attractive **Kaslo** with many Victorian-style buildings visit the 1898 sternwheeler SS *Moyie* on Kootenay Lake and ask the locals how to find nearby Fletcher's Falls. These secluded, impressive falls are just a short drive or walk off

the main road. Near Silverton, Sandon is a mining **ghost town**. In **New Denver** is a memorial centre (☎ 250-358-7288) which commemorates the displacement of thousands of Japanese-Canadians who were moved to internment camps in the area during WWII. Admission is $4/2.

In winter the attraction of this area is skiing. You can go downhill at **Morning Mountain**, north-west of town, off Hwy 3A, or at **Whitewater Ski Area** (☎ 250-354-4944, ☎ 1-800-666-9420), 19km south-east, off Hwy 6. The latter also has well developed cross-country skiing; for wilderness skiing head for Kokanee Glacier.

Places to Stay & Eat

In Nelson, convenient camping is available at the downtown *City Tourist Park* (☎ 250-352-9031, cnr High & Willow Sts) for $13. The central HI *Dancing Bear Inn* (☎ 250-352-7573, fax 250-352-9818, dbear@insidenet.com, 171 Baker St) is a very thoughtfully renovated hostel that's comfortable, immaculate and offers kitchen and laundry facilities. Prices are $17/20 for members/nonmembers and there are family rooms and doubles ($34).

For B&Bs ask at the Visitor Info Centre or contact Lake City B&B Registry (☎ 250-352-5253), which has rooms starting at $40/55 for singles/doubles. There are many motels along the highway at the northern end of town, and some hotels downtown. The *Heritage Inn* (☎ 250-352-5331, 422 Vernon St) offers free breakfast and has a pub, restaurant and night club. Rooms are from $54/59.

For breakfast don't miss *Mimi's* (☎ 250-352-7113, 702 Vernon St) Belgian waffles or omelettes. The *Book Garden* (☎ 250-352-1812, 556 Josephine St) at Victoria St is a comfortable café with a nice patio.

NAKUSP & AROUND

Quiet Nakusp, sitting on Upper Arrow Lake, is the main town in the valley south of Revelstoke, east of the Okanagan Valley. The dry, picturesque valley follows a chain of lakes between the Monashee and Selkirk mountain ranges. This is a very attractive portion of the

province which benefits from not having the high profile and hence major attention of some of the better-known districts. The Nakusp Visitor Info Centre (☎ 250-265-4234, fax 250-265-3808, ☎ 1-800-909-8819), 92 W 6th Ave, is open year-round.

The *McDonald Creek Provincial Park (☎ 250-825-3500)*, 10km south of town on Hwy 6, has camping from $15. The *Selkirk Inn (☎ 250-265-3666, ☎ 1-800-661-8007, 210 6th Ave)* is a moderate place for spending the night at $40/45.

About 12km north-east of Nakusp, off Hwy 23, are the tranquil **Nakusp Hot Springs** (☎ 250-265-4528). They're open daily year-round and have a cramped campground with full facilities including showers for $14. Ask at the Info Centre about trails to undeveloped hot springs in the woods.

South-west of Nakusp, Hwy 6 heads to Vernon in the Okanagan Valley, going over the 1189m Monashee Pass. Near Vernon, the road goes through beautiful country scenery of small farms and wooded hills. There are campgrounds and a few small provincial parks along this route.

South-east of Nakusp, Hwy 6 heads to Castlegar and Nelson, through the Slocan Valley past rugged **Valhalla Provincial Park** with hiking trails and wilderness camping mainly accessed by boat; canoes can be rented. **Slocan Lake** provides excellent canoeing and the Slocan River, from the town of Slocan south to the Kootenay River, has Grade 3 rapids in its upper sections for the whitewater canoeist and less-demanding water farther down. *Valhalla Lodge & Tipi Retreat (☎ 250-365-3226)* at Slocan Lake has teepees for rent at $98 for two people for two nights including a boat trip to the site, a canoe, communal kitchen and a sauna. More conventional rooms cost $59 a night.

North, Highway 23 runs along pretty Upper Arrow Lake to the free ferry at Galena Bay to connect with Revelstoke.

CASTLEGAR

Castlegar, a sprawling town with a population of 7200, sits on the Kootenay River at the southern end of Lower Arrow Lake, at the junction of Hwys 3 and 3A. Recent development has robbed the town of any charm or character it may once have had; stop instead in Nelson where the more limited growth has been achieved with a sense of environmental harmony and history. The Visitor Info Centre (☎ 250-365-6313, fax 250-365-5778), 1995 6th Ave at 20th St, is open year-round. The Greyhound Bus Depot (☎ 250-365-7744) is at 365 Columbia Ave.

This is an area where many members of the Russian Christian pacifist sect, the Doukhobors, settled at the beginning of the 1900s. Borscht is available at every restaurant. The reconstructed **Doukhobor Historic Village** (☎ 250-365-6622) on the east side of the Columbia River off Highway 3 is little more than a couple of buildings and the small museum can be given a miss. Next door there is a restaurant serving Doukhobor specialities.

Seventeen kilometres north-west of Castlegar, on Lower Arrow Lake, is the 2.25 sq km **Syringa Creek Provincial Park** (☎ 250-825-3500), open from April to October. It has hiking, fishing, swimming, sailing and beaches. The *campground* is open May to October with sites for $13.

TRAIL & AROUND

Trail is an industrial town 27km south-west of Castlegar, at the junction of the Crowsnest Hwy and Hwy 3A. It's home to Cominco, the world's largest smelter of silver, zinc and lead, whose enormous mishmash of buildings dominates the skyline. Those, together with the houses squeezed along the cliffs by the Columbia River, give the town a strikingly different character.

The Visitor Info Centre (☎ 250-368-3144, ☎ 250-368-6427), 843 Rossland Ave, is open from 9 am to 5 pm daily in summer, and weekends only other times. The Greyhound Bus Depot (☎ 250-368-8400), right downtown, is at 1355 Bay St.

There are free tours of the **Cominco smelter** which can be booked through the Visitor Info Centre. The many Italian migrants who came here at the end of the

1800s to work in the mines have left their mark and their descendants in Trail.

There are several provincial parks close by. Try **Nancy Greene Provincial Park**, south-west; or **Champion Lakes Provincial Park**, north-west of Trail, off Hwy 23. Both have hiking, swimming, fishing and camp sites. The *Villagers Inn* (☎ *250-367-7664, 1867 Highway Drive)* has a restaurant and basic rooms from $42/49.

South-west, the once ore-rich mines of **Rossland** that fed Trail can be seen. There is a small mining museum, gold-mine tours in the ancient volcano, a tearoom and the tourist office in town.

Farther west, the lovely **Christina Lake** is a good place to stay for a day or two, especially if you are camping, and the nearby small town of **Grand Forks** is known for borscht and sunshine. Russian food is offered through the area and campgrounds and motels can be easily found along Hwy 3.

North-East British Columbia

North-east BC is a largely undeveloped, sparsely populated region dominated by the Rocky Mountains to the west and south, and by the Interior Plain to the north and east.

Two major highways connect this region with other parts of the country: east-west the Yellowhead Hwy (Hwy 16) runs between the Alberta border and Prince Rupert in the Pacific Northwest; Hwy 97 connects the south of the province with Dawson Creek where it becomes part of the Alaska Hwy and heads north-west toward the Yukon. The two highways meet at Prince George, the largest town in the region. The VIA Rail line follows the Yellowhead Hwy.

Like the south-east corner of the province, the area around Dawson Creek is on Mountain Standard Time.

PRINCE GEORGE
Prince George was established as Fort George by Simon Fraser for the North West

Company in 1807. Now known as 'The Gateway to the North', it is not an interesting or attractive town but does serve as a useful crossroads point.

The town of 75,000 people sprawls over a large area. To serve the through traffic there are dozens of motels and hotels. Pulp and paper is an important industry whose recent hard times have proved difficult for the town. The university, with a speciality in Native Indian affairs, has helped to diversify the city.

Orientation & Information
Hwy 97 from Cache Creek cuts through the centre of town on its way north to Dawson Creek (406km) and the Alaska Hwy. Hwy 97 between Cache Creek and Prince George is also known as the Cariboo Hwy and is part of the Goldrush Trail, which begins north of Hope. The Yellowhead Hwy (Hwy 16) runs east-west through town: westward is the long, winding route to Prince Rupert (734km); eastward, it goes through Jasper (377km) to Edmonton. It's 781km to Vancouver.

The downtown area is small, with little character. The main roads running east-west are 2nd, 3rd and 4th Aves, parallel to the train tracks. The main north-south thoroughfare is Victoria St, which also forms part of the Yellowhead Hwy; Patricia Blvd, which becomes 15th Ave, is also a major street.

The Visitor Info Centre (☎ 250-562-3700, fax 250-563-3584, ☎ 1-800-668-7646), 1198 Victoria St, on the corner of Patricia Blvd, is open from 8.30 am to 5 pm daily (closed Sunday outside of summer). A second Info Centre (☎ 250-563-5493) sits 4km south-west of downtown at the junction of Hwy 97 and the Yellowhead Hwy (Hwy 16) and operates daily during summer.

The main post office (☎ 250-561-5184) is at 1323 5th Ave on the corner of Quebec St. Mosquito Books (☎ 250-563-6495), 1600 15th Ave, and Books & Company (☎ 250-563-6637), 1685 3rd Ave, both have a good selection of travel guides and maps. There's a coin laundry at 231 George St near the corner of 2nd Ave. It's open from 7 am to 7 pm daily. There is a vast shopping area at the intersection of Victoria and Patricia Sts.

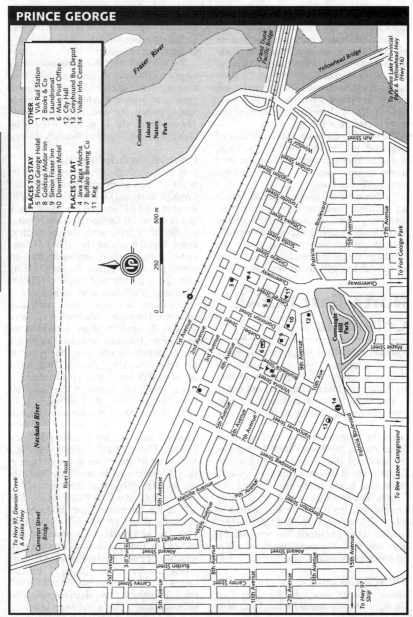

PRINCE GEORGE

PLACES TO STAY
5 Prince George Hotel
8 Goldcap Motor Inn
9 Simon Fraser Inn
10 Downtown Motel

PLACES TO EAT
7 Java Jigga Mocha
7 Buffalo Brewing Co
11 Keg

OTHER
1 VIA Rail Station
2 Books & Co
3 Laundromat
6 Main Post Office
12 City Hall
13 Greyhound Bus Depot
14 Visitor Info Centre

Things to See & Do

The **Fraser-Fort George Regional Museum** (☎ 250-562-1612) in Fort George Park, south-east of the downtown area on the corner of 20th Ave and Queensway, is a small museum with a good section on pioneers and European settlement and development. There are a few Carrier, Cree and Kwakiutl artefacts and a hands-on section geared to kids. Open from 10 am to 5 pm daily May to September; noon to 5 pm Tuesday to Sunday other times. Admission is $4.25/2.25 adults/children.

There are many parks in Prince George. One close to the downtown area is **Cottonwood Island Nature Park**, north between the railway tracks and the river. **Northwood, Inc**, a wood products company, runs free tours through the Visitor Info Centre. Canadian Forest Products has an all-day tour (☎ 250-561-3947) on which you go into the woods to see the complete pulp and timber production process. These tours are a great way to see what all the stink is about – literally. The small **Prince George Railway and Forestry Museum** (☎ 250-563-7351) is just that. Located in Cottonwood Island Nature Park, it's open May to September.

Around Prince George there are dozens of lakes and rivers with good fishing. Some have camp sites; most have boats for hire. Pick up the booklet *Prince George & Area Hiking Guide* from the Visitor Info Centre. **Hart Highlands** (☎ 250-962-8006), Winslow Drive, is the closest downhill ski area being within the city limits. There's also good skiing at **Mt Tabor** (☎ 250-963-7542), about 25km east of town. Cross-country skiing is available close to downtown on **Cottonwood Island** or farther out at **Eskers Provincial Park** north-west of town.

Places to Stay

Blue Spruce Campground (☎ 250-964-7272) is about 6km south-west of town, off the Yellowhead Hwy. It has full facilities and sites from $15 for two people. *Bee Lazee Campground* (☎ 250-963-7263), 15km south on Hwy 97, has full facilities including free hot showers, pool and laundry, with sites from $13. And as the name may suggest, it has a honey farm.

B&Bs The Visitor Info Centre has lists of B&Bs. Readers recommend *Adrienne's B&B* (☎ 250-561-1662, 1467 Fraser Crescent) off 15th Ave, which is reasonably close to the downtown area. Singles/doubles are $40/50. Another favourite is *Mead Manor B&B* (☎ 250-964-8436, 4127 Baker Rd) with rooms for $50/60.

Hotels The basic *Prince George Hotel* (☎ 250-564-7211, 487 George St) has singles/doubles for $46/60. The *Simon Fraser Inn* (☎ 250-562-3181, ☎ 1-800-292-8333, 600 Quebec St) has rooms from $60, which includes coffee. It has a bar downstairs with off-track betting and free parking.

Motels The *Downtown Motel* (☎ 250-563-9241, ☎ 1-800-663-5729, 650 Dominion St) has basic rooms from $40/42. The *Goldcap Motor Inn* (☎ 250-563-0666, ☎ 1-800-663-8239, 1458 7th Ave) is popular with business travellers. Rooms cost $69/76. Out on the Hwy 97 strip, *Grama's Inn* (☎ 250-563-7174, 901 Central St) off Hwy 97 is friendly (although there's no sign of Grama), has a coffee shop and charges from $45/50.

Places to Eat

There are several places downtown that you can walk to. Recommended is *Java Jigga Mocha* (cnr George St & 3rd Ave), which serves fruit juices, varieties of coffee from $1 and soups from $3 as well as delicious cakes. There are tables outside and it also sells second-hand books.

Fast-food restaurants line Victoria St. The busy *White Spot* (820 Victoria St) has pastas for $8 and also serves sandwiches and burgers. The *Buffalo Brewing Co* (611 Brunswick St) is heaven for those weary of dreary Canadian lager. Pizza and burgers average $8. For dinner try the popular *Keg* (☎ 250-563-1768, 582 George St) on the corner of 6th Ave, which serves steak dishes from $17 and seafood from $18.

Getting There & Away

Air Prince George airport (☎ 250-963-2405) is on Airport Rd off Hwy 97, 8km south-east from downtown. Air BC (☎ 250-561-2905) and Canadian Regional (☎ 250-563-0521) both serve Calgary and Vancouver. The Airporter bus (☎ 250-563-2220) serves the hotels and motels and charges $8.

Bus The Greyhound Bus Depot (☎ 250-564-5454) is at 1566 12th Ave, near the junction of Victoria St and Patricia Blvd. There are buses to Prince Rupert (12½ hours, $90), Dawson Creek (six hours, $50), Whitehorse (28 hours, $211), Jasper (five hours, $47), Kamloops (eight hours, $65) and Vancouver (12½ hours, $90).

Train The VIA Rail station (☎ 1-800-561-8630) is at 1300 1st Ave near the top of Quebec St. The *Skeena* runs three times a week west to Prince Rupert (12 hours) and another three times a week east to Jasper (six hours). The runs are made in daytime for maximum scenic viewing. The BC Rail station (☎ 250-561-4033) is south-east of town, over the Fraser River, at Terminal Blvd, off Hwy 97. The train runs three times a week south to North Vancouver (14 hours).

Getting Around

Prince George Transit (☎ 250-563-0011) operates local buses. The one-way fare in the central zone is $1.50.

PRINCE GEORGE TO SMITHERS

From Prince George the Yellowhead Hwy (Hwy 16) heads west to Smithers, Terrace and Prince Rupert, from where most people pick up ferries either south to Vancouver Island and Washington State or north to Alaska. The road travels through a corridor of forest interspersed with lakes, rivers and farmland. (See also the Prince Rupert to New Hazelton section later in this chapter for details.)

The first settlement of any real size is **Vanderhoof**, mainly a service centre for the area and most noted for its annual international airshow held the fourth weekend in July. East of here, Hwy 27 heads 66km

north to **Fort St James National Historic Site** (☎ 250-996-7191), a former Hudson's Bay Company trading post on the south-eastern shore of Stuart Lake. The nearby provincial parks at Paarens Beach and Sowchea Bay have camp sites (no showers).

The other towns along the highway have the usual run of campgrounds and motels. Burns Lake is the centre of the lakes district, a canoeing and recreation area. You can get a taste of the wilderness by heading north to **Babine Lake**. There are hiking trails in **Red Bluff Provincial Park**.

Smithers, in the pretty Bulkley Valley, is another centre for outdoor activity. There's hiking, climbing and skiing on Hudson Bay Mt, 24km south of the junction with the Yellowhead Hwy, and whitewater rafting and canoeing on the Bulkley River. The Visitor Info Centre (☎ 250-847-9854, fax 250-847-3337), 1425 Main St, is open from 9 am to 6 pm daily in summer; 9 am to 4 pm weekdays other times. Motels line the highway. If the weather is good the road toward Terrace provides spectacular scenery.

PRINCE GEORGE TO DAWSON CREEK

As you travel north from Prince George the mountains and forests give way to gentle rolling hills and farmland, until near Dawson Creek the landscape resembles more the prairies of Alberta. For the first 150km the road passes **Summit, Bear** and **MacLeod** lakes with provincial parks and camping along the way. North of MacLeod Lake, Hwy 39 heads north to Mackenzie which sits on the southern shores of the immense **Williston Lake**. Nearby there is downhill and cross-country skiing at **Powder King Ski Resort** (☎ 250-997-6323) on Azu Mountain.

From **Chetwynd** you can take Hwy 29 north past Hudson's Hope (a 20 minute drive from the eastern arm of Williston Lake) to join the Alaska Hwy north of Fort St John.

DAWSON CREEK

Dawson Creek, a city of 11,100 people, 412km north of Prince George on Hwy 97, is notable as the starting point – 'Mile 0' –

for the Alaska or Alcan (short for Alaska-Canada) Hwy. The Alaska Hwy from Dawson Creek goes via Watson Lake and Whitehorse in the Yukon all the way to Fairbanks in Alaska.

The Dawson Creek Visitor Info Centre (☎ 250-782-9595, fax 250-782-9538), 900 Alaska Ave, can give you the details. It's open daily in summer from 8 am to 8 pm; in winter 9 am to 5 pm weekdays. The *Mile 0 Campground (☎ 250-782-2590)* is actually 2.5km along the Alaska Hwy. It has full facilities and charges from $10. The best place to eat is the *Alaska Café & Pub (10213 10th St)*, downtown near the 'Mile 0' marker. Pasta dishes start at $6. It also has accommodation (☎ 250-782-7998) from $39/45. *Northwinds Lodge (☎ 250-782-9181, ☎ 1-800-665-1759, 632 103rd Ave)* is central, has extensive free parking and rooms from $44/48.

DAWSON CREEK TO THE YUKON
Heading north-west from Dawson Creek, the landscape again changes as the prairies are left behind and the Alaska Hwy crosses the Peace River on its way into the foothills of the Rocky Mountains. Except for Fort St John and Fort Nelson, most of the towns on the highway usually have little more than one or two service stations, campgrounds or lodgings.

Fort St John's main function is as a service centre for the oil and gas industries and the surrounding farms. The Visitor Info Centre (☎ 250-785-6037, fax 250-785-7181) and the Fort St John-North Peace Museum are together at 9323 100th St, the town's main street. **Fort Nelson** has one museum at the western end of town, and shops, restaurants and motels strung out along the highway. At **Mile 244** (393km from Dawson Creek), past Fort Nelson, the Liard Hwy (Hwy 77) heads north to the Northwest Territories, Fort Simpson and Nahanni National Park.

At **Stone Mountain Provincial Park** there are hiking trails with wilderness camping and a *campground* with sites for $9.50. The moose in the park can often be seen eating nonchalantly by the side of the road. The 'stone mountain' in question is Mt St Paul (2127m).

Muncho Lake Provincial Park, 935km north of Dawson Creek, has several lodging and camping areas plus wildlife (mainly goats), swimming in the emerald-green lake, and hiking trails. 'Muncho' means 'big lake' in the Tagish language and at 12km long it's one of the largest natural lakes in the Rockies. This 88,420-hectare park (☎ 250-787-3407) is part of the northernmost section of the Rockies which, ending at Liard River 60km north-west, do not continue northward into the Yukon and Alaska. The mountains which do extend northward, the Mackenzies, are geologically different.

SOUTH OF PRINCE GEORGE
South of Prince George, Hwy 97 follows the Goldrush Trail through the northern reaches of the gold rush district known as Cariboo Country.

Quesnel
Quesnel's setting at the confluence of the Fraser and Quesnel rivers, and the carefully cultivated flowers along the riverfront trails can't disguise the fact that this is first and foremost a logging town. The pulp mills dominate the townscape and the smells coming from them permeate the air. The observation tower at the north end of town looks over the most concentrated industrial area for

---

Barking Up the Right Tree

Between 1858 and 1861 the Cariboo Trail, now Hwy 97, was pushed north from Kamloops to Quesnel. It was lined with ramshackle towns hastily built by gold prospectors from around the world. In 1862 a Cornishman, Billy Barker, hit the jackpot, making $1000 in the first two days of his claim. Soon Barkerville sprang up to become the largest city west of Chicago and north of San Francisco. The big boom was instrumental in British Columbia becoming a crown colony in 1858.

BRITISH COLUMBIA

wood products in North America. However, it's worth stopping at the Visitor Info Centre (☎ 250-992-8716, fax 250-992-9606), 703 Carson Ave, which is open from 8 am to 8 pm daily in summer and 9 am to 4 pm weekdays other times. The area's main attractions are the Alexander Mackenzie Trail and the gold rush trail to Barkerville Historic Park and Bowron Lake Provincial Park.

Barkerville Historic Park

This restored gold rush town (☎ 250-994-3332) is 89km east of Quesnel at the end of Hwy 26.

Today, you can see Barkerville as it was, albeit with a whole lot more fudge for sale than when the miners were here. There are over 100 buildings here including a hotel, stores and a saloon. In the Theatre Royal, dancing shows are staged in a family-friendly manner the miners would have hooted at. The park is open from 8 am to 8 pm daily June to August and admission is $6/4 adults/children. At other times of the year the park is open and free but most of the attractions are closed which may actually make for a more atmospheric visit.

There are three *campgrounds* (☎ 250-398-4414) with sites for $12, and facilities include showers. The *St George Hotel* (☎ 250-994-0008) is inside the park and dates from the 1890s. The rooms are filled with antiques and breakfast is included for rates that start at $120/134. You can also stay at Wells, 8km west of Barkerville, which has a commercial *campground* and several *motels*. There's no bus to Barkerville.

Bowron Lake Provincial Park

There is an excellent circular canoe route in Bowron Lake Provincial Park (☎ 250-398-4414), 30km north-east of Barkerville. A number of lakes, separated by rapids and portages, form a connecting route around the perimeter of the park. The 116km route takes an average of seven to 10 days to complete and no more than 50 individuals are allowed to start the route each day. Canoeists must register at the park registration centre before heading out and pay a fee of $55 for one or

$70 for two before heading out. Mountains in and around the park are about 2000m high. Access to the park is on a gravel road that leaves Hwy 26 just before you get to Barkerville. There are tent sites for $9.50. Attractive *Becker's Lodge* (☎ 250-992-8864, ☎ 1-800-808-4761), made from logs, has rooms (from $46), a restaurant, camping and canoe rentals.

Alexander Mackenzie Trail

Heading north-west from Quesnel, this refurbished route follows ancient trails from the Fraser River west to Bella Coola, on the Pacific Ocean. Alexander Mackenzie made the first recorded crossing of continental North America here in 1793 in his search for a supply route to the Pacific Ocean. His graffiti can still be seen carved in a rock near Bella Coola. This 420km trail winds its way through forest and mountains and is a tough 16-day walk. At least one food drop is required. You can do some of the more accessible segments for a few days, for example, the section through the southern end of Tweedsmuir Provincial Park and day hikes from Quesnel. For detailed trail guides contact Alexander Mackenzie Trail Association, PO Box 425, Station A, Kelowna, V1Y 7P1.

Pacific Northwest

North-west BC is a huge, little-developed, scarcely populated region whose remoteness is one of its main attractions. This largely inaccessible area is one of the last true wilderness regions of North America. Various Native peoples have long inhabited the area and to this day they make up a considerable percentage of the permanent residents. The land is dominated by forest, several mountain ranges, and scores of lakes and swift rivers. The Yellowhead Hwy (Hwy 16) runs east to Prince George; the mostly gravel Cassiar Hwy heads north to the Yukon.

PRINCE RUPERT

After Vancouver, Rupert, as it's called, is the largest city on the BC coast. The town was

begun in 1906 by developer Charles Hays, who saw in the vast harbour the potential for a town to rival Vancouver. Tragedy intervened in the form of the *Titanic*, which Hays unwisely booked passage on (he died) and WWI which stripped the region of young men. The town never developed into the vast metropolis Hays envisioned and instead became a fishing centre for the Pacific Northwest. Its port – nowhere near the size once imagined – handles timber, minerals and grain shipments to Asia. The Asian economic crisis has dealt Rupert a blow not helped by the collapse of fishing.

Once known as the world's halibut capital, it has adopted a new title, the 'City of Rainbows', which is one way of saying that it rains a lot. The area has one of the highest precipitation rates in all of Canada. Despite this, the town's setting can look magnificent and when it's not raining, misty, foggy or under heavy cloud, you'll appreciate it. Surrounded by mountains, sitting at the mouth of the Skeena River, looking out at the fjord-like coastline, the area is ruggedly beautiful.

Prince Rupert is a good starting point for trips to Alaska and the Queen Charlotte Islands. Many people, mainly young, arrive here in summer looking for work; and this town with around 17,000 inhabitants fills its needs quickly. Remember, too, that with the influx of tourists, accommodation in July and August can be difficult to find.

Orientation & Information

Prince Rupert is on Kaien Island and is connected to the mainland by a bridge. The Yellowhead Hwy passes right through the downtown area, becoming McBride St then 2nd Ave which, along with 3rd Ave, forms the downtown core. McBride St divides the city between east and west. Cow Bay is a historic waterfront area of shops and restaurants just north of downtown. The ferry terminal is in Fairview Bay, 3km south-west of the centre of town.

The Visitor Info Centre (☎ 250-624-5637, fax 250-627-8009, ☎ 1-800-667-1994) shares space with the impressive new Museum of Northern BC at 100 1st Ave W.

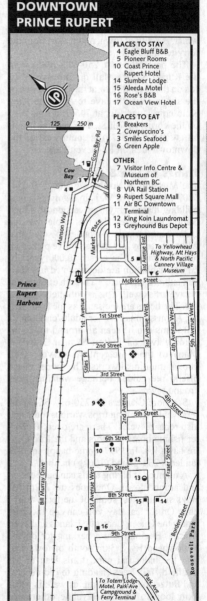

DOWNTOWN PRINCE RUPER

PLACES TO STAY
4 Eagle Bluff B&B
5 Pioneer Rooms
10 Coast Prince Rupert Hotel
14 Slumber Lodge
15 Aleeda Motel
16 Rose's B&B
17 Ocean View Hotel

PLACES TO EAT
1 Breakers
2 Cowpuccino's
3 Smiles Seafood
6 Green Apple

OTHER
7 Visitor Info Centre & Museum of Northern BC
8 VIA Rail Station
9 Rupert Square Mall
11 Air BC Downtown Terminal
12 King Koin Laundromat
13 Greyhound Bus Depot

BRITISH COLUMBIA

It's open from 9 am to 8 pm Monday to Saturday and 9 am to 5 pm in winter. There's a smaller one at Park Ave Campground, which is south of town, about 1km from the ferry terminal.

The post office (☎ 250-627-3085) is in the Rupert Square Mall on 2nd Ave West. It's on the second floor at the back of one of the shops – you'll have to ask. The King Koin coin laundry is at 745 2nd Ave West on the corner of 7th St. The general hospital (☎ 250-624-2171) is south-west of the downtown area, in Roosevelt Park.

Things to See & Do

The **Museum of Northern BC** (☎ 250-624-3207), 100 1st Ave W, is in a gorgeous new building that is a stylised version of a First Nation longhouse. The incredible massive cedar beams exude a wonderful smell that will chase away any moths you've picked up on your travel. The area's 10,000 years of human habitation are documented in excellent exhibits and there's a wealth of excellent Native art as well. This is definitely a must-see. The hours are the same as the Info Centre. Admission is $5/1 for adults/children.

Totems can be seen all around town, including two on Fulton St near 3rd Ave. Many of them are replicas of very well known traditional works. The tourist office offers free guided heritage **walking tours** around town.

Seashore Charters (☎ 250-624-5645) offers whale-watching trips, various tours and also rents bicycles. There are over 70 charter fishing boat operators and the Info Centre has a list. In 1997, some happy tourists landed a 234-pound (106kg) halibut.

A number of **hiking trails** can be found in and around town. One goes up 732m **Mt Hays** situated just south of the ferry terminals. On a clear day you can see local islands, the Queen Charlotte Islands and even Alaska. Beginning at a parking lot on the Yellowhead Hwy, 3km south of town just past the industrial park, trails lead to **Mt Oldfield**, **Tall Trees** (leading to old cedars) and **Butze Rapids**. The rapids walk is a flat 4km loop to Grassy Bay, the others are

more demanding. The Info Centre has details on these and others.

Along Wantage Rd (take the turning after the civic centre), you can visit the **Oldfield Creek Hatchery** (☎ 250-624-6733), a small salmon hatchery. It's open daily in summer from 8 am to 4 pm and there are tours.

About 20km south of Prince Rupert, **North Pacific Cannery Village Museum** (☎ 250-628-3538) at 1889 Skeena Drive in the town of Port Edward, gives a history of fishing and canning along the Skeena River. The fascinating complex was used from 1889 to 1968 and is built over the water. It should be high on your list of sights and can easily occupy half a day. The miserable conditions of the workers are documented along with the workings of this industry that helped build the region. A definite highlight is the most extraordinary one-person stage show in BC that traces the evolution of fish processing. There is a *café* with excellent breakfasts and salmon dinners from $12 and *B&B* accommodation (☎ 250-628-3375) in an old bunkhouse from $50.

The village is open from 9 am to 6 pm daily May to September as well as many additional weekends through the year. Admission is $6/3 for adults/children. Check with the Info Centre for schedules of bus service from Prince Rupert to the village.

About 16km east of town **Diana Lake** and **Prudhomme Lake** are two provincial parks where you can picnic, swim, fish, hike or take out a canoe. Canada's first **grizzly bear preserve**, the remote, rugged Khutzeymateen Valley, is 80km north along the coast. Two to 10-day ecotours by boat are available from Prince Rupert.

Places to Stay

Camping You can camp beside the lake at *Prudhomme Lake Provincial Park* (☎ 250-798-2277), open April to November, for $9.50. The municipal *Park Ave Campground* (☎ 250-624-5861, 1750 Park Ave) near the ferry terminal, has 87 sites, hot showers, laundry and flush toilets. A tent site for two people costs $10.50; in summer on ferry nights it's best to book ahead.

B&Bs There are over a dozen B&Bs in Prince Rupert. One with a good location is *Eagle Bluff B&B* (☎ 250-627-4955, 201 Cow Bay Rd), down by the marina. It has five rooms beginning at $45/55 for a single/double with shared bath. Also central is *Rose's B&B* (☎ 250-624-5539, 943 1st Ave West), the pink place, with rooms for $40/50. Rose speaks French and provides kitchen facilities.

Hotels The cheapest place in town is *Pioneer Rooms* (☎ 250-624-2334, 167 3rd Ave E) and is the nearest thing in Prince Rupert to a travellers' hostel. It's an excellent and immaculate central place with a range of prices. A bed in a dorm is $20, a single $25 and a double $40. There's a cooking area and you're free to use the barbecue and back yard. The friendly *Ocean View Hotel* (☎ 250-624-6259, 950 1st Ave W) has undergone a complete renovation. Rooms with shared bath in this historic building start at $45 and there are private facilities available as well. The *Coast Prince Rupert Hotel* (☎ 250-624-6711, ☎ 1-800-663-1144, 118 6th St) has good views and comfortable rooms from $89/99.

Motels *Aleeda Motel* (☎ 250-627-1367, 900 3rd Ave West) has rooms for $50/60. Close by, the *Slumber Lodge (909 3rd Ave West)* offers free breakfasts in its price of $60. *Totem Lodge Motel* (☎ 250-624-6761, 1335 Park Ave) is good, but because it's close to the ferry terminal gets booked out early, and rooms cost $65.

Places to Eat

With fishing a major local industry it's not surprising to find seafood on just about every menu. Salmon and halibut are headliners. Top billing goes to the storied *Smiles Seafood* (☎ 250-624-3072, 113 George Hills Way) on the waterfront at Cow Bay. It serves a variety of fresh ocean fare but steaks and sandwiches, too. A salmon dinner goes for $15. Flip over the placemat for a look at the 1945 menu when a hamburger could be had for 25¢. It's open daily. Nearby, *Cowpuccino's* (☎ 250-627-1395, 25 Cow Bay Rd) is a mellow coffee house

that maintains the neighbourhood's schtick in its name and cow-spotted dumpsters.

For fish and chips try the *Green Apple* (☎ 250-627-1666, 310 McBride St) on the corner of 3rd Ave East, which serves popular chowders. A good neighbourhood pub worth trying for a meal and a beer is *Breakers* (☎ 250-624-5990, 117 George Hills Way), a busy place in Cow Bay that has a long menu with good fresh fish specials.

Cheap food can be found at many places in the Rupert Square Mall, including the *Happy Orange*, which has huge sandwiches for $5.

Getting There & Away

Air Prince Rupert airport is on an island across the harbour from town. You must check in for your flight at your airline's downtown terminal two hours before flight time so that you can catch a shuttle bus and ferry (combined ticket $11) to the airport; no last minute showing up here. Air BC (☎ 250-624-4554), 112 6th St, flies to Vancouver. Canadian Airlines (☎ 250-624-9181) at 200-500 2nd Ave, also flies to Vancouver. Harbour Air (☎ 250-627-1341) serves small communities all over northern BC.

Bus The Greyhound Bus Depot (☎ 250-624-5090) at 3rd Ave between 7th and 8th Sts, has left-luggage lockers. Buses to Prince George (10½ hours, $87) depart twice daily.

Train The VIA Rail station (☎ 1-800-561-8630) is at 1150 Station St, by the harbour. There are three trains a week to/from Prince George and Jasper.

Ferry From Prince Rupert, Alaska State Ferries heads north through the Alaskan Panhandle. First stop is Ketchikan, but you can go north past Wrangell, Petersburg and Juneau to Skagway, where the Klondike Hwy comes south from Whitehorse in the Yukon.

Alaska State Ferries (☎ 250-627-1744), also called Alaska Marine Hwy, has its office at the ferry terminal. The one-way fare to Skagway (34 hours) is US$124/62 adults/children, US$286 for a car and from US$78 for a two-person cabin. Meals and

BRITISH COLUMBIA

berths are extra. If you're travelling by car or RV you should book well ahead. You can go standby but you may not get on.

The cruise along the Inside Passage is quite beautiful as you pass small Native villages, islands, inlets and see a wealth of wildlife that can include seals, killer whales or larger whales. The ferries themselves are very restful with decent food. Passengers without cabins can grab reclining loungers on heated outside decks for non-stop view delights.

BC Ferries (☎ 250-624-9627, ☎ 1-888-223-3779) sails the *Queen of the North* down the Inside Passage to Port Hardy on Vancouver Island on daytime schedules (15 hours) from mid-May to mid-October. The voyages are quite spectacular for scenery and wildlife. Reservations for vehicles are an excellent idea. The fare is $104/52 for adults/children and $214 for a car.

If you're coming from Port Hardy and you intend to continue north to Alaska by ferry then you should note that the schedules of BC Ferries and Alaska State Ferries do not coincide and you may get the chance to spend at least one night in Prince Rupert.

BC Ferries also sails between Prince Rupert and Skidegate in the Queen Charlotte Islands (6½ hours). In summer there are daily sailings, in winter just one or two a week. The one-way fare is $24/12 for adults/children and $90 for a car.

Getting Around
For information about the local buses contact Prince Rupert Transit (☎ 250-624-3343), 225 2nd Ave W. The one-way fare on buses is $1 and a day pass costs $2.50.

There is very limited service to Fairview Bay and the ferry terminal is about 3km from the centre. Call for details. The ferry terminal has a free phone for cabs or call Skeena Taxi (☎ 250-624-2185).

PRINCE RUPERT TO NEW HAZELTON
Prince Rupert sits near the mouth of the **Skeena River** and east out of town the Yellowhead Hwy (Hwy 16) follows the river, with some magnificent scenery of lakes,

forests and mountains, and camping in provincial parks along the way. There are rest areas where you can stop for a while and take it all in.

Terrace, 147km east of Prince Rupert, sitting in a valley surrounded by mountains, is a logging, service and transport centre. Hwy 16 becomes Keith Ave through town. The Visitor Info Centre (☎ 250-635-2063), 4511 Keith Ave, just south and east of downtown, is open daily in summer from 9 am to 8 pm and has lots of information on the region. The Greyhound Bus Depot (☎ 250-635-7676) is nearby at 4620 Keith Ave.

In **Kitimat**, south of Terrace, at the end of Hwy 37, there are free tours of the Alcan Aluminum Smelter (☎ 250-639-8400). At **Nisga'a Memorial Lava Bed Provincial Park**, north of Terrace, you can go fishing or hiking, but there's no camping.

The Hazelton area is the centre of some interesting **Native Indian sites**. West of town there are totems at Kitwanga and farther north the **Kitwanga National Historic Site** (☎ 250-559-8818) which marks the location of the country's only Indian fort. North of the restored pioneer-era Hazelton, is **K'san**, one of the province's most significant Native Indian attractions (☎ 250-842-5544). The recreated village of the Gitksan people features longhouses, a museum, various outbuildings and totem poles. Admission is $2 and the guided tours ($6) by Natives with entrance to the longhouses are very informative. East of town, **Moricetown Canyon** in the Bulkley Valley is where local Native Indians may be seen fishing this traditional salmon river.

CASSIAR HWY
Between Terrace and New Hazelton, Hwy 37 goes to Meziadin Junction and Stewart (221km). The portion of Hwy 37 extending north from Meziadin Junction is known as the Cassiar Hwy and meets the Alaska Hwy in the Yukon 569km north.

The Cassiar is a mostly gravel road and passes through some beautiful countryside. There aren't many service stations along the way, so if you're driving, make sure the vehicle is in good working condition and take

spare parts and extra gasoline. Flying gravel can crack the windscreen or headlights and dust can severely restrict your vision so treat approaching vehicles with caution, especially logging trucks.

Stewart & Hyder

From Meziadin Junction it's 67km west to Stewart on the Alaskan border. On the way you pass **Bear Glacier**, 49km from Stewart; there's a rest area where you can view the glacier. From Stewart the road goes straight through to Hyder in Alaska. There are no immigration or customs. Hyder is almost a Canadian community. Businesses accept Canadian money as well as US currency, although the cost of items using US dollars is often cheaper. This is the gateway to the **Misty Fiords National Monument** in Alaska. At **Fish Creek**, about 3km past Hyder, between late July and September you can see salmon swimming upstream to spawn and bears coming to feed on them.

In Stewart, the Visitor Info Centre (☎ 250-636-9224, fax 250-636-2199) is open mid-May to September. The *Lions Rainey Creek Campground* (☎ 250-636-2537) on 8th Ave has sites for $10. There are only two motels and one hotel, all with similar prices; book for all three at the *King Edward Hotel* (☎ 250-636-2244, ☎ 1-800-663-3126) on 5th Ave. Singles/doubles cost from $70/80.

Spatsizi Plateau Wilderness Park

This vast wilderness of more than 675,000 hectares includes the Spatsizi Uplands, the Stikine Plateau and the headwaters of the Stikine River. The park is undeveloped and isolated. From the Tatogga Junction on Hwy 16, drive north 361km on the Cassiar Hwy (Hwy 37) to Ealue Lake Rd where you turn east and drive 22km. At this point there is a rough road on an old rail track that extends 114km to the park entrance. From here access to the park is only on foot, by horse or canoe. You can also arrive via float plane.

In the park, Gladys Lake Ecological Reserve is home to Stone's sheep, mountain goats, moose, grizzly and black bears, caribou and wolves. The trails are often little more than vague notions across the untouched landscape. There are no campgrounds, although there are some primitive cabins on Cold Fish Lake for the use of people arriving by float plane. For more information, contact the BC Parks District Manager (☎ 250-847-7320, fax 250-847-7659), Bag 5000, Smithers, V0J 2N0.

In **Iskut**, 290km north of Stewart on Hwy 33, there are services that are the closest to the park. The *Red Goat Lodge* (☎ 250-234-3261, ☎ 1-888-733-4628) has a campground with $20 sites, motel rooms from $65/85 a single/double and an HI hostel with beds from $20.

Mt Edziza Provincial Park

This park has a volcanic landscape featuring lava flows, cinder cones and fields and an extinct shield volcano. It's accessed by gravel road from Dease Lake to Telegraph Creek and has hiking trails and wilderness camping. The park is mostly west of Hwy 37 and is linked to Spatsizi Plateau Wilderness Park. The park is undeveloped and the contact information is the same as Spatsizi.

Stikine River

The Stikine River, which cuts through the glacier-capped Coast Mountains to Alaska and the Pacific Ocean, is one of the best rivers for wilderness whitewater canoeing. In the upper reaches some rapids are deadly Grade V. The section west of the Cassiar Hwy as far as Telegraph Creek is considered unnavigable and you must pre-arrange to be picked up when you reach the Pacific Ocean.

ATLIN

This small, remote town in the north-western corner of the province is reached by road via the Yukon. Take Hwy 7 south off the Alaska Hwy; from the junction of the two highways it's 98km to the town. It sits at the edge of Atlin Lake, which is surrounded by the huge icefields and glaciers of the Northern Coast Mountains. The small **museum** (☎ 250-651-7552) has area information and is open mid-May to early September. Atlin Provincial Park is to the south.

QUEEN CHARLOTTE ISLANDS

The Queen Charlotte Islands, sometimes known as the Canadian Galapagos, are a dagger-shaped archipelago of some 154 islands lying 80km off the BC coast and about 50km from the southern tip of Alaska. As the only part of Canada that escaped the last Ice Age, the islands are rich in flora and fauna markedly different from those of the mainland. Essentially still a wilderness area, the Queen Charlottes are warmed by an ocean current from Japan and hit with 127cm of rain annually. All these factors combine to create a landscape of 1000-year-old spruce and cedar rainforests, abundant animal life and waters teeming with marine life.

The islands have been inhabited continuously for 10,000 years and are the traditional homeland – Haida Gwaii – of the Haida nation, generally acknowledged as the prime culture in the country at the time of the arrival of Europeans. The arts of the Haida people – notably their totem poles and carvings in argillate (a black, glass-like stone) – are world renowned. They were also fearsome warriors who dominated the west coast.

Today the Haida are still proud, defiant people. In the 1980s they led an internationally publicised fight to preserve the islands from further logging. A bitter debate raged, but finally the federal government decided to save South Moresby and create South Moresby Gwaii Haanas National Park. Logging still goes on in other parts of the Queen Charlottes.

The three main towns are all on Graham Island. Queen Charlotte City (QCC) is the main commercial and tourism centre and is near the ferry dock. Skidegate is a waterfront Haida community and Masset, on the north coast, is a Haida community, commercial centre and home to a closed army base. The total population of the islands is 6000. From the Skidegate ferry dock to QCC is 3km, to Masset 135km.

Information

The islands' relative remoteness coupled with the lure of the land and Native Indian culture

---

Forbidden Feast

The potlatch (a Chinook jargon word derived from the Nootka word *patschmatl* meaning 'to give' or 'gift') was a feast or ceremony common among the Native Indians of the Pacific Northwest coast, especially the Kwakiutl. Its main purpose was to validate the status of the chief or clan, although individuals also used it to try to enhance their social ranking. The potlatch involved the public exchange of gifts and destruction of property in a competitive display of affluence. A significant social event such as a wedding or funeral was used as an occasion for a potlatch.

The potlatch was prohibited by the federal government in 1884, when the Kwakiutl, at the cost of their own impoverishment, used it to shame and humble their former enemies. However, the practice continued in secret; the ban was lifted in 1951 and small-scale potlatches again take place. They are especially popular among the Haida.

---

has put the Charlottes on the travellers' map. In conjunction, a number of hostels and services have sprung up to meet the needs of the intrepid. Despite this, it's still all but mandatory to sort out your accommodation in advance and book ahead. It's also important to remember that the Queen Charlottes are a rural and remote place. If you plan to visit the Gwaii Haanas National Park Reserve and Haida Heritage Site – and that's the number one reason for coming to the islands – then understand that a visit takes several days as there are no roads and access is entirely by boat or float plane. Don't be one of the dullards who hop off the ferry expecting to see everything in a few hours and then depart. You won't.

Tourist Offices The Visitor Info Centre (☎ 250-559-8316, fax 250-559-8952) is located in a lovely building on the water on Wharf St in Queen Charlotte City (QCC). It is open from 10 am to 7 pm daily mid-May

to early September and 10 am to 2 pm for about three weeks on either side of that period. There is a second location in Sandspit at the airport that is open from 9 am to 5 pm daily mid-May to early September and 9 am to 1 pm for three weeks on either side of that period. These centres have a wealth of knowledge about the islands and the main office has some good natural history displays. They also have lists of places to rent kayaks, canoes and other gear including diving equipment.

The *Guide to the Queen Charlotte Islands* is encyclopaedic and updated annually. It is widely available for $3.95.

Money There are only two ATMs on the islands. One is in the City Centre Store in QCC, the other in the Northern Savings Credit Union (☎ 250-626-5231) in Masset. The links to the mainland are often down and the ATMs don't work, so bring lots of cash.

Post The post office (☎ 250-559-8349) is in the same shopping complex as the City Centre Store.

Laundry There's a coin laundry in the City Centre Store complex in QCC. It also has showers, the only public ones at this end of Graham Island.

Medical Services Queen Charlotte Islands General Hospital (emergency ☎ 559-4506, general information ☎ 250-559-4300) is in QCC. For major emergencies, patients are generally sent to Prince Rupert by air ambulance.

Graham Island

About 80% of the population lives on Graham Island, the only island with any real road system.

Near the ferry terminal in Skidegate is the **Haida Gwaii Museum** (☎ 250-559-4643) with good displays on the area's history, including an excellent collection of Haida works and totem poles. Open from 10 am to 5 pm daily May to September, Wednesday to Saturday other times. Admission is $3/1.50 for adults/children.

The Raven and the First Men by Haida artist Bill Reid.

The Yellowhead Hwy (Hwy 16) heads 110km north from Queen Charlotte past Tlell and Port Clements (the famous golden spruce tree on the banks of the Yakoun River was cut down by a deranged forester in 1997) to Masset. There's good birdwatching at the **Delkatla Wildlife Sanctuary**, off Tow Rd, north of town. Farther along the road, there are several miles of rugged beaches which are the destination for bongo drum-toting backpackers who try to set up house in little shacks made of driftwood. The cold and lack of services soon take their toll. If you try this, make certain your credit card has enough room left to escape.

Much of the east side of the island between Port Clements and Masset is devoted to **Naikoon Provincial Park** (☎ 250-557-4390). The park combines bogland, dunes and wind and wave beaches. There is a hike (5km one way) to the wreck of the barge *Pesuta* from the Tlell River bridge at the south end of the park. North, a 21km loop traverses a good bit of the park to and from Fife Beach from the end of Tow Hill Rd. The beaches in this area feature strong winds, pounding surf and driftwood from across the Pacific.

Totem Poles

Totem poles are found along the North Pacific coast, roughly between southern British Columbia and Alaska. Carved on logs of western red cedar by the Haida, Tlingit, Tsimshian and Kwakiutl tribes, totem poles show various animal and human forms stacked on each other, depicting different animal spirits as well as revered and respected supernatural beings.

Although Captain Cook noted totem poles as early as 1778, they didn't become abundant until the native peoples decided to display the wealth they acquired from involvement in the fur trade, around the mid-19th century. Traditional totem poles varied greatly in height, though rarely exceeded 18m. Modern poles can be much taller – the tallest totem pole in the world, at Alert Bay, BC, is 52m.

Totem poles identify a household's lineage in the same way as a family crest might identify an Englishman with a particular lineage, although the totem pole is more of a historical pictograph depicting the entire ancestral history. Like a family crest, totem poles also carry a sense of prestige and prosperity.

If it were possible to 'read' a totem pole, it would be from top to bottom – from present to past. Despite its position, the top figure, which represents the pole's owner, is actually the least important figure on the pole. The largest figure, usually the one at the bottom, is the most important. Loosely associated with individuals and events, the figures have no fixed meanings. A figure might be used to represent a particular person, or it may mark a memorable or adventurous event attributed to a particular creature or spirit. It could also represent a legend.

Because birds, fish and mammals figure so prominently on totem poles, it's possible to identify them without really knowing what they mean. A beak is a dead giveaway for a bird – **raven** has a straight, mid-sized beak and **hawk** has a short down-turned beak that also curves inward. **Eagle** also has a short down-turned beak and looks a lot like the mythical thunderbird, which has curled horns on its head. **Hokw-hokw** is a mythical beast with a very long, slender beak used to burst skulls. **Beaver** looks a lot like **bear**, except for a pair of large incisors and a crosshatched tail.

A few animals appear as if viewed from overhead. **Killer whale** is a good example of this – its fin protrudes from the pole as its head faces downwards. Long-snouted **wolf** also faces downwards, as does **frog**. Pointy-headed **shark** (or dogfish), with a grimacing mouth full of sharp teeth, and the **humpback whale** both face upwards.

The culture of totem poles was largely squashed after the Canadian government outlawed the potlatch ceremony in 1884. Few totem poles remain today because most cedar logs begin to decay within 60 to 80 years, though totem poles at Ninstints and Skedans in the Queen Charlotte Islands are over 100 years old.

New totem poles are rarely constructed for tribal purposes, and instead are more frequently carved for non-traditional use as public art. Modern totem poles commissioned for college campuses, museums and public buildings no longer recount the lineage of any one household, but instead stand to honour the First Nations and their outstanding artistry.

Traditionally, a totem pole recorded the genealogy of a particular household.

Gwaii Haanas National Park Reserve & Haida Heritage Site

This huge and wild park encompasses Moresby and scores of smaller islands at the south end of the Queen Charlottes. Ancient Haida villages can be found throughout the park. The most famous – and photographed – is **Ninstints** where rows of totem poles stare eerily out to sea. It was declared a UN World Heritage site in 1981. Other major sights include **Skedans** on Louise Island and **Hotspring Island** where you can soak away the bone-chilling cold in natural springs.

Access to the park and sights is only by boat or plane. A visit requires a fair amount of advance planning and usually requires several days. The easiest way to get into the park is with a tour company. The Visitor Info Centre has lists of operators, many of whom are located in Vancouver and Victoria. On the islands, Queen Charlotte Adventures (☎ 250-559-8990, ☎ 1-800-668-4288), PO Box 196, Queen Charlotte, V0T 1S0, has one to 10-day trips using power boats, kayaks or sail boats. Prices start at $125 for a one-day trip to Skedans. The owners have an office on Wharf St in QCC and are very active in protecting the ecology of the preserve. South Moresby Air Charters (☎ 250-559-4222, ☎ 1-888-551-4222) on 3rd Ave in QCC, has flights on float planes into the park. Half-day trips to Ninstints cost from $250 to $310 per person.

Independent travel within the park is not easy and you must come very well prepared. You also must obtain a reservation for park access from BC Tourism (☎ 250-387-1642, ☎ 1-800-663-6000 in North America, ☎ 250-663-6000 in Vancouver) which costs $15 per person to a maximum of $60 for a group. A few of the limited number of park reservations may be available each day from the Visitor Info Centre in QCC at 8 am, but this is not guaranteed. There are plans to introduce an entry fee on top of the reservation fee. Finally, all park visitors must attend mandatory orientation sessions before entering the park. Lasting 90 minutes, they cover ecological, safety and cultural issues and are held at 8 am and 8 pm daily at the QCC Visitor Info Centre and at 11 am in Sandspit from May to September.

Places to Stay

Wilderness camping is possible in the forests and on the beaches throughout the islands. Naikoon Provincial Park (☎ 250-557-4390) has two excellent campgrounds. *Misty Meadows* is just off Hwy 16 at the south end of the park, *Agate Beach* is on the beach of the same name on the north coast off Tow Hill Rd. Both campgrounds have toilets, firewood and water and charge $9.50 a night.

Just west of QCC, *Hayden Turner Campground* has beach access and forest trails. The unserviced, primitive sites are free. Masset has a *municipal campground* (☎ 250-626-3968) on Tow Hill Rd 1km from town. It has full facilities including a coin laundry and showers and tent sites start at $6.

In Queen Charlotte City, *Spruce Point Lodge* (☎ 250-559-8234, 609 6th Ave) has good views and rooms from $55/65 a single/double. Ask about hostel accommodation. *Charlotte's Web Guest House* (☎ 250-559-4744, 3122 2nd Ave) has rooms with unusual décor and charges from $65 including breakfast. The *Sea Raven Motel* (☎ 250-559-4423, 3301 3rd Ave) is a modern place 3km from the ferry dock.

In Masset, local celebrity David Phillips runs the *Copper Beech House* (☎ 250-626-5441, 1590 Delkatla Rd) on the water. This rambling old house features rooms from $50/75 a single/double that come complete with a teddy bear on every bed. Get Phillips to cook for you and you might not leave. Also ask about hostel accommodation in return for chores (like washing dishes).

Places to Eat

The islands' few restaurants are centred in QCC Many close from October to April. *Harry Martins Eatery* (☎ 250-559-4773) on Wharf St serves organic coffee and numerous vegetarian and organic dishes that average $9. Around the corner, *Hanging by a Fibre* (☎ 250-559-4463) has good cappuccino and baked goods. The best place for fresh local seafood is the *Hummingbird*

BRITISH COLUMBIA

Café (☎ 250-559-8583) at the Sea Raven Motel. The smoked salmon Caesar salad is a delight ($11.95). ***Saunder's Bakery & Deli** (☎ 250-559-4625, 312 2nd Ave)* bakes a special multi-grain loaf good for several days of life in a backpack. In Masset, the local favourite for fresh seafood is *Café Gallery (☎ 250-626-3672)* on Collison Ave.

Getting There & Away

BC Ferries sails between Prince Rupert and Skidegate (6½ hours). In summer there are daily sailings, in winter just one or two a week. The one-way fare is $24/12 for adults/children and $90 for a car. Some of the sailings are at night, others by day. Arriving in Skidegate, as you sail between two islands you have a vista of rows of mountains receding into the mists; it's wild and verdant.

There are frequent daily sailings across the short distance between Graham Island, where most people live, and Moresby Island

where the airport is. The ferry runs between Skidegate Landing and Alliford Bay and costs $3/1.50 adults/children and $8.50 for a car and driver.

At Sandspit airport (☎ 250-637-5313), Canadian Regional (☎ 250-637-5660, reservations ☎ 1-800-665-1177) has daily flights to/from Vancouver.

Getting Around

There is no public transportation, although hitching is common. You'll have to weigh up the high cost of local car rental with the cost of bringing a vehicle on the ferry. Budget (☎ 250-637-5688) and Thrifty (☎ 250-637-2299) have offices at the airport and QCC. Note that the many gravel roads can take a toll on windshields, so if you're renting sort out breakage coverage in advance. For a taxi at the airport and QCC, try Eagle Cab (☎ 250-559-4461).

The paved roads on Graham Island are good for cycling.

Yukon Territory

Some say God was tired when He made it;
Some say it's a fine land to shun;
Maybe; but there's some as would trade it
For no land on Earth – and I'm one.

From *The Spell of the Yukon* by Robert Service

The Yukon is a triangular slice of northern Canada wedged between the Northwest Territories and Alaska. To the south is British Columbia; the north is bounded by the Beaufort Sea in the Arctic Ocean. It's a sub-Arctic region about one-third the size of Alaska. Mountain ranges, including some that continue from the Rockies, almost entirely cover the Yukon.

For the visitor, the Yukon offers many outdoor activities – camping, hiking, climbing, canoeing and fishing – amid a scenic wilderness of mountains, forests, lakes and rivers. Every year more and more tourists are discovering the Yukon's dramatic beauty during the short summer tourist season.

Poet Robert Service and writer Jack London both lived and worked in the Yukon. Their words are highly respected and often recited throughout the territory.

History

In the 1840s Robert Campbell, a Hudson's Bay Company explorer, was the first European to travel the district. Fur traders, prospectors and whalers followed him. In 1870 the area became part of the region known as the Northwest Territories. But it was in 1896 that the biggest changes began. Gold was found in a tributary of the Klondike River near what became Dawson City and all hell broke loose. The ensuing gold rush attracted hopefuls from around the world. The population boomed to around 38,000 – quite a bit higher than today's 1300 – and transport routes were opened up. Towns grew overnight to support the rough-and-ready wealth-seekers, but it was the suppliers and entertainers, rather than the prospectors, who raked in most of the money.

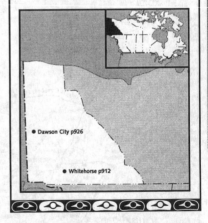

YUKON TERRITORY

In 1898 the Yukon became a separate territory with Dawson City the capital, but the city declined as the gold ran out. The construction of the Alaska Hwy in 1942 opened up the territory to development. In 1953 Whitehorse became the capital, for it had

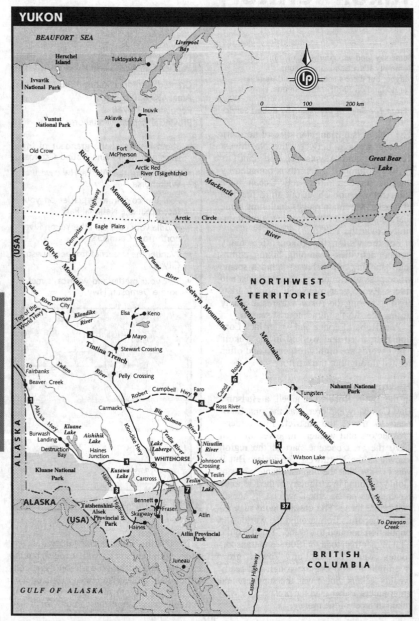

YUKON TERRITORY

the railway and the Alaska Hwy. It now acts as the main distribution and transport centre of the Yukon.

Climate

Summers, spanning June, July and August are short but warm, even hot. Many places are only open from May to September because outside of these months, visitors are few. Winters are long, dark and cold and many of the summer residents head south for the frigid duration.

Average daylight hours in Whitehorse during July are 19; during January six.

Information

Tourist Offices The Yukon has six main tourist offices, called Visitor Reception Centres (VRCs): these are at Beaver Creek, Carcross, Dawson City, Haines Junction, Watson Lake and Whitehorse. They're all open from mid-May to mid-September. They are open 8 am to 8 pm daily in season. Tourism Yukon (☎ 867-667-5340, ☎ 867-667-3546, info@touryukon.com), PO Box 2703, Whitehorse, Y1A 2C6, sends out free information on the territory. Its free magazine *Canada's Yukon*, published annually, has information on activities, events, accommodation and travel. It also distributes an excellent free highway map.

Books Widely available in the territory, *Yukon* is an excellent guide with an emphasis on adventure travel that's written by Dieter Reinmuth, the delightful owner of the Dawson City hostel.

Holidays In addition to the national holidays, Yukon celebrates its Discovery Day on the third Monday of August when much of the territory outside of Dawson City shuts down.

Dangers & Annoyances If you're drinking water from lakes or streams boil it for at least 10 minutes. This water may contain the intestinal parasite *Giardia lamblia* which causes giardiasis. If you're going to be outdoors take plenty of insect repellent.

Although most communities have local emergency numbers, there are two that work anywhere in the territory. For the RCMP dial ☎ 867-667-5555; for medical emergencies dial ☎ 867-667-3333. Hospitals open 24 hours are only found in Whitehorse and Watson Lake. In smaller communities there is usually a doctor or nurse on call after hours.

Activities

The Yukon VRCs can supply you with general descriptions and specific information on hiking, canoeing, rock-hounding, gold prospecting, climbing, skiing, fishing and various adventure tours. There are outfitters and tour companies to cover all these activities. You don't need an organised trip and don't need to be wealthy to enjoy camping, hiking or canoeing in the Yukon.

Hiking The most well known trail is the Chilkoot Trail but Kluane National Park also has excellent hiking from short and easy to long and demanding. The Tombstone Mountain area north of Dawson is also good. The North Fork Pass is called the classic hike of the region. Also above the treeline in alpine terrain is the MacMillan Pass at the NWT border accessible by the north Canol Rd from Ross River. Great hiking can also be found in the Firth River area of Ivvavik National Park but this is accessible only by air and has no services.

Canoeing Canoeists have the whole gamut of choice, from easy float trips down the fast-flowing waters of the Yukon River and its tributaries to challenging whitewater rivers.

Gentle float trips down the Yukon from Whitehorse for a few hours or 16 days all the way to Dawson are popular. Many people start or end at Carmacks, the halfway point, making an eight day trip. Boat rental and return charges for such an eight day, one-way trip are about $200 and transport can be arranged.

Kayaking & Whitewater Rafting The Alsek and Tatshenshini rivers are ranked among the best and wildest in North America.

They're found in BC, south of Kluane accessible only from Haines Junction. Trips can be booked in Whitehorse. Other major areas are the Lapie (near Ross River) and Takhini rivers.

Wildlife Spotting Tourism Yukon publishes an excellent *Wildlife Viewing Guide* that details what critters you can expect to see along the territory's major highways. Bears, moose, caribou, wolves and many more furred and feathered critters can be seen in the summer.

For an unforgettable introduction into the world of Yukon hunting, pick up the government publication *Hunting Regulations Summary*. Besides telling you how to bag a moose or a mountain goat it has a section on determining the sex of caribou that will stay with you long after other memories of your trip have faded.

Accommodation
The Yukon government's series of campgrounds is good, with many along the highways; most have drinking water. There are also numerous private grounds which offer hook-ups, showers and laundry facilities; some of these campgrounds are geared strictly to the large recreational vehicle (RV) market. Accommodation prices rise during the short tourist season, so expect to pay more than for comparable accommodation in the south.

Getting Around
The major towns in the Yukon are connected by air and bus (see the Getting There & Away sections for Whitehorse and Dawson City for details).

Road Driving your own vehicle is the best way to get around, and there are car and RV rental outlets in Whitehorse.

The road system in the Yukon is fairly extensive, if rough. Remember that most roads are gravel. Most of the Alaska and Klondike highways are paved but not necessarily smooth and some parts may be gravel or muck, especially where the never-ending maintenance is taking place. Make

certain you are able to change a tyre and that you have one and preferably more spares in good condition.

Gasoline prices along the highways are pretty high, so plan your budget accordingly. Generally, along the main routes, there's a service station every 100km, but in some areas there may be nothing for 200km or more. Three places where gasoline is not so expensive are Dawson Creek in British Columbia, Whitehorse and Dawson City.

Headlights are required to be on at all times on all roads.

A good circular trip is to travel the Klondike Hwy (Hwy 2) from Whitehorse to Dawson City, then take the Top of the World Hwy (Hwy 9) to the Alaska border. From the border, take the Taylor Hwy (Hwy 5) south to Tetlin Junction in Alaska where you can follow Hwy 2 to Fairbanks. On the way back take the Alaska Hwy (Hwy 1) south-east past Beaver Creek, Kluane National Park and Haines Junction to Whitehorse. This trip, not including a side jaunt to Fairbanks, is 1465km.

For information about road closures due to calamities like floods or major construction, call ☎ 867-667-8215.

WHITEHORSE
Whitehorse, on the banks of the Yukon River, is by far the largest town in the territory. In fact its official city limits cover 421 sq km, making it one of the largest urban-designated areas in Canada. Despite this, the central core is quite small and the total population is only around 20,000.

The town sits on the Alaska Hwy between Dawson Creek in British Columbia (1430km), where the highway starts, and Fairbanks in Alaska (970km). Despite its growth, Whitehorse still has something of a frontier feel about it although the people are condescendingly known as 'southerners' by those living in the more northerly areas of the territory.

Orientation
Whitehorse stretches for several kilometres along the banks of the Yukon River. The

Alaska Hwy passes through the city although it bypasses the city centre. Downtown is designed on a grid system and is easy to walk around. The main traffic routes through downtown are 2nd and 4th Aves.

Information

Tourist Offices The VRC (☎ 867-667-3084), with information on Whitehorse and the Yukon, is in a new building downtown on the corner of 2nd Ave and Hanson St. It's open from 8 am to 8 pm daily mid-May to mid-September.

Post & Communications The post office downtown is at Shopper Drug Mart, on the corner of 3rd Ave and Main St. It's open Monday to Friday from 8 am to 6 pm, and Saturday from 9 am to 5 pm. Computer Doc (☎ 867-667-6362), 305A Main St, has Internet access by the hour.

Bookshops Mac's Fireweed Books (☎ 867-668-6104), 203 Main St, sells a good selection of books on the history, geography and wildlife of the Yukon plus a section on Native Indian culture of the region.

Jim's Toy & Gift (☎ 867-667-2606), 4137 4th Ave, has a wide variety of maps and guidebooks. Topographical maps in 1:250,000 scale are recommended. Six are required to cover the Yukon River from Whitehorse to Dawson City.

Laundry The Public Laundromat (☎ 867-668-5558) is in the Stop-In Family Hotel at 314 Ray St and is open 8 am to 11 pm daily.

Medical Services Whitehorse General Hospital (☎ 867-393-8700), 5 Hospital Rd, is on the eastern side of the river. To get there, take 2nd Ave east over the Yukon River, then turn north on Hospital Rd.

Emergency For police, medical and fire emergencies in Whitehorse dial ☎ 911.

Things to See

In the town itself there isn't much to see, and what there is can be done in a day. For a view of the city, river and mountains beyond, there's a steep footpath at the western end of Hanson St.

SS Klondike National Historic Site The SS *Klondike* (☎ 867-667-4511) was one of the last and largest sternwheel riverboats used on the Yukon River. Built in 1937, it made its last run upriver in 1955.

Now restored as a museum and drydocked near the junction of South Access Rd and 2nd Ave, it's open daily 9 am to 6 pm from mid-May to mid-September. Admission is $3.50/2 for adults/children and includes a guided tour.

MacBride Museum This museum (☎ 867-667-2709), on the corner of 1st Ave and Wood St, is in a log cabin with a turf roof. It contains a collection of materials from the indigenous cultures, the fur trade, gold-rush days and the construction of the Alaska Hwy. It also has displays of Yukon wildlife. It's open daily 10 am to 6 pm from mid-May to the end of September and admission is $4/2.

The Old Log Church The church (☎ 867-668-2555), on the corner of Elliot St and 3rd Ave, was built by the town's first priest in 1900. Known as the only wooden cathedral in the world, it is also the oldest building in town. Inside are artefacts from early churches around the territory. It's open early June to the end of August, Monday to Saturday from 9 am to 5 pm, and Sunday from noon to 4 pm. Admission is $2.50/1. Sunday services at 10.30 am are mostly attended by Native Indians and include hymns in the Gwich'in language.

'Log Skyscrapers' Look for these small two and three-storey wooden cabins on Lambert St between 2nd and 3rd Aves. One is used as the office of the local member for federal parliament.

Yukon Beringia Interpretative Centre During the last Ice Age, some 20,000 years ago, a region encompassing the Yukon, Alaska and eastern Siberia was untouched by

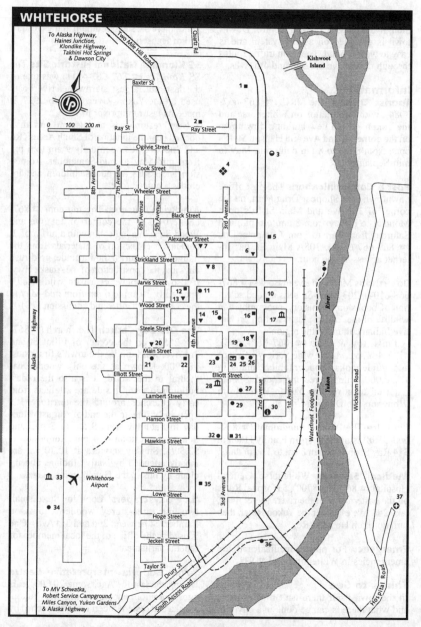

WHITEHORSE

To Alaska Highway,
Haines Junction,
Klondike Highway,
Takhini Hot Springs
& Dawson City

Kishwoot
Island

Two Mile Hill Road

Quartz Rd

Baxter St

Ray St

0   100   200 m

Ray Street

Ogilvie Street

8th Avenue

7th Avenue

Cook Street

Wheeler Street

6th Avenue

5th Avenue

Black Street

3rd Avenue

Alexander Street

Strickland Street

Jarvis Street

4th Avenue

Wood Street

Steele Street

Main Street

Elliott Street

Elliott Street

2nd Avenue

1st Avenue

Lambert Street

Hanson Street

Hawkins Street

Rogers Street

Whitehorse
Airport

Lowe Street

3rd Avenue

Hoge Street

Jeckell Street

Taylor St   Drury St

To MV Schwatka,
Robert Service Campground,
Miles Canyon, Yukon Gardens
& Alaska Highway

South Access Road

Waterfront Footpath

Yukon River

Wickstrom Road

Hospital Road

YUKON TERRITORY

Alaska Highway

1

1
2
3
4
5
6
7
8
9
10
11
12
13
14
15
16
17
18
19
20
21
22
23
24 25 26
27
28
29
30
31
32
33
34
35
36
37

WHITEHORSE

PLACES TO STAY		13	Tung Lock	24	Main Post Office
1	Sourdough City RV Park	14	No Pop Sandwich Shop	25	Murdoch's Gem Shop
2	Stop-In Family Hotel	18	Talisman Café	26	Mac's Fireweed Books
5	Roadhouse Inn	20	Sam 'n' Andy's	27	Log Skyscrapers
10	98 Hotel			28	The Old Log Church
12	Stratford Motel	**OTHER**		29	Klondyke Medical Building
16	Westmark Whitehorse	3	Greyhound Bus Depot	30	Visitor Reception Centre
	Hotel	4	Qwanlin Mall	32	Yukon Conservation
22	Town & Mountain Hotel	9	Kanoe People		Society
31	Hawkins House B&B	11	Jim's Toy & Gift	33	Yukon Transportation
35	High Country Inn	15	Yukon Historical &		Museum
			Museums Association	34	Yukon Beringia
PLACES TO EAT		17	MacBride Museum		Interpretative Centre
6	Antonio's Vineyard	19	Coast Mountain Sports	36	SS Klondike
7	Alpine Bakery	21	Computer Doc	37	Whitehorse General
8	The Chocolate Claim	23	Hougen Centre		Hospital

glaciers. Known as Beringia, the land was home to huge woolly mammoths and many tribes of human hunters. This large new museum (☎ 867-667-8855) re-creates that time with interactive displays and reconstructions of some of the animals. This is the most interesting local sight and is open 8 am to 9 pm daily mid-May to mid-September. Call for hours at other times. Admission is $6/4. The museum is on the Alaska Hwy just south of the airport. From downtown take the airport bus and then walk south for five minutes.

Yukon Transportation Museum Located close to the Yukon Beringia Interpretative Centre, the transportation museum (☎ 867-668-4792) covers the perils and adventures of getting around the Yukon by plane, train, truck and dog. Best bets are the photos showing the horrendous conditions of the construction of the Alaska Hwy and the displays on the many plane crashes. It's open 10 am to 6 pm daily May to August and has very limited hours (call first) the rest of the year. Admission is $3.50/2. A good-value $6 ticket also covers the Beringia centre.

Yukon Gardens These gardens (☎ 867-668-7972) are on South Access Rd close to the Alaska Hwy, about 3km south-west of town. The gardens, covering almost nine hectares, have large displays of wild plants

and flowers that can only be found in the north, plus vegetables and fruit trees. The gardens have been temporarily closed for road construction. Call for new hours and admission details.

Yukon Game Farm The preserve (☎ 867-633-2922) is about 25km north-west of town, off the Klondike Hwy on the Takhini Hot Springs Rd. A fine selection of northern animals such as elk, caribou, Dall sheep, moose, mountain goats, musk ox and others can be seen on the rolling 280-hectare spread. Call ahead for details about the best time to visit. The preserve can be visited as part of a Gray Line bus tour (☎ 867-668-3225) from Whitehorse for $15/7.50 adults/children.

Takhini Hot Springs About 10km off the Klondike Hwy (Hwy 2) north of town in a quiet wooded area are the hot springs (☎ 867-633-2706). The springs are open 8 am to 10 pm daily. Admission is $4/3. There is a B&B nearby and camping at the site.

Activities

For a good walk close to the centre, **Bert Law Park** is on a small island next to the Robert Service Campground and is connected by an old military bridge. A winding footpath leads around the natural wooded area. Around Whitehorse you can go hiking

YUKON TERRITORY

and cycling, particularly at **Mt McIntyre Recreation Centre**, and at **Grey Mountain** east of town and **Miles Canyon** south of town. All along the **Ibex River Valley** is good for cycling. The hiking trails become cross-country ski trails in winter.

Whitehorse is the starting place for the popular canoe and kayak trips to Carmacks or on to Dawson City. It's an average of eight days to the former and 16 days to the latter. Kanoe People (☎ 867-668-4899), on the corner of 1st Ave and Strickland St but right at the river's edge, can arrange any type of trip. To Carmacks costs $195/255 in a canoe/kayak, to Dawson City is $325/450. These prices include an orientation session. Kanoe People has several more trips as well. Prospect Yukon (☎ 867-667-4837), 3123A 3rd Ave and Up North (☎ 867-667-7905), across the river from the MacBride Museum on Wickstrom Rd, offer similar services. At the latter, German is spoken.

Organised Tours

The Yukon Historical & Museums Association (☎ 867-667-4704) at Donnenworth House, 3126 3rd Ave between Wood and Steele Sts, conducts guided walking tours daily during the summer of the downtown area for $2.

The Yukon Conservation Society (☎ 867-668-5678), 302 Hawkins St, offers free nature walks in the area daily during the summer.

Gray Line Yukon (☎ 867-668-3225), in the Westmark Whitehorse Hotel, has several tours. The 4½ hour city tour takes you around the city and out to the Yukon Game Farm for $27/13.50 adults/children.

The MV *Schwatka* (☎ 867-668-4716) sails daily in summer on tours of Schwatka Lake and the Yukon River. This was once the most hazardous part of the river journey but it has now been tamed (or ruined) by a dam. The cruises cost $18/8.50 and you can combine them with the Gray Line city tour for $46/23.50.

If you'd like to do something more adventurous then there are plenty of opportunities. Rocky Mountain Voyageurs (☎ 867-633-

4836) floats re-created gold-rush rafts down the Yukon River daily from May to September. The 2½-hour trips cost $48/35 and it picks up at area hotels. Atsua Ku Riverboat Adventures (☎ 867-668-6854) is a First Nation-owned company that offers three-hour tours down the Yukon River with talks about Native and gold-rush history and natural details. The cost is $49. For an extra $50 you can camp downstream in an old logging camp and enjoy some meals and hikes.

Places to Stay

Camping *Robert Service Campground* (☎ 867-668-3721) is 1km south of town on South Access Rd. It's open late May to early September and has toilets, showers and firepits. A tent site is $9. *Sourdough City RV Park* (☎ 867-668-7938), at the northern end of 2nd Ave past the Greyhound Bus Depot, has a laundry and free showers. It's mainly for RVs but you can put up a tent on the patches of grass behind the office for $10. *Pioneer RV Park* (☎ 867-668-5944), 8km south of Whitehorse on the Alaska Hwy, has drinking water, laundry and showers. Tent sites are $8.

You can camp at *Takhini Hot Springs* (☎ 867-633-2706), about 30km north-west of town off the Klondike Hwy, for $8, and walk to the hot springs. South of Whitehorse on the Alaska Hwy there are *Yukon Government Campgrounds* (☎ 867-667-5648) at Wolf Creek (16km) and Marsh Lake (50km); sites cost $9.

Hostels The *Roadhouse Inn* (☎ 867-667-2594, 2163 2nd Ave) has hostel rooms with bunks and shared washrooms for $20 a person. Singles/doubles are $50/55 at this central place. But note that one reader had his belongings stolen.

B&Bs *International House B&B* (☎ 867-633-5490, 17 14th Ave) in Porter Creek, north of downtown, has rooms from $60/65 a single/double. Readers report favourable experiences here. The deluxe Victorian-style *Hawkin's House* (☎ 867-668-7638, 303 Hawkins St) has four distinct rooms

each with private bath and balcony at $110 a double.

Hotels & Motels *98 Hotel* (☎ *867-667-2641, 110 Wood St)* is basic but central and cheap, with rooms for $45 with bathroom. It is best known for its bar. The well kept *Stop-In Family Hotel* (☎ *867-668-5558, 314 Ray St)* charges $70/85 with private bathroom. There's a laundrette and 24 hour restaurant attached.

The *Town & Mountain Hotel* (☎ *867-668-7644, 401 Main St)* has rooms with free local calls from $79. There's a licensed restaurant and a piano bar. The central *Stratford Motel* (☎ *867-667-4243, 401 Jarvis St)* is good, with rooms from $69 and some with kitchenettes.

The *High Country Inn* (☎ *867-667-4471,* ☎ *1-800-554-4471, 4051 4th Ave)* has rooms in a high-rise from $99/149. The service is very friendly and it has a full range of facilities. The excellent pub has outdoor seating. The top hotel in town is the *Westmark Whitehorse Hotel* (☎ *867-668-4700,* ☎ *1-800-544-0970, cnr 2nd Ave & Wood St)*, which has 181 rooms at $135 a single or double, and is home to the Frantic Follies revue.

Places to Eat

The popular *Talisman Café* (☎ *867-667-2736, 2112 2nd Ave)* between Steele and Main Sts is comfortable and good for any meal. Breakfast can be had for about $6. Lunch and dinner fare ranges from Middle Eastern to Mexican and vegetarian and there are good salads. Lunch will set you back $6 to $8, dinner about $10. This is also a fine place for an afternoon cappuccino.

The *No Pop Sandwich Shop* (☎ *867-668-3227, 312 Steele St)* is a longtime favourite with residents. Tasty sandwiches with interesting names like Beltch, Roman or Tel Aviv cost around $4.50. It has a patio out back.

The Chocolate Claim (☎ *867-667-2202, 305 Strickland St)* is known for tasty breakfasts and lunches from $4. It has its own bakery, makes excellent cappuccino and as the name implies, produces fine chocolates.

Busy *Sam 'n' Andy's* (☎ *867-668-6994, 506 Main St)* specialises in Mexican food and you can have a beer with your meal in the garden out front. The nachos are a perennial fave and you can expect to 'el chowo downo' for about $12.

Of the several Chinese restaurants, *Tung Lock* (☎ *867-6678-3298, 404 Wood St)*, open daily until midnight in summer, is recommended. Seafood is emphasised but there is a wide selection. It has all the usual Chinese standards from $8 and there are a few western dishes tossed onto the menu as well.

The town's best place for a meal, *Antonio's Vineyard* (☎ *867-668-6266, 202 Strickland St)* has an excellent Italian-accented dinner menu that averages $15 for items such as fettuccini Alfredo and fresh salmon.

Most of the hotels have restaurants or dining rooms. The *Alpine Bakery* (☎ *867-668-6871, 411 Alexander St)* has great bread baked from organic ingredients. The preserves made with Yukon berries are also a treat. For major stocking up, *Extra Food* (☎ *867-667-6251, 303 Ogilvie St)*, in the Qwanlin Mall, is the largest supermarket and has a huge bulk-foods section.

Entertainment

Strictly for the tourists is *The Frantic Follies*, an 1890s-style revue with comedy skits, dancing girls and the poetry of Robert Service. The show is held nightly in the *Westmark Whitehorse Hotel* through the summer and tickets cost $18/9.

If you want a taste of what the locals do for entertainment head for the *Saloon* at the Roadhouse Inn where you can hear country and western music most nights. Also popular is the pub at the *High Country Inn* which has good bar food, a very relaxed patio and pints of beer from Whitehorse's own Chilkoot Brewing Co, an excellent microbrewery.

Shopping

Murdoch's Gem Shop (☎ 867-667-7403), 207 Main St, has a huge selection of locally mined gems. For camping gear, Coast Mountain Sports (☎ 867-667-4074), 208

Main St, has a large selection of outdoor equipment and clothes.

Getting There & Away

Air Whitehorse airport is east of town off the Alaska Hwy, five minutes from downtown. Canadian Airlines (☎ 867-668-3535) has services to/from Vancouver. Charter carrier Canada 3000 (☎ 1-877-973-3000) has scheduled services in summer to/from Vancouver and Anchorage, Alaska.

Air North (☎ 867-668-2228, ☎ 1-800-661-0407) connects Whitehorse with Dawson City, Inuvik and Fairbanks, Alaska. First Air (☎ 1-800-267-1247) flies to Fort Simpson, NWT, and on to Yellowknife.

You can charter planes from Alkan Air (☎ 867-668-2107). In summer there is a charter service from Frankfurt, Germany which explains why sometimes you may think you're actually in the Bavarian Alps, what with everyone speaking German.

Bus Whitehorse is the northern end of the road for Greyhound (☎ 867-667-2223), 2191 2nd Ave, which has services south to Dawson Creek (20 hours, $165), Prince George (28 hours, $211), Vancouver (45 hours, $300) and Edmonton (29 hours, $230).

Norline Coaches (☎ 867-668-3355) runs three times a week (twice a week in winter) to Dawson City from the Greyhound Bus Depot for $79.50. The ride takes 6½ hours.

Gray Line of Alaska (☎ 867-668-3225, ☎ 1-800-544-2206) operates Alaskon Express buses to Skagway, Haines Junction, Tok, Anchorage, Fairbanks and Haines in Alaska and other communities along the way. Some journeys involve an overnight stop so you'll need to add on the cost of accommodation. The Anchorage route includes an overnight stop in Beaver Creek, takes two days and costs US$195.

Alaska Direct Busline (☎ 867-668-4833, ☎ 1-800-770-6652) has buses to Anchorage (17 hours) and Fairbanks (14 hours) and points in between such as Haines Junction and Beaver Creek that run at least once a week in summer. The bus to Skagway is a

daily (four hours, $49). The Whitehorse office and station is at 509 Main St.

For complete details of services to Skagway, including connections with the White Horse & Yukon Route train, see the Skagway section later in this chapter.

Car Cars can be rented from the following rental companies; be sure to confirm details like mileage charges and damage insurance coverage in advance:

Avis
   (☎ 867-667-2847, ☎ 1-800-879-2847) 306 Ray St
Budget
   (☎ 867-667-6200, ☎ 1-800-268-8900) 4178 4th Ave
Norcan
   (☎ 867-668-2137, ☎ 1-800-661-0445) 213 Range Rd
Rent-A-Wreck
   (☎ 867-668-7554, ☎ 1-888-786-6666) 120 Copper Rd

Klondike Recreational Vehicles (☎ 867-668-2200), 107 Copper Rd, rents all shapes and sizes of RVs and you can get them equipped with canoes. It also has one-way rentals to/from Kamloops, BC.

Getting Around

Bus Whitehorse Transit System (☎ 867-668-7433) operates buses Monday to Saturday; there are no buses on Sunday or public holidays. The one-way fare is $1.25 but a day pass for $3 allows unlimited travel. If you're going to the airport take the Hillcrest bus from Qwanlin Mall.

Taxi Among the local cab companies is Yellow Cab (☎ 867-668-4811). A trip from the airport into town is about $10.

Bicycle Kanoe People (☎ 867-668-4899), on the corner of 1st Ave and Strickland St, rents mountain bikes.

ALASKA HIGHWAY

The Alaska Hwy, the main road in the Yukon, is about 2400km long and starts in

Dawson Creek, British Columbia. It enters the Yukon in the south-east and passes through Watson Lake, Whitehorse, Haines Junction and Beaver Creek en route to Fairbanks, Alaska. The road is Hwy 97 in BC, Hwy 1 in the Yukon and Hwy 2 in Alaska.

A joint project between the USA and Canada, it was built in 1942 as part of the war effort and was originally known as the Alaska-Canada Military Hwy. Now, each summer, it's very busy (some even say clogged) with visitors, mainly driving RVs. At times there are 10 of these homes-on-wheels for every car or truck. Services for gasoline, food and lodging occur at regular intervals along the highway.

The highway is nearly all paved except for a few stretches where road construction is taking place. On these stretches the biggest problems are dust and flying stones from other vehicles so slow down and keep well to the right. Potholes, too, can be a problem. A spare tyre, fan belt and hose are recommended. Many people attach a bug-and-gravel screen or headlamp covers.

Hitching on the highway is good but be prepared for the occasional long wait – it's a good idea to carry a tent, some food, water and warm clothing. And don't consider hitching outside of the short summer season.

Watson Lake

Originally named after Frank Watson, a British trapper, and now billed as the 'Gateway to the Yukon', Watson Lake is the first town in the territory as you head north-west on the Alaska Hwy from British Columbia. The town stretches out along the highway. The VRC (☎ 867-536-7469), at the junction of the Alaska and Robert Campbell highways, has an excellent video show on the history of the territory and the Alaska Hwy. The centre is open mid-May through mid-September daily from 8 am to 8 pm.

The town is most famous for its **Signpost Forest** just outside the VRC. The original signpost of 'Danville, Illinois' was put up in 1942 by the homesick Carl Lindlay, a US soldier working on the construction of the Alaska Hwy. Other people added their own

signs and now there are over 22,000 and you can have your own sign made on the spot.

Twenty-six kilometres west of Watson Lake is the junction with the Cassiar Hwy which heads south into British Columbia.

Teslin

Teslin, on the Nisutlin River about 280km west of Watson Lake, began as a trading post in 1903 set up to serve the Tlingit people. The Alaska Hwy brought both prosperity and death in the forms of diseases which decimated the Native population. The **George Johnston Museum** (☎ 867-390-2550) has photographs, displays and artefacts on the Tlingit people and from the gold-rush days. It's open May to September daily from 9 am to 7 pm, and admission is $2.50/1. There's canoeing and camping at nearby Teslin Lake.

Johnson's Crossing & Canol Rd

About 53km north of Teslin is Johnson's Crossing at the junction of the Alaska Hwy and Canol Rd. During WWII, the US army built the Canol pipeline at the same time as the Alaska Hwy, to pump oil from Norman Wells in the Northwest Territories to Whitehorse. The only services on Canol Rd (Hwy 6) are in Ross River at the intersection with the Robert Campbell Hwy (Hwy 4). The road ends near the Northwest Territories' border; to go any farther you have to hike the Canol Heritage Trail (see the Northwest Territories chapter).

Haines Junction

Haines Junction, just outside Kluane National Park and Reserve, is reached by the Alaska Hwy from Whitehorse (158km) or by the Haines Hwy (Hwy 3) from Haines in Alaska (256km). The VRC (☎ 867-634-2345), on Logan St, is in the Kluane National Park headquarters building. It's open mid-May to mid-September daily from 8 am to 8 pm.

Haines Junction, big on the map, tiny in three dimensions, has a post office, service stations, two campgrounds, several motels and lodges and B&Bs. The *Village Bakery & Deli* (☎ 867-634-2867), opposite the VRC, is a good place to eat and keeps the same hours

The Alaska Highway

The construction in 1942 of the Alaska Hwy is considered one of the major engineering feats of the 20th century. Canada and the USA had originally agreed to build an all-weather highway to Fairbanks from the south as early as 1930, but nothing serious was done about it until WWII. Japan's attack on Pearl Harbor, then its bombing of Dutch Harbor in the Aleutians and occupation of the Aleutian islands of Attu and Kiska, increased Alaska's strategic importance. The US army was told to prepare for the highway's construction a month before Canada's prime minister, WL Mackenzie King, signed the agreement granting the USA permission to do so.

The route chosen for the highway followed a series of existing airfields – Fort St John, Fort Nelson, Watson Lake and Whitehorse – known as the Northwest Staging Route.

Thousands of US soldiers and Canadians, including Native Indians, built the gravel 2450km highway between Dawson Creek in British Columbia and Fairbanks in Alaska. They began work on 9 March 1942 and completed it before falling temperatures (in what was to be one of the worst winters in recorded history) could halt the work. Conditions were harsh: sheets of ice rammed the timber pilings; floods during the spring thaw tore down bridges; and bogs swallowed trucks, tractors and other heavy machinery. In the cold months the road crews suffered frostbite while in the summer they were preyed on by mosquitoes, blackflies and other biting insects.

In spite of these hardships the single-lane pioneer road was completed at the remarkable average rate of 12km a day, the road crews meeting, a little over eight months after construction began, at Contact Creek close to the British Columbia and Yukon border. The highway cost US$135 million to construct, an incredible sum then even as it is now. It was officially opened on 20 November at Soldiers' Summit (Mile 1061) overlooking Kluane Lake in the south-west corner of the Yukon.

The reason the original road had so many curves and slopes is that with the bulldozers right behind them, the surveyors didn't have time to pick the best route.

In April 1946 the Canadian part of the road (1965km) was officially handed over to Canada. In the meantime private contractors were busy widening, gravelling and straightening the highway; levelling its steep grades; and replacing temporary bridges with permanent steel ones. In 1949 the Alaska Hwy was opened to full-time civilian travel. For the first time

as the centre in summer. *The Raven* (☎ 867-634-2500) is on the Alaska Hwy and has comfortable rooms from $110/125.

Paddlewheel Adventures (☎ 867-634-2683) arranges tours using canoes, bikes, llamas, horses and more. Kluane Glacier Tours (☎ 867-634-2916) has 40-minute aerial tours of the glaciers in Kluane National Park that start at $90. Haines Junction is a transfer point for Gray Line Alaskon Express buses (☎ 1-800-544-2206) to/from Whitehorse, Haines, Alaska, and points in Alaska such as Anchorage and Fairbanks.

Kluane National Park & Reserve

This rugged but accessible wilderness UN World Heritage Site covers 22,015 sq km in the extreme south-western corner of the Yukon adjacent to Alaska's Wrangell-St Elias National Park. Kluane means 'many fish' and is pronounced 'klu-AH-nee'.

There are two VRCs run by Parks Canada. In Haines Junction (☎ 867-634-7201) the facility is shared with the provincial VRC. It is open 9 am to 5 pm daily from May to September. There are very limited winter hours. It has some nature displays and a renowned slide show. A second

The Alaska Highway

year-round overland travel to Alaska from the south of the continent was possible.

The completion of the highway opened the north-west to exploitation of its natural resources, changed settlement patterns and altered the Native Indian way of life forever. Thousands died as a result of diseases introduced by soldiers and workers. Others received their first real monetary wages thanks to jobs brought by the road.

The name of the highway has gone through several incarnations. In its time it has been called the Alaskan International Hwy, the Alaska Military Hwy and the Alcan (short for Alaska-Canada) Hwy. More irreverently, in the early days it was also known as the Oil Can Hwy and the Road to Tokyo. Officially, it is now called the Alaska Hwy but many people still affectionately refer to it simply as the Alcan.

The Alaska Hwy begins at the 'Mile 0' cairn in Dawson Creek in north-eastern British Columbia and then runs to Fairbanks, AK. Actually the highway officially ends at Delta Junction (Mile 1422) about 155km south-east of Fairbanks (Mile 1523).

Milepost signs were set up in the 1940s to help drivers calculate how far they had travelled along the road. Since then improvements, including the straightening of the road, mean that its length has been shortened and the mileposts can't be used literally. On the Canadian side the distance markers are in kilometres. Mileposts are still much in evidence in Alaska, and communities on both sides of the border still use the original mileposts for postal addresses and as reference points.

Until the mid 1970s conditions along the highway were extremely difficult. The highway is now almost completely surfaced except for stretches where road crews are doing maintenance work on potholes and frost heaves (raised sections of pavement caused by water freezing below the road), and there are services every 50km or so. Millions of dollars are spent annually on maintaining and upgrading the road.

Although it's possible to travel the highway year-round most visitors go between May and September when the weather is warmer and road conditions less hazardous. All of the attractions, services and accommodation are open then too. During this time the traffic noticeably increases, particularly the number of RVs. In winter the road is left mostly to logging, oil and mining trucks.

centre is at Sheep Mountain. It is open 9 am to 4.30 pm daily May to September.

The park consists primarily of the still growing St Elias Mountains and the world's **largest nonpolar icefields**, remnants of the last Ice Age. Two-thirds of the park is glacier. Interspersed are valleys, glacial lakes, alpine forest, meadows and tundra. There are also odd natural phenomenon called 'Nunataks' – see boxed text 'There's Life Out There'.

The Kluane Ranges averaging 2500m are seen along the western edge of the highway. In behind, hidden, are the icefields and, largely blocked from view, the towering

Icefield Ranges with 5950m **Mt Logan**, Canada's highest mountain and 5488m **Mt St Elias**, the second highest. Glimpses of the interior peaks can be had at the km 1622 viewpoint on the way into the park from Whitehorse and from around the Donjek River bridge.

A green belt area in and around the Kluane Ranges is where most of the animals and vegetation live.

Turquoise **Kluane Lake** is the Yukon's largest. A short worthwhile side trip can be gained by taking the fork to the east as the road approaches the south end of the lake.

There's Life Out There

Kluane National Park is home to some extraordinary phenomena called 'Nunataks', which is an Inuit word for 'land attached'. They are small outcroppings of rock poking through the 44,000 sq km of icefields found in the park and surrounding region.

Small and from a distance lifeless, these outcrops have recently been discovered to harbour hundreds of species of plants and animal life. The lichens, mosses and small flowing plants such as forget-me-nots are thought to have blown in. Pikas, small rodents that live among the rocks, eke out a precarious existence on the plants and the corpse of the odd bird that's flown in and then doesn't have the strength to escape over the miles of ice.

Scientists have made some remarkable archaeological finds, including evidence of humans living among the rocks 12,000 years ago. There is a strong belief that Nunataks may have helped preserve life through the last Ice Age.

Pika

A few minutes drive takes you to the almost disappeared **Silver City** where you can poke around by the edge of the lake among the ruins and remains of a trading post and Northwest Mounted Police barracks.

The park scenery makes for excellent hiking either along marked trails or less defined routes. There are about a dozen in each category, some following old mining roads, others traditional Native Indian paths. They range from about an hour in length to 10 days or so. The hiking leaflet has a map and lists the trails with distances and starting points. Detailed trail guides and topographical maps are available at the VRCs.

Hiking in the park is strictly controlled. Overnight trekkers need back-country permits costing $5 per person per night. At Sheep Mountain there are additional restrictions on hiking. This is the starting point for the popular 30km Slims West trek to **Kaskawulsh Glacier** – one of the few that can be reached by foot. This is a difficult and world-class route that takes from three to five days to complete. All hikers must have a bear-proof food canister from the VRC. There are only 50 and they are given out on a first-come, first-served basis. There is also a mandatory orientation talk.

In Haines Junction, there is an easy 4.8km loop trail on the Dezadeash River at the day-use area. The Auriol Trail starts 7km south of the town and is a 15km loop into the hills that takes you above the tree line for some good views. It takes four to six hours.

Fishing is good and wildlife abounds. Most noteworthy are the thousands of Dall sheep which can be seen on Sheep Mountain even from the road in April, May and September. There are also moose, grizzly bears, a small herd of caribou and 150 varieties of birds, among them the rare peregrine falcon and eagles.

Famous among mountaineers, the internationally renowned Icefield Ranges provide excellent climbing.

The only *campground* technically within the park is at Kathleen Lake, 24km south of Haines Junction off the Haines Hwy. It's open from mid-June to mid-September and costs $10 for a site with pit toilets and firewood. There are a couple of other *campgrounds* just outside the park on the highway, one at Kluane Lake. They are seldom full. There is commercial accommodation at Kathleen Lake.

Winters are long and harsh while summers are short; generally temperatures are comfortable from mid-June to mid-September, which makes that the best time to visit.

Soldiers' Summit

Near the Sheep Mountain Visitor Centre, from the parking lot off the highway, a 500m path leads up to Soldiers' Summit, site of the official opening of the Alaska Hwy, on 20 November 1942. From the site there are good views overlooking Kluane Lake.

Destruction Bay

This small village of about 50 people sits on the shore of Kluane Lake about 108km north of Haines Junction. Like Burwash Landing and Beaver Creek, it started off as a camp and supply depot during the construction of the Alaska Hwy. It was given its present name after a storm tore through the camp. You can go boating or fishing on the lake and the village has a service station, *campground* and *motel*.

Burwash Landing

Sixteen kilometres north of Destruction Bay, Burwash Landing is most noted for the **Kluane Museum** (☎ 867-841-5561) and its very good animal exhibits. There are also displays on natural history and the Southern Tutchone people or Dan as they call themselves (they are part of the family of Dene, or Athapaskan peoples). The museum is open mid-May to early September daily from 9 am to 9 pm and

Dall ram

admission is $3/1.50. The church and school of the early mission can be visited and there is also a gasoline station and store.

Beaver Creek

Beaver Creek, Canada's westernmost town, is on the Alaska Hwy 457km north-west of Whitehorse close to the Alaska border. The VRC (☎ 867-862-7321), open 8 am to 8 pm daily from mid-May to mid-September, has information on the Yukon and Alaska. The Canadian customs checkpoint is just north of the town; the US customs checkpoint is about 30km farther west. The border here is open 24 hours. The *Beaver Creek Hostel & Campground* (☎ 867-862-7903) has low-cost accommodation from $10 to $15 per person.

Tatshenshini-Alsek Wilderness Provincial Park (British Columbia)

Tucked along the southern Yukon border west of Hwy 3 this remote and rugged 2.4 million-acre park (☎ 250-847-7320) is also part of the regional UN World Heritage Site designation. Together with Kluane and the adjacent national parks of Alaska it makes up one of the world's largest protected areas. It is home to thousands of bald eagles, rare glacier bears and numerous species, almost all of which far outnumber the 1200 human visitors a year. The park can be viewed and some trails along abandoned roads accessed along the Haines Hwy (Hwy 3) south of Haines Junction to Klukwan, Alaska. The Kluane National Park office in Haines Junction has information. There are no facilities of any kind in the park.

Services are nil but whitewater rafting trips down the Grade III and IV rapids of the 'Tat' are run by companies from Haines, Alaska (see the section below for details). These trips should be booked well in advance. Half the daily permits are issued to private parties but there is a waiting list of several years for these. The standard float trip down the Tat is six days after putting in at Dalton Post.

HAINES (ALASKA)

This town of 1200 is at the end of Hwy 3 from Haines Junction. It is a good base for

exploring Tatshenshini-Alsek Wilderness Provincial Park and Glacier Bay National Monument in the USA. It is also a key link in the 594km circle route from Whitehorse that includes Haines Junction and Skagway, Alaska.

The Haines Visitor Bureau (☎ 907-766-2234, ☎ 1-800-458-3579, fax 907-766-3155) is at the junction of 2nd and Willard Sts. It is open 8 am to 8 pm weekdays, 9 am to 6 pm weekends from May to September and has lists of many outfitters and adventure tour organisers including Chilkat Guides (☎ 907-766-2491) and Alaska Discovery (☎ 907-586-1911). Ten-day raft trips down the Tatshenshini-Alsek River system to the coast of Glacier Bay cost from $2100 per person.

The best way to get from Haines to the Yukon is by taking a ferry to Skagway and from there transferring to Whitehorse. However, you can put together your own circle tour without a car by taking the Gray Line Alaskon Express (☎ 1-800-544-2206) to/from Haines Junction (four hours, US$74) where there's a transfer point for buses to/from Alaska and Whitehorse.

Chilkat Cruises (☎ 907-766-2100, ☎ 1-888-766-2103) and Haines-Skagway Water Taxi (☎ 907-766-3395, ☎ 1-888-766-3395) offer daily passenger-only ferries from mid-May to mid-September between Haines and Skagway that take one hour and cost about $20. The Alaska Marine Highway (☎ 907-766-2113, ☎ 1-800-642-0066) usually runs one car and passenger ferry each day between the two towns in the summer.

ATLIN (BRITISH COLUMBIA)
The small, remote town of Atlin, 182km south-east of Whitehorse in British Columbia, is reached by road via the Yukon – take Hwy 7 south off the Alaska Hwy. The scenery is great, with forests in Atlin Provincial Park and snowcapped mountains around Atlin Lake. (See also the British Columbia chapter.)

ROBERT CAMPBELL HIGHWAY
From Watson Lake, this 588km gravel road (Hwy 4) is an alternative route north to Dawson City meeting the Klondike Hwy near Carmacks. Named after Robert Campbell, a 19th century explorer and trader employed by the Hudson's Bay Company, it is a scenic and less travelled road with few services.

Ross River, 362km from Watson Lake at the junction with the Canol Rd (Hwy 6), is home to the Kasha people and a supply centre for the local mining industry. It has a campground and a couple of motels. There's also a small government campground 13km farther west at Lapie Canyon. Little used Canol Rd goes north-east to the NWT border and the beginning of the lengthy **Canol Heritage Hiking Trail** (see the Northwest Territories chapter for more information).

Faro, 10km off the Robert Campbell Hwy on the Pelly River, was created in 1968 to support the huge (largest in the Yukon) copper, lead and zinc mine in the Anvil Mountains. Since then the mine has opened and closed several times depending on the world markets. There are motels, a campground nearby and some walking trails around town. Sheep Trail is an 8km return trip, others lead to a waterfall or Mount Mye. Wildlife is abundant particularly Fannin (Dall) sheep. The road between Faro and the Klondike Hwy, and even down to Whitehorse, can be busy with trucks from the mine.

KLONDIKE HIGHWAY
The 716km Klondike Hwy from Skagway in Alaska, through the north-western corner of British Columbia to Whitehorse and Dawson City, more or less traces the trail some 40,000 gold seekers took in 1898. The highway, open year-round, is paved most of the way but there are some long stretches of gravel where construction is taking place. Watch for flying stones when the Faro mine is operating and truck traffic is heavy. Smoke and forest fires may be encountered through the summer but the road is rarely closed. The stretch from Skagway to Carcross is a scenic marvel of lakes and mountains in a myriad of greens and blues.

Skagway (Alaska)

Skagway is a fascinating little town which, while in the USA, can only be reached by car using the Klondike Hwy from the Yukon through British Columbia. It is also the starting point for the famed Chilkoot Trail and the White Pass & Yukon Route narrow gauge railroad. Alaska Marine Highway ferries link the town with Haines, Alaska and points south as far as Prince Rupert, BC and Bellingham, Washington. It is also an increasingly popular stop for the cruise ships plying the scenic waters of Alaska. John Muir described Skagway during the gold-rush era as 'like an anthill stirred with a stick'. You'll recall this quote on summer afternoons when cruise ships dump as many as 7000 day-tripping passengers on its narrow streets.

Skagway's compact downtown has stores, a bank, camping, hotels, restaurants and more. The Skagway Visitor Center (☎ 907-983-2858, fax 907-983-3854) is open 8 am to 5 pm daily year-round. It has complete area details including the excellent brochure *Skagway Walking Tour*. The office is on 5th Ave near Broadway St but may move to the Arctic Brotherhood Hall near the corner of 2nd Ave and Broadway St.

The US National Park Service (☎ 907-983-2921) has a good information office in the old train station on the corner of 2nd Ave and Broadway St. It is open 8 am to 8 pm daily from June to August; closing at 6 pm in May and September. It has one of its usual brochures covering the **Klondike Gold Rush National Historical Park** which covers Skagway and the US portion of the Chilkoot Trail. It also has frequent walking tours of the town. Parks Canada (☎ 867-667-3910 in Whitehorse) has a small office across the street in summer.

All places in Alaska are on Alaska time which is one hour earlier than the Yukon. For much greater coverage of Skagway and Haines, see Lonely Planet's *Alaska*.

Getting There & Away From Skagway to Whitehorse on the Klondike Hwy (Hwy 2) is 180km. The road is modern and paved and customs at the border is a low-key affair.

The White Pass & Yukon Route (☎ 907-983-2217, ☎ 1-800-343-7373) is primarily a tourist train offering round-trip sightseeing tours of this truly gorgeous route into Canada that parallels the original White Pass trail to the gold fields. The trains were once the only link to Whitehorse, but now they terminate in Fraser, BC, just over the Canadian border. The three-hour round trips cost US$78/39 adults/children. However, you can also combine a one-way journey on the train with a connecting bus to travel to/from Whitehorse and Skagway. This trip takes four hours and costs US$95/47.50. The trains operate from mid-May to mid-September.

One train a day goes 32km beyond Fraser to Lake Bennett which provides a good connection for hikers at the Canadian end of the Chilkoot Trail. There are plans to extend some runs over the now unused but very scenic stretch to Carcross in 1999.

Several bus companies offer services between Skagway and Whitehorse. Alaska Direct (☎ 867-668-4833, ☎ 1-800-770-6652) charges $49 and US$35, Alaska Overland (☎ 867-667-7896) charges $40 and US$30 and Gray Line's Alaskon Express (☎ 907-983-2241, ☎ 1-800-544-2206) charges US$56.

Skagway is the northern terminus of the Alaska Marine Highway's (☎ 907-465-3941, ☎ 1-800-642-0066) inside passage route through south-east Alaska and on to Prince Rupert, BC and Bellingham, Washington. This gorgeous voyage can be a highlight of any trip and should be reserved well in advance of the busy summer season. The schedules vary widely from day to day, but generally the trip to Prince Rupert takes about 34 hours and costs one-way US$124/62 adults/children, US$286 for a car and from US$78 for a two person cabin. Meals and berths are extra. You can go standby but you may not get on.

See Haines earlier in this chapter for details on passenger ferries to/from that town.

Chilkoot Trail

Skagway was the landing point for many in the gold-rush days of the late 1890s. From

there began the long, slow, arduous and often deadly haul to the Klondike gold area near Dawson City. Jack London was one of these people and his book *The Call of the Wild* depicts the harsh realities of the time. One of the main routes from Skagway, the Chilkoot Trail over the Chilkoot Pass is today popular with hikers.

The well marked, 53km trail begins near Dyea, 13km north-west of Skagway, then heads north-eastward following the Taiya River to Bennett in British Columbia, and takes three to five days to hike. You must be in good physical condition to attempt it and come fully equipped. Weather conditions are unpredictable so take a few layers of clothes and be ready to constantly peel them off then pile them back on again.

The most strenuous part of the trail is the hike up to Chilkoot Pass. Along the trail you can see hardware, tools and supplies dumped by the gold seekers. At several places there are wooden shacks where you can put up for the night, but these may be full. There are also 10 designated campgrounds.

At the Canadian end you can either take the train from Lake Bennett back to Skagway or you can catch a bus on the Klondike Hwy to Whitehorse or Skagway. Chilkoot Water Charters (☎ 867-821-3209) has a water shuttle ($50) on the lake to Carcross where you can also connect with buses.

The Chilkoot Trail is a primary feature of the **Klondike Gold Rush International Historic Park**, a series of sites managed by both Parks Canada and the US National Park Service that stretch from Seattle, Washington to Dawson City. See the Skagway section above for details on contacting both services, which issue a basic hiker preparation guide for the trail. In addition, Parks Canada sells an all-but-mandatory guide and map ($2) to the trail. The waterproof National Geographic Chilkoot Trail map (US$8) is also good.

Hikers using the Canadian portion of the trail must obtain one of the 50 trip permits available each day. Parks Canada (for reservations ☎ 867-667-3910, ☎ 1-800-661-0486) charges $35 for each permit plus $10 for a reservation. The permits must be picked up from the small Parks Canada office in Skagway on Broadway St near 2nd Ave. Each day eight permits are issued on a first-come first-served basis.

Carcross

Carcross, 74km south-east of Whitehorse, is the first settlement you reach when coming to the Yukon from Skagway on the Klondike Hwy. The site was once a major seasonal hunting camp of the Tagish people and the town's name is an abbreviation of Caribou Crossing – so called because caribou herds used to cross the narrow strip of land between Bennett and Lares lakes. The VRC (☎ 867-821-4431) is in the old train station. The centre is open 8 am to 8 pm daily from mid-May to mid-September.

Two kilometres north of town, **Carcross Desert**, the world's smallest, is the exposed sandy bed of a glacial lake that retreated after the last Ice Age. Strong winds allow little vegetation to grow.

Whitehorse to Carmacks

North of Whitehorse between the Takhini Hot Springs Rd and Carmacks the land is dry and scrubby though there are some farms with cattle and horses. The road skirts several lakes where you can go swimming, boating and fishing. The largest is lovely **Lake Laberge** with a beach, 40km north of Whitehorse, followed by **Fox Lake**, 24km farther north, and **Twin Lakes**, 23km south of Carmacks. Each has a *campground* with shelters and pump water. Near Carmacks the mountains become lower, rounded hills and the land more forested. On the way to Dawson, service stations have taken to selling cinnamon buns the size of bear cubs.

Carmacks

Sitting on the banks of the Yukon River, Carmacks was once a fuelling station for riverboats and a stopover on the overland trail from Whitehorse to Dawson City. It's now a small community of around 400 people with a service station, campground, hotel, motel and other services. Originally known as Tantalus, the name was changed to Carmacks to

honour George Washington Carmack who, along with two Native Indians, Skookum Jim and Tagish Charley, discovered gold at Bonanza Creek near Dawson City in 1896 and sparked the Klondike gold rush.

North of town about 25km, the **Five Finger Recreation Site** has stairs (a hell of a lot of stairs) which lead to a path overlooking rocky outcrops in the Yukon River which caused no end of trouble for riverboats.

Stewart Crossing

Stewart Crossing, once a supply centre between Dawson City and Whitehorse, sits at the junction of the Klondike Hwy (Hwy 2) and the Silver Trail (Hwy 11), another route taken by prospectors but this time in search of silver. Canoeists can put in here for the very good, five day **float trip** down the Stewart River to the Yukon River and on down to Dawson. Though you travel through wilderness, and wildlife is commonly seen, it is a trip suitable for the inexperienced. Canoeists should organise and outfit in Whitehorse or Dawson City (see under Activities in those city sections).

The Silver Trail

The Silver Trail heads north-eastward to three old, small mining and fur-trading towns: Mayo, Elsa and Keno City. The road is paved almost as far as Mayo. There are some good accessible outdoor possibilities in the area as well as campgrounds and other lodgings although there are no services in Elsa. Just 26km beyond Mayo is **Mount Haldane** with a 6km trail to the top and superb views. The round trip with an hour at the top takes about six hours. **Keno Hill** in Keno City (pop 50), with its signposts and distances to cities all over the world, offers good views of the mountains and valleys. There are hiking and driving trails in the vicinity, ranging from 2km to 20km long, providing access to old mining areas and alpine meadows.

Tintina Trench

Tintina Trench can be seen from a lookout 60km south of Dawson City. The trench is one of the Yukon's most important geological

---

The Yukon Cracks Up

The river which gives the Yukon Territory its name begins in a web of tributaries near the Llewellyn Glacier in north-west British Columbia. Although the majority of its 3200km length and its delta are in Alaska, the stretch of the Yukon in the Yukon itself is fabled for its historic and natural wonder.

From Whitehorse to Dawson City the river was both a vital and dangerous link from the 1890s until after WWII. Its turbulent waters are opaque with glacial silt and mud, which hide submerged hazards. Each April or May the break-up of the frozen waters produces earth-shaking floes that see truck-sized chunks of ice tossed about like toys. Dawson City celebrates this impossible to schedule event each year and there is a contest to guess when the first cracks will appear. The break-up is not all fun and games however. In 1979 an ice jam at Dawson City backed up water and flooded the town.

---

features and the sides of the valley reveal visible evidence of plate tectonics.

DAWSON CITY

Dawson City, a compact town with a population of about 2000, at the confluence of the Yukon and Klondike rivers just 240km south of the Arctic Circle, became the heart of the gold rush. Once known as 'the Paris of the North', it had deluxe hotels and restaurants, plush river steamers and stores stocking luxury items. Today it is the most interesting of the Yukon towns, with many attractions remaining from its fleeting but vibrant fling with world fame and infamy. Many of the original buildings are still standing and Parks Canada is involved in restoring or preserving those considered historically significant. Regulations ensure that new buildings are built in sympathy with the old.

Aside from being a unique and fun place there is a lot to see and although small, a two or three day visit is not a bad idea.

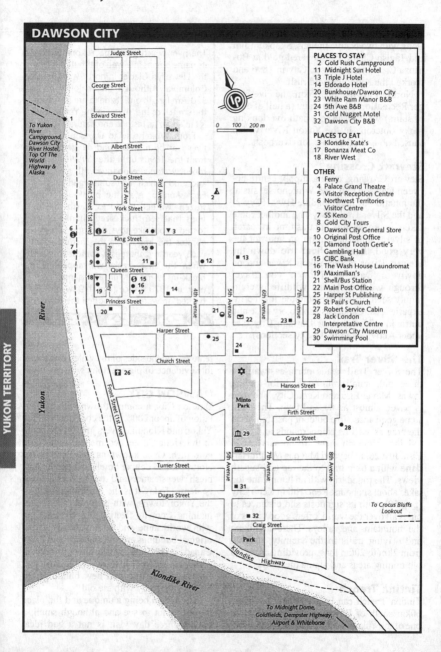

DAWSON CITY

PLACES TO STAY
2 Gold Rush Campground
11 Midnight Sun Hotel
13 Triple J Hotel
14 Eldorado Hotel
20 Bunkhouse/Dawson City
23 White Ram Manor B&B
24 5th Ave B&B
31 Gold Nugget Motel
32 Dawson City B&B

PLACES TO EAT
3 Klondike Kate's
17 Bonanza Meat Co
18 River West

OTHER
1 Ferry
4 Palace Grand Theatre
5 Visitor Reception Centre
6 Northwest Territories
   Visitor Centre
7 SS Keno
8 Gold City Tours
9 Dawson City General Store
10 Original Post Office
12 Diamond Tooth Gertie's
   Gambling Hall
15 CIBC Bank
16 The Wash House Laundromat
19 Maximilian's
21 Shell/Bus Station
22 Main Post Office
25 Harper St Publishing
26 St Paul's Church
27 Robert Service Cabin
28 Jack London
   Interpretative Centre
29 Dawson City Museum
30 Swimming Pool

To Yukon River Campground, Dawson City River Hostel, Top Of The World Highway & Alaska

0   100   200 m

YUKON TERRITORY

River

Yukon

Judge Street
George Street
Edward Street
Albert Street
Park
Duke Street
York Street
King Street
Queen Street
Princess Street
Harper Street
Church Street
Hanson Street
Firth Street
Grant Street
Turner Street
Dugas Street
Craig Street

Front Street (1st Ave)
2nd Avenue
3rd Avenue
Paradise
Alley
4th Avenue
5th Avenue
6th Avenue
7th Avenue
8th Avenue

Minto Park

Park

Klondike Highway
Klondike River

To Crocus Bluffs Lookout

To Midnight Dome, Goldfields, Dempster Highway, Airport & Whitehorse

Summer sees a massive influx of tourists and seasonal workers. RVs roam the streets like caribou in search of good grazing. Many people are drawn by Dawson City's edge-of-civilisation feel and it's not uncommon to see bands of unusual travellers wandering the streets, some dressed as Druids, others playing bagpipes for money.

The town is built upon permafrost, which begins just a few centimetres down. Buildings have foundations of planks resting on gravel and many show the effects of the seasonal heaving of the ground. Outside of town, there are eerie trails of tailings that look like the work of mammoth gophers but in reality are the leavings of the gold dredges which sucked up the swampy earth at one end and left it behind sans gold as they made their circuitous paths across the land.

Some 100 years after the original gold rush, as many as 100 enterprises, some employing just one or two people, are still mining for gold in the region around Dawson City.

Orientation & Information

Dawson City is small enough to walk around in a few hours. The Klondike Hwy leads into Front St (also called 1st Ave) beside the Yukon River. Just north of town, a free ferry crosses the Yukon River to the starting point of the Top of the World Hwy.

On the corner of Front and King Sts is the good VRC (☎ 867-993-5566). It's open 8 am to 8 pm daily from mid-May to mid-September. There is also a counter staffed by Parks Canada. Many of the town's attractions are National Historic Sites for which there is a fee. Parks passes cover much of the area sites and are good value at $15/7.50.

Opposite the VRC is the Northwest Territories Visitor Centre (☎ 867-993-6167), open 9 am to 8 pm daily from June through August, which has maps and information on the territories and Dempster Hwy.

The CIBC Bank (☎ 867-993-5447), 978 2nd Ave, is the town's only bank and has one ATM. It sometimes quits working, so come well stocked with cash.

The main post office (☎ 867-993-5342), on 5th Ave between Princess and Harper Sts, is open Monday to Friday from 8.30 am to 5.30 pm. If you're having any mail delivered, this is where you pick it up. Harper Street Publishing (☎ 867-993-6671), 354 Harper St, has Internet access.

Gold City Tours (☎ 867-993-5175) on Front St opposite the riverboat SS *Keno* is a travel agency and tour company. Maximilian's (☎ 867-993-5486) on the corner of Front and Queen Sts is an excellent small bookstore with lots of titles of local interest. It also has out-of-town newspapers and an array of gift items. The Wash House Laundromat is on 2nd Ave between Queen and Princess Sts. It's open daily.

For a medical emergency, dial ☎ 993-4444; for police dial ☎ 993-5555.

Things to See & Do

Unless otherwise noted, the hours listed below are for the tourist season from May to September. Other times, Dawson City is cold, quiet and most attractions are closed.

Diamond Tooth Gertie's Gambling Hall This hall, on the corner of Queen St and 4th Ave, is a re-creation of an 1898 saloon, complete with small-time gambling, honky-tonk piano and dancing girls. It's open 7 pm to 2 am daily and admission is $5. Note that the casino's winnings go towards town restoration, so go ahead, lose a bundle.

Palace Grand Theatre The large, flamboyant opera house/dance hall, on the corner of 3rd Ave and King St, was built in 1899 by 'Arizona Charlie' Meadows. There are guided tours of the theatre daily at 2 pm for $5/2.50 adults/children.

At night the Gaslight Follies (☎ 867-993-6217) presents remarkably corny stage shows vaguely (*very* vaguely) based on the gold-rush era. Shows are every night (except Tuesday) at 8 pm and cost from $15/7.50. The box office is across the street.

Dawson City Museum This museum (☎ 867-993-5291) situated on 5th Ave houses

YUKON TERRITORY

Tipped Scales and Greased Palms

Pity the poor gold miner during the Klondike gold rush; having survived the odds to stake a claim and having managed to beat the odds and actually find some gold, the miner would head to Dawson City where the odds were impossible because the deck was stacked against him.

One of the major scams was practised by the gold buyers who would 'tip the scales' in their favour when it came time to weigh the hapless miner's gold. In the scores of dubious saloons bartenders would encourage payment in gold. These characters would invariably have heavily greased hair. Before inspecting a miner's nuggets they would wipe their hands in their hair, knowing that a few of the nuggets would stick to the grease on their palms. The bartenders would then wipe their hands in their pockets and by the end of the night have a sizable haul. From this practice came the phrase 'grease my palms'.

With whatever they had left, miners often went to one of the gambling joints where stacked decks were just one of the hazards. In the town's back alleys, the hundreds of prostitutes had their own schemes to separate a miner from his assets. Given all this, it's no surprise that almost every miner left the Yukon as poor as when he'd arrived.

a collection of 25,000 gold-rush artefacts and displays on the district's people which capture the feel of the gold-rush era. It's open 10 am to 6 pm daily and admission is $4/3.

SS Keno The SS *Keno*, one of the area's last riverboats, is on display as a National Historic Site off Front St in the Yukon River. Renovation was nearing completion in 1998, after which tours will be offered.

Robert Service Cabin Called the 'Bard of the Yukon', Robert W Service lived in this typical gold-rush cabin on 8th Ave from 1909 to 1912. Don't miss the captivating recitals of Service's poems by Tom Byrne at 10 am and 3 pm. The cabin itself is free for viewing 9 am to 5 pm daily. The recitals cost $6/3, although cheapskates listen for free from the street.

Jack London Interpretative Centre In 1898 Jack London lived in the Yukon and wrote many of his popular animal stories. He is best known for *Call of the Wild* and *White Fang*. At the cabin and interpretative centre on 8th Ave you can hear recitals and talks about his works at noon and 2.15 pm daily. The site is open from 10 am to 6 pm and admission is by donation.

Midnight Dome To the north the quarried face of this hill overlooks the town, but to get to the top you have to travel south of town to the Crocus Bluffs (about 1km) and turn left off the Klondike Hwy onto New Dome Road. Continue for about 7km. The Midnight Dome, at 880m above sea level, offers good views of the Ogilvie Mountains, Klondike Valley, Yukon River and Dawson City. The hill gets its name from the fact that on 21 June the midnight sun barely sinks below the Ogilvie Mountains to the north before rising again.

Mine Sites There are two National Historic Sites outside of town which relate to the early gold mining days. Dredge No 4, 12km south of the Klondike Hwy on Bonanza Creek Road, is a massive dredging machine which tore up the Klondike Valley and left the piles of tailings which remain as a landscape blight. Thirteen kilometres south of town on the highway is the Bear Creek Mining Camp, site of the large community and shop complex which sprang up around the Klondike gold dredges in 1905 and lasted for 60 years.

Both sites cost $5/2.50 each, so you can see the value of the Parks Pass.

Ship Graveyard When the Klondike Hwy was completed, the paddlewheel ferries were

THE SPELL
OF THE
YUKON

I WANTED THE GOLD, AND I SOUGHT IT;
I SCRABBLED AND MUCKED LIKE A SLAVE.
WAS IT FAMINE — SCURVY — I FOUGHT IT;
I HURLED MY YOUTH INTO A GRAVE.
I WANTED THE GOLD AND I GOT IT —
CAME OUT WITH A FORTUNE LAST FALL, —
YET SOMEHOW LIFE'S NOT WHAT I THOUGHT IT,
AND SOMEHOW THE GOLD ISN'T ALL.

The Yukon's most famous poem

Historic street of Dawson City, Yukon

The annual Gold Panning Championship, Yukon

Recital of the poetry of Robert Service, Dawson City, Yukon

Breaking through 7m-thick ice, Buchanan Bay, Ellesmere Island, Nunavut

thrown out of a job. Several were sailed just downstream from town and left to rot on the bank. Now overgrown, they make a fascinating destination for a short hike. Take the George Black Ferry across the river, then walk north though the campground for 10 minutes and then a further 10 minutes north along the beach.

Activities

Dawson Trading Post (☎ 867-993-5316) rents out canoes and offers wilderness camping trips. One of the main do-it-yourself canoe float trips goes from Dawson three days downstream to Eagle City, Alaska. This trip is good for inexperienced canoeists.

There are numerous trails of all lengths and difficulties; the VRC has details.

Organised Tours

Parks Canada runs excellent walking tours of the town at 9.30 am and 1 pm daily. Among the highlights are tours of some of the restored buildings as well as fascinating little nuggets of information such as details of the now nondescript Paradise Alley which runs between Front St and 2nd Ave and which was once home to 900 prostitutes. The tours cost $5/2.50 but are included in the Parks Pass. Alternatively, you can rent audio tape tours for the same price.

Gold City Tours (☎ 867-993-5175) on Front St opposite the SS *Keno* has two bus tours. One ($34) includes a city tour and trip to the Bonanza Creek gold mine site where you can do some panning. The other ($10), which runs at night, goes up Midnight Dome.

You can combine a river cruise on a tiny old sternwheeler with an orgy of salmon eating at a place called Pleasure Island (☎ 867-993-5482). It has a little office on Front St with full details.

Special Events

Beginning in 1996, the Yukon began a series of gold-rush centennial celebrations centred on Dawson City. That year the theme was 'Year of Discovery'. Each year there is another theme; in 1999 it was 'The 4Rs Readin', 'Ritin', 'Rithmatic and Railroad' in celebration of the first school and in 2000 it is 'Takin' on New Steam' in honour of the railroad. Based on their success as marketing tools, Yukon Tourism seems likely to continue the series until at least 2096 when the theme may well be 'Milking the Tourist' in honour of 100 years of centennials.

The premier annual event in Dawson City is the Discovery Festival in honour of you-know-what that happened in 1896. Over several days there are parades, picnics, a really neat demonstration of gold smelting and a bang-up demolition derby. Don't miss the pancake breakfasts sponsored by the curling club.

Places to Stay

The growing competition to supply accommodation for Dawson City's visitors has kept prices stable. Accommodation fills up in July and August so booking early, especially for B&Bs, is a golden idea. The VRC will make bookings for you and tirelessly search for vacant rooms on busy weekends. Like the town's attractions, there is little choice outside of May to September.

Camping *Yukon River Campground* on the western side of the river has toilets, drinking water and shaded sites for $8. It's about 250m up the road to the right after you get off the ferry. Try for a site on the beach. You can also pitch a tent at the hostel – see the next section.

Right downtown, *Gold Rush Campground RV Park* (☎ 867-993-5247, cnr 5th Ave & York St) is really a big parking lot for RVs with full facilities and spots from $15. One kilometre south of town, *Dawson City RV Park* (☎ 867-993-5142) has sites with full facilities from $15.

Hostel Dieter Reinmuth runs the good HI-affiliated *Dawson City River Hostel* (☎ 867-993-6823) across the river from town and five minutes up the hill from where the ferry docks. It operates between mid-May and early September, has cabins for two to six people, tent sites and a cooking area. It's rustic and funky, has a killer view from the

deck and there is a new communal hot bath house. There's also no electricity and you have to pay cash. It's $9 for a tent site for one person or $6.50 a person for more. Beds are $13/16 for members/nonmembers. Bicycles and canoes are for rent. A free shuttle meets the Norline bus from Whitehorse.

B&Bs The VRC keeps a folder listing the B&Bs in the Dawson City area and it will make bookings. Rates are a near uniform $69/79 for singles/doubles.

White Ram Manor B&B (☎ 867-993-5772), the pink house on the corner of Harper St and 7th Ave, is a friendly, easy-going place with a laundry, kitchen and hot tub to ease those aching muscles. They'll also pick you up from the airport. *Dawson City B&B* (☎ 867-993-5649, 451 Craig St) at the southern end of town can provide lunch, dinner and transport to/from the airport. Another worth trying is the *5th Ave B&B* (☎ 867-993-5941, 702 5th Ave), near the museum. There are kitchen facilities.

Hotels & Motels The *Gold Nugget Motel* (☎ 867-993-5445, cnr Dugas St & 5th Ave) is comparably low-brow, but cheap with rooms from $46/50. The *Dawson City Bunkhouse* (☎ 867-993-6164, fax 867-993-6051) is a frontier-style place on Princess St near the corner of Front St. Rooms with shared bath are $45/50, private bath $75/80. Note that the solid wood construction means that it can get noisy at night as guests liquored up at the nearby saloons go clomping about.

More upmarket is the *Midnight Sun Hotel* (☎ 867-993-5495, fax 867-993-6425, cnr Queen St & 3rd Ave). It has a licensed restaurant, a bar and singles/doubles for $108/118. The *Triple J Hotel* (☎ 867-993-5323, fax 867-993-5030, cnr Queen St & 5th Ave) occupies the whole block and has motel rooms for $107/117 or log cabins with kitchenettes. *Eldorado Hotel* (☎ 867-993-5451, ☎ 1-800-661-0518, fax 867-993-5256, cnr 3rd Ave & Princess St) is open year-round, has a staff dressed in silly period costumes and has fine rooms from $112/122; much less in winter.

Places to Eat

Klondike Kate's (☎ 867-993-6527, cnr King St & 3rd Ave) does very good breakfast specials for $5 with unlimited coffee. The lunches and dinners are served inside or on the patio and are popular with locals. Pasta platters average $12, excellent sandwiches go for $8. It also has a few cabins for rent.

Best of several places along Front St, *River West* (☎ 867-993-6339), near Queen St, has excellent coffees, bagels and sandwiches ($4.50). It also sells health foods. *Bonanza Meat Co* (☎ 867-993-6567), on 2nd Ave near Princess St, sells deli items and has excellent sandwiches from $4 on freshly baked bread. *Dawson City General Store* (☎ 867-993-5475, cnr Queen & Front Sts) is the largest supermarket north of Whitehorse and the staff retain their humour in the face of tourists screaming 'Where's the Pringles!'

Many of the hotels have their own dining rooms for steak, seafood or pastas.

Getting There & Away

Air The airport is 19km east of town off the Klondike Hwy. Air North (☎ 867-993-5110, ☎ 1-800-661-0407) flies to Whitehorse, Fairbanks, Old Crow and Inuvik. Fares and schedules vary widely by season. For tickets and transport to the airport contact Gold City Tours (☎ 867-993-5175).

Bus Norline Coaches (☎ 867-993-6010, in Whitehorse ☎ 867-668-3355) runs buses to Whitehorse (6½ hours, $79.50) three times a week from June to August and twice a week other times. Buses stop at the Shell station on the corner of 5th Ave and Princess St.

Ask at the VRC about other Whitehorse services that tend to pop up seasonally. Also, you can find out if the on-again, off-again service up the Dempster Hwy to Inuvik is running.

Car The George Black Ferry (☎ 867-993-5441) runs 24 hours a day daily when the Yukon River is not frozen. It is free and the seven minute trip is worthwhile even if you just go for a ride.

DEMPSTER HIGHWAY

The Dempster Hwy (Hwy 5 in the Yukon, Hwy 8 in the Northwest Territories) starts 40km south-east of Dawson City off the Klondike Hwy. It heads north over the Ogilvie and Richardson mountains beyond the Arctic Circle and down to Inuvik in the Northwest Territories near the shores of the Beaufort Sea.

The highway, opened in 1979, makes road travel along the full length of North America possible. Inuvik is a long way from Dawson City – along 741km of gravel road – but the scenery is beautiful: mountains, valleys, rivers and vast open tundra. The highway is open most of the year but the best time to travel is between June and September when the ferries over the Peel and Mackenzie rivers are able to operate. In winter ice forms a natural bridge over the rivers. The road is closed during the spring thaw and the winter freeze-up; these vary by the year and can occur from mid-April to June and mid-October to December respectively.

Accommodation and vehicle services along the route are few. There is a gas station at the southern start at the *Klondike River Lodge* (☎ 867-993-6892). It will rent jerry cans of gas you can take north and return on the way back. It is 370km to the next services which are in Eagle Plains. The *Eagle Plains Hotel* (☎ 867-993-2453) is open year-round. The next service station is a farther 180km at Fort McPherson in the Northwest Territories. From there it is 216km to Inuvik. The area's largest private employer is Fort McPherson Tent and Canvas (☎ 867-952-2179) which makes popular travel bags.

The Yukon government has three basic *campgrounds* – at Tombstone Mountain (73km from the start), Engineer Creek (194km) and Rock River (447km); and there's a Northwest Territories government *campground* at Nitainlaii Territorial Park 9km south of Fort McPherson. For maps and information on the road ask at the Northwest Territories Visitor Centre (☎ 867-993-6167) in Dawson City.

The road is a test for drivers and cars. Travel with extra gas and tyres and expect to use them. For road and ferry reports call ☎ 867-979-2678, ☎ 1-800-661-0752.

TOP OF THE WORLD HIGHWAY

At the northern end of Front St in Dawson City the free ferry crosses the Yukon River to the start of the scenic Top of the World Hwy (Hwy 9). Open only in summer, the gravel road extends 108km to the Alaska border. The small customs and immigration checkpoint is open from June through mid-September daily from 9 am to 9 pm; you can't cross outside these times. From the border, the Taylor Hwy (Hwy 5) runs south 108km through Alaska to meet the Alaska Hwy at Tetlin Junction.

VUNTUT NATIONAL PARK

Vuntut, a Gwich'in word meaning 'among the lakes', was declared a national park in 1993. It is north of the village of Old Crow, the most northerly settlement in the Yukon. Each spring a porcupine caribou herd of 160,000 follows its migration route north across the plain to calving grounds near the Beaufort Sea. In Canada these calving grounds are protected within Ivvavik National Park and extend into Alaska where they are part of the Arctic Wildlife National Refuge.

With its many lakes and ponds, Vuntut National Park is visited by around 500,000 waterbirds each autumn. Archaeological sites contain fossils of ancient animals such as the mammoth, plus evidence of early human occupation.

The only access to the 4345 sq km park is by chartered plane from Old Crow, which itself is reachable only by air. The park has no services or facilities of any kind. For more information, contact the Canadian Heritage Yukon District (☎ 867-667-3910), No 205-300 Main St, Whitehorse, Y1A 2B5.

IVVAVIK NATIONAL PARK

With a name meaning 'a place for giving birth to and raising the young', Ivvavik, situated along the Beaufort Sea and adjoining Alaska, covers 10,170 sq km. The park is dominated by the British Mountains and its

vegetation is mainly tundra. It's on the migration route of the porcupine caribou (see the Vuntut National Park section) and is also a major waterfowl habitat. Its facilities are nonexistent.

Access is by charter plane from either Old Crow or Inuvik. For information contact Parks Canada (☎ 867-979-3248), Box 1840, Inuvik, NT, X0E 0T0.

Off the coast is **Herschel Island**, the Yukon's first territorial park. A former whaling station, it is rich in bird and other wildlife. A desolate and foggy place, it was an important settlement for the Thule people, who mostly died out after westerners arrived with diseases. Pauline Cove is a protected harbour and there is camping there during the short summer season. There are fire rings, wind shelters, outhouses and limited water. Access is by chartered plane, usually from Inuvik 250km south-east. For more information contact the Yukon Department of Renewable Resources (☎ 867-667-5648), Box 2703, Whitehorse, Y1A 2C6.

Northwest Territories

Canada's northern territories make up a vast tract of land stretching from the northern boundaries of the provinces to within 800km of the North Pole and from the Atlantic Ocean to the Pacific Ocean. A third ocean, the Arctic, links Alaska and Greenland across the many islands of the far north.

For the most part, this land of the midnight sun is as reputation has it – a barren, treeless tundra that's nearly always frozen. But it is definitely not all this way. There are mountains and forests, abundant wildlife and, even if the season is short, warm summer days with 20 hours of light.

In 1999 this vast region underwent a major political change with the creation of Nunavut (see the following chapter) in the east that comprises 2.2 million sq km, leaving what is still known as the Northwest Territories (NWT) with 1.17 million sq km in the west.

The designation of the Northwest, Nunavut as well as the Yukon as territories rather than provinces is a political one. Because they have relatively small populations, the territories have not been given full status in parliament. And as if to reinforce the northern status of these places, their shared area code of ☎ 867 spells out T-O-P on the dial.

Around Mackenzie River and Great Slave Lake the people call themselves the Dene, or Athapaskans. Together with the Inuit, who live mainly in Nunavut, they are the original northern peoples. The term Eskimo is not appreciated by the Inuit and has fallen out of use. The term Inuit simply means 'people'.

Tourism in NWT and Nunavut is not for the faint-hearted. Except for the parts of the NWT accessible by car, travellers need plenty of planning, money and time for a trip to these remote areas. A glance at a globe will easily show how far these territories are removed from other places; a factor central to both their rewards and difficulties for the visitor.

Much of what is now known as the Northwest Territories lies below the tree line. It is

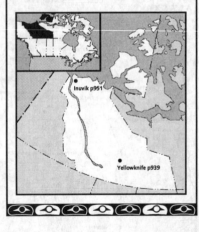

a land of thousands of lakes surrounded by forests and tundra. In the rolling hills left by retreating glaciers there are rich supplies of oil, gas, diamonds and gold which fuel the economy.

Given, however, the ever fluctuating fortunes in natural resources, NWT is relying more each year on tourism as a money

earner. Increased accessibility, together with the lure of pristine wilderness, means a continuing rise in the number of visitors to the territories. Other sources of income include fish, fur and handicrafts.

The territory is home to the mighty Mackenzie River, which runs 1800km from Great Slave Lake in the south-east to the Beaufort Sea and Arctic Ocean in the north-west. Near its end it fans out into one of the world's largest deltas with hundreds of channels and islands over an area of 16,000 sq km. The Dene call the river Deh Cho or Big River.

Yellowknife is both the capital and the main city. Inuvik is the centre for First Nations people above the Arctic Circle. Both are reachable by car.

History

The earliest known inhabitants of the Northwest Territories, the Dene, or Athapaskans, came to the region from Asia somewhere between 10,000 and 40,000 years ago. The Inuit

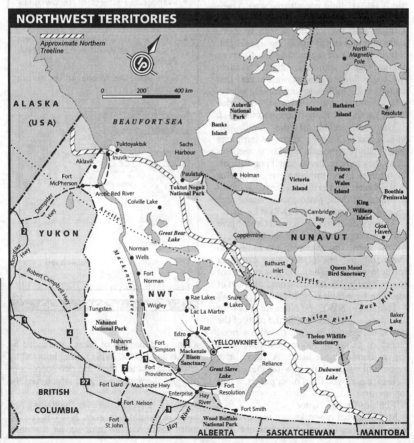

are thought to have arrived between 4000 and 8000 years ago.

The Vikings were the first Europeans to see the Northwest Territories, arriving in about 1000 AD. Later the search began for the legendary Northwest Passage – a sea passage from the Atlantic Ocean to the Pacific Ocean and the shortest route to China and its riches. Canada was thought of as merely a stopping-off point on the way to Asia. From 1524, British, French and Dutch adventurers all joined the search for a waterway through the continent. Many died but the north was mapped out in the process.

The first successful navigation was made in 1906 by Roald Amundsen. Since then, several others have done it, mostly in military vessels. Today the route is used little except as a supply line during the very short summer thaw.

With the prospect of wealth being made from whaling and the fur trade, Europeans, such as Alexander Mackenzie, began to explore in earnest during the 18th and 19th centuries. In their wake came missionaries who built churches, schools and hospitals. Until 1870, when the Canadian government took over, administration of the territories was shared between the Hudson's Bay Company and the British government.

Following the discovery of oil in the 1920s near Fort Norman, a territorial government was set up. In the 1930s the discovery of radium around Great Bear Lake marked the beginning of more rapid change and 20th century development. WWII brought airfields and weather stations. The discovery of gold in 1934 near Yellowknife swelled the town's numbers and in 1967 it became the capital.

In the 1950s the federal government began health, welfare and education programs. The 1960s saw accessibility to the territories increase, with roads being built and more airplanes connecting more places. The search for oil, gas and minerals changed some areas rapidly. The modernisation and development of the region has meant the near-total disappearance of traditional Native lifestyle.

With the establishment of Nunavut, the remaining portion of the NWT faces many questions about its future. Unlike Nunavut, which is largely populated by the Inuit, the western territory's population is split almost equally between Native and non-Native people. There are nine official languages, English, French and seven Native. This non-homogenous mix makes for fractious politics, especially with major decisions about the future course of the territory looming. Not the least of these is a name. A government survey in 1996 showed that over 90% of the people preferred keeping Northwest Territories as the name. However various political factions are still agitating for change, some reflecting various aboriginal groups at the expense of others and one – possibly fed up with the entire question – advocating Bob.

Climate

Winters are long and extremely cold, but summers in the south are surprisingly warm, with temperatures averaging almost 20°C, which, coupled with the long daylight hours (due to high latitude), makes travelling very pleasant. The climate is dry, the average annual rain/snowfall being less than 30cm. Most visitors travel in July and August but June is generally warm, too, with breezes and fewer bugs. A popular NWT T-shirt depicts the four seasons as 'June, July, August and Winter'.

By the beginning of July around the Yellowknife area, the sun sets at about 12.30 am and while the air cools down, it never really gets dark. In winter there is an average of 6½ hours of daylight and the average temperature is -28°C.

Flora & Fauna

Much of the NWT is covered by coniferous forests filled with trees that become increasingly scraggy as you head north. Above the treeline the tundra is covered with low and very hardy perennials which squeeze their entire growing season into a couple of months. Many boast delicate flowers which can transform the otherwise featureless landscape into a colourful carpet.

Major herds of bison can be found around Great Slave Lake and in Wood Buffalo National Park. In addition, there are great numbers of moose, bears, caribou, and many smaller mammals. It's not uncommon to see all of these as you drive the desolate roads of the territory. Most notable among the hundreds of bird species from around the world that summer in the NWT are the whooping cranes in Wood Buffalo National Park. They are part of the small flock of surviving members of the species that winter in Aransas National Wildlife Refuge in Texas.

National & Territorial Parks

The NWT has all or part of four national parks. Nahanni National Park Reserve is in the Mackenzie Mountains in the far southwest. Aulavik National Park on the north of Banks Island, and Tuktut Nogait National Park Reserve in the north-east are remote and untouched. Wood Buffalo National Park straddles the border with Alberta and is the only one accessible by road.

There are also more than 20 parks run by the territorial government for recreation, and a number of wildlife sanctuaries. The territorial parks have had much upgrading in recent years and improvements and expansion continue as tourism increases.

Information

Tourist Offices For information on all parts of the territory contact NWT Tourism (☎ 867-873-7200, ☎ 1-800-661-0788, fax 867-873-0294), Box 610, Yellowknife, X1A 2N5. The good, free booklet *Explorers' Guide* is published annually and contains much useful information. The free *Explorer's Map* is also worthwhile.

Time Almost the entire NWT is on Mountain Time.

Activities

For a lot of visitors, a trip to the Northwest Territories means canoeing, fishing, hiking and camping in the national and territorial parks during the short summer season. For others it's to observe the wildlife or even to trek across the tundra. These activities permit the visitor to see the area's uniqueness and rugged beauty. There is every manner of package tour and all-inclusive guided trip for visitors to pursue these outdoor activities, but many things can also be done independently, which is much cheaper.

Canoeing This is the premier way of travel throughout the NWT and you'll note that almost every car and every yard sports a canoe. Here the possibilities are just about endless and almost every town of any size has at least one local outfitter for equipment, guiding and advice. The Nahanni River in the national park of the same name is popular for trips organised out of Fort Simpson. Many of the lakes and tributaries around Great Slave Lake are easily accessible by car and allow adventures of any length desired.

Boating Kayaking is popular almost any place you find canoes. Sailing boats may be rented in Yellowknife for journeys in and around Great Slave Lake.

Fishing Arctic char, various trout and northern pike are just a few of many species of fish found in abundant waters in the lakes and rivers. A fishing licence is mandatory and costs $15/30 Canadian resident/nonresident for three days and $20/40 for the season. Licences are sold at convenience stores, gas stations, tackle shops and even police stations.

Winter Sports Cross-country skiing is a primary means of travel everywhere in the NWT. It is matched in popularity by snowmobiling over the vast tracts of frozen rivers and lakes.

Hiking Experienced hikers will find no shortage of places to hit the trail or in most cases make their own. The Canol Heritage Trail from the Yukon is a rugged multi-day adventure through mountains and valleys. Other excellent places include the parks and along the Ingraham Trail (Hwy 4) east of Yellowknife. Basically you are only limited by your experience, but don't be overly

ambitious because help is rarely available and the weather can suddenly change much for the worse. Hiking is also restricted by several factors; the bush can be very dense and there are the three Bs to contend with – bugs, bears and bison.

Independent Travel

Increasing numbers of travellers are visiting the territories and more of them without a prebooked excursion. Facilities and small, modest tour or outfitting businesses are slowly increasing with them. The only area for this, though, is the region around Great Slave Lake and along the Liard Trail (Hwy 7) from the BC border.

There are four main areas which can be explored independently. With a car, the Ingraham Trail (Hwy 4) can be explored in any length from a day to several weeks. Many people use one or more of the established canoe routes which vary in difficulty from easy tracks suitable for novices to more demanding routes. Although the lakes and waters are calm, be prepared for portages.

The second area to investigate is the Mackenzie River for canoe and boat trips. These can be done from several places but the primary one is Fort Simpson. Some people spend weeks going with the current all the way to the Beaufort Sea. This area is not for the inexperienced. The waters are swift and there are absolutely no designated camp sites.

The third area is Nahanni National Park. Although most of the trips here are highly organised, prearranged and expensive, it can be done. An airplane or helicopter can be hired to reach the park where there is camping and hiking. The headquarters for excursions is Fort Simpson.

The fourth area is Wood Buffalo National Park where there are both novice and advanced hiking trails and a range of canoe routes. There are outfitters in Fort Smith who will rent equipment or organise various camping adventures into the park.

Organised Tours

Well organised package tours have long been the principal means of seeing some aspect of the NWT. The *Explorers' Guide* has lists of companies, their addresses and the types of tours they offer.

Accommodation

Most parks and their campgrounds are open from mid-May to mid-September. Campgrounds tend to be small, simple and cheap, often with no attendant.

Yellowknife is the only place with much choice of accommodation and includes a number of fine B&Bs. Motels or hotels can be found in all towns of any size and territorial campgrounds are situated along the highways and at town sites. There are no HI hostels in the NWT and budget accommodation of any kind is lacking, thus many people choose to camp or use an RV.

More adventurous and covering a range of prices are the many lodges scattered throughout the territory. Very isolated, these seasonal places are often reached only by float plane from Yellowknife and require a minimum stay of a week or more. Meals are included and there are a range of activities such as fishing, canoeing, hiking and hunting on offer.

Getting There & Around

Air Yellowknife is the transportation hub of the NWT and has access to the rest of Canada through Edmonton. Owing to the paucity of roads, most communities of any size have some form of scheduled air service that usually goes through Yellowknife. Air fares are high and a lack of competition and traffic keep them that way.

Bus The sole bus link to the rest of the world is provided by Greyhound (☎ 1-800-661-8747) from Edmonton to Hay River. From here there is service by Frontier Coachlines (☎ 867-874-2566) to Yellowknife and other places served by road such as Fort Smith, Fort Providence and Fort Simpson.

Car The Mackenzie Hwy (Hwy 1) north from Edmonton is paved as far as the junction with Hwy 3 north of Enterprise. From here, Hwy 3 is paved as far as Rae, after

which the remaining 98km to Yellowknife is unpaved. Hwy 2 is paved from Enterprise to Hay River and a stretch of Hwy 5 is paved east to Fort Smith. The rest of the roads are unpaved and are a varying combination of gravel, dirt and mud. Generally all the numbered highways are passable for cars, but it's a good idea to check on local conditions before setting out as even the paved roads have wash-outs and other calamities.

For road conditions, call ☎ 867-874-2208, ☎ 1-800-661-0750. Free ferries link several roads with the most important one being the Mackenzie River crossing for Hwy 3 near Fort Providence. Travel is interrupted for several weeks during the spring thaw and winter freeze-up when neither the ferries or ice bridges are usable. For ferry information, call ☎ 867-873-7799, ☎ 1-800-661-0751.

Driving in the NWT is not especially easy, distances are long and the drives can be monotonous as there is almost no radio reception and the scenery can get rather mundane. Also there are numerous hazards to be prepared for. You will soon note that most cars in the NWT have damaged windshields from the many stray rocks, so come to terms with the fact that you won't be in the minority for long. All the roads are hard on tyres, especially the coarsely paved ones. Bring at least one full-service spare (not one of those miniature jobs) and know how to change a tyre. Note the distance between services and monitor your gas.

Locals usually carry the following items: first-aid kit, tow rope, flare, axe, knife, matches, water, food and blankets or sleeping bags, and you should too. In addition you might want to fit some form of protector over your lights.

YELLOWKNIFE

Rising out of the wilderness in a region once occupied by the Slavey people, the city gets its name from the copper-bladed knives they used. Although gold was first found here in 1898 by Klondike-bound prospectors, it was not until the discovery of richer veins, first in 1934 and again in 1945, that Europeans were attracted to the area in large numbers.

Yellowknife has a population of around 17,000 and is by far the largest town in the NWT, of which it is the capital. A modern, fast-growing settlement on the northern shores of Great Slave Lake, 1508km from Edmonton by road, Yellowknife is essentially a government town. It also acts as the commercial and service centre for the region and people from all over Canada now live and work here. Visitors use Yellowknife as a base for camping and fishing trips as well as for exploring the rocky landscape and nearby lakes.

Orientation

Yellowknife sits on the northern shores of Great Slave Lake and is connected with the south by Hwy 3 which runs 343km to the junction with the Mackenzie Hwy (Hwy 1). The city is divided into the new (south) and old (north) parts of town, which are connected by Franklin Ave (50th Ave), the main thoroughfare. The new part of town has the shops, businesses, services and hotels. Hilly, residential Old Town wedged between Back Bay and Yellowknife Bay is far more interesting to stroll around and stay in with its history, variety of housing, floatplane bases and views.

Frame Lake, about the size of central Yellowknife, lies along downtown's western edge. The 5.6km walking trail around it is a popular jogging spot and pleasant evening stroll.

The city street naming convention is a confounding mix of streets which run roughly east to west, and avenues which run roughly north to south. Worse, the planners managed to use the same range of numbers for their street and avenue names.

Information

Tourist Office The Visitor Information Centre (☎ 867-873-4262, fax 867-873-3654) is at 4807 49th St near 49th Ave (confusing, eh?). There is a wealth of regional information here; the staff is knowledgeable and there are good displays on the area's history. You can get maps, canoe routes and a guide to settlements across the territory, as well as

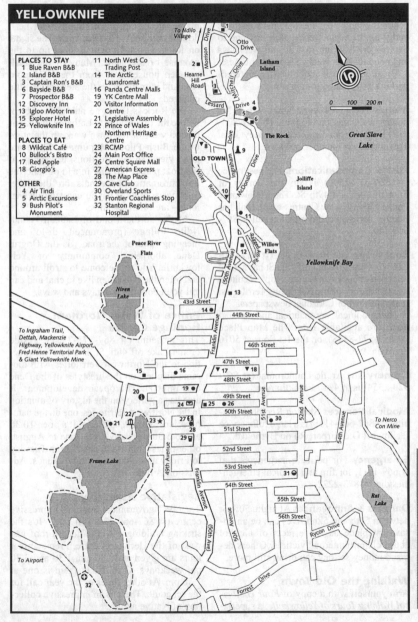

YELLOWKNIFE

PLACES TO STAY
1 Blue Raven B&B
2 Island B&B
3 Captain Ron's B&B
6 Bayside B&B
7 Prospector B&B
12 Discovery Inn
13 Igloo Motor Inn
15 Explorer Hotel
25 Yellowknife Inn

PLACES TO EAT
8 Wildcat Café
10 Bullock's Bistro
17 Red Apple
18 Giorgio's

OTHER
4 Air Tindi
5 Arctic Excursions
9 Bush Pilot's Monument

11 North West Co Trading Post
14 The Arctic Laundromat
16 Panda Centre Malls
19 YK Centre Mall
20 Visitor Information Centre
21 Legislative Assembly
22 Prince of Wales Northern Heritage Centre
23 RCMP
24 Main Post Office
26 Centre Square Mall
27 American Express
28 The Map Place
29 Cave Club
30 Overland Sports
31 Frontier Coachlines Stop
32 Stanton Regional Hospital

NORTHWEST TERRITORIES

fishing, canoeing and motoring guides. The centre is open 8.30 am to 6.30 pm weekdays and 9 am to 6 pm weekends from June to September; 8.30 am to 5.30 pm weekdays and noon to 4 pm weekends at other times.

By all means ask about the free metered-parking pass issued to tourists.

Money There are several banks with ATMs downtown. American Express (☎ 867-873-2121), 5014 Franklin Ave, is in Key West Travel and has member services.

Post & Communications The post office (☎ 867-873-2500) is on the corner of Franklin Ave and 49th St. The Yellowknife Public Library in the Centre Square Mall has Internet access. For information call ☎ 867-669-3403.

Bookshops The Book Cellar (☎ 867-920-2220) in Panda II Mall off 48th St has a good selection of books on Native people's culture and the history of the Northwest Territories. It also has major Canadian newspapers.

Topographical, aeronautical and nautical maps are available from The Map Place (☎ 867-873-8448), on the 1st floor at 5016 Franklin Ave.

Laundry The Arctic Laundromat (☎ 867-920-2354) is at 4310 Franklin Ave.

Medical Services Stanton Regional Hospital (☎ 867-669-4111) is a large full-service facility off Old Airport Rd on Byrne Rd.

Emergency For police emergencies dial ☎ 669-1111; for fire and medical emergencies dial ☎ 873-2222.

Dangers & Annoyances At night, 50th St between 50th and 52nd Aves can be an unsavoury place as the effects of alcohol abuse claim numerous victims. Others demand money so they can drink still more.

Walking the Old Town

Arm yourself with a copy of *Four Historical Walking Tours of Yellowknife*, a superla-tive illustrated booklet showing the town's many interesting old buildings, and head down Franklin Ave to Old Town. The sights on Ragged Ass Rd actually live up to the promise of the name. Many of the small wooden houses date from the 1934 gold rush and in many ways the area seems little changed.

The Rock is the large nub of land right before the tiny bridge to Latham Island. For a good view of the town walk up the steps to the **Bush Pilot's Monument**. There are good views in all directions, especially of the float planes buzzing in and out and the polychromatic houseboats on the lake. Summer sunsets – if you can stay up that long – are often stunning.

At the northern end of Latham Island, **Ndilo Village** (pronounced 'di-lo' and meaning 'end of the road') is the Dogrib Dene aboriginal community of Yellowknife. You're welcome to stroll around and often the older men like to chat and can tell you about the old days and ways.

Prince of Wales Northern Heritage Centre

This museum (☎ 867-873-7551), beside Frame Lake off 48th St, is a fine introduction to the Northwest Territories with diorama displays on the lifestyles of the Dene and Inuit and European development. It also has a gallery on the history of aviation in the Northwest Territories, one on the natural sciences and a cafeteria. It's open 10.30 am to 5.30 pm daily from June to August; other times from 10.30 am to 5 pm Tuesday to Friday and noon to 5 pm weekends. Admission is free.

Legislative Assembly

The NWT government built this impressive centre (☎ 867-669-2200) in 1993. It's the striking building with the domed roof just west of the Heritage Centre. Free summer tours are given at 10.30 am, 1.30 and 3.30 pm weekdays. On Sunday there is one at 1.30 pm. At other times of the year call for the schedule. There is an impressive collection of Native art.

Fred Henne Territorial Park

In Fred Henne Territorial Park (☎ 867-920-2472), off the Mackenzie Hwy opposite the airport, there is sandy **Long Lake Beach** and the 4km-long **Prospector's Trail**. The excellent walk leads over rocky outcrops, through some bush and around muskeg and by a lake – a real little microcosm of the far north topography. Get the map from the park office and get well oriented because it's not hard to lose the path.

Activities

The Visitor Information Centre maintains a lengthy list of guides and outfitters.

Overland Sports (☎ 867-873-2474), 5103 51st Ave, rents canoes, kayaks and winter sports gear. A basic canoe goes for $30 a day or $150 a week. Narwhal Ltd (☎ 867-873-6443) has canoes and kayaks for the same prices. It also will help you organise your trip and offers lessons.

Sail North (☎ 867-873-8019) charters sailing boats for trips on Great Slave Lake. It can provide crews, provisions and other services.

There's no shortage of fishing guides and one of the better known ones is Bluefish Services (☎ 867-873-4818). It has a myriad of trips for anglers including ones where you catch your fish and then cook them at a picnic on an island. Four hours of battling northern pike on Great Slave Lake costs $65. It also has birdwatching tours.

If the frigid waters of the local lakes aren't quite inviting, the city operates the Ruth Inch Swimming Pool (☎ 867-920-5683) at 6001 Franklin Ave. The 25m pool has a wave machine and there are whirlpools and a steam room. A single admission is $4.25/2.50 adults/children. Smelly backpackers can opt for just a shower for $2.50.

Organised Tours

There is a vast range of short and long tours offered in and around Yellowknife. Among them are walking tours, boat trips, kayak adventures, photography safaris, fishing expeditions and more.

Raven Tours (☎ 867-873-4776) offers a variety of options. It has a basic three hour bus tour of the city and nearby gold mine

---

The Northern Lights of Yellowknife

A hot show when the weather is cold, the aurora borealis – the famed 'Northern Lights' – can be seen from the NWT, Nunavut and the Yukon. The best time to see it is during the fall and winter. It appears in many forms – pillars, streaks, wisps, haloes of vibrating light and sometimes looks like the rippling folds of a curtain. Most often, the aurora borealis glows faintly green or pale rose, but during periods of extreme activity it can flare into bright yellows and crimsons.

The visible aurora is created by solar winds (streams of charged particles from the sun) flowing through the earth's magnetic field in the polar regions. These winds are drawn earthwards, where the particles collide with electrons and ions in the ionosphere which creates the visible aurora.

The Inuit and other groups attach a spiritual significance to the aurora. Some consider it to be a gift from the dead to light the long polar nights, while others believe it to be a storehouse of events past and future.

Up to 5000 Japanese tourists a year visit Yellowknife during the otherwise slow winter season to see the show from a special viewing platform 50km east of town. The lights are thought to bring good luck. Canada Ex (☎ 867-669-9200) has numerous tour packages during the peak viewing season.

Despite the stellar boost aurora viewing gives the Yellowknife economy, long-time NWT residents say the very best viewing can be found at Fort Smith on the Alberta border.

NORTHWEST TERRITORIES

for $25. A four hour van trip goes down the Ingraham Trail to Cameron Falls for $38. It has many other special interest tours and aurora viewing in the winter.

Ecologist Jamie Bastedo of Cygnus Eco-tours (☎ 867-873-4782) leads recommended nature walks. The two hour Niven Lake trip features Yellowknife birdlife and a beaver colony and costs $30. Bastedo is the author of *Blue Lake and Rocky Shore*, an excellent nature guide to the Yellowknife area.

Great Slave Sledging Company (☎ 867-920-4542, ☎ 867-873-8249) has winter dog-team expeditions from 30 minutes to two months. A one to two hour trip costs $40/20 adults/children. Mush!

For a view of town, the vast area gold mines and Cameron Falls, Arctic Excursions (☎ 867-669-7216), 3503 McDonald Drive in Old Town, offers 30-minute aerial tours for $50. The chance to see how a float plane works is worth the price alone. If you're lucky, it'll use its old De Havilland Beaver, a plane that's been a workhorse of the north for 50 years. It also offers charter flights for wilderness travel that start at about $150 per person.

Special Events

For exact dates of these annual events, contact the Visitor Information Centre.

March
Caribou Carnival
Three days of festivities as the locals shake off winter with fireworks, games and contests. A highlight is the 240km dog-sled race on Great Slave Lake.

July
Festival of the Midnight Sun
A seven day celebration of local art and culture.
Folk on the Rocks
Held a few days after the arts festival, this event draws folk musicians and entertainers from all over North America as well as Inuit and Dene musicians and dancers.

Places to Stay

Camping The closest campground to town is at *Fred Henne Territorial Park*, which

has full facilities including showers and toilets. A site costs $12. If you're arriving by bus ask the driver to drop you off at the entrance. Downtown is easily walkable in under 40 minutes using the trail around Jackfish and Frame lakes. For those with transport, you can also camp at *Prelude Lake Territorial Park* or *Reid Lake Territorial Park* along the Ingraham Trail for $12; both have toilet and washing facilities. They are 31km and 61km respectively from Yellowknife. You can check on availability at all three parks by calling ☎ 867-920-2472.

B&Bs The Visitor Information Centre has a list of B&Bs and will make reservations for you. The following homes are all in the delightful Old Town area.

Very good value is *Island B&B* (☎ 867-873-4786, 34 Morrison Drive), which has a comfortable living room with a view of Back Bay. Rooms cost $60/80 a single/double. Nearby, *Captain Ron's B&B* (☎ 867-873-3746, 8 Lessard Drive) has smoke-free rooms from $72/88.

Also on Latham Island, *Blue Raven B&B* (☎ 867-873-6328, fax 867-920-4013, 37-B Otto Drive) has nice rooms from $60/75. On The Rock by the float-plane terminal, *Bayside B&B* (☎ 867-920-4686, fax 867-920-7931, 3505 McDonald Drive) has great views of Yellowknife Bay and rooms from $60/70. Just around the corner, *Prospector B&B* (☎ 867-920-7620, fax 867-669-7581, 3506 Wiley Rd) is almost a hotel with well equipped rooms from $75/90 and a noted restaurant for fresh-fish dinners.

Hotels & Motels Rates at the following places fall outside the high season.

The *Igloo Motor Inn* (☎ 867-873-8511, fax 867-873-5547, 4115 Franklin Ave), halfway between downtown and the Old Town, is a friendly place and charges $95/104. At the *Discovery Inn* (☎ 867-873-4151, fax 867-920-7948, 4701 Franklin Ave) rooms are $98/113 for corporate rates. *Yellowknife Inn* (☎ 867-873-2601, ☎ 1-800-661-0580, fax 867-873-2602), on Franklin

Ave between 49th and 50th Sts, is the largest hotel in town. Rooms with all the amenities cost $130 a single or double. Looming over everything is the high-rise *Explorer Hotel* (☎ 867-873-3531, ☎ 1-800-661-0892, fax 867-873-2789, 4823 48th St), with standard modern rooms from $157/172. This is where the Queen stays when she is in town.

Places to Eat

Yellowknife has many places to eat, from fast-food joints on Old Airport Rd to greasy spoons downtown to one of the finest restaurants in the north in Old Town.

Upstairs in the Panda II Mall, the *Picnic Nook* (☎ 867-873-6292) is a lunchtime favourite with locals, who wolf down the $4 sandwiches. Just downstairs, *Ryan's Family Restaurant* (☎ 867-873-2363) has lunches for about $7 and a popular Oriental buffet. The *Red Apple* (☎ 867-873-2324, cnr Franklin Ave & 47th St) has a broad diner-style menu but is acclaimed for its rib-sticking breakfasts.

The best local Italian cooking is at *Giorgio's* (☎ 867-669-2023, 5022 47th St), where the owner's mother, Cosimina Meraglia, runs the kitchen. Expect to spend about $20 per person.

The famous *Wildcat Café* (☎ 867-873-8850, cnr Wiley Rd & Doombos Lane), in the Old Town, is set in a 1937 log cabin. The Wildcat serves all day inside, and on nice days out on the pleasant patio. The changing menu is centred on northern foods like caribou and various fresh fish. The desserts made with local wild berries are a delight. Prices range from $7 to $20.

For a meal that may inspire you to make a return journey to Yellowknife, find a place at *Bullock's Bistro* (☎ 867-873-3474, 4 Lessard Drive) in the Old Town. Here only the freshest fish make the day's changing menu, you have a choice of preparations and everything right down to the incredible garlic-ginger salad dressing is just plain exquisite. Book at one of the tables or nab a stool at the counter where you can engage in cheery banter with the staff and watch the cook work her magic. There is a good range of beers you serve yourself from the cooler and they taste even better if you get a table outside. Expect to pay about $15 per person. Call to check the hours, which vary.

Extra Foods is a large supermarket in the YK Centre Mall on 48th St near Franklin Ave.

Entertainment

The *Cave Club* (☎ 867-920-7011, 5108 Franklin Ave) is a fun subterranean bar. The staff and patrons are lively and live bands span the music spectrum from country to blues to rock. If you want to consummate romance, snog-off to one of the dark booths in the back.

Shopping

Yellowknife is the distribution centre and major retailer of craft items from around the territories. One of the best places to see a range of works is at The North West Company Trading Post (☎ 867-873-8064), near Old Town at 5005 Bryson Drive. The huge store has a large selection and the staff are good at explaining things. Many more outlets for Native works can be found in the various malls downtown.

Getting There & Away

Air Yellowknife is the hub of air service for much of the NWT and western Nunavut. Air fares are not subsidised for visitors and thus can be breathtakingly high. Flights to Edmonton provide the major link to the rest of Canada. First Air (☎ 867-873-6884, ☎ 1-800-267-1247) has consolidated its position as the monopolistic airline of the north by buying NWT Air from Air Canada. It has services to/from Edmonton, Fort Resolution, Hay River, Fort Simpson, Whitehorse, Inuvik and various Nunavut destinations such as Cambridge Bay, Resolute, Rankin Inlet and Iqaluit.

Canadian North (☎ 867-873-4484, ☎ 1-800-661-1505), a division of Canadian Airlines, has services to/from Edmonton, Norman Wells, Inuvik and various Nunavut destinations such as Cambridge Bay, Resolute, Rankin Inlet and Iqaluit.

Smaller airlines serve towns in the NWT and they sometimes offer good special fares. Note that services can be sporadic and companies come and go. Northwestern Air (☎ 867-873-8739) serves Fort Smith, Buffalo Air (☎ 867-873-6112) flies to Hay River with DC-3s. Air Tindi (☎ 867-669-8260) serves Fort Simpson.

Bus Frontier Coachlines (☎ 867-874-2566) has services to/from Enterprise and Hay River (eight hours) that connect with Greyhound buses (☎ 1-800-661-8747) to/from Edmonton. The bus stop in Yellowknife is on the corner of 53rd St and 52nd Ave in front of Bruno's, a scruffy café. However, this location seems to move around a lot, so check with Frontier.

Getting Around
Much of Yellowknife is easily walked. From downtown to Old Town is about 15 minutes. The walk to the airport, however, can take about an hour.

Bus The City of Yellowknife Public Transit System is operated by Arctic Frontier Carriers (☎ 867-873-4437). Fares are $2/1.50 adults/children. Route No 1 serves the airport, Old Airport Rd, downtown on Franklin Ave and on to Old Town. This bus runs hourly from roughly 7 am to 7 pm weekdays and for just a few hours Saturday.

Car It's possible to rent a car in Yellowknife; it's also not cheap. Mileage charges rapidly wipe out the seemingly reasonable daily rates, especially given that all the places worth driving to are fairly far. Take care to determine what your liability will be given the high likelihood of windshield and other flying rock damage.

Avis
  (☎ 867-920-4719) 329 Old Airport Rd
National/Tilden
  (☎ 867-920-2970) 5118 50th St
Rent A Relic
  (☎ 867-873-9839) 356 Old Airport Rd
Yellowknife Motors
  (☎ 867-873-4414) cnr of 49th Ave & 48th St

Bicycle Bikes can be rented from the Visitor Information Centre for $20 per day.

AROUND YELLOWKNIFE
Detah
The small Dogrib Dene village of Detah is 25km by road south-east of town across Yellowknife Bay. You can get a look at the traditional way of life, talk to people and see some interesting handiwork. You will also hear the commonly used Dogrib language. There are no formal tourist facilities.

The Ingraham Trail
The 71km Ingraham Trail (Hwy 4) extends east of Yellowknife to **Tibbitt Lake**, where fittingly, there is a stop sign at the end of the road. About the first 25km is paved and the rest is kept in good condition. The route reveals superb, hilly, rocky Canadian Shield topography dotted with lakes. There are great views and good fishing, hiking, canoeing, camping and picnicking. It's best with a car but cycling is possible.

At **Prelude Lake**, 30km east of Yellowknife, there is camping, a beach and a 2.5km nature trail. This is a busy weekend, family-oriented spot. **Cameron Falls** is a popular hike and there are two trails, a 1.2km one from **Hidden Lake** and another, 4km long, that is just before **Bailey Bridge**.

At **Reid Lake**, 59km from Yellowknife, you can camp, swim or canoe. The *Reid Lake campground* is busy on weekends but otherwise it's very quiet – this is, after all, one of the more remote campgrounds in the country. There's a good beach and walking trail and some fine camp sites on the ridge. Ask for site No 22.

The road ends at **Tibbitt Lake**, which is fine for fishing and is also the start of some fine canoe routes including one to **Pensive Lake**.

Blachford Lake Lodge
Surrounded by lakes, *Blachford Lake Lodge* *(☎ 867-873-3303, fax 867-920-4013)* is a good example of the remote lodges which dot the NWT. They have a variety of fishing and nature tours and accommodation ranging

from small rustic cabins to a rather plush lodge. There is a range of packages, but five days in the summer is $875/1150 per person with/without meals. This includes transportation over the 95km distance to/from Yellowknife by float plane. If you do some chores, you get a 20% discount.

ALBERTA BORDER TO YELLOWKNIFE

The first stretch of the Mackenzie Hwy follows the Hay River which flows north into Great Slave Lake. At the border with Alberta, the North of 60 Information Centre (☎ 867-920-1021) is open 8 am to 10 pm daily from mid-May to mid-September. As well as road and travel information it has a display of arts and crafts. Nearby is a campground with a kitchen shelter and water. The area between the border and Fort Providence provides the visitor with a good introduction to the uncluttered wildness of the territories. There are some good stops along the way with campgrounds and walking trails.

About 75km north of the border is **Twin Falls Gorge Territorial Park** (☎ 1-800-661-0788). Here 33m Alexandra Falls, named after Princess Alexandra of Britain, is not to be missed. A short trail leads to a platform overlooking the high and wide falls. Nearby, stairs lead down to the water and rocky ledges by the lip of the falls. A farther 2km north is the parking lot for the smaller, but still impressive, 15m Louise Falls where there is overnight camping for $10 a night. A 45 minute walking trail along the Hay River gorge links the two falls and is a very pleasant hike especially beginning at Louise and heading towards thunderous Alexandra. Just a few kilometres farther north is **Escarpment Creek**, a good picnic place with views of the gorge.

Enterprise, with a population of about 60, is the first settlement in the Northwest Territories that you come to. There's an Esso service station (☎ 867-874-6424), a store and a *motel*. From Enterprise the Mackenzie Hwy is paved most of the way as far as the junction with Hwy 3 which leads to the Mackenzie River ferry at Fort Providence.

This portion of the road is also called the Waterfall Route. (North-east out of Enterprise, Hwy 2 takes you to Hay River.)

North of Enterprise is the picnic site of **McNallie Creek Falls** with a waterfall tumbling into a water-worn bowl of rock. About 9km north the **Hart Lake Fire Tower** provides views as far as Great Slave Lake.

Before the village of Kakisa, which is 9km off the highway, is **Lady Evelyn Falls** with a walking path to views and the river right beneath the falls. There is good fishing and a very fine *campground* with tall trees presided over by the roar of the falls. A site is $12 and it's usually full on weekends.

Some 105km after Enterprise, Hwy 3 branches north for 31km to the free ferry (☎ 1-800-661-0751) over the Mackenzie River. It operates from roughly mid-May to mid-December. There is an ice bridge in the winter and there is no crossing at all for two to three weeks during the freeze-up and spring thaw.

Fort Providence, a Slavey community of 700, lies on the banks of the Mackenzie River, 6km from the ferry and 312km south of Yellowknife. The site was settled in 1861 when a Roman Catholic mission was established, followed soon after by a Hudson's Bay Company trading post. In town there are benches atop the 10m cliffs overlooking the river. Past the beautiful wooden church the road leads to the dock. From here you can walk along the shore of the inlet to a small beach and picnic area. The road continues past the large rock to the town cemetery.

The fishing is very good and pike, walleye and maybe grayling can be caught from shore.

Two kilometres off Hwy 3 on the access road to town, there is a good *campground* by the river; it has pit toilets and drinking water. Also on the outskirts the charmless *Big River Motel* (☎ 867-699-4301) has a service station, café and rooms from $60. In town, the larger *Snowshoe Inn* (☎ 867-699-3511) charges $90/110 a single/double. The bus station is at the Snowshoe Inn.

North out of Fort Providence, Hwy 3 follows the western boundary of the **Mackenzie**

Bison Sanctuary for nearly 100km. The sanctuary holds the largest herd of free-ranging pure wood bison in the world, some of which can occasionally be seen by the side of the road. Hiking is not recommended as there are no trails, it's easy to get lost and the bison can be ill-tempered (possibly due to the enormous swarms of bugs around each animal).

The dusty but paved and straight road passes through scraggly forests and hilly terrain into the twin Dogrib communities of **Edzo** (214km from Fort Providence) and **Rae**. There is no reason to stop at Edzo although there is a campground just south of town. In Rae there is a service station (☎ 867-392-6955) and basic variety store. From here to Yellowknife (98km) you see the rounded, copper-coloured rock outcrops that form part of the Canadian Shield. This portion of Hwy 3 is unpaved, slow, winding and pretty rough.

HAY RIVER

The town of Hay River, with a population of 3200, sits on the southern shore of Great Slave Lake, 38km north of Enterprise on Hwy 2. This is the heart of Big River Country which encompasses the area and communities by the Mackenzie, Hay and Slave rivers and Great Slave Lake. Although it's a bit of a detour, it is a good place to stop even if you're using the Mackenzie Hwy.

Hay River has two distinct areas; the old part of town is at the north end on Vale Island. The newer section of town is to the south and will be seen first on arrival by Hwy 2. This is the commercial centre with all the restaurants and stores. The Visitor Information Centre (☎ 867-874-3180) is here on the corner of Mackenzie Hwy and McBryan Drive. It is open 9 am to 9 pm daily from May to September.

There are a few things to see around this small but busy town. It's a major distribution centre where barges load up for trips to settlements along the Mackenzie River and up to the Arctic coast. There is a significant commercial fishery here including packing and shipping, primarily of whitefish and lake trout. The broad sandy **beach** on Vale Island is attractive and you can fish in the surf. A nature trail winds along the Hay River.

Across the Hay River, the Dene Reserve operates the **Dene Cultural Institute** (☎ 867-874-8480). This excellent centre offers tours of the Dene village and has good displays on their culture. It is open 9 am to 5 pm weekdays and 1 to 5 pm Saturday from June to mid-September.

Places to Stay

The *Hay River Campground* (☎ 867-874-3772) on Vale Island has sites for $12; facilities include hot showers and a barbecue area. The beach is here and they will always find an empty spot for you no matter how full.

Nearby, *Harbour House B&B* (☎ 867-874-2233) has great views at the end of the beach road. Rooms are good value at $45/65 a single/double and there is a large kitchen. In town, *Cedar Rest Motel* (☎ 867-874-3732) is near the bus station and has rooms from $55/62.

Places to Eat

There is a surprising amount of choice here, with several places around the commercial centre. The local favourite is the *Boardroom Restaurant* (☎ 867-874-2111, 891 Mackenzie Hwy). Open daily, the choice is large given that the menu lists Mexican, Chinese, Italian and northern specialities.

Getting There & Away

Buffalo Airways (☎ 867-874-3333) and First Air (☎ 867-874-2847, ☎ 1-800-267-1247) fly to Yellowknife from the airport which is on Vale Island. Canadian North (☎ 867-874-2434, ☎ 1-800-661-1505) flies to Edmonton.

Greyhound (☎ 867-874-6966, ☎ 1-800-661-8747) has daily services to Edmonton (16 hours, $130). Frontier Coachlines (☎ 867-874-2566) serves Yellowknife and other places served by road such as Fort Smith, Hay River, Fort Providence and Fort Simpson. The bus station is at 39-141 Mackenzie Hwy.

PARADISE VALLEY

Some 24km south of Hay River just off Hwy 2, *Paradise Garden Camp Ground* (☎ 867-

874-6414, fax 867-874-4422) is a delightful place on a sweeping bend of the Hay River. In summer it sells beautiful organic produce and has a lovely and often sunny campground (sites $12) with a good kitchen where you can prepare those vegetables.

FORT SMITH

This town of 2400 sits astride the Alberta border on Hwy 5, 333km east of Hay River. There is a Visitor Information Centre (☎ 867-872-2515), 56 Portage Ave. Among the sights are the **Northern Life Museum** with local history and a trail to the evocatively named Rapids of the Drowned. **Fort Smith Mission Historic Park** is the site of the 1912 Catholic mission. A pelican nesting viewpoint is south of town.

There is a *campground* at Queen Elizabeth Territorial Park on the banks of Slave River close to town on the west side. At Liz's Corner Store is the *Fort Smith International Hostel* (☎ 867-872-3097, 376 Cedar Ave). In addition to $15 beds, canoes can be rented here. *Pinecrest Hotel* (☎ 867-872-2320) has comfortable rooms for $75/85 as well as a bar and restaurant.

Nearby is the entrance to Wood Buffalo National Park, for which the town acts as a supply centre. Get your food in town as there is nowhere to buy it in the park.

WOOD BUFFALO NATIONAL PARK

The second largest national park in the world at 45,000 sq km, Wood Buffalo National Park was established in 1922 to protect the few hundred surviving wood bison of the herds which had once numbered in the millions. Now a UN World Heritage Site, much of the vast park is inaccessible. It is a land of endless boreal forest dappled with a myriad of bogs and criss-crossed with the shallow delta channels of the Peace and Athabasca rivers.

There is camping at **Pine Lake**, 60km south of Fort Smith. In the winter there is an ice road linking the park to Fort MacKay in Alberta. The park visitor information centre (☎ 867-872-2349) on the corner of McDougal Rd and Portage Ave in Fort Smith is well equipped to help you make sense of

this fascinating and confounding park. It is open 8.30 am to 5 pm weekdays year-round and 10 am to 5 pm weekends in July and August. For more information on the park see the Alberta chapter.

WEST OF GREAT SLAVE LAKE

From the junction of Hwy 3, the Mackenzie Hwy (Hwy 1) continues 300km west to Fort Simpson and beyond. At about two-thirds of the way to Fort Simpson, stop at **Sambeh Deh Falls** with waterfalls, a gorge and campground.

There is a free ferry (☎ 1-800-661-0752) across the Liard River just south of Fort Simpson. It runs mid-May to mid-October, replaced by an ice bridge in winter and with the usual lack of any connection during the freeze-up and thaw.

Fort Simpson

Established in 1804 as a fur-trading post, Fort Simpson was once district headquarters for the Hudson's Bay Company. Today, most of the 1200 people in Fort Smith are Dene with some Métis and non-Native people. This is the major town of the Deh Cho region, as the region around the Mackenzie is known. With its tour operators and charter airlines, it is also the main access point for Nahanni National Park, 145km west of Fort Simpson.

Arriving from the south, the Visitors Centre (☎ 867-695-3182) is at the entrance to town. It's open 8 am to 8 pm daily mid-May to mid-September. There is camping ($10) in town at Fort Simpson Territorial Park. It is fairly well equipped with water, pit toilets and a playground. Among the handful of small lodgings, *Nahanni Inn* (☎ 867-695-2201, fax 867-695-3000) has modestly equipped rooms from $100. It also has a lounge and restaurant.

First Air (☎ 867-695-2020, ☎ 1-800-267-1247) stops in Fort Simpson on its flights linking Whitehorse and Yellowknife. Air Tindi (☎ 867-669-8260) serves Yellowknife. Frontier Coachlines (☎ 867-874-2566) serves Hay River.

From Fort Simpson the Mackenzie Hwy continues 222km north to the small Dene

community of Wrigley overlooking the Mackenzie River. Hunting, trapping and fishing remain the basis of this mainly log-cabin village. A winter ice road connects Norman Wells.

Independent travellers and those on budgets insufficient for Nahanni National Park trips might consider contacting the North Nahanni Naturalist Lodge (☎ 867-695-2116, fax 867-695-2118). Run by a Dene family, the lodge offers very interesting trips ranging from three hours to overnight. One goes north along the Mackenzie 32km to the lesser known **North Nahanni River** which runs through the Mackenzie Mountains. A five hour trip covering a lot of territory through national park-like scenery along the North Nahanni and the isolated Tetcela rivers costs from $150. There are also boat trips to Dene outposts which are otherwise inaccessible in summer. Stops are made along the way at houses, old cabins and hunting camp sites. Trips start at the Ndulee Ferry Crossing on the Mackenzie Hwy 78km north of Fort Simpson.

Liard Highway

From a point 65km south of Fort Simpson the Liard Hwy (Hwy 7) branches west off the Mackenzie Hwy along the Liard River valley for Nahanni Butte and Fort Liard. The Mackenzie Mountains can be seen to the west. The road then travels south into British Columbia to Fort Nelson making a circle through BC, the NWT and Alberta possible. From Fort Simpson to Fort Nelson is 487km.

Across from Nahanni Butte and 110km south from the Liard Trail starting point is **Blackstone Territorial Park** with information, hiking trails, camping and views of the Liard River. It is open June to August. Many trips from the national park end here.

Fort Liard

At this largely traditional town of 500 there is a two storey log building erected by Roman Catholic missionaries in 1921. However, archaeological discoveries have shown humans in the area at least 9000 years ago. Among the Dene crafts here the birch bark

baskets made by women and adorned with porcupine quills are noteworthy.

The weather is surprisingly mild and the town has undergone a bit of a boomlet since the opening of the Liard Trail in the early 1980s. Some of the infrastructure for Nahanni National Park visits is based here and there is a small *campground*. The *General Store and Motel* (☎ 867-770-4441) is just that. There's also a service station (☎ 867-770-3122). The BC border is 38km south.

NAHANNI NATIONAL PARK

This magnificent wilderness park in the south-western corner of the District of Mackenzie, close to the Yukon border, is one of the major draws of the NWT and attracts visitors from around the world. Nahanni National Park protects a superb portion of the Mackenzie Mountains and the turbulent South Nahanni River with its spectacular canyons. It is visited mainly by canoeists wishing to challenge the white waters (considered among the best on the continent) of this renowned 322km Canadian Heritage River. The park has been designated as a UN World Heritage Site because of its dramatic, pristine nature.

Other highlights include the waterfalls, particularly **Virginia Falls**, which at 96m is about twice the height of Niagara Falls, and also the sulphur hot springs at **Rabbitkettle** and **Wildmint**. A vast area to the north of the national park called **Ram Plateau** has been proposed to become a territorial park.

Much has been written about the park and the whole area has been a place of lore since the early 1900s when the discovery of the decapitated corpses of two brothers looking for gold led to tales of enormous mountain men, wild native tribes and other mighty fanciful horrors. The best one probably involved the tribe led by Amazon white women.

Numerous other miners who died of possibly unnatural reasons or just disappeared only added to the area's wild reputation. Various place names in the park such as Headless Range, Broken Skull River and Deadmen Valley recall this colourful legacy.

Even if you don't see enormous white women, any fetish for wildlife is bound to be met by the park's large population of bears, mountain goats, moose, wolves and more.

Visiting the Park

With no road access, getting into the park is not cheap. The only way to reach it is by airplane or helicopter, usually as part of a tour although you can do your own self-guided trip.

There are basically two types of visits. The first is on the water. Six-day to three-week canoe or rubber-raft trips eastward take in many of the park's main sites. Adventurers with intermediate paddling skills can do the river on their own. The 'classic' average trip is 14 days with nine days paddling and five days for hiking and delays. Of course, you could get flown in and canoe back for just a day or two. All canoeists and rafters end up at Blackstone Territorial Park on the Liard River.

The second type of visit is a fly-over sightseeing tour with or without a landing to allow hiking. These trips range from a simple 30 minute flight to a couple of days for some more serious hiking. The basic here is the one day hike around Victoria Falls. All visitors on a self-guided trip must register with the park office. For camping, there are seven primitive areas set aside with tables as well as fireplaces.

The main park office (☎ 867-695-3151, ☎ 867-695-2310) for information and permits is in Fort Simpson. Write to Superintendent, Nahanni National Park, Box 348, Fort Simpson, NT, X0E 0N0. The day use fee for the park is $10, with higher fees for overnight stays. There is a very strict quota system in effect for visitors whether on tours or independent so contacting the park in advance for the latest details is essential. There is a much smaller seasonal information office at Blackstone Territorial Park.

Organised Tours

The park information office can offer advice and details on short one or two-day trips or the longer tours. Either way, most leave from Fort Simpson. For short park tours and independent river trips see the following Getting There & Away section.

The long, guided canoe and raft trips are excellent but expensive. Prices and nature of the excursions are similar, averaging from $2200 to $3600 and beyond. Different times of the season offer different advantages so ask for details to best match your interests. Because access to the park is limited, trips should be prebooked, preferably months in advance. The canoe trips are best for people with some basic experience although you needn't be an advanced whitewater paddler. Raft trips are more relaxing, provide more time to enjoy the scenery and are suitable for all ages. See the Getting There & Away section below for details of operators.

Getting There & Away

The lines are blurred between the various Nahanni tour operators, outfitters, guides and charter aircraft services. The following are the major firms that specialise in Nahanni travel. There is a complete listing in the free NWT Tourism *Explorer's Guide*.

Western NWT Tour Planning (☎ 867-695-2955, fax 867-695-3456) organises guided trips throughout the Nahanni region. For information, write to: Box 643, Fort Simpson, NT, X0E 0N0.

Nahanni River Adventures/Whitewolf Adventure Expeditions (☎ 867-668-3180, ☎ 1-800-297-6927, fax 867-668-3056) has a variety of guided trips by canoe and raft. For information, write to: Box 4869, Whitehorse, YT, Y1A 4N6.

Black Feather Wilderness Adventures (☎ 613-722-8375, ☎ 1-800-574-8375, fax 613-722-0245) has guided trips of two and three weeks from Fort Simpson. For information, write to: 1960 Scott St, Ottawa, Ontario, K1Z 8L8.

Nahanni Wilderness Adventures (☎ 403-637-3843, ☎ 1-888-897-5223) has guided trips from one to three weeks. It also does canoe outfitting, route planning and other logistical assistance for independent travellers. For information, write to: Box 4, Site 6, RR No 1, Didsbury, Alberta, T0M 0W0.

Nahanni Wilderness Camps (☎ 867-667-2712, fax 867-667-4868) has tent camps in the Mackenzie Mountains for guided and unguided hikers. For information, write to: Box 5364, Whitehorse, YT, Y1A 4Z2.

Deh Cho Air (☎ 867-770-4103, ☎ 1-888-897-5223) is based in Fort Liard and has day trips to Virginia Falls as well as air services for independent travellers. For information, write to: General Delivery, Fort Liard, NT, X0G 0A0.

Wolverine Air (☎ 867-695-2263, fax 867-695-3400) has day trips to Virginia Falls and the Ram Plateau and air charter services. For information, write to: Box 316, Fort Simpson, NT, X0E 0N0.

South Nahanni Airways (☎ 867-695-2007, fax 867-695-2943) can carry large charter groups into the park. For information, write to: Box 407, Fort Simpson, NT, X0E 0N0.

Blackstone Aviation/Goleeah Air (☎ 867-695-2111, fax 867-695-2132) has the advantage of operating charter flights from Blackstone Territorial Park which is where many of the river trips end, thus allowing you to start from where you will finish. For information, write to: Box 151, Fort Liard, NT X0G 0A0.

MACKENZIE RIVER VALLEY

North-west NWT is wide and flat. The Mackenzie River, swollen by water draining from one-fifth of Canada lazily wends its way across the countryside, and in places it is over 3km wide. This is popular canoe and kayak country with some hearty souls taking advantage of the long summer days to paddle from Fort Providence to Tuktoyaktuk on the Arctic Ocean, a distance of 1800km.

Norman Wells

On the northern shore of the Mackenzie River halfway between Fort Simpson and Inuvik, this town of 800 has long been an oil town. There's a *campground* in town and several hotels, including the *Yamouri (☎ 867-587-2744, fax 867-587-2262)*, which has simple rooms from $100. Canadian North (☎ 867-587-2361, ☎ 1-800-661-1505) stops on its flights between Yellowknife and Inuvik.

North-Wright Airways (☎ 867-587-2333) serves the even more isolated communities along the river. The only road access to Norman Wells is by ice road in the winter.

The town's main attraction is the **Canol Heritage Trail**, a hiking trail designated a National Historic Site which leads 372km southwest to the Yukon border. From there, a road leads to Ross River and the Yukon highway system. The trail was built at enormous monetary and human cost during WWII to supply oil to Whitehorse. Shortly after completion, however, the huge project was abandoned in 1947 because the war was over and there were many cheaper ways to get oil to Whitehorse. Today the trail is lined with derelict army camps and equipment and should really be designated as a monument to North American taxpayers, who forked over $300 million (1945 dollars) for its construction.

The route traverses peaks, canyons, barrens and there's lots of wildlife. There are numerous deep river crossings along the trail and no facilities although you can sleep in some of the old Quonset huts. Canol Rd (Hwy 6) from Whitehorse meets the trail on the Yukon border. Hiking the whole length takes three to four weeks and most people need to arrange food drops along the way. The **Norman Wells Historical Centre** (☎ 867-587-2415) is open from 10 am to 10 pm in summer and has full details about the history of the trail.

Inuvik

Inuvik, with a population of 3300, is the NWT's second largest town, although it was only founded in 1955 as a supply centre. It lies on the East Channel of the Mackenzie River about 90km south of the Arctic coast. The town has the typically somewhat shoddy appearance of northern towns. It is the centre for tourism and logistical base for the Western Arctic. The main street is Mackenzie Rd and you can walk the length of town in about 20 minutes. There are few street numbers.

For nearly two months each year, from the end of May, it has 24 hours of daylight every day. This is a situation that people soon adapt to as locals say that the best way

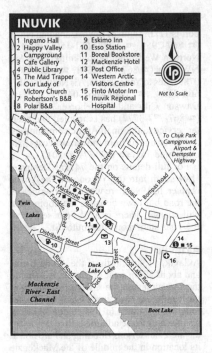

INUVIK

1 Ingamo Hall
2 Happy Valley Campground
3 Cafe Gallery
4 Public Library
5 The Mad Trapper
6 Our Lady of Victory Church
7 Robertson's B&B
8 Polar B&B
9 Eskimo Inn
10 Esso Station
11 Boreal Bookstore
12 Mackenzie Hotel
13 Post Office
14 Western Arctic Visitors Centre
15 Finto Motor Inn
16 Inuvik Regional Hospital

Not to Scale

to tell a new arrival in town is that they have aluminum foil on their windows. The first snow falls sometime around the end of August. The population is roughly divided between Inuit, Dene and non-Native people. Note that crafts, including locally made parkas, are for sale.

Western Arctic Visitors Centre (☎ 867-777-4727, in winter ☎ 867-777-7327) is on Mackenzie Rd at the east end of town. It is open 9 am to 9 pm daily mid-May to mid-September.

There are two banks in town. Boreal Bookstore (☎ 867-777-3748) is a charming little place run by Bob Rowe that has a great selection of northern books and topographical and river maps. The post office (☎ 867-777-2252) is at 187 Mackenzie Rd. The public library (☎ 867-777-2749) has free Internet access. Inuvik Regional Hospital (☎ 867-777-2955) is near the visitors centre.

Things to See & Do The main sight in town is the unusual **Our Lady of Victory Church** with a lovely interior by local artists. One glance at its design will explain why people generally call it the 'Igloo Church'. Close by, **The Carving Corner** is an amiable place where locals artists hang out creating works from ivory and rock. **Chuk Park**, 6km south of town, has a good lookout tower for viewing the sub-Arctic terrain.

The best reason to come to Inuvik is to get out of town on one of the Arctic tours. Most involve flights that pass over the **Mackenzie Delta**, a spectacular place of water, squalls, wildlife and the occasional abandoned trapper's hut on the emerald-green banks. Tours involving flying begin at about $150 for three hours and are worth it for the aerial views alone regardless of the delights of the destination.

Arctic Nature Tours (☎ 867-777-3300), next to the Igloo Church, has a wide range of tours to untouched places like Herschel and Banks islands. The most popular trip is to the village of Tuktoyaktuk. Beaufort Delta Tours (☎ 867-777-4881), 163 Mackenzie Rd, has van tours of Inuvik for $20 as well as longer river tours. It also has the full range of regional tours.

Canadian Arctic Adventure Tours (☎ 867-777-4006) specialises in snowmobile expeditions during the long winters. Western Arctic Adventures (☎ 867-777-2594) rents canoes and kayaks from $200 per week and makes logistical arrangements for independent travellers.

Special Events The Great Northern Arts Festival (☎ 867-777-3536) is a major show of Native art held the third week of July every year. Many of the artists travel from tiny remote villages to display and sell their works. There are workshops where visitors can learn about the art as well as dozens of artists demonstrating their skills.

Places to Stay *Chuk Park Campground* (☎ 867-777-3613), about 6km before town on the Dempster Hwy, is open from June to

October and provides hot showers and firewood; the office is open 24 hours a day for the duration. Sites cost $15/12 with/without electricity. The campground has a good view of the delta and the breeze keeps the mosquitoes down a bit. In town, *Happy Valley Campground* has similar rates and a coin laundry.

In town, ***Robertson's B&B*** *(☎ 867-777-3111, 41 Mackenzie Rd)* has laundry and kitchen facilities and rents out bikes and canoes. ***Polar B&B*** *(☎ 867-777-2554, fax 867-777-3668, 75 Mackenzie Rd)* has similar facilities and rents canoes and kayaks. Both charge $75/85 a single/double.

There are three hotels in Inuvik, all charging about $120 for a room. The very friendly ***Mackenzie Hotel*** *(☎ 867-777-2861, fax 867-777-3317, cnr Mackenzie Rd & Distributor St)* has OK rooms and is right in the centre. The ***Eskimo Inn*** *(☎ 867-777-2801, ☎ 1-800-661-0725, fax 867-777-3234)* on Mackenzie Rd has modern rooms. At the east entrance of town, ***Finto Motel Inn*** *(☎ 867-777-2647, ☎ 1-800-661-0843, fax 867-777-3442)* has nice grounds and locally produced dinner theatre in summer.

Places to Eat & Drink Musk ox and caribou burgers are on just about every menu in town. Big Macs these ain't. For less meaty fare, ***Cafe Gallery*** *(☎ 867-777-2888, 28 Mackenzie Rd)* has a bakery with muffins which feature locally grown blueberries, and local artwork. Next door, ***Tamarack Health Foods*** *(☎ 867-777-2730)* has organic and other foods. The ***Green Briar Restaurant*** in the Mackenzie Hotel has fresh Arctic foods and a very popular prime rib special on some nights for a mere $10. It also has a popular pub and *The Zoo*, a dance club.

The striking ***Ingamo Hall*** *(☎ 867-777-2166, 20 Mackenzie Rd)* has lunches on Thursday for village elders. Visitors are welcome and you can hear some great stories. For a wild time, *The Mad Trapper (☎ 867-777-3825, 124 Mackenzie Rd)* traps locals and visitors alike in an often raucous pub setting.

Getting There & Away Mike Zubko airport is 12km south of town. Canadian North (☎ 867-2951, ☎ 1-800-661-1505) flies to Norman Wells and Yellowknife. First Air/NWT Air (☎ 867-777-2341, ☎ 1-800-661-0789) flies to Yellowknife. Air North (☎ 867-668-2228, ☎ 1-800-661-0407) flies to Dawson City and Whitehorse. Aklak Air (☎ 867-777-3777) has scheduled and charter service to the small Arctic communities. A cab for one to/from the airport costs $25; try United Taxi (☎ 867-777-5050).

For full details on the 741km Dempster Hwy south into the Yukon, see the Yukon chapter. In 1998 there was no bus service on the road but town boosters are hoping that will change. There is a 24 hour self-serve Esso gas station on Distributor St.

Aklavik

Aklavik, 113km north of the Arctic Circle and about 50km west of Inuvik, is home to the Inavaluit and the Gwich'in who, over the centuries, have traded and sometimes fought each other in this region. Aklavik was for a time the administrative centre for the area, but serious flooding and erosion at its location in the middle of the Mackenzie Delta prompted the federal government to move in the 1950s to a new site at Inuvik. Over 700 people have remained in town, refusing to move to drier land. The Mad Trapper Jamboree, held at Easter, keeps alive the memory of Albert Johnson, the Mad Trapper of Rat River. He murdered other trappers for their gold fillings, but was finally gunned down in a shoot-out at Eagle River in 1932 by the Mounties, after he'd killed one of their officers.

For local information, call the hamlet office (☎ 867-978-2351). The Inuvik tour companies visit Aklavik. Road access is limited to winter ice roads.

ARCTIC REGION

Inuvik is the base for exploring the tiny villages and remote and wild expanses and islands of the NWT. By comparison to these sparsely settled lands, Inuvik seems like a metropolis.

Tuktoyaktuk

About 137km north-east of Inuvik in Kugmallit Bay on the Arctic coast is Tuktoyaktuk, commonly known as Tuk. Originally the home of the whale-hunting Karngmalit or Mackenzie Inuit, it's a land base for some of the Beaufort Sea oil and gas explorations. Pods of beluga whales can be seen in July and August. In the land around Tuk are *pingos* – huge mounds made of earth and ice caused by frost heaves.

There is an old military base here dating from the Cold War as well as old whaling buildings and two charming little churches dating from the time when the Catholic and Anglican churches battled to proselytise the Native people. Land access is limited to winter ice roads and most tourists arrive in summer as part of half-day trips from Inuvik. These invariably feature a chance to bare your foot and plunge it into the Arctic Ocean, an experience akin to soaking your toes in a bucket of ice water. The hamlet office (☎ 867-977-2286) can provide more information on the area and services.

Paulatuk

This small Karngmalit community of 110 is on the Arctic coast at the southern end of Darnley Bay near the mouth of the Hornaday River, about 400km east of Inuvik. The town's name means 'soot of coal' and one of the main local attractions is the **Smoking Hills**, which contain smouldering sulphide-rich slate and seams of coal. For more de-

tailed information, contact the hamlet office (☎ 867-580-3531).

Paulatuk is the closest inhabited place to **Tuktut Nogait National Park Reserve**, a wild and untouched place about 60km east that is a major staging ground for caribou migration. There are no services or facilities here. For information, contact Parks Canada (☎ 867-777-3248, fax 867-777-4491), Box 1840, Inuvik, NT, X0E 0T0.

Banks Island

Lying in the Arctic Ocean to the north of Paulatuk, Banks Island may have been first inhabited 3500 years ago. Wildlife is abundant and this is one of the best places to see musk ox. The island has two bird sanctuaries where you can see flocks of snowgeese and seabirds in the summer. **Sachs Harbour**, an Inavaluit community of about 140 that's Native name is Ikaahuk, is the only settlement on the island.

Aulavik National Park, on the north of the island, covers 12,300 sq km. It has the world's largest concentration of musk ox as well as badlands, tundra and archaeological sites. Arctic Nature Tours (☎ 867-777-3300) in Inuvik runs tours of various lengths to the island. *Kuptana's Guest House (☎ 867-690-4151)* has rooms from $175 including meals. It also organises nature tours. For more information, contact the Sachs Harbour hamlet office (☎ 867-690-4351) and Parks Canada (☎ 867-777-3248, fax 867-777-4491), Box 1840, Inuvik, NT, X0E 0T0.

Nunavut

A decades-old dream of the Inuit people to have their own self-governing territory became reality on 1 April, 1999 when the new territory of Nunavut was created out of what had been the eastern Arctic region of the Northwest Territories.

Nunavut means 'Our Land' in Inuktitut, the language of the Inuit who make up 83% of the population scattered over the vast stretches of tundra and polar islands that cover an area twice the size of Ontario. A gentle people with a maritime tradition, the Inuit are in an uneasy transition between their traditional lives of subsistence hunting of whales and seals and modern lives in towns with schools and jobs. More than 80% live in government housing and there is unemployment and other social problems. Alcohol is severely restricted everywhere and banned entirely in many communities. But after years of existing under the rule from Ottawa and Yellowknife, capital of the NWT, there is a palpable excitement as the citizens prepare to determine their own destinies.

Nunavut is a wild and isolated place. You can journey from the waters of Hudson Bay all the way to the North Pole. Your only real limitations are stamina, time and money, especially money. For once the hackneyed phrase 'adventure of a lifetime' truly applies for people who experience the extraordinary sights of places like Ellesmere and Baffin islands.

History

Nunavut has been inhabited for over 4000 years. The first recorded arrival of westerners was an expedition led by Martin Frobisher which landed at Baffin Island in 1576 while looking for the Northwest Passage. Other explorers followed, including John Franklin who disappeared with 128 crew in 1845.

For the next 150 years, the Canadian government was primarily interested in the eastern Arctic for its mineral wealth and strategic position. Large-scale government programs

HIGHLIGHTS

Granted Territorial Status: 1999
Area: 2.2 million sq km
Population: about 25,000
Provincial Capital: Iqaluit

- Hike the pristine Auyuittuq National Park
- Explore the magnificent desolation of the lands around Resolute
- Stay up all night during endless summer days above the Arctic Circle

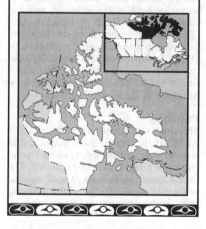

in the 1960s settled most of the Inuit in villages away from their nomadic lives. These programs were often administered rather forcefully. At about this time, the federal government in Ottawa first considered granting the region greater autonomy.

In 1982, 56% of the voters in the NWT approved splitting the territory and creating Nunavut. There were then several years of wrangling over where to draw the division and how to split up the bureaucracy and infrastructure spoils. In 1993, the Canadian Parliament approved the Nunavut Land

Not all Darkness at Noon

Town	24 Hours of Sunshine	Average July Temp	24 Hours of Darkness	Average January Temp
Cambridge Bay	20 May to 23 July	8°C	30 November to 11 January	-30°C
Iqaluit	maximum 20 hours	8°C	maximum 19½ hours	-25°C
Pond Inlet	5 May to 7 August	8°C	12 November to 29 January	-30°C
Rankin Inlet	maximum 18 hours	8°C	maximum 21 hours	-30°C
Resolute	29 April to 13 August	5°C	6 November to 5 February	-33°C

Claims Agreement Act which paved the way for the official creation of Nunavut six years later.

Climate
This is the Arctic and much of Nunavut north of Hudson Bay is covered by ice much of the year. See the table above for details on the temperatures and seasonal periods of daylight for five key towns.

Flora & Fauna
Given a growing season whose number of weeks stays in the single digits, only the toughest of plants survive. These are mainly perennials that stay low to the ground and can survive months of freezing before thawing for some quick growth. Obviously things don't grow very quickly and shrub stems the diameter of a thumb have been found with 400 years of growth rings.

Caribou, musk ox, wolves, hares and other smaller animals live on the tundra. The seas and islands of the far north are home to seals, walruses, three kinds of whales – beluga, bowhead and narwhal – and the Arctic icon, the polar bear.

Information
Nunavut Tourism (☎ 867-979-6551, ☎ 1-800-491-7910, fax 867-979-1261) publishes *The Arctic Traveller*, an excellent annual resource with comprehensive listings of tour and charter operators in the territory. Write to: PO Box 1450, Iqaluit, X0A 0H0.

The Nunavut Handbook is an impressive and encyclopaedic annual guide that is written and produced by longtime residents. It is sold throughout Nunavut or can be ordered in advance from Nortext Multimedia Inc, Box 8, Iqaluit, X0A 0H0.

Time Nunavut covers three times zones from Mountain Time in the west to Eastern Time in the east.

Activities
Canoeing is good on the Kazan and Thelon rivers, which are Canadian Heritage Rivers. Kayaking is a natural, given that it's the Inuit who invented the *qajaq*. The season for any kind of water activities is quite short. Fishing is excellent with such limited competition for the Arctic char and huge lake trout. There are a myriad of hiking possibilities, but none of them are easy and most require an expedition.

Independent Travel
Only the most experienced of Arctic travellers should consider truly independent travel in Nunavut. The logistics and conditions are just too hard and unforgiving. However, there is a growing opportunity for people who wish to organise their own trips using local guides as opposed to being part of a package trip. Many towns now have associations of local guides who charge similar prices.

Outside of Iqaluit, Arctic towns don't often use street names. If you're looking for something just ask. Banks and ATMs are limited to Iqaluit, Cambridge Bay and Rankin Inlet. Credit cards too may find limited acceptance outside of these three towns. Services are often restricted to one

NUNAVUT

NUNAVUT

Approximate Northern Treeline

GREENLAND

Ellesmere Island

Ellesmere Island National Park

Queen Elizabeth Islands

BEAUFORT SEA

0   200   400 km

North Magnetic Pole

Baffin Bay

Devon Island

Bylot Island

Aulavik National Park

Melville Island

Bathurst Island

Resolute

Pond Inlet

Banks Island

Clyde River

Broughton Island

Holman

Victoria Island

Prince of Wales Island

Boothia Peninsula

Baffin Island

Auyuittuq National Park Reserve

Pangnirtung

Tuktut Nogait National Park

Cambridge Bay

King William Island

Igloolik

Melville Peninsula

Kekerton Historic Park

Coppermine

Gjoa Haven

Hall Beach

Circle

IQALUIT

Bathurst Inlet

Spence Bay

Pelly Bay

Repulse Bay

Qaummaarviit

Great Bear Lake

Arctic

Queen Maud Bird Sanctuary

NUNAVUT

Cape Dorset

Kimmirut

Back River

Hudson Strait

Mackenzie Bison Sanctuary

Thelon River

Thelon Wildlife Sanctuary

Baker Lake

Coral Harbour

QUEBEC

Rae

Baker Lake

Chesterfield Inlet

YELLOWKNIFE

Reliance

Dubawnt Lake

Rankin Inlet

Great Slave Lake

Whale Cove

Hudson Bay

Hay River

Fort Smith

Wood Buffalo National Park

NWT

Arviat (Eskimo Point)

ALBERTA   SASKATCHEWAN   MANITOBA

of the ubiquitous Northern stores, a chain of general stores selling everything from food to snow shoes at jaw-dropping prices.

Expect weather delays even in July. You may be stuck somewhere for several more days than you had planned so budget your time and money accordingly.

Organised Tours

The vast majority of visitors to Nunavut will be part of some organised tour whether it's a luxury boat cruise, adventure or nature tour or

marathon trek. *The Arctic Traveller* has full details of the various types of tour operator. Expect to pay in the thousands of dollars.

Accommodation

There are few organised campgrounds. There may be a designated spot but plan to be completely self-sufficient. Outside of Iqaluit, choice of lodging is very limited as well. Expect to pay on average $200 a night in some very rough-edged hostelries (some lacking even windows, others requiring you

to share your room) which includes all meals. The food at these commercial establishments and on many tours tends to be very protein heavy. If you have special needs, make arrangements for them long before you leave home. Once you're out on the ice is not the time to announce 'I'm a vegan'.

Getting There & Around

Air Planes are the only way to get to Nunavut and around once you are there. Iqaluit is linked to Montreal and Ottawa and Rankin Inlet to Winnipeg. Yellowknife in the NWT is a hub for services to the high Arctic and western towns. Outside of the monopolistic services provided by First Air (☎ 867-979-5329, ☎ 1-800-267-1247) to the larger towns, you will have to charter a plane for trips anywhere. Air fares are very expensive – a 'cheap fare' from Yellowknife to Iqaluit costs $700.

Car There are no roads of any kind to any place in Nunavut from any other part of Canada. Each town has a few kilometres of roads around it and if necessary you can usually rent a truck from somebody. There may be one taxi, but most people just stick out a thumb and get a ride from somebody else.

BAFFIN REGION

This region is centred on Baffin Island but stretches north as far as Ellesmere Island way up at the peak of the Canadian Arctic, not far from Greenland's north-western edge. Not one tree grows here but many flowers bloom during the short summer. The northern areas are almost completely uninhabited.

Iqaluit

This town, formerly called Frobisher Bay, is on the east coast of Baffin Island in the eastern section of the territories. In 1984 the town changed its name back to Iqaluit (pronounced 'ee-KAL-oo-it'), its original Inuit name meaning 'the place of fish'. Whatever you do, avoid the English-language habit of inserting a u after the q because the name means something actually ruder than 'big

Inuit soapstone

butt'. It is the new capital of Nunavut and has a population of 4000. There is not much to see or do here but a variety of side trips is possible and there are a number of hiking trails marked by *inukshuks* (human-like figures made of rocks), which take you past archaeological sites and out into the tundra. Most people coming here stop off as part of a package tour en route to somewhere else.

Information The Unikkaarvik, or Baffin Regional Visitor's Centre (☎ 867-979-4636, fax 867-979-1261), has information on the entire territory and several displays on local life and culture there and at the adjoining museum. There are numerous stores – some selling local art – as well as two banks. Baffin Regional Hospital (☎ 867-979-7300) is the only full-service facility in Nunavut.

Qaummaarviit Historic Park The park is 12km by boat or winter dog-sled from Iqaluit. It preserves a settlement of the Thule people who lived here for over 750 years. Many of their sod houses and other artefacts are still there. The visitors centre can put you in touch with someone for transport and a tour.

Activities Eetuk Outfitting and Equipment Rental (☎ 867-979-1984, fax 867-979-1994) is one of the largest firms of its kind in Iqaluit and can custom-design any kind of Arctic journey. Inuit Sea Kayaking (☎ 867-979-2055, ☎ 1-888-850-0059, fax 867-979-2414) arranges trips around South Baffin Island.

Special Events Toonik Tyme (☎ 867-979-5617) is a week-long festival in late April that celebrates Inuit culture. There are games and contests that include igloo-building.

Places to Stay & Eat Because there are several local restaurants, local hotels usually don't include meals in the price of a room. *Pearson's Arctic Homestay (☎ 867-979-6408)* is run by a colourful former mayor and has B&B rooms for $100 per person. The *Toonoonik Hotel (☎ 867-979-6733, fax 867-979-4210)* charges $100/125 a single/double and there is a dining room. The *Navigator Inn (☎ 867-979-6201, fax 867-979-0427)* has good rooms from $139/154 and has a good restaurant popular with locals who especially love the Saturday all-you-can-eat pizza night.

Getting There & Away The airport (☎ 867-979-5046) is close to town. Canadian North (☎ 867-979-6470, ☎ 1-800-979-6470) flies to Rankin Inlet and Yellowknife. First Air (☎ 867-979-5810, ☎ 1-800-267-1247) services numerous towns in Nunavut as well as Yellowknife, Ottawa and Montreal. In summer it has a flight to Nuuk, the capital of Greenland.

Pangnirtung

Pang, as it's often referred to, is a town with about 1100 residents, beautifully set alongside a fjord amid mountains at the entrance to Auyuittuq National Park. It lies at the southern end of Pangnirtung Pass, 40km south of the Arctic Circle, and acts as the jumping-off point for park visitors.

The Angmarlik Visitor's Centre (☎ 867-473-8737, fax 867-473-8685) gives visitors a chance to meet locals and has displays on Thule and Inuit life as well as local infor-

mation on guides and outfitters. The town has a reputation for its woven tapestries which can be seen and purchased at shops or the Uqqurmiut Centre for Arts and Crafts.

Things to See & Do Two walking trails begin in town. One, following the Duval River, takes about three hours. The other, following the Ikuvik River uphill, offers a fine view of the fjord and takes about six hours. Good boots are recommended for both trails.

About 50km south of town is the **Kekerten National Historic Park**, an old whaling station. A trail leads around parts of the island past the remains of the 19th century houses, tools and graves. An interpretative centre provides background information. From Pangnirtung a round trip by boat with time in the park takes 12 hours.

Places to Stay There's camping at the *Pisuktinu-Tungavik* campground or you can stay at the *Auyuittuq Lodge (☎ 867-473-8955, ☎ 867-473-8611)* for $120 per person without meals; however, the lodge also has a dining room.

Getting There & Away From Iqaluit, First Air (☎ 867-473-8960, ☎ 1-800-267-1247) and Air Nunavut (☎ 867-979-4018) fly to Pang.

Auyuittuq National Park Reserve

Covering an area of 21,500 sq km, this is Canada's third largest national park and one of the world's few national parks north of the Arctic Circle. Pronounced 'ah-you-EE-tuk', the word means 'the land that never melts'. Most of the park is a beautiful, pristine wilderness consisting of mountains, valleys, fjords and meadows. Most visitors go for the hiking along 97km **Akshayuk Pass** – between late June and early September when it's free of snow. Climbers flock to Mount Thor (1500m), which has the tallest, uninterrupted cliff face on earth.

Parks Canada (☎ 867-473-8828, fax 867-473-8612) has an office in Pangnirtung with full information on the park. The fee for entering the park is $15 a day and if you need

to be rescued, you better have insurance because they'll give you a bill.

There are two primitive *campgrounds* in the park: at Overlord and Summit Lake. Both are on the Akshayuk Pass and there are an additional seven emergency shelters along the route.

Getting There & Away You can access the south end of the park from Pangnirtung, 25km away. For most of the year that means a $75 snowmobile ride to Overlord. After the thaw in mid-July, you hike for two days. The visitors centre in Pangnirtung can supply names of outfitters.

Pond Inlet

With scenery that includes mountains, glaciers and icebergs, this town of 1200 at the northern tip of Baffin Island is also the access point for **Bylot Island**. Just off the coast, this island bird sanctuary is a summer nesting ground for snow geese and home to other birds like murres and kittiwakes. The waters around the island are also rich in marine life. There are plans to make it a national park.

Nattinnak Centre (☎ 867-899-8226, fax 867-899-8246) in Pond Inlet has information on the area and outfitters. There is a *campground* near town and the *Sauniq Hotel (☎ 867-899-8928, fax 867-899-8364)* charges $230 per person with meals.

Resolute

The logistical centre for the far north, Resolute was founded after WWII when the Canadian government established an air base and moved several families of Inuit here to protect territorial claims. The land is like a moonscape with endless vistas of grey-brown rocks. The remains of several crashed airplanes are near the airport and the remains of centuries-old Thule villages are near the beach. The main reason for visiting Resolute, which is on the southern tip of Cornwallis Island, is as part of a trip to natural destinations such as Bathurst and Ellesmere islands or the magnetic and geographic North Poles. It is almost at the 75° N latitude.

Besides local hiking, if you have a few days in Resolute – which with its 200 people is not blessed with many activities – you should try to visit **Beechey Island** southwest of Resolute. This desolate place was where the ill-fated Franklin expedition wintered in 1845-46 before vanishing forever. There remain many traces of these men and their unsuccessful rescuers.

Jessco Logistics (☎ 403-282-2268, fax 403-282-2195) handles logistics and support for Arctic travel from its summer base in Resolute. It also runs tours through its Arctic Watch subsidiary. Terry Jesudason organises all forms of travel from Resolute and she manages the *Tudjaat Inns North (☎ 867-252-3900, fax 867-252-3766)*, a delightful family-style lodge which charges $185 per person including good home-cooked meals. Ask for the world-famous pecan pie. Jesudason is the best person to know in town.

Getting There & Away Because of its important status as a logistical centre, Resolute is well served by air. Canada North (☎ 867-252-3880, ☎ 1-800-665-1177) flies jets to Cambridge Bay and Yellowknife. First Air (☎ 867-252-3981, ☎ 1-800-267-1247) flies to these towns plus Iqaluit and it does charters. Kenn Borek Air (☎ 867-252-3845) serves small High Arctic towns such as Pond Inlet and does charters.

Ellesmere Island National Park

This national park, way up at the northern tip of Ellesmere Island at the top of the world, is for wealthy wilderness seekers only. Visitors camp and walk. It features **Cape Columbia**, the northernmost point of North America, **Mt Barbeau**, one of the highest peaks on the eastern side of the continent, **Lake Hazen** and numerous glaciers. Around the park are thermal oases where plants and animals are able to survive despite the harsh climate. Various adventure tour companies stage through Resolute on the way to the park. For an idea of the costs, just the chartered plane from Resolute costs about $18,000 for 10

Two North Poles

The North Pole, the imaginary point at the northern tip of the Earth's axis and about 800km north of Ellesmere Island, lies in neutral territory – an area of permanently frozen water without national jurisdiction. However, the Magnetic North Pole, the direction to which a compass needle points at an angle to true north, is in Canada. Exactly where it is, however, varies by the day. Generally just north of Bathurst Island west of Cornwallis Island at about 100° longitude, the pole moves in elliptical circles that can extend over 100km in a 24 hour period. On a yearly basis the pole has been wandering in a north-west direction.

You can visit both poles from Resolute. The magnetic pole is about 500km by air and flights there are common in spring and summer. The scenery is quite similar to Resolute – lots of rocks and ice – and given that there is definitely nothing there when it comes to finding the exact location of the pole this is really just an excuse to go on a jaunt over the High Arctic.

In contrast, the geographic North Pole thankfully stays put. Reaching the pole for most people involves a series of charter plane flights to pre-position fuel and supplies for the 1700km journey from Resolute north. Because of the instability of the weather, a one hour visit to the endless expanse of ice at the pole can involve seven to 10 days of travel and delays. The cost ranges from $9000 to $14,000 per person.

people. For park information, contact Parks Canada (☎ 867-473-8828, ☎ 867-473-8612) in Pangnirtung.

KITIKMEOT REGION
This seemingly limitless area of tundra encompasses the Arctic coast of the mainland as well as nearby islands.

Cambridge Bay
In the south-east of Victoria Island, this town of 1400 is the administrative centre for the region and home to a large military early warning radar station. Explorers in search of the Northwest Passage often took shelter here and you can see the remains of Roald Amundsen's schooner *Maud* in the harbour. **Mt Pelly** is a 15km walk from town and has good views from its 220m peak. This is a good place to see musk ox. South across Queen Maud Gulf to the **Queen Maud Bird Sanctuary**, the world's largest migratory bird sanctuary.

The Arctic Coast Visitor's Centre (☎ 867-983-2224, fax 867-983-2302) has displays about exploration of the North-west Passage and organises tours. The *Arctic Islands Lodge* (☎ 867-983-2345, fax 867-983-2480)

has rooms that are swanky by Nunavut standards and which cost $205 per person with meals.

KIVALLIQ REGION
In the south, the Kivalliq Region consists of a vast, rocky, barren plateau, part of the Canadian Shield, with only 4800 people; to the east its official boundaries incorporate much of Hudson Bay and James Bay. Most of the Inuit population lives in settlements along the western shores of Hudson Bay. Much of the region consists of flat tundra laced by streams, rivers and lakes. It is good for fishing and canoeing.

Rankin Inlet
Founded in 1955 as a mining centre, Rankin Inlet, with a population of about 2000, is Keewatin's largest community and the government and transport centre for the district. From here you can go fishing in the bay or in the many rivers and lakes. **Meliadine Park**, 5km from town, is popular for hiking and berry-picking.

In Hudson Bay, about 50km from Rankin Inlet, is **Marble Island**, a graveyard for James Knight and his crew who were seeking the

NICHOLAS REUSS

Ivory Gull, Buchanan Bay, Ellesmere Island, Nunavut

NICHOLAS REUSS

First blizzard of winter, Resolute, Cornwallis Island, Nunavut

New ice forming, Buchanan Bay, Nunavut

Iceberg from the air, Baffin Bay, Nunavut

Northwest Passage in the 18th century. Some 19th century whaling ships are there too. You can also hike to the **Ijiraliq Archaeological Site**, at the mouth of the Meliadine River, and explore the 15th century underground houses of the Thule Inuit.

The Kivalliq Regional Visitors Centre (☎ 867-645-5091, fax 867-645-5067) has area information and historical displays. There are stores and services. The *Nanuq Inn* (☎ 867-645-2513, fax 867-645-2393) has simple rooms for $99/152 a single/double without meals.

Getting There & Away First Air/NWT Air (☎ 867-645-2961, ☎ 1-800-267-1247) flies to Yellowknife, Winnipeg and Iqaluit. Canadian North (☎ 867-645-2746, ☎ 1-800-665-1177) flies to the same destinations. Its commuter affiliate Calm Air flies to numerous small communities in the Kivalliq Region including Arviat, Baker Lake and Repulse Bay.

Arviat

Arviat, formerly called Eskimo Point, is Nunavut's most southerly settlement. This was originally the site of a summer camp used by several groups of Inuit who lived along the western coast of Hudson Bay and on the mainland tundra. The town now has a population of about 1100 and people still make a living from fishing, hunting and trapping. The Margaret Aniksak Visitors Centre (☎ 867-857-2698) has local information and displays of art from the vibrant community.

From Arviat you can arrange a trip south to **McConnell River Bird Sanctuary** where, from June onwards, about 400,000 snow geese nest, together with snowy owls, Arctic terns, falcons and others.

Baker Lake

Geographically, Baker Lake lies at the centre of Canada. It's good for fishing and is the departure point for canoe or raft trips on the Kazan and Thelon rivers.

From Baker Lake you can arrange a visit west to **Thelon Game Sanctuary**, founded in 1927 by the federal government to save the then-endangered musk ox.

The Akumalik Visitors Centre (☎ 867-793-2456) is open in summer only and has area information.

Repulse Bay

Sitting on the Arctic Circle at the southern end of Melville Peninsula, Repulse Bay is a natural harbour. For centuries whaling ships set off from here. You can go whale watching to see beluga or narwhal whales (August is the best time) or take a boat out fishing. The Arviq Hunters and Trapper Association (☎ 867-462-4334, fax 867-462-4335) arranges nonlethal whale-watching trips.

Language

English and French are the two official languages of Canada. You'll notice both on highway signs, maps, tourist brochures and all types of packaging. In the west, French isn't as prevalent but in Quebec, English can be at a premium. Indeed, roadside signs and visitor information will often be in French only. Outside Montreal and Quebec City, the use of some French, or your own version of sign language, will be necessary at least some of the time.

Many immigrants use their mother tongue, as do some groups of Native Indians and Inuit. In some Native Indian communities though, it's now only older members who retain their original indigenous language. Few non-Native Indian Canadians speak any Native Indian or Inuit language but some words such as igloo, parka, muskeg and kayak are commonly used.

The Inuit languages are interesting for their specialisation and use of many words for what appears to be the same thing; eg the word for 'seal' depends on whether it's old or young, in or out of the water. There are up to 20 or so words for 'snow' depending on its consistency and texture.

CANADIAN ENGLISH

Canada inherited English primarily from the British settlers of the early and mid-1800s. This form of British English remains the basis of Canadian English. There are some pronunciation differences; Britons say 'clark' for clerk, Canadians say 'clurk'. Grammatical differences are few. The Canadian vocabulary has been augmented considerably by the need for new words in a new land and the influence of the Native Indian languages as well as the pioneering French.

Canada has never developed a series of easily detectable dialects such as those of England, Germany, or even the USA. There are, though, some regional variations in idiom and pronunciation. In Newfoundland,

for example, some people speak with an accent reminiscent of the west country of England (Devon and Cornwall) or Ireland, and some use words such as 'screech' (rum) and 'shooneen' (coward).

The spoken English of the Atlantic Provinces, too, has inflections not heard in the west, and in the Ottawa Valley you'll hear a slightly different sound again, due mainly to the large numbers of Irish who settled there in the mid 1800s. In British Columbia some expressions reflect that province's history; a word like 'leaverite' (a worthless mineral) is a prospecting word derived from the phrase 'Leave 'er right there'.

Canadian English has been strongly influenced by the USA, particularly in recent years via the mass media and the use of US textbooks and dictionaries in schools. Most spellings follow British English such as centre, harbour, cheque etc but there are some exceptions like tire (tyre) and aluminum (aluminium). US spelling is becoming more common, to the consternation of some. Perhaps the best known difference between US and Canadian English is in the pronunciation of the last letter of the alphabet. In the USA it's pronounced 'zee', while in Canada it's pronounced 'zed'.

Canadian English as a whole has also developed a few of its own distinctive idioms and expression. The most recognisable is the interrogative 'eh?' which sometimes seems to appear at the end of almost every spoken sentence. Although to many non-North Americans, Canadians and Americans may sound the same, there are real differences. Canadian pronunciation of 'ou' is the most notable of these; words like 'out' and 'bout' sound more like 'oat' and 'boat' when spoken by Canadians.

Canadian English has also added to the richness of the global English language too with words like kerosene (paraffin), puck

(from ice hockey), bushed (exhausted) and moose and muskeg from anglicised Native Indian words.

For those wishing to delve deeper into the topic, there is the excellent *Oxford Dictionary of Canadian English*.

CANADIAN FRENCH

The French spoken in Canada is not, for the most part, the language of France. At times it can be nearly unintelligible to a Parisian. The local tongue of Quebec, where the vast majority of the population is French, is known as Québecois or *joual*, but variations on it occur in all parts of the province. However, many English (and most French) students in Quebec are still taught the French of France. Despite this, where many around the world schooled in Parisian French would say *Quelle heure est-il?* for 'What time is it?', on the streets of Quebec you're likely to hear *Y'est quelle heure?* Most Quebeckers will understand a more formal French – it will just strike them as a little peculiar. Remember, too, that broken French can sound as charming as the French speaker's broken English if said with a friendly attitude. Other differences between European French and the Quebec version worth remembering (because you don't want to go hungry!) are the terms for breakfast, lunch and dinner. Rather than *petit déjeuner*, *déjeuner* and *diner* you're likely to see and hear *déjeuner*, *diner* and *souper*.

If you have any car trouble, you'll be happy to know that generally, English terms are used for parts. Indeed the word *char* for car may be heard. Hitchhiking is known not as *auto stop* but as *le pousse* (the thumb).

Announcers and broadcasters on Quebec TV and radio tend to speak a more refined, European style of French as do the upper class. Visitors to the country without much everyday French-speaking experience will have the most luck understanding them. Despite all this, the preservation of French in Quebec is a primary concern and fuels the separatist movement.

New Brunswick is, perhaps surprisingly, the only officially bilingual province. French

is widely spoken, particularly in the north and east. Again, it is somewhat different from the French of Quebec. Nova Scotia and Manitoba also have significant French populations but there are also pockets in most provinces.

The following is a short guide to some French words and phrases which may be useful for the traveller. The combinations 'ohn/ehn/ahn/' in the phonetic transcriptions are nasal sounds – the 'n' is not pronounced; 'zh' is pronounced as the 's' in 'measure'. Quebec French employs a lot of English words; this may make understanding and speaking the language a little easier.

For a far more comprehensive guide to the language get a copy of Lonely Planet's *French phrasebook* – it's a handy pocket-size book for travellers.

Greetings & Civilities

Hello. (day)
  bohn-joor   *Bonjour.*
Hello. (evening)
  bohn-swar   *Bonsoir.*
Hello. (informal)
  sa-lew   *Salut.*
How are you?
  commohn sa vah?   *Comment ça va?*
                     (often just *Ça va?*)
I'm fine.
  sa vah bee-ahn   *Ça va bien.*

Basics

Yes.
  wee   *Oui.*
No.
  nohn   *Non.*
Please.
  seel voo pleh   *S'il vous plaît.*
Thank you.
  mehr-see   *Merci.*
Welcome.
  bee-ahn ven-oo   *Bienvenu.*
Excuse me.
  par-dohn   *Pardon.*
Pardon/What?
  commohn?   *Comment?*
  kwah?   *Quoi?* (slang)

You're welcome.
　　zhe voo-zohn　　*Je vous en prie.*
　　pree
How much?
　　kom-bee-ahn?　　*Combien?*

Language Difficulties

I understand.
　　zhe com-prohn
　　Je comprends.
I don't understand.
　　zhe neh com-prohn pah
　　Je ne comprends pas.
Do you speak English?
　　parlay vooz anglay?
　　Parlez-vous anglais?
I don't speak French.
　　zhe neh parl pah frohn-say
　　Je ne parle pas francais.

Getting Around

Where is ...?
　　oo eh ...?
　　Où est ...?

What time does the ... leave/arrive?
　　a kel ur pahr/ahreev le ...?
　　A quelle heure part/arrive le ...?

bus	oh-toh-booss	*autobus*
train	trahn	*train*
plane	a-vee-ohn	*avion*

train station
　　gar　　*gare*
platform
　　kay　　*quai*
bus station
　　sta-seeyon　　*station d'autobus*
　　d'ohtoh-booss
one-way ticket
　　beeyay sam-pluh　　*billet simple*
return ticket
　　beeyay alay　　*billet aller et retour*
　　eh reh-tour
bicycle
　　veh-loh　　*vélo*
boat cruise
　　kwa-zyeh　　*croisière de bateau*
　　de ba-toh

Signs

BILLETERIE	TICKET OFFICE
COMPLET	NO VACANCY
ENTRÉE	ENTRANCE
HALTE ROUTIERE	REST STOP
SORTIE	EXIT
STATIONNEMENT	PARKING

petrol (gasoline)
　　eh-sohns/gaz　　*essence/gaz*
lead-free (petrol)
　　sohn plom　　*sans plomb*
self-serve
　　sairvees lee-br　　*service libre*

Directions

I want to go to ...
　　zhe vur ahlay a　　*Je veux aller à ...*
left
　　a go-sh　　*à gauche*
right
　　a drwat　　*à droit*
straight ahead
　　too drwat　　*tout droit*
near
　　prosh　　*proche*
far
　　lwahn　　*loin*
here
　　ee-see　　*ici*
there
　　lah　　*là*

Accommodation

Do you have any rooms available?
　　ehs-ker voo zah-vay day shombr leebr?
　　Est-ce que vous avez des chambres libres?

hotel
　　o-tell　　*hôtel*
youth hostel
　　o-bairzh de zheuness
　　auberge de jeunesse
a room
　　oon shombr　　*une chambre*

a double room
  oon shombr doobl
  une chambre double
with a bathroom
  ahvek sahl de bahn
  avec salle de bain
with a kitchenette
  ahvek kwee-zee-net
  avec cuisinette

Around Town

bank	
bohnk	*banque*
beach	
plazh	*plage*
the bill	
la-dis-yohn/	*l'addition/*
le reh soo	*le reçu*
bridge	
pohn	*pont*
convenience store	
day-pahn-nur	*dépanneur*
department store	
mag-a-zahn	*magasin*
grocery store	
ay-pee-seh-ree	*épicerie*
museum	
mew-zay	*musée*
opening hours	
oh-rair	*horaires*
post office	
bew-roh de post	*bureau de poste*
the police	
la polees	*la police*
show/concert	
spek-tahk'l	*spectacle*
toilet	
twah-leh	*toilet*
tourist office	
bew-ro doo	*bureau du tourisme*
too-rism	
travellers cheque	
shek vwoy-yazh	*cheque voyage*

Food

bakery	
boo-lohn-zheree	*boulangerie*
buffet meal	
tab'l-doht	*table d'hôte*

fresh fish store	
pwa-sohn-eree	*poissonnerie*
restaurant	
rest-a-rohn	*restaurant*
snack bar	
kass krewt	*casse croûte*
bread	
pahn	*pain*
cheese	
fro-mahj	*fromage*
vegetables	
lay-gyoom	*légumes*
fruit	
frwee	*fruit*

I'm a vegetarian.
  zhe swee vayzhayteh-ryahn/ryen
  Je suis végétarien/végétarienne (m/f)

Drinks

water	
oh	*eau*
milk	
leh	*lait*
beer	
bee-yair	*bière*
wine	
vahn	*vin*
red wine	
vahn roozh	*vin rouge*
white wine	
vahn blohn	*vin blanc*

Useful Words

big	
grond	*grand*
small	
peh-tee	*petit*
much/many	
boh-coo	*beaucoup*
cheap	
bohn mar-shay/	*bon marché/*
pa sher/	*pas chère/*
seh cheep	*c'est cheap*
expensive	
share	*cher*
before	
ah-vohn	*avant*
after	
ah-preh	*après*

LANGUAGE

tomorrow
 de-mahn   *demain*
yesterday
 yeah   *hier*

Numbers

1	uhn	*un*
2	der	*deux*
3	twah	*trois*
4	cat	*quatre*
5	sank	*cinq*
6	sease	*six*
7	set	*sept*
8	weet	*huit*
9	neuf	*neuf*
10	dees	*dix*
20	vahn	*vingt*
21	vahn-teh-un	*vingt et un*
25	vahn sank	*vingt-cinq*
30	tronht	*trente*
40	car-ohnt	*quarante*
50	sank-ohnt	*cinquante*
60	swa-sohnt	*soixante*
70	swa-sohnt dees	*soixante-dix*

80	cat-tr' vahn	*quatre-vingt*
90	cat-tr'vahn dees	*quatre-vingt-dix*
100	sohn	*cent*
500	sank sohn	*cinq cents*
1000	meel	*mille*

Emergencies

Help!	
oh say-coor	*Au secours!*
Call a doctor!	
a-pay-lay uhn med-sahn!	*Appelez un médecin!*
Call the police!	
a-pay-lay la poh-lees!	*Appelez la police!*
Leave me alone!	
leh-say-mwa tron-kill!	*Laissez-moi tranquille!*
I'm lost.	
zhe muh swee ay-ga-ray	*Je me suis égaré/ égarée.* (m/f)

Glossary

Acadians – The first settlers from France who lived in Nova Scotia.

Atlantic Provinces – This refers to Newfoundland, Nova Scotia, Prince Edward Island and New Brunswick. See Maritime Provinces entry later.

aurora borealis – Also called the northern lights, they are charged particles from the sun which are trapped in the earth's magnetic field. They appear as other-worldly coloured, waving beams.

badlands – A dry, barren, arid region of unusual, irregular features of erosion and prehistoric fossils. In Canada, this region is mostly found in southern Alberta.

bakeapple – Also called the golden bakeapple and a speciality of Newfoundland, it's a type of berry which is often used for jam or pies.

beaver fever (giardiasis) – The bacteria which causes this disease is found in many freshwater streams and lakes. It affects the digestive tract and can be avoided by boiling drinking water.

boîtes à chanson – Generally cheap, casual and relaxed folk clubs, popular in Quebec.

boondoggle – A futile or unnecessary project or work.

boreal – Refers to the Canadian north and its character, as in the boreal forest, the boreal wind etc.

Bluenose II – A well-known, widely travelled replica of Canada's famous sailing vessel.

brew pub – A pub that brews and sells its own beer.

cabin fever – A traditional term still used to indicate a stir-crazy, frustrated state of mind due to being cooped up indoors over the long northern winter. By extension, it's used to denote the same feelings due to being forced to remain in the house, cottage, or tent for a period of time because of inclement weather or bad health.

calèche – Horse-drawn carriages which can be taken around parts of Montreal and Quebec City.

Canadian Shield – Also known as the Precambrian or Laurentian Shield, it is a plateau of rock that was formed 2.5 billion years ago and covers much of the northern region of the country.

ceilidh – Pronounced 'KAY-lee'; a Gaelic word meaning an informal gathering for song, dance and story. It is sometimes known as a house party; especially popular in Prince Edward Island.

clearcut – This is an area where loggers have cut every tree, large and small, leaving nothing standing.

coulees – Gulches, usually dry.

Cowichan – The name of a Native Indian people originally from the Lake Cowichan area on Vancouver Island (BC); also the name given to the hand-knitted, 100% wool sweaters they produce.

dome car – The two-levelled, glass-topped observation car of a train.

Doukhobours – A Russian Christian pacifist sect, some of whom settled in Canada during the 19th century.

First Nations – A term used to denote Canada's aboriginal peoples. It can be used instead of Native Indians or Native people.

flowerpots – Unusual rock formations, these irregular geological forms are created by erosion effects of waves. Examples can be seen at Tobermory in Ontario and at The Rocks in New Brunswick.

fruit leather – A blend of fruit purees dried into thin sheets and pressed together. It's great for backpacking and hiking.

gasoline – Petrol, known as gasoline or simply gas (gaz in Quebec). Almost all gasoline in Canada is termed unleaded and comes in regular and more costly higher-octane versions.

Haligonians – Residents of Halifax, Nova Scotia.

hoodoos – Fantastically shaped pillars of sandstone rock formed by erosion found in badland regions mainly in southern Alberta.

igloo – The traditional Inuit houses made from blocks of ice.

information chalets – Tourist information booths found in Newfoundland.

Innu – Another name for the Montagnais and Naskapi peoples.

inukshuk – Inuit preferred to trap caribou in water where they could be hunted from a kayak. For this reason they built stone figures called 'inukshuks', next to lakes to direct the animals into the water.

Inside Passage – The sea route from the Alaskan Panhandle to Washington state that runs between the coast of mainland British Columbia and the chain of islands off the coast.

interior camping – This refers to usually lone, individual sites accessible only by foot or canoe. When found in provincial or national parks, pre-registering with park authorities is required for your own safety.

Liveyers – European descendants who lived in small villages along the Strait of Belle Isle in Labrador.

Lotto 649 – The country's most popular, highest-paying lottery.

Loyalists – They were residents of America who maintained their allegiance to Britain during the American Revolution and fled to Canada.

mall – A shopping centre, usually enclosed and containing a range of retail stores. The larger ones generally include a number of low-cost fast-food places at which to eat.

Maritime Provinces – Also known as the Maritimes, this refers to the three provinces: New Brunswick, Nova Scotia and Prince Edward Island.

Mennonites – A religious Utopian group originating in Europe who are mostly found in the Kitchener-Waterloo region of southern Ontario.

Métis – Canadians of French and Native Indian stock.

Mounties – Royal Canadian Mounted Police (RCMP)

mukluks – Moccasins or boots made from sealskin and often trimmed with fur; usually made by Inuit people.

muskeg – Undrained boggy land most often found in northern Canada.

Naskapi – A group of Native Indians, also called the Innu. They are found in north-eastern Quebec.

Newfie – A term applying to residents of Newfoundland, or 'The Rock' as it is sometimes known.

no-see-um – Any of various tiny biting insects which are difficult to see and which can annoy travellers when out in the woods or along some beaches. No-see-um netting, a very fine mesh screen on a tent, is designed to keep the insects out.

Ogopogo – A monster, similar to the Loch Ness monster, thought to reside within the waters of Okanagan Lake (BC). It has never been photographed.

outports – Small, isolated coastal villages of Newfoundland, connected with the rest of the province by boat.

permafrost – Permanently frozen subsoil that covers the far north of Canada.

portage – The process of transporting boats and supplies overland between navigable waterways. It can also refer to the overland route used for such a purpose.

petroglyphs – Ancient paintings or carvings on rock.

potlatch – A competitive ceremonial activity among some Native people, usually those found along the coast of BC, which traditionally involved a lavish distribution of gifts and destruction of property to emphasise the wealth and status of the chief or clan. It now refers to a wild party or revel.

public/separate schools – The two basic school systems. Both are free and essentially the same but the latter is designed for Catholics and offers more religious education.

pysankas – Ukrainian term for painted Easter eggs.

qiviut – The wool of the musk ox that was traditionally woven into garments by some Inuit groups in the far north.

Québecois – The local tongue of Quebec where the vast majority of the population is French; also known as *joual*. The term also refers to the residents of Quebec although it is only applied to the French, not English Quebeckers.

rock hounds – Rock collectors.

rubby – A derelict alcoholic who is often homeless. The term comes from rubbing alcohol which is often mixed with cheap wine for drinking.

RV – Recreational vehicle (commonly a motorhome).

screech – A particularly strong rum once available only in Newfoundland, but now widely available across Canada, but in diluted form.

sourdough – Refers to a person who has completed one year's residency in northern Canada.

spelunking – The exploration and study of caves.

steamies – Hot dogs in Quebec which get their name from the way they are cooked.

sub-compact cars – These are the smallest cars available either for purchase or rent. They are smaller than compacts, which are one size down from standard cars.

sugar-making moon – A former Native Indian term for the spring date when the maple tree's sap begins to run.

sugar shack – The place where the collected maple sap is distilled in large kettles and boiled as part of the production of maple syrup.

taiga – The coniferous forests extending across much of subarctic North America and Eurasia.

trailer – In Canada, as well as in the USA, this refers to a caravan or a mobile home (house trailer). It can also refer to the type of vehicle used for transporting goods.

trap line – A marked area along which a trapper will set traps to catch fur-bearing animals.

tundra – The vast, treeless Arctic plains, north of the treeline and with a perpetually frozen subsoil.

voyageur – A boatman employed by one of the early fur-trading companies. He could also fill the function of a woodsman, guide, trapper or explorer.

Acknowledgments

THANKS

Many thanks to the travellers who used the last edition and wrote to us with helpful hints, useful advice and interesting anecdotes:

Abdullah, Julie Adamson, Amy Agorastos, Richard Alderton, Dave & Janet Allan, Nicole Allen, Bjorn Anders Radstrom, Myles Anderson, Nils F Anderson, Eduardo Angel, Thierry Antoine, Stephanie Appert, Rosalind Archer, BH Atkins, Ace Bailey, Steve Bailey, Jason Baker, Georgia Banks, Michele Barber, Nina Barnaby, Anke Bartels, Cathy Bartlett, Maria Basaraba, Janet Beale, Richard Beeson, Piet Bels, Caryl & Brian Bergeron, David Berridge, WJ Best, Nancy Evelyn Bikaunieks, Jude A Billard, PR Birch, Frida Caroline Bjerkan, Julia Black, Sarah Blackwell, David Bonham, Christopher Booth, Michael Borger, Kevin Boyle, Michael Briggs, Ashley Bristowe, Sean Brooks, B Gavin Brown, Eliza C Brown, Maxine Brown, Annette Buckley, Jonathan Butchard, Jean Butler, Claire Butler & Shayne Beard, Blaine Campbell, Sharyn Carey, Chris Carlisle, Edson Castilho, Vagner Castilho, Robert Catto, Jacky Chalk, Sally Chambers & Robin Longley, Natalie Chow, Niall GF Christie, Steven Christie, Isabel Chudleigh, Steve & Wendy Churchill, Marlene Cirillo, Mike Coburn, M Cohen, Paul Collins, Maurice Conklin, Danielle Conrad & Patrick Spink, Philip Coo, Katherine Cook, Jeremy Copeland, Agustin Cot, Ernest Carwithen & Elsa Coudon, Catherine Cowan, Brian Cox, Brian Crawford, Phil Crew, Ken Crossman, Dany Cuello, Cathy Ann Cwycyshyn, Martina D'Ascola, Mary-Camillus Dale, Margaret Darby, Huw Davies, Louise Davies, Alan & Leanne Dawson, Raffa Deganutti, Petra Dengl, Pierre Devinat, Martin Dinn, Kerry T Diotte, Monique Dodinet, Allan Doig, Sandra Dollar, Guy Douglas, Tilman Duerbeck, Tilman D Ÿrbeck, Nadja Eberhardt, Donna Ebert, Hermann Ebsen & Marion Kuehl, Peter Eden, Henning Eifler, Nicholas A Enright, Tore Fagervold, Paul Falvo, Sandra Farley, Peter Fennick, Gina Field, Nadine Fillipoff, Mandy Fletcher, Michael Fletcher, Suzan Fraser, Constance Frey, Ingo Friese, Donna Fruin & Dean Clark, Juan Garbajosa, Jennifer Gardner, William Gardner, Pam Gaskin, Costanza Gechter, Verstrepen Geert, Mathieu Georges, Marg Gibson, Philip Gilbert, James Gilmour, Travel Girl, Michele Glover, Nigel Goodall, Kristy Goodchild, Paul Goudreau, Eileen Grant, Anthea Grasty, Nonna & Wellum Gross, Joseph Gumino, Natalie Haines, Daryl Hal, Ruth Halsall, Graeme Paul Hamilton, Lutz Hankewitz, Janelle Hardy, Brian Harland, Lorraine Hart, Bernice Hartley & Margaret Reed, Julia Warner & John Harvie, Lilly Haupt, Andy Hay, M Hayden, Roland Heere, Laura Henderson, Amy Higginbotham, Tim Hildebrandt, TE Hillman, Ann & Derrick Hilton, Kelley Hishon, Chris Hocking, Pettina Hodgson & Rob Haub, Abigail Hine & Sarah Hollingham, Henry Hon, JP Hope, Margaret Hothi, Paul Hubbard, Jane Hunt, Paul Hutt, Heidi Ilhren, Carolyn Irvine, Marian Jago, Esther M Jensen, Henrik C Jessen, Carolyn Johnson & Craig Barrack, Lloyd Jones, Margaret Jorstead, Jill Kasner, Innes Keighren, Pat Kelly, Kieran Kelmar, John Kemp, Don Kerr, Roger Kershaw, Katrin Wohlleben & Tarik Khelifi, Barbara Kiepenheuer, Simone Kingston, Wim Klasen, Frank Klimt, Jennifer Klinec, Dayalh Kmeta, Christopher M Knapp, Carla Knoll, Tim Kong, George & Airi Krause, David Kreindler, Dave Kruse, Peta & Pierre Kruse, M Kulowski, Sr, Pierre L'Ecuyer, Tobias & Johannes Laengle, Marie-Helene Lagace, Emmanuel Lambert, Micky Lampe, Denise Lamy, Katrin Lange, Dany LaRochelle, Hans Latour, Lee Lau, Ron Laufer, Al Lawrence, David Lawrence, Belinda Lees, Deborah Leo, Sarah Leonard, Stephen Leslie, Mike B Leussink, Fabienne Lévy, Linda, Morten Lindow & Barbie Bojcun, Edgar H Locke, Clive Long, Helen Lorimer, Helen Lowe, Kris Ludwig, Mark Lunn, Peter Lunt, Fiona Lyle, Carol MacDonald, Stirling & Peta MacDonald, Laurie MacDougall, Eddie Magnussen, Eddie Magnusson, Jens Mahlow, Maya Malik, James Martin, Alexander Matskevich, Brent Matsuda, Nancy Matthews, JR McDermott, Irma M McDougall, Laura McEachern, Tom McKown, Fran McQuail, Judith McRostie, Ryan Medd, N Merrin, Nicole Middleton, Betty JeanMiller, Ian Mitchinson, Peter W Monteath, Tanya Montebello, Heather Montgomery, Gordon A Moodie, Philip Mooney, Stuart Morris, Ian Mortimer, Ian Moseley, Dominique Mouttet, Johan Muit, James Mules, Mary Mullane, Andrea Mullin, Liane Munro, Gary Murphy, Shioko Nagaoka, Jessica Nash, Andrew Newman-Martin, Brian P Nicholas, Brian P Nichols, Andrew Noblet, John O'Brien, Etain O'Carroll, Fidelma O'Connor, Magnus Fredrikson & Jan-éke Olsson, Ann & Bruce Palmer, Dennis Paradine, Craig Park, Ed Parker, Dick Parson, Richard Pedder, Chris Penny, Marc Peverini & David Mifsud, Uli Pfeiffer, Chris Phillips, Jean-François Pin, Lucy Platt, Helen Pleasance, Erhard Poser, Tyrone Power, Antonella Precoma, Annette Prelle, Kevin &

NicholaPrested, Howard Prior, Greg Proctor, David Quinn, Michel Quintas, Linda Rammage, Pierre Renault, Janice G Richards, Jane Robinson, Yetta Robinson, Bernhard Rock, Scott Rogers, Candace Ross, T Carter Ross, Duncan Routledge, Carol Rudram, Sheila & Dieter Salden, Arnaud Samson, PaulSands, Rick & CarolSarchet, André J Sauvé, Neil Schlipalius, Simon Schlosser & Hanne Kjeldehl, Sebastian Schmitz, Ruth Schulze, Oliver Schusser, Florian Schweiger, James Scott, Tim Searle, Anthony Sell, Andy Serra, SW Sherwood, Denis Shor, Peggy Shyns, Melissa Simmons, Andrew Sinclair, Bronwyn Sivour & Ivan Gorman, Alan Smith, Heather Smith, Heidi Smith, Jonathan Smith, Stephen Smith, Mary Smyth, Ann Soper & Craig McKinnie, Jill & David Spear, Kent Spencer, Jenn Stanley, Gavin Staton, Bryun Stedman, Andrew Steele, Mary Steer, John Steinbachs, Rebecca Stevens & Andrew Sansbury, N Stevenson, Prof & Mrs JMW Stewart, Stephen Streich, Arunasubramanian, Eric Swan, O O'Rourk-Swinney, Muei Hoon Tan, Kat Tancock, ChristineTarrach, Mike Telford, Rachael Templeton & John Jansen, Reinierten Veen, Frank Theissen, Pia Thiemann & Fabienne Hoffmann, Jo & Alan Thomas, Gary & Judy Thompson, Kerry Tobin & Alan Jones, Larissa Tomlinson, Véronique Torche & B Nanser, Pierre Tremblay, Richard Twigg, F Ubliani, Philip & Rosemary Ulyett, Sam Unruth, Maurice Valentine, Jos van den Akker, Rob & Marian Van den Heuvel, Jeroen Van Heel, Jeroen & Sendy van Heel, Hulya van Tangeren, Nicole Vandenberg, Elizabeth Evans, J & S Veringer, R Vermaire, Otto & Herma Vermeulan, Nichy Vyce, Sally Wade, Aron Wahl, Ron W Wallace, John & Helen Wardle, Sylvia Warner, VA Waters, Linda M Watsham, Tara Watt, Jayne Weber, Bert Weissbach, Sarah Rose Werner, Susan Westwood & Nick Hayward, Jennifer Whitman, Mattias Wick, Leonore Wigger, Diederik JD Wijnmalen, Andrew Willers, Bernard & Edith William, Katheen Williams, Olugbala Williams, Pauline Williams, Paul Williamson, Chris Wilson, Alex Wilson, Catrin Cousins & Elizabeth Cole, Jenn Wood, Robyn & Colin Wright, Chandi Wyant, Ingrid Wyles, Mary Yearsley, Y Yerbury-Nodgron, Victoria Young, Wanieta Young & Daiana Pellizzon, Joyce & Harold Zuberman

LONELY PLANET

Phrasebooks

Lonely Planet phrasebooks are packed with essential words and phrases to help travellers communicate with the locals. With colour tabs for quick reference, an extensive vocabulary and use of script, these handy pocket-sized language guides cover day-to-day travel situations.

- handy pocket-sized books
- easy to understand Pronunciation chapter
- clear & comprehensive Grammar chapter
- romanisation alongside script to allow ease of pronunciation
- script throughout so users can point to phrases for every situation
- full of cultural information and tips for the traveller

'... vital for a real DIY spirit and attitude in language learning'
– *Backpacker*

'the phrasebooks have good cultural backgrounders and offer solid advice for challenging situations in remote locations'
– *San Francisco Examiner*

Arabic (Egyptian) • Arabic (Moroccan) • Australian *(Australian English, Aboriginal and Torres Strait languages)* • Baltic States *(Estonian, Latvian, Lithuanian)* • Bengali • Brazilian • British • Burmese • Cantonese • Central Asia (Uyghur, Uzbek, Kyrghiz, Kazak, Pashto, Tadjik • Central Europe *(Czech, French, German, Hungarian, Italian, Slovak)* • Eastern Europe *(Bulgarian, Czech, Hungarian, Polish, Romanian, Slovak)* • Ethiopian (Amharic) • Fijian • French • German • Greek • Hebrew • Hill Tribes • Hindi & Urdu • Indonesian • Italian • Japanese • Korean • Lao • Latin American Spanish • Malay • Mandarin • Mediterranean Europe *(Albanian, Croatian, Greek, Italian, Macedonian, Maltese, Serbian, Slovene)* • Mongolian • Nepali • Pidgin • Pilipino (Tagalog) • Portugese • Quechua • Russian • Scandinavian Europe *(Danish, Finnish, Icelandic, Norwegian, Swedish)* • South-East Asia *(Burmese, Indonesian, Khmer, Lao, Malay, Tagalog Pilipino, Thai, Vietnamese)* • South Pacific Languages • Spanish (Castilian) *(also includes Catalan, Galician and Basque)* • Sri Lanka • Swahili • Thai • Tibetan • Turkish • Ukrainian • USA *(US English, Vernacular, Native American languages, Hawaiian)* • Vietnamese • Western Europe *(Basque, Catalan, Dutch, French, German, Greek, Irish, Italian, Portuguese, Scottish Gaelic, Spanish (Castilian), Welsh)*

Lonely Planet Journeys

JOURNEYS is a unique collection of travel writing – published by the company that understands travel better than anyone else. It is a series for anyone who has ever experienced – or dreamed of – the magical moment when they encountered a strange culture or saw a place for the first time. They are tales to read while you're planning a trip, while you're on the road or while you're in an armchair in front of a fire.

These outstanding titles explore our planet through the eyes of a diverse group of international writers. JOURNEYS books catch the spirit of a place, illuminate a culture, recount a crazy adventure or introduce a fascinating way of life. They always entertain, and always enrich the experience of travel.

FULL CIRCLE
A South American Journey
Luis Sepúlveda (translated by Chris Andrews)

'A journey without a fixed itinerary' with Chilean writer Luis Sepúlveda. Extravagant characters and extraordinary situations are memorably evoked: gauchos organising a tournament of lies, a scheming heiress on the lookout for a husband, a pilot with a corpse on board his plane ... *Full Circle* brings us the distinctive voice of one of South America's most compelling writers.

WINNER 1996 Astrolabe – Etonnants Voyageurs award for the best work of travel literature published in France.

GREEN DREAMS
Travels in Central America
Stephen Benz

On the Amazon, in Costa Rica, Honduras and on the Mayan trail from Guatemala to Mexico, Stephen Benz describes his encounters with water, mud, insects and other wildlife – and not least with the ecotourists themselves. With witty insights into modern travel, *Green Dreams* discusses the paradox of cultural and 'green' tourism.

DRIVE THRU AMERICA
Sean Condon

If you've ever wanted to drive across the USA but couldn't find the time (or afford the gas), *Drive Thru America* is perfect for you.

In his search for American myths and realities – along with comfort, cable TV and good, reasonably priced coffee – Sean Condon paints a hilarious road-portrait of the USA.

'entertaining and laugh-out-loud funny'– *Alex Wilber, Travel editor, Amazon.com*

SEAN & DAVID'S LONG DRIVE
Sean Condon

Sean and David are young townies who have rarely strayed beyond city limits. One day, for no good reason, they set out to discover their homeland, and what follows is a wildly entertaining adventure that covers half of Australia.

'a hilariously detailed log of two burned out friends' – *Rolling Stone*

Lonely Planet Travel Atlases

L onely Planet has long been famous for the number and quality of its guidebook maps. Now we've gone one step further and produced a handy companion series: Lonely Planet travel atlases – maps of a country produced in book form.

Unlike other maps, which look good but lead travellers astray, our travel atlases have been researched on the road by Lonely Planet's experienced team of writers. All details are carefully checked to ensure the atlas corresponds with the equivalent Lonely Planet guidebook.

- full-colour throughout
- maps researched and checked by Lonely Planet authors
- place names correspond with Lonely Planet guidebooks
- no confusing spelling differences
- legend and travelling information in English, French, German, Japanese and Spanish
- size: 230 x 160 mm

Available now: Chile & Easter Island • Egypt • India & Bangladesh • Israel & the Palestinian Territories • Jordan, Syria & Lebanon • Kenya • Laos • Portugal • South Africa, Lesotho & Swaziland • Thailand • Turkey • Vietnam • Zimbabwe, Botswana & Namibia

---

Lonely Planet TV Series & Videos

L onely Planet travel guides have been brought to life on television screens around the world. Like our guides, the programs are based on the joy of independent travel, and look honestly at some of the most exciting, picturesque and frustrating places in the world. Each show is presented by one of three travellers from Australia, England or the USA and combines an innovative mixture of video, Super-8 film, atmospheric soundscapes and original music.

Videos of each episode – containing additional footage not shown on television – are available from good book and video shops, but the availability of individual videos varies with regional screening schedules.

Video destinations include: Alaska • American Rockies • Australia – The South-East • Baja California & the Copper Canyon • Brazil • Central Asia • Chile & Easter Island • Corsica, Sicily & Sardinia – The Mediterranean Islands • East Africa (Tanzania & Zanzibar) • Ecuador & the Galapagos Islands • Greenland & Iceland • Indonesia • Israel & the Sinai Desert • Jamaica • Japan • La Ruta Maya • Morocco • New York • North India • Pacific Islands (Fiji, Solomon Islands & Vanuatu) • South India • South West China • Turkey • Vietnam • West Africa • Zimbabwe, Botswana & Namibia

The Lonely Planet TV series is produced by: Pilot Productions
The Old Studio
18 Middle Row
London W10 5AT, UK

Lonely Planet On-line

Whether you've just begun planning your next trip, or you're chasing down specific info on currency regulations or visa requirements, check out Lonely Planet On-line for up-to-the minute travel information.

As well as mini guides to more than 250 destinations, you'll find maps, photos, travel news, health and visa updates, travel advisories, and discussion of the eco-logical and political issues you need to be aware of as you travel. You'll also find timely upgrades to popular guidebooks which you can print out and stick in the back of your book.

There's also an on-line travellers' forum where you can share your experience of life on the road, meet travel companions and ask other travellers for their recommendations and advice.

And of course we have a complete and up-to-date list of all Lonely Planet travel products including travel guides, diving and snorkeling guides, phrasebooks, atlases, travel literature and videos, and a simple on-line ordering facility if you can't find the book you want elsewhere.

Lonely Planet Diving & Snorkeling Guides

Known for indispensible guidebooks to destinations all over the world, Lonely Planet's Pisces Books are the most popular series of diving and snorkeling titles available.

There are three series: **Diving & Snorkeling Guides**, **Shipwreck Diving** series and **Dive Into History**. Full colour throughout, the **Diving & Snorkeling Guides** combine quality photographs with detailed descriptions of the best dive sites for each location, giv-ing divers a glimpse of what they can expect both on land and in water. The **Dive Into History** series is perfect for the adven-ture diver or armchair traveller. The **Shipwreck Diving** series provides all the details for exploring the most interesting wrecks in the Atlantic and Pacific oceans. The list also includes under-water nature and technical guides.

LONELY PLANET

Guides by Region

Lonely Planet is known worldwide for publishing practical, reliable and no-nonsense travel information in our guides and on our Web site. The Lonely Planet list covers just about every accessible part of the world. Currently there are 16 series: Travel guides, Shoestring guides, Condensed guides, Phrasebooks, Read This First, Healthy Travel, Walking guides, Cycling guides, Watching Wildlife guides, Pisces Diving & Snorkeling guides, City Maps, Road Atlases, Out to Eat, World Food, Journeys travel literature and Pictorials.

AFRICA Africa on a shoestring • Cairo • Cairo City Map • Cape Town • Cape Town City Map • East Africa • Egypt • Egyptian Arabic phrasebook • Ethiopia, Eritrea & Djibouti • Ethiopian (Amharic) phrasebook • The Gambia & Senegal • Healthy Travel Africa • Kenya • Malawi • Morocco • Moroccan Arabic phrasebook • Mozambique • Read This First: Africa • South Africa, Lesotho & Swaziland • Southern Africa • Southern Africa Road Atlas • Swahili phrasebook • Tanzania, Zanzibar & Pemba • Trekking in East Africa • Tunisia • Watching Wildlife East Africa • Watching Wildlife Southern Africa • West Africa • World Food Morocco • Zimbabwe, Botswana & Namibia
Travel Literature: Mali Blues: Traveling to an African Beat • The Rainbird: A Central African Journey • Songs to an African Sunset: A Zimbabwean Story

AUSTRALIA & THE PACIFIC Auckland • Australia • Australian phrasebook • Australia Road Atlas • Bushwalking in Australia • Cycling Australia • Cycling New Zealand • Fiji • Fijian phrasebook • Healthy Travel Australia, NZ and the Pacific • Islands of Australia's Great Barrier Reef • Melbourne • Melbourne City Map • Micronesia • New Caledonia • New South Wales & the ACT • New Zealand • Northern Territory • Outback Australia • Out to Eat – Melbourne • Out to Eat – Sydney • Papua New Guinea • Pidgin phrasebook • Queensland • Rarotonga & the Cook Islands • Samoa • Solomon Islands • South Australia • South Pacific • South Pacific phrasebook • Sydney • Sydney City Map • Sydney Condensed • Tahiti & French Polynesia • Tasmania • Tonga • Tramping in New Zealand • Vanuatu • Victoria • Walking in Australia • Watching Wildlife Australia • Western Australia
Travel Literature: Islands in the Clouds: Travels in the Highlands of New Guinea • Kiwi Tracks: A New Zealand Journey • Sean & David's Long Drive

CENTRAL AMERICA & THE CARIBBEAN Bahamas, Turks & Caicos • Baja California • Bermuda • Central America on a shoestring • Costa Rica • Costa Rica Spanish phrasebook • Cuba • Dominican Republic & Haiti • Eastern Caribbean • Guatemala • Guatemala, Belize & Yucatán: La Ruta Maya • Havana • Healthy Travel Central & South America • Jamaica • Mexico • Mexico City • Panama • Puerto Rico • Read This First: Central & South America • World Food Mexico • Yucatán
Travel Literature: Green Dreams: Travels in Central America

EUROPE Amsterdam • Amsterdam City Map • Amsterdam Condensed • Andalucía • Austria • Baltic States phrasebook • Barcelona • Barcelona City Map • Belgium & Luxembourg • Berlin • Berlin City Map • Britain • British phrasebook • Brussels, Bruges & Antwerp • Brussels City Map • Budapest • Budapest City Map • Canary Islands • Central Europe • Central Europe phrasebook • Corfu & the Ionians • Corsica • Crete • Crete Condensed • Croatia • Cycling Britain • Cycling France • Cyprus • Czech & Slovak Republics • Denmark • Dublin • Dublin City Map • Eastern Europe • Eastern Europe phrasebook • Edinburgh • Estonia, Latvia & Lithuania • Europe on a shoestring • Finland • Florence • France • Frankfurt Condensed • French phrasebook • Georgia, Armenia & Azerbaijan • Germany • German phrasebook • Greece • Greek Islands • Greek phrasebook • Hungary • Iceland, Greenland & the Faroe Islands • Ireland • Istanbul • Italian phrasebook • Italy • Krakow • Lisbon • The Loire • London • London City Map • London Condensed • Madrid • Malta • Mediterranean Europe • Mediterranean Europe phrasebook • Moscow • Mozambique • Munich • the Netherlands • Norway • Out to Eat – London • Paris • Paris City Map • Paris Condensed • Poland • Portugal • Portuguese phrasebook • Prague • Prague City Map • Provence & the Côte d'Azur • Read This First: Europe • Romania & Moldova • Rome • Rome City Map • Russia, Ukraine & Belarus • Russian phrasebook • Scandinavian & Baltic Europe • Scandinavian Europe phrasebook • Scotland • Sicily • Slovenia • South-West France • Spain • Spanish phrasebook • St Petersburg • St Petersburg City Map • Sweden • Switzerland • Trekking in Spain • Tuscany • Ukrainian phrasebook • Venice • Vienna • Walking in Britain • Walking in France • Walking in Ireland • Walking in Italy • Walking in Spain • Walking in Switzerland • Western Europe • Western Europe phrasebook • World Food France • World Food Ireland • World Food Italy • World Food Spain
Travel Literature: A Small Place in Italy • After Yugoslavia • Love and War in the Apennines • On the Shores of the Mediterranean The Olive Grove: Travels in Greece • Round Ireland in Low Gear

LONELY PLANET

Mail Order

Lonely Planet products are distributed worldwide. They are also available by mail order from Lonely Planet, so if you have difficulty finding a title please write to us. North and South American residents should write to 150 Linden St, Oakland, CA 94607, USA; European and African residents should write to 10a Spring Place, London NW5 3BH, UK; and residents of other countries to Locked Bag 1, Footscray, Victoria 3011, Australia.

INDIAN SUBCONTINENT Bangladesh • Bengali phrasebook • Bhutan • Delhi • Goa • Healthy Travel Asia & India • Hindi & Urdu phrasebook • India • Indian Himalaya • Karakoram Highway • Kerala • Mumbai (Bombay) • Nepal • Nepali phrasebook • Pakistan • Rajasthan • Read This First: Asia & India • South India • Sri Lanka • Sri Lanka phrasebook • Tibet • Tibetan phrasebook • Trekking in the Indian Himalaya • Trekking in the Karakoram & Hindukush • Trekking in the Nepal Himalaya
Travel Literature: The Age of Kali: Indian Travels and Encounters • Hello Goodnight: A Life of Goa • In Rajasthan • A Season in Heaven: True Tales from the Road to Kathmandu • Shopping for Buddhas • A Short Walk in the Hindu Kush • Slowly Down the Ganges

ISLANDS OF THE INDIAN OCEAN Madagascar & Comoros • Maldives • Mauritius, Réunion & Seychelles
Travel Literature: Maverick in Madagascar

MIDDLE EAST & CENTRAL ASIA Bahrain, Kuwait & Qatar • Central Asia • Central Asia phrasebook • Dubai • Farsi (Persian) phrasebook • Hebrew phrasebook • Iran • Israel & the Palestinian Territories • Istanbul • Istanbul City Map • Istanbul to Cairo on a shoestring • Jerusalem • Jerusalem City Map • Jordan • Lebanon • Middle East • Oman & the United Arab Emirates • Syria • Turkey • Turkish phrasebook • World Food Turkey • Yemen
Travel Literature: Black on Black: Iran Revisited • The Gates of Damascus • Kingdom of the Film Stars: Journey into Jordan

NORTH AMERICA Alaska • Boston • Boston City Map • Boston Condensed • British Colombia • California & Nevada • California Condensed • Canada • Chicago • Chicago City Map • Deep South • Florida • Great Lakes • Hawaii • Hiking in Alaska • Hiking in the USA • Honolulu • Las Vegas • Los Angeles • Los Angeles City Map • Louisiana & The Deep South • Miami • Miami City Map • Montreal • New England • New Orleans • New York City • New York City City Map • New York City Condensed • New York, New Jersey & Pennsylvania • Oahu • Out to Eat – San Francisco • Pacific Northwest • Puerto Rico • Rocky Mountains • San Francisco • San Francisco City Map • Seattle • Southwest • Texas • Toronto • USA • USA phrasebook • Vancouver • Virginia & the Capital Region • Washington DC • Washington, DC City Map • World Food Deep South, USA • World Food New Orleans
Travel Literature: Caught Inside: A Surfer's Year on the California Coast • Drive Thru America

NORTH-EAST ASIA Beijing • Beijing City Map • Cantonese phrasebook • China • Hiking in Japan • Hong Kong • Hong Kong City Map • Hong Kong Condensed • Hong Kong, Macau & Guangzhou • Japan • Japanese phrasebook • Korea • Korean phrasebook • Kyoto • Mandarin phrasebook • Mongolia • Mongolian phrasebook • Seoul • Shanghai • South-West China • Taiwan • Tokyo • World Food – Hong Kong
Travel Literature: In Xanadu: A Quest • Lost Japan

SOUTH AMERICA Argentina, Uruguay & Paraguay • Bolivia • Brazil • Brazilian phrasebook • Buenos Aires • Chile & Easter Island • Colombia • Ecuador & the Galapagos Islands • Healthy Travel Central & South America • Latin American Spanish phrasebook • Peru • Quechua phrasebook • Read This First: Central & South America • Rio de Janeiro • Rio de Janeiro City Map • Santiago • South America on a shoestring • Santiago • Trekking in the Patagonian Andes • Venezuela
Travel Literature: Full Circle: A South American Journey

SOUTH-EAST ASIA Bali & Lombok • Bangkok • Bangkok City Map • Burmese phrasebook • Cambodia • Hanoi • Healthy Travel Asia & India • Hill Tribes phrasebook • Ho Chi Minh City • Indonesia • Indonesian phrasebook • Indonesia's Eastern Islands • Jakarta • Java • Lao phrasebook • Laos • Malay phrasebook • Malaysia, Singapore & Brunei • Myanmar (Burma) • Philippines • Pilipino (Tagalog) phrasebook • Read This First: Asia & India • Singapore • Singapore City Map • South-East Asia on a shoestring • South-East Asia phrasebook • Thailand • Thailand's Islands & Beaches • Thailand, Vietnam, Laos & Cambodia Road Atlas • Thai phrasebook • Vietnam • Vietnamese phrasebook • World Food Thailand • World Food Vietnam

ALSO AVAILABLE: Antarctica • The Arctic • The Blue Man: Tales of Travel, Love and Coffee • Brief Encounters: Stories of Love, Sex & Travel • Chasing Rickshaws • The Last Grain Race • Lonely Planet Unpacked • Not the Only Planet: Science Fiction Travel Stories • Lonely Planet On the Edge • Sacred India • Travel with Children • Travel Photography: A Guide to Taking Better Pictures

FREE Lonely Planet Newsletters

W̲e love hearing from you and think you'd like to hear from us.

Planet Talk

Our FREE quarterly printed newsletter is full of tips from travellers and anecdotes from Lonely Planet guidebook authors. Every issue is packed with up-to-date travel news and advice, and includes:

- a postcard from Lonely Planet co-founder Tony Wheeler
- a swag of mail from travellers
- a look at life on the road through the eyes of a Lonely Planet author
- topical health advice
- prizes for the best travel yarn
- news about forthcoming Lonely Planet events
- a complete list of Lonely Planet books and other titles

To join our mailing list, residents of the UK, Europe and Africa can email us at go@lonelyplanet.co.uk; residents of North and South America can email us at info@lonelyplanet.com; the rest of the world can email us at talk2us@lonelyplanet.com.au, or contact any Lonely Planet office.

Comet

O̲ur FREE monthly email newsletter brings you all the latest travel news, features, interviews, competitions, destination ideas, travellers' tips & tales, Q&As, raging debates and related links. Find out what's new on the Lonely Planet Web site and which books are about to hit the shelves.

Subscribe from your desktop: www.lonelyplanet.com/comet

Index

Text

Bold indicates maps

Bold indicates maps.

O

P

Q

Bold indicates maps.

Boxed Text

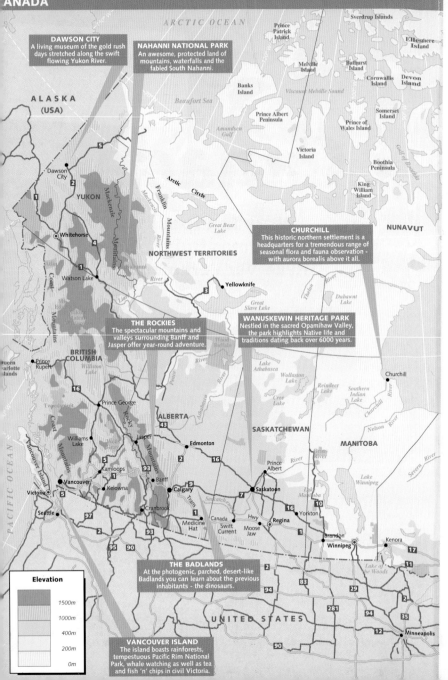

ARCTIC OCEAN

DAWSON CITY
A living museum of the gold rush days stretched along the swift flowing Yukon River.

NAHANNI NATIONAL PARK
An awesome, protected land of mountains, waterfalls and the fabled South Nahanni.

Sverdrup Islands

Prince Patrick Island

ALASKA (USA)

Beaufort Sea

Banks Island

Melville Island

Bathurst Island

Cornwallis Island

Devon Island

Ellesmere Island

Viscount Melville Sound

Prince Albert Peninsula

Amundsen Gulf

Victoria Island

Somerset Island

Prince of Wales Island

Boothia Peninsula

Gulf of Boothia

Dawson City

Arctic

Circle

Franklin Mountains

Mackenzie River

King William Island

YUKON

Mackenzie

Great Bear Lake

NUNAVUT

Whitehorse

CHURCHILL
This historic northern settlement is a headquarters for a tremendous range of seasonal flora and fauna observation - with aurora borealis above it all.

NORTHWEST TERRITORIES

Watson Lake

River

3

Yellowknife

Great Slave Lake

Thelon River

Dubawnt Lake

Queen Charlotte Islands

Prince Rupert

BRITISH COLUMBIA

Williston Lake

THE ROCKIES
The spectacular mountains and valleys surrounding Banff and Jasper offer year-round adventure.

Wood Buffalo

River

WANUSKEWIN HERITAGE PARK
Nestled in the sacred Opamihaw Valley, the park highlights Native life and traditions dating back over 6000 years.

Lake Athabasca

Wollaston Lake

Reindeer Lake

Southern Indian Lake

Churchill

Churchill River

16

Prince George

Coast Mountains

Tweedsmuir

Rocky Mountains

Cree Lake

Nelson River

Williams Lake

ALBERTA

43

Jasper

Athabasca River

SASKATCHEWAN

MANITOBA

Severn River

5

Edmonton

Kamloops

93

2

16

River

Vancouver Island

Vancouver

Banff

Kelowna

Calgary

Prince Albert

Saskatchewan River

Lake Winnipeg

Victoria

5

Trans

Saskatoon

7

River

Lake Manitoba

10

PACIFIC OCEAN

Seattle

97

Cranbrook

1

Canada

Swift Current

Hwy

Moose Jaw

16

Regina

Yorkton

Medicine Hat

1

Brandon

Kenora

2

93

Winnipeg

17

95

90

THE BADLANDS
At the photogenic, parched, desert-like Badlands you can learn about the previous inhabitants - the dinosaurs.

Lake of the Woods

11

2

83

29

2

Elevation

1500m

1000m

400m

200m

0m

94

UNITED STATES

281

94

35

12

Minneapolis

90

VANCOUVER ISLAND
The island boasts rainforests, tempestuous Pacific Rim National Park, whale watching as well as tea and fish 'n' chips in civil Victoria.

D0315316

Canada

Mark Lightbody
Thomas Huhti
Ryan Ver Berkmoes

W9-AXZ-250

LONELY PLANET PUBLICATIONS
Melbourne • Oakland • London • Paris

MAP LEGEND

BOUNDARIES

International
State
Disputed

HYDROGRAPHY

Coastline
River, Creek
Lake
Intermittent Lake
Salt Lake
Canal
Spring, Rapids
Waterfalls

ROUTES & TRANSPORT

Freeway
Highway
Major Road
Minor Road
Unsealed Road
City Highway
City Road
City Street, Lane
Pedestrian Mall
Tunnel
Train Route & Station
Metro & Station
Tramway
Cable Car or Chairlift
Walking Track
Ferry Route

AREA FEATURES

Building
Park, Gardens
Cemetery
Market
Pedestrian Mall
Urban Area

MAP SYMBOLS

✪ CAPITAL	National Capital	✈	Airfield	▲	Mountain or Hill
◉ CAPITAL	State Capital	✈	Airport	🏛	Museum
● CITY	City		Ancient or City Wall	←	One Way Street
● Town	Town	⁘	Archaeological Site	)(	Pass
● Village	Village	❂	Bank	★	Police Station
○	Point of Interest		Beach		Post Office
			Border Crossing	❖	Shopping Centre
■	Place to Stay		Castle or Fort	⚑	Ski field
▲	Camping Ground		Cave		Stately Home
	Caravan Park		Church		Swimming Pool
	Hut or Chalet		Cliff or Escarpment	☎	Telephone
		○	Embassy		Temple
▼	Place to Eat	⊕	Hospital	❶	Tourist Information
	Pub or Bar		Lighthouse	●	Transport
		❋	Lookout		Zoo

Note: not all symbols displayed above appear in this book

LONELY PLANET OFFICES

Australia
Locked Bag 1, Footscray, Victoria 3011
☎ 03 9689 4666 fax 03 9689 6833
email: talk2us@lonelyplanet.com.au

USA
150 Linden St, Oakland, CA 94607
☎ 510 893 8555 TOLL FREE: 800 275 8555
fax 510 893 8572
email: info@lonelyplanet.com

UK
10a Spring Place, London NW5 3BH
☎ 020 7428 4800 fax 020 7428 4828
email: go@lonelyplanet.co.uk

France
1 rue du Dahomey, 75011 Paris
☎ 01 55 25 33 00 fax 01 55 25 33 01
email: bip@lonelyplanet.fr
www.lonelyplanet.fr

World Wide Web: www.lonelyplanet.com *or* **AOL keyword: lp**
Lonely Planet Images: lpi@lonelyplanet.com.au